Encyclopedia of
PRISONS
& Correctional Facilities

EDITORIAL BOARD

Encyclopedia of
PRISONS
& Correctional Facilities

Mary Bosworth, Editor
Wesleyan University

Volume 1

A SAGE Reference Publication

SAGE Publications
Thousand Oaks ▪ London ▪ New Delhi

For information:

Sage Publications, Inc.
2455 Teller Road
Thousand Oaks, California 91320
E-mail: order@sagepub.com

Sage Publications Ltd.
1 Oliver's Yard
55 City Road
London EC1Y 1SP
United Kingdom

Sage Publications India Pvt. Ltd.
B-42, Panchsheel Enclave
Post Box 4109
New Delhi 110 017   India

Printed in the United States of America

Library of Congress Cataloging-in-Publication Data

Bosworth, Mary.
Encyclopedia of prisons and correctional facilities / Mary Bosworth.
 p. cm.
Includes bibliographical references and index.
ISBN 0-7619-2731-X (cloth) (set)
 1. Prisons—United States—Encyclopedias. 2. Correctional institutions—United States—Encyclopedias. I. Title.
HV9471.B675 2005
365'.973'03—dc22

2004021802

This book is printed on acid-free paper.

04   05   06   07   10   9   8   7   6   5   4   3   2   1

Acquisitions Editor:	Jerry Westby
Editorial Assistant:	Vonessa Vondera
Production Editor:	Denise Santoyo
Developmental Editor:	Yvette Pollastrini
Copy Editors:	Kate Peterson, Pam Suwinsky, and Judy Selhorst
Typesetter:	C&M Digitals (P) Ltd.
Indexer:	Teri Greenberg
Cover Designer:	Michelle Lee Kenny

Contents

VOLUME I: A–O
1–662

VOLUME II: P–Z
663–1064

List of Entries

Reader's Guide

Authors

Jack Henry Abbott
Cesare Beccaria
Jeremy Bentham
Meda Chesney-Lind
Donald Clemmer
Constitutive Penology
Convict Criminology
Angela Y. Davis
John J. DiIulio, Jr.
Michel Foucault
Elizabeth Frye
David Garland
Rose Giallombardo
John Howard
John Irwin
George Jackson
Robert Martinson
Jerome Miller
Norval Ramsden Morris
Anthony Platt
Nicole Hahn Rafter
David Rothman
Gresham Sykes

Health

Dental Care
Disabled Prisoners
Doctors
Gynecology
Health Care
HIV/AIDS
Hospice
Mental Health
Medical Model
Optometry
Overprescription of Drugs

Physicians' Assistants
Psychiatric Care
Psychological Services
Psychologists
Ruiz v. Estelle
Self-Harm
Suicide
Women's Health

History

Alcatraz
Attica Correctional Facility
Auburn System
Cesare Beccaria
Bedford Hills Correctional Facility
Jeremy Bentham
Bridewell
Zebulon Reed Brockway
Convict Lease System
Katharine Bement Davis
Dorothea Dix
Elmira Reformatory
History of Correctional Officers
History of Prisons
History of Religion in Prison
History of Women's Prisons
Irish (or Crofton) System
Juvenile Reformatories
Labor
Josephine Shaw Lowell
Alexander Maconochie
Massachusetts Reformatory
Medical Experiments
Panopticon
Parchman Farm, Mississippi State Penitentiary
Pennsylvania Prison Society
Pennsylvania System
Plantation Prisons

Prison Ships
Slavery
Mabel Walker
Willebrant

Inmates

Jack Henry Abbott
Celebrities in Prison
Angela Y. Davis
Stephen Donaldson
Elizabeth Gurley Flynn
Gerald (Gerry) Gault
Gary Gilmore
John Gotti
George Jackson
Malcolm X
Kate Richards O'Hare
Timothy McVeigh
Leonard Peltier
Politicians
Ethel and Julius Rosenberg
Jack Ruby
Karla Faye Tucker

Institutions

ADX (Administrative Maximum): Florence
Alcatraz
Alderson, Federal Prison Camp
Angola Penitentiary
Attica Correctional Facility
Auburn Correctional Facility
Bedford Hills Correctional Facility
Bridewell Prison and Workhouse
Co-correctional Facilities
Community Corrections Centers
Corcoran, California State Prison
Eastern State Penitentiary
Elmira Reformatory
Framingham, MCI
Huntsville Penitentiary
INS Detention Facilities
Leavenworth, U.S. Penitentiary
Lexington High Security Unit
Marion, U.S. Penitentiary
Massachusetts Reformatory
New Maxico Penitentiary
Newgate Prison
Norfolk Prison
Oak Park Heights, Minnesota Correctional Facility

Panopticon
Parchman Farm, Mississippi State Penitentiary
Patuxent Institution
Pelican Bay State Prison
Rikers Island Jail
San Quentin State Prison
Sing Sing Correctional Facility
Stateville Correctional Center
Terre Haute U.S. Penitentiary Death Row
Walla Walla Washington State Penitentiary
Walnut Street Jail

Juvenile Justice

Boot Camp
Meda Chesney-Lind
Children
Child Savers
Cook County, Illinois
Detained Youth and Committed Youth
Group Homes
Juvenile Death Penalty
Juvenile Detention Centers
Juvenile Justice and Delinquency
    Prevention Act
Juvenile Justice System
Juvenile Offenders: Race, Class, and Gender
Juvenile Reformatories
Mens Rea
Jerome G. Miller
Parens Patriae
Patuxent Institution
Anthony Platt
Status Offenders
Waiver of Juveniles Into the Adult Court System
Youth Corrections Act

Labor

Ashurst-Sumners Act
Boot Camp
Hard Labor
Hawes-Cooper Act
Labor
Plantation Prison
Prison Industry Enhancement
Certification Program
Prisoner Pay
Prisoner Unions
Privatization of Labor
UNICOR

List of Sidebars

List of Contributors

Agozino, Biko
Cheyney University of Pennsylvania

Albin, Kimberly
Northeastern University

Allen, Jennifer M.
Western Illinois University

Anderson, Kate
University of Cincinnati

Andrus, Tracy
Prairie View A&M University

Angiello, Elizabeth
*The State University of New Jersey,
    Rutgers Newark*

Arrigo, Bruce
University of North Carolina at Charlotte

Austin, Andrew
University of Wisconsin–Green Bay

Baker, Melissa
University of Ottawa

Bakker, Hans
University of Guelph

Banks, Cyndi
Northern Arizona University

Barker, Vanessa
New York University

Baro, Agnes
Valdosta State University

Barton, Alana
Edge Hill University College

Belbot, Barbara
University of Houston–Downtown

Bernat, Frances P.
Arizona State University West

Blakely, Curtis R.
Southern Illinois University–Carbondale

Blevins, Kristie R.
University of Cincinnati

Blight, Jake
Office of General Counsel, High Court of Australia

Bloom, Barbara E.
Sonoma State University

Bosworth, Mary
Wesleyan University

Bosworth, Michal
Independent Scholar

Brennan, Lori
Fordham University

Brewster, Dennis R.
Auburn University

Brockett, Ramona
Northern Kentucky University

Brooks-Klinger, Jeneve
Fordham University

Brown, Dorothy M.
Georgetown University

Brown, John D.
CEO, Blockhouse

Brown, Michelle
Indiana University

Brown-Dean, Khalilah
Yale University

Bruckert, Chris
University of Ottawa

Bush-Baskette, Stephanie
The State University of New Jersey, Rutgers Newark

Bussert, Todd
Law Offices of Todd A. Bussert

Byers, Bryan D.
Ball State University

Cadigan, Robert T.
Boston University

Camp, Scott D.
Independent Scholar

Campbell, Kathryn M.
University of Ottawa

Capps, Jason S.
University of Kansas

Carleton, Francis
University of Wisconsin at Green Bay

Carrabine, Eamonn
University of Essex

Carter, David
University of Cincinnati

Cash, Staci A.
Independent Scholar

Chanenson, Steven L.
Villanova University, School of Law

Chavez, R. Scott
National Commission on Correctional Health Care

Cohn, Ellen G.
Florida International University

Cohn, Felicia
University of California, Irvine

Coldren, James "Chip"
John Howard Association, Chicago

Cole, Mihael Ami
University of Ottawa

Coleman, Michelle
University of Cincinnati

Collica, Kimberly
Monroe College–Bronx

Collier, Linda J.
Delaware Community College

Conte, Sara
Tennessee Department of Corrections

Culp, Richard
John Jay College of Criminal Justice

Dammer, Harry S.
University of Scranton

Davies, Kim
Augusta State University

De Angelis, Joseph
New York University

Deasy, Kathy S.
Independent Scholar

Decker, Scott H.
University of Missouri–St. Louis

Dell, Colleen Anne
Carleton University

DeMichele, Matthew T.
Western Michigan University

Denov, Myriam
University of Ottawa

Derbitsky, Harry
ACT Training Inc

Desautels, Amy E.
Fordham University

Dobbs, Rhonda R.
Florida State University

Dodge, L. Mara
Westfield State College

Dodson, J. Talmadge
University of Arkansas at Little Rock

Dragan, Henry
Northeastern Illinois University

Faiver, Kenneth L.
Faiver, Campau & Associates

Farrell, William
Indiana University–Southeast

Fasano, Charles A.
John Howard Association, Illinois

Fields, Charles B.
Eastern Kentucky University

Fillmore, Catherine
University of Winnipeg

Finn, Mary A.
Georgia State University

Fisher-Giordano, Marianne
Grambling State University

Flavin, Jeanne
Fordham University

Freedman, Estelle B.
Stanford University

Freiberger, Kimberly L.
Virginia Commonwealth University

Frigon, Sylvie
University of Ottawa

Frost, Natasha
James Cook University

Fuller, John Randolf
Eastern Michigan University

Furst, Gennifer
John Jay College of Criminal Justice

Garcia, Venessa
Kean University

Gaucher, Robert
University of Ottawa

Girshick, Lori B.
Warren Wilson College

Golden, Deborah M.
D.C. Prisoners' Legal Services

Grant, Anna Alice
Griffith University

Greene, Dana
City University of New York

Greene, Susan
University of California, Santa Cruz

Guerette, Rob T.
*The State University of New Jersey,
    Rutgers Newark*

Guevara, Anthony B.
Fordham University

Hamm, Mark S.
Indiana State University

Hanbury, Barbara
York College of Pennsylvania

Haney, Craig
University of California, Santa Cruz

Hannem-Kish, Stacey
University of Ottawa

Heege, Carrie A.
Ball State University

Heffernan, Esther
Edgewood College

Helfgott, Jacqueline B.
Seattle University

Hemmens, Craig
Boise State University

Henry, Stuart
Wayne State University

Hinkle, William G.
Ivy Tech State College

Hogeveen, Bryan R.
University of Alberta

Houston, James G.
Grand Valley State University

Hume, Wendelin M.
University of North Dakota

Hunter, Wanda T.
University of Arkansas at Little Rock

Immarigeon, Russ
Civic Research Institute

Inderbitzin, Michelle
Oregon State University

Ireland, Connie S.
California State University, Long Beach

Jaroslawicz, Isaac M.
The Aleph Institute

Jenkot, Robert B.
University of Alabama

Jesseman, Rebecca
*Corrections Research Division, Public Safety &
    Emergency Preparedness Canada*

Kaim, Marc
Fordham University

Kauffmann, Kelsey
Independent Researcher and Writer

Kelly, Russell
University of Central Lancashire

Kendall, Kathleen
University of Southampton

Keys, David
Plattsburgh State University of New York

Kilty, Jennifer M.
University of Ottawa

King, Ryan S.
American University

Klein, Melissa J.
Fordham University

Knepper, Paul
University of Sheffield

Kobil, Dan
Capital University Law School

Karl R. Kunkel
Southern Missouri State University

Kupchik, Aaron
Arizona State University

Law, Victoria
New York Public Interest Research Group

Lee, Maggy
University of Essex

Leighton, Paul
Eastern Michigan University

Lenning, Emily
Western Michigan University

Light, Stephen C.
State University of New York–Plattsburgh

Linn, Kenneth
Acting Chairman, FedCure

Lobo-Jost, Gregory
Fordham University

Long, Lydia M.
University of Houston–Downtown

Loo, Dennis D.
California State Polytechnic University, Pomona

Lucko, Paul
Murray State University

Macaluso, Mike
Western Michigan University

Maillicoat, Stacy
California State University, Fullerton

Mamiya, Lawrence H.
Vassar College

Martin, Kathryn E.
University of California, Santa Barbara

Mazloom, Richard
Marist College

McCorkle, Jill
University of Massachusetts, Amherst

McKinnon, Kristi M.
University of San Francisco

McManimon Jr., Patrick F.
Kean University

McShane, Marilyn
University of Houston–Downtown

McWhorter, Richard L.
Prairie View A&M University

Mellow, Jeff
Bloomfield College

Mentor, Kenneth
Fayetteville State University

Miller, Alexis J.
Middle Tennessee State University

Miller, Marc L.
Emory Law School

Milovanovic, Dragan
Northeastern Illinois University

Minaker, Joanne
Grant Macewan College

Mitchell Robinson, Deborah
Valdosta State University

Morris, Monique W.
National Council on Crime and Delinquency

Mosley, Thomas S.
University of Maryland, Eastern Shore

Muzzatti, Stephen L.
Ryerson University

Nation, Denise
University of Cincinnati

Newbold, Greg
University of Canterbury, New Zealand

Nurse, Anne M.
The College of Wooster

Odo, Jonathan
University of Maryland Eastern Shore

Oleson, J. C.
Old Dominion University

Onwudiwe, Ihekwoaba D.
University of Maryland Eastern Shore

Onyeozili, Emmanuel C.
University of Maryland Eastern Shore

Owen, Barbara
California State University, Fresno

Owen, Stephen S.
Radford University

Parsons-Pollard, Nicolle
Virginia Commonwealth University

Patenaude, Allan L.
University of Arkansas at Little Rock

Patino, Vanessa
National Council on Crime and Delinquency

Pealer, Jennifer A.
University of Cincinnati

Perkinson, Robert
University of Hawaii at Manoa

Petersilia, Joan
University of California, Irvine

Petrunik, Michael
University of Ottawa

Phillips, Nickie
John Jay College of Criminal Justice

Piper, Katherine
Wesleyan University

Pollack, Shoshana
Wilfrid Laurier University

Potter, Hillary
Metropolitan State College of Denver

Pratt, Monica
Families Against Mandatory Minimums

Price, Mary
Families Against Mandatory Minimums

Purvis, Darcy J.
University of California, Irvine

Raguso, Francine C.
Montclair State University

Rasche, Chris
University of North Florida

Richards, Stephen C.
University of Wisconsin–Oshkosh

Roark, Eric
Iowa State University

Robert, Dominique
University of Ottawa

Roberts, Albert R.
The State University of New Jersey, Rutgers

Roberts, H. Seth
Independent Scholar

Roberts, John W.
University of North Carolina

Robinson, Douglas Neil
Valdosta State University

Roots, Roger
University of Nevada, Las Vegas

Ross, Jeffrey Ian
University of Baltimore

Rothe, Dawn
Western Michigan University

Roy, Jennifer
Eastern Michigan University

Ryan, T. A.
University of South Carolina

Salisbury, Emily J.
University of Cincinnati

Samarco, Vince
Saginaw Valley State University

Santos, Michael
Inmate and Independent Scholar

Schlager, Melinda D.
New Jersey State Parole Board

Schneider, Chris
Northern Illinois University

Schneider, Jennifer E.
The State University of New Jersey, Rutgers

SchWeber, Claudine
University of Maryland, University College

Scott, Gregory S.
DePaul University

Sharp, Susan F.
University of Oklahoma

Shelden, Randall G.
University of Nevada–Las Vegas

Spiropoulos, Georgia
University of Cincinnati

St. Germain, Ryan
Fordham University

Steiner, Benjamin
Boise State University

Steinmann, Rick
Lindenwood University

Stemple, Lara
Executive Director, Stop Prisoner Rape

Stone, Josh
Northern Illinois University

Sudbury, Julia
University of Toronto

Sullivan, Charles
*National CURE (Citizens United for
   Rehabilitation of Errants)*

Sullivan, Larry E.
John Jay College of Criminal Justice

Sullivan, Pauline
*National CURE (Citizens United for
   Rehabilitation of Errants)*

Sumner, Jennifer Macy
University of California, Irvine

Sumter, Melvina
Old Dominion University

Tatumb, B.
Grambling State University

Taylor, David B.
Niagara University

Tewksbury, Richard
University of Louisville

Thomas, Jim
Northern Illinois University

Thompson, Douglas
Chicago State University

Trager, Jennifer S.
University of Cincinnati

Trounstine, Jean
Middlesex Community College

Ulsperger, Jason
Southern Arkansas University

Urbina, Martin G
University of Wisconsin–Milwaukee

Vancee, Stephen
National Center on Institutions and Alternatives

Van Voorhis, Patricia
University of Cincinnati

Vaughn, Michael S.
Georgia State University

Waid, Courtney A.
Florida State University

Walker-Richardson, Rosaletta
Middle Tennessee State University

Wallace, Lisa Hutchinson
University of Alaska–Fairbanks

Ward, David A.
University of Minnesota

Waters, Laura Jean
Fordham University

Webb, Clive
University of Sussex

Webb, Kelly R.
Eastern Kentucky University

Weiss, Robert P.
Plattsburgh State University of New York

Welch, Kelly
Florida State University

Welch, Michael
The State University of New Jersey, Rutgers

Westerberg, Charles
Beloit College

Wilkinson, Molly
Dona Ana Branch Community College

Williams, Ernest R.
Medical Director, Institutional Health Services,
  Orange County Health Care Agency

Williams III, Frank P.
Prairie View A&M University

Wilson, Robin
Correctional Service of Canada

Yates, Pamela
Correctional Service of Canada

Yearwood, Douglas L.
Governor's Crime Commission, North Carolina

Zaitzow, Barbara
Appalachian State University

Zgoba, Kristen Marie
The State University of New Jersey, Rutgers

Chronology

1858	Joliet Penitentiary opens in Illinois
1868	British transportation of convicts to Australia ends
1870–1919	**Reformatory era**
1870	American Prison Congress (forerunner of American Correctional Association)— *Declaration of Principles* enacted
1871	*Ruffin v. Commonwealth* establishes that convicted felons not only forfeit liberty but are slaves of the state; this provides the legal justification for courts to maintain a hands-off doctrine
1873	The first women's prison, the Indiana Reformatory Institution, opens
1876	Zebulon Brockway initiates America's first parole system in Elmira Reformatory
1878	First probation law is passed in Massachusetts
1880	Louisiana State Prison opens at Angola
1890s–1930s	**Progressive era**
1891	Congress passes the Three Prisons Act, establishing federal prison system
1895	Gladstone Commission in United Kingdom ushers in new era of punishment
1899	First juvenile court established in Cook County, Illinois
1904	Parchman Farm opens in Mississippi
1914	Passing of the Harrison Act leads to incarceration of people convicted of narcotic-related offenses
1919	Volstead Act
1920	The American Civil Liberties Union founded
1926	Stateville Penitentiary is founded in Illinois
1927	The federal government opens its first women's institution, the Federal Industrial Reformatory and Industrial Farm for Women at Alderson, West Virginia
1928–1931	Wickersham Commission
1929	Hawes-Cooper Act passed to regulate interstate sale of prisoner-made goods
1930s–1960s	**Medical model**
1930	The Federal Bureau of Prisons is established
1933	The Federal Bureau of Prisons establishes first prison medical center at FMC Springfield
1934	Alcatraz opens
1942	Relocation centers open to confine Japanese and Japanese Americans during World War II
1946	Last of relocation centers closes
1949	Geneva Convention relative to the Treatment of Prisoners of War adopted
1950	Youth Corrections Act passed to create rehabilitative treatment for offenders under the age of 22 in the federal system and the District of Columbia
1958	Gresham Sykes publishes *The Society of Captives*
1960s–1970s	**Community model**
1961	*Monroe v. Pape* resurrected 19th-century post–Civil War legislation (Title 42 Section 1983) allowing federal litigation against those acting under color of state law for depriving of civil rights; provides the basis for prisoner civil rights litigation
1963	Alcatraz closes and U.S. Penitentiary Marion opens
1964	*Cooper v. Pate* overturns *Ruffin*, formally recognizing the constitutional rights of prisoners
1965	Congress passes Title IV of the Higher Education Act, which provides for Pell grants for prisoners to pursue college education
	President Lyndon Johnson creates the President's Commission on Law Enforcement and the Administration of Justice
1966	*In re Kent,* "essentials of due process" required for juveniles
	The Black Panther Party (BPP) forms in Oakland, California
1967	*In re Gault,* Supreme Court rules that juvenile offenders are entitled to state-provided counsel and due process guarantees

	Report of the President's Commission on Law Enforcement and the Administration of Justice is published with 200 recommendations for changes to the criminal justice system
1970	Eastern State Penitentiary closes
	Through the efforts of Jerome Miller, Massachusetts becomes to first state to start closing all of its reform schools; all are closed by 1972
1971	Attica rebellion
	The first black warden is appointed in the federal prison system
	David Rothman publishes *The Discovery of the Asylum: Social Order and Disorder in the New Republic* that critically reevaluates the treatment of the mentally ill in the United States
1972	*Furman v. Georgia,* Supreme Court effectively voids 40 death penalty statutes and suspends the death penalty as "cruel and unusual punishment"
	President Richard M. Nixon declares the initial "war on drugs"
	ACLU founds the National Prison Project to strengthen prisoners' rights
1974	*Wolff v. McDonnell* allows inmates certain due-process rights in prison disciplinary hearings
	Robert Martinson's article "What Works?" appears in *The Public Interest*
	The Juvenile Justice and Delinquency Prevention Act passed
1975	Michel Foucault publishes *Surveiller et Punir*, translated into English as *Discipline and Punish* in 1977
1976	*Gregg v. Georgia* reinstates death penalty
	Estelle v. Gamble deliberate indifference to medical needs violates constitutional rights
	Maine is first U.S. state to abolish parole
	The first female officer is appointed to work in a male federal prison at Lompoc, California
1977	Leonard Peltier imprisoned
	Coker v. Georgia establishes that death penalty is an unconstitutional punishment for rape of an adult woman when the victim is not killed
	Gary Gilmore is put to death by firing squad, the first person executed since the reinstatement of the death penalty
1979	*Bell v. Wolfish* signals a return to a hands-off approach by the courts
	Prison Industry Enhancement Certification Program repealed Depression-era limitations on the interstate commerce in prison-made goods
	Organization "Stop Prisoner Rape" is founded by survivors of prison rape
	The Bureau of Justice Statistics is founded within the U.S. Department of Justice
1980s–present	**Crime control model**
1980	*Ruiz v. Estelle* establishes that conditions of confinement in entire Texas state prison system are unconstitutional
	New Mexico Prison riot
1981	The first woman warden of a men's federal prison is appointed at Butner
	Pat Carlen publishes *Women's Imprisonment* in Britain, one of the first critical sociological studies of a women's prison
1982	President Ronald Reagan declares a "war on drugs"
	Federal Bureau of Prisons establishes residential staff training program at Glynco, Georgia
	Federal Bureau of Prisons establishes first mandatory literacy program
1984	Congress passes the Sentencing Reform Act of 1984, as part of the Comprehensive Crime Control Act and creates the U.S. Sentencing Commission
	Velma Barfield becomes the first woman executed since reinstatement of the death penalty
	Congress passes Young Offender Act
	Hudson v. Palmer, Supreme Court rules that prison administrators are obligated to provide an environment for inmates and prison employees that is both secure and sanitary

	The state of Tennessee ushers in the new age of privatization by contracting Hamilton County Jail facility to be run by Corrections Corporation of America
1985	Nicole Hahn Rafter publishes *Partial Justice: Women, Prisons and Social Control*
1986	Congress passes first Anti-Drug Abuse Act that increases prison sentences for the sale and possession of drugs, eliminates probation or parole for certain drug offenders, increases fines, and provides for the forfeiture of assets
1987	*McCleskey v. Kemp,* Supreme Court rules that racial disparities not recognized as a constitutional violation of "equal protection of the law" unless intentional racial discrimination against the defendant can be shown
	Cuban detainees, from the Mariel boat lift, riot at the Atlanta and Oakdale, Louisiana, federal prisons
1988	*Thompson v. Oklahoma* establishes that executions of offenders ages 15 and younger at the time of their crimes is unconstitutional
	Congress passes the Civil Liberties Act and apologizes to Japanese American community for wartime detention in relocation centers
	Congress passes second Anti-Drug Abuse Act that introduces differential treatment for crack and powder cocaine and mandatory imprisonment for simple possession of more than 5 grams of crack cocaine
	California State Prison, Corcoran, opens; it is later dubbed "America's most violent prison"
1989	*Penry v. Lynaugh,* Supreme Court rules that executing persons with mental retardation is not a violation of the Eighth Amendment
	Number of black people incarcerated becomes greater than number of whites across the United States penal system for the first time
	Stanford v. Kentucky and *Wilkins v. Missouri,* Court rules that Eighth Amendment does not prohibit the death penalty for crimes committed at age 16 or 17
	John Braithwaite publishes *Crime, Shame and Reintegration*, which proposes a new approach to punishment based on restorative justice
1990	David Garland publishes *Punishment and Modern Society*
	Wilson v. Seiter establishes that prisoners must demonstrate that prison staff acted with "deliberate indifference" to prove "cruel and unusual" conditions
	The Solicitor General of Canada publishes *Creating Choices*, the first government report on women's prisons that is based on feminist or women-centered principles
1992	Washington State becomes the first jurisdiction to enact legislation known as "three strikes you're out"
1994	Congress passes the Violent Crime Control and Law Enforcement Act
	California brings in three-strikes legislation
	The Federal Bureau of Prisons opens its supermaximum secure facility, ADX Florence
	New Jersey passes Megan's Law requiring public notification of presence of former sex offenders in the community
1995	Pell grants are abolished for prisoners as a result of the Violent Crime Control and Law Enforcement Act
	Alabama, Arizona, Florida, Indiana, Iowa, Maryland, Oklahoma, and Wisconsin reinstate chain gangs
	Religious Freedom Restoration Act expands rights of prisoners to practice their religion in prison
1996	Congress passes the Prison Litigation Reform Act (PLRA) to limit prisoner litigation
	Congress passes the Illegal Immigration Reform Immigrant Responsibility Act that expands the capacity of the Immigration and Naturalization Service to detain foreigners
	California Supreme Court rules in *People v. Superior Court* that judges may dismiss allegations of prior felonies in second- and third-strike cases "in the interest of justice"

1997	Congress passes the National Capital Revitalization and Self-Government Improvement Act abolishing the D.C. system of corrections
	Critical Resistance established in Berkeley, California
1998	Allen Hornblum publishes *Acres of Skin: Human Experiments at Holmesburg Prison* that reveals extent of medical experiments on prisoners
1999	Number of people incarcerated in the U.S. is, for the first time, greater than 2 million
	Eleven of the Puerto Rican nationalists imprisoned since the 1980s are granted presidential pardons by President Bill Clinton
2000	Attica Brothers Legal Defense Fund wins a $12 million settlement for survivors of the Attica rebellion
	Illinois Governor George Ryan announces a moratorium on capital punishment in Illinois
2001	USA PATRIOT Act passed, in response to the September 11, 2001, terrorist attacks on the United States
	Enemy combatants are placed at Camp X-Ray at Guantanamo Bay, Cuba without trial or access to lawyers for an indefinite period of time
2002	*Ring v. Arizona,* Supreme Court rules that only a jury may pass a death sentence
	Atkins v. Virginia, Supreme Court rules that executing persons with mental retardation is unconstitutional
	Camp Delta, a permanent detention center for enemy combatants, opens at Guantánamo Bay, Cuba
2003	Congress passes Prisoner Rape Elimination Act designed to end prisoner rape
	Illinois Governor George Ryan commutes the death penalty of 160 inmates on death row
2004	First military tribunals held for inmates from Guantánamo Bay
	Abuse of prisoners at Abu Ghraib prison in Baghdad, Iraq, by U.S. military personnel becomes public
	Blakely v. Washington, Supreme Court rules that judges may not use their discretion to enhance sentences; activists believe this decision may affect the federal sentencing guidelines, particularly as they have been applied to those convicted of drug offenses

Introduction

The United States confines more people per capita than any other equivalent industrialized, democratic country. It is also one of the last remaining such nations to practice capital punishment, and one of only a handful of countries anywhere that executes juveniles. Sentences are longer in the United States than in most places, and the numbers of people of color behind bars is particularly disproportionate to their presence in society. In 1999, the United States crossed a threshold when, for the first time, the nation's penal institutions held more than 2 million people. In fact, prisons, jails, and detention centers have been filling since the 1980s at a rate faster than most can handle. As a result, overcrowding is rampant, even with growing numbers of privately run facilities being established and new state and federal institutions being opened each year.

This encyclopedia is a timely and necessary publication for anyone wishing to understand why confinement has become so commonplace in the United States. As many of the entries detail, prisons have become big business in the United States, spawning not just private prison companies but also a multitude of small businesses that service penal facilities (maintenance, laundry, food, clothing, etc.). In some communities, prisons provide one of the only sources of employment. In others, they have taken away almost all of the young men.

As increasing numbers of men, women, and children are being locked up—the prison, the jail, and the detention center are becoming part of many people's lives. The collateral effect of incarcerating more than 2 million is enormous. Many of us now know someone behind bars. More than that, however, prisons are part of our collective cultural imagination. We, as a society, seem to find it hard to imagine a different solution to criminal behavior.

Yet, as the historical entries in these two volumes demonstrate, the prison has not been used so extensively for very long. Moreover, as other authors show, there are numerous alternative possible ways of dealing with those who break the law.

This encyclopedia draws together up-to-date statistics and academic research to sketch out the scope of prisons and punishment in the United States. Its goal is to provide information on all the different types of penal facilities currently being used while keeping a broad focus on the prison itself. Authors strive, where possible, to address issues of race and gender and to make clear how current and historical policies and practices have affected communities and individuals differently.

All of the entries are written in an accessible and engaging style that aims to be appealing for a wide readership. We hope that high school students, visitors to the public library, those who are confined, and criminal justice practitioners, and academics can all find matters of interest to them here. By including race and gender in each entry, the authors have sought to provide a critical assessment of their topic that reveals the differential impact of criminal justice policy.

Though the primary focus of the encyclopedia is on the United States, where possible authors have included comparative information about what is happening elsewhere around the world. There are also specific entries on a handful of other English-speaking penal systems, to provide a sense of comparison.

THEMES

With nearly 400 entries, the two volumes truly provide an encyclopedic analysis of prisons and correctional facilities. To help the reader make sense of the wealth of information included in this collection, it is possible to characterize all of the topics into 12 distinct, yet overlapping, themes.

First, a number of entries are concerned with *prison architecture*. In them, authors map out the historical development of the physical design of penal institutions, showing how changing ideas and goals of punishment, along with the arrival of specific populations, and overcrowding, influence the way in which prisons are built. Likewise, how a correctional facility is designed shapes how prisoners are treated. To illustrate the effect of design, a number of specific prisons are described in some detail.

Theories of punishment constitute the second major theme in the encyclopedia. Specific entries describe goals of punishment, from deterrence to incapacitation. Accounts of particular methods of dealing with offenders, such as the capital punishment, explain how certain practices correspond to particular ideas about what punishment can achieve.

Entries on *prison populations* provide detailed accounts of specific groups of people within penal establishments. Particular attention is given to those groups that are particularly overrepresented such as African Americans and Latino/as. Women prisoners and the elderly are also dealt with separately, as are juvenile offenders.

A number of authors tackle *prison reform*, describing specific groups and organizations that are currently active, as well as individuals who have been crucial to attempts to ameliorate conditions within prison. Entries on abolition and activism point to alternative ideas about punishment that do not involve confinement.

Juvenile justice is another key theme. As with the entries on adult prisons, authors examine treatment of young offenders in historical and contemporary settings. Attention is paid to specific legal cases that particularly affected the treatment of juveniles and to key institutions where they were housed.

Staff are crucial to any penal institution. To that end, a number of entries examine the historical development of correctional officers as well as their present work conditions. Attention is paid to the issue of professionalism, as well as to staff training.

To convey how prisons attempt to address offending behavior, a number of authors focus on a range of *treatment programs*. Topics in this field include psychological services, drug treatment programs, Alcoholics Anonymous, work, education, and vocational courses. There are also a number of entries on related issues such as prison health care, mental health care, HIV/AIDS, and gynecology.

As the penal system in the United States has become increasingly overcrowded, many aspects of it have been handed over to private companies. As a result, *privatization* is another common strand of this encyclopedia. Entries provide information about the move to the private sector overall, as well as describing specific parts of prison life that are now run by corporations. Entries are also included on the two biggest private prison companies in the United States.

Ever since the first penitentiaries, prisoners have been put to *labor*. In a number of entries, authors describe the historical development and changing nature of prison work. They also detail how penal systems train inmates in employable skills to help reduce reoffending rates.

Where possible, each entry in this encyclopedia includes an examination of *race, gender, and class*. Some entries concentrate specifically on these issues, to describe racial dynamics, racism, or specific groups of inmates.

Prisons and other correctional facilities are shaped by the context of *sentencing policy and laws*. Authors describe significant legal cases that have changed penal policy, as well as explain the relevance of constitutional amendments to prison policy. Sentencing guidelines, sentencing laws, and the rationale for different types of sentences are also considered.

Finally, certain entries center on issues of *security and classification*. These include examinations of classification systems, along with description and analysis of prison discipline. The different levels of security are also explained individually, while examples of key types of institutions are outlined. Related topics include entries on specific types of punishment such as probation, parole, community corrections, electronic monitoring, and house arrest.

ORGANIZATION

The entries are organized alphabetically. Each one is cross-referenced to point the reader to related topics that they might find relevant. The essays also all include a list of further readings to help the reader in any additional research. The index provides a guide to the topics covered in specific entries as well as those listed under alternative names.

SIDEBARS AND ILLUSTRATIONS

The encyclopedia contains 25 sidebars and a number of illustrations, including graphs, tables, and photos. In the sidebars, prisoners share their firsthand accounts of life behind bars.

APPENDIX

The appendix lists institutions in the federal prison system. Included in this list are the address and location of each facility, along with brief descriptions of the programs and treatment each place offers. It gives an overview of one of the largest and most important prison systems in the United States

to provide a greater sense of the opportunities available for those behind bars.

CHRONOLOGY

A detailed timeline is listed at the start of each volume. This chronology dates key legal cases, publications, and the founding of certain penal establishments in the United States.

CONCLUSION

While a collection of this size is not designed to be read cover to cover, it is hoped that readers will find the information in each entry absorbing enough to lead them onto another. To that end, readers should take note of the cross-references listed below each entry to direct them to other, related areas. As with all reference books, this collection is designed not just to inform but also to explain and analyze. Reflecting the work of many different individuals, at various stages in their careers and from a number of different places, this encyclopedia aims to provide the most comprehensive overview of issues related to prisons, punishment, and confinement in the United States today.

Acknowledgments

There are many people to thank for helping to pull together this collection of entries. First of all, I have been incredibly fortunate in my editorial team. Jeanne Flavin, Jim Thomas, Esther Heffernan, and Stephanie Bush-Baskette really went above and beyond the call of duty. Not only did they help put together the list of topics, but also they helped me edit some of the thornier pieces of prose that I received. Most important, they did all this with good humor, generosity of spirit, and speed. They particularly stepped into the breach when I experienced the joyful surprise of my daughter Ella arriving one month early and thereby disrupting the scheduled completion of this encyclopedia.

At Sage, I would like to thank Rolf Janke and Jerry Westby for asking me to edit these two volumes. Working with them is always a pleasure. Vonessa Vondera managed to keep the list of contributors and all other organizational matters in order, allowing me to stay focused on editing, while Kate Peterson and Pam Suwinsky have done a wonderful job correcting minor errors and smoothing out stylistic flaws during the copyediting process. Denise Santoyo ensured that all the final issues were resolved so that the encyclopedia could actually be published.

Although there have definitely been moments in its completion where I swore never to be involved in a project of this size again, it has been a fascinating experience that I am pleased to have undertaken. Not only has the encyclopedia enabled me to make contact with most of the interesting people in my field of prisons research, but also I have learned a lot from reading each entry. To that end, I would like to thank the more than 250 authors who are responsible for the entries that I have edited. Drawn from across the United States, as well as from the United Kingdom, Australia, New Zealand, and Canada, they have sought to define their allotted topics in ways that are accessible to a general readership while remaining rigorously academic. This dual task of an encyclopedia is not always easy, yet it is important. Each author also strove to include information about race and gender in order to avoid generalizing.

Others who have helped include Chelsea Adewunmi, who transcribed all of the prisoner entries and helped edit them, while also organizing all my computer files so I could be sure of which entries I still needed to chase up. I also appreciate the assistance of Michal Bosworth, Marianne Fisher-Giordano, Paul Lucko, and Shoshana Pollack, all of whom read through some entries and gave suggestions for changes. The various prisoners who have contributed the information for the sidebars also need to be acknowledged, particularly Seth Ferranti, who organized a number of men to write about their experiences.

Finally, I'd like to thank Anthony for helping out on the home front and for always being enthusiastic about this project. He kept reminding me of the utility that encyclopedias play in disseminating information from the confines of the academy to the general public. I'd like to dedicate this to Ella, who is wriggling on my knee, saying "ooh ooh ooh" as I type this one-handed. She has made the finishing-up stage of this encyclopedia much more amusing than it might otherwise have been, if a little slower than planned.

About the Editor

Mary Bosworth is Assistant Professor of Sociology at Wesleyan University in Connecticut. She has published extensively on a number of different aspects of imprisonment. Her first book, *Engendering Resistance: Agency and Power in Women's Prisons* (1999), analyzes contemporary women's imprisonment in England in light of feminist theory. In contrast, her second book, *The U.S. Federal Prison System* (2002), is designed as a resource for prisoners and their families as well as prisons researchers and practitioners. In it, Bosworth combines academic literature with government reports and firsthand prisoner accounts to explain and analyze key aspects of the federal prison system.

In addition to these two books, Bosworth has published numerous journal articles and book chapters on topics from the history of women's imprisonment in France to methodological issues in prisons research. She is currently coediting (with Jeanne Flavin) a collection of essays on race, gender, and punishment that will be published in 2005.

After finishing her PhD at the University of Cambridge in 1997, Bosworth started working in the United States in the Sociology and Anthropology Department at Fordham University in New York City. In 2002, she moved to the Sociology Department at Wesleyan University. She has been a visiting library fellow at the School of Criminal Justice at Rutgers University and a visiting scholar at the Maison Suger in Paris. In the summer of 2004, she was a visiting scholar at the Crime Research Centre at the University of Western Australia, and at the Institute d'études européennes at the Université de Montréal, where she conducted a comparative study of the detention of immigrants and foreigners in light of recent legislation. In fall 2004, she became a visiting scholar at the Oxford University Centre for Socio-legal Studies and at Wolfson College to continue this research. In December 2003, Mary Bosworth gave birth to her first child, Ella Michal Bosworth-Gerbino.

A

◪ ABBOTT, JACK HENRY (1944–2002)

Jack Henry Abbot is remembered as a complex and controversial figure in the history of U.S. prisons. In 1978, Abbott, while in prison, initiated a lengthy correspondence with author Norman Mailer, who was at the time writing *The Executioner's Song* (1979), a fictionalized biography of executed murderer Gary Gilmore. Abbott and Gilmore served time together in the Utah state penitentiary. Mailer not only was eager to learn more about Gilmore but also took an interest in Abbott's own writings. He was, apparently, impressed by Abbott's ability to convey the stark reality of prison life and was instrumental in having Abbott's letters published in the prestigious *New York Review of Books*. Self-educated, Abbott delved into the revolutionary philosophies of Mao and Stalin and wrote critically about violence and racism in America and in its prisons.

In the Belly of the Beast

Abbott's collection of writings culminated in the publication of the autobiographical text *In the Belly of the Beast* (1981). The book, featuring an introduction by Mailer, was commercially successful and highly acclaimed by critics. In it Abbott chronicles his life as a state-raised convict. He spent the better part of his first 12 years being shuttled among foster homes before being sent to the Utah state reformatory. At age 18, he was released, but only six months later he was sent to the Utah penitentiary to serve time for writing bad checks. Three years later, he stabbed one inmate to death and injured another in a prison brawl, adding more time to his sentence. In 1971, at the age of 25, he escaped briefly and robbed a bank, an offense that added a 19-year federal sentence on top of state time. In the *New York Times Book Review,* critic Terrence Des Pres called Abbott's book "awesome, brilliant, perversely ingenuous; its impact is indelible, and as an articulation of penal nightmare it is completely compelling" (Worth, 2002, p. B2).

When Abbott was being considered for parole, Mailer wrote a supportive letter on his behalf: "Mr. Abbott has the makings of a powerful and important writer" (Worth, 2002, p. B1). Mailer pleaded for Abbott's release, guaranteeing him gainful employment; subsequently, Abbott was transferred to a New York halfway house in early in June 1981 where he worked as a researcher earning $150 a week. Abbott was quickly embraced as a curious celebrity, appearing on nationally televised news programs and attending dinners with New York's literary elite.

THE MURDER OF RICHARD ADAN

Just six weeks after his release, Abbott's fame turned tragic when, during a confrontation outside a restaurant, he stabbed a man to death. His victim, Richard Adan, was a 22-year-old aspiring actor working nights as a waiter. The murder brought intense criticism of Mailer, who was ridiculed for having romanticized Abbot for his literary talent while failing to recognize the ex-con's capacity for violence. Mailer said he "felt a large responsibility" for the death of Adan, insisting that he "never thought Abbott was close to killing and that's why I have to sit in judgment on myself. I just was not sensitive to the fact" (Worth, 2002, p. B1).

After the deadly incident, Abbott eluded police and fled New York City. Following a month-long manhunt, he was apprehended in Louisiana and extradited to New York where he was convicted of first-degree manslaughter and sentenced to 15 years to life. In 1990, Abbott was sued in civil court by Adan's widow, who was awarded $7.57 million in damages. The award included Abbott's future earnings as well as the $100,000 he had already earned from *In the Belly of the Beast* and $15,000 he had earned from the rights to a film about the murder and another book he had written titled *My Return* (1987). Abbott had already been barred from using any of the proceeds of *My Return* under New York State's so-called Son of Sam law that prevents offenders from profiting from their crimes.

CONCLUSION

In 2002, corrections officers at the Wende Correctional Facility (New York) found Abbott, age 58, hanging from a bed sheet, an apparent suicide. After learning of Abbott's death, Mailer lamented: "His life was tragic from beginning to end. I never knew a man who had a worse life. What made it doubly awful is that he brought a deadly tragedy down on one young man full of promise and left a bomb crater of lost possibilities for many, including most especially himself" (Worth, 2002, p. B1).

—*Michael Welch*

See also Celebrities in Prison; Convict Criminology; Deterrence Theory; Federal Prison System; Gary Gilmore; John Irwin; George Jackson; Juvenile Justice System; Juvenile Reformatories; Parole; Prison Culture; Prisoner Writing; Prisonization; Rehabilitation Theory; Solitary Confinement; Special Housing Unit

Further Reading

Abbott, J. H. (1981). *In the belly of the beast: Letters from prison.* New York: Vintage.

Abbott, J. H., with Zack, N. (1987). *My return.* Buffalo, NY: Prometheus.

Worth, R. F. (2002, February 11). Jailhouse author helped by Mailer is found dead. *New York Times,* pp. B1, B2.

◪ ABOLITION

The term *abolition* emerged during the 1830s to define a means of ending slavery. According to abolitionists slavery could be wiped out only by abandoning it and all the structures dependent on it altogether. In contrast, other antislavery activists at the time known as *gradualists* sought to end slavery by buying slaves and setting them free. Gradualism did little to reduce or eliminate the slave system since it did not target the root of the practice. Similar divisions exist within the field of criminal justice. Unlike other reformers who want to change, improve, or better the existing justice system, abolitionists wish to do away with it altogether. Reformers who are not abolitionists usually lobby for more humanitarian treatment of offenders, while seeking to reduce prison terms, or alter criminal law in some manner. Such a course calls for modifications— often substantial—without challenging the institutional or philosophical base on which the system is constructed. In contrast, abolitionists want to either eradicate whole elements of the current punishment system or bring an end to it entirely. They also advocate for a variety of alternatives.

Contemporary abolitionism dates from the countercultural political movements of the 1960s and 1970s. As a relatively new force on the penal landscape it is still evolving. Initially defined by its opposition to incarceration as a means of punishment and thus identified as *prison abolition,* in the mid-1980s the abolitionist position became one of *penal abolitionism*. Penal abolitionists—activists, ex-prisoners, academics, religious actors, politicians, inmates and their families, laborers, students—are opposed to an adversarial criminal justice system that promotes and supports revenge, punitive imprisonment, retribution, and coercion. They are also equally concerned with victims and offenders since they believe that the current systems fail both parties as well as the community.

HISTORY OF THE MOVEMENT

Penal reformers began to criticize methods and practices of punishment almost as soon as the modern criminal justice system was established at the end of the 18th century. The rise of a resolute abolitionist ideology, however, is a far more recent phenomenon. Seeds for such a movement grew within the academy and at the grassroots level in the United States and Europe during the 1960s and 1970s when dramatic social and political upheaval led many to call the mainstream and its institutions, including the criminal justice system, into question.

Academics and students during this period began to examine what crime was, where it came from, and how society dealt with it. In the process, they created numerous approaches to criminology, defining themselves and associating their ideas with a variety of titles—radical, structural, feminist, peace-making, neo-Marxist, left realist—all of which fell under the heading of *critical criminology*. Critical criminologists were (and remain) deeply concerned with issues of class, race, economic structures, inequity, power, social control, and gender. These scholars chronicled the harm, inefficacy, and problems of the criminal justice system calling into question its ideological, philosophical, and theoretical foundation. They also disputed the role of "professionals" in resolving such problems, calling instead for the inclusion of inmates, ex-convicts, and those most affected by penal policy. At the ninth World Conference of Criminology, held in Vienna, academics presented themselves as *abolitionists* for the first time.

As such ideas were being explored and expanded within the academy, abolitionist activism of another sort was taking shape on the ground. In the late 1960s, a prison reform movement was brewing in Scandinavia. The National Swedish Association for Penal Reform, known as KRUM, was founded in 1966. After just a few years this reform organization developed into the first unequivocally abolitionist body. Their assembly was composed of prisoners, ex-prisoners, lawyers, social workers, sociologists, inmate's families, and psychiatrists thus representing a novel cohort. As members worked on humanitarian and "treatment" issues inside correctional facilities, they began to believe that mere reform would not suffice. It would not be enough simply to alter or amend the system in certain ways since these would not change its fundamental principles and customs that were deeply troubling and profoundly entrenched. The modern-day penal model, as they saw it, was flawed and not receptive to reform. This experience served to clarify and radicalize their approach to social change. They began to generate new ideas, strategies, and sentiments about prison rather than attempt to modify specific penal policies. By 1971, the group defined its mission as one "to abolish imprisonment and other types of forced incarceration." As the Swedish group evolved, similar groups materialized: KROM in Norway, KRIM in Denmark, and KRIM in Finland. An abolitionist movement had been born.

RELIGION, ABOLITIONISM, AND NORTH AMERICA

Though a global movement, abolitionism in Canada and the United States exhibits many distinct characteristics. In this part of the world, religious groups and individuals driven by faith have been an integral part of abolitionist activity from the start. In fact, abolitionism is, in many ways, the latest chapter of an enduring tradition of activism going back more than 200 years. The Quakers, specifically, who are closely associated with the creation of the penitentiary at the end of the 18th century, were active in establishing the North American abolitionist movement during the last quarter of the 20th century.

For example, Fay Honey Knopp, a Vermont Quaker and prison minister, founded the Prison Research Education Project (PREAP) in 1976. During that same year, PREAP published *Instead of Prison: A Handbook for Abolitionists,* which was designed as a "how to" manual. The volume served to organize and galvanize penal activists around North America. By the 1980s, PREAP was renamed the Safer Society Program and Press and continued to work in a variety of ways toward an alternative punishment landscape. An abolitionist trend was emerging and traveling north.

The Canadian Quaker Committee on Jails and Justice, an active penal reform organization, officially declared support for the elimination of prisons in 1981. Within a year it grew beyond the continent to become ICOPA, International Circle of Prison Abolitionists. In the spring of 1983, the first of ICOPA's prison abolition conferences was held at the University of Toronto. This unprecedented gathering was the first of what have become annual events. The conference, which moves around the world, offers a means for the abolitionists to transcend their geographic borders and share ideas, cultivate strategies, and educate others. The meetings are financially supported by the International Foundation for a Prisonless Society. Since 1987, the "P" in ICOPA has stood for "penal" instead of "prison" reflecting the growing complexity and nuance of the abolitionist approach.

IF NOT PRISON—THEN WHAT?

Abolitionists reject the existing retributive paradigm and work to overthrow it. They seek to create and promote alternative responses to crime and punishment based on forgiveness by encouraging practices that reduce domination and harm, mandate citizen participation and establish a central role for the victim. They regard offenders as valued community members and believe that the processes of justice may help to solidify social cohesion, prevent crime, and reduce victimization. As the paragraphs below demonstrate, scholars and activists promote a number of different ways of trying to eradicate the current system.

Abolitionists such as Louk Hulsman (1991) and Heinz Steinert (1991) argue that criminal events are unexceptional and should be dealt with as we do a wide range of other community problems including floods, fire, and public health. In other words, we should view crime as a conflict that is a normal part of life and living together, rather than as a remarkable occurrence. Others, including Richard Quinney and Harold Pepinsky, speak of "making peace" on crime and violence. Their approach is primarily a theoretical one in which they hope to change the language and retributive thinking around crime and punishment. They support practices that work to foster peace between affected parties—victims, offenders, survivors, and family members—and within the community.

Theology is central to many in the penal abolition movement, including Ruth Morris, Howard Zehr, and Dan Van Ness, who argue for religious or faith-based responses to crime and justice. Using the Bible and religious tenets as their basis, these activists promote programs centered around mercy, pardon, restoration, amnesty, and healing. There are yet others, such as Sebastian Scheerer and Herman Bianchi, who favor the processes of civil courts over criminal ones. For them, disputes should be settled between the parties directly involved in the criminal event rather by a state-run "monopoly" that defines and resolves such occurrences.

Many abolitionists, including Stanley Cohen, Thomas Mathiesen, and Nils Christie, also address quite specifically the logistics of how to replace revenge-based punishments. Reflecting their criticisms of structured and rule-bound institutions such as prisons and courts, their strategies focus on the importance of decentralization. They assert that communities rather than the state must control the justice process. Responsibilities must therefore shift from professionals to citizens who take an active role in community affairs. Most important, society should stop relying on incarceration. Instead we must release the vast majority of those who are currently incarcerated while diverting new offenders from possible prison sentences into alternative programs. They also identify the need to cultivate new language to foster new ways of thinking and doing justice. The term abolitionism itself, based as it is in the prison paradigm, is problematic and may need to be changed.

CONCLUSION: THE FUTURE OF ABOLITIONISM

Abolitionists work to liberate societies from a static repressive penal system that reflects and sustains prevailing unjust power relations. They seek to imagine what else can be both within and beyond the realm of criminal justice. Scholars argue that the dawn of the new millennium marks a crossroads for penology. Prisons are draining the fiscal coffers, do not appear to deter crime, hold disproportionate numbers of people of color and the poor, and have failed to deliver on virtually every promise. The rehabilitation-retribution cycle has come around so many times that each commands nothing more than cynicism and resignation.

Many abolitionists have embraced and champion an emerging innovative approach directed toward resolving and responding to criminal events known as *restorative justice*. Restorative justice is touted as the harbinger of a much needed paradigm shift and prison alternative. Yet many urge caution, arguing that the movement cannot use notions associated with or integral to retributive justice since these keep it wedded to the same formula of repression, guilt, victims, and punishment. For example, critics ask, is restorative justice aiming to "restore" the community, victim, and offender back to the racist unequal standing that prevailed prior to the criminal event? Or can it do something more radical and far reaching?

Penal abolitionism is a global movement whose supporters are unified not by a single ideology or theory but rather a shared goal. For abolitionism to have a future it must be flexible and welcome new ideas. It must remain dynamic, responding to and evolving with the world it aims to change. Criminal justice may indeed be ready for change but the future is difficult to predict. Thirty years ago, penologists foretold the end of the prison only to witness the largest expansion and incarceration boom ever seen. The prison seems particularly adept at sustaining itself. That which intends to replace or reduce its use has historically been absorbed into the penal repertoire serving to expand and deepen the culture of control rather than diminish it. The challenge thus remains for abolitionists to imagine new possibilities and find ways of putting them into practice.

—*Dana Greene*

See also Capital Punishment; Community Corrections Centers; Convict Criminology; Critical Resistance; Angela Y. Davis; Determinate Sentencing; Elizabeth Gurley Flynn; Elizabeth Fry; John Howard; Indeterminate Sentencing; Intermediate Sanctions; Juvenile Justice System; Juvenile Reformatories; Fay Honey Knopp; Legitimacy; Parole; Quakers; Racism; Resistance; Restorative Justice; Slavery

Further Reading

Abel, R. L. (1991). The failure of punishment as social control. *Israel Law Review, 25,* 740–752.

Bianchi, H., & van Swaaningen, R. (Eds.). (1986). *Abolitionism: Towards a non-repressive approach to crime.* Amsterdam: Free University Press.

Christie, N. (1986). Suitable enemies. In H. Bianchi & R. van Swaaningen (Eds.), *Abolitionism: Towards a non-repressive approach to crime* (pp. 42–54). Amsterdam: Free University Press.

Cohen, S. (Ed.). (1986). *Contemporary crises: Law, crime and social policy, 10.* [Special abolitionism issue]. The Hague, Netherlands: Martinus Nijhoff.

Cohen, S. (1991). Alternatives to punishment—The abolitionist case. *Israel Law Review, 25,* 729–739.

Galanter, M. (1991). Punishment: Civil style. *Israel Law Review, 25,* 759–791.

Hulsman, L. (1991). The abolitionist case: Alternative crime policies. *Israel Law Review, 25,* 681–709.

Mathiesen, T. (1974). *The politics of abolition.* Oslo: Scandinavian University Books.

Pepinsky, H. E., & Quinney, R. (Eds.). (1991). *Criminology as peacemaking.* Bloomington: Indiana University Press.

Steinert, H. (1991). Is there justice? No—Just us. *Israel Law Review, 25,* 710–728.

Van Ness, D. W., & Strong, K. H. (2002). *Restoring justice* (2nd ed.). Cincinnati, OH: Anderson.

West, G. W., & Morris, R. (Eds.). (2000). *The case for penal abolition.* Toronto: Canadian Scholars' Press.

◪ ACCREDITATION

Accreditation is both a process within and a goal of corrections. The contemporary structures now in place for institutions and agencies to be accredited indicate an increasing professionalism within the field of corrections. Just as universities must be accredited in order to award degrees and to be perceived as legitimate places of learning, penal facilities seek accreditation from the American Correctional Association (ACA) to indicate that they are offering their services at a particularly high level. Unlike other processes of accreditation, however, there is no negative effect of failing to be certified.

One of the premises of modern institutional corrections is that offenders are sent to prison as punishment rather than for punishment. Through the accreditation process, correctional professionals are able to assess and improve all aspects of confinement within an institution and the conditions for those persons working within its walls. Yet accreditation is not a panacea that will eradicate the beliefs or behaviors of those persons who seek to punish inmates, or otherwise abuse their authority, nor will it change years of legislative neglect. Accreditation addresses the totality of correctional confinement conditions and their affects on inmates and staff by accentuating the positives and identifying areas for improvement.

THE PROCESS OF ACCREDITATION

Correctional facilities, field services, and agencies may become certified as having met or exceeded a comprehensive set of standards established by the ACA through a series of self-audits, reviews, site visits, and formal hearings, which may take up to 18 months to complete. Once it has been awarded, accreditation lasts for three years. ACA endorsement may be given to pretrial detention and incarceration facilities for adults as well as to juvenile institutional services and community corrections services (probation, parole, and intermediate sanctions) for both adult and juvenile offenders. There are also accreditation standards for health care services within corrections.

Accreditation requires far more than applying a new coat of paint or adding a second dessert on Sundays. First, the agency conducts a self-evaluation of its policies, finances, physical plant, staffing, training and professional development, health care,

inmate programs, and emergency services. This evaluation seeks to measure how well the agency is already complying with ACA standards (many of which are merely sound correctional practices) and which areas need improvements. The self-evaluation permits the agency to begin the process of improvement prior to a formal audit. During the 12 to 18 months that typically elapse between a self-evaluation and a formal audit, agencies work toward full compliance with ACA standards.

The formal audit is conducted by the Commission on Accreditation for Corrections, whose 25 members are drawn from juvenile and adult correctional associations, architects, health care associations, and interested persons outside of corrections. The commission sends three to five members to investigate the agency or institution under review. To be accredited, the institution must demonstrate 100% and 90% or better compliance with mandatory and nonmandatory standards, respectively. After its visit, the commission produces a final report in which the members either recommend ACA accreditation or describe the additional efforts that are required to meet the relevant standards.

Once an agency is accredited, it must submit annual reports listing compliance with existing standards and efforts to comply with new standards as they arise. It will be reinvestigated every three years. There are no direct penalties for an agency that fails to meet the requirements for accreditation by the ACA. Instead it is granted six to twelve months to meet those standards and provided with technical assistance to improve its level of compliance. It is then reevaluated by an accrediting team.

THE GOALS OF ACCREDITATION

Correctional agencies seek to provide more than just places of custody while responding to both internal and external influences. External pressures force correctional agencies to provide safe, humane custody within the fiscal and legislative boundaries imposed on them. Internal pressures are imposed by three constituent groups, each with its own needs: (1) inmates (medical, physical, psychological, rehabilitative), (2) correctional staff (preservice, inservice, and ongoing training; professional development; pay; morale), and (3) administrative/managerial staff (policy, procedures, defense against lawsuits, reduced liability, fiscal resources). In addition to meeting the needs mentioned here, the accreditation process also aims to evaluate existing strengths and weaknesses of the correctional agency and to develop measurable and attainable goals for reducing or removing those weaknesses.

THE BENEFITS OF ACCREDITATION

The Arkansas Department of Correction (ADC) offers a case in point on how the accreditation process can assist an agency that desires to improve itself. The Arkansas prison system was one of the worst in the United States during the 1970s. Confinement conditions in the plantation style prisons were harsh and brutal. Inmates worked long hours in the fields and cattle barns to return at night to barracks where trustees ruled in the absence of correctional officers and many other free-world staff members. Classification and programs were limited in number and scope. From an administrative perspective, the prison system was in poor condition as few administrative and fiscal controls existed and those that did were often disregarded.

After being declared unconstitutional as a result of *Holt v. Sarver* (1970), ADC made enough substantial improvements to warrant release from federal monitoring in 1973 and was declared to be constitutional in 1982. Since that time, ADC has continued to improve itself to the point that it applied for the self-evaluation leading to its first accreditation in 1981. Today, all of ADC's 17 units and 4 work release centers are ACA accredited, and one senior manager serves as an accreditation commission member helping other correctional professionals learn from their experiences. Indeed, ADC's Boot Camp was named "Best of the Best" by the ACA during 1998.

CONCLUSION

Increasingly, in the United States, correctional personnel and the agencies that employ them can claim professional status. This is due, in part, to the accreditation process associated with the ACA.

Today, correctional staff at all levels can point toward national minimum standards in education, training, and performance while agencies can identify minimum standards in administration and finances, operational policies and procedures, emergency procedures, programming, services, and physical plants as areas that an external, regulating organization has certified them as "professional." Compliance with these standards is ongoing among most agencies and reaccreditation occurs in a three-year cycle. Failure to meet or exceed those standards can result in decertification of this professional status. As noted previously, while there are no direct penalties for failing to be accredited or reaccredited, the loss of professional standing within corrections is often accompanied by intensified scrutiny by the courts when dealing with inmate litigation, increased liability, and decreases in staff morale. The costs of not being accredited far outweigh the costs to become accredited.

—*Allan L. Patenaude*

See also Actuarial Justice; American Correctional Association; Governance; Managerialism; Plantation Prisons; Professionalization of Staff; Staff Training; Trustee

Further Reading

American Correctional Association. (1993). *Standards for the administration of correctional agencies* (2nd ed.). College Park, MD: Author.
American Correctional Association. (2002). *Standards for adult correctional institutions* (4th ed.). College Park, MD: Author.

Legal Case

Holt v. Sarver, 309 F. Supp. (E.D. Ark., 1970).

◪ ACTIVISM

Prison activism is a broad-based social movement that addresses injustices in the criminal justice system. Thousands of individuals and organizations are moved to action by the current U.S. prison crisis and are working to change or abolish the system. Their work takes different forms and has varying goals that are not always in accordance with each other. There are large human rights organizations, such as Amnesty International and Human Rights Watch, that include prison issues in their broader work, as well as smaller local and national organizations, such as the Prison Moratorium Project and the Prison Activist Resource Center, devoted solely to reforming or abolishing the prison system. Organizations range from religious to political to youth based. Some focus on a single issue, such as freeing political prisoners, the lack of Pell grant availability for prisoners, or prisoner disenfranchisement, while others aim at changing the entire system.

Action takes a variety of forms. Some advocate groups work both in the courts, helping inmates with their individual legal battles, and in Congress, lobbying for the protection of prisoners' rights and policy changes. Others run workshops in prisons in areas such as poetry and visual arts. There are books-to-prisoner programs to supplement poorly stocked prison libraries. Postrelease organizations work to fill the void left by the state by offering education, job training, and placement opportunities to recently released prisoners. Many groups work on public education, exposing the myths about crime in the United States and the disproportionate impact of race, gender, and class in the criminal justice system.

HISTORY

Prisons originated out of a desire to reform the punishment of criminals. At the end of the 18th century, corporal and capital forms of punishment came to be seen as inhumane, and the "criminal" as one who could be reformed. However, while changes to the prison system throughout history are usually referred to as "reforms," the goals of early reformers were not necessarily aligned with the approach of prison activists today, many of whom seek to abolish the prison altogether. Rather, historical prison reformers such as the Pennsylvania Quakers were often just as concerned with improving the security or efficiency of prisons as they were with ameliorating conditions inside them.

Two figures in the first half of the 20th century stand out as prison activists. Clarence Darrow, the criminal defense lawyer who represented Eugene Debs before the Supreme Court, theorized on the criminalization of the poor. He argued that the only difference between those in prison and those not in prison was their financial situation. In 1902, during a speech to inmates at Cook County Jail in Chicago, Illinois, Darrow argued for the abolition of prisons. Taking particular contention with the death penalty, Darrow represented more than 200 defendants in capital cases, losing only one. Another figure from the early 1900s is Thomas Mott Osborne, former mayor of Auburn, New York. In 1913 he spent a week as an Auburn Prison inmate and published a book about his eye-opening experience. From that experience, Osborne worked to transform prisons into effective rehabilitative institutions, becoming a progressive warden at Sing Sing for a time. After working for the system, Osborne founded the Mutual Welfare League, which focused on postrelease opportunities for inmates.

The second half of the century saw a large growth in prison activism. For example, Caryl Chessman, executed by the State of California in 1960, left behind a legacy of prison activism. In his 12 years on death row in San Quentin, Chessman fought for, and won, a number of civil rights for prisoners, especially in the area of access to books and the right to write. It was these rights that radical prisoners in the 1970s like George Jackson (author of *Soledad Brother)* depended on to develop and express their views and galvanize the public and other prisoners.

In the 1970s, prison activism became more radical, as a movement to abolish prisons grew out of the Black Power and antiwar movements. Groups and individuals began to point to the racism within prison and the disproportionate application of incarceration on the poor. Especially in California, there were a number of politicized prisoners, some of whom were political prior to their incarceration and others who changed while in prison. George Jackson, who was incarcerated at the age of 18 for robbing a gas station and during the next 10 years became one of the leaders of the anti-prison movement, was a key figure in U.S. prison activism. His book, *Soledad Brother: The Prison Letters of George Jackson* (1970), shed light on the brutality of the U.S. prison system and was internationally read. He and other prisoners challenged the popular discourse that portrayed prisoners as uneducated, immoral, violent predators.

Though in principle the activists of the 1970s were seeking to abolish or to change all prisons, in practice their focus was almost exclusively on men's institutions. These days, however, a number of organizations exist that concentrate solely on women's experiences. Groups like Critical Resistance and Women's Advocate Ministry as well as individuals like Angela Davis and Kathy Boudin have done a great deal to illuminate the conditions in women's prisons and to set out an agenda to reform or abolish women's facilities.

ABOLITION VERSUS REFORM

Within activist circles there is an ongoing debate between those who advocate for reform and others who advocate for abolition, also known as "decarceration." Both sides believe that the prison is in crisis. However, prison abolition groups work to reduce and eventually eliminate prisons by restructuring society so that punitive forms of social control are not necessary. In contrast, reform advocates strive to improve conditions within prisons. They also seek alternative forms of punishment, such as electronic monitoring or mandated treatment, and make prisons more effective rehabilitation centers, all the while maintaining the current framework of punishment as the dominant form of social control.

Reform groups wish to make prisons humane and rehabilitative as well as to reduce the numbers of incarcerated people. They try to ameliorate the prison system so that it focuses on rehabilitation and offers opportunities for inmates to obtain treatment, education, and skills. This task is difficult, however, as support for rehabilitation within the criminal has dwindled since the late 1970s. There is little money for educational and job training programs that help reduce recidivism rates. Reform groups see these programs, along with drug treatment programs, as important opportunities for inmates and solutions that will eventually reduce the number of people in prison. For example, after prisoners became ineligible for Pell grants in 1995,

college-in-prison programs became regrettably rare despite their proven success at reducing recidivism rates and improving opportunities for inmates. The absence of such programs is one of the many points of action for reform groups.

In addition to improving services within prison walls, reform groups often seek to reduce the number of people incarcerated. To that end, they support alternative punishments, including mandated drug treatment, community service, house arrest, and other intermediate sanctions. Prison reform groups also try to improve current conditions within prisons by targeting such issues as prisoner rape, denial of civil rights, conditions in supermaximum facilities, and poor health care.

Abolitionists argue that restructuring services within prisons and the criminal justice system serves only to reentrench the inequalities that these institutions create. Rather than finding a replacement for prison, they work to develop solutions outside the criminal justice system, focusing on justice rather than punishment. Intermediate sanctions are not acceptable to abolitionists, because they operate within the current criminal justice system, putting the state in control of people's lives, and still rely on the looming threat of a prison sentence as the consequence of noncompliance. While alternatives such as electronic monitoring keep people out of prison, abolitionists argue that they continue to locate and punish poor people and people of color in disproportionate numbers. Instead of the "criminal" as a category, which is located in a particular place in our society, namely among the poor and people of color, abolitionists prefer to use the category "lawbreaker," which most people have been at some point in time.

An example of an abolition strategy can be found in the decriminalization of drug sale and use. Abolitionists argue that drug addiction should be understood as a medical problem, not a criminal one, and rather than reserving treatment for affluent drug abusers and punishing those who cannot afford treatment, quality, voluntary, appropriate treatment should be available to all who seek it. This redefinition of the drug crisis would reduce the prison population and free up resources to be used for health care and treatment.

DEATH PENALTY

Though from the inception of American colonies individuals and groups have sought to abolish the death penalty, their efforts became more organized in 1845, when the American Society for the Abolition of Capital Punishment was founded. Since then, work has occurred at both the state and national levels in faith-based, political, and legal organizations. These groups fight both for the abolition of the death penalty and for individuals facing execution. For example, Mumia Abu-Jamal spent years on death row until the work of many individuals and organizations lobbying on his behalf succeeded in a commutation of his death sentence. Some who sought to save Abu-Jamal's life became involved because they saw the death penalty as unethical, while others were drawn to his struggle because of his specific position as a political prisoner on death row.

Death penalty lawyers have become particularly important in anti-death penalty activism. They seek to reverse death sentences after defendants have been convicted and sentenced. While their activism takes place in the courtroom and deals intricately with the law, death penalty lawyers do more than merely point to the injustices of their defendant's initial trial; they tell their defendant's story. They move past the crime to reconstruct their clients as human beings in the eyes of the court.

The replacement of life imprisonment for Abu-Jamal's death sentence highlights an important debate within the death penalty abolition movement: What should replace a death sentence? Often, organizations or individuals argue for a sentence of life imprisonment as the appropriate alternative to the death penalty. However, some, such as Angela Davis, see the abolition of the death penalty and the abolition of prisons as interdependent.

PRISONER ACTIVISM

Anti-prison activism and prison reform work is not done only by groups external to the system. Prisoners play a key role in prison activism. Because of the total institution within which they are confined, resources available to prisoners for this kind of work are limited. Often there are restrictions on organizing within prisons, and inmates are written up or otherwise penalized for actions such as petition writing. However, despite tight constraints on them, many find ways to organize and exert agency in a collective manner. Various forms of prisoner activism include the organizing of political or identity groups, pursuing lawsuits that push for protection or expansion of prisoner rights, publishing writing that exposes injustices within the system to the public, strikes, and rioting.

Female prisoners are thought to be less political than their male counterparts. However, research shows that women face considerable additional barriers to organizing. First, more than 75% of female prisoners are mothers, most of whom were the primary caregivers to their children before incarceration. For these women, the consequences of resisting the status quo may be too high. The risk of adding extra time to their sentences or having their visiting and/or phone privileges suspended may not be worth it due to its effect on the lives of their children. Moreover, since the female prison population is much smaller, they do not receive the media attention or outside support that many men's causes receive. When they do organize, women tend to lobby for different issues than do men. In particular, they often seek remedies for medical care and parental rights. Because organizing efforts often rely on outside support in the forms of legal advice and media attention, such silence surrounding women's activism greatly weakens female prisoners' efforts.

CONCLUSION

Attempts at prison reform and abolition have existed since the prison was first established. Efforts have been made from within and outside the prison walls. Though calls for the end to incarceration have so far been unsuccessful, many groups and individuals have made significant changes to how prisons are run. Such people provide a crucial monitoring role to ensure that basic levels of humanity and justice are maintained behind the bars of the nation's total institutions.

—*Katherine Piper*

See also Abolition; Attica Correctional Facility; Black Panther Party; Capital Punishment; Critical Resistance; Angela Y. Davis; Families Against Mandatory Minimum Sentences; George Jackson; Legitimacy; Malcolm X; Nation of Islam; November Coalition; Quakers; Resistance; Riots; San Quentin State Prison; "Stop Prisoner Rape"; Women's Advocate Ministry Women Prisoners

Further Reading

Bosworth, M. (1999). *Engendering resistance: Agency and power in women's prisons.* Aldershot, UK: Ashgate.

Cummins, E. (1994). *The rise and fall of California's radical prison movement.* Stanford, CA: Stanford University Press.

Davis, A. Y. (2003). *Are prisons obsolete?* New York: Seven Stories.

Diaz-Cotto, J. (1996). *Gender, ethnicity and the state: Latina and Latino prison politics.* Albany: State University of New York Press.

Foucault, M. ([1975] 1991). *Discipline and punish* (A. Sheridan, Trans.). London: Penguin.

Haines, H. H. (1996). *Against capital punishment: The anti-death penalty movement in America, 1972–1994.* New York: Oxford University Press.

Jackson, G. ([1970]1994). *Soledad brother: The prison letters of George Jackson.* Chicago: Lawrence Hill.

Shakur, A. (1987). *Assata: An autobiography.* Chicago: Lawrence Hill.

Useem, B., & Kimball, P. (1989). *States of siege: U.S. prison riots, 1971–1986.* New York: Oxford University Press.

ACTUARIAL JUSTICE

Actuarial justice refers to a theoretical model current in the criminal justice system that employs concepts and methods similar to actuarial mathematics. Actuaries evaluate future risks such as unemployment, illness, and death. Their projections are the backbone of the insurance and financial security industries. In these fields, actuarial techniques are used to produce insurance percentage rates needed to establish premiums to cover expected losses and expenses. In the justice system, proponents of an actuarial approach attempt to evaluate risk and dangerousness of offenders and treatment programs. Actuarial justice also underpins crime prevention strategies and policing.

CHARACTERISTICS OF ACTUARIAL JUSTICE

There are at least four characteristics associated with actuarial justice:

Deviance is normal. Crime is now perceived as an inevitable social fact. We no longer try to eliminate it, for it is perceived as a direct consequence of living in society. Like traffic accidents, for example, crime is understood to be something that has a significant probability of happening. We try to prevent it and minimize its consequence, by judging the risk that various situations and individuals pose. In this view, crime has lost its moral component. It has been normalized as a by-product of modern societies.

Risk profiles rather than individuals. One of the fundamental characteristics of actuarial justice is its reliance on the concept of risk. The actuarial lens reconstructs individual and social phenomena as risk objects. Hence, the unit of analysis in the criminal justice system is not the biographical individual anymore but rather one's risk profile. Through actuarial techniques, individual identity is fragmented and remade into a combination of variables associated with different categories and level of risk.

Managing rather than transforming. Changing individuals was the key project of the disciplinary model. The goal was to transform criminals into law-abiding citizens through therapy or other correctional interventions aimed at altering their personalities. Within actuarial justice, transforming individuals is no longer the exclusive goal, in part because it is difficult and resource consuming. The objective shifts to managing the risks that offenders represent. To do so, offenders are identified, classified, and organized in terms of a risk profile. Management therefore comes to be at the heart of the system. Institutional paths are provided for different categories of offender according to the risk they pose. Diagnosis and treatment have more and more given way to managerialism.

The future rather than the past. Finally, actuarial justice has a prospective outlook. It is primarily interested in estimating and preventing the occurrence of forthcoming behaviors rather than with sanctioning them or understanding and addressing their past causes. The focus of actuarial justice is mainly on incapacitating and regulating future behaviors.

Actuarial justice is a set of tendencies in the criminal justice system that still needs to be documented in order to be defined more clearly. Even if actuarial justice is more easily delineated by opposition to the rehabilitative and retributive models, the preceding characterization should not lead one to think that these two models have been superseded by actuarial justice. Neither should these models be conceptualized as a sequence. As it will be shown below, they coexist within the criminal justice system (O'Malley, 1992). One step in the quest to comprehend actuarial justice is to identify its theoretical underpinnings as well as its intellectual, political, and social conditions of possibility.

EMERGENCE OF ACTUARIAL JUSTICE

The origin of actuarial justice, and actuarial practices more generally, traces back to our capacity to perceive and think about phenomena at a group or social level. Before the late 18th to early 19th centuries, averse events were mainly perceived as personal misfortunes. Along with the birth of statistics, the capacity to conceptualized events socially made it possible to observe patterns that affect people on a larger scale. Therefore, new realities came into view: birth and death rates, patterns of accidents, unemployment rates, and so on. It allowed for the emergence of a new form of power focused on the population as a set of characteristics or profiles. In the language of Michel Foucault, it is called government or bio-power. Actuarial practices are a manifestation of that particular form of power.

Despite these early foundations, the idea of actuarial justice became articulated as such only at the end of the 1980s. According to Malcolm Feeley and Jonathan Simon (1994), there are three main reasons why these ideas became popular at this time. First, this particular line of thought was already

present in other fields of the law, namely, tort law. In effect, in tort law strict liability and no-fault gained ascendancy over the notion of individual responsibility. Causality and guilt are not an issue in tort law; the preoccupation is with managing of a pool of averse events. Second, the supplanting of the individual justice logic by the system-thinking and rational management logic contributed to the development of actuarial justice. In effect, we now think of justice in terms of a complex system in search of efficiency and not as the operation of a judge who impartially weigh an individual moral implication in a crime. Finally, the utilitarian idea of deterrence weakened the resistance against actuarial justice in the sense that it replace the traditional moral and individualistic view of crime and punishment by an economic conception of individual guided by the calculation of costs and pleasures.

On the political level, liberal and conservative stances both contributed to the rise of actuarial justice, through their emphasis on management. The first sought to regularize procedure through due process; the second encouraged the use of extended imprisonment and thereby increased the correctional population prompting the use of actuarial techniques for efficient management.

ACTUARIAL JUSTICE IN PRACTICE

Instances of actuarial justice in practice can be found in many parts of the criminal justice system. For example, these days it is common to refer to crime as a risk to be addressed by an insurance base model of control. Accordingly, tools such as target hardening, statistical profiling, opportunity minimization, and loss prevention are put in place. To minimize the occurrence of negative events, proponents of crime prevention and the police rely on risk classification. "Bad risks" are then prevented from entering into some form of social relation as happens in the selective incapacitation of high-risk offenders. In addition, crime prevention aims at modifying the context where aversive events might take place. Hence, the target of control shifts from the criminals to the potential victims and their environments. Finally, another sign that crime prevention is increasingly influenced by actuarial justice is that when people are unable to avoid risk, strategies are implemented to systematically pass it along. Thus, for example, supermarkets often calculate the price of goods to include the foreseeable loss incurred by shoplifting.

Actuarial justice also permeates corrections to form what has been called the "new penology." This correctional model encompasses all the characteristics listed earlier: the normalization of deviance and the focus on risk, management, and the future. Under these ideas, the practices of parole have changed substantially. While originally, readmitting someone to prison while he or she was on parole demonstrated the failure of the correctional system because it showed that the person had not been successfully treated during the incarceration, in the actuarial justice model it has become a sign that the system efficiently controls risks. The criminal is neutralized before he or she commits further crime. Similarly, under an actuarial model, the criminal justice system has become increasingly reliant on long prison terms and three-strikes laws. Not only do these measures aim at punishing offenders for past behaviors, but they mostly seek to contain future crime.

The development of actuarial justice literature was, until recently, mostly based on research done with male offenders. It is then reasonable to ask if this model is relevant to the situation experienced by juveniles and women in the criminal justice system. Research shows that it is applicable to a certain point. Hence, Kimberly Kempf-Leonard and Elicka Peterson (2000) demonstrated that some parts of the juvenile justice system are permeated by the actuarial justice model. Such a shift seems to challenge the *parens patriae* orientation. It is largely the case at the prehearing detention stage, when the type of detention facility is chosen and when community-based services are used. In these instances, risk assessment and management as well as cost-effectiveness seem to prevail over the "best interest of the child." In the same vein, Kelly Hannah-Moffat (1999) demonstrated that the actuarial justice vocabulary and logic are increasingly present in women's imprisonment, alongside the disciplinary and retributive models.

CONCLUSION

Actuarial justice is a conceptual model of the criminal justice system that is preoccupied with managing future risks rather than transforming individual and eliminating deviance. Even if its origin can be traced to the late 18th century, the actuarial justice model developed in the 1980s under the impulse of the system thinking and the management logic as well as the utilitarian philosophy. Both the right- and left-wing politics participated in its development. The actuarial model is pervasive in every part of the criminal justice system from crime prevention to sentencing and corrections. In conclusion, while actuarial justice and the notion of risk suggest neutrality and objectivity, actuarial practices are marked by gender, culture, and subjectivity. Invested with an aura of science and rationality, actuarial practices hide the political processes behind the construction of crime, the identification of segments of the population as high-risk offenders, and the exclusion resulting from the "necessary" protection measures. Finally, actuarial justice isolates the criminal justice system from the social finalities that were once measures of its worth.

—Dominique Robert

See also Deterrence Theory; Michel Foucault; Incapacitation Theory; Just Deserts Theory; Legitimacy; Managerialism; Rehabilitation Theory

Further Reading

Feeley, M., & Simon, J. (1992). The new penology: Notes on the emerging strategy of corrections and its implications. *Criminology, 30*(4), 449–474.

Feeley, M., & Simon, J. (1994). Actuarial justice: The emerging new criminal law. In D. Nelken (Ed), *The futures of criminology* (pp. 173–201). London: Sage.

Glaser, D. (1998). Who gets probation and parole: Case study versus actuarial decision making. In P. O'Malley (Ed), *Crime and the risk society* (pp. 439–450). Dartmouth, UK: Ashgate.

Hannah-Moffat, K. (1999). Moral agent or actuarial subject: Risk and Canadian women's imprisonment. *Theoretical Criminology, 3*(1), 71–94.

Kempf-Leonard, K., & Peterson, E. S. L. (2000). Expanding realms of the new penology: The advent of actuarial justice for juveniles. *Punishment and Society, 2*(1), 66–97.

O'Malley, P. (1992). Risk, power and crime prevention. *Economy and Society, 21*(3), 252–275.

Reichman, N. (1986). Managing crime risks: Toward an insurance based model of social control. *Research in Law, Deviance and Social Control, 8,* 151–172.

Simon, J. (1987). The emergence of a risk society: Insurance, law and the state. *Socialist Review, 95,* 61–89.

Simon, J. (1988). The ideological effect of actuarial practices. *Law and Society Review, 22,* 771–800.

◪ ADULT BASIC EDUCATION

Adult basic education (ABE) is an umbrella term that includes a number of prison courses. Most programs are designed to help inmates obtain literacy skills and/or a high school or general equivalency diploma (GED), though some institutions also offer classes in life skills, anger management, interpersonal relationship, and financial budgeting along with vocational and occupational skills programs. Research suggests that all of these courses help offenders gain legal employment and decrease their rate of rearrest, reconviction, and reincarceration. They also reduce their disciplinary problems while incarcerated.

PROGRAMS

As part of their ABE programs, most states require inmates to take literacy classes if they fall below a certain level of capability. In Arizona, for example, all inmates are meant to be tested on arrival with the Test for Adult Basic Education (TABE), and those who fall below an eighth-grade score in reading, language, or math on the TABE must attend Functional Literacy classes for 120 days. Since 1991, all inmates in the federal system are meant to have a GED in order to participate in any institutional jobs above entry-level positions. In New York State, they must read at least at a ninth-grade level.

In addition to basic literacy programs, states offer vocational and occupational training programs to teach inmates how to search and apply for jobs. Many jurisdictions also offer life skills programs as part of their basic education. Such courses are meant to assist inmates in mending family relationships

and in dealing with issues such as anger management. Tennessee, for example offers a life skills program to mothers incarcerated at the Tennessee Prison for Women known as the Child Visitation Program. This course allows young children (between the ages of three month and six years) to spend an entire weekend with their mother on the prison grounds to encourage family bonds. Before women may participate in the program, they have to be discipline free and complete a parenting skills class. During the weekend visit, mothers are allowed to stay in a single cell with their child and to eat meals and interact with their child in a family atmosphere.

Life skills programs also strive to help inmates reintegrate into society when they are released. South Dakota, for example, runs a program called FORWARD for inmates within one year of their release date. In addition to addressing family issues, this course helps individuals set occupational goals and teaches them how to budget.

DISCIPLINE AND RECIDIVISM

Research has shown that participants in adult basic educational programs recidivate approximately 29% less than nonparticipants. Correctional administrators have also found that those inmates who participate in adult basic educational programs including life skills and vocational and occupational training have less disciplinary violations compared to inmates not enrolled in these programs. This is believed to be because participants are not idle and therefore are less likely to be involved in violent situations. Correctional administrators also believe that these programs foster a sense of accomplishment and hope for inmates who would normally not have a positive outlet. As a result, administrators are able to use these programs as rewards and incentives for good behavior among the inmates.

CONCLUSION

Adult basic education programs help inmates succeed after release in a number of ways. Not only do most courses offer instruction in reading, writing, and basic arithmetic, they also often teach reasoning and analytic skills. Courses that stress life skills such as balancing a checkbook, setting a budget, and applying for a job are also common. Altogether, ABE courses, like most prison education, seek to help prisoners readjust to life outside the prison, and help them to avoid coming back.

—*Alexis J. Miller and Rosaletta Walker-Richardson*

See also Art Programs; College Courses in Prisons; Creative Writing Programs; Drama Programs; Education; English as a Second Language; General Educational Development (GED) Exam and General Equivalency Diploma; Pell Grants; Recidivism; Rehabilitation Theory

Further Reading

Cecil, D. K., Drapkin, D. A., Mackenzie, D. L., & Hickman, L. J. (2000). The effectiveness of adult basic education and life-skills programs in reducing recidivism: A review and assessment of the research. *Journal of Correctional Education, 51*, 207–226.

Harlow, C. W. (2003). *Education and correctional populations* (Bureau of Justice Statistics special report). Retrieved from http://www.ojp.usdoj.gov/bjs/abstract/ecp.htm

Jenkins, H. D., Pendry, J., & Steurer, S. J. (1993). *A post release follow-up of correctional education program completers released in 1990–1991.* Baltimore: Maryland State Department of Education.

Porporino, F. J., & Robinson, D. (1992). The correctional benefits of education: A follow-up of Canadian federal offenders participating in ABE. *Journal of Correctional Education, 43*, 92–98.

Tewksbury, R. (1994). Literacy programming for jail inmates: Reflections and recommendation from one program. *The Prison Journal, 74*, 398–414.

Walsh, A. (1985). An evaluation of the effects of adult basic education on rearrest rates among probationers. *Journal of Offender Counseling, Services & Rehabilitation, 9*, 69–76.

◪ ADX (ADMINISTRATIVE MAXIMUM): FLORENCE

Administrative Maximum (ADX), the highest security federal penitentiary, is located on a government reservation in Florence, Colorado. When Florence was built, it was the Bureau of Prisons' (BOP) first *correctional complex*. On the grounds adjacent to ADX are minimum-, medium-, and maximum-security prisons.

HISTORY

ADX is the third in a line of federal high-security penitentiaries that began with Alcatraz (1934–1963). From 1963 to 1978, BOP officials dispersed problem prisoners among several standard penitentiaries rather than concentrating "the worst of the worst" in one small special purpose prison.

The return to the concentration model began with the transfer of the system's most serious disciplinary problems to the federal penitentiary at Marion, Illinois, which opened in 1963. Ten years later, in 1973, a Control Unit within Marion was established in which inmates moved only in restraints and escorted by several officers. No congregate activities were allowed for these prisoners who were regarded as the most dangerous and disruptive in the federal system. The movement to a regime in which the entire prison was run in a Control Unit mode followed the killing of two officers in separate incidents in the Control Unit on the same day, October 22, 1983. In each case, three officers were escorting a prisoner who was able to remove his handcuffs, secure a knife, and attack the escort group; in addition to killing two officers, four others were seriously injured. Several days later, the body of the 25th Marion inmate to die at the hands of his fellow prisoners was found.

On October 28, BOP Director Norman A. Carlson ordered that "indefinite administrative segregation" regime, popularly called a "lockdown," be initiated in all units of the prison. Henceforth, prisoners were moved one at a time from their individual cells under the escort of three officers and only after they had been handcuffed and leg chains had been attached. All congregate activities including going to the dining hall for meals, to work, to the yard and recreation areas, and to education classes and religious services in the chapel were terminated. All basic services including food were provided to prisoners, who were confined to their cells for 23 hours, leaving one hour for solitary exercise.

What came to be officially labeled as the "high-security" program quickly produced complaints from prisoners and several prisoners' rights groups on the grounds argued that these conditions of confinement violated the inmates' protection against "cruel and unusual (psychological) punishment." A legal challenge was mounted in the Federal District Court of Southern Illinois, which subsequently ruled against the prisoners. This ruling was affirmed by the 7th Circuit Court of Appeals and by the U.S. Supreme Court when it denied a writ of certiorari. These decisions provided the constitutional basis for what came to be known as the "Marion model."

Officials from many states visited the prison to make certain that the new "supermax" prisons they were planning took into account the policies and procedures that had been tested in the courts. Marion carried out its function as what the press called the "new Alcatraz," until its successor at Florence, Colorado, came on line in November 1994.

PHYSICAL DESIGN

ADX is the first federal penitentiary specifically designed to house only maximum-security prisoners. It has a rated capacity of 490 prisoners, all of whom are held in single cells in nine completely separate units. Three units *are* designated for general population prisoners. A Control Unit serves the need for long-term disciplinary segregation while a Special Housing Unit (SHU) is used for short-term disciplinary segregation and a High Risk Unit holds inmates who require protective custody. Two units house prisoners whose improved conduct allows them to be placed first in an Intermediate or Transitional Unit and then in a Pre-Transfer Unit. Increased privileges and opportunities for greater association with other prisoners are allowed in these two units; piecework is available for prisoners in the Pre-Transfer Unit. All inmate movement in ADX is under escort and is controlled by 1,400 electronic doors and 168 closed-circuit television cameras.

Because the regime at ADX was planned for prisoners who would be locked up 23 hours a day, cells are larger than those found in standard prisons. Cells measure 7 feet by 12 feet and contain a shower, sink, and toilet; a concrete slab provides the base for a mattress and another concrete abutment from a wall serves as a table for food trays and writing, next to a concrete stool attached to the floor. A 12-inch black-and-white television set in each cell provides programming from the major commercial networks and the institutional cable system. Each cell has a window 2 feet long and 5 inches wide that looks into a small exercise yard surrounded by concrete walls. Cells are entered first through a solid-steel door with a small window and then through a grill door with a food tray slot in the bars. Inmates in the general population, Control Unit, SHU, and High Risk Unit eat in their cells; men in the Intermediate Units eat together in a common area in each unit; and those in the Pre-Transfer Unit eat in a separate dining area outside their unit.

INMATE SERVICES

Religious services and courses on stress management, anger management, and drug abuse are offered on closed-circuit TV. When requested, chaplains representing a variety of religions and two psychologists are available to meet with inmates through the barred door of the inmate's cell. Self-study courses in the areas of basic adult education and English as a second language are offered. To meet the constitutionally protected right for all prisoners to have access to basic legal materials, requests from unit law libraries are brought to the inmate's cell. Inmates in the Pre-Transfer Unit can work in the institution's clothing industry.

Depending on security considerations, indoor and outdoor exercise areas are available to individuals, pairs, or small groups. The Control Unit and the SHU have individual, enclosed exercise areas. Chain link screens covers all outdoor exercise areas. No universal gyms, free weights, or any other athletic equipment are provided. The amount of time allowed for recreation varies from 7½ hours a week in the Control Unit to 28½ hours a week in the Intermediate, Transition, and Pre-Transfer Units.

Visits by family, lawyers, or approved visitors are conducted in a concrete booth through a glass partition with conversations carried on through a telephone monitored by staff, except for attorney-client visits. Inmates are allowed five social visits a month, each lasting a maximum of seven hours; due to its remote location and the severing of family ties through long years of imprisonment, few inmates have visits as often as ADX rules allow. Control Unit and SHU prisoners are allowed one 15-minute telephone call each month. High Risk and general population prisoners begin with two calls monthly. Inmates in the Transition and Pre-Transfer Units are allowed up to four calls in the same time period.

Food, snacks, stamps, athletic shoes, and other items can be selected from a commissary list; using their own funds, inmates can purchase these items up to maximum of $175 a month. Men in disciplinary segregation are denied this privilege whereas inmates in the Pre-Transfer Unit are able to go directly to the commissary.

WHO GETS TO ADX AND WHY

ADX houses an older population compared to other federal penitentiaries—the average age is 40. It takes time to accumulate a record of misconduct serious enough for a prisoner to work his way up to Florence through the disciplinary segregation units of other prisons. The racial/ethnic composition of the population in the year 2000 was 41.5% Caucasian, 14.5% Hispanic, 40% African American, 2% Native American, and 1.5% Asian/Pacific Islanders. Approximately 10% are not U.S. citizens. The offenses for which prisoners are currently serving sentences that average 40 years in length are bank robbery (33%), murder (23.4%), drug offenses (13.6%), firearms/explosives (8.9%), and kidnapping (5.6%). Other offense categories include crimes related to terrorism, violations of the RICO (Racketeer Influenced and Corrupt Organizations Act) statute (racketeering), Continuing Criminal Enterprise, and Threatening Government Officials.

Approximately 95% of the prisoners are transferred to ADX as a result of misconduct in other prisons: assaulting other inmates (16.3%), murdering other inmates (15.9%), escape (8.8%), attempted murder of another prisoner (7.7%), assaulting staff with weapons (4.7%), and rioting (2.9%). Other justifications for transfer include gang leadership, taking staff hostage, murder and attempted murder of staff, and drug distribution. Among the 5% of the

inmates directly committed from courts are the high-profile offenders who have always brought attention to these exceptional federal prisons. Al Capone and Machine Gun Kelly were held at Alcatraz. John Gotti and assorted spies were housed at Marion. ADX housed the Oklahoma City bomber, Timothy McVeigh, until his transfer for execution and now holds Theodore Kaczynski (the Unabomber), Robert Hansen (ex-FBI agent who sold secrets to Russia), Ramzi Yousef (convicted in the 1993 World Trade Center bombing), and members of Al-Qaeda.

THE STEP-DOWN PROGRAM

The great majority of prisoners move through ADX via its Step-Down program. After being found guilty of misconduct in disciplinary hearings in other institutions, prisoners sent to the Control Unit receive a specific number of months to serve at ADX. A serious offense, for example, assaulting a staff member, will result in a term of 48 months before the inmate can enter the Step-Down program. Most prisoners begin their time at ADX in general population units, where after establishing a record of clear conduct for at least 12 months, they can move to the Intermediate Unit for a minimum of 7 months. They may then proceed to the Transitional Unit for another 5 months of nonproblematic behavior and finally to the Pre-Transfer Unit where, after another year with no misconduct reports, they are eligible for transfer to a standard penitentiary. Thus, it takes a minimum of 36 months for an ADX prisoner to work his way through the various steps. While there are exceptions, most prisoners including those who begin their terms in the Control Unit move through ADX in five years or less.

The Step-Down program puts the responsibility for moving through the prison on the prisoner, rather than asking staff to predict the future conduct of men who are being held under a high level of restraint and who do not experience the normal association between prisoners and between prisoners and staff. This policy ensures that prisoners move through ADX to other prisons in order to free up space for new "management problems." Exceptions to movement into the Step-Down program are cases in which "intelligence" has revealed that while they have engaged in no obvious misconduct, prisoners have been giving orders to others to engage in various illegal activities. Included in this group are leaders of prison gangs, drug cartels, and organized criminal enterprises. Other exceptions to the Step-Down program are prisoners who have killed staff, spies, traitors, terrorists, and celebrity prisoners.

THE SUPERMAX CONTROVERSY

Alcatraz and Marion always housed less than 1% of the federal prison population; ADX holds less, 1/2 of 1%, but the drama associated with these prisons and the offenders sent to them has continued to provide the substance of controversy for prisoners' rights groups, for corrections' professionals, and for the electronic and print media. As soon as it opened, ADX became known as the "Alcatraz of the Rockies" because its operations emphasize highly controlled movement and limited privileges and program opportunities compared to other federal prisons. Although the question of whether the conditions of confinement at Marion and ADX are appropriate and necessary or whether they constitute "cruel and unusual punishment" has been litigated in the federal courts, the debate over how much punishment is too much continues at ADX. Ward and Werlich (2003) have reported basic data for Alcatraz and Marion prisoners including most of those who moved on to ADX. The data include measures of the incidence of mental health problems, the inmates' conduct records in other prisons, and the inmates' criminal records after they were released from their sentences. No systematic research on the effects of long-term confinement under conditions of super maximum custody has been reported for any state prison.

CONCLUSION

The mission of ADX is to "safely house the Federal Bureau of Prisons' most violent, disruptive and escape-prone inmates in an environment which provides the inmate an opportunity to demonstrate improved behavior and the ability and motivation to eventually reintegrate into an open population." From the date of its opening at the end of November 1994 to the end of 2002, no inmate has been murdered, no escapes have been attempted, and no staff have been seriously assaulted at ADX. An additional justification for concentrating, in the words of one Alcatraz warden, "all the rotten apples in one barrel" is that the removal of highly disruptive inmates allows other prisons to operate more open and diverse institutional regimes. However, because ADX and other supermax prison apply the maximum punitive measures sanctioned by the federal courts, they require oversight by agency administrators, legislators, researchers, and the press.

—*David A. Ward*

See also Alcatraz; Control Unit; Disciplinary Segregation; Alexander Maconochie; Marion, U.S. Penitentiary; Panopticon; Pelican Bay State Prison; Special Housing Unit; Supermax Prisons

Further Reading

Ward, D. A. (1995). A corrections' dilemma: How to evaluate supermax regimes. *Corrections Today, 57*(4), 104–108.

Ward, D. A., & Werlich, T. G. (2003). Alcatraz and Marion: Evaluating super-maximum custody. *Punishment and Society, 5*(1), 53–75.

◪ AFRICAN AMERICAN PRISONERS

African Americans are incarcerated in the nation's jails and prisons in disproportionate numbers. At present, black inmates account for more than half of those in U.S. penal facilities even though they make up only 13% of the nation's total free population. The causes and effects of the rate at which the black community is confined constitute some of the most urgent problems facing U.S. society today.

RATES OF IMPRISONMENT

According to the most recent figures, there are approximately 912 male state and federal prison inmates per 100,000 U.S. residents, and 61 female inmates per 100,000. If these figures are then broken down by race, there are 3,437 African American men per 100,000 and 191 African American women per 100,000 locked up as compared to 450 white male and 35 white female inmates for every 100,000 residents. These figures mean that African American men are being incarcerated at a rate approximately eight times that of white men, and black women are confined at approximately five times that of white women. Though more men than women are in prison, African American women have been incarcerated at a greater rate than African American men during the previous two decades.

Further differentiations based on race and ethnicity can be made when age is also considered. For example, across the country an estimated 10% of all African American men ages 25 to 29 are in prison. In some jurisdictions, this figure is as high as 50%. Overall, an African American male has a 29% chance of spending time in prison at some point in his life, as compared to a white male, who has a 4% chance, and a Latino male, who has a 16% chance.

HISTORY

Prior to the abolition of slavery in the United States, African Americans were rarely incarcerated in penitentiaries. Instead, punishment was administered to them on the slave plantations where they were imprisoned and controlled by their owners. When slavery was abolished, Jim Crow laws and the convict leasing system led to a rapid growth in the number of African Americans behind bars. Particularly in southern states where the majority of the black population was located, many African Americans were forcibly returned to work for former slave-owners as plantation owners leased offenders to pick cotton and perform other tasks.

As early as the 1890s, the convict lease system came under scrutiny because of accounts of brutal treatment of the inmate workers. Yet it was not until the 1930s that all states finally abolished this system—and made their governments the sole overseers of convict labor. Indeed, even in those states that officially did away with leasing, other structures grew to replace it that continued many of its racist

traditions. For example, in many states, chain gangs—where convicts labor outdoors while chained to each other—partially replaced the leasing system. African Americans were once again overrepresented among the members of the chain gangs. This method of punishment existed in many states until the 1960s. It was reinstated first in Alabama in 1995, quickly followed by Florida and Arizona. Despite public outcry from and litigation by groups such as the American Civil Liberties Union, this practice now exists in many other states as well.

In the 1970s, racial disparities among U.S. prisoners began to increase. Though prison admissions for all convicted felons grew rapidly in this decade, the number of African American persons being sentenced to prison grew fastest of all. Indeed, since the beginning of national-level data collection on prison populations in 1926, the incarceration rate of African Americans has seen an overall steady increase, while during this same period the incarceration rate of white prisoners declined.

CAUSES AND EFFECTS OF THE OVERREPRESENTATION OF AFRICAN AMERICAN PRISONERS

Criminologists have identified several causes of the overrepresentation of African Americans in the U.S. prison system, including: the rate at which blacks commit crime, criminal justice policies such as policing and sentencing, socioeconomic factors, and racial bias. Weitzer and Tuch (2002), for example, found that race was a key factor in police decisions to stop and interrogate suspects. Others have found that, compared to any other group, young, black men are more likely to be denied bail and sentenced to the harshest prison terms.

One of the most common explanations for the dramatic increase in the imprisonment of African Americans is found in the so-called war on drugs. Many observers believe that the combination of law enforcement focus on combating drug sales and use and the relatively insignificant number of treatment resources available to individuals with lower incomes has led to the rise in the African American prison population. Likewise, current drug laws that punish crack cocaine use much more harshly than powder cocaine have been shown to be particularly detrimental to minority communities, where crack cocaine is more readily available. Not only has the increase in drug-related prison sentences been greater among blacks than whites, but so too has been the rate of incarceration for drug offenses for African Americans.

There are numerous collateral consequences of incarcerating high numbers of African Americans. Some of the most troubling effects include the economic, emotional, and social impact on the children of prisoners; the lack of support for the partners of inmates; the inability of ex-felons to secure gainful employment; and in some states, their loss of the right to vote. Though children are adversely affected by the incarceration of their parents, no matter what their race or ethnicity, when large sections of the community are being confined at the rate that is occurring across black communities in the United States, the impact on black children is even greater. Entire generations of young people are currently growing up without the presence of male role models or fathers.

WOMEN

Between 1986 and 1991, there was an 828% increase in the number of black women incarcerated for drug offenses in state prisons. This was the greatest increase of any demographic group in the United States. In most state and federal prisons, the percentage of black women in the incarcerated female population now equals or exceeds the percentage of black males in the incarcerated male population. Drug offenses constitute the primary offense for which black women are incarcerated, even though most women's role in the illicit drug markets is fairly minor and is most often related to their involvement with a male and is a result of their drug dependency.

Although most inmates are the parents of at least two children under the age of 18 years at the time of their imprisonment, women are, more often than men, the primary caretaker of their children prior to incarceration. Due to the overrepresentation of black women in the female prison population, the increase

and large number of imprisoned black women exacerbates the impact on black children of having a parent who is incarcerated.

Research suggests that the presence of black women in the prison systems must be investigated separately from that of black males. Although they experience similar situations due to race, the intersection of race and gender provides for very different experiences in the criminal justice system.

COPING

All prisoners, including African American prisoners, seek out various support systems to cope with their incarceration. Many African American male prisoners choose religion, including converting to Islam, particularly, the Nation of Islam, during their incarceration as a way to deal with incarceration. In some prison systems with large African American populations, such as New York State, Islam is the most common religion behind bars.

Another form of coping in prison is through the formation of comparable alliances in which people group together for security. Research demonstrates that such alliances are typically formulated along racial lines and that this custom is more prevalent among male prisoners than female prisoners. Such alliances may take the form of prison gangs, which are typically divided by race. Two of the most common gangs in which young black men participate are the Bloods and the Crips. Gangs are far less common in women's prisons. Prisoners also form non-gang-related groups, such as religious organizations or sports teams.

CONCLUSION

Despite the decrease in crime in recent years, it is anticipated that if the current sentencing policies remain in effect, particularly for drug-related offenses, the number of African Americans sent to prison will continue to increase and the racial disparities within the prison population will continue to increase. Fortunately, this state of affairs is beginning to gain more attention from academicians, policymakers, and the general public. With this new interest, it is anticipated that measures, such as youth delinquency prevention efforts, can and will be implemented to alleviate the overrepresentation of African Americans in U.S. prisons and, accordingly, assuage the negative outcomes brought about by this epidemic.

—Hillary Potter

See also Asian American Prisoners; Bloods; Chain Gangs; Convict Lease System; Crips; Gangs; Hispanic/Latino(a) Prisoners; Immigrants/Undocumented Aliens; Nation of Islam; Native American Prisoners; Plantation Prisons; Racism; Religion in Prison; Resistance; Slavery; War on Drugs; Women's Prisons

Further Reading

Bosworth, M., & Bush-Baskette, S. (Eds.). (2005). *Race, gender and punishment: Theorizing differences.* Boston: Northeastern University Press.

DeBerry, C. E. (1994). *Blacks in corrections: Understanding network systems in prison society.* Lima, OH: Wyndham Hall.

Kennedy, R. (1998). *Race, crime, and the law.* New York: Random House.

Mann, C. R. (1993). *Unequal justice: A question of color.* Bloomington: Indiana University Press.

Mauer, M. (1999). *Race to incarcerate.* New York: New Press.

Russell, K. (1998). *The color of crime: Racial hoaxes, white fear, black protectionism, police harassment and other macroaggressions.* New York: New York University Press.

Walker, S., Spohn, C., & DeLone, M. (2002). *The color of justice: Race, ethnicity, and crime in America.* Belmont, CA: Wadsworth.

Weitzer, R., & Tuch, S. (2002). Perceptions of racial profiling: race, class and personal experience. *Criminology, 40,* 435–456.

ALCATRAZ

The United States Penitentiary (USP) Alcatraz was one of the most famous and controversial prisons in American history. Located on Alcatraz Island in San Francisco Bay, California, it was operated from 1934 to 1963 by the Federal Bureau of Prisons. Before that, the U.S. Army had maintained a military prison on the site for nearly 70 years. USP Alcatraz housed some of the country's most notorious criminals, including Al Capone and Machine Gun Kelly.

Reputed to be the most secure prison in the United States at the time, it was popularly known as "The Rock" and "America's Devil's Island."

HISTORY

The Bay Area's original inhabitants, the Ohlone tribe of Native Americans, may have visited the rocky, 12-acre island to fish and gather food in the centuries before the arrival of Europeans, but apparently they established no permanent settlements there. Nor did the Spanish occupy the island after explorer Juan Manuel de Ayala sailed through the Golden Gate in 1775 and named it after the many *alcatraces*, or pelicans, that he saw nesting there.

In the 1850s, however, the U.S. Army established a fort on Alcatraz, to defend one of the most important seaports in the newly admitted state of California. Over the next half-century, the site gradually evolved into an important disciplinary barracks for military prisoners.

By the 1860s, the Army had begun using a portion of the fortress to incarcerate soldiers convicted in courts-martial, as well as a few civilians suspected of sympathizing with the Confederacy during the Civil War. In the 1870s and 1880s, the Army added more cell space on the island, and during the Spanish-American War (1898–1900) the population of military prisoners approached 450. The transition from military post to military prison culminated in 1907, when Alcatraz ceased entirely to operate as a fort. That year, the Army redesignated the site as the Pacific Branch of the U.S. Military Prison, and over the next two years it demolished the citadel that had anchored the fort's defenses, erecting in its place a large, permanent cellhouse. The Army finally closed the prison in 1933 because it was too expensive to operate, the salt air was causing the buildings to deteriorate, and the Army deemed the facility's highly public location to be an embarrassment.

ALCATRAZ BECOMES A FEDERAL PRISON

About the same time that the Army was preparing to withdraw from Alcatraz, the United States was in the throes of one of the most wrenching crime waves in its history. The imposition of Prohibition in 1920, and the onset of the Depression less than 10 years later, gave rise to an unprecedented explosion of organized criminal activities, gangland wars, bank robberies, and kidnappings that terrorized the nation. As soon as the Army left Alcatraz, the U.S. Department of Justice moved in to transform the facility into a high-profile super-prison to hold the toughest underworld figures and make a bold statement about the federal government's war on crime.

The responsibility for managing the new USP Alcatraz fell to the Federal Bureau of Prisons (BOP). The Justice Department had established the BOP only a few years earlier, in 1929, to provide more consistent, centralized, and professional control over the handful of far-flung federal prisons that then existed. It would serve as the prison for the prison system—for those very few inmates who had proven too disruptive, violent, or escape prone to be managed even at such maximum-security penitentiaries as USP Atlanta or USP Leavenworth. Alcatraz would accept few direct commitments of inmates from the courts. Instead, nearly all its inmates would be designated to Alcatraz only after having committed serious infractions at lower-security institutions.

CONDITIONS INSIDE

After several months of retrofitting the prison with improved bars, locking systems, metal detection devices, and other security enhancements, the BOP began transferring inmates to Alcatraz in August 1934. Once there, they were housed one man to a cell, both to protect them from each other and to prevent them from working together to undermine institution security. There was a high staff-to-inmate ratio, and the movement of inmates in the cellhouse, dining area, workshops, and recreation yard was highly restricted and constantly monitored. By the late 1930s, there was a special cellblock, called the Treatment Unit, where inmates could be held in isolation as punishment for serious infractions. Alcatraz initially attempted to impose

Photo 1   *Alcatraz*

a "silent system," whereby inmates were seldom permitted to speak with each other, and to severely limit the number of visits or correspondents that inmates could have, except with their attorneys— although both of those policies were loosened within the first few years of operation. Also, all prisoners were to receive the same treatment—with no special privileges or status for celebrity inmates, as sometimes had occurred at other prisons.

Yet Alcatraz was scarcely the dungeon of popular imagination. Sanitation standards were unusually high, there was a full-service hospital staffed by officers from the U.S. Public Health Service, and even the inmates conceded that the food was both plentiful and good—if only because the BOP did not wish to antagonize a potentially explosive inmate population with unappetizing fare. Alcatraz even maintained an "inmate mail box," a precursor of modern inmate grievance systems, which enabled prisoners to air complaints through uncensored, unmonitored letters to judges, members of Congress, the attorney general, or other officials outside the BOP. Inmates could both occupy their time and earn money by working in a laundry that washed clothes for military bases up and down the West Coast, reconditioning furniture for use in federal offices, making uniforms for prisoners in various BOP facilities, manufacturing cargo nets and anti-submarine nets for use by the Navy during World War II, or carrying out janitorial assignments throughout the prison.

Although Alcatraz did not offer the sorts of classroom-based educational and vocational training opportunities available at other BOP facilities, the prison did arrange for a correspondence school program for the inmates, through the University of California. Inmates also had access to a 15,000-volume library, musical instruments, art and writing supplies, a commissary, athletic equipment, an outdoor recreation yard, and a small auditorium where they could attend religious services and regular showings of motion pictures. By the 1940s, inmates could listen, via earphones, to radio broadcasts piped directly into their cells—although their selections were limited to stations and programs approved by the warden.

The BOP kept the inmate population at Alcatraz as low as possible—only about 1% or 2% of its total inmate population—to ensure the intensive control necessary to manage its most intractable prisoners. Alcatraz never held more than 302 inmates at any one time, even though it had the capacity to house many more. More typically, the Alcatraz population hovered at around 250, and often slipped below 200. Throughout its entire history, USP Alcatraz incarcerated a total of 1,557 inmates.

ESCAPES AND DISORDER

A further indicator of the prison's stability was that there were only 14 escape attempts, altogether involving fewer than 40 inmates. All but three of the would-be escapees drowned in San Francisco Bay, were shot to death, or were recaptured. The only inmates unaccounted for were Frank Morris and brothers John and Frank Anglin, who used drills they had fashioned in the prison's machine shop to break into the utility corridor behind their cells, escaped via the roof of the cellhouse on June 11, 1962, and attempted to paddle their way to freedom aboard small life rafts they had constructed using rubber raincoats that they had glued together and inflated—leaving behind papier-mâché heads sticking above the blankets in their cots to cover their

disappearance. Although sailors on a merchant ship thought they spotted a body floating in the bay the next morning, and despite surveillance of their families for the Justice Department for many years, there were no confirmed sightings of the men after their escape—either dead or alive.

One of the escape attempts metastasized into the lone serious disturbance in the prison's history: the so-called Alcatraz Blastout of May 2–4, 1946. Exploiting a flaw they had noticed in institution security procedures during a time of day when most inmates were at their work assignments and the cellhouse was virtually empty, six inmates who had remained in the cellhouse for various reasons were able to take nine officers hostage, confine them in cells, and grab their keys and billy sticks. They then broke into a gallery above the cellhouse, where they obtained firearms. Having thus taken control of the cellhouse, the inmates hoped to use the keys to break out or, failing that, to incite a full-fledged riot. Even with they keys, however, they were unable to get out. The other 200 inmates on the island, meanwhile, refused to join the uprising and instead were moved by staff into the recreation yard where they waited peacefully until the incident was over. A 42-hour siege ensued, which finally ended when U.S. Marines dropped grenades into the cellhouse. Two BOP officers were killed (one by friendly fire), and three of the six inmates were killed. The other three inmates were recaptured, and two of them eventually were executed for their participation in the disturbance.

CONCLUSION

The BOP had never been comfortable with USP Alcatraz, and as early as 1939 had begun to nudge the Justice Department and Congress into replacing the facility. The prison's dramatic location in picturesque San Francisco Bay, complete with tour boats circling the island to give gawkers a better view, was always a public relations headache for the BOP. Day-to-day operational expenses were enormous, as all supplies (including fresh water) had to be barged to the island, and the transferring of inmates (as well as staff and their families) to Alcatraz often involved costly coast-to-coast transportation. By the 1950s, deterioration of the physical plant was proceeding at such an alarming rate that erecting entirely new structures would have been more cost effective than attempting renovations. Also, at this time, the public demand for tough prisons was evolving into a greater emphasis on the sort of rehabilitative and normative approaches long advocated by senior prison administrators.

In the late 1950s, Congress finally appropriated funds to begin work on a new BOP penitentiary in Marion, Illinois, that would replace USP Alcatraz as the highest-security prison in the federal system. USP Marion would be built specifically to house high-risk inmates and would feature the most up-to-date prison designs and building materials—rather than being a repurposed, retrofitted structure like USP Alcatraz. Also unlike Alcatraz, Marion would be located in a rural portion of the Midwest—far from tourists and other casual onlookers, but with easier access to more parts of the country.

USP Marion, however, did operate according to the same philosophy as Alcatraz: that a large prison system needed to maintain a highly restrictive facility where it could concentrate its most dangerous inmates so that they could not disrupt programs and operations, or threaten staff and inmates, at less restrictive facilities. In 1962, while USP Marion was still under construction, the BOP started transferring inmates to other U.S. penitentiaries. It transferred the last 21 inmates in March 1963, and closed USP Alcatraz. The site remained vacant until American Indian activists, accompanied by family members and other supporters, occupied the island from 1969 to 1971 as part of a political protest. In 1973, the National Park Service acquired Alcatraz and turned it into a prison museum and wildlife sanctuary that quickly—and ironically—became a popular tourist destination.

—*John W. Roberts*

See also ADX Florence; Deterrence Theory; Escapes; Federal Prison System; History of Prisons; Alexander Maconochie; Labor; Marion, Rehabilitation Theory; U.S. Penitentiary; Supermax Prisons

Further Reading

Bureau of Prisons. (1949). *Handbook of correctional institution design and construction.* Washington, DC: U.S. Department of Justice, Bureau of Prisons.

Keve, P. (1991). *Prisons and the American conscience: A history of U.S. federal corrections.* Carbondale: Southern Illinois University Press.

King, R. D. (1999). The rise and rise of supermax: An American solution in search of a problem? *Punishment and Society, 1*(2), 163–186.

Roberts. J. W. (Ed.). (1994). *Escaping prison myths: Selected topics in the history of federal corrections.* Washington, DC: American University Press.

Roberts, J. W. (1996). Work, education and public safety: A brief history of federal prison industries. In J. W. Roberts, *Factories with fences: The history of federal prison industries* (pp. 10–35). Sandstone, MN: Federal Prisons Industries.

Ward, D. A. (1994). Alcatraz and Marion: Confinement in super maximum custody. In J. W. Roberts (Ed.), *Escaping prison myths: Selected topics in the history of federal corrections* (pp. 81–95). Washington, DC: American University Press.

◼ ALCOHOL TREATMENT PROGRAMS

Most state prisons and all federal prisons offer some type of substance abuse education or treatment programs to help inmates overcome their addiction to alcohol and other drugs. It is thought that these programs may also help to reduce recidivism. With 36.41% of all men and 27.86% of all women in prison reporting alcohol use leading up to or during their offense, it seems that there may be a connection between drinking and crime. Nonetheless it is unclear whether prison-based alcohol treatment programs are effective, since less than 25% of both state and federal prison inmates take part in them.

TYPES OF ALCOHOL TREATMENT

There are several different types of alcohol treatment available in correctional settings. While some individual and family counseling may be offered, the vast majority of treatment occurs in group settings because it is more cost effective. In addition, some alcohol treatment programs combine various treatment modalities, but most are based on disease, educational, or social learning/cognitive behavioral models. These models are discussed in turn below.

Disease Model

Proponents of the disease model believe that alcoholics have a disorder rendering them incapable of controlling their drinking. Unlike nonalcoholics, they cannot drink in moderation. Treatment from this perspective is designed to teach alcohol abusers to recognize their disease and its consequences. Abstinence is considered the only appropriate strategy.

Self-help and "12 step" programs are based on the disease model. Participants in these types of programs generally attend group sessions a few times a week. Treatment length may range from a few weeks to a year, and individuals are persuaded to avoid environments conducive to drinking and encouraged to use their support systems when faced with difficult situations. Support from other recovered alcoholics is an important element to this category of therapy.

Evaluations of the disease model are generally mixed. While some research supports this treatment modality, the majority of research and meta-analyses suggest it is not very effective. For example, one of the most common treatments based on the disease model is Alcoholics Anonymous (AA). Many prisons contain AA programs, and some courts offer "good time" credit to inmates for successfully completing an AA program. Still, data indicate there is a low rate of program completion and that offenders who are coerced into entering AA programs to gain good time or other rewards often have worse outcomes than those who received no treatment. However, results are more promising for offenders who join AA groups because they are earnestly looking for treatment.

Educational Model

Alcohol treatment programs based on educational models have their foundation in the idea that people drink to excess because they are unaware of the damaging effects of alcohol. Educational programs seek to inform offenders about harmful health and behavioral consequences of alcohol use with the goal of preventing relapse upon release. These types of alcohol programs are found in all federal prisons and many state prisons. They are usually conducted in group meetings, and treatment length varies.

Overall, studies show that education-based substance abuse programs are less effective with higher-risk offenders, because their focus is on informing participants of the destructive effects of alcohol rather than teaching them how to change behaviors and thought patterns. However, like those based on the disease model, evaluations of educational treatment programs have produced mixed results. Results range from no effect to some evidence of success. One educational program demonstrating evidence of some effect is the In-Focus day treatment program, which was implemented at an Oregon women's prison. While this program contains a strong substance abuse education component, it also contains other elements such as basic life skills training and relapse prevention.

Social Learning/Cognitive Behavioral Models

Some of the most promising approaches to alcohol treatment are based on social learning and cognitive behavioral models. Treatment from these perspectives is based on the notion that behaviors and the thoughts associated with them are learned not only directly but also vicariously by watching and imitating others.

Goals of social learning and cognitive behavioral treatment include teaching offenders more prosocial skills, behaviors, and cognitions. The new behaviors and ideas are then reinforced, often through the use of contingency contracts or token economies, in which participants earn rewards and praise for demonstrating the desired action. Successful programs generally adhere to the principles of effective reinforcement in which it is thought that rewards should be consistent, immediate, and contingent on the desired behavior.

Most cognitive behavioral programs also use role-playing and practicing. These exercises allow participants to become more comfortable with new behaviors so they will be more likely to employ them in their natural environments. Evaluations of properly implemented social learning/cognitive behavioral programs—those based on the principles of effective correctional intervention—consistently reveal high levels of success as compared to other types of treatment. The majority of these types of prison-based programs are set in therapeutic communities.

THERAPEUTIC COMMUNITIES

Therapeutic communities (TCs) are another way of dealing with alcohol (and substance) abuse. TCs seek to change the viewpoints and even personality of offenders by group therapy and occupational improvements. The primary agent of change is the community of offenders. A therapeutic community may utilize any number of the above treatment modalities. One of the most common is a combination of the self-help and cognitive-behavioral approaches (e.g., relapse prevention).

Most prison therapeutic communities have separate quarters, housing inmates in treatment away from the general population. This kind of physical barrier results in treatment participants interacting only among themselves. The environment in most communities is more like an inmate's life on the outside than the typical prison cell or dorm, and inmates usually have input into the operation of the program. Participants typically remain in therapeutic communities for 9 to 12 months, during which time they are constantly in treatment. There are several group meetings per week, and inmates are trained to confront and help each other at any time of the day or night.

Prison therapeutic communities have produced promising results for offenders when compared to milieu therapy, individual counseling, or no treatment at all. As with any type of program, results depend on the elements of each particular case study. Programs that incorporate some cognitive behavioral/social learning techniques appear to be most successful and cost effective. For example, the Amity Program, a therapeutic community in California, employed cognitive behavioral techniques and 12-step techniques. Evaluations of this program showed some effectiveness in reducing the number of rearrests and reincarcerations for participants.

CONCLUSION

Alcohol is a factor in the commission of many crimes, so it is important to offer effective treatment to offenders. There are a variety of possible approaches to dealing with alcohol abuse, each of which is derived from specific psychological and educational models. Regardless of the particular model of treatment administered in the program, the most successful programs share some common characteristics. For example, the most effective programs almost always include some cognitive behavioral and/or social learning techniques. Treatment should also be long term and targeted for high-risk and high-need offenders. Finally, alcohol treatment programs should include an aftercare component for the greatest chance of success.

—Kristie R. Blevins and Jennifer A. Pealer

See also Alcoholics Anonymous; Drug Treatment Programs; Federal Prison System; Group Therapy; Health Care; Individual Therapy; Medical Model; Rehabilitation Theory; Therapeutic Communities

Further Reading

Bureau of Justice Statistics. (1997). *Substance abuse and treatment, state and federal prisoners, 1997.* Washington, DC: U.S. Department of Justice.

Bureau of Justice Statistics. (1998). *Alcohol and crime.* Washington, DC: U.S. Department of Justice.

Miller, W., & Hester, R. (2002). Treatment for alcohol problems: Toward an informed eclecticism. In R. Hester & W. Miller (Eds.), *Handbook of alcoholism treatment approaches* (3rd ed.) (pp. 1–13). Boston: Allyn & Bacon.

Pearson, F. S., & Lipton, D. S. (1999). A meta-analytic review of the effectiveness of corrections-based treatments for drug abuse. *The Prison Journal, 79,* 384–410.

Phipps, P., Korinek, K., Aos, S., & Lieb, R. (1999). *Research findings on adult corrections programs: A review.* Olympia: Washington State Institute for Public Policy.

Van Voorhis, P., Braswell, M., & Lester, D. (Eds.). (2000). *Correctional counseling and rehabilitation.* Cincinnati, OH: Anderson.

Wexler, H. K. (1995). The success of therapeutic communities for substance abusers in American prisons. *Journal of Psychoactive Drugs, 27,* 57–66.

Wexler, H. K., Melnick, G., Lowe, L., & Peters, J. (1999). Three-year reincarceration outcomes for Amity in-prison therapeutic community and aftercare in California. *The Prison Journal, 79,* 321–336.

ALCOHOLICS ANONYMOUS

Alcoholics Anonymous (AA) was begun in 1935 in Akron, Ohio, by two men—a stockbroker (Bill W.) and a surgeon (Dr. Bob S.). By 1950, there were 100,000 recovering alcoholics in the AA organization worldwide. Today, the group has millions of members, and AA meetings are held in the community and in correctional facilities across the United States. Essentially, AA is a self-help and support group that views alcoholism as an incurable disease. Because it is thought that there is no cure for the condition, lifetime abstinence is the only alternative to progression of the disease.

AA MEETINGS AND IDEOLOGY

AA meetings are designed to enable those who wish to become and stay sober to convene with the purpose of discussing their drinking problems and telling their stories. AA meetings in the community are generally open to both men and women, while AA programs in correctional facilities are, for obvious reasons, limited to the single-sex members of the facility population. Most institutional AA meetings are composed of only males or females.

AA meetings may be open or closed. Open meetings are open to alcoholics, their families, and those interested in solving a drinking problem or assisting someone who has a drinking problem. In contrast, closed meetings are reserved for alcoholics to discuss problems related to their drinking and actions taken to maintain sobriety. Such closed meetings are commonly found in correctional facilities.

In addition to general discussions of problems and sobriety maintenance, participants also discuss the 12 steps of AA, which offer a way to live a sober life. Many AA meetings in correctional facilities discuss the 12 steps and how the steps can help them overcome their disease. A perusal of the 12 steps reveals the strong religious aspect of the program. For example, members must first admit that they are powerless over their addiction and in order to overcome the addiction, they must believe that a higher power will assist them in removing character flaws including the addiction. Furthermore, the members must maintain the relationship with the higher power through prayer and meditation and asking for forgiveness. The 12 steps are as follows:

1. Admitting they are powerless over the addiction.

2. Believing in a higher power.

3. Making a decision to turn life over to the higher power.

4. Making a moral inventory of ourselves.

5. Admitting our wrongs.

6. Being ready to have the higher power remove character flaws.

7. Asking the higher power to remove the flaws.

8. Make a list of people we have wronged.

9. Make amends to people we have wronged without causing additional suffering.

10. Continue taking personal inventory and admitting any wrongdoings.

11. Through prayer and meditation improve our relationship with the higher power.

12. Convey these messages to other alcoholics and practice these principles in our lives.

AA AND OTHER TREATMENT PHILOSOPHIES

While AA does not view itself as a psychological model of therapy, there are some therapeutic goals embedded within its traditions. For example, members must deal with denial, find healthy role models through AA sponsorships, and develop coping techniques. In addition, AA meetings challenge members' "stinkin' thinkin'" or antisocial thoughts.

Thus, while the AA organization seeks to remain nonprofessional, there are some remnants of other treatment modalities (e.g., behavioral and cognitive approaches) found within some AA programs.

AA IN PRISONS

The Federal Bureau of Prisons and many state departments of corrections offer AA groups in their penal institutions as a supplement to other programs in cognitive and behavioral interventions for alcohol abuse. Typically, AA sessions are either self-directed by a "model" inmate (i.e., one who has been through treatment and AA and has been sober for a number of years) or offered by an outside provider.

As with outside AA groups, prison inmates must find a sponsor to assist them through the 12-step programs and to act as a role model. Usually, the sponsor is a recovering alcoholic and has been sober for a number of years. He or she may be in or outside the prison. If a member of the outside community, this person can be especially important when the inmate is released.

CONCLUSION: THE EFFECTIVENESS OF AA

While many correctional facilities continue to adhere to the 12-step model of AA, research on its effectiveness has not been promising. A recent meta-analysis of 355 published studies and 48 dissertations on AA found that those who participated in AA were significantly less likely to be abstinent than those who did not participate in treatment. Furthermore, the study found that individuals who were coerced into AA, as many offenders are, have worse outcomes than if they had not received treatment. More promising results were found for those who joined AA voluntarily. Accordingly, forcing offenders into AA as a condition of their sentence, or to earn "good time" credit, may be doing more harm than good. Other types of alcohol treatment programs, such as those based on cognitive behavioral models, have proven to be more successful with offenders.

—*Jennifer A. Pealer and Kristie R. Blevins*

See also Alcohol Treatment Programs; Group Therapy; Individual Therapy; Narcotics Anonymous; Rehabilitation Theory; Relision; Therapeutic Communities

Further Reading

Kownacki, R. J., & Shadish, W. R. (1999). Does Alcoholics Anonymous work? The results from a meta-analysis of controlled experiments. *Substance Use & Misuse, 34,* 1897–1916.

Latessa, E. J. (Ed.). (1999). *Strategic solutions: The International Community Corrections Association examines substance abuse.* Arlington, VA: Kirby Lithographic.

Van Voorhis, P., Braswell, M., & Lester, D. (Eds.). (2000). *Correctional counseling and rehabilitation.* Cincinnati, OH: Anderson.

White, R., Ackerman, R., & Careveo, L. E. (2001). Self-identified alcohol abusers in a low-security federal prison: Characteristics and treatment implications. *International Journal of Offender Therapy and Comparative Criminology, 45,* 214–227.

◪ ALDERSON, FEDERAL PRISON CAMP

The Federal Industrial Reformatory and Industrial Farm for Women at Alderson was opened in 1927 in 200 acres in the hills of West Virginia under the administration of warden Mary Belle Harris and a dedicated staff of women. Set in an open rural area, it had 14 "home-like" cottage-style buildings, each of which housed 30 women and a live-in warder. There was also a prison nursery. According to a detailed classification scheme, inmates were employed in an "industrial" farm and power sewing room and offered educational and treatment programs developed by and for women. They were also allowed to participate in inmate-led clubs. During its first years, Alderson became not only the showpiece women's reformatory, visited by Eleanor Roosevelt and other dignitaries, but also an example of broader progressive prison reform. It was viewed by many as providing a national and international model for women's reformatories. It is presently used by the Federal Bureau of Prisons (BOP) as a minimum-security camp for women.

BACKGROUND

Prior to the establishment of Alderson, the federal government contracted with other jurisdictions to house women convicted of federal crimes. Despite earlier efforts to provide prison space at the federal level for women, contracting remained the policy until a series of legislative acts significantly increased the number of women in federal courts. For example, the Selective Service Act of 1917, criminalizing prostitution near U.S. Army camps, brought new prisoners and federal funds for women's institutions. Likewise, the Harrison Drug Act and the Prohibition Amendment led to unexpected numbers of women being sentenced to federal prison.

During this period, a number of influential women were imprisoned for prohibited suffrage protests or, in the case of Kate Richards O'Hare, for violating the Espionage Act of 1917. Their subsequent public appeals for reform of women's prisons strengthened the efforts to open a model women's reformatory at the federal level. Following the election of a Republican administration, aware of the role that the suffrage movement had played in their victory, Mabel Walker Willebrandt was appointed the first woman assistant attorney general. With responsibility for federal prisons, Willebrandt moved to provide not only a central administration for the male federal prisons, but, joined by a coalition of women's organizations, prison reform groups, and a network of influential women who administered state boards of corrections and reformatories, she successfully brought legislation for the construction of Alderson through Congress on June 5, 1924. With the gift of land at Alderson, provided in the hope that a model prison run "entirely by women" would bring thousands of visitors to West Virginia (including "experts from abroad"), the $2.4 million prison construction began with the aid of male prison labor.

MARY BELLE HARRIS

Mary Belle Harris, named in 1925 as superintendent, was responsible for the construction and development of the reformatory and remained its

articulate defender for 16 years until her retirement in 1941. Harris, a graduate of the University of Chicago with a doctorate in Sanskrit and philology, had been recruited after a career of teaching by Katharine Davis, a fellow graduate, to be superintendent of the women at the New York Workhouse, and subsequently superintendent of New Jersey's state reformatory for women. With the passage of Selective Service Act, Harris became the assistant director of the Section on Reformatories and Houses of Detention, responsible for the women and girls convicted and detained as prostitutes.

DEVELOPMENT

Almost from the beginning, Harris found herself in conflict with Sanford Bates and James Bennett, the male directors of the BOP, who saw women as an "insignificant" but continuing problem in a male-dominated correctional system. The relative autonomy of Alderson and its influential supporters threatened their efforts to develop uniform BOP policy and control. Harris, in her reports, not only defended Alderson's programs but also complained, for example, when the BOP adopted her classification methods but attributed them to others. She argued for the reformative value of Alderson's progressive programs against the assertion that Alderson's programs were not adequate for "gun molls," "madams," and "confirmed drug users," who required the steel cells and armed guards of male maximum-security facilities. Harris's approach was continued until 1949 by her replacement Helen Hironimus, her former secretary, who included pictures of babies in her reports to remind the central office of the "other" inmates at Alderson, maintained Alderson's tradition as a reformatory by and for women.

However, by the 1950s, administered by women wardens without Harris's vision, Alderson was described by an inmate as "just another penitentiary." Efforts were limited to maintain a progressive "women's world" at Alderson against the pressures for uniform BOP policies that reflected dominant male perceptions of correctional needs and concerns. Other dimensions of the movements for women and civil rights also affected the institution. The 1950s struggle for equal pay for equal work and a 40-hour workweek resulted in the elimination of the live-in warders positions and the development of the staffing and housing patterns of male institutions. Civil rights decisions put an end to racial segregation in Alderson's cottages. In response to overcrowding, the cottage kitchens and dining rooms were replaced by a central facility. With equal employment opportunities, positions in other BOP facilities opened for women, but in turn a man was appointed warden of the BOP's "women's institution" in 1976.

Over time, the public view of Alderson shifted from that of a "grand experiment" to an institution that housed notorious women. Infamous prisoners included the widow of Machine Gun Kelly, Axis Sally, and Tokyo Rose, all of whom were sentenced for treason after World War II, as well as the accused communist Elizabeth Gurley Flynn. Alderson came into view again with the media coverage of the escape of Lynette "Squeaky" Fromme, the failed assassin of U.S. President Gerald Ford, from Alderson's open grounds.

CONCLUSION

With the present classification of Alderson as one among a number of minimum-security camps governed by uniform policies and practices, women have become increasingly treated "like men." Harris's assertion that Alderson's policies and programs, while developed by and for women, were models for wider progressive penal reform came to little. Alderson's subsequent history reflects the changing political realities that have shaped correctional policies and practices as well as the perceptions, presence, and position of women within those realities.

—*Esther Heffernan*

See also Sanford Bates; James V. Bennett; Celebrities in Prison; Classification; Cottage System; Katharine Bement Davis; Federal Prison System; Elizabeth Gurley Flynn; Mary Belle Harris; History of Prisons; History of Women's Prisons; Kate Richards O'Hare; Prison Farms; Prison Nurseries; Sex Offenders; Mabel Walker Willebrandt; Women Prisoners; Women's Prisons

Further Reading

Brown, D. M. (1984). *Mabel Walker Willebrandt: A study of power, loyalty and law.* Knoxville: University of Tennessee Press.

Flynn, E. G. (1963). *The Alderson story: My life as a political prisoner.* New York: International Publishers.

Giallombardo, R. (1966). *Society of women: A study of a women's prison.* New York: John Wiley.

Harris, M. B. (1936). *I knew them in prison.* New York: Viking.

Heffernan, E. (1994). Banners, brothels, and a "ladies seminary": Women and federal corrections. In J. Roberts (Ed.), *Escaping prison myths: Selected topics in the history of federal corrections.* Washington, DC: American University Press.

Lekkerkerker, E. C. (1931). *Reformatories for women in the United States.* Batavia, Holland: Bij J. B. Wolter's Uitgevers-Maatschappij.

SchWeber, C. (1982). The government's unique experiment in salvaging women criminals: Cooperation and conflict in the administration of a women's prison—The case of the Federal Industrial Institution for Women at Alderson. In N. H. Rafter & E. A. Stanko (Eds.), *Judge, lawyer, victim, thief: Women, gender roles and criminal justice.* Boston: Northeastern University Press.

◪ AMERICAN CIVIL LIBERTIES UNION

The American Civil Liberties Union (ACLU) is a nonprofit, nonpartisan organization founded in 1920 by Roger Baldwin, Crystal Eastman, and Albert DeSilver. It was created to protect the liberties granted by the U.S. Constitution's Bill of Rights, plus the 13th, 14th, 15th, and 19th Amendments. These civil rights amendments generally protect and provide for freedom of speech, association, and assembly; freedom of the press; and freedom of religion. The Bill of Rights also established the right to equal protection under law that includes equal treatment regardless of race, sex, religion, or national origin and the right to due process characterized by fair treatment by the government whenever loss of liberty or property is at stake. Finally, the right to privacy includes freedom from unwanted government intrusion into private and personal affairs.

HISTORY

The formation of the ACLU coincided with a range of social issues that arose from U.S. involvement in World War I. One of the most pressing issues was over conscription. It soon became clear that a draft was inevitable, raising the problem of how to deal with conscientious objectors. Different organizations attempted to aid the nonexempted conscientious objectors, many of whom received harsh treatment in prison and had their mail censored by the postmaster general. Further legal scrutiny came as the Espionage Act limited or outlawed such constitutionally protected issues as freedom of the press and association.

After World War I, the ACLU shifted its effort and concern from conscientious objectors to protecting labor. Specifically, leftist movements including the communist party, the socialist party, the unions, and also mainstream labor movements were now seen as a threatening move toward the entrenched political mainstream. Roger Baldwin, who had been involved in protecting the rights of conscientious objectors and had even served jail time himself for refusing to submit to the draft, decided that organizations that once focused on the war now must focus on labor. It was at this point in 1920 that Roger Baldwin with Albert DeSilver formed the ACLU.

Fear of growing numbers of Communists and other people with political associations considered radical combined with a series of mail bombs drove Attorney General A. Mitchell Palmer to provide legislation that would justify government actions known as "Palmer raids." Palmer raids were conducted on groups or individuals with radical political association where property or persons were detained without ever being charged or having seen a judge or jury. At first, the public appeared to support Palmer raids, but after the newly formed ACLU published accounts of them and accused the government of violating the Fourth, Fifth, Sixth, and Eighth Amendments of the Bill of Rights, public support diminished. Although the ACLU initially formed to protect labor, it became readily apparent that the ACLU would soon work to protect the rights of people whose constitutionally protected freedoms were being violated.

CRIMINAL JUSTICE

The ACLU tackles many general issues under the umbrella of criminal justice including but not limited to juvenile justice, the death penalty, indigent defense, racial bias, police practices, search and seizure, sentencing, prisons, prisoner rights, and the war on drugs. The wing that deals specifically with prisons is known as the National Prison Project.

From their first protests against the Palmer raids of the 1920s, the ACLU has ranged widely in its legal activities constantly dealing with topical subjects. In 1925, in what is known as the *Scopes* case, for example, the ACLU secured a lawyer to defend a Tennessee biology teacher charged with violating a ban prohibiting the teaching of evolution. In the 1930s, the ACLU had two major cases including the *Ulysses* case and also the case against "Boss" Hague. The *Ulysses* case forced an anticensorship ban that resulted in the ban of James Joyce's novel *Ulysses* to be lifted while the "Boss" Hague case found that a ban on union organizers' meeting in Jersey City was unconstitutional. During World War II, the ACLU stood against the internment of Japanese Americans, and during the Cold War it battled against loyalty oaths. The ACLU was active in the civil rights movement as early as 1954 when it joined the fight for school desegregation that ultimately resulted in the *Brown v. Board of Education* decision, which declared segregated schools to be a violation of the 14th Amendment. In 1973, the ACLU supported the decriminalization of abortion in *Roe v. Wade*, and in 1997 in *ACLU v. Reno* it managed to have the Communications Decency Act struck down after it was found to violate free speech. Currently, the ACLU is actively involved in challenges against the Prison Litigation Reform Act, the USA PATRIOT Act, and the incarceration of suspected Al-Qaeda operatives at U.S. Naval Base Guantánamo Bay.

While these are some of the most well-known cases, the ACLU constantly addresses ongoing issues such as AIDS, capital punishment, lesbian and gay rights, immigrants' rights, prisoners' rights, reproductive freedom, voting rights, women's rights, and workplace rights. It also defends controversial groups including American Nazis, the

Ku Klux Klan, and the Nation of Islam in order to prove that the freedoms of the U.S. Constitution apply to all U.S. citizens.

CONCLUSION

The ACLU is the nation's largest public interest law firm. It is run by a national board of directors, who set policy for a 50-state network of staffed, autonomous affiliate offices. The national office in New York coordinates the efforts of more than 60 ACLU staff attorneys and 2,000 volunteer attorneys who handle approximately 6,000 cases a year. Any individual or group can contact the ACLU if the person or group feels civil liberties have been violated. With the exception of the Department of Justice, the ACLU appears before the Supreme Court more than any other organization.

—Lori Brennan

See also Citizens United for Rehabilitation of Errants; Enemy Combatants; National Prison Project; November Coalition; Prison Litigation Reform Act 1996; Prisoner Litigation; Prisoner of War Camps; USA PATRIOT Act 2001

Further Reading

American Civil Liberties Union. (2004). ACLU home page. Retrieved from www.ACLU.org

Donohue, W. A. (1994). *Twilight of liberty: The legacy of the ACLU.* New Brunswick, CT: Transaction Publishers.

Garey, D. (1998). *Defending everybody: A history of the American Civil Liberties Union.* New York: TV Books.

Walker, S. (1999). *In defense of American liberties: A history of the ACLU.* Edwardsville: Southern Illinois University Press.

◪ AMERICAN CORRECTIONAL ASSOCIATION

The American Correctional Association (ACA) is the official organization devoted to overseeing the development and implementation of improved correctional methods and operational standards. It has more than 20,000 members globally. To achieve its goals, the ACA works with practitioners, academics, and the state. Each year, it holds two annual conferences. It also publishes a directory of facilities, regular reviews of "best practice" in the United States, and two journals: *Corrections Today* and *Corrections Compendium.* In addition, the ACA hosts on-site training sessions and offers insights and input on policy decisions and recommendations to the state. Most important, the ACA is the only institutional accreditation body in the field of U.S. correctional operations.

HISTORY

In 1870, the predecessor to the ACA, the American Prison Association, was established by what was then called the National Prison Association and elected future U.S. President Rutherford B. Hayes as its first president. Highlighting a broadening conception of punishment, in 1954 the Congress of Correction adopted the current title emphasizing a new preoccupation with improving inmates and returning an altered, more adjusted citizen back to communities. This shift reflected a growing liberalization toward punishment that encouraged academics, policymakers, and (to a lesser extent) practitioners to view the potential benefits of incarceration for both society and inmates. Indeed, this thought began to balance more punitive sorts of punishment and displaced dominant trends that merely sought to warehouse and punish law violators.

At the founding meeting in 1870 in Cincinnati, Ohio, and through collaboration between national and international correctional experts, the American Prison Association created the Declaration of Principles. These principles, according to the ACA, clearly "state the beliefs and values underlying the practice of their profession." The central focus for correctional services was identified as the *moral regeneration* of the criminal. In the original statement, these early correctional leaders recognized the importance of returning well-adapted—or, as it was hoped, resocialized—offenders to society possessing the *individual will* to refrain from criminal opportunities and redirect their energies toward more industrious endeavors. From its origins, members of the organization saw the potential for reducing recidivism (i.e., reoffending) by strengthening attachments between inmates and several social institutions such as the family, education, religion, and community.

ACCREDITATION AND THE DECLARATION OF PRINCIPLES

While the originators of the ACA made significant developments to the delivery of punishment, current members are continually working to improve correctional policy and service. With such improvements in mind, the ACA renewed and revised the Declaration of Principles (revisions completed in 1930, 1960, 1970, 1982, and 2002) to lead rational practices, clarify philosophical goals, and encourage multijurisdictional cooperation (i.e., local, state, national, and international).

In the Declaration of Principles, the ACA includes seven foundational concepts to direct "sound corrections policy and effective public protection." The seven principles are humanity, justice, protection, opportunity, knowledge, competence, and accountability, and taken cumulatively they serve as professional beacons steering practitioners to better understand and execute their purpose and mission. The ACA, in an effort to ensure compliance to these principles, offers an accreditation program (by the Standards and Accreditation Department) to evaluate and upgrade correctional administration, programs, and services. For a correctional facility to be accredited by the ACA, it must submit to a four-prong process, centered on a comprehensive on-site, official ACA audit. More than 1,500 facilities have successfully passed through this process since 1978.

The accreditation program offers correctional facilities several benefits. Through accreditation, facilities receive improved training and development, receive assessment of program strengths and weaknesses, receive protection from lawsuits, increase staff morale and professionalism, and establish standardized measurable criteria for evaluation and improvement. Correctional facilities must be a recognized government agency or private entity conforming to appropriate regulations. All

agencies seeking accreditation must meet a series of institutional requirements. The agencies are facilities confining pretrial or presentenced adults or juveniles, sentenced adults or juveniles, or supervision of adults or juveniles sentenced to community corrections and have a single administrative official accountable for all agency operations. ACA principles and the accreditation program, therefore, work to ensure that correctional facilities emphasize due process, fairness, public safety, and humane conditions.

CONCLUSION

The ACA develops, evaluates, and adjusts correctional policy in the United States and abroad. It is working hard to instill a professional attitude combined with an ever-vigilant eye toward ensuring the moral/ethical foundation for current punishment strategies. Though not all correctional facilities have been accredited by the ACA, most strive to meet its goals. As a result, the ACA creates a standard that penal administrators try to meet.

—Richard Tewksbury
and Matthew T. DeMichele

See also Accreditation; Governance; Managerialism; Rehabilitation Theory; Staff Training

Further Reading

American Correctional Association. (2004). ACA home page. Retrieved from www.aca.org

ANGOLA PENITENTIARY

The Louisiana State Penitentiary (LSP) at Angola houses approximately 5,000 men and is arguably the South's most infamous prison. Commonly called Angola, this prison was one of the South's most cruel and brutal prison farms in the 19th and early 20th centuries. More recently, it has become the oldest maximum-security prison ever accredited by the American Correctional Association.

Angola is a prototype of the Southern plantation model of imprisonment. It was first used as a prison in 1880 when the prisoner lessee S. L. James purchased the land from Isaac Franklin's widow and transferred prisoners there from the old walled penitentiary in Baton Rouge. Franklin had been one of the largest slave traders in the South. Angola was only one of seven plantations in the estate at the time of the purchase; the estate consisted of 10,015 acres. Although it is commonly thought that the Louisiana State Penitentiary was named Angola because the original slaves who worked the property came from Angola, Africa, there is no documentation to support this belief. Still an operating farm today, Angola occupies 18,000 acres and is the largest maximum-security prison in the United States. Requiring no walls, it is surrounded on three sides by the Mississippi River and on the fourth by the rugged Tunica hills. It has been home to a former university president, famous prisoner musicians, and an award-winning prison journalist.

HISTORY

After the Civil War, Louisiana turned to a lease arrangement for many of its convicts, most of whom were black former slaves. By the end of 1866, 75% of all Louisiana prisoners were black, and as of July 1, 2002, the proportion remained at this level. Mark T. Carleton (1971) observes that from the early lease system, through state control until the 1970s federal court intervention, race and profit were the defining factors of Louisiana's philosophy of punishment. S. L. James reputedly became one of the richest men in Louisiana from the lease profits. The state resumed control of the institution with an eye toward those same profits.

Under the lease system, which expired in 1901, convicts worked on private property—both Major James's and that of other plantation owners who subcontracted their labor—for the profit of the lessee, Major James. They worked the land, farming and cutting timber, performed as household servants, and repaired and built levees in the never-ending struggle to contain the Mississippi. They were contracted to railroad companies to rebuild the lines destroyed during the Civil War. Consequently—and contrary to public belief—the majority of

prisoners were not housed at Angola but were located throughout the state.

Although today it is an institution only for men, women were the first prisoners transferred to Angola after S. L. James purchased the property in 1880. Women worked in the fields during the James lease and did domestic work in the employees' households. They remained part of the prison until 1961.

STATE CONTROL

When the convict lease expired in 1901, the state resumed control of the prisoners and immediately built new housing, consisting of wooden cabins. The women's quarters were built in the center, at least one mile from other structures in compliance with the Board of Control regulations providing for the separation of males and females. At the time of transfer, there were 1,142 prisoners. Well into the 1920s and 1930s, not more than 25% to 30% of all state prisoners were housed at Angola. Throughout those years, men and some women were working at levee camps, road camps, and other plantations around the state.

The resumption of state control was probably not obvious to inmates since their daily work life changed little and most officials and employees of the James era were retained. The state also pursued the profit motive using primarily black convicts for farming, timber operations, and working on the various levee camps and road camps that the state eventually contracted. As well, the state maintained three other plantations some distance from Angola. White male convicts and all female convicts were sent to Angola except those few of the former who were sent to the camps for clerical or "mental" work. Women continued to do field work under state control, hoeing sugar cane and sorting tobacco. The tobacco barn was located next to the women's quarters, thereby expediting those tasks. There was no effort to rehabilitate inmates due to the underlying assumption that it was neither necessary nor possible to so transform black men and women.

A succession of wardens and general managers struggled to make Angola a profitable enterprise by getting the most out of its inmate labor force. Henry

Fuqua, general manager, fired most of the professional guards and instituted convict trustees in their place in 1917. As salaries for officers and guards constituted almost 50% of the 1913 budget, Fuqua's action was certainly cost efficient. In comparison, supervision costs for the 2002–2003 budget are projected at 63.9% for a typical adult institution.

Due in part to decisions like Fuqua's, Angola gained a national reputation as the worst large prison in America. Newspapers described floggings administered to prisoners to make them work harder and more efficiently. Women were not excluded from such punishments and sometimes received as many lashings as any of the men. A 1951 incident in which 37 white inmates slashed their Achilles tendons focused national attention on Angola's problems and brought about a brief period of reform under the direction of Governor Robert Kennon. The main prison complex (still in use today) was constructed replacing the wooden out-camp buildings, many dating to the turn of the 20th century. A new reception center was built, along with quarters for women inmates, and professional penologists brought modern ideas to penitentiary operations. Convict trusty guards were greatly reduced for a few years, and the basics of rehabilitation were initiated. The women were finally moved to St. Gabriel in 1961.

A severe budget cut in 1962 ended most of these reforms and took Angola back to the conditions of earlier times. By the early 1970s, Angola once again became known as the bloodiest prison in America. This time, reform came through federal court intervention. Judge Gordon West's court order of June 10, 1975, mandated sweeping changes in all aspects of Angola's operations—population, security, classification, discipline, medical care, housing, physical plant, and mental health.

Under federal court supervision for almost 25 years and with the necessary legislative support, Angola was finally turned into a relatively safe, secure, and productive maximum-security prison. In 1975, at the time of the court order, Angola was one of two state prisons in Louisiana. It is now part of a system of state institutions, including medium-security prisons and parish jails holding shorter-term inmates.

CONTEMPORARY ANGOLA

Angola is the only maximum-security prison in Louisiana. Home to 90 men on death row, Angola is also Louisiana's official execution site. In 2001, approximately 3,300 of Angola's population were serving life without parole, and another 1,400 were "virtual" lifers with sentences longer than they can live to serve. Due to the length of their sentences, the majority of men presently housed at Angola will likely die there. To care for the old and dying, Angola has developed a Hospice Program that is purportedly a model for other prisons. In it, prisoner volunteers perform hospice functions for their dying convict friends.

Since most Angola prisoners never leave, the prison provides a variety of vocational, religious, recreational, and self-help programs. Newly arrived prisoners are required to do 90 days of agricultural work in the fields and many of them do so for decades. Other employment includes maintaining day-to-day operations of the institution, work at the (license) tag shop, silk screen shop, print shop, metal fabrication shop, and the mattress, broom, and mop factory.

Education programs include basic literacy, general equivalency diploma (GED) preparation, vocational education (culinary, auto mechanics, body and fender repair, carpentry, and graphic arts), and the New Orleans Baptist Theological Seminary (NOBTS), Angola Campus, that offers associate and bachelor degrees. NOBTS is the only college program offered to prisoners in Louisiana (other than correspondence) and as of 2002, NOBTS has awarded degrees in Christian ministry to more than 100 convicts since 1995. The graduates are then sent out to other state prisons to minister to their fellow convicts.

The prison sponsors approximately 30 self-help organizations including Toastmasters, Jaycees, Vets Incarcerated, and the Lifers' Organization in addition to a variety of faith-based and religious programs. Boxing, volleyball, softball, football, and basketball are just some of the intramural athletic activities. Angola also has the sole surviving prison rodeo in the United States, the only licensed prison radio station in the nation, and the only prison museum in the southern United States operated within an active prison.

CONCLUSION

The Louisiana correctional system has improved greatly since the intervention of the federal courts in 1975. Ironically, as Angola has become a much safer prison than it ever was, Louisiana's incarceration rate has skyrocketed to the highest in the nation and the Western world. Almost coterminously with the federal court's intervention, Louisiana eliminated the possibility of parole for lifers. The war on drugs and the state's partnership with federal authorities require Louisiana to make violent offenders serve 85% of their time. The unanticipated impact on Angola is that it is becoming the most expensive state-run old-age home in the United States. Inmates seldom leave Angola. Most of the men presently confined at Angola will face the convict's worst nightmare: They will die there.

—Marianne Fisher-Giorlando

See also African American Prisoners; Convict Lease System; Elderly History of Prisons; Inmates; Hospice; Labor; Plantation Prisons; Prison Farms; Prison Movies; Prison Music; Racism; Slavery

Further Reading

Bergner, D. (1998). *God of the rodeo: The search for hope, faith, and six-second ride in Louisiana's Angola Prison.* New York: Crown.

Butler, A., & Henderson, C. M. (1990). *Angola: Louisiana State Penitentiary. A half-century of rage and reform.* Lafayette: Center for Louisiana Studies, University of Southwestern Louisiana.

Butler, A., & Henderson, C. M. (1992). *Dying to tell: Angola crime, consequence, conclusion at Louisiana State Penitentiary.* Lafayette: Center for Louisiana Studies, University of Southwestern Louisiana.

Carleton, M. T. (1971). *Politics and punishment: The history of Louisiana State penal system.* Baton Rouge: Louisiana State University Press.

Foster, B., Rideau, W., & Dennis, D. (Eds.). (1995). *The wall is strong: Corrections in Louisiana.* Lafayette: Center for Louisiana Studies, University of Southwestern Louisiana.

Louisiana Department of Public Safety and Corrections, Corrections Services. (2002). *Institutions: Louisiana State Penitentiary at Angola.* Retrieved from http://www.corrections.state.la.us/LSP/

Prejean, H. (1993). *Dead man walking. An eyewitness account of the death penalty in the United States.* New York: Random House.

Rideau, W., & Wikberg, R. (Eds.). (1992). *Life sentences: Rage and survival behind bars.* New York: Times Books.

Sinclair, B. W., & Sinclair, J. (2000). *A life in the balance: The Billy Wayne Sinclair story.* New York: Arcade.

Tattersal, P. (n.d.). *Conviction: A true story.* Montclair, NJ: Pegasus Rex.

◪ ARGOT

Argot is a 19th-century French word originally derived to classify meaning or jargon among criminals. Beggar and thieve guilds used this type of language to communicate within their particular subgroups. More generally, argot is a vocabulary and group of idioms, with semantic meanings used by a specialized group of people, within a social system. These are organized, professional groups, particularly members of the criminal subculture who operate outside the boundaries of the law. This language is not considered part of the standard cultural vocabulary. It is determined by social factors and used with the specific intention to render communications unintelligible to those outside the group.

PRISON ARGOT

Prison argot is a complex and ever changing vocabulary that is used by inmates or former inmates to communicate both inside and outside the prison walls. Examples of this language can be demonstrated in terms such as *crushing* or *crushing out*, which were coined for escapees in the years 1904 and 1925, respectively. Another phrase, "back-gate parole," from 1929, refers to an inmate who died in prison.

Argot is a shared meaning among the prisoners sanctioning their relative status and rights similar to that of a guild. Secrecy can be maintained from the prison staff and other inmates outside the group. Not all of these terms remain secret as demonstrated above, in fact, many would be recognizable to people with no real connection to the correctional system. However, there are multitude of phrases, terms, and symbols unknown to those outside prison. Even those who are within the system, such as guards and other inmates, may be unaware of the complex language system being used.

IDENTITY AND LANGUAGE

Prison argot varies both regionally and ethnically within prison populations. Due to the ethnic variations in the United States, prison populations house differing percentages of inmates from varying regional and ethnic backgrounds. This leads not only to East Coast, Midwest, and West Coast variations in prison argot but also to differences in language between ethnic groups. Furthermore, subgroups or gangs within those prison populations can have more specific vocabularies and symbols. It is an assimilatory process for the prisoners combining argot terms with their language (most generally English, Spanish, Native American, and black English) creating a comprehensible language that is both lexically and grammatically particular.

Prison argot performs important tasks for the inmates by establishing identity and allegiance to other inmates allowing them to communicate privately, even while under surveillance. It creates clear and observable social types that have defined roles. For example, in one Santa Fe, New Mexico, prison, there are approximately 88 terms describing prisoners both inside and outside the prison walls. In the eyes of the inmate, it is very important to know exactly who another person is. Eighteen of these terms were specific in relationship to race— Anglo, Chicano, and so on.

When a prisoner arrives at the correctional facility all possessions are stripped away. The argot term that is associated with him or her is important in establishing an identity and allegiances. An inmate can discern another in a variety of ways, through tattoos, hand symbols, gang symbols, and argot terms. The distinct language of argot brings cohesiveness into prison life through specific word patterns and placements. While there is cohesiveness for the individual in particular groups, argot also contributes to the segregation and exclusion of other inmates.

Beyond establishing identity and allegiance, prison argot aids prisoners to operate their "business" privately without interference from prison staff or other inmates. Those partaking in ventures that are illegal or that break prison rules may use prison argot in an attempt to keep secret their affairs. Subgroups, cliques, or gangs in the prison population, such as the Bloods or Crips, can maintain this secrecy even further by keeping their codes private and by using *cants*. Cants are vocabulary normally associated with gangs and are similar to and employed along with argot, but the language is temporary, changes abruptly and is modified as needed. This ensures the safety and secrecy of the vocabulary of the language by having the capability to change significantly important words. If the interpretation of a word becomes known by one outside the group, the group can either change the meaning of the word altogether or establish a new word as a replacement. Argot vocabulary changes may also arise out of heightened security within the prison walls.

CONCLUSION

Prison argot can result in and is attributed to poor communication among prisoners and staff. It has been the cause many dilemmas inside the correctional facility including, but not limited to, racial problems, murders, employee unrest, major security violations, riots, and inmate assaults. Prisons have currently seen an increase in argot languages, as more subcultures bring their symbols and dialects into correctional facilities and the prison population expands, these distinct argot languages will continue to increase along with the possibility of increased problems such as the ones mentioned above.

—Mike Macaluso

See also Aryan Brotherhood; Aryan Nations; Bloods; Donald Clemmer; Crips; Deprivation; Gangs; Rose Giallombardo; Importation; John Irwin; Prison Culture; Prisonizations Riots; Resistance; Gresham Sykes; Tattooing

Further Reading

Encinas, G. (1984). *Prison argot.* Lanham, MD: University Press of America.

Mauer, D. (1964). *Whiz mob.* New Haven, CT: College & University Press.

Wittenberg, P. (1996). Language and communication in prison. *Federal Probation, 60,* 45–50.

◪ ART PROGRAMS

Art programs have long been a component of correctional recreation and a significant part of prison culture. Programs include self-directed hobby shop projects, formal arts and/or crafts programs, art therapy, and education-oriented art classes. Benefits of art programs include reduced idleness and disciplinary infractions as well as the opportunity for self-expression. They are beneficial to correctional management and offender adaptation, rehabilitation, and reintegration.

HISTORY AND CURRENT PRACTICE

The history of prison art is largely undocumented, but it is likely that prisoners have produced art since the earliest forms of confinement. The first recreation and art programs in the United States were offered at the Elmira Reformatory in 1876. In the late 19th through mid-20th centuries, art programs existed in U.S. prisons but were atypical. Following World War II, the American Correctional and National Correctional Recreation Associations acknowledged the significance of prison recreation. With the rise of correctional rehabilitation in the 1960s and 1970s, art programs flourished as a component of the leisure education model, which viewed recreation as therapeutic/rehabilitative. Programs were supported by the National Endowment for the Arts Artist in Residence Program and Project CULTURE (Creative Use of Leisure Time Under Restrictive Environments), administered through the American Correctional Association and funded by the Law Enforcement Assistance Administration (LEAA).

Today, art programs are offered in county, state, and federal correctional facilities in the United States and around the world, though the "get tough" approach in the 1980s and 1990s, rising incarceration rates, and diminished resources have reduced the number of programs in U.S. prisons. Most art programs are sustained through outside grants, artist-in-residence programs, and volunteers.

TYPES OF PROGRAMS

Correctional art programs offer a broad range of activities including fine arts, crafts, ceramics, jewelry making, wood carving, horse hair weaving, mural painting, poetry, creative writing, drama, music, dance, and in some prisons, public art, video production, and photography. Some programs offer opportunities for prisoners to exhibit and/or publish their work. Correctional art programs can be categorized into four general (non-mutually exclusive) types: (1) self-directed hobby shop projects; (2) formal creative arts and/or crafts programs; (3) art therapy; (4) education-oriented art classes tied to correctional education departments. Many prisons have a hobby shop in which prisoners may (usually for a monthly or quarterly fee) engage in individual and/or supervised projects in conjunction with or independent of formal art programs.

PROGRAM BENEFITS

Prison art programs, in conjunction with other factors and opportunities, are associated with reduced recidivism and disciplinary infractions, increased self-esteem, development of life skills, and reduction of idleness. Studies suggest that art programs provide a means through which prisoners can constructively serve their time, develop positive leisure activities and habits, and learn skills beneficial to institutional adaptation, rehabilitation and reintegration process. Art programs serve a correctional management function in that prisoners who are involved in art activities are less idle and less likely to be involved in institutional misconduct.

CONTROVERSY AND CHALLENGES

Several issues have hindered the proliferation of art programs in prison. First, the "principle of least eligibility"—the idea that prisoners should not be offered the opportunity to engage in leisure activities—has ensured that art programs are the first to be cut during budget crises. Second, many art supplies, materials, and tools are considered contraband and/or are threats to institutional security and management. It is a challenge for prisoners and art instructors to reconcile creativity and institutional constraints, and for correctional managers to balance the costs (control of contraband) and benefits (reduction of idleness) of art programs with respect to security and management.

Institutional constraints, the prison subculture, and the human desire to produce art have created a unique genre of "outsider" art involving the use of unorthodox materials. These materials may include soap, cigarette ashes, shampoo, bible pages, melted chess pieces, toilet paper, cigarette packages, matches, wood scraps, hair, and potato chip bags. Art may also be used as a commodity, for example, trading drawings, cards, poems, decorative envelopes for cigarettes, services, and other items. While seen as innovative by the art community, the use of certain materials and the practice of trading artifacts challenges correctional security and management.

Figure 1   *"My World": 6 × 9 of Concrete and Steel*

SOURCE: Illustration by Martin Potter (1997).

Many art programs provide outlets for prisoners to sell and/or exhibit their work. This practice has also generated controversy, specifically in the case of high-profile serial killers such as John Wayne Gacy, Arthur Shawcross, and Richard Ramirez, who have sold and exhibited their work. As a result, some art exhibits in museums and galleries have banned or cancelled art shows featuring the work of violent offenders, some programs no longer allow violent offenders to show/ sell their work, and in cases where prisoners are allowed to sell their work a portion or all of the proceeds are donated to crime victim advocacy agencies.

CONCLUSION

With or without formal art classes, prisoners will find ways to produce art. Programs provide prisoners with a constructive outlet and life skills, which, in turn, enable them to adapt better to the prison environment, to do time constructively, to deal with emotions, and to reintegrate upon release. Correctional art programs supplement work, education, and other available recreational activities to provide a range of options for prisoners. Most departments of corrections in the United States and around the world recognize that such options are beneficial to prison staff and offenders because they provide a constructive outlet for prisoners and are an important part of programming and institutional management.

—*Jacqueline B. Helfgott*

See also Creative Writing Programs; Drama Programs; Education; Literature; Prison Culture; Prison Music; Recreation Programs; Rehabilitation Theory; Resistance

Further Reading

American Correctional Association. (1996). *Creative therapies and programs in corrections.* Lanham, MD: Author.

Gussak, D., & Virshup, E. (1997). *Drawing time: Art therapy in prisons and other correctional settings.* Chicago: Magnolia Street Publishers.

Kornfeld, P. (1997). *Cellblock visions: Prison art in America.* Princeton, NJ: Princeton University Press.

Szekely, G. (1983). Art education in correctional settings. *Journal of Offender Counseling, 6,* 5–28.

Taft, P. B. (1979). The alchemy of prison art. *Corrections Magazine, 3,* 13–19.

Williams, R. M. (2002). Entering the circle: The praxis of arts in corrections. *Journal of Arts Management, Law, and Society, 31,* 293–303.

◪ ARYAN BROTHERHOOD

The Aryan Brotherhood is a violent, male white supremacist prison gang that is affiliated with the national hate-based organization Aryan Nations. The gang is said to follow the principles of "Identity" or "Christian Identity." Proponents of Christian Identity believe that Armageddon is either upon us or fast approaching when whites and nonwhites must fight to the death in an ultimate "race war."

Aryan Brotherhood members are involved in extortion and drug operations, predominantly selling methamphetamines in prison. Aryan Brotherhood violence and criminal activity, however, does not just occur behind prison walls. Members of this gang were involved in the murder of James Byrd in Jasper, Texas, the killing of Saselzley Richardson in Elkhart, Indiana, and the dog mauling death of Diane Whipple in San Francisco, California. In prison, as well as posing a risk to others, primarily nonwhite inmates, members of Aryan Brotherhood are also known to be violent toward staff members.

OVERVIEW OF HISTORY AND BELIEFS

The Aryan Brotherhood is believed to have begun in San Quentin Prison, California, during the 1960s. Since then, membership has spread nationally with known groups in Texas, Florida, Montana, New Mexico, and various other states. The most notorious of them all is the Aryan Brotherhood of Texas, or ABT. Aryan Brotherhood members follow a system of rules and regulations, which are set out by the leadership, or "commissions." Groups known as "councils" oversee daily gang operations.

All members of the Aryan Brotherhood are Caucasian and are either serving or have completed some sort of prison sentence. Many sport neo-Nazi symbols as tattoos including the swastika, Nazi lightning bolts, "AB" (for Aryan Brotherhood),

and the number "88" (for "Heil Hitler–since "H" is the eighth letter of the alphabet). Some men also may be tattooed with shamrock clover leafs, and various Celtic symbols to symbolize their Anglo-Saxon roots.

Members of the Aryan Brotherhood believe that whites are superior to all others. They base their ideas in Christian Identity, which they claim is an alternative "religion" based on five main propositions: (1) White people are the Israelites of the Old Testament; (2) those of Jewish descent are the direct offspring of a mating of Eve and Satan; (3) Adam and Eve were the first *white* people; (4) all non-whites are an entirely different species than whites; and (5) the war between whites and nonwhites, Armageddon, is in the foreseeable future.

HOW DOES THE ORGANIZATION WORK?

It is difficult to join the Aryan Brotherhood. Those who wish to take part in the gang are placed on probation for approximately one year. They must also take a "blood in, blood out" oath that usually requires them to commit a violent act such as an aggravated assault or murder in order to be initiated into the gang. Once an individual has joined, he is a member for life. Blood must spill in order to be admitted and released from membership.

There are numerous "outreach" programs funded by other white supremacy groups, which provide smuggled literature to Aryan Brotherhood inmates. These publications include *The Way,* published by the Aryan Nations; *Taking Aim,* published by the Militia of Montana; and *Jubilee,* an Identity-affiliated publication. White supremacy and Christian Identity reading material is widely traded throughout prisons, and members are encouraged to recruit and convert as many white inmates as possible. There are even internal publications penned by inmates for other inmates preaching white supremacy, such as *Thule* and *Prisoner of War.*

THE FBI FILES AND PROSECUTIONS

The FBI investigated the Aryan Brotherhood gang in the California penal system from 1982 to 1989 (FBI File No. 183–7396, 1982). The FBI files were closed in 1989 when the U.S. Attorney in Los Angeles declined prosecution, in large part due to the difficulty of finding reliable witnesses. Prosecution of Aryan Brotherhood members would be hard to obtain with testimony from inmates who were subject to threats (and acts) of violence by gang members against "snitches." Moreover, it is difficult to find former members to speak out against the Aryan Brotherhood since the group subscribes to a "Blood in, Blood Out" code in which blood must be spilled to join or leave.

Yet in October 2002, a Los Angeles federal grand jury issued an extensive indictment against 40 Aryan Brotherhood members and associates, alleging violations of RICO (Racketeer Influenced and Corrupt Organizations Act), violent crimes, murders, drug trafficking, extortion, and gambling. Search warrants were executed in California, New York, Illinois, Colorado, Connecticut, Florida, Georgia, Louisiana, Massachusetts, Pennsylvania, Nebraska, and Washington in connection with Aryan Brotherhood activities. Thirty of the 40 individuals indicted were in prison, with the remainder conspiring with them from the outside, again, on a nationwide basis.

CONCLUSION: THE FUTURE OF THE ARYAN BROTHERHOOD

Prisons, by nature, are filled with strife and conflict among individuals with violent tendencies. As a result, there are many perceived benefits for inmates to affiliate for social contact, exploitation, and personal protection. As long as these needs are met through gang affiliation, prison gangs such as the Aryan Brotherhood likely will continue to flourish in American prisons.

—Carrie A. Heege and Bryan D. Byers

See also Aryan Nations; Bloods; Crips; Gangs; Prison Culture Timothy McVeigh; Racism; Violence; Young Lords

Further Reading

Anderson, H. (2002). *Feds charge 40 Aryan Brotherhood figures*. Retrieved from www.upi.com

Anti-Defamation League. (2002). *Anti-Defamation League: Fighting anti-Semitism, bigotry and extremism since 1913*. Retrieved from www.adl.org

Christian Apologetics. (2002). Christian Apologetics home page. Retrieved from www.apologetics.com

Convicts and Cops. (2002). Convicts and Cops home page. Retrieved from www.convictsandcops.com

FBI Files, No. 183–7396, Aryan Brotherhood. (1982). Paperless archives home page. Retrieved from www.paperlessarchives.com/ab.html

Montana Human Rights Network. (2002). Montana Human Rights Network home page. Retrieved from www.mhrn.org/news/898pris

Pelz, M. E. (1988). *The Aryan Brotherhood of Texas: An analysis of right-wing extremism in the Texas prisons*. Unpublished doctoral dissertation, Dissertation Abstracts International.

Pelz, M. E., Marquart, J. W., & Pelz, C. T. (1991). Right–wing extremism in Texas prisons: The rise and fall of the Aryan Brotherhood of Texas. *The Prison Journal, 71*(2), 23–37.

Yang, D. W. (2002, October 17). *Racketeering indictment targets Aryan Brotherhood*. United States Attorney, Central District of California press release. Retrieved from http://www.atf.treas.gov/press/fy03press/field/1018021a_racketeering.htm

◪ ARYAN NATIONS

Founded in the mid-1970s, Aryan Nations, until recently, occupied a settlement in Hayden Lakes, Idaho, where its leader, Richard Girnt Butler, propagated his theological hate ideas. In the 1960s, Butler built a church on his 20-acre compound, equipped with a church-school and paramilitary training ground. He named it the "Church of Jesus Christ Christians," and it attracted a small congregation. These days, Aryan Nations is estimated to have about 1,000 supporters nationwide. Former Silicon Valley entrepreneurs Carl Story and Vincent Bertollini have been its primary financiers.

IDEOLOGY OF HATE

Butler's theology is typical of Identity preachers. He openly adulates Hitler, aligning Aryan Nations with other white supremacists and neo-Nazi groups. According to Butler, Jews are not the true descendants of the Biblical Israelites; rather, that distinction belongs to persons of Northern European ancestry. Known as the British theory, the Christian Identity movement purports that Aryans, not Jews, are God's chosen people. The vilification of Jews and blacks constitutes further characteristics of the theology of hate.

The Aryan Nations is also antigovernment. It promotes the use of violence as the means to make America a promised land reserved for the Aryan people. Paramilitary violence can be equally used to establish Christ's kingdom in the national racist state of America. It proposes to eliminate what has been labeled ZOG—Zionist Occupation of Government. In addition, it believes that the United Nations will take over the American government and establish a world government under the supervision of the world body.

The Turner Diaries

During the 1980s, under the leadership of Butler, supporters of Aryan Nations merged with members of the neo-Nazi National Alliance and some Ku Klux Klan splinter groups to establish the Silent brotherhood, known generally as the Order. The Order, a right-wing white supremacy group, may have taken its name from the *Turner Diaries*. In the futuristic novel, the hero's supporters were largely responsible for planning and executing an attack aimed at crippling the American government, in hopes of creating a sovereign Aryan homeland to be established in the Pacific Northwest. In December of 1984, the Order's plans were halted due to the death of its leader, Robert J. "Bob" Mathews, who died during a confrontation with federal agents on Whidbey Island, Washington.

The murderous violence associated with groups such as Mathews's the Order is not typical of Aryan Nations. For example, Butler has taken pains to disassociate himself and Aryan Nations from militant activity. However, all right-wing groups have similar ideologies and are philosophically bound by religious beliefs. The basic principle of the Identity movement and those within the extreme right include the doctrine of the intrinsic superiority of the white race

PRISON ACTIVITIES

White supremacy groups have been at the forefront of the rise in race-based violence in U.S. prisons. Among the most notorious is a group known as the Aryan Brotherhood. Surfacing at California's San Quentin Penitentiary during the 1960s, this group has strong ties to Aryan Nations. Today they are present in prisons throughout America. In addition to perpetrating racial violence, they purportedly are also involved in extortion and drug trafficking.

Members of the Aryan Brotherhood are usually extremely violent. Examples of such individuals include John Stojetz, who was convicted in 1997 for the murder of a 17-year-old African American inmate. Likewise, Donald Riley, who was convicted in 1994 for the killing of an African American marine, was also a veteran of the Desert Storm war in Iraq. Finally, there is reportedly strong evidence suggesting that six of the eight inmates who have been murdered by other inmates at Pelican Bay State Prison in California since 1996 were part of a dispute that developed within the Aryan Brotherhood.

CONCLUSION

In 2000, Butler and his organization lost a major legal battle, which not only bankrupted Aryan Nations but also forced its leadership to sell the group's compound and name. In September 2001, the group named Harold Ray Redfeairn to succeed the aging Butler. It also announced that the organization would relocate its headquarters to Ulysses, Pennsylvania, where its director of information, August Kreis, lived.

The Anti-Defamation League (ADL), an organization that monitors hate groups and their activities, has warned that the new brand of Aryan Nations constitutes a significant threat because of its public call to violence. Since Butler's demise, nascent groups are struggling for power and to prove their right to the leadership inheritance. They have intensified their anti-Semitic, homophobic, and racist rhetoric that have been the bedrock of their philosophy. One such group, Church of Jesus Christ Christian/ Aryan Nations in Ulysses, Pennsylvania, has openly favored the use of violence to achieve the Aryan Nations ideology. Led by August Kreis, the Pennsylvania faction scheduled a July 26–28, 2002, Aryan Nations Congress, which included speakers such as James Wickstrom, Gary Blackwell, Barry Harris, and Hal Turner.

The new trend in Aryan Nations movement violence is rooted in the Christian Identity movement of Phineas Priests. According to the ADL, the Phineas Priesthood is not a formal organization, but rather it is used by individual extremists to describe themselves in order to neutralize their prior criminal activities. Richard Kelly Hoskins, a believer in the anti-Semitic culture, borrowed the idea from the biblical Phineas, who murdered an Israelite and Midiante who had consummated together. This theology of hate is interpreted by Hoskins and others to mean that they have been divinely given the mission to kill Jews and non-white people.

—*Ihekwoaba D. Onwudiwe*
and Thomas S. Mosley

See also Aryan Brotherhood; Deprivation; Gangs; Importation; Timothy McVeigh; Racism; Violence

Further Reading

Anti-Defamation League. (1982). *Hate groups: A record of bigotry and violence.* New York: Author.

Anti-Defamation League. (2002). ADL home page. Retrieved from www.adl.org/presrele/extremism_72/4178_72.asp

Ridgeway, J. (1990). *Blood in the face: The Ku Klux Klan, Aryan Nations, Nazi skinheads, and the rise of a new white culture.* New York: Thunder's Mouth.

Simonsen, E. S., & Spindlove, J. R. (2000). *Terrorism today: The past, the players, the future.* Upper Saddle River, NJ: Prentice Hall.

Smith, L. B. (1994). *Terrorism in America: Pipe bombs and pipe dreams.* Albany: State University of New York Press.

White, R. J. (1991). *Terrorism: An introduction.* Belmont, CA: Wadsworth.

⬛ ASHURST-SUMNERS ACT 1935

The Ashurst-Sumners Act of 1935 barred the sale of prison goods in interstate commerce, preventing states from selling goods produced from inmate labor to customers in other states. It sought to stop inmate-manufactured goods from flooding the market and undermining free labor. It also required that any products prisoners made would be marked accordingly for outside places that permitted their importation. Though the laws regulating inmate labor have changed since the act was implemented, many of the issues it raised remain relevant today.

HISTORY

From 1929, a series of federal laws was introduced that restricted prison labor. Before that time, states were entitled to regulate their own inmate workforce. For example, many states in the early 19th century contracted inmates to local farmers and industries in exchange for money and goods under a system known as convict leasing. These women and men worked for no pay. Though initially such programs were popular with the public, they were eventually abandoned due to numerous criticisms. In particular, outside laborers who felt unable to compete with the cheap inmate labor force began to organize to end the leasing system. By 1891, a number of states to regulate the utilization of prison labor for revenue. Likewise, by 1894, prison contract labor as well as the practice of leasing inmates to private industries had largely been regulated.

In 1929, the federal government responded to pressure to end prisoner labor by introducing the Hawes Cooper Act. This act introduced some restrictions on the sale of inmate goods. However, it stopped far short of a total ban, permitting instead each state to determine whether or not it wanted to ban the sale of goods made by prison labor. It was not until 1935, with the passage of the Ashurst-Sumners Act, that Congress managed to regulate inmate-manufactured goods in some detail.

THE ACT

The Ashurst-Sumners Act was divided into two sections: (1) the illegal shipment of inmate-manufactured goods and (2) goods to be marketed. In the first section, the act specified:

It shall be unlawful for any person knowingly to transport or cause to be transported . . . merchandise manufactured, produced, or mined wholly or in part by convicts or prisoners, or in any penal or reformatory institution, from one State . . . into any State . . . where said goods, wares, and merchandise are intended by any person interested therein to be received, possessed, sold, or any manner used, either in the original package or otherwise in violation of any law of said such State. . . . Nothing herein shall apply to commodities manufactured in the Federal penal and correctional institutions for use by the Federal government. (18 U.S.C. 396c [1935])

By prohibiting the selling or transfer of inmate-made goods for profit or trade, this part of the act made it difficult for states to employ their inmates at work other than that required for institutional maintenance.

The second section of the act set up strict guidelines for how those institutions that continued to manufacture goods by inmates could dispose of their products to foreign buyers:

All packages containing any goods, wares, and merchandise manufactured, produced, or mined wholly or in part by convicts . . . when shipped or transported in the interstate of foreign commerce shall be plainly and clearly marked, so that the name and address of the shipper, the name and address of the consignee, and nature of the contents, and the name and location of the penal or reformatory institution where produced wholly or in part may be readily ascertained on an inspection of the outside of such packages. (18 U.S.C. 396c [1935])

Despite the restrictions set in place by the Ashurst-Sumners Act, many labor organizations and business leaders felt it did not go far enough. In response to their concerns, Congress amended the Ashurst-Sumners Act in 1940, renaming it the Sumners-Ashurst Act. This act made it a federal crime to transport convict-made goods in interstate commerce for private use, regardless of laws in the states. It continued to allow, however, for inmate manufactured goods either to be bought by the state where they were made or to be purchased by other state agencies for state use.

CONCLUSION

Since 1979, Congress has granted exemptions to the restrictions on interstate commerce of inmate-manufactured goods through the Justice System Improvement Act of 1979 for "Prison Industry Enhancement" pilot projects. Earlier, it made an exception during World War II by enacting an emergency clause to the Ashurst-Sumners Act that allowed the manufacture and transfer of inmate goods to the military and those abroad.

These days, the shape of prison labor is in flux. Many states now require that inmates work. Though inmates mainly produce items for state purchase, some work for private companies, producing a range of goods from underwear to furniture. Outside labor organizations still fear the negative impact such programs could have on them, while others still debate the various merits of employing inmates at all. Much, in other words, has changed, while also remaining the same.

—*Kristi M. McKinnon*

See also Hard Labor; Hawes-Cooper Act 1929; Labor; Prison Industrial Complex; Prison Industry Enhancement Certification Program; Privatization; UNICOR

Further Reading

American Correctional Association. (1986). *Study of prison industry: History, components, and goals.* Washington, DC: National Institute of Corrections.

Ashurst-Sumners Act/Sumners-Ashurst Act, 18 U.S.C. 1761 (1935/1940).

Bureau of Justice Assistance. (2001). *Emerging issues on privatized prisons.* Washington, DC: Office of Justice Programs.

Durham, A. M. (1989). Origins of interest in the privatization of punishment: The nineteenth and twentieth century American experience. *Criminology, 27*(1), 107–139.

Foner, P. S. (1955). *History of the labor movement in the United States.* New York: International Publishers.

Hawes Cooper Act, 49 U.S.C. 60 (1929).

▉ ASIAN AMERICAN PRISONERS

Asian Americans are one of the smallest minority groups in U.S. prisons. Statistical analyses show they are often included in the "other" category with Native Americans and Alaska Natives. Regardless, Asian Americans must be studied because of their increasing involvement in crimes, and their growing numbers behind bars.

WHO ARE ASIAN AMERICANS?

Asian Americans in the United States include Asian Indians (which embraces the countries of

Bangladesh, Bhutan, India, Nepal, Pakistan, Sri Lanka, and Tibet), Cambodians, Chinese, Filipinos, Indonesians, Japanese, Koreans, Pacific Islanders (combined from the Polynesian Islands, such as Guam, Hawaii, Samoa, Tahiti, and Tonga), Thai, and Vietnamese. Even though there are enormous differences between these groups in their histories, cultures, and beliefs, the criminal justice system combined these populations to be treated as one ethnic group. Overall, Asian Americans account for 4% of the population in the United States.

HISTORY

Since the 1800s, Asians have emigrated to the United States from their separate countries in large clusters. All groups suffered various forms of discrimination. In 1882, for example, the U.S. government denied Chinese immigrants access to the United States through the Chinese Exclusion Act, only abolishing the Act in 1943 when the two nations became allies in World War II. Further laws were established to prohibit Asians from marrying individuals from another ethnicity, restricting the amount of land they could own, and assessing additional state and local taxes against them. Finally, the U.S. government responded to the bombing of Pearl Harbor by forcing Japanese Americans to leave their homes and businesses for internment camps for the duration of World War II.

CRIME

Asian Americans involved in illegal activities are often part of organized crime and gangs. The illegal activities of these groups include gambling, prostitution, extortion, money laundering, counterfeiting, and robberies. Crimes in Asian American communities are believed to be underreported for a variety of reasons. Recent immigrants may be reluctant to report crimes based on their own experiences in their homeland because of corruption in their homeland's criminal justice system, while victims may fear retribution for reporting the crime. The police in many cities, particularly those with large Asian populations such as New York City and San Francisco,

have instituted a range of outreach programs to try to combat these problems. Most agencies, however, are hampered by language problems, inadequate community relations, and limited resources.

PRISON STATISTICS

There have always been very few Asian American prisoners in the United States. For example, in 1880, of the 12,681 foreign-born prisoners only 526 were Chinese. In the past 20 years, Asian Americans continuously have had the least number of inmates in both federal and state prisons in the United States of all the minority groups. The *Sourcebook of Criminal Justice Statistics* in 1980 reported that of the more than 300,000 prisoners in the United States, only 699 prisoners were Asian Americans. In 1985, this number had more than doubled to reach 1,575. By 1990, there were 464 Asian Americans in the federal prisons and 2,016 in the state prisons out of a total of more than 700,000 prisoners in the United States. While in 1995 of the more than 1 million prisoners in the federal and state prisons in the United States, Asian Americans accounted for around 6,000 prisoners. Finally, the 2000 *Sourcebook of Criminal Justice Statistics* reported that more than 8,000 prisoners in the federal and state prisons were Asian Americans, yet the total number of prisoners in the United States reached more than 2 million.

CONCLUSION

It is important to remember that the groups that are combined as Asian Americans are not homogeneous in their histories, cultures, or beliefs; rather, these populations have their own autonomy. Still, more research needs to focus on Asian Americans because of their mounting involvement in criminal activities, thereby increasing the number of Asian Americans in U.S. prisons. For example, from 1980 to 2000, the number of Asian American prisoners jumped from almost 700 prisoners to more than 8,000 prisoners in both the federal and state prisons in the United States.

—*Kathryn E. Martin*

See also African American Prisoners; Gangs; Hispanic/Latino(a) Prisoners; History of Prisons; Immigrants/Undocumented Aliens; Native American Prisoners; Prison Culture; Race, Class, and Gender of Prisoners

Further Reading

Chin, K. (1996). *Chinatown gangs.* New York: Oxford University Press.

Christianson, S. (1998). *With liberty for some: 500 years of imprisonment in America.* Boston: Northeastern University Press.

Hendricks, J., & Byers, B. (Eds.). (2000). *Multicultural perspectives in criminal justice and criminology.* Springfield, IL: Charles C Thomas.

Huff, C. R. (Ed.). (2002). *Gangs in America* (3rd ed.). Thousand Oaks, CA: Sage.

Kleinknecht, W. (1996). *The new ethnic mobs.* New York: Free Press.

Russell, K. (1998). *The color of crime.* New York: New York University Press.

Tarver, M., Walker, S., & Wallace, H. (2002). *Multicultural issues in the criminal justice system.* Boston: Allyn & Bacon.

☑ ATTICA BROTHERS LEGAL DEFENSE FUND

The Attica Brothers Legal Defense Fund was formed by a group of political activists and attorneys who banded together to help the prisoners charged with criminal offenses in the wake of the infamous Attica Prison riot. The riot, which began on Thursday, September 9, 1971, ended four days later when the state of New York opened fire for six minutes, killing 29 prisoners and 10 employee hostages, six of whom were officers, and wounding 140 others. The shooting occurred when 1,200 inmates gathered in the D-yard of Attica State Prison, holding 38 prison officials hostage.

EVENTS LEADING UP TO AND DURING THE RIOT

In July 1971, just two months before the riot, inmates at Attica had sent a manifesto, which demanded humane treatment, to the governor and the Corrections Commissioner of New York. The commissioner responded that month by visiting the

prison and sending a prerecorded speech that promised reform. However, many speculate that this response was too late and that the mounting tensions had already made the prison disturbance inevitable. Although it is unclear whether the riot had been prearranged, many prisoners had been organizing and planning nonviolent protests such as a prisonwide sit-down strike.

After the riot, 250 prisoners were held in solitary confinement and 1,200 were beaten and/or denied medical treatment for their participation in the uprising, though all deaths were a result of the state's shooting. According to Richard X. Clark (1973), a former inmate and a leader in the Attica revolt, none of the hostages were badly injured during the riot itself.

THE COURTS' RESPONSE TO THE ATTICA RIOT

In December 1972, the state of New York handed out the largest series of inmate indictments seen to date, totaling 42 in all. Sixty-two inmates were charged with 1,489 felony counts in connection with the riots, including kidnapping, assault, sodomy, and murder. In striking contrast, the original grand jury did not indict any correctional officers, state troopers, or state officials for the way in which the riot was handled. The New York State Special Commission, nine citizens appointed by Chief Judge Stanley Fuld of the New York Court of Appeals and the presiding justices of the four Appellate Division Departments, was asked to investigate the underlying causes and consequences of the Attica riot. The commission, which was funded through the state government, did verify that prison officials were physically and emotionally retributive toward the inmates immediately following the riot, yet there were no immediate charges filed for these reprisals.

THE FOUNDATION AND WORK OF THE DEFENSE FUND

The purpose of the Attica Brothers Legal Defense Fund was to support and defend the inmates who were thereafter indicted by the state of New York. Appalled by this seemingly inconsistent behavior, and in support of the inmates' call for prison reform, more than 75 lawyers from across the nation rallied to defend the inmates who came to be known as the "Attica Brothers." The collaboration of these attorneys, first called the Attica Defense Committee and later renamed the Attica Brothers Legal Defense Fund, was formed by October 1, 1971. Some of the fund's lawyers were appointed by the state and received payment through the state, while others worked *pro bono*. Expenses were eventually covered by civilian contributions that were solicited through direct mail.

In all, the indictments resulted in eight trials, seven acquittals, and only one conviction. The Attica Brothers Legal Defense Fund estimates that the prosecution spent at least $4 million by 1974 alone. In all, the state spent $189 million investigating and prosecuting the Attica incident. Ten of the inmates charged with felonies pleaded guilty, but eventually most of the original 1,489 charges were dropped. On December 31, 1976, New York Governor Hugh Carey granted pardons and clemency to all 62 of the inmates who had been charged with a crime. While this was a victory for the Brothers of Attica, the Defense Fund felt that it was not enough and claimed that the prosecution should have put some focus on the criminal acts of state officials as well. Consequently, a whistle-blowing attorney managed to document the inequitable behavior of the prosecution and, as a result, a second grand jury indicted Gregory Wildredge, a state trooper. Governor Carey also pardoned Wildredge in 1976 before he went to trial.

After the Defense Fund's success, five of the fund's lawyers—Elizabeth Fink, Joseph Heath, Dennis Cunningham, Michael Deutsch, and Daniel Meyers—continued to work on a federal civil rights action that would eventually reward the Attica Brothers with a settlement of $12 million, the largest inmate settlement that the United States has ever seen. This settlement was won in 2000, more than 30 years after the riot. Many of the inmates named in the suit did not live to receive their portion of the settlement.

CONCLUSION

The lawyers who were the Attica Brothers Legal Defense Fund distributed financial advice to the Brothers before disbanding in 2000, shortly after the awards from the settlement were distributed. They left behind a significant legacy. The landmark decision in the case against the Attica prisoners changed the way that the state of New York deals with hostage situations as well as affecting how calls for prison reform were heard across the country.

—Emily Lenning

See also ACLU; Activism; Attica Correctional Facility; Litigation Riots; Violence

Further Reading

Clark, R. X. (1973). *The Brothers of Attica*. New York: Links Books.
New York State Special Commission on Attica. (1972). *Attica: The official report of the New York State Special Commission on Attica*. New York: Praeger.
Wicker, T. (1994). *A time to die: The Attica Prison revolt*. London: University of Nebraska Press.

◼ ATTICA CORRECTIONAL FACILITY

Attica Correctional Facility, a maximum-security state prison for male inmates, is located in rural upstate New York, not far from the city of Buffalo. Opened in 1931, Attica is best known for the September 1971 riot that resulted in the death of three prisoners and one correctional officer, and more important for the forcible retaking of the prison in which state law enforcement officers caused the deaths of 10 employee hostages—6 of whom were correctional officers—and 29 inmates.

The Attica riot was a crucial event in U.S. penal history for three reasons. First, the reform efforts by prisoners, many of which were later implemented by correctional officials nationwide, led to significant changes in ideas about prison management and prisoner rights. Second, the massive use of force by the state in retaking the prison was an exceptional show of strength and brutality that revealed the

Photo 2   *Attica*

stark power relations underlying corrections in the United States. Finally, a large and complex body of litigation arose in response to the riot and the state's retaking of the facility. These civil suits wound their way through the courts for more than 30 years due to the perseverance of prisoners, hostages, and their families in using the courts as a means of redress. In short, the 1971 events and their aftermath raise important questions about use of force by agents of the state and about the legitimacy of the criminal justice system and the legal process.

THE 1971 RIOT

At 8:50 A.M. on Thursday, September 9, 1971, a group of Attica prisoners broke through a security gate and gained control of part of the prison. In the process, they assaulted and fatally injured a correctional officer. They took 43 officers and prison staff hostage and established residence in a large, enclosed yard. At the time of the riot, the prison held 2,243 mostly black and Latino inmates, 1,281 of whom were in the yard during the four-day uprising.

Throughout the four-day occupation of the yard, inmates sought to have their grievances heard by prison administrators and state officials. They drew up a list of politicians, journalists, and religious leaders thought to be sympathetic to their concerns, and they asked that persons on the list be brought to Attica to act as observers. Corrections Commissioner Russell G. Oswald repeatedly entered the prisoner-held yard to hear their demands and inform them of his willingness to grant as many as possible. Representatives of the 33-member observers group also entered the yard to discuss the inmates' concerns.

After several days of negotiations with state officials, the concerns of the prisoners culminated in "15 Practical Proposals" that included such issues as

> minimum wage for prisoner labor,
>
> freedom of religious and political activity,
>
> an end to censorship of mail,
>
> increased rehabilitation programs,
>
> a healthier diet,
>
> better medical care,
>
> a formal procedure for hearing inmate grievances,
>
> better recreational facilities and equipment, and
>
> an end to solitary confinement punishment.

Even as negotiations were proceeding, state law enforcement officials prepared for a possible forcible retaking of the facility. The observers committee, sensing a breakdown in the negotiations, and becoming concerned about the large number of heavily armed state police officers massing outside the prison, publicly appealed to Governor Nelson Rockefeller to come to Attica. Several influential observers who knew the governor on a professional basis spoke to him by telephone at his Hudson Valley estate, beseeching him to come to the prison to forestall a potentially large loss of life. The governor refused.

RETAKING THE PRISON BY FORCE

At 7:40 on the morning of September 13, 1971, Commissioner Oswald issued an ultimatum to the prisoners in D-yard. He gave the prisoners one hour to release all of the hostages and convey their willingness to assist in restoring order to the prison, noting that he had personally listened to their demands and agreed to many of them. At 9:00 A.M., prisoners brought eight hostages to the catwalk surrounding the yard, with knives held to their throats. Word was received at 9:30 A.M. that the prisoners in the yard had rejected the commissioner's ultimatum.

Sixteen minutes later, at 9:46, tear gas was dropped on the yard from a helicopter. New York State Police officers—along with correctional officers, deputy sheriffs, and state park police—began firing from the catwalks overlooking the inmates and hostages. Riot-equipped state police officers armed with shotguns entered the yard and began shooting even though their visibility was restricted by clouds of tear gas and by the gas masks worn over their faces. The melee lasted for approximately six minutes. In this time, 450 shots were fired, striking 128 persons. When the shooting stopped, 10 hostages and 29 inmates were dead or dying. Scores more were injured, many seriously.

Prisoners were made to strip naked and lie on the ground. Some were beaten, tortured, or shot. The naked inmates were forced to run a gauntlet of officers, who beat them with clubs as they passed through the rows.

In the aftermath of the retaking, state officials initially reported that the rioting prisoners had caused all the deaths and injuries. However, medical officials soon contradicted this view, by claiming that deaths and injuries occurring during the retaking had resulted from gunshot wounds fired by state troopers and other law enforcement officers. In addition, few provisions for medical care had been made, which greatly delayed any treatment of the injured.

CRIMINAL AND CIVIL LITIGATION

A large body of criminal and civil litigation resulted from the Attica riot and the subsequent retaking of the facility by the state: criminal prosecutions of prisoners involved in the riot and of officers involved in the retaking, an early round of civil suits by inmates, civil damage suits by hostages and their families, inmate wrongful death and injury suits,

and a federal class action civil rights suit brought by inmates.

It first appeared that many inmates and law enforcement officers had committed criminal offenses during the riot and retaking. Prisoners faced charges of assault, kidnapping, and murder for abduction of the hostages, the death of the correctional officer who received fatal injuries early in the uprising, and the killing of three prisoners during the four-day siege. Many of the police and correctional officers who had participated in the retaking were charged with assault and murder for their part in the shootings and for beating and torturing of inmates. State police were also accused of allegedly obstructing investigation of the shooting by destroying and withholding evidence.

Sixty-two prisoners were subsequently indicted, of whom eight were convicted. One was convicted of murder and sentenced to 20 years to life for the fatal assault on the correctional officer in the first moments of the riot. One correctional officer was indicted but the charges were dismissed.

In December 1976, New York Governor Hugh Carey announced his decision to "close the book" on Attica by terminating all criminal prosecutions. The governor stated that the prosecutions had been one-sided and that the state had failed in conducting the criminal investigations. He noted that the retaking of the prison had been improperly planned and carried out and that the state had failed to properly collect evidence and investigate all crimes allegedly committed by inmates and law enforcement agents. "The state itself should not sanction the maintenance of legal proceedings out of harmony with the principles of equal justice," he wrote. The governor pardoned the seven indicted inmates and commuted the sentence of the prisoner who had been convicted of murder. In addition, he announced that there would be no further prosecution of state police or other officers for their part in the forcible retaking of the facility.

With the criminal cases out of the way, attention was directed once again to the civil litigation. Prisoners had filed several civil suits soon after the 1971 events. In the most important of these, *Inmates of Attica Correctional Facility v. Rockefeller,* the U.S. Court of Appeals for the Second Circuit ruled that the actions of police during and after the retaking constituted cruel and unusual punishment in violation of the Eight Amendment to the Constitution of the United States. In a round of other civil suits resolved in later years, the courts awarded $1.5 million to nine inmates or their estates. Resolution of some of these cases was not achieved until nearly 20 years after the event.

Twenty-eight former employee hostages and their families also filed civil damage suits against the state in the New York State court of claims. In 1981, the state court of appeals dismissed all but one of the hostage suits because the hostages or their families had accepted workers' compensation checks soon after the 1971 events. In the remaining case, the widow of prison clerk Herbert Jones was awarded $1.62 million in 1981.

Finally, in what was to become one of the longest-lasting civil suits in American legal history, inmates filed a class action suit in U.S. district court in 1974 (an earlier class action suit filed in 1971 had been dismissed). The suit alleged that prison officials, police, and Governor Rockefeller had violated the civil rights of prisoners during the retaking of the prison by using excessive force and inflicting unnecessary suffering and death. The class action suit was not resolved until 25 years later when a U.S. federal judge ruled in January 2000 that New York State must pay 502 prisoners or their estates $8 million for death or injuries incurred during the 1971 retaking of the prison.

Even after the resolution of the inmate class action suit, other concerns remained. In 2001, Governor George Pataki announced the creation of a bipartisan task force to study complaints by former Attica employees or families of employees who had been killed or injured during the riot and retaking. As of 2003, the task force had not issued a report.

CONCLUSION: THE LEGACY OF ATTICA

The 1971 events at Attica Correctional Facility are commonly referred to as the "Attica riot." However, the primary reason that Attica is remembered today is the many deaths and serious injuries that resulted from the massive use of force by state law enforcement officers in retaking the prison from the inmates. Prisoners had rioted many times before in American history, but never had there been such a concentrated barrage of firepower used by officials to quell an uprising, and never before had there been such a large loss of the lives of prisoners and prison employees. Subsequent judicial rulings have affirmed that the force used by the state in retaking the prison was excessive and that acts of brutality and racism occurred. In addition, the torturous process of criminal and civil litigation arising from the Attica events casts doubt on the legitimacy of the legal process.

—*Stephen C. Light*

See also Attica Brothers Legal Defense Fund; Correctional Officers; Discipline System; History of Prisons; Jailhouse Lawyers; Leavenworth U.S. Penitentiary; Legitimacy; Litigation; Managerialism; Marion, U.S. Penitentiary; Prisoner Litigation; Racism; Resistance; Riots; San Quentin State Prison; Sing Sing Correctional Facility; Violence

Further Reading

Bell, M. (1987). *The turkey shoot: Tracking the Attica cover-up*. New York: Grove.

Hill, M. (2003, April 17). 32 years later, Attica victims say they wait for justice. *Boston Globe Online*. Retrieved from http://www.boston.com/dailynews

Light, S. C. (1995). The Attica litigation. *Crime, Law & Social Change, 23*, 215–234.

New York State Special Commission on Attica. (1972). *Attica: The official report of the New York State Special Commission on Attica*. New York: Bantam.

Weiss, R. P. (Ed.). (1991). Attica: 1971–1991, a commemorative issue. *Social Justice, 18*(3).

Wicker, T. (1975). *A time to die*. New York: Quadrangle.

◪ AUBURN CORRECTIONAL FACILITY

Auburn Penitentiary, which gave its name to the "Auburn system" of imprisonment that influenced penal regimes throughout America and the world, opened in Auburn, New York, in 1819. Today, it is one of the 71 state prisons in New York. Until the 1970s, it was called Auburn Prison but is currently known as the Auburn Correctional Facility.

HISTORY

William Brittin was hired to oversee the building of the facility, and, upon its opening, became the warden. Its architecture resembled that of the first New York state prison, Greenwich Village's Newgate, with large rooms housing 8–12 inmates instead of singular cells. By 1817, the main building and the south wing were complete and ready to accept prisoners. These early prisoners were put to work finishing the construction of the remaining sections of the building.

Eventually, Captain Elam Lynds, a veteran from the War of 1812, was hired as principle keeper at Auburn. While Lynds was well liked by prison authorities, prisoners objected to his strict military-style rule. Discontent grew to such an extent that, in 1818, the inmates rioted and the military had to be called in to quell the rebellion. This riot led to new state legislation, enacted in 1819, that, ironically, authorized much harsher treatment of prisoners, including flogging. In addition, the legislation called for the construction of a north wing at Auburn to be composed of small cells to be used for solitary confinement. The government then appointed three men to run Auburn: William Brittin, the agent and keeper of Auburn; John Cray, the overseer of discipline and police; and Elam Lynds, the head of finances. While all three men agreed that the prison should be self-supporting, their philosophies of punishment varied greatly, which led to conflicts among them. By 1821, Brittin became ill and left Auburn. Conflicts led Cray to resign, thus leaving Lynds as the sole agent and keeper of the prison.

Around this time, New York State was developing a new plan for the organization of prisons based on a philosophy of solitary confinement and silence, using the Pennsylvania prison model. The legislature decided that prisoners would be separated into three classes with the most troubling offenders placed in solitary confinement. By the end of December 1821, some of the solitary cells in the north wing of Auburn were complete and 80 prisoners were moved in. The cells were 3 feet wide and 7 feet long. Prisoners were kept in complete isolation and were not permitted to work or speak.

Their only distraction was a Bible. Within one year's time, 5 of these men had died and over 40 were declared mentally ill.

THE RISE OF THE SILENT CONGREGATE SYSTEM

After the year's experiment with solitary confinement, there was a general consensus that this type of imprisonment did not work. New programs were created by New York State that allowed prisoners to work together during the day and to be confined in isolation at night. The system was based on the belief that through isolation, quiet reflection, and hard work, prisoners could reform. Silence was required so that prisoners could not exchange criminal ideas.

The new system, implemented under Lynds, was very regimented. The prison was run on a strict schedule and the rules of silence were stringently enforced. Six days a week, prisoners marched in lockstep (a march which involved a shuffling slide step with one hand on the shoulder of the next man, with all heads turned toward the keeper in order to maintain silence) from their cells to a common dining room, where a small meal was eaten, and then to the prison workroom. After a full day of silent work, prisoners returned to their cells for a solitary dinner. On Sundays, prisoners left their cell only to attend church services. Otherwise, they were left to reflect in solitary confinement and were allowed to speak only to the prison chaplain. Rule breakers were subject to severe punishments; Lynds was partial to flogging and he and his staff all carried leather whips. Inmates were not allowed any contact with the outside world. Efforts to make the prisoners as indistinguishable as possible included dressing them all in the same black-and-white striped uniform, and identifying them only by their numbers.

Because of the congregate style of the workroom, supervision became a challenge. Corridors were constructed around the workrooms. The walls separating the workroom and the corridors had small holes and slits in them so that the guards could stand in the corridors and see the activity in the room without being seen. These corridors also served another purpose as they permitted outsiders to come to the prison and, for a small fee, wander through the corridors to view the prisoners, thus creating an extra source of revenue for the prison.

Elam Lynds's system of silent congregate labor became a model for other prisons, gaining popularity for two reasons. Not only was silent congregate labor consistent with the philosophy of silence of the Pennsylvania prison system, but the congregate workshops made the labor economical. Manufacturers began contracting for labor with Auburn and other prisons like it. This arrangement benefited both industry and the prison; that is, industry got cheaper labor and the prison acquired work for prisoners to do. Auburn became self-sufficient, and sometimes even able to produce a profit. Only in later years, as local laborers and unions protested the use of cheap prison labor, did the labor component become less successful. By 1890, Auburn switched from the contract system to the state use system, whereby the inmates produced supplies for use within the prison and other state facilities.

PRISON REFORM

In 1913, Thomas Mott Osborn was appointed to lead a commission on prison reform in New York State. Osborn determined that to understand the workings of a prison, it was necessary to live there. He voluntarily committed himself to Auburn prison for a week, living under the same conditions as the prisoners. At this time, silence and strict discipline were still used as the main components of prison life. The week left Osborn with many new ideas about running a prison. He concluded that the current prison system only damaged the inmates. Believing that inmates should have as much freedom as possible within the prison, Osborn advocated for a system of self-government. He also felt prison society should be as close to regular society as possible to teach inmates how to live in a civil society. Osborn was very critical of Auburn and the silent congregate labor system. Instead of instilling a sense of responsibility and initiative, he was convinced that Auburn's system created tensions and encouraged bad behavior. He recommended closing Auburn and implementing a new system of indeterminate sentencing.

Auburn was not shut down but instead became the location for an experiment in a new type of prison. Osborn worked with the warden and other staff, helping the prisoners to create a Mutual Welfare Inmate League, a type of self-government within the prison. As a result, prisoners participated in group activities such as concerts and sports. Prisoner grievance committees were established to deal with internal problems. The experiment at Auburn led to the establishment of similar programs at other prisons, which, for the most part, resulted in failure. Furthermore, once Osborn was no longer at Auburn the self-government system collapsed under criticism that the prison lacked adequate control over inmates. The Mutual Welfare Inmate League at Auburn was disbanded in 1929 after a prison uprising.

WOMEN

In the first years of Auburn, while the state concentrated on how to deal with male offenders, women were housed in the attic where the windows had been sealed, leaving the area with little light and air. For the most part, the women were left to their own devices and did not have to conform to the silent system. They were employed to do tasks such as spinning and knitting. By 1832, female offenders were moved to the remodeled south wing of Auburn. Women continued to be housed in very poor conditions until they were transferred out of Auburn to a new female unit at Sing Sing.

THE MODERN ERA

One hundred years after it first opened, the facility at Auburn remained largely the same as when it was first constructed. Auburn was marked by substantial overcrowding and idleness, the latter due to a decline in the amount of work available for prisoners. Poor living conditions led to riots breaking out at Auburn in 1921 and in 1929. Riots once again broke out in 1970 after the prisoners' request to conduct a Black Solidarity Day, a result of the civil rights movement, was denied. A number of the inmates who were involved in this riot were sent to Attica Prison and later were involved in the devastating riot that occurred there.

During the 1920s, Auburn started producing license plates for the New York Department of Motor Vehicles, a practice that continues today. Today, this workshop generates about $9,000,000 a year, which helps offset the cost of running the prison. In addition, over the years, Auburn has developed other academic and vocational instruction, such as industrial training through Corcraft Industries. The correctional facility also has counselors to help inmates deal with drug and alcohol problems.

CONCLUSION

Auburn Penitentiary shaped policy and practice in prisons in the United States and throughout the world. Best remembered for the congregate system, Auburn was also noteworthy for opening the State Lunatic Asylum for Insane Convicts in 1859 that was specifically designed to house mentally ill convicts. In addition to being the first prison to have an insane asylum for convicts, Auburn is also credited with being the first prison in the world to have an electric chair. The first execution took place on August 6, 1890. More than 50 men and women were executed at Auburn, with the last execution taking place in 1963.

Today, none of the original 1800s structures of the Auburn Penitentiary remain, even though a prison continues to operate on the same site. At present a maximum-security prison, Auburn houses about 1,800 men. In addition to holding long-term prisoners, Auburn has recently become a transfer facility for inmates moving between facilities. Auburn is a central feature of the surrounding community; since the 1820s it has provided one of the main sources of employment in the town. While many changes in the way prisons are run have occurred, the influence of Auburn still can be seen in the administration of modern prisons.

—*Laura Jean Waters*

See also Auburn System; Campus Style; Cottage System; Convict Leasing; Hard Labor; High-Rise Prisons; History of Labor; History of Prisons; History of Women's Prisons; New Generation Prisons; Newgate Prison; Panopticon; Pennsylvania System; Rehabilitation Theory; Sing Sing Correctional Facility; Telephone Pole Design; Walnut Street Jail

Further Reading

Christianson, S. (1998). *With liberty for some: 500 years of imprisonment in America*. Boston: Northeastern University Press.

Eriksson, T. (1976). *The reformers: An historical survey of pioneer experiments in the treatment of criminals* (C. Djurklou, Trans.). New York: Elsevier Scientific.

Miskell, J. N. (1991). *Auburn? The relationship between Auburn and the prison*. Paper presented to the members of the Cayuga County Historical Society at Cayuga. Retrieved from the New York Correction History Society Web site, http://www.correctionhistory.org/auburn&osborn/miskell/miskell_index.html

Shichor, D. (1995). *Punishment for profit: Private prisons/public concerns*. Thousand Oaks, CA: Sage.

◪ AUBURN SYSTEM

The Auburn system refers to a 19th-century model of penal discipline in which penitentiary inmates worked together in silence. This strategy of prison management competed with, and ultimately replaced, the earlier Pennsylvania system in which prisoners were kept in solitary confinement for the duration of their sentence.

During the day in the Auburn system, inmates were employed in prison industries where they worked collectively. At night, they were kept in separate cells. This approach is often referred to as the congregate or silent system. It was based on the belief that hard labor and silence would help offenders reform. In penitentiaries run using this strategy, prisoners caught trying to communicate were punished harshly by the prison keepers.

HISTORY

Overcrowding at the Newgate Prison in New York led the legislature in 1816 to approve the building of a new state prison in Auburn. Originally, Auburn was designed as other prisons with congregate sleeping. However, concerns over a lack of discipline at Newgate led to the legislature authorizing a new punishment for the most violent inmates. As in the Pennsylvania system, these men would be locked up in solitary cells where they could not communicate with one another. Unlike the

Pennsylvania system, where inmates worked at handiwork in their cells, individuals in solitary confinement at Auburn were not permitted to do anything at all. Within two years, however, prison officials became concerned about the high rates of insanity and suicide they were witnessing. The situation became so bad that the prisoners held in solitary were pardoned and released by the governor. Twelve of these men soon committed new crimes and were convicted and returned to the prison. Solitary confinement, it seemed, did not work. As a result, prison administrators began to reconsider how the institution should be run.

In 1831, a new warden of Auburn, Elam Lynds, and his deputy, John Cray, instituted an alternative system of management called the congregate system. The congregate or Auburn silent system of prison management was seen as a rival to the Pennsylvania or separate system even though it incorporated some of its strategies. Like the Pennsylvania system, for example, no communication between inmates was allowed at Auburn. However, while prisoners in the Pennsylvania system were kept completely separate from one another, in the Auburn system, men worked and ate together. They were simply not permitted to speak to one another or to communicate in other ways. Administrators of both systems believed that silence would not only prevent inmates from influencing one another, but it would also help reform them. It was believed that silence and hard work would make them think about the crimes they had committed and help them repent and turn to God.

To maintain the silence, harsh discipline was used in the Auburn system. Any infraction was punished immediately by flogging. Individuals who denied that they spoke would be flogged for lying. Still, guards had to be ever vigilant to keep prisoners from talking. At night, the guards would remove their shoes and tip toe up and down the cellblocks listening for whispering among the inmates. In addition, John Cray, Warden Lynds's deputy, designed the "lockstep" as a way to allow the guards to better prevent talking and thus maintain discipline. The lockstep was a formation for marching inmates through the prison. Each inmate had to walk with a shuffling side step lined up one behind the other with his hand on the shoulder of the man in front of him and turned toward the guards with his eyes cast down. The lockstep march allowed the guard to enforce silence because he could see the face of each inmate. Inmates were monitored nearly constantly or so they may have thought. Officials even watched prisoners from a 2,000-foot passageway through peepholes behind the workshops at Auburn to be sure they worked hard and refrained from talking or other communication.

The men worked in silence from sunup until sundown every day except Sunday. On Sunday, still silent, they were required to attend chapel followed by dinner and returned to their cells. In their cells, they were to remain silent with only a Bible to distract them unless they were lucky enough to receive a visit from the chaplain.

WOMEN

While the male inmates were held to the strict silent system at Auburn, penal administrators did not enforce it as stringently with the women prisoners. It was commonly believed that it would be much more difficult to keep women from speaking to one another. Furthermore, women, it was thought, were naturally more sociable and keeping them silent might damage their nervous systems. As a result, though women were required to work at tasks such as knitting and spooling wool, silence was not strictly imposed.

Even though the women at Auburn were not prohibited from speaking, observers have noted that the conditions of their confinement were much worse than those for men. Women were kept in an unventilated attic above the kitchen. In response to widespread criticism, a matron was finally hired in 1832 to oversee the female inmates, and four large apartments were constructed in the south wing of the prison for women. Female offenders lived here until a new wing for them was opened at Sing Sing in 1838.

RIVALRY WITH THE PENNSYLVANIA SYSTEM

Reverend Louis Dwight, the secretary of the Boston Prison Discipline Society, and others supported the Auburn silent system against its rival the Pennsylvania separate system. Although physically harsher, the Auburn system proved to be much more successful and longstanding than the Pennsylvania system. The reasons for the success were primarily economic. In both systems, inmates were required to be industrious in silence, working six days a week for up to 10 hours a day. However, under the Auburn system, the silent inmates were forced to work together in what were essentially prison-run factories that helped support the costs of the prison. Inmates housed under the silent system made everything from boots, harnesses, carpenters' tools, buckets, and brooms to clocks, wagons, buttons, carpets, and rifles. The prison managers would take bids on the convict labor to companies, which would supply raw material for the inmates to use to make goods that the companies would sell. By paying the inmates little or nothing for their work, the prison managers could cover the cost of the prisons and had the potential to make the prison a profitable enterprise.

CONCLUSION

The profitability of the Auburn system contributed to its implementation in many prisons throughout the world during the 1800s. The silent system was adopted by Coldbath Fields Prison in England during the 19th century. Other prisons were built as congregate prisons including Sing Sing in New York, which opened in 1825, and Kingston Penitentiary in Ontario, which opened in 1835.

While silent congregate labor was adopted by many prisons including Eastern Penitentiary, which had practiced the separate system, the Auburn system eventually died out as well. In 1894, the New York legislature ended contract labor system for inmate work in New York. By the early 1900s, inmates were permitted to speak, and the striped inmate uniforms and lockstep were gone. Still, today though, we see remnants of this system in current ideas about inmate labor and the specialized uniforms required in some prisons.

—Kim Davies

See also Auburn Correctional Facility; Convict Leasing; Eastern State Penitentiary; Hard Labor; History of Labor; History of Prisons; History of Women's Prisons; John Howard; Labor; Newgate Prison; Pennsylvania System; Quakers; San Quentin State Prison; Sing Sing Correctional Facility

Further Reading

Clear, T. R., & Cole, G. F. (1992). *American corrections.* Belmont, CA: Wadsworth.

Nagel, W. G. (1973). *The new red barn: A critical look at the modern American prison.* New York: Walker.

New York State Department of Correctional Service. (1998, April). Auburn Correctional Facility. *Docs Today.*

Teeters, N. K., & Shearer, J. D. (1957). *The prison at Philadelphia Cherry Hill.* New York: Columbia University Press.

Tewksbury, R. (1997). *Introduction to corrections.* New York: McGraw-Hill.

Zedner, L. (1998). Wayward sisters: The prison for women. In N. Morris & D. J. Rothman (Eds.), *The Oxford history of the prison: The practice of punishment in Western society* (pp. 329–362). New York: Oxford University Press.

⬛ AUSTRALIA

Australia is a member of the Commonwealth. Between 1788 and 1829, Britain annexed the whole continent. In 1901 the various colonies united in a federation but retained important links with Britain. The British monarch remains Australia's head of state, a largely ceremonial position. The Australian Federation has six states and two territories, all of them self-governing. The six federating states have a different status constitutionally, from the territories, since they originally derived their power from acts of the British Parliament. These six states, when agreeing to form a nation, delegated certain powers to a central federal Australian parliament: for example, they delegated their external affairs powers but retained their criminal justice powers. There are eight separate criminal justice systems, eight different police forces (the Australian Capital Territory, however, is policed by the Australian Federal Police), and eight separate correctional systems.

STRUCTURE

Correctional systems are the responsibility of state and territory governments, not the federal government.

There are no federal prisons in Australia as there are in the United States. Instead, the small number of federal prisoners who exist are housed in state prisons.

There are many regional and administrative differences and variations between each of the eight correctional systems in Australia. However, in general, each state or territory government has either a government department or a separate government-funded agency that undertakes the administration of corrections, both custodial and community, for that state or territory.

In 2001, the year for which the most recent figures are available, national expenditure on corrective services was $1.46 billion Australian dollars (AUD). Of this total, $1.3 billion (87%) was spent on prisons and correctional centers. Costs per prisoners are different for each jurisdiction, but in 2001 they ranged from $195.90 (AUD) to $108.40 (AUD) per prisoner, per day.

That same year, there were 119 operational adult correctional facilities in Australia that together held an average of 21,138 people per day. A further 1,178 people were serving periodic detention orders, which usually consists of weekend detention only. This practice allows certain prisoners to live at home and maintain work commitments during the week.

Australian prisons hold those awaiting trial or sentence (on remand), as well as those who have been sentenced to a period of incarceration, frequently within separate parts of the same facility. After arrest, offenders can usually only be held for a certain period of time by police until they must be brought before a court. If a court decides to deny them bail and remand them to custody, they will then be moved to a prison. There is no equivalent to the American jails in the one-tiered Australian correctional system.

JUVENILE JUSTICE

In all Australian states and territories, juvenile justice is the responsibility of a separate government department, which usually also administers any custodial facilities for young offenders. In most cases, the juvenile justice systems service offenders aged between 10, which is the age of criminal responsibility in Australia, and 17 years. Eighteen years is the age of legal adulthood in Australia, when persons can vote, consume alcohol, and drive a car. In some jurisdictions, offenders aged 18 years are also held in juvenile detention facilities if they were sentenced prior to turning this age. In some jurisdictions, juveniles may be transferred to adult prisons upon reaching 18 years and in others offenders aged 17 years may be placed in adult prisons if serving a long sentence. There were 604 juvenile offenders detained in custody on June 30, 2001. Juvenile justice in Australia has a range of diversionary measures and policies, including imprisonment as a last resort, which ensures that only around 1% of juveniles in contact with the criminal justice system are actually imprisoned.

HISTORY

Australia was inhabited for thousands of years by the indigenous peoples, Australian Aboriginals, who lived a nomadic and tribal existence with strong connections to the land. They had a complicated system of tribal law and wide and varied communities and languages. Australia was then settled by Europeans, primarily the British, in the 18th century.

From the mid-17th century, British prisoners were transported to America. When the American War of Independence caused the cessation of transportation, British prisoners were housed in disused ships due to the crowding within British prisons. As these "hulks" also became too crowded, it was agreed to commence transportation to the new colony of New South Wales.

British transportation of prisoners to Australia occurred from 1787 to 1868, and included men, women, and children. Though some free settlers came with the first fleet as soldiers, ministers, and so on, most only began to arrive in increasing numbers from 1793. As an incentive to emigrate, these settlers were entitled to apply for a convict on arrival, although this appears not to have occurred until sometime in the early 1800s. Despite the harsh conditions in the new colony, once convicts had served their sentence many elected to remain in Australia as settlers, either because they could not afford the cost of the travel back to Britain or because of better opportunities in the new land.

Australian correctional systems developed from a transplanted system of British criminal justice. Despite having autonomy for their own system since federation in 1901, prisons and their administration in Australia have continued to mirror the development of corrections in the United Kingdom; however, increasingly, Australian policy is also influenced by practices in the United States.

DEVELOPMENT OF CORRECTIONS, 1970s–1990s

Since the 1970s, Australia, like many countries in the world, has experienced significant growth in the use of imprisonment. At the same time, there has been a continuing controversy over the effectiveness of imprisonment as a method of dealing with crime.

During the 1970s, prisoners' rights and public information of what was occurring behind the walls of the prisons became important issues. There were a number of governmental inquiries during this time as well as a substantial number of prisoner riots throughout all of the nation's correctional systems. A number of prisoners and ex-prisoners also made their grievances known through litigation.

In the mid-1970s, prisoners in many Australian states fought successfully to retain their status as citizens while incarcerated, to be permitted to marry, to hold bank accounts, to vote in elections, and to sue and be sued. Administrative law provisions were also strengthened during these years through the appointment of Parliamentary Commissioners (ombudsmen), who could examine the actions of correctional officials either on their own account or following complaints from prisoners. The first of these ombudsmen were appointed in Western Australia in 1972. These commissioners created a powerful check and balance on the exercise of power within correctional institutions. Recently, Western Australia has appointed a prison inspector (based on

the United Kingdom model) with additional powers designed to increase oversight of correctional administration, practice, and process. Queensland, too, has recently instituted an external body, the Crime and Misconduct Commission, to oversee staff conduct.

In the 1970s and 1980s, women correctional officers began to be employed in prisons for men and social workers and welfare officers were introduced to all penal institutions. During this time, although there was an abandonment of the aim of rehabilitation, correctional centers began to emphasize accountability and humane containment in prisons. These ideals were challenged, however, with the advent of the HIV/AIDS epidemic and a significant rise in deaths in custody in the mid- and late 1980s. As a result of the noticeable increase of deaths in custody, the Australian governments agreed to the formation of the Royal Commission Into Aboriginal Deaths in Custody (RCIADIC), which had significant implications in the development of the various correctional systems.

Finally, the 1990s saw the reemergence of punitiveness in punishment, resulting in rising incarceration rates. Privatization of corrections has been the most visible response to increasing imprisonment rates. Five of the eight jurisdictions currently operate private prisons in Australia. Currently, approximately 17% of Australia's correctional centers are privately operated.

PRISON DEMOGRAPHICS

Every year on June 30, each state and territory in Australia undertakes a national prisoner census. Each state supplies the centralized Australian Bureau of Statistics (ABS) with a range of information on prisoner demographics, including characteristics related to most serious offense and length of sentence. The ABS then outlines the number of prisoners in custody on that night, by state and correctional center as well as daily averages for each month in the preceding year (e.g., July 1, 2001, to June 30, 2002). These figures provide an excellent snapshot of changes in the Australian correctional system over time.

Gender

Currently, the majority of prisoners, 93% (20,960), in Australia are male. The imprisonment rate for men is currently 285 per 100,000 adult male population and for female prisoners is 20 per 100,000 adult female population. While males continue to dominate the prison population globally, the proportion of prisoners who are female has increased in Australia in the past 10 years from 5% in 1991 to 7% in 2001.

There are now separate prisons for women in all states. However, given the small number of women incarcerated in each Australian jurisdiction, there are generally only one or two options in terms of where they can be housed. As a result, in most cases, women's prisons are built to accommodate all security levels within the one center. Also, due to the large geographic areas of some states, some prisons house both males and females, albeit in segregated areas.

Women are generally incarcerated for shorter periods of time than men. In most Australian jurisdictions, women have the right to have their children remain in custody with them from birth until a designated age—generally this is somewhere from three years to five years old. The correctional centers often have designated living units for these women with larger cells to accommodate a cot.

Type of Prisoner

Eighty-one percent (18,123) of all Australian prisoners are serving a sentence, and 19% (4,335) are remanded in custody either awaiting or involved in a trial or awaiting sentencing. Thirty-five percent of sentenced prisoners are serving a fixed-term sentence. Fifty-three percent are serving a maximum-minimum sentence, that is, those prisoners are eligible for release after serving a minimum term (set by the court) in custody and who must be released once the maximum term (also set by the court) has been served.

Most Australian prisoners are sentenced under the laws of the state or territory where the offense was committed. Only about 5% of all Australian prisoners are federal prisoners held under Commonwealth laws. Most of these are imprisoned for offenses relating to drugs, particularly trafficking and importation offenses.

Indigenous Imprisonment

Indigenous people are overrepresented in the nation's prison systems and are a significant factor in rising incarceration rates. They are estimated to be 2.4% of Australia's total population but make up 20% of the country's prison population. There are currently 4,445 indigenous prisoners in Australia. They are approximately 15 times more likely to be imprisoned than nonindigenous people. They have an imprisonment rate of 1,829 prisoners per 100,000 adult indigenous population compared to an imprisonment rate of 150 per 100,000 for nonindigenous persons. After substantive and ongoing research in this area, it is now more widely recognized that the overrepresentation of Aboriginal people in the Australian criminal justice system is the result of underlying structural issues, including racism, poverty, and destruction of their culture.

Imprisonment Rates

The prisoner population in Australia increased by 50% between 1991 and 2001. The adult imprisonment rate increased from a national average of 117 to 150 per 100,000. Within Australia, in the six states and two territories, imprisonment rates vary substantially, with some jurisdictions below the national average and others well above.

Offense Composition

Nearly half (48%) of all currently sentenced prisoners are convicted of offenses involving violence or the threat of violence, including murder (7%), other homicide (3%), assault (11%), sex offenses (10%), other offenses against the person (1%), and robbery (13%). Sentenced prisoners convicted of a property offense as their most serious offense currently represent 26% of all sentenced prisoners, including 12% for break and enter. A further 9% are serving sentences for drug offenses as their most serious offense and 4% of sentenced prisoners were convicted and incarcerated for driving offenses.

GENERAL PRISON CONDITIONS

Each jurisdiction has its own correctional legislation and policies relating to the administration of punishment. However, there is also a national body, the National Correction Minister's Council, with a representative from each of the states and territories as well as New Zealand, that meets annually to discuss issues of concern, exchange ideas, and review existing national guidelines. This national body allows for some degree of standardization across the country particularly in relation to the maintenance of national guidelines and various international obligations.

Australia is a signatory to some of the United Nations conventions relating to punishment and has developed its own Minimum Standard Guidelines. These guidelines are based on the United Nations Standard Minimum Rules for the Treatment of Prisoners and related recommendations as well as the Council of Europe Standard Minimum Rules. They do not have the status of legislation, and the level of implementation is debatable. Court action has been attempted by inmates relying on the Standard Minimum Rules regarding time out of cell, exercise, standard of food, and overcrowding, but all cases have been unsuccessful as the courts have ruled that the Minimum Standard Guidelines are guidelines only and are not legally enforceable.

Housing

There are two types of custody in Australia, open and secure. Open custody is generally where prisoners are accommodated in very low security facilities. Most of the low/open security facilities are called "prison farms" and are generally located in geographically remote areas. They are usually not surrounded by fences, other than normal stock fencing, or locked in cells/units. Prisoners in these institutions are free to come and go within most areas of the facilities and are placed there on a trust basis because they are not considered a risk to themselves, other prisoners, staff, or the wider community. Secure custody refers to more traditional prisons and correctional centers that are surrounded by walls, fences, and electronic security, within which movement is strongly curtailed by staff. In these, prisoners must usually be escorted from one part of the prison to another or prisoner movement is electronically controlled by opening and closing various gates and doors and the provision of airlocks.

In general, most prisoners in Australia occupy a one- or two-person cell. In most jurisdictions, shower/toilet facilities are located within each cell. There remain some dormitory-style accommodations with shared shower facilities in various correctional centers in some of the more remote centers. Most inmates are expected to complete their own washing, cooking, and cleaning within their living areas and cells. Living arrangements vary from individual small huts on many of the prison farms to secure units, which range from 4 to 50 cells. Each unit generally has a kitchen and communal living and exercise areas. Some have individual laundry facilities as well. Most prisons also have staff administration areas, sporting facilities, and separate facilities for education, prison industries, and religious services. They also offer correctional programs such as anger management, sex offender treatment programs, and the like and individual therapy such as counseling. Many of the proffered programs are now being adapted for various discrete groups such as indigenous persons and those of non-English-speaking background.

Clothing

Prisoners are supplied with clothing by the prison for the duration of their term, including footwear. Usually, they are supplied with shorts, T-shirts, underwear (although some women's prisons allow women to purchase their own underwear), tracksuits for winter, and one pair of canvas sneaker type shoe. Usually, these are in one designated color, for example, in one state all male prisoners wear brown, in another green. If prisoners damage the clothing, they are generally responsible for replacing it at their own cost.

Food

In most jurisdictions, the type of food is related to the level of security in which prisoners are housed. However, it is now common that each living unit has its own kitchen and ingredients are supplied for prisoners to make their own meals. Often a prisoner will be assigned the role of unit cook and expected to prepare and cook for the others in that unit. In higher-security units or older centers without individual-unit kitchens, meals may be delivered precooked usually by the central prison kitchen, staffed by prisoners.

Prison Industries

The majority of correctional centers now have designated prison factories. Industries that exist in secure custody include bakeries, laundries, woodworking, metal working, and tailor shops. Industries in open custody include nurseries, dairies, and farming. These prison factories often generate income for the prison. The money either becomes part of that center's individual budget (offsetting other expenditure) or is returned to the central department that oversees that state's correctional facilities and is reallocated as part of the larger overall correctional funding for that state. There is, however, strict legislation in most states/territories that monitors the types of industries prisons are able to undertake and how they can be run. Prison factories must not compete with other industries in the general community.

Money in Prison

The wages prisoners earn as a result of employment within the prison industries vary, depending on the jurisdiction and the type of work in which they are involved. Inmates can also study full time in some jurisdictions and are given a small wage as a full-time student. If they do not choose to work or if the prisons are unable to provide employment for all who request it, prisoners receive a small amount of unemployment funding. Prisoners have an account at the prison and, in most jurisdictions, family members are allowed to deposit up to a certain amount of money each month. Prisoners are expected to buy some food, beverages, cigarettes, and personal hygiene items with this money and there is a limit on what can be spent each week. In some centers, prisoners can buy a TV or radio for their cells from this money.

Staff

There are no nationally collated numbers of staff who work in corrections currently available in Australia. Each state and territory is responsible for the recruitment, selection, and training of its staff. Recently, nationally endorsed competency standards have been developed for correctional employees throughout Australia but how each state incorporates these competency standards into its own training is quite individualized.

Apart from the normal staff associated with a prison, there are also external personnel who provide assistance. These include teachers, who may come to the prison for a set number of weeks to offer a particular course; prisoner support organizations, for example, indigenous elders/mentors; and official visitors such as ombudsman or the prison inspector, who arrive to discuss concerns or grievances with prisoners.

NATIONAL ISSUES OF CONCERN

While there is much variance in Australian corrections there are also matters that cross over all jurisdictions due to their importance or commonality. Issues of national concern in recent history include deaths in custody, mandatory sentencing, and privatization. These issues have resulted in practical changes across Australian correctional systems, although the implications and associated implementation are often different for each jurisdiction.

Deaths in Custody

Australia remains the only Western country to have established at the highest level (national) an inquiry into deaths in custody. Known as the Royal Commission Into Aboriginal Deaths in Custody (RCIADIC), this inquiry was established following a rapid increase in Aboriginal deaths in custody in the mid-1980s. Despite the focus on indigenous deaths, the inquiry has had wide-ranging implication for the handling of all deaths in custody. A key recommendation of the RCIADIC was that all deaths in custody should be monitored and that data should be routinely collected about them. Indeed, there have been remarkable advances made in the recording and reporting of deaths in custody as well as changes to organizational processes and architectural design that seem to have reduced the number of deaths. For example, the total custodial deaths in Australia in 1987 were 93 compared to a total of 56 people dying in prison custody in 2001. However, there has been little research that has analyzed the wider *national* social, structural, and organizational issues concerning the prevention of further deaths in custody rather than at a jurisdictional level. In particular, many deficiencies remain in police, correctional, and coronial practices.

Mandatory Sentencing

Mandatory sentencing first occurred within Australia in the late 1990s following international trends, particularly from the United States. It was introduced within the Northern Territory and Western Australia in relation to property offenses, especially break and enter offenses; however, there remained extensive debate throughout Australia about the introduction of such laws. The legislation within the Northern Territory was repealed after a change of government in early 2000, and the Western Australian legislation was also recently amended due to perceptions that such legislation continued to exacerbate the overrepresentation of indigenous Australians within Australian criminal justice systems.

Privatization

The decade of the 1990s saw the reemergence in Australia of organizations providing correctional programs for governments in Australia. While the private provision of correctional programs, especially medical services and some specialist rehabilitation programs, had been occurring for some time, it was in 1990 that Australia's first privately operated prison (Borallon) commenced operation.

Since then approximately 10% of Australia's prisoners have been incarcerated in privately managed prisons. The private operators are responsible for the full range of prisons from high- to medium- and low-security facilities. Three major companies are involved: Corrections Corporation of Australia (CCA), Australasian Correctional Management (ACM), and Group 4 Securitas (Group 4). The first two companies are consortia with strong U.S. connections, and Group 4 Securitas is European. All three have access to advice and information about the private operation of prisons from their overseas operations. There are no wholly owned Australian companies operating private Australian prisons.

Until very recently, the detailed contracts between state governments and the private providers have not been accessible to the public because of commercial-in-confidence provisions that make it impossible to know precisely how much the state pays private corporations to run its penal facilities. This has made discussion about the relative cost advantages of the private operators compared with government operations extremely difficult. Administrative integration of a multioperator system is an ongoing challenge and has produced problems of controlling the appropriate flow of information about prisoners through the correctional system.

There have, however, also been some advantages. The introduction of newer and different models of prisoner management, modeled on the overseas experiences, has meant that many older prisons within Australia have been closed and that many of the public correctional systems have adopted similar models of prisoner management. In particular, unit management and the wider provision and utilization of prison industries have occurred within publicly owned prisons since privatization.

CONCLUSION

Australian corrections remain a somewhat fragmented system. Australian correctional systems have only recently come together to share information on what works and what does not. Recent innovations, including large-scale capital works and increased demands for accountability in state criminal justice systems, have substantially changed penal practice to the point where, while continuing to mirror overseas development, Australian corrections is now developing its own unique processes and structures.

—Anna Alice Grant

See also Canada; Contract Facilities; England and Wales; Federal Prison System; Food; Jails; Juvenile Justice System; Labor; Native American Prisoners; New Zealand; Private Prisons; Race, Class, and Gender of Prisoners; State Prison System; Suicide; Truth in Sentencing; Wackenhut Corporation; Women Prisoners; Women's Prisons

Further Reading

Australian Bureau of Statistics. (2004). Australian Bureau of Statistics home page. http://www.abs.gov.au/

Bevan, C. (Ed.). (1984). *Minimum standard guidelines for Australian prisons.* Canberra: Australian Institute of Criminology.

Carcach, C., & Grant, A. (1999). Imprisonment in Australia: Trends in prison populations and imprisonment rates 1982–1998. In *Trends and issues in crime and criminal justice No. 130.* Canberra: Australian Institute of Criminology.

Dalton, V. (1999). Australian deaths in custody & custody related police operations. In *Trends and issues in crime and criminal justice No. 105.* Canberra: Australian Institute of Criminology.

Dawes, J., & Grant, A (2000). An expensive decision: Corrections in Australia. In Australian Institute of Criminology, *Handbook of Australian criminology.* Cambridge, UK: Cambridge University Press.

Finnane, M. (1997). *Punishment in Australian society.* Melbourne: Oxford University Press.

Harding, R. (1997). *Private prisons and public accountability.* Buckingham, UK: Open University Press.

Johnston, E. (1991). *Royal commission into Aboriginal deaths in custody, national report, Volumes 1–5.* Canberra: Australian Government Publication Service.

Roche, D. (1999). Mandatory sentencing. In *Trends and issues in crime and criminal justice No. 138.* Canberra: Australian Institute of Criminology.

Royal Commission Into Aboriginal Deaths in Custody. (J. H. Muirhead, chair). (1991). *Interim report.* Canberra: Australian Government Publication Service.

Productivity Commission. (2002). *Report on government services.* Canberra: Australian Government Printer.

Wimshurst, K., & Harrison, A. (2000). The Australian criminal justice system: Issues and prospects. In D. Chappell & P. Wilson (Eds.), *Crime and the criminal justice system in Australia: 2000 and beyond.* Sydney: Butterworths.

B

◪ BATES, SANFORD (1884–1972)

Sanford Bates was one of the preeminent penologists in the United States. He was particularly known for his support of rehabilitation and many related reforms and innovations. He had more than 50 years administering local, state, and federal prison and parole systems, including a stint as director of the Federal Bureau of Prisons from 1930 to 1937.

BACKGROUND

Sanford Bates, born July 17, 1884, practiced law from 1906 to 1918 in Boston and served two 2-year terms in the Massachusetts legislature. He entered penology reluctantly. First, the Republican administration in Boston persuaded Bates to act as street commissioner. A few months later, the city needed a commissioner of penal institutions and appointed Bates, over his objections. By the time he retired as commissioner of the New Jersey Department of Institutions and Agencies in 1954 at the age of 70, Bates had served successively as penitentiary commissioner of his native Massachusetts (appointed by then-Governor Calvin Coolidge), and parole commissioner of New York State and superintendent of Federal Prisons. He was director of the Federal Bureau of Prisons from 1930 to 1937, and then

went on to serve as executive director of the Boys Clubs of America, Inc. until 1940.

His performance earned him a reputation both nationally and internationally. For example, he was elected president of the American Prison Association as well as the International Penal and Penitentiary Commission. He headed a five-year survey of sentencing, probation, and parole in connection with the American Bar Foundation's study of criminal justice. President Harry Truman appointed Bates to the U.N. Commission on Crime Prevention. Bates died on September 8, 1972, at the age of 88.

CONTRIBUTIONS

Bates's 50 years of service left a mark on the study and practice of penology. While commissioner of penal institutions in Boston, he introduced a prison school and partial self-government for inmates. During his decade as commissioner of the Massachusetts State Department of Correction, Bates revised the parole system, introduced printing and foundry work to the available prison industries, established merit pay for prison employees and a state wage for prisoners, founded model institutions for male and female "defective delinquents," and created the first crime prevention bureau connected with a prison department. He also offered inmates university extension courses and arranged for county prisoners to be examined by state psychiatrists.

During his seven-year tenure of director of the Federal Bureau of Prisons, 15 institutions were added to the system, including not only Alcatraz (a famous maximum-security prison) but also libraries, medical departments, bureaus of social work, and training programs for guards. In both New York and New Jersey, Bates established model parole systems. In New Jersey, he transferred many prisoners from maximum-security prisons to work farms and experimented with using inmate labor on public outdoor projects.

One of Bates's most significant contributions was ridding the penal system of politics. At the time he became director of the federal prison system, federal prisons were, as one scholar observed, "virtual hostages of the patronage process." Wardens were lightly supervised by the Department of Justice while dedicated to maintaining good ties to their sponsors in Congress to whom they owed their jobs. By contrast, Bates sought to base hiring and promotion on merit, not patronage. While he recognized the importance of maintaining good ties with Congress, he noted in a March 26, 1929, letter to Attorney General William D. Mitchell that "I should confidently expect the backing of my superiors in withstanding that happily infrequent kind of pressure which comes sometimes from the unreasonable demands on persons whose chief aim in life is political." His position was particularly noteworthy given that he himself had been a politician in a state known for its patronage.

In his book *Prisons and Beyond*, articles, and letters, Bates articulated a guiding philosophy for the management of prison inmates. Although seeing inmates as individuals and advocating a humane system of incarceration and parole seem unremarkable today, at the time this view was unusual. Bates's philosophy reflected not only his commitment to reformation but also his belief that the Bureau of Prisons should be a role model for other states to emulate. His accomplishments prompted the Chairman Wickersham of the president's law enforcement commission to voice regret that the commission's last report had not differentiated between federal and state institutions when it denounced the present prison system as antiquated, inefficient, and failing either to reform offenders or to protect society. Wickersham acknowledged that the revolutionary changes Bates had introduced in the system of penal management, control, custody, and training of offenders were inadequately recognized.

CONCLUSION

Sanford Bates shaped ideas about and practices of punishment in the United States during and after his lifetime. As director of the Federal Bureau of Prisons, he left his mark on a national system of prisons that itself guided many state systems. A lifelong civil servant, he demonstrates the impact one individual can have on broader policies and procedures. To that end, he is one of a number of prison reformers and workers who have shaped the current U.S. penal system

—*Jeanne Flavin*

See also Alcatraz; James V. Bennett; Zebulon Reed Brockway; Katharine Bement Davis; Federal Prison System; Kathleen Hawk Sawyer; Rehabilitation Theory; Mabel Walker Wildebrandt

Further Reading

Bates, S. (1934, February 4). The prison: A complex problem. *New York Times*, p. SM1.
Bates, S. (1936). *Prisons and beyond*. New York: Macmillan.
Keve, P. (1991). *Prisons and the American conscience.* Carbondale: Southern Illinois University Press.
Keve, P. (1994). The sources of excellence. *Federal Prisons Journal, 3*(3), 11–14.

▮ BECCARIA, CESARE (1738–1794)

Cesare Bonesana Marchese Beccaria, was a key figure in the history of criminology and in the field of punishment. Typically, he is identified as the founder of the classical school of criminology, and as one of the first modern proponents of deterrence. In 1764, he anonymously published his ideas in a treatise titled *Dei Delitti e delle Pene (On*

Crimes and Punishments). This text subsequently influenced the development of systems of punishment in most contemporaneous European nation states, and in the United States as well. It was translated into French in 1766 and a later edition, with an introduction by Voltaire, found its place in the salons and courts of Europe within movements of reform identified with the rising bourgeoisie and "enlightened" aristocrats. Praised for its clarity, eloquence, and humanity, *On Crimes and Punishments* was translated into English in 1767. Beccaria's views were hailed by Jeremy Bentham as the foundation of his work and were cited as an influence on the thought of William Blackstone. In the newly forming United States, John Adams, Benjamin Franklin, James Wilson, Thomas Jefferson, and others recorded the use of Beccaria's insights in their efforts to shape both the federal constitution and new state judicial and criminal legislation and penal sanctions.

Along with many of his contemporaries, Beccaria believed that members of a society were bound by a social contract that legitimated laws for the security of their persons and property. He also argued that human behavior was driven by a utilitarian approach in which people sought to avoid pain and seek pleasure and happiness. His own summary of his views, as a "general axiom," was that "in order that punishment should not be an act of violence perpetrated by one or many against a private citizen, it must be essential that it be public, speedy, necessary, the minimum possible in the given circumstances, proportionate to the crime, and determined by the law" (Beccaria, 1995, p. 113). His eloquent arguments against the use of torture and for the abolition of capital punishment were widely quoted in his day and retain their relevance today.

Somewhat ironically, more recent neoclassical criminology has been identified with a "get tough on crime" stance that only partially reflects Beccaria's initial plea for penal reform. Thus, contemporary scholars stress the role of rational choice in criminal behavior, the use of determinant rather than discretionary sentencing, and the deterrent rather than rehabilitative function of corrections.

BACKGROUND

Beccaria was born into an aristocratic Milanese family of moderate wealth. After graduating from the University of Pavia with a doctorate in law in 1758, he joined a literary academy frequented by other young men from the Milanese elite. Subsequently, he followed his mentor and friend Pietro Verri into a new "Academy of Fists," whose members' heated debates on scientific, literary, social, and economic issues and reforms, stimulated Beccaria's interest in and writing on monetary reform. He later responded to Verri's suggestion that he turn his talents and eloquence to a study of the existing criminal law. With the supportive assistance of the members and following extensive editing by Verri, since initially Beccaria knew little about the criminal system, the manuscript developed from a pile of notes. Fear of the reaction of the authorities to his critique led to his decision to publish it anonymously at first. After the fame of his work spread there were demands for his presence, but after a short visit to Paris in 1766, where he was hailed as a benefactor of humanity, he returned to Milan where he remained, despite an invitation by Catherine the Great to implement his recommendations in Russia. Active first as a professor of economics, and later in a series of governmental positions in Lombardy, he continued to write on subjects in political economy and remained active until his death in 1794.

It was not until 1791, when Beccaria was appointment by Emperor Leopold II to a commission for the formulation of a new criminal code for Lombardy that he was involved directly in an effort to bring his recommendations into law. The members subsequently split over the question of the abolition of capital punishment, and after long debates and in the face of political instability after the French Revolution the commission's work was never implemented. Beccaria did not live to see his work bear fruit in his own land. However, in the new United States his work had greater impact.

PENAL REFORM

In an early edition of *On Crimes and Punishment*, an allegorical engraving shows Justice turning from an executioner brandishing a shorn head to a pile of chains, a shovel, and a mallet resting at her feet. In his widely read and debated chapter on the death penalty when public executions or their threat were widely used as the punishment for crime, Beccaria (1995) argued that when "a man who sees ahead of him many years, or even the remainder of his life, passed in slavery and suffering before the eyes of his fellow citizens . . . the slave of those laws by which he was protected, [the example] will make a stronger impression on him than would a spectacle which hardens more than it reforms him" (pp. 70–71).

Even before the formation of the United States, John Adams, in his successful defense of the British soldiers tried after the Boston Massacre in 1770, quoted Beccaria: "If I can but be the instrument of preserving one life, his blessing and tears of transport shall be sufficient consolation to me for the contempt of all mankind" (Maestro, 1973, p. 137). Likewise, Beccaria's influence was apparent in the efforts to restrict the use of the death penalty in the new state codes and the apparent agreement, in a country where the institution of slavery was widespread and accepted, that penal slavery was an appropriate substitute for death.

In Pennsylvania, influenced by Beccaria's thought, Benjamin Franklin, Benjamin Rush, and others in 1786 revised the criminal code limiting the death penalty to murder, rape, arson, and treason and substituted in its place "hard labor, publically and disgracefully imposed." This practice, however, that placed chained prisoners with shaven heads cleaning and repairing the streets of Philadelphia evoked disturbances that led the authorities by 1790 not only to move the punishment from public view but also to substitute private solitary labor. With the construction of cells for solitary confinement, the Walnut Street Jail became hailed as the birthplace of the American penitentiary—a reversal of Beccaria's basic argumentation.

In Virginia, Thomas Jefferson with others began the revision of the criminal law in 1778 citing Beccaria's opposition to the death penalty and recommending the substitution of hard labor on public works. Their legislative efforts lost. When the bill limiting the death penalty to crimes of treason and murder successfully passed in 1796, following the experience in Philadelphia, the alternative punishment of "slavery and suffering" rather than death, led in Virginia to the construction and use of the prison rather than public works.

CONCLUSION

Beccaria's influence was not only felt during the classical period when many of his insights, summarized in his "general axiom," including the rule of law, judicial codes, and public trials, were embodied in legislative and judicial reforms following both the American and French Revolutions but also in continuing efforts in abolish capital punishment. In the United States, his arguments that public slavery at hard labor was a greater deterrent to crime than public executions became, in the twist of political events and control, the impetus for the development of the solitary cells of the penitentiary while retaining the goal of hard labor. Finally, in the more recent rational choice revival of neoclassical criminology the works and insights of Beccaria have again found their advocates.

—Esther Heffernan

See also Jeremy Bentham; Capital Punishment; Chain Gangs; Determinate Sentencing; Deterrence Theory; Hard Labor; Benjamin Rush; Slavery; Walnut Street Jail

Further Reading

Beccaria, C. (1963). *On crimes and punishments* (H. Paolucci, Trans.). New York: Bobbs-Merrill. (Original work published 1764)

Bellamy, R. (Ed.). (1995). *Beccaria: On crimes and punishment and other writings*. Cambridge, UK: Cambridge University Press.

Maestro, M. (1973). *Cesare Beccaria and the origins of penal reform*. Philadelphia: Temple University Press.

◪ BEDFORD HILLS CORRECTIONAL FACILITY

In the world of corrections, Bedford Hills Correctional Facility, a maximum-security prison in the state of New York, is well known for its historical past and the innovative correctional program it currently offers its inmates. However, Bedford Hills is relatively unknown to the general public, principally because its inmates are women.

HISTORY

In New York's earliest correctional history, women were housed at men's prisons or in local jails. Between 1838 and 1877, a building at Sing Sing Prison served as the state's women's facility. When overcrowding became an issue in the men's section of Sing Sing, women were moved to county jails in Brooklyn, Buffalo, and Rochester. The condition of women inmates did not improve in these places as local jails were hardly a suitable place for state-sentenced inmates facing years of confinement.

As reformatories were being established with the promise to salvage young men's lives through education and parole, legislators were pressed to give women the same consideration. Eleven years after the world-renowned Elmira Reformatory opened, the Hudson House of Refuge for Women opened in 1887. With the success of the Hudson House, in 1892, the New York State Legislature passed a bill authorizing a woman's reformatory in Westchester County, to be built at Bedford Station on the Harlem Railroad line.

Seven years later, the New York State Reformatory for Women at Bedford opened, with the first inmates arriving on May 11, 1901. The reformatory was to house women, aged 16 to 30, who had been convicted of minor offenses. Bedford was controlled by a Board of Managers, appointed by the governor. Dr. Katharine Bement Davis was named Bedford's first superintendent. Davis's innovations at Bedford won her national and international acclaim as a champion of women's suffrage.

The first inmates at Bedford Hills worked half a day cooking; making clothing, baskets, and hats; and working in the laundry building. The women milked cows, raised chickens and pigs, farmed in vegetables, planted trees, shoveled coal, painted cottages, and put up fences. They built an artificial pond and harvested the ice during winter. They also learned to make concrete, building thousands of square feet of walkways, stairways, and floors.

The other half of the day was spent in traditional education classes, as well as courses in carpentry, stenography, typing, chair caning, painting, mechanical drawing, cobbling, and bookbinding. Gymnastics classes, inmate productions of Gilbert and Sullivan musicals, and summer recreation were also a part of Davis's fresh-air treatment of the inmates.

In 1927, Bedford, as part of a reorganization of New York's state government, was placed under the newly created Department of Correction. In 1933, women from the state prison in Auburn were moved to a group of buildings adjacent to the reformatory. The entire complex was renamed the Westfield State Farm. Although the reformatory and prison were within one-quarter mile of each other, they operated as two distinct institutions separated by a road and fence.

In 1970, Westfield State Farm was reorganized as women were removed from the prison section and replaced with male inmates. The reformatory became a general confinement facility for women. This new complex constituted a single institution called the Bedford Hills Correctional Facility. The men and women inmates were separated with the exception of coed activities such as creative writing classes and dances.

In 1973, the male prison was administratively separated from Bedford Hills and was renamed Taconic. As the state female inmate population rose to unprecedented numbers, Taconic was converted to a medium-security prison for women, which remains today distinct from the Bedford Hills maximum-security facility.

BEDFORD HILLS TODAY

Today's Bedford Hills is dramatically different to its reformatory predecessor. Currently, Bedford Hills is the only maximum-security women's facility operating in the state of New York. In addition, it is the receiving and classification center for all women sentenced to prison.

Living conditions are different also. When reformatories were being built for women, the architecture was soft, keeping with the image that women were passive and congenitally domestic. The original unfenced facility consisted of cottages, each with its own kitchen and flower garden. The women were placed in cottages according to age, marital status, and behavior.

Today at Bedford Hills, within the confines of massive security fencing, prisoners live in a variety of styles and ages of buildings. Some live in three-story brick buildings built in the 1960s, while others live in modern dormitories. Fiske Cottage, built in 1933 and a remaining link to the past, serves as an "honor house" with individual rooms to which the inmates hold the keys.

New mothers at Bedford Hills live with their babies in the Nursery, the oldest prison nursery in the United States, for up to 18 months. In addition, this is currently the only women's facility to offer its inmates a Family Reunion Program, consisting of overnight, private visits with spouses, children, and other family members of the inmates. The Children's Center is an innovative program designed to make children feel comfortable while visiting their mothers. Both the Nursery and the Children's Center are staffed by inmate child care workers. Other programs include education and advocacy in custody and foster care situations and education workshops to improve parenting skills.

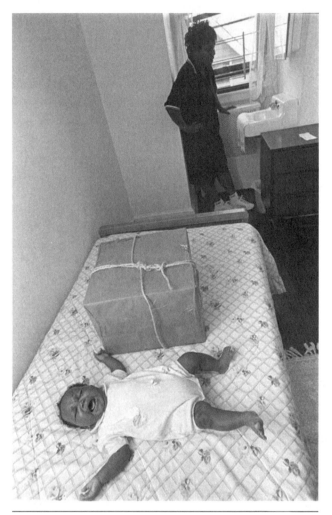

Photo 1   *Bedford Hills*

THE CHILDREN'S CENTER

The Children's Center offers a wide variety of services to women sentenced at Bedford Hills. The main goal of the center is to assist the women in strengthening and preserving their families, in particular their relationships with their children. The center is funded by the Department of Correctional Services and programs are administered by Catholic Charities, in the diocese of Brooklyn. Prisoners primarily conduct the programs, with responsibilities being to plan activities and arrange for workshops, as well as teaching and initiating the programs.

There are various centers within the broader scope of the Children's Center. These include the Children's Center, Parenting Center, Nursery, Infant Day Care Center, Prenatal Center, and Child

Advocacy Office. Each of them will be discussed below.

The Children's Center consists of a well-equipped playroom, with games, age-appropriate toys, building blocks, easels for painting, and a children's library. During holidays, the center is seasonally decorated with matching craft activities. This is currently the only prison in the United States where children and their mothers may visit unescorted.

Within the Parenting Center are 20 different programs and services provided to the inmates. Programs include child development associate courses, where inmates earn credentials as child development associates to work in an accredited nursery school; mental hygiene programs; parenting courses; and bilingual parenting training.

Services include holiday activities, a mother's group, nursery aids, a transportation clinic, and a toy library.

Women who are pregnant upon arriving at Bedford Hills will deliver their children in a hospital located outside the prison and will then return to live with their children in the Nursery, located in the facility medical building. Keeping mother and child together has always been acknowledged and respected at Bedford Hills, understanding that the child's best interest is paramount. In addition, it is believed that inmates who maintain strong bonds with their families during their incarceration period have a greater chance of rehabilitation with a lower chance of recidivism. Parenting, educational, vocational, and substance abuse treatment programs in combination with bonding with their children help the women at Bedford Hills to establish a strong foundation for a lifestyle change.

In February 1990, the Infant Day Care Center opened at Bedford Hills. The purpose of this program is to care for children of inmates who are attending school or engaged in work assignments. This center is staffed by prisoners who have been trained through the child development associate courses. Outside volunteers, known as the "Grandmothers' Group," spend time in the center assisting staff and mothers.

The Prenatal Center was established as recognition of this most critical time in a woman's pregnancy. This center provides pregnant inmates with the opportunity to receive parenting classes and substance abuse classes, as well as sewing, crocheting, and other handwork/craft classes.

Finally, the Child Advocacy Office was established to address all child-related problems. Mothers meet individually with trained child advocates and contacts are made with family members, schools, and various social agencies. In addition, cases involving out-of-state transportation and other unusual problems are directed to this office.

CONCLUSION

Bedford Hills Correctional Facility has come a long way since its humble beginnings as a reformatory for New York's female misdemeanants. Today, as the state's only maximum-security prison for women, it functions as a caring community whose residents aid and support each other. Bedford Hills and its innovative programs, particularly the Children's Center with its various programs for mothers and children, have received numerous awards in recent years. Representatives from across the country, as well as China, England, France, and Scotland, have paid official visits to view firsthand the facility and programs.

—Deborah Mitchell Robinson
and Douglas Neil Robinson

See also Alderson, Federal Prison Camp; Children; Katharine Bement Davis; Fathers in Prison; Gynecology; History of Women's Prisons; Maximum Security; Mothers in Prison; Parenting Programs; Prison Nurseries; State Prison System; War on Drugs; Women Prisoners; Women's Advocate Ministry; Women's Health; Women's Prisons

Further Reading

Family and Corrections Network. (1993). The children's centre—Bedford Hills Correctional Facility. In *Report from the Fourth North American Conference on the Family and Corrections, Quebec City, Quebec, Canada.* Palmyra, VA: Author.

McCarthy, T. C. (1997). *Correction's Katharine Bement Davis: New York City's suffragist commissioner.* Retrieved from http://www.correctionhistory.org/html/chronicl/kbd/kdb11.html

New York State Department of Correctional Services. (1998). Albion Correctional Facility. *DOCS Today, 7*(9), 22–25.

New York State Department of Correctional Services. (1999). Bedford Hills Correctional Facility. *DOCS Today, 2*(5), 12–15.

◪ BENNETT, JAMES V.
(1894–1978)

James V. Bennett was the second director of the Federal Bureau of Prisons (BOP), serving longer than any other (1937 to 1964). Bennett played a role in establishing the centralized bureaucracy for overseeing the operation of federal prisons, the BOP, while working for the U.S. Bureau of Efficiency. In 1928, he produced a report, *The Federal Penal and Correctional Problem,* that described the deteriorating conditions caused by severe overcrowding at the three existing penitentiaries of the time—Leavenworth (Kansas), Atlanta (Georgia), and McNeil Island (California). He identified three acts taken after 1920—the Prohibition Act, the Harrison Narcotic Act, and the Automobile Theft (Dyer) Act—as contributing to the rising number of federal inmates. Instead of proposing to expand the three existing federal prisons, Bennett reasoned that additional federal prisons should be built to reduce transportation costs and to preserve prison sizes that could be managed easily by one warden.

Prior to joining the Bureau of Efficiency and later the BOP, Bennett had graduated from Brown University (1918) and served as a cadet aviator in the Army Air Corps during World War I. Bennett received his law degree in 1926 from George Washington University. He was hired by the first director of the BOP, Sanford Bates, in 1929, shortly after the formal establishment of the BOP.

Bennett argued in 1935 that one of the key issues facing prison management was inmate idleness. One of his key contributions prior to assuming the directorship of the BOP was serving as the initial commissioner of prison industries, which since 1978 has been known by the trade name UNICOR. Under his leadership, legislation was written and enacted by Congress that established Federal Prison Industries, Inc. as a separate corporate entity in 1934. As a corporate entity, prison industries had its own board of directors and working capital that was separate from the federal appropriations process. President Franklin D. Roosevelt and Sanford Bates established the policy that prison industries should be broadly diversified and provide little competition to any one industry in the private sector, and Bennett followed this policy as commissioner of prison industries and later as director of the BOP.

As director of the BOP, Bennett enacted a progressive philosophy regarding the treatment of staff and inmates, especially early in his career. Some of the accomplishments of Bennett may have been initiated during the Bates administration. For example, during the first month of Bennett's administration, all BOP personnel became part of the civil service. This replaced the political patronage system that had existed previously.

Bennett also established the BOP tradition of associating major job promotions with transfers in the 1940s. To combat local empire building and provincialism, as well as potential resistance to central office policy and directives, transfers were tied to accepting a position at a different prison. Some staff initially resisted. These days, however, it is commonly thought that the promotion-tenure link transformed the BOP from a collection of idiosyncratic prisons to a coordinated system under the control of central office.

Bennett and Bates opposed controlling inmates with the simple use of brute force. Sometime during the 1930s, either before or after Bennett assumed the directorship, the BOP disallowed the previous practice of allowing guards to carry billy clubs at penitentiaries. Bennett established the first halfway house used by a correctional agency in the United States to ease the adjustment of inmates back into society. Bennett also created the first "open prison" at Seagoville, Texas. This prison did not have a perimeter wall, fence, guard towers, or the other custody devices most typically associated with prisons. As Bennett noted in a paper delivered to the Institute of Illinois Academy of Criminology in 1955, "The emphasis throughout is on self-reliance, self-respect, and trustworthiness" (Roberts, 1980, p. 33).

Bennett took a leave of absence in 1945 to organize civilian German prisons for the American military at the end of European hostilities in World War II. He received numerous awards for his federal career, including the president's Award for Distinguished Federal Civilian Service, which was presented by President Dwight D. Eisenhower.

Bennett's last official day at the BOP was on his 70th birthday. Critics argue that Bennett became less effective in the latter stages of his career, and then-Attorney General Robert Kennedy had denied his request to extend his stay. Nonetheless, looking over his entire career at the BOP, Paul Keve (1991, p. 214) argued that he was a leader of integrity with sound management practices.

—*Scott D. Camp*

See also Ashurst-Summers Act 1935; Sanford Bates; Katharine Bement Davis; Federal Prison System;

Mary Belle Harris; Hawes-Cooper Act 1929; Kathleen Hawk Sawyer; History of Prisons; UNICOR; Volstead Act 1918

Further Reading

Bennett, J. V. (1964). *Of prisons and justice: A selection of the writings of James V. Bennett.* Washington, DC: U.S. Government Printing Office.

Keve, P. W. (1991). *American conscience: A history of U.S. federal corrections.* Carbondale: Southern Illinois University Press.

Roberts, J. W. (1980). View from the top: The Bureau of Prisons' five directors discuss problems and ethics in corrections. *Federal Prison Journal, 1*(4), 27–46.

The opinions expressed are those of the author and do not necessarily represent those of the Federal Bureau of Prisons or the Department of Justice.

◪ BENTHAM, JEREMY
(1748–1832)

Jeremy Bentham, credited for conceptualizing the "roundhouse" panopticon prison, was a philosopher and essayist whose contributions to criminal justice theory over 60 years extended far beyond his prison designs. A prodigious, even obsessive, author, Bentham wrote on numerous topics spanning criminology, moral philosophy, law, and politics. Born of wealthy parents in London, he studied to be a lawyer like his father and grandfather. However, he eventually discarded this plan and instead began to write social and political critiques. His wealthy background and a later substantial inheritance allowed him to pursue his interests in relative comfort.

Bentham wrote during a time of social upheaval, both in Britain and on the continent. The French and U.S. revolutions, expanding British imperialism, and the problems of crime in England in addition to what Bentham viewed as a breakdown in the moral fabric of society and law, stimulated much of his work. Considered both a philosophical and political radical, many of his reformist ideas were not accepted until the early 19th century.

BENTHAM'S PHILOSOPHY

Bentham is often considered to be one of the founders of Utilitarianism even though he did not originate the core ideas. Utilitarians argue that ethical behavior is determined by the consequences of an act. As a result, according to Bentham, both human actions and government policies should be guided by a "utility principle" in which actions should be intended either to produce good or to reduce harm. Such a view was not based simply on numbers or "majority rules." Rather, the goal or end of an act should be weighed with a calculus that, on balance, will result in the greatest social good or the least social harm, even if it causes individual discomfort. Ethical rules are derived from the principle of the greatest universal utility, summarized by John Stuart Mill (1957) after studying Bentham:

> Pleasure and freedom from pain are the only things desirable as ends; and that all desirable things (which are as numerous in the utilitarian as in any other scheme) are desirable either for pleasure inherent in themselves or as means to the promotion of pleasure and the prevention of pain. (pp. 10–11)

Although recognizing and emphasizing the role of individual choice, Bentham did not believe that people should make choices simply on the basis of their own personal self-interest or pleasure. Rather, a society's "greatest felicity" occurred in conditions that required a shared moral climate, and individuals were obligated to make those choices guided by a common social good. To use a contemporary example, some observers have argued that, for utilitarians, if racism makes the majority of a society "happy," then it can be morally justified. However, this violates the fundamental premise of Utilitarianism, which is that principles of justice are a primary utility, and choices that violate this utility are unjust or immoral.

BENTHAM'S CONTRIBUTIONS TO CRIMINAL JUSTICE

Introductory criminology texts usually divide criminology of the later 18th and early 19th centuries into classical and neoclassical views, placing Bentham in the latter. Although somewhat arbitrary, the distinction is useful for two reasons. First, it helps us understand how writers in the first part of the 19th century shifted from earlier 18th-century views of criminal law as primarily for punishment. Second, it illustrates how criminal law and correctional policies respond to social changes as they evolved.

The distinction between the two schools reflects an emphasis in application rather than any fundamental differences in philosophy. Both classical and neoclassical theorists attempted to examine crime in a way that would allow for a "rational" formulation of policy. The classical school is often associated with Cesare Beccaria (1819), who believed that "the degree of punishment, and the consequences of crime, ought to be so contrived as to have the greatest possible effect on others, with the least possible pain to the delinquent" (p. 75).

The intent of this "just measure of pain" was to deter the offender from future offenses as well as to prevent others from similar acts by indicating that punishment was swift and certain and "cost" more than gains from the crime itself. Both schools focused on crime as a violation of law, moving away from the view of crime as "sins against nature," which dominated criminal law well into the 18th century (and still guides some 21st-century thinking). Both held that the best way to reduce crime was to punish offenders, both for retribution and deterrence. Both opposed excessive punishment and, for the most part, capital punishment, corporal punishment, transportation and prison ships, and torture. Both also argued that the punishment must fit the crime and that punishments should be calibrated according to the nature of social harm of the offense.

The primary difference lies in Bentham's and his followers' reform-oriented views of how punishments should be applied. For Bentham and those influenced by his work, existing criminal law and corresponding punishments were unjust, because they did not account for individual differences. Unlike the classical school, which reacted to crime after it occurred by punishing offenders and thus reducing crime through deterrence, Bentham believed that society could proactively address crime before it occurred by emphasizing moral choices and creating a just system of laws. He advocated indirect means of preventing crimes, such as education, religious sanctions, discouraging "encouragement to crime," and promoting an enlightened, benevolent society (Bentham, 1843).

Like, Beccaria (1819), Bentham believed in the deterrent power of punishment. He felt that the severity of punishment should be increased as the deterrent value decreased. But Bentham also advocated alternatives to conventional punishment, arguing that not all offenses require incarceration or harsh responses. He suggested that "private punishment," or "forfeitures" and other restrictions could be a strong deterrent. Also, unlike classical theorists, who argued that all offenders should be treated alike, regardless of circumstance, Bentham suggested taking the context of a crime and the nature of the offender into account when inflicting punishment.

THE PANOPTICON

One of the key ways in which Bentham sought to deal with crime was through transforming prison policies. Over the decades, he specified a number of principles to guide sentencing and prison administration. Among these included holding wardens responsible for prisoner injuries by fining them for prisoner deaths, increasing sentencing latitude of judges, a presaging of bail and home confinement, and the recognition that some punishments, such as transportation, fell heaviest on the poor and lower classes.

In addition to such policy suggestions, Bentham is perhaps best known to criminology students for his design of the panopticon prison, a round, multitiered open structure with a guard tower in the center. He developed his ideas for this model following a trip to Russia with his brother in 1785 in a venture to help Empress Catherine the Great modernize the Russian government, including the penal system. In a series of letters and articles over the years (Bentham, 1970), Bentham conceptualized a single round building with a floor-to-ceiling guard tower in the center surrounded by tiers of cells. Each cell would have a window for fresh air and light and be easily and safely accessible to staff. Most significantly, this new technology would allow a single guard to have visual access of every cell and prisoner. Keeping prisoners under surveillance, he believed, would make prison control safer, more effective, more humane, and efficient by increasing discipline while reducing staff resources required to maintain it. Prisoners in the panopticon would work rather than sitting idle, and, in the process, would not only learn the benefits of discipline but also make a profit for the prison itself.

Catherine ultimately rejected the idea, and no panopticons were ever built in England. Indeed, only a handful of true panopticons were ever constructed anywhere, although for many decades prison architecture was influenced by the radial design. In the United States, the Western Penitentiary in Pennsylvania was constructed in 1826 guided by Bentham's model. In 1925, Stateville Penitentiary opened with four panopticon units. A fifth was planned, but was replaced with a "long house," reportedly because of the cost of building the roundhouses. Three of Stateville's four panopticon units were torn down in the 1980s. The fourth was upgraded and remains functional, largely for historical reasons. It is reputedly the only remaining operational panopticon in the world.

CONCLUSION: THE LEGACY

Due to a number of problems with the panopticon design, particularly in the expense of building and maintaining it, Bentham's model never became the mainstream institution that he had hoped. This does not mean, however, that his ideas faded from either criminological imagination or from the realm of policy. Rather, the panopticon continues today to influence thinking and practice in a number of ways. In practical terms, constant surveillance, usually through technology, is crucial to most penal institutions. Likewise, labor remains a key part of many institutions. More conceptually, the panopticon was famously used by French philosopher Michel Foucault as an example of how power operates in modern society.

Bentham's other insights into prison construction and management provided the basis for reform well into the 19th century. His ideas of alternative punishments and reform laid out the philosophical framework for later development of probation and parole, advocating community responsibility for offenders. Although he is rarely read today by criminologists, his legacy remains. His view that social justice and just law are intertwined, and that both are necessary for humane and effective prisons, make him worth studying.

—*Jim Thomas*

See also Cesare Beccaria; Deterrence Theory; Michel Foucault; Elizabeth Fry; David Garland; History of Prisons; John Howard; Panopticon; Rehabilitation Theory; Stateville Correctional Center

Further Reading

Beccaria, C. (1819). *An essay on crimes and punishments.* Philadelphia: Philip H. Nicklin. (Original work published 1764)

Bentham, J. (1823). *An introduction to the principles of morals and legislation.* London: W. Pickering.

Bentham, J. (1843). *The works of Jeremy Bentham* (Vol. 1). Edinburgh, Scotland: William Tait.

Bentham, J. (1970). *The collected works of Jeremy Bentham* (J. H. Burns & H. L. A. Hart, Eds.). London: University of London–Athlone Press.

Bentham, J. (2001). *The panopticon letters.* Cartome Archives. Retrieved from http://cartome.org/panopticon2.htm

The Bentham Project. (2004). *Jeremy Bentham.* Retrieved from http://www.ucl.ac.uk/Bentham-Project/info/jb.htm

Foucault, M. (1979). *Discipline and punish: The birth of the prison.* New York: Doubleday.

The Internet encyclopedia of philosophy. (2001). Jeremy Bentham. Retrieved from http://www.iep.utm.edu/b/bentham.htm

Mill, J. S. (1957). *Utilitarianism.* New York: Bobbs-Merrill.

◪ BISEXUAL PRISONERS

Bisexuality is defined as sexual attraction, potential attraction, or sexual behavior toward members of both sexes. Bisexuality, though, like homosexuality, remains an elusive term. Is a married man who engages in periodic homosexual activity gay? Does one incident of same-sex activity render a person gay? Defining bisexuality among prison inmates is especially challenging. Is sexual orientation defined by acts committed prior to incarceration or by acts committed during incarceration? If someone engages in same-sex sex during incarceration, but returns to heterosexuality upon release, is that person gay or bisexual?

ATTITUDES TOWARD BISEXUALS IN PRISON

Much like the outside society, attitudes toward bisexuals in prison are typically unfavorable. One recent study has shown that male inmates tend to be more homophobic than women and that black inmates are more tolerant toward homosexuality than whites. Some facilities may segregate the more effeminate male homosexuals from the general population for their own protection or to discourage sexual behavior. This is because homosexual inmates have been found to be at greater risk of sexual victimization than heterosexual inmates. Due to actual or perceived potential victimization, some homosexual and bisexual prisoners may request protective custody to avoid harassment or assault from other inmates.

METHODOLOGICAL PROBLEMS

Numerous methodological challenges arise when studying sexuality among prisoners. Using a narrow, essentialist definition of bisexuality may not capture the full scope of sexual identity. Likewise, focusing on sexual behavior alone may not reveal desires that are unrequited. Gauging sexual behavior among inmates requires self-report or observational data. Yet observational data may be problematic since observations alone cannot reveal the sexual orientation of the participant, but only their behavior. In addition, it may be difficult to distinguish between consensual or coerced sex. Researchers have found that when interviewed, correctional officers claim they cannot always differentiate between consensual and nonconsensual sex because extortion techniques employed by inmates may not be immediately apparent. For example, an inmate may "willingly" engage in sexual activity as a means of survival or protection from other inmates, with such behavior appearing to the correctional officer as a consensual act.

Self-report measures also have some problems. Due to the stigmatizing nature of homosexuality and bisexuality, many people will underreport their sexual orientation or desire. Inmates may be reluctant to admit engaging in sexual activity for various reasons such as embarrassment or fear of being taken advantage of by other inmates. In attempting to gauge sexual orientation, more comprehensive studies have addressed sexual behavior prior to incarceration as well as behavior engaged in while incarcerated.

BISEXUALITY AMONG MALE INMATES

Due to the difficulty in defining homosexuality and bisexuality, the estimated number of homosexual and/or bisexual prisoners varies. Estimates of the number of male bisexual prisoners range from 11% to 15% while the proportion of male homosexual prisoners is thought to fall somewhere between 6% and 10%. Perhaps most confoundingly of all, the overall percentage of male inmates in medium-security facilities reported to engage in consensual homosexual activity in prison ranges from 2% to 65%. While in one study, only 2% reported engaging in same-sex behavior themselves, the vast majority of inmates indicated that it is their perception that consensual sex occurs every day.

BISEXUALITY AMONG FEMALE INMATES

As with men, there are no accurate estimates of bisexual female inmates. Early studies claimed that women establish "pseudo-family" or friendship relationships that center on emotional attachment and may involve sexual activity. In contrast to men's sexual behavior in prison, which is often characterized by domination and aggression, women were thought to reproduce the gender roles of the outside society. Those involved in a pseudo-family may take on either the "masculine" or "feminine" role within the relationship. The relationships are viewed as intimate, with each partner providing companionship and emotional support.

More recent studies indicate that women prisoners involved in sexual relationships do not adhere to any particular gender roles. In fact, like many male prisoners, the impetus for sexual involvement is often the economic exchange for food or other commissary items. The study concludes that mistrust leads to reluctance to become involved with other inmates.

CONCLUSION

Few studies explicitly address bisexuality in prison. Notwithstanding the methodological concerns involved in identifying bisexual prisoners, continuing research is necessary to develop practical policy recommendations that address the dangers and consequences of coercive sexual behavior as well as health concerns rising from unprotected sex among inmates. Understanding prisoners' sexuality will also help explain the prison experience more clearly.

—Nickie Phillips

See also Homosexual Prisoners; Homosexual Relationships; Lesbian Prisoners; Lesbian Relationships; Prison Culture; Rape; Resistance; Sex—Consensual; Transgender and Transsexual Prisoners Violence

Further Reading

Alarid, L. (2000). Sexual orientation perspectives of incarcerated bisexual and gay men: The county jail protective custody experience. *The Prison Journal, 80*(1), 80–95.

Bisexual Resource Center. (2003). *Bisexuality.* Retrieved from http://www.biresource.org/pamphlets/bisexuality.html

Donaldson, S. (2001). A million jockers, punks, and queens. In S. Sabo, T. Kupers, & W. London (Eds.), *Prison masculinities* (pp. 118–126). Philadelphia: Temple University Press.

Eigenberg, H. (2000). Correctional officers and their perceptions of homosexuality, rape, and prostitution in male prisons. *The Prison Journal, 80*(4), 415–433.

Faith, K. (1993). *Unruly women: The politics of confinement and resistance.* Vancouver: Press Gang.

Greer, K. (2000). The changing nature of interpersonal relationships in a women's prison. *The Prison Journal, 80*(4), 442–468.

Hensley, C. (2000). Attitudes toward homosexuality in a male and female prison: An exploratory study. *The Prison Journal, 80*(4), 434–441.

Hensley, C. (2001). Consensual homosexual activity in male prisons. *Corrections Compendium, 26*(1), 1–4.

Hensley, C. (2002). *Prison sex: Practice & policy.* Boulder, CO: Lynne Rienner.

Kunzel, R. (2002). Situating sex: Prison sexual culture in the mid-twentieth-century United States. *GLQ: A Journal of Lesbian and Gay Studies, 8*(3), 253–270.

Saum, C., Surratt, H., Inciardi, J., & Bennett, R. (1995). Sex in prison: Exploring the myths and realities. *The Prison Journal, 75*(4), 413–430.

Wooden, W., & Parker, J. (1982). *Men behind bars: Sexual exploitation in prison.* New York: Plenum.

■ BLACK PANTHER PARTY

The Black Panther Party (BPP) was formed in October 1966, in Oakland, California, by Huey P. Newton and Bobby Seale. At the time, it was the most prominent revolutionary black power organization. At its peak, the BPP maintained between 10,000 and 30,000 members across more than 30 chapters in North America.

The BPP stressed black cultural pride and promoted educational programs and other community activities. Its political and economic ideology rested on Marxist revolutionary tenets that called for black power, armed resistance, the release of all blacks from jails, and payment of compensation to African Americans for centuries of exploitation.

Early BPP members sought to protect blacks against the police's unnecessary punitive use of force. Members patrolled urban ghetto areas with firearms and law books to prevent police brutality and petit-apartheid practices such as police harassment, illegal arrests, stop and frisks, selective enforcement of the law, racial profiling, and so on. Conflicts between the BPP and the police in the late 1960s and early 1970s led to armed confrontations in California, New York, and Chicago and the arrest and imprisonment of Huey Newton, who was accused of murdering a police officer. The Federal Bureau of Investigation (FBI) engaged in a massive campaign against the BPP, which promoted internal quarrels within the organization and finally led to its demise. While the national influence of the BPP began to wane after 1971, its organizational life span continued until 1982.

THE BPP AND IMPRISONMENT

Between 1967 and 1970, the FBI used state and local police departments, illegal wiretaps, and agent provocateurs to penetrate and destabilize the BPP. In 1967, one of the key BPP leaders, Huey Newton, was jailed on charges of killing an Oakland policeman. In New Haven, Connecticut, the FBI rounded up 14 Panthers including Bobby Seale and Erika

Huggins and charged them with conspiracy and murder, kidnapping, and conspiracy. Other members of the BPP jailed between 1971 and 1982 include Mumia Abu-Jamal, Sundiata Acoli, Herman Bell, Marshall Eddie Conway, Mark Cook, Bashir Hameed, Robert Seth Hayes, Teddy Jah Heath, Mundo We Langa, Abdul Majid, Russell Shoats, Jalil Abdul Muntagin, Baba Odinga, Ed Poindexter, and Albert Nuh Washington.

Angela Davis, a black radical activist and scholar and member of the BPP, was also incarcerated in connection with an armed takeover of a California courtroom in 1970. In 1970, Geronimo ji Jaga Pratt, a decorated war hero received a sentence of 25 years to life in prison on charges of murdering a white couple. He served 27 years before his sentence was overturned. The police had withheld information that the victim had actually accused another man of the offense and Pratt was innocent.

Ironically, incarcerating such people often provided them the opportunity to read widely and sharpen their ideologies. It also enabled the party to recruit new members from among the other prisoners. There was, in other words, a relationship between activists inside and beyond the prison walls, which sentences of confinement could not disrupt.

THE ROLE OF WOMEN IN THE BPP

Black women in the United States have a long history of participation in community-based political and civil rights movements. The BPP was no exception, and women played significant roles and held leadership positions in it until 1981 when the BPP's last Oakland-based community program shut down. According to a 1969 survey, about two-thirds of the general membership of the BPP were women. As early as 1970, the BPP formally called for equality and liberation of women.

Some of the women party members included Kathleen Neal Cleaver, Matilaba, Connie Mathews, Assata Shakur, Zayd Shakur, Shelley Bursey, and Erika Huggins. Each played significant roles in national leadership positions. For instance, Shelley Bursey worked with the newspaper; Kathleen Cleaver, a communications director, ran for state political office on the auspices of the BPP, and Matilaba published drawings in the newspapers. Others like Connie Mathews became the international coordinator, Assata Shakur was exiled in Cuba, while Erika Huggins served jail time.

In the black communities, women were actively responsible for running freedom schools established by the BPP. They also ran the organization's free health clinic, antidrug campaigns, and community-run Breakfast for Children Program. The last of these community programs closed in Oakland in 1981.

THE DEMISE OF THE BPP

Most scholars of American social movements have attributed the decline of the BPP and other social movements of the 1960s to multiple factors that include internal disputes, state political repression, ideological errors, an inexperienced and youthful membership, strategic mistakes, and the cult of authoritarianism. Some argue that the BPP eventually collapsed in part because of oligarchization in which there was an unequal organizational relationship and misuse of power and control by a numerical minority. Tensions between the leadership over the proper direction for black liberation, the role of the armed struggle and electoral politics, the issue of alliances with white radicals, and competing visions of political ideology all served to divide members from one another. The party was also split over organizational strategy and how best to associate with other black organizations. Some scholars estimate that, by the middle of 1971, BPP membership had declined to merely 1,000.

In addition to internal quarrels, the BPP was further eroded by the combined repression of the local, state, and national governments. In 1968, FBI Director J. Edgar Hoover described the BPP as the greatest internal threat to American security. During the COINTELPRO era, the FBI sought to shut the BPP down and more than 300 of its members were jailed or forced into exile. David Hilliard reports the significance of the FBI in his 1993 autobiography: "They employ every kind of deviousness to put us at one another's throat, make us appear like gangsters and thugs, niggers killing niggers" (Hilliard & Cole, 1993, p. 221). The FBI's COINTELPRO was instrumental in using various tactics of "repressive acts of barbarism" such as harassment, arrest and detention, surveillance, snick-jacketing, forged letters, paid informants, and undercover police agents to suppress the members of the BPP that eventually led to the assassination of party leaders (see Jones, 1998, p. 371).

CONCLUSION: THE LEGACY OF THE BPP

As a leading black leftist revolutionary organization in the liberation struggle in America, the BPP captured the imagination of many young people in the United States and in other oppressed revolutionary groups abroad. The legacy of the BPP can be seen in four major areas: the saliency of armed resistance, a tradition of community service, a commitment to the self-determination of all people, and a model of political action for repressed people.

The BPP demonstrated a willingness to have alliances with other leftist organizations and maintained a desire to incorporate women into the organization's hierarchy. Even in its embryonic stage, the BPP advocated for the rights of women and homosexuals. In short, the BPP represented an early model of multiculturalism in American history. Its impact transcended American borders as its tactics, ideology, and politics became a frame of reference for others and were embraced by oppressed movements in both domestic and international arenas.

Despite its ultimate demise, due to internal disputes and government repression, the BPP contributed politically, socially, and economically to the American political landscape. Party members led the movement to squash police brutality, which resulted in the emergence of civilian police review boards. The Black Panthers' ideas, such as free breakfast programs, may have contributed to the policy of free meals to poor children in American schools today.

—*Ihekwoaba D. Onwudiwe*
and Emmanuel C. Onyeozili

See also Abolition; Activism; Critical Resistance; Angela Y. Davis; George Jackson; Nation of Islam; Political Prisoners; Racism; Resistance

Further Reading

Campbell, K. (1996). Where are the civil rights icons of the '60s? *Ebony, 51*(10), 108–112.

Cleaver, K. N. (1999). Women, power, and revolution. *New Political Science, 21*(2), 231–236.

Freedman, J. (1983). *Social movements of the sixties and seventies.* New York: Longman.

Herb, B. (1995). *Black Panthers for beginners.* New York: Writers and Readers Publishing.

Hilliard, D., & Cole, L. (1993). *This side of glory: The autobiography of David Hilliard and the story of the Black Panther Party.* Boston: Brown.

Johnson, P. (1997). The last revolutionary. *Essence, 28*(7), 103–106.

Johnson, R. A. (1975). The prison birth of black power. *Journal of Black Studies, 5*(4), 395–414.

Jones, E. C. (1998). *The Black Panther Party reconsidered.* Baltimore, MD: Black Classic.

Knapper, K. (1996). Women and the Black Panther Party. *Socialist Review, 26*(1/2), 25–31.

Robert, M. (1962). *Political parties: A sociological study of the oligarchical tendencies of modern democracy.* New York: Free Press.

◪ BLOODS

The "Bloods" gang was founded by Sylvester Scott and Vincent Owens in Piru Street, Compton, Los Angeles, in the 1960s in response to another group known as the "Crips." As a criminal organization, the Bloods are known to be involved in murder, theft, robberies, extortion, and drug sales. Originally consisting mostly of African Americans and some Latinos, the group evolved to include a full range of ethnicities including white, Asian, and Caribbean persons.

Individuals who wish to join the Bloods must "Blood in" by either spilling their own blood or that of someone else. This must be done by some violent act including battle between the recruit and another gang member or by an act against a non–gang member. As in any organization, a recruit must demonstrate loyalty and obedience to the group starting with this first act.

INTERNAL ORGANIZATION AND COMMUNICATION STRATEGIES

The Bloods are part of separate cliques or "sets" depending on where they are located and their primary goals. In this way, they compare to the college fraternity system, which has a national charter and many different chapters across the country.

Organizational communication within a complex group such as the Bloods is paramount. Traditionally, street gangs communicate through graffiti as well as through other signals and markings. These markings can include specific tattoos, hand gestures, and language. The most common tattoo is two burned dots over a single burned dot to resemble a dog's paw in blood. Blood members may also call one another "dog." The hand gestures can vary by "set" or when members are under legal supervision to deny affiliation and divert attention and trouble for the gang by law enforcement.

As with other gangs, the Bloods also identify themselves through a particular color: red. Gang colors can be displayed through hats, bandanas, and most commonly, a beaded necklace displaying a pattern with the appropriate colors. The word *Blood* has even been turned into and acronym the reads: Blood Love Overcomes Our Depressions.

BLOODS IN PRISON

Having started as a street gang, the Bloods are now an important prison organization, where they provide group safety and identity for their members as well as an outlet for aggression and criminal activity. As with other prison gangs, Bloods engage in various forms of violence, including physical assaults on corrections officers and sexual assault. They also seek to intimidate rival gang inmates in order to establish a sense of fear and territory. Much of their activity in prison centers on assuming and maintaining control of certain businesses particularly drugs and other forms of contraband.

The prison provides a fertile recruitment site for the street gangs. Indeed, although prisons attempt to control gangs they often facilitate their growth. Traditional methods of control drive gang recruitment underground rendering staff unable to protect inmates from threats and intimidation to join a particular gang. Drug trade inside prison expands the gang's reputation and wealth, thus strengthening its position and power both on the street and behind the

walls. Bloods have long used the drug industry to fund their activities on the streets, and easily adapt it to the prison situation.

Due to the current war on drugs, increasing numbers of Bloods are entering prison. When incarcerated, these men often form "super gangs" such as the United Blood Nation (UBN) that started in Riker's Island Detention facility. This set includes independent Bloods from California, as well as members of New York sets including Nine Trey Gangsta Bloods (NTG), Miller Gangsta Bloods (MGB), Valentine Bloods (VB), Mad Dog Bloods (MDB), One Eight Trey Bloods (183), Mad Stone Bloods (MSB), Gangsta Killer Bloods (GKB), and Blood Stone Villains (BSV). The super gangs are controlled by a strict code of conduct. Bloods require that all members come to the aid of a fellow Blood above all other actions. They have a hierarchy for control that resembles the institutional hierarchy. There is a leader in the prison as well as in cellhouses. People known as enforcers keep members in line at the tier level.

CONCLUSION

Initially formed in Los Angeles to combat their rivals the Crips, Bloods have migrated to major cities throughout the United States including Chicago, New York, Philadelphia, Miami, and cities in Texas. Blood activity in Texas and Florida—especially Miami—rose very quickly because these states border Mexico, Central America, and South America, which are major distribution centers for drugs in the United States. Bloods are also concentrated in parts of New York City and certain parts of New Jersey. Because New Jersey and New York have so many different ports and many ways for the importation of narcotics through various drug cartels or organizations, the Bloods are able to grow and move the drugs on the street. Jersey City, Newark, and Camden are a few of the major Blood territories that resulted from the rise of the UBN

Once thought to be a criminal organization primarily aimed at counterbalancing their rivals, the Crips, the Bloods have expanded to the major urban areas across the country. Their strength and power are increasing and present a formidable challenge to prison authorities. Latest estimates are that 25% of state correctional facilities have members of the Bloods organization, and that number grows annually.

—Patrick F. McManimon Jr.

See also Aryan Brotherhood; Aryan Nations; Crips; Deprivation; Gangs; Importation; Prison Culture; Racial Conflict Among Prisoners

Further Reading

Moore, J. W. (1978). *Gangs, drugs and prison in the barrios of Los Angeles.* Philadelphia: Temple University Press.

Sanders, W. B. (1994). *Gangbangs and drive-bys: Grounded culture and juvenile gang violence.* New York: Aldine de Gruyter.

Silberman, M. (1995). *A world of violence: Corrections in America.* Belmont, CA: Wadsworth.

◪ BOOT CAMP

Boot camps were first established in the United States in 1983 as an alternative to traditional forms of incarceration. Most are residential facilities for juvenile delinquents or adult criminals with military-style structure, rules, and discipline. Boot camp programs are expected to reduce prison crowding and related costs. They are also intended to reduce recidivism and antisocial behavior. Finally, it is commonly believed that they can deter individuals from future offending while also helping to rehabilitate them through the imposition of discipline.

THE CURRENT SITUATION

There are currently more than 75 juvenile boot camps and military-structured programs in 39 states (Rogers, 2002). Modeled after boot camps for adult offenders, the first juvenile boot camps emphasized military discipline and physical conditioning. Offenders often enter the programs in groups and are commonly referred to as platoons or squads. While in the program, they are required to wear military style uniforms and engage in strenuous physical fitness activities, educational programs, treatment programs, and military drills (Mackenzie, Gover, Armstrong, & Mitchell, 2001). Offenders sentenced to boot camps are generally young, first-time, nonviolent felons. Most states, for example, restrict participation to offenders between the ages of 17 and 25, although a few have maximum age limits of between 25 and 30 years of age.

In general, boot camps are selective about the type of offenders admitted into the program. Juveniles undergo psychological, medical, and physical evaluations to determine eligibility. In their study, Mackenzie et al. (2001) found that the majority of the juveniles are young men around 16 years of age. On average these young offenders had been only 13 years when they were first arrested. Most had previously been committed to institutions.

DO BOOT CAMPS WORK?

Criminologists and criminal justice practitioners have evaluated the success of boot camps along a number of parameters. They have examined whether or not they reduce recidivism, prison overcrowding, or cost. They have also looked at the impact of military training on offenders, whether boot camps have helped inmates to adjust, and whether these institutions have had any success addressing the drug problem. So far there is no compelling evidence that boot camp participants recidivate less than the groups with which evaluators have compared them. Likewise, their effect on prison overcrowding is weak at best.

Overcrowding

According to Doris L. Mackenzie and Claire C. Souryal (1991), for boot camps to reduce prison crowding successfully, there must be a sufficient number of eligible offenders entering and completing the programs; and these individuals must be drawn from a population of prison-bound offenders, not from those who would otherwise be sentenced to probation. It is difficult for most programs to meet the first qualification, because they are simply too small to affect crowding. Meeting the second qualification greatly depends on who decides which offenders are placed in boot camp programs.

In some states (Georgia, South Carolina, Texas, and Arizona), as in Florida, judges sentence offenders directly to boot camp. If these offenders are denied entry or are dismissed, they are sent back to the court for resentencing. This type of decision-making structure suggests that a higher proportion of boot camp entrants are selected from those who would otherwise receive probation. Consequently, their incarceration in boot camp will have no effect on prison overcrowding rates at all.

Reduction of Cost

Do boot camp programs reduce costs? It is difficult to interpret the cost data from different states or to make meaningful comparisons across states because of differences in methods of accounting. However, in most states it seems that boot camps cost as much or more per day than traditional incarceration. In Oklahoma, for example, the staff-inmate ratio in boot camps was about four times greater than that for the general prison population, indicating that boot camps would be much more expensive than prison.

In Mississippi and Georgia, the boot camp programs are about as costly as a similarly sized unit in the prisons they adjoin. Cost figures vary from state to state and illuminate the higher costs of operating boot camps over the traditional methods (i.e., probation). For example, in the state of Texas the cost per youth in 1998 for probation supervision was $8.90 a day as compared to $88.62 for residential placement and $85.90 for a youth assigned to a detention facility (Criminal Justice Policy Council, 1999). According to Jerry Tyler, Ray Darville, and Kathie Stalnaker (2001), juvenile boot camps usually are more costly than most other traditional options, and with rare exceptions recidivism rates are extremely disappointing. Unfortunately, the limited data available do not show the effectiveness one might expect from the money and resources channeled into these programs.

Military Training

Boot camp programs are modeled after military basic training and aim to instill self-discipline, respect for authority, and fear of the criminal justice system in the offender. Offenders are required to wear military uniforms, march to and from activities, and respond rapidly to the commands of the drill instructors. Daily activities range from strenuous physical fitness to challenge programs (e.g., ropes courses). The military-style discipline of youths in boot camp programs has been controversial. The military has a very different mission than the correctional system. The ultimate goal of the military is to train young men to kill the enemy. Why would a method that has been developed to prepare people to go into war, and as a tool to manage legal violence, be considered useful for deterring or rehabilitating offenders? The militarism of boot camps, the use of hard labor, and efforts to frighten offenders away from crime may be counterproductive to appropriate behavior. Although boot camps do not provide training in the use of weapons or physical assault, they promote an aggressive model of leadership and a conflict-dominated style of interaction that could exacerbate tendencies toward aggression.

Inmate Adjustment

There have been mixed results about the impact of boot camps on juvenile offenders. Donald J. Hengesh (1991) argued that boot camps should be seen as a foundation for change, not an instant cure. They are designed to provide young offenders a sound foundation on which to build new lives. Hengesh pointed out that most offenders entering boot camps lack basic life skills, are in poor physical condition, have dropped out of high school, and have had considerable exposure to the criminal justice system. They lack self-esteem and have established track records of being quitters or losers whenever they are faced with obstacles or problems. Boot camps, according to Hengesh, are designed to equip these youthful offenders with the foundation to offset these problems, because boot camps teach responsibility through continuous strict conformity to program rules and by holding offenders accountable for their behavior.

In their study, Michael Peters, David Thomas, and Christopher Zamberlan (1997) found that youths in boot camps showed impressive improvements in academic skills and significant numbers of youths found a job while in aftercare. Boot camps provide opportunities for personal development, learning technical and living skills, and drug treatment (Anderson, Laronistine, & Burns, 1999). According to Mackenzie et al. (2001), there were no reported differences between juveniles' anxiety and depression in two types of facilities (i.e., boot camps and traditional facilities) during their first month of confinement. Offenders in boot camps perceived their environment to be more positive, less hostile, and less conducive to freedom than juveniles in traditional facilities. Scales measuring changes over time found that juveniles in boot camps became less antisocial and less depressed than those in traditional arrangements.

Drugs

While it is clear that many offenders sentenced to boot camps need drug treatment and education, it is not clear whether these programs are the most effective way to provide it.

In Illinois, drug education and treatment are mandatory. During orientation, the offender's drug and alcohol history is evaluated, and based on the evaluation, the offender is placed at the proper level of treatment. The duration of treatment varies from 2 to 10 weeks, depending on the individuals. New York operates a six-month program, and all inmates, regardless of substance abuse background, attend alcohol and substance abuse treatment classes for approximately 200 hours. Texas offers a two-phase program that is part mandatory and part voluntary. The focus is on drug education and individual counseling, which lasts for approximately five weeks. Florida and South Carolina's programs focus exclusively on drug education, and participation is mandatory. In South Carolina, drug education classes meet for four hours each weekend during the first month. In Florida, inmates participate in a substance abuse workshop that meets for 15 days.

The efficacy of these programs has yet to be established.

CONCLUSION

Boot camp programs have been embraced by politicians who are looking for a quick fix for crime and the public who are demanding protection from violent young offenders. However, as a crime preventive strategy, there is little evidence that they work to reduce crime. Indeed, some evidence suggests that boot camps could accelerate rather than reduce crime.

Except in the case of violent offenders, there is evidence that many Americans support a broadened use of noninstitutional sanctions that would reduce system contact and costs. The most effective treatment programs are made available outside of the formal institutions of the juvenile justice system. These tend to be skill-oriented nonpunitive programs.

—Jonathan Odo, Emmanuel C. Onyeozili,
and Ihekwoaba D. Onwudiwe

See also Deterrence Theory; Just Deserts Theory; Juvenile Justice System; Rehabilitation Theory

Further Reading

Anderson, J. F., Laronistine, D., & Burns, J. (1999). *Boot camps: An intermediate sanction.* Lanham, MD: University Press of America.

Criminal Justice Policy Council. (1999). *Oranges to oranges: Comparing the operational costs of juvenile and adult correctional programs in Texas.* Austin, TX: Author.

Cronin, R. C., & Han, M. (1994). *Boot camps for adult and juvenile offenders: Overview and update.* Research report. Washington, DC: National Institute of Justice.

Hengesh, D. J. (1991, October). Think of boot camps as a foundation for change, not an instant cure. *Corrections Today, 53.*

Mackenzie, D. L., Gover, A. R., Armstrong, G. S., & Mitchell, O. (2001, August). *A national study comparing the environments of boot camps with traditional facilities for juvenile offenders* (Research brief). Washington, DC: National Institute of Justice.

Mackenzie, D. L., & Piquero, P. (1994). The impact of shock incarceration programs on prison crowding. *Crime & Delinquency, 40*(2), 222–249.

Mackenzie, D. L., & Souryal, C. (1991). Boot camp survey: Rehabilitation, recidivism reduction outrank punishment as main goals. *Corrections Today, 53*, 90–96.

Morash, M., & Rucker, L. (1990). A critical look at the idea of boot camp as a correctional reform. *Crime & Delinquency, 36*(2), 204–222.

Parent, D. G. (1993). Boot camps failing to achieve goals. *Overcrowded Times: Solving the Prison Problem, 4*(4).

Peters, M., Thomas, D., & Zamberlan, C. (1997). *Boot camps for juvenile offenders.* Washington, DC: U.S. Office of Juvenile Justice and Delinquency Prevention.

Rogers, D. (2002, June). Juvenile boot camps. *Law Enforcement Technology, 29*(6), 88, 90, 93–95.

Taylor, W. J. (1992, July). Tailoring boot camps to juveniles. *Corrections Today, 54.*

Tyler, J., Darville, R., & Stalnaker, K. (2001). Juvenile boot camps: A descriptive analysis of program diversity and effectiveness. *Social Science Journal, 38,* 445–460.

U.S. General Accounting Office. (1993). *Prison boot camps: Short-term prison costs reduced, but long-term impact uncertain.* Washington, DC: Author.

◪ BRIDEWELL PRISON AND WORKHOUSE

Bridewell was the first correctional institution in England and was a precursor of the modern prison. Built initially as a royal residence in 1523, Bridewell Palace was given to the city of London to serve as the foundation for as system of Houses of Correction known as "Bridewells." These institutions, eventually numbering 200 in Britain, housed vagrants, homeless children, petty offenders, "disorderly women," prisoners of war, soldiers, and colonists sent to Virginia. Bridewells were relatively self-contained and distinct from county jails that functioned to hold those awaiting trial or punishment.

CHALLENGES OF A GROWING SURPLUS POPULATION

Sixteenth-century England was a period of enormous change. The unraveling of feudalism and the emergence of capitalism saw rising food prices, a change in official religions, dissolution of the monasteries, and the disbandment of private armies. These events released agricultural laborers, unemployed soldiers, and redundant monastic servants to seek work in the growing towns and cities. Those who could not find work roamed from town to town as homeless vagabonds; others were forced, by sickness or misfortune, into an impoverished life of debauchery, begging, and theft. In London alone, with a population of 75,000 in 1550, 12,000 desperately poor immigrants from around the country arrived, threatening to envelop the metropolis in vice and crime: "Citizens found themselves besieged in their streets by the leper with his bell, the cripple with his deformities and the rouge with

Photo 2 *The Bridewell concept carried over to the United States. Here Chicago's Bridewell, also known as Cook County Jail, shows men being forced to work in the prison's quarry.*

SOURCE: *Chicago Daily News.*

his fraudulent scheme" (O'Donoghue, 1923, p. 137). Concern for the poor soon became mixed with fear of these "savages," "beasts," and "incorrigibles." "Respectable" citizens—and especially the new merchant classes—wanted "to protect themselves from the unscrupulous activities of this vast army of wandering parasites" (Salgado, 1972, p. 10), and demanded that something be done to make the city streets safe for the conduct of business.

THE DISRESPECTABLE UNDESERVING POOR

Based on ideas in Lutheran writing and models in Flemish Europe, in 1552, the ill-fated Protestant Bishop of London Nicholas Ridley requested that Bridewell Palace be donated to the city for the purpose of housing and transforming the problem of the streets. At Ridley's urging, a committee of city aldermen and commoners distinguished between the *respectable deserving poor* and the *disrespectable undeserving poor*. The *respectable poor* included those suffering from sickness and contagious diseases, wounded soldiers, curable cripples, the blind, fatherless and pauper children, and the aged poor. These people were the responsibility of the more fortunate and would be segregated by their class and condition, given immediate assistance, including shelter, treatment, adequate maintenance, and in the case of the children, education and training, in a variety of houses and hospitals around the city. Such "respectable" citizens were seen as having fallen upon hard times through no moral fault of their own, by reason of failure in business, ill health, or other misfortunes.

In contrast, the *disrespectable poor*, including vagabonds, tramps, rogues, and a variety of dissolute, "loose" and immoral women, harlots, unfaithful wives, and prostitutes, were thought to be worthless. Most vilified was the "robust beggar," whose career was seen as a choice for a soft and easy life. Such people were to be punished with imprisonment and whipping, before being trained to honest work in a prison, which should also be a house of work, with opportunities for the amendment of character. The "stubborn and foul" would make nails and to do blacksmith's work; the weaker, the sick, and the crippled might make beds and bedding. The premises would also be used to train poor and resistant children into various trades. According to Ridley, Bridewell was intended "to deal with the poverty and idleness of the streets, not by statute, but by labor. The rogue and the idle vagrant would be sent to the treadmill to grind corn, but the respectable poor—whether young, not very strong, or even crippled—would be taught profitable trades, or useful occupations" (O'Donoghue, 1923, pp. 150–151). Training children for work was thought to be an early form of crime prevention.

THE BRIDEWELL SYSTEM

Bridewell was self-contained, managed by city of London aldermen and commoners who appointed its judges and court personnel, including clerks, treasurers, governors (warders), beadles, and sheriff, and set its system of punishment. By regulation, beadles (early police) were directed to patrol the streets of the city, clearing them of beggars, vagrants, and idlers, whether men, women, or children, who were conveyed to Bridewell, to be dealt with by its court. Beadles were empowered to search all suspicious houses, alehouses, skittle-alleys, cock-pits, dancing saloons, gambling dens, and the like. The appointed officers were authorized to convey to Bridewell the keepers of such places as well as the "ruffians and masterless men" arrested therein.

Typically, a presiding judge would hear the case against those "raked in" from the streets whose crimes would include begging with no visible means of subsistence and pilfering from stores. In any year, Bridewell handled some 1,300 persons (an average of 26 a week), who were usually sentenced to no more than a month of confinement. Destitute beggars and vagrants were often sentenced to four days and "a good washing," before being returned to their parishes. Individuals were usually "punished and set to work." "Punishment of course meant the lash—laid on with spirit by an unsentimental brute of a hempman—and it was carried out in a small room, hung with black . . . in the presence of some governors. . . . After receiving their deserts in public, they were sent down stairs to beat hemp or gather up old rags and wastepaper of the government monopolist, or to scour out the city ditches" (O'Donoghue, 1929, pp. 10–13) or set to grind corn on a treadmill.

Punishment at Bridewell had multiple dimensions. The standard whipping (also called flogging) with willows or holly rods of up to 100 stripes or lashes was administered to men, women, and children on their backs as part of an initial punishment. Later this punishment was extended to those who did not work enthusiastically and to anyone who broke various internal rules. After being whipped, people were often displayed in a public pillory where they were pelted with dirt, stones, and dead dogs and cats. Bridewell also had a pair of stocks, and a block, on which the "women of the streets" would have to beat out certain amounts of hemp a day with heavy mallets.

In addition to corporal punishment individuals could be confined in a variety of places within Bridewell, including a dungeon, known as "the hole," and the "Little Ease," which was a cell so small and low that a prisoner had to spend hours there in a squatting position. There were also torture chambers where people were tied by their hands fully stretched above their heads with manacles (so that their toes just touched the cell floor). Another torture (also called the manacles) was known as the "Scavenger's Daughter." This comprised a hoop of iron that compressed the human body into a small ball at the turn of a screw. Finally, there was the "gibbet," which, although rarely used and only for serious offenses, involved suspending a victim in an iron cage where he or she, if already dead, was left to rot, or if alive, to die of starvation and exposure.

Those who stayed in the Bridewell slept on straw beds in filthy, vermin-infested, dark and foul-smelling conditions and were fed meager portions of putrid food. This was after many had been separated from any money or property they may have had, which went toward the livelihood of the governors. Bridewell did not segregate its inmates by age, or by guilt or innocence, although women had their own quarters under the charge of a matron, and political and religious prisoners were separated from the rest, as were injured soldiers. All were allowed visitors from family and associates, and although direct communication with the outside world was prevented, carriers and costermongers served this function.

CONCLUSION: BRIDEWELL'S CONTRIBUTION TO PENAL REFORM

Bridewell is usually seen to be the precursor of the modern prison. Although its system of Houses of Correction did not immediately replace the preexisting forms of corporal and capital punishment, over time they were supplemented by attempts at education and training, particularly for the young. In workhouses, the object was reform of the prisoner, who was to be passed through its workshops and discharged as soon as work could be found in domestic service, workshops, or at sea. Indeed, Bridewell functioned as a kind of labor exchange for youths. Many of the boys and girls were educated in music and many boys had masters on the premises from whom they learned an apprenticeship in such trades as glove making, felt making, beaver hat making, and silk weaving, for up to 7 to 10 years. The work was long and the sustenance meager but the apprentices, as many as 100 at a time, were protected by the governors from harsh treatment by their masters. They were usually kept clean and dressed in new clothes for special occasions. In some cases, they left with financial support from well-wishers to make decent livelihoods employing their own apprentices.

William Penn's "Great Law" of Pennsylvania in 1682 fused the hard labor of the workhouse (Bridewell) with the confinement of detention jail (Newgate) to form the modern prison system. Chicago's Cook County Jail, which employed inmates at quarrying and hard labor, was known as "the Bridewell." The idea that offenders could be reformed through work and training continues to be part of modern penal theory. Likewise the notion that there are deserving and undeserving poor is often cited as an explanation for penal practices. Though clearly there are many differences between the early workhouses in Britain and contemporary prisons, connections can be made, suggesting that any historical account of punishment should include these foundational institutions.

—*William G. Hinkle and Stuart Henry*

See also Cook County, Illinois; Corporal Punishment; England and Wales; Flogging; Michel Foucault; Hard Labor; History of Prisons; John Howard; Labor; Panopticon; State Prison System; Walnut Street Jail

Further Reading

Copeland, A. J. (1888). *Bridewell Royal Hospital, past and present: A short account of it as palace, hospital, prison, and school; with a collection of enteresting* [sic] *memoranda hitherto unpublished.* London: Gardner, Darton.

Hibbert, C. (1963). *The roots of evil.* Harmondsworth, UK: Penguin.

O'Donoghue, E. G. (1923). *Bridewell Hospital; palace, prison, schools, from the earliest times to the end of the reign of Elizabeth.* London: Lane.

O'Donoghue, E. G. (1929). *Bridewell Hospital; palace, prison, schools, from the death of Elizabeth to modern times.* London: Lane.

Salgado, G. (1972). *Cony-catchers and bawdy baskets.* Harmondsworth, UK: Penguin.

⚑ BROCKWAY, ZEBULON REED
(1827–1920)

Penologist and prison reformer Zebulon Reed Brockway ushered in a new age of social control in America, one ostensibly based on enlightened and rational scientific principles. He is perhaps best known for his criticism of determinate sentencing and his advocacy of its replacement: the *indeterminate sentence.*

In contrast to the determinate sentence, the principle of indeterminacy permits prisoners to complete their rehabilitation in the community if experts judge them sufficiently reformed. Brockway believed the determinate sentence was an "active cause of crime" because prisoners who were not yet rehabilitated could be released. Indeed, there was no incentive to reform. He felt the indeterminate sentence was a better alternative because it gave correctional authorities several concrete tools with which to reach the rehabilitative ideal. He thought it replaced the "law of force" with the "law of love," instilling in prisoners "confidence," "courage," and "moral excellence," which Brockway identified as "the very essence of virtue." Because the prisoner had to earn the right of release by obeying the rules of the institution, he believed indeterminate sentences made self-interest work to the advantage of prison authorities by enhancing discipline. They also permitted the examination of inmates by panels of experts, thus allowing prison authorities to time the release of reformed persons into society and to monitor them in the community.

Born in Lyme, Connecticut, in 1827, Brockway spent his life in the service of repressive social control institutions. He began his career as a guard at the Connecticut State Prison at Wethersfield in 1848. By 1861, after positions in numerous prisons, he had scaled the ladder of the correctional hierarchy to the powerful position of superintendent of the House of Corrections in Detroit. It was at this post that he first tried his hand at reform, participating in the construction of an indeterminate sentencing law that was aimed at first-time offenders. Although Michigan courts struck down the legislation, Detroit foreshadowed things to come.

During the 1870s, Brockway worked closely with several reformers, including Enoch Wines, who drafted the Declaration of Principles delivered at the National Congress of Penitentiary and Reformatory Discipline in Cincinnati in 1870. Brockway's major contribution at the congress was his paper "The Ideal of a True Prison for a State," wherein he argued that penitentiaries properly have two functions: (1) the protection of society by the prevention of crime, and (2) the reformation of criminals. He argued against relying on force and fear as tools of control. Well-run institutions, for him, did not need to intimidate or coerce inmates. Rather than punishment to achieve compliance, he advocated systems of rewards. The role of corrections was to provide education and training and to teach inmates self-respect and self-control. Brockway advocated separate facilities for women, which he argued should be under the management of women. He advocated a medical model whereby penitentiaries were to be transformed into reformatories focused on classification, rehabilitation, and prevention; in other words, society would treat the criminal, not the crime.

ELMIRA

Brockway moved from Detroit to New York in 1876 to head up a new state reformatory at Elmira, where he served as superintendent until 1900. At Elmira, Brockway was given wide latitude to pursue his ideas. He experimented with halfway housing arrangements, educational programs in trade and industry, and rigid military style training. Among his most important innovations was an incentives scheme based on the marks system. Used by correctional facilities in Ireland and pioneered by Captain Alexander Maconochie of the Norfolk Island penal colony in Australia, the marks system required inmates to begin their sentences with a number of strikes against them. If they consistently followed prison rules, strikes would be removed. Once all strikes were removed, they were free to leave. Brockway adopted a scheme using privileges for proper conduct in the 1880s, producing the first working parole system in the United States. His success at implementing the principle of indeterminacy led to the adoption of similar programs throughout the country.

CONCLUSION

Elmira Reformatory and the "Father of American Corrections" could not boast of a spotless record. Brockway's methods came under scrutiny in the 1890s when prisoners began to report physical and psychological abuse. On Governor Roswell Flower's orders, the State Board of Charities conducted an extensive investigation and found evidence of inhumane treatment, including shackling, starvation, inadequate medical attention, beatings with paddles and leather straps, and psychological tortures, such as solitary confinement. A second investigation, requested by Brockway, was inconclusive, and on this basis the governor dismissed the case against Brockway. In 1899, newly elected Governor Theodore Roosevelt appointed a new management team that usurped Brockway's power. Brockway left Elmira the next year. He was 73 years old. He continued to lead an active life, publishing an autobiography in 1912 and serving as mayor of Elmira. He died in 1920.

—Andrew Austin

See also American Correctional Association; Classification; Corporeal Punishment; Determinate Sentencing; Education; Elmira Reformatory; Good Time Credit; Indeterminate Sentencing; Irish (or Crofton) System; Juvenile Reformatories; Alexander Maconochie; Massachusetts Reformatory; Medical Model; Parole; Parole Boards; Rehabilitation Theory

Further Reading

Brockway, Z. R. (1871). The ideal of a true prison system for a state. In E. C. Wines (Ed.), *Transactions of the National Congress on Penitentiary and Reformatory Discipline*. Albany, NY: Weed Parsons & Company.

Brockway, Z. R. (1910). The American reformatory prison system. *American Journal of Sociology, 15*, 454–477.

Brockway, Z. R. (1969). *Fifty years of prison service: An autobiography*. Montclair, NJ: Patterson Smith. (Original work published 1912)

Colvin, M. (1997). *Penitentiaries, reformatories, and chain gangs: Social theory and the history of punishment in nineteenth-century America*. New York: St. Martin's.

Morris, N. (2001). *Maconochie's gentlemen: The story of Norfolk Island and the roots of modern prison reform*. Oxford, UK: Oxford University Press.

Pisciotta, A. W. (1994). *Benevolent repression: Social control and the American reformatory-prison movement*. New York: New York University Press.

Shelden, R. G. (2001). *Controlling the dangerous classes: A critical introduction to the history of criminal justice*. Boston: Allyn & Bacon.

Wines, E. C. (Ed.). (1871). Declaration of principles adopted and promulgated by the congress. In *Transactions of the National Congress on Penitentiary and Reformatory Discipline*. Albany, NY: Weed Parsons & Company.

☑ BUREAU OF JUSTICE STATISTICS

The Bureau of Justice Statistics (BJS) is a division within the U.S. Department of Justice, whose primary task is to compile, analyze, publish, and disseminate data on crime and justice. It was founded in 1979, and since then has gathered statistical information about criminal offenders, victims of crime, and the criminal justice procedures and processes used by state and federal governments. Legislators and criminal justice practitioners use the information accumulated by the BJS to create new programs and policies aimed at combating crime and to ensure that the U.S. justice system is efficient and fair. According to the Bureau of Justice Statistics Strategic Plan FY 2003–2004 (BJS, 2002, p. 1), the "BJS's paramount goal is to improve the quality of our national intelligence on crime and justice and to enhance the quality of the debate concerning societal policies."

THE PRIMARY TASKS OF THE BJS

The BJS publishes annual information on criminal victimizations, offenders under correctional supervision, and federal statistics on criminal offenders and case processing. One of the annual publications is the *National Crime Victimization Survey* (NCVS). The NCVS data, which are collected by the Bureau of the Census from approximately 150,000 victims of crime, describe the effects and consequences of victimization. Information within the NCVS reveals how victims and offenders meet and the specifics of the crime, such as weapons, costs of the crime, and place and time of the offense.

In addition to the annual NCVS, the BJS releases intermittent publications on administrative and management issues in policing and corrections, practices and policies among prosecutors, and criminal and civil court processes in state courts. It also produces various work on felony convictions, characteristics of correctional populations, budgeting and expenditures in criminal justice, employment information, and other research on criminal justice topics.

HOW TO ACCESS BJS INFORMATION

Information disseminated by the BJS is available to criminal justice policymakers and scholars in a number of ways. First, BJS findings can be requested through the National Criminal Justice Reference Service (NCJRS). The NCJRS provides copies of reports to interested parties and maintains a mailing list. The NCJRS will provide referrals to other sources of criminal statistics for anyone interested in these data.

Second, research information from the BJS can also be downloaded from the Internet through the National Archive of Criminal Justice Data (NACJD). The NACJD provides secondary data for quantitative research in order to facilitate studies in the field of criminal justice. The NACJD will also provide technical assistance to individuals interested in performing quantitative research.

Third, the Federal Justice Statistics Resource Center (FJSRC) maintains data collected from federal policing, judiciary, and correctional agencies on criminal suspects and defendants processed in the federal system. Researchers can download criminal justice data sets and search for statistics on federal offenses and offenders on the FJSRC Web site, which operates in conjunction with the BJS.

Fourth, the BJS sponsors the National Clearinghouse for Criminal Justice Information Systems (CJIS). The CJIS acts as a clearinghouse for information on criminal justice resources and grant opportunities. It provides information on criminal justice software programs, information technology, best practices, case studies, and federal and state criminal justice system activities. Finally, the Infobase of State Activities and Research (ISAR)

provides information about research and publication activities in individual states. The BJS provides publications on state-related criminal justice programs to the ISAR.

REPORTING PROBLEMS FACED BY THE BJS

Although the BJS attempts to provide accurate statistical information in a timely manner, statistical research of any sort raises a number of problems. The NCVS, for example, is often criticized because of the methodology used in the survey. The NCVS is mailed to victims of crimes or, in some cases, administered over the phone. The rates of response may vary from year to year and may be influenced by a number of factors such as race, gender, type of victimization, education, socioeconomic class, whether or not the victimization was reported to the police, and so forth. In other words, an educated individual who understands the purpose of the NCVS or is familiar with the survey from coursework in a college or university may be more likely to return or participate in the survey because he or she realizes the information is confidential and is not likely to lead to individual identification. However, someone who was victimized in an extremely personal and/or traumatic manner, such as rape, and who is not familiar with the purpose of the NCVS may not return or participate in the survey for fear of personal identification or because of embarrassment, anger, worry, or other emotional or personal reasons. The lower the response rate, the less able the researcher is to generalize the results to an entire population.

The NCVS also raises questions about respondent trustworthiness. Because the survey asks for information that is extremely personal and of a traumatic event, individuals may not fully disclose the extent of type of their victimization, the factors that led up to or instigated their experience, or the disposition of the case. A victim's choice whether to fully disclose may be intentional or unintentional. A person may intentionally choose not disclose the information because of factors such as fear, anger, or humiliation about the victimization or the circumstances surrounding the victimization. He or she may unintentionally not release the information because the victim cannot remember or does not know the answers to the information requested in the survey. The respondent may also intentionally or unintentionally provide answers to the survey that may be misleading. This may be the case in situations in which the individual manipulates the answers to meet their perception of socially accepted behaviors, to look good in the eyes of the researcher, or to disguise his or her own role in the offense or victimization.

Other statistical information used in BJS publications comes from a variety of state and federal resources (prosecutor's offices, corrections departments, prisons, etc.). These data may also be susceptible to error because of the recording procedures used by the various agencies. The agencies may also maintain the statistics for their own purposes and not necessarily the reasons provided by the BJS. Finally, the figures provided by agencies may be manipulated by administrators to secure more funding, to draw attention to particular programs or needs, or to look good to other agencies.

Fortunately, the BJS has worked continuously to maintain internal and external quality standards for validity and reliability in its statistical reports. One quality standard used by the BJS is an examination of data needs with regard to legislative mandates. Reviews are consistently held to determine whether additional reports should be added to the publications list or if reporting procedures should be modified to meet legislative priorities. The BJS also requires agencies to conform to particular reporting procedures and data collection requirements. In addition, the BJS annually compares statistics gathered from state and federal agencies and in the NCVS with those published in the Uniform Crime Reports available yearly from the Federal Bureau of Investigation (FBI).

CONCLUSION

The BJS works closely with the American Statistical Association (ASA) and other agencies to verify and critique the statistics programs used by the BJS. Other agencies provide experienced researchers to analyze the data collected while focus groups of experts discuss new policy initiatives, advice from public interest groups on how to make statistical information more accessible to the public and academic researchers, and information on the suitability of BJS statistics in legislative decisions. Because of all of these strategies, the BJS is able to provide valid and reliable statistical information to criminal justice policymakers, state and federal criminal justice systems, and the public on criminal offending, victimization, case processing, and the feasibility and success of programs, legislation, and initiatives in criminal justice.

—Jennifer M. Allen

See also Accreditation; Federal Prison System; Increase in Prison Population; National Institute of Corrections; Truth in Sentencing

Further Reading

Agresti, A., & Finlay, B. (1997). *Statistical methods for the social sciences* (3rd ed.). Upper Saddle River, NJ: Prentice Hall.

Babbie, E. (1999). *The basics of social research* (8th ed.). Belmont, CA: Wadsworth.

Beck, A. J., & Harrison, P. M. (2002). *Prisoners in 2001*. NCJ 195189. Washington, DC: U.S. Department of Justice, Office of Justice Programs.

Bureau of Justice Statistics. (2002). *Bureau of Justice Statistics strategic plan FY 2003–2004*. Washington, DC: U.S. Department of Justice, Office of Justice Programs. Retrieved from http://www.ojp.usdoj.gov

Felson, R. B., & Ackermann, J. (2001). Arrest for domestic and other assault. *Criminology, 39,* 655–675.

Harlow, C. W. (1999). *Prior abuse reported by inmates and probationers* (NCJ 172879). Washington, DC: U.S. Department of Justice, Office of Justice Programs, Bureau of Justice Statistics.

Rennison, C. (2001). *Violent victimization and race, 1993–98* (Bureau of Justice Statistics special report, NCJ 176354). Washington, DC: U.S. Department of Justice, Bureau of Justice Statistics.

Scalia, J. (2001). *Federal drug offenders, 1999 with trends 1984–99* (NCJ 187285). Washington, DC: U.S. Department of Justice, Office of Justice Programs.

CAMPUS STYLE

The idea in architecture that form should follow the function or purpose of the building is apparent in prison design. Massive impersonal cellblocks reflect eras when themes of punishment and control dominated. In contrast, the development of campus-like facilities, usually in rural areas, with small living units and other services in buildings distributed within open spaces reflected a belief that treatment and reintegration should be key correctional goals. Earlier juvenile and women's institutions in some states and at the federal level were built in campus style with cottages, including kitchens, dining rooms, and in some facilities, nurseries, designed to provide a homelike and domestic environment. The design assumed that both juveniles and women could be best reformed through education and work and by the example set by staff members in a humane setting.

During the 1960s, when ideas about treatment, unit management, and reintegration dominated corrections, both states and the federal correctional systems began to build campus-like minimum- and medium-security facilities with scattered housing units for adult male prisoners. These units, staffed with unit managers and treatment personnel, usually provided rooms for 30 or 40 inmates. They were built with wood, light, and color for a more normalized environment. Dining halls, school buildings, and recreational facilities, work, administrative and health areas were often arranged in a more centralized open plaza area, with secure fencing surrounding the entire layout.

HISTORY

Although campus-style prisons proliferated in the United States in the 1960s and 1970s, penal institutions with similar forms had been built earlier, including the New Jersey Reformatory at Annandale completed in 1929 and the Missouri Intermediate Reformatory at Jefferson City completed in 1932. The Illinois women's prison at Dwight opened in 1930, and in 1958 the Michigan Training Unit at Ionia was opened. At the federal level, the Federal Industrial Reformatory and Industrial Farm for Women was opened in 1927 on more than 500 acres of land in Alderson, West Virginia, with 14 cottages, each with a kitchen and dining room and rooms for approximately 30 women, a school building, industries building, laundry, and a working farm in what was described as a "beautiful, open, campus-like setting" (Keve, 1991, p. 83).

An instructive example of the changes that occur in philosophy and architecture in the transition from an adult female to an adult male institution occurred at the federal facility at Seagoville, Texas. It opened in 1940 in farmland, with a capacity for 400 women on a cottage plan similar to that of Alderson and a fence described as built to keep cows in and people out. In 1942, with the advent of World War II, it became a detention center for Japanese, German, and Italian families. In turn, in 1945 Seagoville became the "showcase" federal minimum-security open facility for men with the campus-like setting providing a "climate" for changing attitudes, while the domestic kitchens and dining rooms were removed from the cottages.

CHANGING PENAL IDEAS AND DESIGN

During the 1960s, as they had earlier for juveniles and women, ideas about the goals of prison turned toward rehabilitation and reintegration, and prison architecture, in turn, changed. Critics began to argue that traditional penal institutions, often huge fortress-like buildings designed to be menacing, did little to prepare individuals to move into successful lives outside of these institutions. In contrast, campus-style prisons were believed to provide a more normalized setting that would assist people in returning to the community. Inmates could be housed in smaller groups within units that could provide a range of specialized programs and living conditions, while unit management could increase both contact and knowledge by staff of individual treatment needs. Distributing other daily activities elsewhere on the campus, rather than providing all the amenities in a single building, was viewed as a more realistic experience of community living. In these institutions, prisoners frequently left their cells to visit the dining halls, or to go to work, recreation, and school buildings. Health services and visiting and chapel areas were also housed in separate buildings.

Campus-style prisons were purposefully designed to provide a different look and feel to traditional penal institutions. Rather than bars of steel, clanging doors, and the rattle of keys, they tended to use wooden doors, laminate surfaces, carpeting, and brightly colored paint. All of these changes in style were thought to make these institutions appear more like the world outside of prison.

CAMPUS-STYLE INSTITUTIONS

In *The New Red Barn,* William Nagel (1973) discussed several new campus-style prisons he and his group visited during their examination of prisons in the United States for the American Foundation's Institute of Corrections in the early 1970s. They visited juvenile institutions in Georgia, Wisconsin, Washington, and Texas as well as the Robert F. Kennedy Youth Center in Morgantown, West Virginia. This federal facility for youthful offenders opened in 1969 in a rolling campus provided with modern teaching equipment, a well-designed chapel, an impressive gymnasium and swimming pool, and extensive classification and treatment programming in its living units. Nagel also described a campus-style facility opened in 1972 for adults at Vienna, Illinois, that later included the local community college within its grounds. He thought the housing units, built around an open area that included churches, shops, schools, and a library, looked like garden apartments. He noted that many of these facilities including those located in Fox Lake, Wisconsin; Ionia, Michigan; and Vienna, Illinois; had very bright and attractive dining areas.

As was their goal, campus-style prisons present a more humane design that can make the prison experience a little easier. They are also more flexible for programming, classification, and unit management. Their building style can serve a variety of functions more cost effectively, while prisoners and staff members have the opportunity to be outside, enjoy fresh air, and experience the changing seasons. A visit to a campus prison may lead some to believe that security is less than in other prison designs, but while some are open facilities, others are very secure. In many states, campus-style prisons have double fences, which deter and prevent escapes by offenders, lessening the fears of neighboring residents, while others are active in providing community services.

CONCLUSION

While some campus-style prisons were built in the early 20th century, they proliferated in the 1960s and 1970s in the United States. Penal philosophy focusing on the reintegration of prisoners into society after they served time in prison led to construction of many campus-style prisons by the end of the 1970s. Changing public attitudes, movements to "get tough on criminals," and extensive overcrowding has led in most prison systems to changing styles of prison architecture, exemplified in the growth of the supermax prison. Campus-style prisons remain, however, as the humane symbols of their era.

—Kim Davies

See also Alderson, Federal Prison Camp; Auburn System; Classification; Cottage System; Eastern State Penitentiary; High-Rise Prisons; Metropolitan Detention Centers; Minimum Security; Panopticon; Prison Farms; Supermax Prisons; Telephone Pole Design; Unit Management; Women's Prisons

Further Reading

Clear, T. R., & Cole, G. F. (2000). *American corrections* (5th ed.). Belmont, CA: Wadsworth.

Goffman, E. (1961). *Asylums: Essays on the social situation of mental patients and other inmates.* New York: Doubleday, Anchor.

Johnston, N. (1973). *The human cage: A brief history of prison architecture.* New York: Walker.

Keve, P. (1991). *Prisons and the American conscience: A history of U.S. federal corrections.* Carbondale: Southern Illinois University Press.

Nagel, W. G. (1973). *The new red barn: A critical look at the modern American prison.* New York: Walker.

◪ CANADA

Canada has two separate penal systems at the federal and provincial/territorial levels. The federal system imprisons individuals who commit the most serious offenses and are sentenced to two years or more, as outlined in Section 731(1) of the Criminal Code of Canada. All federally sentenced persons fall under the jurisdiction of the Correctional Service of Canada (CSC). In contrast, provincial and territorial correctional facilities incarcerate people who receive a sentence of less than two years. They also hold accused persons on remand

awaiting trial, those who fail to pay a fine, federally sentenced individuals appealing their conviction and/or sentence and individuals who apply to serve their provincial time in a federal institution under the Exchange of Services Agreement.

Although there are considerable differences between the federal and provincial/territorial systems, there are also some striking operational similarities between them. For example, CSC's total operational expenditure in 2000–2001 was $1.3 billion, while at the provincial/territorial level it was $1.2 billion. Of these totals, $879.3 million or 80% of the total federal operating expenditure was directed toward custodial services, and in comparison $948 million or 69% of the total provincial/territorial operating funds were allocated to custodial services. These figures translate into an average daily inmate cost of $189.21 at the federal level and $137.44 at the provincial/territorial level. Furthermore, in 2000–2001 the two systems employed a similar number of full-time equivalent staff: 12,572 federal staff and 13,084 provincial/territorial staff.

On average, Canada's rate of incarceration is much lower than in the United States, but substantially higher than in many Western European countries. Each year, the federal system processes a much smaller number of persons than the provincial/territorial systems. For example, 7,723 individuals were admitted to federal custody in 2000–2001 as compared to 227, 279 who were sent to provincial/territorial institutions. Nonetheless, the average number of persons incarcerated at any given time was much more comparable between the two systems, with 12,732 individuals in 68 federal prisons and 18,815 in 143 provincial/territorial institutions. Nationally, in 2000–2001 there was a federal incarceration rate of 54 persons per 100,000 Canadian adults, and a provincial/territorial rate of 80 per 100,000 adults. In the provinces and territories, the rate varied extensively from 684 per 100,000 adults in the Northwest Territories, to 150 in Saskatchewan, and 47 in Nova Scotia. Due to the variations within the provincial/territorial systems, this entry will focus mainly on the federal institutions and the policies of the CSC.

HISTORY

Four models of punishment characterize the history of corrections in Canada: deterrence, rehabilitation, incapacitation, and rehabilitation. Each model has directed the policies and practices in different time periods, and at times have overlapped. In general, CSC's approach to the incarceration of men and women has been one and the same; however, the history of women's imprisonment varies somewhat from that of men's, as it has been influenced by dominant conceptions of femininity, the sexual division of labor, and popular theories of female crime. There has also been a similar, although less pronounced, specific history to the incarceration of Aboriginal peoples.

Deterrence

From the 1600s through to the 1820s, Canadian offenders were dealt with according to ideas of deterrence. As a result, severe physical punishment, such as flogging and mutilation, were common. The deterrence model continued to dictate the response to crime through the 1820s and 1830s; however, this period also introduced what was believed to be milder strategies of punishment, including incarceration and hard manual labor.

As in other countries, 19th-century penal reformers sought to find more humane methods of dealing with offenders than corporal punishment. As part of this movement, the first Canadian penitentiary was built in 1835 in Kingston, Ontario, and the federal Department of Justice (DOJ) was established in 1868. The Kingston penitentiary sought to deter criminals through the threat of incarceration and train those within it in socially acceptable behavior that would prevent them from engaging in future crime. By 1868, the DOJ took over responsibility for Kingston as well as the two penitentiaries in St. John, New Brunswick, and Halifax, Nova Scotia. The creation of the DOJ changed ideas about criminals and their conduct since its officials believed in the necessity of humane treatment and reform. It was still some time, however, before the prison completely replaced earlier strategies of corporal punishment. Likewise, it was not until the

1930s that offender rehabilitation was seriously considered. Around the same time, in 1938, Canada's federal correctional system and the CSC were established.

Rehabilitation

The period from post–World War II to the early 1960s is typically identified as the rehabilitation era in Canada. Two reports helped shape this time and one facilitated its demise. First, the 1937 report of the Royal Commission on the Penal System of Canada, chaired by Mr. Justice Archambault, concluded that the primary goal of the correctional system should be the reformation of the offender in conjunction with community protection. A second report submitted in 1956 by the Justice Department Committee, and chaired by Mr. Justice Fauteux, reaffirmed rehabilitation as the primary objective of corrections, arguing that the offender was damaged during developmental years and could be treated within the prison system.

By the mid-1960s, growing skepticism surfaced about the effectiveness of rehabilitation programs in Canadian penitentiaries. In response, *The Report of the Canadian Committee on Corrections,* also known as the *Ouimet Report* was released in 1969. As with previous studies, the committee strongly supported rehabilitation, except this time in the community rather than correctional facilities. Shortly afterward, an article by Robert Martinson in the United States (1974), titled "What Works—Questions and Answers About Prison Reform," was selectively adopted into Canadian penal ideology to support the demise of prison rehabilitation programs. In place of rehabilitation, deterrence resurfaced as the correctional aim of the Canadian penitentiary system.

By the late 1970s, offender rehabilitation was nearly obsolete from Canada's prison system. In 1977, a federal government task force officially rejected the medical model approach to offender rehabilitation and replaced it with the program opportunity model, which stated that offenders were ultimately responsible for their behavior. The opportunity model placed the responsibility of rehabilitation on the prisoner with no compulsory intervention from treatment officials.

Incapacitation

Largely in response to the perceived failure of prisoner rehabilitation, throughout the 1970s and into the 1980s Canadian corrections sought mainly to incapacitate offenders while emphasizing punishment and deterrence. This was a short-lived approach, however, and was soon replaced with the idea of selective incapacitation of high-risk, dangerous offenders that partially grew out of a study conducted by the RAND Corporation in the United States.

The aim of the RAND study was to help administrators differentiate between low-risk and high-risk offenders. Follow-up research created a seven-point item scale to distinguish between those offenders who posed the greatest danger and should be incapacitated and others who could be released after shorter sentences. This scale was then used by officials to designate offenders as high, medium, and low risk. Ultimately, such ideas of selective incapacitation led to the construction of classification tools to identify offender risks and needs, both within the prison and the community.

Reintegration

The idea of offender reintegration built on the concept of selective incapacitation of high-risk offenders and rehabilitation in the community. Through the 1980s, the federal system maintained its commitment to various forms of community-based sanctions. Some suggest that the rising cost of incarceration greatly influenced this focus on less expensive community reintegration options.

In the late 1980s and early 1990s, due in part to this new focus on community reintegration, the public and penal administrators became increasingly concerned about community safety. In response, the CSC began to model its offender assessment and treatment techniques on its own risk/need research. Institutional and community risk/need assessment scales were implemented in the early 1990s, and since that time CSC has risen as an international leader in the field. Its classification tools collect information on factors to determine criminal risk and identify offender needs, which in turn underlie its management of prisons and prisoner populations and well as offenders reintegrating into the community.

CURRENT POLICY

Since the late 1990s, the guiding ideology of CSC has incorporated the four models of punishment that characterize the history of Canadian corrections. CSC currently stresses offender reintegration, with primacy afforded to community protection (thus selective incapacitation), and maintenance of incarceration for punishment/deterrence with deceased attention on institutional offender rehabilitation. This is relayed in CSC's mission statement, first produced in 1997. It reads:

> The Correctional Service of Canada, as part of the criminal justice system and respecting the rule of law, contributes to the protection of society by actively encouraging and assisting offenders to become law-abiding citizens, while exercising, reasonable, safe, secure and humane control.

CSC's current attention toward reintegration, and thus decreased incarceration, is supported at-large within the community. However, how CSC's ideology transfers into policy and practice is called into question on many fronts when the offender population and its characteristics are considered.

POPULATION CHARACTERISTICS

These days, the typical federal prisoner in Canada is poor, male, single, undereducated, and a substance abuser. He also has an unstable employment history and is disproportionately likely to be from a racial minority group. In terms of the female population, over 50% are mothers, the majority of them are the primary family caregiver, and an overwhelming percentage have a background of sexual abuse and violence. In 2000–2001, women made up 5% of federal (and 9% of provincial/territorial) admissions, while Aboriginal peoples comprised 17% of federal (and 19% of provincial/territorial) admissions. Given that indigenous people make up only roughly 3% of Canada's total population, their numbers in the penal facilities of either system are clearly elevated.

Men and women differ in the age at which they are federally incarcerated. In 2000–2001, 47% of male and 56% of female prisoners were between 20 and 34 years of age. At a higher percentage but with similar proportional difference between the sexes, 58% of Aboriginal males and 66% of Aboriginal females were between the ages of 20 to 34. There is diversity as well in the percentage of men and women serving their first federal sentence. Sixty-two percent of males and 82% of females were serving their first penitentiary sentence, and a comparably lower 57% of Aboriginal males and 72% of Aboriginal females were. Finally, men and women also differ in terms of how long they are incarcerated. The average length of sentence for 31% of males was between 3 and 6 years, whereas it was under 3 years for 36% of females. Likewise for Aboriginal males, the most common sentence was 3 to 6 years (33%) and for 35% of Aboriginal females it was under 3 years.

CSC periodically assesses its prisoner population to determine individuals' risk to the public and to the security of the institution, staff, inmates, and themselves. On April 29, 2001, the majority of males were classified as medium security (59%), followed by minimum (21%) and maximum (14%). This varied significantly for women, of whom the majority were classified as minimum (44%), followed closely by medium (40%) and then maximum (9%). Most male and female Aboriginal offenders were classified as medium (62%), followed by minimum (17%) and maximum (16%).

In 2000–2001, the most common offense of all federally sentenced persons was a Schedule I, which includes the most serious crimes with the exception of murder. Fifty-nine percent of men and 44% of women, and 67% of Aboriginal males and 56% of Aboriginal females, were imprisoned for a Schedule I offense. The second most common offense differed between the sexes. Sixteen percent of men in general and 21% of Aboriginal men specifically were imprisoned for a sex offense, while 24% of women and 22% of Aboriginal women were incarcerated for a drug offense.

Examining the prisoner population from the operational standpoint of CSC, the average annual cost of incarcerating an individual in 2000–2001 at the federal level was $88,427. Broken down by sex, this figure corresponds to an amount of $66,381 for men and $110,473 for women. Women are more expensive to imprison largely because of their fewer numbers and the legal requirement to provide program and service equity with males. In comparison, the average annual cost of supervising an individual in the community (e.g., parole) in 2000–2001 was $16,800.

In 2000–2001, there were also 81 escapes from federal facilities, while at the provincial level there were 1,110. Although this appears to be a dramatic difference, as a percentage of all custodial admissions it translates into a rate of 1% at the federal level and 0.5% at the provincial/territorial level. Finally, that same year there were 43 deaths in federal facilities and 49 in provincial/territorial institutions. As a percentage of all custodial admissions, this translates into 0.6% of all federal admissions and in comparison only 0.02% of all provincial/territorial admissions. Of the provincial/territorial deaths, 28 were suicides and 2 were murders while federally there were 9 suicides and no murders.

WOMEN PRISONERS

For the most part, CSC's treatment of female prisoners has and continues to be subsumed under its treatment of male prisoners. This being said, there is also a history specific to female prisoners in Canada. As relayed, this history has been influenced by dominant conceptions of femininity, the sexual division of labor, and popular theories of female crime.

Historically, women were incarcerated in men's institutions in Canada. Women who were sentenced to prison were thought to be "unnatural," since it was generally viewed as unfeminine for women to be involved in crime. Thus, the few incarcerated women were granted little attention in terms of care and treatment within the men's institutions. For example, women were incarcerated in makeshift sections of the institutions and they did not have access to programming.

In 1934, the first separate facility for federal female prisoners was opened, the Prison for Women, across the road from the Kingston penitentiary. At the foundation of the prison's operation was acceptance of a traditional role for women, emphasizing their domestic position in society. Women were taught, for example, to be better seamstresses and home-makers and to act like proper ladies. Efforts at reforming the female criminal into a traditional caregiver continued until the 1960s.

In the mid- to late 1960s, the public advent of feminism initiated the identification of women who committed crimes as offenders (i.e., Adler's 1975 liberated female criminal) and this assisted with the placement of females on the corrections agenda. This is similar to the U.S. experience, where serious acknowledgment of the unique experiences of women prisoners surfaced in the early 1960s. In Canada, even though CSC was claiming to acknowl-edge differences between males and females, it did little to account for this understanding in its policies and practices.

The 1970s and 1980s were witness to a signifi-cant shift in CSC's response to the female prisoner. No longer was attention focused on differences between females and males, but rather, it was placed on formal equality between the sexes. The problem with this was that the standard against which the female was compared was the male, which disregarded the specific and unique needs of the federal female prisoner in general, and within specific populations in particular (i.e., Aboriginal women). Some practices during this period also remained consistent with the traditional patriarchal view of women prisoners, such as institutional pro-gramming at the Prison for Women that supported normative standards of femininity (e.g., hairdress-ing courses, child care training).

In the early 1990s, apparent progress was made by CSC in its acknowledgment of the unique needs of federal female prisoners *and* their equitable treatment in comparison to males. Goff (1999) summarized:

In essence this approach recognizes that female offenders and male offenders are different, hence they should have programs, services and facilities designed to meet each group's specific needs. A key component in this ideology is the women-centred approach to corrections, which argues that policies must be restructured to reflect the variety of realities experienced by women and men. (p. 169)

Examples of the translation of this approach into practice were the creation of the position of Deputy Commission for Women and the construction of five regional institutions and a healing lodge for federally sentenced women to replace the one cen-trally located prison in Kingston, Ontario. However, such actions were criticized for continuing to apply the male standard to the female prisoner. It was argued that the ideal of the woman-centered approach was not translated into practice.

An example of CSC's current application of the male standard to the female prisoner is its Offender Intake Assessment (OIA). The OIA is a form of risk/needs measurement that was introduced by the CSC in 1994 as a part of all federal prisoners' institutional intake. The OIA was not specifically constructed to measure female risk and needs, and so women's experiences are not at the core of the instrument. Many are therefore critical of the mea-surement tool, noting some research has concluded that the tool imposes harsher conditions of impris-onment on women (e.g., increased security classifi-cation), does not account for women's roles as mothers and caretakers, and negatively affects women's treatment options in prison and upon release. This criticism is not specific to Canada, as it is raised in U.S. corrections as well. In early 2000, CSC initiated work in the area of female-specific risk/needs assessment, but the findings are yet to be publicly released.

ABORIGINAL PRISONERS

Aboriginal peoples in Canada have suffered and continue to experience a number of forms of racial oppression. This is largely a consequence of capi-talist development in Canada, which continues to be highly dependent on the perpetuation race, gender, and class divisions. As with African Americans in the United States, Aboriginal peoples are more likely to be incarcerated upon conviction, denied bail, and held in custody longer in comparison to non-Aboriginal peoples. Until recently, there has been limited attention allotted to race and the federal prisoner by the CSC. The incarceration of Aboriginal peoples, as relayed at the start of this entry, shows they are disproportionately represented within the system, have greater chances of being incarcerated for a second time, and have higher institutional security classifications. This all points toward the need for specific attention to Aboriginal prisoners. Some advances have been made by CSC in recent years, and include the construction of the Healing Lodge for federally sentenced females (Okimaw Ohci), Aboriginal-specific health strategies in HIV/AIDS, endorsement of NativeSisterhood within the prison system, and the establishment of 24 halfway houses for Aboriginal males across Canada. Again, although CSC has acknowledged that Aboriginal prisoners have unique experiences and circumstances in comparison to non-Aboriginal prisoners, there remains a need for ensuing informed policy and practice.

Similar to the history of female prisoners in Canadian corrections, the acknowledgment of the uniqueness of Aboriginal in comparison to non-Aboriginal prisoners to date has come at an expense. In particular, Aboriginal offenders have often come to be thought of as a homogeneous group. For example, CSC's OIA does not account for diversity within the Aboriginal offender population (e.g., Inuit, Metis, First Nations). Furthermore, risk and need assessment tools individualize offender risk and need, decontextualizing these from the social and political structures, and so the tools are not able to account for the impact of colonial oppression, which cannot be individualized.

CONCLUSION

Canada's two systems of incarceration, federal and provincial/territorial, have numerous similarities as well as differences in their operations and prisoner populations. At the federal level, which is likewise characterized by similarities and differences, the history of corrections can be chronicled through four models of punishment: deterrence, rehabilitation, incapacitation, and reintegration. These models offer insight into CSC's approach to imprisonment during various time periods, which assists in understanding the CSC's historic and current policies and practices. CSC's current ideology, conveyed in its

mission statement and evident in its operations, relays the need for increased attention specific to female and Aboriginal prisoners.

—*Colleen Anne Dell*

See also Australia; Classification; Deterrence Theory; England and Wales; Federal Prison System; Incapacitation Theory; Just Deserts Theory; Robert Martinson; Medical Model; Native American Prisoners; Rehabilitation Theory; Rehabilitation Act 1973; Restorative Justice; State Prison System; Prisoners; Women; Women's Prisons

Further Reading

Bonta, J., LaPrairie, C., & Wallace-Capretta, S. (1997). Risk prediction and re-offending: Aboriginal and non-Aboriginal offenders. *Canadian Journal of Criminology. 39*, 127–144.

Carrigan, D. (1991). *Crime and punishment in Canada, a history*. Toronto: McClelland & Stewart.

Correctional Service of Canada. (2001). *Basic facts about federal corrections*. Ottawa, ON: Public Works and Government Services Canada.

Culhane, C. (1985). *Still barred from prison: Social injustice in Canada*. Montreal, QU: Black Rose Books.

Faith, K. (1993). *Unruly women: The politics of confinement and resistance*. Vancouver: Press Gang.

Goff, C. (1999). *Corrections in Canada*. Cincinnati, OH: Anderson.

Hannah-Moffat, K., & Shaw, M. (2000). *An ideal prison? Critical essays on women's imprisonment*. Halifax, NS: Fernwood.

Jackson, M. (2002). *Justice behind the walls*. Vancouver, BC: Douglas & MacIntyre.

Martinson, R. (1974). What works—Questions and answers about prison reform. *Public Interest, 35*, 22–54.

Nielsen, M. (2000). Canadian correctional policy and Native inmates: The control of social dynamite. In R. Neugebauer, *Criminal injustice: Racism in the criminal justice system* (pp. 341–354). Toronto: Canadian Scholars' Press.

Winterdyk, J. (2001). *Corrections in Canada: Social reactions to crime*. Toronto: Prentice Hall.

◪ CAPITAL PUNISHMENT

Capital punishment refers to the use of the death penalty as punishment for certain crimes. In America, almost 20,000 persons have been legally put to death since colonial times, with most of the executions occurring in the 19th and 20th centuries. In recent years, opposition to the death penalty has become more vocal in many states, leading some criminologists to predict its eventual demise.

HISTORY

The United States has had a system of capital punishment in place since colonial times. The first recorded legal execution in the American colonies occurred in 1608 in Virginia, when Captain George Kendall was executed for the crime of spying for Spain. Since then, the crimes eligible for a death sentence have changed. For example, prior to the American Revolution, the list of capital crimes included idolatry, witchcraft, blasphemy, murder, manslaughter, poisoning, bestiality, sodomy, adultery, manslaughter, bearing false witness in capital cases, conspiracy, and rebellion. Now, the application of the death penalty is overwhelmingly confined to murder. It is noteworthy, however, the colonial Americans used the death penalty less often than courts do today despite the greater number of eligible crimes.

During the 19th century, the number of executions increased significantly, with more people put to death between 1800 and 1865 than in the entire 17th and 18th centuries combined. Changes were also enacted that included the introduction of the concept of degrees of murder and the removal of executions from the public realm. In some states, discretionary death penalty laws replaced those that mandated the death penalty for anyone convicted of a capital crime. In addition, the jurisdiction of executions was changed from local to state control. Individual towns were no longer responsible for capital punishment. Instead, the state became the executioner. Finally, the number of offenses punishable by death was reduced and some states began abolishing the death penalty. The number of executions decreased immediately following the Civil War. However, in the last two decades of the 19th century, the number increased again to approximately 1,000 each decade.

Abolitionist efforts grew during this time period as well. Michigan eradicated the death penalty in

1846 for all crimes except treason. Five other states also enacted abolitionist legislation. By 1901, however, three of these states had reestablished capital punishment.

During the first two decades of the 20th century, the United States entered what is known as the Progressive period of social reform. More states abolished the death penalty or severely restricted its use. Six states (Kansas, Minnesota, Missouri, Oregon, South Dakota, and Washington) abolished the death penalty entirely, and three others limited its use to rare offenses such as treason (Arizona, North Dakota, and Tennessee). However, concern about communism and the threat of revolution led to the reinstatement of capital punishment in five states by 1920, and the number of executions across the country overall increased. The 1930s hold the record for the greatest number of executions in one decade in U.S. history, averaging 167 executions per year. The combination of organized crime during the Depression and the writings of criminologists who suggested that the death penalty was necessary to deter violence increased its popularity during this period. By 1950, only three states that had previously abolished capital punishment had not reenacted statutes allowing the death penalty.

During the 1950s, public support for capital punishment began diminishing again, although there were periods of strong support for it. International support for the death penalty was declining. Two cases were particularly noteworthy at this time for the debate surrounding capital punishment. First, the prosecution of Julius and Ethel Rosenberg garnered public support for capital punishment. The Rosenbergs were accused of engaging in espionage for the Soviet Union. Although there was public debate about their sentences as well as widespread international protest, the Rosenbergs were executed in 1953. A Gallup poll taken five months after their executions indicated strong support in the United States for capital punishment, with 70% of people supporting the death penalty. Less than one year later, however, another case occurred that led to strong opposition to the death penalty. Caryl Chessman, who had been sentenced to death in 1948, published the first of four books from death row in California. In them he claimed innocence, and his case became the focus of worldwide opposition to capital punishment. Chessman's execution was stayed eight times before his death sentence was carried out in 1960. National and international efforts to intervene brought the case into the spotlight. Following his execution, opinion polls indicated decreasing support for capital punishment. Four states abolished the death penalty within five years (Iowa, Michigan, Oregon, and West Virginia).

By the mid-1960s, a number of constitutional challenges to capital punishment had been raised. In the case of *Trop v. Dulles* (1958), the U.S. Supreme Court set forth the argument of evolving standards of decency that became important in later constitutional challenges to the death penalty. Eventually, three cases led to a moratorium on executions. *Maxwell v. Bishop* (1970) raised the issue of racial discrimination in the application of capital punishment, and *Witherspoon v. Illinois* (1968) called into question the use of "death-qualified juries" (or the practice of removing potential jurors for cause if they were opposed to the death penalty). *United States v. Jackson* (1968) focused on the requirement that a jury recommend death for federal kidnapping cases. The last execution prior to the 1972 national moratorium on executions occurred in Colorado in 1967.

FURMAN V. GEORGIA AND ITS AFTERMATH

In 1972, the Supreme Court ruled on the case of *Furman v. Georgia,* instituting a complete moratorium on executions in the United States. The *Furman* case focused on the arbitrariness and capriciousness of capital punishment that resulted from unrestrained discretion of juries. While the Supreme Court did not rule that the *practice* of the death penalty was unconstitutional, it did find that existing statutes (involving the *process* of sentencing) were unconstitutional. Death penalty statutes in 40 states and the federal government were overturned, and 629 death sentences were vacated. The *Furman* decision not only instituted a moratorium on executions but also established the "death is different

doctrine." This doctrine has led to the policy of treating capital cases as different from all other crimes, requiring what has been referred to as "super-due process" (Radin, 1980). Super-due process refers to the special procedures that are required in capital cases. It includes guided discretion, automatic appeal, and the suggestion that states review all capital cases to ensure that sentencing was proportional for similar crimes.

States immediately devised new capital punishment statutes. The new statutes either removed all discretion by mandating death sentences for all capital offenses or instituted standards of guided discretion. In *Woodson v. North Carolina* (1976), the Supreme Court rejected statutes that imposed mandatory death sentences. The Supreme Court then upheld the death sentence in *Gregg v. Georgia* (1976). The *Gregg* ruling provided for guided discretion, bifurcated trials, automatic appellate review of all death sentences, and proportionality review to detect sentencing disparities. The first execution following reinstatement of capital punishment was in Utah in January of 1977. Since then, nearly 900 persons have been legally executed in the United States.

THE SUPREME COURT AND CAPITAL PUNISHMENT

Since the *Gregg* decision, the Supreme Court has heard cases on a variety of issues related to capital punishment, including constitutionality, procedural issues, mitigating and aggravating circumstances, and who is eligible for execution. As the composition of the Court has changed, the decisions it has rendered have also changed. This is particularly evident in decisions related to the constitutionality of death penalty statutes and procedural issues. In *McCleskey v. Kemp* (1987), the Supreme Court revisited the issue of racial discrimination in application of the death penalty. Using social science research, *McCleskey* argued that a marked pattern of discrimination based on the race of the victim existed in capital cases. The Supreme Court found, however, that statistical analysis indicating a pattern of racial discrimination in death sentencing did not make the death penalty statute unconstitutional. Instead, the Court stated, discrimination must be proven in individual cases. In *Pulley v. Harris* (1984), the Supreme Court ruled that states were not required to provide proportionality review of death sentences to determine fairness of sentencing. In a series of cases, the Supreme Court upheld the removal of potential jurors for cause if they were opposed to the death penalty. The Supreme Court ruled in *Herrera v. Collins* (1993) that federal courts did not have to hear claims of actual innocence based on newly discovered evidence.

There have also been a number of constitutional challenges to aggravating circumstances included in state death penalty statutes. Aggravating factors must be present to seek the death penalty, but the states differ as to what is considered an aggravating factor. Aggravating factors fall into three broad categories: those that focus on the characteristics of the offender (e.g., prior conviction for a violent crime), those that focus on the characteristics of the crime (e.g., occurring during the commission of a felony); and those that focus on the characteristics of the victims (e.g., law enforcement or multiple victims). The courts have also allowed the defense to present limited information about mitigating factors, circumstances that may be considered to reduce culpability. The Supreme Court has upheld the use of vaguely defined aggravators, allowed the use of victim impact statements, and required that mitigating factors be considered only if supported by evidence.

The Supreme Court has rendered a number of decisions regarding eligibility for a death sentence. In *Thompson v. Oklahoma* (1988), the Court ruled that an individual age 16 at the time of the offense can be sentenced to death. In *Ford v. Wainwright* (1986), the Supreme Court addressed the issue of prisoners who go insane while on death row, ruling that to be eligible for execution the offender must be able to understand the punishment and the reason for its application. The Supreme Court's rulings on degree of participation in the offense have been less clear, however. In 1982, the Court ruled in *Enmund v. Florida* that an offender who neither killed nor intended to kill could not be sentenced to death. However, in 1987 the Court refined its

position in *Tison v. Arizona,* stating that the lack of killing or intent to kill were irrelevant if the offender was a major participant in the crime and showed a "reckless indifference" to life.

Finally, the Supreme Court applied the "evolving standard of decency" interpretation to execution of the mentally retarded in *Penry v. Lynaugh* (1989). Penry, who was sentenced to death in Texas, had the mental capacity of a seven-year-old child. He appealed his sentence arguing that the Eighth Amendment ban of cruel and unusual punishment prohibited execution of the mentally retarded. His appeal was denied. The Court's opinion stated that because no evidence of a national consensus against execution of the mentally retarded existed, there was no basis to suggest the Eighth Amendment was violated. The Supreme Court pointed out that only two states prohibited execution of the mentally retarded at that time, and national opinion polls provided little evidence of consensus on this matter. In 2002, the Supreme Court again agreed to hear the *Penry* case, signaling their desire to revisit the issue of mental retardation and capital punishment. Although Penry's sentence was commuted for another reason prior to the arguments, the Supreme Court revisited the issue in *Atkins v. Virginia.* In the *Atkins* case, the court reversed its earlier decision based on the "evolving standard of decency" issue. By the time that the *Atkins* case was argued, 18 states had enacted legislation banning the execution of mentally retarded individuals, six within the year the case was argued. Furthermore, national opinion polls provided evidence of a growing consensus that mentally retarded individuals should not face execution. Thus, in June 2002 the Supreme Court handed down its decision to ban execution of mentally retarded individuals.

In June 2002, another ruling of the Supreme Court had far-reaching implications. In *Ring v. Arizona,* the Court determined that a judge may not decide critical sentencing issues and impose the death sentence as this violates the right to trial by jury. Arizona and eight other states had statutes that allowed judges, not juries, to determine sentencing in capital cases. As many as 800 death sentences may be affected by this ruling.

CAPITAL PUNISHMENT IN THE UNITED STATES TODAY

As of late 2002, 38 states, the federal government, and the U.S. military have death penalty statutes in place. The District of Columbia and 12 states (Alaska, Hawaii, Iowa, Maine, Massachusetts, Michigan, Minnesota, North Dakota, Rhode Island, Vermont, West Virginia, and Wisconsin) do not authorize the death penalty. More than 3,500 individuals in the United States are currently under a sentence of death. The vast majority of these are men, with 52 women awaiting execution in late 2002. More than 860 persons have been executed since 1976, including 10 women.

The use of the death penalty is not applied equally across all jurisdictions allowing it, however. In terms of per capita execution rates, Delaware has the highest per capita execution rate, followed by Oklahoma, Texas, and Virginia. Almost half of all executions have occurred in just two states (Texas and Virginia); Texas accounted for 37% of all executions between 1992 and 2002. More than 80% of executions post-*Furman* have occurred in the South. Other states and the U.S. military have death penalty statutes but have not executed anyone since the reinstatement of capital punishment.

THE FEDERAL DEATH PENALTY

The federal death penalty law also was struck down in 1972 by the *Furman* decision. In 1988, Congress enacted the Drug Kingpin Statute allowing execution for murder committed in the course of a drug conspiracy. The federal death penalty was further expanded in 1994 to include more than 60 offenses. Offenses not related to homicide include treason; espionage; large-scale drug trafficking; authorizing or attempting to kill an officer, juror, or witness in a Continuing Criminal Enterprise case; and using the mail system to deliver injurious articles with the intent to kill.

The federal government has executed two individuals since reinstatement of the federal death penalty. The first federal execution since 1963 was the 2001 execution of Timothy McVeigh, convicted of the 1995 Murrah Building bombing in Oklahoma City. Later in 2001, Juan Raul Garza was also executed. Garza was the first person executed under the federal drug kingpin law that allows execution for murders related to drug trafficking. As of late 2002, there were 26 men awaiting execution on Terre Haute Penitentiary Death Row.

In 1996, Congress focused on speeding up the appellate process in capital cases with the Anti-terrorism and Effective Death Penalty Act. This law restricts the federal appeals process by dismissing subsequent petitions when a claim has been rejected and through rejection of new claims unless rendered valid by a Supreme Court decision or based on compelling new evidence not previously available.

The federal death penalty has been strongly criticized. In 2000, the Justice Department released a report citing serious racial and geographic disparities in the application of the federal death penalty. Over 40% of the cases where the death penalty was sought originated in five jurisdictions. Furthermore, the report indicated that racial minorities were the accused in nearly 80% of federal cases in which the death penalty was requested. Other research has suggested that whites are more likely to avoid a federal death sentence by entering guilty pleas. In 2002, two district court judges ruled that the federal death penalty was unconstitutional. U.S. District Judge William Sessions of Vermont ruled that the federal death penalty is unconstitutional because of the evidence allowed in the guilt phase of the trial (*United States v. Fell*), while U.S. District Judge Jed Rakoff (New York) cited the probability that innocent individuals have been executed in declaring the 1994 federal death penalty law unconstitutional.

METHODS OF EXECUTION

Methods of execution have changed over time and vary slightly from state to state. By the end of 2002, all states except Nebraska allow lethal injection as a method of execution. Ten states, including Nebraska, authorized electrocution. Five states still authorized the use of the gas chamber, three states authorized hanging, and three authorized the use of firing squads.

Lethal injection was first authorized in Oklahoma in 1977, although the first execution by lethal injection did not occur until 1982 in Texas. Since 1977, the majority of executions have relied on this method. In lethal injection, three drugs are administered intravenously to the condemned person. First, sodium thiopental, an anesthetic, renders the individual unconscious. Pancuronium bromide is then administered. This drug induces muscle paralysis and stops breathing. Finally, potassium chloride is administered to stop the heart. Although developed as a more humane mode of execution, lethal injection has resulted in several botched executions. In several cases, technicians have had difficulty locating usable veins. The injection equipment has malfunctioned in other cases, either coming loose or becoming blocked. In several cases, the prisoners had severe reactions to the chemicals, resulting in convulsions.

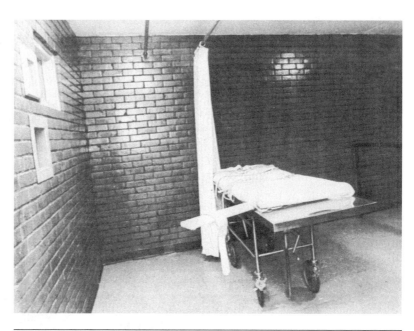

Photo 1   *Capital Punishment*

Until the latter part of the 20th century, electrocution was regularly used for executions. The electric chair, first used in 1890, sends a large jolt of electricity into the body for approximately 30 seconds. Then, medical personnel determine whether the prisoner's heart is still beating. If it is, another jolt is administered. This process continues until the person is pronounced dead. A number of electrocutions have required repeated jolts, and there are numerous documented cases of the condemned individual burning. In a Louisiana execution in 1947, an electrocution malfunctioned and was halted. The Supreme Court ruled that a second execution attempt did not constitute cruel and unusual punishment, and the prisoner was subsequently electrocuted successfully (*Louisiana ex rel. Francis v. Resweber*).

The gas chamber was developed in the 1920s as a more "humane" method of execution. The condemned individual is restrained in a chair in a sealed chamber, under which there is a container of sulfuric acid. A signal is then given, and sodium cyanide crystals are released into the chamber. The prisoner inhales the hydrogen cyanide gas that is released, resulting in asphyxiation. This method has been criticized as overly cruel, since the condemned individuals often struggle and appear to suffer. Today, it is allowed only in Arizona, California, Maryland, and Missouri. All four states, however, authorize lethal injection as well. It is also authorized in Wyoming if other methods are declared unconstitutional.

Two other methods of execution remain legal but are rarely used. Three states still authorize hanging as of 2002, but this method has been used only three times since reinstatement of capital punishment with the *Gregg* decision in 1976. In addition, two states authorize the use of firing squads. The use of a firing squad is also allowed in Oklahoma if other methods are declared unconstitutional. However, only two executions by firing squads have occurred since 1976. The firing squad execution of Gary Gilmore in January 1977 in Utah was the first post-*Furman* execution in the United States.

CONCLUSION: CONTEMPORARY DEBATES ON CAPITAL PUNISHMENT

Discussion of the death penalty has centered on several topics including the costs of maintaining it and whether or not capital punishment is a deterrent to homicide. The research on costs suggests that capital punishment is far more expensive than life without parole, due in part to the expenses related to trials as well as with the cost of the appeals process. The "death is different" doctrine requires more intensive investigation by both prosecutors and defense attorneys, although prosecutors generally have more funding available. Research on the deterrence aspect is mixed, but most studies indicate that the death penalty is not a general deterrent.

Beginning with the work of Cesare Beccaria, many criminologists have argued that instead of being a deterrent the death penalty actually has a brutalizing effect, increasing violence through example. Ernest Van den Haag, one of the few supporters of a deterrence argument, has suggested that since the death penalty is the most severe punishment it should have the greatest deterrent effect. However, research does not support his contention. States that have abolished capital punishment have not seen a rise in murders, and comparisons of contiguous states with and without capital punishment do not indicate any deterrent effect. International opinion about the American system of capital punishment has also been an area of interest. The United States and Japan are the only industrialized nations that still maintain a system of capital punishment. This, in conjunction with execution of juveniles and foreign nationals, has led to extensive international criticism, particularly from Western Europe.

Two other issues related to capital punishment have marshaled considerable interest: racial and economic inequities in the system and wrongful convictions. The *Furman* ruling was based on inequitable application of capital punishment, and reinstatement was designed to reduce the arbitrariness and discrimination inherent in the system. The continued pattern of minority death sentences, at both state and federal levels, has generated serious concern. Regional patterns of executions have been identified as a serious problem with more than 80% of post-*Furman* executions occurring in the South, while only 44% of all homicides occurred in that region. A 1990 U.S. General Accounting Office study concluded that race of the defendant was a factor in the decision to prosecute a case as a capital case.

Furthermore, since 1973 more than 100 persons have been released from death rows across the United States, 12 as a result of DNA analysis. In Illinois, the release of 13 men from death row led to Governor George Ryan declaring a moratorium on executions in January 2001. Two years later, in January 2003, he then commuted the sentences of all of those on death row to life in prison. As of this writing, the long-term impact of this unusual decision is unclear. Opponents of the death penalty hope for a gradual erosion of this practice in the United States. Only time will tell.

—*Susan F. Sharp*

See also Cesare Beccaria; Death Row; Deathwatch; *Furman v. Georgia*; Gary Gilmore; Juvenile Death Penalty; Timothy McVeigh; Julius and Ethel Rosenberg; Terre Haute Penitentiary Death Row; Karla Faye Tucker; Violent Crime Control and Law Enforcement Act 1994

Further Reading

Acker, J., Bohm, R., & Lanier, C. (Eds.). (1998). *America's experiment with capital punishment: Reflections on the past, present, and future of the ultimate penal sanction.* Durham, NC: Carolina Academic Press.

Bedau, H. A. (Ed.). (1982). *The death penalty in America: Current controversies.* New York: Oxford University Press.

Bohm, R. M. (1999). *Deathquest: An introduction to the theory and practice of capital punishment in the United States.* Cincinnati, OH: Anderson.

Death Penalty Information Center. (2001). *The death penalty in 2001: Year end report.* Washington, DC: Author. Retrieved from http://www.deathpenaltyinfo.org/YearEnd Report2001.pdf

Dieter, R. C. (1997). *Innocence and the death penalty: The increasing danger of executing the innocent.* Retrieved from http://deathpenaltyinfo.org/

Liebman, J. S., Fagan, J., Gelman, A., West, V., Davies, G., & Kiss, A. (2002). *A broken system, Part II.* Retrieved from http://www.law.columbia.edu/brokensystem2/report.pdf

Liebman, J. S., Fagan, J., & West, V. (2000). *A broken system: Error rates in capital cases, 1973–1995.* Retrieved from http://justice.policy.net/jpreport/finrep.PDF

Radelet, M., Bedau, H. A., & Putnam, C. (1992). *In spite of innocence.* Boston: Northeastern University Press.

Radin, M. J. (1980). Cruel punishment and respect for persons: Super due process for death. *Southern California Law Review, 53,* 1143–1185.

Snell, T. L. (2001). *Capital punishment 2000.* Washington, DC: U.S. Department of Justice/Office of Justice Programs.

Legal Cases

Atkins v. Virginia, 536 U.S. 304 (2002).

Enmund v. Florida, 458 U.S. 782 (1982).

Ford v. Wainwright, 477 U.S. 399 (1986).

Furman v. Georgia, 408 U.S. 238 at 287–289 (1972).

Gregg v. Georgia, 428 U.S. 1 53 (1976).

Herrera v. Collins, 506 U.S. 390 (1993).

Louisiana ex rel. Francis v. Resweber, 329 U.S. 459 at 474 (1947).

Maxwell v. Bishop, 398 U.S. 262 (1970).

McCleskey v. Kemp, 481 U.S. 279 (1987).

Penry v. Lynaugh, 492 U. S. 302 (1989).

Pulley v. Harris, 465 U.S. 37 (1984).

Ring v. Arizona, 536 U.S. 584 (2002).

Thompson v. Oklahoma, 487 U.S. 815 (1988).

Tison v. Arizona, 481 U.S. 137 (1987).

Trop v. Dulles, 356 U.S. 86 (1958).

United States v. Fell, 217 F. Supp.2d 469 (D. Vermont 2002).

United States v. Jackson, 390 U.S. 570 (1968).

Witherspoon v. Illinois, 391 U.S. 510 (1968).

Woodson v. North Carolina, 428 U.S. 280 (1976).

◩ CELEBRITIES IN PRISON

With few exceptions, celebrities in the United States do not go to prison. Their wealth, power, and influence afford them many privileges, including the leniency of the criminal justice system. It is, therefore, worth examining the rare cases in which celebrities are incarcerated, to see why they received such unusual treatment.

Celebrity by definition is a social construct that is usually shaped in large part by the media. People become celebrities because some aspect of their lives is thought to be newsworthy. Such figures typically include individuals who enjoy success in professional athletics, entertainment, politics, and business. Fame can also be a result of notoriety, as some of the subsequent sections will address. It should be noted that few women achieve celebrity status in prisons like men both because of the relative rarity of women in positions of power and influence in our patriarchal society, and because crime is largely a male activity. People of color are also unequally represented in the subsequent sections; sometimes they are overrepresented, and other times they are underrepresented. This is due to the systemic racism of our society generally, and in the criminal justice system specifically.

CELEBRITY CONVICTS

This category includes incarcerated actors, politicians, musicians, and athletes. In most instances, these individuals are imprisoned only after numerous run-ins with the law. Their fame usually affords them a certain amount of leniency from the courts, until they have offended numerous times. Notable examples include boxer Mike Tyson, who was imprisoned on a rape charge; televangelists Jim and Tammy Faye Bakker, who were incarcerated for fraud and conspiracy; and actor Robert Downey, Jr., and musician Bobby Brown, who both spent time behind bars for drugs. In addition, night club owner Steve Rubell was incarcerated for tax evasion, Louisiana Governor Edwin Edwards and Ohio Congressman James Traficant, Jr., were sentenced to prison for racketeering, and former NFL player and music entrepreneur Suge Knight was locked up for assault and a probation violation. Most recently, businesswoman Martha Stewart recieved a 5-month sentence for lying to investigators about her sale of InClone Systems stock in late 2001.

EX-CON CELEBRITIES

Ex-con celebrities are usually individuals who were incarcerated before they became famous and have subsequently reached celebrity status in some area of endeavor (usually) unrelated to their crimes and incarceration. Often, their demographic characteristics and the circumstances of their crimes closely approximate those typical of the incarcerated population. This category includes comedian Tim Allen, who was sentenced to prison for drugs; boxer Ralph "Sonny" Liston, who was found guilty of larceny and robbery; and activist and community leader Malcolm X and musician Merle Haggard, both of whom did time for burglary. Author Piri Thomas was incarcerated for attempted murder, while boxing promoter Don King served a sentence for manslaughter, actor Mark Walhberg spent time in prison for an assault charge, and author and security consultant Frank Abagnale was convicted of forgery and fraud.

CONVICT CELEBRITIES

Convict celebrities include individuals who, while quite ordinary in many respects, found themselves elevated to the status of celebrity because of media coverage of their crimes. In this category, we find individuals who lived most of their lives prior to the crime for which they were incarcerated in relative obscurity. They are, in other words, famous exclusively because of the media coverage of their crime. Their newsworthiness can be attributed to a number of factors, most commonly the seriousness of their crime or the victimization of a public figure. Their notoriety may also derive from several factors such as their relatively privileged social standing, location, rarity, and prurience. In many respects, the experiences of these individuals are the darkest embodiment of artist Andy Warhol's "15 minutes of fame." This category is the most diverse and populous, and includes an assortment of serial killers such as Charles Manson, high-priced sex trade workers such as Sydney Barrows and Heidi Fleiss, bombers such as Ted Kaczynski (the Unabomber), criminal bankers such as Charles Keating and Michael Milken, and assassins or would-be assassins such as Mark David Chapman and John Hinckley, Jr. It also covers celebrity stalkers such as Robert Hoskins and statutory rapists such as the teacher Mary Kay Letourneau.

In many instances, celebrity convicts are housed in modern, well-equipped, and (relatively) comfortable medium- or minimum-security institutions (colloquially, and somewhat inaccurately, referred to as "country club prisons"). In instances when their sentences take them to institutions more typical of the vast number of state and federal prisons in the United States, they are rarely housed with the general population, and are often extended "privileges" that the average inmate is denied, such as unrestricted commissary, additional exercise time, specially prepared meals, unencumbered use of audiovisual equipment, and deferential treatment by guards and administrators and are often not even required to wear standard prison-issue uniforms. Furthermore, subsequent to their release celebrity convicts rarely have difficulty obtaining a living-wage job, finding a place to live, accessing vital social services, or reestablishing contact with family and friends. Rather, they return to their opulent surroundings and lavish lifestyles, largely unfettered by the stigma commensurate with ex-con. Conversely, the release of the average inmate marks his or her return to the same state of relative economic deprivation, racism, patriarchy, and alienation that were correlates of her or his incarceration.

IN-HOUSE CELEBRITIES

Unlike the convict celebrities, the crimes of in-house celebrities, while sometimes heinous, are only tangentially connected to their fame. Rather, they enjoy some measure of celebrity status because of what they have done while incarcerated. These individuals typically come to the attention of journalists, writers, or scholars (primarily criminologists) and have their lives and/or time in prison chronicled in print. Among them we can count "Stanley" and Sidney Blotznam, Chic Conwell, Harry King, and Gary Gilmore. While considerably less common among this category for a number of reasons, not the least being restrictive prison practices, we must also count inmates who have authored their own books or otherwise produced scholarly or artistic offerings while incarcerated. Among them are Jack Henry Abbott, author of *In the Belly of the Beast: Letters From Prison* (1981); the Lifers Group (10 inmates from the Rahway State Prison), who recorded a self-titled rap CD in 1991; and Sanyika Shakur, author of *Monster: The Autobiography of an L.A. Gang Member* (1993).

POLITICAL CONVICT CELEBRITIES

Political convict celebrities include people who, while ostensibly incarcerated for street crimes, are generally thought to have been persecuted by the criminal justice system because of their political dissidence. This group of people includes historical as well as contemporary figures. For example, feminist, social reformer, and anarchist Emma Goldman was incarcerated in both New York and Missouri and was eventually deported from the United States in 1919. Other notables include labor activists and anarchists Nicola Sacco and Bartolomeo Vanzetti, who were incarcerated and eventually executed in 1927 for allegedly robbing and mortally wounding a paymaster and guard in Massachusetts, and communist leader Gus Hall, who was imprisoned for allegedly conspiring to teach and advocate the violent overthrow of the government. Native American activist Leonard Peltier, who was convicted of killing two FBI agents during a shoot-out, and freelance journalist and community activist Mumia Abu-Jamal, who was found guilty of killing a Philadelphia police officer, are further examples. We can add to this category Eugene V. Debs, who was sentenced to 10 years for an antiwar speech and ran for president as a Socialist Party candidate, from his cell in USP Atlanta. Finally, we should not forget the more than 100 members of the Industrial Workers of the World persecuted for their protests of World War I and sentenced to USP Leavenworth.

CONVICT CRIMINOLOGY CELEBRITIES

A final category of celebrities in prison should include a number of criminologists whose scholarship and activism has been informed not only by rigorous academic training and study but as well by their own experiences with incarceration. While not all convict criminologists are former inmates, several have self-identified as such, including Richard G. Hogan, John Irwin, Richard S. Jones, Alan Mobley, Daniel S. Murphy, Greg Newbold, Stephen C. Richards, Charles M. Terry, and Edward Tromanhauser. The rigorous scholarship and commitment to social justice of these academics have provided unique insight on penal policies and practices.

CONCLUSION

People in prison and jail are deprived of liberty, access to many goods and services, consensual heterosexual relationships, autonomy, security, and numerous other things that noninmate populations take for granted. In some instances, such as in the case of celebrity convicts, fame may function as a bulwark against some of the pains of imprisonment.

In other cases, as with political convict prisoners, individuals may achieve notoriety precisely because of the harsh treatment they have received in prison. In any case, considering incarceration through the lens of celebrity allows us to differentiate between types of inmates and treatment people receive. It also reveals the significant impact of media attention on our understanding of incarceration.

—*Stephen L. Muzzatti*

See also Jack Henry Abbott; Convict Criminology; Angela Y. Davis; Gary Gilmore; Malcolm X; Politicians

Further Reading

Abbott, J. H. (1981). *In the belly of the beast: Letters from prison.* New York: Vintage.

Chambliss, W., & King, H. (1984). *The boxman: A professional thief's journey.* Toronto: John Wiley.

Keve, P. W. (1991). *Prisons and the American conscience: A history of U.S. federal corrections.* Carbondale: Southern Illinois University Press.

Lifers Group. (1991). *The Lifers Group* [CD]. Burbank, CA: Hollywood Basic.

Mailer, N. (1979). *The executioner's song.* Boston: Little, Brown.

Ross, J. I., & Richards, S. C. (Eds.). (2003). *Convict criminology.* Belmont, CA: Wadsworth.

Shakur, S. (1993). *Monster: The autobiography of an L.A. gang member.* New York: Penguin.

Shaw, C. R. (1930). *The jack roller: A delinquent boy's own story.* Philadelphia: Albert Saifer.

Shaw, C. R., with Moore, M. E. (1931). *The natural history of a delinquent career.* Chicago: University of Chicago Press.

Sutherland, E. H. (1937). *The professional thief.* Chicago: University of Chicago Press.

◪ CELL SEARCH

Prison officials may search prisoners' cells at any time because the U.S. Supreme Court has ruled that prisoners are not protected by the Fourth Amendment of the U.S. Constitution. Indeed, though a number of federal circuit courts in the late 1970s were willing to recognize that prison inmates had a *limited* right to be free from *unreasonable* search and seizure, by the mid-1980s the U.S.

Supreme Court had determined otherwise. Thus, the Court stated that "a prisoner has no reasonable expectation of privacy in his prison cell entitling him to the protection of the Fourth Amendment against unreasonable searches" (*Hudson v. Palmer,* 1984).

PRIVACY AND CONFINEMENT

The Fourth Amendment of the U.S. Constitution states that "the right of the people to be secure in their persons, houses, papers, and effects, against unreasonable search and seizure, shall not be violated." To arrive at the conclusion that prisoners do not have this protection, the Supreme Court applied the *Katz* privacy test to establish the reasonableness of a prisoner's Fourth Amendment claim. Under this test, a person can invoke the Fourth Amendment prohibition against unreasonable search and seizure only if he or she demonstrates an actual expectation of privacy and only if society is prepared to recognize this expectation as reasonable (*Katz v. United States,* 1967). After applying this two-pronged standard, the Court held that "society is not prepared to recognize as legitimate *any* subjective expectation of privacy that a prisoner might have in his prison cell" (*Hudson v. Palmer,* 1984).

By using privacy as the standard to determine the reasonableness of a Fourth Amendment claim, the Court noted that the Fourth Amendment right to privacy is "fundamentally inconsistent" with incarceration. As a result, the interest of a prisoner's privacy within the prison cell must yield to the accepted belief that "the loss freedom of choice and privacy are inherent incidents of confinement" (*Bell v. Wolfish,* 1979).

SECURITY AND CONFINEMENT

An expectation of privacy within a prison cell must be one that society is prepared to recognize as legitimate before prisoners can effectively invoke Fourth Amendment concerns. In prison, the Supreme Court decided that the right to privacy is always curtailed by the institution's responsibility for security. To this end, the Court clearly held in *Hudson v. Palmer* (1984) that prison administrators are obligated to provide an environment for inmates and prison employees that is both secure and sanitary. While society *might* value the ability of prison inmates to enjoy some degree of Fourth Amendment protection, that is, privacy, this possibility is outweighed, and effectively cancelled out, by the more prominent social demand that prisons represent a secure and sanitary environment. The Court saw no way to reconcile the "privacy rights" of inmates with the more pertinent social concern of prison security and sanitation. "It would be impossible to accomplish the prison objectives of preventing the introduction of drugs, weapons, and other contraband into the premises if inmates retained a right of privacy in their cells" (*Hudson v. Palmer* 1984).

CELL SEARCHES

Because prisoners are not protected by the Fourth Amendment, prison cell searches may occur at random times in a frequent and unannounced basis. They need not adhere to the dictates of an established plan or method of search. Furthermore, random shakedown searches may be done regardless of whether the prisoner is present to observe the search of his or her cell.

The Court's willingness to allow prison cell searches to occur randomly, frequently, unannounced, without any established guidelines, and in the absence of the prisoner signifies an almost never recognized deference to governmental agents (prison administrators) to decide for themselves the rights of another (prisoner). As the Court concluded in *Bell v. Wolfish* (1979), "Prison administrators [are to be] accorded wide ranging deference in the adoption and execution of polices and practices that in their judgment are needed to preserve internal order and discipline and to maintain institutional security."

In effect, the Supreme Court has mandated that prison administrators and not courts should determine the extent to which cell searches are consistent with a balancing of prisoner concerns and the security of penal institutions. Thus, under *normal* circumstances no judicial body should supersede the decisions made by prison administrator regarding cell searches when matters of institutional security are at stake.

Shakedown cell searches while potentially detecting illegal contraband can also harass and destroy the property of prison inmates. On this issue, the Supreme Court is a little more critical, holding that the "intentional harassment of even the most hardened criminal cannot be tolerated by a civilized society" (*Bell v. Wolfish*, 1979). The Court further stated "that prisoners do not have a reasonable expectation of privacy does not mean that he is without remedy for calculated harassment unrelated to prison needs, nor does it mean that prison attendants can ride roughshod over inmates' property rights with impunity" (*Hudson v. Palmer*, 1984).

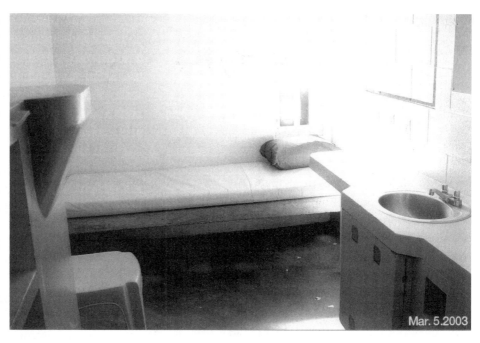

Figure 2   *View of a Prison Cell*

Notwithstanding the Court's strongly wording warnings against the harassment of prisoners and the needless destruction of inmates' personal property, the Court has retained that "despite the importance of avoiding the destruction or loss of prisoner property, such loss or destruction does not violate the United States Constitution. Even if an officer intentionally destroys a prisoner's personal property during the challenged shakedown search, the destruction does not violate the due process clause where an adequate post-depravation remedy exists under state law" (*Bell v. Wolfish*, 1979). Given that the state in which the prisoner is located has a legal remedy to address claims of harassment and property destruction the U.S. Constitution offers prisoners *no* protection from such violations.

CONCLUSION

While prisoners have seen their rights increase in a number of important areas—medical assistance, legal assistance, religious rights, due process rights, free speech rights, and the ability to use the mail system—the same cannot be said of Fourth Amendment protections. Prison administrators need not consider a prisoner's Fourth Amendment concerns as they carry out cell searches in whatever manner and fashion they deem necessary. The Supreme Court's decision that prisoners are not constitutionally entitled to privacy protections in the confines of their cell cannot mystically remove privacy concerns from the prisoner. The impasse created between a socially recognized "reasonable expectation of privacy" and the privacy expected by prisoners is likely to escalate, as the absolute treatment of the issue by the Court is bound to create future tension.

—Eric Roark

See also Contact Visits; First Amendment; Fourth Amendment; Prison Litigation Reform Act 1996; Strip Search

Further Reading

Amnesty International. (1999). *Rough justice for women behind bars.* New York: Author.

Goring, D. (1984). Supreme Court review: Fourth Amendment–prison cells: Is there a right to privacy? *Journal of Criminal Law and Criminology, 75,* 609. (Northwestern School of Law)

Legal Cases

Bell v. Wolfish, 441 U.S. 520 (1979).
Block v. Rutherford, 468 U.S. 576 (1984).
Hudson v. Palmer, 468 U.S. 517 (1984).

◪ CHAIN GANGS

In the middle of the 19th century, the practice of chaining prisoners together while they worked became customary in England and Australia. The iron chains weighing from six to seven pounds were riveted together by blacksmiths, inspected daily to prevent tampering, and remained attached to prisoners for the length of their sentences, between six months and two years. From its inception, the rationale of chaining convicts transcended the utilitarian notion of security. Instead, chain gangs are spectacles of punishment; being chained—especially in public—is degrading and dehumanizing.

HISTORY

In the United States, following the Civil War, Reconstruction required manual labor to rebuild the South's economy and infrastructure. While convicts in the North worked in prison factory shops, their Southern counterparts—who were disproportionately black—labored outside prison walls on the plantations and in public works projects. During this time, chain gangs were widespread in Alabama, Arkansas, Florida, Georgia, Louisiana, Mississippi, North Carolina, Texas, and Virginia where sentences ranged from a few weeks to 10 years. They were used extensively throughout the convict leasing system in the South where private businesses compensated the state for use of its prisoners. Prisoners wearing striped uniforms were chained together in crews of five to seven and transported to work sites in caged wagons holding up to 18 men. At night, all of the chains were attached to a steel rod running the length of the sleeping area.

During Reconstruction, chain gangs demonstrated the unbroken line between slavery and the use of convict slave labor. The appeal of chain gangs was not limited to free labor, it also satisfied the racist sentiment that blacks should be shackled to the land. Testimonies of brutality and oppression often surfaced from the Southern prison camps. It was even rumored that unlucky hitchhikers were arrested and railroaded to chain gangs, thus serving as a valuable source of free labor. Sadistic armed guards often took delight in shooting at the feet of prisoners. Deploying the lash, "whipping bosses"—akin to the slave driver on antebellum plantations—routinely disciplined prisoners on chain gangs. According to a corrections officials of that era: "A Negro is punished to 'teach him respect for a white man,' or for 'inciting insurrection,' or because he 'tried to run away,' or because 'he is just a bad nigger'" (Barnes & Teeters, 1946, p. 631). Especially under intense heat, sick, malnutritioned, and injured convicts accused of malingering were typically whipped until they returned to work; even worse many prisoners were beaten to death and clandestinely buried in quicklime.

PUNISHMENT

The most brutal punishments imaginable were inflicted on members of the chain gangs who were assigned to road camps of the South. Floggings were routinely administered to promote discipline. In addition, many were placed in the sweatbox that was just large enough for a man to stand erect when the door was closed. The only ventilation in the box was provided by a breathing slot, that was one inch high and four inches long, a little below the height of the average man. Often the boxes were placed in direct sun. Men were confined in them from a few hours to a few days. Swelling of the legs in extreme cases necessitated the victims being hospitalized for a week or more. It was not unusual for a convict to die of suffocation. Larger sweatboxes were designed to punish several prisoners collectively. In 1941, a grim report chronicled the appalling treatment of Georgia's prisoners forced into the sweat box in which "a Negro convict had died of suffocation in a sweat-box 7½ feet square, where he, together with 21 other prisoners, was incarcerated for 11 hours. There was only a six-inch opening in the roof of the box for the purposes of ventilation" (Barnes & Teeters, 1946).

REFORM

Eventually, the brutality of chain gangs was criticized publicly. In the 1930s, the story of Robert E. Burns shocked the common conscience. His book, *I Am a Fugitive From a Georgia Chain Gang,* which was made into a movie, brought critical attention to the inhumane chain gangs in the South. While a fugitive in New Jersey, Burns—aided by the courtroom tenacity of lawyer Clarence Darrow—successfully fought extradition to Georgia. His trial precipitated and amplified public outrage concerning chain gangs, prompting state officials across the South to discontinue the practice. Economic developments also contributed to the demise of chain gangs. Following World War II, American servicemen returning from war needed jobs in civil service, construction, and highway maintenance, prompting government officials to scale down their use of convicts.

THE REEMERGENCE
OF CHAIN GANGS

In the 1990s, the prohibition on chain gangs eventually gave way to resurging "tough on crime" campaigns proclaiming the need for greater forms of retribution and deterrence. As public anxiety over crime escalated, political leaders advocated the return to earlier penal practices, such as requiring prisoners to wear prison striped uniforms and stripping them of amenities (e.g., television, weightlifting, and cigarettes) as well as reintroducing

Photo 3 *Women's Chain Gang, Maricopa County, Arizona, 2003*

chain gangs. The year 1995 became a watershed when state and county corrections departments in Alabama, Arizona, Florida, Indiana, Iowa, Maryland, Oklahoma, and Wisconsin reinstated chain gangs.

In Alabama, prisoners were shackled at the ankle in three-pound leg irons and bound together by eight-foot lengths of chain, forced to work the fields with shovels and swing blades for 12 hours a day. Other chain gangs spent their days breaking rocks into pea-sized pellets, a demeaning chore imbued with pure punishment since the state has no use for crushed rock. Ron Jones, prison commissioner of Alabama, referred to the public spectacle in offering a rationale for recent chain gangs: "Deterrence . . . the sight of chains would leave a lasting impression on young people" (Bragg, 1995, p. 16). Commissioner Jones even proposed that women inmates also be shackled to chain gangs; however, the measure was rejected by the governor. Jones further boasted that guards armed with shotguns loaded with double-aught buckshot supervise the chain gang, obligated by law to shoot if a prisoner attempts to escape. "People say it's not humane, but I don't get much flak in Alabama," said the commissioner (Bragg, 1995, p. 16).

RACE

As is so often the case with corrections, blacks are overrepresented in chain gangs. Alabama Congressman Alvin Holmes opposed chain gangs for this reason, arguing: "The only reason they're doing it is because an overwhelming majority of the prisoners are Black. If the majority were White, they wouldn't have the chain gang" (Jackson, 1995, p. 12). Representative John Hilliard also joined the campaign to halt the use of chain gangs: "I think it's a reminder of the way it used to be, putting the African-American male in chains" (Jackson, 1995, p. 12). Serving two years for receiving stolen property, one inmate who spends his days on the chain gang breaking rocks complained, "They're treating us like . . . slaves" (Jackson, 1995, p. 16).

In Queen Anne's County (Maryland), the antebellum notion of chain gangs has taken a futuristic twist. Corrections officials have proposed the use of "chainless" chain gangs by attaching stun belts to prisoners assigned outdoor work detail, leaving convicts writhing in the dirt if they attempt to escape or engage in violence. Supporters of that practice claim that the belts reduce the costs of supervision. They also argue that "there is no long-term physical damage to a prisoner who is stunned" (Kilborn, 1997, p. 11). Amnesty International, however, has challenged the practice, arguing that stun belts are cruel, inhuman, and degrading and can be used to torture prisoners.

CRITICS

Civil libertarians and human rights advocates took exception to chain gangs, charging that the practice violates the Eighth Amendment's prohibition on cruel and unusual punishment. According to Alvin J. Bronstein, executive director of the National Prison Project of the American Civil Liberties Union, "People lose touch with humanity when you put them in chains. You are telling him he is an animal" (Bragg, 1995, p. 16). Amnesty International also weighed into the controversy, arguing that chain gangs violate international treaties on human rights; specifically, the use of leg irons is outlawed under

the United Nations Standard Minimum Rules for the Treatment of Prisoners. Similarly, it is reasoned that chain gangs also violate the principle of acceptable penal content whereby sanctions are acceptable only if lawbreakers can endure them and still maintain their human dignity. In 1995, the Southern Poverty Law Center filed suit in federal district court, arguing that chain gangs are barbaric and inhumane.

In reinstating chain gangs, corrections officials insist that they have the support of citizens. Still, many people question the logic, utility, and overall fairness of chain gangs. "If these guys are so dangerous, they shouldn't be out on those crews. And if they're not dangerous, why put them in chains?" asked Mary Chambers, a Maryland resident. Chambers added: "You have people in there for drunk driving. Maybe they have a problem. But do you put them in chains?" (Kilborn, 1997, p. A-18).

The controversy over chaining extends beyond chain gangs to include inhumane restraining practices employed not as security measures but also for disciplinary purposes. In Alabama, for example, inmates filed a class action suit challenging the use of the hitching post at the Fountain Correctional Center where those who refuse to (or are late for) work were handcuffed to a triangular rail about four and a half feet off the ground. Prisoners were hitched as long as five hours at a stretch, exposed to the blazing sun, and often go for as long as seven hours without water, food, and access to a toilet. The practice has been monitored by the American Civil Liberties Union Prison Project, which asserts that there are alternative, humane ways to discipline balky inmates (i.e., isolation cells and/or loss of privileges). Furthermore, there are reports of racism insofar as the hitching post appeared to be reserved for black inmates. In 1997, a federal magistrate ruled that the Alabama corrections officials should not be allowed to hitch inmates to posts, commenting: "Short of death by electrocution, the hitching post may be the most painful and tortuous punishment administered by the Alabama prison system" (Nossiter, 1997, p. A14). State corrections officials have appealed the magistrate's opinion. But the Southern Poverty Law Center, which represents the inmates, promises to continue its legal battle against the hitching posts, calling the practice a form of torture. In her ruling, Magistrate Vanzetta Penn McPherson fittingly likened the hitching post to the pillory of colonial times.

CONCLUSION

Given that the history of the modern chain gang is traced to slavery, it is important to recognize the limitations of the nostalgia inherent in much of the emerging penal harm movement. Supporters of the "get tough" movement claim that prisons are not harsh enough to fulfill the retributionist goal of imposing punishment, instilling discipline, and deterring lawbreakers from future offenses. Moreover, they insinuate that corrections coddles inmates and—by way of circular reasoning—imply that high rates of recidivism are the result of inadequately punitive institutional conditions. While adhering to traditional notions of retribution, the get-tough movement is inspired by nostalgic visions of criminal justice.

Get-tough proposals commonly include "three strikes" legislation and correctional boot camps as well as a return to hard labor and chain gangs. Sentiments of nostalgia signaled a backlash to the modern, and liberal, penal institution where inmates are afforded certain constitutional protections, participate in institutional programs, and are permitted to keep personal belongings while incarcerated (e.g., cigarettes, civilian clothes, coffee, snack food, televisions). Sounding the alarm of perceived lawlessness and growing social disorder, the nostalgic version of corrections punctuates the supposed need to regain control of inmates and prisons, as well as a return to a simpler and racist society. Referring to the reemergence of chain gangs, Congressman Holmes remembers that as a child in Alabama he never saw a white man on a chain gang: "The only people you ever saw were Black. The whole purpose of having the chain gang is racist to the core. There are certain Whites in key positions who want things back the way they used to be" (Jackson, 1995, p. 14). Critics of chain gangs insist that by turning back the clock to revive nostalgic forms of punishment, corrections officials reinforce racist stereotypes of lawbreakers.

—*Michael Welch*

See also Boot Camp; Convict Lease System; Corporeal Punishment; Deliverance Theory; Eighth Amendment Electronic Monitoring; Hard Labor; History of Prisons; Labor; Race, Class, and Gender of Prisoners; Slavery; Three-Strikes Legislation

Further Reading

Allen, H. E., & Abril, J. (1997). The new chain gang: Corrections in the next century. *American Journal of Criminal Justice, 22*, 1–12.

American Correctional Association. (1995). *Historical overview: Chain gangs in the United States, 1880s–1995.* Washington, DC: Author.

Ayers, E. (1984). *Vengeance and justice: Crime and punishment in the 19th century American South.* New York: Oxford University Press.

Barnes, H., & Teeters, N. (1946). *New horizons in criminology* (3rd ed.). New York: Prentice Hall.

Bragg, R. (1995, March 26). Chain gangs to return to roads of Alabama. *New York Times,* p. 16.

Burns, R. (1932). *I am a fugitive from a Georgia chain gang.* New York: Vanguard.

Chain gangs for women cause furor. (1996, April 28). *New York Times,* p. 30.

Clear, T. (1994). *Harm in American penology.* Albany: State University of New York Press.

Corsentino, M. (1997). Inmate chain gangs are an improper form of punishment. In C. Cozic (Ed.), *America's prisons: Opposing viewpoints* (pp. 12–127). San Diego, CA: Greenhaven.

Inmates fight "work or be shackled" policy. (1993, September 5). *New York Times,* p. 43.

Ives, G. (1970). *A history of penal methods.* Montclair, NJ: Patterson Smith. (Original work published 1914)

Jackson, B. (1995, September 18). Is the Alabama prison system's return to the chain gang unfair to blacks?" *Jet,* pp. 12–16.

Kilborn, P. (1997, March 11). Revival of chain gangs takes a twist: Stun belts emerge as the latest tool to keep inmates in line. *New York Times,* p. A18.

Lichenstein, A. (1993). Good roads and chain gangs in the Progressive South: The Negro convict is a slave. *Journal of Southern History, 59*(1), 85–110.

Nossiter, A. (1997, January 31). Judge rules against Alabama's prison "hitching posts." *New York Times,* p. A14.

Pens, D., & Wright, P. (1998). The resurgence of chain gangs. In D. Burton-Rose (Ed.), *The celling of America: An inside look at the U.S. prison industry* (pp. 70–77). Monroe, ME: Common Courage Press.

Sellin, J. T. (1976). *Slavery and the penal system.* New York: Elsevier.

Spivak, J. (1932). *Georgia nigger.* New York: Harcourt, Brace.

Steiner, J., & Brown, R. (1972). *The North Carolina chain gang.* Chapel Hill: University of North Carolina Press.

Welch, M. (1999). *Punishment in America: Social control and the ironies of imprisonment.* Thousand Oaks, CA: Sage.

Welch, M. (2004). *Corrections: A critical approach* (2nd ed.). New York: McGraw-Hill.

Welch, M., Weber, L., & Edwards, W. (2000). "All the news that's fit to print": A content analysis of the correctional debate in the *New York Times. The Prison Journal, 80*(3), 245–264.

☑ CHAPLAINS

Chaplains have been part of the U.S. prison system since its beginnings. From the first penitentiary set up by Quakers in the Walnut Street Jail in Philadelphia, the clergy have been able to enter penal institutions to provide religious training, counseling, and support. Since this time, the role of the prison chaplain has diversified and become much more complex.

Eighteenth- and 19th-century proponents of the Pennsylvania system sought to reform offenders through a combination of solitary confinement and Bible reading. Inmates in this system were housed in separate cells; their only human contact was the occasional visit of a clergyperson or prison guard. At that juncture, prison chaplains were the earliest paid noncustodial staff; they provided education and counseling in addition to religious programs. One of the first chaplains, named William Rogers, began teaching the Bible at the Walnut Street Jail in 1787, where he was also responsible for Sabbath schools as well as providing reading and writing instruction.

Though the tasks of a prison minister have changed since these early beginnings, the contemporary job retains some of the influences of its origins. Chaplains are meant to provide succor to their inmate flock, while also performing the role of security officer. They are, in short, aiming to rehabilitate within a punitive environment. It is this paradox that shapes much of the job.

WHO IS THE PRISON CHAPLAIN?

Prison chaplains are ordained clergypersons who minister within an institutional setting. They may be employed full time or part time, and some even volunteer to provide an array of religious services and programs to meet the inmates' spiritual needs. To some extent, the prison ministry differs little from that provided to local church congregations, except that it takes place in a correctional environment. However, at a closer look, there are some crucial differences. First, the prison chaplain must work with offenders of all faith traditions present in the institution. Second, of course, the prison environment places the prison chaplain into a potentially dangerous and volatile situation. Moreover, recent "get tough on crime" policies, such as sentencing guidelines, mandatory minimums, truth in sentencing, and the war on drugs, have increased levels of frustration, stress, and disciplinary problems in prisons because of overcrowding. In this overheated environment, prison chaplains may be more preoccupied with their personal safety and security than are their counterparts who provide religious ministry to local community church congregations.

Although state and federal correctional department personnel hiring policies may differ, there are several universal qualifications for a prison chaplain position. Most agencies require that a minister has graduated from an accredited four-year college or university or from a school of theology or divinity. In addition, a prison minister is expected to be a representative of his or her faith community, to have obtained ecclesiastical endorsement by his or her denominational body, and to have performed a minimum of two units of Clinical Pastoral Education (CPE) and pastoral counseling training and experience.

CHAPLAIN FUNCTIONS

Prison chaplains have many diverse responsibilities. Primarily, of course, they are responsible for managing religious activities within the correctional facility. They must ensure, therefore, that all offenders are afforded the opportunities to practice the faith of their choice. In general, they do this by coordinating religious programming, providing prison ministry and crisis intervention, and by ensuring the implementation and delivery of religious programs and services.

As religious program coordinators, prison chaplains are the primary advisors on and implementers of religious program policy. As such, they clarify issues involving various faith practices, religious articles, religious diets, and other religious standards while ensuring that these services are provided to the fullest extent possible within the usually restrictive correctional environment. In addition, prison chaplains are expected to develop and maintain up-to-date religious activity schedules and ensure that information about various opportunities for religious activities is available to all inmates. Finally, they must develop plans, policies, procedures, and budget recommendations to deliver pastoral care in the prison setting.

As part of their ministry, all chaplains are required to teach the central and inclusive doctrines common to major faith groups without degrading the tradition of others. They also provide regular religious worship services, pastoral counseling, and spiritual guidance, as well as individual and group counseling. In addition, they are expected to lead, host, and coordinate Bible studies, worship services, and general spiritual development and growth seminars. Finally, prison chaplains assist offenders in obtaining literature and other materials necessary to practice their faiths.

Prison chaplains play an important role in helping offenders adjust to prison and deal with the prison environment. In this role, they provide crisis intervention in emergency situations, offering counseling to offenders in times of need, such as during divorce or the illness of an immediate family member. They also frequently counsel those who have difficulty coping with the day-to-day issues that result from the pains of imprisonment. In addition, the prison chaplain provides inmates with notification of the death of a loved one, as well as maintains contact, support, and pastoral visitation when offenders are hospitalized in other medical correctional facilities.

Prison chaplains must coordinate and supervise all inmate religious programs and services. This

Religion and Diversity in Prison

Religion in prison is one of the best experiences that a believer in Jesus Christ can have. Because there are so many different races and ethnicities of people in the same place, inmates get to experience how people of different cultures worship. Similarly, the chaplains have the chance to experience ethnic groups on a level that I believe would never happen in another setting. Through exposure to other cultures, you learn to live with people with different faiths and understand certain behaviors that you may not agree with but are justifiable according to another's religion. However, even though you learn how to deal with people on a new level through this experience, a level you may have never learned on the outside, it would be better to learn it on the outside where you are free, rather than on the inside where you really don't have a choice.

Jesse McKinley Carter, Jr.
FCI Fairton, Fairton, New Jersey

means that the minister must ensure that an array of religious programming, from traditional Protestant and Catholic services to a variety of services for other world religions, such as Islam, Judaism, Native American, Quaker, Wicca, Buddhism, Hinduism, and Sikh, is available. Programs range from worship services, pastoral counseling, spiritual guidance, Bible study, prayer groups, and Christian Fellowship to temple, Native American sweat lodges, Wiccan services, Spanish Bible study, and Siddha meditation practice. The prison chaplain also maintains a chapel library, which includes books, magazines, audiocassettes, and videos to accommodate the religious rights and diverse needs of all offenders.

THE MULTIPLE REALITIES OF PRISON CHAPLAINCY

Prison chaplains encounter multiple realities working in the correctional environment. Not only do they have to work with people of different faiths and provide counseling to all, they also must perform a number of administrative and security-based tasks. Like all prison employees, the prison chaplain is first and foremost a correctional officer. He or she is also a community liaison officer, administrative assistant, and human resource specialist. Accordingly, prison chaplains do not spend all or even most of their time providing religious instruction or advice. The prison chaplain is expected to be visible in all areas of the institution, make regular rounds through the correctional facility, assist with inmate management, serve on the adjustment committee, be on call for emergencies, and be ready to assist correctional officers as needed.

There is a considerable amount of paperwork attached to the everyday management of religious services. Like all prison employees, prison chaplains have many administrative tasks. They must maintain records, prepare reports on pastoral care, develop lists of activities to distribute to offenders, document pastoral counseling and services provided in the offender record, and compile various ad hoc reports as requested by prison administrators. They also help inmates with requests for visits, clothes, and commissary money. As well, prison chaplain are usually expected to be a source of information to prison staff, participate in staff retreats and meetings, and attend educational and professional training seminars.

Prison chaplains are responsible for community development, coordinating resources from the community to meet the spiritual needs of offenders in the correctional facility. As such, they speak to religious, civic, and other community groups to promote the prison ministry and to enlist financial and volunteer support. Prison chaplains work closely with representatives of the various faith communities to encourage community participation in correctional facility religious programs and to ensure that volunteer activities are conducted in a diverse yet secure manner. They also recruit, coordinate, supervise, and provide formal and informal training for all volunteers.

CONTRACT CHAPLAINS

Both compassion and the U.S. Constitution compel departments of corrections to provide basic religious services, including opportunities for spiritual growth, to the prison population. In spite of this, in a law-and-order era with overcrowded prisons, many states have decided that they can survive with fewer chaplains in tight fiscal times. Faced with mounting costs and tighter budgets, state legislators and correctional administrators across America have reduced the number of prison chaplains and, in some cases, eliminated all of the positions as a cost-saving strategy. In many instances, funds have been allocated to provide full-time chaplain positions on a contractual basis, which do not carry benefit packages or job security.

At first glance, contracting out chaplain services might appear to be a sound management and fiscal decision; however, there are numerous compelling reasons that existing prison chaplain positions should be retained and those eliminated reinstated. First, religious volunteers, who primarily promote their own faith tradition, may overlook some religious groups. Because offenders retain the right to worship freely in their own faith, a failure to provide these services can lead to increased tensions, grievances, and possible lawsuits from offenders who feel they have no outlet for religious worship. Prison chaplains understand the complexity of the constitutional issues involved, and therefore work to provide worship opportunities for all inmates.

Second, fewer prison chaplains may also mean fewer volunteers, since a primary role of the prison chaplain is the recruitment of volunteers from local church congregations. Third, volunteers as well as staff may be at greater risk of harm, as the prison chaplain is responsible for ensuring that volunteers follow appropriate security policies and procedures. Finally, without prison chaplains, the stresses of everyday life in prisons increase, since under normal circumstances chaplains provide counseling to inmates to help them adjust to prison and deal with the inherent tensions of the prison environment as well as handle grief when crisis situations arise. The elimination of these services risks amplifying the stress levels of both inmates and staff, as well as increasing the likelihood of conflict, disciplinary problems, and/or violence.

CONCLUSION

Prison chaplains provide offenders of all faith groups with reasonable and equitable opportunities to pursue religious beliefs and practices consistent with the security and orderly running of the prison facility. As such, they conduct and facilitate religious services; provide pastoral care, religious programming, and spiritual guidance; and provide an impartial religious leadership to meet the diverse needs of the different faith groups in the prison environment. Prison ministry continues to be an integral part of correctional programming, as demonstrated by the routine weekly religious programs such as worship services, pastoral counseling, Bible study, Sunday services, and visitation ministry provided by prison officials.

—Melvina Sumter

See also Contract Ministers; History of Religion in Prison; Islam in Prison; Judaism in Prison; Native American Spirituality; Quakers; Rehabilitation; Religion in Prison; Santería

Further Reading

American Correctional Association. (1983). *The American prison: From the beginning–a pictorial history*. College Park, MD: Author.

Clear, T., & Cole, G. (1997). *American corrections* (4th ed.). Belmont, CA: Wadsworth.

Clear, T., Stout, B., Dammer, H., Kelly, L., Hardyman, P., & Shapiro, C. (1992). *Prisoners, prisons and religion: Final report*. Newark, NJ: Rutgers University, School of Criminal Justice.

Clear, T. R., & Sumter, M. (2002). Prisoners and religion: Religion and adjustment to prison. *Journal of Offender Rehabilitation, 3*(4), 129–161.

Duncombe, D. D. (1992). The task of prison chaplaincy: An inmate's view. *Journal of Pastoral Care, 46*, 193–209.

Johnson, E. L. (1968). *Crime, correction, and society*. Homewood, IL: Dorsey.

LeFevere, P. (1995). N.Y. prison ministry could face big cuts. *National Catholic Reporter, 31*(19), 5.

McCarthy, C. (1996). Truth about prisons could change things. *National Catholic Reporter, 32*(35), 18–19.

Shaw, R. (1995). *Chaplains to the imprisoned: Sharing life with the incarcerated*. Binghamton, NY: Haworth.

Stout, B., & Clear, T. (1992, Winter). Federal prison chaplains: Satisfied in ministry but often undervalued. *Federal Prisons Journal*, pp. 8–10.

Sumter, M. T. (1999). *Religiousness and post-release community adjustment*. Doctoral dissertation, Florida State University, Tallahassee, School of Criminology and Criminal Justice.

Sundt, J. L., & Cullen, F. T. (1998). The role of the contemporary prison chaplain. *The Prison Journal, 78*(3), 271–298.

Tappan, P. W. (1960). *Crime, justice and correction*. New York: McGraw-Hill.

CHESNEY-LIND, MEDA (1947–)

Meda Chesney-Lind, professor of women's studies at the University of Hawaii at Manoa, was a pioneer in juvenile justice and feminist criminology in the early 1970s, a time when, as she says, feminist research was considered a "career killer" (Chesney-Lind, 2000, p. 3). She has written scores of journal articles and book chapters and has authored or edited four books addressing female offending and incarceration. Her contributions to the discipline have been recognized by awards from several professional associations including the American Society of Criminology and the Academy of Criminal Justice Sciences. She is a vocal advocate for girls and women, particularly those involved in the criminal justice system. Her scholarship on the sexist treatment of girls in the juvenile justice system and, more recently, soaring rates of women's imprisonment, has focused national attention on these issues.

SCHOLARLY WORK AND THEMATIC IDEAS

Chesney-Lind revolutionized the field of juvenile justice by drawing attention to the unequal ways in which young women and young men were treated. In articles published in criminology and women's studies journals, she pointed out that young women were more likely than boys to be arrested and incarcerated for status offenses. Status offenses, which include such activities as running away from home, truancy, incorrigibility, curfew violations, and being sexually active, are considered offenses only because the perpetrator is a minor; they would not be considered offenses if the actor was an adult. Chesney-Lind argued that status offenses were a means by which parents and the state were able to police and enforce a particular ideal of femininity for young women. As a result of the growing awareness of the problem of disparate treatment of male and female delinquents, many states have attempted to address the double standard.

Girls, Delinquency, and Juvenile Justice (coauthored with Randall Shelden, 1992, 1998) and *The Female Offender: Girls, Women, and Crime* (1999) expose the problems associated with applying male-oriented criminological theories to girls and women. Historical data and numerous contemporary studies show that mainstream theories and approaches based on adults (especially adult males) do not explain female delinquency. Instead, factors such as histories of troubled family backgrounds (marked by poverty, divorce, parental death, abandonment, alcoholism, and frequent abuse) may contribute to their delinquency. These backgrounds may prompt young women to run away from home where they may engage in prostitution, petty property crimes, and drug use. As a result, statutes originally developed to "protect" girls have criminalized their survival strategies.

Chesney-Lind recommends that counseling for delinquent and at-risk young women should address these multiple problems and should include educational and occupational support. Furthermore, programming should address the needs of young women who do not live with their families and provide them with access to caring adults and communities. Chesney-Lind's research also examines racial issues and injustices; girls' involvement in gangs and violence, and sentencing. More recently, Chesney-Lind has coedited a book with Marc Mauer, *Invisible Punishment: The Collateral of Consequences of Mass Imprisonment,* that explores some of our most infamous criminal justice policies (e.g., "three strikes and you're out," "a war on drugs," "get tough on crime" attitudes that included mandatory sentencing, and prison privatization) and details the detrimental impacts and social consequences these (and other) policies have had on our families and communities.

CONCLUSION

Meda Chesney-Lind is arguably the preeminent scholar of female delinquency. Her research has focused national attention on the growing number of women and girls entering the correctional system and has aided in the call for seeking alternative solutions to women's incarceration. Her continued research and active voice in policy issues will endure to facilitate arguments against gender-blind and racialized policies and practice on crime-related issues. Meda Chesney-Lind's contributions have pointed out noteworthy contradictions and gaps in the literature on girls and women in the criminal justice system. Her scholarly work sets the scene for additional research and policy making and has contributed to recognition of the contributions of feminist criminology.

—Kimberly L. Freiberger

See also Juvenile Justice System; Nicole Hahn Rafter; Status Offenders; Women Prisoners; Women's Prisons

Further Reading

Chesney-Lind, M. (1977). Judicial paternalism and the female status offender: Training women to know their place. *Crime & Delinquency, 23,* 121–130.

Chesney-Lind, M. (1986). Women and crime: The female offender. *Signs: Journal of Women in Culture and Society, 12*(1), 78–96.

Chesney-Lind, M. (1999). *The female offender: Girls, women, and crime.* Thousand Oaks, CA: Sage.

Chesney-Lind, M. (2000). Reflections on an accidental career. *Women & Criminal Justice, 11*(4), 3–4.

Chesney-Lind, M. (2002). Meda Chesney-Lind home page. Retrieved from www.chesneylind.com

Chesney-Lind, M., & Brown, M. (1999). Girls and violence: An overview. In D. J. Flannery & C. R. Huff (Eds.), *Youth violence: Prevention, intervention, and social policy* (pp. 171–199). Washington, DC: American Psychiatric Press.

Chesney-Lind, M., & Hagedorn, J. M. (Eds.). (1999). *Female gangs in America: Essays on gender, and gangs.* Chicago: Lakeview.

Chesney-Lind, M., & Mauer, M. (Eds.). (2002). *Invisible punishment: The collateral consequences of mass imprisonment.* New York: New Press.

Chesney-Lind, M., & Shelden, R. G. (1998). *Girls, delinquency, and juvenile justice* (2nd ed.). Belmont, CA: Wadsworth.

CHILD SAVERS

The child savers were a group of reformers in 19th-century Chicago who created the first juvenile court in the United States and developed the model for a separate juvenile justice system that is widely in use around the world today. The child savers hoped to care for and reform delinquent, neglected, and dependent children, helping them to lead lives of conformity and thereby preventing future crimes.

ORIGINS

Anthony Platt literally wrote the book on child savers. In *The Child Savers* (Platt, 1977), he describes the child saving movement as being driven by middle- and upper-class women who had the means, the time, and the political connections to work on philanthropic endeavors. These women were primarily the white, Anglo-Saxon Protestant wives and daughters of prominent men in Chicago; as such, they were highly educated and had the leisure time, the resources, and the support to pursue interests outside of their own households.

Working to create new institutions for wayward children seemed to be a natural expansion of the traditional female role as the child savers expanded their duties in the domestic sphere out into the community. Because raising children was largely viewed as women's work, there was little resistance to the child savers as they embraced the role of providing care for and correcting children in need of supervision.

IMPACT ON CHILDREN AND JUVENILE JUSTICE

The child savers created the first juvenile court in Chicago in 1899. It explicitly recognized children and adolescents as more malleable than adults, more open to rehabilitation, and less culpable for their crimes. The juvenile court was based on the idea of *parens patriae,* where the state—through wise and benevolent judges—would serve as a surrogate parent to children in need of help and supervision. Judges had wide discretion to determine and to act in the "best interest of the child." The process was meant to be less adversarial than criminal courts, so it was assumed that children did not need due process protections. Children had virtually no rights as their fate was in the hands of the judge.

As it was created, the juvenile court focused on both prevention and control. A primary goal was to control and rehabilitate juvenile delinquents, protecting the community from further crimes. In addition, the juvenile court served a social work function, supervising and caring for dependent and neglected children in the hopes of preventing them from turning to crime to meet their basic needs. Children deemed in need of supervision were frequently sent to reformatories outside of the city where they could learn working-class skills and middle-class, conforming values.

THE LEGACY OF THE CHILD SAVERS

The child savers undoubtedly had good intentions. They created an innovative juvenile justice system that almost immediately became a model for similar systems in every state and many countries. They managed to separate juveniles from adults in court and in correctional facilities and to change the way the public thought about poor children and adolescent offenders. Critics, however, argue that the child saving movement may have done more to benefit middle- and upper-class women than it did for children. The child savers carved out new roles and careers in social work for women, creating new legitimate opportunities for women to work in the public sphere.

At the same time, the child saving movement placed more restrictions on children's behavior, furthering government control over children's activities that previously would have been overlooked or dealt with more informally in the community. With additional power and responsibility to enforce these new rules and correct such youthful misbehavior, the juvenile justice system particularly focused on poor, immigrant children as those in need of reformation. In many ways, girls were more closely monitored than boys, as the child savers took an active interest in patrolling and reforming the moral and sexual behavior of girls.

The social distance between the child savers and the children they targeted was significant, and scholars, including Anthony Platt and Thomas Bernard, have suggested that the child saving movement reinforced the sense of moral and intellectual superiority of the reformers over their charges. In addition, critics argue that the child saving movement was largely a symbolic movement that ultimately served to reinforce social institutions, controlling the poor and helping them to adapt to lives in an unjust system.

CONCLUSION

Many people continue to support the basic ideas of the child savers. Yet 100 years after its creation, the juvenile court is under attack as juveniles are again being tried as adults for serious offenses and judges' discretion has been replaced in many states by determinate sentencing. The best interest of the child has been replaced with the goal of holding young offenders accountable for their actions and meting out like punishments for like crimes.

The child savers had an enormous impact on how we think about and how we treat delinquent, neglected, and dependent children. Their legacy, both the good and bad, will continue to shape our vision of juvenile offenders long into the future as we struggle to find the balance between prevention, rehabilitation, punishment, and protection of the community.

—*Michelle Inderbitzin*

See also Cook County, Illinois; Cottage System; Juvenile Justice and Delinquency Prevention Act 1974; Juvenile Reformatories; *Parens Patriae*; Anthony Platt; Status Offenders

Further Reading

Ayers, W. (1997). *A kind and just parent: The children of juvenile court*. Boston: Beacon.

Bernard, T. J. (1992). *The cycle of juvenile justice*. New York: Oxford University Press.

Chesney-Lind, M., & Shelden, R. G. (1998). *Girls, delinquency, and juvenile justice* (2nd ed.). Belmont, CA: Wadsworth.

Feld, B. (1999). *Bad kids: Race and the transformation of the juvenile court*. New York: Oxford University Press.

Platt, A. M. (1977). *The child savers: The invention of delinquency* (2nd ed., enlarged). Chicago: University of Chicago Press.

◪ CHILDREN

Children may be involved in the U.S. prison system in two ways: directly by their confinement in juvenile institutions and adult prisons or indirectly by the incarceration of their parents. On any given day in the United States, approximately 107,000 juveniles are incarcerated in juvenile institutions and adult facilities. Children in another estimated 336,300 households in the United States had at least one parent in jail or prison in 1999.

INCARCERATED CHILDREN

Children are incarcerated in both juvenile institutions and in adult prisons. In 1998, the number of delinquency cases in juvenile court reached 1.8 million; increasing 44% from 1989. This expansion of the number of children brought before the juvenile court for delinquent offenses in turn spurred an increase in the number of juveniles being incarcerated. The number of children incarcerated in juvenile institutions peaked in 1990 when 570,000 such juveniles were housed in these facilities. The total number of juvenile offenders in custody across the United States has decreased since that time. According to the Census of Juveniles in Residential Placement, as of October 29, 1997, the number of juveniles being housed in correctional facilities had been reduced to approximately 105,790.

One of the most controversial aspects of incarcerating children involves housing them in adult facilities. Prior to the Juvenile Justice and Delinquency Prevention Act of 1974 (Public Law 93–415, 42 U.S.C. 5601) juveniles were often housed in the same facilities as adult offenders. This act did not, however, entirely eliminate the presence of juveniles under the age of 18 in the adult criminal system.

Currently, there are several ways in which juveniles can be housed in correctional institutions with adults. First, juveniles can be sent to adult court through a judicial waiver in which the judge decides to transfer a case from juvenile to adult court, usually as the result of a transfer hearing. Second, in some states juveniles are automatically waived to the adult court based on the crime they allegedly committed. Most of these statutorily excluded offenses involve murder or other person-related offenses. The age at which statutory exclusions may be applied to juveniles differs among states. For example, those charged with a capital crime in Florida are automatically tried in adult court while children aged 14 and older in North Carolina are also automatically tried in adult court if charged with a capital offense. In New Mexico, juveniles must be aged 15 and older and charged with murder, while in Mississippi they have to be aged 17 and older and charged with a felony. Finally, some jurisdictions allow the prosecutor discretion to decide in which court (adult or juvenile) to prosecute the individual.

As with so much of the criminal justice system, race seems to play a role in the number of juveniles transferred to adult court. Between 1988 and 1997, the number of black youths who were transferred to adult court increased by 35%. Yet the number of white youths transferred increased by only 14%. Furthermore, black youths were more frequently transferred for person-related offenses, while white youths were transferred for property offenses.

JUVENILES IN ADULT PRISONS

When juveniles are transferred to the adult system, they are often incarcerated in adult facilities, despite their age. Of the approximately 107,000 youths incarcerated daily in the United States, 14,500 are confined in adult facilities. Forty-four of the 50 states and the District of Columbia allow children 17 years of age and younger to be housed in adult correctional facilities. While a small portion of these juveniles were being held as juvenile offenders (21%), the majority (75%) were held as adult offenders. Seventy-nine percent of the incarcerated youth were 17 years old, while 18% were 16.

Juveniles housed in adult jails experience a rate of suicide that is 7.7 times higher than their counterparts in juvenile detention centers. Incarcerated juveniles in adult facilities are frequently the victims of rape or attempted rape. Ten percent of the juveniles in adult prisons versus 1% of the juveniles in juvenile facilities reported that another inmate in their facility tried to sexually victimize them. Juveniles in adult correctional facilities are also often the targets of staff assaults. One in 10 juveniles in adult prisons was reportedly the victim of staff assaults. Juveniles also face victimization from their fellow adult inmates, presumably because of their youthful age. Finally, young people housed in adult facilities reported being attacked with a weapon by a fellow inmate at a rate 50% higher than their counterparts in juvenile detention centers.

CHILDREN OF INCARCERATED PARENTS

The number of children with at least one parent incarcerated in prison has risen in response to the growing rate of incarceration in the United States. Between 1991 and 1999, the number of children with a parent in state or federal prison increased from 936,500 to 1,498,800. This number continues to grow by 5.7% each year. Of the 72 million children in the United States during 1999, approximately 2% had a parent incarcerated in a penal institution. Twenty-two percent of these children were under the age of five.

While the majority of incarcerated parents are fathers (97%), the number of mothers continues to expand. Since 1990, the number of women incarcerated has grown by 106%. In addition, minority children are affected more than white children by parental incarceration. African American children were nine times more likely to have a parent incarcerated; Latino children, three times more likely.

Placement

Before their confinement, approximately 64% of the parents lived with their children. Once their parent is incarcerated, the home environment of many of these children changed. After their incarceration, 85% of parents, most of whom were fathers, reported that the child's other parent (the mother) now held the responsibility for raising the child. Not all children remained with one of their natural parents, however. Some were placed in the homes of other family members, most commonly, their grandparents. Fifty-three percent of children whose mothers were incarcerated and 14% whose fathers were incarcerated lived with their grandparents. Children are also often placed with extended family members. Given the emotional and financial burden of raising other people's children, many of these children find themselves being constantly shifted between family members.

Some children are placed in the foster care system, which may raise a number of problems. First, in families where there are multiple children, siblings are often separated from one another in placements, adding to the trauma of having lost a parent. Second, a majority of parents who are incarcerated will eventually be released, yet efforts to reunite them with their children are minimal in most jurisdictions. The impact of parental incarceration on permanency planning can be profound. For instance, social workers often have a difficult time contacting the parent and thus permanency planning strategies and hearings may take place without any input from the parents. Following the Adoption and Safe Families Act of 1997, incarcerated parents now have less time than ever to make their case for keeping their children.

Visits

Maintaining contact between incarcerated parents and their children is difficult and often ignored by correctional officials. While 60% of the mothers and 40% of the fathers in prison reported having weekly contact with their child, the primary means of such contact was via telephone or mail. Fifty-seven percent of state inmates and 44% of federal inmates reported never having had a personal visit with their child.

Financial constraints make all means of contact more difficult. Since the primary means of telephone access for most prisoners is expensive collect calls, many are simply unable to communicate with their children. In addition, many of the parents in the state (62%) and federal (84%) prisons are incarcerated at facilities more than 100 miles from their homes, making the financial and logistical issues insurmountable. Finally, correctional institutions often lack

appropriate parent-child visiting facilities. The visiting process in many institutions is often very invasive and frightening for children. The physical contact between parents and children may also be limited, depending on the institution, while the physical environments of visitation areas are most uninviting given the institutional atmosphere.

EFFECTS OF A PARENT'S INCARCERATION ON CHILDREN

There are numerous effects of parental incarceration on children. Aside from the initial trauma of having a parent arrested (which many of them witness), children must also deal with the physical separation from their parent. The loss of physical parental contact, as well as the general disturbance of the family structure, serves to uproot the child's sense of family. Many also suffer serious economic hardships when their parent is incarcerated due to the reduction of family income. The emotional consequences of parental incarceration, however, may be even more severe. Children usually experience an emotional attachment to their parent, regardless of whether they were living with that parent prior to their incarceration. After incarceration, children often become angry, anxious, and depressed or even experience post-traumatic stress disorder as a result of parental incarceration. They may blame themselves for their parent's incarceration. These emotional issues often manifest themselves in behaviors that place them at risk for delinquency. For instance, many children turn to alcohol and drug abuse, teen pregnancy, and truancy in an effort to alleviate the effects of the incarceration. Finally, children with incarcerated parents are five times more likely to engage in criminal and/or delinquent activities than are their peers without incarcerated parents.

EFFORTS TO MAINTAIN PARENT-CHILD CONTACT

There have been some efforts by nonprofit agencies, state agencies, and correctional officials to foster the parent-child relationship. Many efforts have been programmatic in nature, such as Girl Scouts Beyond Bars, which has been implemented in four states, as well as the creation, at the federal level, of the Resource Center for Children of Prisoners, jointly organized in 2001 by the Child Welfare League of America, the American Correctional Association, and the National Center on Crime and Delinquency. The most common efforts, however, are visiting programs designed to provide incarcerated parents more contact with their children. The efforts of correctional institutions are vastly different, but some of the more common visiting initiatives include interactive videoconferencing, an allotted number of overnight stays per month, week-long summer camps, and weekend camping trips.

CONCLUSION

The discussion of the relationship between children and prisons can be divided into two separate issues: the direct incarceration of children and the incarceration of their parents. While conceivably the most influential aspects of prisons on children results from their own incarceration in adult and juvenile correctional facilities, the effects of the incarceration of their parents has serious repercussions for many children in the United States today.

—Lisa Hutchinson Wallace

See also Children's Visits; Families Against Mandatory Minimums; Fathers in Prison; Juvenile Detention Centers; Juvenile Justice System; Juvenile Reformatories; Mothers in Prison; Parenting Programs; Prison Nurseries; Prisoner Reentry; Visits

Further Reading

Austin, J., Johnson, K. D., & Gregoriou, M. (2000). *Juveniles in adult prisons and jails.* Washington, DC: Office of Juvenile Justice and Delinquency Prevention.

Bartlett, R. (2000). Helping inmate moms keep in touch: Prison programs encourage ties with children. *Corrections Today, 62*(7), 102–104.

Bilchik, S., Seymour, C., & Kreisher, K. (2001). Parents in prison. *Corrections Today, 63*(7), 108–111.

Federal Resource Center for Children of Prisoners. (2003). *What happens to children?* Retrieved August 2, 2003, from www.cwla.org/programs/incarcerated/cop_03.htm

Griffin, P., Torbet, P., & Syzmanski, L. (1998). *Trying juveniles as adults in criminal court: An analysis of state transfer provisions.* Washington, DC: Office of Juvenile Justice and Delinquency Prevention.

Johnson, E. I., & Waldfogel, J. (2002). Parental incarceration: Recent trends and implications for child welfare. *Social Service Review, 76* (3), 460–479.

Juvenile Justice and Delinquency Prevention Act of 1974, 42 U.S.C. 5601.

Kauffman, K. (2001). Mothers in prison. *Corrections Today, 63*(1), 62–65.

Mazza, C. (2002). And then the world fell apart: The children of incarcerated fathers. *Families in Society, 83*(6), 521–529.

Moses, M. C. (1995). *Keeping incarcerated mothers and their daughters together: Girl Scouts Beyond Bars* (NCJ 156217). Washington, DC: National Institute of Justice.

Mumola, C. J. (2000). *Incarcerated parents and their children* (BJS special report, NCJ 182335). Washington, DC: U.S. Department of Justice, Bureau of Justice Statistics.

Parent, D. G. (1993). Conditions of confinement. *Juvenile Justice, 1*(1), 2–7.

Puzzanchera, C. M. (2001). *Delinquency cases waived to criminal court, 1988–1997.* Washington, DC: Office of Juvenile Justice and Delinquency Prevention.

Sickmund, M. (2000). *State custody rates, 1997.* Washington, DC: Office of Juvenile Justice and Delinquency Prevention.

Ziedenberg, J., & Schiraldi, V. (1998). The risks juveniles face. *Corrections Today, 60*(5), 22–26.

◪ CHILDREN'S VISITS

There are currently approximately 1.9 million minor children with a parent in prison and millions more who have experienced the incarceration of a parent at some point in their lives. African American children are almost nine times more likely than white children to have a parent in prison, and Hispanic children are three times as likely. The majority of these children are under 10 years old.

Criminological literature suggests that visits improve the postrelease success of prisoners, reducing their recidivism as well as the chances of future incarceration of their children. Likewise, research shows that visits help maintain family ties and increase the likelihood that a family will reunify after release from prison. Child welfare experts assert that lack of contact between parent and child following separation can harm a child's development and perpetuate family patterns of destructive behavior.

SCALE AND SCOPE OF PARENTAL CONTACT

Although most children have some contact with their incarcerated parents by phone or mail, more

Family Visits

Being in the visiting room is like waiting in an airport or bus station. The scene is constructed of the same nondescript uncomfortable chairs and vending machines encompassed by a feeling of boredom. All the prisoners are in their khakis and boots. Their clothes look pressed and their boots are shining because they are trying to look good for their people. But all the prisoners look identical because everything in federal prison is supposed to be uniform.

You know you should be happy to get a visit in prison but the environment of the visiting room is so depressing. Usually a bunch of kids are running around and all the mommies look sad because their man and breadwinner is locked up. Families usually gather around their loved one but they can't touch them because prison regulations stipulate one hug and kiss upon arrival and one on departure. Plus, you have guards all around you checking you out to make sure you're not smuggling drugs into prison or anything. If you get too close to your girl the guards will come up and call you to the side to humiliate you and tell you "if they have to warn you about excessive touching again, your visit will be terminated."

So you sit there trying to be happy seeing your family and friends and eating vending machine food but there is so much surveillance and the visiting room is so loud with everybody yelling that it ends up being a big hassle. Your people drove God knows how many hours to see you, so you feel obligated to stay and to make conversation, but your family is falling asleep from the trip and the whole affair is really rather tiring and then the visit ends. You leave, and proceed to the necessary strip search routine as you hope that the cops won't hassle your family.

Seth Ferranti
FCI Fairton, Fairton, New Jersey

than half never visit them in prison. Children who do visit do not see their incarcerated parents regularly or frequently. Long distances to most correctional facilities, lack of transportation, and limited financial resources are the most common reasons why children do not visit their parents in prison. Prisons are often located in remote, rural areas, typically more than 100 miles from the urban areas where most of the prisoners' children reside. Public transportation rarely services these areas and many families do not own a car or have the resources to rent one.

Prisoners' relationships with their children's caregiver also influences whether children will come to see them while they are incarcerated. Approximately 90% of children with an imprisoned father live with their mother, while only about 20% of children whose mother is in prison live with their father. When a mother goes to prison, often the father is absent. Most children of incarcerated mothers live with a grandparent or other relative. Visiting rooms in men's prisons are typically crowded with mothers who bring children to visit their fathers. However, visiting rooms at women's facilities are noticeably sparse with only a few grandmothers, sisters, or other relatives who are able to bring children to visit their mothers.

There has been a seven-fold increase in the number of incarcerated mothers over the past two decades, while the percentage of children who visit their mothers has declined from 92% in 1978 to less than 50% in 1992. The number of children with a mother in prison nearly doubled from 1991 to 1999 and two-thirds of these mothers were their children's primary caregiver before incarceration.

Some caregivers are angry with the parent and may not believe he or she deserves to see the child. In some cases, children do not want to visit their incarcerated parent. In other cases, parents may be ashamed or embarrassed about their criminal activity, may not tell their children where they are, or do not want their children to see them in a prison. Prisoners and caregivers alike debate whether to have children visit because of the stressful entry process, unfriendly environment, and tearful goodbyes.

THE VISITING PROCESS

Prior to a visit, prospective visitors must file paperwork and review prison rules. Children under

18 years old must have their original birth certificate and be accompanied by an adult; sometimes the legal guardian is required. Clothing restrictions are common and when violated, may prevent the child from visiting. It is not uncommon for visitors to wait two or three hours before being admitted through the prison gates. Once inside, each visitor must pass a security checkpoint to prevent contraband such as drugs or weapons from entering the facility. Uniformed guards escort visitors through a metal detector and often search, frisk, and/or ask them to remove shoes or babies' diapers.

Some prisons have a playroom where children can be entertained with toys, games, and books; however, visiting most often takes place in an open area such as a cafeteria, with tables and surrounding stools bolted to the floor. Children are typically elated once they see their parents and siblings often vie for their attention. Naturally, children's reactions depend on how old they are, how long it has been since they have seen their parent, and their individual circumstances.

While rules vary across institutions and their levels of security classification, parents are generally allowed to give each child one hug and one kiss hello and goodbye. Parents can usually hold babies, but children are not allowed to sit on their lap. Guards closely oversee family interactions and reprimand prisoners or visitors who violate regulations. If a child or parent misbehaves, the visit may be terminated and future visits jeopardized. Prison officials see visits as a privilege that can be revoked in order to motivate good behavior among prisoners.

The length of visits varies by institution and can range from 20 minutes to two hours. Occasionally, children's visits that are part of a parenting education program run longer. Children, parents, and caregivers all report that saying goodbye is the hardest part. The child-unfriendly environment coupled with emotional goodbyes make some parents and caregivers decide against future visits.

Incarcerated parents with children in foster care make up approximately 10% of those in prison with children. These individuals must depend on child protective services (CPS) workers to arrange for their children to visit. Availability of funds and willingness of a CPS worker or foster parent to transport the child, as well as their attitudes toward children visiting parents in prison, all influence whether and how often visits take place. Even though CPS mandates visits as part of all reunification plans, research finds that most children in foster care are not taken to see their parents in prison.

IS VISITING BENEFICIAL OR HARMFUL TO CHILDREN?

There is an ongoing debate about whether prison is an unhealthy environment in which to bring children to be with a parent. Some fear it normalizes the harshness of prison and believe children should remain afraid of it. Others worry that older children might come to see serving time as a right of passage. Many wonder if having to say goodbye again and again only exacerbates the trauma of separation.

Denise Johnston, M.D., a national expert on children of incarcerated parents, maintains that visits are not harmful. She recognizes that sad goodbyes are a natural response and indicative of an affective bond. Furthermore, a visit immediately following parent-child separation reassures children that their parents are alive and safe. Visits ease fears children may hold about prisons and dispel frightening illusions instilled by media images. In the visiting room, children do not feel the stigma of having an incarcerated parent and can connect with other kids who share similar circumstances. Visits allow a child to return to his or her own life feeling more secure.

Most children of incarcerated parents get little or no emotional support to help them process their feelings. Children's ages, their situation before their parent's incarceration and relationship with their caregiver all influence their reactions to the separation. While research on this population is limited, studies consistently find that children of incarcerated parents often have problems in school with concentration, aggressiveness, withdrawal, or excessive crying. Some children too young to understand the criminal justice process blame themselves, inferring that they must have done something wrong to deserve abandonment. Visits mitigate the anxiety of separation, improve mental health for both child and parent, and are a critical step toward family reunification.

CHILDREN VISITING PROGRAMS

There are various programs across the nation that support child-parent visitation in prisons. For example, the Bedford Hills Correctional Facility in New York has the nation's oldest, complete prison program where newborns can live with their mothers up to one year, and children visit on weekends and during the summertime. Girl Scouts Beyond Bars is a mother-child visitation program started in Maryland in 1992 that has expanded to several states across the country. Operation Prison Gap in New York and Families With a Future in California help transport children to visit their incarcerated parents. While there is relatively little information about these children, their numbers are growing and they are perhaps the most at-risk population of children in the nation.

CONCLUSION

There are significant collateral costs to incarcerating parents. At the current rate, two out of three prisoners will recidivate, each costing taxpayers more than $20,000 per year in prison. Children of incarcerated parents are 50% more likely than other children to become entangled in the criminal justice system, continuing intergenerational cycles of crime and incarceration. Visits are a low-cost intervention with proven advantages for family reunification and crime prevention.

—*Susan Greene*

See also Children; Fathers in Prison; Mothers in Prison; Parenting Programs; Prison Nurseries; Visits

Further Reading

Bloom, B., & Steinhart, D. (1993). *Why punish the children?* San Francisco: National Council on Crime and Delinquency.

Hairston, C. F. (1990). Mothers in jail: Parent-child separation and jail visitation. *Affilia, 6*(2), 9–27.

Hairston, C. F. (1991). Family ties during imprisonment: Important to whom and for what. *Journal of Sociology and Social Welfare, 18,* 87–104.

Johnston, D. (1995). Parent-child visitation in the jail or prison. In K. Gabel & D. Johnston (Eds.), *Children of incarcerated parents.* New York: Lexington Books.

Katz, P. C. (1998). Supporting families and children of mothers in jail: An integrated child welfare and criminal justice strategy. *Child Welfare, 77*(5), 495–512.

Mumola, C. J. (2000). *Incarcerated parents and their children* (BJS special report, NCJ 182335). Washington, DC: U.S. Department of Justice, Bureau of Justice Statistics.

Reed, D. F., & Reed, E. L. (1997). Children of incarcerated parents. *Social Justice, 24*(3), 152–169.

Wright, L. E., & Seymour, C. B. (2000). *Working with children and families separated by incarceration.* Washington, DC: CWLA Press.

◪ CITIZENS UNITED FOR REHABILITATION OF ERRANTS

Citizens United for Rehabilitation of Errants (CURE) is one of the most active prison reform groups in the United States. The organization began in San Antonio, Texas, on January 2, 1972, when volunteers drove hundreds of miles in dilapidated buses to the state prisons. Riding on the buses were families who had not seen their loved ones in years. In the 1973 legislative session in Austin, one of the buses was used to bring families to help in passing legislation that banned prisoners from having disciplinary power over other inmates. Initially, the prison system had assisted CURE with the bus service, but they stopped cooperating when this bill became law. As a result, CURE decided to become a statewide advocacy organization and moved to Austin in 1974.

Besides prison reform, CURE began to focus on jail, parole, and probation problems. It helped ensure the appointment of the first black, woman, and Hispanic to the parole board as well as the creation of commissions on jail standards and probation. This last agency, the Texas Adult Probation Commission, became the vehicle for a substantial increase in community corrections.

All these victories were a prelude to *Ruiz v. Estelle,* the most comprehensive lawsuit ever filed and the longest ever argued on a prison system.

When the historic order came from Federal Judge William Wayne Justice, it would be at the end of CURE's first decade of existence and it would reform most of the Texas prison system.

1982–1991: IN TRANSITION

After testifying and helping to facilitate *Ruiz*, CURE moved from confrontation to cooperation in encouraging the state to comply with the court order and not to appeal it. In 1983, the Texas Legislature responded by shifting millions of dollars from proposed prison construction to community corrections. The governor was removed from the parole process that not only streamlined the procedure but also led to many more releases.

During the rest of the decade, other state chapters were also established. Forty states now have chapters, and the volunteer leaders are either families of prisoners or former prisoners. Training for these volunteers occur at conferences on leader development that are held every few years. In 1991, CURE established national issue chapters that focus on specific goals such as treatment for sex offenders, reforming the sentences for "lifers," and bringing together the federal prisoners and their loved ones. Like the state chapters, the leaders of the issue chapters are either former prisoners or families of prisoners.

In August 1985, CURE expanded to a national organization and opened an office in Washington, DC. At the federal level, CURE helped to (1) extend the WIC (Women, Infants and Children) Program to pregnant prisoners, (2) increase the Prison Industry Enhancement (PIE) Program to all states, and (3) create an Office of Correctional Education within the U.S. Department of Education.

1992–2003

In 1994, Congress passed the Violent Crime Control Act, which increased the number of crimes for which capital punishment could be applied, gave millions more dollars to states to build prisons, and discontinued Pell grants for prisoners.

CURE's only victories during this period were the creation of an Office of Correctional Job Training and Placement and Specter grants for prisoner education. Within CURE, this depressive picture seemed to be reflected too. From 1997 to 2000, six CURE leaders died. Two passed unexpectedly and one was executed by the state of Texas. However, eventually, the organization seemed to build from these ashes. Equitable Telephone Charges, CURE's highly successful national campaign to reduce the costs of inmate phone calls, was launched. This was followed by For Whom the Bells Toll, a project to have religious communities toll their bells on the day of an execution.

There were also four far-reaching reforms approved by Congress. First, all deaths in custody would have to be reported to the U.S. Department of Justice and annual statistics compiled on them. This legislation was similar to the bill CURE had passed in Texas in the 1983 reform session. Second, mental health courts were created. Similar to drug courts, this allows a judge to divert a mentally ill offender from jail into treatment. Third, the section of the U.S. Department of Justice that sues prisons and jails for unconstitutional conditions received its first staff increase in its 20-year history. Fourth, the U.S. Department of Veterans Affairs was mandated to assist incarcerated veterans with reentry.

Finally, almost 200 people participated in the First International Conference on Human Rights and Prison Reform that was held in October 2001 in New York City. Most of the 24 countries that were represented prepared and delivered report cards to their ambassadors to the United Nations. These cards reported on the status of human rights in the prisons in their countries.

CONCLUSION

At the time of writing, CURE is considering expanding internationally. Whether this happens or not, the organization has tried and many times succeeded in providing "a place at the table" for prisoners and their loved ones when prison policies are decided.

Governors, legislators, prison directors, and wardens have had to at least consider formal positions taken by this organized, totally independent, volunteer group. Whether CURE is the name of this type of prisoner consumer organization or movement remains to be seen. But CURE leaders are convinced that an organization like CURE should be keeping an eye on every prison and jail in the world.

—Pauline Sullivan and Charles Sullivan

See also Families Against Mandatory Minimums; John Howard; November Coalition; Parole; Pell Grants; Prison Reform Groups; *Ruiz v. Estelle*; Truth in Sentencing; Violent Crime Control and Law Enforcement Act 1994

◪ CIVIL COMMITMENT OF SEXUAL PREDATORS

In the 1990s, public outrage over habitual sexual offenders prompted some states to enact sexual predator statutes. These statutes empower states to confine and treat sexual offenders indefinitely once they have completed their criminal sentence. The legislative rationale for these statutes is that states must protect their citizenry from persons who have a history of sexual deviance pursuant to the states' *parens patriae* and police powers duties. The legislation provides for the civil commitment of dangerous offenders who may lack a mental disease or defect but who are highly likely to sexually reoffend upon their release from prison.

CIVIL COMMITMENT STATUTES

In 1990, Washington became the first state to enact a sexual predator statute. Missouri became the latest state to enact such a statute in 2002. Other states that provide for the involuntary civil commitment of sex offenders include Arizona, California, Colorado, Connecticut, Florida, Illinois, Iowa, Kansas, Massachusetts, Minnesota, Nebraska, New Jersey, New Mexico, North Dakota, Oregon, South Carolina, Tennessee, Texas, Utah, Virginia, and Wisconsin. The statutes in all states presume that sexual predators have a mental abnormality or disability and that they are persons who lack the ability to control their sexual deviancy.

These civil commitment statutes have similar procedural processes governing the postprison confinement of sexual predator offenders. A local prosecutor will be notified that a sexual offender is about to be released from prison. If a prosecutor decides to pursue civil commitment, he or she will begin an involuntary civil commitment hearing or trial to determine if the offender is too dangerous to be released. The commitment proceeding can be held before a judge or jury, and if the prosecutor proves beyond a reasonable doubt that the offender is a sexual predator then the offender will be committed to a secure facility. The commitment is indefinite, and the offender will be held until such time as it is shown that the offender is no longer a threat to the community.

CONSTITUTIONAL CHALLENGES

Constitutional challenges to sexual predator statutes have questioned whether the statutes satisfy due process. Substantive due process prohibits a state from limiting an individual's fundamental rights unless the state has a compelling state interest. In addition, the state statute has to be narrowly tailored to achieve that interest. In regard to sexual predator statutes, states argue that the state must protect the community from the substantial harm that a sexual predator can inflict on victims of rape and sexual assault. Opponents of sexual predator statutes argue that the statute's presumption is not based on a showing of a mental illness or defect, the traditional focus of civil commitment laws, but on a showing of a mental "abnormality," an overbroad characterization. In addition, opponents argue that an individual's procedural due process rights are violated when fact finders presume habitual offending propensities based on past conduct without adequate procedural protections to ensure that such commitments are not indefinite.

Civil commitment is traditionally based on the need to confine and treat persons who suffer from a mental illness and release persons when they are no longer a danger to themselves or others. Because civil confinement of sexual offenders does not depend on the ability of the state to provide treatment, opponents of sexual predator laws argue that the statutes do not comport with the expanded rights of the mentally ill that has occurred over the past 30 years.

Sexual predator statutes have also been challenged under the Constitution's double jeopardy and *ex post facto* provisions. Opponents of these laws argue that an individual should not continue to be "punished" upon completion of a prison sentence. Since the statutes were enacted after many sex offenders had committed their offenses, opponents also argue that the laws cannot be applied to these individuals.

ONE STATE'S EXAMPLE: KANSAS

The U.S. Supreme Court upheld the constitutionality of Kansas's Sexually Violent Predator Act in two cases. In *Kansas v. Hendricks*, 521 U.S. 346 (1997), a divided court found that because the statute is "civil" and not part of the criminal law system the statutes cannot violate the Constitution's double jeopardy and *ex post facto* clauses. In *Kansas v. Crane*, 534 U.S. 407 (2002), the U.S. Supreme Court clarified the definition of a sexual predator and held that involuntary civil commitment of a sexual offender is permissible if a sex offender is shown to lack control over his or her behavior. The Court stated that a finding of "total" lack of control is not required, but the state cannot commit a person without a showing that the individual suffers from a volitional impairment (e.g., pedophilia) and has serious problems with controlling his or her behavior.

CONCLUSION

Sexual predator statutes that provide for the civil commitment of sexual offenders who cannot control their sexual offending behavior are, in general, constitutional. These statutes must provide substantive and procedural processes that establish that an offender suffers from a mental abnormality and lacks control over the deviant sexual behavior beyond a reasonable doubt. States cannot automatically transfer sexual offenders to a secure facility involuntarily at the expiration of a prison sentence without due process. Nonetheless, because these statutes are civil in nature other constitutional concerns that might exist if the statutes were part of the criminal law do not apply.

—*Frances P. Bernat*

See also Incapacitation Theory; Indeterminate Sentencing; Just Deserts Theory; Megan's Law; Sex Offender Programs; Sex Offenders; Truth in Sentencing

Further Reading

Gillespie, A. C. (1998). Note: Constitutional challenges to civil commitment laws: An uphill battle for sexual predators after *Kansas v. Hendricks*. *Catholic University Law Review, 47,* 1145–1187.

Hamilton, G. S. (2002). Casenote: The blurry line between "mad" and "bad"—Is "lack-of-control" a workable standard for sexually violent predators? *University of Richmond Law Review, 36,* 481–508.

Maskovich, J. (2001). Case note: *Kansas v. Crane*—Its effects on *State v. Ehrlich* and Arizona's sexually violent persons statute. *Arizona Law Review, 43,* 1007–1013.

Matson, S., & Lieb, R. (1997). *Sexual predator commitment laws* (Document No. 97–10–1102). Olympia: Washington State Institute for Public Policy.

Spierling, S. E. (2001). Notes and comments: Lock them up and throw away the key—How Washington's violent sexual predator law will shape the future balance between punishment and prevention. *Journal of Law and Policy, 9,* 879–928.

Washington's new violent sexual predator commitment system: An unconstitutional law and an unwise policy choice [Comments]. (1990). *University of Puget Sound Law Review, 14,* 105–141.

☷ CLASSIFICATION

Classification is fundamental to correctional practice. It is incumbent upon any correctional agency, institution, or community to identify (classify) who is (a) at risk of reoffending, (b) likely to incur problems adjusting to prison, and (c) in need of specific services. Determining whether an offender is able to participate in various types of treatment programs, examining such traits as ethnicity, age, gender, and intelligence, also falls under the rubric of correctional classification.

Offenders are not all alike but differ according to risk, treatment needs, intelligence, gender, ethnicity, financial needs, family considerations, personality, employment, employability, and other factors. Failure to assess for and plan for such differences may imperil the safety of prison facilities and communities. At the same time, ignoring assessments, which help to match offenders to appropriate treatments and

Type of System	Purpose: Institutional Corrections	Purpose: Community Corrections
Risk Assessments	Predict institutional misconducts	Predict new offenses
Needs Assessments	Identify offender needs for programming referrals	Identify offender needs for programming referrals
Risk/Needs Assessments	Seldom used in institutions	Predict new offenses with needs that are also risk factors
Responsivity Assessments	Assessments of IQ, maturity, personality, and other attributes likely to interfere with an offenders' ability to participate in certain programs.	Assessments of IQ, maturity, personality, and other attributes likely to interfere with an offenders' ability to participate in certain programs.

Figure 1 *An Overview of Correctional Classification Approaches*

services, increase the likelihood that offenders will commit new offenses upon release.

HISTORY AND DEVELOPMENT OF "OBJECTIVE" CLASSIFICATION

Prior to the 1960s, correctional classification typically involved a clinical process, where decision makers based their determinations on professional judgment of an offender's dangerousness, treatment amenability, treatment needs, or his or her likelihood of absconding or escaping. Critics faulted this process as inequitable, subjective, and discretionary. More recently, classification has begun to use actuarial or objective assessment and testing procedures. Research finds that properly constructed and validated tests are far more accurate than professional judgment.

The common features of objective correctional classification systems are as follows:

1. They are usually administered systematically to all offenders in a correctional institution or program, usually at the point of intake and at regular intervals thereafter.

2. They result in a "typology" of offenders in an agency, where each "type" on the typology categorizes offenders according to similar needs or risk levels.

3. Some level of staff training is required to administer the system.

4. The classification process is governed by agency policy, which set forth uniform and efficient procedures, applying the same criteria to all offenders in an expeditious way.

There are four types of classification systems currently in use: (a) risk assessment systems, (b) needs assessment systems, (c) risk/needs assessments, and (d) systems for testing amenability to treatment. The latter falls under the notion of offender *responsivity* in which agencies are seeking to identify those individual attributes or learning styles that could affect an offenders' ability to participate in certain interventions, including those he or she might need.

As shown in Figure 1, each one of these three broad categories of classification system serves a different purpose. As a result, "What do you want the classification system to do?" is a question that needs to be answered prior to selecting or constructing classification systems (Hardyman, Austin, & Peyton, 2004). Keeping these functions clear helps to prevent misuse of a classification system. Unfortunately, agencies often use systems for the wrong purpose. For example, institutional systems typically do not predict new offenses in the community.

RISK ASSESSMENT

Risk assessments are designed to predict new offenses or prison misconduct. As early as the 1970s, the U.S. Parole Commission was employing the Salient Factor Score (SFS) to classify parolees into high, medium, and low levels of risk of reoffending, while institutions were developing models designed through the early National Institute of Corrections (NIC) Model Prisons to classify incarcerated offenders according to maximum, medium, and minimum custody.

The factors considered in the NIC institutional classification systems appear in Figure 2. A host of validation studies found such systems, including their later versions, to be predictive of institutional misconduct, particularly serious misconduct. Individual states have modified these systems somewhat, but the basic structure of the NIC model has stayed intact and is the most common system in institutional use.

This classification instrument is administered to all inmates upon admission and then readministered every six months to one year thereafter. Classification specialists score each item, add the scores, and consult guidelines to determine what custody level matches the score. It is noteworthy that the factors listed in Figure 2 are *static* factors—they do not change over time. Reclassification assessments attempt to correct for this. Items such as prison misconduct, time to serve, accomplishments in institutional treatment programs can reduce or increase one's custody assignment. Similarly, some systems change scores or weight on the static items for purposes of reclassification. With the item not count for as many points on the reclassification instrument as it does on the intake classification system, custody assignments can drop.

Institutional custody classification systems offer no recommendations for programming and correctional treatment. Similarly, they do not predict recidivism in the community. Therefore, it would not be entirely correct to assume that offenders classified at minimum custody are the best candidates for work release, early release, or furloughs. Instead, community risk assessment instruments are needed for this purpose.

At roughly the same time that the custody classification systems were appearing in institutions, the

Intake Classification System:	**Reclassification**
Past institutional violence	Past institutional violence
Severity current offense	Severity current offense
Severity prior convictions	Severity prior convictions
Escape history	Escape history
Prior felonies	Prior felonies
Stability (age, ed. employ.)	Stability (age, ed. employ.)
Time to release.	Prison misconduct
	Program/work performance
	Time to release.

Figure 2   *Factors Considered on Institutional Custody Classification Systems*

U.S. Parole Commission implemented the SFS. SFS items (shown in Figure 3) are entirely static, meaning that an offender scored as poor risk is unlikely to be reclassified as low risk at a later date. As with the NIC system, the SFS has little information to offer practitioners about treatment needs. Just the same, it has been revalidated and found to work with both men and women offenders.

- Prior convictions/adjudications
- Prior commitment(s) > 30 days
- Age at current offense
- Commitments during past 3 years
- Correctional escape
- Heroin/opiate dependence

Figure 3   *The Salient Factor Score (Hoffman, 1994)*

Agencies using these two models find them useful in classifying offenders according to risk. They inform what is widely considered to be the most important function of corrections—community and institutional safety. Even without additional tools to inform treatment or responsivity considerations, these models, particularly the community risk models, have changed the face of correctional practice and made programs such as intensive probation, a host of intermediate sanctions, and alternatives to incarceration possible.

NEEDS ASSESSMENTS

Classifying offenders into separate institutional custody levels or community supervision levels on the basis of risk alone cannot determine what should be done for them in terms of treatment, facilitating adjustment to prison, or preventing problems while in prison. Needs assessment systems attempt to offer such treatment-relevant implications. In both community and institutional corrections, needs assessment instruments supplement risk assessment instruments. Most are not designed to inform custody or level of supervision.

Needs assessments serve a number of purposes including (a) systematic and objective identification of offender needs; (b) linking offenders to needed programs to promote behavioral change and prevent physical, psychological, or social deterioration (if incarcerated); (c) provide a tool for individualized case planning; and (d) allocate agency and programming resources. When used in institutional settings, needs assessments conform to what Levinson (1988) termed as "internal classification."

The needs that are most likely to be identified by these instruments include health, intellectual ability, mental health, education, employment, and drug and alcohol abuse. Like risk assessment models, needs assessments are designed to be administered at intake and at regular intervals throughout the correctional terms.

Usually, correctional case managers or counselors using this kind of classification system rate each need according to the extent to which, if any, the problem interferes with daily functioning. In response to the alcohol abuse item, for example, a case manager might be prompted to indicate where there is (a) no alcohol abuse; (b) occasional abuse, some disruption of functioning; or (c) frequent abuse, serious disruption, needs treatment. Understandably, some have faulted such items as requiring too much subjectivity and likely to lead to problems with the reliability of the instrument.

More acceptable approaches would more closely follow guidelines established by the American Correctional Association that emphasize the importance of providing objective criteria for each level of need, and informing determinations with the best available information (e.g., assessments, presentence investigations, medical reports, and psychological evaluations). More recently, agencies have begun to use established screens, especially for mental health, substance abuse, and education.

Needs assessments were never designed to be the final assessment of a serious problem such as substance abuse; instead, they are intended to triage offenders, identifying those who need more intensive assessments. For more detailed assessment, agencies tend to use established screens and assessments to supplant the less formal needs assessment instrument. Substance abuse, for example, may be assessed by instruments such as the Substance Abuse Subtle Screening Inventory (SASSI), Adult Substance Use Survey (ASUS), or Addiction Severity Index. Mental health screenings have used the Minnesota Multiphasic Personality Inventory-2 (MMPI-2), Symptom Checklist 90 (SCL90), or MCMI III to name just a few.

Another alternative that is discussed in unpublished agency documents (e.g., states of Texas and Colorado), rather than in the published media, involves the use of algorithms or scoring rules for combining an assessment with behavioral indicators of an offender need requiring treatment. The Colorado Department of Corrections, for example, developed scoring rules for combining results of the MCMI III with indicators pertaining to past hospitalization, medications, past treatment, and history of self-destructive behavior to indicate whether the offender is low, moderate, or high need for mental health services. Taking this a step further, the state of Texas links similar need categories to treatment/programming recommendations. The importance of guiding case managers to available services commensurate with assessment results should not be overlooked. Many assessments sit in files and do not get used.

RISK/NEEDS INSTRUMENTS

In a growing number of community correctional agencies, risk and needs assessments are being combined into a single instrument. Such classification models constitute what Bonta (1996) referred to as the third, and most recent, generation of correctional classification strategies. The most commonly used system of this nature is the Level of Service Inventory-Revised (LSI-R), a system developed in Canada during the late 1980s and 1990s. States and federal jurisdictions have developed alternatives to the LSI, but published accounts of their validation are scarce.

The classification items comprising the LSI-R scores are shown in Figure 4. Most of these items are dynamic, pertaining to offender needs that can change over time, especially when agencies successfully target and program for those needs. The LSI-R does not target all of the offender's needs that an agency may wish to address, however. For example, housing, child care, and self-esteem are not listed. In fact, any dynamic need included on the LSI-R is also a risk factor, or to use a term coined by the assessment's authors, a *criminogenic need* (Andrews, Bonta, & Hoge, 1990). Therefore, the LSI and other instruments like it are composed of both static current and prior offense variables and by dynamic needs that are also risk factors.

• Criminal history	• Leisure/recreation
• Education/employment	• Companions
• Financial	• Alcohol/drug
• Family/marital	• Emotional/personal
• Accommodations	• Criminal sentiments

Figure 4   *Level of Service Inventory-Revised (Andrews & Bonta, 1995)*

Given its dynamic features, the LSI-R scores can change over time; this is an important feature of this mode of classification technology. Agencies can administer the assessment at later points in time to determine whether an offender's participation in needed treatment programs resulted in a reduction in his or her overall risk score. At the same time, the most recent scores are the most valid predictors of future offending.

Studies of the LSI-R suggest that, for men, reduced scores result in lower rates of recidivism and increased scores result in higher rates. However, recent analysis of the validity of this measure for women has been more equivocal. The success of classification systems, may, in other words, be determined in part by gender.

As their title implies, risk/needs instruments serve two functions: They classify offenders into high-, medium-, and low-risk categories, and they identify the needs that are contributing to an offender's risk profile. These features make such classification models extremely useful to agencies providing treatment services designed to change offender behavior. From meta-analysis contributed to by the same authors (Andrews, Bonta, & Hoge, 1990; Andrews, Zinger, Hoge, Bonta, Gendreau, & Cullen, 1990) emerge two of several principles of effective intervention (treatment) that are highly relevant to the use of dynamic risk assessment instruments—the risk principle and the need principle.

First, the *risk principle* maintains that intensive and extensive services are more effective among high-risk offenders; low-risk offenders usually respond better when they receive either no interventions or minimal intervention. Research bears this out. Second, the *need principle* maintains that in order to reduce offender recidivism, programs must address offender characteristics (or needs) that are related to future offending. As noted earlier, these needs are called criminogenic. They include substance abuse, antisocial attitudes, and antisocial peers, to name a few. To distinguish criminogenic from noncriminogenic needs, noncriminogenic needs are not associated with criminal behavior. A program can and should treat a noncriminogenic need such as physical health, but it must be understood that such treatment is not likely to lead to a reduction in the offender's future offending.

RESPONSIVITY

During the 1970s and 1980s, a number of correctional psychologists worked to evaluate and develop psychological assessments to facilitate the notion of differential treatment. Grounded, as all classification research is, in the notion that offenders are not all alike, the assessments developed by these scholars classified offenders according to personality or conceptual/cognitive maturity. These and later studies found differential adjustments to prison and differential responses to specific types of correctional interventions.

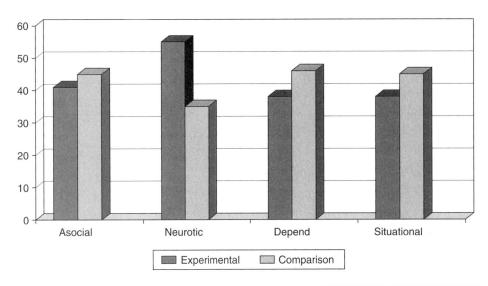

Figure 5   *Percentage Returning to Prison Following Cognitive Skills Programming by Specific Personality Types (Van Voorhis et al., 2002)*

One of the latest studies of psychologically informed differential treatment employed the Jesness Inventory (Jesness, 1996) to classify adult male parolees into the following four personality styles, which have roots in the earlier scholarship on differential treatment:

Asocial aggressive: Offenders with internalized antisocial values, beliefs, and attitudes. Crime is a lifestyle.

Neurotic: Highly anxious offenders, whose criminal behavior represents the acting-out of an internal crises. Crime for these offenders often has more of a personal meaning than an instrumental one. Dysfunctional, self-defeating coping responses play a role in getting these individuals into trouble.

Dependent: These offenders tend to be immature and easily led. They get into trouble through their own naïveté and in the course of being too easily led by other offenders.

Situational: These offenders have pro-social values, and less extensive criminal careers. They get into criminal behavior on a situational basis that they are unable to cope with or through substance abuse.

When these parolees were assigned to Ross and Fabiano's (1985) cognitive skills program (Reasoning and Rehabilitation), some types were clearly more successful than others. The treatment implications for findings such as these suggest that the cognitive skills program was most appropriate for asocial, immature, and situational offenders. Neurotic program participants, on the other hand, faired worse than members of the comparison group who did not participate in the program. They perhaps should be screened out of the program into a program more suitable to their needs. Such a practice would involve practitioners in doing exactly what the classification systems are designed to do—match offenders to programs they can benefit from. Alternatively, the program, itself, could be altered to better accommodate or work with neurotic personality attributes.

Today, differential treatment is encompassed in one of the principles of effective intervention, the *responsivity principle*. The responsivity principle maintains that programs should consider different learning styles, motivation levels, personality types, intellectual functioning, housing, child care and other considerations that are likely to become barriers to the success of some types of interventions. That is, even when an offender, even a high-risk offender, might need a specific type of program on the basis of having a related risk factor, he or she may still not be able to attend because of intellectual consideration, child care needs, or other responsivity-related characteristics. Assessing and screening them from inappropriate to more appropriate programming would increase their chances of success.

CONCLUSION: THE NEXT STEPS

At present, several concerns are receiving the attention of researches and practitioners alike. First, at both national and state levels, agencies have voiced concern for the validity of these systems among women offenders. In fact, a recent nationwide survey of state directors of classification revealed that 36 states still had not validated their custody classification systems on women offenders. Efforts to do so in seven states quickly revealed that existing systems either were invalid for women or overclassified them, thereby placing them in higher custody levels than warranted on the basis of their ultimate prison adjustment. Use of invalid classification systems, of course, is considered to be professionally unethical.

Second, the development of new assessments for specific types of offenders, such as psychopaths and sex offenders, and for specific criminogenic needs is resulting in numerous additional assessments to inform case management and supervision of these individuals. These include, for example the (a) Hare Psychopathy Checklist-Revised; (b) Sex Offender Need Assessment Rating (SONAR), (c) Static 99, (d) Spousal Assault Risk Assessment Guide (SARA), and (e) Criminal Sentiments Scale.

A final issue does not involve the assessment systems but rather the practitioners who use them. Particularly relevant to dynamic risk assessments and needs assessment, the systems are often not used to make case management decisions. The implementation of such systems, in many agencies, appears to have stopped at the point of administering the assessment. The next step, using the assessment results to guide program referrals is either not understood by case managers or is not possible due to insufficient program resources. Clearly, the next level of research and development would be to develop case management systems to use these models to their full potential.

—*Patricia Van Voorhis*

See also American Correctional Association; Community Corrections; Correctional Officers; Discipline System; Federal Prison System; Governance; Intermediate Sanctions; Managerialism; Maximum Security; Medical Model; Medium Security; Minimum Security; Prerelease Programs; Psychology Services; Security and Order; State Prison System; Supermax Prisons; Unit Management; Women's Prisons

Further Reading

American Association of Correctional Psychologists (Standards Committee). (2000). Standards for psychology services in jails, prison, correctional facilities and agencies. *Criminal Justice and Behavior, 27,* 433–493.

Andrews, D., & Bonta, J. (1995). *The Level of Service Inventory-Revised (LSI-R)*. North Tonawanda, NY: MultiHealth Systems.

Andrews, D., & Bonta, J. (2003). *The psychology of criminal conduct* (3rd ed.). Cincinnati, OH: Anderson.

Andrews, D., Bonta, J., & Hoge, R. (1990). Classification for effective rehabilitation: Rediscovering psychology. *Criminal Justice and Behavior, 17,* 19–52.

Andrews, D., Zinger, I., Hoge, R., Bonta, J., Gendreau, P., & Cullen, F. (1990). Does correctional treatment work? A psychologically informed meta-analysis. *Criminology, 28,* 369–404.

Bonta, J. (1996). Risk, needs assessment, and treatment. In A. Harland (Ed.), *Choosing correctional options that work: Defining the demand and evaluation the supply* (pp. 18–32). Thousand Oaks, CA: Sage.

Butcher, J., Dahlstrom, W., Graham, W., Tellegen, A., & Kaemmer, B. (1989). *Manual for the restandardized Minnesota Multiphasic Personality Inventory: MMPI-2. An interpretive and administrative guide.* Minneapolis: University of Minnesota Press.

Clements, C. (1986). *Offender needs assessment.* College Park, MD: American Correctional Association.

Feeley, M., & Simon, J. (1992). The new penology: Notes on the emerging strategy of corrections and its implications. *Criminology, 30,* 449–474.

Hanson, R., & Harris, A. (2000). *The Sex Offender-Need Assessment Rating (SONAR): A method for measuring change in risk levels* (User Report No. 2000-01). Ottawa, ON: Solicitor General Canada.

Hanson, R., & Thornton, D. (1999). *Static 99: Improving actuarial risk assessments for sex offenders* (User Report No. 1999-02). Ottawa, ON: Solicitor General Canada.

Hare, R. (2004). *Hare Psychopathy Checklist-Revisited* (2nd ed.). North Tonawanda, NY: MultiHealth Systems.

Hardyman, P., Austin, J., & Peyton, J. (2004). *Prisoner intake systems: Assessing needs and classifying prisoners.* Washington, DC: National Institute of Corrections.

Hardyman, P., & Van Voorhis, P. (2004). *Developing gender-specific classification systems for women offenders.* Washington, DC: National Institute of Corrections.

Hoffman, P. (1983). Screening for risk: A revised Salient Factor Score (SFS-81). *Journal of Criminal Justice, 11,* 539–547.

Hoffman, P. (1994). Twenty years of operational use of a risk prediction instrument: The United States Parole Commission's Salient Factor Score. *Journal of Criminal Justice, 22,* 477–494.

Jesness, K. (1974). *Classifying juvenile offenders: The Sequential I-Level Classification Manual.* Palo Alto, CA: Consulting Psychologists Press.

Jesness, K. (1996). *The Jesness Inventory manual.* North Tonawanda, NY: MultiHealth Systems.

Knopp, P., Hart, S., Webster, C., & Derek Eaves, M. (1997). *Spousal Assault Risk Assessment Guide (SARA).* North Tonawanda, NY: MultiHealth Systems.

Levinson, R. (1988). Developments in the classification process. *Criminal Justice and Behavior, 15,* 24–38.

MacKenzie, D. (1989). Prison classification: The management and psychological implications. In L. Goodstein & D. MacKenzie (Eds.), *The American prison: Issues in research and policy* (pp. 163–189). New York: Plenum.

Megargee, E., & Bohn, M. (1979). *Classifying criminal offenders: A new system based on the MMPI.* Beverly Hills, CA: Sage.

Megargee, E., Carbonell, J., Bohn, M., & Sliger, G. (2001). *Classifying criminal offenders with the MMPI-2.* Minneapolis: University of Minnesota Press.

Miller, G. (1985). *The Substance Abuse Subtle Screening Inventory manual.* Bloomington, IN: SASSI Institute.

Millon, T. (1998). *Millon Clinical Multiaxial Inventory III (MCMI-III) corrections report.* Minnetonka, MN: NCS.

National Institute of Corrections. (1982). *Classification, principles, models, and guidelines.* Washington, DC: Author.

Palmer, T. (1978). *Correctional intervention and research.* Lexington, MA: D. C. Heath.

Palmer, T. (2002). *Individualized intervention with young multiple offenders: The California Community Treatment Project.* Hampton, CT: Garland.

Quay, H. (1984). *Managing adult inmates: Classification for housing and program assignments.* College Park, MD: American Correctional Association.

Quay, H., & Parsons, R. (1972). *The differential behavioral classification of the juvenile offender.* Washington, DC: U.S. Department of Justice.

Ross, R., & Fabiano, E. (1985). *Time to think: A cognitive model of delinquency prevention and offender rehabilitation.* Ottawa, ON: Air Training and Publications.

Van Voorhis, P. (1994). *Psychological classification of the adult, male prison inmate.* Albany: State University of New York Press.

Van Voorhis, P. (2000). An overview of offender classification systems. In P. Van Voorhis, M. Braswell, & D. Lester (Eds.), *Correctional counseling & rehabilitation* (2nd ed.). Cincinnati, OH: Anderson.

Van Voorhis, P., & Brown, K. (1996). *Risk classification in the 1990s.* Washington, DC: National Institute of Corrections.

Van Voorhis, P., & Presser, L. (2001). *Classification of women offenders: A national assessment of current practices.* Washington, DC: National Institute of Corrections.

Van Voorhis, P., Spruance, L., Listwan, S., Ritchey, P., Pealer, J., & Seabrook, R. (2001). *The Georgia Cognitive Skills Experiment outcome evaluation: Phase I.* Cincinnati: University of Cincinnati.

Wanberg, K., & Milkman, H. (1998). *Criminal conduct and substance abuse treatment.* Thousand Oaks, CA: Sage.

⬛ CLEMENCY

Clemency is a broad term for intervention that reduces the punishment for a crime. Also called *executive clemency,* because it normally results from the decision by the executive officer of a state (the governor) or the federal system (the president), it includes pardons, reprieves, and commutations. Clemency is considered essential to the criminal justice system, because in theory, if not always in practice, it serves as an executive check to balance perceived injustices in sentencing.

The power of the sovereign to forgive crimes dates at least from the time of Solon in seventh-century Athens. It was a mainstay of English common law and was used variously to show mercy as well as to provide incentive to privateers and other criminals to join battles on behalf of the crown. In the United States, Alexander Hamilton provided the rationale for the constitutional foundations in the *Federalist Papers:*

> [The president] is also to be authorized to grant "reprieves and pardons for offenses against the United States, *except in cases of impeachment.*" Humanity and good policy conspire to dictate, that the benign prerogative of pardoning should be as little as possible fettered or embarrassed. The criminal code of every country partakes so much of necessary severity, that without an easy access to exceptions in favor of unfortunate guilt, justice would wear a countenance too sanguinary and cruel. (Hamilton, 1788/1961, p. 447)

TYPES OF CLEMENCY

Because state and federal statutes vary, definitions of the forms of clemency also vary. In general, *commutation* refers to reducing the punishment for an offense. One common example is the reduction of the sentences of abused women who murdered their abusive partners, or the reduction in sentence of relatively minor drug offenders who received sentences disproportionate to their crime under harsh mandatory sentencing statutes.

A *pardon* nullifies an original sentence and can occur while an offender is incarcerated, or while on parole or probation. A pardon can also be issued after a full sentence has been completed, or even granted posthumously, as occurred when New York Governor George Pataki pardoned comedian Lenny Bruce. There are several types of pardons. An *absolute,* or *full pardon,* ends the punishment of an offender and fully restores the offender's civil rights. A *conditional pardon* requires an offender to meet a set of prespecified conditions that can include restitution, counseling, therapeutic programming, or other conditions. Like parole or probation, a conditional pardon can be revoked if the offender fails to comply with the specified conditions. A *partial pardon* absolves a limited range of the offenses. For example, the original conviction might be upheld, but the severity of the offense is mitigated by factors that lessen the severity of the original charges and that were not recognized during the original judicial proceedings.

Amnesty, also called a *general pardon,* is a blanket pardon of a class of offenders and can include persons who have not yet been convicted of a crime. Amnesty precludes future punishment for the offense. An example occurred when President Jimmy Carter, in one of his first acts of office in 1979, granted amnesty to young men who, during the Vietnam War era, failed to register for the draft or who sought refuge in another country to avoid military service. In the past decade, President Bill Clinton gave amnesty to qualified Central American aliens residing in the United States, and in 2004 President George W. Bush proposed a de facto limited amnesty program for unregistered immigrant workers.

Other than by a full pardon, clemency actions, unlike exoneration, usually do not clear the offender's record of the conviction, and the recipient generally still bears the legal stigma. However, governors or the president can *exonerate* an offender, which expunges the conviction and

Clemency

For federal prisoners, only the president has the power to grant clemency. It is a power the recent presidents exercise rarely. Indeed, ever since Ronald Reagan's term in the early 1980s, acts of clemency have become less frequent, where only a handful of federal prisoners receive any form of relief through this extraordinary act of the executive branch of government.

There are a few different types of clemency, including amnesty, pardons, and commutations of sentence. Prisoners who want clemency usually try for a commutation of sentence. Ordinarily, a prisoner must exhaust all other possibilities for relief before submitting a petition for clemency. Federal prisoners can request the clemency petition from their case managers, or directly from the U.S. Pardon Attorney, whose office is responsible for reviewing all such petitions.

I submitted a petition for clemency in 1993. I had then completed over five years in prison, during which time I had earned an undergraduate degree, maintained a clean disciplinary record, and contributed to programs inside and outside of prison walls. I solicited and received letters of support from leading penologists around the United States. I have worked hard to earn freedom, and the hopes of receiving a commutation of sentence sustained me through thousands of lonely prison nights, in a dark, dank prison cell. Two years after I submitted my petition, however, I received a form letter from my case manager informing me that my petition had been denied. Now I am in my 17th year of this sentence, and I contemplate the possibility of filing a second petition. The political climate today, however, feels much colder than in 1993, and I am less than sanguine about President Bush granting me relief. Regardless of what an individual does to redeem himself, today's kinder, gentler America wants its pound of flesh.

Michael Santos
Federal Prison Camp, Florence, Illinois

removes the blame for the offense. Exonerations most often occur following wrongful convictions and the presumed offender was found innocent (as opposed to "not guilty") of the offense.

Although a form of clemency, a *reprieve* generally does not reduce or alter a sentence, although this may eventually occur. Instead, it temporarily defers punishment. This most often occurs in capital cases usually for the purpose of allowing courts to reconsider the offender's appeal.

GRANTING CLEMENCY

Although courts may grant reprieves or commute sentences, this requires that offenders go through the legal process to appeal their case. Executive clemency, by contrast, occurs at the individual discretion of the president or a governor.

For federal crimes, Article II, Section 2, Clause 1 of the U.S. Constitution gives the president the irreversible power to grant pardons or commutations for federal offenses, except in the case of impeachment. The president cannot grant clemency to those convicted of crimes in a state court. However, presidential clemency power does extend to convicted offenders in Washington, D.C., federal territories, and the U.S. military.

A governor of a state in which a state offense has been committed may also issue clemency, but this power varies dramatically by state. Governors in 35 states have sole authority to make clemency decisions, but in five states, boards make clemency decisions and in the rest the authority is shared between the governor and an advisory board (Michigan Battered Women's Clemency Project [MBWCP], n.d.).

Both state and federal procedures require that those wishing to appeal for clemency undergo a formal application process. At the federal level, The Office of the Pardon Attorney in the Department of Justice provides forms and guidelines for eligibility and processing. After review, these are submitted to the president. State clemency requests are also reviewed by a board or similar committee, and then submitted to the governor.

Pardons, the most common form of clemency, are traditionally granted at the end of an executive's term of office or during the holidays in December. Although accurate figures are not maintained, most estimates indicate that about 2,000 pardons are granted to state offenders annually, a figure that most observers see as fairly stable over the past decade. At the federal level in the past century, however, the number of pardons and other forms of clemency has varied dramatically among the presidents, ranging from less than 5% of clemency requests granted under the first President Bush to about one-third granted by President William Howard Taft.

Until the end of the Civil War in 1865, presidential pardons were granted sparingly. Only three presidents, James Monroe (419), Andrew Jackson (386), and Abraham Lincoln (343) granted more than 300, and the majority of President Lincoln's pardons were given to Union soldiers. This changed dramatically after the Civil War and peaked in the mid-20th century with a "pardon explosion" by Presidents Calvin Coolidge (1,545), Herbert Hoover (1,385), Franklin D. Roosevelt (3,687), and Harry S. Truman (2,044). Although President Bill Clinton's pardons during his eight-year tenure in office were controversial, the number of pardons he issued, 456, was roughly the same as those granted during the terms of Presidents Gerald Ford in a bit over two years (409) and Ronald Reagan in eight (406). President Clinton pardoned about half of those granted by President Richard Nixon (956), who served barely six years in office. However, despite the explosion in the federal prison population, the number of annual clemency applications between 1953 and 1999 edged toward 1,000 only twice, suggesting that relatively few convicted felons are granted, let alone apply for, clemency (Jurist Legal Intelligence, 2004a, 2004b).

THE CONTROVERSY OF PARDONS

Although those receiving clemency cut across class and race divisions, there is a perception that clemency tends to be given to high-status offenders who are wealthy or politically connected. This perception occurred early in the history of clemency in the United States, when wealthy patrons were accused of granting clemency for political or monetary reasons. President Lincoln was alleged to have used pardons of Union soldiers to improve morale of Northern troops, and President Warren G. Harding was suspected of participating in "pardons for cash" schemes.

More recently, President Clinton was accused of pardoning of Marc Rich, who had fled the country, in return for contributions from Rich's wife. Gerald Ford was accused of politicking when he granted a postimpeachment pardon to former President Nixon, and the first President Bush was alleged to have pardoned six Iran-Contra defendants to avoid embarrassing revelations about high-level political involvement in trading "arms for hostages."

In addition, the governors or other high officials of some states have been accused of or charged with pardons for cash. Although not uncommon in the 19th century, the practice apparently has since declined. However, In the 1920s, Texas Governor Miriam A. Ferguson pardoned more than 2,000 offenders in her first term, with the price alleged as high as $5,000, and in 1923, Oklahoma Governor John Walton was removed from office for selling pardons. More recently, in 1979 Tennessee Governor Ray Blanton also was implicated in a pardon-selling scheme, although he was not indicted.

Governors have also been accused of using clemency for ideological or political motives. In 1986, outgoing Governor Toney Anaya commuted the sentences of New Mexico's five death row inmates, and Ohio changed its pardon statutes after departing Governor Richard F. Celeste pardoned 67 prisoners in 1991. Wisconsin Governor Tommy Thompson was accused of granting an unjustifiable pardon to the son of a close political colleague prior to leaving office in 2000. Perhaps the most controversial clemency action in recent decades was the blanket commutation of 167 death row inmates by Illinois Governor George Ryan in his final days in office, which the governor justified on the bases of the state's demonstrably flawed system of justice in capital cases.

CONCLUSION

Clemency has been widely criticized in recent years. Some citizen groups claim that it unfairly reduces prison sentences imposed on serious offenders and is unfair to victims. Other groups feel it should be granted more liberally, especially in cases where offenders killed an abusive partner, when an offender is old or terminally ill, or when other extenuating circumstances not recognized at trial mitigate the seriousness of the offense. The controversies arising from high-profile cases have eroded the public's confidence in the integrity of the system, and the continued concerns with crime and increased sentences increase the suspicion that clemency is "soft on crime." Yet clemency remains a final remedy for sentences that were originally unfair or for which punishment serves no further purpose. Despite the controversies, clemency gives hope to prisoners and helps reduce some of the injustices in the criminal justice system.

—*Jim Thomas*

See also Compassionate Release; Federal Prison System; Furlough; Pardon; Parole; Parole Board; State Prison System

Further Reading

Glaberson, W. (2001, February 16). States' pardons now looked at in starker light. *New York Times*. Retrieved from http://www.nytimes.com/2001/02/16/national/16STAT .html?ex=1080622800&en=776f3bf5c096c91b&ei=5070

Hamilton, A. (1999). No. 74. *The federalist papers*. New York: Mentor Books. (Original work published 1788)

Jurist Legal Intelligence. (2004a). Retrieved from http://jurist .law.pitt.edu/pardons5a.htm. Pittsburgh, PA: University of Pittsburgh School of Law.

Jurist Legal Intelligence. (2004b). Retrieved from http://jurist .law.pitt.edu/pardonsex9.htm. Pittsburgh, PA: University of Pittsburgh School of Law.

Michigan Battered Women's Clemency Project. (n.d.). *Clemency for battered women in Michigan: A manual for attorneys, law students and social workers*. Retrieved from http://www.umich.edu/~clemency/clemency_manual/ manual_chapter02.html. Ann Arbor, MI.

Texas Board of Pardons and Paroles. (2002). Retrieved from http://link.tsl.state.tx.us/tx/BPP/eclem.html#WHAT%20I S%20EXECUTIVE. Austin, TX.

U.S. Department of Justice. (2003). *Office of the Pardon Attorney*. Retrieved from http://www.usdoj.gov/pardon/

◾ CLEMMER, DONALD

Donald Clemmer was one of the first to study and document the psychological effects prison life can have on inmates. He is best known for *The Prison Community* published in 1940 in which he coined the word *prisonization* to explain how individuals adapt to incarceration. In this text, he also explored the relationship of individual inmates to prison groups. Clemmer's study was the result of a career that spanned more than 30 years working in prisons, and it became the foundation for further research on the social and psychological effects of prison.

WORKING IN CORRECTIONS

Clemmer served as the first director of the District of Columbia's Department of Corrections in 1946 until his untimely death on September 18, 1965. Before obtaining this position, Clemmer also worked more than 15 years in Illinois prisons, the federal penitentiary in Atlanta, and the Federal Bureau of Prisons.

During his time in the District of Columbia, Clemmer was always in search of new ways to rehabilitate inmates in the hope that they would not return to prison. Clemmer's philosophy was emphasized in the *Personnel Handbook* for the Department of Corrections in 1949, "That is, while custody and discipline may be regarded as of importance, so also is training of inmates wherever possible, as well as their proper feeding, clothing, and medical care" (Oakey, 1988, p. 173). Clemmer was also instrumental in increasing the number of psychologists and psychiatrists on the staff of the Department of Corrections and he served as a strong advocate for the treatment of addictions such as alcoholism. He was hailed as a humanitarian when he abolished the use of "the hole" or solitary confinement as a form of punishment. During Clemmer's reign, there were very few problems at his facilities, which many attribute to his humane treatment of the inmates and staff.

The Prison Community

The Prison Community was based on many years of research at the Illinois State Penitentiary. Its central idea, known as prisonization, is described by Clemmer as a process by which an individual will take on the traditions, moral attitudes, customs, and culture of the penitentiary population. According to Clemmer, prisonization occurs to all inmates, to varying degrees, immediately upon entering the prison doors and explains why individuals take on the language, dress, inferior position, and rules of prison life to survive. Whether individuals will completely assimilate to the prison culture occurs depends on many factors including their personality types, the length of the sentence to be served, their relationships with family and friends outside of prison life, and their desire to isolate themselves from prison groups.

According to Clemmer, inmates adapt to life in prison by relinquishing self-esteem and independence to the prison system. Prisoners are known by numbers rather than name, they give up their clothing for a prison uniform, and they assume a subordinate role to prison staff. Paradoxically, the essential qualities inmates surrender are necessary for their later successful reintegration into the community upon release. Consequently, the degree to which people assimilate to their life inside prison affects the chances the inmate has in being reintegrated into society upon release.

PRISONER GROUPS

In *The Prison Community*, Clemmer also addresses the relationship of inmates to primary and informal groups while incarcerated. Until this study, it was assumed that prisoners have strong alliances with various prison groups just like those in the free world. However, Clemmer claims that most inmates are either not intimately associated with a group or are only superficially affiliated with groups. A very small minority of inmates were found to associate with primary groups and those relationships were discovered not to develop in the same manner as primary groups outside of prison because they lack a fundamental unity. Clemmer explains that primary groups outside of prison develop based on the "warmth of person-to-person relationships" while inmate relationships are often based on the "convict code," which dictates not snitching on another inmate or participating in any acts that would assist the prison staff.

CONCLUSION

Clemmer's work contributed to penology by inspiring further research into ways of reducing the prisonization process and increasing the inmate's chances for reintegration into society. Other researchers have also used Clemmer's study as the basis for understanding prison culture as it relates to females inmates, prison gangs, prison race relations, and effective rehabilitation. Although its ideas are no longer accepted in their entirety, it remains a key text in prison studies.

—*Nicolle Parsons-Pollard*

See also Deprivation; Rose Giallombardo; Importation; John Irwin; Prison Culture; Prisonization; Gresham Sykes; Visits

Further Reading

Clemmer, D. (1940). *The prison community*. New York: Holt, Rinehart & Winston.

Cohen, S., & Taylor, L. (1972). *Psychological survival: The experience of long-term imprisonment*. New York: Pantheon.

Cordilia, A. (1983). *The making of an inmate: Prison as a way of life*. Cambridge, MA: Schenkman.

Cressey, D. R. (Ed.). (1961). *The prison: Studies in institutional organization and change*. New York: Holt, Rinehart & Winston.

Goffman, E. (1961). *Asylums: Essays on the social situation of mental patients and other inmates*. Garden City, NY: Doubleday.

Irwin, J. (1970). *The felon*. Englewood Cliffs, NJ: Prentice Hall.

Jacobs, J. B. (1977). *Stateville: The penitentiary in mass society*. Chicago: University of Chicago Press.

Mathieson, T. (1990). *Prison on trial: A critical assessment*. London: Sage.

Oakey, M. H. (1988). *Journey from the gallows: Historical evolution of the penal philosophies and practices in the nation's capital*. Lanham, MD: University Press of America.

Sykes, G. M. (1958). *The society of captives: A study of a maximum security prison*. Princeton, NJ: Princeton University Press.

CO-CORRECTIONAL FACILITIES

Co-correctional facilities house women and men in the same institution under the direction of one administration. Some allow a significant amount of interaction between the sexes, while others have no direct interaction between female and male inmates at all. These prisons are also sometimes referred to as coed institutions.

When the first prisons were established in the United States, the small number of women offenders were housed with the men. By late in the 19th century, however, all prisons had been desegregated by gender. Co-correctional prisons resurfaced as a correctional strategy 30 years ago to serve as an innovative method for better program delivery to prisoners. It was also hoped that they would be cost-effective since they could use vacant sleeping and living quarters in women's prisons.

HISTORY

The first prisons in the United States incarcerated women and men, and adults and children together. This mixed-gender, mixed-age setting was not always the most conducive environment for the prisoners, particularly for women and children since rape and other acts of intimidation and violence occurred regularly in them. As a result, reformers began to advocate for gender segregation during the 19th century. In 1873, the first women's prison opened in Indiana. Women-centered facilities such as Indiana Women's Prison provided job opportunities for professional women, who served in positions as matrons, administrators, and other prison staff. These female workers were expected to act as positive role models for the inmates.

Almost one century later in 1971, a co-correctional facility was opened in Forth Worth, Texas, for adults sentenced to the federal prison system. During the 1970s, five federal co-correctional facilities opened, and by 1977 fifteen state co-correctional prisons had been established. Through the 1980s and 1990s, many more co-correctional facilities were set up. According to the American Correctional Association's 2002 *Directory of Adult and Juvenile Correctional Departments, Institutions, Agencies, and Probation and Parole Authorities,* 54 adult and 38 juvenile state co-correctional facilities were in operation in the United States during 2001. Eighteen of these are part of the federal prison system.

The level of interaction between female and male inmates varies among co-correctional facilities. In many, there is virtually no direct contact between the sexes, while others have contact at all times except during sleeping hours.

CURRENT PRACTICE

In the modern era, co-correctional facilities do not have the same problems of the sexually integrated prisons over a century ago. Instead, prisoners enjoy an environment that is more comparable to that of society outside the prison than is evident in same-sex institutions. Being able to interact with members of the opposite gender on a daily basis is thought to reduce disruptive and predatory homosexual activity, lessen violence between prisoners, and promote a better self-image of the inmates.

Co-correctional institutions generally try to facilitate cross-gender relationships, to assist with rehabilitation and effective reintegration into the community outside prison for offenders. Supporters of this approach to prison management claim that these facilities improve access to programs for all offenders, particularly women, who often receive less educational and vocational training than men.

As they did in the beginning, co-correctional facilities enable administrators to redistribute prisoners into systems with more space. Thus, some prison administrations deal with the increased numbers of women by using available space in men's prisons, while others transfer men into low-capacity women's prisons to relieve some of the overcrowding among the men's institutions. The Federal Bureau of Prisons also sometimes uses these facilities to house prisoners at risk of victimization in other institutions, including former police officers and judges, and "blatant" homosexual persons.

Last, the programs may enable women prisoners to be in more geographically desirable locations, closer to their places of origin. Because there are few women prisoners, many states have only one or two prisons exclusively for them. Co-correctional facilities provide women with greater opportunities to be near their children and other family members.

SOME PROBLEMS WITH CO-CORRECTIONAL FACILITIES

Even though supporters of coed prisons believe that women would be afforded more opportunities by being housed with male inmates, co-correctional programs have also been criticized for relegating the small numbers of women within them to a subordinate position. For example, the availability of recreational, vocational, medical, and educational programs for women in co-correctional facilities is often deficient because most correctional institutions are designed for men, not women. When women are introduced into a prison that had housed only men, adjustments have to be made to address their needs. Women cannot merely be added to a male prison environment without appropriate adjustments in the delivery of services. When co-correctional programming has been found to be in keeping with the needs of women offenders, male inmates who dictate the level of participation by women in these programs may hinder female inmates' involvement in the services offered by the prison administration. Similarly, some women find it traumatic to live in an environment with men because of their tendency to have histories of sexual and other abuse.

Another concern of opponents to the co-correctional model is the way in which coed facilities perpetuate traditional gender roles. This problem can be seen in the manner in which labor assignments are distributed. Evidence suggests that women tend to perform domestic work such as cleaning the living areas, while men are more likely to be assigned to landscaping duties outdoors. Similarly, female prison staff members have been shown to have fewer opportunities for advancement in co-correctional facilities as in women's prisons, due also to the male-dominated field of corrections.

As a result of a male inmate-dominated co-correctional prison environment, women inmates may be less likely to take on leadership roles. As it is, critics argue that women prisoners tend to concentrate on relationships and caretaking of others, as opposed to focusing on their personal improvement. By integrating men into the milieu, women will continue to employ this characteristic and cater to the male inmates' needs, putting their own needs second.

Women and men adjust to and serve their time in prison differently. Interaction among men in prison tends to be more aggressive and violent than that of women. Therefore, combining women and men in one institution may bring about coercion and exploitation that women would not have suffered in a single-sex institution. Women in integrated settings are more likely to be disciplined for prison code violations. Also, men tend to have more freedom to move around the facility than women.

Though some believed that homosexual activity would decrease when a prison is gender integrated, there is little evidence to support this view. Prison administrators and staff have been criticized for the enforcement of homophobic and sexist policies and procedures in co-correctional facilities. Though homosexual behavior is forbidden, just as in same-sex facilities, some heterosexual behavior, such as hand holding, is often allowed in co-correctional prisons. Furthermore, when heterosexual sex is punished by corrections officials, women are more likely to be disciplined, even in cases where the male inmate has been identified.

In same-sex facilities, inmates sometimes demand that another person provide sexual services to other inmates who are willing to pay for it. Such prostitution also occurs in sex-integrated facilities with women serving as the sex workers, and men acting as "pimps." Not only does this interaction among the inmates promote the transmission of sexually transmitted diseases, it may result in pregnancies. Given the high numbers of women who have experienced sexual abuse prior to incarceration, such activity in prison may revictimize already damaged individuals.

CONCLUSION

The efforts of co-corrections supporters to make prison resemble the society outside the prison walls have positive and negative effects. The gender roles played out by prisoners tend to correspond with those traditionally established roles in U.S. society, where males portray patriarchal characteristics. Unfortunately, these interactions may also demonstrate the dysfunctional relationships experienced by the female and male prisoners prior to their incarceration, causing disruption in institutional functions. This distraction in programming may interfere with the successful integration of inmates back into general society, as opposed to the expected outcome of better use of resources, more programming for women, and improved rehabilitation methods.

—*Hillary Potter*

See also Federal Prison System; History of Women's Prisons; Homosexual Relationships; Lesbian Relationships Rape; Sex—Consensual; "Stop Prisoner Rape"; Women's Prisons

Further Reading

Anderson, D. C. (1978). Co-corrections. *Corrections Magazine, 4*(3), 32–41.

Davis, J. R. (1998). Co-corrections in the U.S.: Housing men and women together has advantages and disadvantages. *Corrections Compendium, 23*(3), 1–3.

Massachusetts Correction Department. (1975). *A study of a co-educational correctional facility.* Boston: Author.

Rafter, N. H. (1992, Spring). Equality or difference? *Federal Prisons Journal, 3*.

SchWeber, C. (1984). Beauty marks and blemishes: The coed prison as a microcosm of integrated society. *The Prison Journal, 64*(1), 3–14.

Smykla, J. O. (1980). *Co-ed prison.* New York: Human Services Press.

Smykla, J. O., & Williams, J. J. (1996). Co-corrections in the United States of America, 1970–1990: Two decades of disadvantages for women prisoners. *Women and Criminal Justice, 8*(1), 61–76.

◪ COLLEGE COURSES IN PRISON

Research indicates that prison college programs are among the best tools for reducing recidivism. Individuals who take college courses while in prison improve their chances of attaining and keeping employment after release. They are less likely to commit additional crimes that would lead to their return to prison. The effectiveness of these programs led to their widespread adoption for several years. However, nearly all programs were discontinued during the 1990s and few college programs are currently available in prison settings. The history of these programs, and the debate about their merits, demonstrates the counterproductive effect that political influence can have on efforts to combat crime.

HISTORY

The University of Southern Illinois began the nation's first prison-based college program in 1953. Other programs followed, but since the development of these programs was dependent on limited funding, only 12 postsecondary correctional education programs existed by 1965. The funding situation changed significantly that year as the U.S. Congress passed Title IV of the Higher Education Act. This act gave inmates and other low-income students the right to apply for federal financial aid in the form of federal Pell grants to be used for college courses.

Title IV provided the funding that was needed to ensure the financial stability of corrections education programs. As a result, by 1973, 182 college programs were operating in U.S. prisons. By 1982 (which was the last year an official count was made), 350 programs were active in 45 states and approximately 27,000 inmates received some form of postsecondary education. Although the numbers had increased significantly, this represented just 9% of the total prison population at the time.

Prisoners applied for Pell grants under the same criteria as those outside prison. Pell grants are noncompetitive, need-based federal funds that are available to all qualifying low-income individuals who plan to enroll in college degree programs. For qualifying individuals in correctional facilities, the average Pell grant award was less than $1,300 per year. The total percentage of the program's annual budget that was spent on inmate higher education was 1/10 of 1%. Although the cost was relatively low, the idea of providing Pell grants to prisoners remained controversial and many argued for the elimination of these grants.

The beginning of the end for college programs in prison was in 1991, as Republican Senator Jesse Helms of North Carolina introduced an amendment to eliminate federal funds for education to inmates. Several members of the U.S. House of Representatives introduced similar amendments. Like Helms, they claimed that federal money was being spent at the expense of "law-abiding" students who were enrolled in college outside of prison. Although these amendments failed, this argument would return the next year with the passage of the Higher Education Reauthorization Act, which determined that Pell grants for prisoners could be used only for tuition and fees. The 1992 bill also made those on death row, or serving life without parole, ineligible for Pell grants seeming to acknowledge the importance of education for those who would eventually be released from prison.

Despite evidence supporting the connection between higher education and lowered recidivism, the U.S. Congress included a provision in the Violent Crime Control and Law Enforcement Act of 1994 that eliminated Pell grants for prisoners. This law had a devastating effect on prison education programs. In 1990, there were 350 higher education programs for inmates. By 1997 only 8 programs remained. Ironically, at the same time as the federal government abolished Pell grants for prisoners, many states were undergoing a dollar-for-dollar tradeoff between corrections and education spending. New York State, for example, steadily increased its Department of Corrections budget by 76% to $761 million. During the same period, the state decreased funding to university systems by 28%, to $615 million. Much of the increase in corrections spending was the result of longer prison terms and the need for increased prison construction.

In the 1993–1994 school year, more than 25,000 students in correctional facilities were recipients of Pell grants. Although these grants were not the only source of revenue for these programs, they provided a predictable flow of money that enabled the continued functioning of classes. Since there were no replacement funds, programs were forced to abandon efforts to provide college courses in prison.

BENEFITS OF CORRECTIONS EDUCATION

In 2002, there were more than 1.4 million prisoners in federal and state facilities. That same year, more than 600,000 inmates were released, either unconditionally or under conditions of parole. Many of those released will be rearrested and will return to prison. Costs of this cycle of incarceration and reincarceration are very high. Many studies suggest that corrections education has the potential to greatly reduce these costs. For example, a 1987 Bureau of Prisons report found that the more education inmates received, the lower their rate of recidivism. Those who earned college degrees were the least likely to reenter prison. For inmates who had some high school, the rate of recidivism was 54.6%. For college graduates, the rate dropped to 5.4%. Similarly, a Texas Department of Criminal Justice study found that while the state's overall rate of recidivism was 60%, for holders of college associate degrees it was 13.7%. The recidivism rate for those with bachelor's degrees was 5.6%. The rate for those with master's degrees was 0%.

Even small reductions in recidivism can save millions of dollars in costs associated with keeping the recidivist offender in prison for longer periods of time. Additional costs are apparent when we consider that the individual, had he or she not committed another crime, would be working, paying taxes, and making a positive contribution to the economy. When we add the reduction of costs, both financial and emotional, to victims of crime, the benefits are even greater. Finally, the justice system as a whole, including police and courts, can save a great deal of money when the crime rate is reduced.

The Changing Minds study (Fine et al., 2001), which was conducted at Bedford Hills Correctional Facility, New York's only maximum-security prison for women, was the first major study to examine the impact of college in prison since Pell grants were eliminated. As other research had shown before, Changing Minds demonstrated that college prison programs transform lives, reduce recidivism, create safer prisons and communities, and significantly reduce the need for tax dollars spent on prisons. Only 7.7% of the inmates who took college courses at Bedford Hills returned to prison after release, while 29.9% of the inmates who did not participate in the college program were reincarcerated. The authors calculated that this reduction in reincarceration would save approximately $900,000 per 100 student prisoners over a two-year period. If we project these savings to the 600,000 prison releases in a single year, the savings are enormous.

The success demonstrated in the Bedford Hills study has led to the creation of the Center for Redirection Through Education. This organization continues to work to develop college programs in prisons throughout New York State. Other states are also working to develop postsecondary education programs but they continue to face funding problems.

In most cases, options are limited to single courses with no expectation of earning a full degree.

CHALLENGES

Students in prison education programs evidence a wide range of potential and have had varying educational experiences. Inmates who choose to enroll in college courses are not necessarily any different from the typical university student. As in any college-level course, the range of abilities can include very gifted students, students who face challenges, and students who have various motives for enrolling in college courses.

The educator's challenge is compounded by the uniqueness of prison culture and the need for security. Prisons adhere to strict routines and provide a controlled environment for education classes. These routines may not be ideal for teaching or learning. College programs may also adhere to schedules that conflict with the requirements of correctional institutions. Another issue is that inmates are often moved from one facility to another with little or no notice. This movement interrupts, or ends, the individual's educational programming. Along with structural issues related to security, social factors may further limit learning opportunities. For example, prison culture can vary from one facility to another, or even in different parts of a single facility. The support and expectations of fellow prisoners can be an important determinant of prison culture. Prison administrators may also have varying degrees of support for education—especially if they see education as a threat to the primary functions of security and control. If the culture of the facility is not supportive of the individual's educational goals, and willing to work toward integrating education into the dominant goal of creating a safe and secure facility, it may be difficult for individuals to reach their goals.

CONCLUSION

Most studies indicate that an individual who takes college classes while in prison is less likely to return to prison than someone who has not received the same educational opportunities. There is some question as to why these courses lower recidivism. Many of the benefits of a college education are hard to measure. As such, it may be difficult to show a clear relationship between educational opportunity and recidivism. However, an intervening factor, the ability to find and hold a job, appears to relate to college courses in prison since college education increases the likelihood of postrelease employment, which, in turn, reduces the chance of recidivism.

The vast majority of incarcerated individuals will eventually be released. The growth in the incarcerated population over the past 20 years has created unprecedented release rates since there are just so many people in prison. Due to strict sentencing guidelines, these women and men have often served long terms and are released only when their terms have been completely served. Many are released unconditionally, without parole or other postrelease supervision. Each of these individuals will be expected to begin leading a productive, law-abiding life outside prison walls. Access to a quality education can increase their chance of success.

—Kenneth Mentor

See also Adult Continuing Education; Education; General Educational Development (GED) Exam and General Equivalency Diploma; Recidivism; Rehabilitation Theory; Violent Crime Control and Law Enforcement Act 1994

Further Reading

Batiuk, M., Moke, P., & Rounree, P. (1997). Crime and rehabilitation: Correctional education as an agent of change— A research note. *Justice Quarterly, 14*(1).

Bureau of Justice Statistics. (2002). *Key crime and justice facts at a glance.* Retrieved from http://www.ojp.usdoj.gov/bjs/glance.htm

Currie, E. (1985). *Confronting crime: An American challenge.* New York: Pantheon.

Fine, M., Torre, M. E., Boudin, K., Bowen, I., Clark, J., Hylton, D., Martinez, M., Roberts, R. A., Smart, P., & Upegui, D. (2001). *Changing minds: The impact of college in a maximum security prison.* New York: Graduate Center of the City University of New York. Retrieved from http://www.changingminds.ws/

Gerber, J., & Fritsch, E. (1993). *Prison education and offender behavior: A review of the scientific literature.* Huntsville: Texas Department of Criminal Justice, Institutional Division.

Greenwood, P. W., Model, K. E., Rydell, C. P., & Chiesa, J. (1996). *Diverting children from a life of crime: Measuring costs and benefits.* Santa Monica, CA: RAND.

Haigler, K. O., Harlow, C., O'Connor, P., & Campbell, A. (1994). *Literacy behind prison walls.* Washington, DC: National Center for Education Statistics.

Harer, M. (1995). *Prison education program participation and recidivism: A test of the normalization hypothesis.* Washington, DC: Federal Bureau of Prisons.

LoBuglio, S. (2001). Time to reframe politics and practices in correctional education. In J. Comings, B. Garner, & C. Smith (Eds.), *Annual review of adult learning and literacy* (Vol. 2). San Francisco: Jossey-Bass.

Steurer, S., Smith, L., & Tracy, A. (2001). *Three State Recidivism Study.* Prepared for the Office of Correctional Education, U.S. Department of Education. Lanham, MD: Correctional Education Association.

Stevens, D., & Ward, C. (1997). College education and recidivism: Educating criminals meritorious. *Journal of Correctional Education, 48*(3).

Taylor, J. M. (1992). Post secondary correctional education: An evaluation of effectiveness and efficiency. *Journal of Correctional Education, 43*(3).

Taylor, J. M. (1993, January 25). Pell grants for prisoners. *The Nation.*

Tolbert, M. (2002). *State correctional education programs.* Washington, DC: National Institute for Literacy. Retrieved from http://www.nifl.gov/nifl/policy/st_correction_02.pdf

U.S. Department of Education, Office of Correctional Education. (1994). The impact of correctional education on recidivism 1988–1994. Washington, DC: U.S. Department of Education.

U.S. Department of Education, Office of Correctional Education. (1995). *Pell grants and the incarcerated.* Washington, DC: U.S. Department of Education.

Worth, R. (1995, November). A model prison. *Atlantic Monthly.*

◪ COMMISSARY

Prison commissaries help ease some of the deprivations of imprisonment, by allowing inmates with sufficient funds to buy products from a fairly broad range of items. They stock food and other goods. Items include shoes, radios, food, stamps, photocopy and phone credits, and, in some institutions, over-the-counter medication such as Tylenol, ibuprofen, and allergy medicine. Prison commissaries vary in their prices, variety, and accessibility, although some attempt is usually made to ensure consistency between establishments in the same correctional system. In most prisons, individuals may visit the commissary only once a week, although in jails those awaiting trial may be able to make purchases more frequently. Housing units within a facility usually visit the store at different times to minimize contact and conflict between different inmates. Although, increasingly, commissaries are being privatized, profits from commissary purchases often go back into an inmate fund for such items as cable television, leisure time activity equipment, and other resources for the general population. Thus, the benefits of prison commissaries may be felt by more than just those individuals who buy products from them.

Commissary

The commissary is where prisoners can buy all types of stuff—sneakers, sweatsuits, radios, junk food, toiletries, stationery supplies, batteries, and anything else that is allowed in prison, which isn't much. Unlike shopping on the street, there is little selection. For example, in here there is one brand of peanut butter, and if you don't like that brand then too bad. In prison you don't have any choice and that's how the administration wants it. Different compounds have different things on the commissary but they are all pretty much the same.

At most federal institutions you have a limit on how much you can spend. It is usually $275.00 a month and is referred to as your spending limit. As soon as you spend it you can't spend any more until you revalidate on the first of the next month. You can also put money on your inmate ID card, which can be used for the laundry machines, photocopiers, vending machines, or to buy photo tickets that can be used on special days in recreation to get your picture taken. The commissary sells stamps but you are limited to buying only three books at a time (sixty stamps).

At most prisons there are also thriving underground economies for obtaining services and goods unavailable at the commissary. With certain goods like mackerels, cigarettes, or stamps, you can buy services such as laundry, ironing, or room cleaning, or buy drugs or foods smuggled out of the chow hall like green peppers or onions. You can also buy hooch, prison alcohol that others make from juice and sugar they buy at the commissary. Also, if you have to pay off a gambling debt you can tell the person to give you a list and you will buy it at the commissary.

Seth Ferranti
FCI Fairton, Fairton, New Jersey

HISTORY

In the first gaols and workhouses of the 17th and 18th centuries, inmates had to provide their own food, clothing, and equipment. Either friends or family members would bring them in such items, often providing meals on a daily basis, or else they would have to procure them by other means. The warden or gaoler often supplemented his income by running errands to buy items for those who were incarcerated, or by employing his wife to cook their meals.

Unlike these earlier institutions, penitentiaries began to provide all the food, clothing, and basic items of clothing and the like that inmates would need during their period of confinement. No additional items were allowed. It was not until the 20th century that penal institutions returned to the practice of allowing inmates to supplement their food and possessions. This time, however, rather than running errands in the community, they set up a store within the prison itself: the commissary.

HOW DO COMMISSARIES WORK?

To buy items at the commissary, an individual must have a commissary account. This account is usually established when an individual first arrives in prison. In most institutions, friends and family members may send in postal orders to deposit funds in an inmate's commissary account. Likewise, inmates may deposit any wages earned from prison labor in the account. Most systems no longer allow prisoners cash during their sentence. No matter how much money an individual has in his or her commissary account, prisons usually limit the amount of money someone may spend at the commissary each month. Jails may be more flexible, since people who have not yet been convicted retain more privileges than those who have been.

In the federal prison system, individuals may spend between $150 to $300 at the commissary per month, depending on where they are held. The current most common amount that a prisoner may spend is $175. Certain items, like stamps, are not included in this sum. During the holidays in December, most institutions expand the sum inmates may spend. Unspent monies may not be carried over to the next month.

POSITIVE AND NEGATIVE ASPECTS OF COMMISSARIES

Commissaries play an important role in most penal establishments, by providing additional items that inmates may need or desire. Though everyone will be given the bare necessities, government-issue products such as shampoo, toothpaste, and toilet paper are not always to everyone's liking. Commissaries usually offer alternatives that may be the regular brands that prisoners used prior to incarceration.

Being able to choose items, however mundane, enables some prisoners to cope with the monotony and restrictions of prison life. Items in most commissaries, however, cost at least the same as they would outside, and, in some cases, more. This can be difficult for most people to afford, unless they have additional monies sent in, because prison wages are extremely low. In addition, commissaries may not stock ethnically specific items, such as hair products for African Americans, or foreign language magazines for non-English speakers. In some states, prisoners have filed suits, mostly unsuccessfully, to challenge both the prices and the items available in the prison store.

Like many other aspects of contemporary prisons, commissaries are increasingly being leased to private companies. These companies, such as Covenco, Inc. in Pennsylvania, which contract with state and federal departments of corrections, endeavor to make a profit. Thus, the range of items they make available, and the prices they ask for them, will often reflect their own desires, rather than those of the prisoners. These same companies also usually offer similar services outside of prison, operating vending machines in schools, or providing food to hotels and other businesses.

Finally, commissaries play a role in the maintenance of order and discipline in penal institutions, in a number of ways. First, some of the items for sale in prison stores such as canned fruit or fruit juice can be used by skilled prisoners to make hooch or prison alcohol. Any product, in fact, could be used for trade between inmates, and thus may become contraband. Although everyone is entitled to spend the same amount per month, not everyone will have access to the funds to do so. In this case, the commissary can lead to conflict and competition between individuals. Also, inmates commonly prey on others for their items, particularly newly arrived prisoners. Sometimes gang members must "donate" their commissary goods to a reserve pool for others who cannot afford to buy what they need. Finally, in recognition of the emphasis most individuals place on their ability to shop at the commissary, the right to buy items from a prison or jail commissary can be taken away as a disciplinary measure, for minor infractions.

CONCLUSION

Commissaries play an important and complex role in most penal institutions. Though items are often overpriced and may not always be precisely what individuals are looking for, being able to buy things, however small, is prized by most inmates as a means of retaining some autonomy in a restrictive environment. Many of the items for sale in the prison store help people maintain contact with the outside, such as cards and stamps. Other goods such as books, magazines or foodstuffs can be used to help provide a little variety in their everyday life behind bars.

—Mary Bosworth

See also Contraband; Deprivation; Federal Prison System; Food; Hooch; Prison Culture

Further Reading

Bosworth, M. (2002). *The U.S. federal prison system.* Thousand Oaks, CA: Sage.

Burton-Rose, D., Pens, D., & Wright, P. (Eds.). (1998). *The celling of America: An inside look at the U.S. prison industry.* Monroe, ME: Common Courage.

Santos, M. (2004). *About prison.* Belmont, CA: Wadsworth.

Sykes, G. M. (1958). *The society of captives: A study of a maximum security prison.* Princeton, NJ: Princeton University Press.

COMMUNITY CORRECTIONS CENTERS

Community corrections centers include halfway houses, work release centers, and restitution centers. Individuals housed in these places usually work in the community and participate in court-ordered programs such as drug treatment or family counseling. Centers hold inmates either as an alternative to incarceration or at the end of their prison sentence for a period of readjustment to community life. Community residential corrections programs are the most underutilized component of the corrections continuum.

HISTORY

Halfway houses for released prisoners were first established during the 1800s in Boston and New York to aid former offenders in their readjustment to the community. While other cities and states gradually introduced similar establishments, it was not until 1975 that all states in addition to the federal government had approved legislation approving the use of halfway houses. The passage by Congress of the Prisoner Rehabilitation Act of 1965 made it possible for the U.S. Bureau of Prisons to delegate the care, custody, and control of inmates to a community treatment center or contract facility. Contract facilities are nonprofit, or private, facilities owned and operated by a nongovernment entity for the same purpose and operated much the same as a government-operated community residential center. Shortly after passage of the Prisoner Rehabilitation Act of 1965, many states followed suit and began to use community residential centers to help integrate probationers and inmates into the community as part of the service of their sentence or as a condition of probation.

THE PURPOSE OF A COMMUNITY CORRECTIONS CENTER

Community corrections facilities serve two roles: halfway in prison and halfway out. That is, for offenders who are on probation or appearing for sentencing for the first time, a halfway house offers an alternative to the judge who believes that the offender, at the time of sentencing, will not be well served by going straight to prison. However, in his or her opinion the offender needs a period of time to benefit from stronger controls, regular employment, counseling, and perhaps other programs such as drug treatment. The sentencing judge may then place the offender on probation with the condition that he or she may serve the first 90–120 days in a halfway house. While in the program offenders are required to find employment (if they are unemployed), participate in required programs such as drug treatment or education. In addition, they must follow rules and regulations that restrict their activities. They will also usually meet once or twice with the probation officer assigned to his or her case to discuss rules and concerns. Once offenders have completed their stay in the program without incident and are ready to leave, they are usually entitled to live at home under the supervision of a probation officer.

Halfway out of prison refers to the inmate's release from prison prior to the expiration of sentence in order to secure employment, have time to become reintegrated with his or her family, and experience a period of decompression after serving perhaps years in the regimented environment of prison. When an inmate is transferred to a work release facility or halfway house, he or she is usually placed on furlough for a period of time to travel by public transportation to the designated facility. Once there, she or he will undergo a period of classification and in-house assignments in order for the staff to properly classify the inmates and determine whether there are issues that indicate the inmate should be returned to custody. This usually does not happen because the inmate must meet the criteria of (1) being within 90–120 days of release from custody, (2) no history of violence or organized crime or sexual offenses, and (3) good adjustment in prison. Thus, before inmates are accepted into a residential facility, they must be screened by the institutional staff and the halfway house staff. Providing a residential service for those who are halfway out of prison addresses the issue of prisonization and inmates' needs for a period of adjustment to the community before being allowed to go on parole. If someone has regular employment, has a place in his or her family, and/or a place to live, the parolee stands a much better chance to complete the demands of parole or succeed upon mandatory release.

Finally, a minority of residents of halfway houses are pretrial inmates. These include individuals suspected of crimes and awaiting trial who have been deemed not dangerous enough or not enough of a risk of flight to be held in prison, and too dangerous or too much of a risk of flight to be released into the community unsupervised pending trial. For these people, a community residential center provides the supervision necessary, while shielding the inmate from the potential harm resulting from spending time in jail.

STAFFING

All community corrections centers operate under the purview of a central office or board of directors. The government facility is part of the community programs division of the department of corrections, or if a local corrections center, part of the jail division of the sheriff's department. Nonprofit centers are also operated under the supervision of a board of directors whose members are selected by the parent agency. In the case of some centers, after the initial board is selected, members of the board will select replacements. As a consequence, the director of the facility will report to either a supervisor in the central office or the board itself.

Other than the director, there is some variation in staffing a community corrections center. At minimum, there should be one case manager for every 30 to 50 inmates, an employment placement officer, and an adequate staff to provide security and supervision. The supervision staff should have at minimum one supervisor for every 25 inmates on all three shifts, 365 days a year. In addition to security and supervision of inmates, officers may have to drive inmates to employment interviews, supervise organized recreation, and perform sundry tasks related to the orderly management of the facility, such as passing out laundry, counts, and supervising sanitation. Many community corrections centers also have on staff, or on contract, a licensed social worker or psychologist to develop and run counseling programs and to assist with classification and reclassification of inmates

PRIVATIZATION

The privatization of halfway houses is not new, but the practice was reinvigorated in the mid-1970s when Canon and Company opened a for-profit facility in Inglewood, California. The facility was operated just as a government-operated or nonprofit facility and was quite successful. However, it closed due to the lack of contract funding during the Reagan years.

Not long after Canon and Company opened, Eclectic Communications Corporation of Santa Barbara and Behavioral Systems of the Southwest opened halfway houses as private corporations. In the mid-1980s, Corrections Corporation of America opened for business as a private corporation in both institutional and community corrections. At present Corrections Corporation of America holds a 52% market share of privately held beds in the United States and a 43% share of global private corrections beds, including community corrections centers.

PROGRAMMING IN A COMMUNITY CORRECTIONS CENTER

The programs of community corrections centers vary from jurisdiction to jurisdiction and whether they are a government, nonprofit, or private facility. For example, a work release center operated by the state department of corrections may focus almost exclusively on employment and security. As a part of case management, the inmate may be referred to a community drug treatment program for counseling. On the other hand, many programs are designed for offenders with a history of substance abuse and the entire program will revolve around counseling and related programs, including employment.

On the whole, community corrections centers offer a relatively wide range of program opportunities such as referring inmates to local community colleges for completion of a general equivalency diploma (GED) or for vocational training, in-house counseling sessions either by staff or contract social workers or psychologists, and other enrichment programs such as assistance from officers from the department of employment assistance. In addition, the orientation may include sessions on how to find a job, how to get along with a supervisor, how to use the local transportation system, and how to manage money.

It is important to stress that the community corrections center can be used as a means to increase control of the offender, that is, remove him or her from the freedom of community life to a program that can provide stricter controls short of imprisonment. They can also be used as a transition device between the strict regimentation of prison to the relative freedom of parole. Either way, the community benefits and in addition, the offender usually must pay a portion of his or her paycheck each week as reimbursement for room and board. Part of each paycheck is also used to make court-ordered payments such as restitution or child support payments.

EFFECTIVENESS OF COMMUNITY CORRECTIONS CENTERS

The effectiveness of community corrections centers is difficult to address. If one is asking if they are effective as a rehabilitation agent, the answer is, probably not. Perhaps we should think of community corrections centers as a tool for reintegration rather than a means of rehabilitation. Edward Latessa and Lawrence Travis (1991) looked at a matched sample of probationers and halfway house residents and found no difference in postrelease behavior. They conclude that halfway house placement may be better for some offenders but that such

a placement might best be based on the offender's need rather than on a desire to increase the penalty. David Hartman, Paul Friday, and Kevin Minor (1994) looked at predictions of successful halfway house discharge and recidivism and concluded that program completion is more important than the completion of specific components and that successful program completion can be associated with lessened recidivism. Finally, Karol Lucker (1997) examined the role of privatization in community corrections and concluded that, despite defects of private offender treatment, the abolition of private halfway houses is neither warranted nor likely.

GENDER-SPECIFIC ISSUES

Many community corrections centers are single-sex facilities though some also house both men and women. There usually are no problems related to inappropriate behavior between men and women in coed facilities because most inmates are focused on job, family, and just getting out. Still, when problems occur they usually result in both inmates being remanded (back) to custody.

Merry Morash and Pamela Schram (2002) report that on average 31.4% of women inmates are released through prerelease centers and 10.7% are released from prison through a halfway house. In one of the few pieces of research about women in community corrections, David Dowell, Cecilia Klein, and Cheryl Krichmar (1983) reviewed a group of female residents of a halfway house in Long Beach, California, and compared them with a similar group of parolees who did not receive the benefit of halfway house services. They conclude that release through a halfway house reduced both the number and severity of offenses committed after the women were released from the facility. Thus, while gender-specific research is sketchy in regard to successful outcomes of confinement in community corrections centers, overall research indicates that they are at least cheaper than prison and do less harm than imprisonment.

Determining whether community corrections centers are more successful for men or women is difficult due to definitions of success and to the absence of research. Nonetheless, many argue that since female offenders have special needs, community corrections centers should address those needs through programs that include substance abuse, parenting classes, counseling that addresses codependency, and even therapy for abuses suffered at a younger age. In addition, many community corrections centers are designed to control male offenders and the intent is to separate and observe behaviors.

CONCLUSION

Community corrections centers aim to provide offenders with opportunities to adjust to the demands of community life under the supervision of staff. While research into their effectiveness is inconclusive, for the most part they appear to do less harm to the individual than incarceration. In the spectrum of punishment options currently available in the United States, community corrections centers fall somewhere in the middle, alongside probation, fines, community service, and restitution. Since they are cheaper and more humane to operate than prisons, and because they allow the possibility for enhanced family contact, many argue that community corrections centers should be used more frequently, to house a greater variety of nonviolent offenders.

—*James G. Houston*

See also Classification; Drug Treatment Programs; Electronic Monitoring; Furlough; Intermediate Sanctions; Minimum Security; Parole; Prerelease Programs; Prisoner Reentry; Security and Order

Further Reading

Clear, T. (1998). Challenges for corrections in the community. In J. Petersilia (Ed.), *Community corrections: Probation, parole, and intermediate sanctions.* New York: Oxford University Press.

Corrado, R. R., Odgers, C., & Cohen, I. M. (2000). The incarceration of female young offenders: Protection for whom? *Canadian Journal of Criminology, 42*(2), 189–208.

Dowell, D., Klein, C., & Krichmar, C. (1983). Evaluation of a halfway house for women. *Journal of Criminology, 13*(1), 217–226.

Hartman, D. J., Friday, P. C., & Minor, K. I. (1994). Residential probation: A seven-year follow-up study of halfway house discharges. *Journal of Criminal Justice, 22*(6), 503–515.

Latessa, E., & Travis, L. F., III. (1991). Halfway house or probation: A comparison of alternative dispositions. *Journal of Crime and Justice, 14*(1), 53–75.

Lucker, K. (1997). Privatizing discretion: Rehabilitation treatment in community corrections. *Crime & Delinquency, 43*(3), 243–260.

Morash, M., & Schram, P. J. (2002). *The prison experience: Special issues of women in prison.* Prospect Heights, IL: Waveland.

◤ COMPASSIONATE RELEASE

Compassionate release of prisoners is appropriate when circumstances unforeseen at sentencing make continued incarceration unjust, and when no other adequate legal mechanisms exist to effect sentence reduction. Where recognized, compassionate release may be justified by a wide variety of postsentence developments. These can include extraordinary and compelling medical circumstances (such as imminent death, debilitating illness or injury, or mental illness), changes in the law that reduce the sentence but are not retroactive, unwarranted sentence disparity, extraordinary assistance to the government, compelling change in family circumstances, or sentencing error that was not discovered in time to be corrected using available legal procedures (American Bar Association [ABA], 2003, pp. 3, 4).

A system for early release for compassionate reasons can be administered by the courts, corrections systems, parole authorities, or a combination of agencies. It may involve sentence reductions, medical furloughs, early parole, or other administrative or judicial methods. However accomplished, compassionate release recognizes that in certain cases continued incarceration has ceased to serve legitimate penological ends. It expresses a moral judgment that whatever the reasons for imposing sentence, they are overborne by subsequent events that render continued incarceration unjust and inappropriate.

CURRENT PRACTICE

Compassionate release is comparatively rare today due to the widespread adoption of fixed or mandatory sentencing schemes and the abolition of parole by many states and the federal government. For example, in the mid-1980s, Congress passed the Sentencing Reform Act abolishing parole and authorizing sentencing guidelines, and adopted a number of laws providing for mandatory minimum sentences. Similarly, in the states the advent of "truth-in-sentencing" laws eliminated some of the existing compassionate release mechanisms—for example, those accomplished through parole—or created conditions incompatible with earlier, more flexible approaches to sentencing reduction. Thus, indirectly and perhaps unintentionally, changes in sentencing law have effectively curtailed the practice of reducing sentences on compassionate grounds (ABA, 2003, p. 2).

States generally have provisions ranging from the explicit to the general that may be used for humanitarian requests. In a 1995 survey, it was found that about only half of the states provide compassionate release mechanisms for the terminally ill (ABA, 1995, p. 6). Others have general methods such as clemency, furlough, and parole that may be used to serve compassionate ends (Aldenberg, 1998, p. 557; ABA, 1995, p. 6; Russell, 1994, p. 836, n. 10; Volunteers of America, 2001, p. 5). The federal government's compassionate release statute, 18 U.S.C. § 3582(c)(1)(A), provides relatively broad authority to the Federal Bureau of Prisons to submit a motion to the sentencing judge for sentence reduction based on "extraordinary and compelling circumstances" (Price, 2001, p. 189).

In some cases, compassionate release is confounded by political concerns, adherence to the principle that respects the finality of sentences, or a lack of guidance about the appropriate grounds for relief (Price, 2001, p. 190, n. 6). Decision makers are constrained to be conservative in their application of compassionate release by a tough-on-crime atmosphere, or fear that those released may reoffend (Aldenberg, 1998, p. 553; Greifinger, 1999, p. 236). Many compassionate release programs are limited to cases where the prisoner is just about to die and require determinations that he or she is unlikely to reoffend or become a threat to public safety (Russell, 1994, pp. 826–827). This means that, where mechanisms exist, as a practical matter they are used sparingly.

In 1996, a study of state and federal release programs by the U.S. Department of Justice's Office of Justice Programs found only 20 jurisdictions had released prisoners pursuant to early-release authority (ABA, 2003, p. 4, n. 5; U.S. Department of Justice, 1996–1997, p. xiv). A survey of the use of sentence reductions in the federal system found that only 226 people had been released from federal prison between the years 1990 and 2000 (Price, 2001, p. 191). Not only is the federal statute rarely invoked, it is limited generally to those circumstances where the prisoner is near death, despite the apparently broad use of the power contemplated by Congress (Price, 2001, pp. 188, 189). In recent years, the Bureau of Prisons has somewhat expanded the scope to include prisoners suffering diseases that have resulted in "markedly diminished public safety risk and quality of life" (Price, 2001, p. 191).

CONCLUSION

For some in the criminal justice community, compassionate release defeats the aims of tough-on-crime sentencing. Expanding the use of compassionate release might create a back door through which offenders may avoid serving their sentences. Others support the reinstatement and expansion of compassionate release mechanisms, arguing that rule-bound sentencing systems do not adequately account for compelling postsentence developments. In light of its determination that most sentencing systems cannot routinely accommodate the variety of "truly exceptional" postsentence developments that may warrant reconsideration of incarceration, the ABA House of Delegates recommended in 2003 that jurisdictions evaluate existing procedures. The ABA urged jurisdictions to develop and implement mechanisms for sentence reductions in cases of extraordinary and compelling postsentence developments and develop criteria ensuring that the procedures that are developed can be easily used by prisoners and their advocates (ABA, 2003, p. 1).

—Mary Price

See also Clemency; Furlough; Pardon; Parole; Sentencing Reform Act 1983; Truth in Sentencing

Further Reading

Aldenberg, W. B. (1998). Bursting at the seams: An analysis of compassionate-release statutes and the current problem of HIV and AIDS in U.S. prisons and jails. *New England Journal on Criminal & Civil Confinement, 24,* 541–597.

American Bar Association. (1995). *Compassionate release of terminally ill prisoners.* Draft Report of the ABA Corrections and Sentencing Committee's Compassionate Release Working Group. (On file with the author)

American Bar Association. (2003). *ABA House of Delegates Resolution 103B (February 2003).* Retrieved from www.abanet .org/leadership/recommendations03/103B.pds

Greifinger, R. B. (1999). Commentary: Is it politic to limit our compassion? *Journal of Law, Medicine & Ethics, 27,* 234–237.

Price, M. (2001). The other safety valve: Sentence reduction motions under 18 U.S.C. § 3582(c)(1)(A). *Federal Sentencing Reporter, 13,* 188–191.

Russell, M. P. (1994). Too little, too late, too slow: Compassionate release of terminally ill prisoners—Is the cure worse than the disease? *Widener Journal of Public Law, 3,* 799.

U.S. Department of Justice, Office of Justice Programs. (1996–1997). *Update: HIV/AIDs, STDs and TB in correctional facilities.* Washington, DC: Author.

Volunteers of America. (2001). The GRACE Project. *Incarceration of the terminally ill, Current practices in the United States.* Alexandria, VA: Author.

◪ CONJUGAL VISITS

Conjugal visits, sometimes referred to as family visits, are a privilege afforded to some married lower-security-risk inmates in a limited number of jurisdictions in only a handful of states. These programs allow spouses, and sometimes the couples' children, to visit for several hours at a time in complete privacy for the purpose of maintaining interpersonal relations. Heterosexual intercourse may occur during these conjugal visits.

HISTORY

American penal institutions first officially introduced conjugal visiting programs in 1918 in Mississippi. Evidence, however, suggests that this policy had been implemented unofficially long before it was legally permitted, to induce inmates to work harder in the fields. Thus, it seems that the origins of conjugal visitation were rooted solely in the management of inmates and the administrative needs of the institutions rather than in any desire to fortify family bonds. Initially, these conjugal visits were intended to be exclusively sexual in nature and did not require inmates to be married. In fact, records suggest that prostitutes occasionally met with those eligible to enjoy heterosexual relations within prison.

CURRENT PRACTICE

In the period immediately following the legalization of conjugal visiting, there were no correctional facilities appropriate for private sexual encounters between partners, so inmates would have to meet in their cells and hang a sheet to provide some visual privacy from others. Today, institutions offering conjugal visits provide various settings for privacy. Certain institutions use campgrounds on the premises of correctional institutions, where families may even stay together overnight. Others make available private rooms within prison walls themselves. The type of setting for family relations depends on several factors, including the level of security of the institution—even though they are limited almost exclusively to individuals held in lower-security institutions—the type of facility the prison or jail is using, and the resources available to the institution.

THE CASE FOR CONJUGAL VISITS

Conjugal visiting programs have been instituted in a limited number of correctional facilities to offset some of the negative psychological effects of being imprisoned. Their primary justification is that inmates who maintain relatively normal familial interactions are more likely to have lower recidivism rates and are easier to manage while serving their sentences.

In addition, conjugal visitation policies have sometimes been justified as a way to reduce the amount of homosexual activity that occurs between inmates who have no other sexual outlets. This reasoning is predicated on the presumption that inmates have uncontrollable sexual desires that, if not channeled into heterosexual interactions, will result in consensual homosexual contact or homosexual rape. One problem with this justification has been that acts of rape have more to do with power and control of another inmate than with sexual pleasure or desire. Another challenge to this reasoning has been that not all inmates prefer heterosexual relationships, and many may intentionally seek out homosexual contact exclusively.

Conjugal visits have been praised by individuals and groups that seek to keep children of inmates closely bonded with their institutionalized parents. Extensive research exists on the negative psychological impacts of having a parent imprisoned. The findings of these studies have provided the impetus for many of the conjugal visitation programs predominantly in women's prisons that allow children to visit their mothers overnight or throughout weekends. Certain specialized programs, like the one initiated by the Girl Scouts of America, have established programs with some women's correctional institutions that allow mothers and their daughters or sons to work together on projects that can result in badges of merit or other forms of positive recognition. As an incentive for incarcerated women, conjugal visits with children are sometimes granted for the successful completion of parenting courses provided by correctional institutions. Some institutions even provide nurseries on the institution's premises where expectant mothers can prepare to give birth and then stay for up to 18 months after the birth of her child, with the expectation that she continue to fulfill expectations of conduct. Few problems have been documented as a result of these programs, although unfortunately these kinds of program incentives are chiefly offered only to female inmates.

CHALLENGES TO CONJUGAL VISITATION

There are several problems with conjugal visits that have been brought to light by their opponents. First, since so few inmates are eligible for them, the fairness of these programs has been challenged. These visits are available only to male or female inmates who are legally married, which by definition excludes the possibility of visitation by gay or lesbian partners or those who are involved in common law marriages. On these grounds, conjugal visits have been the target of constitutional challenges.

In addition, the kinds of facilities that would be appropriate for these visits are scarce, largely due to limited resources, often making them unavailable. Likewise, research has found deficits in security, abuses of power by correctional officers, and the abuse of inmates by jealous convicts, among other problems. Other problems are more ideological in nature, such as the logic of offering a program that offers enjoyment to inmates, or the sexual nature of many of these visits. Finally, conjugal visits may produce children who may not be financially supported or parented because the mother or father is incarcerated.

CONCLUSION

It is commonly believed that children who maintain healthy relationships with both parents will grow up to be more stable and more likely to be law-abiding individuals. It is also believed that inmates who are allowed to maintain an active position within their families will have a smoother transition to civilian life upon eventual release. As a result, some hypothesize that family conjugal visits may prove to be an effective long-term crime prevention method.

—Kelly Welch

See also Children; Children's Visits; Donald Clemmer; Deprivation; Homosexual Prisoners; Homosexual Relationships; Lesbian Relationships; Mothers in Prison; Pains of Imprisonment; Parenting Programs; Prisonization; Rape; Sex—Consensual; "Stop Prisoner Rape"; Gresham Sykes; Visits; Wives of Prisoners

Further Reading

Johns, D. (1971). Alternatives to conjugal visits. *Federal Probation, 35,* 48–50.

Nebraska Department of Corrections. (1995). *Annual report.* Lincoln: Author.

Ross, R., & Fabiano, E. (1986). *Female offenders: Correctional afterthoughts.* New York: McFarland.

Stumbo, N., & Little, S. (1991). Campground offers relaxed setting for children's visitation program. *Corrections Today, 53*, 136–144.

◪ CONSTITUTIVE PENOLOGY

Constitutive penology is an extension of postmodernist constitutive criminological theory. Its proponents argue that societal responses to crime are interrelated with the wider society, particularly through "crime and punishment" talk. Discursive distinctions are constructed and continuously reinterpreted (iterated) through penal policy pronouncements, practical actions, discussions in the popular culture, and the proclamations, rules, and practices of institutional structures such as the criminal justice system, correctional institutions, and punishment and rehabilitation. These abstract distinctions obscure the numerous ways in which penological discourse and practices permeate the wider society. They also disguise the connections between the theory and practices of penology and the impacts, costs, and consequences that these have for our societal system. Constitutive penologists call for (1) the integration of prison and related penological practices with society, (2) a demystification of the penological society, and (3) the development of more holistic responses to criminal harm.

Constitutive penologists also argue that conventional penology provides the discursive reference for actions that create, develop, and sustain prison. Discursive structures are embodied with ideological material, which provides the backdrop for socially constructed meaning. Whether penology is taken in its broadest sense to mean the systematic study of penal systems, or the more narrowly focused investigation of the effectiveness of sentencing in preventing reoffending, or even the microscopic examination of penal institutions and their routine practices of violence and discrimination, all research sustains the continued existence of the penological society, dubbed the "incarceration nation." Thus, debates over being in or out of prison, over building more or less penal institutions, about overcrowding and overspending, about

alternatives to and challenges, all continuously assume the taken-for-granted existence of the very structures that need to be questioned and explained. In short, they reinforce the prison as a necessary reality.

CRITIQUE OF CONVENTIONAL PHILOSOPHIES OF PUNISHMENT

Constitutive penologists see penal policy as part of a way of talking about dealing with offenders (discursive process) whereby aspects of existing practice are selected, emphasized, refined, and given linguistic form and formally discussed, while other aspects are ignored, subordinated, dispersed and relegated to the informal, are framed as aberrant, or seen as "noise." Conventional penologists generally distinguish between six general philosophical approaches that underpin their policies and inform sentencing practice: (1) incapacitation/social defense, (2) punishment/retribution/just deserts, (3) deterrence, (4) rehabilitation/treatment, (5) prevention, and (6) restitution/reparation. For a constitutive penologist, any one of these "philosophies" constructs a false separation between the penal system and society. For example, incapacitation does not separate offenders from society since being *in* prison is being *in* society; prison is physically, structurally, and symbolically integrated into the broader community. Rather than "walls of imprisonment," there is continuity between being "in" or "out." The incarcerated are not incapacitated, since they do additional and, in many cases, more serious forms of offensive behavior inside prison as a reaction to their confinement. Metaphors for the lawbreakers such as "slime," "dirt bag," "asshole," and "scumbag" often both objectify the humans who perpetrated the harms and provide the very "logical" penal response that encourages the development of a pool of suspects, shielding other more invisible and powerful "excessive investors" in harm production from potential incrimination while maintaining the need for social structures of control.

Constitutive penologists also point out that we pay the economical and social costs of massively expanded prison programs. Socially, the "new penology" of incapacitation has accentuated the issue of race in American society, since one in three African American males aged 20–29 are in prison, on probation, or on parole. This permeates the minority perspective of those people of color *outside* prison who withdraw sentiment for, and commitment to, society's formal institutions, especially from government and law enforcement. It simultaneously corrupts the majority white population's views on minorities, thereby contaminating day-to-day interaction; through this, the institutions and structures of society reinforce the justification for implicit and institutionalized racism. Thus, argue constitutive penologists, incapacitation has a major impact on the nonwhite *and* white populations. Once moral sentiment is withdrawn, people feel morally justified in violating all kinds of rules based on the rationalization that "whites" and other dominant groups in general cannot be victims of specific crimes, since their racist violations of minorities make them the aggressors. Minorities are merely taking back what was seen as rightly taken from them, including dignity, self-determination, property, and even life itself.

Finally, incapacitation feeds the false security of social order and the "safer with them behind bars" mentality. The paradox is that for each constitutive brick of incapacitation we release another swirl of freedom for "accident makers" (Bhopal), "liberators" (Iran-Contra), "job creators" (GM's Jeffrey Smith), "risk takers" (Boesky, Milken), and "fabricators" (Enron). We feel safer in our homes and workplaces, yet it is often in these routine places that we are most victimized.

Constitutive penologists apply a similar analysis to the other penal policies. For example, they claim that advocates for punishment/retribution/just deserts foster the idea that there are circumstances where it is acceptable to harm others on the basis that harmful acts should be followed by other harmful acts, as though it was self-evident that this equation of proportion and reaction was justified. Likewise, deterrence communicates the idea that we should seek ways to avoid making our own acts appear like those that are punishable for fear that we too will be punished. Ideas of rehabilitation/treatment, argue constitutive penologists, suggest

that both the harms committed and the victim who suffers are less important than manipulating aspects of the individual offender's personal or situational environment to prevent them from harming again. This conceptual separation of victims, offenders, and environments overlooks the interconnected and coproduced nature of social "reality," failing to see that we are locking the offender into the very social role that the policy intends to expunge.

Finally, constitutive penologists criticize the more radical philosophies of restitution/reparation. They acknowledge that this approach at least brings the victim back in to share their experience of being harmed with the individual/agency that allegedly caused the harm. They also point out that insofar as the community and control institutions have a facilitative role, then less harm is being done by this kind of mediated intervention. However, they argue that the hidden message of restorative justice is that getting together and talking about a problem can fix it, without recognizing that the very structural situations in which folk are enmeshed are not part of the transformational mix. Neglected is an understanding that the emerging "mediation-discourse" is itself the basis of reducing differences into least common denominators, which can mean "equitable" solutions, downplaying the uniqueness of the disputant's own constructions. In other words, bureaucratic discourse that promotes "mediation" and "resolutions" overlooks differences in discursive practices that privilege some over others and their associated underlying ideologies; rarely is the outcome of restorative justice that institutions of society see themselves as a contributing force.

AN ALTERNATIVE SEMIOTIC APPROACH

Constitutive penologists are concerned with how criminologists may, despite their best intentions, replicate the very system they try to understand and critique. Criminologists do this by constructing ideal typical classifications that disguise how policy makers, practitioners, targeted agents, and theorists de-emphasize some aspects of the reality of prison practice as aberrant, unofficial, informal, or untypical in order to make claims about its operational identity. To avoid legitimating the prison while analyzing penal policy, constitutive penologists argue that it is necessary to use a semiotic approach that deconstructs the role that language use plays in the construction of the penal system and its attendant philosophies and institutions. Transformation of crime and societal responses to it, they argue, requires a reintegration of crime and societal responses with the whole of which each is a part, and they indicate that a change in the whole is necessary to bring about a change in any of its parts. This is a holistic exercise, in many ways analogous to the hologram where illumination of any part reproduces the whole; the "part" resides in the whole, but each part represents the whole.

An alternative direction would provide an opportunity for the development of a new "replacement discourse." Replacement discourse is not merely another package of ways to talk and make sense of the world, but a language of "transpraxis." It connects the way we speak with our social relations and institutions, so that we are continuously aware of the interrelatedness of our agency and the structures it reproduces through the constitutively productive work of our talking, perceiving, conceptualizing, and theorizing. "Transpraxis is a deliberate and affirmative attempt not to reverse hierarchies but, instead, to affirm those who victimize, marginalize and criminalize while renouncing their victimizing, marginalizing and criminalizing practices. Transpraxis is an effort to validate the act of resistance. The key to transpraxis is speech, words, grammar and how we talk about (and then act upon) emancipation" (Arrigo, 2001, p. 220). Constitutive penology asks us to rethink the discursive structures within which we situate our research on the penal question.

Constitutive penologists have suggested several directions and alternative notions for the development of social justice: social judo; replacement discourse; transpraxis; newsmaking criminology; narrative therapy; reconceptualizing crime as "harms of reduction" and "harms of repression"; recovering subjects; an understanding of the social formation more in terms of historically contingent and relatively stabilized configurations of coupled iterative loops (constitutive inter-relational [COREL] sets),

which can be seen as the basis of contingent "structures" with effects; and forms of an empowered democracy in a political economy identified by Unger as "superliberalism."

Social judo responds to the state's continued investment in violence to counter harms (called criminal justice), which thereby escalates the overall prevalence of violence in society. It argues for creative responses whereby those investors in harm have their power turned against themselves. It is a policy of undermining excessive investors in harms. In its maximal beneficial form, conflict is an occasion to reexamine given societal relations, institutions, and structures and their tendencies toward harm. Reconceptualizing harm in terms of "harms of reduction," whereby a person is reduced from some standing, and "harms of repression," whereby a person is denied her or his ability to attain a position sought without it being at the expense of the other, provides a suggestion for an alternative way of perceiving harm. It takes us beyond the restrictions of the legalistic definition of crime.

The notion of COREL sets offers an alternative nonreductionist way of historically conceptualizing the interconnectedness of prison and prison policy with the social formation, and for shedding light in a political economy on the various forms of excessive investment to impose power on others in the form of harms of reduction or repression. Constitutive penology, then, would make as its first priority the development of a social formation, which minimizes harms of reduction and repression. They argue that it is in the very resolution of conflicts that we need creative initiatives that transform the process whereby the conflict reproduces harm that sets in place new conflict. They believe that this cycle of conflict production must end. Constitutive penologists have advocated a multifaceted approach to "criminal" justice policy. Their "radical accusatory" policy implicates the entire society for its contributions to harm; their "reformist remedial" policy is much in accord with Unger's superliberalism, which advocates an empowered democracy. A social justice approach would implicate the individual, community, and societal levels consistent with "transformative justice."

CONCLUSION

A genuinely alternative, replacement discourse would envelop not just the declarations of policy but the ways its practitioners and policy makers distinguish their reality from the totality and point toward ways these can be reintegrated. It would require a "bringing back in" of the underemphasized, informal, unofficial, marginalized practices (the unspoken) that are part of the totality of the prison business. Only with such a comprehension of the totality and the contribution of these excluded parts to the reality-making process, argue constitutive penologists, is it possible to provide an alternative understanding of the phenomena of crime and crime control in our society. Only from such an understanding of the total constitutive process is it possible to generate a replacement discourse that begins the deconstruction of penology, the correction of corrections, and the ultimate reconstruction of penal policy that is its own demise.

—*Dragan Milovanovic and Stuart Henry*

See also Abolition; Activism; Deterrence Theory; Michel Foucault; Incapacitation Theory; Just Deserts Theory; Rehabilitation Theory; Resistance

Further Reading

Arrigo, B. (1999) (Ed.). *Social justice/criminal justice.* Belmont, CA: Wadsworth.

Arrigo, B. (2001). Praxis. In E. McLaughlin & Muncie J. (Eds.), *The Sage dictionary of criminology* (pp. 219–221). London: Sage.

Bosworth, M. (1999a). Agency and choice in women's prisons: Toward a constitutive penology. In S. Henry & Milovanovic D. (Eds.). *Constitutive criminology at work: Applications to crime and justice* (pp. 205–226). Albany: State University of New York Press.

Bosworth, M. (1999b). *Engendering resistance: Agency and power in women's prisons.* Aldershot, UK: Ashgate.

Burnside, J., &. Baker, N. (Eds.). (1994). *Relational justice: Repairing the breach.* Winchester, UK: Waterside.

Duncan, M. (1996). *Romantic outlaws, beloved prisons.* New York: New York University Press.

Henry, S., & Milovanovic, D. (1991). Constitutive criminology: The maturation of critical theory. *Criminology, 29,* 293–315.

Henry, S., & Milovanovic, D. (1996). *Constitutive criminology: Beyond postmodernism.* London: Sage.

Henry, S., & Milovanovic, D. (Eds.). (1999). *Constitutive criminology at work: Applications to crime and justice.* Albany: State University of New York Press.

Matza, D. (1969). *Becoming deviant.* Englewood Cliffs, NJ: Prentice Hall.

Maurer, M. (1997). *Intended and unintended consequences: State racial disparities in imprisonment.* Washington, DC: Sentencing Project.

Milovanovic, D., & Henry, S. (1991). Constitutive penology. *Social Justice, 18,* 204–224.

Morris, R. (1994). *A practical path to transformative justice.* Toronto: Rittenhouse.

Morris, R. (2000). *Stories of transformative justice.* Toronto: Canadian Scholars Press.

Schehr, R., & Milovanovic, D. (1999). Conflict mediation and the postmodern: Chaos, catastrophe, and psychoanalytic semiotics. *Social Justice, 26,* 208–232.

Unger, R. (1987). *False necessity.* New York: Cambridge University Press.

◪ CONSULAR VISITS

Pursuant to the guidelines established by the Vienna Convention on Consular Relations (VCCR) in 1963, any criminal justice or correctional institution detaining a foreigner must notify him or her of the right to have his or her consulate notified about the confinement. The United States, which ratified the convention in 1969, considers the right to consular visitation within correctional institutions so fundamental that the U.S. State Department requires it for all international detainees (other than those suspected of terrorism), even if an inmate's country of origin has not signed the VCCR. Following the detainee's request to have the consulate informed of the arrest and confinement, the custodial criminal justice institution may permit a locally stationed consul to visit the detainee in the institution without hindering access or communication.

WHAT DOES A CONSUL DO?

The consul is an official representative of a particular government who lives in a foreign country to help the home nation's citizens within that country and to represent the home country's interests in various affairs. Generally, consuls should provide advice to the detainee on a range of matters. For example, they should furnish a list of possible sources of legal representation from the confining nation and provide information about the local legal system. They may also offer humanitarian assistance in addition to any other practical assistance required by the detainee. The consul may arrange for financial assistance in the form of a loan and may notify the detainee's family about the detention. However, consuls may not provide a detainee any direct aid or legal advisement.

The assistance a consul may provide a foreign national is limited. The consul may not demand the release of the detainee, provide legal advice, pay for legal services, get bail, pay fines, offer financial support beyond a prisoner loan, conduct an investigation, or get the detainee legal or institutional treatment that exceeds that of other inmates or other nationals. The consul's role is simply to provide indirect assistance to the detainee and represent the foreign government's interests in criminal cases.

If the confinement is ongoing or long term, consular visits may continue. The frequency of these visits will depend on various factors such as the length of sentence, how far the prison is from the consul's office, and the seriousness of the situation. Most important, visits require the consul to obtain the necessary local government's approval and prison clearance prior to any official visit. Some institutions are more restrictive than others, particularly those of higher security. Most consular visits do not occur more than once a year following initial visits at the beginning stages of incarceration.

SPECIAL CIRCUMSTANCES: DUAL NATIONALITY

Some detained foreigners maintain dual national status. If a dual national is detained in a country of one of his citizenships, the assistance a consulate is able to provide will likely be further restricted by the detaining nation, in accordance with a strict interpretation of international law. It is possible, however, that the local authorities will allow the consul to provide some limited assistance. The decision to do this is made entirely by the country

detaining the law violator, leaving the consul from the other country of citizenship very little control.

CONCLUSION

Article 36 of the VCCR specifies that notifying detainees about their consular rights should be provided "without delay" by local or national authorities. This requirement was intended to prevent any type of interrogation prior to a consular visit, if this is what the detainee would like. However, there is some evidence that this mandate has been interpreted rather broadly by responsible authorities within U.S. institutions, resulting in consular notification that often follows detention by varying amounts of time. Similarly, changes in policy since the terrorist attacks of September 11, 2001, have meant that foreigners suspected of terrorism may be held indefinitely without charge and without access to a lawyer or any other kind of a representative, including their consul.

The extent to which U.S. law enforcement agencies may have breached their consular notification obligations has been evidenced in a recent lawsuit. In *Sorensen v. City of New York,* a Danish national sought punitive and compensatory damages for the failure of the New York Police Department to inform her immediately upon arrest that she had the right to consular notification and visitation. This court case revealed that more than 50,000 foreign nationals had been arrested in New York City during a one-year period of time, but official records showed that only four of these individuals had been notified of their consular rights. Thus, even though the United States has fully supported the tenets of the VCCR, consular officials are sometimes unable to provide the crucial assistance to foreigners at the stages of the criminal justice process when it would be most beneficial.

—Kelly Welch

See also Contact Visits; Cuban Detainees; Enemy Combatants; Foreign Nationals; Immigrants/ Undocumented Aliens; Long-Term Prisoners; Minimum Security; Political Prisoners; Prisoner of War Camps; Security and Control; USA PATRIOT Act 2001; Visits

Further Reading

Human Rights Watch. (2002, December). *Ending the abusive treatment of prisoners.* Retrieved from http://www.hrw .org/prisons/

Vienna Convention on Consular Relations and Optional Protocols. 1963, April 24). *U.N.T.S.* Nos. 8638–8640, *596*, 262–512.

◪ CONTACT VISITS

Contact visits generally permit an inmate to visit with a friend or relative for a limited amount of time in the same room, rather than to communicate through a glass window. Most correctional facilities set strict visiting hours and policies and require that visitors be approved prior to their arrival, to give the institution reasonable time to conduct a background check of the visitor. Contact during these visits is usually closely monitored, allowing only minimal, if any, physical contact, such as handholding or a brief hug.

Contact visits are considered a privilege and can be revoked for any number of reasons. In higher-security institutions, or in the case of death row inmates, those in disciplinary detention, or those who are being kept in protective custody, contact visits are usually not allowed since it is thought that security concerns outweigh the benefits provided by allowing contact visits. Some states such as Michigan also severely restrict visits for inmates of any security level.

CONTACT VISITATION POLICIES

Correctional institutions that allow inmates contact visits have numerous and very specific rules and regulations that control the process. These rules, which include the number of individuals that may be on an inmate's visiting list and the frequency with which he or she may receive visits, generally vary according to the facility's security requirements, its traditions, and its availability of resources, including visiting space and personnel. Contact visits are most often afforded only to lower-security-risk inmates, although each institution may make exceptions depending on individual circumstances and the mandates of the jurisdiction.

Most correctional facilities require that eligible inmates provide lists at the outset of their incarceration of those whom they want to visit them. Usually, individuals may include parents, spouses, children, friends, attorneys, and religious leaders. However, prisoners are allowed to include only a small number of people on their visiting lists; they are usually forced to prioritize their contacts by those closest to them or those most likely to come. Most institutions conduct background checks on these individuals before they are allowed to visit to ensure that they present no security challenge and are not likely to pass contraband, such as drugs or weapons, to the inmates with whom they are in contact. Felons, parolees, and former inmates are generally not permitted to have contact visits with inmates.

BENEFITS OF CONTACT VISITS

The primary justification for allowing inmates contact visits is to decrease the potential negative psychological effects of being imprisoned. It has been suggested that contact with loved ones and others who are "on the outside" can decrease the effects of what Donald Clemmer (1939) has termed prisonization and what Gresham M. Sykes (1958) has called the pains of imprisonment. It is believed that if inmates are able to connect with those who are not institutionalized, they will be better able to adjust to their release. An inmate who has maintained contact with individuals outside of prison may have a group of people to help him or her start a new life upon release. The loved ones who came to visit may help him or her live a law-abiding life by providing financial assistance or by aiding in a job search.

Contact visits also allow children and incarcerated parents to maintain some relationship with each other. Children are often allowed to see their parents in jail or prison, and being allowed to touch or embrace them may be especially meaningful. Such physical contact could have implications for the child's sense of security and identity as well as the parent's success in transitioning to freedom once released back into society.

Some even suggest that the efficiency of correctional institutions may be enhanced by allowing contact visits since inmates look forward to them so much. They may act as an incentive for good behavior or participation in rehabilitation, educational, or life skills programs. Institutions that have contact visit policies seem to run more smoothly, because their inmates have a powerful motivation to comply with facility rules.

SOME PROBLEMS CAUSED BY CONTACT VISITS

Because visitors are the primary source of smuggled contraband, including drugs, weapons, and money to inmates, contact visits present special problems for correctional institutions. Although correctional officers and other staff attempt to ensure that visitors do not have materials that can be passed along to the inmates by conducting background checks and by searching their belongings, it is not possible to prevent all of this illegal activity. Even if visitors do not smuggle contraband to inmates, it is possible that they act as partners in crime by helping the inmate continue criminal activity from inside the correctional institution. In other situations, inmates might take advantage of sympathetic visitors by encouraging them to carry out some illegal action for the inmate. Some inmates may become depressed if they do not have anyone to come to see them. The isolation for these individuals is exacerbated by witnessing others getting out of work responsibilities or other obligations to meet with their friends and loved ones.

CONCLUSION

Contact visits are considered by many to be a successful method for jail and prison inmates to maintain bonds and associations with the world outside of the institution, making transitions upon release much smoother. These policies have also been touted as effective means for better controlling growing inmate populations. However, the very aspect that makes contact visits so valuable to inmates and correctional facilities also presents several problems, including the potential for contraband to flow from visitor to inmate and increased criminal activity within the institution. Even so, the benefits of contact visits appear to outweigh their risks, suggesting that better methods of screening and searching visitors is in order to ensure the highest security possible.

—Kelly Welch

See also Children; Children's Visits; Donald Clemmer; Conjugal Visits; Contraband; Deprivation; Drug Offenders; Long-Term Prisoners; Minimum Security; Mothers in Prison; Parenting Programs; Visits; Prisonization; Security and Control; Gresham Sykes; Wives of Prisoners

Further Reading

Dickinson, G., & Seaman, T. (1994). Communication policy changes from 1971–1991 in state correctional facilities for adult males in the United States. *The Prison Journal, 74*, 371–382.

Wilkinson, R. A., & Unwin, T. (1999). *Visiting in prison: Prison and jail administration's practices and theory.* Columbus: Ohio Department of Rehabilitation and Correction.

Wright, L. E., & Seymour, C. B. (2000). *Working with children and families separated by incarceration: A handbook for child welfare agencies.* Washington, DC: CWLA Press.

◪ CONTRABAND

Contraband refers to any item in the possession of an inmate that was not directly issued by the institution or purchased through appropriate channels such as the commissary or a hobby-craft program. In most facilities, each prisoner has only a few square feet of space to store personal property. By limiting the type and quantity of personal property prisoners may keep in their possession, administrators try to reduce the possibility for contraband while also maintaining order in the institution.

WHY IS CONTRABAND A PROBLEM?

Above all, prison administrators want uniformity in the prison system. Prison should be classless, without distinction or wealth or poverty. People must, therefore, wear the same clothing, eat from the same menu, and have comparable living quarters.

In their efforts to maintain order and sameness among the prisoner population, administrators issue a specific quantity of clothing to each inmate. If this clothing is altered in any way, such as a patch or the insertion of pockets, the clothing becomes defined as contraband. It may then be confiscated, and the inmate may face disciplinary action. For example, if an individual purchases a sweatshirt from the commissary with personal funds and then marks the sweatshirt with a name or symbol, the item becomes contraband.

Each prisoner is entitled to food, shelter, and clothing as provided by the institution. The prisoners may purchase specific items for personal use or consumption from the commissary, but only in limited quantities. They are not allowed to hoard items, to transfer ownership, or to relocate government-issued supplies from specifically authorized areas to nonauthorized ones. For example, although vegetables may be served and authorized in the food services department, kitchen foods immediately become contraband if they are transferred to the living quarters for consumption there.

WHY IS CONTRABAND IMPORTANT TO PRISONERS?

Just as administrators strive to create homogeneity within the confines of each institution, the prisoners struggle to preserve some aspect of their individuality. Their names have been replaced with numbers; they have been stripped of their freedom, their clothing, and their identities. As a result, acquiring something that is not government issue brings some flavor, some variety to the monotony of daily prison life.

Prisoners may also alter clothing or property for utilitarian reasons. For example, the prison commissary may sell athletic apparel without pockets. Prisoners are required, however, to carry their prison identification with them at all times. Some, therefore, sew pockets into their clothing to hold such items. The commissary may also sell battery-operated radios or reading lights. Prisoners may

modify these items with electrical adapters so they can avoid the costly purchase of batteries.

Prisoners may purchase contraband food from those who hustle it out of the kitchen in order to eat on their own schedule rather than on those imposed by the prison authorities. They may use contraband fruit, sugar, and yeast as ingredients for a prison-made wine or hooch. Finally, they may modify structured elements of the prison such as a pipe or piece of steel into a weapon for use against others; they may collect rope as a tool for escape or for suicide.

WHERE DOES CONTRABAND COME FROM?

Contraband comes from inside and outside the prison walls. Prisoners may be limited to possession of five books, five magazines, $20 worth of stamps, or individual paperwork that does not measure more than three inches in height when stacked flat. Everything in excess of these standards is defined as contraband and subject to confiscation. Prisoners must, in other words, regularly send items home or discard property they have accumulated through the mail over time.

Other, more insidious forms of contraband may be smuggled into the institutions with the help of guards or visitors. Some guards may bring drugs, alcohol, weapons, or other prohibited items into the prison. Visitors may also try to pass such items during contact visits. This type of contraband is considered a serious breach of institutional security. Anybody found in possession of such items will be subject to criminal prosecution.

CONCLUSION

Obviously, not all contraband items present the same threat to the security and order of the institution. Prisoners caught with drugs or weapons may face further prosecution, while administrators have a variety of sanctions at their disposal with which to punish those who have been caught with items of a less threatening nature such as food. For these kinds of illicit items, prisoners may lose their commissary, visiting, or telephone privileges.

Despite the sanctions association with contraband, it remains a common part of prison life. Some guards use their discretion and overlook minor contraband violations, such as extra clothing or books. Others enforce prison rules strictly, confiscating all items and writing up prisoners for disciplinary infractions. Due to the large numbers of inmates compared to staff, it is impossible to catch all illicit items. As a result, contraband continues to play a significant role in most prisoners' experiences of incarceration.

—Michael Santos

See also Commissary; Correctional Officers; Deprivation; Hooch; Importation; Prison Culture; Resistance

Further Reading

Jones, R. A., & Schmid, T. (2000). *Doing time: Prison experience and identity among first-time inmates.* Greenwich, CT: JAI.

Ross, J. I., & Stephens, S. C. (2002). *Behind bars: Surviving prison.* Indianapolis, IN: Alpha.

Santos, M. (2004). *About prison.* Belmont, CA: Wadsworth.

Sykes, G. M. (1958). *The society of captives: A study of a maximum security prison.* Princeton, NJ: Princeton University Press.

◪ CONTRACT FACILITIES

The practice of contracting with private agencies for correctional services grew substantially in the late 20th century, coinciding with a steady growth in the size of the correctional population. Contract facilities have become increasingly common in English-speaking countries, particularly in the United States, the United Kingdom, and Australia. Also referred to as partial privatization or outsourcing, the practice has faded in, out, and back into popularity over the course of history. Under a contract system, correctional services are funded by the government agency responsible for custody of inmates but delivered by a third party. The government maintains control over the type and quality of services provided but delegates the service delivery to a private entity. Contracts are typically arranged with nonprofit agencies, for-profit companies, or other government units.

While the contracting out of particular services such as medical care, food service, maintenance, education, and mental health services is widespread in corrections, the contracting out of entire correctional facilities is limited and has remained a controversial practice, particularly when for-profit companies are involved. Concerns that private companies may sacrifice conditions of confinement in order to make money and general ethical concerns about the delegation of punishment underlie an ongoing debate over contract facilities. In practice, the respective advantages and disadvantages of using contract facilities tend to vary considerably depending on the individual ability of contractors, the capacity of governments to oversee contracts, and the extent of provisions covered under the contracted agreement.

HISTORY

Government contracting with the private sector in the United States dates as far back as 1785 when the nascent federal government contracted with private stagecoach operators to deliver mail and passed subsequent legislation that required the bidding process to be publicly advertised. The U.S. experience with contracting for prisons and correctional facilities dates to the early 19th century. Borrowing from European workhouse models, the earliest American prisons (such as Philadelphia's Walnut Street Jail) contracted out the labor of convicts to private entrepreneurs. While the practice extended well into the 20th century, it became increasingly controversial due to abusive treatment of inmates, insider contracting arrangements, and concerns that prison labor was unfairly depressing wages and cutting into the private sector job market. By 1940, federal and state laws severely restricted the market for prison-made goods.

In the juvenile justice field, contract facilities have been providing services to juvenile delinquents since the early 20th century. Unlike the adult contract system, contracts for juvenile facilities have been primarily with religious, charitable, and other nonprofit agencies rather than for-profit businesses. As a result, the practice of placing juvenile delinquents in privately run facilities has proceeded with far less controversy than has been the case in the adult corrections arena. In the 1970s, the movement to deinstitutionalize status offenders from the youth correctional system created a demand for more contracted services and spawned considerable research on the effectiveness of contract facilities. As adult correctional populations increased during this time, at least 18 states passed "community corrections acts" designed to transfer resources and funding from state departments of correction to local governments and to provide community residential services to offenders. Many jurisdictions turned to private contractors to operate these facilities.

During the 1980s, governments throughout the world came under increased pressure to cut costs and reduce the public workforce while still meeting their legally mandated responsibilities to provide various public services. Advocates for "reinventing government" sought to lower costs and improve the quality of services by making many traditional government programs, such as corrections, open to competitive bidding by the private sector. A new model of contracting for correctional facilities emerged that differed fundamentally from the earlier century's model. Under the old model, contract facilities received funding by selling the labor of inmates. Under the new system, private contractors are paid simply to keep prisoners under custody, or for providing other services (such as education and counseling) that are specifically spelled out in a contract.

THE GROWTH OF CONTRACT FACILITIES

The primary advantage of using contract facilities rests in the speed with which additional prison capacity can be obtained and the possibility of increasing bed space without public capital expenditure. Unprecedented growth in the number of prisoners in the United States led to considerable overcrowding in public facilities; by 1989, two-thirds of the states were operating under court orders or consent decrees due to conditions of confinement suits brought on by overcrowding. By 1990, nine state systems were operating at more than 150% of capacity, 15 states were operating at between 125% and 150% of capacity, and the federal prisoner population was at roughly 190% of its rated capacity.

Burgeoning prisoner population rates were accompanied by rapidly rising correctional costs. State and local government annual operating costs for correctional facilities ballooned eight-fold between 1978 and 2000, from $5 billion to nearly $40 billion. Total capital outlay for new prison construction in the states averaged nearly $2 billion each year during the 1990s. Many jurisdictions could not issue bonds, the primary method of funding large, capital projects such as prisons and jails, without going directly to the voters—a time-consuming process with an uncertain outcome. In some cases, states were at or approaching debt ceilings, and expenditure on new prisons precluded spending on other needed capital projects. The entire process of planning, designing, permitting, building, staffing, and opening a new government-owned facility can take several years. Private entities, on the other hand, invest private capital into new facilities and can cut a substantial amount of time off the development process. Moreover, by contracting with another government jurisdiction or private provider that has existing unused bed space, governments can forestall capital investment in new prisons and quickly relieve immediate problems of prison overcrowding.

The demand for increased capacity caused by prison overcrowding and the relative expediency of using contract facilities combined to fuel rapid growth in the private prison industry in the United States. Between 1988 and 1998, the number of contracted prison beds increased from 3,000 to 132,000. By 1998, there were 158 private correctional facilities contracting for the placement of about 5% of the total U.S. correctional population. But by the end of the 1990s, incarceration rate growth began to cool off, prison capacity began to more closely approximate need, and the rate of growth in contract facilities declined accordingly.

AVOIDING PROBLEMS WITH CONTRACT FACILITIES

Simply contracting with a nongovernment entity to provide correctional services does not guarantee that contract facilities can actually provide correctional services at less cost or greater quality than government programs. The body of research comparing public and private facilities finds that cost savings in contract facilities are most likely to occur in jurisdictions where the wages and benefits of public employees exceed the national average and that, on the whole, contract facilities provide a quality of inmate care on parity with public facilities. However, research also shows that many problems in contract facilities are prompted by poorly written contracts or by inadequate contract monitoring by government agencies.

Prior to entering into the contract process, government agencies should consider whether they have the capacity to manage and monitor contracts with private entities adequately. While the use of contract facilities may streamline government operations, it does not relieve government from the ultimate responsibility for custody and care of inmates. At minimum, successful contracting requires that governments assign full-time staff to the tasks of contract management. Contract development should begin with a competitive bidding process that permits bids by nonprofit as well as for-profit organizations. Many government jurisdictions also allow government agencies, including divisions within the contracting jurisdiction, to compete head-to-head with nongovernment bidders. Commonly referred to as "market testing," this practice was pioneered in the United Kingdom and has had the collateral effect of prompting government-operated facilities to adopt cost-saving strategies in order to remain competitive with the private sector.

Contracts should be thorough and specific to ensure accountability, detailing all areas of operations, including: staffing patterns, care and treatment provided to inmates, and policies and procedures for dealing with serious incidents. Quantifiable performance standards should be established to set acceptable levels for all operations along with procedures for government access to the contractor's facility, records, and staff. The contract should also specify the payment structure and billing policies to be used. Most contract facilities operate under a per diem payment system, whereby the provider is paid only for actual bed days used. The length of the agreement should be kept as short as possible by requiring that the contract be rebid every three to five years.

The contract should also describe courses of action to be taken should the contractor fail to live up to any contract provisions, be found to be deficient in any operational areas, change its management structure, or go out of business. Such stipulations should include a corrective action process to deal with deficiencies, a dispute resolution process for handling disagreements between the government and the contractor, and a system of liquidated damages that details financial penalties, to be deducted from contract payments, when serious deficiencies occur or previously identified compliance problems are not corrected. Finally, the contract should specify grounds for termination of the agreement, including grounds for termination for cause and termination by mutual consent.

CONCLUSION

Contract facilities, it seems, are here to stay. Their standards must, however, be carefully monitored, by criminologists, government agencies, and private businesses alike. Ongoing research and documentation will ensure that conditions in these institutions does not fall below comparable ones in state-run facilities.

—*Richard Culp*

See also Community Corrections Centers; Corrections Corporation of America; Convict Lease System; Privatization; Wackenhut Corporation

Further Reading

Austin, J., & Coventry, G. (2001). *Emerging issues on privatized prisons.* Washington, DC: U.S. Department of Justice, Bureau of Justice Assistance.

Collins, W. (2001). *Contracting for correctional services provided by private firms.* Washington, DC: U.S. Department of Justice, Office of Justice Programs, Corrections Program Office.

Cooper, P. J. (2003). *Governing by contract: Challenges and opportunities for public managers.* Washington, DC: Congressional Quarterly Press.

Jensen, C. (Ed.). (1987). *Contracting for community corrections services.* Sacramento: California State University, Center for California Studies.

◪ CONTRACT MINISTERS

Contract ministers are employed by all prison systems in the United States to offer pastoral care to inmates whose religious beliefs may not be adequately covered by the staff prison chaplain. Increasing numbers of these contract workers are being hired, as some jurisdictions have decided not to employ full-time chaplains. At their best, contract ministers can offer a broad range of religious options and care to the inmate community. They may also, however, operate at somewhat of a disadvantage, since they are not part of the full-time prison staff. In general, contractors are expected to respect the interfaith ethos of prison ministry and it is understood that proselytism in all forms is forbidden.

STAFF CHAPLAINS IN PRISON MINISTRY

All federal and most state prisons in the United States have at least one chaplain on staff who ministers to the diverse religious needs of the inmate community. With the passage of the Religious Freedom Restoration Act (RFRA) of 1993, which prohibits the state from taking any action that would substantially burden a prisoner's religious exercise, some state prisons that previously did not have a chaplaincy program have since employed a staff chaplain. The RFRA challenged the notion that a prisoner's right to religious observation could be refused because of perceived security threats and has now placed the burden of proof on the state or institution to prove any such threat.

A prison chaplain is responsible for providing all inmates with sufficient opportunities for religious worship, religious education, counseling, and crisis intervention. Besides providing these direct services, the prison chaplain is also in charge of administrative functions such as hiring contractors and coordinating prison volunteers as well as representing corrections to the larger community. Most prison chaplains are required to hold a master's in divinity degree, possess at least two years of pastoral care experience, and be endorsed by their own religious tradition. However, in some state prisons, lay people may also qualify for a chaplaincy position after completing a prison chaplaincy training program.

Prison chaplains' professional code of ethics obliges them to emphasize an impartial and interfaith approach to their prison ministries. For instance, they are meant to discourage the usage of their own denominational title (e.g., Rabbi, Father, Imam) within the prison setting, in favor of the more generic title of Chaplain. In addition, they must ensure that the diverse religious worship needs of all prisoners within the institution are being met. To meet these diverse needs, a prison chaplain may hire contractors (i.e., qualified clergy from a particular denomination) to perform religious worship services.

THE USE OF CONTRACTORS IN PRISON MINISTRY

There are a variety of possible scenarios in which a chaplain may be required to use outside contractors. In some situations, a contractor may be hired to conduct religious worship services that fall outside of the chaplain's own denomination. For example, a Protestant chaplain may hire a contract imam to perform worship services for the Islamic inmates if there is no Muslim chaplain on staff to meet this need. Outside contractors of the same faith background as the chaplain may also be recruited in the following instances: the prison chaplain is a lay person who is not allowed to perform certain, liturgical duties; there is an inordinately large number of inmates of that faith background who require multiple worship services a week; or the prison's physical layout is such that separate worship services are needed such as in a high-rise building.

A signification portion of most U.S. prison chaplaincy budgets are earmarked for the hiring of contractor services. However, due to budgetary considerations, contractors are recruited in most cases only when there is a critical mass of inmates requiring their services. For example, a prison chaplain could not divert resources to hiring a contract rabbi if there was only one Jewish inmate in the institution. Instead, the staff chaplain would have to meet the religious worship needs of the Jewish inmate by either coordinating a volunteer rabbi or the inmate's own rabbi to come in and perform the necessary liturgical duties for the inmate.

A CASE STUDY OF A CONTRACT MINISTER

Paul Rodgers is president of the American Correctional Chaplains' Association and the full-time chaplain at Dodge Correctional Institution, a state prison in Waupan, Wisconsin. In his role as chaplain, Rodgers uses contractors to fill the unmet religious worship needs of various groups of inmates. The faith backgrounds and worship needs of incoming inmates are generally determined by having them fill out a Religious Preference Form when they enter the institution.

Although the majority of inmates at Dodge Correctional Institution come from mostly Protestant backgrounds (i.e., mainly Lutheran and Methodist), there is a sizable enough Catholic population that Rodgers contracts Catholic priests to meet the religious worship needs of the Catholic inmates on a weekly basis. Rodgers himself is Catholic, but as a layman chaplain cannot perform mass or serve the Eucharist.

There are only 25–40 Jews among the 20,000 men and women who are incarcerated in the state of Wisconsin. In addition, Muslims, Buddhists, Native Americans, and those belonging to other religious groups represent only a small fraction of the state's total prisoner population. To meet the needs of these religious minorities, the state of Wisconsin's corrections system hires individual contractors to travel throughout the state to a number of prisons to perform religious services for these underserved groups. Chaplain Rodgers, as well as other prison ministers, also use volunteer clergy from these various faith traditions to help serve the religious minorities within Wisconsin's state prison system.

CONCLUSION

Contractors as well as volunteers help to meet the worship needs of prisoners at many penal institutions. Even though staff prison chaplains are obliged to foster an interfaith, impartial environment and to provide counseling and crisis intervention to inmates of all faith traditions, contract ministers are often required to assist them, if the prison holds a particularly diverse population. By supplementing the work of prison chaplains, contractors and volunteers ensure that a prisoner's right to religious observation are upheld.

—*Jeneve Brooks-Klinger*

See also Chaplains; History of Religion in Prison; Islam in Prison; Judaism in Prison; Native American Spirituality; Religion in Prison; Quakers; Volunteers

Further Reading

Beckford, J., & Gilliat, S. (1998). *Religion in prison: Equal rites in a multi-faith society.* Cambridge, UK: Cambridge University Press.

Cowart, J. (1996). *The prison minister's handbook: Volunteer ministry to the forgotten Christian.* San Jose, CA: Resource Publications.

Rodgers, P. (2003, January). *A message from our president.* Retrieved from http://www.correctionalchaplains.org

Shilder, D. (1999). *Inside the fence: A handbook for those in prison ministry.* Staten Island, NY: Alba House.

U.S. Department of Justice, Federal Bureau of Prisons. (2001). *Chaplains' employment, responsibilities, and endorsements* (PS3939.07). Washington, DC: Author.

◪ CONTROL UNIT

The National Institute of Corrections defines a *control unit* as

a highly restrictive, high custody housing unit within a secure facility, or an entire secure facility, that isolates inmates from the general population and from each other due to grievous crimes, repetitive assaultive or violent institutional behavior, the threat of escape or actual escape from high-custody facility(s), or inciting or threatening to incite disturbances in a correctional institution. (Riveland, 1999, p. 6)

Control units are also referred to as administrative maximum penitentiaries, intensive housing units, intensive management units, maxi-maxi units, maximum control facilities, restrictive housing units, secured housing units, and special housing units. These days they exist in almost all penal systems.

HISTORY

Since the inception of prisons, correctional administrators have always had to determine what to do with those inmates who did not conform to institutional rules. Both the Auburn and Pennsylvania models of the penitentiary that developed in the 19th century relied heavily on isolation to foster inmate reform and obedience. In these systems, women and men were held in isolation for long periods of time and forbidden to communicate with one another. They were also forced to labor. Unlike today, recalcitrant prisoners could also be whipped. Once corporal punishment was outlawed, correctional officials began more frequently to remove recalcitrant inmates from the general population often placing them in solitary confinement, more commonly referred to as "the hole" or "the box." Inmates in solitary confinement were unable to interact with others and placed on restricted diets for a period of time determined by the correctional administration. In two landmark cases, *Wolff v. McDonnell* (1974) and *Sandin v. Conner* (1995), the U.S. Supreme Court further delineated the due process rights afforded inmates before they could be placed in isolation for a set period of punishment in response to violation of an institutional rule.

The Federal Bureau of Prisons is often credited with the development of super-maximum secure facilities when it opened Alcatraz in San Francisco Bay to hold habitual felons. When Alcatraz closed in 1963, its inmates were spread throughout the bureau's remaining federal penitentiaries. In 1978, in response to the high level of violence in the federal prison system, U.S. Penitentiary in Marion, Illinois, opened a high-security control unit. As a result of continued violence at Marion, the entire prison was converted to lockdown, otherwise known as indefinite administrative segregation. In 1994, the Federal Bureau of Prisons opened the Administrative Maximum Penitentiary in Florence, Colorado, that now houses the federal prison system's most serious and chronic troublemakers.

State correctional systems soon followed the federal prison system's example and developed segregated housing areas or units within existing prisons, or built separate prisons for this purpose. A recent survey by the National Institute of Corrections reports that 30 states are operating one or more such facilities or units. Nationally, there are at least 57 control units/facilities, providing more than 13,500 beds. Similarly, Canada reported that between 1991 and 2001, its percentage of segregated prisoners more than doubled to represent 5.5% of federally sentenced prisoners. Such facilities are usually justified by a perceived need to manage an increasing number of violent and seriously disruptive inmates.

POPULATION CHARACTERISTICS

Who exactly is housed in control units is unclear. Although the U.S. Department of Justice provides statistics on the number of penal facilities by security level (maximum, medium, minimum), it does not provide separate information on those held in control units or super-maximum secure prisons. Indeed, given that most prisoners are confined in control units only for short periods of time, accurate information might be difficult to obtain.

Compounding the problem, there are few empirical studies of inmates housed in control units in the United States or Canada. Since most of the research that does exist focuses on a small number of control units in a handful of correctional institutions, the demographic information of the samples may not be representative of the larger control unit population. With these caveats in mind, studies indicate that in both Canada and the United States men housed in control units have an average age of 29. Over half are Caucasian and about one-quarter are black.

Not unexpectedly, information about women in control units in the United States and Canada is also very limited. Once again, from the limited body of literature that exists, it appears that segregation is practiced similarly in men's and women's prisons, with two exceptions. First, women may have greater freedoms within control units than men since they are usually allowed reading materials and personal toiletries such as make-up. They are also usually permitted to congregate for meals. Somewhat paradoxically, however, women are more likely to be placed in control units for relatively minor infraction most of which appear merely to be conduct that violates their gender roles, such as swearing, tattooing, and "mouthing off." The demographic characteristics of women housed in segregation in Canada and the United States indicate an average age of 31. In Canada, women housed in segregation are 67% Aboriginal, 23% Caucasian, and 10% black.

PLACEMENT IN CONTROL UNITS

In both the United States and Canada, inmates are placed in control units at the discretion of correctional administrators for one of three purposes. Those who are charged with a serious rule violation may be moved to a control unit while the investigation of their crime and disciplinary hearing takes place. If they are found guilty of violating a serious rule (one that involved the threat or use of violence), they may be returned to the control unit to serve a specified number of days or months as imposed by the hearing officer. When control unit confinement is a sanction for prisoners found guilty of violating serious prison rules, it is called disciplinary segregation or punitive segregation. In some instances, when a rule violation also contravenes state laws, as is the case in assaults, homicides, and drug trafficking, prisoners may be convicted for these additional crimes.

Inmates suspected of playing a role in an incident or potential incident within the prison, and who have not yet been formally charged, may also be detained in a control unit until the investigation is complete. This type of isolation is referred to as administrative segregation or administrative detention.

Last, inmates may be placed in a control unit when prison officials believe they are dangers to themselves or will be victimized by others. Control units thus provide protective custody to vulnerable inmates, such as those who have been threatened or experienced physical or sexual assaults, those who are unable to function in the general population perhaps because of their mental or physical disabilities, and those who serve as informants for the administration. Inmates who are repeatedly involved in serious institutional rules (assaults, predatory behavior, inciting riots, or attempting escapes) could be segregated until the administration believed that they were no longer a threat to institutional security.

WHAT ARE CONTROL UNITS LIKE?

Control units are basically a miniature prison within the larger institution. They vary widely in the degree of restrictions placed on those living in them, but their primary purpose is always to control inmate behavior. Those held for protection are likely to have more privileges afforded to them than are those held for administrative or disciplinary purposes.

Regardless of the reason for their confinement, control unit inmates typically remain in their small cells for 22–23 hours a day. The cells are often equipped with solid steel doors that prevent any communication between prisoners. Remote-controlled electronic sliding doors and intercom systems further reduce the direct interaction and contact between inmates and correctional staff. No communal dining, exercise, or religious services are provided. If inmates are offered programs/services such as education or substance abuse treatment, these are typically brought to the inmates via counseling staff or through television or cable programming. Work opportunities are almost nonexistent. Human contact is often limited to medical staff, clergy, and counselors who visit the inmate. Noncontact visits with approved visitors are permitted for some inmates housed in control units.

THE CASE FOR AND AGAINST CONTROL UNITS

Current policies in most jurisdictions allow for inmates to be housed for administrative reasons and protection for indefinite periods of time. A few studies have examined the effects of short-term periods of isolation (60 days or less) and report that inmates adapt initially by increased pacing and sleeping, and then typically shift into reading, physical exercise, or meditation to deal with the lack of stimulation. Individuals housed in control units evidence more internalized problems, interpersonal distress, and psychiatric symptoms than those in the general population. However, at least one study found no empirical evidence that these symptoms deteriorated after confinement in control units for periods less than 60 days. The effects of longer terms of solitary confinement have not been studied, although personal accounts suggest that it is stressful and may limit inmates' coping abilities.

The use of control units has been criticized by several organizations including Amnesty International, Human Rights Watch, the American Friends Service Committee, and the National Lawyers Guild, and some have formed campaigns to shut down all control units. These groups raise concerns about the negative psychological impact that such confinement may have on inmates. There is consensus that inmates with serious mental health problems should not be placed in control units. The high constructional and operational costs due to the enhanced security features and intensive staffing necessary to deliver services and programs to inmates individually are also a source of concern for some critics.

In contrast, correctional administrators usually tout three benefits of control units. First, they reduce the level of violence in other correctional institutions throughout a correctional system. The threat of transfer to control units serves as a deterrent to violence, and thus makes the inmate population more manageable. Second, control units house only the most violent prisoners who have demonstrated that they cannot be held at other prisons without jeopardizing the safety of other inmates and correctional staff. However, there is some evidence that in practice broader criteria for entry are employed. Last, the reduction of violence that results from use of control units allows the security at other prisons in that system to be relaxed. No empirical data have been collected to test these claims.

CONCLUSION

In recent years, control units have become commonplace in many penal systems. Given the controversies that still rage over their effectiveness and impact on psychological health, clearly more research needs to be done. Until it is clearer what this modern form of solitary confinement actually achieves, there is a fairly strong case that its use should be kept to an absolute minimum.

—*Mary A. Finn*

See also ADX (Administrative Maximum) Florence; Alcatraz; Disciplinary Segregation; Lexington High Security Unit; Marion, U.S. Penitentiary; Maximum Security; Mental Health; Pelican Bay State Prison; Protective Custody; Solitary Confinement; Special Housing Unit; Supermax Prisons; Violence

Further Reading

American Friends Service Committee. (1997). *National campaign to stop control unit prisons.* Retrieved from http://www.afsc.org/crimjust/controlu.htm

Barak-Glantz, I. L. (1983). Who's in the "hole"? *Criminal Justice Review, 8,* 29–37.

Korn, R. (1988). The effects of confinement in the high security unit at Lexington. *Social Justice, 15*(1), 1–8.

LIS, Inc. (1997). *Supermax housing: A survey of current practice.* Longmont, CO: U.S. Department of Justice.

Martel, J. (2001). Telling the story: A study in the segregation of women prisoners. *Social Justice, 28*(1), 196–215.

Riveland, C. (1999). *Supermax prisons: Overview and general considerations.* Washington, DC: National Institute of Corrections.

Shafer, C. (1998). It's like living in a black hole: Women of color and solitary confinement in the prison-industrial complex. *New England Journal on Criminal and Civil Confinement, 24*(2), 385–416.

Zinger, I., Wichmann, C., & Andrews, D. A. (2001). The physical effects of 60 days in administrative segregation. *Canadian Journal of Criminology, 43*(1), 47–83.

Legal Cases

Sandin v. Conner, 515 U.S. 472; 115 S. Ct. 2293; 132 L. Ed. 2d 418; 1995 LEXIS 4069.

Wolff v. McDonnell, 416 U.S. 966; 945 S. Ct. 1987; 40 L. Ed. 2d 556; 1974 LEXIS 346.

■ CONVICT CRIMINOLOGY

There are a significant number of former prisoners studying criminology and becoming professors. As a result of their experiences of arrest, trial, and years of incarceration, they have profound insight that promises to update and inform what we know about crime and correction. Since 1997, ex-convict criminology and criminal justice professors have organized sessions at annual meetings of the American Society of Criminology, Academy of Criminal Justice Sciences, and American Correctional Association. These professors discuss academic response to and responsibility for deteriorating prison conditions.

THE NEW SCHOOL OF CONVICT CRIMINOLOGY

The conference presentations were used to build a working group of ex-convict and nonconvict critical criminologists to invent the "new school of convict criminology." This is a new criminology led by ex-convicts who are now academic faculty. These men and women, who have worn both prison uniforms and academic regalia, served years behind prisons walls, and now as academics are the primary architects of the movement. As ex-convicts currently employed at universities, the convict criminologists openly discuss their personal history and distrust of mainstream criminology.

Regardless of criminal history, all the group members share a desire to go beyond "managerial" and "armchair" criminology by conducting research that includes ethnography and the inside perspective. In contrast to normative academic practice, the "convict criminologists" hold no pretense for value-free criminology and are partisan and proactive in their discourse. This includes merging convict, ex-convict, and critical voices in their writing. As Rideau and Wikberg (1992) wrote, "That's the reality, and to hell with what the class-room bred, degree toting, grant-hustling 'experts' say from their well-funded, air-conditioned offices far removed from the grubby realities of the prisoners' lives" (p. 59).

CONVICT CRIMINOLOGISTS

The ex-convicts can be described, in terms of academic experience, as three distinct cohorts. The first are the more senior members, full and associate professors, some with distinguished research records. A second group of assistant professors is just beginning to contribute to the field. The third, only some of whom have been identified, are graduate student ex-convicts.

While all these individuals provide convict criminology with unique and original experiential resources, some of the most important contributors may yet prove to be scholars who have never served prison time. A number of these authors have worked inside prisons or have conducted extensive research on the subject. The inclusion of these "non-cons" in the new school's original cohort provides the means to extend the influence of the convict criminology while also supporting existing critical criminology perspectives.

Convict criminologists recognize that they are not the first to criticize the prison and correctional practices. They pay their respects to those who have raised critical questions about prisons and suggested realistic humane reforms. The problem they are most concerned with is that identified by Todd Clear in the foreword to Richard McCleary's *Dangerous Men* (1978/1992): "Why does it seem that all good efforts to build reform systems seems inevitably to disadvantage the offender?" The answer is that, despite the best intentions, reform systems were never intended to help convicts. Reformers rarely even bothered to ask the convicts what reforms they desired. The new school "con-sultants" correct this problem by entering prisons and directly asking the prisoners what they want and need.

ETHNOGRAPHIC METHODOLOGIES: INSIDER PERSPECTIVES

Convict criminologists specialize in "on site" ethnographic research where their prior experience with imprisonment informs their work. They interview in penitentiary cellblocks, in community penal facilities, or on street corners. Their method is to enter jails and prisons and converse with prisoners. This may include a combination of survey instruments, structured interviews, and informal observation and conversation. As former prisoners they know the "walk" and "talk" of the prison, as well as how to gain the confidence of the men and women who live inside. Consequently, they have earned a reputation for collecting quality and controversial data.

Ex-convict academics have carried out a number of significant ethnographic studies. John Irwin, for example, who served a prison sentence in California, drew on his experience to write the *The Felon, Prisons in Turmoil, The Jail,* and *It's About Time* (with James Austin). Richard McCleary, who did both state and federal time, wrote his classic *Dangerous Men* based on his participant observation of parole officers. Charles M. Terry,

a former California and Oregon state convict, wrote about how prisoners used humor to mitigate the managerial domination of penitentiary authorities. Greg Newbold, having served prison time in New Zealand, wrote *The Big Huey, Punishment and Politics,* and *Crime in New Zealand* to analyze crime and corrections in his country. Stephen C. Richards and Richard S. Jones, both former prisoners, used "inside experience" to inform their studies of prisoners returning home. Finally, Jeffrey Ian Ross and Stephen C. Richards coauthored *Behind Bars* and coedited *Convict Criminology.*

LANGUAGE AND POINT OF VIEW

The convict criminologists all share an aversion to the language used in most academic research writing on crime and corrections. Typically, researchers use words such as *offender* and *inmate.* In comparison, convict criminology prefers to use *convicts, prisoners,*

Prison Writing

Officially, the Federal Bureau of Prisons supports the writing of prisoners, but there are a number of ambiguous policy and program statements that allow the administration to come out of nowhere, start writing you shots, and put you in SHU. My experience is a perfect example of what happens to prison writers.

I started out getting published in underground magazines. My first published pieces were poems and essays on prison life. Then I started writing about prisoners with special talents like musicians, basketball players, and other types of phenomenal athletes. Back then my writing never created a stir with the administration. Sometimes I would even show my case manager or counselor the pieces I had published.

Then one time I wrote a piece that was published in *Don Diva* magazine, a thuglife publication based in New York City. The piece harshly criticized the war on drugs and I compared the future drug war trials to the Nuremburg Trials. As soon as the administration found out about this article I was shipped right out of the low security prison I had resided in for three years with no problems to a higher security prison where I was harassed and retaliated against for the next six months.

But I persevered and to this day I am still writing and getting published. I have heard other stories about writers in prison too. For example, Dannie Martin, a.k.a. Red Hog, who was thrown in and out of the hole for years, has finally got out and now has an agent and several books under his belt. I believe that prison writing is a good profession to try to start while in prison because when you get out you have viable options, plus it's better than working at McDonald's.

Seth Ferranti
FCI Fairton, Fairton, New Jersey

or simply *men* or *women.* The distinction is important because it illustrates the different point of view of researchers and authors who have never been incarcerated with those that have. *Offender* and *inmate* are managerial words used by police, court officials, and criminal justice administrators to deny the humanity of defendants and prisoners. To the ear of a former prisoner, being referred to as an offender or inmate is analogous to a man being called a boy, or a women a girl. Clearly, the struggle feminists fought to redefine how women were addressed and discussed taught an important lesson to the convict criminologists: Words are important.

RESPECT FOR CONVICT AUTHORS STILL IN PRISON

A number of the convict criminologists continue friendships and working relationships with writers in prison, some of whom are well published in criminology. This includes Victor Hassine, a prisoner in Pennsylvania who wrote *Life Without Parole;* Wilbert Rideau, a convict in Louisiana who wrote *Life Sentences* (with Ron Wikberg); and Jon Marc Talyor, serving time in Missouri and the author of numerous newspaper and journal articles. The ex-convict academics use correspondence, phone calls, and prison visits to communicate with these prisoners in order to stay current with prison conditions.

The convict authors write serious commentaries on prison life. Unfortunately, much of their research and writing, while critically informed, based on their experiences inside prisons, may be only partially grounded in the academic literature. After all, many of these authors lack or have difficulties obtaining the typical amenities that most scholars take for granted. For example, they may not have access to a computer for writing, to a university library, and or to colleagues educated in criminology. They struggle to write by hand, or with broken or worn out machines, and lack of supplies. They may be unable to procure typewriter ribbons, paper, envelopes, stamps, and so on. In addition, their phones calls are monitored and recorded, and all their mail is opened, searched, and read by prison authorities. In many cases, they suffer the retribution of prison authorities, including denial of parole, loss of "good time" credit, physical threats from staff or inmates, frequent cell searches, confiscation of manuscripts, trips to the hole, and disciplinary transfers to other prisons.

In comparison, convict criminologists have academic resources and credibility to conduct a wide range of research and writing. These resources allow them to use developments in theory, methodology, and public policy to hone their discourse. As academics they know the scholarly literature on prison, including theory, methodologies, and how issues have been debated over the years. This knowledge provides them with the opportunity to generalize from research findings and to understand better how prison conditions compare over time, from state to state, or country to country.

RECENT POLICY RECOMMENDATIONS

Convict criminologists have come up with several policy recommendations. First, the group advocates dramatic reductions in the national prison population through diversion to probation or other community programs. Today, many men and women are sentenced to prison for nonviolent crime. These people should be evaluated as candidates for early release, with the remainder of their sentence to be served under community supervision. The only good reason for locking up a person in a cage is if he and she is a danger to the community. A prisoner should have an opportunity to reduce his or her sentence by earning good-time credit for good behavior and program participation. Unfortunately, many state correctional systems, following the federal model, have moved toward determinate sentencing. This "truth in sentencing" has limited provisions for good-time reductions in sentences, and no parole.

One problem with reducing the prison population is predicting who might commit new crimes. Despite numerous attempts, we still have no reliable instruments to predict the potential risk of either first-time or subsequent criminal behavior by either free or incarcerated individuals. The problems are many, including "false positives," which predict a person to be a risk who is not. Conversely, "false negatives" are persons predicted not to be dangerous who turn out to be so. Even so, the fact that our science is less than successful at devising classification schemes and prediction scales is not an adequate rationale for failing to support reductions in prison admissions and population.

Second, convict criminologists support the closing of large-scale penitentiaries and reformatories, where prisoners are warehoused in massive cellblocks. Over many decades, the design and operation of these "big house" prisons has resulted in murder, assault, and sexual predation. A reduced prison population housed in smaller institutions would be accomplished by constructing or redesigning prison housing units with single cells or rooms. Smaller prisons, for example, with a maximum of 500 prisoners, with single cells or rooms, should become the correctional standard when we begin to seriously consider the legal requirement for safe and secure institutions. As a model, we should turn to European countries that have much lower rates of incarceration, shorter sentences, and smaller prisons.

Third, we need to listen carefully to prisoner complaints about long sentences, overcrowding, double celling, bad food, old uniforms, lack of heat in winter and air-conditioning in summer, inadequate vocational and education programs, and institutional violence. The list grows longer when we take a careful look at how these conditions contribute to prisoners being poorly prepared for returning home and the large number that return to prison.

Fourth, we have strong evidence that prison programs are underfunded, since administrators and legislators continue to emphasize custody at the expense of treatment. Prisoners should be provided with opportunities for better-paid institutional employment, advanced vocational training, higher education, and family skills programs. It is true that most institutions have "token" programs that serve a small number of prisoners. For example, a prison may have paid jobs for 20% of its prisoners, low-tech training, a general equivalency diploma (GED) program, and occasional classes in life skills or group therapy sessions. The problem is that these services are dramatically limited in scope and availability.

We need to ask convicts what services and programs they want and need to improve their ability to live law-abiding lives rather than assume and then implement what we believe is good for them. One recommendation is that prisoners be provided with paid employment, either inside or outside of the prison, where they will earn enough to pay for their own college tuition. At the very least, all prisons should have a program that supports prisoners to complete college-credit courses by correspondence.

At the present time, most U.S. prisons systems budget very little for prisoner programs. Instead they spend on staff salaries and security. This is because prison administrators are evaluated on preventing escapes and maintaining order in their institutions. So the prisons are operated like zoos where human beings live in cages, with few options to develop skills and a new future.

Fifth, convict criminology advocates voting rights for all prisoners and felons. The United States is one of the few advanced industrial countries that continues to deny prisoners and felons voting rights. We suggest that if convicts could vote, many of the recommendations we advocate would become policy because the politicians would be forced to campaign for convict votes. State and federal government will begin to address the deplorable conditions in our prisons only when prisoners and felons become voters. We do not see prisoners as any less interested than free persons in exercising the right to vote. To the contrary, if voting booths were installed in jails and prisons, we think the voter turnout would be higher than in most outside communities.

Sixth, we advocate that prisoners released from prison have enough "gate money" that would allow them to pay for three months' worth of rent and food. The ex-cons could earn some of this money working in prison industries, with the balance provided by the institution. All prisoners exiting correctional institutions should have clothing suitable for applying for employment, eyeglasses (if needed), and identification including a social security card, state ID or driver's license, and a copy of their institutional medical records. They should be given credit for time served on parole supervision. Finally, we need to address the use of drug and alcohol testing as the primary cause of parole violations.

Seventh, our most controversial policy recommendation is eliminating the snitch system in prison. The snitch system is used by "guards" in old-style institutions to supplement their surveillance of convicts. It is used to control prisoners by turning them against each other and is therefore responsible for ongoing institutional violence. If our recommendations for a smaller population, housed in single cells or rooms, with better food and clothing, voting rights, and well-funded institutional programming were implemented, the snitch system would be unnecessary. In a small prison, with these progressive reforms, prison staff would no longer be forced to behave as guards, instead having the opportunity to actively "do corrections" as correctional workers. The staff would be their own eyes and ears, because they would be actively involved in the care and treatment of prisoners.

Finally, we support the termination of the drug war. Military metaphors continue to confuse our thinking and complicate our approach to crime and drug addiction. For example, the theory of judicial deterrence, discussed as a rationale for sentencing in nearly every criminal justice textbook, is derived from the Cold War idea of nuclear deterrence. This idea evolved into mutually assured destruction (MAD), which was the American rationale for building thousands of nuclear bombs to deter a possible Soviet nuclear attack. The use of deterrence and war has now bled over from the military strategic thinking to colonize criminal justice. The result is another cold war, this one against our own people. We advocate an end to the drug war, amnesty for drug offenders, and a reexamination of how our criminal justice priorities are set.

PROS AND CONS OF CONVICT CRIMINOLOGY

The first strength of convict criminology is that it is based on a bottom-up, inside-out perspective that gives voice to the millions of men and women convicts and felons. The second is that the group is composed of men and women who have served prison time in many different environments including the Federal Bureau of Prisons, various state systems, different countries, and at different levels of security. Altogether, the founding members of the group have served more than 50 years in prison. Finally, it should be remembered that it would have been much easier for the ex-convict professors to conceal their past and quietly enjoy their academic careers. Instead, they decided to "come out of the closet," develop their own field of study, and take up the fight against the liberal-conservative consensus that continues to ignore the harm done by mass incarceration in the United States.

There are two glaring weaknesses of this new field. First, most of the ex-convict professors are white males. This is the result of two facts: Very few minorities leave prison prepared to enter graduate school, and over 90% of prisoners are male. To some extent, this problem is being addressed through active recruitment of minorities and women into the group. For example, the group does include feminist non-con criminologists who conduct prison research.

Second, because the group is partisan and activist it is clearly biased in its approach to research and publication. On the other hand, the convict criminologists would argue that given the prejudice most people, academics included, have against criminals, convicts, and felons, the idea of value-free prison research is at best a polite fantasy. The only solution to this dilemma is for all researchers who contribute to the literature to discuss their biases openly, including former criminal justice personnel.

CONCLUSION

Convict criminology is a new way of thinking about crime and corrections. The alumni of the penitentiary now study in classrooms and serve as university faculty. The old textbooks in criminology, criminal justice, and corrections will have to be revised. A new field of study has been created, a paradigm shift occurred, and the prison is no longer so distant.

—*Stephen C. Richards and Jeffrey Ian Ross*

See also Jack Henry Abbott; Celebrities in Prison; Constitutive Criminology; Angela Y. Davis; Education; Gary Gilmore; John Irwin; George Jackson; Literature; Malcolm X; Prison Culture; Prisoner Writing; Resistance

Further Reading

Austin, J., Bruce, M. A., Carroll, L., McCall, P. L., & Richards, S. C. (2001). The use of incarceration in the United States. American Society of Criminology National Policy Committee. *Critical Criminology: An International Journal, 10*(1), 17–41.

Austin, J., & Irwin, J. (2002). *It's about time: America's incarceration binge* (3rd ed.). Belmont, CA: Wadsworth.

Irwin, J. (1970). *The felon.* Englewood Cliffs, NJ: Prentice Hall.

Irwin, J. (1985). *The jail.* Berkeley: University of California Press.

McCleary, R. (1978/1992). *Dangerous men: The sociology of parole.* New York: Harrow and Heston.

Newbold, G. (1982/1985). *The big Huey.* Auckland, New Zealand: Collins.

Richards, S. C., & Jones, R. S. (1997). Perpetual incarceration machine: Structural impediments to post-prison success. *Journal of Contemporary Criminal Justice, 13*(1), 4–22.

Richards, S. C., & Ross, J. I. (2001). The new school of convict criminology. *Social Justice, 28*(1), 177–190.

Rideau, W., & Wikberg, R. (1992). *Life sentences: Rage and survival behind bars.* New York: Times Books.

Ross, J. I., & Richards, S. C. (2002a). *Behind bars: Surviving prison*. New York: Alpha.

Ross, J. I., & Richards, S. C. (Eds.). (2002b). *Convict criminology*. Belmont, CA: Wadsworth.

Terry, C. M. (1997). The function of humor for prison inmates. *Journal of Contemporary Criminal Justice, 13*(1), 23–40.

CONVICT LEASE SYSTEM

Convict leasing refers to a particular means of putting inmates to work that originally developed in the South following the end of the Civil War, but was eventually used all over the United States. In this system, persons convicted of criminal offenses were sent to sugar and cotton plantations, coal mines, turpentine farms, phosphate beds, brickyards, sawmills, and cotton mills. They were leased to businessmen, planters, and corporations in one of the harshest and most exploitative labor systems known in American history. Though this practice no longer strictly exists in the United States, remnants of it can be found in joint venture programs where prisoners work for the profit of private corporations.

HISTORY

Convicts have been used as a source of cheap and profitable labor for centuries. The ancient Greeks and Romans both put convicted criminals to work on state-operated public works. In the Middle Ages, convicts were routinely sold into slavery, especially galley slavery. By the late 15th and 16th centuries, workhouses were established to confine beggars and vagabonds, to put them to work grinding corn, making nails, spinning fabric, or other labors.

This same trend occurred in the American colonies. In 1699, Massachusetts "declared that rogues and vagabonds were to be punished and set to work in the house of correction" (Rothman, 1971, p. 26). Other colonies followed suit. Inmates of the first American prisons were forced to labor as part of their incarceration. The Walnut Street Jail, which began to accept prisoners in 1790, set its inmates to work under what we now call the piece-price system. With the rise of the penitentiary system in the early 1800s, convict labor was a central focus of reform.

THE AMERICAN CONTEXT

The early debate over the merits of the Pennsylvania and Auburn systems focused on the uses of convict labor and, ultimately, on profitability. The Pennsylvania system reflected a plan for solitary confinement of inmates. Each inmate worked alone in his cell without contact with other inmates. Work was mostly menial and unprofitable for the institution. The Auburn system combined separate confinement with silent, collective work. This system became the model for most prisons in the United States.

A few years after the first prison opened in Auburn, New York, in 1817, a local citizen was given a contract to operate a factory within the prison walls. Prisoners were also leased out to private bidders to be housed, fed, and worked for profit. This practice provided the beginnings of the lease system.

Eventually, three systems of convict labor emerged in the 19th century: the contract system, the state use system, and the convict lease system. The contract system dominated prisons in the northern part of the country. Under this system, the state feeds, clothes, houses, and guards the convict. To do this, the state maintains an institution and a force of guards and other employees. The contractor pays the state a stipulated amount per capita for the services of the convict and sells the final product on the open market. In the lease system, the state enters into a contract with a lessee who agrees to receive the convict; to feed, clothe, house, and guard him; to keep him at work; and to pay the state a specified amount for his labor. The state does not maintain an institution to house prisoners. In the state use system, the state conducts a business of manufacture or production but the sale of the goods produced is limited to state agencies. Today, the state use system is the most commonly used of the systems.

RELATIONSHIP BETWEEN SLAVERY AND CONVICT LEASING

The convict lease system was inexorably intertwined with the post–Civil War economic recovery of the South. Emancipation moved the Southern economy from a slave society based on forced labor to a caste society based on more overt, coercive techniques. The antebellum South was a labor-intensive, agricultural society. The convict lease system helped restore the basis of agricultural profitability by alleviating the shortage of labor. The legal system provided a cheap labor force of experienced agricultural workers and helped to control the black population.

In Southern states, prisons were not used extensively prior to the Civil War. After the war, the South was faced with severe economic, political, and social problems. At the time, the North and the South both incurred vast increases in prison populations due to the large numbers of returning servicemen and the postwar recession. The situation was more acutely felt in the war-ravaged South as prisons, railroads, factories, and much of the land itself had been almost totally destroyed in many areas. The destruction of the economy coincided with the emancipation of black slaves, creating a further strain on economic and social institutions. The South's solution to this problem was to create a system of convict leasing, as well as to found a number of plantation-style penitentiaries. Both served to perpetuate race and class divisions while profiting the state.

The lease system worked in concert with the new criminal codes of the postwar South, which, in a series of laws known as the Black Codes, piled up heavy penalties for petty offenses against property while at the same time weakening the protection afforded blacks in court. Prior to the Civil War, blacks were not sent to prison in great numbers. When a slave did commit a crime, the matter was usually resolved locally. A range of corporal punishments (flogging, beating, etc.) was typically used for petty criminal acts, while more serious offenses were dealt with through shootings or lynchings. After the war, the implementation of vaguely worded laws (vagrancy, loitering, etc.) meant that just about any former slave could be arrested and sentenced to prison.

The "pig law" of Mississippi, passed in 1876, illustrates the nature and effect of the Black Codes well. This bill "declared the theft of any property valued at more than ten dollars, or of any kind of cattle or swine, regardless of value, to be grand larceny," which was punishable by up to five years in the state prison (quoted in Shelden, 1980, p. 6). After its adoption, the number of state convicts in Mississippi increased from 272 in 1874 to 1,072 by the end of 1877. The number in Georgia increased from 432 in 1874 to 1,441 in 1877 (Woodward, 1971, p. 213).

Such laws caused not only a dramatic increase in prison populations but also a shift in the racial make-up of who was incarcerated. McKelvey (1977) noted: "In the Deep South [African Americans] soon exceeded 90% of the total prison population, making the traditions and methods of the old slave system seem more logical patterns for southern penology than the costly methods of the north (p. 198). Shelden (1980, p. 5) noted that the black population at the main prison in Nashville, Tennessee, went from 33% in 1865 to 67% in 1867 and remained at 60% well in to the 20th century.

LEASING, CAPITALISM, AND VIOLENCE

The lease system rapidly became a large-scale business. Leases of 20 and 30 years were granted by legislatures to powerful politicians, Northern syndicates, mining corporations, and individual planters. The Tennessee Coal and Iron and Railroad Company (later to become a subsidiary of the U.S. Steel Corporation), dealt in convict "futures" in the same way brokers dealt in wheat and corn futures. Most problematically, as McKelvey (1977) noted, under the lease system, "there was no check, as in the North, where cells rapidly became crowded and compelled the construction of costly bastilles if convictions were too frequent" (p. 211).

In effect, under the leasing system, convicts became the slaves of the lessee as the latter had complete control over their food, clothing, discipline, and especially working conditions. Though the lessee was nominally responsible for the health and well-being of his convict-workers, abuses, brutality, and degradation became part of the system as lessees deprived convicts of necessary care and resorted to brutal punishments to extract more work from them. A grand jury investigation of the penitentiary hospital in Mississippi reported that inmates were

> all bearing on their persons marks of the most inhuman and brutal treatment. Most of them have their backs cut in great wales, scars and blisters, some with the skin peeling off in pieces as the result of severe beatings . . . they were lying there dying, some of them on bare boards, so poor and emaciated that their bones almost came through their skin, many complaining for want of food. . . . We actually saw live vermin crawling over their faces, and the little bedding and clothing they have is in tatters and stiff with filth. (quoted in Woodward, 1971, p. 214)

As a result of such treatment, the mortality rate for convicts rose dramatically. In the South, for instance, the rate of mortality was 41.3 per thousand convicts, while the rate for Northern prisons was only 14.9 (McKelvey, 1977, p. 183). The average annual death rate among Negro convicts in Mississippi from 1880 to 1885 was almost 11%; for white convicts it was half that. The death rate among prisoners of Arkansas was reported in 1881 to be 25% annually (Woodward, 1971, p. 141). In Louisiana between 1870 and 1901, 3,000 black convicts died under the lease system (Carelton, 1971, p. 46).

THE END OF THE LEASE SYSTEM

The reformist literature portrayed the lease system as being worse than slavery. An unidentified Southern man succinctly summarized the situation in 1883: "Before the war, we owned the Negroes. If a man had a good negro, he could afford to take care of him. He might even get gold plugs in his teeth. But these convicts: we don't own 'em. One dies, get another " (quoted in Carleton, 1971, p. 46).

Nonetheless, the lease system disappeared largely because of economic objections of both labor and business, rather than because of humanitarian objections. Free labor complained that convict labor deprived free men of jobs and businesses complained of unfair competition. McKelvey (1968) noted: "But the lease system was doomed by its decreasing usefulness to the state, and it was

not abandoned until profitable substitutes were perfected." These other systems included plantations, industrial prisons, and the chain gang, which still exists today (McKelvey, 1968, p. 185).

CONCLUSION

Today, private companies are once again increasingly using inmate labor. Though convict leasing is no longer practiced, some critics point to the similarities between it and current joint venture schemes. Other similarities can also be found in the racial constitution of the prison population, where African Americans remain disproportionately incarcerated. Though the abuses of the past are unlikely to be repeated, the problematic history of convict leasing is important to recall when evaluating the role of private businesses in prison work programs.

—William Farrell

See also Auburn Correctional Facility; Auburn System; Contract Facilities; Hard Labor; John Howard; Labor; Parchman Farm, Mississippi State Penitentiary; Plantation Style Prisons; Pennsylvania System; Privatization; Slavery; Walnut Street Jail

Further Reading

Cable, G. (1889). *The silent South.* New York: Scribner's.

Carelton, M. (1971). *Politics and punishment: The history of the Louisiana State penal system.* Baton Rouge: Louisiana State University Press.

Crowe, J. C. (1956). The origin and development of Tennessee's prison problem. *Tennessee Historical Quarterly, 15*(2), 122–130.

Farrell, W. J. (1994). *Prisons, work and punishment.* Dubuque, IA: Kendall-Hunt.

Green, F. (1949). Some aspects of the convict lease system in the Southern states. In *Essays in Southern history* (Vol. 31). Durham: University of North Carolina Press.

Mancini, M. (1996). *One dies, get another: Convict leasing in the American South, 1866–1928.* Columbia: University of South Carolina Press.

McKelvey, B. (1968). *The emergence of metropolitan America, 1915–1966.* New Brunswick, NJ: Rutgers University Press.

McKelvey, B. (1977). *American prisons: A history of good intentions.* Montclair, NJ: P. Smith.

Meier, A., & Radwick, E. (1970). *From plantation to ghetto.* New York: Hill and Wang.

Miller, M. (1974). At hard labor: Rediscovering the nineteenth century prison. *Issues in Criminology, 9,* 91–114.

Rothman, D. (1971). *The discovery of the asylum.* Boston: Little, Brown.

Sellin, T. (1976). *Slavery and the penal system.* New York: Elsevier.

Shelden, R. (1980, Winter). From slave to caste society: Penal changes in Tennessee, 1840–1914. *Tennessee Historical Quarterly, 39.*

Shelden, R. (1981). Convict leasing: An application of the Rusche-Kirchheimer thesis to penal changes in Tennessee, 1830–1915. In D. Greenberg (Ed.), *Crime and capitalism.* Palo Alto, CA: Mayfield.

Wilson, W. (1933). *Forced labor in the United States.* New York: International Publishers.

Woodward, C. V. (1971). *Origins of the new South.* Baton Rouge: Louisiana State University Press.

◪ COOK COUNTY, ILLINOIS

Cook County, Illinois, founded the first juvenile court in the United States in 1899. Today, the juvenile court has become a model for dealing with various social and psychological problems besetting youths in the United States.

HISTORY: THE FIRST JUVENILE COURT

The first juvenile court was established in Illinois largely due to the collaborative efforts of the Chicago Women's Club, the Chicago Bar Association, and the Illinois State Conference of Charities. The club convinced the Chicago Bar Association to draft a juvenile court bill, which was subsequently passed by the Illinois House. The bill was the 1899 Illinois Juvenile Court Act, which suggested that the state should care for dependent and/or neglected children who had been abandoned or lacked proper parental care, support, or guardianship. The early juvenile court functioned as an administrative agency of the circuit or district courts, and it was mandated as such by legislative action. By 1945, almost all states had developed similar juvenile court systems.

The Illinois Juvenile Court Act contained a number of important features. For the first time it defined a delinquent as under the age of 16. It also mandated that children must be kept separate from adult institutions, while prohibiting altogether the detention of children under age 12 in jail or police custody. It established special, informal procedural rules in juvenile court by employing a social work approach rather than a law enforcement or prosecutorial one in which probation officers handled the intake phase. The act also introduced private hearings in limited courts of record, where notes might be taken by the judges to reflect judicial actions. It granted original jurisdiction and individualized justice (based on each child's needs) in all cases concerning people under the age of 16. In this manner, the law divested the adult courts of all jurisdiction over children and reflected the concept of *parens patriae* (the duty of the state to act as the children's parents) as a functional approach.

The juvenile court as conceived in Cook County emphasized rehabilitation instead of punishment. In contrast to earlier practices, it relied on probation officers in diagnosis and processing for adjudicatory hearings instead of criminal prosecutors. In effect, the courts hoped to redeem all salvageable children while leaving only those not amenable to correction to be waived to adult criminal court processing.

THE SITUATION TODAY

Today, Cook County, Illinois, is still at the forefront in juvenile corrections. The historical Chicago Area Project, instituted in the early 1930s and based on social disorganization theory and the ecological approach that was developed by researchers at the University of Chicago, is still a model. As a demonstration program, the project was designed to discover a procedure for the treatment of delinquents and the prevention of delinquency in those Chicago neighborhoods that sent disproportionately large numbers of boys to the Cook County Juvenile Court. The project currently operates out of the Division of the Illinois Department of Corrections, and through research, has contributed immensely to the field of American criminology and corrections.

The Chicago Area Project has empowered many neighborhoods through involving community volunteers, community organizations, local churches, and other institutions in the process of program development and implementation. In cooperation with neighborhood residents, the project has affected social and environmental transformations by providing facilities, professional guidance, and child welfare programs.

Numerous other community-based youth-oriented diversion and delinquency prevention programs have based their activities on the Chicago Area Project. Just one example can be found in the Atlanta Operation Weed and Seed that started in the 1980s. Like the Chicago Area Project, it is a neighborhood empowerment program designed to work with community organizations and volunteers, local churches, and other institutions to revamp socially disorganized neighborhoods and empower them to become self-reliant. It was initiated in collaboration with Atlanta University, and grant funds came from both federal and state governments. It offered counseling, social services, and back-to-school or work curriculum as essential ingredients of the project.

Other correction-related juvenile programs in Cook County include the 4-H program and the Center for Conflict Resolution (CCR). A youth development program of the University of Illinois Cooperative Extension Service (CES), about 60,000 Cook County children and teenagers are enrolled annually in 4-H clubs. Through hands-on learning experiences in the arts and sciences and community service projects, and participation in official club meetings and activities, the clubs help these children grow and develop. CES also works with the Juvenile Detention Center to provide stress management, crisis coping, and leadership skills and self-esteem workshops for the detainees.

The CCR is one of the numerous distinguished programs in Cook County. Since 1992, it has been engaged with the Cook County State's Attorney's Office to provide mediation services for both the minors charged with crimes and the victims of those crimes. In cases involving criminal damages, criminal trespass, battery, assault, and simple theft, mediation is often used as an alternative to adjudication process. It is also employed in cases where victims seek restitution or want the juvenile to perform community service, or when the victim and the juvenile still have an ongoing relationship. On average, CCR mediates about 150 cases annually.

Finally, Cook County vigorously enforces the Safe School Zone Act passed by Illinois legislature in 1985. The act requires that 15- and 16-year-olds charged with delivery of a controlled substance within 1,000 feet of a school be tried in adult court. In 1987, the act was merged with the Juvenile Court Act, thereby making drug offenses higher-level crimes, especially when they are committed within the school safe zone. In 1989, the "Safe Zone Act" was extended to public housing developments in the state. It is, however, particularly in Cook County that this law is vigorously enforced.

CONCLUSION

Cook County, Illinois, made a lasting impact on juvenile corrections in the United States. Until 1898, children were arrested, charged, tried, and sentenced to adult prisons. Illinois was the first state to pass a bill that separated juveniles from adults, and Cook County was the first to direct the juvenile court toward meeting the goals of the juvenile bill. The pioneering roles of the Chicago Area Project and the 4-H program in delinquency prevention and control clearly place Cook County in the annals of juvenile justice and correctional history. Recently, however, many of the ideas of the first juvenile reformers have come under attack as more and more states choose to waive young offenders to adult courts, and even to incarcerate them in adult prisons. Whether the views and practices of Cook County will survive these changes remains unclear.

—Emmanuel C. Onyeozili, Jonathan C. Odo,
and Ihekwoaba D. Onwudiwe

See also Child Savers; Juvenile Detention Centers; Juvenile Justice System; Juvenile Offenders: Race, Class, and Gender; Juvenile Reformatories; Massachusetts Reformatory; *Parens Patriae*; Waivers Into Adult Courts

Further Reading

Abadinsky, H. (2003). *Probation and parole: Theory and practice.* Upper Saddle River, NJ: Prentice Hall.

Clement, M. (1997). *The juvenile justice system: Law and process.* Boston: Butterworth-Heinemann.

Empy, L. T. (Ed.). (1979). *Juvenile justice: The Progressive legacy and current reforms.* Charlottesville: University Press of Virginia.

Krisberg, B. (1988). *The juvenile court: Reclaiming the vision.* San Francisco: National Council on Crime and Delinquency.

Krisberg, B., & Austin, J. F. (1993). *Reinventing juvenile justice.* Newbury Park, CA: Sage.

Platt, A. M. (1974). *The child savers: The invention of delinquency.* Chicago: University of Chicago Press.

Rosenbaum, D. P., Lurigio, A. J., & Davis, R. C. (1998). *The prevention of crime: Social and situational strategies.* Belmont, CA: West/Wadsworth.

Shaw, C. R., & McKay, H. D. (1942). *Juvenile delinquency and urban areas.* Chicago: University of Chicago Press.

◪ CORCORAN, CALIFORNIA STATE PRISON

One of the 33 state prisons in the California archipelago, California State Prison, Corcoran (CSP-C) houses approximately 6,000 minimum-, medium-high-, and maximum-security inmates. Corcoran provides a variety of educational and vocational programs, as well as an acute care hospital and a substance abuse program. But Corcoran, dubbed "America's most violent prison," has achieved media notoriety not for its innovations in corrections but for claims of serious human rights violations.

OVERVIEW OF THE FACILITY

Corcoran is located in California's Central Valley, approximately midway between Fresno and Bakersfield. Opened in February 1988, Corcoran Prison was built on 942 acres that was once Tulare Lake. It is designated as a Level I, Level III, Level IV, General Population, and Security Housing Unit/Protective Housing Unit institution.

Minimum-security Level I facilities are characterized by open dormitories without a secure perimeter. At Corcoran, five Level I dormitories house about 884 inmates. A substance abuse program was activated in January 2001, providing alcohol and drug treatment for 190 Level I inmates. Medium-high Level III facilities usually have individual cells, fenced perimeters, and armed coverage.

At Corcoran, about 1,000 inmates occupy five Level III buildings. Maximum-security Level IV facilities are characterized by cells, fenced or walled perimeters, electronic security, and armed officers both inside and outside the installation. At Corcoran, about 2,000 inmates occupy 10 buildings in Level IV general population.

Another 2,000 Level IV inmates at Corcoran occupy two special housing unit (SHU) facilities. Corcoran was the first California prison with a separate facility built to house SHU inmates exclusively. Special units within the SHU facilities accommodate handicapped inmates, those with HIV, and prisoners requiring protective housing.

In addition to the Levels I, III, and IV facilities, Corcoran Prison maintains an acute care hospital (ACH) with 75 beds. The ACH is a maximum-security facility, providing acute medical, surgical, mental health crisis, and specialty outpatient services to inmates. Corcoran also employs about 600 inmates through prison industry authority (PIA) programs. Inmates work in Corcoran's manufacturing yards, institutional laundry, 400-acre agribusiness center, warehouse/freight distribution center, or industrial maintenance and repair facilities.

ALLEGATIONS OF HUMAN RIGHTS VIOLATIONS

Throughout the late 1990s, prison activists and journalists reported that serious human rights violations were occurring at Corcoran Prison on a regular and ongoing basis. Otherwise incredible claims of "gladiator fights" and state-sanctioned rape seemed plausible when several whistleblowers, all former Corcoran guards, substantiated the accounts. In 1998, state legislative hearings concluded that a pattern of brutality existed at Corcoran. An independent panel confirmed that 24 of the 31 serious or fatal shootings at Corcoran between 1988 and 1995 had involved unjustified use of deadly force. Investigations by the state attorney general and the Federal Bureau of Investigation (FBI) followed, and although all were acquitted, several guards were prosecuted in a series of high-profile trials.

ASSAULTS

According to reports, a group of rogue Corcoran guards (calling themselves the "Sharks") met a bus-load of new prisoners in 1995. The Sharks mistakenly believed that these prisoners had been involved in the assault of a correctional officer at another California correctional institution, Calipatria Prison. The officers dressed in dark jumpsuits and riot gear. They covered their badges with tape so they could not be identified. Then they pulled the shackled prisoners off the bus and subjected them to an anonymous hail of fists, steel-toed boots, and metal batons that continued for more than 30 minutes. Other examples of coordinated assaults have been reported. Corcoran prisoners recount similar events that took place as early as 1988.

RAPE

Corcoran guards were accused of orchestrating inmate rapes. According to former Corcoran guard Roscoe Pondexter, officials knowingly placed 118-pound Eddie Dillard into a cell with 220-pound Wayne Robertson, despite the fact that Robertson was listed in prison records as Dillard's enemy. They did so because Robertson, known as the "Booty Bandit," regularly raped prisoners as a favor for Corcoran guards. He was employed as a tool of punishment; in exchange, he was rewarded with extra privileges.

Dillard maintains that Robertson raped him repeatedly over a three-day period. A full rape examination was ordered, but inexplicably cancelled. Although Dillard's claims were corroborated by Pondexter's testimony, investigative reports, and Robertson's own boasting, the four Corcoran guards who were tried for intentionally placing Dillard into the cell with Robertson were acquitted in November 1999.

GLADIATOR FIGHTS

Corcoran guards were also accused of staging fights among rival gangs in the SHU yards, then shooting at them when fights broke out. Under the California Department of Corrections (CDC) "integrated yard policy," rival gang members were assigned to common exercise yards in order to destabilize ethnic

gangs. But, whistleblowers alleged, the resulting "gladiator fights" were regulated by Corcoran guards for amusement and blood sport.

On April 2, 1994, Preston Tate was taken from his SHU cell to participate in a gladiator fight. Predictably, Tate and his cellmate were attacked by two rival inmates. After several seconds of flailing punches, guards fired 37 mm wooden baton rounds, then fired a single 9 mm round, blowing Tate's skull open.

Tate's shooting, combined with testimony from former Corcoran guards, prompted U.S. Attorneys to indict eight Corcoran guards on charges of violating the civil rights of prisoners in 1998. In June 2000, all eight guards were acquitted. The CDC did, however, pay $825,000 to Tate's parents in a civil settlement, the CDC's largest settlement for a shooting death.

CONCLUSION

Since opening in 1988, Corcoran Prison has retained a reputation for being a brutal and violent institution. Allegations of orchestrated assaults, coordinated rapes, and gladiator fights were made throughout the 1990s, sparking local and federal investigations and leading to the prosecution of several correctional officers. These officers were acquitted, but there is no question that Corcoran has been stained by a legacy of institutional violence. Although conditions have certainly improved at Corcoran, the advocacy group California Prison Focus maintains that Corcoran remains plagued by prisoner abuse, staff misconduct, medical neglect, and safety violations to this day.

—*J. C. Oleson*

See also Correctional Officers; Disciplinary Segregation; Gangs; Marion, U.S. Penitentiary; New Mexico Penitentiary; Pelican Bay State Prison; Racial Conflict Among Prisoners; Rape; San Quentin State Prison; Special Housing Unit; Violence

Further Reading

Arax, M. (2000, June 10). 8 prison guards are acquitted in Corcoran battles. *Los Angeles Times,* p. A1.

California Prison Focus. (2004). *Corcoran State Prison 2001–2002: Inside California's brutal maximum security*

prison. Retrieved from http://www.prisons.org/Corcoran02
.htm

Quinn, T. (Ed.). (1999). *Maximum Security University: A documentary history of death and cover-up at America's most violent prison*. San Francisco: California Prison Focus.

Wisely, W. (1998, October). Corcoran Prison: Sex, lies, and videotape. *Prison Legal News*, pp. 8–11.

◪ CORPORAL PUNISHMENT

Corporal punishment refers to physical penalties that cause pain or disfigure the body. It is usually contrasted with practices such as imprisonment, probation, or parole, which control but are not meant specifically to harm the body. Of course, incarceration may cause discomfort and potentially subject inmates' bodies to violence such as rape, but it is not the same as whipping or flogging where the judicial sentence directly requires acute pain as the payment for an offense. While executions obviously harm the body by putting someone to death, legally they must not involve torture or unnecessary pain and suffering.

HISTORY AND EXAMPLES OF CORPORAL PUNISHMENT

Corporal punishments predate the birth of the prison. Indeed, early jails and prisons were designed merely to hold offenders until their corporal punishment could be carried out. A common strategy until around 1800 was to hold an offender in the stocks. Just as every community now has a jail, historically every village had stocks. For this punishment, offenders were placed in hinged heavy timbers with holes cut in them to hold arms and/or legs, so that they were "powerless to escape the jests and jeers of every idler in the community" (Earle, 1896/1995, p. 37). Stocks could be used to hold offenders prior to another penalty or as a form of punishment itself.

Another method commonly used at this time was the pillory. The pillory was similar to the stocks in design (and ubiquity) but held "the human head in its tight grasp, and thus holds it up to the public gaze" (Earle, 1896/1995, p. 44). Individuals held in this structure were further humiliated by the public

who would throw at them "rotten eggs, filth, and dirt from the streets, which was followed by dead cats, rats" and "ordure from the slaughter-house" (Andrews, 1890/1991, pp. 85, 86). They might also have their ears nailed to either side of the head hole or cut off entirely ('cropped') for additional ridicule. Some communities put offenders in the pillory during public market days to increase their exposure.

Whipping posts were usually similar to the pillory in design, although they also could be little more than a post to which an individual was secured. Some communities tied an offender to a whipping cart and walked him or her through town "till his body became bloody" (Earle, 1896/1995, p. 70). This technique, which was popular until the 1800s, could be done with a variety of implements such as reeds, birch rods, and whips; famously the cat-o'-nine-tails was made of a rope that was unraveled and knotted at the ends to inflict maximum discomfort.

Finally, more permanent methods of corporal punishment existed such as branding, maiming, and amputation. Branding involved burning a sign into someone's flesh that forever labeled him or her a criminal. Often the sign would vary depending on the crime. Maiming could take many forms and was usually aimed symbolically at addressing the crime: A blasphemer would have his tongue cut out or fixed to the side of his cheek, thieves would have a hand cut off, and so on. In extreme cases, offenders' hearts could be cut out, or their limbs amputated.

GENDER AND CLASS

As with most forms of social control, corporal punishment was never applied equally across social classes or groups. Aristocrats, for example, were usually exempt from such practices, while certain techniques—such as the dunking stool and scold's bridle—were almost exclusively reserved for women for gendered crimes like gossiping or being argumentative. The dunking stool was used occasionally for men accused of slander or for quarrelsome married couples. It usually resembled a see saw onto which the offender could be placed in a chair that was then plunged into cold water "in order to cool her immoderate heat" (Andrews, 1890/1991, p. 4). The bridle was "a sort of iron cage, often of great weight; when worn, covering the entire head; with a spiked plate or flat tongue of iron to be placed in the mouth over the tongue" so "if the offender spoke she was cruelly hurt" (Earle, 1896/1995, p. 96). This device locked in the back, and women would either be led around town or attached to a post. The bridles were sometimes ornamented to give the wearer's face a bestial appearance. The women staked out in the public square could expect "painful beatings, besmearing with feces and urine, and serious, sometimes fatal wounding–especially in the breasts and pubes" (Held, 1985, p. 150).

CORPORAL PUNISHMENT AND EXECUTIONS

Until the 19th century, abuse and torture were integrated into the death sentence to maximize a person's suffering. For example, an English sentence for treason in 1691 required the offenders to be

> hanged by the neck, to be cut down while ye are yet alive, to have your hearts and bowles taken out before your faces, and your members cut off and burnt. Your heads severed from your bodies, your bodies divided into quarters . . . and disposed of according to the king's will and pleasure; and the Lord have mercy upon your souls. (quoted in Johnson, 1998, p. 14)

Depending on the jurisdiction and the time, offenders were burned to death, broken on the wheel (breaking the major bones of their body with an iron rod while tied to a large circle symbolizing eternity), impaled, disemboweled, and beheaded. They could also be drawn and quartered by being tied to four horses that pulled in different directions. After executions, the corpse might be gibbeted and displayed hanging in chains. As medical schools sought after corpses to teach anatomy and improve surgical success, poor offenders were sentenced to be dissected, sometimes in a public hall. The previous practice of robbing graves for cadavers provoked hostility in villages, which occasionally burned down medical schools in retaliation for the

digging up the recently deceased and the "deliberate mutilation or destruction of identity, perhaps for eternity" that dissection entailed (Richardson, 1987, p. 29). The strong reaction reveals how dissection and the potential evisceration of a person's body were seen as punishment even after death.

FOUCAULT AND THE BIRTH OF PRISON

The transition to prison from corporal punishments and the spectacle of execution is the subject of *Discipline and Punish* by French philosopher Michel Foucault (1979). This book famously starts with a gruesome description of the 1757 execution of Damiens, who had been convicted of regicide. Before he dies, Damiens's flesh was torn with red-hot pincers, he was partly burned and eviscerated, and then, unsuccessfully drawn and quartered. The executioner finally had to cut Damiens's body apart and then burn the pieces. The second type of punishment that Foucault describes is a "House of young offenders" 80 years later, based on a strict timetable or schedule. Using these two examples, Foucault (1979) argues that punishment underwent major changes between 1760 and 1840 "from being an art of unbearable sensations, punishment has become as economy of suspended rights" (p. 11). According to him, in less than 100 years, public spectacle disappeared, physical pain was downplayed, the prison replaced corporal punishment, and punishment became hidden and part of "abstract consciousness."

Foucault argues that spectacles of pain associated with corporal punishment were rooted in the sovereign's power to wage war against his enemies and were intended to terrorize citizens into obedience. Such displays, however, were inefficient systems of social control and with the rise of capitalism states sought to find better ways of appropriating bodies rather than killing them. The new goal, which Foucault views as creating "docile bodies," advanced through mechanisms of surveillance and control that were typified by the prison but existed in many other social institutions as well: "Prisons resemble factories, schools, barracks, hospitals, which all resemble prisons" (Foucault, 1979,

p. 228). The result is generalized surveillance and the formation of a disciplinary society based on a strict organization of space, timetables, performance standards, repetitive exercises, and drills. The end of corporal punishment is thus not seen as a humanitarian step but a transformation to more totalizing forms of power and domination. Foucault (1979) ominously states:

> Historians of ideas usually attribute the dream of a perfect society to the philosophers and jurists of the eighteenth century; but there was also a military dream of society; its fundamental reference was not to the state of nature, but to the meticulously subordinated cogs of a machine, not to the primal social contract, but to permanent coercions, not to fundamental rights, but to indefinitely progressive forms of training, not to general will, but to automatic docility. (p. 169)

CONTEMPORARY ARGUMENTS

Because many non-Western countries practice corporal punishment, Westerners somewhat ethnocentrically tend to see this penalty as primitive or barbaric. Even so, occasionally politicians in the United States, United Kingdom, or Australia attempt to reintroduce corporal punishment as part of a "tough on crime" agenda. Likewise, people commonly debate whether public school teachers should be allowed to spank or cane students for disciplinary reasons. The most important current advocate of corporal punishment is criminologist Graeme Newman. In his text *Just and Painful* (1995), he makes a case for corporal punishment that also serves as a critique of prison, which he sees as overused, violent, and expensive.

Newman's suggestion is to implement corporal punishment in the form of electric shocks to be used instead of prison for minor offenses; he sees the combination of shock and prison to constitute torture, which is not the case for a one-time infliction of pain. Shocks would be done in a public punishment hall, after which the offender would be released. For Newman, the pain of punishment can be matched to the severity of crime by controlling the number of shocks, the voltage, and duration of the jolts. Acute physical pain, Newman argues, is experienced more similarly by people than the

chronic pain of a prison sentence, which will vary between institutions and even for individuals in the same prison. While men, women, whites, and minorities "respond to and interpret pain differently, there is every chance that they actually feel pain in about the same way" (Newman, 1995, p. 60). Newman further argues that minority overrepresentation in punishment is a "silent statistic," but if blacks were punished in public to the differential extent they are now, "it would be *too much.* It would force us to be accountable for the excesses of prison" (p. 62, emphasis in original).

While some see Newman's system as humiliating to the offender, he argues that many forms of punishment such as boot camps are built on degrading activities like cleaning toilets with toothbrushes. He argues that the obviously painful nature of corporal punishment would force society to take responsibility for it, in contrast to prison violence and rape, which usually we feel is not our concern. Corporal punishment in the form of electric shocks could also be administered more cheaply than prison, and would not require a primary wage earner or parent to be imprisoned. It would, therefore, cause less disruption to people's lives.

Newman (1995) notes that his book is "a polemic, intended to inflame and provoke" (p. 2). The point is thus less political advocacy of corporal punishment than an attempt to have people think more deeply about why and how society punishes offenders. He fears that many who say they support his position do so for the wrong reasons, while others reject it because of complacency with mass incarceration or cultural arrogance about "barbaric" Islamic countries that practice corporal punishment.

Newman, however, agrees with criticisms from human rights organization about practices in non-Western countries that combine corporal punishment with incarceration. For example, Amnesty International (2002a) notes, "Caning is used in Malaysia as a supplementary punishment for at least 40 crimes even though it contravenes international human rights standards." Newman would not support such sentences, because he believes the criminal should be incarcerated *or* experience corporal punishment; it is the combination of the two that he sees as torture, which is a process and different from a one-time infliction of pain. Thus, he would also agree with Amnesty International in condemning Saudi Arabia for sentencing two defendants charged with drug crimes to "to 1,500 lashes each, in addition to 15 years' imprisonment. The floggings were scheduled to be carried out at a rate of 50 lashes every six months for the whole duration of the 15 years" (Amnesty International, 2002b).

CONCLUSION

Corporal punishment has been involved in some of the spectacular excesses of the criminal justice punishment, but it is a type of punishment of interest to people across schools of punishment. Retributivists are attracted by the increased ability to create "just deserts" by matching the crime with a wide range of corporal punishments. Utilitarians, going back to Jeremy Bentham's vision of a spanking machine (Farrell, 2003), see potential for more uniform and precise punishments than incarceration can offer.

In spite of widespread "tough on crime" rhetoric, the public has ambivalent feelings about the deliberate infliction of physical pain as the official sentence. In addition, sentencing women, especially white women, to corporal punishment would present another barrier. Women's demands for equal rights have sometimes resulted in a backlash in the form of harsher sentences, a phenomenon referred to as "equality with a vengeance." Yet executions of women are more troublesome to many than the execution of men. And the Alabama prison commission was fired by the governor in 1996 when he suggested women join the predominantly black men on the state's chain gangs (Gorman, 2001, p. 405).

Corporal punishment, like the chain gang, will continue to attract interest because there is something about the notion of "punishment for punishment's sake, that appeals to an electorate scared of crime [and] fed up with what it sees as coddling" (Gorman, 2001, p. 406). Both, however, are inconsistent with the trend described by Foucault as moving away from spectacle to the surveillance-based society.

—Paul Leighton

See also Jeremy Bentham; Capital Punishment; Chain Gangs; Flogging; Michel Foucault; History of Prisons; Alexander Maconochie

Further Reading

Amnesty International. (2002a). *Malaysia: Caning should be abolished.* Retrieved from http://web.amnesty.org/library/index/ENGASA280032002

Amnesty International. (2002b). Saudi Arabia. *Annual report 2002.* Retrieved from http://web.amnesty.org/web/ar2002.nsf/mde/saudi+arabia!Open

Andrews, W. (1991). *Old time punishments.* New York: Dorset. (Original work published 1890)

Earle, A. M. (1995). *Curious punishments of bygone days.* Bedford, MA: Applewood. (Original work published 1896, Chicago: H. S. Stone)

Farrell, C. (2003). World corporal punishment Web site. Retrieved from http://www.corpun.com/

Fillingham, L. A. (1993). *Foucault for beginners.* New York: Writers and Readers.

Foucault, M. (1979). *Discipline and punish.* New York: Vintage.

Gorman, T. (2001). Back on the chain gang: Why the Eighth Amendment and the history of slavery proscribe the resurgence of chain gangs. In P. Leighton & J. Reiman (Eds.), *Criminal justice ethics.* Upper Saddle River, NJ: Prentice Hall.

Held, R. (1985). *Inquisition: A bilingual guide to the exhibition of torture instruments.* Florence: Qua D'Arno.

Johnson, R. (1998). *Death work: A study of the modern execution process* (2nd ed.). Belmont, CA: Wadsworth.

Newman, G. (1985). *The punishment response.* Albany, NY: Harrow and Heston.

Newman, G. (1995). *Just and painful: A case for the corporal punishment of criminals.* Albany, NY: Harrow and Heston. The full text of the first edition is available online through http://www.albany.edu/~grn92/jp00.html.

Richardson, R. (1987). *Death dissection and the destitute.* New York: Routledge & Kegan Paul.

■ CORRECTIONAL OFFICER PAY

Historically, prison guards were paid poorly for their work and were subjected to poor working conditions. Today, the pay and position of the correctional officer has improved dramatically in many jurisdictions. However, differences in pay still exist between states and by gender.

HISTORY OF OFFICER PAY

Historically, the position of prison guard has had low social status. Subject to poor working conditions and low pay, it was a field that few aspired to and often entered only as a last resort. Usually, guards lived on the prison grounds and were thus continually interacting with prisoners. Such a relationship often compromised their capacity to be viewed as authority figures and limited their ability to enforce punitive and rehabilitative models.

Even so, attempts were made almost from the beginning to increase the social status of the prison guard. During the development of the penitentiary in New York, for example, guards were required to wear uniforms and to behave in a professional manner. Additional attempts to professionalize the role of the officer were made in the 19th and 20th centuries, as many states changed the job title from "prison guard" to "correctional officer."

CURRENT LEVELS OF PAY

In addition to changing the social status of the correctional officer, attempts were made throughout the 20th century to increase the compensation provided to officers for their work. Compensation for correctional officers is based on a number of factors, including type of facility, location, rate of starting salary, number of years of service, turnover rates, frequency of promotion opportunities, training opportunities, job performance, and educational level. In 2002, the median yearly income level for correctional officers was $32,670, with the lowest 10% earning less than $22,010 and the highest 10% earning more than $52,370 (Bureau of Labor Statistics, 2003b). A survey of 25 states in the central United States illustrates how salaries can vary dramatically from state to state. In 2001, the average salary for officers in North Dakota ranged from $21,000 for entry-level officers to $38,352 for experienced officers. In contrast, Wyoming correctional officers begin their careers at a higher salary of $23,844, but the maximum salary level after five years' experience is lower compared to North Dakota's, at $33,876 yearly (Correctional Officers Salaries, 2002).

In comparison to the salaries in the central United States, correctional officers in California receive significantly higher salaries. In 2004, a job announcement by the California Department of

Corrections listed a yearly salary range of $34,284 to $58,620. In 2003, 391 officers earned more than $100,000 due to overtime pay (Gladstone, 2004). Salaries have increased dramatically for California officers since the 1980s, when the median yearly salary for a correctional officer was $14,400. The California Correctional Peace Officers Union has been largely responsible for the increases in the pay structure for California prison guards. Its lobbying efforts have also increased the benefits available to guards, which include medical coverage and a retirement plan that allows employees to retire at age 55 after 30 years of service and receive a stipend equal to 75% of their yearly pay. While the California Correctional Peace Officers Union has made a number of positive contributions for correctional officers in its jurisdiction, it has also been criticized for its lobbying efforts and contributions to political campaigns. These efforts have prioritized budget decisions toward officer pay over other services to prisoners within the correctional system (Pens, 1998).

GENDER

In addition to pay variations by state, research suggests that female officers are compensated at a lower rate than male officers. According to the U.S. Department of Labor, female correctional officers earned 78.6% of the wages of their male counterparts in 2002 (Bureau of Labor Statistics, 2003a). Women are also less likely to hold positions in management or administrative posts, even in female-occupied facilities. Like many other male-dominated occupations, women in corrections tend to occupy lower-ranking positions. Women are also more likely to be found working in state facilities, where wages are lower compared to federal facilities.

CONCLUSION

The compensation for working in prisons has evolved significantly throughout history. Prison guards in early prisons received limited monetary compensation and were required to live with the inmates within the prison walls. As an occupation of lower status, in early correctional history the position of prison guard had few benefits. Today, the salaries and benefits for correctional officers vary widely from jurisdiction to jurisdiction. While the career can be financially lucrative in some facilities, such is not the case for all who work in this field. However, the expanding growth of the prison system in the United States, coupled with the political forces of prison guard unions, have led to increased opportunities for employment as well as improvements in pay and benefits.

—Stacy Mallicoat

See also Accreditation; American Correctional Association; Correctional Officers; John J. DiIulio, Jr.; Governance; History of Correctional Officers; Managerialism; Professionalization of Staff; Staff Training

Further Reading

Britton, D. M. (2003). *At work in the iron cage: The prison as a gendered organization.* New York: New York University Press.

Bureau of Labor Statistics. (2003a). *Highlights of women's earnings in 2002.* Washington, DC: U.S. Department of Labor.

Bureau of Labor Statistics. (2003b). *Occupational outlook handbook, 2002–3 edition: Correctional officers.* Washington, DC: U.S. Department of Labor.

Correctional officers salaries. (2002). *Correctional officer salaries—North Dakota and surrounding states.* Unpublished report prepared by the North Dakota Legislative Council staff for Representative Ron Carlisle.

Gladstone, M. (2004, March 6). Negotiator works both sides. *San Jose Mercury News,* p. 3A.

Martin, S. E., & Jurik, N. C. (1996). *Doing justice, doing gender: Women in law and criminal justice occupations.* Thousand Oaks, CA: Sage.

Morris, N., & Rothman, D. J. (1997). *The Oxford history of the prison.* New York: Oxford University Press.

Pens, D. (1998). The California prison guards' union: A potent political interest group. In D. Burton-Rose (Ed.), *The celling of America: An inside look at the U.S. prison industry.* Monroe, ME: Common Courage.

◪ CORRECTIONAL OFFICER UNIONS

The first correctional officer unions were established in the mid-20th century. In the early 21st century, more than 50% of prisons have officer unions working to improve the conditions of their members. In some states, such as California, correctional officer unions have become extremely powerful, able to lobby governments into pursuing certain correctional building programs and methods of punishment. Even so, most are prohibited by law from going on strike because of the chaos that a strike would cause behind prison walls.

As with other labor organizations, correctional officer unions seek to bargain for better working conditions, better pay and benefits, and guaranteed job security. They also work toward appropriate training techniques and encourage enhanced technology while seeking to improve communication between higher management and employees. Unions offer their members information about medical issues and taxes, and if there is a legal issue arising out of employment, they will cover legal fees and/or provide representation. Union members usually make contributions to a legal benefit plan to help pay for such services. Correctional officer unions argue that if management improved working conditions, increased pay, and provided the required training, the turnover rate for correctional officers would decline.

HISTORY OF UNIONS

In the past, correctional officers received assistance from labor unions that represented all workers. These labor unions and correctional unions include AFL-CIO, AFSCME, Central Impact 82, CSEA of New York, Massachusetts Correction Officers Union, Pennsylvania State Corrections Officers Association, and Public Employees Federation Union, to name only a few. These groups bargained for better pay and conditions for all laborers, but they were not always able to deal specifically with the issues facing those who worked in prison. Consequently, correctional officers realized that they needed their own representatives.

California

The California Correctional Peace Officers' Association (CCPOA) is one of the major and most organized correctional unions in the United States. Founded in 1957 to bargain for better working conditions, training, and pay for employees in corrections, CCPOA strove to make the occupation more professional by providing appropriate training for the officers. It also began extensive background checks for all potential corrections employees and implemented policies and procedures that provide correctional facilities with the required safety equipment needed.

CCPOA has improved the working conditions of its members and has reduced the once-tremendous turnover rate for correctional officers. Statistics show that during the 1970s and 1980s, the state's turnover rate was 25%. Today it is down to 8%, in large part because of the effort that has been put into making the conditions better for correctional employees.

CCPOA has been particularly influential in politics, in large part because it has donated considerable sums to legislators' campaigns. As a result, it seems to wield considerable influence in crime and policy issues, leading some to claim that the CCPOA is the main reason for the success of the "three strikes" laws. In addition to addressing law-and-order issues, CCPOA has also lobbied for more mainstream union issues, such as the right to collective bargaining, home loan assistance for officers, benefits for officers and families of deceased officers, improved health plans, and income tax credits. Similarly, CCPOA has asked that peace officers may carry concealed weapons across state lines. In recent years, CCPOA succeeded in obtaining grant money to improve the juvenile justice system, thereby hiring more correctional officers, and in creating the National Corrections and Employees Week, which is celebrated the week beginning May 4.

PRIVATIZATION

The recent shift in some states and the federal system toward privatizing parts of their penal system has considerably weakened some prison officer unions. Private prison companies generally will not hire employees who are members of a union, nor allow employees to unionize later. Consequently, it is difficult for many private prison employees to lobby against their relatively low wages and poor

benefits. While organizations such as CCPOA have so far managed to persuade legislators to restrict the number of private facilities in their state, other unions have not been as successful. The long-term effect of privatization on prison officer unions is unclear, yet it seems already to have created a dual system of pay and conditions, with private employees losing out relative to their public counterparts.

CONCLUSION

Unions aim to improve conditions of the correctional officers by improving their wages, conditions with management, and emotional stability within the workforce. Research suggests that states that have a separate union for correctional officers have a lower turnover of officers in their prison systems. Officer unions are powerful because they are very active in politics; even though most officer unions are not allowed to strike, they still have the power to make changes.

—*Wanda T. Hunter*

See also Correctional Officer Pay; Correctional Officers; Governance; History of Correctional Officers; Managerialism; Prisoner Unions; Privatization; Professionalism; Staff Training

Further Reading

Barling, J., Fullagar, C., & Kelloway, K. (1992). *The union and its members: A psychological approach.* New York: Oxford University Press.

California Correctional Peace Officers Association. (2002). *Welcome to the California Correctional Peace Officers Association.* Retrieved October 23, 2002, from http://www.ccpoanet.org/

Clement, D. (2000). *Private vs. public: The prison debate.* Minneapolis, MN: Fedgazette.

Logan, C. (1990). *Private prisons: Cons and pros.* New York: Oxford University Press.Union of Canadian Correctional Officers. Retrieved from http://www.ucco-sacc.csn.qc.ca/

◪ CORRECTIONAL OFFICERS

Correctional officers are responsible for the security of the penal institutions in which they work and the safety of the inmates housed within their walls. Their duties include enforcing the rules and regulations of the facility, responding to inmate needs, diffusing inmate conflicts, and supervising daily movement and activities within the institution.

As of June 2000, state and federal prisons employed 430,033 individuals. Nearly two-thirds of these people were involved in direct contact with the inmate population and responsible for their safety and security. These figures represent a 24% increase from the number of correctional staff since 1995. The greatest increases in correctional employment are found in private institutions (364%), followed by federal (32%) and state (18%) facilities (Stephan & Karberg, 2003).

The increased need for correctional officers is a direct result of the growing numbers of correctional facilities that have been established throughout the United States in the past few decades. In many communities, the new jobs that have been created represent previously unavailable employment opportunity, security, and stability. However, a career in corrections is not without its problems. Work as an officer is dangerous, given the population that they are responsible for supervising. A stressful work environment, burnout, and high attrition rates place a heavy load on the occupation. These factors, coupled with the intense growth of the industry, have left many prisons understaffed, which in turn can place officers who are working at the prison at risk. As of June 2000, the number of inmates to correctional officer ratio in federal facilities was 9:1, with state facilities reporting a 4.5:1 ratio (Stephan & Karberg, 2003). The demands of the job can also present strain for the personal life of the officer, as people are often forced to relocate based on job availability.

HISTORY

While the primary duty of the correctional officer has always been to maintain the security of the prison setting, changes in correctional philosophy throughout history have impacted the role of the correctional officer within the prison. During the early 19th century, for example, the penitentiary was designed to isolate offenders from society and from each other. At the time, the responsibilities of the officer were limited to maintaining the keys of the facility. Guards at this time were all men, as the majority of prisoners were male. The job as a prison guard had little status, and officers generally lived in the prison under poor conditions receiving little pay for their work.

As the penitentiary system evolved, so did the role of the correctional officer. Officers began to wear uniforms and operate within a paramilitary structure. They often used corporal punishment against the inmates to demand compliance. Though the central nature of this practice was reduced in the late 19th century, physical sanctions remained as a component of treatment within the reformatory movement.

GENDER, RACE, AND ETHNICITY

During the early correctional period, women were not employed as prison guards. Instead, those few women who worked in penal facilities were employed in office work and domestic positions. Only a handful worked as matrons in the women's wing of a state penitentiary. It was not until Indiana led the way and established a women-only prison in 1873 that the field of corrections work opened for women guards, and even then, positions were available only in women's institutions. Like their male counterparts, these early female keepers were required to live within the prison walls and were poorly compensated for their work.

The introduction of the women's reformatory movement saw not only a shift in the philosophy of the prison but also a shift in the social class of the guards. Whereas the early female keepers tended to be drawn from the working classes, the mid-19th century saw an influx of middle- and upper-class white women into the correctional system. Their role was to "guide and discipline the fallen women and serve as examples of virtuous middle class femininity" (Britton, 2003, p. 58)

Other than those women employed by women's prisons, the workforce of the prison has historically been male. It took the 1972 Title VII amendment to the

Civil Rights Act to allow employment opportunities for women as correctional officers. This same legislation also signaled the end to all women's facilities, as men became entitled to apply to work with female prisoners.

Like many other parts of the labor force at the time, men's prisons were slow to incorporate women into their correctional staff. Administrators tried to get around equal opportunity's legislation by claiming that women were excluded on the basis of a bona fide occupational qualification. However, lower court decisions in *Gunther v. Iowa* (1980) and *Harden v. Dayton Human Rehabilitation Center* (1981) held that the bona fide occupational qualifications could not be used to deny prison employment opportunities to women.

In addition to being largely male, early correctional officers were exclusively white. Just as women were denied opportunities for employment in corrections, so too were African Americans, Latinos, Asian Americans, and Native Americans. Indeed, as with gender, much of the racial discrimination in correctional employment paralleled the racial discrimination in mainstream society. When opportunities of employment did arise, the job duties for guards of color were limited to guarding inmates of color.

Today, the ranks of correctional officers are diversifying. In 1999, women made up 23.5% of the correctional workforce while African Americans accounted for 24.9% of correctional officers, and Latinos constituted 8.7% of the population (Bureau of Labor Statistics, 2003). However, given that the majority of prisons are located in rural areas, the workforce remains predominantly white. This relationship results in issues of racial conflict within the prison, given that the majority of inmates are from inner-city environments, where racial diversity is much more prevalent.

WORKING CONDITIONS

The types of facilities in which correctional officers work and the inmates they supervise vary by jurisdiction. At the local level, correctional officers are responsible for the custody of offenders awaiting court proceedings, or who are involved in community-based correctional programming in the jail setting. The population of the jail is in constant change, with more than 11 million people processed through local jails each year (Bureau of Labor Statistics, 2003).

Correctional officers are also employed at the state and federal levels, where at year end 2002, they were responsible for 1,440,655 adult inmates, representing a 2.6% increase in the prison population from the previous year (Harrison & Beck, 2003). In contrast to the jail setting, the purpose of the state and federal prison facilities is general population confinement. Prisons are typically more stable places to work than jails, as inmates typically spend longer periods of time in them and work and live to a strict routine. Of course, inmates can also be housed in privately operated prisons. Private prisons housed 6.5% of the U.S. prison population, or 93,771 prisoners, at year end 2002 (Harrison & Beck, 2003). The duties of an officer in a private prison are similar to those supervising inmates in state and federal facilities.

In addition to jurisdictional variations, the prison setting varies by security setting, ranging from minimum- to low-security confinement, up to maximum-security and even super-maximum secure prisons. Such jurisdictional and security differences impact the correctional officer due to the differing operational practices of the facility and the procedures for dealing with the needs of inmates.

For example, while maximum or supermax facilities often involve little to no physical contact between the inmate and the officer, lower-security prisons usually require more direct supervision and interaction with the prison population. In the former, officers increasingly tend to supervise inmates through video camera surveillance systems. Communication with inmates occurs via an intercom system, rather than engaging in face-to-face encounters, which may put the officer at risk. Access to the cell may be controlled electronically, allowing an officer to remain in an enclosed booth. If an inmate is let out of his cell, he is handcuffed and shackled and usually escorted by at least two officers wearing shank-resistant body armor. In a recreation yard setting, control is typically maintained by an armed guard stationed in a surveillance tower.

In comparison, medium- and minimum-security facilities place the officer in the center of the inmate population. Guards are unarmed and outnumbered in these facilities. Unable to use physical force as a primary mechanism to maintain order, guards must rely on their interpersonal skills and develop relationships with the inmates to maintain control on a daily basis.

The physical layout of the prison, as well as policies on inmate movement, also help the officer maintain control of the facility. When larger-scale disturbances arise, the use of force has varied. Historically, tear gas was used to subdue prisoners during times of crisis. The use of violent force to retake the Attica prison in 1971 resulted in the loss of life for 29 inmates and 10 employees, six of whom were guards. Today, advances in technology have increased the variety of nonlethal agents that can be used to control noncompliant inmates.

Prisons are responsible for meeting the daily needs of the inmate population, including nutrition, shelter, clothing, and rehabilitative, psychological, and recreational programming, and correctional officers must ensure that all of these services are provided. The prison setting regulates every aspect of an inmate's life through the labor of its correctional officers, who are responsible for supervising their movement and activities throughout the prison. The work of a correctional officer is unlike that of any other occupation as "prison officers are involved with the totality of inmates' lives, supervising and surveilling their meals, showers, communications and a multitude of normally private aspects of personal and sexual behavior" (Britton, 2003, p. 3).

It is common to hear accounts of correctional officers feeling imprisoned, just like the inmates. For example, Ted Conover's (2000) ethnographic exploration into the work of a correctional officer at Sing Sing found that "prison work was about waiting. The inmates waited for their sentences to run out, and the officers waited for retirement . . . it was a life sentence in eight-hour shifts" (p. 21).

Research consistently demonstrates that correctional officers are subject to high levels of stress. They have similar rates of divorce, death, and suicide to police officers. The major sources of stress for correctional officers result from role ambiguity and role conflict. Role ambiguity refers to the uncertainty officers may experience regarding the duties, responsibilities, and expectations of their position. Related to role ambiguity is role conflict. Role conflict occurs when the reality of job conflicts with the strict "rule based" method under which officers receive their training. The use of discretion to make decisions often places correctional officers in a no-win situation, as they are stuck between appeasing administrators and inmates. Additional sources of stress include a perceived lack of authority, poor communication, lack of administrative support, inadequate equipment, lack of training, and inconsistencies in staff discipline. Left untreated, stress can result in absenteeism, physical illness, emotional issues, and drug and alcohol abuse.

In addition to stress related to their job, the physical health of correctional officers is sometimes placed at risk by the nature of their employment. Notwithstanding the threats of injury or death while on the job, correctional officers must deal with the possibility of additional risks to their physical health. Exposure to the inmate population and their health needs in turn leaves the correctional officer potentially exposed to various health concerns such as influenza, tuberculosis, hepatitis, and HIV and AIDS. As of 2001, 2.0% of state prisoners and 1.2% of federal prisoners were identified as HIV-positive. While only a small proportion of the prison population, the confirmed rate of AIDS among prisoners (.49%) is three times that of the general population (.14%). In addition, 1 in 12 deaths in prison is AIDS related (Marushack, 2004). While officers are aware of these risks and engage in practices to minimize their potential risk, research has shown that many correctional officers ignore other health risks caused through smoking, poor nutrition, lack of exercise, and a failure to attend to preventive medical care (Wright & Northrup, 2001).

TYPOLOGY OF CORRECTIONAL OFFICERS

Like every occupation, correctional officers have different personality styles that affect their working relationships. The ability of correctional officers to perform their job successfully often depends on how they enforce the rules and regulations of the facility. Research by Britton (2003) found that "no effective officer does the job completely by the book. Many prison rules are explicitly contradictory and many others are unnecessarily petty. Enforcing all rules uniformly would undoubtedly lead to widespread discontent and perhaps even mass disorder" (p. 64). With the central role that correctional officers play in the organization of the prison and the impact they have on the life of the inmate, understanding the different approaches of correctional officers is useful in the management from an organizational and interpersonal level.

Research on correctional officers divides the occupation into two general philosophical categories: custodial officers and human services officers. Custodial officers see themselves as rule enforcers of the prison structure and follow a "by the book" philosophy (Owen, 1988). Human services officers take a more personal approach to their work, focusing on a counseling or rehabilitative philosophy (Johnson, 1996). Research by Owen (1988) distinguished an additional category: the "lazy-laid back officer" that referred to those who were simply going through the motions of the job with little investment in their role in the prison or their potential impact on inmates.

Expanding on previous research, Farkas (2000) developed a typology of correctional officers to understand the relationship between individual characteristics of the officer and the social setting of the prison. Drawing from data obtained in interviews, five types of correctional officers were generated: rule enforcer, hard liner, people worker, synthetic officer, and loner.

The rule enforcer is the most common type of correctional officer. Reflective of the by-the-book classification by Owen (1988), the rule enforcer is described as one who embraces the ideology, norms, and values of the prison structure. Militaristic in nature, the rule enforcer is concerned with maintaining control within the prison and is highly suspicious of the motives of inmates. The typology of the hard liner is a subsidiary of the rule enforcer. While the hard liner is similar to the rule enforcer, they distinguish themselves through their abuse of power.

The people worker style is similar to the human services worker characteristic illustrated in previous research. People workers are focused on maintaining a positive and communicative relationship with the inmates. Central to the people worker style is the officer's use of discretion. Due to their role in the prison, correctional officers are endowed with a high level of freedom in their rule enforcement. The people worker focuses on their interpersonal skills rather than punishment as a method for resolving conflicts. The synthetic officer is a combination of the rule enforcer and the people worker. While they follow a strict interpretation of the rules and regulations of the facility, they are also interested in understanding the individual needs of the inmates and circumstances of the situation. The synthetic officer is one "who treats inmates fairly and with respect but enforces all the rules and doesn't take all the crap inmates try to give you" (Farkas, 2000, p. 442). The loner is one who tries to fit in with the normative structure of the organization, yet feels alienated from the prison, coworkers, and inmates.

PATHWAYS, QUALIFICATIONS, TRAINING, AND COMPENSATION

The pathway to working as a correctional officer is different from most other occupations. According to Britton (2003), few children grow up with the aspirations of becoming a prison guard. Many correctional officers report that working in the prison was a profession that they drifted into, rather than as part of an occupational plan. For many, their interest in a career in corrections was fueled through their university coursework in criminal justice. For others, they came to prison work as a result of their military or other policing experience. Yet few come to the job knowing what to expect and draw conclusions from media representations of corrections. While many officers reported that while the media portrays the occupation of the correctional officer as one subjected to constant violence, the reality of life on the job was "a lot better than what's portrayed in the movies" (Britton, 2003, p. 92).

Qualifications for employment as a correctional officer vary with the type of institution. Most state facilities require correctional officers to be at least 18 or 21 years old, have a high school diploma or equivalent, and have no felony convictions (Bureau of Labor Statistics, 2003). For example, a position as a correctional officer with the California Department of Corrections requires applicants to be at least 21 years of age, possess either a high school diploma or its equivalent, and have a history of law-abiding behavior. Applicants must also be in good physical and emotional health and be legally eligible to own and possess a firearm (California Department of Corrections, 2003). To work for the Federal Bureau of Prisons requires either four years of college study, a bachelor's degree, or three years of full-time experience completed in a policing or corrections-related field.

Training programs for correctional officers vary with the type and jurisdiction of the facility. Federal officers complete 200 hours of training, 80 of which are based at the institution in which they will be employed and 120 hours of specialized training. Federal correctional officers also receive opportunities for additional specialized training throughout their careers (Britton, 2003). State training systems vary by state and are often less rigorous. In Texas, correctional officer trainees undergo 120 hours of classroom training (Hallinan, 2001). Correctional officers are instructed in subjects related to their job duties, including CPR/first aid, use of force/defense tactics, chemical agents and firearms training, crisis intervention, report writing, institutional standards, inmate/staff communications, safety and security procedures, and other related topics.

Correctional officers also participate in on-the-job training, whereby they shadow another officer to become familiar with the daily routine of the prison. At the Sing Sing Penitentiary in New York, correctional officers spend four weeks training with another officer before they receive solo assignments. The on-the-job training becomes the most important experience in preparing officers to work as a correctional officer (Conover, 2000). An important, though informal, component of the on-the-job training involves learning about the day-to-day activities of the prison from the inmates themselves. Inmates, like guards, have an interest in keeping order within the prison walls and often know the routine better than the newly trained guard.

Like working conditions, the pay scale for correctional officers has improved over recent years. Overall median annual incomes for correctional officers in 2000 were $31,170, with the lowest 10% earning less than $20,010 and the highest 10% earning greater than $49,310. For correctional officers employed in federal facilities, the median income equaled $37,430, with state correctional officers' median incomes equaling $31,860 (Bureau of Labor Statistics, 2003). According to the Federal Bureau of Prisons, the starting salary for correctional officers at the GS-5 level in 2003 was $28,909, not accounting for regional differences (Bureau of Prisons, 2003). In addition, correctional officers employed in the state or federal system receive medical and retirement benefits.

CONCLUSION

Though low pay and poor working conditions characterized the history of the correctional officer, the occupation has greatly improved. Today, the occupation benefits from racial, class, and gender diversity. Nonetheless, the career is not without its problems as officers are exposed to high levels of on-the-job stress, as well as threats to their personal safety. In spite of these concerns, employment opportunities as a correctional officer will continue to increase as a result of the expanding prison industry.

—Stacy Maillicoat

See also Correctional Officer Pay; Governance; History of Correctional Officers; History of Women's Prisons; Legitimacy; Managerialism; Professionalization of Staff; Reformatories; Staff Training

Further Reading

Belknap, J. (1995). Women in conflict: An analysis of women correctional officers. In B. R. Price & N. J. Sokoloff (Eds.), *The criminal justice system and women: Offenders, victims and workers* (2nd ed.) (pp. 195–227). New York: McGraw-Hill.

Black, S. (2001). Correctional employee stress and strain. *Corrections Today, 63*(6).

Britton, D. M. (2003). *At work in the iron cage: The prison as a gendered organization.* New York: New York University Press.

Bureau of Labor Statistics. (2003). *Occupational outlook handbook, 2002–3 edition, correctional officers.* Washington, DC: U.S. Department of Labor.

Bureau of Prisons. (2003). *Salary table 2003-GS.* Retrieved from http://www.bop.gov/

California Department of Corrections. (2003). *Career opportunities.* Retrieved from http://www.corr.ca.gov

Cheek, F. E., & Miller-Marie, D. (1983). The experience of stress of correction officers: A double blind theory of correctional stress. *Journal of Criminal Justice, 11*(2), 105–120.

Conover, T. (2000). *New Jack: Guarding Sing Sing.* New York: Random House.

Farkas, M. (2000). A typology of correctional officers. *Internal Journal of Offender Therapy and Comparative Criminology, 44*(4), 431–449.

Goffman, E. (1961). *Asylums: Essays on the social situation of mental patients and other inmates.* New York: Anchor.

Hallinan, J. T. (2001). *Going up the river: Travels in a prison nation.* New York: Random House.

Harrison, P. M., & Beck, A. J. (2003). *Prisoners in 2002.* Washington, DC: U.S. Department of Justice, Office of Justice Programs, Bureau of Justice Statistics.

Johnson, R. (1996). *Hard time: Understanding and reforming the prison.* Belmont, CA: Wadsworth.

Marushack, L. (2004). *HIV in prisons, 2001.* Washington, DC: U.S. Department of Justice, Office of Justice Programs, Bureau of Justice Statistics.

Owen, B. A. (1988). *The reproduction of social control: A study of prison workers at San Quentin.* New York: Praeger.

Ray, G. (2001). The emotions hidden behind a badge. *Corrections Today, 63*(6).

Stephan, J. J., & Karberg, J. C. (2003). *Census of state and federal correctional facilities, 2000.* Washington, DC: U.S. Department of Justice, Office of Justice Programs, Bureau of Justice Statistics.

Wright, L. N., & Northrup, M. K. (2001). Examining the health risks for corrections professionals. *Corrections Today, 63*(6).

Zimmer, L. E. (1986). *Women guarding men.* Chicago: University of Chicago Press.

Zimmer, L. E. (1989). How women reshape the prison guard role. *Gender and Society, 1,* 415–431.

Zupan, L. (1992). The progress of women correctional officers in all-male prisons. In I. Moyer (Ed.), *The changing roles of women in the criminal justice system* (pp. 230–249). Prospect Heights, IL: Waveland.

Legal Cases

Gunther v. Iowa, 612 F.2d 1079 (1980).

Harden v. Dayton Human Rehabilitation Center, 520 F. Supp. 769 (1981).

■ CORRECTIONS CORPORATION OF AMERICA

Corrections Corporation of America (CCA) is a private corrections corporation that was formed in 1983 in Nashville, Tennessee, by Thomas Beasley, with financial support from the venture capital firm of Massey Burch, the financiers of Kentucky Fried Chicken. The company manages 60 correctional facilities in 21 states, housing 54,000 inmates, and employing more than 14,000 people.

CCA began the current era of prison privatization with the first county-level award from Hamilton County, Tennessee, in 1984. In 1985, the company made an unsuccessful attempt to manage the entire prison system of Tennessee. Today, CCA is the largest private provider of correctional services to government agencies. It boasts the sixth largest corrections system in the nation, trailing only Texas, California, the Federal Bureau of Prisons, New York, and Florida. CCA currently has contracts with the Federal Bureau of Prisons, the Immigration and Naturalization Service (INS; in 2003 this agency was renamed the U.S. Citizenship and Immigration Services, USCIS, and placed under the governance of the Department for Homeland Security), and the U.S. Marshals Service. It also has contracts with 21 state governments and the District of Columbia.

Facilities run by CCA house prisoners at all security levels (minimum, medium, and maximum), though the most of the CCA prisons house medium-security inmates. Both men and women are housed in CCA facilities. The Arizona Department of Corrections contracts with CCA to house all of its female prisoners.

ACCOUNTABILITY

Private prison companies such as CCA should not be thought of as prison systems themselves, but as agents of public prison systems. In all cases, governments are ultimately responsible for the care and well-being of prisoners. Through regulatory and accountability measures, governments seek to evaluate the programs that private prisons operate.

The chief organization offering accreditation to correctional facilities is the American Correctional

Association (ACA). The ACA assesses administrative and fiscal controls, staff training and development, safety and emergency procedures, sanitation, and rules and discipline. CCA seeks ACA accreditation for all of its facilities. Currently, about 85% of CCA facilities are ACA accredited.

In addition to seeking accreditation, CCA has built strong ties with the public sector corrections community and political officials. CCA has connected itself to the public sector corrections community by hiring several former high-ranking government officials, including J. Michael Quinlan, former director of the Federal Bureau of Prisons. Public-private connections between CCA and political officials have been noted by those monitoring campaign contributions. For example, during the 2000 election cycle, CCA made more than 600 campaign contributions worth roughly $500,000 to state-level candidates in 13 southern states.

PROBLEMS WITH CCA FACILITIES

Correctional facilities run by CCA have had their share of problems. Critics have accused CCA prisons of being understaffed with poorly trained guards, unsanitary, and unsafe. There have been multiple cases of these kinds of charges reported in the press. In addition, CCA came under heavy criticism after a report was filed in 2000 for the Wisconsin legislature that found unacceptable conditions such as insect and rodent infestations and evidence of guards smuggling drugs and weapons into CCA prisons that house inmates from Wisconsin.

CCA has also come under attack for its recent strategy of building prisons on spec, where correctional facilities are constructed before any government contract is in place, thereby avoiding contracting laws to which federal and state governments are subject. This practice, some argue, enables companies like CCA to exert undue influence on how, where, and when new prisons are built.

CONCLUSION

While there are compelling examples of both positive and negative impacts of CCA on the corrections landscape, one thing is certain: CCA continues to win contracts from national and state governments. As long as inmate populations continue to grow beyond the capacity of governments to house them, and there is increased public pressure to cut corrections budgets, it is likely that CCA and its competitors will gain an increasing share of the corrections market.

—*Charles Westerberg*

See also Accreditation; American Correctional Association; Contract Facilities; INS Detention Facilities; Privatization; Privatization of Labor; Wackenhut Corporation

Further Reading

Clare, E., Adrian, J., Bottomley, K., & Liebling, A. (1997). *Privatizing prisons: Rhetoric and reality.* Thousand Oaks, CA: Sage.

Geis, G., Mobley, A., & Shichor, D. (1999). Private prisons, criminological research, and conflict of interest: A case study. *Crime & Delinquency, 45,* 372–388.

Neufeld, R., Campbell, A., & Coyle, A. (Eds.). (2003). *Capitalist punishment: Prison privatization and human rights.* Atlanta, GA: Clarity.

Shichor, D., & Gilbert, M. J. (Eds.). (2000). *Privatization in criminal justice: Past, present, and future.* Cincinnati, OH: Anderson.

◪ COTTAGE SYSTEM

During the first three decades of the 20th century, a dozen states built women's prisons using a cottage style architectural design. Instead of traditional cellblocks, female prisoners were housed in small units scattered across a rural "campus" setting. These cottages generally held 25 to 30 women in single or double rooms. To cut costs, some states (Maine, Kansas, and Ohio) developed dormitory style cottages housing 50 to 100 women.

Each cottage, designed to foster women's rehabilitation by promoting the "idea of family life," typically contained its own kitchen, dining room, and sitting room. In these idealized domestic settings, female prisoners received training in sewing, cooking, serving, and other domestic arts. Special cottages for pregnant, mentally defective, and/or inmates with venereal disease were common, as was racial segregation. Most reformatories classified cottages by security level: minimum, medium, and maximum.

HISTORY

Cottages represented a radical departure from traditional prison design. During most of the 19th century, women were incarcerated alongside men in separate annexes, wings, or units either within or attached to their state's male penitentiaries. After the Civil War, women activists began to campaign for entirely separate women's prisons. These reformers were convinced that female offenders would be reformed only within a more domestic and homelike setting.

In 1873, Indiana established the nation's first completely independent, all female-staffed, women's prison. However, it followed a traditional cellblock design. New York's House of Refuge at Hudson (1887) and Western House of Refuge at Albion (1893) were the first women's institutions (albeit, for younger women) to incorporate cottage units alongside a typical "custodial" prison building.

Between 1900 and 1935, this new type of women's prison, officially labeled reformatories, was established in 17 states. The New Jersey State Reformatory for Women at Clinton, opened in 1913, was the first to rely exclusively on cottage housing. Subsequently, eight states mandated that their women's reformatories be built according to a cottage plan: Minnesota (1916), Ohio (1916), Connecticut (1917), Kansas (1917), Maine (1917), Arkansas (1920), Pennsylvania (1920), and North Carolina (1929).

During these early decades, African American women remained relegated to the more traditional women's prisons. In 1923, African American women represented two-thirds (65%) of female prisoners incarcerated in state penitentiaries, whereas they were only 12% of those sentenced to the new reformatories. Reformatory advocates fully subscribed to the dominant racist ideology that portrayed African American women as more "masculine," violent, aggressive, hardened, promiscuous, and immoral than white women. Consequently, African American women were regarded as unsuitable subjects for the reformatory's goal of transforming female offenders into proper ladies.

In addition to their cottage style architecture, women's reformatory prisons broke radically with traditional male prisons in their commitment policies, incarcerating both felons and misdemeanants. Unlike men, women could be sentenced to a reformatory for such misdemeanor offenses as disorderly conduct, public drunkenness, vagrancy, adultery, fornication, and petit larceny. In Illinois, for example, misdemeanor commitments represented 73% of all reformatory commitments in the 1930s, 38% in the 1950s, and 12% in the 1970s.

DISCIPLINE AND DAILY LIFE

To outside observers, the cottage style women's reformatory appeared far more benign than men's prisons: quaint cottages scattered across a campus style setting. However, the conditions of women's incarceration could be even more restrictive. Surveillance within the small cottages was often more intense and invasive than that experienced by men housed in far larger, more anonymous, cellblock units. Because women's reformatories initially lacked fences, walls, and guard towers, prisoners had to be strictly supervised. Ironically, they often enjoyed little freedom of movement across their bucolic campus settings.

Few studies exist of the evolution of the women's reformatory prison or its cottage ideal. The Illinois State Reformatory for Women at Dwight (1930–1972) provides a rare glimpse into cottage living. Reformers insisted that the cottage system was the heart of the reformatory's rehabilitative philosophy. They argued that cottage living facilitated individualized treatment, training in appropriate gender-role behaviors, and resocialization in-group living skills. Within this ideology, "home" was imbued with tremendous transformative power all its own.

Yet, in reality, cottage living provided only the most tenuous relationship to a real home. Cottage life rarely matched the tranquil domestic visions of the reformatory's founders. Prisoners were graded daily on their attitude, work, and "citizenship" (i.e., cooperation). They could be disciplined for such rule infractions as wearing inappropriate clothing, improper etiquette, unladylike language, and poor attitudes. These minor violations adversely affected women's chances of parole.

Staff, known as warders or matrons, also lived in the cottages. They were typically older, widowed, white women from small farming towns, who coveted the room and board that came with their modest salaries. Their only qualification was a high school degree. Deep divisions frequently emerged between cottage and professional staff of psychologists and sociologists. Psychiatric labels gave cottage warders little guidance in how to handle the numerous day-to-day problems they confronted. Responsible for managing and disciplining 20 to 30 adult women 24 hours a day, warders often resented the introduction of special diets or individualized treatment programs. Despite the existence of so-called minimum-security cottages, staff convenience dictated that daily routines were often the same in all cottages.

Disciplinary files reveal that cottage warders and their "girls" competed daily over who would "run the cottage." For example, in 1944 one warder in Illinois reported: "In one day here, I have found inmate Frances Grayson, second cook, runs the kitchen as she pleases. I heard her say she would butter up Warder Miller as she had Mrs. Orr and she would run the kitchen." This warder had no intention of allowing "her girls" to do as they pleased. She gave the woman a demerit for impudence. One week later she wrote another note explaining that at dinner she had seen one prisoner pass a handkerchief to another, who later used it to sneak a piece of cake upstairs. As the warder dryly remarked: "I noticed Crystal's bust being terribly large, but didn't say anything." Both inmates received two days in isolation as punishment for this minor infraction (Dodge, 2002, pp. 201–202).

CONTRAST WITH MEN'S PRISONS

Male prisoners were hardly ever disciplined for sneaking a few cookies, a piece of cake, or single sandwich. Although it was also against regulations for men to exchange any items of personal property,

their cells were not inspected on a daily basis. When "shakedowns" did occur, correctional officers searched men's cells for weapons, drugs, and major contraband. In contrast, one former female prisoner recalled bitterly, "They weren't searching our rooms for knives or weapons, they were searching our bras and panties, searching our pockets for candy and gum, counting our barrettes and hair bands" (Dodge, 2002, p. 233).

The much greater staff-inmate ratio in men's institutions, as well as the architecture of men's prison with 500-man cellblocks, central cafeteria, and factory-size industrial work sites, mitigated against the possibility of such tight control. Yet architecture and scale cannot alone account for these differences. As in the free world, women were expected to tolerate and acquiesce to a level of social control that would be deemed unacceptable by men.

UNIQUELY REPRESSIVE CHARACTER

By the 1930s, most reformatories had come to resemble traditional women's prisons in the strictness of their disciplinary regimes, their lack of programs, and in their difficulty in attracting qualified personnel. The most distinct aspect of the reformatories, their cottage architectural design, soon gave way to far less expensive dormitories and more traditional cellblocks as the reformatories expanded and economics triumphed over ideology. Even when cottages remained in use, more economical centralized dining halls replaced individual-cottage kitchens. This shift to a more repressive system typically coincided with an increasing proportion of African American commitments. For example, in Illinois their percentage grew from 30% in the 1930s to 65% in the 1960s.

Instead of offering a wide array of individualized treatment services, security concerns dominated cottage life. Over the decades, rules and regulations grew increasingly restrictive. Even though the Illinois State Reformatory for Women was one of the best equipped and staffed of the nation's 17 reformatories in the 1930s, few inmates doubted that they were in anything other than a prison. The intimate cottage settings allowed for an unprecedented level of surveillance and control. From the

1930s to the 1960s, rules governed every aspect of women's lives, dictating how they must fold and wear their clothes, sit at the dining room table, and style their hair. Cottage staff vigilantly monitored every word and action, policing women's language, attitudes, dress, table manners, and associations. They carefully recorded all incidents that occurred on their shifts, from a prisoner's failure to eat her breakfast toast to open defiance, physical fights, "unladylike" language, possession of contraband goods, or suspected "unwholesome" friendships.

At the Illinois reformatory, as at many mid-20th-century women's prisons, lesbianism represented the greatest transgression of proper feminine behavior. Staff vigilantly monitored all inmate friendships, as the following notes from the 1950s indicate: "Warder questions the relationship of Lucille Edelberg and Pearl Fells. Warder feels that it is not what it should be to be referred to as wholesome." "Mrs. Lee advised me to watch Ola Mae Hahn, due to sex reasons; as yet I have seen nothing out of the way" (Dodge, 2002, p. 234). Even the most innocuous behaviors—walking or sitting regularly with another woman—were suspect. Exchanging or sharing contraband—whether candy, cosmetics, or clothing—was interpreted as a sign of a potential lesbian relationship. Any physical contact or show of affection was grounds for punishment. Gossip, rumors, and unsubstantiated allegations were routinely included in women's files.

In such a repressive setting, "domestic training"—trumpeted as the heart of women's rehabilitation—became merely a hollow simulation. Creativity and decision making are essential elements of real home making. However, in a prison environment, obedience, not decision making, was the "skill" that was taught. Menus, recipes, routines, timing, and procedures were all set by the institution. Any deviation or mistake could be cause for a demerit.

CONCLUSION

Despite its many advocates, the cottage model was never universally realized. Only 17 states established women's reformatories, mostly in the northeast and midwest. The movement barely touched the south or west. Many states continued to build custodial women's prisons that were either physically attached to, or a short distance from, their male penitentiaries. Fifteen states as late as 1976 still relegated women to a corner of the state prison for men. The 1970s also witnessed a return to the model of "coeducational" prisons. In 2002, one quarter (26%) of the 118 state penal institutions housing women were co-correctional facilities that incarcerated both men and women in separate housing units.

Thus, by the 1970s the ideal of a gender-specific women's reformatory had been cast aside. Modern women's prisons are once again under the authority of centralized departments of corrections. Male correctional officers and administrators, anathema to an earlier generation of female reformatory advocates, dominate women's corrections in most states. Architecturally, modern women's prisons are indistinguishable from men's: the homelike cottage ideal abandoned by the mid-20th century. Yet even at its height, the cottage system, conceived as a more humane model of incarceration for female offenders, resulted in a uniquely oppressive and repressive institution.

—*L. Mara Dodge*

See also Alderson, Federal Prison Camp; Bedford Hills Correctional Facility; Campus Style; History of Women's Prisons; Lesbian Prisoners; Lesbian Relationships; Massachusetts Reformatory; Mothers in Prison; Prison Nurseries; Women's Prisons

Further Reading

Carlen, P. (1983). *Women's imprisonment: A study in social control.* London: Routledge & Kegan Paul.

Dobash, R. P., Dobash, R. E., & Emmerson, S. (1986). *The imprisonment of women.* London: Basil Blackwell.

Dodge, L. M. (2002). *"Whores and thieves of the worst kind": Women, crime, and prisons, 1835–2000.* DeKalb: Northern Illinois University Press.

Freedman, E. B. (1981). *Their sisters' keepers: Women's prison reform in America, 1830–1930.* Ann Arbor: University of Michigan Press.

Rafter, N. H. (1992). *Partial justice: Women, prisons, and social control* (2nd ed.). New Brunswick, NJ: Transaction Publishers.

CREATIVE WRITING PROGRAMS

Creative writing programs in U.S. prisons began in the late 1960s and early 1970s in response to the burgeoning prisoners' rights movement. The 1971 Attica riot was particularly influential in prompting the formation of prison arts programs of which writing courses were usually a part. For their supporters, these programs are inherently constructive and potentially rehabilitative. While financial support for writing programs has waxed and waned, these programs continue to survive due the work of individual writers and activists.

HISTORY

The first significant effort to offer creative writing programs in American prisons was initiated by PEN (Poets Playwrights Essayists Editors and Novelists) in 1971. PEN was established in 1921 as a means of using professional writers to advocate for world peace, and its Freedom to Write committee has helped prisoners abroad since 1960. In 1971, PEN created the PEN Prison Writing Committee to advocate for and instigate creative writing programs in America. This group lobbied state and federal governments, as well as individual departments of corrections, to reduce censorship, provide access to typewriters, and improve prison libraries. PEN also persuaded other writers to read, teach, and mentor inmates. In 1973, PEN launched its first annual literary competition for prisoners and encouraged the formation of a number of journals devoted to prison writing.

The efforts by PEN precipitated individual authors to offer creative writing workshops in prisons across the country. Two such men whose work in prisons has been most influential are Joseph Bruchac and Richard Shelton. In the early 1970s, Bruchac, the author of more than 20 books of poetry and fiction, began teaching creative writing in a number of prisons, often at his own expense. Bruchac was awarded an NEA grant in 1975 that enabled him to expand his programs through the publication and distribution of the *Prison Project Newsletter,* a periodical that served as a forum for thousands of aspiring prison writers and workshop instructors throughout the nation.

Richard Shelton has also offered creative writing workshops in a number of Arizona state prisons since the early 1970s. The author of a series of poetry collections, including *The Tattooed Desert, Of All the Dirty Words,* and *You Can't Have Everything,* Shelton founded the Arizona State Prison Creative Writing Workshops (ASPCWW). Since 1974, ASPCWW has continuously run at least one and sometimes several creative writing classes in Arizona state prisons. The program has been supported since 1991 by a grant from the Lannan Foundation.

CALIFORNIA ARTS-IN-CORRECTIONS

In the late 1970s, California officials adopted the framework set forth by PEN and writers such as Bruchac and Shelton and became the first state to commit substantial funds for a system-wide arts program. This system shaped subsequent arts programs throughout the country.

The California Arts-in-Corrections program, initiated by Eloise Smith and Page Smith, still relied on the work of individual writers and activists, but it signaled a deeper commitment from the state to the arts and the benefits that arts-related instruction could bring. At the time of its founding, Eloise Smith stated that their goal was "to provide an opportunity where a man can gain the satisfaction of creation rather than destruction, earn the respect of his fellows, and gain recognition and appreciation from family and outsiders . . . provide the professional artist as a model of creative self-discipline, and show the making of art as work which demands quality, commitment, and patience" (Cleveland, 2000, p. 3). In 1981, Eloise Smith and Verne Stanford convinced the state to offer the program to all of the California state prisons as the Arts-in-Corrections program.

Despite studies that demonstrate that prison arts programs reduce recidivism, the California Arts-in-Corrections program in 2003 faced elimination due to a proposed $46 million cut to the state's prison education program. "This is a program that takes people whose lives are often hopeless, and it gives them an avenue for personal change," said Jim Carlson, a former manager of the program. "It must be retained."

THE DECLINE OF CREATIVE WRITING PROGRAMS AND HOW UNIVERSITIES INTERVENED

Since the 1980s, growing conservatism across the United States has precipitated cuts in funding to a number of creative writing programs. For example, the National Endowment for the Arts dramatically cut funds to prison journals in 1982, and by 1984 every significant prison writing journal temporarily dissolved. In response, writers who believed in the value of teaching creative writing in prisons were forced to return to volunteering their services or to turn to academic institutions for support. Two groups that have effectively harnessed the financial support of universities are the Prison Creative Arts Project and SPACE.

The Prison Creative Arts Project, founded by Buzz Alexander at the University of Michigan in 1990, offers theater, writing, and visual art workshops in prisons and juvenile detention centers throughout Michigan. The project offers University of Michigan students the opportunity to teach in state prisons as part of a class. The group offers instruction, exhibitions, and advocacy.

Space in Prison for the Arts and Creative Expression (SPACE) was founded in 1992 by a group of women from Brown University interested in working in the Women's Division of the Rhode Island Adult Correctional Institution. The program offers theater, creative writing, and visual arts workshops to inmates. The group also produces a journal and trains others to respond to the issues of incarcerated women, particularly issues of disrupted families, histories of abuse, and challenges to feminine identities.

CONCLUSION

There is a mixed future for prison creative writing programs. Funding is still scarce, yet increasing numbers of anthologies by and about the lives of American prisoners are being published. These texts include *Disguised as a Poem: My Years Teaching Poetry at San Quentin* by Judith Tannenbaum, *Doing Time: 25 Years of Prison Writing* edited by Bell Gale Chevigny, *Prison Writing in 20th Century America* edited by H. Bruce Franklin, and *Couldn't Keep It to Myself: Testimonies From Our Imprisoned Sisters* edited by Wally Lamb. Books such as these make accessible the wealth of artistic production from U.S. prisoners and point to the ongoing importance of creative writing programs in prisons. They also offer testimony to the efforts of writers and activists from the past three decades whose belief in the power of writing helped influence the lives of inmates.

—*Vince Samarco*

See also Adult Basic Education; Art Programs; Drama Programs; Education; General Educational Development (GED) Exam and General Equivalency Diploma; Literacy; Prison Pell Grants Literature

Further Reading

Chevigny, B. G. (Ed.). (2002). *Doing time: 25 years of prison writing—A PEN American Center Prize anthology.* New York: Arcade.

Cleveland, W. (2000). *Art in other places.* Westport, CT: Praeger.

Franklin, H. B. (Ed.). (1998). *Prison writing in 20th century America.* New York: Penguin.

Lamb, W. (Ed.). (2003). *Couldn't keep it to myself: Testimonies from our imprisoned sisters.* New York: Regan.

PEN American Center Archives, Princeton University. (2004). Retrieved from http://libweb.princeton.edu/libraries/firestone/rbsc/aids/pen.html

Tannenbaum, J. (2000). *Disguised as a poem: My years teaching poetry at San Quentin.* Boston: Northeastern University Press.

☑ CRIME, SHAME, AND REINTEGRATION

In his book *Crime, Shame and Reintegration*, published in 1989, Australian criminologist John Braithwaite puts forth a theoretical model for dealing with crime at the individual and community levels. Braithwaite integrates many traditional sociological theories of crime into a single view explaining why some societies have higher crime rates, why certain people are more likely to commit crime, and how communities can deal effectively with crime for the purposes of prevention.

According to Braithwaite, high rates of predatory crime in a society are indicative of the failure to shame those acts labeled as criminal. Braithwaite argues that the breakdown of community ties in modern urban communities has meant that perpetrators of crime are not made to feel ashamed of their actions, and thus continue victimizing others without remorse.

The concept of shame is the linchpin of this theory. Braithwaite suggests that if perpetrators were made to feel guilty about their actions, they would be deterred from committing further crime. He bases this assumption on the belief that those who are closely tied to family and community anticipate a negative reaction to the violation of community norms. Foreseeing the shame that they would feel, they are deterred from committing crime. However, according to this theory, shaming must be done in such a way as to be reintegrative, bringing the offender back into the community, rather than disintegrative, which would push the individual even farther out of the community. For Braithwaite, reintegrative shaming is the key to effective deterrence and crime prevention.

BACKGROUND TO THE THEORY

Braithwaite integrates the major tenets of five different theoretical traditions in 20th-century criminology into his theory of reintegrative shaming. He explains how labeling, subcultural, control, opportunity, and learning theories fit into his work. Crime, shame, and reintegration is not then an attempt to rewrite criminology, but to synthesize several seemingly disparate theories into a singular explanatory system.

Crime

Braithwaite begins with the notion, taken from control theory, that individuals are naturally drawn to commit criminal acts for personal gain and hedonistic pleasure. Proponents of control theory assume that it is more important to look at why certain people do not commit crime, rather than why some do. It is assumed that, without a particular set of restraints, the average person would commit criminal or immoral acts.

Criminological research has established that various personal and circumstantial characteristics are positively correlated to criminality. Being male, between the ages of 15 and 25 years, unmarried, unemployed or without steady employment, of lower socioeconomic status, living in a city, and having low educational attainment are all indicative of a statistically higher propensity for crime. The opposite is also true. Individuals who are female, younger than 15 or older than 25, married, of a higher socioeconomic status, living in a rural area, and having greater than secondary school education would be found to be at a significantly lower risk of committing a criminal act.

According to Braithwaite, the very characteristics that lead one person to have a higher propensity for criminality also lessen his or her relationship with family and community and leave a person less susceptible to the deterring power of shame. Those characteristics associated with a lower risk of criminality correlate to increased contact with family and community, which in turn increases a person's susceptibility to shame. For example, an individual who is married with children has responsibilities to his or her family that may constrain him or her from making risky or poor choices, whereas a single individual does not necessarily have such ties to family and responsibilities. Those who are more integrated into the community and involved in relationships with others are less likely to commit crime because they appreciate the shame and embarrassment that would result from violating community norms and values. Furthermore, those who are firmly integrated into a community feel personal responsibility for the safety and well-being of those around them. In contrast, those who are not integrated into a community or involved in meaningful relationships with others are more likely to commit crime because they do not feel a sense of responsibility to those around them, and they are not constrained by feelings of shame.

Briathwaite uses these beliefs to argue that cohesive, communitarian societies, such as Japan, which are characterized by networks of interdependent relationships, are likely to have lower rates of crime than more individualistic, fragmented societies, such as the United States. In Japan, he claims, honor and responsibility to family and community are emphasized. The Japanese place their community and family above themselves. In contrast, people in the United States and other Western nations are socialized to value individuality and personal accomplishment and fulfillment over the needs of family and community. According to Braithwaite, it is this distinction of values that accounts for Japan's much lower rates of violent and predatory crime.

Shame

For Braithwaite, shame is the ultimate deterrent against the violation of societal norms, for those who have a stake in a particular community. As already stated, he differentiates between shaming that is stigmatizing and shaming that is followed by reintegration. Reintegrative shaming is characterized by a ceremony in which the criminal act committed is denounced and community members express their disapproval of it. The shaming ceremony is then followed by efforts to "reintegrate the offender back into the community of law-abiding or respectable citizens through words or gestures of forgiveness or ceremonies to decertify the offender as deviant" (Braithwaite, 1989, pp. 100–101). An example of reintegrative shaming in practice can be found in New Zealand family group conferencing, which is frequently used to deal with cases of juvenile delinquency. In this strategy, the victim and offender meet in the presence of family and concerned community members to work out an appropriate restitution and consequence for the crime. In Canada, a similar process of circle sentencing is sometimes used by Aboriginal communities.

Shame that is stigmatizing, or disintegrative, occurs when the act and the actor are denounced as unworthy of the community. There are no efforts to reintegrate the offender, and he or she is rejected by the community. Disintegrative shaming is exemplified in the traditional criminal justice system by the court and sentencing process. Here, the offender is stigmatized by his or her conviction and literally, as well as symbolically, sent away from the community to prison.

Shaming that is reintegrative is not "soft" or "easy" on the offender. Although it can be done in love and with caring, reintegrative shaming can also be degrading, cruel, and punishing. The difference between reintegrative and disintegrative shaming is not in the quality of the shaming, but in its aim and in the processes that follow. Disintegrative shaming emphasizes the evil of the actor, while reintegrative shaming acknowledges the act as an evil thing, done by a person who is *not* inherently evil. Reintegrative shaming is followed immediately by gestures of reconciliation and inclusion, before the deviant identity is established as a master status.

Reintegration

As a follow-up to his theory of crime and reintegration, Braithwaite wrote an article with Stephen Mugford in 1994 titled "Conditions of Successful Reintegration Ceremonies," which identified 14 characteristics that must be present for a reintegration ceremony to be successful. They noted that structurally successful reintegration ceremonies usually include two aspects: confrontation with the victim, which leads to effective shaming, and inclusion of the people who respect and care most about the offender. Reintegrative shaming is most effective when those who are closest to the offender and/or to the situation participate.

Braithwaite believes that offenders must be able to view their act outside of their own perspective to see the harm that it has caused. The victim's perspective is invaluable in breaking down the offender's justification of the act, to enable him or her to see it as a crime. The victim may have the most impact on an offender in a face-to-face encounter, but those who do not wish to meet the person who harmed them may also communicate through letters, video conferencing, or a written statement. Shaming and reintegration are found to be most effective when those who support and care for the offender take part. This is because offenders are more likely to give regard to family and community members who have been involved in their lives than to people whom they do not know.

An individual's community may not be geographic, but instead composed of various individuals who have a common concern for the individual. For example, in New Zealand and Australia, Maori and Aboriginal people often bring relatives or friends of an offender from far away, so that those people can support the offender in his or her reintegration. Most important, those involved in the shaming and reintegration process must be able to impart to the offender the idea that they are denouncing the act that he or she committed, but restoring him or her to the community as a full member.

CRIME, SHAME, AND REINTEGRATION IN PRACTICE

Community measures and reintegrative shaming do not form an extensive part of the U.S. criminal justice system. They remain far more popular in New Zealand and Australia. However, in recent years, alternative measures that use the theoretical principles presented here have sprung up in the United States and Canada. Community conferencing, victim-offender mediation, and sentencing circles are examples of these new measures. Such measures are often referred to as *restorative justice.*

Community conferencing is one alternative to the traditional justice system in cases of juvenile offending. The victim and his or her supporters, the offender and his or her supporters, and other concerned community members gather in the presence of a community facilitator to discuss the incident and what should be done about it. The community conference is usually resolved when all parties agree on an acceptable restitution or punishment, at which point the reintegration can begin.

Victim-offender mediation is similar to a community conference, but it is usually not opened to concerned citizens. The victim and one or two supporters meet with the offender and one or two supporters in the presence of a trained mediator. The mediation is usually ended with the signing of a contract for restitution or community service. Victim-offender mediation may be used as a diversion from the traditional criminal justice system, or following the imposition of a custody sentence for a juvenile or adult offender.

Sentencing circles originated among Canadian Aboriginal peoples. The sentencing circle, available to juvenile and adult offenders, is similar to a community conference, in that it is opened to concerned community members, but it differs in that a judge presides over the circle and it is conducted in lieu of a formal trial. The sentencing circle differs from community conferencing and victim-offender mediation in that it may result in a custodial sentence, fine, or any option that would be available in a criminal sentencing hearing. A common thread among these alternative measures is that the offender has to first acknowledge his or her guilt in order to be eligible for these processes.

CONCLUSION

Braithwaite's theory has been criticized for its unquestioning assumption that Western societies are built on a consensus about what is right and what is wrong. His theory places little value on the beliefs and morals of subcultures while assuming that there is an overarching societal consensus on the laws of the land. Often, his theory obscures the fact that there are subcultures within the dominant culture that may or may not support the "dominant" consensus. For example, although violence against women is defined as criminal by the law and by many in society, prevailing patriarchal norms lead others to feel that there is nothing wrong with the abuse of a female partner or spouse. Similarly, those who grew up prior to the age of anti-drinking and driving sentiment often feel that it is perfectly acceptable and sociable to "take one for the road." They do not feel shame for their actions and are unlikely to respond well to a shaming ceremony. In such cases, reintegrative shaming may not work, since the crimes are not universally abhorred.

The use of prison, for Braithwaite, is inherently disintegrative and counterproductive, especially given the fact that most offenders return to the community. He thus supports the use of community alternatives to imprisonment or, at the very least, the use of proactive community reintegration following a term of incarceration.

—Stacey Hannem-Kish

See also Australia; Canada; Community Corrections Centers; Deterrence Theory; Faith-Based Initiatives; Intermediate Sanctions; New Zealand; Prisoner Reentry; Rehabilitation Theory; Restorative Justice

Further Reading

Braithwaite, J. (1989) Crime, shame and reintegration. Cambridge, UK: Cambridge University Press.

Braithwaite, J. (2000). Shame and criminal justice. Canadian Journal of Criminology, 42(3), 281–298.

Braithwaite, J., & Mugford, S. (1994). Conditions of successful reintegration ceremonies. British Journal of Criminology, 34(2), 139–171.

Daly, K. (2002). Restorative justice: The real story. Punishment and Society, 4(1), 55–79.

Immarigeon, R. (1992). Prison-based victim-offender reconciliation programs. In B. Galaway & J. Hudson (Eds.), Restorative justice: International perspectives. Monsey, NY: Criminal Justice Press.

Presser, L., & Gaarder, E. (2000). Can restorative justice reduce battering? Some preliminary considerations. Social Justice, 27(1), 175–195.

Umbreit, M. (1994). Victim meets offender: The impact of restorative justice and mediation. Monsey, NY: Criminal Justice Press.

Watts, R. (1996). John Braithwaite and "Crime, Shame and Reintegration": Some reflections on theory and criminology. Australian and New Zealand Journal of Criminology, 29(2), 121–141.

CRIPS

The Crips are among the best-known gangs in the United States. Along with their rival group the Bloods, Crip sets exist in cities throughout the United States, and thus have attained status as a supergang. Due to their involvement in the drug trade, and as a result of increased policing of gang-related activity, many Crip members are currently imprisoned.

HISTORY AND DEVELOPMENT

The Crips began in Los Angeles in the late 1960s. Raymond Washington and Stanley "Tookie" Williams are generally cited as the initial organizers of the group. The first name taken by the Crips was the "Baby Avenues" for the street on which Washington lived. There is some dispute about the origins of the name "Crip" itself. Some suggest that the initial name was Cribs and it evolved into Crips. Others suggest that the initial name was "Crypts" taken from the Vincent Price movie, Tales From the Crypt. Other reports suggest that one of the members was a cripple and walked with a cane.

Whatever its origins, Crip gangs spread quickly throughout South Central Los Angeles into other parts of the city and Los Angeles County, composed primarily of young, male African American residents of these neighborhoods. These groups took the color blue as their primary symbol, and similar to the longer-standing Hispanic gangs in southern California, wore bandanas that identified their membership.

Members of the Crips fought against other youths in neighborhoods in and around where they lived. It did not take long for youths in other neighborhoods to form groups for protection; these groups soon took a name. The groups opposed to the Crips came to be known as the Bloods, and early gangs were known as Piru Bloods, for the street near which many of the youths lived. These gangs chose red as their color. Wearing this color symbolized both membership in the Bloods and opposition to the Crips.

The development of the Crips reveals the importance of oppositional groups in gang activity. As Malcolm Klein (1995) has observed, gangs cannot exist in a vacuum. Thus, because of the role that external rivals play in both increasing solidarity internally and spreading the growth of the group, the Crips could not exist long without a rival. The rivalry between the Bloods and Crips has been important in fueling the growth of both groups.

Equally important to that growth, however, has been the impressive movement of Crip and Blood gangs into popular culture. Even though black gangs in the Los Angeles are fewer in number than their Hispanic counterparts, they receive the most attention. This notoriety is in part due to their involvement in violence, but can also be tied to their emergence in popular culture. This can be seen most directly in the depiction of Los Angeles Crips and Bloods in movies such as *Colors* and *Boyz in the Hood*, books such as *Do or Die*, and music videos. Through these vehicles, gang style and aspects of gang culture were spread to other American cities. There are even reports from several European cities, including Amsterdam and Munich, that youth groups that emulated Crip gang styles were emerging.

Crip gangs were very turf oriented and engaged in a considerable amount of violence. As they engaged in these activities, they were able to grow in number and size. When crack cocaine became available in the 1980s, Crip gang members became actively involved in the distribution of this drug. What is not clear, however, is the extent to which the Crip gang as an organizational entity was responsible for or behind the sales of the drug. There is solid evidence that Crip gang members were extensively involved in the sale of crack; however, the evidence that Crips controlled distribution of the drug is less solid.

ROLE IN OTHER CITIES

While Crip gangs trace their origins to Los Angeles, there are Crip sets in dozens of other American cities. The presence of such gangs in Cleveland, Indianapolis, Orlando, Atlanta, Charlotte, and St. Louis (among other cities) raises an interesting question about the Crips. Part of the reason that they have been identified as a supergang is that presence in other cities across the country. But how did this come to be? Maxson and Klein (1994) determined that most gang migration can be explained through traditional migratory patterns that involve family movement and employment patterns. Rather than gangs being "franchised" much like a fast food restaurant according to a plan and purpose, migration of Crip gangs appears to be due to the normal migratory patterns of Americans enhanced by the

presence of cultural messages through music videos, movies, and cultural symbols.

Ron Huff studied gangs in Cleveland in the early 1990s (Huff, 1996). He found four groups of gangs active in Cleveland: Folks, Vice Lords, Crips, and other independent gangs. The two largest groups of Crip gangs he interviewed included the Rolling 20s and Shot Gun Crips, groups related at least by name to Crip gangs in Los Angeles. Individuals in these gangs displayed versatile crime patterns and considerable levels of organizational variation. The Crip gangs in Cleveland were composed largely of young black males, whose predominant activity was hanging out and engaging in drug sales. Member of these groups had high levels of arrest, indicating extensive involvement in crime.

Decker and Van Winkle's research in St. Louis (1996) uncovered a large number of Crip gangs, 16 in all. The remainder of the gangs were associated with Blood gangs. The largest of the Crip gangs included the East Coast Crips, Long Beach Crips, Rolling Sixties Crips, and Hoover Crips. There was little if any evidence that Crips from Los Angeles had come to St. Louis to "franchise" Crips, rather the power of cultural transmission was more likely to account for the presence of these Los Angeles gang names in St. Louis.

ROLE IN PRISONS

As an increasing numbers of Crip gang members were sent to prison for their involvement in crime, a proportion of gang activity shifted from the street to the prison. In prison, street gang rivalries often are played out in a similar manner as that on the street. Yet there are differences as well. In prison, for example, gangs usually involve older, more criminally involved members than do street gangs. Likewise, ethnicity or race can be more important than street gang membership for the purposes of forming affiliations. One of the other ways that prisons are important for street gangs is the manner in which individuals change prior to their return to the street. Most prison releasees are older and have a wider range of criminal networks and ties than street gang members.

Often information is passed from the street to the prison and from prison to the street. In this way, contact is maintained between street and prison gang members, reinforcing criminality and influence in both directions. Prison is also a location in which the transmission of gang culture and membership can be expanded. Individuals from different locations around a state can be exposed to Crip gang members and when they return to their communities, bring aspects of the gang with them to their friends and neighborhoods.

In attempting to understand the role that Crips play in prison, it is important to distinguish between the state and federal prison systems. In state prison systems, gang members can maintain ties among members and with their community much more effectively. Federal prisons are a much different story. Because of the wider regional and national draw of federal prisons, there is a greater mix of individuals. Consequently, the ability of a local gang to dominate prison life is diminished.

CONCLUSION

One of the original cofounders of the Crips, "Tookie" Williams, is currently awaiting execution in San Quentin's death row. Incarcerated since 1981, Williams has undergone a dramatic change of heart about his involvement in gangs. He is now a vocal opponent of gang violence and publishes books for children warning of the risks of becoming involved in drugs and criminal activities. Due to his activities since entering prison he has been nominated for the Nobel Peace Prize.

—Scott H. Decker

See also Abolition; Activism; African American Prisoners; Bloods; Capital Punishment; Control Unit; Death Row; Deathwatch; Gangs; Prison Movies; Racial Conflict Among Prisoners; Racism; Resistance; San Quentin State Prison; War on Drugs; Young Lords

Further Reading

Curry, G. D., & Decker, S. H. (2003). *Confronting gangs: Crime and community*. Los Angeles: Roxbury.

Decker, S. H., & Van Winkle, B. (1996). *Life in the gang: Family, friends and violence*. New York: Cambridge University Press.

Huff, C. R. (1996). The criminal behavior of gang members and nongang at-risk youth. In C. R. Huff (Ed.), *Gangs in America* (2nd ed., pp. 39-74). Thousand Oaks, CA: Sage.

Klein, M. W. (1995). *The American street gang: Its nature, prevalence, and control.* New York: Oxford University Press.

Maxson, C., & Klein, M. (1994). *The scope of gang migration in the United States.* Washington, DC: National Institute of Justice.

Maxson, C., Klein, M., & Cunningham, L. (1992). *Street gangs and drug sales* (Report to the National Institute of Justice). Washington, DC: National Institute of Justice.

Shelden, R., Tracy, S., & Brown, W. (2001). *Youth gangs in American society.* Belmont, CA: Wadsworth.

◪ CRITICAL RESISTANCE

Critical Resistance is a grassroots organization that "fights to end the prison industrial complex by challenging the belief that policing, surveillance, imprisonment and other forms of control make our communities safer" (Critical Resistance, 2002c, p. 1). The national office of Critical Resistance is in Oakland, California, and there are local chapters in Springfield, Massachusetts; New Haven, Connecticut; Oakland, Sacramento, and Los Angeles, California; Washington, D.C.; New York City; and Sydney, Australia. Its work includes organizing local campaigns, movement building through large national and regional gatherings, and public education through film festivals, publications, and media work.

HISTORY

In 1997, a multiracial and intergenerational group of grassroots activists, scholars, students, and former prisoners met in Oakland, California, to generate a movement against mass incarceration and prison construction in the United States. Initially, the organizers decided to host an international conference that would bring together diverse constituencies affected by mass imprisonment, from prisoners and their families, to homeless advocates, sex worker organizations, antiracist, and LGBT (lesbian, gay, bisexual, and transgender) activists. This conference, titled "Critical Resistance: Beyond the Prison Industrial Complex," was held at the University of California, Berkeley, in September 1998 and was attended by more than 3,500 participants. In conjunction with the conference, several thousand high school students staged a walkout to demand "Schools Not Jails." The Youthforce Coalition, dedicated to opposing criminalization and incarceration of youths of color and calling for funding for schools and youth programs, was an outcome of this event. Critical Resistance East, a Northeast Regional Conference held in New York in Spring 2001, and Critical Resistance South, held in New Orleans in April 2003, continued the work of building a national movement.

THEORIZING THE PRISON INDUSTRIAL COMPLEX

Both prison intellectuals and academic scholars have contributed to Critical Resistance's theoretical development. A key achievement of the group has been to popularize the concept of the "prison industrial complex." As Angela Y. Davis argues, the massive growth in imprisonment is linked not to efforts by the state to curb crime, but rather to broader political and economic trends. The rolling back of the welfare state, coupled with the downsizing and relocation of manufacturing, Davis argues, has generated a social crisis in industrialized nations. Aggressive policing and harsh prison sentences have replaced social investment, affirmative action, and welfare as the primary response to the social problems generated by desperate socioeconomic conditions. At the same time, the function of the prison has shifted from rehabilitation to incapacitation. A key goal of prisons in industrialized nations appears now to be the removal of large numbers of the poor, disenfranchised, and racially marginalized from the streets. In so doing, prisons reproduce and exacerbate the social problems from drug use to unemployment that plague communities of color and indigenous communities in particular.

The phrase "prison industrial complex" refers also to the profit element in mass incarceration. Critical Resistance has drawn attention to prison corporations such as Wackenhut and Corrections Corporation of America that build and operate private prisons. The private prison industry in the United States alone earns up to $2 billion a year, and subsidiaries in other locations, from South Africa to Britain, also provide immense profits. Whether public or private, prisons are also a source of earnings for a host of companies that supply necessities from food and telephone services to stun guns and razor wire or employ the cheap and disciplined prison labor force. This interdependence between the state and capital has ensured the centrality of prisons to the global economy.

ENVIRONMENTAL AND ECONOMIC IMPACT OF PRISON CONSTRUCTION

In Spring 2001, Critical Resistance filed a historic environmental lawsuit against the California Department of Corrections with the aim of preventing the construction of a new $596 million, 5,160-bed prison in California's Central Valley. In filing the lawsuit, Critical Resistance, in partnership with the California Prison Moratorium Project, brought together a coalition of groups that had previously not worked together, including environmentalists, farm workers unions, Latino and immigrant advocates, and antiprison activists. The lawsuit demonstrated the increasing importance of rural communities in the prison industrial complex. Many rural town councils have viewed prison construction as a solution to economic stagnation. However, Critical Resistance used research by Ruth Wilson Gilmore to show that prisons have not actually been as economically beneficial to such communities as previously thought. In addition, Critical Resistance highlighted the negative environmental impacts of prison siting, including the destruction of farmland, the drain on water supplies, and the threat to local endangered species.

Critical Resistance views legal action as part of a wider strategy to shift public opinion against prison expansion. The campaign has generated a national debate about the failure of the "prisons as public works" policy. In addition, the lawsuit has thus far delayed construction.

ABOLITION

Central to Critical Resistance's work is an abolitionist commitment. According to Critical Resistance, abolition is "a political vision that seeks to eliminate the need for prisons, policing, and surveillance by creating sustainable alternatives to punishment and imprisonment" (Critical Resistance, 2002b, p. 1). Rather than promoting alternatives to incarceration that operate within the remit of the criminal justice system, Critical Resistance calls for sustainable alternatives that generate safety and security, while refusing to rely on law enforcement. These measures include community-based economic development, educational programs, community forums, drug treatment, and medical care. In Delano, California, for example, Critical Resistance worked with a range of community and labor organizations to identify programs, including youth facilities, additional investment in schools, and job creation that could serve as an alternative form of economic development to prison construction.

CONCLUSION

As an abolitionist organization, Critical Resistance rejects reformist agendas that expand the remit of the prison industrial complex. Rather than seeking to improve conditions by allocating additional resources to corrections budgets, Critical Resistance calls for a reduction in corrections spending by releasing prisoners including nonviolent offenders, addicts in need of treatment, and elderly prisoners and reducing the number of prisoners returned to prison for minor parole violations. Critical Resistance argues against investing more money into the prison system, and instead calls for the diversion of funds from social control into social welfare and community development.

—*Julia Sudbury*

See also Abolition; Activism; Corrections Corporation of America; Angela Y. Davis; Families Against Mandatory Minimums; Incapacitation; Increase in Prison Population; Prison Industrial Complex; Privatization of Prison; Race, Class, and Gender of Prisoners; Resistance; Three-Strikes Legislation; Truth in Sentencing; Wackenhut Corrections Corporation; War on Drugs

Further Reading

Critical Resistance. (Ed.). (2000a). Critical Resistance to the prison-industrial complex. *Social Justice, 27*(3).

Critical Resistance. (2002b). *What is abolition?* Retrieved from http://www.criticalresistance.org

Critical Resistance. (2002c). *What is Critical Resistance.* Retrieved from http://www.criticalresistance.org

Davis, A. Y., & Shaylor, C. (2001). Race, gender and the prison industrial complex: California and beyond. *Meridiens, 2*(1), 1–25.

Gilmore, R .W. (In press). *Golden gulag,* Berkeley: University of California Press.

Sudbury, J. (2000). Transatlantic visions: Resisting the globalization of mass incarceration. *Social Justice, 27*(3), 133–149.

◪ CUBAN DETAINEES

Today there are more than 1,000 Cuban nationals detained in federal prisons under special terms of confinement. Most of these men and women arrived in the United States in 1980 and are held as a result of special legislation and state powers that were enacted specifically to confine them. Most cannot be released since Cuba will not accept them back, and the United States will not grant them immigrant status.

WHO ARE THE CUBAN DETAINEES?

The Cubans came to the United States as part of the Freedom Flotilla that brought more than 120,000 refugees to the United States from the tiny port city of Mariel, Cuba, in 1980. Most of these people, soon to be called "Mariel Cubans" or "Marielitos" came to the United States because of economic problems in Cuba. A relatively small number of "anti-socials," political prisoners, and petty criminals were also forced to leave by the Cuban government. The overwhelming majority of Mariel Cubans were law-abiding citizens. They included farmers, mechanics, fishermen, truck drivers, seamstresses, accountants, construction workers, plumbers, carpenters, and professional athletes.

Ultimately, more than 90% of the refugees were processed by the U.S. Immigration and Naturalization Service (INS) and passed along to their families or to private relief groups across America. During the INS processing, however, officials began to notice some Cuban men who were more hardened and rougher in appearance than others. Research also suggests that a disproportionate number of these men were minorities. Based solely on their appearance, the INS concluded that the Cuban government had taken advantage of the Freedom Flotilla by emptying its prisons of hard-core criminals. Though Castro denied the allegation, the media began characterizing the Marielitos as "murderers," "vagrants," "homosexuals," and "scum."

WHY WERE THEY INCARCERATED?

The INS identified 350 Cuban men who were considered to have criminal backgrounds in Cuba. This figure represented less than one half of 1% of the total number of Cubans who came to the United States via the port of Mariel in 1980. By comparison, in the same year approximately 6,000 out of every 100,000 U.S. residents committed a major-index crime, as reported in the *Uniform Crime Reports*. Criminality within the general U.S. population was, therefore, roughly 17 times greater than that among members of the Freedom Flotilla. Nevertheless, this small group of Cuban criminals inspired the belief that a number of émigrés were dangerous people who could not be trusted. They became the first cohort of Mariel Cubans incarcerated in U.S. prisons. Others cohorts would follow, including a small number of women among them, and their imprisonment would also be affected by the stigmatized image of the "dangerous Marielito."

In addition to the 350 criminals, some 7,600 Freedom Flotilla émigrés had questionable backgrounds and were classified by the INS as "excludable entrants." Such people were allowed to enter U.S. society under the strict conditions of INS parole under which their parole could be revoked without explanation. Over the next several years, the INS revoked hundreds of paroles and detained Cubans in federal prisons because they had no visible means of support or fixed addresses, because they did not have an appropriate sponsor, or because they required medical treatment. Other Cubans were sent to prison for violating curfew or travel restrictions,

or for failing to participate in relocation programs. Still others were imprisoned for petty crimes. The INS revoked paroles for a range of infractions including driving without a license, shoplifting, or possession of small amounts of marijuana and cocaine. All of these men were given "indefinite sentences," meaning that they did not know when, if ever, they would be released from federal custody.

By 1987, the INS had criminalized enough male Mariel Cubans to fill two prisons: the Federal Detention Center at Oakdale, Louisiana, and the U.S. Penitentiary at Atlanta, Georgia. While it is generally assumed that maximum-security prisons exist to punish society's most dangerous criminals, this was not true for the Mariel Cubans. The maximum-security prison at Atlanta was used to warehouse the disadvantaged. A 1986 congressional report found that *absolutely none* of the nearly 1,900 Mariel Cubans locked up in Atlanta was serving a criminal sentence. That is, the detainees had already served their sentences for criminal transgressions, or they had committed no crimes at all.

HOW WERE THE DETAINEES TREATED?

The congressional report found that the Cubans at the Atlanta Penitentiary were incarcerated in the worst overcrowded situation in the federal prison system. Most were housed eight men to a cell for 23 hours a day. Suicide and psychological depression were rampant. In one year, nine Cubans committed suicide and there were 158 suicide attempts. There were more than 2,000 serious incidents of self-mutilation, 9 homicides, and 10 deaths from heart attacks and other natural causes. Ten percent of the Cubans were classified as mentally retarded, mentally disordered, or psychotic. The report concluded that the Cubans were forced to live in conditions that were "brutal and inhumane . . . without any practical hope of ever being released."

WHAT HAPPENED AS A RESULT?

In November 1987, the Cuban detainees responded to their conditions and legal uncertainties by mounting the longest and most destructive prison riot in American history. Using chains, blowtorches, and homemade machetes, they seized Oakdale and Atlanta with military precision, taking more than 200 hostages, and burning the prisons to the ground. In all, the Cubans destroyed more than $6 million worth of federal resources. During the siege, the detainees held machetes to the throats of hostages and threatened to burn them alive with gasoline. After two weeks, officials negotiated an end to the riot by promising the Cubans a "full, fair and equitable review" to determine eligibility for release into mainstream American society.

CONCLUSION

Following the riots, the INS approved nearly two-thirds of the detainees for release. Because of the riots, the Cubans were guaranteed more rights than at any other time since their arrival on the Freedom Flotilla. Yet for all that happened, nothing much changed. The policy of indefinite detention still remains. (In 2003, the INS was renamed the U.S. Citizenship and Immigration Services, USCIS, and placed under the governance of the Department for Homeland Security.) Today, 1,700 Mariel Cubans are still being indefinitely detained in federal prisons where they are segregated from other prisoners and treated with special restrictions because they are thought to be extremely dangerous. Confined to their cells for 23 hours a day, they are given no access to education. Most cannot speak or read English. They have few skills that would help them assimilate into American society. In recent years, Cuban detainees have waged several small-scale disturbances. For many, depression, lethargy, and resort to suicide and self-mutilation have become a way of life.

—*Mark S. Hamm*

See also Enemy Combatants; Federal Prison System; Foreign Nationals; Immigrants\Undocumented Aliens; INS Detention Facilities; Political Prisoners; Prisoner of War Camps; Santería; Relocation Centers; Resistance; Riots; USA PATRIOT Act 2001; Violence

Further Reading

Cohen, S. (2001). *States of denial: Knowing about atrocities and suffering.* Malden, MA: Blackwell.

Dow, M. (2004). *American gulag: Inside U.S. immigration prisons.* Berkeley: University of California Press.

Hamm, M. S. (1995). *The abandoned ones: The imprisonment and the uprising of the Mariel boat people.* Boston: Northeastern University Press.

Welch, M. (2001). *Detained! Immigration laws and the expanding I.N.S. jail complex.* Philadelphia: Temple University Press.

D

DAVIS, ANGELA Y. (1944–)

Angela Yvonne Davis is an African American activist and scholar who was charged and arrested for an alleged role in the August 7, 1970, failed escape of three inmates at the Marin County courthouse in California. Davis was accused of supplying guns used in the inmate escape and conspiring to free Soledad Brother George Jackson. While evading arrest on these charges, she became the third woman in U.S. history to be placed on the FBI's Most Wanted List. Arrested in New York on October 13, 1970, she spent 16 months in jail prior to being granted bail after a California Supreme Court decision ruled on a death penalty case that changed her bail status. A jury found Davis not guilty of all charges on June 4, 1972. Since then, she has continued to work for prisoners' rights throughout the world.

BIOGRAPHY

Davis was born on January 26, 1944, in Birmingham, Alabama. While growing up, her family lived in a section of Birmingham known as "Dynamite Hill" because of the frequent bombings by racist whites attempting to prevent the neighborhood from being integrated. As a youngster, however, Davis spent summers in New York where her mother worked on her master's degree. Summers in New York were a striking contrast to life in Alabama. In New York, African American children could swim in public pools and eat in restaurants—activities restricted to whites only in Alabama.

During high school, Davis took part in an experimental program that allowed African American students from southern states to attend integrated northern high schools. Consequently, she spent two years at Elizabeth Irwin High School, a small private progressive school in New York City. Davis then went to Brandeis University where she graduated summa cum laude in 1965 with a major in French literature. After graduating from Brandeis, she spent two years studying philosophy on a scholarship in Frankfurt, Germany, before returning to the United States in 1967 to pursue her master's degree in philosophy at the University of California, San Diego (UCSD), where she worked with Herbert Marcuse, a Marxist philosopher who believed it was important not just to theorize but to act.

During her time at UCSD, Davis joined the Communist Party. She also became involved in the black power movements. Then, in 1969 after receiving her master's degree and while working on her doctorate, Davis signed a contract to work at the University of California, Los Angeles (UCLA). When asked by an administrator if she were communist,

Davis answered affirmatively. In a public battle, the California Board of Regents attempted to dismiss Davis despite her successful teaching, arguments about academic freedom, and a California Supreme Court ruling in her favor. The regents were eventually successful.

SOLEDAD BROTHERS

At the same time that she was struggling to keep her teaching position at UCLA, Davis learned about the Soledad Brothers, three African American inmates who were accused of killing a white prison guard. Davis became the cochairperson of their defense committee and began an intense correspondence with one of them, George Jackson.

On August 7, 1970, Jackson's younger brother Jonathan attended the trial of James McClain, an inmate charged with assaulting a guard. According to some present in the courtroom, Jonathan stood up, took four guns out of his coat, and announced he was taking over. After conferring with Ruchell Magee and William Christmas, two inmates also present as witnesses in the case, the three men took hostages and left the courtroom. They made it to a rented van where a shootout left McClain, Christmas, Jonathan Jackson, and the judge dead and others injured.

A warrant was issued for Davis's arrest on August 11, 1970. Though she was not at the trial, she was charged, along with the only inmate survivor, Ruchell Magee, of murder, a capital offense, as well as kidnapping and conspiracy. It was alleged that she had given guns to Jonathan. Davis went into hiding and managed to evade law enforcement until her arrest in October 1970 and was extradited to California. She remained imprisoned until February 23, 1972, when she was released on $102,500 bail due to a California Supreme Court decision abolishing capital punishment.

The trial against Davis began on February 28, 1972. After 104 prosecution witnesses, 12 defense witnesses, and 203 items of evidence, the trial ended on June 4, 1972. It was clear to her supporters that the evidence against her was nonexistent. Following three days of deliberation, the jury (11 whites and 1 Mexican American) agreed and found Davis not guilty of all charges.

CONCLUSION

Drawing on her own experiences as a political prisoner, an African American, and a woman, Davis is deeply involved in the movement for prison reform worldwide. Most recently, she was one of the leading organizers of a conference called "Critical Resistance: Beyond the Prison-Industrial Complex" held in 1998 at the University of California, Berkeley. Critical Resistance is now a national organization that "seeks to build an international movement to end the Prison Industrial complex by challenging the belief that caging and controlling people makes us safe" (Critical Resistance, 2003).

—*Kim Davies*

See also Abolition; Activism; Black Panther Party; Critical Resistance; Elizabeth Gurley Flynn; George Jackson; Kate Richards O'Hare; Prison Industrial Complex; Racial Conflict Among Prisoners; Racism; War on Drugs

Further Reading

Aptheker, B. (1999). *The morning breaks: The trial of Angela Davis* (2nd ed.). Ithaca, NY: Cornell University Press.

Critical Resistance. (2003). Critical Resistance home page. Retrieved March 15, 2003, from http://www.critical resistance.org

Davis, A. Y. (1971). *If they came in the morning: Voices of resistance.* New York: New American Library.

Davis, A. Y. (1974). *Angela Davis—An autobiography.* New York: Random House.

Davis, A. Y. (1981). *Women, race, and class.* New York: Random House.

Davis, A. Y. (1989). *Women, culture, and politics.* New York: Random House.

Davis, A. Y. (1998). *Blues legacies and black feminism: Gertrude "Ma" Rainey, Bessie Smith, and Billie Holiday.* New York: Pantheon.

James, J. (1998a). *The Angela Y. Davis reader.* New York: Basic Books.

James, J. (1998b). *Resisting state violence: Radicalism, gender, and race in U.S. culture.* Minneapolis: University of Minnesota Press.

Nadelson, R. (1972). *Who is Angela Davis? The biography of a revolutionary.* New York: Peter H. Wyden.

Timothy, M. (1975). *Jury woman: The story of the trial of Angela Y. Davis.* San Francisco: Glide Publications.

DAVIS, KATHARINE BEMENT
(1860–1935)

Katharine Bement Davis was a nationally and internationally recognized pioneer in penology and prison reform. She was one of the first women to hold the top office in corrections in one of the largest cities in America and, in addition, she contributed ideas about the causes of crime and the effectiveness of treatment. Davis was a highly public figure, who spoke passionately about her work in the field and influenced policymakers and practitioners alike on the design and operation of prisons and reformatories.

Katharine Davis was born in Buffalo, New York, in 1860. Her parents were reformers. In the 10 years following her high school graduation she worked as a teacher before leaving that profession to pursue a degree at Vassar College. She then was granted a political economics fellowship and went on to obtain a doctorate at the University of Chicago. Returning to Vassar, she taught for several years before being appointed in 1901 to run the first female reformatory, Bedford Hills Correctional Facility, in Westfield, New York. She remained as superintendent of Bedford Hills for 13 years.

CORRECTIONAL INNOVATIONS

As female offenders were moved from men's prisons to their own institutions, Davis introduced the cottage system design for women's facilities. Unlike the warehouse-style prisons built for men, she viewed the cottage as more in keeping with the personality and temperament of women and as structurally more conducive to their good health. Davis even wrote an article titled "The Fresh Air Treatment for Moral Disease." She believed the cell-stacked architecture of prisons such as New York City's "Tombs" was "fundamentally wrong" because it shut out outside air and sunlight, which she considered "the greatest of all medicines for the mental, moral, and physical human sufferer" (Davis quoted in Marshall, 1914, p. SM6).

The women at Bedford were required to participate in schoolwork and to learn trades. They were also encouraged to work and engage in recreation outdoors, thus they were assigned farming chores. This environment was said to have a positive effect on all participants, even those who suffered from mental illnesses. As another innovation, a nursery was established within the reformatory where new mothers and their children could stay together for up to two years. This nursery program was later reactivated at Bedford as a highly acclaimed rehabilitation program in the 1980s.

Funding from grants and foundations enabled Davis to hire a prison psychologist. Performing routine psychiatric assessments for incarcerated women, Bedford Hills helped to lay the foundations of modern diagnostic prison procedures.

CRIMINOLOGICAL INNOVATIONS

Davis was a proponent of criminal theories that presented offenders as of subnormal intelligence and defective. An advocate of the medical model, she was concerned about the number of prostitutes, their lack of education and skills, and their high rates of disease. Fines for prostitution, she argued, usually placed the female offender further in debt to her male pimp and were therefore counterproductive.

In much of her criminology, Davis was highly influenced by the concerns of her day, particularly those about cultural adaptation to life in the melting pot of America. She pointed out the many Italian names on the rosters of incarcerated women and speculated that they emigrated with "their own primitive ideas of vengeance" (Davis quoted in Marshall, 1914, p. SM6). She lamented that some of the women murderers at Bedford were caught up in the conflicts of their culture when their own codes make them "victims of the racial custom of revenge" (Davis quoted in Marshall, 1914, p. SM6).

While others at this time were proponents of eugenics principles, Davis was more cautious. As a staunch advocate for the scientific study of crime, particularly the clinical assessment of the offender, Davis persuaded John D. Rockefeller, Jr., to donate $50,000 to establish the Laboratory of Social Hygiene directly across from the reformatory, one of the first institutes for studying female criminality.

Davis believed in the beneficial effect of cultural programs and introduced them into the prison.

Prisoners attended lectures, celebrated birthdays, and went on picnics. She hosted a tea reception for inmates in her quarters each New Year's Day. One of her most widely noted policies was the concept of an "honor cottage." Used as a means of encouraging good behavior, the honor cottage was reserved for inmates who had worked their way to the highest classification levels. Residents were allowed self-government and created their own rules. Gillin (1926) quoted one observer as saying, "The matron of the house has general oversight, but the girls in the honor cottage have as much freedom as a girl at a good boarding-school. The cottage is made as attractive as possible with ferns, pretty furniture, individual sleeping rooms, a pleasant sitting-room, and a sewing room where they make their own clothing" (p. 658).

Davis was also a supporter of early parole, preferring that inmates be released into country environments. She was of the opinion that the temptations of the city encouraged bad habits; thus, parole in the countryside gave the inmates a better chance to succeed. In addition, she actively sought parole and work and living arrangements that would most encourage adjustment into productive society.

Primarily because of her work at Bedford Hills, Davis became the first female corrections commissioner in New York City in 1914. She was responsible for the infamous Tombs prison, Raymond Street and Queens County jails in Brooklyn, the workhouse on Blackwell's Island, two other workhouses on Hart's and Rikers Islands, the New York City Reformatory for Male Misdemeanants, and the detention house for women. The Tombs was a source of concern because she felt the style of construction did not allow the building to be properly "flushed" and cleaned. It was woefully overcrowded and internal temperatures were difficult to regulate. She was also concerned about providing medical care and a separate facility for "inebriates."

CONCLUSION

Throughout her professional life, Davis researched successful programs around the country and in Europe. Disillusioned by the workhouse and penitentiary models, she encouraged judges to consider individual needs when sentencing and worked toward

developing individualized treatment plans for offenders. She summarized her optimistic philosophy as follows: "The needs of society and the individual can be best served by a system of correction based upon the character and requirements of the person rather than on the nature of the criminal act" (Davis quoted in Marshall, 1914, p. SM6). True to her optimism, she believed that the best model for improving corrections would be an apolitical process with all sectors of public welfare and justice working together.

The legacy of Katharine Bement Davis is found in the many employees she instructed, the policymakers she influenced, and the correctional concepts she championed. Another well-known reformer, Mary Belle Harris, was a protégé whom Davis originally recruited to run the workhouse on Blackwell Island and to implement her progressive practices. As an indication of the extent to which her work and ideas were respected, Davis was appointed a cabinet member of New York City and chairwoman of the city's parole board.

—*Frank P. Williams III*

See also Alderson, Federal Prison Camp; Bedford Hills Correctional Facility; Cottage System; Mary Belle Harris; Katherine Hawk Sawyer; History of Women's Prisons; Medical Model; Parole; Prison Nurseries; Psychological Services; Psychologists; Rehabilitation Theory; Mabel Walker Willebrandt; Women's Health; Women in Prison; Women's Prisons

Further Reading

Gillin, J. L. (1926). *Criminology and penology.* New York: Century.

Harris, J. (1990). *They always call us ladies.* New York: Zebra.

Marshall, E. (1914, January 11). New York's first woman commissioner of correction. *New York Times,* p. SM6.

McKelvey, B. (1936). *American prisons.* Chicago: University of Chicago Press. (Reprinted Montclair, NJ: Patterson Smith, 1968)

Morton, J. (1992). Looking back on 200 years of valuable contributions. *Corrections Today, 54*(6), 76–78, 80, 82, 84–87.

◪ DEATH ROW

Death row refers both to the physical space where those awaiting execution are held and the general population who have been sentenced to death. Capital punishment is as old as written law. It was the ascribed punishment for 25 different crimes under Hammurabi's Code (c. 1700 B.C.). Since condemned individuals are typically confined between the moments of judgment and execution, some form of "death row" must be equally ancient. Through the centuries, however, death row has evolved from a rudimentary cell located near the place of public execution to a highly specialized, segregated unit within a modern penal facility.

THE EVOLUTION OF DEATH ROW

Historically, executions were public spectacles (and remain so in countries such as Saudi Arabia, Iran, and Nigeria). But throughout the 19th century, many Western countries began conducting executions in private, behind prison walls. In 1834, Pennsylvania removed its executions from the public gaze; Massachusetts, New Jersey, and New York followed in 1835. The last public hanging took place in England in 1868, in the United States in 1937, and the last public execution by guillotine took place in France in 1939. As these executions became private, the process was streamlined. In prisons built during the early 20th century, visiting facilities and the living quarters of the condemned were often placed very close to the execution chamber, sometimes merely paces away.

GLOBAL TRENDS

Amnesty International reports a gradual international trend toward the abolition of capital punishment. They state that as of August 2002, more than half the countries in the world have abolished capital punishment in law or in practice. Members of the European Union (EU), for example, enforce a mandatory ban on capital punishment. Citizens from abolitionist countries are not executed for their crimes unless they are committed under a retentionist jurisdiction. But offenders from countries retaining capital punishment may face execution. In 1998, 76% of all known executions occurred in just three countries: China, the Democratic Republic of Congo, and the United States of America.

Although 12 states and the District of Columbia have abolished the death penalty, the United States remains a solid retentionist nation. Thirty-eight different states authorize the death penalty, as does the U.S. military and the federal government. Since the death penalty was reinstated in 1976 by the U.S. Supreme Court, 842 people have been executed in America, including 3 in the national execution chamber at Terre Haute, Indiana.

THE RISE AND FALL (AND RISE) OF DEATH ROW IN THE UNITED STATES

The numbers of men and women on death row fluctuates in size over time. Their proportions are a function of the number of people condemned to die and the expediency with which executions are conducted. Of these two factors, however, the number of people condemned to die has the greatest effect on the population of death row. Obviously, the number awaiting execution shrinks dramatically when states abolish capital punishment.

American states began limiting or abolishing the death penalty as early as 1846. During the early 20th century, many U.S. states abolished or restricted capital punishment, but there was a resurgence in the practice from the 1920s to the 1940s. Throughout the 1950s and 1960s, however, public support for the death penalty waned. Capital punishment was legislatively abolished in England in 1965. It was briefly struck down in the United States, as well.

In 1972, in the watershed case of *Furman v. Georgia,* the U.S. Supreme Court held that the death penalty (as then applied) constituted cruel and unusual punishment under the Eighth Amendment of the U.S. Constitution. States halted their executions. Consequently, numbers on death row shrank from 334 (in 1972) to 134 (in 1973) as the sentences of condemned men nationwide were commuted. But just four years later, the American death penalty was resurrected. In 1976, in *Gregg v. Georgia,* the U.S. Supreme Court declared that, under new state legislation, executions could resume. At this point, death row began to grow once again. By 1977, when Gary Gilmore ushered in the modern era of American capital punishment with his execution before a Utah firing squad, the numbers on death row had already ballooned to 423.

Since Gilmore's death, the size of death row has steadily escalated. At the end of 2002, there were 3,692 condemned individuals waiting to die in America. Yet the size and composition of death row may continue to change. Throughout the late 1990s, DNA evidence suggested that innocent people could be found on death row, triggering intense public debate about the propriety of capital punishment, leading to legislative reform and executive action.

THE DEMOGRAPHICS OF DEATH ROW

Death row prisoners tend to fall into certain demographic categories. They tend to be adult males, often come from impoverished backgrounds, and disproportionately belong to racial minorities. Many endure long periods of incarceration before their execution. In the following section, each of these issues shall be dealt with in turn.

Age

Most death row prisoners are adults. Since 1990, only seven countries are known to have executed juveniles (individuals under the age of 18 at the time of their crimes): the Democratic Republic of Congo, Iran, Pakistan, Yemen, Nigeria, Saudi Arabia, and the United States of America. Only the United States and Iran formally authorize the practice with U.S. barring execution of those who are less than 16 years old. The execution of juveniles in the U.S. is relatively uncommon. Although juveniles account for 15% of murder arrests, they account for only about 2% (81) of prisoners on death row and about 2.6% (21) of individuals executed since the death penalty was reinstated.

Class

Death row prisoners disproportionately come from impoverished backgrounds. Poverty may correlate positively with aggravating factors such as prior criminal history or predictions of future dangerousness, leading juries to impose death sentences. Affluence, on the other hand, may correlate positively with mitigating factors—close relationships with family and friends, well-articulated remorse, or status in the community—decreasing the likelihood of receiving a death sentence. Perhaps more important, wealthy capital defendants can afford sophisticated "dream team" legal representation, while disadvantaged defendants are often represented by overworked or inexperienced public defenders who may not even want the case. Even Supreme Court justices acknowledge that poverty influences the dispensation of capital punishment. In the *Furman* decision, Justice Douglas wrote, "One searches in vain for the execution of any member of affluent strata of this society."

Race

Race plays a significant role in the shaping of death row. Both the race of the defendant and the race of the victim may influence the imposition of a death sentence. Although whites constitute about 75% of the American population, they account for only 57% of those executed since the death penalty was reinstated and about 45% of those on death row. On the other hand, while blacks constitute only 12% of the American population, they constitute 43% of death row and account for 35% of those executed. Seventy-six percent (19) of the 25 prisoners on federal death row and 6 of the 7 prisoners on the U.S. military's death row are minorities. But research indicates that the race of the victim may play a more significant role on who is condemned to death than the race of the defendant. The murder of a white victim is more likely to result in a capital conviction than the murder of a nonwhite. More than 80% of capital cases in America involve a white victim, although only 50% of murder victims are white nationwide.

In *McCleskey v. Kemp* (1987), the U.S. Supreme Court considered research that demonstrated systemic racial discrimination in the imposition of capital punishment. After controlling for many nonracial variables, the research indicated that Georgia defendants charged with killing white victims were 4.3 times more likely to get the death penalty as defendants charged with killing blacks. While the Court did not challenge the legitimacy of

McCleskey's data, it rejected his claim that these findings amounted to an unconstitutional risk of prejudice in death penalty decision making. Warren McCleskey was executed in 1991.

Gender

Death row is composed primarily of males. Some countries, such as Russia, explicitly made women ineligible for capital punishment. Other countries did so in practice. Although women comprise about 51% of the U.S. population and account for about 20% of criminal homicides, they account for only about 10% of murder arrests, 2% of death sentences at trial, about 1.4% of prisoners on death row, and about 1.2% (10) of those who have been executed since capital punishment was reinstated. Legal scholars explain this screening-out effect by citing gender discrimination in the attitudes of judges and jurors and by claiming gender discrimination is inherent in existing death penalty statutes.

Time Spent on Death Row

Historically, little time elapsed between sentencing and execution. Under England's Murder Act of 1752, executions were carried out just two days after sentencing; after 1834, only three Sundays elapsed before the sentence was carried out. These days, however, because of the "super due process" safeguards required under *Gregg,* contemporary death row prisoners in America spend years (not days or weeks) awaiting execution. The average duration from sentence to execution is now more than 12 years, and some prisoners have spent more than 20 years on death row.

CONDITIONS OF CONFINEMENT

Typically operated as a prison within a prison, characterized by lockstep security and minimal freedoms, death row represents the hardest time a prisoner can do. "Death row is the most total of total institutions, the penitentiary most demanding of penitence, the prison most debilitating and disabling in its confinement. On death row the allegorical pound of flesh is just the beginning. Here the

whole person is consumed. The spirit is captured and gradually worn down, then the body is disposed of" (Johnson, 1998, p. 71).

Time on death row often drags. Because a sentence of death is supposed to be both definitive and final, death row prisoners do not participate in rehabilitative activities such as education, therapy, or job skills training. Nobody wants to invest resources in developing an individual who will be executed in a month or a year or a decade. Plagued by tedium, some death row prisoners throw themselves into their appeals, honing their skills as jailhouse lawyers. Others write voluminous correspondence, immerse themselves in religious study or literature, or turn to handicrafts and art projects as a pastime. Many seek to lose themselves in television.

The physical environment of death row closely resembles that of super-maximum secure facilities. Because it is thought that death row prisoners "have nothing to lose," security is tight. Prisoners are usually confined to small single-occupancy cells for up to 23 hours a day and are monitored carefully. Movement is restricted: Meals are typically served to death row prisoners in their cells, and religious and legal services are often delivered to the cell (either by closed-circuit programming or book request). Prisoners are afforded opportunity to exercise for several hours per week, allowed to visit with family members and lawyers, and are usually permitted to have some personal possessions in their cells.

The elite correctional officers assigned to death row attempt to emphasize professionalism and compassion, and strive to maintain the dignity of the prisoner throughout the process. Actual execution procedures are rehearsed to precision, minimizing the likelihood of mishap or error. These staff also supervise inmates in their final days on deathwatch.

These maximum-security facilities are expensive. When coupled with the appellate processes required under *Gregg*'s super due process requirements, it is more expensive to execute a prisoner than to incarcerate him for a life sentence. A 50-year life sentence costs the government approximately $1 million. On the other hand, the average execution costs somewhere between $2 and $3 million, and high-profile executions may cost more than $20 million.

There are also tremendous (psychological) costs for the prisoners on death row. The austere deprivation of super-maximum secure conditions was characterized by the *Madrid v. Gomez* court as pressing "the outer bounds of what humans can psychologically tolerate," and the oscillating hope and despair of death row can be torturous.

DEATH ROW SYNDROME AND VOLUNTEERS

In his essay "Reflections on the Guillotine," Albert Camus (1961) wrote:

> The devastating, degrading fear that is imposed on the condemned for months or years is a punishment more terrible than death. . . . Torture through hope alternates with pangs of animal despair. The lawyer and the chaplain, out of mere humanity, and the jailers, so that the condemned man will keep quiet, are unanimous in assuring him that he will be reprieved. He believes this with all his being and then he ceases to believe it. He hopes by day and despairs by night. As the weeks pass, hope and despair increase and become equally unbearable. (p. 200)

The anxiety of this sustained uncertainty may have legal as well as philosophical consequences. In *Soering v. United Kingdom,* the European Court of Human Rights held that extraditing a German national to the United States to face the death penalty would amount to a violation of the European Convention on Human Rights' prohibition against "torture or to inhuman or dehumanizing treatment or punishment." While the execution that Soering faced did not, itself, constitute a violation, a combination of the dehumanizing conditions of death row, the protracted delays between sentence and execution, and the stress of living under the ever-looming shadow of execution amounted to a violation of the European Convention. While the concept of a "death row syndrome" has met with little acceptance within the United States, it has achieved legitimacy in the international legal community.

Confronted with the prospect of enduring years, perhaps decades, of death row syndrome, some condemned prisoners exercise the little autonomy they retain, terminating their legal appeals, and "volunteer" for execution. Twelve percent of those executed since the death penalty was reinstated were volunteers, including Gary Gilmore (the first post-*Furman* execution by an American state) and Timothy McVeigh (the first federal execution after *Furman*).

COMMUTATION AND ABOLITION

Troubled by inequities and errors in capital sentencing, numerous organizations have called for a moratorium on the death penalty. Human rights groups such as Human Rights Watch and the American Civil Liberties Union along with religious organizations such as the American Jewish Congress and Catholic Charities USA lobby states to change their laws. They are further supported by a range of professional societies such as the American Bar Association and the American Society of Criminology and by dozens of city and county governments.

After 13 death row prisoners were exonerated in the post-*Furman* era, former Governor George Ryan of Illinois declared a moratorium on all executions in January 2000. An appointed commission evaluated Illinois's death penalty, recommending that it either be overhauled or abolished. Then, in January 2003, Ryan commuted the sentences of all 156 death row prisoners in Illinois to life in prison. Although extremely controversial in the United States, Ryan's action was mirrored elsewhere. In February 2003, President Kibaki of Kenya lifted the death sentence for 28 prisoners and commuted the sentences of 195 others to life imprisonment.

Other sociolegal changes are transforming the face of death row. Although about 70% of Americans favor the death penalty for a person convicted of murder, support decreases when life imprisonment without parole (LWOP) is introduced as an alternative. Given this choice, public support for the death penalty drops to the 45–50% range, and about 40–45% favor LWOP penalties. This divided public opinion is altering contemporary judicial practice. While the use of the electric chair was upheld as constitutional by the Florida Supreme Court in 1997, it was condemned as an unconstitutionally cruel and unusual form of punishment by the Georgia Supreme Court in 2001. In 2002, in *Atkins v. Virginia,* the U.S. Supreme Court held that the execution of mentally retarded prisoners violated the Eighth Amendment's prohibition against cruel and unusual punishment. Since an estimated 12–20% of condemned prisoners are mentally retarded, the holding could exert a profound impact on the composition of death row.

DEAD MAN WALKING: FROM DEATH ROW TO EXECUTION

When a prisoner's scheduled execution date nears, he or she is usually transferred from death row to a holding cell near the execution chamber. The prisoner remains in this cell under "deathwatch" during the 24 to 72 hours before execution. He or she is kept under continuous supervision, denied physical contact with others, granted a final meal, and prepared for execution.

In some states, the condemned may select between the five methods of execution: lethal injection, electrocution, gassing, hanging, and firing squad. In practice, the lethal injection has become the de facto standard in U.S. executions, used in 76% of the executions conducted since *Furman* and all but one of the executions since January 2001. Lethal injection is available in 37 states and employed by the U.S. military and federal government. Electrocution, in contrast, is available in 10 states and is the only means of execution available in Nebraska. Lethal gas is an option in 5 states, while hanging and the firing squad are available only in 3 states. After the prisoner is pronounced dead, a postmortem examination is conducted and then the body is released, usually according to the prisoner's wishes.

CONCLUSION

Death row has evolved from primitive origins to a highly specialized component of the modern U.S. penal system. Despite an international trend toward abolition, after the *Furman* and *Gregg* decisions

abolished and rehabilitated capital punishment, America's death row has grown steadily in size. Prisoners on death row tend to be poor adult males, and minorities are overrepresented. Death row conditions are severe. Delays between sentencing and execution yawn into decades, and alternating states of hope and despair lead some prisoners to suffer from "death row syndrome." Recent social events have led some organizations to call for a moratorium on capital punishment and have triggered changes within the executive and judicial branches of government.

—*J. C. Oleson*

See also Capital Punishment; Corpareal Punishment; Deathwatch; *Furman v. Georgia*; Gary Gilmore; Timothy McVeigh; Supermax Prisons; Terre Haute Penitentiary Death Row Karia Faye Tucker

Further Reading

Amnesty International. (2003). Web site against the death penalty. Retrieved March 25, 2003, from http://www .web.amnesty.org/rmp/dplibrary.nsf/index?openview

Bohm, R. M. (1999). *Deathquest: An introduction to the theory and practice of capital punishment in the United States.* Cincinnati, OH: Anderson.

Camus, A. (1961). Reflections on the guillotine. In *Resistance, rebellion, and death* (pp. 173–234) (J. O'Brien, Trans.). New York: Knopf.

Death Penalty Information Center. (2003). Retrieved from http://www.deathpenaltyinfo.org/

Gillespie, L. K. (2003). *Inside the death chamber: Exploring executions.* New York: Allyn & Bacon.

Hood, R. (1989). *The death penalty: A world-wide perspective.* Oxford, UK: Clarendon.

Johnson, R. (1998). *Death work: A study of the modern execution process* (2nd ed.). Belmont, CA: Wadsworth.

NAACP Legal Defense and Educational Fund. (2003, Winter). *Death row U.S.A.* Retrieved from http:// www.deathpenaltyinfo.org/DEATHROWUSArecent.pdf

Von Drehle, D. (1995). *Among the lowest of the dead: The culture of death row.* New York: Times Books.

Legal Cases

Furman v. Georgia, 408 U.S. 238 (1972).

Gregg v. Georgia, 428 U.S. 153 (1976).

Madrid v. Gomez, 889 F. Supp. 1146 (N.D. Cal. 1995).

McCleskey v. Kemp, 481 U.S. 279 (1987).

Soering v. United Kingdom, ECHR (1989). Series A, No. 161.

◪ DEATHWATCH

The term *deathwatch* is defined as the period of time, typically the last 24 to 48 hours, before a condemned inmate is executed. In many U.S. states, the deathwatch period is one of "virtually solitary confinement under unmitigated solitary confinement" (Johnson, 1998, p. 93). In other states, such as Arkansas, however, the condemned may have unlimited access to his or her attorney(s) and spiritual advisor along with limited access to his or her family members. What is constant across jurisdictions is the intense scrutiny and detailed records that are maintained during the deathwatch, as well as the inevitable death of the inmate.

A deathwatch commences once the condemned person is transferred from his or her cell on death row to the deathwatch cells. Large enough for a single individual, these cells are typically located adjacent either to death row or to the death chamber (in those facilities where the death chamber is located a separate building or in a separate facility as in a number of states). The deathwatch concludes once the inmate's death is certified and the body removed from the facility by the coroner or buried on the grounds of the prison.

PAST PRACTICES

When executions used to be conducted in public places, such as at England's Tyburn Fair, the need for the condemned to be alive for the open journey from the prison to the scaffold was paramount. The deathwatch of this period was minimal and sought only to ensure that the person did not take his or her own life. Consequently, some prison officials provided condemned inmates with laudanum (an early opium-based narcotic) or strong liquor to ensure compliance with prison rules and lower his or her resistance during the execution process.

Gradually, in response to a series of different factors, including public outrage when an execution was not carried out justly or efficiently, capital punishment was removed from the public arena. The transfer of executions behind prison walls changed the nature of the death penalty within the penal process. Penal practices no longer engendered significant public debate, and the mechanics of death became highly routinized and sterile.

CURRENT PRACTICES

One might wonder, since the condemned inmate is going to die anyway, what purpose is served by a deathwatch in a modern, state-sanctioned execution? The reasons for having the deathwatch are threefold: (1) to ensure the safety of the condemned and correctional personnel prior to the execution, (2) to ensure that the execution proceeds without difficulty, and (3) to avoid litigation against both the individuals involved and the state that sanctioned the execution.

Time spent on death row is more rigidly structured than in other areas of a prison. While some argue that the routine provides stability to a particularly stressful experience, no amount of predictability can mitigate the manner in which inmate reactions are polarized by violent outbursts on one end and despondency at the other end. The reactions of the condemned on death row are more unpredictable than usual since some people may believe they have nothing to lose since the state is planning to kill them. Actions that were ignored one day as trivial might be akin to a spark touching gasoline on the next day. Some inmates may despair, or withdraw into themselves, while others find new focus in religious prayer and meditation. Very few condemned men or women, at least in the last part of the 20th century, become "gallows-thieves" by attempting to cheat the executioner by taking his or her own life.

Condemned inmates facing the last one or two days of their lives know where the journey ends, but not what happens along the way. Their waking hours are occupied with visits from family members, attorneys, and spiritual advisers in preparation of the final moment. While they are preoccupied with these matters, a small number of correctional staff observe and record every event and utterance that occurs throughout the deathwatch; they are the deathwatch team.

This team engages the condemned in directed conversation during those moments not otherwise occupied. The purposes of such conversations are twofold. First, they provide limited comfort to the individual while preparing him or her emotionally for the eventuality of death. Officers assigned to the deathwatch provide information concerning the next steps in the execution process. Thus, the condemned is aware of both the process of the execution and of any changes in the routine from that which he or she experienced while on death row. Second, such conversations are the ultimate form of dynamic security whereby staff members monitor the inmate's anxiety levels and try to ensure that he or she remains calm. The ultimate goals are to ensure that the execution is free of behavioral mishaps (resistance) on the part of the condemned and that no harm is caused to the inmate or any member of the deathwatch and execution teams prior to the carrying out of the death sentence. Regardless of the manner in which it is provided, the goals of providing such information are to help the individual accept the inevitable and to ensure that the execution proceeds without difficulty.

Today, the deathwatch team maintains constant vigilance and records every occurrence in the last hours of the condemned's life. This record keeping has the contradictory goals of ensuring and documenting that the prison system treats the condemned humanely prior to his or her execution while precluding any litigation that might interfere with subsequent executions. The remaining part is the manifestation of Foucault's *surveiller* ("to oversee" in French) that he identified in the practices and regimentation of the factory floor, the armed forces, and the prison. While he noted that these institutions offered the best expressions of such oversight, he would have agreed that the deathwatch provided the penultimate expression of the state's power and its ability to ensure that the individual is constantly subjected to and reminded of that power through the routinization and record keeping inherent in the deathwatch.

CONCLUSION—WALKING THE LAST STEPS TOGETHER

Yet, one might wonder, why would a correctional officer participate as a member of the deathwatch team? Nearly every jurisdiction that invokes capital punishment has its own execution routine, including who serves on the deathwatch and execution teams. In some states, the deathwatch and execution teams are one and the same, whereas other states may have separate teams for these two different functions. In Arkansas, for example, correctional officers serving on the combined deathwatch-execution team are all volunteers and have served together for nearly a decade at the Cummins Unit (where the death house is located). Two contributing factors to the longevity of this team include the effective leadership of the captain who leads this team and the mandatory critical incident stress debriefing that occurs the morning following every execution.

Following the last meal and the issuance of a clean set of prison clothes, the condemned may spend time with his or her spiritual adviser and/or attorneys, who are escorted out of the area shortly before the execution is to take place. In the final moments of the deathwatch, officers and members of the execution team escort the prisoner into the death chamber and secure him or her onto the gurney or chair. The deathwatch team (but not the execution team) departs from the death chamber once these tasks are completed. The duties of the deathwatch team members are not completed, however, until their observations are recorded and that deathwatch log submitted.

While moving executions behind prison walls removed them from the public eye, the deathwatch has remained a part of the modern execution process. The nation-state must not only ensure that justice is carried out, but it must also be seen to be carried out by both the condemned and the public. The deathwatch is merely one of the many sets of eyes that ensure that the process is complete.

—*Allan L. Patenaude*

See also Capital Punishment; Death Row; Eighth Amendment; Michel Foucault; Terre Haute Penitentiary Death Row

Further Reading

Anderson, F. W. (1982). *Hanging in Canada: Concise history of a controversial topic*. Surrey, BC: Frontier Books.

Bohm, R. M. (1999). *Deathquest: An introduction to the theory and practice of capital punishment in the United States*. Cincinnati, OH: Anderson.

Engel, H. (1996). *Lord High Executioner: An unabashed look at hangmen, headsmen, and their kind.* Toronto: Key Porter.

Foucault, M. (1975). *Surveiller et punir: Naissance de la prison.* Paris: Éditions Gallimard.

Gatrell, V. A. C. (1994). *The hanging tree: Execution and the English people, 1770–1868.* Oxford, UK: Oxford University Press.

Jackson, B., & Christian, D. (1980). *Death row.* Boston: Beacon.

Johnson, R. (1998). *Death work: A study of the modern execution process* (2nd ed.). Belmont, CA: Wadsworth.

Martinez, A. (1997, Spring). Corrections officer: The "other" prisoner. *The Keeper's Voice, 18*(1). Retrieved from http://www.acsp.uic.edu/iaco/kv1801/180108.shtml

DENTAL CARE

Prisoners are entitled to dental care while incarcerated because of the U.S. Constitution's Eighth Amendment that forbids the use of cruel and unusual punishment by the government. In the view of the U.S. Supreme Court, this civil liberty applies to prisoners incarcerated in federal, state, and local facilities. This means that the government may not demonstrate "deliberate indifference to [the] serious medical needs" of prisoners (*Wynn v. Southward,* 251 F.3d. 588, 593 [2001]). Such serious medical needs can include dental care.

In *Wynn,* for example, a prisoner alleged that when he was moved to an isolation unit, the attending prison official deliberately misplaced, among other things, his dentures. As a result, according to this prisoner, he suffered "bleeding, headaches, inability to chew his food, humiliation, shame, and 'disfigurement'" (*Wynn v. Southward,* 251 F.3d. 591 [2001]). The Seventh Circuit Court of Appeals subsequently ruled that Wynn should have the opportunity to demonstrate at trial that prison officials "knew of and deliberately disregarded [his] dental needs" (*Wynn v. Southward,* 251 F.3d. 593 [2001]). This same court also held, as per precedent, that "dental care is one of the most important medical needs of inmates" (*Ramos v. Lamm,* 639 F.2d 559, 576 [1980]).

The U.S. Supreme Court stated in *Estelle v. Gamble* (429 U.S. 97 [1976]) that "an inmate must rely on prison authorities to treat his medical needs." If prison officials demonstrate "deliberate indifference to serious medical needs," then an Eighth Amendment violation has been proven. It is also true, however, that "because society does not expect that prisoners will have unqualified access to health care, deliberate indifference to medical needs amounts to an Eighth Amendment violation only if those needs are 'serious'" (*Hudson v. McMillian,* 503 U.S. 1, 6 [1992]).

ADEQUACY OF DENTAL CARE FOR PRISONERS

Some scholars question the quality of dental care afforded prisoners. Demonstrably, for example, patients who are not incarcerated are better protected by legal principles surrounding the issue of medical malpractice. Outside prison walls, medical personnel are held to the standard of negligence. Within a prison facility, however, a prisoner is protected from medical malpractice only by the more relaxed standard of deliberate indifference. According to some, the nature of this standard does little to safeguard prisoner-patients, since "behavior that amounts to negligence can never equal the culpability required for a finding of deliberate indifference" (Vaughn & Carroll, 1998, p. 12). Similarly, the federal courts have made it clear that prisoners can invoke a constitutionally guaranteed right to medical care only if "serious medical needs" are at stake (Vaughn & Carroll, 1998, p. 12). Those who are not incarcerated, conversely, need not demonstrate such a need before seeking medical assistance (although a severe lack of economic resources can significantly constrain their access to medical care). In addition, medical care may not be as good quality in prison, since "prison medical personnel suffer from limitations in resources, staff, and facilities" (Vaughn & Carroll, 1998, p. 27).

Critics of the level of medical care available to those who are incarcerated worry that the courts have embraced what Michael Vaughn and Leo Carroll (1998) refer to as the "principle of less eligibility" (p. 3). This principle suggests that the "conditions of penal confinement must be harsher than the living standards of the working classes and people on welfare" (p. 37). These same critics put forth an alternative and more egalitarian vision of medical care for prisoners in which they point out that physicians have a professional responsibility to provide the same level of medical care for all human beings, regardless of social status.

CONCLUSION

Federal, state, and local prisoners enjoy a constitutional right to adequate dental care. Prisoners who believe they have been improperly denied such medical care, however, must demonstrate not only that the medical implications of such a denial are serious but also that the prison official or officials in question denied care with deliberate indifference. Meeting these two legal standards can be quite difficult for prisoners.

Prisoners afflicted with medical disorders also face a host of additional hurdles to obtaining the level of medical care that many of those who are not incarcerated can expect. The Eighth Amendment to the U.S. Constitution, then, provides a floor below which the level of medical care provided to prisoners may not fall. Some believe that this floor is unduly low, while others suggest that prisoners should be least eligible for scarce social goods.

—*Francis Carleton*

See also Doctors; Eighth Amendment; *Estelle v. Gamble;* Gynecology; Health Care; Legitimacy; Mental Health; Optometry; Physician's Assistant

Further Reading

Dvorchak, R. (1989, June 18). Medicine behind bars. *Los Angeles Times*, p. 2.

Friedman, M. (1992). Special project: Cruel and unusual punishment in the provision of prison medical care— Challenging the deliberate indifference standard. *Vanderbilt Law Review, 45,* 921.

Prout, C., & Ross, R. (Eds.). (1988). *Care and punishment: The dilemmas of prison medicine.* Pittsburgh, PA: University of Pittsburgh Press.

Short, R. (1979). *The care of long-term prisoners.* London: Macmillan.

Vaughn, M., & Carroll, L. (1998). Separate and unequal: prison versus free-world medical care. *Justice Quarterly, 15.*

Watts, T. (1990). *Health and mental care in prisons and jails: A bibliography.* Monticello, IL: Vance Bibliographies.

Legal Cases

Estelle v. Gamble, 429 U.S. 97 (1976).
Hudson v. McMillian, 503 U.S. 1, 6 (1992).
Ramos v. Lamm, 639 F.2d 559, 576 (1980).
Wynn v. Southward, 251 F.3d. 588, 591, 593 (2001).

■ DEPRIVATION

The concept of deprivation, associated with the work of Donald Clemmer (1940) and Gresham Sykes (1958), explains prison culture and inmate conduct as primarily the result of the deprivations prisoners experience while incarcerated. In this view, prisoner culture is a fairly normal response to an abnormal environment. Their work was later challenged by others, beginning with John Irwin (1980), who contended that, instead, prison life was shaped by ideas, attitudes, and experiences inmates brought with them, or "imported," from their street culture. Today, most prison sociologists recognize that the two factors of deprivation and importation work together to shape people's prison experiences.

OVERVIEW

Proponents of the deprivation model argue that upon entering prison, individuals inevitably assimilate into a subculture, undergoing a process known as *prisonization.* Through these adaptation mechanisms, prison culture is formed in opposition to the prison administration and officers, whom inmates view as responsible for the prison rules that restrict their choices. According to Sykes (1958), there are five key deprivations that result from institutional regulations: the deprivation of liberty, goods and services, heterosexual relations, autonomy, and lack of personal security.

DEPRIVATIONS

The deprivation of liberty is the most fundamental aspect of confinement. It refers not only to the ways

Friendships and Coping in Prison

Contrary to some observers, friendship among prisoners exists, and a few friendships may even be forged in steel. However, most are based on some form of self-gratification, security consciousness, or peer pressure. It is only through time, trials, and tribulations that friendship develops among prisoners.

The most common and successful friendships are formed similar to those in a free society, where people of similar nature, skills, interests, or education bond. Depending on the nature of the institution (federal or state), or the security level (maximum, medium, minimum), friendships are also forged on the basis of race, geographical location, and social ties inside and outside of prison. Regardless of a prisoner's immediate emotional needs, most friendships are tempered and controlled by the authoritarian nature of prison control and by peer and clique pressures. These pressures tend to shape relationships on the basis of racial prejudice, sexual orientation, and even fear and security.

Friendship among prisoners thus becomes a pseudo-bond that must continually be tested and nurtured and allowed to breathe to prove its qualities. Among prisoners, the ties that reinforce bonding include shared gratifications, security, and protection, the need to belong, sex, fear, and sometimes even greed.

If nurtured, prison friends can lead to respect and equality while incarcerated. The ultimate test of friendship, however, is longevity, and whether the relationship endures beyond the prison walls.

Geoffery Truss
Dixon Correctional Center, Dixon, Illinois

characterize a state of involuntary servitude, reducing the inmate self-esteem further and deepening the overall resentment against the administration. Freedom is further curtailed by the restrictions on personal possessions, access to family and other loved ones, and normal routines. The choice of with whom to cell, how to spend leisure time, when to eat, what to wear, and what property can be possessed add to the deprivation of free choice. In this "total institution" (Goffman, 1961) virtually all aspects of daily live are regulated.

The loss of heterosexual relationships is not restricted to the absence of physical intimacy in

in which prisoners have their freedoms curtailed but also to the conditions of their confinement. Prisoners are restricted to the boundaries of the institution, and their movement is further restricted within the institution by a system of passes and physical barriers. For significant portions of the day, they may also be locked in a cell or dormitory. Such loss of liberty has deep psychological impact on most people as they are cut off from their family and friends. Their links to the community and their support usually weaken over time serving as a constant reminder of this deprivation and deepening their level of distress.

While incarcerated, inmates are unable to control the quality, quantity, or nature of goods and services they receive. Although they usually receive adequate food, medical care, and housing, they have little choice in how basic services are delivered. As a result, most inmates become bored. They also are often frustrated or dissatisfied with the available choices of diet and commissary items. Low pay and lack of variety

prisons but also to the restriction of all physical contact. In high-security facilities, for example, wives, lovers, and children are able to visit only behind a glass barrier. Even in lower-level institutions, physical contact is usually limited to hand-holding and an embrace upon arrival and departure during visits. The deprivation of normal physical contact with another human being, critically important to psychological well-being, adds a level of stress and dehumanization to the prison experience. There is little opportunity for a healthy outlet for a basic human need.

Deprivation of autonomy refers to the ability to make basic decisions about one's life or daily activities. Regardless of their crime or security level, prisoners are governed by rules and regulations over which they have no control. Guards constantly monitor and search them and in many cases regulate their communication with others on the outside by censoring mail, surveilling behaviors, and monitoring outgoing telephone conversations. There are few issues over which a confined person retains any control.

The deprivation of personal security is, in many respects, the most troubling loss some people suffer. Prisons contain other individuals who may be violent or hostile. Even if there is no immediate threat, the very possibility of it is anxiety provoking. In some prisons, inmates are tested by others to see how far they will go to defend themselves and their meager possessions. Someone who fails to fend off attackers may be viewed by others as vulnerable and thus be revictimized. This often requires aggressive adaptation strategies that, while judged unacceptable on the streets, can become routinely necessary inside the walls.

PAINS OF IMPRISONMENT AND INMATE CULTURE

Proponents of the deprivation model view the pains of imprisonment as directly connected to people's response to their incarceration. For example, higher-security-level prisons are more likely to have more restrictions, and therefore high-security inmates have fewer choices and freedoms those in lower-security institutions. These restrictions often lead to seemingly antisocial behavior and resistance to prison rules and policy. Other factors, such as the percentage of inmates incarcerated for violent crimes, the proportion of minority offenders, the age of the institution, and the length and types of sentences that cause increased levels of deprivation, are also thought to lead to greater tension in penal facilities, and thus increase what some see as dysfunctional behavior. Finally, some studies have shown that the degree of overcrowding within an institution affects the level of misconduct and increases solidarity among the inmate population, because the lack of personal space exacerbates the painful conditions of confinement. This, in turn, creates adaptive behavior to find both physical and psychological comfort zones to reduce the impact created by these conditions.

The deprivations that prisoners face are not limited to the loss of physical liberty or to violence or overcrowding. The feelings of deprivation arise in other, more banal, ways. Loneliness, boredom,

and discomfort are more emotionally profound, and the individual's self-image begins to diminish. The attack on a person's pride and dignity constantly diminishes his or her on view of self and leads to the inculcation of the values and goals of the inmate subculture. By engaging in seemingly abnormal and antisocial behaviors, the prisoner is able to obtain goods and services, a position within the prisoners' social hierarchy, some degree of autonomy and self-respect, and security. The inculcation of the norms and values of the inmate subculture, which conflict with prison rules and regulations, increases the likelihood that inmates will adhere to and support the inmate code of conduct.

According to the early deprivation theorists, inmate subculture upheld a particular inmate code that existed in opposition to all aspects of the prison administration: Inmates were not meant to interfere in other prisoners' business; they were meant to "stay cool," do their own time, not exploit others; and not to be weak. In this model, the inmate population was thought to be strongly loyal to the group norms and values.

WOMEN

Although most of the early studies of prison culture concentrated solely on men's prisons, a handful of authors have examined women's incarceration. Two works in particular examined whether women's prisons were shaped by the deprivations that female inmates faced. David Ward and Gene Kassebaum published *Women's Prison* in 1965, and Rose Giallombardo released *Society of Women* one year later. Unlike the comparable literature on men's prisons, which explained prison life as either a result of deprivation or a reflection of "bad guy" street culture, these authors developed a combination of both. Thus, while women were affected by their choices inside, the way they responded to them was generally shaped by ideas and expectations they brought with them from beyond the prison walls. More recent theorists (Bosworth, 1999; Jones & Schmid, 2000) have moved beyond this dichotomy. They suggest a more critical or phenomenological approach that examines prison adaptation and culture as the result of a dialectical process of identity transformation. Changes to prisoners' sense of self, these authors contend, reflect, but are not dependent on, the street culture or prison deprivations.

CONCLUSION

Correctional institutions have changed drastically since the early studies of deprivation. Today, inmate populations consist of multiple subgroups, each of which subscribes to a variety of social norms and values that are often in competition with one another. The changes are a result of increases in racial and ethnic minority populations, religious and political stratification, and the growth of gangs. In addition, due to civil rights and inmate litigation institutions are held to higher standards of accountability.

As a result of the demographic shifts, sociologists no longer believe in a homogeneous inmate subculture. Instead, it is thought that the various groups have their own norms and values and each group is in competition with the others for power. Also, institutional management has changed. Inmates enjoy more freedom of movement, transfers to reduced-security institutions are common practice, and communication with friends and family for most people is encouraged and increasing. Many prisoners have more freedom to purchase items from outside the institution. Though prison remains a place of great restriction, these changes have all altered and, in some case, significantly reduced the "pains of imprisonment."

—*Patrick F. McManimon, Jr.*

See also Donald Clemmer; Contraband; Gangs; Rose Giallombardo; Governance; Importation; Inmate Code; Legitimacy; Prison Culture; Prisonization; Racial Conflict Among Prisoners; Resistance; Riots; Security and Control; Gresham Sykes; Violence

Further Reading

Bosworth, M. (1999). *Engendering resistance: Agency and power in women's prisons.* Aldershot, UK: Ashgate.

Cao, L., Zhao, J., & Van Dine, S. (1997). Prison disciplinary tickets: A test of the deprivation and importation models. *Journal of Criminal Justice, 25*, 103–113.

Carroll, L. (1974). *Hacks, blacks and cons: Race relations in a maximum security prison.* Lexington, MA: D. C. Heath.

Clemmer, D. (1940). *The prison community.* New York: Holt, Rinehart & Winston.

Giallombardo, R. (1966). *Society of women: A study of a women's prison.* New York: John Wiley.

Goffman, E. (1961). *Asylums: Essays on the social situation of mental patients and other inmates.* New York: Doubleday, Anchor.

Irwin, J. (1980). *Prisons in turmoil.* Boston: Little, Brown.

Jones, R. A., & Schmid, T. (2000). *Doing time: Prison experience and identity among first-time inmates.* Greenwich, CT: JAI.

Sykes, G. M. (1958). *The society of captives: A study of a maximum security prison.* Princeton, NJ: Princeton University Press.

Ward, D., & Kassebaum, G. (1965). *Women's prison: Sex and social structure.* Chicago: Aldine.

◪ DETAINED YOUTH AND COMMITTED YOUTH

Detained youth and *committed youth* are legal terms used to describe the incarcerated status of a juvenile offender, under the age of 18 who has been charged with breaking the law. There are several ways in which youths may be detained or committed. The most common ways include (a) holding them while they await adjudication or placement or (b) committing them to state custody in residential programs and/or juvenile correctional institutions after a court disposition or adjudication. Today, there are more than 130,000 juveniles in residential placements across the United States. Most are sent to juvenile correctional facilities for nonviolent offenses.

An adjudicated delinquent is a young person who has been found guilty of a violation of federal or state law, or local ordinance. Under some federal and state statutes, youthful offender status is extended to young adults aged 18–25 in sentencing consideration. However, under some statutes juvenile offenders can be transferred to the adult court as early as age 16. With a growing punitive public sentiment and calls for accountability and public safety, many juvenile justice systems across the country have imposed harsher sanctions for youths. Likewise, many states have increased spending on juvenile justice programs designed to incarcerate youthful offenders. Despite this trend toward harsher sanctions for youths, several public opinion polls reveal that respondents believe the main purpose of the juvenile court system should be to rehabilitate offenders and that juvenile crime can be reduced by prevention and rehabilitation rather than by enforcement or punishment.

THE DECISION PROCESS

When juveniles are arrested, state officials must decide what to do with them. All states have passed age limits and definitions for crimes that determine whether an accused individual will be treated as a juvenile or as an adult. Although the decision to divert youths from the court system ultimately lies with most state attorney offices, workers that handle initial intake assessments also have the discretion to make this recommendation. If the youths are handled judicially, it must then be decided whether they can be released to their parents or if they must be held in a state detention center facility until their court date. They should usually only be placed in detention if they pose a threat to public safety, have a prior criminal history, or because of the seriousness of their offense or other risk factors.

TYPES OF DETENTION

There are many different ways to hold juveniles. Home and secure detention are two common ways to keep youths under state custody. Individuals can be detained in preadjudicatory status (those awaiting court hearing), postdisposition (those awaiting commitment placement), as part of their punishment, or as an alternative to correctional institution (similar to jail status in adult system). Juveniles placed in secure detention have been found to be a risk to public safety, and must therefore be held in a physically secure location. Home detention, as a type of punishment, means that the person is closely supervised in the community, or electronically monitored, and is not allowed to leave the home other than for specified conditions.

TYPES OF COMMITMENT

Committed youths are persons under the age of 18 who have already gone through the court process and have either been found to be delinquent and sentenced to a juvenile facility or have been waived to adult court, sentenced as an adult, or placed in a state or federal prison or jail. Commitment facilities for youth can also house those who are status offenders, those who need to be confined to a mental health facility, or those who voluntarily admit themselves.

In the United States, both public and private facilities provide services to youth offenders. These include detention centers, shelters, assessment and diagnostic centers, boot camps, training schools, ranches, youth camps, halfway houses, and group homes. Public facilities are usually locked local detention facilities or locked state correctional institutions for youth. Private facilities are usually less prison-like, and youths are generally confined by staff security measures. Nationally, the largest portion of state juvenile justice spending is for residential placements.

When making a juvenile justice placement recommendation, the type and seriousness of offense as well as prior record are used to determine commitment level. Facilities range from low to maximum risk. If an individual is considered to be of age, or to have committed a serious crime, as defined by the state legislature, he or she can be waived to adult court and placed in an adult facility. In some states, legislative changes have allowed for the automatic transfer of youths into adult court because of specific offenses.

COMMITMENT PLACEMENT DECISIONS

The juvenile justice agency for most states determine where to confine youths, the types of special programs to enroll them in, and if needed, their specific rehabilitative goals. There are states, however, in which the court chooses the actual institution, security level, or specialized program for each youth. Once committed to an institution, there are different types of sentencing models that states use which define the length of stay for any juvenile in their custody. These include indeterminate only, indeterminate with a minimum, indeterminate up to a maximum, determinate and indeterminate, and determinate-only sentences.

For indeterminate arrangements, youths can be committed for an indefinite period of time (usually until staff determine they have successfully completed their individual case plan), or up to the age of majority. Sentences with minimum time periods specified or maximum time periods specified also fall under indeterminate arrangements. A combination of a fixed sentence with an indeterminate option or a determinate-only sentence that the court specifies length of commitment in advance are other examples of determinate arrangements.

SERVICES PROVIDED TO COMMITTED YOUTHS

In the least restrictive programs (e.g., low-risk residential), youths are generally sentenced for shorter lengths of stay and require fewer special services. As the level of commitment increases, sentences usually increase, youths have less access to the community, and greater security restrictions are placed on them. Staff ratios are smaller and the facilities may have more secure hardware and locked gates.

GENDER

In the United States, there has been a significant increase among female juvenile offenders as compared to males in the juvenile justice system in recent years. Today, females represent a greater proportion of juveniles who are detained as compared to those who are committed, although females also tend to admit themselves voluntarily into residential placements at a greater rate than males. Many females are detained for status offenses, violations that would not be illegal for an adult, such as running away. Despite the growing numbers of female offenders, there are fewer juvenile correctional facilities available to young women since not all commitment facilities can provide services to girls. As a result, judges who are looking to detain or commit females on the basis of graduated sanctions have fewer options of where to send them.

Graduated sanctions are levels of continuum of care for juveniles that aim to place youths in the least restrictive program available while still meeting both their individual needs and the safety of the community. In Florida, the majority of girls were found to be in more restrictive residential placements due to lack of alternatives. Young women also tend to be committed to more private facilities than public facilities. Finally, those who are committed to residential placements tend to be younger on average, compared to their male counterparts.

MINORITY YOUTHS

Minority youths have a greater likelihood of entering the juvenile justice system than white youths. In the United States, there are more black young people in residential placement than whites. This is referred to as disproportionate minority confinement. In fact, minority youths are disproportionately represented at every stage in the juvenile justice process, not just in confinement (commitment). On average, the number of African American youths referred to the juvenile justice system is twice that of their proportion in the general population. The custody rate of African American youths is about five times higher than for whites, while Latino and Native American youths are incarcerated at a rate about 2.5 times higher than whites. While minority youths represent approximately one third of the adolescent population in the country, they account for two thirds of the detained or committed youth population. This disproportion is most apparent among drug offense cases.

When charged with the same offense as a white youth, an African American youth is more likely to be detained preadjudication. African American youths and Latino youths are also held in custody longer than white youths for all offense categories. In addition, there is a greater proportion of minority youths committed to public facilities than private facilities. The pattern of disproportion exists across all offense categories, where the number of white youths referred is substantially greater than the number detained and where the proportion of African American youths detained is greater than the proportion referred. Youths of other races represent about the same proportion in their referral and detention.

CONCLUSION

California, Texas, and Florida, respectively, have the largest numbers of young women and men locked up within the United States. Juveniles in these states account for 25% of the total juvenile population, but over 30% of the juveniles in custody. Because the juvenile population in custody has grown, public facilities are faced with crowding, and many operate above capacity. These conditions and the decisions made in the processing of juvenile offenders have many implications for juvenile justice in the new millennium. For example, many voters in Florida disagree with the direction and priorities of their state's juvenile justice department and do not support shifting dollars from prevention and treatment to more correctional approaches, such as long-term lockups for juveniles. The public and political debate regarding ways to deal with juvenile offenders will continue. While the public may not be as punitive as the political debate would indicate, many youths remain in detained or committed status.

—*Vanessa Patino*

See also Juvenile Detention Centers; Juvenile Justice System; Juvenile Offenders: Race, Class, and Gender; Juvenile Reformatories; *Parens Patriae;* Status Offenses

Further Reading

Florida Children's Campaign. (2001). *Campaign news and updates: Florida Juvenile Justice Benchmark Poll.* Retrieved from http://www.iamforkids.org

Griffin, P. (2000). National overviews. *State juvenile justice profiles.* Pittsburgh, PA: National Center for Juvenile Justice. Retrieved from http://www.ncjj.or/stateprofiles/

Jones, M. A., & Poe-Yamagata, E. (2000). And justice for some: Differential treatment of minority youth in the justice system. *Building Blocks for Youth.* Retrieved from http://www.buildingblocksforyouth.org/justiceforsome/jfs.html

Office of Juvenile Justice and Delinquency Prevention. (2000). *Juvenile offenders and victims: 1999 national report. Chapter 7: Juveniles in correctional facilities.* Washington, DC: U.S. Government Printing Office.

Voices for Florida's Children. (2004). Voices for Florida's Children home page. Retrieved from http://floridakids.org/site/news.php

◪ DETERMINATE SENTENCING

A determinate sentence operates when a judge assigns a convicted offender to a term of imprisonment for a specific time period, for example, three years. Thus, determinacy refers to knowledge at sentencing of the amount of time that the convicted person will actually serve. "Good time" credits (or remission) typically modify that presumption, but even so, offenders enter prison with much better knowledge of how much time they will actually serve than they would if they were given an indeterminate sentence. In the United States, determinate sentencing systems usually provide also for probation as an option. This means that the sentencing choice, which is typically negotiated in exchange for a guilty plea, amounts first to an in-out decision—to prison or to probation—followed by specification of amount of time (usually measured in years) or, in the case of probation, conditions of release.

HISTORY

Determinate sentencing reemerged in the 1970s in the United States in response to widespread dissatisfaction with the indeterminate sentencing that had prevailed for nearly a century. The origins of this policy shift may be traced to leftist (or progressive) critiques that emerged in the 1960s, before becoming a centerpiece of the growing right-wing (or conservative) agenda for crime control. Progressives decried the large disparities in the time being served by inmates, noting the fundamental injustices involved and highlighting the opportunities that unfettered sentencing discretion provided for racism and social class bias. They also identified an immense gap between the rhetoric of rehabilitation that justified indeterminate sentencing and the daily reality of prisons.

However, the critiques of indeterminate sentencing were easily co-opted by those pushing for a crackdown on street crime. Thus, conservative critics lobbied for determinate sentences to increase punishment at the same time as they shifted discretion from judges to prosecutors. Legislatures also began to set new, and higher, sentencing penalties.

Typically, such sentencing revisions initially targeted more serious, more violent crimes. Eventually, however, the effort would often sweep in some lesser offenses including property offenses and drug offenses. In short, the Left had set the stage but the Right put on another play.

IMPACT ON SENTENCING

Several states established determinate sentencing systems by legislative action in the 1970s. Others followed with various forms of sentencing guidelines that sought to systematize the administration of punishment. Some of the early changes improved the situation. Minnesota, for example, adopted presumptive sentencing guidelines, after which racial disparities declined and sentencing severity did not escalate. North Carolina showed similar trends. In most states, however, determinate sentencing vastly increased prison populations while de-emphasizing and degrading probation and related community sentencing options.

The federal system's approach to sentencing guidelines became especially influential, reinforcing the movement toward mandatory minimum sentences particularly in the "war on drugs." However, the federal guidelines, and the approach to determinacy that they fostered, have not occurred without debate. Numerous federal judges have publicly criticized the harsh sentences they are forced to hand down. Federal probation officers have also complained as their discretionary expertise has been greatly diminished.

In addition to developing sentencing guidelines, the federal government and many states such as Illinois and North Carolina began to pass other legislation that upheld determinate sentencing. Some of these policies included mandatory minimum incarceration sentences; repeat offender laws; increased punitiveness toward drug offenses; truth in sentencing laws; elimination or de-emphasis of parole; reductions in good time allowances; sentencing guidelines, or more generally, structured sentencing.

All of these policies, with the possible exception of sentencing guidelines and structured sentencing, led to harsher sentencing and a concomitant burgeoning of prison (and jail) populations. For some, such developments and their associated arguments have compromised the original progressive critiques of indeterminate sentencing out of which the determinate sentences grew. Thus, critics such as Kay Harris (1991), Ruth Morris (1995), and Dennis Sullivan and Larry Tifft (2001) query why we punish and how we could do otherwise. Whether informed by feminist, pacifist, Marxist, or anarchist thought, such critiques direct us to rethink the ethical foundations of the whole punitive enterprise. Whether this leads to calls for penal abolition, for increased voice and participation, or for building a needs-based economy, all point toward peacemaking. All suggest that the fixation with sentencing reform has been epiphenomenal, and has ignored the social structural sources of penal inequities. Sullivan and Tifft (2001) summarized such a view:

> By suggesting the need to consider applying restorative justice principles within larger structural frameworks, we are not simply recommending that we introduce restorative justice practices into our families, schools, and workplaces so that a set of non-retributive processes or procedures can be called forth when someone hurts another and we seek to bring about healing and reconciliation instead of punishing them. . . . Rather, we are talking more about the creation of social arrangements that are from the outset structurally healthy because they are set up to attend to everyone's needs. They are structured in such a way that they do not do violence to anyone or create loss or deficits for anyone by either limiting participation or distributing benefits according to one's position, merit, or desert. (p. 95)

SOCIAL CLASS, ETHNICITY, AND GENDER IMPLICATIONS

Implicitly at least, radical, feminist, and abolitionist critics view determinate sentences as a misguided, harmful, and dangerous penal enterprise. More recently, those who support restorative justice and reintegrative shaming alternatives to conventional criminal justice practices proffer another challenge to determinacy and its foundation in retributive and deterrent ideologies.

Even though the civil rights movement provided the broader social and political context from which determinate sentencing emerged, sentencing reform efforts in the United States tragically contributed to growing racial disparities in sentencing and corrections. Tonry and Hatlestad (1997) aptly characterized this situation as follows:

> The cruelest irony of the modern American sentencing reform movement is that diminution of racial discrimination in sentencing was a primary aim and exacerbation of racial disparities is a major result. The aim was to make it less likely that officials would exercise broad unreviewable discretion in ways harmful to minority defendants and offenders. The result has been the establishment of rigid rules and laws that narrow officials' discretion but that also punish minority offenders disproportionately harshly. Racial disparities in the justice system that are unprecedented in American history, and steadily growing worse, are the result. (p. 217)

At the same time, the mass incarceration project in the United States also greatly increased the numbers of women confined in prisons and jails. In large part, this resulted from application of increases in drug enforcement and penalties, together with changes in the economy that pushed more women toward low-level participation in the drug trade. Again, movement toward determinate sentencing in the 1970s paved the way for such inequities as well as the related phenomenon of prisons continuing the tradition of disproportionately confining those from economically impoverished backgrounds.

So if indeterminate and determinate sentencing both produced inequities and abuses, perhaps this historical record calls for responses to criminal harms that work outside the conventional sentencing frameworks. Restorative justice may serve this role as it poses a significant challenge to punishment and control arguments. More broadly, the criminology-as-peacemaking movement could fill such a role, as would any approach attuned to the problematic relationship between social and economic justice and criminal justice.

Any such efforts, however, will need to attend to powerful historical and contemporary features of the imprisonment project that tend to embed it culturally and structurally. Thus, any nation's stance on penality tends to justify extant structures of sentencing and punishment in ways so ingrained as to resist reform. Similarly, the larger political economic agenda that massive confinement's abeyance function serves obstructs progressive change. In addition, the emphasis of the "new penology" on risk assessment and management further bolsters imperviousness to transformation. Likewise, harsh sentencing and mass incarceration provide an insidious model for governing in an era of diminished progressive political efficacy.

INTERNATIONAL COMPARISONS

While the U.S. experience dominates the criminology literature, the story of determinate and structured sentencing and its relationship to prison populations becomes much richer with attention to the experience of other nations. Major sentencing reforms in the 1980s and 1990s took place in Australia, Canada, Sweden, and the United Kingdom with significant developments elsewhere as well. Such reforms sprang from some of the same sources witnessed in the United States: inconsistency in sentencing imposition and in sentencing implementation as well as concern about confinement itself.

While the United States receives criticism for its lack of attention to sentencing reforms elsewhere—with exceptions such as day reporting centers, community service, and day fines—other nations have shown less reticence in following its lead. Thus, Australia with regard to truth-in-sentencing legislation, Canada and Australia with regard to sentencing guidelines systems, and South Africa, New Zealand, Australia, England, and the Netherlands with regard to intensive probation supervision appear to owe such developments in part to American examples. This brief contrast suggests a possible pattern with regard to sentencing reform diffusion: the United States borrowing progressive reforms, albeit infrequently, while exporting regressive policies.

The overall tendency of sentencing reforms outside the United States has been in the direction of providing greater structuring of decision making but generally with less of the legislative rigidity that characterizes some of the early U.S. experience. In addition, while such reforms often mimic the punitiveness of the America experience, they also provide notable attempts to reduce prison populations and to make more engaged use of authentic community-based options.

As in the United States, sentencing reforms in England have not always yielded the expected results. In contrast, Australia's experience appears more promising for avoiding mass incarceration effects.

Some promising developments in sentencing reform for U.S. consideration come from the experience of Sweden and Germany. Sweden has sought greater fairness and proportionality in sentencing by attention to principles rather than resorting to the more technocratic use of numerical sentencing grids favored in several U.S. jurisdictions. Germany has reduced prison populations by largely replacing short-term incarceration with the equivalent of probation (conditional dismissal).

CONCLUSION

Determinate sentencing has become something of a lightning rod for critiques of the punitive and repressive system of which it forms only a part. Thus, criticisms of it are often less an attack on the practice of letting an offender know for how long he or she will be incarcerated than they are a denunciation of mandatory minimum sentences; expanded drug enforcement, prosecution, and sentencing policies and practices; probation and parole revocation practices; and the growth of mass imprisonment over the past three decades.

Nonetheless, determinate sentencing does not have to be harshly punitive, and could even reduce prison populations. Instead, its impact depends on the scale of punishment. That is, how much pain, or deprivation of liberty, should the state impose? Should one err on the side of excess or on the side of insufficiency? How does one even determine what constitutes excess, insufficiency, or getting it just right?

Various classical schools of penal jurisprudence counsel imposing the minimum punishment necessary to the purpose. That purpose varies according to philosophy. For Cesare Beccaria and Jeremy Bentham and other early proponents of deterrence, the pain should prevent future reoffending. For contemporary scholars who believe in an idea of just deserts, the pain should satisfy some metaphysical standard of moral recompense. What these approaches share is profound respect for liberty, and distrust of centralized authority, especially the state. That explains the strong preference for imposing minimum penalties. It fit with the commitment to greater due process for the convicted and the imprisoned, fairer and less coercive treatment, and a recognition and acceptance of inmates' critiques of indeterminate sentencing and its tendency to shield, sanitize, and legitimize corrections regimes that promised treatment but delivered punishment or worse.

On all of these points, contemporary crime control proponents part company with such conventional Enlightenment thinking. Instead, in the 1970s they sought to marry the movement toward determinate sentencing with increased punishment. They won. Prison populations in the United States (as well as in many other advanced industrial nations) swelled during the last third of the 20th century due to changes in criminal justice policies, especially regarding sentencing. The critique of indeterminate sentencing and the march toward determinate sentencing, shared in part by the left and the right, became a significant source of mass incarceration instead of the basis for greater fairness that progressives sought.

—*Douglas Thomson*

See also Abolition; Activism; African American Prisoners; Australia; Cesare Beccaria; Canada; England and Wales; Indeterminate Sentencing; Incapacitation Theory; Increase in Prison Population; Jeremy Bentham; Intermediate Sanctions; Just Deserts Theory; Parole Board; Prison Industrial Complex Probation; Restorative Justice; Sentencing Reform Act 1984; Truth in Sentencing; War on Drugs

Further Reading

Albonetti, C. (1997). Sentencing under the Federal Sentencing Guidelines: Effects of defendant characteristics, guilty pleas, and departures on sentence outcomes for drug offenses, 1991–1992. *Law & Society Review, 31,* 789–822.

American Friends Service Committee. (1971). *Struggle for justice.* New York: Hill and Wang.

Ashworth, A. (1992). Sentencing reform structures. In M. Tonry (Ed.), *Crime and justice: A review of research* (Vol. 16). Chicago: University of Chicago Press.

Braithwaite, J. (1999). Restorative justice: Assessing optimistic and pessimistic accounts. In M. Tonry (Ed.), *Crime and justice: A review of research* (Vol. 25). Chicago: University of Chicago Press.

Engen, R., Gainey, R., Crutchfield, R., & Weis, J. (2003). Discretion and disparity under sentencing guidelines: The role of departures and structured sentencing alternatives. *Criminology, 41,* 99–130.

Goodstein, L., & Hepburn, J. (1985). *Determinate sentencing and imprisonment: A failure of reform.* Cincinnati, OH: Anderson.

Griset, P. (1991). *Determinate sentencing: The promise and the reality of retributive justice.* Albany: State University of New York Press.

Harris, M. K. (1991). Moving into the new millennium: Toward a feminist vision of justice. In H. Pepinsky & R. Quinney (Eds.), *Criminology as peacemaking* (pp. 83–97). Bloomington: Indiana University Press.

Morris, R. (1995). *Penal abolition, the practical choice: A practical manual on penal abolition.* Toronto: Canadian Scholars' Press.

Shane-DuBow, S., Brown, A., & Olsen, E. (1985). *Sentencing reform in the United States: History, content, and effect.* Washington, DC: U.S. Government Printing Office.

Sullivan, D., & Tifft, L. (2001). *Restorative justice: Healing the foundations of our everyday lives.* Monsey, NY: Willow Tree.

Taylor, I. (1999). *Crime in context: A critical criminology of market societies.* Boulder, CO: Westview.

Thomson, D. (1987). Probation in the USA. In J. Harding (Ed.), *Probation and the community.* London: Tavistock.

Tonry, M. ([1988]1996). *Sentencing matters.* New York: Oxford University Press.

Tonry, M. (1999). Reconsidering indeterminate and structured sentencing. In *Sentencing & corrections issues for the 21st century* (Papers from the Executive Sessions on Sentencing and Corrections, No. 2). Washington, DC: U.S. Department of Justice.

Tonry, M., & Hatlestad, K. (Eds.). (1997). *Sentencing reform in overcrowded times: A comparative perspective.* New York: Oxford University Press.

Wright, R. (2002). Counting the cost of sentencing in North Carolina, 1980–2000. In M. Tonry (Ed.), *Crime and justice: A review of research* (Vol. 29). Chicago: University of Chicago.

Legal Cases

In re Gault, 387 U.S. 1 (1967).
Kent v. United States, 383 U.S. 541 (1966).

◧ DETERRENCE THEORY

Proponents of deterrence believe that people choose to obey or violate the law after calculating the gains and consequences of their actions. Overall, however, it is difficult to prove the effectiveness of deterrence since only those offenders not deterred come to the notice of law enforcement. Thus, we may never know why others do not offend.

GENERAL AND SPECIFIC DETERRENCE

There are two basic types of deterrence—general and specific. General deterrence is designed to prevent crime in the general population. Thus, the state's punishment of offenders serves as an example for others in the general population who have not yet participated in criminal events. It is meant to make them aware of the horrors of official sanctions in order to put them off committing crimes. Examples include the application of the death penalty and the use of corporal punishment.

Since general deterrence is designed to deter those who witness the infliction of pains upon the convicted from committing crimes themselves, corporal punishment was traditionally, and in some places is still, carried out in public so that others can witness the pain. Although outlawed in the United States, public punishment is still used in other countries. For instance, in August 2001, Nigeria introduced *shari'a,* or Islamic law, that allows the application of corporal punishment. That same month, Iran sentenced 20 people to be caned for consuming alcohol. In November 2001, Saudi Arabia lashed 55 youths for harassing women. Likewise, Human Rights Watch reports that under Saddam Hussein's regime in Iraq, those who violated military orders or committed other crimes could be punished by amputation of arms, legs, and ears. Finally, in England and the United States, hangings were once carried out in public. The public and family members were allowed to attend so that they could see what happened to those who broke the law. Today, some advocates call for televised executions as a way of deterring murder.

Specific deterrence is designed—by the nature of the proscribed sanctions—to deter only the individual offender from committing that crime in the future. Proponents of specific deterrence also believe that punishing offenders severely will make them unwilling to reoffend in the future. A drunk driver, for example, would be deterred from drinking and driving because of the unpleasant experience he or she suffered from being arrested, or having his or her license taken away or his or her car impounded. The state must apply enough pain to offset the amount of pleasure derived from drinking.

EARLY CLASSICAL PHILOSOPHERS OF DETERRENCE THEORY

The deterrence theory of punishment can be traced to the early works of classical philosophers such as Thomas Hobbes (1588–1678), Cesare Beccaria (1738–1794), and Jeremy Bentham (1748–1832). Together, these theorists protested against the legal policies that had dominated European thought for more than a thousand years, and against the spiritualistic explanations of crime on which they were founded. In addition, these social contract thinkers provided the foundation for modern deterrence theory in criminology.

Thomas Hobbes

In *Leviathan,* published in 1651, Hobbes described men as neither good nor bad. Unlike religious philosopher Thomas Aquinas, who insisted that people naturally do good rather than evil, Hobbes assumed that men are creatures of their own volition who want certain things and who fight when their desires are in conflict. In the Hobbesian view, people generally pursue their self-interests, such as material gain, personal safety, and social reputation, and make enemies without caring if they harm others in the process. Since people are determined to achieve their self-interests, the result is often conflict and resistance without a fitting government to maintain safety.

Hobbes also pointed out that humans are rational enough to realize that the self-interested nature of people would lead to crime and inevitable conflict due to the alienation and exclusion of some members of society. To avoid this, people agree to give up their own egocentricity as long as everyone does the same thing approximately. This is what Hobbes termed the social contract. To avoid war, conflict, and crime, people enter into a social contract with the government so that it will protect them from human predicaments. The role of the state is to enforce the social contract. Hobbes indicated that if one agrees to the social contract, that individual authorizes the sovereign to use force to uphold the social contract. But crimes may still occur even if after governments perform their duties. In this case, Hobbes argued that the punishment for crime must be greater than the benefit that comes from committing the crime. Deterrence is the reason individuals are punished for violating the social contract, and it serves to maintain the agreement between the state and the people in the form of a workable social contract.

Cesare Beccaria

Building on the ideals of the social contract philosophers, in 1764, Cesare Bonesana, Marchese Beccaria, published his treatise, *Dei Delitti e delle Pene (On Crimes and Punishments)*, in which he challenged the rights of the state to punish crimes. He followed Hobbes and other 18th-century Enlightenment writers that laws should be judged by their propensity to afford the "greatest happiness shared by the greatest number" (Beccaria, 1963, p. 8). Since people are rationally self-interested, they will not commit crimes if the costs of committing crimes prevail over the benefits of engaging in undesirable acts. If the sole purpose of punishment is to prevent crime in society, Beccaria (1963) argued, "punishments are unjust when their severity exceeds what is necessary to achieve deterrence" (p. 14). Excessive severity will not reduce crime, in other words, it will only increase crime. In Beccaria's view, swift and certain punishment are the best means of preventing and controlling crime; punishment for any other reason is capricious, superfluous, and repressive.

Beccaria and the classical theorists believed that humans are rational beings with free will to govern their own decisions. Indeed, he emphasized that laws should be published so that people may know what they represent—their intent, as well as their purpose. Basing the legitimacy of criminal sanctions on the social contract, Beccaria (1963) called laws "the conditions under which men, naturally independent, united themselves in society" (p. 11). He was against torture and secret accusations, and demanded they be abolished. Furthermore, he rejected the use of capital punishment and suggested that it be replaced by imprisonment.

According to Beccaria, jails should be more humane and the law should not distinguish between the rich and the poor. Judges should determine guilt and the application of the law, rather than the spirit of the law. Legislators should pass laws that define crimes and they must provide specific punishments for each crime. To have a deterrent value, punishment must be proportionate to the crime committed. Finally, Beccaria argued that the seriousness of crimes should be based on the extent of harm done to society. As an advocate of the pleasure-pain principle or hedonistic calculus, Beccaria maintained that pleasure and pain are the motives of rational people and that to prevent crime, the pain of punishment must outweigh the pleasure received from committing crime.

Jeremy Bentham

Jeremy Bentham, a contemporary of Beccaria, was one of the most prominent 18th-century intellectuals on crime. In 1780, he published *An Introduction to the Principles of Morals and Legislation*, whereby he proclaimed his famous principle of utility. He argued that "nature has placed mankind under the governance of two sovereign masters, pain and pleasure" (Bentham, 1948, p. 125). Bentham believed that morality is that which promotes "the greatest happiness of the greatest number" (Moyer, 2001, p. 26) a phrase that was also common to Beccaria. The duty of the state in Bentham's view was "to promote the happiness of the society, by punishing and rewarding" (Bentham, 1948, p. 189).

Like Beccaria in Italy, Bentham was troubled by the arbitrary imposition of punishment and the barbarities found in the criminal codes of his time in England. Noting that all punishment is mischief, he maintained, also, that all penalties, per se, are evil unless punishment is used to avert greater evil, or to control the action of offenders. In short, the object of the law is to widen the happiness of the people by increasing the pleasure and lessening the pain of the community. Punishment, in excess of what is essential to deter people from violating the law, is unjustified.

SEVERITY, CERTAINTY, AND CELERITY OF PUNISHMENT

The theory of deterrence that has developed from the work of Hobbes, Beccaria, and Bentham relies on three individual components: severity, certainty, and celerity. The more severe a punishment, it is thought, the more likely that a rationally calculating human being will desist from criminal acts. To prevent crime, therefore, criminal law must emphasize penalties to encourage citizens to obey the law. Punishment that is too severe is unjust, and punishment that is not severe enough will not deter criminals from committing crimes.

Certainty of punishment simply means making sure that punishment takes place whenever a criminal act is committed. Classical theorists such as Beccaria believe that if individuals know that their undesirable acts will be punished, they will refrain from offending in the future. Moreover, their punishment must be swift in order to deter crime. The closer the application of punishment is to the commission of the offense, the greater the likelihood that offenders will realize that crime does not pay.

In short, deterrence theorists believe that if punishment is severe, certain, and swift, a rational person will measure the gains and losses before engaging in crime and will be deterred from violating the law if the loss is greater than the gain. Classical philosophers thought that certainty is more effective in preventing crimes than the severity of punishment. They rejected torture as a means of eliciting confessions, and the death penalty as an effective method for punishing murderers and perpetrators of other serious crimes. Capital punishment is beyond the just powers of the state.

MODERN DETERRENCE RESEARCH IN CRIMINOLOGY

The deterrence hypothesis remains a key intellectual foundation for Western criminal law and criminal justice systems. Today, the idea that sanctions deter criminals has influenced penal sanctions in death penalty cases and other areas of criminal sentencing. Adherents of the deterrence theory have consistently favored policies such as "three strikes" laws, establishment of more prisons, increased penalties, longer sentencing severity, certainty of conviction and sentencing, and the hiring of more police officers. Together, these policies would control and reduce the recidivism (a return to the life of crime) of offenders who have been convicted, and curtail the participation in crime by future offenders.

Yet, despite the merits of the deterrence argument, and until 1968 when criminologists started again to test the deterrence hypothesis, empirical measurement of the theory have been scant. Prior to the 1960s, studies focused only on the philosophical ideas of the deterrence doctrine, its humanitarian orientation, and its implications for punishment. One popular research endeavor that actually tested the deterrence theory in 1968 concluded that homicide might be deterred by both certainty and severity of punishment. In research conducted in 1969, criminologist Charles Tittle found support for the theory and concluded that that the certainty of imprisonment deters crime but that severity can only deter crime when certainty of punishment is reasonably guaranteed. Other studies in the 1970s have also challenged the validity of the earlier empirical findings, arguing instead that variations in police record keeping could account for the results on certainty.

When it comes to celerity of punishment, prior and current studies have generally avoided its inclusion in deterrence measurement. Most important, much of the empirical analysis of the deterrence value has been focused on whether capital punishment deters potential offenders from engaging in homicide acts. Collectively, the empirical results of the death penalty studies have concluded that the death penalty does not deter murder.

CONCLUSION

Because criminal justice policies are sometimes based on the foundations of the deterrence doctrine, debates on the deterrence effect of punishment continue to be waged in criminological research. Programs such as boot camps for teenage offenders and "scared straight" programs continue to rely on the deterrence theory. Across the nation, "get tough" policies are based as well on the actual and threatened incarceration of offenders. In their efforts to have more empirical support, criminologists today are working in the direction of expanding the deterrence concepts from certainty, severity, and celerity to include informal social processes of reward and moral beliefs.

Since some aspects of deterrence and rational choice theories are part of the routine activities theory, deterrence theory has been modified and expanded to include the rational choice perspectives. In summary, support for deterrence theory is much greater than it has been during the past two decades. However, research demonstrates that contemporary criminal justice policies place more emphasis on the severity of punishment than it places on certainty. Death penalty, longer imprisonments, three-strikes laws, mandatory sentencing, and a plethora of other "get tough" policies have not demonstrated greater deterrent effects of punishment than less severe penalties. Indeed, increases in the severity of punishment, rather than reduce crime, may actually increase it. On the other hand, increases in the certainty of apprehension of offenders' conviction and punishment have been found to have possible effects on crime reduction. The current trend toward the use of death penalty in the United States contradicts Beccaria's ideas on certainty and quick punishment.

—*Ihekwoaba D. Onwudiwe, Jonathan Odo,*
and Emmanuel C. Onyeozili

See also Cesare Beccaria; Jeremy Bentham; Boot Camps; Capital Punishment; Corporal Punishment; Flogging; History of Prisons; Incapacitation Theory; Just Deserts Theory; Quakers; Rehabilitation Theory; Truth in Sentencing

Further Reading

Akers, R. L. (2000). *Criminological theories.* Los Angeles: Roxbury.

Andenaes, J. (1974). *Punishment and deterrence.* Ann Arbor: University of Michigan Press.

Beccaria, C. (1963). *On crimes and punishments* (introduction by H. Paolucci, Trans.). New York: Macmillan. (Original work published 1764)

Bentham, J. (1948). *An introduction to the principles of morals and legislation* (with an introduction by W. Harrison, Ed.). New York: Macmillan.

Chiricos, T. G., & Waldo, G. P. (1970). Punishment and crime: An examination of some empirical evidence. *Social Problems, 18*(2), 200–217.

Gibbs, J. P. (1968). Crime, punishment and deterrence. *Southwestern Social Science Quarterly, 48,* 515–530.

Jacoby, J. E. (Ed.). (1994). *Classics of criminology.* Prospect Heights, IL: Waveland.

Moyer, I. L. (2001). *Criminological theory: Traditional and nontraditional voices and themes.* Thousand Oaks, CA: Sage.

Nagin, D. S. (1998). Criminal deterrence research at the outset of the twenty-first century. In M. Tonry (Ed.), *Crime and justice: A review of research* (pp. 1–42). Chicago: University of Chicago Press.

Rennie, Y. (1978). *The search for criminal man: A conceptual history of the dangerous offender.* Lexington, MA: Lexington Books.

Tittle, C. R. (1969). Crime rates and legal sanctions. *Social Problems, 16,* 409–423.

Vold, G. B., Bernard, T. J., & Snipes, J. B. (2002). *Theoretical criminology* (5th ed.). Oxford, UK: Oxford University Press.

Williams, F. P., & McShane, M. D. (1999). *Criminological theory.* Upper Saddle River, NJ: Prentice Hall.

Wilson, J. Q., & Herrnstein, R. J. (1985). *Crime and human nature.* New York: Simon & Schuster.

◪ DIIULIO, JOHN J., JR. (1959–)

For at least two decades, from the mid-1980s through the early years of the 21st century, political scientist John J. DiIulio, Jr., put forth a contentious body of academic research, proposals, and policy on prisons and offenders that agitated or assuaged both conservative and liberal critics of his work. At the beginning of the 21st century, DiIulio turned to writing about faith-based initiatives and became a national adviser on faith-based programming for President George W. Bush.

BIOGRAPHICAL DETAILS

DiIulio completed undergraduate work at the University of Pennsylvania and graduate work at Harvard University. His first major piece of scholarship, *Governing Prisons* (1987), was based partially on his dissertation work in political science at Harvard, where he studied the Massachusetts prison system. After graduation, DiIulio was hired at Princeton University, where he quickly developed a national reputation, initially advising liberal groups, such as the Edna McConnell Clark Foundation, which at the time provided significant funding for jail and prison crowding reduction efforts in various states. Subsequently, DiIulio drifted away from liberal groups, becoming more conservative in his politics and publications.

Currently, DiIulio is the Frederic Fox Leadership Professor at the University of Pennsylvania, a Senior Fellow at the Manhattan Institute, working with the Jeremiah Project, and a Senior Fellow at the Brookings Institute, where he cofounded the Center for Public Management. In addition, he is Senior Counsel with Public/Private Ventures, an employment and training research and practice agency located in Philadelphia.

Governing Prisons

DiIulio's major study, *Governing Prisons,* explored the administration and management of high-custody prisons in California, Michigan, and Texas. In this book, where he argued that little can be achieved within prison walls without order, DiIulio advocated studying prison "not as a mini-society but as a mini-government." As with other governments, he pointed out, prisons are subject to "a vigorous system of internal and external controls" including "judicial and legislative oversight, media scrutiny, occupational norms and standards, rigorous internal supervision and inspections, ongoing intradepartmental evaluations, and openness to outside researchers" (DiIulio, 1987, pp. 235–236) Thus, criminologists should pay particular attention to issues of management in order to understand the meaning and effect of punishment.

DiIulio followed *Governing Prisons* in the 1990s with two further books about corrections. In 1990, he published *Courts, Corrections, and the Constitution*, an edited collection of articles written by researchers and practitioners who studied or managed jails or prisons in Georgia, New Jersey, New York, Ohio, Texas, and West Virginia, and one year later released *No Escape: The Future of American Corrections*. In both books he stressed the importance of managerial practices and external monitoring of penal institutions on how prisons work. Overall, DiIulio concluded that while there is nothing inherent in prisons, prison managers, or prisoners that make prisons work, prison can nonetheless be improved through better management practices. In short, he argued, "Good prison management and prison programs are possible" (DiIulio, 1991).

THE INFLUENCE OF POLITICS

In the mid-1990s, DiIulio formed an intellectual partnership with conservatives William Bennett and John Waters—former and current "drug czars" overseeing the Office of National Drug Control Policy—and moved away from just studying prisons. Together, these men argued that crime is caused by "moral poverty." They also claimed that the United States was witnessing the development of a new type of "super-predator" young offender, who could not be controlled without harsh, punitive intervention.

Moral poverty, they explained, is the effect of absent parents, when the young do not learn right from wrong; "It is the poverty of being without parents, guardians, relatives, friends, teachers, coaches, clergy, and others who *habilitate* children to feel joy at others' joy; pain at others' pain; satisfaction when you do right; remorse when you do wrong." Moreover, they added, "In the extreme, it is the poverty of growing up surrounded by deviant, delinquent, and criminal adults in a practically perfect criminogenic environment—that is, an environment that seems almost consciously designed to produce vicious, unrepentant predatory street criminals" (Bennett, DiIulio, & Waters, 1996, pp. 13–14). Super-predators, in other words, are the result of poor parenting and poor communities. Thus, the web of punishment and surveillance

should be extended to include these people as well as the offenders themselves.

CONCLUSION: A CHANGE OF HEART?

For a while, DiIulio continued to argue that increasing numbers of juvenile offenders were turning into super-predators. He also posited that incarceration practices had more of an impact than commonly acknowledged, especially by liberal crime analysts. However, in the wake of a deepening religious commitment, DiIulio came to regret and revise his "super-predator" comments. He began embracing crime prevention efforts and churches, not prisons. In 2002, President George W. Bush appointed him director of the White House Office of Faith-Based and Community Initiatives, but he resigned less than a year later amid a controversy about comments he made in the press that were critical of Bush policies and practices. Since then, he has not produced any new work on punishment. However, given the growing role of religious organizations in prisons around the country, including the opening of an entirely faith-based penal institution in Texas, it seems that DiIulio foresaw a new shift in the means of governing prisons and offenders.

—*Russ Immarigeon*

See also Correctional Officers; Discipline System; Michel Foucault; David Garland; Governance; Legitimacy; Managerialism; Prison Culture; Riots; Security and Control; Violence

Further Reading

Becker, E. (2001, February 9). As ex-theorist on young "super-predators," Bush aide has regrets. *New York Times*. Retrieved from www.nytimes.com/2001/02/09/politics

Bennett, W. J., DiIulio, J. J., Jr., & Walters, J. P. (1996). *Body count: Moral poverty . . . and how to win America's war against crime and drugs*. New York: Simon & Schuster.

DiIulio, J. J., Jr. (1987). *Governing prisons: A comparative study of correctional management*. New York: Free Press.

DiIulio, J. J., Jr. (1990). *Courts, corrections, and the Constitution: The impact of judicial intervention in prisons and jails*. New York: Oxford University Press.

DiIulio, J. J., Jr. (1991). *No escape: The future of American corrections*. New York: Basic Books.

☑ DISABLED PRISONERS

The overall number of disabled offenders housed in prisons or jails, and the types of disabilities they possess, is not known. We know more about the extent and nature of mental disabilities than we do about physical disabilities among the incarcerated population. Most recent estimates indicate that among state prisoners 16.2% are mentally ill, of which 6.4% to 8% evidence severe mental disorders such as schizophrenia, manic-depressive illness, and major depression; 4% to 10% are mentally retarded; and 10% are learning disabled.

POPULATION CHARACTERISTICS

As in the general community, proportionally more women in prison appear to have mental disabilities than men. Recent estimates indicate that 31.0% ($n = 326,256$) of state inmates and 23.4% ($n = 20,734$) of federal inmates had a physical impairment or mental condition, and 21% of federal and state prison inmates reported that the disability limited their ability to work. Rates of vision and speech impairments are higher among the prison population than the free population. Across type of disabilities, a greater percentage of male inmates than female inmates reported learning and speech impairments, whereas a greater percentage of female inmates than male inmates reported hearing, vision, and physical impairments and mental conditions.

In comparison, a recent survey of sentenced and remanded prisoners (pretrial detainees) in England and Wales found prevalence rates of psychoses of 7% for sentenced male offenders, 10% for remanded male offenders, and 14% for female prisoners. The reported disability rate among Canadian prisoners is 4.1%, with the largest percentage being physical disabled due to disease or illness.

AMERICANS WITH DISABILITIES ACT

The Americans with Disabilities Act (ADA), enacted in 1990 and effective in 1992, defines persons as disabled if they have a physical or mental impairment that substantially limits one or more major life activities such as walking, speaking, seeing, hearing, learning, caring for oneself, performing manual tasks, or working. Mental impairments include mental retardation, organic brain syndrome, mental illness, or learning disabilities. Physical impairments include blindness, deafness, and chronic medical conditions brought on by disease or aging. Examples of such medical conditions include seizure disorders, tuberculosis, AIDS, end-stage renal disease, cardiovascular conditions, and respiratory conditions. Inmates under 21 years of age with an educational disability have a right to special education under the Individual with Disabilities Education Act.

The ADA requires correctional agencies to screen offenders for the presence of disabilities and to establish services/programs to address their needs. However, two separate surveys conducted by the U.S. Department of Justice found that only 70% of state prisons screened inmates for mental health problems at intake, 82.3 % of state inmates reported they were asked about their health history upon admission to prison, and 85% reported they received a medical exam since prison admission.

ACCOMMODATING DISABLED OFFENDERS

Inmates with disabilities present major challenges to the correctional system. The U.S. Department of Justice requires that all public agencies, including prisons, assess their compliance with the ADA and create plans to eliminate barriers to access of services and programs for eligible inmates with disabilities. This often includes modifying rules, policies, or practices so that the disabled are not deemed ineligible based solely on their disability. Correctional facilities must provide physical access for its inmates, visitors, staff, and volunteers with disabilities. Services and activities may be relocated to an area that provides access for the disabled rather than having to engage in renovations or new construction. Many prison systems have separate housing units available for the disabled. For example, mentally ill inmates in the federal prison system and in over half of state correctional systems offer separate housing units in one or more institutions. Eight states and the Correctional Service of Canada operate specialized facilities for the mentally ill.

Inmates and their families or visitors are entitled to effective means of communicating, and auxiliary aids such as assisted listening devices, telecommunications devices for the deaf, taped texts, and qualified readers may be necessary for this communication to occur. Because correctional facilities are responsible for medical care of their inmate population, inmates with disabilities are provided wheelchairs, prescription eyeglasses or hearing aids, readers for personal use or study, and assistance in eating, toileting, and dressing as needed.

CONCLUSION

Prisons and jails are stressful environments and were not designed with the disabled in mind. These two factors combine to make the adjustment of the disabled more difficult. Incarceration can often exacerbate preexisting disabilities, especially those related to mental health. In addition, inmates may develop disabilities while incarcerated through injuries or through aging. In the wake of recent federal recognition of the rights of the disabled, correctional systems will have to be more responsive to inmates who possess qualifying disabilities and costs of incarceration are likely to increase.

—*Mary A. Finn*

See also Education; Elderly Prisoners; Health Care; HIV/AIDS; Literacy; Mental Health; Psychiatric Care; Rehabilitation Theory; Visits

Further Reading

Beck, A. J., & Maruschak, L. M. (2001). *Mental health treatment in state prisons, 2000* (NCJ 188215). Washington, DC: U.S. Department of Justice.

Maruschak, L. M., & Beck, A. J. (2001). *Medical problems of inmates, 1997* (NCJ 181644). Washington, DC: U.S. Department of Justice.

Motiuk, L. L. (1994). Raising awareness of persons with disabilities in Canadian federal corrections. *Forum on Corrections Research, 6*(2), 6–9.

Phillips, R., Dobash, R. P., & Bruce, A. (1994). *Physically disabled prisoners in Scotland.* Edinburgh: Scottish Prison Service.

Rubin, P., & McCampbell, S. W. (1995). *The Americans with Disabilities Act and criminal justice: Mental disabilities and corrections* (NCJ 155061). Washington, DC: National Institute of Justice.

Stationery Office. (1997). *Psychiatric morbidity among prisoners in England and Wales.* Norwich, UK: Author.

◪ DISCIPLINARY SEGREGATION

Disciplinary segregation is a generic term used to identify various forms of separate or segregated confinement where prisoners are housed as a form of added punishment. Persons are usually held in this manner in response to disciplinary infractions that they have been judged to have committed. In addition to separation (and sometimes isolation), disciplinary segregation also commonly includes the imposition of additional restrictions on the movement of inmates within the institution, a decreased level of privileges and programming, and more severe levels of material deprivation.

TYPES OF SEGREGATION

As a generic term, disciplinary segregation subsumes more specific forms of punitive prison confinement. For example, some prisons practice a form of disciplinary segregation known as confinement to quarters (CTQ). Prisoners usually are placed on CTQ status as a result of having violated relatively minor prison rules. Generally, they are not permitted to leave their cells and cannot participate in the normal routines of the prison including work, education or vocational training, or recreation.

Disciplinary segregation also includes various forms of solitary or near-solitary confinement, where prisoners are placed—generally for specific terms of punishment—because they have been found guilty of violating more serious prison rules. Most prisons have separate housing units that are devoted to some form of solitary-like confinement. Terms of such disciplinary confinement typically vary as a function of the severity of the infraction and range from a few days to months and, in extreme cases, a year or more.

More recently, a number of prison systems in the United States have created an especially severe form of disciplinary segregation—imprisonment in so-called supermax facilities. These are often free-standing housing units or entirely separate prisons devoted to this form of disciplinary segregation. In them, prisoners generally are subjected to extreme forms of solitary-like confinement, unprecedented levels of monitoring and surveillance (because of the technological sophistication that is brought to bear in many such units), and very severe restrictions on movement and property. Prisoners often are placed in supermax for long and potentially indefinite periods of confinement. They may be placed in this form of disciplinary segregation for a number of reasons. Either they have committed what are regarded as very serious disciplinary infractions, or they have been judged to pose a very serious threat to the security of the institution, and/or because they have been labeled by prison authorities as gang members or associates.

Finally, administrative segregation ("ad seg") is a form of disciplinary segregation that is used for a variety of reasons in many correctional systems. In some systems, prisoners are placed in ad seg because they are suspected of having violated prison rules and are awaiting a prison disciplinary hearing or other procedure used to adjudicate their case. In some instances, prisoners are placed in ad seg because they represent what is perceived to be a general threat to prison security. And, although it technically falls outside the scope of disciplinary segregation, prisoners may be held in ad seg for their own protection, as a form of protected custody or what, in some prison systems, is known as "safekeeping." Even though these prisoners are not being disciplined for any infractions that they committed, they may be held under conditions of segregated confinement that are similar or identical to those of prisoners who are being punished and may be experienced by the prisoners themselves as punitive in nature.

THE RATIONALE FOR SEGREGATION

The use of segregation, physical restriction, and material deprivation as punishment within a prison in some ways replicates the punitive logic of prison itself—the use of "spatial confinement" to punish wrongdoers. Much as a prison embodies the idea that the persons who have committed crime in the free world should be removed from it, so too does disciplinary segregation reflect a belief that prisoners who have violated prison rules or are otherwise perceived as a threat to the operation of the prison itself are to be "taken away" and separated from the normal day-to-day routines of the environment in which they once lived.

Also like incarceration, in most instances, this kind of disciplinary sanction entails more than just removal or separation. As noted above, there usually are additional restrictions on personal liberties and material conditions that prisoners otherwise would retain during their imprisonment. Thus, although segregation is at the core of the sanction, other aspects enhance its punitive quality. Indeed, the punitiveness of disciplinary segregation and its potentially adverse psychological effect derive in part from these additional restrictions on movement, activities, property, contact with the outside world, and social interaction with fellow prisoners.

One could argue that the underlying *logic* (as opposed to punitive effect) of the use of spatial confinement as punishment, of which disciplinary segregation is part, has been degraded over time. In earlier times, there was an apparent purpose to the isolation that was imposed by incarceration. Originally, all convicts were isolated in a supposed attempt to enhance the prison's capacity to induce their "penance." Later, prisoners ostensibly were segregated to prevent them from contaminating one another with the internalized (and presumably contagious) criminality from which they were thought to suffer. At around the same time, as prisons proliferated in the course of the 19th century, Jacksonian reformers in the United States claimed that prisoners needed to be separated and isolated to protect them from the destructive influences of the surrounding society.

However, as the use of imprisonment greatly expanded over the course of the 19th century and well into the next, the logic of these more extreme forms of spatial confinement was modified and diluted. The large numbers of prisoners who had to be housed for increasingly long periods of time made isolated confinement impractical and, eventually, impossible to sustain on a widespread basis. Congregate labor, commingling, and eventually high levels of social density brought about by overcrowded prison conditions became the norm.

When the project of personality transformation through long-term isolation gave way to managerial control through short-term solitary confinement, prisoners were still segregated, to be sure, but for different reasons. In some instances, segregation supposedly gave prisoners some respite from the turmoil in which they had become involved (in the hopes that they could disengage)—an opportunity to "cool out." Then there was the notion that isolation provided a shock treatment of sorts—a stimulus for the prisoner to come to his or her senses, receive an "attitude adjustment," or otherwise to be persuaded by the painfulness of the segregation to mend his or her ways. The continuing threat of future placement in the harsh environment of segregation was conceived as a lesson learned, a future deterrent.

Of course, none of these goals was regularly or predictably achieved. Moreover, notwithstanding the sometimes noble-sounding justifications, they always seemed to mask a basic, underlying punitive purpose. Nowadays, however, there is no mixed motive or need to disguise the punitive intent of even the most extreme forms of disciplinary segregation. Indeed, to many critics, the most extreme uses of isolation as punishment appear to be designed to achieve only one real purpose—to hurt people. The hurting at times seems so gratuitous that a more draconian end, beyond the simple infliction of pain, suggests itself—the goal is one of breaking a prisoner's spirit so profoundly that the experience will psychologically disable him.

The most extreme forms of disciplinary segregation, especially the supermax type confinement, seem to be practiced with no real concern for how or whether the prisoner will ever be able to readjust to free society, or even to mainline prison life. Indeed, most of these regimes have been implemented without any thought being given to long-term psychological consequences. Even the most extreme and, therefore, most psychologically disabling disciplinary

segregation units often operate without transitional programs or graduated steps in which prisoners are exposed to conditions and experiences that are designed to reacclimatize them to more normal social environments and regain the competencies required for meaningful social interaction. In these cases, which appear to be becoming more common, it seems that the purpose of disciplinary segregation has become one of permanent exclusion from free society.

CONDITIONS AND COMPOSITION OF DISCIPLINARY SEGREGATION

Because forms of disciplinary segregation vary so widely, it is difficult to generalize accurately and meaningfully about the exact conditions of confinement that prevail in segregation units. By definition, prisoners held within them experience greater levels of social isolation, more severe limitations on movement and activity, and degrees of more deprived living conditions. Beyond these general characteristics, however, the exact nature of conditions will depend on the particular prison and the particular level of segregated discipline that is being applied.

Thus, disciplinary segregation includes units such as the Estelle High Security Unit in Texas in which prisoners were subjected to an especially problematic mix of extremely deprived and restricted confinement combined with high levels of noise and chaos. Certain units or "pods" in the California security housing unit at Pelican Bay—the state's most notorious supermax—are so quiet that they give the impression that no one is housed there, while other units in the same facility are boisterously loud. Prisoners in disciplinary segregation units in Florida—known as "close management"—are punished for talking to one another or for being "on the door" while in their cells (where they could otherwise communicate with one another or at least see what was taking place outside their cells).

The cells inside the "administrative maximum" or ADX are really cells within cells; in addition to the solid doors, each one is equipped with an inside set of bars, which, when closed, prevent prisoners from coming to the doors of their cell. In some overcrowded disciplinary segregation units (such as Pelican Bay's supermax), prisoners are double-celled (housed with another prisoner), even though they are confined to their cells for an average of 23 hours per day. And, in one unusual variation of disciplinary segregation, prisoners in the High Security Unit at the Lexington federal penitentiary were kept in a form of "small group" isolation, where they were housed in the same small units and only allowed to interact with each other under conditions of extreme surveillance and deprivation.

GENDER AND RACE

Disciplinary segregation is used in women's prisons as well as in those that house men. Although, in general, fewer women prisoners are perceived to be a threat to the safety and security of the institution, and women generally are thought to adapt to prison confinement in less violent or aggressive ways, some women have been held in disciplinary segregation for very long periods of time. For those who are held in segregation, the conditions of confinement are as severe, psychologically taxing, and potentially harmful as those in men's prisons.

For a variety of reasons, higher numbers of prisoners of color are housed in disciplinary segregation units. In the United States, in particular, African Americans tend to be sentenced to prison in disproportionate numbers and to be given longer prison sentences than whites. For these reasons and perhaps because, in at least some prisons, prison rules are applied differentially to African American prisoners, they tend to be heavily overrepresented in disciplinary segregation units in many prison systems.

DEBATE OVER THE NEED FOR AND EFFECTS OF DISCIPLINARY SEGREGATION

Disciplinary segregation is a long-standing correctional practice. Yet it has been controversial and subjected to criticism since its inception several centuries ago. Prison administrators who defend and employ the practice in varying degrees generally offer at least one common rationale for its continued use—that housing otherwise dangerous or disruptive prisoners in one place, away from others, makes prisons safer overall. Although commonly asserted, and endorsed essentially as "commonsense" by many prison administrators, this rationale still lacks any convincing empirical proof or objective documentation. In some instances where policies of disciplinary segregation have been pursued aggressively, prison infractions and overall violence rates appear to have decreased. However, alternative explanations for these reductions are many and varied. In other instances, disciplinary segregation appears to have contributed to increases in violence and disruption (with the same caveat—that many alternative explanations for the adverse outcomes cannot be eliminated). Moreover, because most forms of disciplinary segregation lack explicit educational or therapeutic components—ones by which prisoners might learn something about the origins of their offending behavior or obtain treatment for the alleged maladies that caused them to infract—they are pursued more as a short-term management strategy rather than a real program of long-term violence control.

On the other hand, critics of the practice argue that much prison violence and disruption stem from adverse or poorly managed prison conditions, not from the inherent and cross-situational violent propensity of prisoners. Removing prisoners who have engaged in violent or disruptive behavior, absent attention being given to correcting or improving criminogenic prison conditions, is not likely to have an appreciable impact on overall levels of prison violence. Moreover, depending on the nature and duration of the disciplinary segregation itself, extremely adverse psychological reactions (including, in some instances, reactions that may make prisoners more rather than less violent) are likely to occur. Opponents of the extensive use of intense forms of disciplinary segregation contend that the costs of the practice—in economic and especially psychological terms—greatly exceed its alleged benefits.

CONCLUSION

Although sometimes prisoners' behavior and state of mind "improve" during and after their confinement in disciplinary segregation, becoming more compliant and less problematic overall, these "spontaneous remissions" appear to be infrequent. Given the fact that no proven penological or consistent therapeutic rationale is systematically pursued through this kind of confinement, the lack of beneficial outcomes is not surprising. Instead, prisoners commonly show patterns of deepening resentment, oppositional resistance, and even various forms and degrees of psychological deterioration. What is surprising is that so few alternative approaches to disciplinary infractions have been designed or implemented in correctional systems. But this, too, may reflect the power of the prison form and the punitive imperative that it implies: Wrongdoing must be responded to with penal punishment, and such punishment—in modern times—entails a form of separation or isolation from others, no matter the long-term consequences.

—*Craig Haney*

See also ADX (Administrative Maximum) Florence; Alcatraz; Control Unit Discipline System; Eighth Amendments; Lexington High Security Unit; Marion, U.S. Penitentiary; Pelican Bay State Prison; Self-Harm; Solitary Confinement; Special Housing Units; Suicide; Supermax Prisons

Further Reading

Bauman, Z. (2000). Social issues of law and order. *British Journal of Criminology, 40,* 205–221.

Christie, N. (1993). *Crime control as industry: Towards gulags, Western style?* London: Routledge.

Feeley, M., & Simon, J. (1992). The new penology: Notes on the emerging strategy of corrections and its implications. *Criminology, 30,* 449–474.

Grassian, S., & Friedman, N. (1986). Effects of sensory deprivation in psychiatric seclusion and solitary confinement. *International Journal of Law and Psychiatry, 8,* 49–65.

Haney, C. (2003). Mental health issues in long-term solitary and "supermax" confinement. *Crime & Delinquency, 49,* 124–156.

Haney, C., & Lynch, M. (1997). Regulating prisons of the future: The psychological consequences of solitary and supermax confinement. *New York University Review of Law and Social Change, 23,* 477–570.

Korn, R. (1988). The effects of confinement in the High Security Unit at Lexington. *Social Justice, 15,* 8–19.

Rothman, D. (1971). *The discovery of the asylum: Social order and disorder in the new republic.* Boston: Little, Brown.

Shaylor, C. (1998). "It's like living in a black hole." Women of color and solitary confinement in the prison industrial complex. *New England Journal of Criminal & Civil Confinement, 24,* 385–416.

Tachiki, S. (1995). Indeterminate sentences in supermax prisons based upon alleged gang affiliations: A reexamination of procedural protection and a proposal for greater procedural requirements. *California Law Review, 83,* 1117–1149.

◪ DISCIPLINE SYSTEM

All correctional facilities have a discipline and punishment system to ensure an orderly and safe environment for staff and inmates. Accordingly, rules and regulations cover almost all aspects of an inmate's daily routine. These rules should be provided in written form to everyone as they arrive at the reception and evaluation center. Anyone who breaks any of the rules and regulations of the penal institution will be subject to a disciplinary hearing within the institution. If the infraction is criminal and serious enough, the person also may be charged with another offense and taken to court.

DEVELOPMENT OF FORMAL DISCIPLINARY SYSTEMS

The use of a dark and isolated cell as a method of punishing violations of prison rules dates back to the earliest prisons in the United States. To enforce the rule of silence in the congregate prison system, inmates were placed in "the hole." These cells were often bare, unlit, and poorly ventilated. Those confined to them were served a diet of bread and water. The duration of their confinement ranged from days to years. Inmates were often placed in solitary confinement arbitrarily and were subject to verbal humiliation, physical beatings, and torture.

At this time, disciplinary procedures were exercised without challenge since inmates were legally considered slaves of the state. Although the case was at no time a legal base point upon which the courts could rely on for doctrine, it seems that many were influenced by the *Ruffin v. Commonwealth* (1871) decision that "the prisoner has, as a consequence of his crime, not only forfeited his liberty, but all his personal rights except which the law in its humanity accords to him." Indeed, most courts maintained their "hands-off" policy about conditions of confinement well into the 20th century. Thus, it was not until the 1960s that federal and state courts began regularly to consider inmate appeals about correctional practices regarding their treatment and violation of their constitutional rights.

The 1941 case of *Ex parte Hull* is generally considered to mark the beginning of the court's intervention in inmates' allegations of mistreatment. In this case, the U.S. Supreme Court declared that inmates have the unrestricted right to the federal court system. Later, in *Coffin v. Reichard* (1944) the court extended federal habeas corpus to include conditions of confinement, stating that inmates retain all the rights of ordinary citizens except those expressly or by necessary implication that are taken from the inmate by the law. This decision, marking the first time in which a federal appellate court ruled that inmates do not lose all their civil rights as a condition of confinement, modified the long-standing interpretation of *Ruffin v. Commonwealth.*

The ruling in *Monroe v. Pape* (1961) permitted access to the federal courts to litigate inmate rights without first exhausting state judicial remedies. Later, in *Cooper v. Pate* (1964), the court ruled that state inmates could sue prison staff for depriving them of their constitutional rights. Hence, both the *Monroe v. Pape* and *Cooper v. Pate* court decisions signaled the end of the hands-off doctrine, and consequently served as the catalyst for an explosion of inmate lawsuits against prison authorities. In response, the rampant physical brutality, rigid authoritarian discipline, and repulsive conditions that had previously characterized disciplinary segregation were dramatically reduced.

DUE PROCESS: ITS SOURCE AND PURPOSE

Inmate disciplinary procedures are governed by the 14th Amendment to the U.S. Constitution. This amendment provides that a state shall not make or enforce any law that abridges the privileges or immunities of citizens of the United States; nor shall any state deprive any person of life, liberty, or property, without due process of law. Most disciplinary actions were exercised without challenge until the Supreme Court ruled in *Wolff v. McDonnell* (1974) that states are required to provide inmates with due process procedures before depriving them of a constitutionally protected liberty interest. The Supreme Court ruled that prison disciplinary procedures must follow certain minimum due process procedures when an inmate faces serious action that could result in the withdrawal of good time or placement in disciplinary segregation. Even so, prison officials are not bound by the same procedures found in criminal court because of the special conditions of incarceration. For example, inmates do not have the right to cross-examine witnesses or present evidence that may be hazardous to institutional safety or correctional goals.

In *Wolff,* the Supreme Court outlined the following due process procedures for states to follow when an inmate is accused of a disciplinary infraction. The inmate (1) must receive advance written notice (at least 24 hours) in order to prepare a defense against the charges; (2) is permitted to seek counsel from another inmate or a staff member when the circumstances of the case are complex or if the prisoner is illiterate; (3) has the right to present documentary evidence and to call witnesses on his or her behalf, as long as the security of the institution is not jeopardized; and (4) has a right to a hearing before an impartial body and has a right to receive a written statement of fact findings concerning the outcome of the hearing.

Following *Wolff,* the Supreme Court has relaxed many of the due process standards in disciplinary proceedings. For instance, it ruled in *Baxter v. Palmigiano* (1976) that in less serious cases where inmates might lose privileges, due process requirements are not required, even when a short-term segregation is possible. The Court also determined that the inmate has no right to counsel in these cases. Similarly, in *Sandin v. Conner* (1995), the Supreme Court ruled that disciplinary actions that are taken to achieve the goal of a safe and secure prison and do not add to the sentence being served or change the conditions of the sentence being served do not create a liberty interest. Therefore, due process is not required. Finally, *Wolff* requirements are not required for disciplinary hearings that result in a 30-day segregation sanction. On the other hand, if the results from the disciplinary hearing change an inmate's release date, the due process protections defined by *Wolff* still apply.

DISCIPLINARY POLICY

The disciplinary policy of any correctional facility is a written document outlining the specific behaviors that are prohibited to inmates. This document should explain the process for considering guilt and determining punishments as well as listing the range of sanctions that usually result from disciplinary infractions. A copy of the disciplinary policy is usually provided to all new inmates on arrival at the reception and evaluation center. The policy should notify them of the rules and regulations they are responsible for adhering to and the possible sanctions associated with being found guilty of a disciplinary infraction.

DISCIPLINARY PROCEDURES

While all state and federal systems must adhere to the Supreme Court rulings listed above, they will vary slightly in terms of their responses to minor and major infractions. Even so, it is possible to generalize about the disciplinary procedures in most institutions.

When an inmate commits a disciplinary infraction, the correctional staff has several options to deal with the rules violation. Usually, the staff member who suspects that a disciplinary infraction has occurred must document it in an incident report, which is then submitted to the shift commander. The incident report specifies the prohibited act allegedly committed by the inmate and includes all the details surrounding the incident witnessed by the employee writing the report. The shift commander has the authority to dispose informally of a minor disciplinary infraction; however, a written record of the informal resolution is maintained. If an informal resolution of a minor disciplinary infraction is not appropriate or successful, the incident report is

forwarded to the chief of security for investigation. Major disciplinary infractions, which cannot be disposed of informally, are reviewed by the shift commander and then forwarded to chief of security for investigation. Investigations for both minor and major disciplinary infractions normally commence within 24 hours of the reported violation.

If an inmate is found not guilty of a disciplinary infraction, the incident and disciplinary report, the disciplinary committee's decision, and all references to the disciplinary infractions should be removed from his or her institutional record unless the disciplinary report also includes an action for which the inmate was found guilty. If a prisoner is found guilty, a copy of the disciplinary report, notice of hearing, request for representation/witnesses form, waivers, the disciplinary committee's decision, and appeal forms are kept in his or her institutional record and central office record. The inmate is also provided with a written statement of the guilty findings, the evidence relied upon, the sanction(s) imposed, and a notice of the right to appeal.

DISCIPLINARY SEGREGATION

Individuals found guilty of some infraction against prison rules are usually placed on disciplinary segregation away from the rest of the population. Inmates on disciplinary segregation are typically housed in single cells or rooms and receive the basic necessities and services such as food, clothing, showers, medical care, and visitation by the prison chaplain. They are also allowed limited exercise, reading materials, and mail. They are not, however, usually eligible for most program privileges, other than religious guidance and necessary medical services.

Disciplinary segregation operational procedures are designed to ensure that an inmate's interactions with correctional staff occur infrequently. Inmates who are placed in disciplinary segregation typically spend 23 hours a day in their cells and are deprived of human contact and touch. Their meals are provided through slots. When they leave the cell, they are restrained and escorted by a minimum of two correctional officers. They also are denied contact visits. While the evidence is not conclusive, medical experts and psychologists suggest that inmates confined in these conditions often suffer some type of mental breakdown. These experts argue that the side effects of total isolation range from delusions, schizophrenia, paranoia, panic attacks, and hallucinations to delirium-like conditions of hearing voices and even whispers. Experts also contend that total isolation leads to depression, cognitive impairments, anxiety, unbearable levels of spontaneous fits of rage and frustration, and difficulty in concentration with memory, which may result in disorientation, mind wanderings, self-torture, mutilation, and/or suicide. Finally, the experts suggest that apathy and lethargy set in, since inmates are tired all the time as a result of being completely idle.

GENDER DIFFERENCES IN DISCIPLINE

Despite lower levels of violence in women's prisons, it seems that staff members often perceive female prisoners as being harder to manage than their male counterparts. Male inmates are often considered to be more cooperative and respectful than female inmates, who are usually portrayed as manipulative and emotional. As a result, staff members are often quick to formally discipline women for certain actions that they might tolerate if they were committed by a man.

Indeed, despite lower levels of violence and serious infractions in women's prisons, empirical evidence indicates that the discipline for female inmates is generally harsher compared to that of male inmates. For example, Dorothy McClellan found in 1994 that in Texas, female offenders were far more likely to be cited for minor rule infractions than their male counterparts. The study findings also revealed that in these cases, the female inmates were punished more severely than males who committed similar offenses. For example, infractions such as cursing were thoroughly enforced in the women's prison, but were usually ignored in the men's prison. Likewise, in contrast to males, female inmates tended to be cited more often for offenses such as disobedience, disrespect, and vulgar language.

CONCLUSION

Prison disciplinary procedures are employed to regulate inmates' behavior while incarcerated in state or federal prison systems. Upon arrival at the reception and evaluation center, in addition to medical screening, psychological testing, and classification, inmates are provided with copies of written rules and regulations that govern their behavior as well as outline rules violations plus the prescribed penalties for violating established rules. As such, when imposing a disciplinary action on an inmate, correctional administrators adhere to the standards outlined in the *Wolff v. McDonnell* case to ensure that the minimal due process standards are met in disciplinary proceedings.

Inmates who are found guilty of major rules infractions typically are separated from the general population and placed in disciplinary segregation for a specified period of time. While not all inmates manifest negative psychological effects from total isolation in disciplinary segregation to the same degree, empirical evidence suggests that a significant number of inmates do suffer some type of mental breakdown. This problem has led many to recommend that trends toward increased use of forms of extremely harsh confinement be reversed. In addition, prisoners should be screened for special vulnerability to isolation and carefully monitored. Finally, while the informal and formal disciplinary procedures are the same for male and female offenders, research indicates that in some prisons the discipline female offenders receive is harsher than that of male offenders.

—Melvina Sumter

See also Classification; Control Unit; Disciplinary Segregation; *Habeas Corpus;* Legitimacy; Managerialism; Security and Control; Section 1983 of the Civil Rights Act; Special Housing Unit

Further Reading

Austin, J., & Irwin, J. (2001). *It's about time: America's imprisonment binge* (3rd ed.). Belmont, CA: Wadsworth.

Cripe, C. A. (1999). Inmate disciplinary procedures. In P. M. Carlson & J. S. Garrett, *Prison and jail administration: Practice and theory.* Gaithersburg, MD: Aspen.

Feeley, M. M., & Rubin, E. L. (1998). *Judicial policy making and the modern state.* New York: Cambridge University Press.

Gray, T. (2002). *Exploring corrections: A book of readings.* Boston: Allyn & Bacon.

Hass, K., & Alpert, G. (1995). *The dilemmas of corrections.* Prospect Heights, IL: Waveland.

McClellan, D. S. (1994). Disparity and discipline of male and female inmates in Texas prisons. *Women and Criminal Justice, 5,* 71–97.

Palmer, J. W., & Palmer, S. E. (1999). *Constitutional rights of prisoners* (6th ed.). Cincinnati, OH: Anderson.

Smith, C. E. (2000). *Law and contemporary corrections.* Belmont, CA: Wadsworth.

Wallace, D. (1992). *Ruffin v. Virginia* . . . a nonexistent baseline of prisoners' rights. *Journal of Criminal Justice, 20,* 333–342.

Legal Cases

Baxter v. Palmigiano, 425 U.S. 308; 96 S. Ct. 1551; 47 L. Ed. 2d 810 (1976).

Coffin v. Reichard, 143 F.2d 443 (6th Cir. 1944) 294.

Cooper v. Pate, 378 U.S. 546 (1964) 260, 262.

Ex parte Hull, 312 U.S. 546, 61 S.Ct. 640, 85 L.Ed. 1034 (1941).

Monroe v. Pape, 365, U.S. 167 (1961) 270.

Ruffin v. Commonwealth, 62 Va. (21 Gratt.) 790 (1871) 172, 243.

Sandin v. Conner, 515 U.S. 472; 115 S. Ct. 2293 (1995).

Wolff v. McDonnell, 418 U.S. 539; 94 S. Ct. 2963; 41 L. Ed. 2d 935 (1974).

◼ DISTRICT OF COLUMBIA CORRECTIONS SYSTEM

Washington, D.C., has a unique governance structure, unlike any other city, since it is not part of any state. Article I, Section 8 of the Constitution gives the national Congress exclusive power to make legislation for this federal city. In the 1990s, the city's prison system deteriorated into disarray and the city as a whole faced severe budget crises. Although previously Congress had handed some control over internal matters to the city government, including running a prison system, it was convinced to act. As a result, Congress passed the National Capital Revitalization and Self-Government Improvement Act of 1997. This act enabled Congress to take control of the prison system, while leaving responsibility for the jail system with the city.

THE DISTRICT OF COLUMBIA DEPARTMENT OF CORRECTIONS

The District of Columbia Department of Corrections (DCDC) was founded in 1946. It is an independent agency within the District of Columbia government, with a director appointed by the mayor. It supervises confinement for the city's pretrial detainees and the misdemeanants. DCDC is also responsible for running the city-owned halfway house.

THE DISTRICT OF COLUMBIA JAIL SYSTEM

Two facilities, controlled by separate administrations, currently serve as jails for the District of Columbia: the Central Detention Facility and the Central Treatment Facility. They are located next to each other, and in fact are physically connected by a bridge. Transfer from one jail to the other is often referred to by both inmates and staff members as "going across the bridge."

The Central Detention Facility is commonly called the DC Jail. It is run directly by the DCDC. Opened in 1976, it was built to house up to 2,200 inmates. Until 2002, the jail population was limited by a court order to a population of 1,674. Since that court order was lifted, it now houses an average population of more than 2,000 people.

The Central Treatment Facility (called CTF) was originally built to serve as an intensive medical and drug treatment facility for the District of Columbia's prison system. It opened in 1992. In 1997, the city signed a 20-year contact with Corrections Corporation of America to administer the day-to-day functions of the CTF. It is built to house a maximum of 898 inmates and houses an average of 800 people per day.

COMPOSITION OF THE DC DEPARTMENT OF CORRECTIONS POPULATION

According to publicly released DCDC statistics, almost 85% of the District's inmates are African American men. African American women make up the next largest group, comprising 8.5% of the population. Hispanic men are 2.8% of the population and Hispanic women, 0.2%. The rest of the inmate population in DC is made of people who are Asian, white, or other racial groups. Broken down by gender, men constitute 91% of the DC corrections population and women are the other 9%.

PRISONS FOR INMATES FROM THE DISTRICT OF COLUMBIA

Historically, the District's 3,000-acre prison complex was located in Lorton, Virginia. In 1997, Congress passed the National Capital Revitalization and Self-Government Improvement Act to correct the serious financial difficulties facing the city. Congress wanted to address unfunded liabilities in the city's pension programs and other budgetary problems and refine the city's court system.

Years of neglect by the city government had turned the Lorton prison complex into an irreparable financial drain on the city's budget. The Revitalization Act mandated that the District close the Lorton prison complex and move its sentenced felons to control of the Federal Bureau of Prisons. In November 2001, the last of the Lorton prisoners was transported out. Now, after a felony sentencing hearing, a DC offender is designated to the Federal Bureau of Prisons and is taken from either of the two local jail facilities to a federal prison.

As a result, people who have been convicted of a felony violation of Washington's municipal code may be sent to prisons as far away as California. The Federal Bureau of Prisons has promised to try to keep 80% of DC inmates within 250 miles of the District and 90% within 500 miles. As this statement is simply one of intent to try, it is not legally enforceable on any level. It should be noted that the nearest federal medical center for women is in Fort Worth, Texas, so ill female inmates must be housed far away from the city and their families.

PAROLE FOR DISTRICT OF COLUMBIA PRISONERS

The parole process for prisoners from Washington, D.C., has also been federalized. Prior to the passage

of the National Capital Revitalization and Self-Government Improvement Act of 1997, the local District of Columbia Board of Parole made decisions about parole for District inmates. With the passage of that act, Congress shifted authority to the U.S. Parole Commission. This policy change was finalized on August 5, 2000. Now, all decisions regarding whether to grant or revoke the parole of a DC inmate are made by the presidentially appointed commission in accordance with the federally established guidelines. This policy change is confusing for those inmates who believe that their parole should be determined according to the old DC guidelines.

In the past, decisions about parole were made on an individual basis by a parole board that was familiar with the city, its culture, and the programs available. Now decisions are made by presidential appointees from around the country. In turn, their decisions are based on relatively inflexible federal guidelines. While there are special guidelines for DC prisoners, these are based on the guidelines originally set up for federal prisoners, who, in general, commit a different class of crimes than those committed by prisoners prosecuted by the city. In addition, the U.S. Parole Commission is not bound by recommendations entered by the DC Board of Parole. Thus, prisoners may have been told that they would be paroled after serving a short amount of time, but after the transition, all decisions are revisited based on the stringent federal guidelines. These days, parole is legally considered a privilege, not a right. Thus, inmates do not have a right to parole at a certain date. At the time of this printing, legal challenges to the imposition of the new guidelines have not been successful.

When offenders are released on parole, unless there are special circumstances, they are released to live in the District under supervision. The Court Services and Offender Supervision Agency supervises the more than 2,615 people who are on pretrial releases, probation, or parole in DC. This agency was created by the Revitalization Act and took over from the previous city-run agency. It is the job of the Court Services and Offender Supervision Agency to ensure that people comply with the terms of their parole, for example, by maintaining a job or remaining drug free. If there is a problem with an offender complying with the terms of parole, the agency can recommend that his or her parole be revoked.

PROBLEMS WITH THE DISTRICT OF COLUMBIA SYSTEM

Many lawsuits have been filed against Washington, D.C., for the unconstitutional conditions in all of its facilities. Two of the most important that are still relevant now that the Lorton Complex closed are *Campbell v. McGruder, et al.* and *Women Prisoners of the District of Columbia Department of Corrections, et al. v. District of Columbia, et al.*

Campbell v. McGruder, et al. was filed in 1971. It was later consolidated with another lawsuit, *Inmates of D.C. Jail v. Jackson, et al.,* which was filed in 1975. Both of these cases are class action lawsuits that were filed on behalf of pretrial detainees and sentenced inmates. Both cases charged widespread constitutional violations in the conditions of the DC Jail in areas such as medical care, environmental conditions, and mental health services. The city proved unable or unwilling to remedy persistent problems, so in 1995 the Court appointed a receiver to run the medical department. The receiver ran the medical services until 2000, when the District was once again allowed by the court to run its own medical services. Now it hires a subcontractor to provide services at the jail. Also, to counteract the effect of overcrowding, the Court implemented a population cap of 1,674 in 1985.

Due to the requirements of the Prison Litigation Reform Act, and the amelioration of some of the unconstitutional conditions that led the court to impose the cap, the population cap was lifted in 2002. Now, the DCDC is free to house as many people as it wants at the jail, regardless of how crowded it becomes. It remains to be seen whether DCDC can meet the requirements imposed by the Constitution with the number of people held in the jail.

The Women Prisoners lawsuit was filed in 1993. It alleged multiple violations of federal law, including discrimination based on gender, lack of appropriate medical care, and sexual harassment of female inmates. While the trial court ruled in many respects for the inmates, the District of Columbia was able to narrow the scope of the judgment somewhat in the appellate process. In the end, the lawsuit forced DCDC to create a policy and programs to limit sexual harassment, institute better obstetrical and gynecological care, and establish programming equity for the women as compared to the men.

Other problems continue. In the city jail system, inmates continue to complain of inadequate medical care, unhealthy environmental conditions, sexual harassment, sexual assault, and a mismanaged central records office. As men and women are placed around the country in the Federal Bureau of Prisons, there are concerns that arise about issues such as access to family, the cultural competence of staff in far-away prisons, and parity of programs.

CONCLUSION

The Washington, D.C., prison system remains in the control of the U.S. Congress, while the jail system is still under local control. Prisoner rights advocates continue to monitor the DC Department of Corrections for both ongoing and new problems. As the transition to federal control of prisoners is completed, advocates also continue to scrutinize and attempt to alleviate problems, especially those caused by the great distance between the prisons and the DC community. As the corrections system for the city remains split between local and federal control, there will continue to be an effort to ameliorate the confusion caused in both inmates and the general public.

—*Deborah M. Golden*

See also Corrections Corporation of America; Federal Prison System; Jails; Parole; Parole Boards; Prison Litigation Reform Act 1996; Privatization

Further Reading

Blecker, R. (1990, May). Haven or hell? Inside Lorton Central Prison: Experiences of punishment justified. *Stanford Law Review,* 1149.

DC Department of Corrections. (2004). DC Department of Corrections home page. Retrieved from http://www.doc.dc .gov/main.shtm

Hasaballa, A. Y. (2001). *The social organization of the modern prison.* Lewiston, NY: E. Mellon.

Kober, G. M. (1927). *Charitable and reformatory institutions in the District of Columbia.* Washington, DC: U.S. Government Printing Office.

Lezin, K. (1996, Winter). Life at Lorton: An examination of prisoners' rights at the District of Columbia correctional facilities. *Boston Public Interest Law Journal,* 165.

Oakey, M. H. (1988). *Journey from the gallows: Historical evolution of the penal philosophies and practices in the nation's capital.* Lanham, MD: University Press of America.

Ogletree, C. J., Jr. (2002, March). Symposium: The bicentennial celebration of the courts of the District of Columbia Circuit: Judicial activism or judicial necessity: The D.C. District Court's criminal justice legacy. *Georgetown Law Journal Georgetown Law Journal,* 685.

Parker, K. C. (2002). Note and comment: Female inmates living in fear—Sexual abuse by correctional officers in the District of Columbia. *American University Journal of Gender, Social Policy & the Law American University Journal of Gender, Social Policy & the Law,* 443.

Photo 1   *Dorothea Dix*

DIX, DOROTHEA LYNDE
(1802–1887)

Dorothea Lynde Dix was a social reformer and advocate for better treatment of the mentally ill. During the 19th century, mentally ill individuals generally were confined in the same facilities as convicted criminals. Between 1841 and 1856, Dix inspected jails, prisons, workhouses, and other institutions housing the mentally ill in the United States and in 13 European countries, collecting evidence of mistreatment of criminals and the mentally ill. She actively worked for the creation of mental hospitals designed to treat the mentally ill and to separate them from convicted offenders, changing the nature of the prison population. In addition, she brought about major improvements in how criminals in prisons and jails were housed and treated.

BIOGRAPHICAL DETAILS

Dorothea Dix was born in Hampden, Maine, on April 4, 1802. Her parents, Joseph and Mary Dix, were inattentive and abusive to Dorothea and her two younger brothers, Joseph and Charles. Her father was an alcoholic itinerant preacher, who rode circuit and was frequently absent from home. Her mother, who suffered from depression and was often bedridden, did not adequately care for the children. By the time she was 10, Dorothea was expected to care for her younger brothers and to stitch religious tracts, which her father sold.

Shortly before the War of 1812 began, the family moved to Vermont, and later to Worcester, Massachusetts. When she was 12, Dorothea and her brothers went to live with their wealthy paternal grandmother in Boston. Madame Dix attempted to educate Dorothea and turn her into a socialite. However, Dorothea had no interest in dancing or fine clothes and was eventually sent to live with her great-aunt, Sarah Duncan, in Worcester. While there, Dorothea opened a small "dame school" for girls between the ages of six and eight. She ran this school until 1819, when she returned to Boston and opened a school for older children in a building on her grandmother's estate. The school flourished and, after her father's death in 1821, allowed her to support her widowed mother. In addition to teaching, she also wrote poetry, children's textbooks, and religious tracts for children.

Dix was not physically strong and suffered from tuberculosis during the 1830s. In 1836, she collapsed and was forced to close her school. Upon her doctors' recommendation, she left for a long holiday in Europe. While visiting friends in England, Dix met prison reformers such as Elizabeth Fry and Samuel Tuke, who were attempting to develop more humane treatments for the mentally ill.

BECOMING A SOCIAL REFORMER

Dix returned to Boston in 1838, after the deaths of her mother and grandmother. Her inheritance from her grandmother, combined with royalties from the sale of her books, gave her financial independence. In 1841, she was asked to teach a Sunday School class for women inmates in the East Cambridge Jail. She was appalled at the conditions in which the inmates lived. Criminals, children, and the mentally ill were crowded together in filthy, unheated cells without furniture or blankets. Many were naked, physically abused, and underfed. This experience greatly affected her and was the impetus for what would become her lifelong passion: a dedication to improving conditions for individuals suffering from mental and emotional disorders.

Dix campaigned for better treatment of inmates in the East Cambridge Jail and eventually obtained a court order requiring the jail to provide heat and proper clothing for the inmates. She then traveled to other parts of Massachusetts, finding similar conditions in jails, workhouses, and other facilities for the mentally ill. In 1843, with the help and support of Dr. Samuel Howe, Director of the Perkins School for the Blind, she presented her evidence to the Massachusetts Legislature and eventually persuaded the legislature to allocate funds to expand the State Mental Hospital in Worcester.

Dix then began investigating the conditions of institutions in other states. She proceeded the same way in each state, first visiting facilities and collecting information on conditions in which the mentally ill were housed, then preparing a "memorial" (a document presenting her evidence and outlining

her concerns), and finally, persuading well-known local politicians to act as lobbyists by delivering her memorials and requesting funding for better accommodations for the mentally ill. In total, she played a key role in the founding of 32 mental hospitals, 15 schools for the "feeble-minded," and a school for the blind. Her efforts also inspired other reformers who also worked to establish or improve hospitals and other institutions for the mentally ill.

In the 1840s, Dix developed a proposal focusing on national long-term care and treatment of indigent mentally ill. She recommended that Congress set aside a land grant, with the income used to care for the mentally ill. Her proposal was supported by President Millard Fillmore, and she lobbied for her plan from 1848 to 1854. In 1854, her bill passed in the House and Senate, but President Franklin Pierce vetoed the bill.

In the late 1850s, Dix traveled to Europe, planning to rest and recover from her failed attempt at national provisions for the mentally ill. However, she soon began crusading for indigent mentally ill throughout Europe. Between 1854 and 1856, she visited 13 different countries and even met personally with Pope Pius IX, persuading him to order improvements in hospital conditions in Rome.

CONCLUSION

Dix returned to the United States in 1856 and continued her work as an advocate for the mentally ill. In 1861, when the Civil War began, Dix was appointed superintendent of U.S. Army Nurses. She recruited women volunteers and organized them into a nursing corps, established field hospitals and other facilities, and tirelessly worked to raise funds for medical supplies. After the war ended, Dix returned to her advocacy work, primarily focusing on Southern states where facilities for the mentally ill had been damaged or destroyed during the war. In 1881, Dix fell ill and retired, moving into an apartment in the New Jersey State Hospital, in Trenton, New Jersey, the first hospital planned by Dix and built through her efforts. She remained there for six years, until her death on July 17, 1887.

—Ellen G. Cohn

See also Elizabeth Fry; Fay Honey Knopp; Medical Model; Mental Health; Rehabilitation Theory

Further Reading

Colman, P. (1992). *Breaking the chains: The crusade of Dorothea Lynde Dix.* White Hall, VA: Shoe Tree Press.

Dix, D. L. (1971). *On behalf of the insane poor: Selected reports.* New York: Arno.

Dix, D. L. (1975). *The lady and the president: The letters of Dorothea Dix and Millard Fillmore.* Lexington: University Press of Kentucky.

Dix, D. L., & Lightner, D. L. (1999). *Asylum, prison, and poorhouse: The writings and reform work of Dorothea Dix in Illinois.* Carbondale: Southern Illinois University Press.

Gollaher, D. (1995). *Voice for the mad: The life of Dorothea Dix.* New York: Free Press.

Tiffany, F. (1971). *The life of Dorothea Lynde Dix.* Michigan: Plutarch.

Wilson, D. C. (1975). *Stranger and traveler: The story of Dorothea Dix, American reformer.* Boston: Little, Brown.

DOCTORS

The purpose of medicine is to diagnose, comfort, and cure; the purpose of prisons, although sometimes rehabilitative, is to punish through confinement. These often mutually incompatible purposes form the background for the interaction of correctional and health professionals and help explain why ethical dilemmas, even in well-managed correctional settings, are inevitable. Medicine is typically practiced in an office, clinic, or hospital where the goals of patient care define the administration and process of care. The role of prison doctors in the practice of medicine should be the same in corrections as it is in the outside world: to provide health care to the patient. Like their peers in the community, prison doctors are bound by certain ethical imperatives, particularly protection of the confidentiality of the patient-provider relationship and the process of informed consent. Correctional medicine, however, is practiced in a space where custody is predominant and health care is viewed, at best, as a necessary support for good administration, and, at worst, as a barely tolerated interference with the authority of the warden or correctional staff.

The provision of humane and effective health care for prisoners is guaranteed by the Eighth Amendment of the U.S. Constitution. Nonetheless, it presents formidable challenges. The extent to which these challenges are faced and met reflect wider societal views, the ethical integrity of prison medical services, and the degree of support prison doctors receive from their colleagues and professional associations.

DUTIES OF PHYSICIANS IN THE CORRECTIONAL SETTING

Correctional physicians have numerous duties. Their most basic task is to provide hands-on health care. This is usually done in the intake areas, during sick call, in infirmaries, and whenever emergency care is required. Physicians also act as consultants with outside providers, hospitals, emergency rooms, and specialists. Should an inmate die while in custody, it is the prison doctor who must ascertain why this happened. He or she must assess the conditions surrounding the death and determine whether the delivery of medical care contributed to its occurring.

Prison doctors are also crucial to the detoxification of inmates. The withdrawal process from drugs or alcohol generally happens in two phases: (1) the initial four to six hours and (2) a more prolonged phase in which an individual may require treatment through the administration of decreasing doses of either the same drug on which he or she was physiologically dependent or a drug that has been demonstrated to be effective in controlling symptoms. Doctors must determine which medications to use to help inmates in this part of the process while also monitoring their reaction to the first stage of withdrawal.

Many individual physicians approve of assisting in executions, even though all major medical societies and organizations (including the American Medical Association [AMA], the American College of Physicians, and the American College of Surgeons) have published their opposition to physician participation in capital punishment on ethical grounds. Twenty-eight states require or permit doctors to be involved in executions. According to the AMA, physicians may certify death and administer a tranquilizer. They may not, however, pronounce death, place an IV for lethal injection, order the drugs to be used, or do anything else to facilitate the execution.

CHALLENGES FACED BY PRISON DOCTORS

A number of factors often create barriers to the provision of physician services in correctional institutions. For example, medical personnel and correctional staff may be incompetent or indifferent to prisoners' health. There is often a shortage of prison doctors, since it is difficult to find highly qualified practitioners willing to trade their income from private practice for prison service salaries. Consequently, prison health services tend to rely heavily on physicians' assistants (PAs) and nurses. The situation may be exacerbated by the location of a facility, low salaries, sexism, and poor working conditions. For example, isolated rural institutions may find it difficult to hire a medical professional. Other institutions may refuse to hire women. Those facilities that employ physicians do not always provide adequate supplies or equipment. Most problematically, the lack of trust inherent in penal facilities makes providing medical care difficult. As a result, inmates do not assume that the medical system is acting in their best interests.

The changing and aging prison population has meant that prison doctors are now dealing with medical problems that were less prevalent 20 years ago, such as those associated with caring for the elderly. They are also required to provide adequate obstetric/gynecological care for the growing number of women prisoners, while treating and preventing the spread of tuberculosis, hepatitis, and HIV/AIDS.

PRIVATIZATION OF HEALTH CARE

As with so much else in the U.S. criminal justice system, prison health care in many facilities has been privatized. When this happens, physicians work as contract employees, rather than for the state. The Physicians' Network Association is one such private company that provides health care to adult and juvenile facilities throughout the United States. Established in 1990, this organization provides physician, nursing, and mental health services to correctional facilities, nursing homes, assisted living centers, and medical clinics.

CONCLUSION

Despite the many challenges facing prison doctors, in many ways, correctional health care is one of the last bastions where a physician can actually practice medicine the way it was taught in medical school. He or she is free from the problems of private practice such as billing, rationing care based on ability to pay rather than need, defensive medicine, cost of operating a practice, and so on. There is no need to worry about whether there will be enough patients to make ends meet. A physician who wants to provide good health care can do so in the prison setting. He or she can continue in the role of caregiver and patient advocate.

—*Ernest R. Williams*

See also Dental Care; Drug Treatment Programs; Elderly Prisoners; Gynecology; Health Care; HIV/AIDS; Hospice; Optometry; Physicians' Assistants; Women's Health

Further Reading

American College of Physicians. (1998). *Ethics manual* (4th ed.). West Philadelphia, PA: Author.

Anno, B. J. (2001). *Correctional health care: Guidelines for the management of an adequate delivery system.* Washington, DC: National Institute of Corrections.

Dabney, D., & Vaughn, M. S. (2000). Incompetent jail and prison doctors. *The Prison Journal, 80,* 151–183.

Dubler, N. N. (1998). The collision of confinement and care: End-of-life care in prisons and jails. *Journal of Law, Medicine and Ethics, 26,* 149–156.

Farber, N. J., Aboff, B. M., Weiner, J., Davis, E., Boyer, E. G., & Ubel, P. A. (2001). Physicians' willingness to participate in the process of lethal injection for capital punishment. *Annals of Internal Medicine, 135*(100), 884–888.

Prout, C., & Ross, R. N. (1988). *Care and punishment: The dilemmas of prison medicine.* Pittsburgh, PA: University of Pittsburgh Press.

Skolnick, A. A. (1998). Prison deaths spotlight how boards handle impaired, disciplined physicians. *Journal of the American Medical Association, 280*, 1387–1390.

◪ DONALDSON, STEPHEN
(1946–1996)

Stephen Donaldson, the first American jailhouse rape survivor to discuss his experience publicly, spent many years of his life working to expose the problem of sexual assault in U.S. correctional institutions. He also served as the president of the group Stop Prisoner Rape from 1988 to his death in 1996.

Donaldson, who was born Robert A. Martin, Jr., in Norfolk, Virginia, lived a life of many firsts. He adopted the name Stephen Donaldson as a pseudonym for his involvement in the gay liberation movement, started the world's first gay student organizations at Columbia University in 1966, and was the first sailor publicly to fight against a discharge from the U.S. Navy for "homosexual behavior."

In 1973, Donaldson was arrested during a Quaker antiwar pray-in at the White House. He refused to pay the $10 bail, which he believed discriminated against the poor, and instead chose to go to jail.

Donaldson was initially placed in a cellblock with other nonthreatening prisoners, including G. Gordon Liddy, who had broken into Democratic Party headquarters in the Watergate complex that year. In his autobiography, Liddy relates what he heard happened to Donaldson when District of Columbia Jail Captain Clinton Cox transferred him to an all-black cellblock. The young, small, and white prisoner was beaten and gang-raped approximately 60 times over the next two days.

Donaldson required rectal surgery to recover from his injuries. Furious at having been set up by Cox, he called a news conference on August 24, 1973, the day of his release from the hospital. He also testified about his experience before the Washington, D.C., City Council. The Washington *Star-News*, writing of Donaldson's experience, called him "a man of uncommon understanding."

Protesting his experience in the Washington, D.C., jail was the beginning of a life of work to end sexual abuse in prison. In 1984, he was named Eastern regional director for People Organized to Stop Rape of Imprisoned Persons, the group that eventually became Stop Prisoner Rape (SPR). He was named president of SPR in 1988.

Donaldson was an indefatigable researcher and prolific writer on the subject of prisoner rape. His articles and editorials appeared in the *New York Times*, *Los Angeles Times*, *Boston Globe*, *Penthouse*, and many other publications. He was the first person to collect statistical data on the incidence of prisoner rape. He joined a team of researchers, headed by Dr. Cindy Struckman-Johnson of the University of South Dakota, that concluded that from 9% to 22% of male prisoners are raped in confinement each year.

Donaldson appeared at many rallies to improve prison conditions, as well as on radio and TV. He was the focus of a 40-minute live TV interview on *Good Morning San Francisco* in 1985, after which the U.S. Parole Commission ordered him not to speak about jails and prisons in the media. He also appeared on *Geraldo* and *60 Minutes* to discuss prisoner rape.

Buddhism was a serious interest for Donaldson, and he taught courses on the subject at Columbia University. He spent a year in India becoming an Advaitist Hindu monk and took the name "Lingananda," as part of his studies.

Seemingly suffering from posttraumatic stress disorder as a result of the 1973 incident, Donaldson was frequently in and out of trouble with the law. He was jailed numerous times, and he was often raped in custody. While incarcerated in the early 1980s, he contracted AIDS from a prisoner who sexually enslaved him. Such victims are called "punks" in prison lingo, and Donaldson—in the Buddhist tradition of embracing what is painful or unpleasant—took the additional name of "Donny the Punk." Under this name, he became well-known in the punk rock music culture in the United States and Europe.

Not long before he died, he wrote a brief for and testified before the U.S. Supreme Court in *Farmer v.*

Brennan, the case that became the legal precedent for handling of both inmate-on-inmate rape and custodial sexual misconduct. In defense of the sometimes explicit content on SPR's Web site, Donaldson also testified as a plaintiff in the case *ACLU v. Reno,* which challenged the Communications Decency Act.

Donaldson died July 18, 1996, in New York City at the age of 49. His death was caused by an "indeterminate virulent infection complicated by an AIDS-defining condition." Several of his essays are featured on SPR's Web site, www.spr.org.

SOURCE: Portions of this biography are drawn from the American Civil Liberties Union's obituary of Stephen Donaldson (http://www.aclu.org).

—*Lara Stemple*

See also Activism; Bisexual Prisoners; Homosexual Prisoners; Prison Monitoring Groups; Rape; Sex— Consensual; "Stop Prisoner Rape;" Violence

Further Reading

Eigenberg, H. (1990). Rape in male prisons: Examining the relationship between correctional officers' attitudes toward male rape and their willingness to respond to acts of rape. In M. C. Braswell, R. Montgomery, & S. Dillingham (Eds.), *Prison violence in America.* Cincinnati, OH: Anderson.

Stop Prisoner Rape. (2004). Stop Prisoner Rape home page. Retrieved from www.spr.org

Struckman-Johnson, C., & Struckman-Johnson, D. (2000). Sexual coercion rates in seven mid-western prisons. *The Prison Journal, 80,* 379–392.

◪ *DOTHARD v. RAWLINSON*

In *Dothard v. Rawlinson* (1977), the U.S. Supreme Court addressed how Title VII of the Civil Rights Act of 1964, which forbids sex discrimination in the workplace, applied to a state prison's employment policies regarding prison correctional officers. At the time, Alabama had a statute that specified that prison guards must be at least five feet, two inches tall and weigh at least 120 pounds. The plaintiff in *Dothard,* a female applicant for a prison correctional officer position within an Alabama maximum-security facility, alleged that this policy, although seemingly neutral with regard to gender,

had a discriminatory impact in practice. Namely, women were far less likely than men to meet the state's minimum physical standards. The weight and height requirements in question disqualified about 40% of female applicants, and only 1% of male applicants. The Court held that once a plaintiff demonstrates that an employment policy has a disparate impact on the basis of sex, the burden of proof then shifts to the employer, who must show that there is a manifest relationship between the specified qualifications and the employment in question. The plaintiff would then have the opportunity to demonstrate that "other selection devices without a similar discriminatory effect would also serve the employer's legitimate interest in efficient and trustworthy workmanship."

In *Dothard v. Rawlinson,* the Court ruled that the plaintiff did indeed establish a prima facie case of sex discrimination and that the state did not demonstrate the validity of using height and weight standards to measure an applicant's ability to serve as a correctional officer. As a result, the minimum height and weight requirements were held to be in violation of Title VII of the Civil Rights Act of 1964. The Supreme Court thus paved the way to open up employment as correctional officers to female applicants.

GENDER AS A BONA FIDE OCCUPATIONAL QUALIFICATION

During the early stages of Dothard's legal attack on Alabama's height and weight requirements, the state adopted a regulation specifying that women could not work as prison guards in maximum-security facilities where they would be in "continual close physical proximity to inmates of the institution." This regulation had the effect of screening women out of about 75% of prison guard positions. Dothard subsequently amended her claim to include the state's open use of gender as an occupational qualification. The question for the Court was whether the explicit use of gender qualifications is "reasonably necessary to the normal operation of that particular business or enterprise." Gender in this case was deemed to be a bona fide occupational qualification that would constitute a legitimate exception to Title VII's general prohibition against sex discrimination in the workplace.

The Supreme Court's ruling that gender was a legitimate factor disabling women from certain tasks on the grounds that the "environment in Alabama's penitentiaries is a peculiarly inhospitable one for human beings of whatever sex" rescued the state from a Title VII violation. The Court pointed out that no attempt was made to segregate male sex offenders from the prison's general inmate population, and hence female guards in such institutions would likely prove unable to function effectively. In short, given Alabama's notoriously brutal prisons, the state could legitimately prohibit women from serving as prison guards in maximum-security prisons in "contact" positions.

The Court in *Dothard* did emphasize that "Alabama's penitentiaries are evidently not typical . . . [and] women guards could be used effectively and beneficially" in many maximum-security prisons. As such, one can understand the impact of *Dothard* as potentially quite narrow, since the Court took pains in this case to interpret the claim of Alabama against the backdrop of what they themselves characterized as a prison system shot through with "rampant violence" and a "jungle atmosphere."

DISSENT IN *DOTHARD*

In his dissent, Justice Thurgood Marshall refused to accept that Alabama's particularly inhospitable maximum-security prisons were in any sense operating "normally." Marshall concluded that "two wrongs do not make a right," and Alabama, if indeed its prisons were in violation of the Eighth Amendment's prohibition against cruel and unusual punishment, should be required to remedy this constitutional deficiency "with all possible speed." Marshall also suggested that the conditions of Alabama's maximum-security facilities posed just as much risk to male guards as to female guards. Marshall then lamented that the Court majority in *Dothard* required from the state no empirical evidence of breakdowns in the "normal" operation of their prisons because of female prison guards. He concluded that mere speculation about what *might* happen should not be able to satisfy the stringent

requirements of a bona fide occupational qualification defense.

DISCRIMINATION AGAINST MALE PRISON GUARDS

In those relatively few cases involving male prison guards and female prisoners, the courts have been more sympathetic to the privacy rights of women inmates. An interesting companion case to *Dothard* can be found in *Torres v. Wisconsin* (1988). In this case, the superintendent of a women's maximum-security facility (Taycheeda Correctional Institution) decided to prohibit men from serving in correctional officer positions that involved a great deal of contact with prisoners. The superintendent argued that the rehabilitation of many female prisoners would be substantially furthered by limiting the access of male correctional officers. Two men filed suit after they were reassigned to positions involving less contact with prisoners, albeit they suffered no loss of pay because of the reassignment. The Seventh Circuit Court of Appeals held that the state successfully carried their burden of demonstrating a legitimate employment issue based on gender.

The court in this case was convinced that the state's goal of rehabilitating female prisoners at Taycheeda Correctional Institution, where about 60% of the inmates had been sexually abused by males in the past, was materially furthered by the superintendent's policy on gender. As in *Dothard*, the court concluded that while there was no available "objective evidence" on the harmful effects of having male prison guards in close contact with female prisoners with a history of sexual abuse, the "totality of the circumstances" presented in the record demonstrated to their satisfaction the legitimacy of the policy in question.

CONCLUSION

The ability of prison facilities to use gender as a job requirement has been narrowed greatly since the *Dothard* ruling. The courts have tended to favor the employment rights of female prison guards over the privacy claims of male prisoners. Conversely, the federal courts have been more willing to limit the employment opportunities for male guards when they are dealing with female prisoners. The overall employment impact on male prison guards has been negligible, however, in part because the vast majority of prisoners in the United States are men.

The general trend has been for the federal courts to find that "very few prisons [were] as 'constitutionally intolerable' as Alabama's maximum-security prison" (Jurado, 1998, p. 27). Many states have no gender requirements for who may serve as a prison guard in maximum-security facilities, ostensibly because no such requirements are warranted on the basis of physical strength, security, or correctional officers' influence on prison conditions. Evidence suggests that correctional officers very rarely use physical force to carry out their job duties but rather rely on interpersonal skills such as negotiation, accommodation, and manipulation to carry out their core job functions. Available evidence also suggests that women correctional officers are not more likely than male officers to be assaulted by inmates. Finally, whether correctional officers are men or women does not seem to have an appreciable impact on prison conditions.

—*Francis Carleton*

See also Correctional Officers; History of Correctional Officers; Managerialism; Professionalization of Staff; Women's Prisons

Further Reading

Farkas, M. A., & Rand, K. (1997). Female correctional officers and prison privacy. *Marquette Law Review, 80,* 995.

Jenne, D., & Kersting, R. (1996). Aggression and women correctional officers in male prisons. *The Prison Journal, 76,* 442.

Jenne, D., & Kersting, R. (1998). Gender, power, and reciprocity in the correctional setting. *The Prison Journal, 78,* 166.

Jurado, R. (1998). The essence of her womanhood: Defining the privacy rights of women prisoners and the employment rights of women guards. *American University Journal of Gender, Social Policy & the Law, 7,* 1.

Parker, K. (2002). Note and comment: Female inmates living in fear—Sexual abuse by correctional officers in the District of Columbia. *American University Journal of Gender, Social Policy & the Law, 10,* 443.

Pogrebin, M., & Poole, E. (1997). The sexualized work environment: A look at women jail officers. *The Prison Journal, 77,* 41.

Legal Cases

Dothard v. Rawlinson, 433 U.S. 321 (1977).
Torres v. Wisconsin, 859 F.2d. 1523 (1988).

◪ DRAFT RESISTORS

A draft resistor or conscientious objector is an individual who, with sincere conviction that is motivated by conscience, cannot take part in either all forms or in particular aspects of war. There have been many examples and ways of resisting armed service throughout the history of the United States. During Vietnam, for example, many young men refused to appear for military obligations and often engaged in a public declaration of resistance by burning their draft card. Others, more silently and anonymously, merely crossed the border. Both then and now, members of the armed forces claimed conscientious objector status.

The U.S. government recognizes two types of conscientious objectors: (1) those who, by reason of religious, ethical, or moral belief, are conscientiously opposed to participation in war in any form and (2) noncombatant conscientious objectors, who are opposed to killing in war in any form but who do not object to performing noncombatant duties (e.g., medic) in the armed forces. In addition, there are four other types of resistors who are not officially recognized: (1) tax protesters, whose conscience does not allow them to pay the military portion of their taxes because of ethical, moral and religious beliefs; (2) selective objectors, whose conscience forbids them to participate in an "unjust" war (e.g., Vietnam); (3) nuclear pacifists, who refuse to participate in a nuclear war, or what they believe would likely become a nuclear war; and (4) noncooperators with the draft, whose conscience does not allow them to cooperate with draft law requirements.

Many resistors, such as Quakers, who are pacifist by doctrine, refuse to serve for religious reasons.

Others do not fight because of a deep sense of their responsibility toward humanity as a whole and from a belief that the government doe not have the moral authority to wage war. Some draft resistors are unwilling to serve in the military in any role, while others may agree to work in noncombat roles. In World War I, for example, numerous resistors drove ambulances, often under fire.

HISTORY

If the citizen soldier can be traced back to the early origins of America, so can the draft resistor. The first known recorded instance of pacifist resistance to military service took place in Maryland in 1658, where one Richard Keene was fined for refusing to be trained as a soldier. Usually, religion underpinned individual resistance to military action. Indeed, James Madison, in his original proposal for a bill of rights, also felt that no person should be compelled to render military service because of religious scruples. It is not clear why his idea was never adopted, but the evidence suggests that the framers of the Constitution favored leaving military exemptions to the jurisdiction of the states.

Conscientious objection first achieved legal status during the Civil War. At this time, President Abraham Lincoln established a system of alternative civilian service, and the revision of the 1864 draft law provided that draftees who objected on religious grounds be considered noncombatants.

From 1948 to 1973, the United States drafted men to fill vacancies in the armed forces. In 1973, the draft ended and the United States converted to an all-volunteer military. Today, a registration is in place, whereby with certain exceptions all 18-year-old men residing in the United States are required to register for the draft.

During the 20th century, conscientious objectors risked punishment and incarceration if they refused to serve in battle. For example, many of those who objected to fighting in World War I on either religious or moral grounds, as well as those who just spoke out against the war, were sent to prison. Most famously, socialist Eugene Debs was convicted of criticizing the conviction of draft resistors and draft opponents and was sentenced to 10 years in prison. Similarly, even though President Franklin D. Roosevelt restored the citizenship rights of more than 1,500 persons who served prison terms for draft violations (or for minor espionage acts) during the war, numerous men were incarcerated for refusing to serve in World War II. Of the 34.5 million men who registered for the draft in the second world war, more than 72,000 applied for conscientious objector status. Of these, 6,000 rejected the draft outright and served prison sentences. Once again, it was not until after the war that President Harry Truman pardoned some 1,500 of these individuals and another 9,000 who had been convicted of military desertion during wartime. During the Vietnam War, more than 209,000 men were formally charged with violating draft laws. Of the 25,000 indictments, 8,750 were convicted and fewer than 4,000 served prison time.

CONTEMPORARY VIEWS

In 1970, the Supreme Court removed the religious requirement and allowed conscientious objection based on a deeply held ethical philosophy with no reference to a deity. One year later, however, the Court refused to allow objection to a particular war that affected tens of thousands of opponents to the Vietnam War causing an exodus of draft evaders, primarily to Canada and Scandinavia.

President Gerald Ford in 1974 instituted a partial clemency program for draft resistors. The program covered the following categories: convicted drafted violators, convicted military deserters and AWOLs (absent without leave), draft violators who had never been tried, and veterans with less than honorable discharges for absence offenses. Persons receiving clemency were required to complete up to 24 months of alternative service and sign an oath of allegiance to the United States. Only 27,000 of the 350,000 eligible individuals applied and 21,800 were given clemency, mostly those living in the United States, not exiles.

In 1977, President Jimmy Carter established two programs to assist war resistors. In January, he issued an unconditional amnesty for draft resistors and later that year, set up a process to pardon military deserters. Together these programs provided amnesty for all draft evaders whether they had pursued legal remedies or not. Unfortunately, there are no accurate figures available for the real number of resistors who benefited from it. In addition, Congress did not adequately fund the program and the period of time under which people could apply was very limited.

CONCLUSION

Claiming conscientious objector status is by no means a thing of the past. There were 117 conscientious objectors during the 1991 Persian Gulf War. More recently, in the war in Iraq several hundred U.S. soldiers initially applied for this status. Likewise, the United States is not alone dealing with this issue. In Israel, for example, many soldiers in the IDF (Israeli Defense Force) have recently been subject to court-martial for their refusal to fight against the Palestinians, seeing it as an army of occupation. There is no such alternative civilian service in Israel, so most serve jail or prison sentences for their acts of conscience. Wherever a state elects to wage war, it seems that there will be those who refuse to serve. The question then becomes how does society respond to their resistance?

—Kelly R. Webb

See also Enemy Combatants; Prisoner of War Camps; Resistance

Further Reading

Brock, P. (Ed.). (2002). *Liberty and conscience: A documentary history of conscientious objectors in America through the Civil War.* Oxford, UK: Oxford University Press.

Eller, C. (1991). *Conscientious objectors and the Second World War.* Westport, CT: Praeger.

Gaylin, W. (1970). *In the service of their country: War resisters in prison.* New York: Viking.

Kohn, S. M. (1986). *Jailed for peace: The history of American draft law violators, 1658–1985.* Contributions in Military History, No. 49. Westport, CT: Greenwood.

Schlissel, L. C. (1968). *Conscience in America: A documentary history of conscientious objection in America, 1757–1967.* New York: E. P. Dutton.

◪ DRAMA PROGRAMS

Theater behind bars has consistently survived in harsh prison environments as well as in more lenient milieus. Prisoners and practitioners report that drama programs involving workshops, classes, or productions enable them to transcend their prison routines and move toward greater empathy. They also help them gain access to literature and to a world outside their confinement while feeling part of a community. Drama helps many to create personal space in an impersonal place; work toward personal, social, or institutional change; and prepare for release and reintegration. However, as prisons seek to make conditions increasingly restrictive for inmates, artists have more difficulty in finding supporters inside, and prisoners have less opportunity for creative outlets.

HISTORY

Prison is a ready-made place for theater because people need to be able to express themselves. Theater has always been a way for ordinary people to feel extraordinary, and for many to transcend their circumstances, physical problems, or emotional lives. In an unfeeling or repressive environment, it is a way to be connected to one's inner self and it is also a way to step into the shoes of a person whose behavior may be radically different from one's own. Entertainment from the outside is one way prisoners gain access to drama but more significant are those programs initiated by inmates or provided by artists and/or teachers from the outside.

While it is difficult to pinpoint a first program or play behind bars in this country, a photo from the State Penitentiary in Canon City, Colorado, held in the archives of the *History of the American West, 1860–1920* in the Denver public library, shows male prisoners enjoying a stage show at the turn of the 20th century. The 1970s and 1980s saw an increase in the relationship between theater and criminal justice. Programs in European countries far surpassed those in American prisons as companies from England, France, Italy, Spain, Ireland, and Germany, for example, sought to create innovative ways to reach prisoners. Theater troupes such as England's Clean Break started because inmates wanted to communicate their experiences with others. Theatre for Prison and Probation began in Manchester, England, as the need grew to teach practitioners to work in prisons. John Bergmann founded Geese Theatre in 1980 in Iowa and expanded his work to include training and performing with prisoners in seven countries. Shakespeare too got a turn as Murray Cox brought *Hamlet* to a secure psychiatric hospital in the United Kingdom, male inmates in a Kentucky maximum-security prison performed *Titus Andronicus,* and women at Framingham Women's Prison in Massachusetts put on *The Merchant of Venice* and *Rapshrew,* an adaptation of *The Taming of the Shrew.*

By the 1990s, as more violence hit America's cities, the country turned toward a "tough on crime" policy and theater programs folded as prison officials feared the wrath of politicians and the scorn of the public for allowing inmates to participate in nonpunitive activities. When the Omnibus Crime Bill, in 1995, took away Pell grants from incarcerated adults—the federal funds that were supporting students behind bars—many college credit programs disappeared. At the same time, many other arts programs were cut across this country.

TYPES OF PROGRAMMING

Drama programs that encourage productions inside tend to fall into two categories. Many artists work with inmates' own stories and help prisoners create plays from them. These kinds of works are original and may involve music and poetry as well. Rhodessa Jones from San Francisco has been creating original pieces for more than 10 years with incarcerated women, incorporating music and dance into her theatrical productions as well. In South African prisons, puppets often play a large role in productions as a way to tell stories, and in Brazil, a dialogue was initiated after a play about the oppressive prison system was performed for an audience that included politicians. Other practitioners work with scripts and develop plays that expand inmates' knowledge of literature, producing the plays

exactly as the author wrote them, or recreating classic texts by allowing prisoners to add some of their own words to the original text.

Theater practitioners also use drama techniques for ends other than performance such as anger management, dealing with drugs, bullying behind bars, stress management, and teaching cooperation versus competition. Buzz Alexander in Michigan created a course to educate theater students at a university to be volunteers behind bars. Charles Dutton, known to TV audiences as the star of the 1990s sit-com *Roc,* first educated himself in solitary confinement by reading plays. When he returned to the general population, he started a prison theater group for inmates to deal with their pent-up energy, and when he was released from prison pursued an acting career at Yale Drama School. Most practitioners who go into prison to do drama work also talk about the fact that they, as teachers, are consistently taught by the inmates, thereby reconnecting with the age-old transformational power of theater.

PROBLEMS IN RUNNING A PRISON DRAMA PROGRAM

The major problems that drama practitioners face come from the nature of incarceration itself. Inmates may enroll in a class or sign up for a production and then get disciplined for weeks and be pulled out or transferred to a different prison. Visits, doctor appointments, and conflicting activities cause inmate-students to miss rehearsals or classes. Literacy can be a problem and often students of many skill levels are enrolled in the same class. However, by reading plays and by using improvisation, groups overcome the discrepancies in abilities.

Most difficult are issues around production. Props and costumes need approval and prison rules must be carefully followed, sometimes meaning extra hours for thorough searches. Any disruption in the prison may mean activities are cancelled. Security always takes precedence over expression and may cause performance cancellations. Tensions between inmates may also surface in the intensity of dramatic performance and because correctional officers sometimes sit in on rehearsals. Issues that must always be addressed are working with the authoritative prison administration, safety, conflicts within the group, the liaison with guards, and time issues.

CONCLUSION

Anecdotal evidence from participants indicates that drama programs in prison are important to the inmates and that the "tough on crime" attitude should not discredit such programs. Black, white, and Latino women were equally involved in classes taught in the Massachusetts Women's Prison and reported that their experiences in class and on stage helped them learn more about other ways of living than those they had learned on the street. In England, evaluations show that prisoners' attitudes changed after their involvement with drama. Many became more self-confident and reported higher levels of self-esteem. Officers reported a good sense of group coherence that promoted a more respectful environment. European Theatre and Prison Conventions have been held in Milan, Manchester, and Berlin, aimed at organizing artists and promoting theater in prison as a viable vehicle for growth and change. What is certain is that these kinds of energies are not going away and may in fact thrive in even the most repressive environments and most secure institutions. While the future of drama programs may be at risk, the outcomes have been so positive to insist that theater behind bars is definitely an underutilized tool in U.S. prisons.

—*Jean Trounstine*

See also Art Programs; College Courses in Prison; Creative Writing Programs; Literacy; Pell Grants; Prison Music

Further Reading

Boal, A. (1995). *The rainbow of desire: The Boal method of theatre and therapy* (A. Jackson, Trans.). London: Routledge.

Cox, M. (Ed.). (1992). *Shakespeare comes to Broadmoor. "The actors are come hither."* London: Jessica Kingsley.

Fraden, R. (2001). *Imagining Medea: Rhodessa Jones and theater for incarcerated women.* Chapel Hill: University of North Carolina Press.

Thompson, J. (Ed.). (1998). *Prison theatre: Perspectives and practices.* London: Jessica Kingsley.

Trounstine, J. (2001). *Shakespeare behind bars: The power of drama in a women's prison.* New York: St. Martin's.

◪ DRUG OFFENDERS

Drug offenders have been the fastest growing segment of the U.S. prison population since the mid-1980s. As a result of the "war on drugs," which focused local enforcement on street dealing and increased sentences for drug crimes, drug offenders now make up a significant proportion of inmates in most state prisons and in the federal corrections systems. The growth in numbers of people serving sentences for drug offenses has disproportionately penalized ethnic minorities, especially young back men. The decision to treat drugs as a law-and-order issue rather than one of public health has also created significant obstacles to effective treatment provisions for drug users.

DRUGS AND CRIME

Crime is one of the attendant problems of drug abuse. According to one estimate, a male drug user may commit 80 to 100 serious property offenses per year to pay for his drugs. A number of ethnographic and longitudinal studies of drug-using criminals also show that high levels of drug (ab)use are associated with high levels of crime, while lower levels of drug use are associated with fewer offenses. However, the connection between drugs and crime is not always straightforward. Not all drug users are predatory offenders; many have no convictions except for illegal possession and remain otherwise "crime-free" for all their drug-taking careers. Moreover, there is evidence to suggest that some types of drugs are less associated with crime than others; offending might have more to do with the lifestyle and personal circumstances of the drug user than anything else. For example, ecstasy use is not generally associated with crime because of the sociodemographic features of users most of whom are occasional drug users with adequate economic resources. They are less likely to have a criminal history or a subsequent criminal career. On the other hand, heroin users are more likely to be working class, unemployed, homeless and poly-addicts. Drugs and crime are strongly associated with this group, but this may be because their sociodemographic background put them at a higher risk of criminality in the first place.

DRUG CONTROL

The current characterization of drug control in the United States as a war on drugs was initiated by the Nixon administration in the early 1970s. Since then, the United States has launched successive "wars" on drugs even at a time when general population surveys showed declining levels of drug use. In each war, law enforcement and punishment have been by and large favored over prevention, treatment, and education strategies.

In practice, the war on drugs has been translated into "get tough" drug laws and harsh mandatory minimum prison sentences. In an increasing climate of zero tolerance, police crackdowns and intensive community policing strategies have also been extended to minor drug users and buyers. Controversial police enforcement activities have included undercover drug buys, increased use of stop-and-search powers especially in drug hot spots, and police arrests for various misdemeanors such as loitering and disorderly conduct.

CONSEQUENCES

The toughened-up approach to drug control has brought a large number of drug offenders into the courts, jails, and prisons. From 1980 to 1998, the total number of criminal arrests nationwide increased by 40% while the number of drug arrests rose by 168%. Of the 38,288 suspects referred to U.S. attorneys for prosecution during 1999, about one-third were involved with marijuana; 28%, cocaine powder; 15%, crack cocaine; 15%, methamphetamine; 7%, opiates; and 3%, other drugs. The majority of these suspects (around 97%) were investigated for drug trafficking (including manufacture, distribution, or possession with intent to distribute illicit drugs), 2% for simple possession, and less than 1% for other drug offenses. According to data collected by the U.S. Department of Justice, the number of drug offenders entering into the prison system has also increased dramatically in the past two decades. Between 1980 and 2000, the number of women and men incarcerated in federal prisons and new commitments to state prisons for drug offenses increased more than tenfold. The average time served in prison by a convicted drug offender rose by over 100% during the same period.

Many minor drug offenders have been caught up in the drug control system. A significant proportion of the prison inmates are low-level drug offenders with no current or prior violence or previous prison time. Almost half of the drug defendants convicted in federal courts during 1999 had no prior convictions; 92% of first-time drug offenders were sentenced to prison. Even statutes that are meant to target the violent and more serious offenders often result in punishing relatively minor drug offenders. For example, as of 1995 more people had been sentenced under California's three-strikes law for simple marijuana possession than for murder, rape, and kidnapping combined.

RACE AND GENDER

There have been other effects of the drug-related prison population explosion. At every level of the criminal justice system empirical analyses suggest that the war on drugs has resulted in worsening racial disproportionality in juvenile institutions, in jails, and in state and federal prisons. Between 1985 and 1995, the number of black state prison inmates sentenced for drug offenses rose by more than 700%. In some states, the racial disparity has been dramatic. In Pennsylvania, for example, drug commitments of black males increased by a staggering 1613% in the 1980s; white males by 477%. In 1990, 11% of Pennsylvanians were black but 58% of state prisoners were black. A similar pattern has been found in Minnesota, North Carolina, and Virginia. It is now clear that blacks and Hispanics are serving most of the mandatory prison terms under the existing drug laws. In 2000, sentenced for drug offenses were 43,300 (out of a total of 178,500) Hispanic state prison inmates and 145,300 (out of 562,000) black state prison inmates.

The impact of the prison population explosion on young black men and minority communities has been well documented. Black women are also over-represented among those sentenced to prison for drug offenses. For example, in 1994, around 8 out of 10 women sentenced for crack cocaine offenses and 1 in 2 women sentenced for drug offenses over-all were black.

EFFECTIVENESS

Conclusions about the effectiveness of drug sentencing are hard to draw. It is difficult to measure the deterrent effect of criminal sanctions on drug selling. Indeed, some critics argue that as long as demand for drugs and the likelihood of marginal gains from drug selling remain high, offenders in socially and economically marginal neighborhoods may continue to perceive strong economic benefits from participation in the drug economy. The incapacitative effect is also limited in high-volume drug offenses since a top drug dealer or major trafficker in prison may simply be replaced by someone else in the organized crime enterprise.

In Britain, the use of imprisonment for drug offenders has remained relatively steady over the past decade—about 10% of the total of drug offenders by the end of the 1990s. Research indicates that drug taking among prison populations prior to incarceration is high, with use in the 12 months before entering prison ranging from 40% to about 70%. Findings from self-report studies show that many continue to use a variety of drugs while in prison. However, many are reluctant to seek help, as they fear they will be targeted during their sentence (e.g., for additional searches).

In the United States, there are similar estimates that as many as 50% to 60% of state prison inmates have a drug problem sufficiently severe to warrant treatment. The provision of drug treatment programs in prison varies, and claims for the effectiveness of treatment for drug and alcohol problems differ dramatically. There is a significant gap between the need and the availability of drug treatment in prison, and any programs that do exist are often determined by the interests and qualifications of the staff and the amount of time allocated to this rather than other requirements. The goal conflict between treatment and custody that has existed since the inception of prisons remains highly pertinent especially at a time when other training and education activities are seen as extravagances that make life too easy for inmates.

CONCLUSION:
AN ALTERNATIVE APPROACH

So is there an alternative approach to the treatment and punishment of drug-using offenders? In 1989, the first American drug court to adopt the so-called Miami drug court model was established to provide court-based treatment programs to treat the offenders' drug addiction. Since then, there has been a burgeoning of dedicated drug courts throughout the United States as well as in Canada, Australia, and the Republic of Ireland. Drug courts are not homogeneous. Some place offenders on a diversionary program prior to adjudication stage, others implement postadjudication treatment courses, and still others deal only with low-level offenders. Many proponents argue that drug court has revitalized rehabilitation within the criminal justice system. They claim that treatment experience begins in the courtroom and continues throughout, making it a comprehensive therapeutic experience for the drug-using offenders. At the same time, sanctions are imposed for continued drug use, and responses increase in severity for failure to abstain. Evaluations of drug courts are promising, although as less tractable offenders enter the programs, rates of compliance may decline and recidivism may rise. Other critics have argued that the drug court produces personalized justice and, with it, a set of attendant dangers since it may produce vastly divergent sentences for similar offenses.

There is no doubt that penal sanctions for drug offenses have been influenced by populist concerns about the evil of drugs and inherent contradictions in the goals of punishment. In this context, the rhetoric of a "war" on drugs is particularly unhelpful because it legitimizes the potential excesses of a law-and-order approach to the problem of drugs while at the same time obscures its social costs and differential impact on particular social groups.

—Maggy Lee

See also African American Prisoners; Deterrence Theory; Drug Treatment Programs; Hispanic/Latino (a) Prisoners; Incapacitation Theory; Increase in Prison Population; Narcotics Anonymous; Rehabilitation Theory; Sentencing Reform Act, 1984; War on Drugs; Women Prisoners

Further Reading

Bean, P. (2002). *Drugs and crime.* Cullompton, UK: Willans.

Bureau of Justice Statistics. (2001). *Federal drug offenders, 1999 with trends 1984–99, NCJ August 2001.* Washington, DC: U.S. Department of Justice.

Burrows, J., Clarke, A., Davison, T., Tarling, R., & Webb, S. (2000). *The nature and effectiveness of drugs throughcare for released prisoners.* Home Office Research Findings 109. London: Home Office.

Chaiken, J. M., & Chaiken, M. R. (1990). Drugs and predatory crime. In M. Tonry & J. Q. Wilson (Eds.), *Drugs and crime.* Chicago: University of Chicago Press.

Currie, E. (1998). *Crime and punishment in America.* New York: Metropolitan.

Federal Bureau of Investigation. (1980). *Uniform Crime Reports for the United States.* Washington, DC: U.S. Department of Justice.

Federal Bureau of Investigation. (1999). *Uniform Crime Reports for the United States, 1998.* Washington, DC: U.S. Department of Justice.

Federal Bureau of Investigation. (2003). *Uniform Crime Reports for the United States, 2002.* Washington, DC: U.S. Department of Justice. Retrieved from http://www.fbi.gov/ucr/02cius.htm

Mauer, M. (2000). *Race to incarcerate.* New York: New Press.

McKenzie, D., & Uchida, C. (Eds.). (1994). *Drugs and crime.* Thousand Oaks, CA: Sage.

National Association of Drug Court Professionals. (1997). *Defining drug courts: The key components.* Alexandria, VA: Author.

Nolan, J. (1998). *The therapeutic state.* New York: New York University Press.

Tonry, M. (1995). *Malign neglect: Race, crime, and punishment.* New York: Oxford University Press.

U.S. Department of Justice, Bureau of Justice Statistics. (2000). *Prisoners in 2000.* Retrieved from www.ojp.usdoj.gov/bjs

Weinman, B. A., & Lockwood, D. (1993). Inmate drug treatment programming in the Federal Bureau of Prisons. In J. Inciardi (Ed.), *Drug treatment and criminal justice.* Thousand Oaks, CA: Sage.

◪ DRUG TREATMENT PROGRAMS

Drug treatment programs are designed to provide offenders with the skills to end drug use and maintain a drug-free lifestyle. Currently, less than half of all U.S. correctional facilities have specific substance abuse programming. Despite rates of substance abuse estimated at a minimum of 75%, treatment capacity is limited to approximately 10% to 15% of the overall population. Due to restricted funding and resources, most programs address substance abuse in general rather than exclusively focusing on the use of illicit drugs. Interest in the development of treatment specific to narcotics is, however, increasing due to high rates of drug offenders, recidivism, and prison overcrowding. The types of treatment available range from traditional institutional 12-step programs such as Narcotics Anonymous to intensive "treatment communities" where the offender is separated from the general prison population. Preliminary program evaluations indicate that some forms of substance abuse treatment are associated with decreased parole breaches, recidivism rates, and addiction relapse.

DEVELOPMENT

Correctional drug treatment programs in the United States originated in the 1930s with "narcotics farms" in Lexington, Kentucky, and Fort Worth, Texas. Treatment in these institutions was based on therapeutic withdrawal using gradually declining doses of methadone. Diversionary programs such as these, which placed offenders in civil substance abuse institutions rather than in correctional facilities, continued to be the primary means of dealing with drug-using offenders until the 1960s. In the 1960s and 1970s, the idea of treating offenders through psychological counseling and programming gained popularity. Treatment options incorporating programs such as detoxification, 12-step programs, counseling, and residential treatment developed and spread. In the late 1970s, however, meta-analyses of existing programs showing limited effects on recidivism led to the adoption of a "nothing works" approach to penal rehabilitation.

Diminished faith in the treatment of offenders resulted in a swift decline in correctional drug treatment programs that lasted until the mid-1980s.

RECENT FUNDING INITIATIVES

The declaration of a "cocaine epidemic" and the "war on drugs" in 1986 led to unprecedented numbers of drug offenders in U.S. prisons. In response, the Anti-Drug Abuse Act of 1986 called for the development of new resources for correctional drug treatment. Initiatives such as projects REFORM and RECOVERY were implemented to provide the research and training needed for the development of nationwide treatment programs. These initiatives originated in the Bureau of Justice Assistance, but were soon passed to the Department of Health and Human Services's newly developed Center for Substance Abuse Treatment. Currently, program funding is provided by a variety of sources, including the Bureau of Justice, Department of Health, research organizations such as the National Institute on Drug Abuse, correctional psychological services, and individual states and correctional facilities.

PROGRAM ADMISSION

Offenders are referred to treatment programs through institutional admissions screening, staff, judge, or case manager recommendation, parole requirements, or, more rarely, through volunteering. Offenders are often initially identified for suitability based on reported substance abuse history, drug-related offenses, or standardized psychological tests such as the Addiction Severity Index. Many institutions also require individual interviews with psychology staff or social workers to confirm motivation and personal suitability for treatment. As a general rule, more intensive programs have more stringent admission criteria. Additional requirements vary by treatment program, but often include documented history of drug use, drug-related recidivism, and a clean institutional disciplinary file. Most programs do not admit inmates who have a history of violent or sexual offenses, mental illness, or in-custody disturbances. Sentence length also determines program participation as some treatment modalities require up to one year to complete or are offered only to inmates approaching parole or release dates.

PROGRAM MODALITIES

Treatment programs vary according to the offender population, resources, and attitude toward rehabilitation of individual prisons and/or their governing states. Larger institutions usually offer a greater range of treatment options. Where more than one option is available, inmates are generally matched during the screening process according to personal needs and suitability criteria. Inmates can be transferred to other prisons in order to access suitable programs, but restrictions such as security level, available beds, jurisdiction, and inter-facility cooperation make the practice comparatively rare.

Diversion

Due to prison overcrowding, programming diverting offenders with nonviolent drug-related offenses or drug abuse problems is an extremely popular option. These programs include community-based incarceration such as halfway houses with mandatory participation in community substance abuse programs, boot camps, intensive probation, and electronic monitoring. Most use urinalysis, the collection of urine samples for drug testing on random or fixed intervals, to monitor offender compliance. A term of incarceration is often imposed if the offender breaches the diversion arrangements, for example, by failing a urinalysis test or by committing a new crime.

The TASC (Treatment Alternatives for Safer Communities) program is a popular example of a diversion offered to drug-using offenders. There are more than 180 TASC projects operating across the United States. TASC provides intensive case management, treatment, and support to drug offenders who do not pose a serious threat to the community. Clients in the TASC program remain in treatment for an average of six to seven weeks longer than average criminal justice clients and are provided with referrals to community resources following program completion. By taking a comprehensive, individual-needs approach, the program aims to provide offenders with the skills and contacts to develop a drug- and crime-free lifestyle.

Treatment Communities

Treatment communities are the most intense treatment option available, although specific practices vary from program to program. Inmates must have a well-documented history of drug abuse issues; self-report is inadequate and the screening process thorough. Treatment communities are characterized by residential settings that separate inmates from the general population. Cornerstone, operating in Oregon, opened as the first correctional treatment community in 1975. The Stay'n Out program in New York, established in 1977, is the most commonly modeled program, having demonstrated reduced rearrest rates among both male and female participants in a 1984 National Institute on Drug Abuse evaluation. Both programs follow a similar approach, with the key difference being the use of primarily ex-addict, ex-offender staff in the Stay'n Out model.

Program length in treatment communities varies from a few months to over a year, with optimal effects shown at participation durations of 9 to 12 months. Treatment communities are designed to offer comprehensive programming to address substance abuse as a lifestyle issue. It is understood, in other words, as a symptom of wider personal problems rather than as a sole cause of offending. Communities operate based on mutual self-help and responsibility. Inmates depend on one another for support and share the responsibility of day-to-day program operation.

Programs such as Cornerstone and Stay'n Out are broken down into phases of increasing responsibility and therapeutic intensity. The introductory phase familiarizes prisoners with daily operations, intermediate phases teach them to deal with substance abuse issues by recognizing relapse triggers and developing life skills, and final phases place prisoners in leadership positions assisting newer participants. Many programs also incorporate a community transition phase in which prisoners are released to community aftercare, monitored, and often encouraged to continue assisting with the program as role models. Programming offered within the community usually includes a combination of individual psychotherapy, group therapy, cognitive-behavioral therapy, life skills training, relapse prevention skills, education, and occupational training.

In the federal system, the Federal Bureau of Prisons offers a number of incentives to prisoners participating in residential drug treatment programs. These incentives include financial compensation to make up for lost work time and sentence reductions of up to one year for inmates who successfully complete residential programs.

Group Counseling

Several treatments fall under the heading of group counseling within correctional institutions. Programs incorporating expression through means such as dramatic role-playing and art are gradually accompanying traditional practices such as cognitive-behavioral therapy in which the offender learns to identify and modify problematic thinking and behavioral patterns. Most group therapy programs use a confrontational approach. Inmates discuss the emotional, cognitive, and behavioral issues associated with their drug use and respond to challenges and suggestions offered by their peers.

Counseling sessions occur at various levels of frequency and intensity. Program frequency varies according to institutional resources and practices. The participants largely determine intensity, as group members must decide how much they are willing to reveal and interact with the others. Members of the prison psychology department often staff groups, although some institutions use private contractors or incorporate community volunteers.

Individual Counseling

Individual psychological counseling is available to all members of the inmate population. However, high counselor workloads limit the duration and frequency of treatment sessions; other modalities would ideally complement personal development.

Treatment specifics depend on the training of the psychologist, but are most typically based in psychoanalysis, reality therapy, cognitive therapy, or behavioral therapy.

Methadone Maintenance

Methadone programs are rare due to the security and policy issues related to providing incarcerated offenders with a narcotic substance. However, the danger of HIV transmission through intravenous drug use among incarcerated heroin addicts garnered support for the establishment of the "Key" program at the Rikers Island facility in New York. The first of its kind in 1987, the Key provides methadone to heroin addicts during their incarceration and arranges referrals to community programs on release. Inmates do not have to be on a methadone program prior to incarceration in order to qualify.

Twelve Step

Twelve-step programs are available in most facilities with substance abuse programs. Narcotics Anonymous and Cocaine Anonymous are based on the Alcoholics Anonymous format but adapted to focus on illicit drug addictions. Twelve-step programs are often staffed by volunteers and ex-addicts from the community; therefore, they can operate at virtually no cost to the institution. They provide a forum of mutual support for offenders as they work through steps from admitting the problem to attempting to make amends for harm done. Some groups provide sponsors in the community to provide additional support, particularly upon community reentry.

Drug Education

Drug education programs have been mandatory in all federal prisons since 1990. Program participation is compulsory for any inmates with drug-related offenses. The education sessions are low intensity and relatively brief, designed only to inform participants of the potential consequences of drug use and motivate them to pursue further treatment. Treatment is intended to be a minimum of 40 hours in duration, usually taking place twice a week for approximately 10 weeks. Education sessions address issues such as reasons for drug use, theories of addiction, types of drugs, effects of drug use on the individual, and effects on the family. These sessions consist of activities such as lectures, movies, group discussions, and written assignments.

Detoxification

Detoxification programs provide therapy for inmates undergoing withdrawal on admission to the institution. Participants may be provided with gradually declining doses of methadone or receive counseling through the prison psychology department or community volunteers. Detoxification programs may also be offered to those ceasing a drug habit maintained within the correctional institution.

TREATMENT PROGRAMS FOR WOMEN

Female offenders are more likely than male offenders to have substance abuse problems. Yet, because women constitute a small minority of the correctional population, the treatment programs that are available to them are most often ones that have originally been designed for men. The problem with such programs is that female substance abusers tend to have very different needs that traditional male programs do not address. First, female drug use is more often correlated with criminality. Therefore, the percentage of women incarcerated for drug-related offenses is higher and it is increasing more quickly than that of male offenders. Second, drug use by female offenders is more likely to be instigated or encouraged by a romantic partner and associated with issues of abuse, psychological problems, and escape. Third, female drug offenders are less likely to have marketable employment skills and are at a higher risk for health problems such as HIV, malnutrition, and sexually transmitted diseases. Finally, due to histories of abuse and dependency, many women may be unable to cope with the adversarial nature of group therapies designed for men.

Programs that address the specific needs of female substance abusers are being developed. The OPTIONS (Opportunities for Prevention and Treatment Interventions for Offenders Needing Support) program in Philadelphia, for example, focuses on issues such as diet, body image, abuse, parenting, empowerment, and self-image that are of greater concern to women. OPTIONS, a treatment community, also operates in a cyclical pattern, eliminating the pressure and competition of the hierarchical system in male programs. Other programs offer innovative modalities such as acupuncture and recreation therapy in place of adversarial group therapies.

Programs such as WINGS (Women Incarcerated Getting Straight) in Alabama and Stepping Out in San Diego, California, also provide treatment specific to pregnant or postpartum women. These programs are usually less intense and focus on health and parenting as well as substance abuse issues. Although many programs for female offenders attempt to integrate postrelease community resources, transitional efforts are often hampered by low education and employment skills and few placement options, particularly for women with children.

CURRENT PROBLEMS FACING DRUG TREATMENT PROGRAMS

The primary barrier to the development and implementation of correctional drug treatment programs is funding. Although successful programs are cost-effective through reductions in justice and health costs, programs face competition for limited funds from other correctional programming. They must deal with political resistance from the zero-tolerance mentality surrounding both drugs and incarceration. In addition, prison overcrowding severely limits the space available for treatment. Programs such as treatment communities rely on separating the offender from influences such as drugs, rivalry, and peer pressure in the general population. With no room to isolate prisoners in treatment, programs must face these additional barriers to rehabilitation.

Programs also face problems of subject selectivity. Not all screening processes are able to weed out volunteers who are looking to improve their record or kill time rather than address real problems. Substance abuse treatment programs are also seen as prime marketing grounds for inmate drug dealers. Most intensive programs target high-risk populations—offenders with long histories of drug abuse and recidivism. Measures of success based on absolute levels of relapse rather than control group comparisons may therefore be interpreted as indications of program failure.

To achieve cost effectiveness, treatment programs cater to the greatest common denominator. Unfortunately, this practice does not address the needs of minorities such as women and people of varying racial and ethnic backgrounds. Despite the overrepresentation of Native and Hispanic offenders with substance abuse issues, for example, only a few programs offer instruction or interaction in languages other than English.

CONCLUSION

Although the developmental trend in correctional drug treatment is fairly recent, the Federal Bureau of Prisons, individual researchers, and the National Institute of Drug Abuse have been involved in program evaluation since the late 1980s. Program success is most commonly measured by reduced rates of recidivism, parole revocation, and drug use relapse. Current data indicate that the most successful programs are of high intensity, such as treatment communities, and incorporate a supervised community transition phase. Duration of treatment is also correlated with success, with an ideal program length of 9 to 12 months. Treatment modalities such as 12-step programs, drug education programs, individual counseling, and group counseling that are infrequent, low intensity, and take place within the general population are generally of negligible efficacy unless part of a more comprehensive overall treatment program that includes some form of postrelease continuity.

Preliminary evaluations indicate that comprehensive drug treatment programs reduce recidivism as well as drug use. Reduced rates of reincarceration can in turn reduce prison overcrowding and justice system expenses. Successful treatment programs are therefore necessary in a nation where the "war on drugs" ensures that both drug offenders and prison overcrowding remain key social concerns.

—Rebecca Jesseman

See also Alcoholics Anonymous; Drug Offenders; Group Therapy; Increase in Prison Population; Individual Therapy; Medical Model; Narcotics Anonymous; Psychological Services; Rehabilitation Theory; Therapeutic Communities; War on Drugs; Women Prisoners

Further Reading

Federal Bureau of Prisons. (2000). *TRIAD Drug Treatment Evaluation Project: Three-year outcome report.* Retrieved from www.bop.gov

Leukefeld, C. G., & Tims, F. M. (Eds.). (1992). *Drug abuse treatment in prisons and jails.* Washington, DC: U.S. Government Printing Office.

Lipton, D. S. (1998). Treatment for drug abusing offenders during correctional supervision: A nationwide overview. *Journal of Offender Rehabilitation, 26*(3 & 4), 1–45.

Substance Abuse and Mental Health Services Administration. (2000). *Substance abuse treatment in adult and juvenile correctional facilities.* Retrieved from www.samhsa.gov/oas/ufds/correctionalfacilities97/index.htm

U.S. Department of Justice, National Institute of Corrections. (1994). *Profiles of correctional substance abuse treatment programs: Women and youthful violent offenders.* Retrieved from www.nicic.org/pubs/1994/011369.pdf

E

◪ EASTERN STATE PENITENTIARY

The Eastern State Penitentiary opened in 1829. Sometimes called the Cherry Hill Penitentiary, it was erected in what was once a cherry orchard. Cherry Hill was designed from the beginning to enable those in solitary confinement to work. Care was taken so that its architectural design would follow the premises of the Pennsylvania system. Its first seven cellblocks were built to radiate from a central rotunda where guards could keep surveillance on prisoners who were housed in their own cells, each with central heat, running water, a toilet, and a skylight. Next to each cell was an outdoor exercise yard surrounded by a wall. Samuel Wood, a Quaker and member of the Philadelphia Society for Alleviating the Miseries of Public Prisons, served as Cherry Hill's first warden. Several of the wardens who followed Wood were also members of the Philadelphia Society.

Cherry Hill became famous as the chief exponent of the separate system. It attracted penal reformers from all over the world who came to see how successfully rehabilitation could be accomplished by means of total and complete separation and to view its modern construction. Ultimately, however, this system was replaced by the silent or congregate system initiated in New York State at Auburn Prison. Nonetheless, elements of the separate system can still be seen in contemporary practices of solitary confinement.

SOLITARY CONFINEMENT

When an inmate arrived at Eastern State Penitentiary, he was placed in a cell and left alone to contemplate his fate without work or reading materials. After a few days, if he had not already requested it, the prisoner was asked if he wanted work to do in his cell. If he had a trade that could be continued inside his cell, he was permitted to pursue it. If he did not, he was allowed to choose one and received instruction from an overseer. Prisoners wore masks or hoods on the few occasions when they were permitted out of their cells to prevent them from communicating with each other. Prisoners did, however, receive visitors.

The Board of Inspectors visited regularly as required by the terms of their appointment. The Philadelphia prison society had an extensive visiting program to encourage contact with the prisoners at Cherry Hill. The society's records indicate that its members made thousands of visits each year. Not only did they provide support and counsel to the inmates, they also accumulated information about prison operations and conditions. They made notes about each visit and the morale and emotional status of the offender. Records indicate that inmates were allowed visits with family members a few times a year.

Advocates of the separate system maintained that physical punishment was unnecessary to control an institution. Because prisoners were isolated from each other, there were few opportunities to get into trouble. If someone was recalcitrant, he was not permitted to work or keep reading materials in his cell. He could also be placed on a restricted diet.

CRITICISMS OF THE REGIME

In 1834, serious allegations surfaced that Warden Samuel Wood had used cruel forms of physical punishment against several prisoners. An investigation by the state legislature in 1835 discovered that Wood had isolated prisoners in a dark, unheated cell with no bedding and only bread and water for exceptionally long periods of time. It was also suggested that he used the shower bath to discipline prisoners by pouring water, at various temperatures, on an inmate from different heights. Another punishment was the tranquilizing chair. Prisoners were strapped to a large chair so tightly they could not move any part of their body. Finally, there was evidence Wood had used the straight jacket and the iron gag. A minority report expressed concern about the severity of punishment; however, the investigators' majority report found that such punishments were not inappropriate, and Wood was not admonished. Over the years, the prison's Board of Inspectors sanctioned the use of limited forms of corporal punishment at Cherry Hill.

THE CHALLENGE OF THE AUBURN MODEL

Unlike the separate system of solitary confinement, the Auburn system required prisoners to work together in large groups during the daytime. Only at night were they isolated in their own cells. To deal with the large numbers of prisoners gathered together, a strict code of complete silence was enforced. Officials instituted extensive surveillance techniques backed by certain and swift punishment once they discovered an infraction. Prisoners marched to and from their cells to the industrial shops or the mess hall in silent lockstep formation. When a prisoner disobeyed the rules, he was subject to immediate corporal punishment, usually a flogging or caning.

With the initiation of the Auburn system began a fierce debate about the meaning of punishment. Adherents to the Pennsylvania system spoke and wrote prolifically about its virtues, as did its detractors who supported the silent system. Both sought to remove offenders from society and prevent them from contaminating each other. They shared the theory that offenders were a "different class" of people (Hirsch, 1992, p. 36). Their similarities, however, ended here. The separate system kept inmates physically segregated 24 hours a day. In contrast, the Auburn system made inmates separate only at nighttime and enforced a rigid code of silence during the day.

Embedded in the two regimens were different beliefs about human nature and the ability of people to change. In the Pennsylvania system, isolation was tempered by the Quaker philosophy. Although there are reports that some wardens at Cherry Hill relied on corporal punishment, there is ample evidence that efforts were made to avoid incorporating it into the regular regime of the penitentiary. The men who devised the Pennsylvania system believed in the capacity of the individual to reform and that corporal punishment threatened rehabilitation. Those who devised the silent system were less inclined to believe that offenders could reform and thus spent little time aiding prisoners' efforts to change.

In 1833, French statesman and author Alexis de Tocqueville and his traveling companion Gùstave de Beaumont chronicled the debate that was waging between the Pennsylvania and New York systems in their book *On the Penitentiary System in the United States.* For Beaumont and Tocqueville, the New York system, with its reduced expectations, was more likely to instill good habits and an industrious nature. Prisoners learned useful trades in a congregate setting that was more like what they would eventually experience upon release. Similarly, after visiting Cherry Hill in 1842 author and social reformer Charles Dickens denounced the Pennsylvania system for its psychological torture. Acknowledging the good intentions of those who supported separation, Dickens wrote that they simply did not know what they were doing. Finally, critics pointed out, prisons built for the separate system were more expensive, and the inmates could not produce the quantity and variety of products that could be produced in the large, congregate shops that resembled assembly-line factories.

CONCLUSION

By the 1850s, the Philadelphia Prison Society had failed to convince the nation that the separate system was best. Cherry Hill was the only penitentiary in the United States that operated under the separate system, and even there the system had been diluted. Overcrowding made it impossible to assign every inmate to a single cell. By 1866, Cherry Hill officials no longer titled their system the separate or silent system, instead designating it the individual treatment system. A congregate workshop was built in 1905. In 1913, the separate system was officially abandoned. Pennsylvania closed the Eastern State Penitentiary in 1971.

Recently, this historic institution has been reborn as a museum. The Pennsylvania Prison Society opened the penitentiary for guided tours in 1994. In 2001, the Eastern State Penitentiary Historic Site, Inc., a nonprofit corporation, took over operation of the facility and extensive preservation efforts. In its new guise as an historic site, Eastern State Penitentiary powerfully demonstrates the early ideas of confinement in the United States.

—*Barbara Belbot*

See also Auburn Correctional Facility; Auburn System; History of Prisons; John Howard; Newgate Prison; Panopticon; Pennsylvania Prison Society; Pennsylvania System; Philadelphia Society for Alleviating the Miseries of Public Prisons; Quakers; Benjamin Rush

Further Reading

Barnes, H. E. (1968). *The evolution of penology in Pennsylvania: A study in American social history.* Montclair, NJ: Patterson Smith. (Original work published 1927)

Beaumont, G. de, & Tocqueville, A. de. (1964). *On the penitentiary system in the United States and its application in France* (Introduction by T. Sellin). Carbondale: Southern Illinois University Press. (Original work published 1833)

Hirsch, A. J. (1992). *The rise of the penitentiary: Prisons and punishment in early America.* New Haven, CT: Yale University Press.

Lewis, O. F. (1967). *The development of American prisons and prison customs, 1776–1845.* Montclair, NJ: Patterson Smith. (Original work published 1922 by the Prison Association of New York)

Lewis, W. D. (1965). *From Newgate to Dannemora: The rise of the penitentiary in New York, 1796–1848.* Ithaca, NY: Cornell University Press.

McKelvey, B. (1977). *American prisons: A history of good intentions.* Montclair, NJ: Patterson Smith.

Teeters, N. K. (1955). *The cradle of the penitentiary: The Walnut Street Jail at Philadelphia, 1773–1835.* Philadelphia: Pennsylvania Prison Society.

Teeters, N. K., & Shearer, J. D. (1957). *The prison at Philadelphia Cherry Hill: The separate system of penal discipline, 1829–1913.* New York: For Temple University Publications by Columbia University Press.

☑ EDUCATION

A range of educational opportunities is available in prisons, jails, juvenile justice facilities, and various community-based settings. Classes are often tailored to the needs of students and seek to provide learning experiences that will help them during their sentence and after release. For example, those entering correctional facilities may require classes in literacy, communication, and other subjects that will ease their transition into a corrections setting. In contrast, those who are nearing release will benefit from learning experiences that prepare them for the transition into a society that is very different from that found in prison, and, depending on their length of sentence, possibly unlike what they left behind. Other courses or learning may be selected based on age, gender, prior education and skills, and other factors.

Education

A U.S. Supreme Court Justice once stated that criminals are sent to prison as punishment, not to be punished. However, many citizens are against educational programs in prisons. Deprivation of education in prisons is a means of punishing prisoners.

These same citizens expect prisoners to be rehabilitated upon their release. Rehabilitation starts with education. Education unlocks many doors in a person's mind, giving a person legitimate skills and opportunities upon release.

Education also changes the way people think. It gives people hope and confidence in a future free of crime and incarceration. To eradicate education in prisons is to abandon prisoners in their quest for successful reintegration into society after they've paid their debt.

Education also plays a key role in prisoners' pursuits for redemption, be it spiritual or secular. How can I redeem myself or prove worthy of freedom if I am not invested with the proper tools to accomplish these objectives? I fail society because my incarceration has failed to prepare me adequately for my return to society. How can you expect me to build a better life and become a better citizen if I'm not given the appropriate blueprints? To deprive a prisoner of education while incarcerated is to render that person useless. We live in a society that emphasizes the importance of education in terms of success.

Finally, who do you want for a neighbor: An educated ex-con focused on positive productivity, or an uneducated ex-con focused on the only avenue you have left open: Crime?

John Rowell
Dixon Correctional Center, Dixon, Illinois

women" (Conrad, 1981, p. 1). Since then prison classes have been an entrenched part of the prison experience.

Inmates in the first prisons were taught the basics of reading and writing by prison staff and, if possible, an employable skill that might keep them away from criminal activity upon release. Later, education departments began to have responsibility for law and leisure libraries as well as vocational training and postsecondary schooling options. In most prisons, they also organize sports and recreational activities.

HISTORY

The earliest U.S. prisons generally sought to educate prisoners through religious instruction. Pennsylvania's Walnut Street Jail tried to reform and teach inmates by encouraging hard work and religious contemplation. Both activities were conducted in solitude. Over time, however, education outgrew solitary Bible reading, culminating in the introduction of a school in 1798, together with a library of 110 books.

The competing Auburn system that provided the model for most penitentiaries in the federal and state systems was far less supportive of prison classes, because of a concern that they might distract inmates from the more important tasks of prison labor. Nonetheless, by 1870 the National Prison Association, which was the forerunner of the American Correctional Association, set out in its Declaration of Principles that "education is a vital force in the reformation of fallen men and

PURPOSE

The U.S. Department of Education defines correctional education as "that part of the total correctional process that focuses on changing the behavior of offenders through planned learning experiences and learning environments. It seeks to develop or enhance knowledge, skills, attitudes, and values of incarcerated youth and adults." Similarly, the U.S. Department of Justice "recognize[s] the importance of education as both an opportunity for inmates to improve their knowledge and skills and as a correctional management tool that encourages inmates to use their time in a constructive manner" (cited in Tolbert, 2002, p. 15). These definitions illustrate the overlapping goals of correctional education: to improve individual skills while helping to manage correctional settings.

Prison-based education programs may provide incentives to inmates in an environment in which rewards are relatively limited. Formal classes and other less structured educational settings offer socialization opportunities with similarly motivated students and educators, who serve as positive role models. Education keeps students busy and provides intellectual stimulation in a place that can be difficult to manage. Programs also provide a "light at the end of the tunnel"—a stabilizing force for the individual who otherwise views his or her situation as somewhat hopeless.

Corrections education often focuses on improving individual skills needed to function productively within correctional facilities. These courses include literacy, special education, English as a second language (ESL), and learning disabilities. Other classes are designed to help inmates with life skills necessary in, and out, of correctional facilities. These include classes in parenting, empathy skills, communication and dispute processing, and cultural awareness. Finally, some classes are designed to instruct prisoners in vocational skills that may lead to employment opportunities upon release. These courses include library science, tutoring, barbering or hairstyling, auto and small engine repair, cooking, laundry and tailoring, carpentry, and building maintenance.

COLLEGE COURSES AND BASIC EDUCATION

Many states have mandatory education laws that require correctional education courses for any inmate who scores below a certain level on a standardized test. At least 26 states have laws that mandate education for a certain amount of time or until a set level of achievement is reached. The level that inmates must reach varies enormously, however. The Federal Bureau of Prisons, for example, requires inmates who do not have a high school diploma or a general equivalency diploma (GED) to participate in literacy programs for a minimum of 240 hours or until they obtain their GED. In New York State, by comparison, prisoners must indicate merely that they can read at a ninth-grade level. Enrollment in correctional education is also usually required if the inmate is under a certain age, as specified by that state's compulsory education law. Thus, in Connecticut, all young women under the age of 18 who are held in the state's only women's facility in Niantic spend the majority of their day in school.

Since the mid-1990s, prison classes other than basic literacy has been under attack both from within and outside the prison. Tertiary education has been particularly vulnerable. Although college classes in prison date to the 1920s, academic or postsecondary courses were rarely offered until 1965, when Congress passed Title IV of the Higher Education Act, a major part of which was the Basic Education Opportunity Grants. Later renamed the Pell grant in honor of Senator Claiborne Pell, the bill's sponsor, this act enabled prisoners and other low-income people to afford college education for the first time.

These days, however, prisoners are no longer guaranteed the right to earn a college degree. Since Pell grants for prisoners were abolished by the Violent Crime Control Act of 1994, few college programs remain in operation throughout the country. In 1990, there were 350 higher education programs for inmates. In 1997, only eight programs remained. Since there was no source for replacement funds, these programs were forced to abandon efforts to provide college courses in prison. Most of what is left of a once successful system of prison higher education is college by correspondence for those who can afford to pay for it themselves. Prisoners are limited even here, by restrictions on audio- and videocassettes and on the number of books they are allowed to have in their cells at any one time. They are also not given access to the Internet. Compounding matters, many universities have established residency requirements for course completion. Fears of alumni disapproval, faculty absences, and an association of the university degree with offenders are all used as excuses by many institutions from stepping into the breach created by the repeal of the Pell grants.

BENEFITS OF EDUCATION
WITHIN AND BEYOND THE PRISON

There are numerous benefits of an education both within and beyond the prison. At the most basic level, enrollment in education classes may raise an inmate's income during his or her sentence. In the federal system, for example, prisoners must have a GED or equivalent in order to work in most prison jobs. Without this qualification, they remain at the lowest pay level in the institution. Those for whom English is not their native language must take ESL classes to be able to read and understand simple instructions in their prison jobs. Many prisons also provide a range of other nonfinancial incentives for inmates who participate in education classes. Opportunities to earn privileges within the facility, increased number of visits, and the accumulation or loss of "good time" credit that can lead to earlier parole are all used to motivate students while simultaneously encouraging certain types of behavior within the facility.

In addition to helping prisoners cope with their sentence, education also appears to have a significant impact on people's tendency to reoffend. For example, the Three State Recidivism Study (Steurer, Smith, & Tracy, 2001) examined the impact of prison education while controlling for the effects of socioeconomic factors, criminal behavior, family life, educational experiences, and work history. This study found that inmates who participated in education programs while incarcerated showed lower rates of recidivism after three years. Measures of recidivism, rearrest, reconviction, and reincarceration were significantly lower in each of the three states. Employment data demonstrated that during each of the three years after release wages reported to the state labor departments were higher for the education participants than nonparticipants.

Likewise, a 1987 Bureau of Prisons report found that the more education an inmate received, the lower the rate of recidivism. Inmates who earned college degrees were the least likely to reenter prison. For inmates who had some high school, the rate of recidivism was 54.6%. For college graduates, the rate dropped to 5.4%. Similarly, a Texas Department of Criminal Justice study found that while the state's overall rate of recidivism was 60%, for holders of college associate degrees it was 13.7%. The recidivism rate for those with bachelor's degrees was 5.6%. The rate for those with master's degrees was 0%. Finally, the Changing Minds study (Fine et al., 1991) found that only 7.7% of the inmates who took college courses at Bedford Hills returned to prison after release, while 29.9% of the inmates who did not participate in the college program were reincarcerated.

Even small reductions in recidivism can save millions of dollars in costs associated with keeping the recidivist offender in prison for longer periods of time. The Bedford Hills study, for example, calculates that the reduction in reincarceration would save approximately $900,000 per 100 student prisoners over a two-year period. If we project these savings to the 600,000 individuals who are released from prison in a single year, the savings are enormous. Additional costs are apparent when we consider that the individual, had he or she not committed another crime, would be working, paying taxes, and making a positive contribution to the economy. When we add the reduction of costs, both financial and emotional, to victims of crime, the benefits are even greater. Finally, the justice system as a whole, including police and courts, saves a great deal of money when the crime rate is reduced.

CHALLENGES

Prison educators face many challenges that are shared by teachers in other settings. Inmates who choose to enroll in corrections-based courses are not necessarily any different from the typical student. As in any class, the range of students can include very gifted students, students who face challenges, and students who have various motives for enrolling in the course.

The correctional educator's challenge is compounded by the unique nature of prison culture and the need for security. Prisons adhere to strict routines that may not be ideal in an educational setting. In addition, inmates are often moved from one facility to another. This movement interrupts, or ends, the individual's educational programming.

These structural issues are accompanied by social factors that can further limit learning opportunities. For example, other prisoners may not support the individual's educational efforts. Although the student may be very motivated to earn an education, he or she remains in an environment in which conflicting demands may limit the opportunity to act on that motivation. In addition, prison administrators may also have varying degrees of support for education—especially if they see education as a threat to the primary functions of security and control.

Since correctional education programs offer courses in a variety of areas, institutions often rely on a range of funding sources. Some sources will provide general funds while others will provide funding for specific programs. As discussed above, Congress placed significant restrictions on corrections-based college courses with the passage of the Violent Crime Control and Law Enforcement Act of 1994. This act eliminated Pell grants for prisoners, with devastating effects. As a result of the elimination of Pell grants for prisoners, nearly every prison-based college program was eliminated. Since this funding often provided the foundation for other educational programs, the elimination of these programs had a ripple effect in correctional facilities. The funding problems were exacerbated with the passing of the Adult Education and Family Literacy Act (AEFLA), which became law in 1998. Funding continues to fall short of need, and the AEFLA has not improved this situation. The AEFLA continues to provide funding but altered the formula for state funding. Prior to 1998, states were required to spend at least 10% of AEFLA funds on educational programming in correctional institutions. The law now requires that they spend no more than 10%. Similar limitations were placed on funding as the Perkins Vocational and Technical Act was amended in 1998 to require that no more that 1% of federal funding for vocational and technical education programs be spent in state institutions, including correctional institutions.

Legislation over the past 20 years, a time in which the prison population has grown at unprecedented levels, has resulted in significant cuts in corrections education funding. This has resulted in the elimination of many programs. Ironically, the "get tough on crime" mentality resulted in the elimination of many programs that were effective in reducing crime. In the 1990s we began to see a dollar-for-dollar tradeoff between corrections and education spending. New York, for example, steadily increased its Department of Corrections budget by 76% to $761 million while decreasing funding to university systems by 28%, to $615 million. Research by the RAND Corporation demonstrates that crime prevention is more cost effective than building prisons and that of all crime prevention methods, education is the most cost effective. However, states were committing an increasing percentage of their budgets to fund longer prison terms and increased prison construction.

CONCLUSION

At the end of 2002, there were 1,440,655 people in federal and state prisons. The vast majority of these individuals will be released and will be expected to become productive, law-abiding members of society. Nearly 600,000 inmates are released each year, either unconditionally or under conditions of parole. Unfortunately, many of those released will be rearrested and will return to prison. Costs of this cycle of incarceration and reincarceration are very high. Corrections education has the potential to greatly reduce these costs as studies consistently indicate that an individual who benefits from education while in prison is less likely to return to prison than someone who has not.

There is some question as to why corrections-based education leads to lower recidivism. Many of the benefits of education are difficult to measure. As such, it may be difficult to show a clear relationship between educational opportunity and recidivism. However, an intervening factor, the ability to find and hold a job, appears to clearly demonstrate the benefits of corrections-based education. Individuals who take courses while in prison improve their chances of attaining and keeping employment after release. As a result, they are less likely to commit additional crimes that would lead to their return to prison. Individuals who benefited from college courses in prison also found better jobs and held these jobs for longer periods of time. It is clear that these factors work together to reduce recidivism—those with more education find stable employment, which makes them less likely to commit crime.

The imprisonment binge over the past 20 years has created a situation where we are beginning to see prison releases at unprecedented levels. Due to strict sentencing guidelines, these prisoners have often served long terms and are released only when their terms have been completely served. As a result, many are released unconditionally, without parole or other postrelease supervision. Each of these individuals will be expected to begin leading a productive, law-abiding life outside prison walls. It is clear that access to a quality education increases the individual's chance of success.

Correctional educators continue to work with their students while facing constant scrutiny and pessimism from the public and from some legislators who question the value of their work and the merits of providing educational opportunities for those who have committed serious crimes. Due to various controversies surrounding corrections education, most prisoners do not participate in prison education programs. The rate of participation has dropped over the past decade during a time in which crime control efforts became increasing punitive. Given the unprecedented prison population, and the equally unprecedented rate of release, corrections education has the potential to save millions of dollars while improving the lives and opportunities of individuals who have served their time and have successfully paid their debt to society.

—Kenneth Mentor

See also Adult Basic Education; Art Programs; College Courses in Prison; Drama Programs; English as a Second Language; General Educational Development (GED) Exam and General Equivalency Diploma; Good Time Credit; Literacy; Music Programs; Pell Grants; Prisoner Reentry; Recidivism; Rehabilitation Theory; Violent Crime Control Act 1994; Vocational Training Programs

Further Reading

Batiuk, M., Moke, P., & Rountree, P. (1997). Crime and rehabilitation: Correctional education as an agent of change—A research note. *Justice Quarterly, 14*(1).

Bureau of Justice Statistics. (2002). *Key crime and justice facts at a glance.* Retrieved from http://www.ojp.usdoj.gov/bjs/glance.htm

Conrad, J. P. (1981). *Adult offender education programs.* Washington, DC: U.S. Department of Justice, National Institute of Justice.

Davidson, H. S. (Ed.). (1995). *Schooling in a "total institution": Critical perspectives on prison education.* Westport, CT: Bergin & Garvey.

Fine, M., Torre, M. E., Boudin, K., Bowen, I., Clark, J., Hylton, D., Martinez, M., Roberts, R. A., Smart, P., & Upegui, D. (2001) *Changing minds: The impact of college in a maximum security prison.* New York: Graduate Center of the City University of New York. Retrieved from http://www.changingminds.ws/

Gerber, J., & Fritsch, E. (1993). *Prison education and offender behavior: A review of the scientific literature.* Huntsville: Texas Department of Criminal Justice, Institutional Division.

Greenwood, P. W., Model, K. E., Rydell, C. P., & Chiesa, J. (1996). *Diverting children from a life of crime: Measuring costs and benefits.* Santa Monica, CA: RAND.

Haigler, K. O., Harlow, C., O'Connor, P., and Campbell, A. (1994). *Literacy behind prison walls.* Washington, DC: National Center for Education Statistics.

Harer, M. (1995). *Prison education program participation and recidivism: A test of the normalization hypothesis.* Washington, DC: Federal Bureau of Prisons.

LoBuglio, S. (2001). Time to reframe politics and practices in correctional education. In J. Comings, B. Garner, & C. Smith (Eds.), *Annual review of adult learning and literacy* (Vol. 2). San Francisco: Jossey-Bass.

Steurer, S., Smith, L., & Tracy, A. (2001). *Three State Recidivism Study.* Prepared for the Office of Correctional Education, U.S. Department of Education. Lanham, MD: Correctional Education Association.

Tolbert, M. (2002). *State correctional education programs.* Washington, DC: National Institute for Literacy. Retrieved from http://www.nifl.gov/nifl/policy/st_correction_02.pdf

Trounstine, J. (2001). *Shakespeare behind bars: The power of drama in a women's prison.* New York: St Martin's.

U.S. Department of Education, Office of Correctional Education. (1994). *The impact of correctional education on recidivism 1988–1994.* Washington, DC: U.S. Department of Education.

◪ EIGHTH AMENDMENT

The Eighth Amendment to the U.S. Constitution forbids "cruel and unusual punishments." The federal courts have sought to address how this is to be applied in the context of prisons. At what point do prison conditions become so egregious and inhospitable that the government has, in essence, inflicted cruel and unusual punishment upon prisoners?

HISTORY

The U.S. Supreme Court first became involved in the field of prisoners' rights in 1964, under the leadership of Chief Justice Earl Warren. By the early 1970s, federal district courts, which had been empowered by the Warren Court to play a key role in evaluating the constitutionality of prison conditions, began to apply the Eighth Amendment to state and federal prisons. As a result, by 1986 "in thirty-seven states correctional administrations or individual prisons were operating under federal court orders" (Rosenberg, 1991, p. 306). Despite the potential for change, however, most agree that the interventions by the federal courts led to minimal improvements in the conditions of life in prison. In any case, since the latter part of the 1980s, the role of these courts has been much reduced by the Supreme Court under the leadership of Chief Justice William Rehnquist.

APPLYING THE EIGHTH AMENDMENT TO PRISONS

Federal courts have developed several standards that are to be used in evaluating a prisoner's claim of an Eighth Amendment violation. First, the punishment in question must be both cruel *and* unusual before the Eighth Amendment can be used to limit the power of the government. Second, prison inmates do retain fundamental Bill of Rights protections, so long as those rights are compatible with the legitimate objectives of incarceration. Third, in the case of *Wilson v. Seiter* the Supreme Court has decided that the threshold question for deciding if the Eighth Amendment has been violated is if prison guards have, as part of their official conduct, engaged in the "serious deprivation of a human need" vis-à-vis prisoners. Furthermore, a prisoner seeking vindication under the Eighth Amendment must demonstrate that the prison official in question had a "culpable state of mind" when depriving a

prisoner of a human need such as food, warmth, or exercise. This means that the prison official(s) must have acted with "deliberate indifference" in depriving a prisoner of a human need—that is, he or she must know that the prisoner will face a serious risk of substantial harm and then fail to act on that knowledge. Such a claim can encompass the state's failure to protect an inmate from other prisoners, as in the case of rape or prison violence. Similarly, the government has a constitutional obligation to provide adequate medical and mental health services to needy prisoners. Prison overcrowding can also create a legal cause of action, if prison conditions subject inmates to a "substantial risk of serious harm." Finally, the government has violated the Eighth Amendment if prison officials inflict "unnecessary and wanton . . . pain." This standard of conduct, however, is qualified by a recognition that harsh punishment may be appropriate as part of the core functions of a correctional facility.

ROLE OF CONGRESS AND THE COURTS IN RECENT YEARS

Congress responded to what it saw as the illegitimate role of federal judges in determining prison policy with the Prison Litigation Reform Act of 1996 (PLRA). This piece of legislation significantly limited the ability of prisoners to bring Eighth Amendment litigation against state and federal facilities by requiring that prisoners exhaust all possible administrative remedies prior to bringing any grievances based on federal law about prison conditions to the courts. Prisoner petition appeals subsequently fell by 5% in 1997, although they rose by 8% in 1998—due, in significant part, to the rapidly growing prison population in the United States. In *Porter v. Nussle,* 534 U.S. 516 (2002), the U.S. Supreme Court ruled unanimously that the term *prison conditions* applies both to general conditions within a prison and to individual instances involving a claim of excessive force employed by a particular correctional officer. Nussle, an inmate, had argued that a single instance of excessive force applied by a guard against an inmate fell outside the PLRA's coverage of "prison conditions," and thus could be brought before a federal court via an Eighth Amendment claim without recourse to administrative remedies within the prison system itself.

The District Court for the Middle District of Alabama, in December of 2002, held that a women's prison designed to house 364 inmates violated the Eighth Amendment by allowing the prison population to reach 1,017. In the view of the court in this case, this extreme form of overcrowding subjected the inmates to a "substantial risk of serious harm." The prison administrators were then ordered to remedy this constitutional defect as quickly as possible, using their own discretion in the fashioning of a solution. The U.S. Supreme Court, however, in *Wilson v. Seiter*, held that placing two inmates in cells designed for a single person does not necessarily violate the Eighth Amendment. Rather, prisoners living under such conditions must demonstrate the "deprivation of a . . . human need [and] a culpable state of mind on the part of prison officials."

While the Supreme Court of late has been decidedly hostile to the rights of prisoners, it has not uniformly struck down all Eighth Amendment claims. In a recent case, *Hope v. Pelzer*, for example, the Court held that an Alabama prison's use of a "hitching post" to place handcuffed prisoners in the hot sun for several hours did indeed constitute the "gratuitous infliction of wanton and unnecessary pain," and thus violated the Eighth Amendment.

A limitation on the Eighth Amendment's application to incarceration facilities is the issue of what constitutes a "punishment." Conditions in jail prior to a trial, therefore, and sexual predators who are confined by the government after serving their term of detention in order to receive treatment, are not covered by the ban on cruel and unusual punishments. In such cases, however, the Fifth Amendment's due process clause would apply, and the courts have developed standards for this claim that are similar to those they have developed for the Eighth Amendment.

CONCLUSION

All of the above limitations on the ability of prisoners to invoke the Eighth Amendment on their own behalf may help to explain the limited impact that litigation has had on prison conditions in the United States. While many scholars agree that Eighth Amendment litigation has helped to ameliorate the very worst conditions in U.S. correctional facilities, several also suggest that many serious problems such as prison overcrowding and sadistic behavior by prison guards remain.

—Francis Carleton

See also Capital Punishment; Chain Gangs; Civil Commitment of Sexual Predators; Correctional Officers; *Estelle v. Gamble;* First Amendment; Fourth Amendment; Health Care; Jailhouse Lawyers; Overcrowding; Prison Litigation Reform Act 1996; Prisoner Litigation; Rape; Riots; Violence; *Wilson v. Seiter*

Further Reading

Bosworth, M. (2002). *The U.S. federal prison system.* Thousand Oaks, CA: Sage.

Developments in the law: The law of prisons: II. The Prison Litigation Reform Act and the Antiterrorism and Effective Death Penalty Act: Implications for federal district judges. (2002). [Special isssue]. *Harvard Law Review, 115,* 1846.

Hallinan, J. (2001). *Going up the river: Travels in a prison nation.* New York: Random House.

Lucero, L., & Bernhardt, J. (2002). Thirty-first annual review of criminal procedure: VI. Prisoners' rights. *Georgetown Law Review, 90,* 2005.

Rich, W. (2002). Editor's letter: Prison conditions and criminal sentencing in Kansas—A public policy dialogue. *Kansas Journal of Law and Public Policy, 11,* 693.

Rosenberg, G. (1991). *The hollow hope.* Chicago: University of Chicago Press.

Third Branch. (1999). Changing trends in prisoner petition filings. *Newsletter of the Federal Courts, 31*(12).

■ ELDERLY PRISONERS

The most common definition of an *elderly inmate* is someone aged 50 and older. The point at which someone becomes elderly has been set at 50 because research has identified a 10-year differential between the overall health of inmates and that of the general population. Most have attributed this to people's lifestyles prior to incarceration during which many used drugs and alcohol to excess, had poor eating habits, and were poor. Even so, there has been difficulty and dissent among scholars, both in corrections and in general, in reaching agreement on who classifies as an "elderly prisoner." The definition of aging is affected by many factors including physical, emotional, social, and economic changes in communities. Similarly, the processes of aging are dependent not only on time but along on the interaction of various factors such as gender, age of parents, susceptibility to disease, environment, diet, and lifestyle.

CURRENT SITUATION

There are approximately 103,132 inmates aged 50 and older in U.S. correctional facilities. Most elderly inmates are male and tend to be held in minimum-security facilities. Changes in sentencing, which have criminalized more practices and lead to longer periods of confinement for many crimes, in conjunction with a move away from early-release practices such as parole, are all contributing to a rapid growth in older inmate populations. In essence, inmates are staying longer and growing older in prisons rather than being older when entering prison.

ELDERLY PRISONER DEMOGRAPHICS

There are three main groups of elderly prisoners. First, there are the first-time inmates imprisoned at an older age. These people are highly likely to be imprisoned for a violent offense and have the most complex needs of the three groups due to their lack of familiarity with the conditions of incarceration. In the second group are repeat offenders who return to prison at a later age. They often have substance abuse problems and associated poor health. In the final group are people who have grown old in prison due to the long sentences they are serving. While prisoners in this group are likely to be well adjusted to the system, they are also very likely to be institutionalized so that their release is very difficult for them to manage. Such people may be at high risk of self-harm and suicide when they return to the community, or they may reoffend in order to be returned

to a penal institution where they will feel more comfortable.

OFFENSE CATEGORY

Most inmates over 50 years of age are imprisoned for violent offenses. Whereas age may be a mitigating factor in sentencing for most other offenses, it will have the least effect for violent offenders. Thus, older persons who commit a violent crime are more likely to be imprisoned than older people committing property or nonviolent crimes.

HOUSING

Most correctional centers are designed to accommodate young and active inmates. Elderly residents report finding the prison environment cold and damp and the stairs and distances difficult to cope with. Since they may be unable to climb stairs, they usually require ramps or wheelchair accessibility to be built. Correctional institutions designed during the 1980s often feature buildings scattered over wide areas. Inmates in these institutions are required to walk long distances to obtain meals, medical services, and other essentials. This may be difficult for elderly inmates.

Research has also found that older inmates express a greater need for privacy and for access to preventive health care and legal assistance, all of which have implications for the design or modification of correctional centers. Currently, prisons are generally designed to provide basic health care and do not have the facilities for the higher health monitoring required for older people. Overcrowding has also meant that inmates often lack of individual space and have only minimal access to services. These factors may be particularly difficult for elderly inmates to manage.

IMPLICATIONS FOR MANAGEMENT

The specific needs of elderly inmates, in particular their need for a high level of care, dramatically increase the cost of incarceration. Growing old is accompanied by an inevitable physical decline. The majority of people over 60 years of age in the community have at least one chronic health condition, use more prescription drugs, have more adverse reactions to medication, and spend twice as much time in medical facilities. The health care costs of the elderly in prison are second only to HIV/AIDS patients.

Elderly inmates in U.S. correctional facilities commonly receive more specialized medical care including chronic care clinics and preventive care. They also usually have an increased frequency of physical examinations. More than half of the correctional departments in the United States report that special nutrition/dietary care and housing and the use of inmate aides to provide nonmedical assistance are available to the elderly in their particular jurisdictions. On the other hand, very few of these agencies have special units for elderly female prisoners. Elderly women will have very different health care and other needs not only in relation to other elderly male prisoners but also to other female inmates in general. Difficulties they face include menopause, osteoporosis, and frequent difficulties with arthritis, cardiac conditions, and memory loss.

It may also be complicated to find ways of keeping older inmates occupied during their term of incarceration. There are few suitable programs and it is often difficult to find specialized and suitably trained staff. Careful staff recruitment and selection for sensitivity to the unique requirements of elderly inmates should be a considered by administrators. Suitable programs may include reading and discussion groups, modified exercise and fitness programs, and modified treatment and rehabilitation programs. Often the reasons for offending are quite different for older people and difficult to address through current rehabilitation programs.

Certain legislation must be considered when developing and implementing policies, processes, and programs for older inmates. Antidiscrimination law, such as the Americans with Disabilities Act, addresses age and can affect issues such as opportunity to work, transport, and access to health care and buildings. It must be carefully considered by correctional administrators.

CONCLUSION

Research shows that while elderly inmates may appear better adjusted to prison life and less disruptive than younger inmates, many have more extensive psychological and emotional difficulties. Older inmates frequently express fear of being victimized by younger prisoners and suffer from greater social isolation within the correctional environment. Such differences from the mainstream prison populations mean that elderly inmates require more physical and personal resources than other types of inmates in correctional centers.

—Anna Alice Grant

See also Clemency; Furlough; Health Care; HIV/AIDS; Hospice; Increase in Prison Population; Indeterminate Sentencing; Just Deserts Theory; Parole; Prison Culture; Prison Industrial Complex; Sentencing Reform Act 1984; Truth in Sentencing; War on Drugs

Further Reading

Aday, R. H. (1994). Golden years behind bars: Special programs and facilities for elderly inmates. *Federal Probation, 58*(2), 47–54.

Correction yearbook. (2000). Retrieved from http://www.cji-inc.com/cyb/download/000ver50.pdf

Hartjen, C., & Rhine, E. (1992). Ageing inmate offenders: Another perspective. In C. Hartjen & E. Rhine (Eds.), *Correctional theory and practice*. Chicago: Nelson Hall.

Kesley, O. W. (1986). Elderly inmates: Providing safe and humane care. *Corrections Today, 48*(3), 56, 58.

Krajick, K. (1979). Growing old in prison. *Corrections Magazine, 5*(1), 33–46.

Kratcoski, P., & Babb, S. (1990). Adjustment of older inmates: An analysis by institutional structure and gender. *Journal of Contemporary Criminal Justice, 6*(4), 264–281.

Kratcoski, P., & Pownall, G. (1989). Federal Bureau of Prisons programming for older inmates. *Federal Probation, 53*(2), 28–35.

LIS Inc. (1997, September). *Prison medical care: Special issues in corrections*. National Institute of Corrections. Retrieved from http://www.nicic.org/pubs/prisons.htm

Mays, G. L., & Wintree, L. T. (1998). *Contemporary corrections*. Belmont, CA: Wadsworth.

Morton, J. (1992). *An administrative overview of the older inmate*. National Institute of Corrections. Retrieved from http://www.nicic.org/pubs/prisons.htm

Morton, J., & Anderson, J. (1982). Elderly offenders: The forgotten minority. *Corrections Today, 44*(6), 14–16, 20.

◪ ELECTRONIC MONITORING

Electronic monitoring emerged in the United States in the early 1980s, at a time when prison overcrowding and costs necessitated the development of alternative strategies for supervising offenders. Electronic monitoring involves the use of telemetric technology to monitor the presence or absence of an offender in a specified monitored location. The surveillance technology is often coupled with community sanctions such as probation or home confinement, also known as house arrest, to ensure compliance with specified conditions such as curfew. The objectives of electronic monitoring, like other alternative correctional measures, are to protect society through offender supervision, decrease the use of incarceration among less serious offenders, punish offenders, and support rehabilitation.

PROGRAMS AND TECHNOLOGIES

Electronic monitoring programs are run by state departments of corrections, local courts and law enforcement agencies, and private contractors, depending on the jurisdiction in which the program is run. There is a great deal of variation in the administration of this penal strategy. For example, programs may target specific populations, and offense types, and vary in their hours of operation. Some charge the offender a fee, while others do not.

Electronic monitoring exists at all stages of the criminal justice system from pretrial to postrelease supervision. Thus, surveillance may be used as (1) an alternative to pretrial detention, (2) a sanction meted out at time of sentencing, (3) an alternative to custody that is offered postsentencing, (4) a tool to ensure compliance with a work release program, or (5) a condition of probation or parole.

There are two main types of monitoring technology currently in use: *continuous signaling* and *programmed contact*. Continuous signaling involves the use of three devices: a transmitter that is worn by the offender on the ankle or wrist, a receiver-dialer attached to a telephone in the monitored location, and a central computer that receives the transmitted information. The transmitter sends signals to the receiver-dialer, which contacts the central computer at the monitoring center whenever there is a change in the offender's status (entering or leaving the monitored location). The offender's approved schedule is stored within the central computer, allowing for a comparison between the signaled change in status and the offender's schedule to ensure compliance and detect violations.

Programmed contact technology involves the use of equipment that initiates periodic telephone calls to the location under surveillance (usually the offender's home) to verify the offender's presence. Verification may occur by having the offender insert a worn device, or wristlet, into a verifier box that is attached to the phone. This is known as an "electronic handshake." Verification may also be established using voice verification technology, video verification, or by having the offender call an 800 number and typing in a random code provided by a device worn by the monitored person to establish ID.

For individuals who do not have a telephone, a drive-by unit may be used for monitoring purposes. A transmitter worn by the offender will send out signals that an officer can receive by tuning a receiving device into the frequency of the monitor. The person will not be aware of when checks are being conducted.

Hybrid electronic monitoring equipment, combining continuous signaling and programmed contact technology, is now also being used. When continuous signaling equipment notes a deviation from the offender's approved schedule, he or she will be contacted by telephone to allow for verification of his or her location.

Electronic monitoring programs may also use alcohol-testing systems to ensure compliance with a condition to abstain from alcohol use. There are four types of alcohol testing systems currently available. The simpler tests provide only an indication that the offender has consumed alcohol, while more sophisticated testing systems measure a person's actual blood alcohol level.

ELIGIBILITY FOR ELECTRONIC MONITORING: WHO IS BEING MONITORED?

Due to the variance in the administration of electronic monitoring programs across the United

States, no one set of eligibility criteria exists. Rather, individual programs define and operate under their own regulations.

Electronic monitoring is currently in use with both adult and juvenile offenders. While both male and female offenders are eligible, the majority of those being monitored are male. Most offenders under this type of surveillance have committed nonviolent offenses. However, there are some monitoring programs that specifically target high-risk offenders who are considered to be at risk for recidivism. These programs increase the level of supervision for selected recently released offenders, allowing correctional officials to watch their reintegration into the community.

To be considered for most electronic monitoring programs, an offender must have a structured living arrangement and either be currently employed or actively seeking work. While some programs accept only those who do not have a history of serious substance abuse, other programs are specifically designed for offenders who have been convicted of driving while under the influence (DUI) or drug law violations.

PREVALENCE OF USE AND EFFECTIVENESS

Currently, electronic monitoring programs are operated in some form in most, if not all, U.S. states. Because such programs are operated at various levels of government and by nongovernment agencies, and their duration is relatively short, it is difficult to obtain accurate information regarding the number of individuals being monitored at any given time. While electronic monitoring programs have grown rapidly, the percentage of offenders being supervised in this way compared to the total number of offenders under some form of supervision is extremely small. Recent estimates suggest that approximately 28,000 to 30,000 people are currently being electronically monitored across the United States, equaling only 0.6% of the total offender population.

Determining the effectiveness of electronic monitoring is complicated by a dearth of experimental studies that evaluate them. Existing evaluations use various indicators of success, including rates of completion and recidivism, and the number of violations accumulated while participating in a program. Success rates for electronic monitoring vary dramatically, ranging from 30% to 100%. These rates are affected by a program's rules and regulations and its approach to dealing with violations, as some programs are very strict and will terminate an offender's participation upon first violation whereas others will assess the violation and provide offenders with warnings. Most revocations from electronic monitoring programs are the result of technical violations, not the commission of a new offense. At present, it is unclear whether electronic monitoring is more effective in terms of successful completion and rates of recidivism than other community sanctions.

SOME STRENGTHS AND WEAKNESSES OF ELECTRONIC MONITORING

Arguably, one of the greatest strengths of electronic monitoring is that it provides an intermediate sanction between the extremes of probation, which offers minimal or limited supervision, and incarceration, which entails total supervision. Surveillance of this nature enables individuals to maintain family and community ties and employment during the sanctioning period. The maintenance of these supports may decrease their likelihood of reoffending, particularly important for juvenile offenders. Offenders placed on electronic monitoring are also able to avoid the stigma of imprisonment.

Electronic monitoring is also a means for avoiding what has been termed "offender contamination," that is, exposing first-time or nonserious offenders to the more experienced offenders found in prisons. Despite the less restrictive nature of surveillance as compared to incarceration, it has been reported as having a stabilizing affect on the lives of monitored offenders, as they become accustomed to a routine of attending work and spending time in the home. Offenders under electronic`surveillance may be made to pay restitution to their victim as a condition of their program. Electronic monitoring programs have also had some success in effectively treating certain types of offenders such as those convicted of DUI, drug, and other nonviolent offenses. Finally, the costs associated with this strategy are far less than the costs of incarceration.

Despite numerous strengths, electronic monitoring also has a number of weaknesses. The technology associated with it has had to be continually upgraded to deal with numerous technical problems such as the incompatibility of phone lines, radio frequency interference, and transmission blockage due to environmental conditions. Although many companies have added tamper detection equipment to their techniques, offenders continue to remove or disable monitoring devices and avoid detection.

The implementation of electronic monitoring programs may, in some instances, widen the net of criminal justice control by punishing individuals who would have otherwise been diverted from the justice system. When used with serious or high-risk offenders, it has been criticized for failing to adequately protect the public, as those who are under surveillance are free to be in the community unescorted.

Although electronic monitoring was initially implemented in response to increasing prison overcrowding, it has had only a minimal impact on decreasing prison populations. It has also been criticized for turning the home into a prison. In doing so, electronic monitoring may have a negative impact on other inhabitants of the household, whose lives are disrupted by numerous phone checks, unannounced home visits from correctional workers, and having a member of their family restricted to the home. Relapse after program completion is also a concern, as offenders must adjust to the process of going from the intensive supervision of electronic surveillance to minimal or no supervision.

THE USE OF ELECTRONIC MONITORING INTERNATIONALLY

Electronic monitoring is in use or has been considered for use in a number of countries around the world including Canada, Singapore, Australia, Sweden, and the United Kingdom. In Canada, it has not been implemented by the federal government,

but rather programs are run at the provincial level in four provinces: British Columbia, Saskatchewan, Newfoundland, and Ontario. Surveillance programs of this nature developed slowly in Canada and are subject to a great deal of variation in program administration. In Canada, electronic monitoring is used to enhance compliance with house arrest and may be initiated by the courts or by corrections depending on jurisdiction.

Like in Canada, electronic monitoring in the United Kingdom has developed slowly. While the strategy was introduced by the Criminal Justice Act of 1991, this sanctioning option was not used until 1994. In the United Kingdom, electronic monitoring has two main uses: (1) part of an order of probation lasting less than six months and (2) a home detention curfew whereby an offender will spend the last two months of a custodial sentence in the home under electronic surveillance. Electronic monitoring is a national program in the United Kingdom and is supervised by the Home Office.

CONCLUSION: THE FUTURE OF ELECTRONIC MONITORING

Electronic monitoring technology continues to be developed to enhance the supervision capabilities of correctional officials. Equipment has now been created that links the individual to the global positioning system (GPS). The coupling of electronic surveillance with GPS removes the restrictions of monitoring the offender in only one or a small number of locations and enables the continuous tracking of offenders. Future advances in monitoring technology involve the creation of tracking devices that may be implanted into the body of the monitored individual. This device would be able to signal the location of the offender at all times and monitor such activities as drug use or alcohol consumption associated with offending.

—*Melissa Baker*

See also Community Corrections Centers; Furlough; Home Arrest; Intermediate Sanctions; Minimum Security; Overcrowding; Pretrial Detainees; Prerelease Programs; Recidivism; Work-Release Programs

Further Reading

Bonta, J., Rooney, J., & Wallace-Capretta, S. (1999). *Electronic monitoring in Canada* (User report). Ottawa, ON: Solicitor General Canada.

Payne, B. K., & Gainey, R. R. (2000). Electronic monitoring: Philosophical, systemic, and political issues. *Journal of Offender Rehabilitation, 31*(3/4), 93–111.

Schmidt, A. K. (1994). Electronic monitoring in the United States. In U. Zvekic (Ed.), *Alternatives to imprisonment in comparative perspective.* Turin, Italy: United Nations Interregional Crime and Justice Research Institute.

Schmidt, A. K. (1998). Electronic monitoring: What does the literature tell us? *Federal Probation, 62*(2), 10–19.

Whitfield, D. (1997). *Tackling the tag: The electronic monitoring of offenders.* Winchester, UK: Waterside.

☫ ELMIRA REFORMATORY

"Elmira" conjures up both the best and the worst of prison history in the United States. Though it is most commonly known for the reformatory that bore its name, Elmira, New York, was originally a prison opened to contain Confederate prisoners of war during the Civil War. It became known as a "death camp" because of the squalid conditions and high death rate in its few years of operation. Approximately one-quarter of the 12,000 Southern prisoners died there between summer 1864 and the war's conclusion in 1865. Today, only a large stone plaque in the current residential area marks the prison once known as "Helmira."

The opening of New York State's Elmira Reformatory at a different site in 1876 marked an important shift in the history of U.S. penology. Built as the first rehabilitation-oriented institution in the country, the ideals of the early-19th-century's penitentiary model, which were embodied in the Pennsylvania and Auburn systems, were supplanted by the new ideals of the reformatory movement. Fixed sentences intended to fit the crime were replaced by the new indeterminate sentence designed to fit the criminal. Mass discipline and physical punishment would give way to individual classification, with privileges as rewards. Instead of releasing the criminal unconditionally after his debt to society was paid, the reformatory's "new parole procedure would assure he did not begin running up a new tab" (Elmira, 1998).

CONSTRUCTION AND DESIGN

In 1869, the New York State Legislature authorized the purchase of 280 acres of land in Elmira. The original plans for the reformatory made provisions for 500 prisoners. Cellblocks would be arranged so that prisoners could be divided by classification, but not completely isolated. Construction soon began, with the majority of physical labor done by inmates from other state prisons. Elmira received its first prisoners in July 1876. Thirty inmates transferred from the Auburn Prison to help finish construction, with others following as the construction progressed. By 1879, the $1.5 million project was nearly completed, and the appearance of the institution reflected its purpose. Zebulon Brockway (1969), superintendent of Elmira from 1876 until 1900, commented:

> The very outward appearance of the reformatory so little like the ordinary prison and so much like a college or a hospital helps to change the common sentiment about offenders from the vindictiveness of punishment to the amenities of rational educational correction. (p. 163)

This thinking spawned a new vocabulary at Elmira. The institution itself was referred to as "the college on the hill" or "a reformatory hospital." Inmates were deemed "students" or "patients" (Blomberg & Lucken, 2000, p. 71).

INDETERMINATE SENTENCES AND INSTITUTIONAL PROGRAMS

Elmira's reformatory program was, originally, intended for first-time felons between the ages of 16 and 30 and was developed by Brockway. It combined the indeterminate sentence, a mark system of classification, and parole. The first indeterminate sentencing law, which also was drafted by Brockway, was enacted in New York in 1877 and applied only to the Elmira Reformatory. This law retained the maximum penalties in the state statutes while typically setting the minimum sentence at one year. The amount of time served between the minimum and maximum was up to the supervisor and,

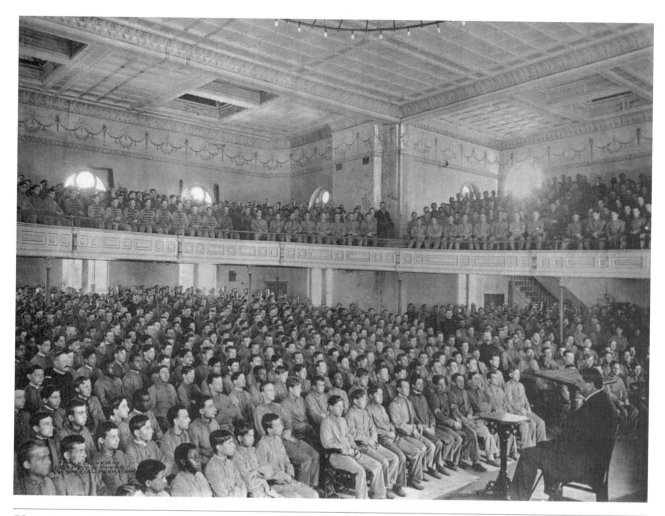

Photo 1   *Elmira*

ultimately, the prisoner himself (Witmer, 1925). According to Brockway (1910),

> The indeterminate sentence was important for reformation in that . . . the indeterminateness of the sentence breeds discontent, broods purposefulness, and prompts to new exertion. Captivity, always irksome, is now increasingly so because the duty and responsibility of shortening it and of modifying any undesirable present condition of it devolves upon the prisoner himself, and, again, by the active exactions of the standard and criterion to which he must attain. (p. 470)

To shorten his sentence, the prisoner was forced to adhere to the reformatory program. Not only did this entail good behavior, but he also was required to earn good marks in work and school. Elmira's

educational program consisted of inmates, college professors, public school teachers, and lawyers teaching a wide range of general subjects, as well as sports, religion, and military drill. In addition, a trade school served to provide inmates with the entry-level skills needed for work in such fields as tailor cutting, plumbing, telegraphy, and printing.

THE MARK SYSTEM

Progress through Brockway's reformation program was traced through a mark system of classification, similar to the merit and demerit system used in military academies. Upon entering the reformatory, an individual was placed in the second of three grades for an observation period of six months. If he failed to comply with the program, he would be demoted to the third grade where he would stay until he proved himself worthy of returning to the second grade. Demotion to the third grade meant increased punishment and the loss of privileges. The inmate would be placed in a red uniform and forced to march in lockstep. In addition, he would be denied writing, mail, and visitation privileges. On the other hand, six months of good behavior in the second grade would earn an inmate promotion to the first grade and the privileges that went along with it.

The first grade entitled the inmate to a comfortable blue uniform, a spring mattress, better food, and extended library and bedtime hours. An additional six months of good behavior in the first grade, coupled with other criteria, such as the inmate's offense of conviction, number of marks earned or lost, attitude, history and future plans, would determine the inmate's eligibility for parole. Parole, which was typically set at a minimum of six months, served as a test to determine how much of the reformation program had been absorbed. Once on parole, the prisoner worked at prearranged employment in the field in which he had been trained, with required "monthly reports certified by the employer and [parole] supervisor." Upon completion of this trial period of freedom, and barring any setbacks on behalf of the prisoner, he would become a free man (Brockway, 1969, p. 324).

CONCLUSION

By the time Brockway retired in 1900, the population of Elmira had grown to roughly 1,500 inmates. Even though the end of his career was marred by investigations into physical and psychological abuse at the institution, many of his original programs had remained in place, most notably the classification system. Brockway would interview each new inmate to discover any potential problems or needs, and then place him in programs that could best reform that inmate. These ideas were expanded in 1917 by Dr. Frank Christian, one of Brockway's successors. The culmination of Brockway's and Christian's work was the building of a reception center at Elmira in 1945, which officially became a part of the main facility in 1970, resulting in the reformatory being renamed the Elmira Correctional and Reception Center.

Even though Elmira is no longer a reformatory, many of the programs that began with Brockway can be seen in the modern institution. The reception center still has an active educational and industrial programs, as do many other prisons across the nation. In addition, although indeterminate sentences and parole have been criticized, they, along with classifications of prisoners and the use of privileges as rewards, still serve key functions in corrections today.

—Josh Stone

See also Zebulon Reed Brockway; Corporal Punishment; Determinate Sentencing; Flogging History of Prisons; Indeterminate Sentence; Irish (or Crofton) System; Juvenile Justice System; Juvenile Reformatories; Alexander Maconochie; Massachusetts Reformatory; Parole

Further Reading

Blomberg, T. G., & Lucken, C. (2000). *American penology.* New York: Aldine de Gruyter.

Brockway, Z. R. (1910). The American reformatory prison system. *American Journal of Sociology, 15*(4), 454–477.

Brockway, Z. R. (1969). *Fifty years of prison service: An autobiography.* Montclair, NJ: Patterson Smith.

Elmira. (1998, October). *DOCS Today.* Retrieved from http://www.geocities.com/MotorCity/Downs/3548/facility/elmira.html

Farr, G. R. (n.d.) *The federal Confederate prisoner of war camp at Elmira.* Retrieved from http://www.rootsweb.com/~srgp/military/elmcivwr.htm

Gray, M. P. (1999). *Elmira, a city on a prison-camp contract.* Retrieved from http://www.gloverfamily.com/civilwar/elmira/elmirahistory.htm

Rotman, E. (1990). *Beyond punishment: A new view on the rehabilitation of criminal offenders.* New York: Greenwood.

Witmer, H. L. (1925). The development of parole in the United States. *Social Forces, 4*(2), 318–325.

◼ ENEMY COMBATANTS

In 2001, the Bush administration coined the term *unlawful combatant* (later renamed *enemy combatant*) to describe certain individuals either captured during the war in Afghanistan or suspected of having links to the terrorist organization Al-Qaeda. Currently, any individual who the administration deems a threat or danger to the United States, including "citizens who associating themselves with the enemy and with its aid, guidance, and direction, or enter into this country bent on hostile acts are enemy belligerents" (U.S. District Court, Lower Manhattan, *U.S. v. Padilla* [2002]), may be defined as an enemy combatant. In other words, U.S. citizens may also be designated as enemy combatants.

As of March 2003, two Americans have been categorized in this way: Jose Padilla and Yassar Esam Hamdi. Padilla was named an enemy combatant in June 2002 after he was "captured" not on a battlefield, but at Chicago's O'Hare Airport. The government says he was planning to detonate a radiological bomb in America. Padilla was transferred to a Navy brig in South Carolina where he has been questioned by military interrogators and denied contact with outsiders, including his attorney. He has not been charged with a crime. Hamdi is an American-born Saudi who was captured in Afghanistan. He is being detained at a Navy brig in Virginia. Provisions for future enemy combatants include a special wing at Goose Creek (SC Navy Brig) to accommodate up to 20 U.S. citizens. Attorney General John Ashcroft is said to have announced additional plans to construct detention camps for U.S. citizens deemed as enemy combatants.

Categorization as an enemy combatant denies a captive access to the rights of the Geneva Convention to which prisoners of war are entitled. Enemy combatants are not permitted contact with lawyers, family, or friends. They may also be denied counsel, detained indefinitely, and held incommunicado, without due process and without review of their designation as enemy combatants by the U.S. Court of Appeals.

ORIGINS OF THE TERM

The term *enemy combatant* derives from two sources: international law and the 1942 U.S. Supreme Court *Ex parte Quirin* (317 U.S. 1) decision that pertained to eight suspected Nazi saboteurs, one of whom was a U.S. citizen. International law

recognizes combatants and noncombatants in Article 3 of the Geneva Convention Rules of War (Hague 4, Chapter 1, Article 3, October 18, 1907). The terminology articulates who qualifies for prisoner of war status in order to establish who is then duly protected with rights. Article 3 states: "The armed forces of the belligerent parties may consist of combatants and non-combatants. In the case of capture by the enemy, both have a right to be treated as prisoners of war." International law standards for noncombatant status are reserved for persons accompanying the armed forces without being members, such as civilian members of military aircraft crews, war correspondents, supply contractors, members of labor units or of services responsible for the welfare of the armed forces (Article 4:4, Hague Convention 3, 1949). *Combatant* is defined by the following standards: "(a) That of being commanded by a person responsible for his subordinates; (b) that of having a fixed distinctive sign recognizable at a distance; (c) that of carrying arms openly; (d) that of conducting their operations in accordance with the laws and customs of war" (Article 4:2, Hague Convention 3, 1949).

In the 1942 *Quirin* case, the Supreme Court defined enemy combatant' with the same terminology as spies were then viewed under international law. That is to say, unlawful combatants were judged to be the same as spies, who engage in secretive passage through military lines, without uniform (a criteria under international law for prisoner of war [POW]) in a time of war for the purpose of waging war by destruction of life or property. This renders such individuals belligerents who are not entitled to the status of POW or offenders against the law of war and therefore subject to trial. Such individuals are subject to trial and punishment by military tribunals. Since *Quirin,* no new case has elaborated or superseded this definition.

IMPLICATIONS FOR THE FUTURE

At the time of writing, the implications of U.S. citizens being detained under military rule and denied constitutional rights continues to the subject of vigorous debate. On September 5, 2002, Senators Carl

Levin and Russ Feingold wrote to Attorney General John Ashcroft and Defense Secretary Donald Rumsfeld seeking clarification of the new category of enemy combatant in eight areas. Specifically, they requested the operative definition along with a document providing a clear and distinct definition (and its sources), the process by which individuals may be given this label, and the criteria used in its determination. They also wanted to know about the rights of U.S. citizens named as enemy combatants, the time line for detention, any documented changes to existing U.S. military regulations implementing the Geneva Convention of 1949, and an un-redacted copy of the president's orders designating Padillo and Hamdi as enemy combatants.

Around this same period, the American Bar Association (ABA) took two unprecedented actions condemning the practice of the Bush administration. In a resolution on August 13, 2002, the ABA denounced the secret detention of people by the Immigration and Naturalization Service (INS). On August 9, 2002, the ABA released a preliminary report addressing the government's ability to detain U.S. citizens as enemy combatants. The ABA cited Section 4001(a) of the 1971 U.S. Criminal Code that states: "No citizen shall be imprisoned or otherwise detained by the US except pursuant to an Act of Congress."

CONCLUSION

Individuals detained and labeled as enemy combatants without the process afforded by the U.S. Constitution or international law have almost no legal rights or safeguards. While supporters of this change of policy point to the need for safeguarding homeland security since the terrorist attacks on the Pentagon and the World Trade Center in New York City on September 11, 2001, critics argue that the current rule of law could become a malleable tool during times of peace and war.

—Dawn Rothe

See also First Amendment; Foreign Nationals; Fourth Amendment; Prisoner of War Camps; Eighth Amendment; USA PATRIOT Act 2001

Further Reading

Avalon Project. (2002). *Convention between the United States of America and other powers, relating to prisoners of war.* Retrieved from http://www.yale.edu/lawweb/avalon/lawofwar/geneva02.htm

Ex parte Quirin 317 U.S. 1 87 L. Ed. 317 U.S. 1 (1942).

Human Rights Watch. (2002). Human Rights Watch home page. Retrieved from http://www.hrw.org

International Criminal Court. (2002). International Criminal Court home page. Retrieved from http://www.iccnow.org/

[President Bush's June 9, 2002, order declaring Jose Padilla, a U.S. citizen, to be an enemy combatant.] (2002). Retrieved from http://news.findlaw.com/hdocs/docs/terrorism/padillabush60902det.pdf

Sonnett, N. R., et al. (2002). *ABA Task Force on Treatment of Enemy Combatants, preliminary report* 10–11. Retrieved from http://abanet.org/poladv/letters/exec/enemycombatantareport.pdf

U.S. Code. 18 U.S.C. 4001(a).

Winthrop, Military Law (2nd ed.). Instructions for the Government of Armies of the United States in the Field Approved by the President, General order No. 100, 4/1863, Sections 4 & 5.

Turley, J. (2002, August 14). Camps for citizens: Ashcroft's hellish vision. *Los Angeles Times.*

◼ ENGLAND AND WALES

Imprisonment is the harshest penalty available to the courts of England and Wales, since the death penalty was abolished for murder in 1969. Currently, around 110,000 offenders are each year committed to the 137 institutions that make up the prison system, providing employment for more than 43,000 staff to keep them there. All of this stands in stark contrast to the situation just over 50 years ago, when, in 1946, there were about 40 prisons, approximately 15,000 prisoners, and around 2,000 staff (Morgan, 2002, p. 1117). The reasons for this striking increase are complex, yet there is considerable consensus that the prison system in England and Wales has been in a state of ever-deepening crisis since the early 1970s.

Even though conclusions drawn from international comparisons should always be treated with caution, it is clear that England and Wales consistently use imprisonment to a greater extent than practically every other country in Western Europe.

In 2002, for instance, 139 persons were incarcerated per 100,000 population in England and Wales, compared to 96 in Germany, 95 in Italy, 93 in the Netherlands, and 68 in Sweden (Walmsley, 2003, p. 5). Such crude comparisons also indicate that England and Wales lie behind the global leaders in imprisonment—Russia, the United States, China, and South Africa—as well as most of the countries in Eastern Europe. Of course, these international differences can only be properly explained through separate and detailed analyses of the political changes, cultural sensibilities, economic landscapes, and social histories that each of these societies has experienced. Such a task is beyond the scope of this entry; instead the more modest ambition is to chart the historical origins of imprisonment and provide an overview of contemporary problems that sustain the prison crisis.

THE ORIGINS OF IMPRISONMENT

Any attempt to identify the exact moment when the prison was born in England and Wales is an exercise doomed to failure. For as Christopher Harding and his colleagues (Harding, Hines, Ireland, & Rawlings, 1985) point out, some form "of detention becomes necessary as soon as disputes over wrongs come to be settled in any but the most immediate and brutal fashion" (p. 3). According to the historian Ralph Pugh (1968, p. 1) the holding of defendants prior to trial was probably the earliest use of imprisonment, a practice that dates from the ninth century in England. At this time, the accused were held awaiting "gaol delivery" (the arrival of traveling courts) usually in makeshift structures such as castle dungeons, hall cellars, town gates, and stables.

Imprisonment in medieval England came to serve three main uses: *custodial* (detaining those waiting trial or sentence), *coercive* (forcing fine defaulters and debtors into making good their misfortune), and *punitive* (as punishment in its own right). The main role of early prisons was to detain rather than punish, with the coercive function used almost exclusively for recovering civil debt. The punitive potential of imprisonment was not thought to be useful until the late 18th century. Until this

point, the customary forms of punishment were primarily corporal or capital including banishment, execution, mutilation, branding, whipping, and forms of public shaming.

As the feudal system began to break down and mercantile capitalism emerged, significant numbers of people migrated from rural areas to the burgeoning towns and cities. This new population was widely viewed as troublesome, and thought to spread crime, poverty, and unemployment. In response, a range of secular institutions that are usually understood to be the precursors of modern imprisonment emerged across Europe in the 16th and 17th centuries. The *hôpital général* in France, the *spinhuis* and *rasphuis* in Amsterdam, and Bridewells and workhouses in Britain were all used to confine the growing numbers of poor, homeless, and dispossessed citizens. Britain and France also transported offenders to their colonies.

It was not until the 18th century that the prison was really established as the best response to crime, as opposed to the former public spectacles of suffering such as capital punishment or flogging. There are competing explanations as to why the prison came to be the dominant response to crime at this time, from capitalism to technological advancements and legal changes. The role of religious reformers such as John Howard and Elizabeth Fry was also crucial. Such figures were opposed to the indiscriminate mixing of men and women in the Bridewells, workhouses, and local gaols. They were also concerned about the lack of segregation between the tried and the untried, the open sale of alcohol, gambling, and the generally filthy conditions, where diseases like typhus were rife.

Guided by religious piety and Enlightenment reason the reformers advocated the benefits of classification, isolation, and sanitation. Howard's widely publicized description of the abuses and distress encountered in these institutions and his comprehensive proposals for change, combined with the American War of Independence of 1776, which left the government with nowhere to send those sentenced to transportation, ultimately led to the 1779 Penitentiary Act. This act promoted a new vision of imprisonment that would unite the punitive and reformative through hard labor and religious instruction in a system where prisoners were classified into groups, and profits from their labor were used to pay staff. Nearly 100 years later, in 1877, the penal system was finally fully brought under centralized state control.

THE MODERN PRISON SYSTEM

The prison system has changed considerably since the 19th century. While the big Victorian prisons hold the majority of prisoners, there is now a range of more recently constructed institutions as well. In many respects, prisons in England and Wales fall into one of two categories. First, there are local prisons and remand centers whose primary task is to receive and deliver prisoners to the courts, and to allocate those serving sufficiently long enough sentences to the second category of institutions. These are Young Offender Institutions and adult training prisons, which are further subdivided into closed and open institutions for men and women. This subdivision reflects a prisoner security classification and the level of security that institutions provide. All prisoners are classified A, B, C, or D according to a scheme devised in 1966 by Lord Mountbatten following a series of notorious prison escapes.

Category A prisoners are those "whose escape would be highly dangerous to the public or police or to the security of the state" and while Mountbatten thought that such prisoners would probably be no more than 120, a recent estimate puts the current figure at some 700 (Morgan, 2002, p. 1143). At the opposite end of the spectrum, Category D prisoners are those "who could be trusted under open conditions." Category B and C prisoners are those in between, who are held in closed conditions providing more or less security. Trial and remand prisoners, with the exceptions of those provisionally categorized as A, are all assumed to be Category B.

Where to house sentenced Category A prisoners has been the subject of long-running controversy. Mountbatten called for the concentration of all such individuals into one single-purpose maximum-security fortress that would not only ensure that high-risk prisoners were kept in secure surroundings but

that security could be relaxed in other regimes. This proposal was quickly rejected on the basis that housing all high-risk prisoners together would mean that maintaining order and providing a constructive regime would be near impossible in a prison composed of "no-hopers." Instead a policy of "dispersal" was adopted, in which maximum-security prisoners are spread around among a few high-security prisons known as dispersal prisons. There are currently five of these institutions plus a further five that have high-security arrangements.

Even though the dispersal policy might have solved the problem of perimeter security since high-security prisons are very difficult to escape from, it has intensified the problems of internal control. For within the prison system the presence of a small number of maximum-security prisoners affects the vast majority of other prisoners who are subjected to much more restrictive and oppressive regimes so that high-security conditions are met.

The system of classification maintains a sharp differentiation between dispersal, training, and local prisons, to the extent that the latter have come to bear the brunt of the chronic overcrowding, squalid conditions, and understaffing, while the dispersal and training prisons have to a large extent been protected. The rationale behind this policy is the assumption that for prisoners serving short sentences there is too little time to achieve results, so that these prisoners all too often bear the brunt of the substantial problems faced in the penal system and where the sense of crisis is most palpable. It is important to recognize that the crisis is composed of the following sets of interrelated issues: an expanding prison population that contributes to overcrowding and decrepit conditions, which does much to undermine the authority and legitimacy of the system while constituting a number of troubling social consequences that are now outlined.

CONTEMPORARY CRISES

The Expanding Prison Population

Since the 1950s, the growth in the prison population has consistently kept apace of available space in penal institutions. This is in marked contrast to the era between the two World Wars, when prisons were routinely half full. For instance, in 1928 there were only just over 11,000 prisoners in a system that could offer 20,000 cells. By 1938 the number of prisoners remained around the 11,000 mark, but many prisons had been closed on the grounds that they were no longer required (Stern, 1993, p. 24). In contrast, during the postwar era there was a fivefold increase in recorded crime from 280,000 in 1938 to 1,334,000 in 1965. During this period, the courts' proportionate use of imprisonment actually decreased as the fine replaced probation as the main form of sentence, yet the prison population tripled—from 11,100 in 1938 to 32,500 in 1968 (Bottoms, 1987, p. 181).

Even though the prison population rose modestly during the 1980s, and reached a peak at around 50,000 in 1988–1989, it then declined in the early 1990s to around 45,000. Between 1993 and 1998, it increased rapidly by some 47% to reach 65,300 and then declined slightly only to increase from January 2001 to reach a new peak of 71,220 in June 2002 (Home Office, 2002). Nevertheless, it is important to recognize that there has been a "twin-track" approach operating across criminal justice policy since at least the mid-1970s, where successive governments have pursued both "soft" and "tough" sentencing options simultaneously. In mid-1980, for instance, 22% of prisoners were serving sentences of more than four years; by mid-2000 this figure stood at 46% of adult male prisoners (Home Office, 2001, p. 76). These changes are partly explained by the introduction of parole in 1967 and subsequent developments in its use, but the important point to note is that long-term prisoners dominate life both numerically and culturally in most training prisons and consequently preoccupy prison administrators, with important consequences for the remaining prisoners.

Overcrowding and Conditions

The prison system in England and Wales is seriously overcrowded. The effects of the sheer numbers contribute to a sense of crisis in many ways. Most obviously, the overcrowding has a deleterious impact on conditions. Prisoners who begin their carceral career, and most do, in a local prison will typically find themselves in the midst of the worse conditions

that the penal system can inflict, where overcrowding has been a daily feature of life within many of these institutions for more than three decades. The dilapidated physical conditions in which prisoners are contained combined with poor sanitation, scarcely edible food, decaying cramped cells, clothing shortages, and brief, inadequate family visits compound this wretchedness. Moreover, since there is neither the space, facilities, nor resources to provide training, work, and educational opportunities when there are too many prisoners to cope with, most people remain idle. Such abject conditions have been condemned by the European Committee for the Prevention of Torture, which concluded in 1991 that the overcrowding, unsanitary facilities, and impoverished regimes found at three Victorian local prisons amounted to inhumane and degrading treatment.

Authority and Legitimacy

Criminologists in Britain routinely portray a crisis of authority and legitimacy in the prison system. Here they refer not only to the long and bitter industrial relations between prison staff and management but also to major changes in the philosophy and organizational form of prison administration. In the postwar era, there has been a shift in the source of authority in prisons from a highly personalized form of charismatic power to systems based on bureaucratic rules and procedures. Further organizational changes have meant that the Prison Service, formerly a Department of State within the Home Office, became a semiautonomous executive agency in 1993 and privatization (the contracting out of public services to the private sector) is now an important and controversial feature of the penal landscape. For its critics, the turn to managerialist issues in the 1980s and 1990s has only served to undermine a sense of mission to the service, save for meeting narrow management objectives and performance indicators.

SOCIAL CONSEQUENCES

Gendered Prisons

As in other judicial systems, English prisons predominantly hold young adult men and most commentators agree that the organization and culture of the prison system reflect this dominance to the extent that there are very different regimes for male and female prisoners. For instance, women prisoners have tended to be thought of as mad or sad rather than bad, and their regimes have reinforced traditional stereotypes of motherhood and domesticity. There are only a dozen or so women's institutions in the English prison system, making it both extremely difficult for women in prison to sustain relationships with friends and family while compounding their overall marginalization in research and policy areas.

Nonetheless, the drastic increases in the female prison population over the past decade and a series of scandals have pushed the issue of women's imprisonment to the forefront of policy debates. For instance, between 1990 and 1998 the female prison population doubled, and reached 3,350 in 2000, the highest level since 1901 (Home Office, 2001). The sense of crisis in women's prisons extends far beyond numbers. For example, since the mid-1990s the media have widely reported on the shocking practices of manacling mothers in labor and degrading methods of drug testing. In addition, Holloway Prison, the largest prison for women, was deemed too filthy to inspect by the Chief Prisons Inspector; and in 2002 more women killed themselves in prison than ever before. Nevertheless, there are some signs that the government is sufficiently concerned about the increase in women prisoners to have published the *Strategy for Women Offenders* with a view to reducing the number of women in prison (NACRO, 2001/02, pp. 27–28).

Ethnicity, Nationality, and Racism

As in the United States, prisoners in England and Wales are disproportionately young, poor, ethnic minorities. They also possess few occupational skills or academic qualifications and are likely to be suffering from psychiatric distress. Recent figures indicate that 19% of male prisoners and 25% of female prisoners are members of ethnic minorities; two thirds of them are Afro-Caribbean (Morgan, 2002, p. 1133). There are a number of reasons for this

overrepresentation. One key factor is nationality, and it has been noted that 9% of the prison population comprises foreign nationals (a growing trend observed across Europe). Another factor is the relative youthfulness of ethnic minorities compared to the white population, which means that overrepresentation is all the more likely to occur (Morgan, 2002, p. 1134).

Elaine Genders and Elaine Player (1989) have provided substantial evidence of racial discrimination within prisons. For example, they found that the best jobs were regularly allocated to white prisoners, as prison officers believed that Afro-Caribbean prisoners were arrogant, lazy, and antiauthority. More recently, the official inquiry into the racist murder of Zahid Mubarek in March 2000 by his fellow cellmate, in Feltham Young Offender Institution, found pervasive institutional racism, leading the Prison Service to invite the Commission for Racial Equality to carry out a formal inquiry into racism in prisons. The first part of the report identified 20 "systematic failures" by the Prison Service to prevent the murder, while the second part commented more widely on racial discrimination in prisons (Commission for Racial Equality, 2003a, 2003b).

CONCLUSION

Clearly, the problems that face the penal system in England and Wales are deep, multifaceted, and controversial. In November 2002, the government released figures predicting that the number of prisoners would increase by 40% over the next decade, taking the population to more than 100,000 for the first time. The escalating prison population means that the system will expand far beyond Western European norms, with English and Welsh prisons continuing to be damaging places as the severe problems that have been documented here will intensify. Under these circumstances, it is unlikely that an overstretched prison system will help offenders lead law-abiding lives, while the question of why some countries persist with imprisonment to a greater extent than others remains more pressing than ever.

—Eamonn Carrabine

See also Australia; Bridewell; Canada; Classification; Federal Prison System; Elizabeth Fry; History of Prisons; John Howard; Legitimacy; Managerialism; New Zealand; Overcrowding; History of Prisons; Racism; Rehabilitation Theory; Resistance; Riots; State Prison System; Women's Prisons

Further Reading

Bosworth, M. (1999). *Engendering resistance: Agency and power in women's prisons.* Aldershot, UK: Ashgate.

Bottoms, A. (1977). Reflections on the renaissance of dangerousness. *Howard Journal of Criminal Justice, 16,* 70–96.

Bottoms, A. (1987). Limiting prison use: Experience in England and Wales. *Howard Journal of Criminal Justice, 26,* 177–202.

Carlen, P. (1983). *Women's imprisonment: A study in social control.* London: Routledge and Kegan Paul.

Cavadino, M., & Dignan, J. (2002). *The penal system.* London: Sage.

Commission for Racial Equality. (2003a). *The murder of Zahid Mubarek: A formal investigation by the Commission for Racial Equality into HM Prison Service of England and Wales, Part 1.* London: Author.

Commission for Racial Equality. (2003b). *Racial equality in prisons: A formal investigation by the Commission for Racial Equality into HM Prison Service of England and Wales, Part 2.* London: Author.

Committee for the Prevention of Torture. (1991). *Report to the United Kingdom government on the visit to the United Kingdom carried out by the CPT from 29 July 1990 to 10 August 1990.* Strasbourg, France: Council of Europe.

Garland, D. (1990). *Punishment and modern society: A study in social theory.* Oxford, UK: Clarendon.

Genders, E., & Player, E. (1989). *Race relations in prison.* Oxford, UK: Clarendon.

Harding, C., Hines, B., Ireland, R., & Rawlings, P. (1985). *Imprisonment in England and Wales: A concise history.* London: Croom Helm.

Home Office. (1966). *Committee of an Enquiry Into Prison Escapes and Security* (Mountbatten Report). London: HMSO, Cmnd. 3175.

Home Office. (2001). *Prison statistics England and Wales 2000.* London: HMSO, Cmnd. 5250.

Home Office. (2002). *Prison population brief, England and Wales: June 2002.* London: HMSO.

Morgan, R. (2002). Imprisonment: A brief history, the contemporary scene, and likely prospects. In M. Maguire, R. Morgan, & R. Reiner (Eds.), *The Oxford handbook of criminology* (pp. 1113–1167). Oxford, UK: Oxford University Press.

National Association for the Care and Resettlement of Offenders (NACRO). (2001/2002). Women offenders. *Safer Society, 11,* 27–28.

Prison Service. (2001). *Prison service: Annual report and accounts, April 2000 to March 2001,* HC 29. London: Author.

Pugh, R. (1968). *Imprisonment in medieval England.* Cambridge, UK: Cambridge University Press.

Sparks, R. (2001). Prisons, punishment and penality. In E. McLaughlin & J. Muncie (Eds.), *Controlling crime* (pp. 201–256). London: Sage.

Spierenburg, P. (1984). *The spectacle of suffering: Executions and the evolution of repression.* Cambridge, UK: Cambridge University Press.

Stern, V. (1993). *Bricks of shame.* London: Penguin.

Walmsley, R. (2003). *World prison population list* (4th ed.). London: HMSO.

Woolf, H., & Tumim, S. (1991). *Prison disturbances April 1990,* Cm 1456. London: HMSO.

✓ ENGLISH AS A SECOND LANGUAGE

English as a second language (ESL) is the term used to describe English-language instruction for nonnative English speakers. Another term used to describe the nonproficient English speaker is limited English proficiency (LEP). All prisoners in the United States should be able to demonstrate proficiency in English. If not, they must enroll in ESL or LEP instruction. In addition to providing language skills needed in the institution, corrections-based ESL and LEP instruction seeks to assist the learner with the basic language skills necessary to perform adequately in general education classes.

Of the total prison population, 8% are non–U.S. citizens. The number of inmates with limited English speaking ability is much higher. According to the Federal Bureau of Prisons, 31.7% of inmates held in federal facilities are classified as Hispanic, 1.6% as Native American, and 1.8% as Asian. These numbers vary greatly by state. For example, 53% of New Mexico inmates are Hispanic. New York has the second highest percentage of Hispanic inmates with over 32%. Five other states have Hispanic prison populations of over 25%. Although Spanish is the most common non-English language in prison, the ethnic background of inmates is changing in ways that reflect recent trends in immigration. As a result, we can expect an even wider range of languages in state and federal prisons. Due of a growing number of illegal immigrants, in some cases entire facilities are being filled with non-English speakers. In this case, the language needs are so complex that ESL instruction is being supplemented, or replaced, with electronic translation technologies.

ASSESSING AND TEACHING

A survey of national of adult literacy in 1992 found that on a scale of 1 (low) to 5 (high), over half of nonnative speakers consistently scored below Level 3. Level 2 was the average level for Hispanics born in the United States, while Level 1 was the average for immigrants from Hispanic countries. Level 3 was the average for Asian-Pacific Islander born in the United States, compared to Level 2 for immigrants from Asia and the Pacific Islands (National Center for Education Statistics, 1992).

Several standardized and commercial tests are used to determine the proficiency level of a potential ESL student. Among these are Test of Adult Basic Education (TABE), Adult Basic Learning Exam (ABLE), Basic English Skills Test (BEST), CASAS ESL Appraisal, and the Henderson-Moriarty ESL Placement (HELP). Some of these tests measure the proficiency of the learner in his or her native language to provide a comparison with the learner's aptitude in English. Other tests measure oral abilities such as listening and speaking (the first two levels of English acquisition), while others measure writing and reading as well (the upper levels of English acquisition). The results of most tests need to be interpreted to properly classify the learner by level. Training on interpretation is required for best results, yet, due to expenses, such training is often not provided to the instructor. As a result, in many cases the learner is not properly classified before enrolling in ESL classes.

Several curricula are available to the nonnative speaker. Some of these, provided by general education material providers, include student workbooks, learning tapes, and instructor manuals. Two other curricula commonly used and available for correctional facilities are "Crossroads Café" and "I Can Read." These programs include videos that the student can use without support from an instructor or tutor. The videos show the learner the written target word, pronounce the word, and connect the word to phrases or objects.

CHALLENGES

Regardless of the curricula chosen, language mastery depends in part on the ability of the learner to interact with others to practice new vocabulary and speech patterns. This is not an easy task for the incarcerated student. Procedural policies of many facilities do not provide for adequate interaction, slowing down the acquisition process. Funding issues in correctional facilities create another problem. Corrections education programs typically have limited educational funds for materials. Administrators are forced to prioritize their expenditures. As a result, materials purchased for use in correctional education programs are concentrated on English-proficient students. This leaves the LEP inmate without adequate resources to improve his or her language skills.

On average, it takes five to seven years for a nonnative speaker of English to become accomplished at most communication tasks. The minimum requirement for a person literate in his or her native language is 750 to 1,000 hours of skills development to satisfy basic needs and to have limited social interaction in English. Due to the nature of correctional facilities, many inmates are transferred or released before that time period has elapsed. As a result, it may be difficult for prisoners to complete their ESL education in a correctional facility. However, even if basic language skills are not fully developed, one of the goals of the ESL educator is to help the individual acquire language skills necessary for survival in the prison society. This can be accomplished in a relatively short period of time.

CURRENT PROGRAMS AND ISSUES IN ESL TRAINING

Many different ESL programs are used in correctional facilities. Several states provide ESL training as part of their adult basic education programming. Since correctional education literacy programs vary from facility to facility, it is difficult to discover what services are provided to inmates. Each state, and in some cases each facility, feels different pressures to develop and administer ESL and LEP programs. Varying levels of integration with other correctional education programs can also lead to problems with information sharing that could lead to increased standardization of delivery.

Since funding for ESL programs does not typically fall into state-mandated education budgets, ESL-specific programs must compete with state funds allocated to general education within the corrections departments. As a result, many facilities rely on outside volunteers or contractors to provide ESL instruction. Community volunteers and school agencies, such as community colleges, offer the majority of ESL programs to the general population. In addition, Laubach International and Literacy Volunteers of America has historically offered special training for low-language-proficiency learners and currently offer materials and guidelines for instruction in corrections-based ESL services.

Most ESL students are grouped with English-proficient students in general classrooms. Many of these students drop out of correctional education for the same reasons they do so in general public facilities' education. Common reasons include problems related to grasping the vocabulary, understanding the subculture expressed through language, and learning the conversational patterns used in normal speaking. Since speech patterns vary among ethnic groups, and these vary from standard English speech patterns, students are likely to make several mistakes speaking English as a second language. In addition to the inherent difficulty of learning a new language, pedagogical approaches by educators may diminish their effectiveness as teachers to non-English speakers. Many of these problems can be addressed through the development of ESL-specific programs or by encouraging educators to work to participate in opportunities for ESL training.

CONCLUSION

Data indicate that corrections education is an effective tool in the effort to reduce recidivism. Less evidence is available regarding a link between ESL programs and crime reduction. We know that correctional institutions function better when prisoners are encouraged to live together and follow the rules. As with other forms of corrections education, ESL and LEP programs provide opportunities for prisoners to learn to "do their time" in a productive way.

Many benefits of ESL instruction are difficult to assess. For example, it is hard to measure large-scale improvement in the ability to effectively function within correctional facilities. Corrections education is consistently shown to be very effective in efforts to reduce recidivism and improve employability after prison. Although the relationship of ESL instruction and crime control has not been clearly demonstrated, there is no reason to believe that ESL instruction does not have the same potential. In many cases, the incarcerated individual will not be able to fully participate in corrections education without first learning to speak English. As such, the benefits of education are denied to those with limited English skills.

The corrections industry, like the justice system as a whole, relies on established procedures, policies, and laws. The incarcerated individual and the institutions in which individuals are incarcerated each benefits from efforts to ensure that policies and procedures are effectively communicated. These policies and practices are often intended to protect the rights of those who interact with the system. Those who do not speak the dominant language of this system are at a distinct disadvantage. Although general impacts are difficult to assess, ESL instruction has the potential to reduce this disadvantage and minimize the loss of rights that may occur when an individual is unable to actively participate in processes that have serious implications.

—Molly Wilkinson
and Kenneth Mentor

See also Asian American Prisoners; Education; Foreign Nationals; General Educational Development (GED) Exam and General Equivalency Diploma; Hispanic/Latino(a) Prisoners; Immigrants and Undocumented Aliens; Literacy

Further Reading

Bureau of Justice Statistics. (2003). *Key crime and justice facts at a glance*. U.S. Department of Justice. Retrieved from http://www.ojp.usdoj.gov/bjs/glance.htm

Burt, M., & Keenan, F. (1995). *Adult ESL learner assessment: Purposes and tools*. Washington, DC: National Center for ESL Literacy Education. (ERIC Digest No. EDO-LE-95–08)

Fillmore, L. W., & Snow, C. E. (2000). *What teachers need to know about language*. Washington, DC: U.S. Department of Education, Educational Research and Improvement. (ERIC Digest No. ED-99-CO-0008)

Haigler, K. O., Harlow, C., O'Connor, P., & Campbell, A. (1994). *Literacy behind prison walls*. Washington, DC: National Center for Education Statistics.

Heilman, K., & Lawson, K. M. (2000, December). Facilitating communication with limited- and non-English-speaking offenders. *Corrections Today*.

National Center for Education Statistics. (1992). *National Adult Literacy Survey*. Washington, DC: U.S. Department of Education, National Center for Education Statistics.

Office of Science and Technology of the National Institute of Justice. (2000, December). Do you speak English? *Corrections Today*.

Richiusa, G. (1997, November/December). Language barriers: Teaching ESL in the corrections system. *American Language Review, 1*(5).

ESCAPES

Each year a small number of men and women escape from their prison or jail. However, the popular perception of the violent and dramatic prison escape as portrayed in television and film is not generally true. Most escapes involve low-security inmates, or walk aways, who receive scant media attention and remain a low priority for understaffed police departments.

ESCAPE RATES

Prison escapes have decreased dramatically since 1994 when a total of 7,598 inmates (all security levels) escaped. In 2001, the total number of escapes (all security levels) was 5,487. When these figures are broken down into security levels, the number of higher-security escapes has decreased by 78% from 1994 to 2001, while the number of low-security or walk-aways has only decreased about 6%. In 1994, of the total number of escapes, 30% were classified as medium to high security, while in 2001, only 9% were classified as such. Such decrease is even more notable in light of the simultaneously growth in the prison population. During this period, the total number of inmates has increased 86% from approximately 1 million to 1.9 million.

WALK AWAYS

Those who seek to escape their prison sentence usually do it merely by walking away. That is to say, they either do not return to prison or simply disappear from work release, transitional supervision centers, halfway houses, furloughs, medical appointments, and so on. From 1994 through 2001, the number of walk aways fell slightly from 5,311 to 4,995. In the same period, the percentage of these escapees who were returned fell from 49% in 1994 to 46% in 2001. Less attention is paid to these kinds of escapes since the people involved usually are thought to pose little threat to the community.

HIGH-SECURITY ESCAPES

The total number of higher-security escapes from federal and state facilities decreased from 2,287 in 1994 to only 492 in 2001. Most high-security escapees are eventually caught and returned to the institution with additional time added to their original sentence. The rate at which escapees are caught and returned to confinement improved from 87% in 1994 to 91% in 2001.

The drop in number of high-profile and high-security escapes and the improved rate at which such individuals are found are attributed to a number of factors including an increased focus on correctional officer selection and education, more rigorous classification schemes, and better perimeter security. Various technological developments have also reduced prisoners' ability to run away from prison such as the installation of motion detectors, metal detectors, and nonlethal stun fencing. In some institutions, visits are now placed under video surveillance to reduce the possibility of contraband or weapons being smuggled into the prison that could be used in an escape attempt.

There have also been many changes and innovations in prison construction over the past decade that have made high-security institutions much harder to escape from. Increases in perimeter fence lighting and the use of razor ribbon around the perimeter of the facility, for example, both act as physical barriers to those wishing to flee. Furthermore, the introduction of the supermax prison, such as Pelican Bay in California, has also affected the escape rate. Inmates in these kinds of institution are isolated from others and have little contact even with staff. They remain in lockdown at all times, in small cells that have only the tiniest of windows with unbreakable glass. Such institutions are nearly impossible to get out of other than by officially sanctioned means of release.

RISK ASSESSMENT AND ESCAPE BEHAVIOR

Reflecting the relative infrequency with which it occurs, there is not much current research being done about escape. To understand those factors that make escapes happen, therefore, we must, for the most part, turn to earlier studies. From this considerable body of work, it seems that there are three separate factors that determine whether inmates will try to escape: (1) static, (2) situational, and (3) psychological.

Static factors include such things as demographic characteristics such as age, race, and gender and well as the criminal's career and time behind bars. Thus, for example, Holt (1974) and Morgan (1967) found that escapees tend to be less than 30 years of age, and Morgan also established that many of the escapees had been incarcerated less than one year prior to their escape attempt.

Not only are certain types of offenses associated with an increased likelihood of escape, but the number of times someone has been incarcerated appears to be relevant. According to Holt (1974), therefore, inmates with property convictions were more likely to escape than those convicted of a crime against a person. These people were also more likely to have had prior escape attempts. More recently, the National Institute of Justice in 1987 stated that the prior escape record of the inmate was indicative of future behavior and could be effectively

applied during the security classification process. Similarly, a 1997 study done by the Correctional Service of Canada indicated that the female inmates with more violent criminal convictions were more likely to attempt escape.

Situational factors associated with escape attempts include substance abuse, family issues, parole problems, and institutional problems. Hilbrand (1969) indicated that the more unstable a person's home life and familial situation, the more likely it is that he or she would try to escape. Family issues in particular are common causes of walkaways, as inmates sometimes feel as though they need to resolve some family conflict and so cannot return to their place of confinement.

An additional situational factor, the threat of institutional violence and assault, also seems to be a factor in people's decision to escape (Loving, Stockwell, & Dobbins, 1959). Not surprisingly, those who feel at risk while incarcerated often try to flee. Other factors that are associated with an increased likelihood of escape include the number of times a person has been involved in incidents of misconduct and related disciplinary actions (Hilbrand, 1969) and whether they participate in institutional programming (Duncan & Ellis, 1973). Such research suggests that subjective factors, such as how content or invested in an institution someone is, will affect the decision to try to leave. Finally, researchers have even examined seasonal factors (Hilbrand, 1969). Not surprisingly, people are more likely to try to leave in the warmer months.

Although a number of scholars have attempted to identify those psychological factors that lead people to escape, there has been no conclusive evidence indicating that any specific characteristics indicate a higher probability of escape (Loving et al., 1959; Shaffer, Bluoin, & Pettigrew, 1985). Some radical psychologists and criminologists see escape attempts as a healthy form of resistance. For these authors, prisoners do not actually have to leave the prison confines to escape. Many other more everyday mechanisms can be used to create some distance between inmates and their surroundings. These strategies run the gamut from legitimate forms of self-expression such as writing and artwork to illicit means of muting the senses like drug use. Firsthand accounts by inmates, as well as critical studies of inmate culture, portray such techniques as attempts to resist the power of the prison and its staff.

CONCLUSION

It is not easy to predict which prisoners will seek to escape and which will not. The complex interconnections between institutional, static, and situational factors as well as a person's history of escape attempts and psychological makeup make any such predictions unreliable. All that can be safely said is that despite various developments in technology, security, classification, and prison management, some inmates will always try to flee from their confinement. Incarceration is very rarely a desirable state and so people will try to escape.

—*Sara Conte*

See also Alcatraz; Classification; Control Unit; Correctional Officers; Furlough; Maximum Security; Medium Security; Minimum Security; Resistance; Staff Training; Supermax Prisons; Work-Release Programs

Further Reading

Anson, R. H., & Harnett, C. M. (1983). Correlates of escape: A preliminary assessment of Georgia prisons. *Criminal Justice Review, 8*(1), 38–42.

Cohen, S., & Taylor, L. (1978). *Escape attempts: The theory and practice of resistance to everyday life.* Harmondsworth, UK: Penguin.

Duncan, D. F., & Ellis, T. R. (1973, May–June). Situational variables associated with prison escapes. *American Journal of Corrections,* 29–30.

Hilbrand, R. J. (1969). The anatomy of escape. *Federal Probation, 33*(1), 58–66.

Holt, N. (1974, May). *Escape from custody* (California Department of Corrections Research Report No 52). Sacramento: California Department of Corrections.

Loving, W., Stockwell, F. E., & Dobbins, D. A. (1959). Factors associated with escape behavior in prison inmates. *Federal Probation, 23,* 3DD, 49–51.

Morgan, D. (1967, March–April). Individual and situational factors related to prison escape. *American Journal of Correction,* 30–31.

Riots, disturbances, violence, assaults and escapes. (2002). *Corrections Compendium, 27*(5), 6–19.

Shaffer, C. E., Bluoin, D., & Pettigrew, C. G. (1985). Assessment of prison escape risk. *Journal of Police and Criminal Psychology, 1*(1), 42–48.

◪ *ESTELLE v. GAMBLE*

The U.S. Supreme Court case *Estelle, Corrections Director et al. v. Gamble,* 429 U.S. 97 (1976) underpins inmate rights to medical treatment in all correctional facilities. This case, generally referred to as *Estelle v. Gamble,* established for the first time that prison and jail inmates have a constitutional right to medical treatment under the Eighth Amendment. Its decision was made applicable to states by the 14th Amendment.

THE CASE

J. W. Gamble, an inmate at the Texas Department of Corrections, was injured while performing job-related duties after a bale of cotton fell on top of him while he was loading a truck on November 9, 1973. Gamble continued to work the rest of the day despite complaining of pain and tenderness in his back. He was diagnosed with lower back strain and prescribed pain medication along with "cell-pass, cell-feed" status for two days, which was later extended into a few weeks. Three weeks later, Gamble complained once again of severe lower back pain, which he claimed was as bad as when the incident first occurred. At this point, he refused to return to work. In response, he was sent to "administrative segregation" on December 3 and taken before the disciplinary committee. Once the disciplinary committee heard of Gamble's intense lower back pain and complaints of high blood pressure, the committee directed him to a doctor, who prescribed him medication. Gamble remained in administrative segregation for the entire month of December.

In January 1974, Gamble was reprimanded for not returning to his assigned job-related duties on the prison farm. Once again, he refused to work because of his back pain. Once again he was remanded to administrative segregation and brought before the disciplinary committee. This time, when he complained of pain and high blood pressure, however, the medical staff testified that he was in "first rate" health and able to return to work. The disciplinary committee then refused Gamble's request for additional medical examination and sentenced him to solitary confinement until he agreed to return to work on the farm. At this point, Gamble filed the said petition.

The complaint first went before the U.S. District Court for the Southern District of Texas where it was dismissed "for failure to state a claim upon which relief could be granted." Later, the U.S. Court of Appeals for the Fifth Circuit reversed and remanded the compliant back to the District Court with explicit instructions to reinstate it. The complaint was then heard by the U.S. Supreme Court on certiorari.

THE ISSUE

Gamble filed civil suit against the warden of his Texas correctional facility and the assisting doctor to that prison under 42 USCS 1983. He argued that his constitutional rights against "cruel and unusual punishment" under the Eighth Amendment had been violated because the prison staff had refused to provide proper medical care when he injured himself while fulfilling work-related duties.

THE HOLDING

Gamble won his case. The Court found that the medical care provided to Gamble was insufficient and that prison staff acted with "deliberate indifference" to his medical problems. The Court held that deliberate indifference to an inmate's acute medical requirements violated the Eighth Amendment's prohibition on cruel and unusual punishment, and was, therefore, actionable as a civil right's grievance under Section 1983. Justice Thurgood Marshall delivered the majority opinion of the Supreme Court.

Justice John Paul Stevens dissented by arguing that the "pro se complaint against the prison's chief medical officer should not have been ordered dismissed." He further argued that "in any event, by its references to "deliberate indifference" and the "intentional" denial of adequate medical care, "the [Court] improperly attached significance to the

subjective motivation of [Gamble] as a criterion for determining whether cruel and unusual punishment had been inflicted, whereas such determination should instead turn on the character of the punishment rather than the motivation of the individual who inflicted it" (429 at 104–105). According to him, the "intent" of the defendant is not necessary as long as the resulting condition results from the lack of proper medical treatment to the inmate. Justice Stevens argued that this ruling would give correctional facilities greater latitude in proving their provision of medical treatment, while placing greater burden on the petitioner, or recipient of the mediocre treatment. He concluded by adding that certiorari should have never been granted in this case and that the decision by the Court of Appeals should have been affirmed.

CONCLUSION

Estelle v. Gamble was the first case in which the Supreme Court considered prisoners' rights to medical treatment with respect to the Eighth Amendment clause banning the use of cruel and unusual punishment. In this case, the Court termed a new standard, which is known as the "deliberate indifference" burden. In employing the deliberate indifference burden, the Court paved the way for inmates to seek resolve for medical malpractice via tort law.

In 1996, Congress passed the Prison Litigation Reform Act (PLRA) to discourage inmates from filing "frivolous" lawsuits and to limit the power of federal courts in conditions litigation. The act also restricted inmates' use of attorneys in tort-related cases. This made it difficult for those seeking awards under the deliberate indifference standard set forth in *Estelle v. Gamble.* As a result, inmates are now faced with great obstacles in filing claims of neglect and substandard conditions. This affects a range of prisoner complaints, including how pregnant women are received in correctional facilities. If an inmate mother loses her child due to the inadequate services by staff, her chances of seeking civil justice are now limited. While the *Estelle* decision was a historical one in assessing inadequate health care, its standard set forth by the Court was quite narrow in establishing deliberate indifference and was furthered restricted with the PLRA.

—*Kristi M. McKinnon*

See also Control Unit; Disciplinary Segregation; Doctors; Eighth Amendment; Health Care; Jailhouse Lawyers; Mothers in Prison; Prison Litigation Reform Act 1996; Prisoner Litigation; Resistance; Solitary Confinement

Further Reading

Palmer, J. W., & Palmer, S. E. (1999). *Constitutional rights of prisoners* (6th ed.). Cincinnati, OH: Anderson.

Thomas, J. (1988). *Prisoner litigation: The paradox of the jailhouse lawyer.* Totowa, NJ: Rowman & Littlefield.

Legal Cases

Cooper v. Pate, 378 U.S. 546 (1964).
Estelle, Corrections Director et al. v. Gamble, 429 U.S. 97 (1976).
Gregg v. Georgia, 428 U.S. 153 (1976).
Haines v. Kerner, 404 U.S. 519 (1972).
Robinson v. California, 370 U.S. 660 (1962).
U.S. Code, 42 USCS 1983.
U.S. Code, 18 USCS 3626.

F

◪ FAITH-BASED INITIATIVES

Faith-based initiatives refer to a widespread effort among governmental and religious nonprofit agencies to incorporate religious activism into various social welfare programs, including the correctional system. Most programs currently in place in the United States are centered around the Christian or Muslim faiths. Faith-based initiatives encompass everything from programs designed to help religious organizations obtain federal funding for outreach activities to the actual implementation of prison ministries.

The faith-based movement has recently been reenergized in the United States by President George W. Bush's strong commitment to it. Following his inauguration, President Bush announced the establishment of the White House Office of Faith-Based and Community Initiatives (OFBCI). During subsequent months, the Bush administration created legislative proposals focusing on the delivery of federally funded social services through faith-based organizations, becoming commonly known as the "faith-based initiative." The principle behind this initiative is that faith-based charities should have an equal opportunity to compete for federal funds to provide public services.

Included among the proposed legislation was HR 7, the Community Solutions Act of 2001. The bill sought to provide tax incentives for charitable contributions by individuals and businesses and expand the "charitable choice" provision of the 1996 welfare reform legislation. The charitable choice provisions prohibit public officials from discriminating against religious social service providers seeking to compete for government positions. By expanding the charitable choice provision, President Bush created a specific and highly controversial way in which government and religious institutions may collaborate to provide social services. As a result, the issue has stirred tremendous debate over the separation between church and state.

RELIGION IN PRISON

Research has indicated that religious activity (e.g., attendance at religious services) in prison reduces adult criminality. Previous studies have also shown that inmates most active in Bible study activities who attend 10 or more studies in a year were significantly less likely to be rearrested during a one-year follow-up period compared to inmates less involved or entirely uninvolved in Bible study activities. Such findings are often used to support faith-based initiatives, even though other research exists that is somewhat more equivocal about the long-term effects of religion on reoffending rates.

Faith-based programs fall under two general headings: those that are federally funded by the government and others that are privately funded institutional programs. Federally funded programs are prohibited from promoting inherently religious activities such as prayer, Bible study, and proselytizing. Programs using federal funds are directed to further the crime reduction objectives established by the U.S. Congress. Privately funded programs are not restricted to the separation of church and state as are federally funded program.

Most faith-based initiatives are offender oriented, attempting to create a prison environment that fosters respect for both a higher power and for others while teaching the moral principles of a specific religion. The goal of these programs is to reduce reoffending through the power of religion. These outreach programs typically include components of Bible study, mentoring, educational classes, and transitional programming for ex-offenders.

Prison Fellowship Ministries, founded by Charles Colson (a former Watergate convicted felon), is an international volunteer Christian ministry that opened the world's first faith-based prison near Houston, Texas, in 1997. This faith-based initiative, the InnerChange Freedom Initiative, has subsequently opened three additional faith-based prisons in Iowa, Kansas, and Minnesota. Among the initiative, the state pays for the cells, guards, and uniforms, while Prison Fellowship finances the religious programs and activities through private funds.

In 2003, the University of Pennsylvania's Center for Research on Religion and Urban Civil Society evaluated the InnerChange Freedom Initiative and reported that graduates from the program have had significantly lower recidivism rates than a matched control group. The news was received with much excitement and celebration by Colson and President Bush. The program was deemed a success.

However, critics of the study are quick to raise concerns regarding the manner in which results were reported. InnerChange began with 177 volunteer prisoners but only 75 of them "graduated." Rather than report on both the successful prisoners ($n = 75$) and those who were kicked or dropped out ($n = 102$), the report highlighted only the successful graduates, something researchers call a "selection bias."

Overall, the 177 participants actually did somewhat worse than the matched control group. They were slightly more likely to be rearrested and noticeably more likely to be reincarcerated (i.e., 24% vs. 20%). Although the University of Pennsylvania study is not guilty of concealing information, it does seem to highlight the graduate-only results before reporting on all the facts.

John J. DiIulio, Jr., a serious advocate of faith-based initiatives who was the first director of the OFBCI and founder of the University of Pennsylvania research center, acknowledges that the study results were not exactly what he had hoped to find. However, he points out that one study is never enough to provide conclusive evidence either way. More research on InnerChange and other similar faith-based initiatives is necessary before answers can become unequivocal.

FUTURE DIRECTIONS

Faith-based initiatives face several future challenges. First, there is the legal issue of employment rules. Being exempt from Title VII of the Civil Rights Act of 1964 allows faith-based organizations to discriminate based on religious orientation. Faith-based initiatives are also restricted when it comes to proselytizing. President Bush's Executive Order states that government funds cannot be used for "inherently religious activity." The U.S. Supreme Court has yet to define the financial parameters for inherently religious activity. These and other legal challenges are sure to come into play as more religious organizations seek federal funding.

The criminal justice field has additional considerations for the future of faith-based initiatives. First, faith-based organizations are encouraged to provide assistance to victims in addition to offenders. Second, the relationship between religious figures and criminal justice administrators should be developed. Religious figures can provide training about the important role criminal justice officials can play in assisting both victims and offenders.

CONCLUSION

Faith-based initiatives are a growing trend in both general social welfare programs and the correctional system. They often use federal funding to assist both victims of crime and offenders in an institutional setting. They tend to incorporate Bible study, educational classes, and mentoring to reduce recidivism among offenders.

The interest in faith-based initiatives continues to grow, particularly because it was one of President Bush's top priorities in the White House. And although the September 11, 2001, terrorist attacks on the United States forced the president to alter his political agenda, with faith-based initiatives taking a back seat to fighting worldwide terrorism, there is still a political movement attempting to pass legislation allowing religious nonprofit agencies to incorporate spiritual beliefs into various social programs using public funds.

Criticism surrounding the issue is likely to continue by many who feel the agenda violates the doctrine of separation between church and state. Additional research investigating the ability of these programs to reduce recidivism is necessary to fully inform the debate over their utility.

—*Emily J. Salisbury and Jennifer S. Trager*

See also Chaplains; Contract Facilities; Contract Ministers; John J. DiIulio, Jr.; History of Prisons; History of Religion in Prison; Quakers; Recidivism; Rehabilitation Theory; Religion in Prison

Further Reading

Colson, C. W. (2001). *Justice that restores*. Wheaton, IL: Tyndale House.

Johnson, B. R. (1997). Religious programs, institutional adjustment, and recidivism among former inmates in Prison Fellowship programs. *Justice Quarterly, 14,* 145–166.

U.S. Department of Justice. (1998). *New directions from the field: Victims' rights and services for the 21st century.* Washington, DC: Author.

◪ FAMILIES AGAINST MANDATORY MINIMUMS

Families Against Mandatory Minimums (FAMM) is a national nonprofit organization that challenges the inflexible and excessive penalties required by mandatory sentencing laws. It is the only advocacy group devoted entirely to sentencing reform.

MANDATORY SENTENCES

Congress enacted mandatory sentencing laws in 1986 because lawmakers believed that rigid, severe drug laws would catch drug kingpins and deter others from entering the drug trade. The laws established drug weight and type as the only factors that judges can consider in determining drug sentences and prescribed fixed and predetermined sentences for these crimes. In 1988, Congress created new mandatory sentences for drug conspiracy (under which drug weight had only to be alleged) and the presence of a firearm during a felony offense, as well as a five-year mandatory sentence for mere possession of five grams of crack cocaine. Most states also enacted mandatory minimum sentences for drug offenses in the 1980s.

As a result of these mandatory laws, judges can no longer consider the severity of the offense, an offender's role in the crime, or the offender's potential for rehabilitation when determining the sentence. This rigidity has led to thousands of low-level offenders and addicts now serving sentences designed for kingpins. In addition, the laws disproportionately affect minorities. African Americans account for 12% to 13% of America's general population, yet they comprise 30% of those receiving federal mandatory drug sentences. Hispanics constitute 12% of the general population but receive 43% of mandatory drug sentences. Mandatory sentences also affect an increasing number of women. In 1997, nearly 72% of federal female prisoners were serving drug sentences. Taking a message for a boyfriend involved in a drug deal or driving him to the bank can lead to conspiracy charges and the woman can be charged for the entire amount of drugs sold.

THE ESTABLISHMENT OF FAMM

Julie Stewart founded FAMM in 1991 when her brother was arrested for growing marijuana and sentenced to five years in prison under mandatory sentencing laws established by Congress in 1986. From this small beginning, FAMM has grown to an organization of more than 28,000 members, including individuals, organizations, prisoners, and their families. Its national office is located in Washington, D.C., while state coordinators maintain chapters in many states. FAMM lobbies for the repeal of mandatory drug sentences and the return to limited judicial discretion, as established in the U.S. sentencing guidelines, which govern all other federal criminal cases. Under sentencing guidelines, judges base decisions on all the facts of the case and select from a range of sentences based on those facts.

CURRENT PROJECTS OF FAMM

FAMM concentrates its efforts in five areas. The Legislative Outreach Project lobbies Congress and the U.S. Sentencing Commission to reform severe federal mandatory sentences and federal sentencing guidelines. State projects advocate sentencing reform in states with particularly harsh sentencing laws and work to prevent adoption of additional mandatory sentences.

The FAMM Litigation project was organized in 1995 to provide litigation assistance of pro bono counsel for cases that involve important or evolving sentencing issues before the U.S. Supreme Court, the lower federal courts, and the state courts. To bring public attention to harsh and disproportionate mandatory sentences on low-level, nonviolent offenders, the litigation project also accepts a handful of cases involving grave injustice, regardless of the legal issue presented. The project is guided by in-house counsel and an advisory board of prominent criminal defense attorneys and law professors, and it is aided by prestigious law firms with pro bono programs.

The FAMM Community Action Network trains and coordinates a national network of members to educate policy makers about sentencing reform.

Through postcards, letters, phone calls, and visits to federal and state lawmakers, members actively influence sentencing policy. The FAMM Communication Project works with all forms of media to educate the public about the excessively punitive nature of mandatory sentencing policies. FAMM's extensive case files of people serving mandatory drug sentences help provide individual examples of injustice.

FAMM's efforts have brought about major improvements to federal and state sentencing systems and generated hundreds of articles in major newspapers and magazines and features on national and local television each year. These help alert citizens about the problems of mandatory minimum sentencing. Up-to-date information can be found on the FAMM Web site, www.famm.org, which provides updated information on mandatory sentencing, puts a face on sentencing laws with its extensive file of prisoners serving lengthy mandatory sentences, and provides a vehicle for citizen action.

CONCLUSION

Each year, one out of four federal drug offenders are sentenced under the more flexible sentencing guidelines rather than mandatory minimum laws, thanks to FAMM's efforts to establish a "safety valve" for first-time, nonviolent offenders who meet specific criteria. FAMM's work to establish more realistic weight measurements of marijuana and LSD offenses produced fairer sentences for nearly 1,000 prisoners and continues to affect hundreds of new cases annually. FAMM's participation in nearly 20 Supreme Court cases and numerous federal appeal cases has led to fairer sentences for hundreds of defendants. FAMM helped file clemency petitions for 21 members who were low-level, nonviolent drug offenders serving lengthy mandatory sentences. In 2000, President Bill Clinton commuted the sentences for 17 of them. FAMM also led a successful effort to amend Michigan's notorious "650 Lifer Law," which required life in prison without parole for anyone convicted of delivery or conspiring to deliver 650 grams of cocaine or heroin—even first-time offenders. In 2002, FAMM completed the job of reforming Michigan's draconian sentences by spearheading a campaign that resulted in a bipartisan majority of Michigan's legislature voting to eliminate most of the mandatory minimums for drug offenses. The reforms allow judges to impose sentences based on a range of factors, replace lifetime probation for the lowest-level offenders with a five-year probationary period, and permit earlier parole for some prisoners.

—Monica Pratt

See also Activism; Citizens United for Rehabilitation of Errants; Critical Resistance; Determinate Sentencing; Deterrence Theory; Incapacitation Theory; Just Deserts Theory; November Coalition; Sentencing Reform Act 1984; Three-Strikes Legislation; Truth in Sentencing; War on Drugs

Further Reading

Families Against Mandatory Minimums. (2002). *Primer on mandatory sentences.* Washington, DC: Author. Retrieved from http://www.famm.org/rs_publications.htm

Leadership Conference on Civil Rights and Leadership Conference Education Fund. (2000). *Justice on trial: Racial disparities in the American criminal justice system.* Retrieved from http://www.civilrights.org/publications/cj

RAND Drug Policy Research Center. (1997). *Are mandatory minimum drug sentences cost-effective?* Retrieved from http://www.rand.org/publications/RB/RB6003/

U.S. Sentencing Commission. (1991). *Special report to the Congress: Mandatory minimum penalties in the federal criminal justice system.* Retrieved from http://www.ussc.gov/r_congress/MANMIN.PDF

◼ FATHERS IN PRISON

Historically, much more attention has been paid to incarcerated mothers than to fathers. This is partly caused by concern about pregnant women in prison and also because of widespread beliefs that the mother-child bond is stronger than that between the father and child. In recent years, however, cultural norms have increasingly emphasized the importance of fatherhood. This, combined with concerns about the welfare of the children of male inmates, has led researchers to collect some of the first large-scale data regarding the fatherhood status of prisoners. Nonprofit groups and prison staff have also increased their efforts to provide services to incarcerated fathers.

The most comprehensive national information concerning fathers in prison comes from surveys conducted by the Bureau of Justice Statistics. Unless otherwise noted, all statistics cited here are taken from its report.

STATISTICS ABOUT FATHERS IN PRISON

About 55% of male inmates in state facilities have children under the age of 18—a percentage that has not changed appreciably over the past 10 years. Out of the incarcerated fathers, approximately 30% have more than one child. Comparable statistics for federal inmates are 63% and 40%, respectively. As a result, at least 1,372,700 minor children in the United States have a father in prison. During the past decade, a rise in the incarceration rate has resulted in an increase in the number of incarcerated fathers with minor children. Because data are not kept on the number of inmate fathers with children age 18 and over, we do not know the total number of incarcerated men with adult children.

Fathers in state facilities are serving an average sentence of 94 months, and those in federal prisons an average of 124 months. The most common offenses committed by those in state prisons are violent in nature, while, in the federal system, they are more likely to have to have been convicted of drug trafficking. In terms of race/ethnicity, approximately half of the fathers in state custody are African American, a quarter are white, and some 19% are Hispanic. At the federal level, 44% are black, 30% are Hispanic, and 22% are white.

While we do not have reliable data on the number of fathers in juvenile detention nationwide, estimates suggest that between 20% and 25% of them have children. This percentage is notable given that nationwide only about 5% of men under the age of 20 are fathers. These men are disproportionately represented in juvenile prison because incarceration and young fathering are concentrated in the same impoverished communities. In addition, regardless of their backgrounds, fathers appear more likely than those without children to engage in delinquent behaviors and to go to prison. National data are not kept on the number of juvenile fathers in county and local custody.

Fathering

In prison you get to think about a lot of things, and one of the most important is how to be a father to children who feel that you have abandoned them. Fathering from prison is one of the most difficult things I believe a man can do in his entire life. How do you explain anything to a child who believes that you don't or didn't ever care for them? They have the right to feel this way because after all, you left them. Your children don't care about what happened to put you here. They think about the fact that you're not there when they need to be held, when they need to feel the love that only a father could give.

I believe that children need both of their parents in order to feel secure in this short life we live in. Children growing up without fathers are missing something important that is a necessity in their lives. Raising your children is something you can never do over again. I've learned to be truthful with my five children. They all have different personalities but that doesn't stop all of them from hurting because I'm not there. I write them every month and try to do what I can to help them. I teach them what they need to know to become productive members of society.

Some fathers never get the chance to see their children because they are imprisoned far away from home. This makes it difficult for children to come to visit. Phoning is also not always an option since it is expensive and, in any case, a phone call from prison only lasts 15 minutes. All of these barriers make it difficult maintain family ties.

Jesse McKinley Carter, Jr.
FCI Fairton, Fairton, New Jersey

FATHER-CHILD CONTACT

Fathers in prison are generally allowed three kinds of contact with their children: mail, phone, and visits. About 40% of inmates report that they have at least one type of contact with their children each week. Most commonly they do this through the mail, with 27% of fathers reporting at least weekly contact. Phone calls are similar, with 25% of father inmates reporting that they talk to their children on a weekly basis. However, it must be noted that a full 43% report no phone contact and 32% do not write letters. One of the reasons for limited phone contact may be the cost. Most states have made arrangements with phone companies to include a surcharge on calls made from prison, raising the rates for already expensive collect calls. Children's caretakers are often on a limited budget and may not be able to afford such calls. Recent lawsuits have improved this situation, but the telephone remains an expensive means of communication. Prison rules that limit the amount of time each inmate is allowed for calls may also affect phone contact rates in some states.

In terms of visits, rules and policies vary by state and by institution. About 21% of incarcerated fathers nationally see their children at least once a month. State inmates are less likely than federal inmates to see children, with about 57% of them reporting that they never see their children. The equivalent percentage at the federal level is 44%. Visiting policy in jails tends to be more stringent than in prisons, with some forbidding visits altogether and others allowing only noncontact ones. At the juvenile level, these policies vary widely. While some institutions allow children to visit, others do not allow them to come into the facility except under special circumstances.

PROGRAMS FOR FATHERS IN PRISON

The recent interest in incarcerated fathers has prompted the creation of programs to provide support services for men and their children. Most states provide parenting classes in at least one of their adult facilities and several states also provide them at the juvenile level. These parent education courses focus on a wide range of topics including self-identity/self-esteem, parenting skills, child development, co-parenting, and legal issues regarding incarcerated fatherhood. In addition to parenting classes, some prisons offer other types of support services. For example, fathers in some prisons are provided with tape recorders to record stories and messages for their children. In others, special areas are set aside for father-child visits.

In addition to these initiatives in prison, there are a range of nonprofit groups that provide services, including parenting classes, to incarcerated fathers and their families. For example, the Osbourne Association in New York provides counseling and parenting classes to incarcerated men. It also staffs children's visiting areas in three prisons and provides information and referrals to the families of prisoners. Men who participate in the program are eligible to receive employment counseling and other social services upon their release. Other nonprofit groups focus on providing transportation for children to visit their fathers. As described below, these services are particularly important because many men are placed in prisons located far from their children.

EFFECTS OF FATHERS IN PRISON

We know less about the effect of incarcerating fathers on their children than we do about the effect of locking up mothers. The research that has been done suggests that the children exhibit symptoms such as nightmares, depression, and poor achievement. Reports from mothers point to negative behavioral changes in children after the father goes to prison. Imprisonment usually strains the relationship between a father and his children, and between a father and the mother of these children. Men miss years of their children's lives, and often become estranged from them. Children grow and change rapidly, and it is extremely difficult to maintain a close relationship from a distance. Imprisoned men also miss years of their wives' and girlfriends' lives, and they can provide them with only limited emotional support. As a result, there are high rates of divorce between inmates and the mothers of their children. Divorce, and the subsequent introduction of new men into the mothers' lives, may put further stress on the children.

Some research suggests that children with imprisoned fathers are more likely to engage in criminal behavior and do poorly in school, but such findings should be interpreted carefully. It is not clear if these outcomes are a direct result of the fathers' imprisonment or whether other factors are involved. For example, it is possible that the increased poverty that results from the loss of an incarcerated father's income could negatively affect the children. It is also possible that problems originating prior to the father's confinement are responsible.

CHALLENGES FACED BY INCARCERATED FATHERS

The structure of the prison system makes it difficult for fathers interested in maintaining a relationship with their children. Men are often placed in facilities far from where their children live. The Bureau of Justice Statistics reports, for example, that 60% of parents in state prisons are placed 100 miles or more from their children. Because the prison system disproportionately draws from poor communities, children's caretakers frequently cannot afford the costs of transporting children to see their fathers. Other disincentives to visiting come from the men themselves. Many are unwilling to expose their children to the prison environment, and some feel shame at being incarcerated.

Other challenges preventing incarcerated men from participating in their children's lives involve the children's caretakers. Caretakers act as gatekeepers, controlling the amount of contact incarcerated men have with their children. Problems or tensions between a man and the child's caretaker may limit his access. Relationship difficulties are sometimes a direct result of men's incarceration—caretakers may be angry about the loss of the man's income and his absence from their lives. Other times, however, problems exist well before the man's confinement. For example, only about 40% of the fathers in state custody and 55% of those in federal custody lived with their children before their incarceration. This suggests that relationships with mothers were already strained. Such tensions may be, at least in part, a result of drug use and other criminal behaviors the men engaged in before their arrest.

As noted above, a significant percentage of men in prison do maintain some type of contact with their children. Visiting is the most direct type of contact and also presents some of the greatest challenges. Most men do not see the children on a regular basis and may be unsure how to act around them. Increasing this awkwardness, children may also be uncomfortable, angry, or tense. While some prisons provide toys or activities, most do not. This means that children, including toddlers, must sit still for long periods of time with nothing to do. Prison security measures mean that children watch as their fathers are counted or ask permission to go the bathroom. This can be embarrassing for both fathers and children. As a result of these factors, visiting hours sometimes turn out to be a disappointment for all involved.

IMPORTANCE OF FATHER-CHILD RELATIONSHIPS

Research suggests that enabling fathers to stay in contact with their children is beneficial. Not only does such contact allow men and their children to develop more realistic expectations of each other, it also helps children to work through feelings of grief and abandonment due to their father's absence.

Most men are eventually released from prison and will try to resume some sort of contact with their children. Denying fathers contact with their children while they are in prison makes the transition to home very difficult, both for them and for their children. Furthermore, there is evidence to suggest that parents who maintain close contact with their children during their incarceration are less prone to recidivism.

REENTRY OF FATHERS INTO THE COMMUNITY

Returning fathers face many challenges when they attempt to reintegrate themselves into their children's lives. They may have been replaced by a new boyfriend or husband. Some children, unused to their father's presence, refuse to accept his authority. Fathers who return expecting to reassume their role as head-of-household may experience resistance from both children and the children's caretakers. For example, many mothers become more independent during a man's incarceration and may resist his attempt to resume a decision-making role in the family.

In our culture, one of the primary roles fathers are expected to fill is provider of financial support. This is a particularly difficult role for newly released men because their prison records disqualify them from some jobs and discourage employers from hiring them for others. For men who want to provide support for their children, the inability to find a job can be deeply disappointing. In addition, some states continue a man's child support obligations while he is incarcerated. This means a father may leave prison with a large child support debt.

CONCLUSION

Each year, an increasing number of fathers spend time in our nation's correctional facilities. A failure to address the impact of prison on these men's children, families, and communities may have serious social consequences. The incarceration of a father can lead to an estrangement from his children, financial and psychological problems for those children and for their caretakers, and a lack of male role models in this man's community. While the issues of fatherhood and incarceration are attracting more attention and research, there is still a great deal to be learned. Increasing our knowledge of imprisonment's impact can help us to formulate appropriate policy responses to this pressing social problem.

—*Anne M. Nurse*

See also Children; Children's Visits; Conjugal Visits; Foster Care; Mothers in Prison; Parenting Programs; Prisoner Reentry; Recidivism; Rehabilitation Theory; Termination of Parental Rights

Further Reading

Hairston, C. F. (1991). Family ties during imprisonment: Important to whom and for what? *Journal of Sociology and Social Welfare, 18*(1), 87–104.

Johnston, D., & Gable, K. (1995). *Children of incarcerated parents.* Lexington, MA: Lexington Books.

Lanier, C. S., Jr. (1991). Dimensions of father-child interaction in a New York state prison population. *Journal of Offender Rehabilitation, 16*(3/4), 27–42.

Mumola, C. (2000). *Incarcerated parents and their children.* Washington, DC: U.S. Department of Justice, Bureau of Justice Statistics.

Nurse, A. M. (2002). *Fatherhood arrested: Parenting from within the juvenile justice system.* Nashville, TN: Vanderbilt University Press.

Shaw, R. (Ed.). (1992). *Prisoners' children: What are the issues?* London: Routledge.

∎ FEDERAL PRISON INDUSTRIES

See UNICOR

∎ FEDERAL PRISON SYSTEM

The federal prison system holds offenders who have been convicted of federal crimes. It is currently one of the biggest prison systems in the country, with more than 175,000 inmates. Most of these women and men are housed in a nationwide system of some 104 establishments. Others are held in community corrections centers, in state and local prisons, or under house arrest.

HISTORY

The U.S. Congress formally established the Federal Bureau of Prisons in 1930. By then, a fairly considerable federal corrections system already existed. Courts had been created in 1789, and seven prisons had been gradually established from the last decade of the 19th century. Individuals found guilty of federal offenses could be fined, given corporal punishment, or held in state, local, or federal facilities. The federal correctional system, although predominantly a 20th-century creation, has its roots, in other words, in the 18th and 19th centuries.

The so-called Three Prison Act, which was passed in 1891, began the process of creating the federal prison system by identifying three sites around the country for its first penitentiaries. Development, however, was slow, and six years passed before ground breaking began on the first of the penitentiaries, USP Leavenworth. All told, it took inmates 25 years to complete Leavenworth Penitentiary.

Leavenworth was followed by Atlanta in 1902 and then, in 1909, by McNeil Island in Washington State, which had originally been founded as a territorial jail in 1875. These three institutions made up the entire system for many years until new laws, such as the Volstead Act in 1918, which introduced Prohibition, caused the federal population to grow exponentially.

The first women's prison in the federal system, FPC Alderson, opened in 1928 almost 40 years after the Three Prison Act. Prior to this time, women convicted of federal offenses were held in state and local penal facilities. Unlike the earlier penitentiaries that had grouped men in single large buildings, Alderson housed women in low-level, freestanding houses set within a rural setting.

Alcatraz, commonly viewed as a precursor to today's supermaximum secure facilities, opened in 1934. Designed to be an impenetrable and inescapable facility, Alcatraz was the destination for the most notorious criminals of the time. Al Capone, George "Machine Gun" Kelly, and Robert Stroud, the so-called Birdman of Alcatraz, all spent time there. When Alcatraz finally closed in 1963, its prisoners were transferred to the modern facility at Marion, Illinois.

Originally, Marion was a Level 5 prison, the highest security rating of the time. A series of violent and lethal attacks by inmates on staff and other prisoners throughout the 1970s and early 1980s culminated in the killing of two staff members on the same day in October 1983. After this event, the prison was re-rated at the previously unheard of security level of 6 and placed on continual lockdown. In 1994, ADX Florence replaced Marion as the destination "of last resort" for those inmates who were labeled dangerous and troublesome in the federal system.

The supermaximum secure prison at ADX Florence has the highest security level in the federal prison system. It holds "inmates who have been officially designated as exhibiting violent or serious and disruptive behavior while incarcerated" (National Institute of Corrections [NIC], 1997, p. 1). Prisoners are housed in solitary confinement and are rarely allowed out of their cells. Very few inmates are sent directly to ADX Florence from the courts. They are

Arriving in Prison

My public defender said, "Take nothing, have what you need sent after you settle." I called the BOP to confirm this, and they said they provide everything, including postage. The three-hour drive was filled with fear and anxiety. Once I arrived, I said goodbye to my friends, we hugged, and I turned and walked away. I couldn't look back, I tried not to cry. This couldn't be real; it had to be a bad dream.

It took three hours to process me, and it was all so surreal. I had to wait for R&D, wait for medical, wait for a female officer. Another prisoner, my mentor, came and took me where I would spend the next 53 months of my life. Leaving R&D, I saw gray concrete buildings and a dirt yard, and this stark and barren landscape mirrored how I felt inside. My mentor was talking, but I was in a fog.

At first sight, the housing unit looked like Costco with brick cubicles. The women inside were kind and generous with words and supplies. Even though I weighed 265 pounds I was assigned to a top bunk. During that first night, I laid in my bunk and quietly cried.

Seven months have passed, and the fog has lifted. Some things are better than I envisioned, others are not. Medical treatment is inadequate and the administration and most staff seem to thrive on dehumanizing and exerting their power and authority. The BOP didn't provide everything, they barely covered the necessities. Family and friends can only send money. We live in constant turmoil. However, most of the women in here make it tolerable. Although this place has changed me, I have faith that eventually my life will go on.

Letha Kennedy
Federal Prison Camp–Victorville, Adelanto, California

laws, such as the Sentencing Reform Act, were passed that ended parole, established determinate sentencing, and created mandatory minimum sentences. As a result of these legal changes, the inmate population grew dramatically, more than doubling between 1980 and 1989, from more than 24,000 to almost 58,000. In response, 20 new prisons opened between 1987 and 1992 alone. The system continued expanding during the 1990s, with the population reaching 175,000 in early 2004 (www.bop.gov).

usually transferred there from other high-security state or federal facilities during their sentence. Wardens wishing to commit prisoners to ADX Florence must make a special request to the North Central Regional Director and provide evidence that the individual "can be controlled only by separation, restricted movement, and limited direct access to staff and other inmates" (NIC, 1997, p. 1). According to the Federal Bureau of Prisons (2000b), "Inmates with severe or chronic behavior patterns that cannot be addressed in any other Bureau institution should be referred to ADX Florence general population, and those who are somewhat less problematic should be referred to USP Marion" (p. 12). If the inmate is designated a "failure" within Marion he may be sent on to ADX Florence.

Within 10 years of the creation of the Bureau of Prisons, the federal prison population and the number of facilities had almost doubled. The inmate population then remained more or less stable until the 1980s. During the second part of the 1980s, various

FEDERAL PRISONS TODAY

According to the most recent weekly population figures, the Federal Bureau of Prisons currently houses just over 175,000 inmates. Approximately 150,000 of these inmates are confined in bureau-operated correctional institutions or detention centers; the rest are held in state, local, and private institutions. Despite a continuing reliance on state and other facilities, the federal prison system remains heavily overcrowded, incarcerating 33% more people at year end of 2002 than it was built to contain (Harrison & Beck, 2003, p. 1).

Overall, the majority (56.5%) of prisoners in federal institutions are white, 40.3% are black, 1.6% are Asian, and 1.6% are Native American. About one-third (32.1%) are known to be of Hispanic ethnic origin. Almost 30% of all prisoners are foreign nationals, with more than 16% from Mexico alone. Since the 1980s, all are adults or juveniles who have been charged as adults. There are no juvenile facilities in the federal system. Women now make up 6.8% of the total population, which is greater than their proportion in state prisons. This figure reflects an increase of 182% in the number of female inmates since 1988. In comparison, the number of male inmates grew by 158% during the same period (Federal Bureau of Prisons, 1998; www.bop.gov).

More so than in most state systems, a disproportionate number of individuals in the federal prison population are serving time for drug offenses. Currently, they constitute 54.7% of the total population. Other crimes include immigration (10.5%), robbery (6.5%), and burglary (4.5%). The most frequent sentence being served by federal inmates is 5 to 10 years (29.5%), with the next common period being 10 to 15 years (17.4%). Very few (2.0%) serve less than 1 year, and not many serve life either (3.2%). At the time of writing, 26 people are on death row. As these figures suggest, the majority of federal inmates are assigned low (38.8%) or medium (25.0%) security levels, and the rest are labeled as minimum (19.4%) or high (10.7%) security; 6.1% of inmates have not been assigned a security level (www.bop.gov).

STAFF

Around 35,000 people work in the Federal Bureau of Prisons. The vast majority of them (71.8%) are men. Likewise, most prison employees are white (64.4%). African Americans make up 21.0% of the total number of staff, while only 11.0% of officers are Hispanic, 2.0% are Asian, and 1.5% are Native American.

The federal system was one of the first to establish a training program for correctional officers in 1930. Even so, a formal, centralized system was not fully implemented until 1982, when the Bureau of Prisons established a residential program at Glynco, Georgia, where, to this day, all staff members receive the same basic training (Keve, 1991, p. 237). All prison workers, from the medical personnel to those running the prison factory, must be coached as correctional officers. They must know how to use firearms and restraining techniques. The only exceptions to this rule are the staff in private facilities,

who are trained separately. They should, however, have equivalent skills to those in the public prisons.

Despite the bureau's early move to attempt to professionalize its employees, the pay and education levels of many staff members remain low. Just over one-third of all staff (34.6%) have only a high school diploma, while fewer than one in five of them (19.2%) have a bachelor's degree (Federal Bureau of Prisons, 2000c, p. 55). Salaries for correctional officers are similar to other areas of law enforcement. According to the Web site of the Bureau of Labor Statistics, for example, federal correctional officer salaries started at $27,000 in 2001. The previous year, the median salary was around $35,000. Like the police, correctional officers may retire after 20 years service for full benefits.

TYPES OF FACILITIES

The Bureau of Prisons operates many different kinds of facilities from penitentiaries to prison camps. Other than the sole supermaximum secure facility at ADX Florence, the highest-security prisons in the federal system are the U.S. penitentiaries (USPs). They have walls, or reinforced fences, and close staff supervision. Prisoners are held in both single-occupant and cell housing. These facilities, which include USP Marion, Leavenworth, and Lewisburg, among others, are designed to hold high-security male offenders. There is no penitentiary for women.

Federal correctional institutions (FCIs) are the most common type of penal institution. These facilities are usually low security with double-fenced perimeters, although there are some medium-security establishments as well. In correctional institutions, prisoners are typically housed in cubicles in dormitory style units with a medium staff-inmate ratio.

Federal prison camps (FPCs) and the three intensive confinement centers (ICCs) in Lewisburg, Lompoc, and Bryan have the lowest security rating of all the federal institutions other than the community corrections centers (CCCs), which are also known as "halfway houses." Because they are classified as minimum security, most of them have no fences, and there is a low staff-inmate ratio. Individuals may be either sent to the camps directly from the court or transferred from other higher-security facilities. They are usually housed in open dormitories. Security is much more relaxed at these institutions than anywhere else. However, they generally offer fewer opportunities for education and recreation because they are primarily work-oriented institutions. This is particularly the case for those prison camps located next to higher-security facilities in the federal correctional centers (FCCs), which the bureau has built since the 1980s. In these institutions, camps are merely part of a series of other institutions, including correctional institutions and penitentiaries.

Administrative prisons make up the final and most varied category of federal institutions. These are designed to hold inmates of all security classifications with special needs or characteristics. They include the federal transfer center (FTC) at Oklahoma City, federal medical centers (FMCs), federal detention centers (FDCs), metropolitan detention centers (MDCs), metropolitan correctional centers (MCCs), the medical center for federal prisoners (MCFP) at Springfield, and the supermaximum secure section of USP Florence, which is known as ADX Florence.

The federal transfer center at Oklahoma City is the first stop for most prisoners as they enter the federal system for the first time. Because this institution holds some high-security prisoners, its conditions are much more restricted than some may expect. Though most inmates spend only a few days at this institution, some are assigned longer periods of time in the work cadre to provide necessary labor. Most visits here, however, will be brief, ranging from a few weeks to a few months.

FMCs are essentially prison hospitals. There are seven of them across the national system, six catering to men only and one (FMC Carswell) to women. Though all prisons offer medical care, if the individual has a chronic or serious illness he or she will usually be placed in an FMC. In addition to holding ill female prisoners, FMC Carswell has a special administrative unit for women deemed to be particularly high-security risks.

FDCs and MDCs hold people awaiting trial, as well as those who have been convicted but who are awaiting sentence. They will also house a small work cadre, like the transfer center, to provide labor for the main institution. They are, in effect, jails and thus have a rapid turnover of population, as most prisoners are held there awaiting transfer. Many detention centers have been contracted out to private companies.

There are three MCCs in the United States, in San Diego, New York City, and Chicago. These high-rise buildings opened within a year of each other, from December 1974 to August 1975, and represented the first shift within the Bureau of Prisons to "new generation" prison building. MCCs cater to a large and varied population. They hold both female and male sentenced offenders and those awaiting trial or sentencing. Inmates serving short-term sentences provide the necessary work details in each facility.

Finally, offenders may be sent to a community-based facility if they have been sentenced to six months or less. Very minor offenders may be held under house arrest. CCCs are essentially halfway houses and are contracted by the Bureau of Prisons to private companies. Only those people who are deemed no risk at all to the community may be sent there without prior time spent in a higher-security institution.

Individuals incarcerated by the Federal Bureau of Prisons will be assigned to a prison's mainline population in any one of the foregoing types of institutions. A certain number will, however, be segregated from the general population in special sections of these institutions such as control units, administrative segregation, disciplinary segregation, or death row. A rare few men (around 0.5%) will spend time in one of the system's highest-security facilities, the Control Unit of USP Marion or ADX Florence.

Each institution is imbued with a different ethos, depending on its security level and population type. Some, such as FMCs, provide specialized treatment for inmates with HIV/AIDS or other physical and mental health issues. Many women's facilities offer specific opportunities to enhance family ties. More than half of all the institutions now have residential substance abuse treatment programs as mandated by the Violent Crime Control and Law Enforcement Act of 1994.

WOMEN IN PRISON

Women make up approximately 7% of the federal prison population. Of the total number of women incarcerated in the system, 58% are white, 39% are black, 2% are Asian, and 1% are Native American. Hispanics account for nearly one out of three female prisoners in federal custody (Federal Bureau of Prisons, 1998, p. 4; Greenfeld & Snell, 1999, p. 7).

More than two-thirds of women (68%) are imprisoned for drug offenses. The next most common category of crime, accounting for only 11% of those incarcerated, is extortion and fraud. Overall, women tend to commit less serious and less violent offenses than men and, in general, have lower security classifications. The majority of them are held either in minimum-security prison camps or in pretrial facilities. There is no medium-security facility for women in the federal system and only one high-security institution (Federal Bureau of Prisons, 1998, pp. 4–5). There are now 20 different prisons that hold female offenders, including prison camps, correctional institutions, FMC Carswell, and various MCCs.

Most women in prison (80%) are primary caretakers of children. More than half (59%) of women in federal prisons have children under the age of 18. Half of those women had lived with their children before entering prison (Greenfeld & Snell, 1999, p. 8). Many female inmates have experienced domestic or other forms of violence, in most cases including sexual assault. Nearly three-quarters (73%) of women in federal prison have completed high school, and 30% to 40% of those high school graduates have attended some college or more. Despite these relatively high rates of education, however, like male prisoners, most women were unemployed before their incarceration (Greenfeld & Snell, 1999, p. 7).

Women in prison abide by the same rules as men except in the areas of health and beauty treatments, pat searches, and transportation. Women generally are allowed more items under health and beauty than are men, and, in light of concerns about sexual harassment, their pat searches are more strictly regulated. Male guards are not permitted to take part in, or be present during, a search of a female prisoner. Women who are transported while pregnant should be held with fewer physical restraints than other prisoners, although a number of reports from human rights organizations suggest that this policy is not always closely followed.

DRUG TREATMENT PROGRAMS

More than half of the total population is doing time for drug offenses, and others are there for drug-related crimes. It is estimated that 80% of state and federal inmates either committed drug offenses, were under the influence of drugs or alcohol at the time of their crime, committed their crime to support their drug use, or had histories of substance use. Under the new sentencing laws, many of these individuals are serving long terms of imprisonment, often for their first offense.

According to a 1999 report to Congress, the Federal Bureau of Prisons "addresses inmate drug abuse by attempting to identify, confront, and alter the attitudes, values, and thinking patterns that lead to criminal and drug-using behavior" (Federal Bureau of Prisons, 1999, p. 1). The Bureau of Prisons differentiates between prisoners who are incarcerated for manufacturing or selling drugs and those who are incarcerated for crimes that were a direct result of their drug use and recognizes that each group requires different counseling and treatment. As a result, the federal system offers three different forms of drug programs through Psychology Services, each of which attempts "to identify, confront and alter the attitudes, values and thinking patterns that led to criminal behavior and drug or alcohol abuse" (Pelissier et al., 2000, p. 5). Currently, drug treatment options include a 500-hour residential drug treatment program, a 40-hour drug education program, and a more loosely organized set of counseling and self-help classes known collectively under the title of "nonresidential" drug treatment.

The residential drug abuse program (RDAP) is the most intensive of the bureau's drug treatment options. First, the inmate participates in a unit based program that generally has a capacity for around

100 people. During this time, he or she spends half of each day learning about drug use and the other half of it in ordinary activities such as work and education with the general population. Prisoners are screened and assessed at the beginning of the RDAP to work out their treatment orientation. To complete the program, they take a variety of classes, including "Criminal Lifestyle Confrontation," "Cognitive Skills Building," "Relapse Prevention," "Interpersonal Skill Building," and "Wellness," before being returned to the general prison population. Afterwards, they must also participate in 12 months of treatment, meeting with "drug abuse program staff at least once a month for a group activity consisting of relapse prevention planning and a review of treatment techniques learned during the intensive phase of the residential drug abuse program" (Pelissier et al., 2000, p. 4). The residential program even reaches beyond prison. Once an inmate is been transferred to a CCC, he or she will meet with privately contracted counselors to reaffirm the lessons of the drug treatment program. These sessions may also include other family members.

RDAPs are the most celebrated and, apparently, successful part of the bureau's current drug policy. According to a recent evaluation, these programs, which last from 9 to 12 months, reduce men's reoffending after three years in the community by 16% and women's by 18%. Thirty-six months after their release, men who have successfully completed an RDAP course also are 15% less likely to use drugs on release, and women are 18% less likely to do so.

Because of these findings, the Bureau of Prisons has introduced a series of incentives to encourage prisoners to participate in RDAPs. Some examples of the opportunities available include a small monetary award for successful completion of program; consideration for placement in a six-month halfway house; and what are referred to as "tangible benefits," such as shirts, caps, and pens with program logos. The most influential incentive, however, was brought in by the Violent Crime and Law Enforcement Act of 1994, which allows up to a one-year reduction in sentence from an inmate's statutory release date. This incentive has obvious attractions, and many prisoners are in favor of it. Others, however, are more critical of this reward. They point out that sentence reductions lead to inconsistent sentencing, in which participants do less time for the same crimes. Specifically, critics suggest that this policy may unintentionally reward inmates with drug problems (Pelissier et al., 2000, p. 6).

The 40-hour drug education program is somewhat less intensive than the residential program. It incorporates lectures, movies, written assignments, and group discussion. Participants usually meet twice a week for approximately 10 weeks, covering the reasons for their drug use and abuse, theories of addiction, physical and psychological addiction, defenses, effects of drug abuse on the family, and different types of drugs and their effect on an individual.

Nonresidential drug treatment can include meetings with Alcoholics Anonymous and Narcotics Anonymous as well as individual and group counseling offered by the Psychology Services. Finally, as part of their more general approach to curbing substance abuse, all federal prisons conduct regular random drug tests of all prisoners. Those with outside assignments are tested most frequently. The bureau's policy appears to have worked. The 2000 *Judicial Resource Guide* (Federal Bureau of Prisons, 2000a) states that "the number of positive test results for the random tests continues to be very low for the last few years—1.3% FY95; 0.9% FY96; 1.0% FY97; and 0.9% FY98" (p. 31).

EDUCATION AND VOCATIONAL TRAINING PROGRAMS

The main thrust of education in the federal system has always been literacy skills and vocational training. Inmates in the first federal prisons were taught the basics of reading and writing by prison staff and, if possible, an employable skill that might keep them away from criminal activity upon release. The first mandatory literacy program in the Bureau of Prisons was established in 1982. All inmates were required to enroll unless they could demonstrate a sixth-grade level of reading and writing. In 1986, the standard was increased to an eighth-grade level, and in 1991 the current requirements of a high school equivalency (general equivalency diploma, GED) were established.

These days, the bureau's commitment to basic literacy has been taken a further step: All promotions in institution jobs above entry level require a GED. Although seemingly a commendable idea, tying education to prison labor so closely places those with little educational experience or those from a foreign or non-English-speaking background in a vulnerable position, rendering them ineligible for many prison jobs.

In addition to creating an employable workforce in prison, reduced reoffending rates have always been another important justification for prison education classes. For that reason, vocational courses and apprenticeships are two of the main strategies that education departments pursue to help prisoners prepare for successful release. Like most aspects of imprisonment, the quality and availability of these courses vary enormously. Some facilities offer a variety of choices from carpentry to cooking. Others, particularly high-security institutions, are much more restricted. In any case, certificates or diplomas will not specify that they were earned in a correctional facility.

WORK

Unlike other correctional systems, work of some sort is mandatory in federal prisons. Upon arrival, prisoners are offered jobs in various aspects of site maintenance, usually in food services. Following a certain amount of time (usually 90 days), they may shift to another area of prison labor, such as grounds maintenance, the prison farm, or work as an orderly. They may also apply for employment in the federal prison industries known as UNICOR. If they do not wish to work, they must enroll in some education or training program. The vast majority work at jobs that contribute to the maintenance of the prison such as grounds, and cooking. Around 25% are employed by the higher-paying prison industries.

CONCLUSION

Since the 1980s, the prison population in the United States has increased dramatically. The U.S. federal prison system currently holds more prisoners than ever before and far more than it can comfortably house. The majority of these women and men are serving time for drug offenses. Disproportionate numbers of them belong to minority communities, and few have significant levels of education or much legitimate work experience. Sentences have become longer, and consequently the average age of the inmate community is growing. All of these factors mean that there are a number of challenges facing the administrators of the federal system. How they respond to them will determine whether federal prisons will break down into disturbances as they have in the past, or whether they will remain relatively peaceful as they are at present.

—Mary Bosworth

See also Alcatraz; Alcoholics Anonymous; Alderson, Federal Prison Camp; Campus Style; College Courses in Prison; Community Corrections Centers; Correctional Officers; Cottage System; Drug Offenders; Drug Treatment Programs; General Educational Development (GED) Exam and General Equivalency Diploma; Group Therapy; History of Prisons; Individual Therapy; INS Detention Facilities; Leavenworth, U.S. Penitentiary; Maximum Security; Medium Security; Minimum Security; Prison Camps; Professionalization of Staff; Psychological Services; Race, Class, and Gender of Prisoners; Racism; Staff Training; Supermax Prisons; Therapeutic Communities; Three Prisons Act 1891; UNICOR; Violent Crime Control and Law Enforcement Act 1994; Volstead Act 1918; War on Drugs; Women in Prison

Further Reading

Amnesty International. (1999). *Not part of my sentence: Violations of the human rights of women in custody.* New York: Author.

Bosworth, M. (2002). *The U.S. federal prison system.* Thousand Oaks, CA: Sage.

Federal Bureau of Prisons. (1998). *A profile of female offenders.* Washington, DC: U.S. Department of Justice.

Federal Bureau of Prisons. (1999). *Substance abuse treatment programs in the Federal Bureau of Prisons: Report to Congress, as required by the Violent Crime Control and*

Law Enforcement Act of 1994. Washington, DC: U.S. Department of Justice.

Federal Bureau of Prisons. (2000a). *Judicial resource guide to the Federal Bureau of Prisons.* Washington, DC: U.S. Department of Justice.

Federal Bureau of Prisons. (2000b). *Security designation and custody classification manual.* Washington, DC: U.S. Department of Justice.

Federal Bureau of Prisons. (2000c). *State of the bureau 1999: Accomplishments and goals.* Washington, DC: U.S. Department of Justice.

Greenfeld, L., & Snell, T. (1999). *Bureau of Justice special report: Women offenders.* Washington, DC: U.S. Department of Justice.

Harrison, P., & Beck, A. (2003). *Prisoners in 2002.* Washington, DC: Bureau of Justice Statistics.

Heffernan, E. (1994). Banners, brothels, and a "ladies seminary": Women and federal corrections. In J. Roberts (Ed.), *Escaping prison myths: Selected topics in the history of federal corrections.* Washington, DC: American University Press.

Keve, P. (1991). *Prisons and the American conscience: A history of U.S. federal corrections.* Carbondale: Southern Illinois University Press.

National Institute of Corrections. (1997). *Supermax housing: A survey of current practice.* Longmont, CO: U.S. Department of Justice.

Pelissier, B., Rhodes, W., Saylor, W., Gaes, G., Camp, S. D., Vanyur, S. D., & Wallace, S. (2000). *TRIAD Drug Treatment Evaluation Project: Final year report of three year outcome, executive summary.* Washington, DC: Bureau of Prisons.

Roberts, J. W. (1996). Work, education and public safety: A brief history of Federal Prison Industries. In Federal Prison Industries, Inc. (Ed.), *Factories with fences: The history of Federal Prison Industries.* Sandstone, MN: Federal Prison Industries.

Witke, L. (Ed.). (1999). *Planning and design guide for secure adult and juvenile facilities.* Lanham, MD: American Correctional Association.

◪ FELON DISENFRANCHISEMENT

Felon disenfranchisement refers to the practice of banning individuals with a felony conviction from voting. These laws are determined at the state level. States have the option of banning a felon from voting while in prison, while on parole, probation, or permanently barring them from voting.

The United States is one of few nations across the world that bans people from voting while they are imprisoned. Countries such as Spain, Greece, Ireland, Switzerland, France, Israel, Japan, and the Czech Republic all allow incarcerated felons to vote. Furthermore, other countries such as Germany and South Africa require prison officials to encourage inmates to exercise the vote. In Puerto Rico, the right to vote is one of the few rights citizens retain during incarceration.

HISTORY

Disenfranchisement provisions have existed since the founding of the United States. Throughout earlier periods in American history, the right to vote was seen as a privilege that only some people deserved. It was not extended to groups such as women, Catholics, the illiterate, and the poor. Supporters of limited suffrage argued that class and social standing should be important determinants of political status. Others asserted that individuals who broke the social contract did not deserve to enjoy the full rights of citizenship, for example, voting. Therefore, legislators viewed criminal disenfranchisement laws as a means of both protecting the ballot box and promoting the community's interests.

Between 1776 and 1821, 11 states adopted provisions that denied the vote to convicted felons: Virginia (1776), Kentucky (1799), Ohio (1802), New Jersey (1807), Louisiana (1812), Indiana (1816), Mississippi (1817), Connecticut (1818), Alabama (1819), Missouri (1820), and New York (1821). The original justifications for these statutes were based on the dual concepts of deterrence and retribution. However, the end of the 19th century marked an important era for the expansion and strict enforcement of criminal disenfranchisement laws. After several constitutional amendments increased blacks' access to the political process, Southern white opposition soared. In response, most states tailored their statutes during the post-Reconstruction era to enhance their impact on African Americans. These news plans penalized blacks without any explicit reference to blacks as a racial group. As a result of this subtlety, states were protected from legal challenges. In particular, they were able to uphold the 15th Amendment's ban on overtly racial policies while still promoting their interests.

Mississippi's plan set the standard for states interested in altering their disenfranchisement provisions. The state's 1869 constitution required disenfranchisement of citizens convicted of *any* crime. However, its 1890 constitution imposed disenfranchisement for a very narrow list of crimes such as bigamy, theft, and burglary. In particular, the disenfranchising crimes were based on those crimes that blacks were believed to commit more frequently, and excluded crimes that whites were believed to commit more frequently.

Realizing the effectiveness of Mississippi's plan, from 1891 to 1910 eleven other states—Louisiana (1898), Virginia (1902), Alabama (1901), North Carolina (1900), Georgia (1908), South Carolina (1895), Tennessee (1891), Florida (1889), Texas (1902), Arkansas (1893), and Oklahoma—adopted similar criminal disenfranchisement policies. The impact of these new statutes, in conjunction with the long-standing tools of poll taxes, literacy tests, violence, and intimidation, significantly reduced the eligible black electorate. For example, in 1897 Louisiana had more than 130,000 African Americans registered to vote, representing nearly 44% of the electorate. After the adoption of disenfranchisement provisions at the 1898 constitutional convention, the number of African Americans registered to vote plummeted to 5,320. In 1904, that number fell to 1,342.

Although the number of whites registered to vote during this time also decreased, the change was not nearly as dramatic. For example, 125,437 whites were registered to vote in Louisiana in 1897. In 1904, the number of white citizens who were registered was 91,716. Overall, the black electorate in Louisiana was reduced by nearly 96%, while the white electorate was reduced by 23%.

As the dual process of migration and urbanization pulled African Americans out of the South and into northern centers, the adoption of criminal disenfranchisement statutes spread across the country. Randall Kennedy documented the disproportionate number of African American men who were arrested in northern cities on what many believed to be false charges. These charges often included things such as burglary, assault, and inciting or participating in riots. Taken together, the evolution of felon disenfranchisement laws slowly eroded the legal enfranchisement that blacks had acquired.

CURRENT PRACTICE

These days, convicted felons constitute the largest single group of American citizens who are permanently prohibited from voting in elections. Currently, 48 states and the District of Columbia ban inmates from voting. In 32 states, individuals on parole or probation cannot vote. In 13 states, a felony conviction can lead to a lifetime loss of voting rights. As a result of these laws, there are more than 4 million American citizens who have permanently lost the right to vote.

Whether a convicted felon can vote depends on the state he or she resides in, not the state he or she was convicted in. Therefore, a felon convicted in the state of New Hampshire would be able to vote in elections while residing in New Hampshire. However, if that individual moved to the state of Virginia, he or she would lose that right.

Individuals with a felony conviction are not banned from holding public office. Therefore, many citizens would be able to hold elected office but would not be eligible to cast a vote in that election. For example, Lyndon LaRouche was able to run for president in 1992 and Jim Traficant was able to run for U.S. Congress in 2001.

RACE AND FELON DISENFRANCHISEMENT

Although the civil rights movement and the prison reform movement were important for making the American polity more inclusive, most states continue to be governed by disenfranchisement laws that were created during an era saturated with racial hostility. Indeed, African Americans and Latino/as account for nearly half of those (ex-) felons permanently banned from voting, with African Americans in particular, representing more than 36% of permanently banned citizens. The rate of black disenfranchisement is nearly seven times the national average, and if current rates of incarceration persist, 3 in 10 of the next generation of black men in this country can expect to lose the right to vote at some point in their lifetime.

As it was historically, the disproportionate impact of these laws is particularly pronounced in a number of southern states. According to a U.S. Census report, the 10 states with the largest black populations combine to account for 58% of the total U.S. black population but account for less than 49% of the total U.S. population. All but one of these states has a lifetime ban on felon voting. In Alabama and Florida, one-third of black men are permanently barred from voting. In Mississippi, Virginia, Texas, and Iowa, one in four black men are permanently disenfranchised.

For most states with lifetime bans on felon voting, ex-felons can usually go through some type of review process to have their rights restored. This process varies significantly across the states. For example, in Alabama an ex-offender must submit a DNA sample to the state's department of forensic science. In Mississippi, an ex-offender must either secure an executive order from the governor or convince a state legislator to introduce a bill on his or her behalf. Therefore, although these options exist in theory they seldom result in the restoration of voting rights. This failure can be attributed to a number of factors including (1) limited knowledge of the process necessary to regain the right to vote; (2) an emphasis on more immediate needs, for example, finding housing, jobs; and (3) the lack of political and financial resources necessary to successfully navigate the restoration process.

CONCLUSION: THE IMPACT OF FELON DISENFRANCHISEMENT

The effect of criminal disenfranchisement laws was seen in the controversial presidential election of 2000. In Florida alone—where the result of the election was determined—there were more than 300,000 ex-felons who were barred from voting. In fact, 31% of all voting-age black men in Florida were disenfranchised. Given that the majority of the

black population traditionally votes Democrat, had these men been able to vote, the result of the election could have been very different.

Thus far, the most successful tool for challenging the felony disenfranchisement laws has been litigation. A number of cases including *Hunter v. Underwood* and *Richardson v. Ramirez* have all successfully challenged the constitutionality of felon disenfranchisement restrictions. Although the laws still exist, these cases have narrowed their scope while also challenging legislators to adopt more uniform standards.

Many attribute the racial and gendered disparities in disenfranchisement rates to the national war on drugs movement ushered in during the 1980s. Thus, repealing the drug laws may reduce the number of people of color who are banned from voting. Given that the prison population continues to soar, unless changes are made in some arena, the United States can expect to see more and more people denied the right to vote in the near future.

—Khalilah L. Brown-Dean

See also Abolition; Activism; African American Prisoners; Hispanic/Latino(a) Prisoners; Racism

Further Reading

Manza, J., & Uggen, C. (2002). Democratic contraction? The political consequences of felon disenfranchisement in the United States. *American Sociological Review, 67,* 777–803.

Mauer, M., & Fellner, J. (1998). *Losing the vote: The impact of felony disenfranchisement laws in the United States.* Washington, DC: Sentencing Project.

Legal Cases

Hunter v. Underwood, 471 U.S. 222 (1985).

Richardson v. Ramirez, 418 U.S. 24 (1974).

⚑ FINE

A fine is a monetary sum ordered by the court to be paid to the state by a convicted offender for the purpose of retribution and deterrence. While the use of fines is a common form of criminal sanction in both the United States and many European countries, the use of fines and their relative successes varies greatly by jurisdiction.

HISTORY

The practice of imposing fines for malfeasance dates back to the Dark Ages (500–1000 A.D.). Both German and Anglo-Saxon societies practiced a system of *wergild,* which required offenders to compensate victims for their damages. One of the earliest records of such practices can be found in the sixth-century legal code of Salic Franks (a tribe in what is now known as France). Under this system, a punishment of 24,000 denars (currency) was assigned for the killing of a woman of childbearing years and the sum of 8,000 denars for a woman past childbearing years.

After the Norman conquest of England in 1066 A.D., the system of wergild was transformed so that the sum paid by the offender (the *bot*) was divided between the king (*wer*) and the victim (*wite*). The amount of compensation was somewhat graded, in that greater compensation was provided for more serious offenses. The practice of wergild is the historical precursor to the modern criminal fine in the United States.

CURRENT PRACTICE IN THE UNITED STATES AND EUROPE

In the United States, fines are generally assigned as the sole sentence for only the most minor offenses, such as traffic violations and infractions. More commonly, fines are used in conjunction with another form of intermediate sanctions, such as community service and probation in misdemeanor cases, or in conjunction with incarceration in more serious cases. For example, a misdemeanor conviction might result in a sentence that includes a fine, community service, and probation, while a felony conviction might result in a sentence that includes a fine as well as a term of confinement in jail or prison. Currently, fines are assigned in 86% of lower court and 42% of superior court sentences. Although research indicates that less than half of all fines are in fact

paid in the United States, more than $1 billion in fines are collected annually.

Currently, the use of fines in the United States is somewhat more limited than in European nations, in part due to the difficulty of enforcing this sanction and in collecting fines from offenders. In addition, there is some concern that the use of flat fines commonly practiced in the United States is unfair to the poor, for whom a predetermined fine may be unduly harsh, and too lenient for the very rich, for whom a predetermined fine may be a minor inconvenience.

Many European nations have solved the equity dilemma through the use of day fines, which have been commonly used since the early 20th century. In Europe, more than 80% of convicted offenders receive a sentence of a fine with no other sanctions. However, the mechanism for calculating day fines varies by country. In Germany, for example, a day fine is calculated by assigning a unit value for the offense. This unit value takes into consideration both the seriousness of the offense and the culpability of the offender. This value is then multiplied by the net daily income of the offender. In the German example, the day fine is roughly the cost for a number of day(s) of freedom. One of the benefits of the use of day fines is that it applies an equivalent multiple (based on the offense) to the income of a given offender; as such, it represents equivalent financial hardship to each offender. It also saves valuable prison resources for more serious offenders. Since this process was introduced, the use of day fines has grown while the use of short-term incarceration has diminished.

A number of states have experimented with day fines in the United States, with mixed results. Some studies have demonstrated that 70% of fines are collected under the day fine model, a substantial increase from the overall national collection rate of only 50%. In other studies, day fines seem to increase collection from the poorest offenders but have resulted in lower total collections overall, which, in practice, may deter some jurisdictions from applying this model. Other studies indicate that the use of day fines seems to have no impact on recidivism, so there appears little incentive to move toward the day fine in the United States.

CONCLUSION

The use of fines in the United States appears to be limited to use as the sole sanction in only the most minor cases or in conjunction with additional sanctions in the majority of cases. While initial evaluations of day fines in the United States demonstrate somewhat mixed results, the use of day fines have had promising results in Europe, namely, greater equity for offenders with varying incomes, a decline in short-term incarceration, and increased revenues.

—*Connie Stivers Ireland*

See also Corporal Punishment; Deterrence Theory; England and Wales; History of Prisons; Incapacitation Theory; Intermediate Sanctions; Increase in Prison Population

Further Reading

Clear, T. R., & Cole, G. F. (2003). Intermediate sanctions and community corrections. In T. Clear & G. F. Cole, *American corrections* (6th ed.). Belmont, CA: Wadsworth/ Thompson.

Cole, G. F., & Smith, C. E. (2001). Corrections. In G. F. Cole & C. E. Smith, *The American system of criminal justice* (9th ed.). Belmont, CA: Wadsworth/Thompson.

Composition, in ancient and medieval law. (2002). In *Columbia encyclopedia* (6th ed.). New York: Columbia University Press. Retrieved December 29, 2002, from www.bartleby.com/65/

Cromwell, P. F., Del Carmen, R. V., & Alarid, L. F. (2002). Nonresidential intermediate sanctions. In P. F. Cromwell, R. V. Del Carmen, & L. F. Alarid, *Community-based corrections* (5th ed.). Belmont, CA: Wadsworth/Thompson.

McDonald, D. C., Greene, J., & Worzella, C. (1992). *Day fines in American courts: The Staten Island and Milwaukee experiments*. Washington, DC: U.S. Department of Justice, National Institute of Justice.

Turner, S., & Petersilia, J. (1996). *Day fines in four jurisdictions*. Santa Monica, CA: RAND.

◼ FIRST AMENDMENT

> *Congress shall make no law respecting an establishment of religion, or prohibiting the free exercise thereof; or abridging the freedom of speech, or of the press; or the right of the people peaceably to assemble, and to petition the Government for a redress of grievances.*
>
> —U.S. Constitution,
> Amendment 1 (ratified 1791).

The First Amendment guarantees a certain level of freedom of speech, religion, association, and access to government throughout the United States. Although it technically applies only to the federal government, it is made applicable to all the state governments (and any subunits of the states) through the due process clause of the 14th Amendment. Like all constitutional rights, however, First Amendment rights are not absolute. For example, freedom of speech does not give anyone the right to yell "Fire!" in a crowded theater, unless there is indeed a blaze. People in prison are subject to additional limitations since the mere fact they are incarcerated means that their rights of association are restricted.

Many states have language in their state constitutions that is similar to the First Amendment. Those states may interpret their own constitutional language to be more protective than the federal standard. Thus, the federal First Amendment sets a floor, not a ceiling, for the rights it mentions. Finally, prison administrations are always free to be more protective of the rights mentioned than either the federal Constitution or the state constitutions.

GENERAL TEST APPLIED BY THE COURTS

The general rule for prison limitations on First Amendment rights is found in the case of *Turner v. Safley* (1987). A rule is acceptable under the U.S. Constitution as long as it bears a "rational relation to a legitimate penological interest." This standard is usually an easy one for a prison system to meet. Safety and the orderly running of a prison are two common examples of widely accepted legitimate penological interests and provide a basis for many of the regulations inside a prison system.

Once a legitimate penological interest for a rule is established, the prison system only has to show that the promulgated regulation is rationally related to that interest. "Rationally related" means that the rule or regulation does not have to be the least restrictive means of dealing with the prison's interest; the rule or regulation does not need to be the most respectful of the First Amendment interest that it possibly could be. Rather, it simply has to be one way of dealing with the legitimate penological interest the prison system has asserted.

Many concerns that prisoners have are related to the freedoms guaranteed by the First Amendment, from religious freedom to freedom of expression. Some issues are litigated regularly in the courts. Although always analyzed within the general *Turner* framework, these areas have their own specific tests. General rules have been developed by the courts. Some of the more common questions that prisoners and prison administrators face will be described below.

RELIGION

The First Amendment prohibits the government both from establishing a mandatory religion and from prohibiting the practice of any particular creed. Generally, these two rights are referred to as the right to freedom of religion. However, as for people outside of prison, inmates do not have absolute freedom to practice their religious beliefs.

In 1972, the U.S. Supreme Court held that a prisoner must be given a reasonable opportunity to practice his or her religion (see *Cruz v. Beto,* 1972). Since then, *Turner* has been decided, so the test the courts must apply is now more detailed. However, an examination of the earlier case is instructive. In the 1972 case, a Buddhist prisoner was prohibited from using the chapel for his religious observance. The Court held that he must be allowed to use the chapel but emphasized that the prison did not have to provide the same services for a minority of one that it provided the larger religious groups.

Post-*Turner* religious freedom cases have borne out that the *Turner* test does in fact provide great latitude for prison officials. *O'Lone v. Estate of Shabazz* (1987) was one such case. In *O'Lone,* Muslim inmates sued because they were being denied the opportunity to participate in Jumu'ah prayers, a requirement of their religion. The prison at which they were housed required work outside of the facility during the day and would not transport them back during the workday. Thus, Muslim prisoners could not go to Jumu'ah prayers, which are held on Friday afternoons. The Supreme Court ruled that the failure of the prison to allow Muslims

to participate in Jumu'ah prayers was acceptable under the First Amendment. The Court reasoned that the work requirement was rationally related to relieving overcrowding and tension and the refusal to transport Muslim prisoners back was rationally related to efficient prison operations.

Within the general framework of religious freedom, religious names and religious food become very important to prisoners who have limited ability to control almost any other area of their life. These areas also cause concern for prison administrators, as name changes and special diets tax their resources. Because these two issues arise so frequently, cause such conflict, and have such importance to prisoners, they are discussed below.

Name Changes

Some people who are in prison change their names to reflect their religious beliefs. Again, courts have applied the test laid out in *Turner* to reach the following set of rules regarding name changes. People in prison have a First Amendment interest in using their religious name in conjunction with the name under which they were committed to the prison. However, people in prison cannot force the prison administration to reorder its filing system. If a state allows people to change their names legally, the prison can require that an inmate pass through that process before it recognizes his or her new name. For more explanation of these types of cases, see *Malik v. Brown* (1995) and *Hakim v. Hicks* (2000).

Religious Meals

Access to religious meals is also analyzed under the *Turner* scheme. A prisoner's request must be based on a belief that is sincerely held and religious in nature (see *DeHart v. Horn,* 2000). While the courts are not permitted to determine if the prisoner is interpreting his or her faith correctly, they can determine if the prisoner actually has a religious belief that compels a special meal. Efficient administration and prevention of jealousy among other prisoners are considered legitimate penological needs. Generally, it is very difficult for prisoners to compel a prison to give them special religious meals by citing the First Amendment; see *DeHart v. Horn,* (2000) (finding that a Buddhist inmate had other means of expressing his Buddhism and holding he was not entitled to vegetarian meals), *Levitan v. Ashcroft* (2002) (remanding for further fact finding and *Turner* analysis the question of whether Catholic inmates could have access to wine for communion), and *Sutton v. Rasheed* (2003) (holding that Nation of Islam texts are religious books and inmates were entitled to have them in the Special Housing Unit).

In short, as these examples demonstrate, religious freedom cases are very hard to win if the only grounds relied on are First Amendment guarantees. As long as prison can point to a penological need and show that the infringement on religious freedom is rationally related to that need, the institution's view will be upheld.

ACCESS TO THE COURTS

The First Amendment also protects the right to petition the government for redress of grievances. In simple terms, all people have the right to complain to government, subject to minimal limitations. Inside the prison context, access to the court's claims is also analyzed under the *Turner* test: whether the limitation is rationally related to a legitimate penological interest.

As a starting point, prisoners retain the right to submit cases to court challenging their sentences or conditions of confinement (see *Lewis v. Casey,* 1996). As the specific examples show below, however, they do not have unlimited rights to access all the possible ways there are to complain to the government.

Grievance Systems

All prisons and jails have a system of filing internal grievances. Usually, this process has several steps and levels of appeal. Filing a grievance inside the prison system is protected under the First Amendment for two reasons. First, a prison grievance is in and of itself an attempt to seek redress from the government, in this case the prison system. It is also protected by the First Amendment because it is a prerequisite for filing a federal court case under the Prison Litigation Reform Act (see

Shabazz v. Cole, 1999, and *Graham v. Henderson,* 1995). Thus, prison rules or customs that block prisoners from filing grievances violate the First Amendment. Again, however, any rule will be analyzed under the *Turner* test to see whether a rule or custom bears a rational relationship to a legitimate penological interest.

Law Libraries

Prisoners also do not have an unlimited right to a law library. Rather, they have the right to information that will help them litigate cases related to their confinement (see *Thaddeus-x v. Blatter,* 1999). To prevail in a lawsuit, a prisoner will have to show not only that he or she was denied access to legal material but also that he or she has been harmed by the denial (see *Lewis v. Casey,* 1996). Thus, a prisoner has to show that he or she would have won the case or been granted the relief otherwise denied if only he or she had access to the law library. Again, this is a high burden. It is again important to note that laws or regulations may require more access to the law library. However, those requirements are not mandated by the First Amendment.

RIGHT TO ASSOCIATION WITH THE OUTSIDE WORLD

The right to associate is protected by the First Amendment. This is derived from the literal right of the people to assemble, which is contained directly in the First Amendment. For those in prison, however, these rights are subject to the *Turner* analysis. This means the prison system can limit a prisoner's contact with the outside world as long as the limits are rationally related to a legitimate penological interest.

In the recently decided case of *Bazzetta v. Overton* (2003), the Supreme Court ruled that a prison system may place severe limitations of visits, even noncontact visits. Essentially, the Court found that orderly running of visitation, preventing the passing of contraband, and protecting children were legitimate penological goals and that these severe regulations did in fact bear a rational relation to those goals. It remains to be seen how this decision will be interpreted by lower courts.

Mail

Letters and publications are a common way for prisoners to communicate with the outside world. While prisoners can receive and send out mail, their right to do so is subject to limitations. Arbitrary censorship of outgoing mail will violate the First Amendment (see *Procunier v. Martinez,* 1974). However, prison authorities can review outgoing letters to make sure that the letters do not contain threats, criminal plans, escape plans, and other threats to the orderly and safe running of the prison.

Arbitrary censorship of incoming mail will also violate the First Amendment, although prison officials can be stricter about incoming mail (see *Thornburgh v. Abbot,* 1989). The reasoning behind this distinction is that only a limited number of categories of outgoing information will affect the orderly running of a prison, but the list of categories of incoming information that could cause a disruption is much longer and harder to quantify.

Press

Prisoners have the right to communicate with the press, but this right is not absolute. Representatives of the press are treated under the First Amendment like any other visitors (see *Pell v. Procunier,* 1974). Prisoners are not entitled to special meetings with or communication with members of the press. Again, the reader is cautioned there are laws and regulations that protect communications with the press more stringently than does the First Amendment.

CONCLUSION

The First Amendment covers many issues that arise in the prison context. While it does prevent prison officials from arbitrarily limiting the freedoms it guarantees, many restrictions remain on freedom of religion, association, and access to the courts. As long as a prison rule or regulation is rationally related to a legitimate penological interest, the rule or regulation is constitutionally sound.

—*Deborah M. Golden*

See also Fourth Amendment; Fourteenth Amendment; Islam in Prison; Jailhouse Lawyers; Judaism in Prison; Nation of Islam; Native American Spirituality; Prison Litigation Reform Act 1996; Prisoner Litigation; Religion in Prison; Section 1983 of the Civil Rights Act; USA Patriot Act, 2001

Further Reading

Barron, J. A., & Dienes, C. T. (2000). *First Amendment law in a nutshell.* St. Paul, MN: West Group.

Boston, J., & Manville, D. E. (1995). *Prisoners' self-help litigation manual* (3rd ed.). New York: Oceana.

Columbia Human Rights Law Review. (2000). *A jailhouse lawyer's manual* (5th ed.). New York: Author.

Columbia Human Rights Law Review. (2002). *A jailhouse lawyer's manual* (5th ed., 2002 supplement). New York: Author.

Developments in the law of prisons: IV. In the belly of the whale—Religious practice in prison. (2002). [Special issue]. *Harvard Law Review, 115,* 1891.

Garvey, J., & Schauer, F. (1996). *The First Amendment: A reader.* St. Paul, MN: West Group.

Mushlin, M. (2002). *The rights of prisoners* (3rd ed.). St. Paul, MN: West Group.

Legal Cases

Bazzetta v. Overton, 123 S. Ct. 2162 (2003).

Cruz v. Beto, 405 U.S. 319, 92 S. Ct. 1079, 31 L. Ed. 2d 263 (1972).

DeHart v. Horn, 227 F.3d 47 (3rd Cir. 2000).

Graham v. Henderson, 89 F.3d 75 (2nd Cir. 1995).

Hakim v. Hicks, 223 F.3d 1244 (11th Cir. 2000).

Levitan v. Ashcroft, 281 F.3d 1313 (DC Cir. 2002).

Lewis v. Casey, 518 U.S. 343; 116 S. Ct. 2174; 135 L. Ed. 2d 606 (1996).

Malik v. Brown, 71 F.3d 724 (9th Cir. 1995).

O'Lone v. Estate of Shabazz, 482 U.S. 342; 107 S. Ct. 2400; 96 L. Ed. 2d 282 (1987).

Pell v. Procunier, 417 U.S. 817, 94 S. Ct. 2800; 41 L. Ed. 2d 495 (1974).

Procunier v. Martinez, 416 U.S. 396, 94 S. Ct. 1800, 40 L. Ed. 2d 224 (1974).

Shabazz v. Cole, 69 F. Supp. 2d 117 (D. Mass 1999).

Sutton v. Rasheed, 323 F.3d 236 (3rd Cir. 2003).

Thaddeus-x v. Blatter, 175 F.3d 378 (6th Cir. 1999).

Thornburgh v. Abbot, 490 U.S. 401, 109 S. Ct. 1874, 104 L. Ed. 2d 459 (1989).

Turner v. Safley, 482 U.S. 78, 96 L. Ed. 2d 64, 107 S. Ct. 2254 (1987).

◪ FLOGGING

While flogging has long been outlawed as a method of punishment in the criminal justice system of the

United States, it is still used in other countries and has gained increasing support among several American penologists in recent years. Historically used instead of capital punishment or imprisonment, it has not proven effective as a deterrent to further aberrant behavior. Still, some contend that it helps maintain social order.

HISTORY

The practice of flogging or whipping for those convicted of wrongdoing has a long history. The Law of Moses, as outlined in the Old Testament Book of Deuteronomy (Chapter 25, verses 2 & 3) reads, "If the wicked man be worthy to be beaten, that the judge shall cause him to lie down, and to be beaten before him . . . forty stripes he may give him, and shall not exceed . . . ." Likewise, in England in the 1500s, the Whipping Act ordered delinquents to be tied to the end of a cart, naked, and beaten with whips through a market town till the body be bloodied.

In colonial America, flogging and other corporal punishments occurred both within the prison as well as in public view. The pillory, stocks, dunking stool, and public whipping post were commonly used. Whipping was not always reserved for those who committed a crime. Mothers of illegitimate children (and the fathers if known) were sometimes publicly flogged, as were blasphemers and drunkards. Upon arrival in America, members of certain religious groups, most notably Quakers, were often tied to a cart and whipped before being forced back on the ship that brought them. The systematic punishment of slaves by flogging and branding is well documented.

Benjamin Rush was one of the first vocal opponents to the public flogging of prisoners. A prominent Philadelphia physician and signer of the Declaration of Independence, Rush founded the Philadelphia Society for Alleviating the Miseries of Public Prisons. In an important pamphlet at the time, Dr. Rush wrote that the reformation of the criminal offenders can never be achieved through public punishment: "Experience proves, that public punishments have increased propensities to crimes. A man, who has lost his self-respect at a whipping post, has nothing valuable to lose in society. Pain has begotten insensibility to the whip; and shame to infamy" (Teeters, 1937, p. 25).

Later, as the American penitentiary evolved, corporal punishment remained a mainstay of prison discipline and inmate control. In some institutions, the cat-o'-nine-tails with wire-tipped leather straps was used, sometimes with a saltwater sponge bath to increase the pain. In San Quentin, inmates were strapped to a ladder, naked, without any protection for their neck and kidneys, and whipped with the "cat." In the late 1800s, the cat-o'-nine-tails was replaced in most prisons by other types of flogging devices, such as the baton and the hose. Sharp-edged paddles were used in the Ohio State Penitentiary.

By the 1940s, flogging as corporal punishment had essentially been abolished in Americans prisons, but it was not until 1968 that the federal courts officially condemned the practice. It has been argued that the framers of the Bill of Rights did not expressly forbid corporal punishment as a violation of the "cruel and unusual punishment" prohibition of the Eighth Amendment. But in 1968 in *Jackson v. Bishop* (404 F. 2d, 571; 579–80), the Eighth Circuit Court of Appeals held that whipping prisoners in the Arkansas prisons with a strap "offends the contemporary concepts of decency" and did not contribute to rehabilitation but instead frustrates the rehabilitative process while creating other correctional problems. "It generates hate toward the keepers who punish and toward the system, which permits it. It is degrading to the punisher and to the punished alike." Although this ruling was limited to the issue of whipping inmates as a disciplinary measure, it has been interpreted by many legal scholars to forbid it entirely. In 1972, Delaware became the last state to abolish public whipping as a criminal punishment.

CONTEMPORARY PRACTICES

Flogging as punishment is still used extensively in many other countries. In Iran, for example, public whipping for relatively minor offenses (e.g., drinking alcohol, disturbing public order) have increased in recent years. In Saudi Arabia, flogging is a punishment handed down by courts on an almost daily basis. Amnesty International reports that in Nigeria, public whippings have been meted out for offenses that have included smoking marijuana, gambling, and carrying women on the back of motorcycle taxis.

Contemporary supporters of corporal punishment argue that lashing an offender is an effective deterrent because of the acute and immediate pain involved. Corporal punishment is seen as a viable response to prisoners who violate prison rules. Since they are already incarcerated and their date of release may seem distant (or nonexistent), some suggest that there is little else with which to maintain order. It is swift and visible to other inmates, as well as a proportionate punishment for certain crimes.

Criminologist Graeme Newman (1995) argued that "corporal punishment should be introduced to fill the gap between the severe punishment of prison and the non-punishment of probation. For the majority of property crimes, the preferred corporal punishment is that of electric shock because it can be scientifically controlled and calibrated, and is less violent in its application when compared with other corporal punishments such as whipping" (p. 54). He suggests that for violent crimes, in which the victim was subjected to pain and suffering, and for which there is no public wish to incarcerate, harsh punishment should be considered, such as whipping; humiliation of the offender is seen as justifiably deserved.

CONCLUSION

Opponents of flogging contend that punishing with pain is barbaric. There are always alternative punishments that can be used in prison, such as solitary confinement and the removal of privileges. Mistreatment of prisoners may encourage abuse from prison supervisors who seek to maintain order through a climate of fear. Finally, it does not deter; when the United States allowed flogging and similar punishments in the past, crime still increased.

—*Kelly R. Webb*

See also Capital Punishment; Corporal Punishment; Deterrence Theory; Michel Foucault; Elizabeth Fry; John Howard; Prison Monitoring Agencies;

Philadelphia Society for Alleviating the Miseries of Public Prisons; Quakers; Benjamin Rush

Further Reading

Amnesty International. (2000). *AI [Amnesty International] Index.* London: Author.

Foucault, M. (1995). *Discipline and punish: The birth of the prison.* New York: Vintage.

Morris, N., & Rothman, D. J. (1995). *The Oxford history of the prison: The practice of punishment in Western society.* New York: Oxford University Press.

Newman, G. (1978). *The punishment response.* Philadelphia: J. B. Lippincott.

Newman, G. (1995). *Just and painful: A case for the corporal punishment of criminals.* Albany, NY: Harrow and Heston.

Teeters, N. K. (1937). *They were in prison: A history of the Pennsylvania Prison Society, 1787–1937.* Chicago: John C. Winston.

Van den Haag, E. (1975). *Punishing criminals: Concerning a very old and painful question.* New York: Basic Books.

◤ FLYNN, ELIZABETH GURLEY (1890–1964)

Elizabeth Gurley Flynn, the daughter of working-class socialists, was born August 7, 1890, in Concord, New Hampshire. A founding member of the American Civil Liberties Union (ACLU) and a prominent Communist Party member, she was incarcerated under the McCarthy era in the federal prison for women at Alderson. Her account of her imprisonment that she published in the book *The Alderson Story: My Life as a Political Prisoner* sheds light on an important period of U.S. penal history.

BIOGRAPHICAL DETAILS

Flynn joined the Industrial Workers of the World (IWW) in 1906 and at the age of 16, and gave her first speech at the Harlem Socialist Club, *What Socialism Will Do for Women.* Subsequent to this speech and due to her political activism, Flynn was expelled from high school. One year later, in 1907, Flynn became a full-time organizer for the IWW. In this capacity, she traveled and took part in the IWW's "free speech" campaigns in several cities as far west as Missoula, Montana, and Spokane, Washington.

Photo 1   Elizabeth Gurley Flynn

Back east, Flynn helped organize campaigns for a wide variety of industrial workers in several different cities: garment workers in Pennsylvania; the textile strike of 1912 in Lawrence, Massachusetts; the strike of 1913 that involved silk weavers in Paterson, New Jersey; restaurant workers in New York; and finally, the iron miners' strike of 1916 in Mesabi, Minnesota. During these years of traveling and organizing campaigns, speaking out, and raising relief and legal defense funds on behalf of industrial workers, Flynn was arrested 10 times but never convicted of any criminal activity.

In 1918, Flynn helped establish the Workers' Liberty Defense Union and served as secretary until 1922. In 1920, she was a founding member of the ACLU and in 1927 to 1930 she chaired the International Labor Defense. Flynn was particularly concerned with women's rights and was a supporter of birth control and women's suffrage. During this time, Flynn also focused her attention on legal defense issues of labor and was a political activist for aliens who were threatened with deportation for their political views and affiliations.

COMMUNISM

In 1936, Flynn joined the Communist Party and made her first speech in 1937 as a Communist in Madison Square Garden. She wrote a feminist biweekly column for the *Daily Worker* and was also active in the women's commission as chair for the next 10 years. In 1940, due to her Communist Party membership, Flynn was removed from the national committee of the ACLU. Two years later, she ran for Congress at large in New York City, and although she lost she nonetheless received 50,000 votes.

In July 1948, 12 leaders of the Communist Party were arrested and falsely accused of advocating the overthrow of the U.S. government by force and violence. Flynn initiated a campaign for their release, but found herself arrested in June 1951 in a second wave of arrests under the infamous anti-Communist witch-hunt. On January 24, 1952, after a nine-month trial, Flynn was found guilty and was incarcerated in the Federal Reformatory at Alderson in West Virginia. Flynn described her experiences in Alderson in *The Alderson Story: My Life as a Political Prisoner.*

ALDERSON

Flynn was escorted by train from New York City to the Federal Women's Reformatory located in West Virginia. She was incarcerated from January 1955 to May 1957 and during these 28 months, she documented her many experiences as a political prisoner. In her writings, Flynn describes the injustices and suffering that she and others endured during confinement.

Upon her arrival, Flynn was labeled prisoner number 11710 and subsequently was fingerprinted for the third time since her original arrest date and sent into quarantine for the next three days. Flynn's living quarters, a small lock-in room, consisted of a toilet, wash bowl, narrow bed, radiator, and small cast-iron chest.

Along with the other women prisoners, Flynn worked at prison labor until 5 P.M. each day. Most of her sentence, Flynn was employed at sewing and mending article of clothing and linens. Others were made to do manual labor jobs that involved a lot of heavy lifting and moving, no matter how young or old and frail. Some were assigned clerical jobs, but most were assigned to duties in the craft store.

Flynn was placed in a maximum-security quarter because they considered her crime of being a Communist as maximum threat. It was thought that if they could keep close supervision on her that she would be restrained from carrying out acts of communicating communism to others. Because of the nature of her crime, Flynn had no expectation of making parole. She was also not entitled to industrial or meritorious good time off, even if she earned it.

In addition to her depiction of anti-Communist sentiment, Flynn's memoir is notable for its depiction of the racial and ethnic prejudice in the daily operations of Alderson. She describes, for example, the segregation of the Negro women and Spanish-speaking women. Flynn was also attuned to the class and gender expectations that were apparent in Alderson's population and regime. As she writes, despite a rather diverse population, "No rich women were to be found in Alderson" (Flynn, 1963, p. 37). Likewise, regardless of age, all inmates were referred to as "girls" and were at times treated as adolescents by the working prison staff.

Flynn was not able to communicate with many people outside of the prison walls and even her visits were restricted. Initially, the FBI reviewed Flynn's list that consisted of personal friends that she wished to correspond with and rejected it. Her visits were limited to once a month and all her visitors had to be a family member or an authorized correspondent. Flynn's sister, Kathie, went to see her on a monthly basis and kept her apprised of the political events taking place on the outside world and filled her in on the latest convictions and releases of others who were found guilty under the Smith Act. Kathie would end their session with new gossip of family and friends, and events from the neighborhood.

Upon her release on May 25, 1957, her sister Kathie, Marian Bachrach, and John Abt and his sister greeted Flynn at the gates. She was to report to a parole officer on the upcoming Monday and would remain on conditional release until July 6, 1957. Flynn promised her comrades whom she met during her stay in Alderson that upon her release, she would write about their experiences in Alderson to speak out about the injustices of censorship,

discrimination, segregation, lack of proper medical care and equipment, and neglect to personal health care needs that she and others experienced. Flynn documented and wrote about her experience in an attempt to educate and rally public support for prison reform.

CONCLUSION

In 1961, Flynn became the national chair of the Communist Party and held this post until her death. In January 1962, the State Department revoked her passport along with four other well-known Communists. At the time, Flynn who had just returned from the Communist Party of the Soviet Union's 22nd Congress.

As usual, Flynn did not take her treatment passively. Instead, she protested that the State Department was a violation of the United Nations Declaration of Human Rights adopted in 1948. In 1964, when this case reached the court, the justices agreed with Flynn and ruled Section 6 of the McCarran Act unconstitutional. Flynn returned to the Soviet Union in August 1964 to represent the Communist Party at an international Party Congress. During this visit, she was hospitalized for a stomach disorder and died on September 5, 1964. She was given a state funeral in Red Square. Her body lay in the Hall of Columns of the Soviet Trade Unions for eight hours while mourners filed past. Flynn's final wishes were carried out when her remains were flown to the United Sates for burial in Chicago's Waldheim Cemetery. She was laid to rest near the graves of Eugene Dennis, Big Bill Haywood, and the Haymarket Martyrs.

—Kimberly L. Freiberger

See also Activism; Alderson, Federal Prison Camp; Angela Y. Davis; Kate Richards O'Hare; Resistance; Women's Prisons

Further Reading

Baxandall, R. F. (1987). *Words on fire: The life and writings of Elizabeth Gurley Flynn.* Douglas Series on women's lives and the meaning of gender. New Brunswick, NJ: Rutgers University Press.

Camp. H. (1995). *Iron in her soul: Elizabeth Gurley Flynn and the American left*. Pullman: Washington State University Press.

Flynn, E. G. (1963). *The Alderson story: My life as a political prisoner*. New York: International Publishers.

Flynn, E. G. (1973). *Rebel girl: An autobiography, my first life*. New York: International Publishers.

Gorn, E. J. (2001). *Mother Jones: The most dangerous women in America*. New York: Hill and Wang.

Zinn, H. (1995). *A people's history of the United States: 1492–present* (updated and rev. ed.). New York: Harper Perennial Library.

⚑ FOOD

The U.S. Supreme Court has consistently ruled that prisoners have the right to an adequate and varied diet, including the right to tailor meals to religious prescriptions and medical needs. However, the provision of food in prison often remains a sore point for inmates. Problems include food and preparation quality, portion sizes, and the temperature at which it is served.

HISTORY

Traditionally, food was used in prisons as a means of reward and punishment. In the 19th century, for example, incoming prisoners were often served bread and water until they had earned the right for such luxuries as meat or cheese. In the Eastern State Penitentiary in Philadelphia, breakfast was sparse and monotonous, consisting of coffee, cocoa, or green tea, and a mix of bread and Indian mush. The primary meal at midday consisted of substantial portions of boiled pork or beef, soup, potatoes or rice, sauerkraut, and tea. Indian mush and tea constituted the evening meal.

Under the medical model of rehabilitation that emerged in the early 20th century, prison food became linked to scientific notions of nutrition. Prison diets were examined for the calorific content rather than used primarily as a means of control. Healthy prisoners, it was believed, would be productive workers and, ultimately, reformed citizens. Even so, some institutions, such as Alcatraz, deliberately offered a daily total of at least 5,000 calories, combined with minimal exercise, to make prisoners more lethargic and less likely to engage in violent behavior.

In recent decades, the science of nutrition has remained crucial to the provision of food in most prisons. Usually, diets are carefully planned and standardized. Some facilities post the weekly menu, including nutritional analyses of each meal listing caloric, fat, cholesterol, and sodium content of each prepared item. In addition, all federal prisons are meant to have a salad bar and offer a "heart healthy" version of the main meal. Fried and baked chicken, for example, or french fries and baked potatoes may be served at the same meal.

State prison systems, however, vary dramatically, in part because contracting food services out to the private sector is becoming increasingly common. As a result, many do not match the federal standards. However, because of both formal and informal pressures, such as prison reform efforts, prisoner litigation challenges conditions, and the nationwide influence of the American Correctional Association in providing minimal standards before individual prisons receive accreditation, prison food has improved dramatically.

SPECIAL MEALS

In most systems, prisoners with medical conditions, such as diabetes, HIV/AIDS, pregnancy, or heart problems, may request special meals. They may also be allowed special snacks, if examined and authorized by a dietician. Similarly, vegans, who eat no animal products, are increasingly becoming recognized as a legitimate group with special dietary needs.

Religious prisoners form another group who require and are usually entitled to special meals. While some prisons provide different meals for each faith group, others, such as the Federal Bureau of Prisons, offer one uniform option known as "common fare" that tries to satisfy the dietary requirements of all religions. In this system, the meat is kosher, pork and its derivatives are never used, and vegetarian options are meant always to be available. To avoid contamination with nonkosher or Halal food, common fare meals are usually served with disposable plates and cutlery. Certain other religious-based food requirements are usually honored throughout the year. Muslims may eat breakfast before dawn and eat dinner after sunset during Ramadan. All Jewish prisoners who submit a request in writing to the chaplain are entitled to kosher food for Passover. Christians will be offered a meatless meal on the mainline menu during Ash Wednesday and on all Fridays of Lent.

Photo 2   *Kithen area of Alcatraz with daily menu posted, 1956*

FOOD AS PUNISHMENT

Other than restricting access to the commissary, food may not, by law, officially be used as punishment. There is no longer any such thing as a diet of bread and water. Inmates even when in disciplinary segregation are entitled to nutritionally adequate meal. Ordinarily, these are from the menu of the day for the institution. However, some supermaximum secure facilities serve what is known as a "food-loaf" or "meal-loaf" to recalcitrant inmates, especially those who continually throw feces or urine on staff. This product is made up of the ingredients of a regular meal, for example, hot dogs, potatoes, and beans, that have been mashed together, baked like a meat loaf, and served. Although nutritionally adequate, and thus not equivalent to a diet of bread and water, in serving, taste, and aesthetics it functions a form of punishment, even if defined as a "dietary adjustment."

COMMISSARY

Prison commissaries stock food and other goods for prisoners to buy. Items include shoes, radios, food, stamps, photocopy and phone credits, and, in some institutions, over-the-counter medication such as Tylenol, ibuprofen, and allergy medicine. Prison commissaries vary in pricing policies, variety, and accessibility. Prices are usually at least market rate, making prisoners dependent on funds from outside. Their prison salaries, often starting at $15 a month, are often insufficient to purchase other than the most basic hygiene items.

THE CULTURAL SIGNIFICANCE OF FOOD

In prison, food creates or ameliorates conflict, establishes social boundaries of power and status, and provides a significant element in prisoner culture. Prison meals establish a routine for prisoners and staff. Inmates are not required to go to meals, and some manage to avoid them all together by living off commissary items and "gifts" from others. For most, however, meals provide a valued opportunity to interact with others.

The scarcity of desirable food in prison creates an illicit market for alternatives. As with other

Prison Food

Prison food sucks. Or at least it does in all the medium joints I've been in. This is because the dudes working in the kitchen don't care about the quality of the food. On most compounds the chow hall is considered the worst place to work, so naturally, they don't want to work in the kitchen. They're not trying to cook good food, but are trying to "hustle" by stealing food like green peppers and onions that they can sell back on the block for a dollar each. The dudes who work on the mainline are just slopping the food on your plate and you better hope you get enough so you won't go hungry later.

The meals consist of a lot of rice, pasta, sandwiches, and garbage meats. They try to mix up the menu selections but the only things they don't ruin are the hamburgers and french fries, and half the time the fries are cold. And forget about getting good fruits. The fruits they serve in here look like the slop they give to pigs on farms. You can't even get a decent apple or pear let alone any exotic fruits. Even if you are on common fare, which is a special religious diet, you are only getting cantaloupe and pears.

A lot of dudes in here live off the chow hall food and I don't see how they do it. If I have commissary food in my locker I don't ever go to the chow hall. I cannot remember the last time I had a nice juicy steak, which I'll never be getting in prison. But if you complain about the food the kitchen administrators will just tell you that you should of thought of that before you came to prison.

Seth Ferranti
FCI Fairton, Fairton, New Jersey

scarce resources, competition generates an underground acquisition and distribution system. Some food can be obtained from the prison commissary or kitchen by theft and cooked in the privacy of one's cell.

Those who can acquire quantities of high-quality food use it as status-enhancing currency by sharing it with friends or impressing outsiders. Those particularly adept at obtaining quality merchandise develop a reputation as a valued peer. Pilfered food can be returned to the cellblock and distributed or sold, sometimes in collusion with staff. For well-connected inmates, a cell can be turned into a mini-cafeteria where food is sold.

SOME PROBLEMS WITH PRISON FOOD

Concerns about food are often related to how and when meals are distributed. The serving line at meals is a constant reminder of the diners' vulnerability and their powerlessness over the daily routine. Sanitary prescriptions in kitchens and dining rooms may or may not be rigidly enforced, and on hot days in poorly ventilated sweltering areas, the servers' perspiration, mingled with steam from the trays, may drip into the food. The prevalent rumors that some inmates "sabotage" food with saliva, feces, or other matter perpetuates the image of uncleanliness. Although there are few documented cases of foreign substances such as feces or saliva added to the food during preparation, the rumors contribute to lack of confidence in prison sanitation, especially for prisoners isolated in segregation units to whom food is delivered. While usually delivered in a covered cart from the central kitchen, food served in this way may be vulnerable to hygiene problems. It also frequently arrives cold.

Another problem with meals in prison is the hour at which they are served and the amount of time available to eat. Most meals occur in prison far earlier than is normal in the free community. Prisoners must, therefore, become accustomed to an entirely new eating schedule that may commence as early as 6 A.M. and end by 4 P.M. Generally, no more than 14 hours may elapse between the evening and breakfast meals. Thus, religious inmates fasting during Ramadan or Passover must sign a waiver form, articulating that they have chosen to go hungry for more than the allowed time period. In total institutions, mealtime is short, usually about a half an hour from entry to exit. If the lines into the dining room or through the "chow line" are slow, the time for eating is reduced proportionately. Inmates are taken to the dining hall from their cellblocks or assignments in lines, with one line entering when the previous group exits. Although variations occur within and across prison systems, dining generally follows a highly structured regimen.

Finally, prison food can be repetitive despite variation in menus. This occurs in part because of poor preparation resulting in meals in which soggy vegetables and overcooked meat, for example, are indistinguishable from one meal to the next. Some institutions attempt to overcome the problems associated with the provision of food by making cooking facilities available to inmates. Women and low-security prisoners may have access to hotplates, microwaves, and other appliances necessary to cook and serve food. Sometimes, sympathetic staff may allow inmates to prepare food in their cells using illicit "stingers" or other heating devices, or ignore contraband food that prisoners have managed to obtain. The bulk of the population, however, is dependent on what the institution kitchens produce for everything other than what they may buy at the prison commissary.

CONCLUSION

The ubiquity of food, its importance both as one of life's small luxuries and a survival need, its relative ease of accessibility compared to other illicit resources, and its seemingly benign nature—"who has ever been stabbed with a sandwich?"—disguise both its practical and symbolic dual character as a conveyor and ameliorator of punishment. The ability to control when and what one eats is a basic aspect of adulthood. It is, therefore, often a flash point for conflict. The restriction of something as mundane as food adds a significant layer of punishment to the prison experience. The consequences derive not simply from deprivation of a discrete resource, but from the disruption of normal eating rituals such as mealtimes. In addition to being a valuable amenity, food functions as a commodity of exchange for other resources. The deprivation of fundamental amenities constantly reinforces loss of individual control.

Prisons are, to a large extent, restricted in the freedom they can give to inmates in preparing their own food because of security fears. Food service staff must account for knives and other potentially threatening implements before ending duty. They must also lock away any products such as yeast, cloves, or other spices that could potentially be used in the production of homemade alcohol (hooch). The variety of ways by which inmates attempt to reassert control may be perceived as maladaptive by administrators and outsiders, but they may also be viewed as creative strategies to increase normalcy in an abnormal environment.

—Mary Bosworth and Jim Thomas

See also Alcatraz; Commissary; Contraband; Deprivation; Eastern State Penitentiary; Prison Monitoring Agencies; Prison Culture; Prison Farms; Religion in Prison; Resistance; Supermax Prisons

Further Reading

Beckford, J., & Gilliat, S. (1998). *Religion in prison: Equal rites in a multi-faith society.* Cambridge, UK: Cambridge University Press.

Burton-Rose, D., Pens, D., & Wright, P. (Eds.). (1998). *The celling of America: An inside look at the U.S. prison industry.* Monroe, ME: Common Courage.

Johnson, N. (with Finkel, K., & Cohen, J. A.). (1994). *Eastern State Penitentiary: Crucible of good intentions.* Philadelphia: Philadelphia Museum of Art.

Marquart, J. W., & Roebuck, J. B. (1987, January). Institutional control and the Christmas Festival in a maximum security penitentiary. *Urban Life, 3/4,* 449–473.

Pens, D. (2001). Food strike puts Washington DOC on spin control. *Prison Legal News, 12*(2), 9.

◪ FOREIGN NATIONALS

It is difficult to determine the exact number of foreign nationals incarcerated in U.S. prisons and jails, since it is not always easy to differentiate legal and illegal immigrants from U.S. citizens. Also, many state records are not accurate enough to provide precise statistics. Even so, certain trends can be identified. First, citizens of Mexico, El Salvador, Honduras, Guatemala, the Dominican Republic, Canada, Cuba, Brazil, Colombia, Jamaica, Ecuador, Haiti, and the Republic of China represent the largest sources of foreign inmates in U.S. prisons. Second, most foreign nationals are imprisoned for drug offenses and immigration act violations.

Finally, since the 1980s, the number of incarcerated noncitizens has been steadily growing. In particular, the number of Arabs in U.S. penal facilities has dramatically increased since the September 11, 2001, terrorist attacks on the United States.

OVERVIEW OF LEGISLATION

Since the mid-1980s, a number of laws have been passed that have caused the numbers of foreign nationals in U.S. prisons to grow. The 1984 Sentencing Reform Act, the 1986 Anti-Drug Abuse Act, the 1991 U.S. federal sentencing guidelines, the 1996 Illegal Immigration Reform and Immigrant Responsibility Act, and the Antiterrorism and Effective Death Penalty Act of 1996 all increased the alien inmate population substantially. These laws and their revised versions have both expanded the definition of various crimes and lengthened the sentences with particular regards to non-U.S. citizens.

The 1984 Sentencing Reform Act requires defendants to serve out 85% of their sentences. This affects foreign nationals' prison sentence length disproportionately because the crimes they commit typically carry longer sentences. About 75% of foreign nationals are convicted of drug offenses, which under federal sentencing guidelines carry harsher statutory minimum terms of imprisonment than other offenses. Given the time-served requirements, noncitizens serve an average of 50 months in U.S. prisons.

Departures from the federal sentencing guidelines influence noncitizens' length of imprisonment mainly by decreasing offenders' sentence length. Annually, approximately 27% of foreign nationals receive departures that are either increases or decreases, from the established federal sentencing guidelines. Approximately 16% received a lesser sentence by offering substantial assistance to the government in prosecuting or investigating other individuals. Another 10% had their sentences reduced through plea-bargaining. On the other hand, another 1% received an upward departure, that is, longer sentences, due mainly to the large quantity of drugs involved or extensive criminal history.

The foreign inmate prison population has been growing at an annual rate of about 15% for the past 20 years. According to the Bureau of Justice Statistics, the overall prison population increased an average of only 10% during the same time period. Given the number of foreign nationals living in the United States, the differences in incarceration rates between U.S. citizens and noncitizens seem problematic. In 2000, the Bureau of Justice Statistics estimated that foreign nationals in federal prisons would continue to increase at a rate of 4% annually through 2005, because of the new deportation procedures incorporated in the 1996 Illegal Immigration Reform and Immigrant Responsibility Act. The 1996 Illegal Immigration Reform and Immigrant Responsibility Act dictated increased law enforcement and also immediate deportation of illegal aliens by the U.S. Immigration and Naturalization Service (INS) after they have served their time. This has resulted in a threefold increase in immigration offenders housed in the federal system. (In 2003, the INS was merged into the Department of Homeland Security and renamed the U.S. Citizenship and Immigration Services, USCIS.)

NATURE OF VIOLATIONS

The majority of foreign nationals in U.S. prisons are sentenced for immigration and drug violations. Most are charged with unlawfully entering or reentering the country, alien smuggling, and misuse of visas. With the passing of the 1986 Anti-Drug Abuse Act, foreign nationals prosecuted for drug crimes increased substantially from 1,799 in 1985 to 7,803 in 2000. The act established mandatory minimum sentences of 5 or 10 years depending on the offense and the amount of controlled substances. Between 1984 and 1994, foreign nationals serving sentences for a drug offense increased by 20%.

Noncitizens convicted of federal drug offenses usually play a minor role compared to U.S. citizens. The majority was sentenced for having less than one kilogram of heroin and for having less than five kilograms of cocaine powder and other types of contraband. They are also less likely to have a known criminal record. Even so, the U.S. government usually prosecutes them more vigorously than

U.S. citizens. Hispanics and people from the Caribbean islands and from Canada are more likely to be serving time for drug offenses versus other racial/ethnic groups.

Between 1985 and 2000, foreign nationals prosecuted in federal courts increased from 4,539 to 23,477. In 1985, foreign nationals made up 14% of federal inmates. Ten years later, they accounted for 21,421, and by the year 2000 that number grew to 37,243. In 1996, foreign nationals who were serving time in federal prisons for immigration offenses totaled 4,411. By 2000, that number had more than tripled to 13,676. At year-end in 2001, there were 19,137 immigration violators detained. Of this number 10,784 had been convicted of criminal offenses and 1,589 had criminal cases pending. Men were more likely than women to be charged with an immigration offense, while Hispanics were the most common offenders, accounting for 87% of all violations. Whites accounted for 4% of all immigration violations followed by blacks, who made up 3% of the total numbers.

TREND IN FEDERAL AND STATE PRISONS

Though most foreign nationals in the federal prison system are there for immigration and drug offenses, they are usually incarcerated in the state prison system for violent crimes and drug offenses. Foreign-born inmates both legal and illegal accounted for 31,300 of the states' prison population in 1991; by 1995 the Bureau of Prisons estimated that approximately 71,294 foreign inmates occupied states prisons (Wunder, 1995). This estimate could be egregiously low as this figure is a very rough estimate. The states' departments of corrections rely on inmates to furnish citizenship information that they at times cannot verify.

About 1 in 23 inmates in state prisons is estimated to be foreign born, originating from approximately 49 countries. Mexican nationals account for the majority, 47%. Other countries that are heavily represented in the state prison system are Cuba, Dominican Republic, Colombia, Jamaica, El Salvador, Guatemala, Trinidad and Tobago, United Kingdom, and Vietnam. Nearly all foreign-born

inmates are males, with 50% between the ages of 25 and 34 years old.

FOREIGN NATIONALS IN EUROPEAN PRISONS

The United States is not the only country that incarcerates disproportionate numbers of foreigners. Foreign nationals and second-generation immigrants are grossly overrepresented among the imprisoned population in countries such as England, France, Italy, Spain, the Netherlands, and Greece. In 1993, for example, 11% of all prisoners in English prisons originated from "West Indian, Guyanese and African ancestry." People of West Indian, Guyanese, and African ancestry between the ages of 18 and 39 make up about 2% of the English population, but they represent 11% of all prisoners in English prisons. The majority are imprisoned for drug offenses and burglaries.

Drug offenses and illegal immigration offenses account for the majority of foreign nationals' stay in European prisons. Three-quarters of foreigners in European prisons are serving some type of prison sentence for unlawful residence and unlawful entry. In Germany, Gypsies from Romania have incarceration rates 20 times those of German citizens. Moroccans' and Turks' incarceration rates are 8 times and 4 times, respectively, the rates of German natives. In the Netherlands, the prison population consists of almost 50% foreign nationals, while foreign nationals make up 29% of France's prison population. According to 1997 figures, German prisons have the most foreign prisoners (25,000), followed by France (14,200), Italy (10,900), Spain (7,700), England (4,800), Netherlands (3,700), Belgium (3,200), Greece (2,200), Austria (1,900), Portugal (1,600), Sweden (1,100), and Denmark (450).

CONCLUSION

A majority of foreign nationals in U.S. state and federal prisons are serving time for immigration and drug offenses. This trend is also evident in

European prisons. Although the exact number of noncitizens in U.S prisons is unknown, it is believed that this number continues to increase at an annual rate of about 15%. According to the Bureau of Justice Statistics, this number will decline to about 4% by 2005. The Bureau of Justice Statistics estimates that nationals from more than 75 countries were convicted in U.S. courts. Mexican nationals and nationals from South America and the Caribbean accounted for the majority of foreign-born inmates serving time in U.S. prisons.

—Denise Nation

See also Enemy Combatants; Immigrants/Undocumented Aliens; INS Detention Facilities; USA PATRIOT Act 2001

Further Reading

Beck, A. J., & Harrison, P. M. (2002). *Prisoners in 2001.* Washington, DC: U.S. Department of Justice, Bureau of Justice Statistics.

Scalia, J., & Litras, M. F. (1996). *Noncitizens in the federal criminal justice system, 1984–1994.* Washington, DC: U.S. Department of Justice, Bureau of Justice Statistics.

Scalia, J., & Litras, M. F. (2002). *Immigration offenders in the federal criminal justice system, 2000.* Washington, DC: U.S. Department of Justice, Bureau of Justice Statistics.

U.S. Department of Justice. (1999). *Survey of inmates in state and federal correctional facilities, 1997.* Washington, DC: Bureau of Justice Statistics.

U.S. Department of Justice, Immigration and Naturalization Service. (2002). *Statistical yearbook of the Immigration and Naturalization Service, 2001.* Washington, DC: Author.

Wacquant, L. (1999). Suitable enemies: Foreigners and immigrants in the prisons of Europe. *Punishment and Society, 1*(2), 215–222.

Wunder, A. (1995). Foreign inmates in U.S. prisons: An unknown population. *Corrections Compendium, 20*(4), 4–18.

◪ FOSTER CARE

Foster care is a complex and difficult system for children of incarcerated parents. As arrest and incarceration usually occur in a swift and confusing manner, parents often have little or no opportunity to plan for the care of their children. Consequently, unless family members are able and willing to care for their kin, these children become part of the foster care system.

Prison policy often makes it difficult for parents to obtain information regarding the placement of their children and the name of their caseworker. Limited contact between child welfare workers and parents challenge the ability of the caseworker to assess the feasibility of parental reunification. Caseworkers find themselves in a double bind. The Adoption and Safe Families Act (1997) requires that state child welfare systems move a child toward permanency within the shortest possible time frame. The law also requires that the child welfare workers meet the requirements of reasonable efforts in providing services that will strengthen families and allow children to return home. Yet, when correctional facilities dictate the amount and type of contact between parents and workers and do not provide needed services, the best casework efforts are thwarted. In the midst of this quandary is the child caught in the foster care system.

STATISTICS

Mandatory sentencing policies and "get tough" legislation has put greater numbers of mothers and fathers behind bars serving longer sentences with no regard for their children. Close to 1.5 million children in the United States have at least one parent serving time in a state or federal prison, while nearly 600,000 more have parents who are being held in county jails

Statistics show that approximately two-thirds of all women incarcerated in state prisons have minor children. Over 70% of those with young children lived with them prior to incarceration. At the same time, about 56% of men in state correctional facilities have minor children and approximately half lived with them prior to incarceration. About 50% of children with incarcerated mothers are cared for by grandparents with low incomes. A further 25% live with their father, and about 12% live with another relative. The remaining 13% reside in foster care. Close to 90% of children of incarcerated men live with their mother. Children of incarcerated parents often move back and forth between foster care and kinship care.

ADJUSTMENT TO FOSTER CARE

While incarcerated parents have to adjust to prison policy and a prison routine, children living in foster care also have to make significant adjustments to their new environment. Foster children bear the burden of adapting to a new set of parents, siblings, and extended family members. Roles and responsibilities connected to age, gender, and birth order are likely to change in their new family setting. Children need to master a new set of rules that revolve around bedtime, meal times, watching television, and doing homework. They often have to adjust to unfamiliar foods and food odors. Foster parents may speak a language they are not familiar with.

For some children, their new neighborhood may look very different from their old neighborhood. Children from urban settings might find themselves in a rural community and children from a rural community may find themselves in a city environment. Such changes of setting may require adjustments to noise, traffic, and outdoor vs. indoor recreation. At school, the children must face a new set of teachers and peers while enduring the stigma often attached to being in the foster care system. The religious practices of their foster family may seem unusual and participation at church services may lead to feelings of guilt. Similarly, some children may be required to change their hairstyle, style of dress, and even their style of communication. These imposed changes may raise identity issues for children that may be further compounded by multiple moves that demand multiple transitions.

UNINTENDED VICTIMIZATION

Children are the unintended victims of parental incarceration. They are traumatized first by the events that precede incarceration and then by the effects of separation, loss, and out-of-home placement. Prior to arrests, many children lead lives characterized by poverty, family violence, and addiction. If they are left with caretakers overwhelmed with economic and emotional responsibilities, they will once again be vulnerable to abuse and neglect. The resulting emotional and behavioral difficulties that these children experience put them at high risk for learning difficulties, substance abuse, delinquent behavior, and teen pregnancy.

PARENTAL ROLES

Incarceration changes established parental roles and weakens the parent-child bond. When parents enter prison they can no longer nurture or care for their children. The daily role that they play in their children's lives drastically decreases. Incarceration removes them from the parental decision-making process, limits their ability for financial support and supervision, and restricts their access to information regarding their children's daily activities and well-being.

Although children of incarcerated mothers and fathers suffer the same general effects of separation and loss, they experience them in different ways. Mother and fathers play different gendered roles in the lives of their children. The nurturing relationship usually delegated to mothers is critical to healthy child development. Absence of this nurturing relationship puts both children and mothers at risk. Those who shared a close and nurturing relationship with an incarcerated mother suffer the long-term consequences of the disruption of a healthy emotional bond that is sometimes replaced with custodial instability.

Although children of incarcerated parents live with mothers at much higher rates, there remain a significant number of children who live with their fathers prior to incarceration. Contrary to popular myths, many incarcerated men have strong emotional ties to their children and are important in their lives. Although their role is different from that of mothers, nonetheless, their role is also critical. Fathers often discipline their children, set guidelines for their daily behavior, and provide structure in their daily lives. They play an important role in their children's development, and children suffer negative consequences from paternal separation.

PARENTAL CONTACT

Prisoners have little or no control over their daily schedules and have limited resources. As a result, their ability to maintain family relationships becomes dependent on prison rules. Visits, phone contacts, and writing letters allow parents to maintain their parental role, if even in a limited manner. Feeling connected to their children prepares them to resume their social roles after release. In recognition of the importance of the family bond, some correctional facilities offer programs that promote the maintenance of healthy parent-child relationships. For example, the MATCH (Mothers and Their Children) program, first established in California in 1978, calls for the strengthening of the mother-child bond through improved visiting conditions, by providing inmates with training in parenting and early childhood education, by improving prenatal care, and by providing referrals to outside social service agencies. PATCH (Pappas and Their Children) is modeled after the California MATCH program.

VISITS

Visits provide a key means for maintaining contact with children. However, prison visits are not always easy. Visiting procedures are often unclear, and corrections officials are not always receptive to time-consuming family visits. Likewise, prisons are not "family friendly." Limitations placed on the frequency of visits as well as geographic proximity to the prison reduces both the number and quality of contacts and adversely affect the parent-child bond.

Children in foster care must rely on their caretakers for transportation to visits, some of whom may be unable or unwilling to travel great distances to facilitate visits. They may fear that the prison atmosphere will upset the child or believe that the parent is a poor influence. When visits do occur, they generally take place in an environment that is not conducive to privacy and communication. Visiting areas may be uncomfortable and noisy and are generally policed. When parent-child visits are beneficial to a child, visitation can ameliorate the stress of separation and increase the likelihood of reunification after incarceration.

PHONE CALLS AND LETTER WRITING

When prison programs allow, incarcerated parents can continue to nurture their children from afar. Frequent letters, phone calls, and birthday cards give children a sense of continued involvement in their parent's lives. Giving advice over the phone and writing letters allow parents to maintain their role if even in a limited manner.

However, communication between family members is often hampered by collect-call telephone policies. Foster parents and kin on the other side of a call from prison often pay three times the amount as a collect call from a public pay phone or call not placed from prison. Letters and packages that are sent from prison are often stamped with a warning. The public stamp as well as the operator announcing a call from a correctional facility stigmatizes the child on the receiving end of the communication.

CONCLUSION

Incarceration threatens the parent-child bond and further fragments already troubled families. It is almost impossible for children in foster or kinship care to feel connected to their parents and for parents to feel adequate. Prison puts families in a situation where they can no longer identify, assess, and respond to each other's needs. Incarceration punishes children as well as their parents by an imposed separation and often jeopardizes their emotional and physical well-being.

Families disrupted by incarceration are a community problem that needs to be resolved by the collaboration of many systems. While some crimes preclude the efficacy of continued contact, we cannot assume that because parents are incarcerated that the parent-child bond must be severed and that parents can no longer play a positive role in their children's lives.

—Francine C. Raguso

See also Children; Children's Visits; Families Against Mandatory Minimums; Fathers in Prison; Mothers in Prison; Parenting Programs; Termination of Parental Rights

Further Reading

Beckerman, A. (1998, September/October). Charting a course: Meeting the challenge of permanency planning for children with incarcerated parents. *Child Welfare, 77*(5), 513–529.

Bilchik, S., Seymour, C., & Kreisher, K. (2001, December). Parents in prison. *Corrections Today, 63*(7), 108–111.

Block, K. J., & Potthast, M. (1998, September/October). Girl Scouts beyond bars: Facilitating parent-child contact in correctional settings. *Child Welfare, 77*(5), 561–578.

Girschick, L. (1999). *No safe haven: Stories of women in prison.* Boston: Northeastern University Press.

Hairston, C. F. (1998, September/October). The forgotten parent: Understanding the forces that influence incarcerated fathers relationships with their children. *Child Welfare, 77*(5), 617–639.

Johnson, T., Selber, K., et al. (1998, September/October). Developing quality services for offenders and families: An innovative partnership. *Child Welfare, 77*(5), 595–615.

Seymour, C. (1998, September/October). Children with parents in prison: Child welfare policy, program, and practice issues. *Child Welfare, 77*(5), 469–493.

Zaplin, R. (1998). *Female offenders.* Gaithersburg, MD: Aspen.

Zealand, E. (1998, Winter). Protecting the ties that bind from behind bars: A call for equal opportunities for incarcerated fathers and their children to maintain the parent-child relationship. *Columbia Journal of Law & Social Problems, 31,* 247.

Photo 3   Michel Foucault

◼ FOUCAULT, MICHEL (1926–1984)

French philosopher Michel Foucault was one of the most influential social theorists of the last quarter of the 20th century. In his works, Foucault used the style and techniques of the historian, the sociologist, and the anthropologist to reveal how power operated in the wider society and in what he describes as "the system of penality." For Foucault, an imposed order affected every level of society, defining the character of general social institutions and organizations such as government, hospitals, asylums, and prisons. Power relations further permeate the individual self, the body, and the mind through which that self was expressed.

BIOGRAPHICAL INFORMATION

Born in Poitiers on October 15, 1926, Foucault moved to Paris to study at the prestigious lycée Henri-IV. In 1946, he was admitted to the Ecole Normale Supérièure where he studied philosophy with Maurice Merlau-Ponty. In 1948, Foucault received his degree in philosophy. He followed this in 1950 with a degree in psychology, and in 1952 was awarded a diploma in psychopathology.

Foucault published his first book, *Madness and Civilization,* in 1960. From this point until his death from an AIDS-related illness in 1984, he maintained an active publishing record, on a dizzying array of subjects. While all of his work has influenced the study of prisons in some form or another, his book *Discipline and Punish,* which analyzes the historical development of the prison, is most often cited. In addition to his academic work, Foucault influenced prison policy through his involvement with the Prison Information Group (GIP) that sought to give inmates a voice in shaping penal practices in France.

FOUCAULT'S MAIN THEORETICAL IDEAS

Foucault sought the explanation of modern life in its historical origins. He believed that the social world of the past was an ordered place and that traces of that order could still be found. Searching for those traces in accounts from that epoch or period was an undertaking much like the work of archaeologists searching for relics and artifacts of ancient societies and cultures. Each specimen had a story to tell, and several of those stories could be combined to give an account of how the pharaohs of Egypt or the Aztecs of South America lived. Similarly, texts, records, accounts, and inventories could tell the story of a social organization such as a prison or correctional system in the same way that an artifact could offer up explanations of how food was prepared, how clothes were made, how animals were hunted and caught, or how battles were fought and won.

Foucault was not so much interested in extinct and ancient civilizations as in how archaeological features of recently passed social institutions and organizations could help explain how modern society came to be like it is. The social archaeology of the 15th or 16th centuries could offer sources and evidence of the origins of modern institutions such as the hospital, the school, or the prison. Knowledge was the key source to be sifted for archaeological discoveries.

In much the same way that an Egyptologist would dig in and around pyramids or burial sites looking for artifacts or cultural symbols such as paintings or ancient scriptures, the *discourse* (i.e., how knowledge was created, discovered, secreted and stored, displayed, replicated, and communicated) was the "site" where Foucault proposed to dig. How knowledge was ordered reflected how power was exercised in the society. Its consequences for individuals and for the society at large would describe for the archaeologist the world in which people had lived, which, in turn, described the origins of so much of modern living. Out of this discourse emerged the knowledge and ways of

knowing that characterize later epochs. We see how the power of religion has given way to the power of science, and how the power of confession has given way to therapy. Interpreting acts of nature as acts of God has given way to scientific experimentation and discovery. Eventually, the sciences of the natural world extended to sciences of the social world such as psychology, sociology, criminology, and penology.

In a series of texts, Foucault examined how ideas about health, madness, discipline and punishment, and sexuality ensured the effective management and control of citizens. According to him, the simple process of recording births and associating that knowledge with the social status, literacy, residence, religion, and beliefs of the mother or both parents led inevitably to more efficient policing of society. Equally, anatomy and the search within organisms for the causes of diseases, which accompanied the growth and spread of clinics and hospitals before and after the French Revolution, delivered knowledge about the body and its functioning that was used to interpret individuals' bodies and their skills and capacities. This knowledge in Foucault's eyes was an essential prerequisite and accompaniment of early capitalism. The supply of fit and healthy workers to the factory system became the driving force for scientific, medical, and clinical advances throughout the 19th century.

If, for Foucault, discourse guides the institutions and organizations in knowing how to look and what to look for, the *Gaze* does the looking. Looking in this sense describes direct visibility of citizens and their actions as well as other forms of recording and accounting. Once again, Foucault asserts, the Gaze is historically contingent, as the amount of detail about individuals' lives recorded and stored has been continuously expanding since the end of the 18th century. These days, an almost unlimited amount of information is gathered from medical records of the state of our internal organs; records of our mental, social, and financial circumstances; and even daily instances of actions like going to work or making a telephone call.

Where to look is determined by another of Foucault's key concepts, *interiorization*. In a different context, this might be understood as the reductionism of science, the constant seeking for causes and explanations by breaking down, looking within the object or process that science is seeking to understand. Contemporary examples include genetic engineering and the Human Genome Project that look within DNA chains to explain actions, behaviors, thoughts, moods, and many other social aspects of human life. Closed-caption television (CCTV), home video security, and satellite observations of smaller and smaller features of everyday life anywhere on earth are another example of how far the Gaze has extended. The Gaze also describes the origin of increasingly pervasive media such as paper-based bureaucracies; computer databases holding and exchanging vast amounts of personal information; and what he called technologies of the self such as social work, psychoanalysis, counseling, and family therapy where the Gaze could look inside relations between family members and at an individual's thoughts and feelings and record or report on them. Foucault argues that this progressive extension inward helps to manage societies as a whole and the communication, action, and thoughts of their citizens.

Discipline and Punish

Foucault applied many of his ideas to the prison in his book *Discipline and Punish: The Birth of the Prison*. Originally published in French in 1975, it was translated into English two years later. Since then it has remained extremely influential in the sociology of punishment and related fields.

The book begins with a graphic description of the 1757 execution of Damiens, who was hung, drawn, and quartered for killing a king before his remains were burned to ashes. Foucault's reason for starting his text with the details of this dismemberment was to show the lengths that the state went to eradicate not only the crime but also the body and soul of the criminal. To punish any crime it was thought necessary to mutilate or destroy the body of the criminal. For lesser criminals, such as thieves, the hand with which they offended was removed. Others were branded in a prominent place with a symbol or letter

indicating their crime or sin for all to see. The "marked" man or woman could not go unnoticed and would be barred from contact with others, and moved on. Later, the punishment for lesser crimes was to remove the "body" entirely by banishment, exile, or transportation to the colonies or some other far-away place. For Foucault, the legal and penal process had an overriding purpose, to display, celebrate, and demonstrate the power of the sovereign in a ceremony where marks of vengeance were applied to the body of the condemned man.

In the next phase, the system of "penality" both engenders and is caused by the emergence of discipline. The exercise of power was to be achieved through the exercise of discipline, producing citizens who were obedient to absolute laws. Justice needed not only to be done, as in public executions, but must be seen to be done in elaborate judicial systems. Here was born the declaratory function of justice and punishment. The people must know the law and know that the law must be obeyed. Legal tests focused less on the "body that carried out the crime, and more on the "mind" and its intentions. The emphasis was not on removal or exclusion from the "body" politic but on the correction of the subject. The power of the state had to be seen to act directly on each individual subject. Foucault refers to a new "technology of power" and "political anatomy of the body." Biology, anatomy, and later, psychology and psychiatry, would see the body to be adjudged, convicted, punished, and disciplined in a different way.

In this way, according to Foucault, the prison was born. Punishment in the form of loss of liberty, or incarceration, leads to the carceral society. In this society, a public display or ceremony expunging the body-criminal from the body-politic was replaced by the definite knowledge that the criminal had been arrested, convicted, and sentenced and that the sentence would be carried out. There was no longer a need for the public witnessing of the punishment or of a ceremonial demonstration of the king's power. The punishment could be enacted behind closed doors, and for a measured and witnessable period of time corresponding with the length of the sentence of imprisonment. The reassurance that the punishment was being carried out and that the needs for retribution, reform, and rehabilitation were being met rested in the architecture of the prison itself.

According to Foucault, prison design was influenced by Jeremy Bentham's model institution, the panopticon. In the panopticon, each object body/convicted offender was assigned a single cell. Cells were arranged in a semicircle on a number of levels. At the focal point of each semicircle was a guard observation post. The guards could see into every corner of each cell. Inmates were aware that they were in full view and being watched at all times. At the same time, the guard observation post was lit from behind the guards so that inmates could barely see the guards from their cells. A supervisory officer could be positioned behind the guards so that one supervisor could observe several guards, each observing several inmates.

This prison design reflected industrial societies' emerging needs for means of dealing with urban crime rates and other social problems. During the second half of the 19th century, this example of prison design became popular across the world. Bentham's panopticon formed the basis for Foucault's notion of the Gaze, the means by which modern societies observe not only their prison inmates but also their citizens in general.

CONCLUSION

Modern prisons retain many of the features and serve most of the functions that Foucault describes. Nonetheless, as society has moved on, so too has the system of discipline and punishment. Foucault depicted in later works, for example, the development of *technologies of the self,* where, to cope with increasingly broad and less absolute definition of crimes and deviance, the power of the state would become more diffuse and more intrusive in its effort to control. New forms of control evolve to see inside the family through child care and social work agencies, to see inside the minds and relations between parents and their children by the extension of compulsory education, to observe relations between parents and adults through attempts to regulate sexuality, abusive relationships, and forms of disempowerment. Foucault described and predicted how the Gaze and its associated discourse was and

would continue to be a core feature of modern society.

—*Russell Kelly*

See also Auburn Correctional Facility; Auburn System; Cesare Beccaria; Jeremy Bentham; Bridewell; Capital Punishment; Corporeal Punishment; Deterrence Theory; Eastern State Penitentiary; Flogging; David Garland; History of Prisons; Incapacitation Theory; Alexander Maconochie; Medical Model; Panopticon; Pennsylvania System; Prison Psychologists; Quakers; Resistance; Walnut Street Jail

Further Reading

Armstrong, D. (1985). Review essay: The subject and the social in medicine—An appreciation of Michel Foucault. *Sociology of Health and Illness, 1,* 111.

Foucault, M. (1967). *Madness and civilization.* London: Tavistock.

Foucault, M. (1970). *The order of things [Les Mots et les choses]* (Trans. unnamed). London: Tavistock.

Foucault, M. (1972). *The archaeology of knowledge.* London: Routledge.

Foucault, M. (1977). *Discipline and punish: The birth of the prison [Surveiller et punir: Naissance de la prison]* (A. Sheridan, Trans.). London: Allen Lane-Penguin.

Foucault, M. (1980a). *The history of sexuality: Vol. 1. An introduction.* New York: Random House.

Foucault, M. (1980b). *Power/knowledge: Selected interviews and other writings 1972–1977* (C. Gordon, Ed.). Hemel Hempstead, UK: Harvester-Wheatsheaf.

Foucault, M. (1991). Governmentality. In G. Burchell, C. Gordon, & P. Miller, *The Foucault effect: Studies in governmentality.* Chicago: University of Chicago Press.

Gutting, G. (1989). *Michel Foucault's archaeology of scientific reason.* Cambridge, UK: Cambridge University Press.

Jay, M. (1986). In the empire of the Gaze: Foucault and the denigration of vision in twentieth-century French thought. In D. Couzens Hoy (Ed.), *Foucault: A critical reader* (pp. 175–204). Oxford, UK: Basil Blackwell.

Martin, L. H., Gutman, H., & Hutton, P. H. (Eds.). (1988). *Technologies of the self: A seminar with Michel Foucault.* London: Tavistock.

McHoul, A., & Grace, W. (1995). *A Foucault primer: Discourse, power and the subject.* London: University College Press.

Rabinow, P. (Ed.). (1986). *The Foucault reader.* Harmondsworth, UK: Penguin.

◪ FOURTEENTH AMENDMENT

Section One of the 14th Amendment (1868) to the U.S. Constitution guarantees all citizens equal protection under the law and states that no citizen can be denied due process of the law. In other words, all citizens will be treated equally under state laws regardless of such factors as race, gender, and religious beliefs and the state has provided to the individual whatever legal process is due under the facts and circumstances of the case. Historically, the due process and equal protection clauses of the 14th Amendment did not relate to prisoners, since they were intended instead to protect the rights of former slaves after the Civil War. In 1871, for example, the Virginia Supreme Court in *Ruffin v. Commonwealth* stated that prisoners had forfeited their liberty as a consequence of their convictions and were, thus, "slaves of the state." The Virginia ruling and others like it prevented prisoners from filing lawsuits for violations of their constitutional rights. U.S. courts interfered little in prison and jail administration and practices until the 1960s.

DUE PROCESS CLAUSE

The due process clause in the 14th Amendment says no state should "deprive any person of life, liberty, or property, without due process of law." Court decisions have made clear that correctional personnel must provide due process provisions and procedural safeguards during inmate disciplinary procedures, but the procedures, as long as they are fair, do not have to mirror due process rights of a defendant on trail. Two significant U.S. Supreme Court cases on this subject are *Wolff v. McDonnell* (1974) and *Sandin v. Conner* (1995).

In *Wolff v. McDonnell,* the Supreme Court established minimum due process requirements for prison disciplinary hearings when the possible outcomes include the loss of "good time" credit or other privileges. According to the court, the inmate must be sent written notification of his or her alleged violation and be given a minimum of 24 hours to prepare for the hearing. The prisoner may call witnesses and submit documents as long as such actions do not cause a security risk. They may also ask for assistance in helping with the case. Inmates, however, do not have the right to a lawyer, nor may they cross-examine adverse witnesses during disciplinary hearings.

A series of subsequent Supreme Court cases have limited prisoner due process rights. In *Meachum v. Fano* (1976), the Supreme Court held that prisoners do not have any constitutionally protected rights to be assigned or transferred to a particular prison, even if the prison conditions are less desirable. In *Montanye v. Haymes* (1976), hearings are not required when transferring a prisoner to another correctional facility. More recently, in *Sandin v. Conner* (1995), the Supreme Court ruled that the 14th Amendment's due process clause does not apply to prisoners unless they are subject to "atypical and significant hardship" beyond what is ordinary in prison life. In the same case, the court ruled that disciplinary segregation of up to 30 days does not in itself constitute a significant hardship and, thus, does not require the due process procedures outlined in *Wolff v. McDonnell.*

An exception to the limitation of due process rights is the Supreme Court ruling of *Vitek v. Jones* (1980). Larry Jones was a prisoner who was involuntarily transferred to a mental institution without a hearing. The Supreme Court ruled that Jones was entitled to due process provisions and procedural safeguards, because of the increased risk of being stigmatized that he would experience in a mental facility and because he may be subjected to forced behavioral modification treatments. It should be noted, however, that the courts rarely limit the discretion of prison administrations in their classification schemes.

EQUAL PROTECTION CLAUSE

The 14th Amendment's equal protection clause prohibits racial, gender, and religious discrimination in correctional facilities. This has not always been the case. Traditionally, racial minorities were often segregated in facilities where conditions and programming did not meet the standards of their white male counterparts because prison administrators claimed that interracial violence would escalate without such segregation. Women, likewise, were often housed in poor conditions.

It was not until the 1960s that court decisions determined that the 14th Amendment's equal protection clause used in the 1950s to limit racial discrimination in the school system could be applicable to correctional facilities. Though the courts have ruled that all prisoners do not have to be treated exactly alike in all circumstances, they have also deemed unconstitutional discrimination and classification schemes that are capricious and arbitrary.

In the case of *Lee v. Washington* (1968), the U.S. Supreme Court upheld a lower court ruling that found Alabama's state statutes mandating complete racial segregation within correctional facilities unconstitutional. The Supreme Court found that segregation violated the 14th Amendment, but, at the same time, also claimed that segregation was constitutional in certain circumstances, specifically the maintenance of security, discipline, and good order. More recent lower court decisions have stated that a generalized fear that racial desegregation will cause violence is not a valid reason to segregate facilities. All other possibilities such as proper supervision of inmates and decreasing the inmate population need to be tried first before segregating inmates.

Courts have also determined that unequal treatment of male and female prisoners is unconstitutional under the equal protection clause. In the first equal protection class action lawsuit filed on behalf of women prisoners in the United States, a federal district court found in *Glover v. Johnson* (1979) that Michigan provided substantially inferior educational and vocational opportunities for women prisoners compared to male prisoners. At that time, job training and college courses were offered in Michigan's male correctional facilities, while home economics classes were the only programs provided for Michigan's female inmates. The court stated that a small female prison population could not be used as an excuse to limit the educational, counseling, job training, and legal education programs for women inmates.

CONCLUSION

In sum, the constitutional rights of prisoners are still limited compared to the rights of U.S. citizens in free society. Nevertheless, since the 1960s, the courts have used the due process and equal protection clauses of the 14th Amendment to ensure that prisoners have access to the courts to address violations of their constitutional rights.

—*Jeff Mellow*

See also Discipline System; First Amendment; Fourth Amendment; Eighth Amendment; Jailhouse Lawyers; Prison Litigation Reform Act 1996; Prisoner Litigation; Thirteenth Amendment

Further Reading

Carlson, P., & Garret, J. (Eds.). (1999). *Prison and jail administration: Practice and theory.* Gaithersburg, MD: Aspen.

Early, B., Zimmerman, J., & Williams, D. (1999). Prisoners' right. *Georgetown Law Journal, 87*(5), 1903–1974.

Feeley, M., & Rubin, E. (1998). *Judicial policy making and the modern state: How the courts reformed America's prisons.* New York: Cambridge University Press.

Muraskin, R. (Ed.). (2000). *It's a crime: Women and justice.* Upper Saddle River, NJ: Prentice Hall.

Legal Cases

Glover v. Johnson, 478 F. Supp. 1075, 1078 (1979).

Lee v. Washington, 390 U.S. 333 (1968).

Meachum v. Fano, 427 U.S. 215 (1976).

Montanye v. Haymes, 427 U.S. 236 (1976).

Ruffin v. Commonwealth, 62 Va. 790 (1871).

Sandin v. Conner, 515 U.S. 472 (1995).

Vitek v. Jones, 445 U.S. 480 (1980).

Wolff v. McDonnell, 418 U.S. 539 (1974).

◼ FOURTH AMENDMENT

The Fourth Amendment is designed to guard against unreasonable federal government searches and seizures of persons, papers, houses, and effects perpetrated against "the people" of the United States. The amendment was established because the colonists despised the general warrants used by the British to curb the illegal smuggling of molasses, which was a primary ingredient in the making of rum. These days, it is frequently invoked in relation to police search and seizure of narcotics or other restricted substances in the war on drugs.

The Fourth Amendment contains two clauses. The first ensures that no unreasonable searches and seizures will be constitutionally tolerated. The second clause, commonly referred to as the "warrant clause," sets forth requirements that police must follow in order to obtain a warrant from a detached and neutral magistrate. The U.S. Supreme Court has interpreted these clauses independently. Thus, a warrant need not necessarily accompany a search or seizure (*Carroll v. United States*, 1925; *Terry v. Ohio*, 1968; *New York v. Burger*, 1987). A search or seizure must, however, be conducted in a reasonable manner, determined by balancing individual rights with those of the police who investigate crime (*Whren v. United States*, 1996). The use of balancing allows the Court to use a great deal of flexibility when addressing various Fourth Amendment claims.

"REASONABLE" SEARCHES

In 1967 (*Katz v. United States*), the Court devised a two-pronged test designed to establish a criteria of reasonableness in Fourth Amendment claims. As former Supreme Court Justice John Marshall Harlan described the *Katz* standard, "My understanding of the rule that has emerged from prior decisions is that there is a two-fold requirement, first that a person have exhibited an actual (subjective) expectation of privacy and second, that the expectation is one that society is prepared to recognize as 'reasonable.'" Thus, the reasonableness of a search, or its constitutionality, is largely a matter of "socially accepted" privacy concerns; anything a person does not try to keep private is not protected by the Fourth Amendment.

The vague nature of privacy has led to a range of legal interpretations of what constitutes a "reasonable" search. For instance, federal agents trespassing on a land-owner's "open field" may confiscate evidence later to be used at trial in a reasonable manner so long as they stay a good distance from his or her personal (family) quarters (*United States v. Dunn*, 1987). On the other hand, a person placing a call on a public phone may not have his conversation reasonably seized, without a warrant, by means of listening devices (*Katz v. United States*, 1967). While these determinations of reasonableness might seem odd if we consider property as a standard of reasonableness—the standard the Court used prior to 1967—they are consistent with the

two-pronged privacy standard made explicit in *Katz*.

EXCLUSIONARY RULE

Although the Fourth Amendment clearly prohibits unreasonable search and seizure it does not provide a specific remedy to alleviate any such constitutional violation. What should happen to evidence that was found through a violation of Fourth Amendment rights? In particular, what should be done when the police break the law in order to catch lawbreakers? In 1914, the Supreme Court answered this question by ruling that "in a federal prosecution the Fourth Amendment barred the use of evidence secured through an illegal search and seizure" (*Weeks v. United States*, 1914). Thus, after 1914 a federal prosecutor could not use evidence deemed by a magistrate to have been collected via a violation of the Fourth Amendment. This standard of suppressing illegally gained evidence at a criminal trial would come to be known as the *exclusionary rule.* This rule was only expanded to include state prosecutions in 1961 (*Mapp v. Ohio*, 1961).

The rationale used by the Court to justify the exclusionary rule and its expansion to include state prosecutions is based on the principle of police deterrence. Presumably the hypothetical "rational" police officer desires to put criminals in prison. Evidence is the primary means to put criminals in prison. Therefore, it logically follows that if police believe their (unconstitutional) actions will result in the inadmissibility of evidence, they will determine that there is no benefit to be derived from engaging in violations of the Fourth Amendment. Of course, such a rationale is primarily dependent on a legal system to apply the exclusionary rule when needed.

STANDING TO ASSERT THE FOURTH AMENDMENT

During the past 20 years, the ability to protest a violation of the Fourth Amendment has become exceedingly difficult. The criminal defendant does not have an automatic right to challenge illegally obtained evidence. Instead, he or she must prove that there is a reason the exclusionary rule should be applied toward criminal evidence. This is commonly referred to as standing to assert the Fourth Amendment.

Since 1980, a criminal defendant must demonstrate a "legitimate expectation of privacy" in the area searched, as a prerequisite of standing to challenge the legality of the search or seizure in question (*Rawlings v Kentucky*, 1980; *United States v. Salvucci*, 1980). By establishing that a criminal defendant must demonstrate a "legitimate expectation of privacy" in the area searched the Court has greatly restricted the circumstances in which the exclusionary rule may even be requested. For instance, passengers in a vehicle may not expect privacy (*Rakas v. Illinois*, 1978), nor may those visiting a house solely for commercial reasons (*Minnesota v. Carter*, 1998); likewise passengers in a taxicab do not have a "legitimate expectation of privacy" (*Rios v. United States*, 1960).

CONCLUSION

As an informed citizen contemplates his or her constitutional right to be free from *unreasonable* search and seizure at the hands of police who are constantly under pressure to search for the evidence of possessory offenses, a few things should be remembered. First, evidence that is effectively contested in a motion to suppress evidence is often, due to the *exclusionary rule,* deemed inadmissible at trial. Second, to appear before a judge at a suppression motion, standing to assert the Fourth Amendment must be established. Third, the ability to gain standing to assert the Fourth Amendment necessarily means that a criminal defendant demonstrate that a "legitimate expectation of privacy" existed in the area were the police searched for and seized the criminal evidence in question.

Violations of law by the police can almost always be challenged in civil court. However, a monetary reward is slight consolation if illegally gained evidence enters into a criminal trial resulting in the defendant's loss of liberty. For those who desire stronger police authority and less crime, this may be a positive restriction of Fourth Amendment rights. Nonetheless, the words of former Supreme Court Justice Louis Brandeis offer a compelling second opinion:

Decency, security and liberty alike demand that governmental officials shall be subject to the same rules of conduct that are commands to the citizens. In a government of laws, existence of the government will be imperiled if it fails to observe the law scrupulously. Our government is the potent, the omnipresent teacher. For good or for ill, it teaches the whole people by its example. Crime is contagious. If the government becomes a lawbreaker, it breeds contempt for the law; it invites every man to become a law unto himself; it invites anarchy. (dissenting opinion *Olmstead v. United States*, 1928)

—*Eric Roark*

See also American Civil Liberties Union; Cell Search; First Amendment; Freedom of Information Act 1966; Increase in Prison Population; Race, Class, and Gender of Prisoners; War on Drugs

Further Reading

Mauer, M. (1999). *Race to incarcerate.* New York: New Press.
Taslitz, A. E., & Paris, M. L. (1997). *Constitutional criminal procedure.* New York: Foundation Press.
U.S. Bureau of Justice. (2004). U.S. Bureau of Justice statistics. Retrieved from www.ojp.usdoj.gov/bjs/

Legal Cases

Carroll v. United States, 267 U.S. 132 (1925).
Katz v. United States, 389 U.S. 347 (1967).
Mapp v. Ohio, 367 U.S. 643 (1961).
Minnesota v. Carter, 119 S. Ct. 469 (1998).
New York v. Berger, 482 U.S. 691 (1987).
Olmstead v. United States, 277 U.S. 438 (1928).
Rakas v. Illinois, 439 U.S. 148 (1978).
Rawlings v. Kentucky, 448 U.S. 98 (1980).
Terry v. Ohio, 392 U.S. 1 (1968).
United States v. Dunn, 480 U.S. 294 (1987).
United States v. Salvucci, 448 U.S. 83 (1980).
Weeks v. United States, 232 U.S. 383 (1914).
Whren v. United States, 116 S. Ct. 1769 (1996).

◪ FRAMINGHAM, MCI (MASSACHUSETTS CORRECTIONAL INSTITUTION)

Massachusetts Correctional Institution– Framingham (MCI–Framingham), located 22 miles west of Boston in Framingham, Massachusetts, is the oldest women's prison in the United States. All women sentenced to serve state time are processed at Framingham before being assigned to wherever they will serve out their sentence. The state's other facility for female inmates is South Middlesex Correctional Center, a minimum-security prison also located in the town of Framingham. The vast majority of female inmates (87%) are housed at Framingham.

Framingham has two units, each with a different level of security. A medium-security facility houses county and state inmates who have been sentenced to serve time in a state Department of Correction (DOC) facility. The maximum-security unit, known as the Awaiting Trial Unit (ATU), is used to hold women facing federal charges. In June 2002, the medium-security unit held approximately 500 women, while the ATU held just over 135 women.

INMATE CHARACTERISTICS

The state's female inmate population differs from the male population in several ways. As of January 1, 2002, the state DOC had 9,610 inmates under its jurisdiction. Six percent of these people were women (535) and 94% (9,075) were men. While approximately 78% of females in the state system are white and 21% are black, the male population is characterized as 66% white and 32% black. The age difference between the populations is reflected not only in the average age of the inmates, 35.7 years for the females and 36.8 years for the males, but also in the range of ages. Males ranged from 16 to 86 years, while females ranged from 18 to 71. Women, generally considered to engage in less violent crime than men, were convicted of more drug crimes (35%) than person offenses (32%). In contrast, nearly half of all male inmates (49%) were incarcerated for person offenses, followed by 20% for drug offenses and 19% for sex offenses.

CONDITIONS

For many years, all of Massachusetts' prisons operated above capacity. In response, the state mandated the DOC commissioner in 1985 to issue a quarterly report on the status of overcrowding in all state and county facilities. From these data, it can be seen that Framingham continues to suffer from serious crowding issues. For example, the ATU has operated at approximately 200% above capacity for more than two decades. The medium-security facility has remained steady at just over 125% capacity according to the state's data for the same time period.

Inmates live in two types of housing at Framingham: cells and dormitories; both are forced to accommodate more inmates than they were designed to hold. Overcrowded dorms are not only noisier and more stressful for inmates, they also place a greater demand on the security staff members whose responsibility is to watch all the inmates in the room. The size of Framingham's inmate population also requires that some women live double-celled, where two women live in a cell space originally built for one.

HEALTH CARE

Health care at Framingham has long been criticized. While a series of hearings and studies in the 1980s called for radical changes, criticism of its inmate care continued to grow. Recently, the University of Massachusetts Medical School was awarded the contract to provide both mental and physical health care services. It is hoped that this local teaching institution will have increased accountability and provide improved services.

The women at Framingham mirror the national profile of female inmates who have more medical problems than male inmates. About 15 inmates at Framingham are pregnant at any one time and approximately 20% of the inmates are HIV-positive, creating a great medical need. Pregnant women, like patients with HIV/AIDS, require regular, ongoing medical services including monitoring and testing. Therefore, poor health care is particularly damaging to these populations.

There has been a recent move to improve mental health services at Framingham, where at least six women have committed suicide since 1995. Compared to male inmates, female inmates have greater mental health care needs. Over 20% of the women at Framingham are actively receiving mental health care.

PROGRAMS

MCI-Framingham offers numerous educational, vocational, and therapeutic programs. Inmates can receive their general equivalency diploma (GED) while incarcerated and participate in college-level classes in a partnership with Boston University. The prison also offers a number of vocational trade programs, including computer technology and building trades. Women in the manicuring program receive the state-mandated 100 hours of instruction and are then eligible to take the state licensing exam. The state's correctional industry, MassCor, employs 18 women at its flag shop at Framingham. The facility has rehabilitative programs including Alcoholics Anonymous, Alanon, and Narcotics Anonymous; HIV/AIDS and sexual and domestic abuse survivor support groups have also been organized by the inmates. In the Choices youth outreach program for girls who are at risk for future offending, inmates share their criminal histories with the girls, hoping to have an impact on them with frank discussions of their own violent experiences.

In addition to helping children unknown to them, inmates can also participate in a number of parenting programs offered to help improve their relationships with their own children. Framingham sponsors a number of innovative therapeutic programs, including Catch the Hope. The project was started in 1991 to provide medical attention and social services to pregnant and postpartum inmates. In addition to substance abuse counseling and preparation for birth and infant custody planning, the program pairs inmates with professional birth attendants who guide them through their labor and delivery. The program also works with postrelease programs that will accept women with their children.

THE "FRAMINGHAM EIGHT"

In 1992, a group of women known as the "Framingham Eight" collectively petitioned the governor and the Massachusetts Advisory Board of Pardons for clemency. Each had been convicted of manslaughter or murder for killing her domestic partner. They argued that they had killed their batterers in self-defense (one woman was battered by her female partner). Boston College Law School Clemency Project organized the Framingham Eight Commutation Project, and the women received an outpouring of public support. Their case brought attention to the plight of battered women and is well known for its successful use of battered women's syndrome as a criminal defense (each of the eight women was eventually released by Governor William Weld). They also inspired a short film, *Defending Our Lives*, that won an Academy Award for Best Short Film—Documentary in 1993.

Just a few years later, another group of Framingham women successfully fought against injustice. In 1998, a group of inmates incarcerated at Framingham won a lawsuit against the DOC for brutality after an early-morning raid in September 1995 where masked correction officers dressed all in black forced more than 110 women from their beds and publicly strip-searched 16 of them in what the DOC called a training exercise. The DOC, while not admitting that it violated any laws, settled the suit by agreeing to discontinue the use of the training techniques and pay the women $80,000 in damages.

CONCLUSION

Framingham, like the larger DOC of which it is a part, has struggled during its history. In addition to the unique challenges female inmates present to prison officials, problems with overcrowding, inmate treatment, and health care services have marked the facility. Informed policy and program decisions are necessary to positively affect this population. Therefore, researchers must focus their efforts on the issues facing women in prison, such as the women living at Framingham.

—*Gennifer Furst*

See also Cottage System; History of Women's Prisons; HIV/AIDS; Massachusetts Reformatory; Mothers in Prison; Race, Class, and Gender of Prisoners; Status Offenders; Women's Health; Women's Prisons

Further Reading

Goldfarb, P. (1996, March). Describing without circumscribing: Questioning the construction of gender in the discourse of intimate violence. *George Washington Law Review, 64,* 582.

Massachusetts Department of Correction. (2001, December 10). *Frequently asked questions.* Retrieved from http://www.state.ma.us/doc/faqs.htm

Massachusetts Department of Correction. (2003). *Quarterly report on the status of prison overcrowding, second quarter of 2002.* Retrieved from http://www.state.ma.us/doc

McGurrin, M. (1993). Pregnant inmates' right to health care. *New England Journal on Criminal & Civil Confinement, 20,* 163.

◪ FREEDOM OF INFORMATION ACT 1966

The Freedom of Information Act (FOIA) was originally enacted in 1966. It established for the first time a statutory right of access by any person to federal agency records unless the information sought was specifically exempted. The act requires certain materials to be made available under the agency's own initiative by publication in the *Federal Register* or in public reading rooms. Disclosure, not secrecy, is the dominant objective of the act.

After President Lyndon B. Johnson threatened a veto, the exemptions were broadened. The act, which went into effect in 1967, is codified as Title 5 U.S.C. § 552 and has been amended five times. At first, agencies interpreted the exemptions broadly and employed a variety of means to discourage FOIA use, including high fees, long delays, and claims that they could not find the requested materials. More recently, however, courts have interpreted most exemptions narrowly and fashioned procedural remedies against agency intransigence.

ADMINISTRATIVE PROCESS

The act specifies certain administrative procedures for processing requests. The initial request may be made to agency headquarters or a regional office and must "reasonably describe" the information sought. A statement of need is not necessary under FOIA, but may prove relevant in convincing an agency official to release the sought after information. Search and copy fees may apply, although it is also possible to have these fees waived. Generally,

there is a 20-working-day statutory time limit for the agency response, but some agencies (particularly the FBI and CIA) may take years to reply. Such delay may usually be construed as a denial, although administrative remedies may be available if this occurs.

Once the relevant federal agency has determined whether the FOIA request will be honored, the agency must provide the individual or group that has lodged the request with a statement of what will or will not be released. The agency must also issue a statement of any reasons it may have for withholding the request and instruct the person about his or her right to appeal the determination. Finally, if necessary, the agency will also explain why it is not in the public interest to waive a fee.

FEES AND FEE WAIVERS

A requestor may incur three types of fees: (1) the cost of the search, (2) the cost of review, and (3) duplication costs. Agencies are required to provide for free the first two hours of search time and the first 100 pages of copying to noncommercial requestors. Multiple requests will not bypass fees.

The act states that if disclosure of the information is in the public interest, so as to contribute significantly to the public understanding of how government works, it may qualify for a fee waiver. However, the burden is on the requestor to prove (a) genuine public interest, (b) value of the records to the public, (c) that the information is not already in the public domain, (d) "expertise" in one's ability and intention to disseminate information, and (e) no personal interest in disclosure. A court can review agency fee action *de novo* (anew).

ADMINISTRATIVE APPEALS

Generally, exhaustion of administrative remedies is required prior to requesting judicial relief (i.e., obey each agency rule relating to data request). The burden of producing evidence of a proper agency appeal is on the requestor. The following items can be appealed: (a) denial of a request in full or in part, (b) adequacy of the agency's search, (c) failure to respond within the time limits, (d) excessive fees, or (e) denial of a request for waiver of or a fee reduction. An appeal usually results in the release of additional documents that were initially withheld.

WHAT IS AN AGENCY?

An agency includes most entities that receive federal funds and operate under federal control. The courts and Congress as well as units in the executive office of the president are excluded, although not necessarily other offices in the executive branch of the federal government. Each entity is examined anew. A subunit of an agency may be sufficiently independent so as to be treated as an agency as may an advisory group (e.g., the Federal Bureau of Prisons is a subagency of the Department of Justice).

WHAT IS AN AGENCY RECORD?

There is a two-pronged test to determine whether a record is an agency record: (1) The agency must either create or obtain the material, and (2) the agency must be in control of the material at the time the FOIA request is made. The government bears the burden of proving that a record remains under the control of an exempt entity. Business records and personal entries created (but mixed) solely for an individual's conveniences that may be disposed of at that person's discretion are not agency records under the FOIA. There is no distinction between records kept manually or in computer storage systems. The requestor need not seek access from the agency that originated the document.

EXEMPTIONS

There are nine exemptions that allow an agency to withhold access to information. The FOIA, in other words, does not apply to the following:

Exemption 1: National Security Information

Matters that are specifically authorized under criteria established by an executive order to be kept secret in the interest of national defense or foreign policy and properly classified as such (e.g., CIA documents).

Exemption 2: Internal Agency Rules

Matters that are related solely to the internal personnel rules and practices of an agency, including agency matters in which the public could not reasonably be expected to have an interest.

Exemption 3: Information Exempted by Other Statutes

Matters specifically exempted by other statutes that leave no discretion on the issue. The statute must require or authorize withholding that incorporates a congressional mandate of confidentiality.

Exemption 4: Business Information

Privileged or confidential trade secrets or commercial or financial information obtained from a person. Information generated by the government does not fall under Exemption 4. One who has submitted information to the government may sue to prevent disclosure of that information. This type suit is known as "reverse FOIA litigation."

Exemption 5: Inter- and Intra-agency Memoranda

Inter-agency or intra-agency memorandums or letters, which would not be available by law to a party other than an agency in litigation with the agency. These claims are generally waived if the documents have been disclosed to third parties or non-federal agencies. This exemption was intended to incorporate the government's common law privilege from discovery in litigation such (a) "executive" privilege, which protects advice, recommendations, and opinions that are part of the deliberative, consultative, decision-making processes of government; (b) "attorney work product" privilege, which protects documents prepared by an attorney that reveal the theory of the lawyer's case or his or her litigation strategy; (c) the "attorney-client" privilege, which protects confidential communications; and (d) a qualified privilege based on Rule 26(c)(7) FRCP for confidential commercial information generated by the government in the awarding of a contract.

Exemption 6: Personal Privacy

Matters that are personal, medical, or similar files, the disclosure of which would constitute a clearly unwarranted invasion of privacy. This policy involves a balancing of interests between the protection of an individual's private affairs with the public's right to government information and the preservation of the basic purpose of the FOIA to open up agency action to the light of public scrutiny. "Similar files" is construed broadly. The identity of the requestor is irrelevant. A prior promise of confidentiality is not determinative. Prior public disclosure can defeat the exemption. The majority view is that this exemption shields lists of names and addresses (e.g., union memberships).

Exemption 7: Law Enforcement Records

Information compiled for law enforcement purposes if their production (a) could reasonably be expected to interfere with enforcement proceedings; (b) would deprive a person of a fair trial or impartial adjudication; (c) could reasonably be expected to constitute an unwarranted invasion of privacy; (d) could reasonably be expected to disclose the identity of a confidential source; (e) would disclose techniques, procedures, or guidelines for law enforcement investigations or prosecutions if disclosure could reasonably be expected to risk circumvention of the law; and (f) could reasonably be expected to endanger the life or physical safety of *any* individual. The threshold test is whether the records are compiled for law enforcement purposes—whether civil or criminal, judicial or administrative. The records are not exempt unless the agency can show potential harm from document release under one or more of the six protected law enforcement interests above (e.g., the release of an informant's name).

Exemption 8: Records of Financial Institutions

Matters related to records for the use of an agency responsible for regulation or supervision of financial institutions. This broadly interpreted exemption is designed to protect the integrity and security of financial institutions and safeguard the relationship between banks and their supervising agencies.

Exemption 9: Oil Well Data

Finally, matters related to geological and geophysical data (e.g., maps of wells). This exemption, the least invoked and litigated of all the exemptions, has been called the "Texas touch." It is often criticized as being redundant to Exemption 4 because it includes confidential business information.

SEGREGABILITY

Section 552(b) of the FOIA provides that any portion of a record that can be reasonably segregated from exempt portions shall be provided to the requestor. Claims by an agency otherwise must be made with the same degree of detail as required for claims of exemption. District courts have broad discretion to determine whether *in camera* inspection (secret judicial scrutiny) is necessary when the agency claims inability to segregate. When the requestor cites this issue in an administrative appeal, it often leads to additional release of information.

LITIGATION STRATEGY

The FOIA may be an attractive alternative or adjunct to civil or criminal discovery because a person need not be a party to a lawsuit nor make a showing of need or relevancy nor bear the government's litigation costs if unsuccessful. Theoretically, the FOIA is a faster way to obtain copies of agency records.

FOIA requestors must exhaust administrative remedies before filing suit to obtain agency records. Even if the FOIA time limits for disclosure have been violated, this does not guarantee a court-established strict deadline. Suits may be filed in federal district court (a) in the plaintiff's home district, (b) where the records are located, or (c) in the District of Columbia (most familiar with FOIA litigation). The statute of limitations is set by Title 28 U.S.C. § 2401(a) at six years. A federal agency must always be named as a party defendant in an FOIA lawsuit. The complaint should be brief and request expedition of the lawsuit (§ 552(a)(4)(D)).

CONCLUSION

The FOIA is meant to provide some kind of check and balance on government actions. Similar acts have been adopted in several countries. The complex laws surrounding such acts often make it difficult for regular citizens to use them successfully.

—*Kenneth Linn*

See also Activism; American Civil Liberties Union; Enemy Combatants; Habeas Corpus; Jailhouse Lawyers; Prisoner Litigation; Prison Litigation Reform Act 1996; Resistance

Further Reading

Clinger, W. (2001). *Citizen's guide on using the Freedom of Information Act and the Privacy Act of 1974 to request government records.* Collingwood, PA: Diane Publishing.

Foerstel, H. (1999). *Freedom of information and the right to know: The origins and applications of the Freedom of Information Act.* Westport, CT: Greenwood.

Kavass, I. (1997). *Justice Department guide to the Freedom of Information Act 1996.* Buffalo, NY: William. S. Hein.

Maida, P. (2001). *Freedom of Information Act guide and Privacy Act overview* (May 2000 ed.). Collingwood, PA: Diane Publishing.

◪ FRY, ELIZABETH (1780–1845)

Elizabeth Fry was a prison reformer who advocated for the humane treatment and rehabilitation of inmates. She incorporated religion, education, and vocational practices into her ideology of reform. She was a strict Quaker who incorporated her religious beliefs into her educational work to inmates. Fry primarily advocated on behalf of women offenders.

BIOGRAPHICAL DETAILS

Elizabeth Gurney Fry was born at Earlham in Norwich, England, on May 21, 1780. She was the third daughter of John Gurney and Catherine Bell, and 1 of 11 children. Her mother died when she was 12 years of age, at which point, in her mother's place, her eldest sister became responsible for tending to the children.

Elizabeth Gurney married Joseph Fry in August 1800. Joseph too, was a devout Quaker, and he hailed from a wealthy family. The newlywed couple settled in London, where Fry found her calling of assisting female prisoners. Fry was acknowledged in 1811 as a Quaker minister. Following her first visit to Newgate Prison in 1813, she dedicated herself to prison reform. Elizabeth Fry died on October 12, 1845, at the age of 65 years. She was the mother to 11 children and left an indelible imprint on prison reform practices.

NEWGATE PRISON

At the time of Fry's first visit to Newgate Prison, all female prisoners were confined in what was later labeled as the "untried side" of the jail. The women's division was made up of two cells and two wards, in a zone of about 190 yards. More than 300 women were crowded into this area, mixing those on trial with those who had been convicted of both mild and the most violent crimes. Children were also confined in this area alongside their mothers.

In April 1817, Fry organized a committee, the Ladies Association for the Reformation of the Female Prisoners in Newgate, which was extended in 1821 into the British Ladies' Society for Promoting the Reformation of Female Prisoners. The committee consisted of nine Quaker women and one clergyman's wife. These 10 women served the female prison population at Newgate, by providing clothing, religious and educational instruction, and employment training and opportunities. They sought to instill the habits of sobriety and order in the women with the hope of rendering them docile and peaceful in prison and beyond.

THE IDEOLOGY OF REFORM

In 1818, under the reign of King George III, and one year after the establishment of her school within Newgate Prison, Elizabeth Fry was called to give evidence before the Committee of the House of Commons on the Prisons of the Metropolis. She was the first woman, other than a queen, to be called into the councils of government in an official manner to advise on matters of public concern. It was during this meeting that Fry set forth her main ideology of penal reform.

Fry suggested that there should be women warders taking care of women inmates. According to her, a single-sex environment would be more conducive to their reformation, as the warders would be positive role models for the women offenders. Second, Fry suggested that there be an entirely separate prison for female inmates. Rather than using a section within the male institution, she thought that women should be held separately in order to address their special needs more thoroughly. She also sought to have the prisoners paid at a fair rate by the government and to be allowed to spend a portion of their earnings upon reception. Fry believed that if the inmates were able to support themselves through legal means upon release, they would be less likely to engage in criminal activity.

Fry wanted inmates to be classified and separated. She argued that first-time and petty offenders should be separated from more chronic and violent inmates. First-time offenders would not have the opportunity to learn the criminogenic lifestyles of the more experienced inmates and would thus be more susceptible to penal reformation strategies. Fry also advocated for the segregation of prostitutes, since she saw them as a special population who were in need of specific moral and religious reformation. She argued that female inmates should be allowed to eat their meals and engage in recreation time as a group, but should remain segregated at night for their mental and physical well-being.

Unlike her prison reform predecessor John Howard, Fry advocated for the elimination of solitary confinement. She realized that prison officials would be unwilling to relinquish this practice completely and therefore made an exception stating that if this practice must continue, it be used only for very short periods of time and in the most horrific of cases. Fry believed that strict Quaker religion should be enforced in prison to help rebuild and restructure the morals of the inmates and to guide their behavior upon release. She also implemented educational and vocational training to better the social position of the women and to help ensure them a viable means of living upon release. Women were taught to cook, sew, clean, read and write, and properly care for their children. Finally, following her Quaker beliefs, Fry argued for the prohibition of

alcohol within the prison since she believed alcohol consumption was related to criminal activity. As a result of Fry's tactics, Newgate Prison experienced a drop in the recidivism rate from 30%–40% to 4%.

WORK OUTSIDE OF NEWGATE

In addition to assisting prison inmates, Fry also helped those who were aboard convict ships. When the women were transferred from Newgate to the convict ships, they often engaged in riotous and destructive behavior. The women were moved in open wagons, which was both humiliating and tended to make them aggressive. Fry advocated that the women be moved in closed hackney coaches, and she volunteered to escort them. The convict ships lay in the harbor for five to six weeks, wherein Fry and the Ladies Association incorporated the caring practices they were bringing to Newgate. Eventually, moving women from their prison to the convict ships was made illegal.

CONCLUSION

Elizabeth Fry's system of governing female inmates was premised on the assumption that women were capable of redemption. This approach was in stark contrast to the strongly held belief at the time that women offenders were more evil than their male counterparts and thus "irreclaimable" (van Drenth & de Haan, 1999, p. 72). Fry influenced penal systems in Canada, the United States, Australia, France, Denmark, and Wales. She was a forerunner in prison reform practices. Her legacy is remembered in such organizations as the Canadian Association of Elizabeth Fry Societies (CAEFS), which assists and advocates on the behalf of women in conflict with the law. Echoes of Fry's interest in women prisoners may also be found in the extensive body of work that concentrates solely on women's experiences of imprisonment around the world.

—*Jennifer M. Kilty*

See also Abolition; Activism; Classification; History of Women's Prisons; John Howard; Fay Honey Knopp; Religion in Prison; Quakers; Women Prisoners; Women's Prisons

Further Reading

Canadian Association of Elizabeth Fry Societies. (2002a). *Goals of the Elizabeth Fry Societies*. Retrieved from http://www.elizabethfry.ca/

Canadian Association of Elizabeth Fry Societies. (2002b). *Origins of the Elizabeth Fry Societies*. Retrieved from http://www.elizabethfry.ca/

Canadian Association of Elizabeth Fry Societies. (2002c). *Principles of the Elizabeth Fry Societies*. Retrieved from http://www.elizabethfry.ca/

Hanks, G. (1981). *Friend of prisoners: The story of Elizabeth Fry*. Exeter, UK: Religious and Moral Education Press.

Pitman, E. R. (1969). *Elizabeth Fry*. New York: Greenwood.

van Drenthe, A., & de Haan, F. (1999). *The rise of caring power: Elizabeth Fry and Josephine Butler in Britain and the Netherlands*. Amsterdam: Amsterdam University Press.

Whitney, J. (1972). *Elizabeth Fry: Quaker heroine*. New York: Benjamin Blom.

◪ FURLOUGH

The word *furlough* has Old English origins and, when used as a verb, basically means to grant a leave. The expanded contemporary use of the word furlough usually refers to a scheduled temporary and nonduty and nonpay status. This period of work may be voluntary. Furloughs in the civilian world may at times be mandatory and of a financial emergency nature such as the widespread furlough of flight attendants who were not needed due to significantly fewer scheduled flights after the September 11, 2001, terrorist attacks.

In a correctional setting, furlough also refers to a temporary and time-limited leave of absence. Typically, an inmate on a furlough will be entitled to an overnight or longer release from prison. Furloughs are used most often to address social and rehabilitative needs of the inmate. They may be granted so that an inmate may be present during a crisis, such as a funeral, in the immediate family (mother, father, stepparents, foster parents, sibling, spouse, and children). Prisoners may also be allowed to leave the confines of their prison temporarily to participate in the development of release plans, to reestablish family and community ties, and to participate in select educational, social, religious, and therapeutic activities that might facilitate their transition to the community.

Anytime that an inmate leaves or enters a facility, there are procedural and security concerns. To address these concerns, each institution typically has established guidelines outlining who might be eligible for furlough and procedures before leaving and upon the inmate's return. They also dictate what costs are expected to be paid by the inmate typically before the furlough is granted. Each of these issues shall be dealt with in turn below.

ELIGIBILITY

In the United States, furloughs are not very common and inmates are carefully screened for risk to the community before permission for a furlough is given. In many other countries, furloughs are more readily and routinely offered. In the United States, usually only minimum-security inmates who are in the last year of their sentence, meet the institution's eligibility criteria, and are approved by the warden are eligible for a leave of absence.

Since research has shown that inmates who maintain ties with their families generally have lower rates of recidivism, activities that may facilitate release transition and strengthen family ties may be deemed appropriate for the granting of a furlough. Some work skill programs may also be considered appropriate for the granting of a furlough. In addition, prisoners may be granted furloughs to participate in classes or treatment that are not available at their institution, such as a residential drug and alcohol rehabilitation program, or to obtain medical services not available at the prison.

Furloughs are considered a privilege. They are, therefore, not routinely given to an entire category of inmates but are instead awarded only to those individuals with a record of behavior making them worthy of the privilege. Women and prisoners in remote areas may be at a disadvantage if vocational or other services are not provided in the communities near the prison since travel time and the difficulty of making arrangements may be too great for the limited time allocated to furloughs. In any case, the warden or disciplinary committee of the institution may decide to revoke or withhold furlough privileges of any inmate.

PROCEDURES

Security procedures mandate that facts pertaining to the reason for a furlough such as the alleged death or terminal illness of a family member must be verified, for instance, by contacting the funeral home or doctor, and then documented on the appropriate institutional forms by designated institutional staff. Inmates will be informed of the conditions of their furlough. Conditions of furlough vary by institution but typically include keeping a copy of the furlough agreement on their person at all times, remaining within the appropriate county limits, avoiding alcohol and illegal drugs, not associating with suspected criminals, and obeying all laws and regulations.

Before anyone leaves a correctional facility to begin his or her furlough, all relevant victims/witnesses should be notified of the starting and ending dates of the furlough as well as specific location. The chief law enforcement officer (sheriff and/or chief of police) of the furlough destination should also be notified before the prisoner leaves. Usually, inmates must also make contact with the appropriate law enforcement official upon their arrival in the community and must later produce a document verifying this contact when they return to the institution.

Of course, there are risks involved in allowing prisoners to be out on furlough. The purpose of the leave of absence may not be accomplished if, for example, employment is not secured. Also, there is the possibility that someone on leave may commit another crime. Occasionally, those out on furlough may simply "walk away" and escape. While some factors such as type of crime for which the inmate was arrested and previous escape history can be used in attempting to predict risk, no prediction formula is completely foolproof.

If the conditions of the furlough agreement are not met or are violated, a range of consequences may result. Failure to accomplish the purpose of the furlough such as by missing a scheduled interview or a minor violation of rules, for example, returning from furlough 10 minutes late, may result in disciplinary action. An individual who commits a felony while on furlough will not be entitled to any further leaves during the remainder of his or her sentence. Anyone who has not contacted the institution with an appropriate explanation and who is more than three hours late in returning shall typically have an escape warrant issued.

Inmates usually have to pay for any nonemergency costs associated with a furlough such as transportation, lodging, and meals. Costs for conducting a urinalysis upon the inmate's return to the institution will also typically be withdrawn from the inmate's personal funds prior to his or her release. Such funds may make it difficult for indigent prisoners to take advantage of the furlough system.

CONCLUSION

Furlough programs are widely but selectively used by most correctional institutions. Such programs are thought to improve inmate morale while furthering the goals of rehabilitation and lessening recidivism. However, not all administrators support them, since furlough programs are labor intensive because all prisoners must be screened before being allowed off the premises. Furthermore, furlough programs are by nature controversial, and thus, potentially risky for prisons, because the public typically does not approve of prisoners being released into the community before their sentence is complete. Even though the low levels at which inmates commit serious crimes while on furlough suggest that such fears are ungrounded, concerns remain high enough that few inmates will be given the opportunity to participate in a furlough while they are confined.

—Wendelin M. Hume

See also Clemency; Community Corrections Centers; Compassionate Release; Parole; Prerelease Programs; Prisoner Reentry; Recidivism; Rehabilitation Theory; Work-Release Programs

Further Reading

Champion, D. J. (1990). *Corrections in the United States.* Englewood Cliffs, NJ: Prentice Hall.

McShane, M. D., & Williams, F. P., III. (Eds.). (1996). *Encyclopedia of American prisons.* New York: Garland.

Petersilia, J. (2003). *When prisoners come home: Parole and prisoner reentry.* New York: Oxford University Press.

Travis, J., Solomon, A., & Waul, M. (2001). *From prison to home: The dimensions and consequences of prisoner reentry.* Washington, DC: Urban Institute.

◪ *FURMAN v. GEORGIA*

Furman v. Georgia was the U.S. Supreme Court case that briefly suspended capital punishment in the United States, for four years, from 1972 to 1976. Although the death penalty was eventually reinstated, *Furman v. Georgia* changed the legal and political landscape surrounding capital punishment.

HISTORY

Prior to the 1960s, courts uniformly supported the constitutionality of the death penalty. However, during the civil rights movement, a number of cases brought by death row inmates successfully challenged many of the legal and social assumptions that underpinned capital punishment. One of the first shifts toward challenging the death penalty actually occurred in the unrelated case of *Trop v. Dulles* (1958) where it was successfully argued that the framers of the Eighth Amendment inserted an "evolving standard of decency that marked the progress of a maturing society."

This decision was applied 10 years later in the case of *United States v. Jackson* (1968) where the court held that the sole discretion given to juries to determine the death penalty was unconstitutional because it forced defendants to waive right to jury trial in order to escape the death penalty. It further appeared in *Witherspoon v. Illinois* (1968) where it was ruled unconstitutional to exclude a juror who had reservations about the death penalty but who could still reach a reasonable decision on a capital case.

In 1971, the cases of *Crampton v. Ohio* and *McGautha v. California* challenged the death penalty on the basis of the due process rights of the Fourteenth Amendment but the Supreme Court disagreed with their claims and gave the jury full discretion in the determination of the death penalty on the basis that it was "humanly impossible" to guide the sentencing discretion of the jury. The next year, *Furman v. Georgia* reopened this challenge by arguing that jury decisions were evidently arbitrary and capricious and therefore "cruel and unusual" contrary to the provisions of the Eighth Amendment. This time, the court agreed by 5–4 majority, thereby voiding the death penalty statutes in 39 states and those of the federal government, commuting 629 pending death sentences across the country and imposing a moratorium on further death sentences until there were adequate safeguards against arbitrary and capricious jury sentencing decisions. Four years later, new death penalty statutes were once again ruled constitutional by the U.S. Supreme Court following the challenge of *Gregg v. Georgia* in 1976.

BACKGROUND TO *FURMAN v. GEORGIA*

In many ways, Furman was a lucky man. This is not just because he saved his own life and those of 629 other death row inmates by appealing against the death penalty and winning but also because he was not the only one whose case was decided on the same day. Instead, he was the first of three appellants to file appeals with the U.S. Supreme Court in 1969 (as his case number indicates, No. 69–5003). As a result, it could have been the name of Jackson as in *Jackson v. Georgia* (No. 69–5030) or that of Branch as in *Branch v. Texas* (No. 69–5031) that would be remembered widely today. In fact, the other two cases should actually be more well known than Furman's because their rulings have endured longer. The cases of Branch and Jackson finally ended the use of death penalty for rape, for which African American men were overwhelmingly executed in America prior to 1972. Their victories were solidified in 1976 when the U.S. Supreme Court clearly prohibited states from punishing rape with death in the case of *Coker v. Georgia*.

These three African American men made history by challenging and defeating a form of punishment that the Supreme Court agreed was cruel and unusual and therefore unconstitutional. Furman and Jackson appealed their cases before the supreme court of Georgia, while Branch appealed before the court of criminal appeals of Texas. All three cases were decided on June 29, 1972.

Furman

Furman was 26 years old with a sixth-grade education. He was found guilty of murder when he entered a house and shot the owner dead through a closed door. He claimed that the gun went off unintentionally when he tripped and fell and that he had no intention of killing anyone. His counsel entered an insanity plea on his behalf, and he was committed to Georgia Central State Hospital for psychiatric observation. The hospital staff unanimously reported that he suffered from mental deficiency with psychotic episodes associated with convulsive disorder. They recommended further psychiatric hospitalization and treatment. But later, the superintendent reported that Furman was not psychotic at the time, that he knew right from wrong, and that he was capable of cooperating with his court-appointed counsel.

Jackson

Jackson was 21 years old when he was convicted of raping a white woman. He was serving a three-year sentence at that time for auto theft and had escaped from a work gang in the area. He entered the house when the woman's husband left for work and threatened her with a pair of scissors that he held to her neck. In addition to raping her, he demanded money. A court-appointed psychiatrist testified that Jackson was not an imbecile or schizophrenic and that he was competent to stand trial because he was only suffering from environmental influences.

Branch

Branch had earlier been convicted of felony theft with borderline mental deficiency and below average IQ of Texas prison inmates. He was convicted of entering the house of a 65-year-old white widow while she slept and raping her, with his hand on her throat. After raping her, like Jackson, he demanded money. Branch then left and warned her not to tell anyone what happened or he would return and kill her.

THE SUPREME COURT

The Supreme Court was asked by the three men to answer the following question: "Does the imposition and carrying out of the death penalty in (these cases) constitute cruel and unusual punishment in violation of the Eighth and Fourteenth Amendments?" Five of

the Supreme Court justices answered the question affirmatively (concurring), while four justices answered the question negatively (dissenting). Justices William Douglas, William Brennan, Potter Stewart, Byron White, and Thurgood Marshall filed separate opinions in support of the judgments, while Chief Justice Warren Burger and Justices Harry Blackmun, Lewis Powell, and William Rehnquist filed separate dissenting opinions. By this narrow 5–4 majority decision, the Supreme Court could have effectively abolished the death penalty in America forever. However, the question before the Court was limited to issues "in (these cases)." That was the loophole that later enabled their decision to be overturned.

CONCLUSION

On June 26, 1997, the Southern Center for Human Rights marked the 25th anniversary of *Furman v. Georgia* by issuing a report that concluded that the promise of reform that emanated from the 1972 judgment did not materialize because the death penalty remains discriminatory, arbitrary, and cruel especially with reference to race, poverty, innocence, mental retardation, mental illness, and children on death row. This report echoed the argument of *McCleskey v. Kemp* (1987) when the Supreme Court was asked to rule the death penalty unconstitutional on the basis of racial discrimination. The petition of McCleskey was rejected by a narrow margin of 5–4 majority, the same margin with which *Furman v. Georgia* was granted.

Only Justice Marshall and Justice Brennan found in the case of *Furman* that the death penalty was unconstitutional. The other three justices who found in favor of *Furman* held that it was only the existing death penalty statues that were unconstitutional. This majority opinion meant that states quickly started rewriting their death penalty cases to get rid of arbitrariness. Only five months after the landmark decision, 34 states proclaimed new death penalty statutes that supposedly conformed to the higher standard set by the Supreme Court in the case of *Furman*.

These new acts were challenged in 1976 by three more cases, *Gregg v. Georgia*, *Jurek v. Texas*, and

Proffitt v. Florida, that were collectively known as *Gregg v. Georgia*. This time, the Supreme Court decided by 5–4 majority that the new death penalty statutes were constitutional, thereby ending the suspension of the death penalty and paving the way for the imposition of new death penalties in America, although the 629 sentences commuted as a result of the *Furman* decision could not be reimposed.

—*Biko Agozino*

See also Capital Punishment; Death Row; Deathwatch; Eighth Amendment; Fourteenth Amendment

Further Reading

Agozino, B. (2003). How scientific is criminal justice? A methodological critique of research on *McCleskey v. Kemp* and other capital cases. *National Black Law Journal*, (Columbia ed.), *17*(1), 85–97.

Baldus, C. D., Woodworth, G. G., & Pulaski, C. A., Jr. (1989). *Equal justice and the death penalty*. Boston: Northeastern University Press.

Berger, V. (1991). "Black box decision" on life or death—If they're arbitrary, don't blame the jury: A reply to Judge Patrick Higginbotham. *Case Western Reserve Law Review, 41*(4), 1067–1093.

Davis, A. (1987). Rape, racism and the capitalist setting. *Black Scholar, 9*(7), 24–30.

Death Penalty Information Center. (2003). *The constitutionality of the death penalty in America.* Retrieved from http://www.deathpenaltyinfo.org/article.php?scid=15&did=410#SuspendingtheDeathPenalty

Higginbotham, P. E. (1991). Juries and the death penalty. *Case Western Reserve Law Review, 41*(4), 1047–1067.

U.S. Department of Justice. (1982). *Capital punishment, 1981* (NCJ-78600). Washington, DC: U.S. Department of Justice, National Prisoner Statistics.

Legal Cases

Crampton v. Ohio, 402 U.S. 183, 210-211 (1971).

Furman v. Georgia, 408 U.S. 238 (1972).

Gregg v. Georgia, 428 U.S. 153 (1976).

Jurek v. Texas, 428 U.S. 262 (1976).

McCleskey v. Kemp, 481 U.S. 279 (1987).

McGautha v. California, 402 U.S. 183 (1971).

Proffitt v. Florida, 428 U.S. 242 (1976).

Trop v. Dulles, 365 U.S. 86 (1958).

United States v. Jackson, 390 U.S. 570 (1968).

Witherspoon v. Illinois, 391 U.S. 510 (1968).

GANGS

As the number of gangs and gang members in the United States continued to escalate during the past two decades of the 20th century and the response by the criminal justice system became harsher, many gang members found themselves in the nation's prison system. A 1999 study of prison administrators in 47 states estimated that about one-fourth (24.7%) of all male prisoners and 7.5% of female prisoners were gang members. In comparison only 9.4% of men and 3.5% women were identified as such in 1991. This percentage change means that there were approximately 47,220 male gang members in the nation's prisons in 1999, up from 43,765 in 1993. Some states have even a greater proportion of gangs in their prison population. In Illinois, for example, about 60% are believed to belong to gangs.

According to the 1999 survey of prison administrators, the most frequently cited gangs overall around the country were the Crips (various factions), Black Gangster Disciples, Bloods/Piru factions, Vice Lords, Aryan Brotherhood, and Latin Kings. Most of these gangs have strong rivalries within the prison system, based almost solely on race. While incarceration may be a short-term solution to the problem of gang violence in the community, in the long run it has resulted in increased gang cohesion and membership recruitment. Many gang members report that prison strengthens their involvement in the group, which is exactly the opposite of the intended effect of incarcerating them, while others join a gang for the first time when they are imprisoned.

HISTORY

Prison gangs first emerged in the west in the state of Washington in 1950 and in California in 1957. Twelve years later, in 1969, they began to appear in Illinois. During the 1970s, states adjacent to California and bordering Mexico, as well as two states to the north of Illinois, had similar organizations develop inside their prison systems. In the 1980s, development continued in Missouri and Kentucky.

Early prison gangs spread either by transfers or rearrests of gang members in another jurisdiction. In these cases, the inmate in a new prison setting sometimes tried to reproduce the organization that gave him or her an identity prior to incarceration. In other cases, charismatic leaders imitated what they had heard about other gangs.

RELATIONSHIP BETWEEN STREET GANGS AND PRISON GANGS

Two major types of gangs exist within the prison system: street gangs imported into the prison and groups that originate within the penal institution itself. There are many indigenous gangs in penal facilities. As a result, we need to be cautious about the common view that prison gangs are "mere extensions" of street organizations, for that is clearly not always the case.

Most indigenous prison gangs developed, at least in part, as a means of belonging and for protection during a term of confinement. Racketeering, black markets for illegal goods and services such as drugs, and racism have also been factors in the development of these organizations. Protection seems to be a key factor. When an individual enters a prison, he or she may be challenged to a fight. If this happens, typically the new prisoner will either join a gang or pay for protection or become a "servant" to other prisoners. It tends to happen more frequently in certain men's prisons than others and is more common in all men's prisons than in women's facilities. In Texas, gangs often recruit like fraternities and often specifically target prisoners who are serving short sentences. This way they can help the group when they leave. They adhere to a very strict code of silence and are committed to the gang for life, reflected in the common expression "blood in, blood out."

In contrast to the recruitment pressures experienced by the unaffiliated convict, the gang member from the street has little trouble in adjusting to the new environment. Besides physical security, the gang in the prison, as on the street, serves important material and psychological functions for its members. It functions both as a communication network and as a convenient distribution network for contraband goods. It also provides a source of identification and a feeling of belonging. Other members comprise one's family and are often referred to "my homes" or just "homes" (short for "homeboy"). Members live, and die, for the gang. The organizations, with their insignias, colors, salutes, titles, and legendary histories, often provide the only meaningful reference group for their members.

Many gang members in prison were leaders in the organization outside. They may still be looked to for guidance, and in many cases, they "call the

shots" as far as gang businesses are concerned. For example, Larry Hoover of the Gangster Disciples reportedly ran his gang for years behind bars in the Illinois prison system (Curry & Decker, 1998, p. 134). It is for this reason that most penal facilities try to determine gang affiliation as people begin their sentence. Being a known gang member, or what is referred to by administrators as a "security control threat," usually draws with it restricted work, recreation, and housing. Most facilities also try to separate members of rival groups.

STRUCTURE AND ORGANIZATION

Most of the criminal organizations within any given urban area have their direct counterparts within the state prison system. In Stateville, Illinois, for example, the inmate system is organized in ways almost identical with the gangs on the streets of Chicago. Likewise, in a nationwide survey, Camp and Camp (1985) found that of 33 state prison officials who indicated they had gangs, a total of 21 said that these gangs had their counterparts in the cities of these states.

Prison gangs, not unlike many on the streets, adhere to a code of secrecy and emphasize power and prestige, both of which are measured in terms of the ability to control other inmates and specific activities within the institution. Money and drugs in particular represent tangible symbols of a gang's ability to control and dominate others, and of its ability to provide essential protection, goods, and services for its members. The gang's capacity to bring status and prestige for the members reinforces group commitment and solidarity.

One of the distinguishing characteristics of the prison gang, unlike most groups on the streets, is the virtual absence of any noncriminal, nondeviant activities. Members in prison usually become completely immersed in being a career prison gangster, leaving little time and less inclination for other than asocial behavior.

Prison gangs have several additional characteristics. They often have a well-defined hierarchical structure. They recruit based on "homeboy" preprison experiences. For many, the prison system is only one of several institutions, along with welfare and the police, that their members may have experienced. Thus, there may be a sort of "anticipatory socialization" to prison. Indeed, ethnographer J. W. Moore (1978) notes that the prison system "is an omnipresent reality in barrio life, and contact with it is continuous and drastic, affecting nearly everybody in the barrio. . . . Prison adaptations are seen by convicts themselves as variants of adaptations to street life" (pp. 40, 98).

THE IMPORTANCE OF RACE

Since most urban gangs are made up of racial minorities, it should not be surprising that race is important among the gangs in prison. Such divisions often lead to inmate-on-inmate violence. Thus, in a 1999 survey of prison administrators, 87% said that gang disturbances were related to racial conflicts.

Virtually every study has found that the several different gangs that exist within the prison system are each made up of specific racial or ethnic groups. For example, one recent study found that in Florida there were six major gangs.

1. The Neta, which consists of Puerto Rican and Hispanic prisoners, was originally established in 1970 in the Rio Pedras Prison, Puerto Rico.

2. The Aryan Brotherhood (AB), for whites only, originated in San Quentin Prison (California) in 1967. Most of the members are white supremacists, with some displaying neo-Nazi characteristics and ideology.

3. The Black Guerrilla Family (BGF) was founded in San Quentin by George Jackson (former Black Panther Party member and author of *Soledad Brothers*) in 1966.

4. The Mexican Mafia consists of Mexican Americans and was formed in the late 1950s at a youth correctional center called Duel Vocational Center. They originally were an extension of a Los Angeles street gang.

5. La Nuestra Familia, a mostly Mexican American gang, originated in Soledad Prison in California in the mid-1960s.

6. The Texas Syndicate (TS), a Mexican American prison gang, was founded in Folsom Prison (California) in the early 1970s in direct response to other gangs, especially the Aryan Brotherhood and Mexican Mafia, who would prey on Texas prisoner (they have developed associations with two other smaller gangs, known as the Texas Mafia and the Dirty White Boys).

Many of the gang conflicts stem from these kinds of racial divisions.

In addition to racial conflict and intolerance, some of the conflicts between prison gangs arise from the many kinds of criminal activities in which they are involved. Most commonly, prison gangs offer the primary source of drugs in prison. They may also control sex, food, clothing, loan sharking, gambling, extortion, and protection.

THE RESPONSE TO PRISON GANGS

Gangs are the one of the most notorious aspects of life behind prison walls, at least within men's prisons. The unaffiliated convict enters the prison fearing that his or her life may be in danger from gangs. Even if he is not immediately concerned with survival, he will face the prospect of being "shaken down" for commissary items and/or sex. The guards can be of little help in protecting him, since in many institutions administrators tend to "look the other way" as rival gangs tend to maintain a certain level of social control and order. In one way or another, the convict must find a strategy for dealing with the gang situation.

Nonetheless, it is important to acknowledge that the gang problem varies from one type of institution to another. The 1999 prison gang survey found that as security levels increase, the gang problem also increases. Prison administrators report a greater number of gang disturbances in maximum-security prisons. Specifically, while about 10% of minimum-security prisons reported a gang disturbance in 1999, over half (59%) of the medium-security prisons had such disturbances, while almost two-thirds (64.7%) of the maximum-security prisons had gang disturbances (Knox, 1999).

Prison administrators have used a number of different techniques to control the gang problem within the prison system. According to the 1999 survey, among the most common recommendations include improving race relations, passing tougher legislation (no specifics given), eliminating weight lifting, monitoring telephones, monitoring mail, providing tuition support for staff to attend more training conferences, and using a full-time ombudsman for prisoners. As for the most common responses to the gang problem, these administrators used the following most often: transfers (used by 80%), the use of informers (54%), segregation (60%), isolating leaders (46%), and monitoring mail and telephone calls (61% and 51%, respectively). It appears that the prison gang problem has become worse over the years. The 1999 survey revealed that the vast majority of prison administrators believe the problem has worsened over the years. Specifically, while in 1992, of prison administrators surveyed, 27% believed the problem has increased, in 1999 almost two-thirds (63%) believed this. Most expected the problem of gang violence to increase in the next five years (Knox, 1999).

CONCLUSION

As inner-city social conditions worsen due to loss of jobs, low wages, poor schools, crumbling city infrastructures, and broken families, the attractiveness of gangs will continue to grow. The "get tough" policies toward gangs that began in the 1980s has had at least one negative result: Many of the gang members sent to prison have recently been released and placed right back into the very conditions that led to their gang affiliation in the first place. In Los Angeles, for example, a rise in gang-related homicides in South Central Los Angeles (255 in 2001, up from 161 in 1998) has been at least partly attributed to the release of these gang members, plus continued deterioration of their neighborhoods. As long as sentencing policies follow traditional conservative thinking, prison officials will continue to be confronted by gangs, as will the communities where these gang members grew up.

—*Randall G. Shelden*

See also Aryan Brotherhood; Aryan Nations; Bloods; Crips; Deprivation; Importation; Prison Culture; Racial Conflict Among Prisoners; Racism; Resistance; Security and Control; Young Lords

Further Reading

Camp, G., & Camp, C. (1985). *Prison gangs: Their extent, nature, and impact on prisons.* Washington, DC: U.S. Department of Justice.

Curry, G. D., & Decker, S. H. (1998). *Confronting gangs: Crime and community.* Los Angeles: Roxbury.

Danitz, T. (1998). *The gangs behind bars.* News World Communications, Inc. Retrieved from www.findarticles.com

Florida Department of Corrections. (n.d.). *Major prison gangs.* Retrieved from www.dc.state.fl.us/pub/gangs/prison

Hagedorn, J. (1990). Back in the field again: Gang research in the nineties. In C. R. Huff (Ed.), *Gangs in America.* Newbury Park, CA: Sage.

Hagedorn, J. (1998). *People and folks* (2nd ed.). Chicago: Lakeview.

Jankowski, M. S. (1990). *Islands in the street: Gangs and American urban society.* Berkeley: University of California Press.

Klein, M. (1995). *The American street gang.* New York: Oxford University Press.

Knox, G. W. (1999). *National assessment of gangs and security threat groups (STGs) in adult correctional institutions: Results of the 1999 Adult Corrections Surveys.* Chicago: National Gang Crime Research Center.

Moore, J. W. (1978) *Homeboys: Gangs, drugs, and prisons in the barrio of Los Angeles.* Philadelphia: Temple University Press.

Shelden, R. G., Tracy, S. T., & Brown, W. B. (2001). *Youth gangs in American society* (2nd ed.). Belmont, CA: Wadsworth.

◪ GARLAND, DAVID (1955–)

David Garland is one of the foremost scholars of punishment in the United States. His oeuvre can be divided into two broad projects. First, he has successfully carved out a domain of study that can broadly be termed the sociology of punishment. Second, he has explored the history of criminology. Both fields of study have been enormously influential.

In his work on criminology, Garland (2002) set out "to trace its historical conditions of emergence, identify the intellectual resources and traditions upon which it drew, and give some account of the process of its formation and development" (p. 14). His work has an obviously historical bent, yet he does not search for inherent causes or unique events. Rather, Garland's approach is historical only so far as he recognizes the contingency of modern phenomena and problematizes their taken-for-granted existence. The point, he says, "is not to think historically about the past but rather to use that history to rethink the present" (Garland, 2001, p. 2) Thus, instead of starting from a preconception that criminology's development would inevitably mirror the course set out by the natural sciences, Garland traces the conditions that made its emergence and expansion possible without attributing cause and effect to these events.

SOCIOLOGY OF PUNISHMENT

Despite Garland's absorbing and significant contributions to the history of criminology, he is best known for his pioneering efforts on the sociology of punishment. In 1999, he became the founding editor of the journal *Punishment and Society,* which brings together interdisciplinary scholarship on this subject. His own work in this area has influenced a generation of scholars and has expanded the scope of understanding, inquiry, and theoretical interpretation of punishment. According to Garland (1990), the sociology of punishment, "broadly conceived, [is] that body of thought which explores the relations between punishment and society, its purpose being to understand punishment as a social phenomenon and thus trace its role in social life" (p. 14).

Garland (1991) encourages scholars to see punishment as a complex institution and evaluate it by "recognizing the range of its penal and social functions and the nature of its social support" (p. 160). His understanding of an expanded sociology of punishment is most clearly revealed in his 1990 book, *Punishment and Modern Society,* which has become a core text for graduate and senior-level undergraduate students. In this work, Garland offers a broad sociological description of punishment in contemporary society using the interpretive tools of Karl Marx, Émile Durkheim, Michel Foucault, and Norbert Elias along with several other social theorists. The result is an intricate investigation of punishment in late modern society that attends to the complexity of its development through what Garland calls a multidimensional interpretive approach. This book attempted to "extend and synthesize the range of interpretive material that currently forms the sociology of punishment, and to build up a more complete picture of how punishment might be understood in modern society" (Garland, 1990, p. 16).

Garland does not view "punishment" as a singular entity. Rather, he conceives of it as composed of a complex set of institutions, discourses, societal forces, and interrelated processes. Moreover, he suggests that punishment does not have a single purpose or serve a particular end. It is precisely because of its "stored up" historical meaning and diverse rationales that a multidimensional approach to understanding punishment's meaning, function, and rationale is paramount. To comprehend penality's nature and character at any given time requires one to "explore its many dynamics and forces and build up a complex picture of the circuits of meaning and action within which it . . . functions" (Garland, 1990, p. 17). Underlying this multifarious approach lies a commitment to discerning "punishment" in a way that exposes its complexity.

In his latest book, *The Culture of Control,* Garland extends his examination of penality to the burgeoning neoliberal crime control complex. He once again employs a multidimensional history of the present that examines the complexity of modern forms of punishment. In this work, Garland (2001) attempts to understand how the contemporary responses to crime and deviance took their present form, "with all their novel and contradictory aspects" (p. 2). Furthermore, his task was to "unravel the tangle of transformative forces that has, for decades now, been reconstituting those responses in surprising and unexpected ways and to understand the practices and policies that has emerged out of these developments" (p. 2). What distinguishes the contemporary forms of penality from those that existed for most of the 20th century? Included among the "contradictory" and "novel" policies and practices that concern Garland in this work are the declining importance of rehabilitation as a sentencing option, a return to punitive sanctions, shifts in the emotional tone of crime policy, the return of the victim, an overriding concern to protect the public, crime as an issue in elections, transformations in criminological thought, privatization, and a perpetual sense of crisis leading to rapid legislative, organizational, and policy reform.

Perhaps the most surprising feature of contemporary penality, Garland points out, is the return and reinvention of the prison. Although prisons now seem firmly entrenched in the criminal justice landscape, this situation is of recent origin. Post–World War II penologists and commissions of inquiry saw prisons as counterintuitive institutions that were ultimately criminogenic. During the 1960s and early 1970s, considerable resources were "expended on the task of creating alternatives to incarceration and encouraging sentencers to use them" (Garland, 2001, p. 14). Unfortunately, the emergence of punitive politics, neoconservative rhetoric, and mass media preoccupation with crime largely reversed this trend such that Western nations are now locking up offenders at a record rate.

Clearly, the contemporary crime control landscape is an amalgam of policy and practice that has defied the most astute expert prediction. In *The Culture of Control,* Garland stops short of forecasting future developments, but instead offers a manner of coming to terms with the ever-changing criminal justice landscape. To understand the emergence and entrenchment of contemporary practice, Garland (2001) suggests that we look beyond rising crime rates and systemwide loss of faith in the welfare sanction, although these forces did play a limited role. Instead, he argues:

> It was created by a series of adaptive responses to the cultural and criminological conditions of late modernity—conditions which included new problems of crime and insecurity, and new attitudes towards the welfare. But these responses did not occur outside of the political process or in a political and cultural vacuum. On the contrary. They were deeply marked by the cultural formation . . . ; by the reactionary politics that have dominated Britain and America during the last twenty years; and by the new social relations that have grown up around the changing structures of work, welfare and market exchange in these two late modern societies. (p. 193)

It is this type of intricate genealogical analysis that sets Garland's analysis of current crime control policy apart.

CRITICISM

Despite the many important contributions he has made to the study of punishment and criminology, Garland is not without his critics. In the face of gross overrepresentations of the politically powerless and minorities of all kinds in carceral institutions in countries such as the United States, Canada, Australia, and New Zealand, Garland seems relatively unconcerned with this element of late-modern penality. Given his concern to push the limits in studies of punishment, this neglect is troubling. Garland's concern to untangle the forces that underlie contemporary crime control policy leads him to focus on practices and structures of penality at the expense of those subjected to them.

Although we cannot expect Garland to investigate and include every possible force and element into his analysis of punishment, nevertheless the systemic targeting of the powerless by state-sponsored forms of social control constitutes a fundamental part of the contemporary penal scene. The underlying rationale for this condition is connected to the systemic marginalization and subordination experienced by the politically, socially, racially, and economically excluded. It is also tied to the systematic targeting of the working classes and ethnic minorities by the policing arm of the state. Inherent biases built into state criminalization and management practices have continually reproduced— despite claims to the contrary—systemic inequality and resulted in these groups being overrepresented at all levels of the justice system (Hogeveen, in press). For example, in Canada Aboriginal youths make up roughly 5% of the adolescent population, yet conservative estimates suggest they constitute 75% of the young offender prison population. Unfortunately, drawing on Garland's work does not allow us to adequately address the fundamental conditions that create and sustain this relationship.

Feminist and gender scholars are also concerned that Garland does not consider punishment a gendered and gendering institution. In recent years, feminists in particular have demonstrated that gender profoundly conditions parental and institutional responses to female criminality. Scholars such as Adrian Howe (1994), Pat Carlen (1990), and Barbara Hudson (1996) have addressed Garland's oversight by calling for a woman-centered penality, which not only "takes into account the maleness of supposedly gender neutral concepts, and requires attention to the lives of female offenders, but is also cognizant of the gendered power relationships in the societies which women and men are committing crimes and enduring penalties" (Hudson, 1996, p. 148). This women-centered scholarship has unravelled how penological reform so regularly reproduces the gender, class, and race inequalities governments set out to rectify.

CONCLUSION

Garland's analysis of historical patterns, emerging social relations, economic conditions, and political culture continuously produces fresh insight into contemporary penality. Though his scholarship ignores how crime control practices contribute to systemic discrimination particularly in terms of race and gender, David Garland has made incalculable contributions to the study of punishment.

—Bryan R. Hogeveen

See also Australia; Jeremy Bentham; Canada; Meda Chesney-Lind; Convict Criminology; Determinate Sentencing; John J. DiIulio, Jr.; England and Wales; Michel Foucault; Increase in Prison Population; Indeterminate Sentencing; Just Deserts Theory; New Zealand; Panopticon; Prison Industrial Complex; Race, Gender, and Class of Prisoners; Racism; Nicole Hahn Rafter; Resistance; Sentencing Reform Act 1984; Truth in Sentencing; War on Drugs; Women's Prisons; Women Prisoners

Further Reading

Beckett, K. (1997). *Making crime pay: Law and order in contemporary American politics.* New York: Oxford University Press.

Carlen, P. (1990). *Alternatives to women's imprisonment.* Buckingham, UK: Open University Press.

Foucault, M. (1977). *Discipline and punish.* New York: Vintage.

Garland, D. (1990). *Punishment and modern society: A study in social theory.* Chicago: University of Chicago Press.

Garland, D. (1991). Sociological perspectives on punishment. *Crime and Justice. 14*(1), 115–164.

Garland, D. (2001). *The culture of control: Crime and social order in contemporary society.* Chicago: University of Chicago Press.

Garland, D. (2002). Of crimes and criminals: The development of criminology in Britain. In M. Maguire, R. Morgan, & R. Reiner (Eds.), *The Oxford handbook of criminology* (pp. 7–50). London: Oxford University Press.

Goldson, B. (2002). New punitiveness: The politics of child incarceration. In J. Muncie, G. Hughes, & E. McLaughlin (Eds.), *Youth justice: Critical readings* (pp. 386–401). London: Sage.

Hogeveen, B. (In press). "The evils with which we are called to grapple": Élite reformers, eugenicists, environmental psychologists, and the construction of Toronto's working-class boy problem, 1860–1930. *Labour/Le Travail.*

Howe, A. (1994). *Punish and critique: Towards a feminist analysis of penality.* London: Routledge.

Hudson, B. (1996). *Understanding justice: An introduction to ideas, perspectives and controversies in modern penal theory.* Buckingham, UK: Open University Press.

Newburn, T. (2002). Atlantic crossings: "Policy transfer" and crime control in the USA and Britain. *Punishment and Society, 4*(2), 165–194.

O'Malley, P. (1999). Volatile and contradictory punishment. *Theoretical Criminology, 3*(2), 175–196.

Simon, J. (2001). "Entitlement to Cruelty": Neo-liberalism and the punitive mentality in the United States. In K. Stenson & R. Sullivan (Eds.), *Crime risk and justice: The politics of crime control in liberal democracies* (pp. 125–143). Portland, OR: Willan.

◪ GAULT, GERALD (GERRY) (1949–)

Gerald Gault was arrested when he was 15 years old on charges of making obscene phone calls to a neighbor. His trial and subsequent appeal led to fundamental changes in the juvenile justice system. Specifically, it ushered in due process rights for juveniles involved in delinquency proceedings.

As a direct result of this case, young people are now entitled to legal counsel, to confront and cross-examine witnesses, to confront their accuser, to refuse to incriminate themselves, and to be given timely notice of charges. While many of these due process rights are closely akin to those afforded to adults, they are not identical.

FACTS OF THE CASE

On June 8, 1964, Gerry Gault and a friend were arrested by the sheriff for making obscene phone calls. At the time of his arrest, Gault was already on probation for involvement in the theft of a wallet. As was common practice at the time, the sheriff took him to the Children's Detention Home without informing his parents. When his mother finally discovered where Gault had been taken and arrived at the home, the probation officer informed her that a hearing would occur the following day in the judge's chamber.

At the hearing, Gault and his parents were not served with a copy of the formal petition that had been filed by the probation officer. In addition, the victim was not present at the hearing, nor was she interviewed by anyone other than the probation officer. No one at the hearing was sworn in and no official records or transcripts of the proceedings were made. The hearing concluded with the judge deciding to "think about" the case. Gault was sent back to the Children's Detention Home. Within a few days, Gault was released from the home to his mother, and another hearing was scheduled to occur in a week. At the second hearing, the judge committed Gault to the State Industrial School for a period of six years, until his 21st birthday, even though there was some dispute as to whether he had merely dialed the number or actually made the obscene comments.

Because there was no right to appeal for juveniles in Arizona, Gault's attorney filed a writ of *habeas corpus* with the Superior Court of the State of Arizona on his behalf. The writ was subsequently denied. Although the Arizona Supreme Court upheld that juveniles were entitled to due process rights during delinquency proceedings,

they failed to require that Gault should be released from his commitment because the procedures used during his delinquency proceedings were, in their opinion, consistent with due process. Their denial of the writ forced Gault's attorney to seek relief from the U.S. Supreme Court. On May 15, 1967, the U.S. Supreme Court disagreed with the Arizona Supreme Court's findings, reversed the case, and ordered that Gerald Gault be released from the State Industrial School. At the time of the U.S. Supreme Court's decision, Gault was already 18 years old. He had spent the last three years in the State Industrial School on a charge that would have resulted in a $50 fine and a maximum of 30 days in jail if committed by an adult.

SIGNIFICANCE OF THE CASE

In re Gault (1967) set forth specific requirements for due process rights afforded juveniles in delinquency proceedings. The specific rights recognized by the U.S. Supreme Court included timely notice of the charges, right to counsel, protection against self-incrimination, and right to confront and cross-examine witnesses.

The first right to which juveniles are now entitled is written notice of the charges against them. Such notice must be adequate and timely and contain information regarding the alleged misconduct. Furthermore, the Court specified that notice must be given to the juvenile as well as to his or her parents or care givers. The second due process right granted to juveniles in this case is the right to counsel. Such counsel shall be provided in all delinquency proceedings, regardless of financial ability. Juveniles as well as their parents must also be informed of their right to counsel, as well as the implications for the waiver of counsel.

The third due process right is the fundamental right against self-incrimination. Juveniles must knowingly give away their Fifth Amendment rights. If their rights are not knowingly given away, then their statements may not be used against them. The Court further said that "admissions and confessions by juveniles require special caution" when evaluating voluntariness. The fourth right that the Court granted juveniles was the right to confront and cross-examine witnesses. A juvenile is entitled to all of the above-described procedural rights during the adjudicatory phase.

CONCLUSION

Although *In re Gault* led to the recognition of a substantial number of due process rights for juveniles, the Court failed to provide all of the rights enjoyed by adults facing criminal sanctions. Specifically, the Court chose not to address the juvenile code of Arizona, which did not provide for appellate review in delinquency matters. Even today, the right of a juvenile to appeal is dependent upon the state statutes. The Court also refused to address the issue of a juvenile's right to a transcript of the adjudication hearing. Juvenile court judges still enjoy an enormous amount of discretionary power.

—*Lisa Hutchinson Wallace*

See also Child Savers; Elmira Reformatory; Determinate Sentencing; Fifth Amendment; Fourth Amendment; *Habeas Corpus*; Indeterminate Sentencing; Juvenile Detention Centers; Juvenile Justice and Delinquency Prevention Act 1974; Juvenile Justice System; Juvenile Offenders: Race, Class, and Gender; Juvenile Reformatories; *Parens Patriae*; Anthony Platt; Rehabilitation Theory; Status Offenders; Waiver of Juveniles Into the Adult Court System

Further Reading

Feld, B. C. (1988). *In re Gault* revisited: A cross-state comparison of the right to counsel in juvenile court. *Crime & Delinquency, 34*(4), 393–424.

In re Gault, 387 U. S. 1, 87 S. Ct. 1248 (1967).

Levidow, B. (1972). Overdue process for juveniles: For the retroactive restoration of constitutional rights. *Howard Law Journal, 17*(2), 402–433.

McMillian, T. (1999). Early modern juvenile justice in St. Louis. *Federal Probation, 63*(2), 4–7.

Regoli, R. H., & Hewitt, J. D. (2003). *Delinquency in society.* Boston: McGraw-Hill.

Siegel, L. J., Welsh, B. C., & Senna, J. J. (2003). *Juvenile delinquency: Theory, practice, and law* (8th ed.). St. Paul, MN: West.

◪ GENERAL EDUCATIONAL DEVELOPMENT (GED) EXAM AND GENERAL EQUIVALENCY DIPLOMA

The General Educational Development (GED) exam assesses skills and general knowledge that are acquired through a four-year high school education. The exam changes periodically, most recently in January 2002, in an effort to keep up with knowledge and skills needed in our society. The exam covers math, science, social studies, reading, and writing. All of the test items are multiple choice except for a section in the writing exam that requires GED candidates to write an essay. The complete exam takes just under eight hours to complete and is typically broken down into several sections that can be taken over time.

In addition to the GED exam, the acronym "GED" is also used to signify the diploma (general equivalency diploma). Research that assesses the value of the GED examines employment and the likelihood of continuing with formal education after earning the GED. Scholars have also examined whether the GED is equivalent to a high school diploma. Past research indicates that employees with a GED are not the labor market equivalents of regular high school graduates. Those who leave school with very low skills benefit from obtaining a GED. However, this advantage is lessened for those who have obtained other employment-related skills. The message gained from much of the research is that it is best to remain in school. While the GED has value, it should not be seen as a replacement for four years of high school.

THE GED AND CORRECTIONS

Though there has been little research examining the impact of obtaining a GED in corrections settings, the majority of those studies that do exist suggest that earning a GED while in prison reduces the likelihood of returning to prison. However, some researchers have criticized the methodology used in studies that focus on recidivism since it may be argued that those who choose, or are chosen, for corrections education programs benefit most from the experience since they have already indicated a willingness to "stay out of trouble." Arguably, these are the people who will benefit most from any efforts to increase their chances of success. It may be difficult to blame corrections education programs that focus on those most likely to benefit from the program.

Another problem regarding an effort to demonstrate the value of a prison GED, in comparison to a high school diploma or GED earned in a traditional setting, is related to the complexity of factors that surround an individual in the labor market. It is possible that the impact of earning a GED in prison is not great enough to overcome the negative effect incarceration can have on employment opportunities. Employers may be reluctant to hire someone who has served time in prison. In fact, a felony conviction can disqualify an individual for employment in some professions. Given the barriers placed before individuals who seek employment after prison, it may be difficult to demonstrate the impact of a single educational experience.

Although the employment-related impacts of the GED earned in corrections settings are difficult to assess, research has consistently demonstrated that corrections education can significantly reduce recidivism. A 1987 Bureau of Prisons report found that the more education an inmate received, the lower the rate of recidivism. Inmates who earned college degrees were the least likely to reenter prison. For inmates who had some high school, the rate of recidivism was 54.6%. For college graduates the rate dropped to 5.4%. Similarly, a Texas Department of Criminal Justice study found that while the state's overall rate of recidivism was 60%, for holders of college associate degrees it was 13.7%. The recidivism rate for those with bachelor's degrees was 5.6%. The rate for those with master's degrees was 0%. The Changing Minds study (Fine et al., 2001), which focused on the benefits of college courses in a women's prison, calculated that reductions in reincarceration would save approximately $900,000 per 100 student prisoners over a two-year period. If we project these

savings to the 600,000 prison releases in a single year, the savings are enormous.

In addition to gains related to recidivism, prison-based education programs provide benefits related to the functioning of prisons. These programs provide incentives to inmates in a setting in which rewards are relatively limited. These classes also provide socialization opportunities with similarly motivated students and educators who serve as positive role models. Educational endeavors also keep students busy and provide intellectual stimulation in an environment that can be difficult to manage when prisoners break rules in search of an activity that breaks the monotony of prison life. Many prisons provide incentives for inmates who participate in corrections education. Opportunities to earn privileges within the facility, increased visitation, and the accumulation or loss of "good time" credit that can lead to earlier parole are used to motivate the student while providing incentives for appropriate behavior within the facility.

Prison educators face many challenges. Inmates who choose to enroll in corrections-based courses are not necessarily any different from students who enroll in GED courses in other settings. The range of abilities can include very gifted students, students who face challenges, and students who have various motives for enrolling in the course. However, the educational setting is very different. Challenges faced by corrections educators are compounded by the uniqueness of prison culture and the need for security. Prisons adhere to strict routines that may not be ideal in an educational setting. In addition, inmates are often moved from one facility to another. This movement interrupts, or ends, the individual's educational programming. These structural issues are accompanied by social factors that can further limit learning opportunities. The student may be very motivated to earn an education but is in an environment in which conflicting demands may limit the opportunity to act on that motivation. For example, other prisoners may not support the individual's educational efforts.

Prison administrators may also have varying degrees of support for education—especially if they see it as a threat to the primary functions of security and control. GED courses may be seen as a burden to prison administrators who believe their primary goal is confinement. However, in many cases administrators are required to provide educational opportunities. At least 26 states have mandatory corrections education laws that mandate education for a certain amount of time or until a set level of achievement is reached. Enrollment in correctional education is also required in many states if the inmate is under a certain age, as specified by that state's compulsory education law. The Federal Bureau of Prisons has also implemented a policy that requires inmates who do not have a high school diploma or a GED to participate in literacy programs for a minimum of 240 hours, or until they obtain their GED.

States typically provide corrections education funding based, in part, on success as measured by the rate of GED completion. In addition to state funding, the federal government provides support to state corrections education through the Adult Education and Family Literacy Act (AEFLA), which became law in 1998. However, funding often fails to keep pace with needs. Legislation over the past 20 years, a time in which the prison population has grown at unprecedented levels, has resulted in significant cuts in corrections education funding. This has resulted in the elimination of many programs. Ironically, the "get tough on crime" mentality resulted in the elimination of many programs that were effective in reducing crime.

CONCLUSION

Studies consistently indicate that an individual who benefits from education while in prison is less likely to return to prison than someone who has not had the benefits of education while in prison. There is some question as to why corrections-based education leads to lower recidivism. This is a complex process, and difficult to measure, but it appears that the ability to find and hold a job consistently functions to reduce the chance that an individual will commit crime. Individuals who increase their education also increase their opportunities. Individuals who take classes while in prison

improve their chances of attaining and keeping employment after release. As a result, they are less likely to commit additional crimes that would lead to their return to prison.

The benefits of earning a GED while in prison are difficult to demonstrate. Individuals may find it difficult to obtain employment after serving time in prison. Potential employers may benefit from education regarding the realities of employing someone who has completed his or her punishment and is attempting to return to a productive life outside prison walls. It may also be time to question the belief that tougher prisons, with limited efforts to educate or otherwise rehabilitate offenders, reduce crime. The get-tough-on-crime mentality has resulted in the elimination of many corrections education programs. Individuals in prison are typically burdened with many educational deficiencies. In many cases, the lack of skills limited options, resulting in criminal acts. Upon release from prison, with limited education and job experience that is well below the level gained by those outside prison, it is no surprise that many individuals will head back down the path that originally led them to prison.

—*Kenneth Mentor*

See also Adult Basic Education; College Courses in Prison; Creative Writing Programs; Education; Literacy; Pell Grants; Recidivism; Rehabilitation Theory; Security and Control; Violent Crime Control and Law Enforcement Act 1994; Vocational Training Programs

Further Reading

Batiuk, M., Moke, P., & Rountree, P. (1997). Crime and rehabilitation: Correctional education as an agent of change—A research note. *Justice Quarterly, 14*(1).

Bureau of Justice Statistics. (2002). *Key crime and justice facts at a glance.* Retrieved from http://www.ojp.usdoj.gov/bjs/glance.htm

Fine, M., Torre, M. E., Boudin, K., Bowen, I., Clark, J., Hylton, D., Martinez, M., Roberts, R. A., Smart, P., & Upegui, D. (2001). *Changing minds: The impact of college in a maximum security prison.* New York: Graduate Center of the City University of New York. Retrieved from http://www.changingminds.ws/

Gerber, J., & Fritsch, E. (1993). *Prison education and offender behavior: A review of the scientific literature.* Huntsville:

Texas Department of Criminal Justice, Institutional Division.

Greenwood, P. W., Model, K. E., Rydell, C. P., & Chiesa, J. (1996). *Diverting children from a life of crime: Measuring costs and benefits.* Santa Monica, CA: RAND.

Haigler, K. O., Harlow, C., O'Connor, P., & Campbell, A. (1994). *Literacy behind prison walls.* Washington, DC: National Center for Education Statistics.

Harer, M. (1995). *Prison education program participation and recidivism: A test of the normalization hypothesis.* Washington, DC: Federal Bureau of Prisons.

LoBuglio, S. (2001). Time to reframe politics and practices in correctional education. In J. Comings, B. Garner, & C. Smith (Eds.), *Annual review of adult learning and literacy* (Vol. 2). San Francisco: Jossey-Bass.

Murnane, R. J., Willett, J. B., & Boudett, K. P. (1999). Do male dropouts benefit from obtaining a GED, postsecondary education, and training? *Evaluation Review, 23,* 475–504.

Steurer, S., Smith, L., & Tracy, A. (2001). *Three State Recidivism Study.* Prepared for the Office of Correctional Education, U.S. Department of Education. Lanham, MD: Correctional Education Association.

Tolbert, M. (2002). *State correctional education programs.* Washington, DC: National Institute for Literacy. Retrieved from http://www.nifl.gov/nifl/policy/st_correc tion_02.pdf

U.S. Department of Education, Office of Correctional Education. (1994). *The impact of correctional education on recidivism 1988–1994.* Washington, DC: U.S. Department of Education.

◪ GIALLOMBARDO, ROSE
(1925–1993)

Rose Giallombardo is best known for her research on the inmate culture of a women's prison. Her 1966 book, *Society of Women: A Study of a Women's Prison,* helped raise questions about the degree to which studies based on field work in men's institutions were applicable to women. Giallombardo argued that women respond to the pains of imprisonment by re-creating traditional family roles among the inmate population. These informal systems sustain women's emotional need for social relationships and are shaped by their perception of female role expectations. Giallombardo's study ensured that gender issues could not be overlooked in prison research. Her findings continue to be cited in subsequent works that examine similarities and differences between male and female prisons and prisoners.

BIOGRAPHICAL DETAILS

Giallombardo completed her doctoral work at Northwestern University in 1965. Her dissertation, based on one year's ethnographic study at the Federal Reformatory for Women at Alderson, was published in 1966 as *Society of Women: A Study of a Women's Prison.* The study has become one of the standard sources for descriptions of women inmate's culture. Her later work, *The Social World of Imprisoned Girls: A Comparative Study of Institutions for Juvenile Delinquents,* published in 1974, summarized her earlier research findings and examined the presence of similar cultural elements within differing juvenile institutional settings. In 1966, Giallombardo edited a widely used reader, *Juvenile Delinquency: A Book of Readings,* revised through 1982, as well as editing *Contemporary Social Issues* in 1975. She held faculty appointments at New York University from 1964 to 1966, and at the University of Chicago from 1967 to 1972. During this period, she was a senior study director at the National Opinion Research Center and a research associate at the Center for Social Organization Studies.

RESEARCH BACKGROUND

Giallombardo placed her research in the context of earlier publications on inmate culture, beginning with Donald Clemmer's 1940 classic ethnographic study, *The Prison Community,* and Gresham M. Sykes's *Society of Captives: A Study of a Maximum Security Prison,* published in 1958. These authors argued that inmate culture develops in an effort to lessen the pains of imprisonment within systems of near total control. The deprivations of prison are viewed as the source of a culture resistant to staff and supportive of an "inmate code" that values loyalty, within a violent environment marked by struggles for power and goods. The tension between inmate solidarity and exploitive alienation gives rise to argot roles—"rats," "merchants and gorillas," "wolves, punks, and fags" and "real men," for example; as well as inmate norms—"do your own time," "don't trust anybody" and "don't snitch"—that reflect this reality. Giallombardo sought to investigate whether similar norms and roles existed in women's prisons.

Society of Women

Giallombardo argued that women's responses to prison reflected their sexual roles and institutional expectations in the larger society. Her work was influenced by a dominant cultural perception that men's status was decided by their occupational positions in the market place, while women's prestige and status derived from their roles as wives and mothers within the home. This view led Giallombardo (1974) to conclude that homosexual "marriage" relationships and the extensive "family groups" and other kinship ties she found at Alderson integrated the women into a social system that represented "an attempt to create a substitute universe within the prison" (p. 2). She asserted that the homosexual relationship, pivotal in the women's lives, was relatively unstable and competitive, while overlapping kinship structures provided stable networks of mutual support for the women.

The presence of both "marriage" and "family" relationships within the prison becomes a critical source for prestige and status for women beyond their ascribed status of inmate, while the absence of these relationships among male prisoners Giallombardo attributes to the inability within ascribed male roles for men to develop the affectionate "legitimate feminine roles" played out in informal supportive kinship networks. (Giallombardo, 1966, p. 186). Giallombardo concluded from her evidence that "the adult male and female inmate cultures *are* a response to the deprivations of prison life, but the *nature* of that response in both prison communities is influenced by the differential participation of males and females in the external culture" (Giallombardo, 1974, p. 3).

One year before Giallombardo's book was published, criminologists David Ward and Gene Kassebaum released a study based on their research at the women's prison in Frontera, California. At first glance, *Women's Prison: Sex and Social Structure* seems somewhat similar to *Society of Women*. However, Ward and Kassebaum provide only a limited analysis of how women cope with imprisonment, focusing almost exclusively on homosexual relationships, which they believe are a result of women's constant search for emotional support. Though they note in passing other responses to incarceration, they conclude that a women's prison is "a society dominated by homosexual ideology and behavior" (Ward & Kassebaum, 1965, p. 93).

Following both Ward and Kassebaum's and Giallombardo's publication of their research, Esther Heffernan's District of Columbia research, *Making It in Prison: The Square, the Cool and the Life,* published in 1972, found more complex and multiple subsystems of adaptation among the women. They included play-family structures, homosexual relationships, and economic and power networks. Heffernan also identified a range of argot roles and patterns of cooperation and resistance that reflected differing reactions to imprisonment based on the woman's previous identification with the norms and goals of conventional life, those of the "criminal underworld," or those for whom prison was "a way of life." These diverse and interrelated systems of adaptation were similar to those identified by John Irwin and Donald Cressey, in their 1962 article, "Thieves, Convicts and the Inmate Culture." Heffernan (1972) concluded that "members of the systems of the square, the cool and the life participate in an inmate system, but their orientation and relationships differ" (p. 164).

CONCLUSION: THE LASTING IMPACT OF GIALLOMBARDO'S RESEARCH

Rose Giallombardo's seminal research in *Society of Women: A Study of a Women's Prison* remains a major cited source, both nationally and internationally, in reading lists on inmate culture. Though most would now reject her rigid ideas of sex roles, this work has influenced all subsequent studies in the field of women's prisons. Cited in scholarly debate over the degree to which imported values or internal reactions to the deprivations of imprisonment play a major role in the development of inmate culture, it was also used to analyze the comparative differences between male and female adaptations to imprisonment as well as to discuss the presence or absence, and the purpose and functioning of, "families" in prison.

More recently, and after a relative absence of comparative ethnographic studies of female prisons along with significant changes both in the position of women in society and in the numbers of imprisoned women and the administration of their facilities, new studies have recently appeared that ask new questions about women's imprisonment. Such works include Barbara Owen's 1998 study, *"In the Mix": Struggle and Survival in a Women's Prison,* and Mary Bosworth's 1999 publication of her British research, *Engendering Resistance: Agency and Power in Women's Prisons.* Both works raise questions stimulated by Giallombardo's earlier work, and modify her conclusions. Finally, the continuing influence of Giallombardo's analysis of gender and kinship structures is further apparent in a 2003 article by Craig Forsyth and Rhonda Evans, "Reconsidering the Pseudo-Family/Gang Gender Distinction in Prison Research."

—*Esther Heffernan*

See also Alderson, Federal Prison Camp; Donald Clemmer; Deprivation; Elizabeth Gurley Flynn; History of Women's Prisons; Homosexual Relationships; Importation; Inmate Code; John Irwin; Lesbian Relationships; Sex—Consensual; Gresham Sykes; Women Prisoners; Women's Prisons

Further Reading

Bosworth, M. (1999). *Engendering resistance: Agency and power in women's prisons.* Aldershot, UK: Ashgate.

Clemmer, D. (1958). *The prison community.* New York: Holt, Rinehart & Winston. (Original work published 1940)

Forsyth, C. J., & Evans, R. D. (2003). Reconsidering the pseudo-family/gang gender distinction in prison research. *Journal of Police and Criminal Psychology, 18,* 15–23.

Giallombardo, R. (1966). *Society of women: A study of a women's prison.* New York: John Wiley.

Giallombardo. R. (1974). *The social world of imprisoned girls: A comparative study of institutions for juvenile delinquents.* New York: John Wiley.

Heffernan, E. (1972). *Making it in prison: The square, the cool and the life.* New York: John Wiley.

Irwin, J., & Cressey, D. R. (1962). Thieves, convicts and the inmate culture. *Social Problems, 10,* 142–155.

Owen, B. (1998). *"In the mix": Struggle and survival in a women's prison.* Albany: State University of New York Press.

Sykes, G. M. (1958). *The society of captives: A study of a maximum security prison.* Princeton, NJ: Princeton University Press.

Ward, D. A., & Kassebaum, G. G. (1965). *Women's prison: Sex and social structure.* Chicago: Aldine.

◪ GILMORE, GARY (1940–1977)

Gary Gilmore was the first person in the United States to be executed after the U.S. Supreme Court's moratorium on capital punishment was established by *Furman v. Georgia* (1972) and then lifted in a series of cases highlighted by *Gregg v. Georgia* (1976). Partly as a result of this, and because of the publication of Norman Mailer's (1979) book *The Executioner's Song,* Gilmore attained status as a minor celebrity in the public eye.

THE CRIMES AND EXECUTION OF GARY GILMORE

Gilmore was in and out of correctional institutions for much of his life. He was released from a term of imprisonment in April 1976, and in July 1976 he committed two homicides on two consecutive days. The first victim was a gas station attendant in Orem, Utah, and the second was a hotel clerk in Provo, Utah. He shot both victims in the head after robbing them. Gilmore was subsequently arrested and charged. In October 1976, his case went to trial.

Gilmore's case differed from contemporary death penalty cases in two ways. First, the trial was very brief—the jury selection, guilt phase, and sentencing phase were concluded within three days. Second, Gilmore elected not to pursue appeals. He requested death by firing squad and did not mount legal challenges to his sentence. By modern standards, his execution by firing squad on January 17, 1977—only five months after sentencing—was exceptionally quick. Gilmore's execution made him the first person to be put to death following the lifting of the Supreme Court's moratorium on capital punishment.

A 1984 study by Robert Jolly and Edward Sagarin notes that the first executions following the *Furman* decision, including Gilmore's, were marked by characteristics that made them suitable for capital punishment, thus lending legitimacy to the reestablishment of the death penalty. For instance, Gilmore's murders appeared to be particularly wanton since the victims were shot execution style during the course of a robbery. In addition, Gilmore's guilt was clearly established, and Gilmore himself essentially asked—some observers might say challenged—the state to execute him.

Gilmore was incarcerated in Utah's death row from the time of his sentence until his execution. During his stay in prison, he attempted suicide by drug overdose, but was unsuccessful. He also entered into a hunger strike to protest unsolicited appeals that were made on his behalf. Gilmore made it clear that he wanted his sentence to be carried out, enhancing public interest in his case.

On the night of January 16, 1977, the United States got ready for the first execution in the past 10 years; Utah prepared for its first state execution in 16 years; and Gary Gilmore spent his last night at Utah State Prison. Reports suggest that, the night before his execution, Gilmore received guests, gave a boxing demonstration, made phone calls, consumed alcohol smuggled into the prison, danced, and gave a final interview.

The execution was set for the morning of January 17, 1977. Earlier that morning, a stay of execution was averted, and the U.S. Supreme Court refused to delay his case further. The execution was conducted by firing squad in a makeshift chamber in the Utah State Prison, and the official time of death was noted as 8:07 A.M. Following his death, the unusual nature of the Gilmore case continued, as some of his organs were removed for transplant; currently, executed inmates are generally considered ineligible as organ donors, in part because of the damages caused by the methods of execution. After autopsy, Gilmore was cremated.

GILMORE'S CELEBRITY STATUS

Executions are often surrounded by publicity and media coverage. In the months leading up to and following Gilmore's execution, his case received considerable national publicity. Gilmore himself became a minor celebrity as the public developed a fascination with both his crimes and the man himself. This public interest was largely fueled by the fact that he would be the first post-*Furman* execution, and also because he wanted to be executed.

The public interest in Gilmore's cases was evidenced by the coverage in the mass media. For instance, *Playboy* conducted a fairly lengthy interview with Gilmore that was published shortly after his execution. Two books have since been published regarding Gilmore's life, crimes, trial, and execution. The first to appear, in 1979, was a lengthy treatment by Normal Mailer, titled *The Executioner's Song*. The second was written by Gilmore's brother, Mikal Gilmore. Published in 1994, it was titled *Shot in the Heart*. Both books were subsequently developed into films. In addition, prior to his execution, Gilmore entered into negotiations to sell his story and some of his letters.

CONCLUSION

Few death row inmates have attained the notoriety of Gary Gilmore. By virtue of being the first person executed in the post-*Furman* era, and due to his insistence that the sentence be carried out, Gilmore's case attracted considerable attention. As such, he holds a place in the history of American corrections and capital punishment.

—*Stephen S. Owen*

See also Jack Henry Abbott; Capital Punishment; Celebrities in Prison; Death Row; Deathwatch; *Furman v. Georgia*

Further Reading

Gilmore, M. (1994). *Shot in the heart.* New York: Doubleday.

Jolly, R. W., Jr., & Sagarin, E. (1984). The first eight after *Furman*: Who was executed with the return of the death penalty? *Crime & Delinquency, 30,* 610–623.

Mailer, N. (1979). *The executioner's song.* Boston: Little, Brown.

Schiller, L., & Farrel, B. (1977). Playboy interview: Gary Gilmore. *Playboy, 24*(4), 69–92, 130, 174–186.

◪ GOOD TIME CREDIT

Good time credits, also sometimes referred to as gain time, or time off for good behavior, allow for the early release of inmates from incarceration. Credits are deducted from a person's original sentence to reduce time served, providing the reward of early release from incarceration. The use of good time credits serves three purposes: population control, discipline, and rehabilitation. The number of credits awarded to prisoners varies from state to state. Credits are reduced or taken away if inmates are found guilty of disciplinary infractions or violations of prison rules. One criticism of good time credits is that they have evolved into a standard practice and are automatically awarded to inmates as a lump sum at the beginning of the prison term, thereby reducing their rehabilitative incentive. The use of good time credits was originally a key part of the rehabilitation process. Today, however, following an increased turn to punitiveness, good time credit is under attack.

HISTORY

The development of good time credits can be traced to the early 19th century, when the first good time law in the United States was enacted in Auburn, New York, in 1817. Other countries provided similar opportunities for inmates to reduce sentence length. For example, the marks system developed by Alexander Maconochie in Norfolk Island, Australia, rewarded good conduct during incarceration through a reduction in sentence length. The Irish reward system developed by Sir Walter Crofton provided a graduated structure of early release in which inmates progressed through a series of stages to earn release from incarceration, known as a ticket of leave. Both strategies were precursors in the development of modern-day parole. The Canadian remission system was also similar to the concept of good time credits. By 1876, 29 states in the United States had enacted good time laws.

PURPOSE

Good time was developed to serve three distinct purposes: discipline, population control, and rehabilitation. Thus, good time laws in the United States were designed primarily to facilitate prison management and to resolve problems with overcrowding.

Prison administrators used good time credits as a management tool to control the behavior of prison inmates. Credits provided powerful motivation for good behavior and an effective means of control, since those who refused to follow the rules or who acted out faced the possibility of the loss of good time credits. Misconduct was punished through a loss of accrued credits, which lengthened the term of incarceration.

Good time credits reduced prison crowding by establishing a safety valve through which administrators could regulate the flow of inmates out of the prison system. They also provided a back-door solution to the problem of prison overcrowding by allowing the early release of inmates from incarceration. Additional credits were occasionally provided during period of extreme overcrowding to accelerate the release process. For example, Michigan responded to a period of prison overcrowding in 1981 and 1982 by rolling back minimum sentence lengths by 90 days to increase the number of inmates released on parole. The early release of inmates from incarceration also made space available for incoming offenders.

Good time was once considered to be an integral part of the rehabilitative process because it allowed punishment to be tailored to the needs of each offender. It provided an incentive to participate in a wide variety of prison programs, including educational and vocational classes. Similarly, good work habits and pro-social skills were rewarded with the hope that they would carry over into the community upon release from incarceration.

ADMINISTRATION

Four forms of good time credits exist: statutory or administrative, earned, meritorious, and emergency credits. Statutory good time is awarded automatically to prison inmates in a lump sum at the beginning of the term of incarceration. The credits are revoked only for a serious violation of prison rules or policy. A system of earned credits provides rewards for positive behavior such as program participation, similar to the original concept of good time credits. Meritorious credits are awarded to inmates who demonstrate exemplary behavior, such as those who donate blood. Emergency credits are used as a response to prolonged periods of overcrowding, during which credits are granted to eligible inmates nearing release from incarceration.

The administration of good time credits is often controversial because it allows prison staff extensive discretionary powers. Decisions to award credits or penalize inmates for misconduct are highly subjective because they are not based on a standardized written policy. Also, there is some variation in how many credits prisoners can earn. Thus, usually inmates earn credits at different rates based on their classification status. For example, prisoners in a lower-level-security housing unit typically earn more credits than those in a high-security housing unit.

RELATIONSHIP TO PAROLE

Parole refers to the discretionary early release of an inmate following a period of incarceration. It was developed to relieve prison crowding while providing supervision of offenders. Indeterminate sentences established minimum and maximum periods of incarceration thereby allowing correctional officials to tailor punishment to the needs of individual offenders. In an indeterminate sentencing system, release from incarceration follows successful completion of treatment. Parole developed in conjunction with indeterminate sentencing to assist in the goal of offender rehabilitation. The offender is eligible for parole release after serving a minimum term minus good time credits.

Dissatisfaction with the concept of rehabilitation produced a shift in emphasis from indeterminate to determinate sentencing. Determinate sentencing was intended to reduce discretion in sentence length by providing a fixed period of incarceration. Under a system of determinate sentencing, inmates were required to serve the entire sentence length prior to release from incarceration. Good time served as the predominant form of release in a determinate sentencing system.

PRESENT STATUS

The Violent Crime Control and Law Enforcement Act of 1994 provided federal funding incentives to encourage individual states to pass Truth in Sentencing (TIS) legislation. Truth in Sentencing increased prison sentences for offenders convicted of violent crimes and reduced discrepancies between original sentence and time served. It required certain inmates to serve an 85% minimum of the original sentence length prior to parole eligibility. It therefore restricted the ability of incarcerated offenders to earn good time credits through participation in prison programs and good behavior. By 1999, 27 states and the District of Columbia met the 85% requirement to qualify for funding through federal TIS grants. Little is known about how recent policies designed to "get tough on crime" such as truth in sentencing will influence rates of misconduct in prison populations and participation in prison programs.

CONCLUSION

Good time credits provide prison administrators with the ability to influence the size of the prison population by reducing time served. For this reason, they continue as one solution to the problem of prison overcrowding despite controversy over the extent of prison officials' discretion in their use and despite the passage of legislation intended to increase time served.

—*Jennifer E. Schneider*

See also Correctional Officers; Determinate Sentencing; Indeterminate Sentencing; Irish (or Crofton) System; Just Deserts Theory; Legitimacy; Alexander Maconochie; Parole; Rehabilitation Theory; Truth in Sentencing; Violent Crime Control and Law Enforcement Act 1994

Further Reading

Bottomley, A. K. (1990). Parole in transition: A comparative study of origins, developments, and prospects for the 1990s. In M. Tonry & N. Morris (Eds.), *Crime and justice: A review of research* (Vol. 12). Chicago: University of Chicago Press.

Chayet, E. C. (1994). Correctional "good time" as a means of early release. *Criminal Justice Abstracts, 26*(3), 521–538.

Davis, S. P. (1990, May). Good time. *Corrections Compendium, 15*(4).

Ditton, P. M., & Wilson, D. J. (1999). *Truth in sentencing in state prisons.* Washington, DC: U.S. Department of Justice, Office of Justice Programs.

Parisi, N., & Zillo, J. A. (1983). Good time: The forgotten issue. *Crime & Delinquency, 29*, 228–237.

✓ GOTTI, JOHN (1940–2002)

John Joseph Gotti was born on October 27, 1940 to John J. Sr. and Fannie Gotti, the fifth of 11 children. By age 12, he was already involved with people thought to be involved with organized crime known as "wiseguys." Gotti formally left school at age 16 to join the Fulton-Rockaway Boys, where he quickly rose to a leadership position. While a member of the Fulton-Rockaway Boys, Gotti was arrested five times between 1957 and 1961. Each time the charges were dismissed or reduced to a probationary sentence.

Gotti was one of the first individuals prosecuted under the Racketeer Influenced and Corrupt Organizations (RICO) statute for a variety of crimes centering on a criminal organization (in this case La Cosa Nostra). To secure his conviction, the prosecution relied on protected witnesses. Ultimately, Gotti was sentenced to one of America's most notorious maximum-security federal prisons, where he eventually died.

EARLY INCARCERATION

Gotti's first incarceration came in 1963, when he and Salvatore Ruggiero were arrested in an automobile that had been reported stolen. He spent 20 days in jail for this offense. Throughout the rest of the early 1960s, Gotti took part in small-scale criminal behavior such as larceny, unlawful entry, and possession of bookmaking records.

Then in 1966 he spent several months in jail for attempted theft.

Once released from jail in 1966, John Gotti became an associate of an organized crime group headed by Carmine and Daniel Fatico. The group operated out of the Bergin Hunt and Fish Club in Ozone Park, Queens, New York. The Fatico group was a part of the Gambino organized crime family. At this point, Gotti began to hijack trucks coming from the John F. Kennedy International Airport until he was arrested by the FBI on November 27, 1967, with Gene and Angelo Ruggiero. He was then convicted of several hijackings and was sentenced to four years at Lewisburg Federal Penitentiary in Pennsylvania. He was released in January 1972.

When Carmine, the Fatico group leader was indicted, Gotti was appointed as acting capo (captain, or leader) of the group. He assumed control of the Fatico group in May 1972. Soon after his rise to power in the Fatico group, the Gambino family underboss (the secondary leadership position) Aniello Dellacroce was also imprisoned, and Gotti began to interact directly with Carlo Gambino, the family boss.

THE GAMBINO CRIME FAMILY

Gotti's relationship with Carlo Gambino was strengthened when he helped arrange the killing of Jimmy McBratney in 1973. McBratney allegedly was involved with the kidnapping and murder of Carlo Gambino's nephew Manny. While the details of the kidnapping are still debated, Gotti's was eventually indicted for McBratney's murder. Gotti pleaded guilty to attempted murder and was sentenced to four years' imprisonment. He spent less than two years at Green Haven Correctional Facility, 80 miles north of Queens, and was released on July 28, 1977. Shortly afterward, he was made a full member of the organized crime group.

While Gotti was imprisoned, the leadership of his "family" changed. Carlo Gambino died, and his nephew, Paul Castellano, was appointed as boss. However, underboss Aniello Dellacroce was next in line for the position. Two factions arose in the organization; Gotti sided with Dellacroce, while Paul Castellano maintained control over the organization.

Through the late 1970s and into the 1980s, Gotti built his "crew" (a fairly stable group that takes part in crimes together) into a strong organization. At the same time, the FBI was accumulating substantial resources in its battle against organized crime. Confidential informants, covert listening devices, and regular surveillance became more frequent.

In 1985, Gotti's crew began to plan the demise of their boss, Paul Castellano. A perceived slight occurred when Aniello Dellacroce died and Castellano refused to attend the funeral. Later Castellano stated he was going to split up Gotti's crew. Instead, Castellano was executed on December 16, 1985, in front of Spark's Steak House in downtown Manhattan, placing John Gotti at the helm of the Gambino family.

Initially known as the "Dapper Don" for his attire, Gotti soon acquired the new nickname of "Teflon Don" when he was acquitted two times. Finally, in 1992, with the help of Sammy "The Bull" Gravano as a government witness, Gotti was convicted on RICO charges.

THE RACKETEER INFLUENCED AND CORRUPT ORGANIZATIONS (RICO) STATUTE

Prosecuting individuals who are involved with a criminal organization (La Cosa Nostra, outlaw motorcycle groups, etc.) is difficult due to the secrecy surrounding such organizations. Historically, the resulting convictions have been for singular crimes such as hijacking one truck, the murder of one person, or the extortion of one business. RICO, however, enables prosecutors a legal means to connect these various crimes to show that each criminal event is tied to the maintenance and growth of a criminal organization. For example, the hijacking of a truck was done to obtain goods to sell at a profit for the group, the murder may have been committed to silence a witness to the hijacking thereby protecting the criminal group, and extortion may have been used to force a storeowner to sell the stolen goods. In all, the three crimes were performed due to association with a corrupt organization. Recently, RICO has been used to prosecute

white-collar criminals as well as the traditional organized crime groups.

CONCLUSION

Gotti was sentenced to life in federal prison. He spent most of his term at the maximum-security facility in Marion, Illinois. Due to the confinement strategy of the administrators at the Marion Facility, Gotti's time in prison was largely uneventful. There were several reports of Gotti being assaulted by other inmates and receiving minor wounds. In the late 1990s, he was diagnosed with throat cancer. During that time, he was scheduled to be sent to the new state-of-the-art maximum-security facility in Florence, Colorado. On September 13, 2000, he was moved to the federal prison hospital in Springfield, Missouri, for treatment. John Gotti died on June 10, 2002, at the age of 61 from complications of head and throat cancer.

—Robert B. Jenkot

See also ADX (Administrative Maximum): Florence; Celebrities in Prison; Classification; Control Unit; Elderly Prisoners; Health Care; Marion, U.S. Penitentiary; Maximum Security; Supermax Prisons; Volstead Act 1918; WITSEC

Further Reading

Capeci, J., & Mustain, G. (1996). *Gotti: Rise and fall.* New York: Penguin/Onyx.

Cummings, J., & Volkman, E. (1992). *Goombata: The improbable rise and fall of John Gotti and his gang.* New York: Avon.

Shawcross, T. (1994). *The war against the Mafia.* New York: Harper.

◪ GOVERNANCE

Governance refers to the methods by which correctional facilities are administered. It usually includes the means by which a social and organizational hierarchy is created, how roles in that organization are formalized, and the manner in which order is maintained within the institutional social system. How prisons are run determines individuals' experiences of incarceration.

BACKGROUND

Two alternative models of prison governance gained prominence in the latter half of the 20th century both of which continue to influence how prisons are run today. The first of these approaches is known as the *control model* and is characterized by a rigid and routinized model of administration that is hierarchical in nature and emphasizes obedience, work, and education. The roots of the control model can be traced to the first penitentiaries in the Pennsylvania system. These institutions controlled prisoners and sought to reform them through regimes of silence and labor. John DiIulio is the contemporary scholar whose work is most often associated with this model of prison governance.

In contrast, the *participatory model,* advocated by scholars such as Hans Toch and John Irwin, stresses a system of inmate democracy. For its supporters, prisons are run best when they use prisoner input to shape their policy and programs. In this system, prisoners may be permitted a voice in the day-to-day operations through representatives on administrative committees. There is also usually a formalized protocol through which prisoner grievances can be heard. According to its supporters, this strategy helps maintain prison order, because all members are invested in it. It also prepares inmates more effectively for their eventual discharge by permitting them to engage in decision making that trains them for the challenges they will face upon release from prison.

CONTROL MODEL

Supporters of the control model believe that deviance occurs because of a lack of discipline and responsibility. As a result, only a social environment of absolute control can teach inmates acceptable patterns of behavior.

The control model is bureaucratic in the classic Weberian sense of the term. According to Max Weber, for a rational bureaucracy to work, there must be prescribed roles that each individual plays, and transactions between different members of the organization must be regulated. This will create stability, thereby reducing conflict between different members of the prison organization (namely, administration and staff) as well as staff and inmates. A clearly defined set of rules and principles that govern everyone's role, and the means by which they can interact reduces the uncertainty that often leads to conflict in prison. Any deviation from the control model, through inmate participation, for example, threatens the balance created by a bureaucratic model and could potentially lead to the emergence of violence, "con bosses," and gang conflict.

Prisons run according to the control model function like paramilitary organizations, with respect and obedience enforced relentlessly through a rigid system of discipline. The assumption is that obedience, work, and education, administered in a supervisory environment of zero tolerance, is the only way to bring about reform in the behavior of the inmates. To make this system work, everyone in the prison must know that the guards are in control.

The Beto Control Model in Texas

The control model of prison governance is best exemplified by the Texas prison system of the 1960s, implemented by Dr. George Beto beginning in 1962 and recounted by John DiIulio in his work *Governing Prisons.* Beto's ideas of prisoner governance were designed in reaction to the barbaric conditions that then existed in many Texas penal institutions. He modeled his administration after that of Joseph Ragen in Illinois's Stateville Prison; an authoritarian regime in which top-down control was employed with the ultimate goal of safety and order. Labor from sunup to sundown was combined with corporal punishment to create a prison system in which many individuals did not survive the length of their term either due to sickness or punishment. Although there are many who have criticized Beto's control model, during his 10-year reign there were only 17 homicides in the prison. This figure contrasts strikingly to the particularly brutal period that preceded Beto in which labor, violence, and disease meant that a sentence to a Texas prison would often amount to capital punishment.

Under Beto's system, officers relied on what were known as "building tenders," which were a modern manifestation of the old "con boss," or inmates who acted as proxies for the guards. These men were empowered to enforce rules both formally and informally. Usually, they enforced most of the petty rule violations themselves and only involved the officers for larger violations. They also acted as a conduit of information to the administration so that they would be able to maintain a system of tight supervision. They were permitted a great degree of discretion, deciding what to report and enforce, on whom to inform, and which officers with whom they were willing to develop a relationship. Most of the guards were from rural areas, and the racial conflict that emerged between the white guards and the black inmates made for a particularly incendiary situation. Moreover, the inmates often enforced rules along racial lines, and minority inmates bore the brunt of an arbitrary and vicious execution of discipline. In Beto's control system, order and compliance was maintained by strict adherence to the authority of the correctional officers, but the ultimate enforcers were the building tenders.

As the prison population continued to grow, Texas was forced to rely more and more on building tenders and reward them with greater freedom and privileges. In the now landmark case *of Ruiz v. Estelle* (1980), the U.S. District Court in Texas intervened and specified a number of areas of prison administration that must be changed to bring the correctional system inline within constitutional guidelines. These included a mandated reduction in the ratio of officers to inmates, steps to be taken to address overcrowding, increased access of inmates to legal representation, the introduction of a more effective classification system, and an end to the use of building tenders. This effectively brought about the demise of the Texas control model.

PARTICIPATORY MODEL

The participatory model is based on a system of classification in which inmates' behavior governs the amount of autonomy they are given. The goal of this model is to match individuals with a level of supervision that is appropriate to their classification. Those who have proven records of behavior can earn more autonomy over their actions, while others who are unwilling to abide by prison rules will face increased restrictions. As such, most models of inmate participation are limited to minimum- and medium-security institutions. Rigid rule enforcement is to be avoided, unless demanded by the situation. This approach is rooted in the work of Cesare Beccaria and Jeremy Bentham, who suggested that punishment must be devised to inflict the least amount of discomfort to the offender while still ensuring that the requisite amount of punishment is delivered.

Proponents of the idea of prisoner participation believe that symbolism of rank should be suppressed so as not to create a perception of subordination by the inmates. In other words, there should not be a system of dress that can be used to identify rank or status within the prison. Inmates should also be free to socialize with one another and form groups to interact with others of a like mind. At its heart, the responsibility model believes that inmates should be subjected to the bare minimum of supervision needed to maintain order in prison.

The responsibility, or participatory, model differs from the control model at the very core of the purpose of prison. Prisoners have rights, and the role of the prison administrator is not to punish, but to supervise and "serve" the inmate. The prison environment is where the inmate lives 24 hours a day; therefore, prisoners should be permitted to play an active role in shaping how it is governed. The participatory model maintains that inmate compliance may be achieved much more efficiently by running a system in which they have input and do not feel powerless to control their own destiny. Subjecting prisoners to constant supervision teaches them only to second guess themselves at every point and does not permit them to adopt an approach that will help them adapt to the outside world after their release. Inmate participation in prison is an effective way to introduce and teach democracy and rights of citizenship to individuals, many of whom have had little interaction with these concepts in the past.

Michigan, California, and Arkansas

The most famous example of a participatory model is the Michigan responsibility model that was founded by Director of Corrections Perry M. Johnson. This model allows inmates to maintain a certain degree of responsibility over their own environment and encourages interaction between staff and inmates to be governed by informal principles rather than by hard-and-fast rules. A classification system was used to ensure that each inmate was placed in an environment that was as minimally restrictive as possible while still maintaining safety, the belief being that an overreliance on security and force would prohibit inmates from learning to practice autonomy over their lives through effective decision making. The central theme in Michigan was that prison should be used as a tool of rehabilitation, and this can be accomplished most effectively by giving inmates the most freedom possible to self-govern, thereby instilling within them responsibility that will remain once they return to society.

The California consensual model is another participatory model of prison governance that emphasizes inmate responsibility and autonomy, although without any focused strategy such as in Michigan. In the California system, prisoner input shapes policy decisions and staff are intended to play a supervisory role, rather than a controlling role as in Texas. DiIulio notes that although California's system of governance lacks an identifiable approach in the same fashion as Texas or Michigan, the central theme is that administration of the prison relies upon the "consent of the governed." Much like Michigan, the California approach chooses to handle prisoners in a more informal manner, ultimately seeking to maintain order within the prison by keeping the peace between major prison gangs that hold significant influence within the prison social system.

In addition to the Michigan and California experiences, Thomas Murton, warden of Cummins Prison in Arkansas, achieved significant success in reforming a racist and violent prison system through inmate democratization. By permitting inmates to participate in the classification process of fellow prisoners, the violence rate within the prison decreased dramatically. After instituting this system, Murton was able to take steps to reintegrate the prison racially as well as implement a number of progressive programs that had been neglected in the past due to the violent nature of the facility. In a short while, Murton transformed an unstable Arkansas facility defined by administrative control through racism, violence, and torture into a participatory institution that had few instances of violence, all the while allowing significant inmate involvement.

Eventually however, democratic approaches such as those implemented at Arkansas run into difficulties, because prison staff tend to feel that they allow inmates "to run the prison." The model was designed to create a system of supervised self-governance by the inmates, but correctional officers perceived it as the administration favoring the rights of the prisoners over the need for them to do their job (i.e., keep the peace). Prisoners also felt that this model gave them power within the administration; therefore, they could be selective in how obedient they were to the demands of correctional officers. In the same way that the building tender system led to the emergence of a brutal hierarchy, the responsibility model also resulted in a hierarchy in which certain privileged inmates were able to exert a great deal of influence over their social environment.

COMPARISON

At the heart of these two models is a tension that strikes at the core of incarceration: What is the purpose of holding people in prison? Is it incapacitation and punishment (control model) or rehabilitation (participatory model)? In the control model, the emphasis is on discipline as a means to keep order within the institution. Supporters of this approach claim that rehabilitation and reform are impossible goals unless the social system within which these inmates exist is kept in order and a hierarchy is enforced. In the wake of federal court intervention in a number of states, in which authoritarian models of control were outlawed or curtailed, many systems witnessed social disruption and violence. This has been referred to by many as the "paradox of reform"; court intervention was supposed to produce a safer atmosphere for prisoners, but the lack of a strategy to replace the control model left a power void that was often filled by prisoner gangs. Moreover, many correctional officers felt demoralized by the reforms and were unable to keep order within the prisons. Proponents of the control model point to this violence as evidence that the control model was the only successful approach, while critics maintain that it was the lack of an effective replacement strategy that caused this unrest in the 1970s and 1980s.

In contrast, those who advocate the participatory model suggest that a system of total control may keep order but neglects to provide for the rehabilitation of the prisoner. By refusing to consider the opinions and visions of inmates, institutions eventually release women and men who are ill-prepared to reenter a society that requires people to be autonomous and participatory in defining the direction of their lives. By rendering inmates decidedly impotent, they also neglect to create a stake for them in the direction of the prison, and instead may cause animosity that makes order more difficult to attain. Proponents of the participatory model point to the disruption in the wake of court reform as an example of the inequality and poor administrative techniques of the control model. They assert that if the only way to keep order is with constant supervision and threats of punishment, then we have failed in our duty to rehabilitate and those people being released are ill-prepared to reenter society.

CONCLUSION

The best way to govern prisons is a point of contention among prison administrators and criminologists. To what extent should inmates participate in any decision-making processes in penal facilities? How much discretion should officers have when doing their job? While answers to these questions remain unclear, what is obvious is that how prisons are run shapes people's experiences of incarceration. More problematic, governance may also influence what happens to inmates after release. As of December 2003, more than 2.1 million Americans are being held in U.S. prisons and jails, and research suggests that over half of them will recidivate within three years of their release from prison. Such figures indicate that no matter which models of governance are currently being used, they are

failing to provide an environment in which successful long-term change can be sought and achieved.

—*Ryan S. King*

See also Activism; Correctional Officers; Deprivation; John J. DiIulio, Jr.; Discipline System; History of Prisons; Importation; Incapacitation Theory; Legitimacy; Managerialism; Maximum Security; Medium Security; Minimum Security; Plantation Prisons; Prison Culture; Rehabilitation Theory; Security and Control; Stateville Correctional Center; Supermax Prisons

Further Reading

Crouch, B. M., & Marquart, J. W. (1989). *An appeal to justice: Litigated reform of Texas prisons.* Austin: University of Texas Press.

DiIulio, J. J., Jr. (1987). *Governing prisons: A comparative study of correctional management.* New York: Free Press.

Irwin, J. (1980). *Prisons in turmoil.* Boston: Little, Brown.

Jacobs, J. (1977). *Stateville: Penitentiary in mass society.* Chicago: University of Chicago Press.

Murton, T. (1976). *The dilemma of prison reform.* New York: Holt, Rinehart & Winston.

Ruiz v. Estelle, 503 F.Supp. 1265 (S.D. Texas, 1980).

Sparks, R., Bottoms, T., & Hay, W. (1996). *Prisons and the problem of order.* Oxford, UK: Clarendon Press.

Wortley, R. (2001). *Situational prison control: Crime prevention in correctional institutions.* New York: Cambridge University Press.

◾ GROUP HOMES

Group homes are nonsecure residential facilities used to house juvenile and adult offenders convicted of a criminal offense, as well as those younger individuals who are facing adjudication in a juvenile court or conviction in an adult court. Group homes are considered to be nonrestrictive, intermediate-level alternatives to secure confinement. Although their programs may vary, their underlying philosophies are similar. The primary purpose of these homes is to provide residents with rehabilitative services such as education, counseling, job training, and social skills while maintaining a level of interaction with the community.

Facilities designed to provide nonsecure community-based confinement for adult offenders are usually referred to as halfway houses. Group homes are typically community-based treatment facilities designed for juvenile offenders. These facilities have become an increasingly common alternative to secure confinement in the juvenile corrections system. In fact, during 1998 alone, of the 634,000 juveniles adjudicated delinquent, 26% were ordered to an out-of-home placement, which includes detention centers, residential facilities, group homes, and foster homes. An estimated 3,000 of those juveniles were placed at a group or foster home (Champion, 2001; Puzzachera, 2002). Group homes may be private or public institutions. Because they rely heavily on the interaction of their residents with the community, group homes are usually community based whatever their administrative orientation.

NONSECURE CONFINEMENT

Group homes provide nonsecure alternatives to incarceration. There is limited direct supervision within the houses, and residents are free to move around them as well as to participate in a variety of activities in the community. Although the residents enjoy a significant amount of liberty, group homes are not without structure. There are numerous rules governing the conduct of the residents that must be obeyed. Typically, such rules entail respect for staff and other residents, a curfew, and active participation in a variety of rehabilitative programs, such as school, work, and counseling. Residents are also frequently required to submit to random urine tests for detection of alcohol and drug use, while staff members constantly monitor their general behavior.

Judges usually place juveniles in group homes for a designated period of time. During their time at the facilities, these juveniles remain under the dispositional control of the judge and program staff are routinely required to report the progress of the juveniles to the judge. The length of time that the juvenile must remain in the home can be extended if he or she is shown not to progress.

It should be noted that group homes are only one form of nonsecure confinement options available for juvenile offenders. Several other nonsecure facilities, such as foster homes, camps, ranches, halfway houses, farms, boarding schools, wilderness programs, and independent living programs, also exist.

KEY COMPONENTS OF GROUP HOMES

The central component of many group homes is their attempt to replicate a noninstitutional, home-based atmosphere. Generally, group homes are characterized by a family-based setting. They use counselors who serve as model parents for the residents on a daily basis. In an effort to maintain the family atmosphere, juveniles are usually housed in groups ranging in size from 10 to 15.

Most group homes are designed to rehabilitate juvenile offenders. Residents are thus provided services such as counseling, education, and vocational training, as well as problem solving and social skills training. Juveniles are expected to participate in some type of educational program. They are usually required to pursue a traditional diploma, general equivalency diploma (GED), or some type of vocational training. Unlike secure confinement alternatives, residents of group homes receive their education at schools or programs within the community. They may be enrolled in individual or specific therapy, such as substance abuse treatment or anger management, and they are usually required to participate in group counseling with their peers and program staff. Most group counseling activities are designed to elicit positive peer influence on behaviors, as well as to teach problem-solving skills. Finally, juveniles are usually required to participate in some form of community activity either in the form of interaction with other residents within the group home itself or in more structured events within the community, such as recreational or creative programs.

PROBLEMS

Group homes are not without problems. First, many have staff who are not properly trained to provide quality care. In many instances, community volunteers are used to aid in the delivery of services to the residents. Second, group homes are not currently subjected to a unified, governing set of rules and regulations, such as those that govern secure confinement facilities. In many jurisdictions, these facilities operate without oversight by government agencies. Finally, not all juveniles are amenable to treatment in the group home setting. Therefore, it is important that juveniles undergo appropriate screening processes before being placed in a group home setting.

The reasoning behind placing juveniles in group homes has also been the subject of some scrutiny. Young women are more typically incarcerated in these homes for status offenses than are males. African American males have also been found to be more disproportionately incarcerated in these institutions than their white counterparts for minor offenses.

CONCLUSION

Group homes are nonsecure confinement options generally used for juvenile offenders. They provide a less restrictive alternative to confinement for treatment purposes. Group home are used frequently as an out-of-home placement for children, particularly young women and African American young men.

—Lisa Hutchinson Wallace

See also Meda Chesney-Lind; Community Corrections Center; Foster Care; Intermediate Sanctions; Juvenile Justice and Delinquency Prevention Act 1974; Juvenile Justice System; Juvenile Offenders: Race, Class, and Gender; Juvenile Reformatories; Parole; Probation; Status Offenders; Waiver of Juveniles Into the Adult Court System

Further Reading

Bowker, L. H. (1982). *Corrections: The science and the art.* New York: Macmillan.

Champion, D. (2001). *The juvenile justice system: Delinquency, processing, and the law.* Upper Saddle River, NJ: Prentice Hall.

McNeely, R. L., & Pope, C. E. (1981). *Race, crime, and criminal justice.* Beverly Hills, CA: Sage.

Puzzachera, C. (2002). *Juvenile court placement of adjudicated youth, 1989–1998.* Office of Juvenile Justice and Delinquency Prevention. Washington, DC: U.S. Government Printing Office.

Rosenbaum, J. L. (1989). Family dysfunction and female delinquency. *Crime & Delinquency, 35,* 31–44.

Siegel, L. J., & Senna, J. J. (1981). *Juvenile delinquency: Theory, practice, and law.* St. Paul, MN: West.

☒ GROUP THERAPY

Group therapy is one of a number of methods used in prison settings to help inmates deal with their mental health problems and addictions. In group therapy, there is the leader and more than one client/member. The size of a group may be larger, to include one or two therapists (co-therapists) and many members. Research suggests that the most efficient size for group therapy is 6 to 10 members and the leader(s), though larger groups do form for various reasons.

DEFINITION

Various types of group therapy exist, including group guidance, growth group, group counseling, and group psychotherapy. Though these terms are sometimes used interchangeably, each method differs in structure and focus and in the qualifications and credentials vary of the group leader. Thus, in group counseling, the leader may be a layperson, a paraprofessional, or a credentialed professional who has been certified or licensed by a state or national program.

Programs based on group guidance typically have a large number of participants. In such groups, the leader functions more as an instructor or facilitator than as someone giving direct, specialized care. These groups usually offer educational and skill development as in the drug education programs available in all U.S. federal prisons. Growth groups, on the other hand, are intended to provide a setting for the participants to become more functional individuals, once again with the leader functioning as instructor, guide, or facilitator.

Group counseling and group psychotherapy are more clinical in orientation. These strategies are often used in therapeutic communities. Group counseling focuses on normal persons with common problems, whereas psychotherapy focuses on dysfunctional persons with disorders. As with individual counseling and psychotherapy, group counseling and psychotherapy can be viewed on a continuum. In practice, they may be blended and move from one orientation to the other as the group members' needs arise.

JUSTICE APPLICATIONS

Several types of group counseling and therapy are employed in the adult and juvenile justice system. Depending on the charges and contributing factors, an adjudged or adjudicated individual may be required to attend various types or multiples of groups. Three of the more popular types of groups that are commonly incorporated into sentencing and plea bargains are 12-step programs, that is, Alcoholics Anonymous, Cocaine Anonymous, or Narcotics Anonymous substance and drug abuse, anger management, and sex offender counseling or therapy programs. With the exception of the 12-step type programs run by laypeople, the other forms of groups are clinical in orientation and thus led by credentialed professionals.

These groups provide cost-effective and efficient service distribution since they usually employ only one leader for many participants. They strive to address the dysfunctions of individuals, while providing opportunities to explore different types of relating with other persons and to learn more effective social skills. Also, they offer opportunities for participants to discuss their perceptions of life situations and experiences and to receive feedback on how others interpret and cope with them. Finally, groups such as these enable their members to experiment with alternative behaviors.

CHALLENGES OF REHABILITATION

The challenges of rehabilitation in correctional confinement are complex because the population of the incarcerated present the therapeutic professionals multiple and diverse pathologies with many qualifying for dual or multiple diagnoses. These pathologies extend beyond the antisocial issues that led to incarceration in the first place. Research indicates that a large proportion of inmates present suffer from significant mental health issues including past abuse victimizations, substance abuses, and learning difficulties, not to mention adjustment issues associated with their confinement. In addition, there are the developmental issues of juvenile offenders, the different socialization of genders, and the belief systems of multiple cultures of the inmates. Perhaps most problematic, though group therapy usually attempts to provide a supportive environment for voluntary members, in correctional institutions groups are used to reform and socialize its members, who may be mandated to attend by the courts or by prison personnel. Finally, the therapeutic professionals are confronted with the additional difficulties of providing services in an environment that may either not understand or be unsupportive of the process of therapy itself.

EFFECTIVENESS OF GROUP THERAPY

The effectiveness of group therapy for adjudged or adjudicated individuals appears to vary. As with other forms of clinical treatments, various studies of "what works" have considered this category of treatment with mixed results. Cognitive-behavioral approaches, which attempt to modify the cognitive processing and the development of psychosocial skills of the individual, have often been shown to be the most successful. This strategy can be readily applied through therapeutic groups.

Some of the differences in the results of the various studies of effectiveness lie in the lack of controls of the consistency of services provided by various methods. Identifying and matching participants with appropriate treatments and the failure of the participants to commit to the effort by either dropping out or a lack of committed effort may decrease the success of treatment. Finally, as with all therapeutic relationships there are concerns with trust and confidentiality, in group therapy this is not only with the leader but also over the other members of the group. These are especially so for the incarcerated, even more than in individual therapy, because of the inmate code that exists in all prisons. This includes how prisoners are required to interact with staff and with other prisoners.

CONCLUSION

Even with strong social support for a more "get tough" approach to punishment, there remains a consistent belief by society that offenders should be rehabilitated before they are released back to the community. Group therapy is just one example of a strategy used in contemporary U.S. penal facilities to help reduce reoffending rates. Though it cannot totally eliminate recidivism, studies suggest such counseling may reduce it. Offering therapy in a group setting helps individuals to realize that their issues and problems are not unique and that they are, therefore, not alone. Though counseling of this nature may not be appropriate for everyone, when it is done well, following a rigorous needs assessment, it provides a cost-effective and practical means of addressing common problems and behaviors in the inmate community.

—*Richard L. McWhorter*

See also Alcoholics Anonymous; Drug Treatment Programs; Individual Therapy; Mental Health; Narcotics Anonymous; Psychology Services; Psychologists; Suicide; Therapeutic Community; Women's Health

Further Reading

Alexander, R., Jr. (2000). *Counseling, treatment, and intervention methods with juvenile and adult offenders.* Belmont, CA: Brooks/Cole.

Burrow, T. (1927). The group method of analysis. *Psychoanalytic Review, 14,* 268–280.

Glicken, M. D., & Sechrest, D. K. (2003). *The role of the helping professions in treating the victims and perpetrators of violence.* Boston: Allyn & Bacon.

Henning, K. R., & Frueh, B. C. (1996). Cognitive-behavioral treatment of incarcerated: An evaluation of the Vermont Department of Corrections' cognitive self-change program. *Criminal Justice and Behavior, 23*(4), 523–542.

Martinson, R. (1974). What works? Questions and answers about prison reform. *The Public Interest, 10,* 22–54.

Palmer, T. (1994). *A profile of correctional effectiveness & new directions for research.* Albany: State University of New York Press.

Sherman, L. W., Gottfredson, D. C., MacKenzie, D. L., Eck, J., Reuter, P., & Bushway, S. D. (1998). *Preventing crime: What works, what doesn't, what's promising.* Washington, DC: U.S. Department of Justice, National Institute of Justice.

ⓜ GYNECOLOGY

Virtually every U.S. jurisdiction provides gynecological and obstetrical services to its female inmates. Under normal circumstances, the practitioner providing these services would be a gynecologist who had completed specialized residency training in the study and treatment of the diseases of the female reproductive system, including the breasts. Generally, this training also includes obstetrics (the care of the pregnant woman) and integrates the medical and surgical care of women's health throughout their life span. The study of obstetrics and gynecology includes the physiologic, social, cultural, environmental, and genetic factors that influence disease in women. Individual obstetrician-gynecologists may choose a wide scope of practice, to include the care of pregnant women and surgical procedures on the reproductive organs, or a more focused practice that limits care to ambulatory (office-based) services. In some cases, other medical practitioners, including nurse practitioners, nurse midwives, physician assistants, and physicians from other specialties such as family medicine or internal medicine, may provide gynecologic or obstetrical services. In prison, the credentials of the health practitioners providing these services to women are uncertain.

Three national organizations accredit correctional health care facilities: the National Commission on Correctional Health Care (NCCHC), the American Correctional Association (ACA), and the Joint Commission on Accreditation of Healthcare Organizations (JCAHO). Accreditation by NCCHC, ACA, or JCAHO is not mandatory in order for an institution to provide medical services to inmates. As one part of the accreditation process conducted by these national organizations, periodic site visits and reviews of inmate health care records are conducted to determine the quality of care provided. However, at these site visits, the use of gynecologic health care parameters, such as the percentage of inmates who have had Pap smears performed, are not routinely used in the review process. As a result, women's health issues are often marginalized in policy decisions.

WOMEN IN PRISON AND THEIR HEALTH PROBLEMS

Over the past 20 years, there has been a greater than fivefold increase in the number of women incarcerated in the United States, with the preponderance in state facilities. A number of health profession organizations and human rights groups have been calling attention to the inadequate health care provided in our prisons and jails. The ratio of incarcerated, HIV-infected women to men is 3:1, in large part a result of their intravenous drug use, sexual abuse, prostitution, and sexual encounters with men of high-risk behavior profiles. For many of the same reasons the female inmate population is high risk for HIV infection, they are also high risk for other sexually transmitted diseases and gynecologic complications, such as cervical cancer.

LAWSUITS

One way in which women have successfully lobbied for an improvement in the quality of obstetric and gynecologic health care within the correctional setting has been through the use of class action lawsuits. At the forefront of this effort is attorney Ellen Berry, who has worked on behalf of women prisoners for 24 years in the California state and federal prisons and several large California county jails. In 1985, Berry filed *Harris v. McCarthy,* on behalf of pregnant women prisoners at the California Institution for Women in response to a range of serious allegations concerning pregnancy care, including a very high rate of miscarriage and fetal demise, birth complications, and untreated medical emergencies. At that time, there was no obstetrician-gynecologist to serve the 1,500 inmates. The settlement agreement in this case required the hiring of an obstetrician-gynecologist and the creation of a Pregnancy Related Health Care Team of an obstetrician-gynecologist, nurse practitioner, registered nurse, and social worker to evaluate and handle each pregnancy case based on the then current American College of Obstetricians and Gynecologists (ACOG) standards. Subsequent cases, including *Jones v. Dyer* (1986) on behalf of pregnant women in the Alameda County Jail and *Yeager v. Smith* (1987) on behalf of pregnant and postpartum

women at the Kern County Jail, were successfully settled, again relying on ACOG guidelines of care.

CONCLUSION

Although class action lawsuits may be instrumental in addressing some deficiencies in the obstetric and gynecologic health care of inmates, more sweeping reform is needed. ACOG guidelines for women's health care that have been adapted to the unique setting of correctional institutions are needed. The use of female-specific health care parameters in the accreditation review process of correctional facilities would improve the standards of care. The accreditation process must also begin assessing the female inmate's access to care and quality of gender-specific, gynecologic care.

—*Kathy S. Deasy*

See also Accreditation; Doctors; Health Care; HIV/AIDS; Mothers in Prison; Parenting Programs; Prison Nurseries; Women's Health; Women's Prisons

Further Reading

Amnesty International. (1999). *"Not part of my sentence": Violations of the human rights of women in custody.* AI Index: AMR 51/01/99. New York: Author.

Berry, E. (1996). Women prisoners and health care. In K. L. Moss (Ed.), *Man-made medicine: Women's health, public policy, and reform* (pp. 249–272). Durham, NC: Duke University Press.

DeGroot, A. S. (2000, May). HIV infection among incarcerated women: Epidemic behind bars. *The AIDS Reader.*

National Commission on Correctional Health Care. (2000). *Standards for health services in prisons.* Chicago: Author.

U.S. General Accounting Office. (1999, December). *Report to Honorable Eleanor Holmes Norton, women in prison, issues and challenges confronting U.S. correctional systems* (Publication GAO/GGD-00–22). Washington, DC: Author.

H

◪ *HABEAS CORPUS*

Habeas corpus is a Latin term that means literally "you have the body." It refers to a judge-issued writ requiring the government to bring a prisoner to court for the court to consider whether the detainee's imprisonment is legal. It is also known as the Great Writ of Liberty because it is designed to prevent unlawful imprisonment.

Habeas corpus concerns due process—whether an inmate's constitutional or statutory rights have been violated. It is most commonly used when a state prisoner appeals his or her conviction to a federal court on the grounds that his or her constitutional rights were violated. Typically, only those who are incarcerated may file habeas corpus petitions. However, a person may file a petition if a court has threatened to jail him or her for contempt of court. In family law, a parent denied custody of his or her child by a trial court may also file a habeas corpus petition. Finally, many inmates on death row file habeas requests, although recently, their capacity to do so has been restricted.

HISTORY

Habeas corpus is mentioned as early as the 14th-century in England, and was formally articulated in the Habeas Corpus Act of 1679. It was considered important enough to be mentioned in the U.S. Constitution and the failure to issue it was one of the American colonists' grievances leading up to the American Revolution: "The Privilege of the Writ of Habeas Corpus shall not be suspended, unless when in Cases of Rebellion or Invasion the public Safety may require it" (Article 1, Section 9). It is one of the few individual rights guaranteed by the original Constitution.

During the Warren Court years (1953–1969), the U.S. Supreme Court expanded the use of the federal role and that of habeas corpus. It did so on the grounds that the Constitution called for the uniform protection of essential liberties, including the rights of criminal defendants. This trend reached its zenith in *Fay v. Noia* (1963) where the Court found that liberal access to federal review constituted a fundamental right. Since the 1970s, however, the Court has chipped away at that position, beginning under the stewardship of Justice Warren Burger (1969–1986). Arguing that federal review produced administrative inefficiencies and resource expenditures, the Burger Court in *Wainwright v. Sykes* (1977) introduced a cost-benefit analysis where the benefits to the individual should be weighed against the costs to the states for multiple appeals to the federal level. Many other changes to habeas corpus have occurred since Justices Sandra Day O'Connor, Antonin Scalia, and Anthony Kennedy joined the Court in the 1980s. The

Rehnquist Court's conservative majority has sharply limited the use of the writ, especially by death row inmates.

HABEAS CORPUS IN TIMES OF POLITICAL TURMOIL

Well before the present era, people's rights to habeas corpus were routinely restricted during times of political turmoil. President Abraham Lincoln suspended habeas corpus during the Civil War in parts of the Midwest to clamp down on members of the Union who supported the Confederate cause, the so-called Copperheads. Congress supported Lincoln's decision, but Supreme Court Justice Roger Taney objected. Lincoln ignored Justice Taney. In *Ex parte Milligan* (1866), the Supreme Court ruled that Lincoln's suspension of habeas corpus was unconstitutional since civilian courts were still functioning and habeas corpus could be suspended only if these courts had been forced to close. Notably, this decision came after the Civil War was already over.

Historically, the Supreme Court has deferred to the executive and legislative branches during times of turmoil, and only after the crisis has faded has it acknowledged the constitutional violations that occurred. During World War I, for example, the Supreme Court upheld the incarceration of those who vocally opposed the war. It was only after the war that the court ruled that people could not be jailed for speaking out against war. Likewise, during World War II, in *Korematsu v. the United States* (1944), the Supreme Court upheld the internment of Japanese Americans. This case was revisited in 1984 by a federal district court that vacated Korematsu's conviction. The court decided this case on the basis of evidence showing that the government had misled the courts on the necessity to intern Japanese Americans. In particular, an attorney, Peter Densho, discovered a memo from a U.S. Department of Justice lawyer named Edward Ennis, written to the U.S. solicitor general Charles Fahey, who was preparing to argue the Korematsu case before the Supreme Court in 1944. In it Ennis said, "We are in possession of information that shows that the War Department's report on the [necessity

for the] internment is a lie. And we have an ethical obligation not to tell a lie to the Supreme Court, and we must decide whether to correct that record" (584 F. Supp. 1406 N.D. Cal). In spite of this document, Solicitor General Fahey did not correct the record in his appearance before the Supreme Court. Even though Korematsu's criminal conviction was nullified in 1984, the Supreme Court's 1944 decision in *Korematsu v. the United States* persists as a legal and historical precedent.

During the Cold War (1947–1991), the court generally refrained from intervening in cases where habeas corpus rights were abridged. On the few occasions when the Court did intervene, it sustained government actions. Only after the McCarthy era was waning did the court state that the right of free association made further prosecution for Communist Party membership infeasible.

Most recently, the passage of the USA PATRIOT Act (2001) has allowed for the indefinite detention of persons certified by law enforcement as national security threats. In other words, probable cause, guaranteed by the Fourth Amendment, does not need to be demonstrated to the courts. This feature, along with other provisions of the act, has sparked considerable debate and opposition since habeas corpus has effectively been nullified under such circumstances. Since the September 11, 2001, terrorist attacks on the United States, more than 100 prisoners captured in Afghanistan have been held at the U.S. military base in Guantánamo Bay, Cuba, classified as "illegal combatants" rather than as prisoners of war. By such classification, the U.S. government has avoided granting habeas corpus rights to these prisoners, effectively holding them incommunicado. This action has sparked international protest.

HABEAS CORPUS APPEALS BY DEATH ROW INMATES

Much of the concern about habeas corpus rights revolves today around death row appeals, with conservatives decrying delays in executions and civil libertarians alarmed at the drastically diminished role for habeas corpus appeals in recent years.

Justice Sandra Day O'Connor, writing for the majority, argued in *Coleman v. Thompson* (1991) that the key costs of multiple habeas corpus appeals were a loss of respect for the states. This effectively moved the debate away from balancing state interests (*Wainwright v. Sykes*) to actually *deferring* to the states, and away from a cost-benefit analysis to asserting a more abstract cost of comity. From one perspective, differences over federalism—what the proper relationship between the federal and state governments should be, with the "new federalists" arguing for a larger state role and diminished federal role—underlie the shifting Court's positions historically over habeas corpus rights.

In *McCleskey v. Zant* (1991), the Court limited death row inmate appeals to one round of federal habeas corpus review. Warren McCleskey was a Georgia death row inmate who has since been executed. He brought his second habeas corpus appeal on the grounds that he had discovered that the government had illegally planted an informant in an adjoining cell to obtain incriminating statements from him. The government had for years denied that this inmate was a plant. The Supreme Court denied McCleskey's appeal on the grounds that a "reasonable and diligent investigation" by McCleskey, in spite of the government's repeated denials, would *somehow* have allowed him to find out that the inmate had been a plant and that he could then have raised this issue at the state level.

In *Herrera v. Collins* (1993), Lionel Torres Herrera, another death row inmate, filed a habeas corpus petition on the grounds that new evidence had come to light demonstrating that he was innocent. The Supreme Court majority declined to remand the case for further proceedings on the grounds that there were no due process errors in his conviction. The Court thus found, in effect, that actual innocence is *not* a basis for a federal habeas claim. Justice Harry Blackmun, in his dissent, stated: "Nothing could be contrary to contemporary standards of decency . . . or more shocking to the conscience . . . than to execute a person who is actually innocent."

Finally, in *Schlup v. Delo* (1995), the Supreme Court held that a claim of actual innocence "would have to fail unless the federal habeas court is itself convinced that . . . new facts unquestionably establish Schlup's innocence." In other words, preponderance of evidence (let alone reasonable doubt) would not be enough. The Rehnquist Court has argued that its rulings will not produce unacceptable results because (1) if an inmate cannot demonstrate a constitutional violation at state trial, he has received a "full and fair trial" (Rehnquist's words); (2) lower state and federal courts will vet injustices in posttrial reviews; and (3) executive clemency is available to those who demonstrate their innocence. Critics point out that proving a constitutional violation and being accorded a full and fair trial are not equivalent, that state and federal courts will not necessarily spot or act on injustices, that most governors are reluctant to commute death sentences in the current political climate, and that some innocent defendants have not been granted executive clemency.

CONCLUSION

Despite its historical and legal importance to the U.S. judicial system, these days fewer and fewer habeas corpus requests are resulting in any effect. In 1995, for example, the Bureau of Justice Statistics conducted an empirical study of habeas reviews that found that only 1% of habeas corpus appeals were granted on the merits, and another 1% remanded to the state courts for follow-through. The study's authors concluded that their data indicated that state courts are performing well in protecting prisoners' federal constitutional rights. That conclusion has merit *if* it is safe to assume that federal review is adequately responding to inmate's constitutional rights. In light of recent changes under the PATRIOT Act, where it seems that some people's due rights are no longer fully protected, it is unclear whether we can always be so sanguine about the courts' responses.

—*Dennis D. Loo*

See also Cell Searches; Death Row; Enemy Combatants; Fourth Amendment; Fourteenth Amendment; Prisoner Litigation Reform Act 1996; Relocation Centers; Thirteenth Amendment USA PATRIOT Act 2001

Further Reading

Clark, A. W. (1994). *Procedural labyrinths and the injustice of death: A critique of death penalty habeas corpus.* Dissertation, Queen's University at Kingston, MAI, 33, No. 05, 1419.

Doyle, M. (1992). *Federal habeas corpus background & issues..* Series title: Major studies and issue briefs of the Congressional Research Service. Supplement 1992, 92–615 A. 4006199277. Washington, DC: Library of Congress, Congressional Research Service.

Federman, C. H. (1996). *The primary of rights and the procedures of federalism: The development of habeas corpus and federal-state relations, 1789–1991.* Dissertation, University of Virginia, DAI, 62, no. 09a, 3170.

Freedman, E. M. (2001). *Habeas corpus: Rethinking the great writ of liberty.* New York: New York University Press.

Gottlieb, D., & Coyne, R. (2001, Winter). Habeas corpus practice in state and federal courts. *New Mexico Law Review, 31*(1), 201–217.

Liebman, J. S., Fagan, J., & West, V. (2000). *A broken system: Error rates in capital cases, 1973–1995* Washington, DC: Justice Project.

Rehnquist, W. H. (1998). *All the laws but one: Civil liberties in wartime.* New York: Knopf.

◪ HARD LABOR

Hard labor is a punishment of ancient origin and widespread adoption. In the United States, the Pennsylvania General Assembly established the first hard labor sentence in the fall of 1786 by directing "motley crews" of prisoners to clean and repair public streets. Imprisonment at hard labor then became a common sentence in the 19th century, in the United States and in many European countries. Today, several penal systems enforce hard labor, officially and unofficially. China, for example, maintains a vast system of hard labor camps under its "reform through labor" system. The central feature of Japan's prison system is compulsory hard labor production for private sector industry subcontracting. While Russia no longer has the old gulag, it still maintains the tradition of penal labor camps. At the Russian Strict Regime Colonies, labor is compulsory and hard, although those who meet production quotas are paid.

HISTORY

Hard labor has played an important role in criminal sentencing history as an alternative to corporal punishment and as a substitute for the death penalty—although, in extreme cases, it was just a sentence of slow death. In America, William Penn's Great Law of 1682 eliminated the death penalty for all cases except premeditated murder, and designated imprisonment with hard labor instead as a means of reforming offenders. This was a high point in the history of hard labor, and even in Pennsylvania the ideals of reformative work did not last long. In practice, over the course of its history, "hard labor" fell along a continuum of severity, with dignified and paid work at the soft end and, at the other pole, work that was futile and degrading, or even a form of torture and gradual death.

Hard labor first appeared as ancient slavery, the prototypical form created by the Romans as a life sentence to slaving in heavy irons at stone quarries and copper, silver, and salt mines. Likewise, penal slavery in gold mines and at monument construction was a sentence for criminals and war captives during the first century B.C. in Egypt, while the Spanish used penal slaves in their copper mines and stone quarries during the 17th and 18th centuries.

After an epoch of penance and fines during feudalism, labor exploitation reappeared in the early 16th century as an adjunct to emerging trade practices. Galley slavery was a common criminal penalty in 16th-century France, and during the 17th and 18th centuries in Spain and the papal states. Spanish American labor systems exploited penal labor in private industry in the 17th century and mandated slave labor in presidios during the next century. By the mid-18th century in Great Britain and on the Continent, hard labor imprisonment was widely used as a substitute for flogging.

Productive work was abandoned in England in the early 19th century, as soon as labor shortages turned into surpluses. Thereafter, hard labor took unproductive and torturous forms such as busting rock, cranking sand, and stepping the "everlasting staircases"—punishments intended to inflict a "just measure of pain" in minutely measured doses.

The labor of prisoners could be used profitably elsewhere, however. Transportation to America and Australia became a major strategy to relieve prison overcrowding at home while developing the labor-starved colonies. A cogent reinterpretation of Australian convict rule by Stephen Nicholas (1989) demonstrates how ordinary British and Irish men and women convicts were part of a global system of forced labor migration into a highly efficient and productive capitalist labor system. And, although their labor was truly hard, Australian convicts experienced incentives and rewards just like free workers. In a twist on the "less eligibility principle," which states that prison conditions must never be more desirable than the living conditions of the lowest paid free worker, prisoners put in fewer hours of hard labor than did free British worker counterparts.

HARD LABOR IN THE UNITED STATES

In one of the most nuanced examinations of hard labor in American penology, Christopher Adamson (1983, 1984) developed a socioeconomic interpretation of hard labor in America, connecting industrial and financial considerations with crime control objectives, especially the reinforcement of legal norms, reformation of the criminal through hard work, and deterrence. While these legal objectives were important in shaping penology, business cycles and the vicissitudes of labor supply helped determine the variable meanings of hard labor and solitary confinement through the first half century of the penitentiary experiment.

Effective deterrence must address the relative living conditions (as determined by the labor market) of free persons, Georg Rusche and Otto Kirchheimer (2003, p. 6) hypothesized. Thus, Adamson's research shows that during cycles of prosperity, prisoners were viewed as resources and hard labor regimes of productive activity prevailed in the United States. On the other hand, during recessions and depressions, prisoners were viewed as threats and placed in solitary confinement without labor or made to perform futile labor on treadwheels, as abject examples to would-be thieves. Thus, after 1800

shortages of skilled labor and European restrictions on emigration led to the widespread adoption of productive and profit-oriented prison manufacturing systems, such as shoemaking, ironworking, carpentry, and weaving. In the aftermath of the War of 1812, America experience a deep business recession, with high levels of unemployment and growing imports of cheap manufactured goods. According to Adamson, hard labor lost is financial value and it ability to meet criminal justice objectives. Prison sentences increased dramatically after 1815 to absorb the growing surplus population, and the severity of penalties increased. With the return to prosperity in the period 1825 to 1840, hard labor was redefined as productive economic activity and the Auburn system of congregate manufacturing reached its apogee.

In addition to the variable meanings of "hard" and whether "labor" was productive or unproductive, prison industry alternated between periods of private control with production for the open market and public administration for state consumption. The most extensive and vicious system of forced penal labor for private profit occurred in the postbellum U.S. South, where labor-starved states of the former Confederacy adopted the convict lease system to extract private profit in a system of penal slavery on cotton plantations, railroads, rice fields, turpentine farms, and coal mines. The 13th Amendment to the U.S. Constitution, which abolished slavery, exempted involuntary servitude of "duly convicted" criminals. The Southern ruling class would probably have preferred free workers, but the freedmen vigorously resisted wage slavery. Forced to labor from dawn to dusk, held in rolling circus cages when not working, provided with grossly inadequate medical care, the average life expectancy of convicts on the lease was five to seven years.

COMPARATIVE EXAMPLES AND CONTEMPORARY PRACTICES

Other notorious forced-labor regimes of the modern era include the Soviet gulags of the Stalin period and South Africa's penal system, akin to the convict lease, that forced blacks into agriculture and mining from the 1880s until the end of the apartheid regime in 1994. Forced labor for reformative and economic purposes has existed in Chinese history since the 17th century. Mao Tse-tung's Communist revolutionary "reform through labor," or *laogai*, and *laojiao*, or "reeducation through labor," systems have sent millions to agricultural labor camps to be "reeducated." Since the late 19th century, Japan has operated a system of prison industrial subcontracting that constitutes hard labor in the extremely exacting regimentation required by its prisoner-workers. Hard labor in U.S. states and Western countries today is rare, with Texas and Mexico as prominent exceptions. In the northern states, Mexico has begun supplementing its laissez-faire petty entrepreneurial prisoner economy with *maquiladora* sweatshop factories. Texas maintains vast state plantations where convicts harvest cotton by hand without monetary compensation. In most of the former Soviet bloc countries, hard labor regimes have been replaced with a corrosive and debilitating idleness, with Poland as a prime example. China, however, still imprisons more than a million on farms and in factories that are said to manufacture for export.

CONCLUSION

Hard labor has existed as a form of punishment for centuries. In some places and eras, it has been used in conjunction with a sentence of imprisonment, while elsewhere and at other times, it has been a punishment in its own right. These days hard labor in Western industrialized states is rare, possibly because of the competition it would pose to other workers. Even so, methods such as the chain gang, which has been introduced in numerous U.S. states, as well as the plantations in Texas and elsewhere in the South, indicate that hard labor remains part of penal policy in America. The question remains, however, is it an effective means of punishment or control? Or does it simply provide a source of income for the state?

—*Robert P. Weiss*

See also Auburn System; Australia; Jeremy Bentham; Chain Gang; Corporal Punishment; Flogging; Labor; Alexander Maconochie; Privatization of Labor; Slavery; Thirteenth Amendment

Further Reading

Adamson, C. (1983). Punishment after slavery: Southern state penal systems, 1865–1890. *Social Problems, 5,* 555–569.

Christie, N. (1994). *Crime control as industry: Towards GULAGS, Western style.* London: Routledge.

Dutton, M., & Zhangrun, X. (1998). Facing difference: Relations, change and the prison sector in contemporary China. In R. P. Weiss & N. South (Eds.), *Comparing prison systems: Toward a comparative and international penology* (pp. 289–336). Amsterdam: Gordon and Breach.

Nicholas, S. (Ed.). (1989). *Convict workers: Reinterpreting Australia's past.* Cambridge, UK: Cambridge University Press.

Rusche, G., & Kirchheimer, O. (2003). *Punishment and social structure.* New Brunswick, NJ: Transaction.

Sellin, T. (1965, October). Penal servitude: Origin and survival. *Proceedings of the American Philosophical Society, 109*(5), 277–281.

Sellin, J. T. (1976). *Slavery and the penal system.* New York: Elsevier.

Solzhenitsyn, A. I. (1974). *The Gulag archipelago: 1918–1956.* New York: Harper & Row.

◪ HARRIS, MARY BELLE
(1874–1957)

Mary Belle Harris was renowned for her work as the head of several women's prisons in the first part of the 20th century. Throughout her career, she maintained that women's institutions must assist inmates to become self-sufficient through work training and education in a supportive, nonpunitive environment. As with other penal reformers of the period. Harris believed that most women's crimes were caused by their dependence on men—economically and psychologically—and thus only in institutions run by women for women, could offenders achieve the skills and strengths necessary for independence. Harris's work and ideas culminated in the development, design, and management of the first federal women's prison at Alderson, West Virginia, from 1925 to 1941.

BEGINNINGS: EDUCATION AND TEACHING IN THE CLASSICS

Mary Belle Harris, born August 19, 1874, was the oldest child of three, and the only daughter, of John Howard and Mary Elizabeth (Mace) Harris. Her mother died in 1880, and her father married Lucy Bailey, a cousin of Mary Mace, who became her beloved stepmother. John Howard Harris was a Baptist minister and president of Bucknell University (1889–1919), where Mary Belle Harris earned a music degree (1893), an A.B. (1894), and an M.A. in Latin and classics (1896). Thereafter, she went to the University of Chicago, receiving a Ph.D. in Sanskrit and Indo-European philology (1900). It was at Chicago that she became friends with Katharine Bement Davis, a woman who was to have a pivotal role in Harris's later career in corrections.

Between 1900 and 1914, Harris taught Latin (one appointment was at the Bryn Mawr School in Baltimore, Maryland, led by Edith Hamilton), studied numismatics at Johns Hopkins University, and traveled to Europe as a teacher-chaperone, working at the American Classical School in Rome. During this time, she also studied numismatics at the Kaiser Friedrich Museum in Berlin. She returned to the United States in 1914.

PRISON REFORM AND ADMINISTRATION

Harris arrived in New York City when Katharine Bement Davis was commissioner of corrections. Davis offered Harris the newly created position of superintendent of women and deputy warden of the Workhouse at Blackwell Island, which she accepted. Thus, on July 1, 1914, at age 40, Mary Belle Harris began the work for which she had not trained, yet would bring her national renown.

In 1914, the workhouse held around 700 women convicted of prostitution, alcoholism, and drugs, who were serving sentences from three days to six months. Harris instituted changes that enabled the women to leave their cells, get some exercise, and do activities that relieved the boredom and petty infractions. Harris opened a library and allowed women to play cards and knit. She fenced off part of the yard so they could exercise. She also renovated the dining room and opened a lounge for staff. Harris's approach at Blackwell Island was to be her trademark: common sense changes that fit women's needs, even when it meant altering the accepted ways or challenging the bureaucracy.

After leaving the workhouse in 1917, Harris became superintendent at the State Reformatory for Women in Clinton, New Jersey, for two years. Over the same period, while on leave from Clinton, she was assistant director of the Section on Reformatories and Detention Houses for the (U.S.) War Department's Commission on Training Camp Activities under Martha P. Falconer. From 1919 to 1924, she was the superintendent of the State Home for Girls (juveniles) in Trenton, New Jersey, In March 1925, Mary Belle Harris embarked on her final and most public leadership role in women's corrections: heading the new federal prison for women in Alderson, West Virginia.

ALDERSON: "A SOCIETY OF WOMEN WORKING TOGETHER UNDER THE GUIDANCE OF OTHER WOMEN"

The Federal Industrial Institution for Women was established by the U.S. Congress in June 1924, and the site of Alderson, West Virginia, was selected in January 1925. Upon the recommendation of Assistant Attorney General Mabel Walker Willebrandt, Harris was appointed superintendent before the construction began. Supported by Willebrandt, Harris played a unique role in working with architects and engineers to ensure that the design and construction conformed to her view, and that of other reformers, of the best environment for rehabilitating women offenders.

The first 15 prisoners—"the early settlers"—arrived at Alderson on April 30, 1927, even though the institution was officially opened on November 24, 1928. The institution earned accolades throughout the United States, and occasionally beyond, largely as a result of Harris's design ideas and regime. As one member of Congress asked during appropriation hearings: "Alderson: That is a

Ladies' Seminary?"[1] Harris instituted physical fitness (baseball games), farming, an inmate self-governing system, and educational and vocational training. She also held county fairs, nature hikes, individualized classification—without any serious disciplinary problems and with few escapes. In keeping with the values of the times, all of these activities were racially segregated.

Despite her successes, Harris's independence to do as she wished in the institution became increasingly challenged once the Federal Bureau of Prisons was established in May 1930. For the next 11 years, until her retirement in 1941, Mary Belle Harris used the Alderson Advisory Board, women's networks, relationships with important personages such as Eleanor Roosevelt, and the press to battle for the ideas she and others had fought for in distinguishing the treatment of women from that of men. Harris and Sanford Bates, the first bureau director, argued about staff selection, a variety of inmate management issues, management of the institution including the physical plant, and most intensively the battle over the role of prison industries and education. In the latter situation, the bureau wanted to increase the output and limit Alderson's ability to limit the amount of time women spent at the sewing machines so these inmates could go to class.

CONCLUSION

After reluctantly retiring from Alderson at the age of 66 in March 1941, Harris returned to Pennsylvania and served on the state's parole board until it was abolished in 1943. She moved to Lewisburg, home of Bucknell University and the First Baptist Church, serving as a trustee of each. In 1953, she traveled throughout Europe and Northern Africa returning to Lewisburg in July 1954. Mary Belle Harris died on February 22, 1957, at the age of 82.

NOTE

1. Rep. Kop asked this of the superintendent of prisons, Captain O'Connor, during the 1929 appropriations hearings.

—*Claudine SchWeber*

See also Alderson, Federal Prison Camp; Sanford Bates; Cottage System; Katharine Bement Davis; Federal Prison System; History of Women's Prisons; Mabel Walker Willebradnt; Women Prisoners; Women's Prisons

Further Reading

Garrett, P. W., & MacCormack, A. H. (Eds.). (1929). *Handbook of American prisons and reformatories.* New York: National Society of Penal Information.

Harris, M. B. (1936). *I knew them in prison.* New York: Viking.

Lekkerker, E. C. (1931). *Reformatories for women in the United States.* The Hague, Netherlands: J. B. Wolters.

Strickland, K. G. (1968). *Correctional institutions for women in the United States.* Ph.D. dissertation, Syracuse University, New York.

Torrey, W. (1928, September 16). Women at Alderson prepare for useful careers. *Washington Star, 7,* 1.

U.S. House of Representatives. (1929, January 7–15). *Hearings before the Special Committee on Federal Penal and Reformatory Institutions.* 70th Congress, 2nd Session.

◪ HAWES–COOPER ACT 1929

The Hawes-Cooper Act (H.R. 7729) was passed on January 19, 1929, and mandated that prison-made goods and merchandise transported from one state to another were to be subject to the existing laws of the importing state. The act took effect five years after passage and was repealed in 1978.

HISTORY

Work by inmates in the earliest American penitentiaries was initially justified by the idea that hard labor was reformative in nature. Whether by individual labor in a solitary cell (as in Philadelphia's Eastern State Penitentiary) or through congregate labor in enforced silence (as in the Auburn system), work was thought to be integral to the reformation of the criminal. Gradually, as a result of increased public and government attention to the costs of prison operations, many institutions began to examine ways whereby a prison could also achieve some degree of self-sufficiency.

During this time, many states begin to use prison labor in various ways. The "contract system," where inmates worked within the prison manufacturing goods and merchandise for private concerns, was a popular way of making prisoners work. Under this system, the manufacturer supplied the raw materials and prison officials supervised the inmates. Because the private manufacturer purchased the goods at an agreed on price, this was also called the "piece-price system." Also common, particularly in the South was the "lease system," which began in Kentucky in 1825. In this system, prisoners were rented to contractors to work often outside the prison itself. They were generally poorly paid (if at all) and worked in unsafe and often squalid conditions.

Over time, it became increasingly clear that much of the free market labor could not compete with the lower cost of (and lower-priced) products manufactured in or outside of prison by forced inmate labor. By the late 1800s, prison reformers, who opposed the exploitation of inmates who were forced to work, and labor unions, fearing unfair competition, increased their opposition to prison labor and prison-made goods. In response, several states enacted new laws between the 1880s and 1920s to restrict or outright prohibit the sale of goods and merchandise made by inmates within their states. In 1887, for example, the New York Legislature, with the Yates Law, abolished all prison labor contracts and manufacturing, limiting prison industries to handicrafts that could only be sold within the state. New Jersey, Ohio, and Illinois eliminated these contracts as well and beginning in 1893, Pennsylvania passed a number of restrictive laws and by 1897, prison industry ceased to exist at all in that state.

With the increased use of the automobile by the average American and the necessity for more public access, road construction and maintenance provided other opportunities for inmate labor. Known as chain gangs in the South, prisoners were employed to build bridges, clear land, and repair buildings as well. By 1923, only Rhode Island prohibited inmates (primarily from the county jails) from working on public highways. The use of chain gangs diminished when soldiers returned from World War II and these jobs reverted to the public sector.

Prison labor became particularly controversial during the Depression, as prison populations increased dramatically and organized labor reasserted its influence in the American workplace, arguing that prison labor and prison-made goods held an unfair competitive advantage. While prison officials and others opposed any new restrictions on prisoner labor, nevertheless many states adopted legislation that severely curtailed the ability of prisons to effectively employ the huge labor pool of incarcerated offenders. Congress followed suit and, in 1929, passed the Hawes-Cooper Act, the first of what would be several federal laws regulating or restricting the production and sale of prison-made goods.

THE ACT

The act reads (in part): ". . . That all goods, wares, and merchandise manufactured, produced, or mined, wholly or in part, by convicts or prisoners, except convicts or prisoners on parole or probation, or in any penal and/or reformatory institutions, except commodities manufactured in Federal penal and correctional institutions for use by the Federal Government, transported to any State or Territory of the United States and remaining therein for use, consumption, sale or storage, shall . . . be subject to the operation and effect of the laws of such State or Territory . . . and shall not be exempt otherwise by reason of being introduced in the original package or otherwise."

There were several other laws in this area passed by Congress placing restrictions on interstate commerce that made it increasingly more difficult to employ inmates in productive labor. For example, the Ashurst-Sumners Act, passed in 1935, made the shipping of prison-made goods to a state that prohibited the receipt, possession, sale, or use of such goods a violation of federal law. Although this strengthened the restrictions outlined in Hawes-Cooper, opponents were not satisfied because the prior act still relied on the states to ban such commerce. Five years later in 1940, the Sumners-Ashurst Act made it a federal crime to transport prison-made goods in interstate commerce for private use, regardless of whether the states involved had laws restricting it. Ultimately, 30 states also passed legislation restricting the sale of prison-made goods.

In addition to the restrictions placed on the shipment of goods made by state inmates, Congress addressed federal purchases and contracts with the Walsh-Healy Act in 1936. This basically banned prison labor on federal procurement contracts where the amount of the contract exceeds $10,000. During World War II, however, these prohibitions of inmate labor were temporarily suspended as prison industries produced much needed war materials. Some prisons became somewhat self-supporting and some even made profits, but after the war the restrictions were again imposed. This continued until the 1970s, when a general disillusionment regarding the purpose and effectiveness of prisons emerged and prison industry was once again identified as a mechanism to address these concerns.

THE ACT IS REPEALED

The Hawes-Cooper Act was repealed in 1978, and in 1979 Congress further relaxed restrictions on prison labor with the passage of the Justice System Improvement Act (or Percy Amendment). This permitted waivers of the Sumners-Ashurst and Walsh-Healy restrictions provided that (1) prisoners are paid the prevailing wage (sometimes union scale), (2) local labor unions are consulted and their approval given, (3) local nonprisoner labor is not affected, (4) participating prisoners must do so voluntarily, and (5) goods produced are in an industry where there is no local unemployment. The Justice System Improvement Act also created the Private Sector/Prison Industry Enhancement Certification Program (known as the PIE program), which began the process of allowing private companies to employ prison labor in many areas. The Comprehensive Crime Control Act of 1984 contained provisions that also encouraged the expansion of prison industries, and by 1985 the federal government and about half of the states had some private sector ventures.

By the end of 1994, the PIE program had 74 companies (e.g., J.C. Penney, Honda, Eddie Bauer) employing more than 1,600 inmates manufacturing a variety of goods, from bird feeders to circuit boards. Others were employed in service industries (e.g., Best Western Hotels and TWA) including data

processing, airline reservations, and telemarketing. Of the $46 million in gross wages paid since 1979, inmate laborers have retained 56%, with the remainder going to room and board (19%), taxes (12%), victim restitution (6.6%), and family support (6.4%).

CONCLUSION: CURRENT INMATE LABOR

There are currently four basic program models of inmate-involved labor in use:

1. *Employer model.* Private company owns and operates a business that uses inmate labor to produce goods or services; business has control of hiring, firing, and supervision of the inmate labor force (e.g., telemarketing firms that train and employ inmates to do telephone surveys).

2. *Investor model.* The private sector capitalizes or funds a business to be operated by the state correctional agency; aside from the financing, the business will play no other role.

3. *Customer model.* Outside company purchases a significant percentage of the output of a state-owned and -operated business, which is located within the prison.

4. *Manager model.* Private sector manages a business owned by the correctional agency; the company does not supply any material or funding, nor does it purchase any of the products. This is a personnel-supplying system, which provides managers, supervisors, and technicians.

Critics of these and similar programs are quick to point out that this results in a prisoner being paid much less than the "prevailing wage" as mandated by the program. There is also the problem that many of these industries develop skills that are not transferable to the private sector upon the inmate's release. A number of supporters and prison reformers, however, are convinced that such programs are invaluable in teaching prisoners marketable skills, even though many prison industries involve labor-intensive, low-skill work, and that there is some rehabilitative success. An often-cited 1991 study of the U.S. Bureau of Prisons found that only 6.6% of federal inmates employed in prison industries reoffended or violated parole compared with 20% for nonemployed prisoners. Whatever the perspective, it remains the case that more prisoners are idle than employed in prison industry, and the question of prison labor continues to divide the free and incarcerated worlds alike.

—*Charles B. Fields*

See also Ashurst-Sumners Act 1935; Chain Gangs; Convict Lease System; Federal Prison System; Hard Labor; History of Prisons; Labor; Prison Industry Enhancement (PIE) Certification Program; Privatization; Privatization of Labor; UNICOR

Further Reading

Lichtenstein, A. (1996). *Twice the work of free labor: The political economy of convict labor in the new South.* New York: Verso.

Schaller, J (1982). Work and imprisonment: An overview of the changing role of prison labor in American prisons. *The Prison Journal, 62*(2), 3–12.

U.S. Department of Justice, Law Enforcement Assistance Administration. (1977). *Study of the economic and rehabilitative aspects of prison industry.* Princeton, NJ: ECON.

◪ HAWK SAWYER, KATHLEEN

Kathleen Hawk Sawyer was appointed director of the Federal Bureau of Prisons by Attorney General William Barr (1991–1993) on December 4, 1992. The attorney general of the United States, as head of the Department of Justice, is the chief law enforcement officer of the federal government and represents the United States in legal matters generally. The office of the attorney general has responsibility for the Bureau of Prisons. The attorney general recommends a director of the Bureau of Prisons to the U.S. president, and upon approval by the president, Congress confirms the choice.

A career public administrator in the Department of Justice for the Federal Bureau of Prisons, Kathleen Hawk Sawyer was the bureau's sixth director since 1930. She has a doctorate of education in counseling and rehabilitation from West Virginia University. Preceding her career with the Bureau of Prisons, Hawk Sawyer was employed at the Sargus Juvenile Facility in St. Clairsville, Ohio, where she established a psychological counseling program for pre- and postadjudicated youths and their families.

FEDERAL BUREAU OF PRISONS TENURE

Hawk Sawyer began her career with the Federal Bureau of Prisons in 1976 when she became a psychologist at the Federal Correctional Institution (FCI) in Morgantown, West Virginia, which housed approximately 400 male juvenile offenders. In 1983, she was designated chief of psychology services. During that year, she also served as a senior instructor for the Bureau of Prison's Staff Training Academy in Glynco, Georgia, as a training instructor in vocational and occupational training programs.

In 1985, Hawk Sawyer became associate warden for programs at the FCI-Fort Worth, Texas. This facility was a co-correctional institution that housed 1,000 inmates. In 1986, the bureau appointed Hawk Sawyer as chief of staff training for three training centers: Glynco, Georgia; Aurora, Colorado; and Fort Worth, Texas. In 1987, she became warden at the FCI-Butner, North Carolina, which housed 800 male offenders.

Hawk Sawyer became the assistant director for the Program Review Division at the Central Office, Washington, D.C., in May 1989, which led to her appointment as director in 1992. In 1997, President Bill Clinton awarded her with the Distinguished Executive Award, the highest award offered to professionals in the Senior Executive Service.

CAREER GOALS

As director, Hawk Sawyer sought to reduce the recidivism rate by offering more work and education opportunities to federal prisoners. In her decisions, she was influenced by the Post Release Employment Project, a long-term evaluation of the impact of prison industrial work that found former prisoners who had worked in prison industries were 35% less likely to recidivate one year after release than comparison group members who had not. The report also found that prisoners who had worked in prison industries were more likely to be employed during the first year after release and earned higher wages during the first year of release than others who had not had the same opportunities. In response to the study, Hawk Sawyer increased the number of inmates working for UNICOR (Federal Prison Industries) from approximately 16,000 inmates at the end of 1992 to 22,000 inmates mid-2003. She also focused on modernizing the educational opportunities offered to inmates by offering secondary education at every institution.

Hawk Sawyer also brought in a number of residential substance abuse treatment programs while director. Reflecting in part her background in psychology, these programs, which were available at 47 facilities in 2001, use a cognitive restructuring approach. They also incorporate a pro-social values program that focuses on inmates' emotional and behavioral responses to difficult situations and emphasizes life skills for respect of self and others. All federal prisons offer drug education programs.

CONCLUSION

During her distinguished career and as the first female director of the Bureau of Prisons, Kathleen Hawk Sawyer initiated major changes in the field of corrections, particularly in the fields of work, education, and treatment. She retired from the Bureau of Prisons as director in April 2003 and was replaced by Harley Lappin, the mid-Atlantic regional director for the bureau.

—*Barbara Hanbury and John D. Brown*

See also Sanford Bates; James V. Bennett; Drug Treatment Programs; Federal Prison System; Mary Belle Harris; Psychological Services; Mabel Walker Willebrandt

Further Reading

Anonymous. (1999). Federal prison official testifies before Congress. *Corrections Digest, 30*, 2–3.

Bureau of Prisons. (2001, July). Kathleen M. Hawk, director of the Federal Bureau of Prisons. Retrieved from www.bop.gov

Bureau of Prisons. (2004). *Federal Bureau of Prisons quick facts.* Retrieved from http://www.bop.gov/fact0598.html

Munley-Norris, T. (2001). Commission salutes corrections' finest (Commission on Accreditation for Corrections). *Corrections Today, 63*, 29.

Sabol, W. J., et al. (2000), *Offenders returning to federal prison, 1986–97* (Bureau of Justice Statistics special report). Washington, DC: U.S. Department of Justice, Bureau of Justice Statistics.

☑ HEALTH CARE

Methods for diagnosing and treating illness are the same, whether the patient lives behind bars or in free society. No convincing legal or ethical argument can be made, on the basis of arrest, conviction, or sentence, to justify denying prisoners a level of health care that is equivalent to the community standard.

Though the principles and criteria governing medical practice for incarcerated persons are identical to community standards, the correctional context introduces important differences. Concern for safety and security is preeminent. Consequently, there may be compromises in privacy and confidentiality. Health care service delivery in correctional facilities is less efficient, given the need to secure all sharp items and medications from possible misuse. Movement and transport are necessarily controlled and restricted, resulting in downtime for health professionals between patients. Patients also have less freedom to choose among providers, though they remain autonomous and free to accept or reject treatment.

Caring for sick prisoners is challenging. Penal institutions were never designed for the purpose of providing health care. Their environment, regimentation, physical plant, and lifestyle are anything but therapeutic. Nevertheless, prisoners do become ill—sometimes quite seriously.

COURT-ORDERED REFORMS

Prior to the mid-1970s, prisons were virtually closed to public scrutiny, and convicts were accorded few rights. Most health care services were provided by other inmates—usually without formal training and with only rudimentary medications and equipment. Professional health care providers were few. Many of these had licensing, competence, or sobriety problems and could not find gainful employment elsewhere. As a result, abuses abounded. Sometimes medical care was denied as a form of punishment or because of the whim of an officer.

Few gave credence to prisoners' complaints. Judges ruled it was not the business of courts to meddle in the internal affairs of prisons and left these matters to the discretion of correctional managers. This state of affairs continued until the 1960s and 1970s, when white, middle-class, affluent, educated, and socially well-connected people were incarcerated for civil disobedience or other activities in civil rights and antiwar demonstrations. These activists generally had greater credibility than the typical inmate, whose only contact with a lawyer may have been with a public defender. Amid voters' rights rallies and Vietnam War protests, legal defense societies were quickly mounted to provide competent defense and advocacy.

Soon class action suits were filed, grouping similarly situated inmates together as plaintiffs seeking redress. Most were filed in federal courts and sought relief under 42 U.S.C. § 1983 of the Civil Rights Act from conditions of cruel and unusual punishment prohibited by the Eighth Amendment. In 1976, the U.S. Supreme Court in *Ruiz v. Estelle* ruled that "deliberate indifference to serious medical needs of prisoners constitutes the 'unnecessary and wanton infliction of pain' proscribed by the Eighth Amendment."

Following *Ruiz v. Estelle,* an avalanche of litigation ensued. Some suits were successful. Many resulted in court-ordered consent agreements and required defendants to implement sweeping changes under the watchful eye of court-appointed monitors. Besides medical and mental health care, reforms addressed overcrowding, brutality, nutrition, and access to courts. The most fundamental health arena changes required access to professional medical evaluation and prohibited interference with ordered medical treatment.

These improvements were costly, and some court-ordered reforms may have been excessive. In 1996, the Prisoner Litigation Reform Act swung the pendulum the other way, rendering access to courts much more difficult for inmate plaintiffs. These days, therefore, it is difficult for inmates to address health care problems through the court process. Instead, they must try to deal with any complaints they have at the institution where they are confined.

MEDICAL STANDARDS AND ACCREDITATION

Following public outcry over prison conditions, the American Medical Association formulated jail and prison health care standards in the late 1970s. These were subsequently adopted by the National Commission on Correctional Health Care. The American Correctional Association's facility-wide standards for various types of correctional institutions also addressed health care issues. Promulgation of standards was accompanied by development of accreditation mechanisms to assess voluntary compliance.

Correctional health care professionals credit the dual influence of court involvement and the standards and accreditation process for improving access to quality medical care for the incarcerated. Prison and jail clinics are generally staffed with an adequate number of competent health professionals; inmates no longer provide health care; treatment is documented in accordance with contemporary standards; many sites have viable quality improvement programs. The quality of health care typically available to prisoners today approximates that required by the standards and follows contemporary community practice. Glaring abuses and deficiencies are largely past.

The National Commission on Correctional Health Care endeavors to upgrade the quality of jail and prison clinical staff by encouraging them to become Certified Correctional Health Professionals and to join the Academy of Correctional Health Professionals. The American Correctional Health Services Association also sponsors programs to facilitate networking among correctional health care providers and raise their knowledge and professional awareness. Prisons and jails once were the refuge of questionably competent medical providers. Today, no stigma is attached to work as a prison doctor or nurse. Good—even outstanding—professionals are being recruited to this work.

RISING COSTS OF CARE

Partly because they are sicker, partly because they have little opportunity for self-care, and partly

Health Care

I have been incarcerated for close to five years now and have been in four different institutions. I was in a serious motorcycle accident when I was sixteen. I broke my left leg in three places, shattered my left ankle, suffered many internal injuries, and injured my back, which caused complete paralysis from the knee down on my left leg. I have had several operations because of these injuries. Since I have been in the federal prison system I have had to beg and plead with the medical staff to get even basic needs met.

I started my time at Carswell's Federal Medical Center in Ft. Worth, TX. I had three surgeries there, two on my back and one on my left leg and ankle. My back surgery was successful. The surgery, which was a fusion of my left leg and ankle, was a whole different story. The orthopedic surgeon that performed the surgeries set my cast crooked after the surgery.

Later, when I was transferred to FCI Dublin, still in my cast, the cast was removed. I was horrified because my foot was permanently crooked, turning inward. It looked deformed and remains that way today. I was devastated, as I still am. Before surgery I wore a leg brace (from the knee down), but my foot was straight. If I wore pants you could not even tell that anything was wrong with me. Now even with pants on it is quite evident that my leg is crippled. I am very self-conscious about it, but at this point there is nothing that can be done. I will try to get it corrected when I get out. I asked medical in Dublin if they could fix it. The head of medical there, told me that I would have to go back to Carswell for a procedure like that because they could not provide the aftercare necessary. Plus they did not want the liability. Needless to say, I decided not to go back to Carswell.

I do have to give credit, where credit is due. The physical therapy department in Carswell was real good, and I had a very caring and competent physical therapist. They also made sure I got my medications, my leg brace, and special shoes.

After FCI Dublin I went to Phoenix Prison Camp, and now I am currently at the Victorville Prison Camp in California. For the most part, with all the prisons I have been in it has been the same old story. There is no order and they are incompetent, with Phoenix and Victorville being the worst. I have been going to doctors for years before my incarceration, and I have never seen nothing like this. You rarely ever if at all, see a doctor. It is usually a physician's assistant or a nurse who cares for our medical needs; anything from a headache to terminal cancer, and it is usually the same treatment—Ibuprofen. I never once saw a doctor the whole time I was in Phoenix, which was over one year. I did write them up for negligence to their regional director, and I did win.

I have been in Victorville for three weeks now and have not yet seen a doctor. It is a task just to get your prescriptions filled here. When I asked the physician's assistant what the problem was, she told me that they were just overwhelmed with work because there are so many inmates. And that, I believe, is exactly it. They are all short staffed and don't have the time to spend on our individual medical needs. I am sure our medical care would improve considerably if there was enough medical staff for the inmate population. But until that happens, we will go without.

The Bureau of Prisons's sole function is not to simply warehouse inmates, but while in their custody, we have the right to receive health care in a manner that recognizes our basic human rights. Our eighth amendment right states that we are not to be subjected to cruel and unusual punishment. To be left sick or in pain is cruel and unusual punishment.

Tara Frechea
Federal Prison Camp Victorville, Adelanto, California

because confinement and idleness promote excessive focus on their bodies, prisoners tend to require more, rather than less, health care. The causes of their illnesses often predate their incarceration and include unhealthy lifestyles, trauma and injury, malnutrition, heavy use of drugs and alcohol, and generally poor access to the health care delivery system.

Following the huge increase in the number of incarcerated in the United States, the cost burden of health care services in corrections has reached staggering proportions. Medical costs are 9% to 12% of the total cost of corrections. In addition to the sheer number of inmates who need medical treatment, several other factors contribute to this high cost: (1) the growing number of elderly prisoners, (2) technological and qualitative improvements (e.g., new, costly medications and procedures), (3) focus of attention by courts and media, (4) communicable diseases such as AIDS and hepatitis C that are difficult and costly to treat, and (5) ravages of substance abuse. Each of these factors requires increased staffing, pharmaceuticals, hospitalization, and liability insurance.

To cope with and attempt to reduce these costs, some correctional jurisdictions turn to privatization to divest themselves of the direct burden of managing and supervising health care programs and of the responsibility for controlling costs. This strategy has had mixed results. For smaller facilities, where acquisition of in-house expertise is often difficult, private companies bring the benefit of patterned approaches to policies and methods. Some large state systems also have gone this route, though they might do as well and at lower cost by employing competent managers and providers. On this point there are differing opinions.

KEY PROGRAMS

Correctional health care provides a number of key programs throughout a person's sentence. The most important of these are described below.

Intake Screening

Correctional facilities perform a brief health screening of each inmate immediately upon arrival to determine whether an emergent or serious health problem exists, whether there is significant risk of suicide or of alcohol withdrawal, and if medications are required. These needs should be attended to within the first few hours of arrival. Within the first 7 to 14 days, inmates undergo physical health assessment and mental evaluation to provide baseline information for their medical records.

Suicide Prevention

Health care providers and correctional staff should be trained in suicide prevention. Research indicates that individuals are most likely to try to take their own lives in the first hours of detention. Self-harm and suicide attempts can take place, however, at any time. Those determined to be at elevated risk for suicide require close supervision and, when clinically indicated, may have their property or clothing restricted. In rare instances, and despite literature criticizing this practice, brief use of restraints may

occur. However, it often suffices to keep patients under observation in a setting where social interaction with others can occur, such as a day room, rather than secluding them in a cell. Isolation tends to exacerbate the loneliness, sadness, and depression already being felt.

Medication

Ensuring that outpatients receive their medications in the doses and at the times prescribed is one of the most important tasks of prison health care personnel. This is also often one of the most difficult jobs to do. Rules vary as to whether inmates are allowed to keep medications in their own possession. Prisons tend to be more lenient on this practice than jails because the inmates are better known to staff. National standards insist that medications be dispensed and administered in full compliance with state and federal pharmacy regulations.

Sick Call

"Sick call" refers to the scheduled opportunity for prisoners to see a health provider face to face. Patients generally initiate nonemergency requests by writing a note for review by a nurse, who subsequently schedules an appointment with an appropriate provider (nurse, physician, dentist, psychologist). All sick call encounters are documented in the medical record.

Segregation Rounds

The health and well-being of persons housed in segregated settings, apart from the general inmate population, pose special concerns. Standards require thrice weekly to daily visits from health care staff to ensure that health problems do not go undetected.

Emergency Response

Every correctional facility has a response plan or strategy for emergencies. If health care staff, typically nurses, are on site when a medical emergency occurs, they are summoned to the scene. However, officers are trained in First Aid and cardiopulmonary resuscitation to serve as first responders until the nurse arrives. Serious illness or injury usually results in a call to the local ambulance and paramedic service, and the patient is taken to a hospital emergency room, accompanied by a correctional officer.

Many correctional facilities now include an automated external defibrillator in their emergency response kits and ensure that nursing staff and officers are trained in its use. This precaution enables fast response to cardiac victims among inmates, staff, or visitors.

Chronic Disease Management

When the number of patients with chronic illness is sufficiently large, it becomes efficient to schedule weekly or monthly chronic disease clinics apart from the times acute and new patients are seen. The appropriate provider calls chronic patients to the clinic for routine testing and follow-up according to the treatment plan. Especially in systems with multiple providers, use of approved chronic disease guidelines can help ensure consistency in treatment and avoid substandard care.

Contagious Disease Control

Close living quarters present elevated risk for spread of contagious illness. Consequently, correctional authorities must take systematic precautions to minimize transmission of infectious disease. AIDS, hepatitis B, hepatitis C, and tuberculosis are major concerns. These diseases abound among prisoners because of previous lifestyles, including needle sharing and substance abuse.

Mental Health Services

Since the 1970s, state mental hospitals have systematically deinstitutionalized (discharged) their patients to receive care in the community. Many of these women and men have been reinstitutionalized into prisons and jails. Such people generally cope poorly under the conditions that prevail in general prison populations. Many require a special intermediate-level mental health unit where antitherapeutic stimuli are minimized.

Dental Care

Prisoners are entitled to basic dental care. Such treatment usually provides them with fillings and routine endodontic and periodontal services. Gold crowns and extraordinary prosthetic or restorative measures are usually not allowed.

Detoxification and Withdrawal

Jails, especially, must identify new arrivals at risk of serious consequences of overdose or withdrawal from alcohol or drugs. Each new inmate is questioned about recent use of intoxicants and whether difficulty was previously experienced when discontinuing these substances. Mild to moderate symptoms can often be managed in the correctional facility, but severe symptoms of withdrawal nearly always require prompt admission to a hospital.

Off-Site Care

While smaller facilities refer all complex and specialty care to off-site providers, large correctional systems find it cost effective to schedule certain specialty clinics on site. Some even provide minor surgeries, dialysis, and inpatient care within the walls. When a prisoner requires medical care beyond the level available in the facility, services are arranged with a community provider or medical specialist. If necessary, the prisoner is admitted to a local hospital. Unless the hospital has a secure unit staffed by a cadre of officers, a correctional officer is assigned to remain by each prisoner's bedside to prevent escape or harm to other persons.

Pregnancy

Many pregnant prisoners are at high risk due to drug abuse, lack of prenatal care, AIDS, recent trauma, and other factors. They require close and specialized monitoring and care. Accommodations may be needed in diet, living conditions, and work assignments. Every effort is made to ensure delivery in a community hospital. Very few correctional facilities in the United States permit incarcerated mothers to be accompanied by their infant and small children, though this practice is more common in other countries.

The Elderly and Disabled

To meet the special needs of the growing number of elderly and disabled inmates, some larger correctional systems are establishing dedicated housing units. These are barrier free, readily accommodate wheelchairs, and afford a more leisurely and less regimented and stressful routine. Like community homes for the aged, they make life more tolerable. Some chronic illness conditions can also be cared for in these units.

End-of-Life Care

Prison systems find it increasingly necessary to cope with dying inmates. Until recently, all but the most sudden and unexpected inmate deaths occurred in community hospitals. Wardens and jail administrators went to extreme lengths to ensure that nobody died in the institution. Instead of peaceful and reassuring surroundings, patients were unnecessarily subjected, during their final days and hours, to frightening sounds, commotion, and unfamiliar faces.

Dying prisoners experience the same kinds of disability, pain, anxiety, fear, confusion, incapacity, and needs as do free citizens who face old age and death. They, too, want closure, need to say farewell, desire to forgive and to be forgiven, appreciate kind words, crave companionship, require assistance, and fear dying alone. Separation from family and friends only exacerbates these problems. A few prisons have established special policies and programs to cover the final phase of life, relaxing visitation rules and other restrictions and utilizing the services of specially trained inmate volunteers to sit at the bedside, assist with activities of daily living, and provide companionship during the last days. Demonstrable benefits of this practice include redemptive and rehabilitative effects for the inmate caregivers themselves. Prisoners in these programs are allowed to die peacefully in a familiar environment and are appropriately permitted to refuse unwanted life-prolonging rescue methods.

Transitional Case Management

Transitional case management approaches have been successfully employed to assist terminally or seriously ill and disabled inmates to cope in the community after release from jail. Using case managers to prepare living and support arrangements prior to release and to afford follow-up guidance and assistance afterward, these programs can reduce recidivism and promote humane living conditions and should be implemented in collaboration with other agencies.

HOW MUCH CARE?

Medical care of inmates is subject to limits, just as it is in the community. Those whose care is paid by public funds or insurance policies cannot demand every expensive procedure, regardless of need. Cost must always be balanced with need so that there are sufficient resources for all.

Inmate status and nature or gravity of the crime—such as gender, race, color, creed, or ethnicity—have no bearing on such decisions. Even expensive procedures such as organ transplants ought not be denied solely because of inmate status. Age and expected years of life remaining, general health condition (including comorbidity), likelihood of successful response to treatment, and patient's wishes are relevant.

A jail or prison ought not deny or withhold a necessary treatment or diagnostic procedure because of lack of funds. Previous failure to access health services while in the community does not justify denial of care. Jails or prisons may defer treatment of short-term inmates until released from custody, provided a determination is made that this will not pose undue risk to the patient.

CONCLUSION

A healthy tension should exist between correctional authorities and the responsible health authority. If open and constructive discussion is repressed or discouraged, the differences in approach, policy, and mission can result in imprudent decisions.

There is no real contradiction between the principles and practice of good correctional programs and good health care programs. Each party needs to be familiar with the content and rationale of the other's policies. Health care professionals should never fail to be their patients' advocates.

—*Kenneth L. Faiver*

See also Dental Care; Doctors; Eighth Amendment; Gynecology; HIV/AIDS; Hospice; Mental Health; Prison Litigation Reform Act 1996; Psychiatric Care; Physicians' Assistants; *Ruiz v. Estelle*; Section 1983 of the Civil Rights Act; Suicide; Women's Health Care

Further Reading

Anno, B. J. (2001). *Correctional health care: Guidelines for the management of an adequate delivery system.* Washington, DC: National Institute of Corrections.

Faiver, K. L. (1998). *Health care management issues in corrections.* Lanham, MD: American Correctional Association.

GRACE Project. (2001). *A handbook for end-of-life care in correctional facilities.* Alexandria, VA: Volunteers of America.

National Commission on Correctional Health Care. (2003). *Standards for health services in prisons.* Chicago: Author.

Ort, R. S., & Faiver, K. L. (1998). Mental illness as a chronic condition: Coping with chronic mental patients in a correctional setting. *Corrections Compendium, 23*(5), 1–6.

Puisis, M. (Ed.). (1998). *Correctional medicine.* St. Louis: C. V. Mosby.

Sanderford-O'Connor, V. (1998). Prerelease program for inmates with HIV: Cost-effective case management. In E. E. Rhine (Ed.), *Best practices: Excellence in corrections* (pp. 249–251). Lanham, MD: American Correctional Association.

Vitucci, N. (2000). Patient or inmate—Do these terms affect how we treat the incarcerated? *CorrectCare, 14*(4), 1, 9.

Legal Case

Ruiz v. Estelle, 503 F. Supp. 1265 (1980).

◪ HIGH-RISE PRISONS

Various architectural styles have been employed in prison design, from the first radial cells of the Pennsylvania model to the recent innovations of new-generation prisons. Classic models such as the Auburn style and the telephone pole design provided the blueprint for most facilities built in the late 19th and early 20th centuries. These facilities, which include Sing Sing and San Quentin, were designed to hold large numbers of men in single cells at night, and in congregate labor during the day. Although popular for most of the 20th century, they presented numerous obstacles for program implementation and delivery, as well as safety.

In response, prison administrators began looking for alternative styles of design to aid in the establishment of smaller facilities, or, at the least, for methods that could facilitate the establishment of smaller, distinct units within larger institutions. Recent design models also tend to rely on enhanced technology. High-rise prisons, also commonly referred to as skyscraper prisons, are just one solution to the problems posed by the early architectural designs described above.

HISTORY AND DESIGN CHARACTERISTICS

Experimentation with high-rise prison facilities began in the 1970s, when the U.S. federal government began to construct metropolitan detention centers for the purpose of detaining persons accused of federal crimes. Soon thereafter, many state and local jurisdictions began to employ the high-rise design in the construction of prisons and jails. Since this time, the majority of facilities built according to the high-rise plan tend to be located in urban areas, presenting accused persons and those charged with their care the unique advantage of proximity to court services and other municipal buildings housing criminal justice–related divisions and departments. The facades of many high-rise institutions are architecturally designed to blend in with the urban landscape in which they are built.

Most high-rise facilities detain offenders prior to trial and sentencing. Many hold women and men, as well as some juvenile offenders. To keep these populations separate, housing units are usually contained within one floor allowing for the housing of multiple security levels in one site (i.e., different security levels on different floors). Likewise, the functional units such as medical, education, or recreation are located on different floors, eliminating contact among subpopulations.

PROFILES OF HIGH-RISE FACILITIES

Several high-rise prisons that can be found in metropolitan settings in the United States are profiled below. Many details of these facilities conform to the theoretical plan originally developed for the building and use of these facilities. Nevertheless, each facility presents its own unique contribution to the inmates and neighborhood that it serves. A discussion of the pros and cons of high-rise institutions follows the profiles of these facilities.

Federal Detention Center–SeaTac

The Federal Detention Center–SeaTac is a 10-story, 502-cell facility. The physical plant is composed of a six-story cell tower, as well as a four-story base that houses administrative offices, health services, laundry facilities, a commissary, and food services. It also accommodates vehicle entry via a sallyport. Security is the main mission of the Federal Detention Center–SeaTac, and this function is represented in the placement of the physical plant, since the facility is removed from the intersection that provides access to the facility's parking and buildings. This remote physical placement of the facility minimizes visual contact between the inmates and the public.

Federal Detention Center–Philadelphia

Located in a historic district in the center of the city, the Federal Detention Center–Philadelphia's exterior is designed to be compatible with the buildings that surround it, visually incorporating the facility into the established fabric of the neighborhood. The physical plant is composed of 11 stories. Interestingly, several stories are below ground level, which facilitates secure transport of detainees via an underground passage to the Justice Byrne Federal Courthouse, which is located across the street from the detention facility. The base of the facility is composed of four stories and houses administrative offices, inmate services, U.S. Marshal offices, and access to the secure passage from the courthouse. The central control room is also located in the facility base, allowing for optimal surveillance of

pedestrian, U.S. Marshal, and service personnel entry. In addition, the control room provides surveillance of vehicular entry via sallyports.

Federal Detention Center–Honolulu

The Federal Detention Center–Honolulu, which is the most recent federal institution to be built according to the high-rise plan, is located near the Honolulu International Airport. It is bound by airport facilities on the east and south, and residential housing from Hickam Air Force Base on the north. Thus, it is located on the fringe of industrial and residential areas of the city of Honolulu. The detention center is composed of 12 stories, with a 10-story main tower and a two-story administrative base. The administrative base houses the central control center, which provides surveillance for the main entrance, the waiting area, the service sallyport, and the main service corridor. The 10-story cell tower is L-shaped, with unit management offices centrally located between the two wings on each floor. The cell tower is composed of 496 general inmate housing cells and 62 special inmate housing cells, for a total of 558 cells and a rated capacity of 670 inmates. A one-story warehouse and receiving building is located adjacent to the main building. This component of the facility provides for storage of general supplies and food products, and also houses the central mechanical plant. The administrative base/cell tower and warehouse/receiving building are separated by sallyports used by service and U.S. Marshal personnel, and closed-circuit television monitoring controls access to the sallyports.

THE CASE FOR AND AGAINST HIGH-RISE PRISONS

High-rise prison facilities may be a viable means to increase penal capacity when space is limited. This is especially relevant when facilities are planned in urban areas. In turn, the building and opening of facilities along the lines of the high-rise model can help to relieve overcrowding at established, traditional facilities.

Nonetheless, many questions regarding the benefits of high-rise facilities remain. For example, although there is less geographic space to monitor, high-rise prisons may not be desirable in terms of optimal management and control. First, these facilities often require more staff as transport from housing units to service levels requires more detailed surveillance and potential problems that staff have not encountered at traditional facilities. Second, the surveillance of inmate activity within the facility is sometimes difficult in times of emergencies and disturbances. For these reasons, most guidelines for facility plans include a capacity of no more than 500 inmates, and a physical height of no more than five stories (inclusive of service floors and housing units).

When considering the interior details of a high-rise facility, the institution's purpose should be clearly assessed so that architectural accommodations can be made. For example, if the high-rise facility will house youthful offenders, one or several floors in the tower should be devoted to the building of classrooms. In turn, if the high-rise facility will house adult offenders, workshops should be included in facility plans.

Finally, individuals housed in high-rise prisons are rarely allowed outdoors. At most, inmates will be allowed to visit recreation areas on the roof. Such spaces have no greenery, or horizon to view. The long-term effects of such a sterile environment have yet to be assessed.

CONCLUSION

Over the past 30 years, the high-rise design has served to change the landscape of detention and corrections in the United States. These institutions have aided in the delivery of correctional services and programming for specific populations (i.e., maximum-security offenders, females, and juveniles) that are often housed together in these facilities. The facilities profiled above depict many facets of the high-rise prison as conceptualized in the mid-1970s. Nevertheless, the theoretical concepts related to the design of the high-rise prison have not been intricately developed or assessed since the mid-1970s,

and the pros and cons of high-rise facilities must be considered before researchers begin empirical assessments related to the details of these unique facilities. Only until the questions surrounding the optimal use of such institutions is assessed can correctional researchers and planners begin to embrace the potential that the high-rise prison may have for detention and corrections in the United States.

—Courtney A. Waid

See also Auburn System; Campus Style; Metropolitan Detention Centers; New Generation Prisons; Panopticon; Telephone Pole Design; Unit Management

Further Reading

Johnston, N. (2000). *Forms of constraint: A history of prison architecture.* Chicago: University of Illinois Press.

Krasnow, P. (1997). *Correctional facility design and detailing.* New York: McGraw-Hill.

Spens, I. (Ed.). (1994). *Architecture of incarceration.* London: Academy Editions.

Waid, C. A., & Clements, C. B. (2001, November). Correctional facility design: Past, present, and future. *Corrections Compendium, 26*(11).

Witke, L. (Ed.). (1999). *Planning and design guide for secure adult and juvenile facilities.* Lanham, MD: American Correctional Association.

☑ HIP HOP

Hip hop was created by youths of African American and Caribbean (including Latin-Caribbean) descent in the early 1970s. At the time, the counter-disco movement was developing, and gangs in the Bronx, New York, were becoming the subjects of books and films that depicted black and Latino youths as savage predators incapable of rehabilitation. Contradicting this stylized and oversimplified presentation of the Bronx as a site of decay was an artform that would emerge into international significance through expressions that include rapping/MCing, deejaying/ mixing, break-dancing, and graffiti. This artistic and cultural movement produced a generation of people—"hip hop America"—who would embrace not only its distinct language, music, and fashion but also its politics, vices, and other social realities.

Hip hop culture became popular during the same time that African Americans were responding to the aftermath of the politically charged civil rights movement of the 1960s. While hip hop was developing in basements of the Bronx, many African Americans were returning from the turbulent war in Vietnam, where 10% of American soldiers used heroin, and 5% were hard-core addicts. Many of these men brought their addiction back to their communities, generating a new kind of criminal— one who would supplement the existing criminal activity that included numbers running, prostitution, fencing, and robbery, and one who would later give way to the onslaught of crack cocaine in the 1990s. Ironically, the infusion of drugs and the accompanying drug economy employed many young black and Latino men and women who would otherwise not participate in the labor market. Thus, Sanyika Shakur (1993, p. 70) reports that in 1993 the gangs in Los Angeles recruited more people than the four branches of the U.S. Armed Forces, and crack dealers employed more than IBM, Clorox, and Xerox combined.

HIP HOP AND THE PRISON INDUSTRIAL COMPLEX

In large part a result of harsh new sentencing laws against drugs, prison populations have grown exponentially in the United States since the 1980s. Hip hop culture, particularly in its music, has lent a "bullhorn" to the prison experience that has become part of the life of so many young women and men of color. Many hip hop artists began to tell prison stories in their music, write prison poetry, wear prison "fashion," and adopt a mentality that embraced incarceration as a right of passage rather than as an experience that should avoided at all costs. When "gangster"/"reality" hip hop (typified by harsh, misogynist lyrics and tales of violence and victimization) began to gain momentum as the dominant expression of anger and resentment among disenfranchised urban youths in the late 1980s, their forms of expression, as well as that of the communities they spoke for, evoked punitive responses from the criminal justice system.

For example, in 2001, California passed Proposition 21, officially titled the Gang Violence and Juvenile Crime Prevention Act, which supported more juveniles being tried in adult court, required that certain youths be confined in local detention and in state correctional facilities, restricted the types of probation available to youths, increased existing penalties by requiring longer periods of confinement, and broadened existing three-strikes categories. On the ballot, Proposition 21 used crime data from the early 1990s and omitted the more recent crime statistics published at the time by the California Department of Justice in 1999, which showed significant declines in juvenile crime and delinquency. In addition to Proposition 21's use of outdated and misleading statistics, its implementation disproportionately affected the number of youth of color subjected to being processed in an adult court, with potentially more severe court sanctions than their white counterparts.

In essence, Proposition 21 built on the false belief that the youths were not able to be rehabilitated and that by relegating them to a slavery of another kind—lengthy incarceration, increased violence and abuse, unemployment, and perpetual disenfranchisement—California would be solving the "problem" of juvenile crime. This legislation was interpreted by many as being a particular assault on hip hop America by including language that allowed for broad interpretations of what constituted "dressing gang-like" (which often includes the prison-inspired sagging pants) as reason enough to be considered worthy of suspicion. Many viewed Proposition 21 as a clear association of California's black, Latino, and Asian youths, and by extension, hip hop culture and fashion, with prison culture and marked culpability.

The massive incarceration and subsequent return of youths from urban areas generated an acculturation of prison culture—wearing the "uniform," the rigid structure that fosters no critical thinking, as well as the divisive, punitive climate—that spread like a disease through much of hip hop America, creating an overexposure to and desensitization to the prison culture. This has led to many adults reenacting prison culture by engaging in abusive relationships and other antisocial behavior, as well as many youths adopting prison mannerisms as a survival mechanism both within and beyond penal institutions.

Perhaps the most significant impact of hip hop's acculturation of prison culture is the acceptance of violence and incarceration as a normal part of the black and Latino youth experience. Most black youths, and the people living in their communities, are law-abiding citizens. Research has confirmed that only 6% of youths are actually chronic, violent juvenile offenders. Still, most stories that end up in commercial hip hop music or on screen are stories of "stick-up kids," "gangsters," and heists, which leads to an internalization, among those who absorb the culture, that these occurrences are normal.

The prevalence of violence and incarceration in rap music is a reflection of the economic, political, and social stratification in many urban communities. However, violence, as expressed through hip hop art, is grossly exaggerated relative to the degree of violence that really takes place within black and Latino communities. It is true that for black males, ages 15–24, homicide and legal intervention are the number one cause of death. However, it is not true that most communities of color are crime-ridden neighborhoods infested with violent youths. It is true that black people experience a disproportionate rate of incarcerated from their communities due to a number of factors that include high unemployment, poor housing, and easy access to guns, liquor, and drugs, and the absence of other resources that make them less vulnerable to these vices.

CONCLUSION

African American youth culture since the 1980s has shared a paradoxical and multilayered relationship with the criminal justice system. The roots of this problematic relationship between people of African descent and the American correctional system lie in the usage of slavery as a penal code from the 1600s through the late 1800s, subsequent Jim Crow laws of the antebellum South, and anti-immigration laws that left many people of color searching for alternative means of qualifying their existence. The generational psychological and emotional effects of enduring

"justice"—punishments that included the whip, the stocks, the pillory, the brand mutilation, lynchings, and jail—has left a mark of distrust and suspicion that is difficult to dissipate within communities of color. The legacy of this brand of justice is reinforced by the societal inequities that continue to be a breeding ground for conditions that lead to racial profiling, disparate sentencing, lengthy incarceration, and the aftermath of this incarceration.

Many criminal justice policies and practices that lead to lengthy incarceration feed on the myth that dark-skinned youths, particularly those who are part of hip hop America, are criminal. Hip hop is not criminal. But hip hop America has been criminalized—unjustifiably perceived as suspect, considered unable to be rehabilitated, and labeled an overall menace to American society. For much of hip hop America, correctional facilities have become the literal and figurative spaces where, as sociologist Stephen Nathan Haymes (1995) once stated, they "develop self-definitions or identities that are linked to a consciousness of solidarity" (p. 35). This adaptation of prison culture as "normal" has placed a scarlet letter on the art and mindset of many youths who see their collective community's prison experience as a necessary part of their lives, which is dangerous and demeaning to their psychological, emotional, and physical development.

—Monique W. Morris

See also African American Prisoners; Drug Offenders; Hispanic/Latino(a) Prisoners; Prison Culture; Prison Music; Racial Conflict Among Prisoners; Racism War on Drugs

Further Reading

George, N. (1998). *Hip hop America.* New York: Penguin.

Haymes, S. N. (1995). *Race, culture, and the city: A pedagogy for black urban struggle.* Albany: State University of New York Press.

Kitwana, B. (2003). *The hip hop generation: Young blacks and the crisis in African American culture.* New York: Basic Civitas.

Sellin. T. (1976). *Slavery and the penal system.* Amsterdam: Elsevier Scientific.

Shakur, S. (1993). *Monster: The autobiography of an L.A. gang member.* New York: Atlantic Monthly.

HISPANIC/LATINO(A) PRISONERS

The terms *Latino/a* and *Hispanic* typically refer to people of Spanish origin. Latinos and Latinas are the fastest-growing minority group in the United States, growing seven times faster than the general population. Between 1980 and 1990, the Hispanic population had increased by half, while the white (non-Hispanic) population increased only 6%.

Such increases in the general population have also occurred behind bars. Between 1985 and 2002, the rate of Latino inmates in state and federal facilities increased from 10% to 18%. As for specific offenses, from 1995 to 2001, the number of Latino offenders incarcerated for property and drug offenses declined, but the rate for those incarcerated for violent crime increased by 81.5%. In 2001, the greatest portion of the 205,300 Latinos incarcerated in state prisons were sentenced for violent crime (50%), followed by drug offenses (23%), and property crime (16%). As for those under the sentence of death, approximately 12% are Latinos, most of them of Mexican origin.

The majority of Latino and Latina inmates are incarcerated in those states that contain a significant number of Latinos and Latinas: Arizona, California, Colorado, Florida, Illinois, Nevada, New Mexico, New York, and Texas. For example, based on the Bureau of Justice Statistics 1998 report, over 50% of New Mexico's inmate population is Latino/a, mostly Mexican. On the other side of the county, approximately one-third of all New York state prisoners are of Latino/a heritage, mostly Puerto Rican. SArizona, California, Colorado, Connecticut, and Texas and the federal prison system each has Latino/a inmate populations of more than 25%.

PRISON CONDITIONS IN THE PAST AND PRESENT

Spanish-speaking prisoners have long been subjected to differential treatment while inside prison walls. Many Hispanic prisoners are pressured to refrain from speaking their native language and also are denied the opportunity to learn the English language when such classes exist. Some have complained that their letters are not mailed out or allowed to be received unless written in English. Similarly, others allege that medical treatment is not given to Latino prisoners either because of the language barrier, discrimination by correctional officers, or use sometimes as punishment for certain behavior.

The 1971 Attica Prison rebellion represented a first crucial step in addressing some of the inequities Latino prisoners faced. On September 9, 1971, over half of the 2,243 prisoners at Attica Correctional Facility rebelled, holding 39 security and civilian personnel hostage. The rebellion ended four days later on September 13, claiming the lives of 29 prisoners and 10 employees, six of whom were guards, and wounding many others. Of the demands made by the prisoners, three in particular were geared specifically toward Latinos. These demands included adequate medical treatment for every inmate and if needed, Spanish-speaking doctors or an interpreter to accompany the inmate to the doctor. Also, Latinos requested a complete Spanish library and the institution of a program that would increase the number of Latino and African American correctional officers. The lack of Spanish interpreters, lawyers, books, and general services were and continue to be a large part of the Latino discontent. The Attica Prison rebellion also paved the way for Latinos(as) to form informal networks within prisons to continue the fight for equality and fairness.

One year after Attica, David Ruiz filed his pioneering *Ruiz v. Estelle* lawsuit, which revealed the unconstitutional conditions in Texas prisons. Though Ruiz claimed in a later 1989 court case that officers responded to his original suit by denying him medical care, interfering with his mail, and wrongly classifying him as a gang member, his action in 1972 dramatically changed prison conditions around the country for all inmates.

These days, many prisons have hired correctional officers who speak both Spanish and English. Some systems offer language training for existing staff. Some systems are exploring the possibility of developing language translation technology, which will automatically translate words and phrases in one language to computer-generated speech and/or text in another language. Such technology may be useful during booking, informing individuals of their rights, screening, and emergency treatment and in large spaces to communicate with inmates during critical incidents.

PRISONER GROUPS

Both Latino and Latina prisoners tend to depend on each other for a sense of belonging and emotional support, and, more important, for physical protection from other inmates. For these reasons, since offenders typically come from the same geographic areas, Latino/a inmates often form informal groups composed of people they knew prior to being incarcerated. Informal networks sometimes provide supplies to their members such as clothing, cigarettes, and food. Furthermore, in some facilities in states such as California, New Mexico, and Texas, informal groups have become organized (and politically driven) in an attempt to challenge the correctional system to improve prison conditions.

The desegregation of some prisons during the 1960s led to the development of racial and ethnic gangs for socialization, protection, political motives, and deviant behavior (e.g., drugs). Some Latino prisoners, for example, joined gangs such as the Mexican Mafia, La Nuestra Familia, or Surenos. In an effort to weaken the power of racial and ethnic gangs, some states have actually separated specific racial and ethnic groups into certain cellblocks as a security measure. However, given the political economy of drugs and crime, gangs continue to present a serious problem to the correctional system.

WOMEN

In 2002, Latinos comprised 18% of all state and federal prisoners. Their incarceration rate of 1,176 per 100,000 residents was 2.6 times higher than the rate for Caucasian men. By contrast, in large part, due to increases in violent crime, lethality, and drug cases, Latinas are now the fastest-growing population of all prisoners. In 2002, Latinas comprised approximately 1% of all state and federal prisoners, and 6%

of all Latino/a prisoners. Latinas are imprisoned at a rate of 80/100,000, which is significantly higher than the incarceration rate for Caucasian women (35/100,000). Also, incarceration rates are highest for Latinas between the ages of 30 and 34 (216/100,000). While incarcerated, Latinas not only confront some of the same issues faced by Latinos, but they also have to endure stereotypical and gender-specific pressures from the prison system and society in general.

CONCLUSION

Based on the existing literature, the Latino and Latina experience in correctional institutions across the United States not only differs from other racial groups such as African Americans and Caucasians, but there is significant variation within the Latino/a population. Even though certain improvements have been made, institutional gaps still remain. First of all, certain groups such as the Puerto Rican Nationalists, the Cuban Marielitos, Mexicans on death row, and South and Central Americans in Immigration and Naturalization Service facilities have received some of the most punitive sanctions in the history of the American criminal justice system. Second, Spanish interpreters, lawyers, and medical, technical, and educational services continue to be a significant concern for Latino/a prisoners. Considering the current situation of ethnic inmates (e.g., language barriers and illness), and the living conditions of some facilities (e.g., overcrowding; limited education, technical, and medical resources), the quality of prison life for Latinos and Latinas needs to be radically improved.

—*Anthony B. Guevara*

See also African American Prisoners; Attica Correctional Facility; Immigrants/Undocumented Aliens; INS Detention Facilities; Native American Prisoners; Puerto Rican Nationalists; Racism

Further Reading

Black, M. S. (1998). Keeping the promise: Research obligations for curriculum study and Latino schooling. *Journal of Curriculum & Supervision, 13*(4), 373–379.

Bureau of Prisons. (2004). BOP home page. Retrieved from http://www.bop.gov

California Prison Focus. (2004). California Prison Focus home page. Retrieved from http://www.prisons.org

Diaz-Cotto, J. (1996). *Gender, ethnicity, and the state: Latina and Latino politics.* Albany: State University of New York Press.

Eisenman, R. (2000). Characteristics of prisoners in the California Department of Corrections: Race, ethnicity, and other aspects. *Mankind Quarterly, 41,* 211–215.

Harrison, P. M., & Beck, A. J. 2003. *Prisoners in 2002.* Washington, DC: U.S. Department of Justice.

Irwin, J., & Austin, J. (1997). *It's about time: America's imprisonment binge* (2nd ed.). Belmont, CA: Wadsworth.

Mann, C. (1993). *Unequal justice: A question of color.* Bloomington: Indiana University Press.

National Institute of Corrections. (2004). NIC home page. Retrieved from http://nicic.org/

Rendon, L. I., & Hope, R. I. (1996). *Educating a new majority.* San Francisco: Jossey-Bass.

Schaeffer, R. T. (2000). *Racial and ethnic groups* (8th ed.). Upper Saddle River, NJ: Prentice Hall.

Skinner, C. (1990). Overcrowded prisons: A nation of crisis. *Crisis, 98*(4), 18–21, 45–46.

Tonry, M. (1995). *Malign neglect: Race, crime, and punishment in America.* New York: Oxford University Press.

Urbina, M. G. (2003). *Capital punishment and Latino offenders: Racial and ethnic differences in death sentences.* New York: LFB Scholarly Publishing.

Urbina, M. G. (2004). Language barriers in the Wisconsin court system: The Latino/a experience. *Journal of Ethnicity in Criminal Justice, 2*(1/2), 91–118.

U.S. Census Bureau. (2003). *The Hispanic population in the United States: March 2002.* Washington, DC: U.S. Department of Commerce.

U.S. Department of Justice. (2004). DOJ home page. Retrieved from http://www.usdoj.gov

Walker, S. (1980). *Popular justice: A history of American criminal justice.* New York: Oxford University Press.

☘ HISTORY OF CORRECTIONAL OFFICERS

The vocation of prison officer has changed from that of *guard,* who is concerned only with matters of security, to the *corrections officer,* who must deal with human relations, institutional procedures, and legal requirements. This transformation has come about via three historical eras: politics, professionalism, and civil rights.

THE ERA OF POLITICS

The formative years of the prison occurred during the age of Andrew Jackson (1820s), whose presidential administration was marked by the spoils system. The basic idea—of rewarding political loyalty with public office—became federal practice, and state officials responsible for prisons adopted it with great enthusiasm. The political era for prison officers began in the early 1800s and continued until well into the 20th century.

In this system, the warden was a political appointee who, in turn, selected all his subordinates—assistant warden, turnkey, yardmaster, and guard. The law gave the warden complete control over the selection and retention of prison officers. Generally, prison officers were required only to be "men of good moral character and temperate habits"; Wyoming provided that guards "be quick to grasp a situation" and Utah specified they were to be "capable of handling men" (Knepper, 1990, p. 233). The superintendent of Arizona's prison at Yuma preferred unmarried men who could live adjacent to the prison and always be on hand in case of emergencies, a hiring "policy" likely in place elsewhere.

The only qualifications required to be a prison officer at San Quentin or Folsom in California were "the physical and mental and moral ability to perform the duties of the offices to which they are appointed and to the satisfaction of the wardens" (Knepper, 1990, pp. 232–233). Vague and minimal language concerning job qualifications ensured that wardens made their selections with few constraints and invariably chose personal and political favorites.

The political system provided one or more well-paid positions in prison governance, along with greater numbers of positions for prison officers that paid reasonably well. In Arizona, guards received $75 a month in 1876. By 1900, they earned $80 a month during their first year and $100 a month after that. At $100 a month, guards' wages compared to skilled positions in mine operations, such as blacksmiths, machinists, engineers, and electricians, and on the railroads, including brakemen and boilermakers. Common laborers in mines and on railroads received $50–$60 a month, while farmhands were compensated as little as $30 per month.

The relatively high salaries for prison work, plus the benefits of sleeping quarters and meals came, however, with long hours and challenging work rules. Arizona's codified rules of conduct for guards in 1895 made them subject to 40 rules—7 more rules than applied to prisoners. It was the guards' responsibility to keep prisoners to the work assigned to them, require personal cleanliness, and restrict movement to designated places. The rules required guards to wear side arms, walk a beat every 15 minutes, and maintain a state of "watchfulness and wakefulness at all times." The warden's expectations extended to the guards' private life as well: The rules prohibited them from "consorting with loud and vicious company," frequenting saloons, and gambling while away from the prison (Knepper, 1990, p. 235).

THE ERA OF PROFESSIONALISM

Professionalism came to prison administration during the Progressive era (1900–1917), decades marked by wide-scale social engineering for egalitarian ends. Progressivism led to growth in the role of government and to cadres of government professionals specializing in everything from civil engineering and landscape architecture to policing and firefighting. Social workers, psychiatrists, and other experts joined prison staffs, and prison officers responded by professionalizing their ranks. The process they initiated around 1900 and continued throughout the 20th century. In corrections, *professionalism* refers to the idea that prison officers do more than "guard prisoners." The profession of prison officer requires specialized knowledge and skills acquired through education, training, and apprenticeship.

By the 1930s, most states included prison officers on civil service lists so that party politics no longer resulted in wholesale turnover of staff. However, the vocation of prison officer faced severe challenges due to a long workday, little training, and what had become a fairly low level of pay.

At the majority of prisons, officers continued to work 10 hours a day or more. Prison officers received little or no formal training but were expected to deal with inmates by intuition and on-the-job experience. When the Wickersham Commission (1928–1931) turned its attention to penal institutions, it found the situation for prison officers to be problematic. Named after its chair, George W. Wickersham, the commission was appointed by President Herbert Hoover to investigate the administration of justice following problems of corruption that had occurred during prohibition. The commission determined that low pay for prison officers made the positions attractive only to those without options or ambition. At somewhere between $1,000 and $1,500 a year, annual pay for prison officers had slipped below the level of "the most incompetent mechanic" (Rothman, 1980, p. 147). Consequently, staff turned over rapidly. Individuals worked for a year or two, then left.

During the 1950s, prison administrators increasingly began to voice the need for staff training and introduced specialized courses for prison officers. State commissions with responsibility for prisons began requiring that prison officers complete training comparable to that of state law enforcement officers. Oklahoma's commissioner of Charities and Corrections, for instance, recommended that all guards at the state's penitentiary complete a training school comparable to the highway patrol and that no guards at the state reformatory should have less than a high school education. This development led in turn to creation of centralized training academies within states and to a national training academy. James V. Bennett of the U.S. Bureau of Prisons became known for his insistence on prison staff selection and training during his more than two decades as director. Early efforts within the federal prison system to train line staff, beginning in 1969, were followed by a national institute for training corrections personnel. The National Institute of Corrections was established five years later.

It was also during the 1950s that prisons began to be called "state correctional institutions," wardens were renamed "superintendents," and guards became "corrections/correctional officers." These name changes were meant to inform the wider public that prisons, and those working in them, did not exist simply to "lock people away" but carried out a significant and meaningful role in society: enabling lawbreakers to fulfill their responsibilities under the social contract. The American Prison Association changed its name to the American Correctional Association (ACA) at its 1954 Congress of

Correction in Philadelphia, Pennsylvania. Founded by prison reformers in 1870, the ACA became throughout the second half of the 20th century a leading proponent of professionalism among corrections workers.

THE ERA OF CIVIL RIGHTS

The civil rights era (1954–1968) concentrated unprecedented energy against racial segregation and discrimination. Marches, protests, boycotts, "freedom rides," "sit-ins," and other forms of nonviolent protest helped bring about federal legislation to extend the benefits of citizenship to more people. Beginning with Black Muslims, prisoners won a series of rights through litigation and defeated the "hands-off" doctrine in which the courts had refused to examine prison administration. When prisoners came to be seen as citizens with rights under the law, it became apparent that prison officers had important legal rights related to their employment and working conditions. During the era of civil rights, women and African Americans claimed the right to pursue corrections as an occupation. Opportunities in corrections employment became available to women and African Americans as never before.

Gender

The first prisons had been designed by men, for men, and no women worked as guards in them, but by 1850, states began providing matrons for growing numbers of women prisoners. Matrons were responsible for the "female ward," typically small numbers of women prisoners confined in the absence of a facility for women. Women were hired to minimize the threat of exploitation, and consistent with the "matron theory" of prisoner reformation, to serve as good examples for female lawbreakers. More often than not, women became matrons as part of a "package deal": The warden or superintendent lived on site and the warden's wife assumed clerical and other administrative responsibilities.

The women's reformatory movement, beginning in 1870, led to the establishment of separate institutions for women lawbreakers. Copying the model of juvenile institutions, these women's prisons were built in rural areas on the cottage plan; inmates lived in small units under the supervision of matriarchal matrons. The title of "matron" survived until the middle of the 20th century, when it was changed to "cottage officer" and "cottage warden."

Women began working in men's prisons following enactment of the 1972 amendments to the Civil Rights Act of 1964. The amendments to Title VII strengthened the antidiscrimination provisions of the act and extended the nondiscrimination provision to public as well as private employers. By the late 1980s, women supervised male inmates in every state prison as well as the Federal Bureau of Prisons. The notion that men and women may be involved in similar work had come to prevail, although correctional staff experienced tensions as women took up their role in the control of inmates. By 1987, there were more than 519 women in correctional officer positions within the Bureau of Prisons, and women began to claim increasing numbers of upper-level management positions. Margaret Hambrick, appointed in 1981 to head the Federal Correctional Institution at Butner, North Carolina, was the first woman superintendent of a federal prison for men.

Title VII also ended many of the restrictions on men working in women's facilities. By the 1990s, the majority of staff positions in women's prisons came to be held by men. In 1996, women inmates in Michigan filed a class-action lawsuit charging that corrections officials had violated the civil rights of women prisoners by allowing men to use staff positions for sexual misconduct against the women under their supervision. The state reached a settlement in which corrections officials agreed to avoid assignment of male corrections officers to women's housing units. While restrictions on male staff supervising women prisoners remain subject to litigation, courts have found that male officers' employment concerns must give way to protect women prisoners' safety and privacy.

Race/Ethnicity

The 1972 amendments, and federal court intervention, opened the doors of prison employment to racial/ethnic minorities as well. In the southern states,

African American correctional officers worked in segregated facilities; part of all-black staff in facilities with all-black populations. These conditions limited leadership positions to a few. In North Carolina, for example, Lewyn M. Hayes became the first black superintendent of a corrections institution. He took charge of the Raleigh Youth Center for Negroes in 1952. The right to work in integrated facilities, and aspire to leadership positions throughout state corrections, did not come until the 1970s. There were no black employees supervising white inmates at Mississippi's Parchman Penitentiary, which had become by 1972, the starkest example of the system of racial segregation practiced in the South. Under pressure of federal court intervention, the superintendent in 1973 attempted to redress racial imbalance among staff with the appointment of an African American assistant warden and promotion of Eddie Holloway, who became Mississippi's first black warden.

Women and African Americans organized their own professional associations to identify areas of concern, make the most of opportunities, and offer support for colleagues. In 1975, at the ACA's annual congress, a Women's Caucus met to address the concerns of women in corrections. As a result, the ACA president in 1978 appointed a task force as a standing subcommittee of the Affirmative Action Committee. The National Association of Blacks in Criminal Justice (NABCJ) organized in 1974 following a meeting at the University of Alabama, at which Bennett Cooper, director of Ohio's Department of Rehabilitation and Correction, called for creation of a permanent national organization to focus on the goal of achieving equal justice for African Americans and other minorities.

CONCLUSION

Significant changes have occurred in the vocation of the prison officer during the 19th and 20th centuries. During the era of politics, all prison staff served "at the warden's pleasure." The era of professionalism institutionalized training requirements. Finally, during the era of civil rights, women and African Americans claimed the right to work in institutional roles that had been denied them. Despite all the changes, however, prison officers are

still grappling with many of the same issues as they ever have. Relatively low salaries combined with low educational levels and repetitive tasks contribute to the job's enduring stigma.

—Paul Knepper

See also American Correctional Association; Correctional Officer Pay; Correctional Officer Unions; Correctional Officers; Federal Prison System; Governance; History of Prisons; Legitimacy; Managerialism; Professionalizatuon of Staff

Further Reading

Farkas, M. A. (1990). Professionalization: Is it the "cure all" for what ails the corrections officer? *Journal of Crime and Justice, 13*, 29–54.

Hawkes, M. G. (1991). Women's changing roles in corrections. In J. Morton (Ed.), *Change, challenge and choices.* Laurel, MD: American Correctional Association.

Keve, P. W. (1991). *Prisons and the American conscience.* Carbondale: Southern Illinois University Press.

Knepper, P. (1990). *Imprisonment and society in Arizona Territory.* PhD dissertation. Tempe: Arizona State University.

Rothman, D. J. (1980). *Conscience and convenience.* Glenview, IL: Scott, Foresman.

Thomas, J. E. (1972). *The English prison officer since 1850.* London: Routledge and Kegan Paul.

Zimmer, L. L. (1989). Solving women's employment problems in corrections: Shifting the burden to administrators. *Women and Criminal Justice, 1*, 55–79.

☑ HISTORY OF THE JUVENILE JUSTICE SYSTEM

See JUVENILE REFORMATORIES

☑ HISTORY OF PRISONS

The presence of prisons is well documented in the annals of ancient history, mentioned in Greek philosophy, biblical sources, and the laws of Rome. The dominant forms of punishment in early times were execution, exile, fines, and the confiscation of property, and for debt, confinement until payment and debt bondage. The use of imprisonment as the major form of punishment, however, has a more recent history.

The difficulty of tracing the emergence of imprisonment itself as a form of punishment lies in the fact that the prison—past and present—has had multiple functions. Prisons have served as places of custody for those to be tried, for those sentenced and awaiting their punishment, as sites for corporal punishment and execution, holding places for debtors, and (infrequently) in earlier times, as places for long-term or lifetime incarceration. For example, Rome's first-century B.C. Mamertine Prison, whose history can be traced back to the third-century B.C., was an underground chamber close to the seat of the courts, used both as a site of confinement and as a

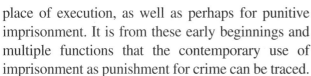
Photo 1   *Sing Sing convicts attending Sunday Service in the prison chapel*

place of execution, as well as perhaps for punitive imprisonment. It is from these early beginnings and multiple functions that the contemporary use of imprisonment as punishment for crime can be traced.

EARLY EUROPE

In early medieval Europe, local prisons scattered across centers of population and seats of jurisdiction retained their multiple functions, while execution, exile, mutilation, enslavement, and fines remained the dominant forms of punishment. However, by the 13th and 14th centuries, canon law and ecclesiastical courts had developed with jurisdiction over lay persons as well as clergy. At the same time, monastic cells became a locus for penitential expiation within an institutionalized disciplinary system in a manner that foreshadowed the function of the prison as a site for moral correction.

In England, by the 12th century, the Tower of London, the Fleet, and other royal prisons held a range of occupants for both coercive and custodial purposes. People could be sentenced under common law or be placed there by the will of the sovereign

for a range of activities, including incursion of debt. At the same time, towns and local nobles responsible for keeping the peace were required to provide local jails for those awaiting trial and sentencing. Jailors charged fees and sold food and clothing to the prisoners. Inmates had to pay any debts incurred during their confinement before they could be released. Conditions in these early jails ranged from relative comfort for those with means to a foul and death-threatening existence for those without.

The numbers of imprisonable offenses increased in England from the 13th century onward. By the 16th century, there were 180 such acts, including vagrancy, illegal bearing of arms, and morals offenses, which carried sentences of penal bondage. People sentenced for these crimes could be placed in "bridewells" or "houses of corrections" that sought to instill habits of discipline, hard labor, and religious observance in a domestic household model. London's Bridewell, the first of many in England, opened in 1556 for the confinement of women and men "idle, criminal and destitute."

For serious crimes, however, execution remained the primary punishment. The sheer number of capital offenses, the severity of that punishment, and an increasing reluctance in the courts to enforce the penalty, led to the royal decree of 1615 that transportation to the colonies could be substituted for the penalty of death, with the stated purpose of combining "justice tempered with mercie" but reflecting economic interests as well. With the Transportation Act of 1718, penal bondage became the primary punishment for a range of offenses, predominantly those against property. Between 1718 and 1776, between 30,000 and 50,000 convicts, men and women, with sentences of bondage for 7 or 14 years or for life, were transported to America. By the 17th and early 18th centuries, the foundations were laid for the penal reforms that led to the development of the modern prison system.

THE RISE OF PENAL REFORM

Two currents were at work in England in the late 18th and early 19th centuries. One was a practical need to respond to the perceived rising crime and increasing disorder of a revolutionary time, to the loss of the American colonies for transportation, and to the increasing overcrowding and deteriorating conditions in local jails and houses of correction. The second was the changing views of the nature of punishment, inspired in part by Cesare Beccaria's essay *On Crimes and Punishments,* published in 1764. Beccaria's influence can be seen in the writings of men like Joshua Hanway and John Dornford, both of whom called for the care of both the body and the soul of the convicted, through solitary confinement, hard labor, and the ministrations of the chaplain.

Perhaps the most influential reformer of the time was John Howard, whose 1777 report on *The State of the Prisons in England and Wales* was widely read in England, Europe, and America. As the new sheriff of Bedfordshire, he was shocked with the conditions in the jails that were now his responsibility. Motivated by what he saw in his own county, he began to inspect all of England's prisons, decrying not only their filth, overcrowding, illness, lack of order and rules, but also the presence within them of acquitted persons unable to pay their jailor's fees. During his survey of the nation's prisons, he also visited the prison hulks at Woolrich, which

were ships that had been pressed into convict service in 1776 as a "temporary expedient" after transportation to America ceased. Despite Howard's criticisms, the "temporary" use of the hulks as places of confinement supplying convict labor for the docks lasted until 1857.

Largely in response to Howard's exposé of prison conditions, England passed the 1779 Penitentiary Act. This act called for the construction of penitentiaries in each of the home counties, based on the principles of solitary confinement, religious instruction, and hard labor.

Millbank Prison, Britain's first vaunted national "penitentiary house," arose on the swampy banks of the Thames. In it, 1,200 convicts were to be housed in cells in six massive pentagons surrounding a central chapel rotunda. Though it was initially hailed as a humane and scientific experiment in the Christian redemptive value of hard labor in separate confinement, Millbank ultimately proved to be a failure. Inadequate pay rendered staff unreliable and hard to recruit, while small cells, built in a confusing maze made for unhealthy inmates, particularly when combined with a medically determined near-starvation diet, made inmates difficult to control. Begun in 1812 at the cost of nearly half a million pounds, and opened in 1816, Millbank had closed by 1844. Despite such initial setbacks in the design and running of penitentiaries, the movement for penal reform continued in England, and extended to the Continent as well as to the United States.

COLONIAL AND REPUBLICAN AMERICA

Like their counterparts in Britain, during the 17th and 18th centuries American colonists punished a wide range of conduct in a variety of ways, including fines, whippings, public shaming, banishment, and public execution. Influenced by Calvinism, the colonists believed that humankind was plagued by original sin that could not be corrected or rehabilitated. However, in some of the smaller, more intimate communities, offenders were viewed merely as wayward neighbors who could, through the use of the pillory and stocks, be cured through reintegrative shaming. If someone reoffended or committed a serious offense, they would be punished harshly. Sanctions included public whipping and banishment and public executions.

Though for all of the colonies, as in England, public executions retained their central role, there was some variation in what conducts were proscribed and how they were punished. Thus for example, under Penn's "Great Law," Pennsylvania mandated hard labor in houses of correction for most offenses, while at the same time in New York about 20% of all offenses, including picking pockets, burglary, robbery, and horse stealing, were punishable by death.

The American Revolution and the repudiation of British rule brought about a reconsideration of the legacy of British justice. Deeply influenced by Enlightenment thinkers, and particularly by Beccaria's argument against the use of the death penalty, key reformers like Benjamin Rush in Pennsylvania and Thomas Eddy in New York advocated the deterrent use of incarceration. By 1820, almost all the new states had limited the use of the death penalty to first-degree murder or other serious crimes. In turn, following Pennsylvania's experiment in the Walnut Street Jail, most of the states, almost as their first public act, built state prisons with incarceration at hard labor as their primary punishment for crime.

As with the first penitentiaries in Europe, these early U.S. prisons were harsh and brutal places. Some, such as Newgate Prison in Connecticut, built in the 1770s, used an underground rock cavern that paralleled conditions in the ancient Roman Mamertine Prison. Repeating the troubles of the earlier houses of correction, inmates in the early state prisons were often inadequately supervised in overcrowded conditions. These prisons frequently spread disease and death but did little to deter crime in the new republic.

THE PENNSYLVANIA SYSTEM

Reflecting the same concerns that had influenced individuals like John Howard in England, reform groups lobbied for solitary confinement. One such influential group was the Philadelphia Society for Alleviating the Miseries of Public Prisons (1787). Following Howard's principles, the Philadelphia Society persuaded the Pennsylvania Legislature to authorize the construction of penal facilities that were based on a particular model of governance

known as the Pennsylvania system. This system, as summarized by a contemporary, Robert Vaux, was based on five principles: (1) prisoners should not be treated with malice, their suffering should work to change their ways; (2) further corruption, or infection, within the prison can be prevented through solitary confinement; (3) solitary confinement can achieve penitence and repentance of the offender; (4) solitary confinement was a true punishment since people are social beings; and (5) solitary confinement was cost effective because it would not take long under isolation for inmates to become rehabilitated and fewer guards would be needed for their supervision.

The "separate system" was first implemented in Philadelphia in 1790, when part of the Walnut Street Jail was reconstructed into a penitentiary. Thirty-six solitary confinement cells were built for serious offenders. The policies of solitary confinement and mandatory labor implemented within the jail were designed to instill discipline and self-control. However, it soon became clear that this separate system was terribly expensive. The labor engaged in by the inmates did not cover the costs of the upkeep of the jail. Furthermore, overcrowding did not allow the administration to isolate inmates. Too many inmates spent time in idle waste so as to make the system virtually ineffective. In the end, the administration returned to hard convict labor and physical punishment in order to maintain control.

Despite the failures at the Walnut Street Jail, the state of Pennsylvania continued to experiment with the separate system, opening the Western Penitentiary in Pittsburgh in 1821 and in 1829 the Eastern Penitentiary in Philadelphia. Like the Walnut Street Jail, these prisons held inmates in isolation to work, read the Bible, reflect on their sins, and follow a code of silence. Cells were slightly larger than the typical cell of the day, and only a small amount of light shone within. Like the earlier Walnut Street Jail, by the 1860s overcrowding in the Eastern Penitentiary did not allow for solitary confinement. Once again, prison administrators returned to the old habits of leasing out convict labor and physically punishing rule breakers in order to maintain control. By 1833, the Western Penitentiary closed its doors.

THE AUBURN SYSTEM

While Pennsylvanian prison reformers advocated that prisoners should be held in solitary confinement for the duration of their sentence, New York prison reformers believed that inmates should labor together in order to minimize operating costs. The Auburn system, or the "congregate system," as it was called, held its inmates in solitary confinement only at night to allow them to contemplate on their sins but required that they labor in group workshops, engaging in factory-like labor. All activities followed strict schedules. Inmates were held to a code of silence from the moment they entered the prison to the moment they exited. In order to control movement, inmates were required to move in unison and in lockstep. During meals inmates sat backs straight, face to back. They were not allowed even eye contact with another inmate at any time. Each inmate wore a striped uniform. As informed upon their entrance to the prison, inmates for all intents and purposes were considered dead to the outside world.

However, as with the other prison reforms, overcrowding, budget concerns, and politics took over the administration of the Auburn Penitentiary. Soon inmate were housed two to three to a cell, segregation by offense or sex became impossible, and discipline was achieved through floggings, as in the past. While the congregate system was cheaper than the separate system, it still proved to be too expensive.

THE SOUTH

Though U.S. prison history is usually characterized as a battle between the Auburn and Pennsylvanian systems, it is important to realize that both of these models initially only influenced penal policy in the northern states. Life was very different in the South. Under slavery there were very few penitentiaries, and those that existed held only a handful of white offenders. South Carolina, for example, did not have a penitentiary until the late 1860s.

Following the Civil War and the abolition of slavery, southern prisons virtually doubled their inmate population as former slaves convicted under the notorious Black Acts were placed in prison or on chain gangs for any number of minor offenses. States also developed complex convict leasing schemes, where offenders were imprisoned in "portable prisons on wheels" as they labored for the state or for private entrepreneurs building roads, picking cotton, mining, or performing numerous other tasks to rebuild the shattered infrastructures of the South.

THE CINCINNATI DECLARATION OF PRINCIPLES

In 1870, the National Prison Association (now called the American Correctional Association) met in Cincinnati in order to address the harsh conditions of prisons throughout the country. The result of this meeting was the Declaration of Principles that set out a series of standards by which prisons should be governed. Most notably, the organization called for rehabilitation to become the primary purpose of the prison. The National Prison Association also declared that rehabilitation of the inmate should be achieved within the prison walls. Furthermore, time lapsed should no longer be the standard by which rehabilitation was determined. In essence, the Declaration of Principles called for the abolition of fixed sentences to be replaced by indeterminate sentences. In this way, the inmate had to prove he or she was rehabilitated before being released back into society.

THE ELMIRA REFORMATORY

The Elmira Reformatory, built in 1876, was the first prison to implement the Declaration of Principles set forth by the National Prison Association. Under the administration of Zebulon Brockway, the Elmira Reformatory sought to identify and treat the root causes of the individual's criminality. Believing in hard work as well as education, Brockway implemented a rigid program of work during the day and academic, vocational, and moral training during the evening. This program rested on a "mark" system of classification, based on earlier practices at Norfolk Island in Australia and in Ireland.

According to the mark system, an inmate could be placed in any one of three grades depending on his work and academic activities and behavior within the reformatory. Inmates entered the Elmira Reformatory at grade two. If they earned nine marks a month for six months, they could move up to grade one, which was the grade required for release. However, if the inmate did not cooperate in his rehabilitation or violated rules, he was demoted to grade three. The inmate had to cooperate for three months before he could be considered for a higher grade. This classification system placed rehabilitation in the hands of the inmate.

PROGRESSIVE REFORMS: REHABILITATION AND THE MEDICAL MODEL

During the Progressive Era (1900–1930), prison reformers introduced many practices that remain today, including probation, parole, indeterminate sentences, the presentence report, treatment programs, and classification systems designed to identify the rehabilitative progressive of the inmate. The code of silence was eliminated, as were the lockstep and the separate system.

Progressive reformers believed in the medical model. They proposed that criminality was caused by individual social, biological, and psychological deficiencies. Hence the diseased inmate could be diagnosed and treated. The medical model ushered in a deepening reliance on indeterminate sentences; inmates were not released until the prison staff, often a social worker or psychologist, determined that they were cured. After World War II, new forms of treatment were introduced, such as group therapy, behavior modification, and counseling.

By the 1970s, the rehabilitation and medical models were losing favor. Rising crime, large-scale prison riots, and the publication of an influential article in 1974 by Robert Martinson that claimed that "nothing works" all contributed to a shift in penal policy. Liberal reformers began to call for the abolition of indeterminate sentencing and the reenactment of determinate sentencing in order to reduce the inconsistencies that had come to plague the penal system. Conservation reformers also lobbied to a return to determinate sentencing, arguing that the system was too lenient. Conservative reformers

won the debate, ushering in a "get tough" on crime philosophy that resulted in habitual offender laws (i.e., three-strikes laws and sex offender laws), mandatory minimums, the reinstitution of the chain gang, and cuts in educational programs.

WOMEN'S PRISONS

Though much of prison reform in America, England, and Europe focused on the imprisonment of the male inmate, female inmates did get some attention. In the early 19th century, for example, fellow nonconformist Elizabeth Fry took over the mantle of John Howard. Unlike Howard, however, she mainly focused on the treatment of women. Fry in 1813 visited and publicized the disorderly conditions for women imprisoned at Newgate Prison in London. Confident of the role of faith, she taught and preached to the women and spoke and wrote widely, including her influential *Observations on the Siting, Superintendence and Government of Female Prisoners*, published in 1827. She stressed the need for the separation of women and children from male inmates, female prisons administered and staffed by women, and a focus on the needs of women for education and discipline. Quaker belief in the value of voluntary public action not only to curb abuse but to propose new reforms was instrumental in founding the Society for the Improvement of Prison Discipline in 1816, as well as stimulating women's prison associations.

In the United States, influenced by the work of Elizabeth Fry, the Women's Prison Association formed in New York in 1844 to improve the treatment of women and to separate them from men. The separation of female inmates was thought necessary because women were more delicate than men, had special needs including familial responsibilities, and were often victims of male inmates and guards. Though some, like Elizabeth Farnham, head matron of the women's wing at Sing Sing (1844–1848), attempted to improve conditions for female inmates fairly early in U.S. penal history, it was not until 1873 that the first female-run prison was opened in Indiana. In 1927, the federal government opened its first women's prison in Alderson, West Virginia.

CONCLUSION

These days, imprisonment has become an increasingly common method of punishment for all sorts of offenders in the United States. Though it has only been used as a punishment in its own right for little more than 200 years, the prison seems to be unassailable. Looking at the history of the development of this institution reminds us not only that it is of relatively recent origin, but also that many practices have been tried before and failed. Thus, as the nation turns to ever greater reliance on solitary confinement in supermaximum-secure prisons like Pelican Bay State Prison in California and ADX Florence in Colorado, we might do well to remember the failures of the Pennsylvania system and its concurrent expense.

—*Venessa Garcia*

See also Alcatraz; Auburn Correctional Facility; Auburn System; Cesare Beccaria; Jeremy Bentham; Bridewell Prison and Workhouse; Zebulon Reed Brockway; Child Savers; Convict Lease System; Corporal Punishment; Cottage System; Flogging; Michel Foucault; Elizabeth Fry; Elmira Reformatory; History of Correctional Officers; History of Women's Prisons; John Howard; Irish (or Crofton) System; Juvenile Reformatories; Alexander Maconochie; Newgate Prison; Panopticon; Parchman Farm, Mississippi State Penitentiary; Pennsylvania System; Philadelphia Society for Alleviating the Miseries of Public Prisons; Plantation Prisons; Quakers; Nicole Hahn Rafter; Slavery; Supermax Prisons; Walnut Street Jail

Further Reading

Foucault, M. (1977). *Discipline and punish: The birth of the prison.* New York: Pantheon.

Johnson, R. (1996). *Hard time: Understanding and reforming the prison.* Belmont, CA: Wadsworth.

Martinson, R. (1974, Spring). What works? Questions and answers about prison reform. *Public Interest, 25.*

Morris, N., & Rothman, D. (Eds.). (1995). *Oxford history of the prison.* New York: Oxford University Press.

Rafter, N. H. (1990). *Partial justice: Women, prisons, and social control* (2nd ed.). New Brunswick, NJ: Transaction.

Rothman, D. J. (1971). *The discovery of the asylum: Social order and disorder in the new republic.* Boston: Little, Brown.

Rothman, D. J. (1980). *Conscience and convenience: The asylum and its alternatives in progressive America.* Boston: Little, Brown.

☑ HISTORY OF RELIGION IN PRISON

"Sin No More," the motto of the New York Prison Association, founded in 1844 and still active as the Correctional Association of New York, evocatively illustrates the religious origins and concepts that laid the foundation of the modern prison. An individual could redeem his or her sin through punishment. Although secular society institutionalized the criminal justice system, religion and religious discourse, whether sincere or formalist, has remained a key part of the correctional realm.

PENITENTIARY

The belief that it was possible to absolve sin through penance was the guiding principle of the early religious prisons and the origin of the term *penitentiary*. Jean Mabillon, a 17th-century French Benedictine monk, was the first to make use of the term penitentiary to designate the monastic prison in which the inmate was to spend his sentence for self-reform through spiritual contemplation and work in silence. Many of the early penitentiary practices, such as flogging and solitary confinement, were used in these religious prisons.

Quakers were the first to advocate prison reform in the United States based on religious principles. In 1787, the Philadelphia Quakers founded the Philadelphia Society for Alleviating the Miseries of Public Prisons. Philadelphia's Walnut Street Jail opened in 1790 where religious services were an integral part of the program for prisoners. Although a number of states built prisons on this model, by the early 19th century atrocious conditions, including overcrowding and congregate living arrangements, prompted reformers to look to new methods and models of confinement. The modern penitentiary was born with the Eastern State Penitentiary in Philadelphia (1829) and the Auburn Prison in New York (1819). Both prisons originally made use of solitary confinement for prisoners and were directed by rigid moralists and religious disciplinarians. Throughout the 19th century, most wardens of these prisons manifested at least outwardly a deep spiritual commitment. Moral instruction was primarily, if not solely, religious, and the prison directors waged a continuous war on sin and social evils.

Through the second quarter of the 19th century, the major champion of the Auburn system of congregate labor and solitary confinement was the puritan New Englander Louis Dwight. Dwight founded the Boston Prison Discipline Society in 1826. The membership of the society was composed largely of Congregational and Baptist ministers. Dwight believed firmly in stern discipline and the inculcation of religious ideas in convicts. Most prisons in the United States until the post–Civil War period followed this model, a model infused with a stern Calvinist idea of the wages of sin.

After the Civil War, American prisons were subjected to the methodology of the social sciences and the professionals who became practitioners in social engineering. But in no way was religion and especially religious rhetoric banished from the corridors of the prison. In fact, Enoch Wines, one of the leading lights of post–Civil War prison reform, who helped compile the ground-breaking *Report on the Prisons and Reformatories of the United States and Canada* (1867), was a Protestant minister. Wines was one of the driving forces behind the National Prison Congress, held in Cincinnati in 1870. The congress, as summed up by Wines, strongly believed in the prison's role in the reformation of character. To accomplish this end, the congress recommended more productive labor, education, and religion in the prisons. The stated principles of the congress propounded reform through religion, education, and industrous work habits. The congress advocated social science methods, but methods still firmly based in religious belief.

THE RISE OF EVANGELISM AND THE SOCIAL SCIENCES

While it is clear that religion was a driving, defining force in prisons through the penitentiary's formative period in the 19th century, faith also found a central place in the prisoner's life during the Progressive period of the prison (1890–1950). It was not the stern Calvinism of olden days, but the Christian evangelical, social uplifting fervor of the social gospel movement. The character of prison reform during this period mirrored that of free-world society. The majority of Progressive reformers were middle-class Protestants who advocated applying Christian precepts to social problems. Moral fervor infused the Progressive prison reform movement with this Protestant spirit. But if the spirit was evangelistic the means were firmly rooted in a misdirected social science methodology that claimed to predict and reform criminal behavior.

As more and more social science professionals and methodologists took the reins of the vast American correctional edifice, official religious rhetoric became more formalist and even less efficacious than in the heyday of Calvinist influence. Though each prison usually had a chaplain, religion itself became more of an individual endeavor among the convicts. Self-reformation became the key for religious change. The increasing secularism that accompanied social science brought an end to institutionalized religion as a tool of reform. In addition, liberal theology advocated a more personal mode of devotion. Religion became just one more individual strategy of survival for the inmate.

THE INFLUENCE OF NON-CHRISTIAN RELIGIONS

Throughout most of the history of the American penitentiary, Christian principles molded the prison. However, as the racial demography of the prison changed during the 20th century so too did its religious makeup. With the great migration of southern blacks to the north and west in the first half of the 20th century, many northern prisons found themselves holding a black majority of prisoners. The militantly nationalistic Black Muslim movement converted many of these convicts. Giving converts discipline, protection, and a sense of purpose, the sect grew rapidly. Perhaps the most famous of these convicts was Malcolm X, who, as Malcolm Little, became a convert to Islam in a Massachusetts penitentiary in the 1950s.

Initially, prison official did not allow Muslims to observe many of the precepts of their religion, including special diets and places and times to hold religious services. In response, a number of convicts asserted their rights and went to the courts, demanding, among other things, copies of the Koran, special meals, and to hold religious services. The U.S. Supreme Court, in 1964, in *Cooper v. Pate* reversed a lower court's dismissal of Black Muslim complaints, recognizing the Black Muslims as a legitimate religious group. This landmark case allowed prisoners for the first time to sue state officials in a federal court. The question of religion in prison thus opened the doors for countless prisoner lawsuits for the remainder of the century.

CONCLUSION

The history of religion in prison illustrates the condemned's quest for self-improvement and salvation. Institutionalized religion is a reflection of a society intent on the moral reformation of character. Religion gave the prisoner a framework in the quest for moral balance. Religion, however, could also be used as a retributive tool. Punishment as penance perhaps best sums up this history.

In the late 20th and early 21st centuries, prisons and prison reform have lost their bearings. The idea of rehabilitation and reformation, which was based on religious principles, fell out of favor in the 1970s and resulted in harsher, truth-in-sentencing laws, the abolishment of parole, and "no frills" prisons. Even so, at the end of the 20th century militant religion has made a comeback in prison in an attempt to resurrect the idea and practice of the ethical transformation of character. A number of moral and penal philosophers have taken up again the concept of religious repentance as an integral ingredient of punishment. Most controversially, a number of Christian prisons have sprung up in various states under the aegis of the Prison Fellowship Ministries, begun in 1976 by Charles Colson, the ex-convict former aide to President Richard Nixon. By many accounts, "graduates" of these prisons fare much better on release, have lower recidivism rates, and lead more productive lives than other ex-convicts. The reasons for these results are still unclear, as are the constitutional questions, but there is no doubt

that religious activity has found a central place once again in the life of the prison.

—*Larry E. Sullivan*

See also Auburn System; Chaplains; Contract Ministers; Islam in Prison; Pennsylvania System; Quakers; Religion in Prison

Further Reading

Corringe, T. (1996). *God's just vengeance: Crime, violence and the rhetoric of salvation* Cambridge, UK: Cambridge University Press.

Etzioni, A., & Carney, D. (1997). *Repentance: A comparative perspective.* Lanham, MD: Rowman & Littlefield.

Fliter, J. A. (2001). *Prisoners' rights: The Supreme Court and the evolving standards of decency.* Westport, CT: Greenwood.

Skotnicki. A. (2000). *Religion and the development of the American penal system.* Lanham, MD: University Press of America.

Sullivan, L. (1990). *The prison reform movement: Forlorn hope.* Boston: Twayne.

☑ HISTORY OF WOMEN'S PRISONS

Women throughout history have been imprisoned with men in refuges, workhouses and houses of correction, jails, debtor's prisons, chain gangs, penitentiaries, reformatories, and correctional institutions. Even so, their presence, and not infrequently that of their babies as well, was (and is) often overlooked in official documents and historical accounts. When it has been noted, often their imprisonment has been a source of concern and controversy. Above all, the numbers of incarcerated women and the conditions of their imprisonment have reflected not only wider socioeconomic realities and changing definitions of crime and forms of punishment but also the perceived nature and position of women at the time.

While there is a long history of women's imprisonment in Europe, Great Britain, and the American colonies, only in the 19th century did women begin to be incarcerated for long periods of time in facilities built for that purpose. Earlier, women and their children could be found in local almshouses and workhouses provided for the care and correction of the poor and the vagrant; in crowded jails awaiting trial and sentencing; or, after sentencing, facing the penalty of death or its alternative, transportation and service in bondage. During the 18th and 19th centuries, Great Britain shipped thousands, women as well as men, initially to the American colonies and, after the American Revolution, to Australia.

HOUSES OF CORRECTION, LOCAL JAILS, AND TRANSPORTATION

During the 16th and 17th centuries, numerous "houses of correction" were established to house women and men found wandering, begging, or engaged in petty thievery or prostitution, for corrective discipline and productive work. London's Bridewell, the first of many in England, opened in 1556 for the confinement of "idle, criminal and destitute women and men." In 1602, the work of all the inmates in the Bridewell was leased to "three gentlemen," who then proceeded to sell the "labor" of the women as prostitutes. The first house of correction constructed specifically for women was Amsterdam's *Spinhuis*. Opened in 1645, it was hailed for its order, cleanliness, and productivity. The women's spinning and sewing was overseen by a warder and his wife in a paternalistic setting whose motto rejected vengeance but affirmed "a compulsion for good," and concluded: "My hand is stern, but my heart is kind."

In Great Britain, men and women were housed together in overcrowded and diseased local jails for many years. In 1813, Elizabeth Fry began visiting the women in London's Newgate Prison with other Quaker women. Most efforts to segregate prisoners by sex are usually traced to this time, and the subsequent public outcry caused by the reformers' reactions to what they saw. Reporting that nearly 300 women—"blaspheming, fighting, dram-drinking, half-naked"—with "their multitudes of children" were crowded into two wards and two cells while they awaited trial or after sentencing, faced death or transportation, Fry and her associates demanded changes in penal policy (Smith, 1962, p. 102). Ten years later in 1823, Parliamentary legislation required the separation of women, the appointment

of a matron for their supervision, and no admission of men into their quarters unless accompanied by a woman officer.

While the 18th century's widening death penalty statutes, primarily for the protection of property, brought an increasing number of condemned women into the jails, the substitution in Great Britain of transportation for its actual use sent women, usually for theft, into the convict ships. Before the American Revolution, more than 30,000 men and women were sent to the colonies. From 1787 to the cessation of transportation in 1852, almost 25,000 women were shipped to Australia. Under the assignment system they were available for service as domestics or laborers, but the government reported in 1812 that they were "given to such of the inhabitants as demanded them, and were in general received rather as prostitutes than as servants" (Dobash, Dobash, & Gutteridge, 1986, p. 33). In response, a "Factory" prison was opened in Parramatta in 1821 to provide shelter and work for women who had not obtained jobs in service. While the original Factory and two others opened later served as a "marriage market" for interested settlers, women also viewed them as a place of protection rather than punishment. The final cessation of transportation forced the government of Great Britain to consider the alternative of long-term imprisonment as a replacement for the transportation that had regularly relieved their jails of women.

PENITENTIARIES OR REFUGES

In the legislatures of the new United States, as earlier in Great Britain's Parliament, there was awareness that capital punishment did not successfully produce a "terror" sufficient to deter an increasing number of property crimes. Influenced by a range of factors, including the writings of Cesare Beccaria, who argued that loss of freedom and public slavery were more effective a punishment than death, the new states built their penitentiaries. During the first part of the 19th century, disputes raged between those who supported complete solitary confinement and others who believed that the congregate silent system was best. Ultimately, the silent system won out, since it enabled prison administrators to put prisoners to work in factory-like conditions, rather than leaving them alone in their cells all day furnished only with a Bible.

Another factor influencing where female offenders were placed can be found in legal scholar William Blackstone's assertion that under English common law a woman's legal existence as a person was suspended in marriage. In particular, under the "protection and influence" of her husband, who may restrain her "of her liberty" for misbehavior, a wife may be excused "in some felonies and other inferior crimes," though not for murder or treason (Blackstone, Sharswood's 1859 ed., Vol. I, pp. 442–444). Courts of the day, in America and Britain, were thus advised to recognize that a wife's criminal actions might occur under the influence of her husband or her need to provide for herself and her children absent her husband's "protection." Within the context of common law, the state as *parens patriae* could assume responsibility to "care and protect" as well as to "restrain" both children and "dependent" women. The state or "benevolent societies" assumed that paternal responsibility and control through the provision of refuges, almshouses, and houses of correction.

However, adult women who as *femme-sole* were legally persons were morally responsible for their actions when charged in a criminal court. Many urban and rural poor women, including freed slaves, had no "civil union" and the men and children in their lives were without legal "existence." As a consequence, they appeared in the courts as fit subjects for penitentiary discipline, as did those women convicted of murder or treason.

In 1833, in the Introduction to Gustave de Beaumont and Alexis de Tocqueville's famous report *On the Penitentiary System in the United States,* Francis Lieber argued that women needed the discipline of the penitentiary even more than men, since a woman in the courts as a *femme-sole* was not only "like a man" but according to "all criminalists" even more dangerous after "renouncing honesty and virtue" (Beaumont & Tocqueville, 1833, p. xiii). Confident that isolation from family, evil companions, and fellow convicts and the use of

terror, silence, and work was of value, an inspector at Sing Sing reported that "no doubt is entertained, but the same discipline which now controls and subdues the male convict may be made equally serviceable with the female" (Beaumont & Tocqueville, 1833, p. xii). In the 1820s, the members of the Boston Prison Discipline Society praised the matron of the women's department of the Baltimore Penitentiary for developing a "system of industry, instruction and religious duty" for her 60 female convicts that saved them from sickness, made them "profitable for the State," and taught them "useful arts" for employment after release (Lewis, 1965, pp. 161, 162).

The reality, however, was revealed in the reports of the congregate penitentiaries where the unwanted women were placed in upper floors, inner rooms, or areas of the penitentiaries where, in competition with the larger numbers of male prisoners, they were deprived of exercise yards, windows, or fresh air. Indeed, just as its value for women was being hailed, the chaplain at the "model" Auburn Penitentiary protested that while the men's conditions were tolerable, for the 20 or 30 women, isolated and left to themselves in a securely locked attic room, it was "worse than death." Similarly, back in England, the governor of the newly constructed Millbank Prison in London reported that women held in solitary confinement in this model penitentiary "became liable to fits" that could be controlled only by the threat to shave and blister their heads. The assumption that women required less food, and thus could be given a reduced diet, had led to an outbreak of scurvy, illness, and death.

WOMEN'S VOICES ON REFORM

At Sing Sing, confident of the value of penitentiary discipline for women, a separate building named Mt. Pleasant, which included a nursery, was built in 1822. Its stormy history reflected the growing tension within prison reform movements between the male members, administrators, and legislators, who were increasingly supportive of solitary confinement, silent systems, and hard labor, and the middle-class women "visitors," who were not.

Predominantly Quaker and Evangelical, these women instead thought that kindness rather than terror was the key to submission and, reflective of women's nature, homelike communal settings rather than solitude were the locus of reformation.

Elizabeth Fry's *Observations on the Siting, Superintendence and Government of Female Prisoners,* published in 1827, became the influential guide for an increasing number of middle- and upper-class women who created their own reformist organizations. The Association of Women Visitors and the British Ladies Society for Promoting the Reformation of Female Prisoners in England and parallel societies in Philadelphia and New York sought control over imprisoned women, while attempting to follow Fry's advice to be "at once wise as serpents and harmless as doves" when facing male administrators and legislators. Fry's vision required a site separated from contact with male inmates or officers, managed by full-time "pious and benevolent" female staff with the assistance of lady visitors who would, through "kind superintendence" and "tender" treatment, develop their system of control and supervision. Her recommendations included classification with progressive motivational stages of privileges, provision for religious instruction, basic education, and continuous useful labor to create both orderly habits and training for later employment as domestics or seamstresses.

After a series of disturbances in Sing Sing's Mt. Pleasant Women's Prison, in 1844 the newly appointed matron, Elizabeth Farnham, influenced by Fry, was determined to transform the discipline that unsuccessfully "subdued" the female convict into one reflecting a "women's world," including the provision of flowers, curtains, a piano, women visitors, and a reading circle. After two years, Farnham was fired for her lack of "discipline."

However, critical changes were beginning to occur that would bring the opportunity for the views of Fry and others on the reformatory management of women prisoners to affect public policy both in Great Britain and the United States. While the penitentiary developed in the United States as the alternative to the "terror" of death, with the refusal

of Australia to accept Great Britain's convicts, England's use of transportation for women ended in 1852. The resultant Penal Servitude Act of 1853 provided that all the rules and regulations for men would also apply to women.

PENAL DISCIPLINE

The heads of both England's and Ireland's prisons attempted to develop integrated systems of penal discipline for their male and female convicts, but Crofton's Irish system, more centralized, coordinated, and well publicized, became the model most influential in the United States. The system incorporated the concept of the "ticket of leave" or parole developed in Australia to release well-behaved convicts into the community before the end of their sentence, and elements of a "mark" system of incentives, not dissimilar to Fry's earlier recommendations, that were associated with the short-lived efforts of Alexander Maconochie to shift from a punitive to a reformative regime in the Australian Norfolk Island penal colony. Crofton's system, viewed positively in the 1850s by members of American prison reform societies, claimed to combine both punishment and reformation within the 3- to 15-year penal servitude sentences through the use of three stages. First, inmates had to endure a punishment period of solitary confinement (shortened for women) to ensure reflective submission and incentive for subsequent reformative discipline. Then they entered a second period of congregate work and successive levels of classification and earned privileges. Finally, they participated in an "intermediate" period of "individualized" supervised work in community settings, prior to early release under the surveillance of the constabulary.

For women, a wing of Dublin's Mountjoy Prison under the supervision of a matron and women officers provided the first two stages. Initially placed in cells for four months of solitary confinement, the women later moved through the levels of classification and increasing privileges in the second stage when they were allowed to participate in a congregate sewing room, schooling and religious instruction, a nursery, and provision for regular "lady visitors." The successful completion of the second stage led to release to two refuges, one for Catholics managed by the Sisters of Mercy and one for Protestants, for work and placement in the community. The Irish system's well-publicized "success stories" tended to obscure the overt and covert resistance of women convicts to their well-disciplined "reformation."

However, viewed and praised by Rhoda Coffin and other influential American reformers, the Irish "reformatory system" became a model for prison management in the United States in the famous 1870 National Prison Association's "Declaration of Principles." The principles reflected the increasingly active role of "benevolent women" in social reform and embodied Fry's earlier vision that there should be separate facilities under "the agency of women." Reformer Coffin and others successfully won legislation in 1869 for the first separate prison for women in the United States, in the wake of sexual scandals at the Indiana Prison and the willingness of the warden to relieve himself of the burden of women. The Indiana Reformatory Prison for Women and Girls opened in Indianapolis in 1873 with women from the state prison and the juveniles housed in separate wings in what was described as a "homelike atmosphere." By 1877, the goal of full administration of the institution by women was achieved when Coffin was appointed head of the board and, in the words of the superintendent, the state "assigned to women the privilege of caring for, elevating and reforming her own sex" (Rafter, 1985, pp. 30–31).

Initially, efforts by women reformers in other states to place women with felony convictions in separate facilities were resisted by legislators and wardens of congregate penitentiaries and prisons who argued that the women inmates' domestic work—sewing, washing, and cooking—were management essentials. Their position was strengthened by the continuing reality that smaller numbers of imprisoned adult women made the provision of a separate system a serious economic burden, starving attempted facilities of needed resources, or in some cases, bringing under one roof all the women supervised by the state.

THE RISE AND DECLINE OF WOMEN'S REFORMATORIES

A critical element of the Irish system of reformative discipline brought to the United States was the administrative use of the incentive of parole to lessen sentence length. Parole was first introduced legislatively in Michigan in 1869 for women, but not men. The Michigan "three years law" for prostitution provided an indeterminate sentence of up to three years in place of a much shorter jail sentence, justified by the need for a longer period to "reform" prostitutes. Based on their good behavior women were released on parole to a newly formed House of Shelter, where they were prepared in a domestic setting to live a "true good womanly life." This gender-specific legislation for "fallen women" legitimized longer sentences for offenses that would not bring men to prison and assumed that women would benefit from differential sentencing and treatment. The result essentially set up a dual system with women with felony convictions remaining in the corners of state prisons while women whose lives did not conform to the dominant beliefs regarding their sexual and domestic responsibilities were brought under the supervision of the state. The House of Shelter combined what historian Nicole Rafter describes as the later model program for women's reformatories, one of a "relaxed prison discipline" combined with that of a "protective home" within a "family-setting," as the appropriate domestic model for the reformation of "fallen women."

The first "women's reformatory" opened in Massachusetts in 1877. After considerable political activity, unsuccessful starts, and persistent resistance, Hannah Chickering, Ellen Cheney Johnson, and others proudly celebrated the construction of the Reformatory Prison for Women at Sherborn (later called Framingham) for women who were "convicted of being vagrants, common drunkards, lewd and wanton and lascivious behavior, common nightwalkers, and other idle and disorderly females" (Lekkerkerker, 1931, pp. 92–94). With large work and school rooms, a chapel and nursery, individual rooms and dormitories and yards for recreation and farming, its founders assured the legislature that by a "direct appeal" to the "self-interest" of these "idle and disorderly females," through the disciplinary use of classification, progressive privileges, shared wages, and conditional release, "voluntary industry, frugality and self reliance may be encouraged and promoted." Echoes can be heard of 16th- and 17-century "houses of correction."

New York followed suit through the politically astute efforts of Josephine Shaw Lowell and Abigail Hopper Gibbons, the first a commissioner of the State Board of Charities and the latter the active head of the Women's Prison Association. The significantly named House of Refuge opened at Hudson in 1887, followed in 1893 by the Western House of Refuge in Albion, New York. With Albion's cottages, including a nursery cottage, the model architecture for a women's reformatory emerged. Cottages promoted "the ideal of family life" with kitchens, dining rooms, and living rooms where, as a report notes, "the family assemble in the evening for diversion" (Rafter, 1985, p. 35). In the rationale for these new institutions, Lowell included not only an affirmation of the Irish system's goal of reformation but also the eugenic need to limit the "unrestrained liberty allowed to vagrant and degraded women" (Rafter, 1985, p. 44).

At the turn of the 20th century, with the emergence within the Progressive movement of professionally educated women, there were new efforts, predominantly in the Northeast and Midwest, to develop reformatories for fallen women. Opened in 1901, New York's Bedford Hills was headed by Katharine Bement Davis. With a doctorate from the University of Chicago, she stressed the scientific study of the backgrounds, characteristics, and methods of treatment for women. The placement of the Rockefeller-funded Laboratory of Social Hygiene at Bedford Hills and the formulation of model legislation for women's reformatories by the National Social Hygiene Association reflected the increasing Progressive concern with the social effects of prostitution. With the outbreak of World War I, fear of venereal disease among the troops led to the first gender-specific federal legislation prohibiting prostitution near army bases and providing federal support for the incarceration of women. Historian

Estelle Freedman estimates that the legislation played a role in the development of at least 20 state women's institutions.

The subsequent passage of federal legislation criminalizing alcohol and narcotic use as well as providing suffrage for women, the appointment of Mabel Walker Willebrandt as assistant attorney general, and the presence of women's organizations active in prison reform brought mounting pressure for the construction of a model federal women's reformatory. The federal government, up to that point, contracted with states to house federal women prisoners. With the exposé by Kate Richard O'Hare, as a federal prisoner convicted under the Espionage Act, of conditions for women in the Missouri State Prison and the reluctance of states to house increasing numbers of women with federal convictions, the groundwork was laid for the significantly named Federal Industrial Reformatory and Industrial Farm for Women at Alderson, West Virginia. Opened in 1927 and staffed by women, the reformatory had, segregated by race, 14 cottages that included a nursery cottage and one named for Elizabeth Fry, as well as a working farm and garment factory, educational programs, forms of self-government, and extensive classification. Eugenia Lekkerkerker, in her classic study *Reformatories for Women in the United States* (1931), described Alderson as "undoubtedly the largest and best equipped reformatory that exists" (p. 127). Alderson was developed, organized, and defended by Mary Belle Harris, a fellow graduate with Davis of the University of Chicago, through 16 conflicted years with the male-administered central office of the Federal Bureau of Prisons (Lekkerkerker, 1931, p. 127).

By the 1930s, the women's reformatory movement had come to an end. States financially unable during the Depression to maintain a dual system brought the women housed in the corner of the state prison to the grounds of the "refuges" or "homes" for women imprisoned primarily for their sexual behavior. At the same time, the administration of both state and federal prison systems became increasingly centralized. While many states accepted the necessity of a separate prison for women, the prisons no longer functioned to serve women, but supported and adopted the custodial values of the male-dominated prison system.

PATRIARCHY, SLAVERY, AND THE NEW SOUTH

While the Northern states developed reformatories for men and women, during the same period in the postbellum South, the passage of the Thirteenth Amendment in 1865 reaffirmed the belief that slavery or involuntary servitude as "punishment for crime" was a "terror-producing" alternative to death. For black women and men freed from domestic slavery, the rapidly developed Black Codes and vagrancy laws legitimated a state slavery that, through the use of convict leasing, provided the labor of both women and men to build the mines and railroads of the New South. In time, Southern states developed their own plantations, exemplified by Mississippi's Parchman Penitentiary, opened in 1900, where the women, most of whom were black, were segregated but vulnerable to sexual assault by male guards and trusties. They canned food, did laundry, sewed clothing, and in time of harvest, worked the cotton fields, reproducing women's roles under domestic slavery. At the same time, white women, with the exception of those *femme-sole* deemed dangerous "like men," were likely to be acquitted or if convicted, in a form of *parens patriae,* pardoned by the governor.

CONCLUSION: EQUAL RIGHTS AND INTEGRATION

In the 1960s, women reformers, often working within the civil rights movement, directly and indirectly shaped women's prisons. Legislation supporting equal employment opportunities had a double effect. Women whose employment options had previously been limited to the world of women's prisons were now able to move into men's prisons and central administration, while men were entitled to guard and administer women's prisons. As racial segregation based on the principle of "separate but equal" was questioned and challenged in the schools, women in the 1970s challenged

gendered disparities in sentencing and the absence of or unequal programs and services for women.

Facing the cost of maintaining separate-but-equal programming for smaller numbers of women, one response at the state and federal level was the "coed" integration of facilities. Driven more by space needs than by programmatic concerns, however, the stated purposes included sharing educational, occupational, and medical resources, as well as "normalizing" relationships. In the face of resistance from staff, divergent disciplinary traditions and controversy on how "normalized" or "sexually exploitive" the relationships became, the reality of increasing numbers of women entering the system at the end of the 1970s curtailed the "experimentation" of co-corrections.

Ironically, the assumed "equality before the law" of sentencing guidelines, mandatory sentences, "three strikes" legislation, and the rejection of indeterminate sentences and parole disproportionately affected women. Like the earlier "war on prostitution," the "war on drugs" that began in the 1980s and still continues brought increasing numbers of women into prison. But rather than the earlier development of differential sentencing and treatment, the response has been increasing uniformity of treatment duplicating, for women, men's facilities and deterrent discipline. "Correctional institutions" may now be separated by gender or be "cogendered," but both are administered and staffed by women and men under the same disciplinary rules. Nevertheless, legacies of the past still remain in buildings, programs, and policies.

—Esther Heffernan

See also Alderson, Federal Prison Camp; Auburn System; Australia; Bedford Hills Correctional Facility; Bridewell Prison and Workhouse; Zebulon Reed Brockway; Classification; Co-correctional Facilities; Cottage System; Katharine Bement Davis; Discipline System; Dorothea Lynde Dix; Elizabeth Fry; Framingham, MCI (Massachusetts Correctional Institution); Mary Belle Harris; History of Prisons; Indeterminate Sentencing; Irish (or Crofton) System; Josephine Shaw Lowell; Alexander Maconochie; Newgate Prison; Kate Richards O'Hare; Parchman Farm, Mississippi State Penitentiary; Pardon; *Parens Patriae*; Parole; Plantation Prisons; Prison Nurseries; Quakers; Nichole Hahn Rafter; Sing Sing

Correctional Facility; Slavery; Thirteenth Amendment; Truth in Sentencing; Miriam van Waters; Mabel Walker Willebrandt; Women Prisoners; Women's Prisons

Further Reading

Beaumont, G. de, & Tocqueville, A. de. (1833). *On the penitentiary system in the United States* (F. Lieber, Trans.). Philadelphia: Carey, Lee and Blanchard.

Dobash, R. P., Dobash, R. E., & Gutteridge, S. (1986). *The imprisonment of women.* Oxford, UK: Basil Blackwell.

Freedman, E. B. (1981). *Their sisters' keepers: Women's prison reform in America, 1830–1930.* Ann Arbor: University of Michigan Press.

Fry, E. (1827). *Observations on visiting, superintending, and government of female prisons.* London: John and Arthur Arch.

Heffernan, E. (1994). Banners, brothels, and a "ladies seminary": Women and federal corrections. In J. Roberts (Ed.), *Escaping prison myths: Selected topics in the history of federal corrections* (pp. 37–79). Washington, DC: American University Press.

Lekkerkerker, E. C. (1931). *Reformatories for women in the United States.* Batavia, Netherlands: J. B. Wolters Uitgevers-Maatschappij.

Lewis, W. D. (1965). *From Newgate to Dannemora: The rise of the penitentiary in New York, 1796–1848.* Ithaca, NY: Cornell University Press.

Rafter, N. H. (1985). *Partial justice: Women in state prisons, 1800–1935.* Boston: Northeastern University Press.

Rafter, N. H. (1990). *Partial justice: Women, prisons, and social control* (2nd ed.). New Brunswick, NJ: Transaction.

Smith, A. (1962). *Women in prison.* London: Stevens.

Zedner, L. (1995). Wayward sisters: The prison for women. In N. Morris & D. Rothman (Eds.), *Oxford history of the prison: The practice of punishment in Western society* (pp. 329–361). New York: Oxford University Press.

◪ HIV/AIDS

At the end of 2000, around 2.2% of all state inmates (24,000 people) and 0.8% of all federal inmates (1,000 people) were infected with HIV. Among state and federal inmates, 0.6% and 0.2%, respectively, had AIDS. According to the Bureau of Justice Statistics (BJS), the rate of confirmed AIDS cases among the nation's prison population in 2000 was about four times the rate in the general population of the United States. Thirteen in every 10,000 persons in the United States general population had confirmed AIDS compared to 52 in every 10,000 prison inmates.

HIV INFECTION AND AIDS

The human immunodeficiency virus (HIV) does not kill a person directly. Instead, it destroys the immune system and makes people infected with HIV vulnerable to infections that are rarely seen in people with normal immune systems. After a person becomes infected with HIV, it may take years for symptoms to develop. During this latency period, many people are unaware they are infected but can still transmit the virus to others. Acquired immunodeficiency syndrome (AIDS) is diagnosed by a physician using certain clinical criteria (e.g., blood test results, AIDS indicator illnesses).

HOW HIV IS AND IS NOT TRANSMITTED

HIV can be spread by oral, vaginal, and anal sex with an infected person. The risk of HIV transmission through oral sex is much smaller than that associated with vaginal and anal sex. HIV is also transmitted by sharing needles or syringes with someone who is infected. Babies born to women infected with HIV may become infected before or during birth, or after birth through breast-feeding. Health care workers may be infected with HIV after being stuck with needles containing HIV-infected blood, or after infected blood gets into a worker's open cut or a mucous membrane (e.g., the eyes or inside of the nose). There has been one case of HIV transmission from acupuncture.

Most HIV-positive inmates became infected prior to their incarceration. HIV transmission through sharing injection equipment and unprotected sex does occur within correctional facilities, although not very frequently. A 1997/1998 article published in *The Canadian HIV/AIDS Policy & Law Newsletter,* for example, described a 1993 study of an HIV outbreak in a Scottish prison, which revealed that 13 inmates who engaged in extensive syringe sharing had become infected in prison. A study of an Australian prison found that at least four injection drug-using inmates had become infected in prison.

Correctional officers and inmates are often afraid of HIV being transmitted through a bite or a sneeze. Neither a small amount of blood being exposed to intact skin nor exposure to sweat, tears, saliva, or airborne droplets has ever been shown to result in HIV transmission. Biting or needlestick injuries pose a low threat of HIV transmission. According to the Centers for Disease Control and Prevention (CDC), 99.7% of needlestick/cut exposures do *not* lead to infection. Biting presents even less of a risk of HIV transmission than does a needlestick. Typically, a biter is more likely to come into contact with the victim's blood than vice versa. The medical literature has reported cases in which HIV appeared to have been transmitted by a bite but all of these cases involved severe trauma with extensive tissue tearing and damage, and the presence of blood. The CDC knows of cases where the hepatitis B virus has been transmitted through tattooing or body piercing, but no instances of HIV transmission through these practices. In the United States, blood is routinely screened for HIV antibodies. Consequently, HIV is very rarely transmitted through transfusions of infected blood or blood clotting factors. HIV is not spread by insects nor through casual contact such as sharing food utensils, towels and bedding, telephones, or toilet seats.

HIV AND AIDS IN PRISONS AND JAILS

The number of HIV infections and AIDS cases dropped from 1999 to 2000; however, this trend was not present in all states. The decrease in the number of confirmed AIDS cases was the first since data collection began in 1991. During 2000, 18 states reported a decrease in the number of HIV-infected inmates while 29 states reported an increase. Nearly one in four inmates known to be infected with HIV are incarcerated in New York; at least 6,000 inmates are infected with HIV in New York. New York also has the highest percent of the custody population that is infected with HIV (8.5%) followed by Maryland (with 4.3% or 998 inmates infected), Florida (with 3.7% or 2,640 inmates infected), and Texas (1.9% or 2,492 inmates infected).

The quality and effectiveness in HIV/AIDS care has improved with the introduction of protease inhibitors and highly active antiretroviral therapy (HAART). As a result, AIDS-related death rates in state prisons have been dropping, from 100/100,000 inmates in 1995 to 14/100,000 in 2000. AIDS-related illnesses are now the third leading cause of death in state prisons (after natural causes and suicides), having been the second leading cause of death since 1991. Death rates vary widely from state to state, however. For example, in 2000, the District of Columbia, Florida, New Jersey, Connecticut, New Hampshire, Pennsylvania, South Carolina, and Alabama all had AIDS-related death rates at least twice the national prison average of 14 deaths/100,000 inmates.

At mid-year 1999, 1.7% of jail inmates (8,615 inmates) were reported to be infected with HIV. Jails in the South and the Northeast account for 80% of all jail inmates known to be infected with HIV. The south held the largest number of inmates infected with HIV, followed by those in the northeast (3,822 and 3,105, respectively). Forty-three of the 50 largest jail jurisdictions held nearly 4,000 inmates who were known to be HIV-positive. Of these, almost one-third were held in New York City jails.

HIV/AIDS raises a number of issues for correctional administration, including those related to testing, housing, education, medical care, confidentiality, and the greater rates of HIV infection among women. Each of these issues is discussed briefly below.

HIV Antibody Testing

HIV infection is diagnosed by an ELISA test that is confirmed by a Western Blot test. Both of these tests detect HIV antibodies rather than HIV itself. It may take as long as several months for antibodies to develop to detectable levels. During this time, an infected person may still pass the virus on to others. All correctional systems provide HIV antibody testing on some basis. In 2000, the most common circumstances under which jurisdictions test inmates are: upon inmate request (46 jurisdictions), upon clinical indication of need (46), upon involvement in an incident (41), or upon intake (41).

Fifteen states test inmates in specific "high risk groups," and a handful of states test inmates upon their release, test all inmates currently in custody, or test inmates selected at random.

Housing

In 1985, 16% of state and federal facilities segregated prisoners with HIV and 75% segregated inmates with AIDS, on the grounds that it would reduce rates of HIV transmission. No reliable studies support this assertion. By 2003, Alabama was the only state to isolate inmates infected with HIV from all other prisoners in both its housing and its prison programs. Most states integrate inmates with HIV infection with the rest of the prison population and permit them to access some, if not all, prison programming. Some states house prisoners throughout the system until their medical condition warrants their transfer to a clinic that provides specialized care. Others—including programs in California, Texas, Florida, and South Carolina—group prisoners known to be infected with HIV into a single facility in an effort to provide state-of-the-art medical care. Some experts are concerned that a quarantine model may give prisoners in the general population a false sense of security and lead to greater transmission within the facility. Also, even in states with special HIV units, the demand for beds may exceed the supply, resulting in a lack of uniformity of care and expertise.

Education and Prevention

Incarceration provides an important opportunity to educate inmates about HIV, sexually transmitted diseases (STDs), and other communicable diseases. A 1997 National Institute of Justice/Centers for Disease Control and Prevention (NIJ/CDC) study found that HIV/STD education and prevention programs were becoming more common in correctional facilities. Few systems, however, had implemented comprehensive and intensive HIV prevention programs in all of their facilities. For example, while over 85% of prison and jail systems provided basic HIV information and explained the meaning of HIV test results, less than half offered education

on more controversial topics such as how to negotiate safer sex or engage in safer injection practices. The NIJ/CDC study found that only 10% of state and federal prison systems and 5% of jail systems offered comprehensive programs in correctional facilities that included instructor- and peer-led programs, pre- and posttest counseling, and multisession prevention counseling.

Correctional administrators in the United States have resisted measures such as condom distribution that might reduce the spread of HIV and other STDs in the facility, citing concerns that condoms might be used as weapons (by filling them with sand or using them to strangle someone) or to conceal contraband. Another concern is that condom distribution implies that sexual activity is permitted when, in fact, it is prohibited behavior. In 2001, only 4% of U.S. jails and 10% of U.S. prison systems permitted condom distribution. Most other industrialized countries (including Canada and most European prison systems) make condoms available to inmates and report few problems.

Medical Care

The introduction of protease inhibitors and HAART in 1996 revolutionized the treatment of HIV/AIDS. These new HIV therapies have reduced morbidity and mortality in the general population, and they are widely available in correctional systems. Still, the treatment of HIV in a correctional setting presents many practical challenges as well as legal and ethical questions.

Barriers to Medical Care

Barriers to medical treatment of inmates remain such as high medication costs; inmate reluctance to seek testing and treatment out of fear, denial, and/or mistrust; and uneven medical competence and treatment standards. Features of correctional facilities such as strict schedules, definitions of "contraband," inmates' extremely limited ability to self-treat even minor medical ailments without reporting to sick call, and the need to constantly balance security concerns over the medical needs of inmates pose several challenges to the delivery of medical services to inmates. Many inmates who are not adequately warned about the complicated drug regimens and the potential side effects may discontinue the treatment. Prison regulations and routines may interfere with inmates' attempts to comply with instructions regarding when and how to take the medication. If an antiretroviral regimen is pursued but fails, it may lead to resistance to other drugs of the same class thus limiting future treatment options and adding to the economic burden HIV imposes on society. Inmates with HIV infection often seek access to therapeutic clinical trials in hopes of obtaining good-quality care from knowledgeable university staff. Because of past abuses, federal regulations discourage—but do not prohibit—research conducted on inmates. Inmates seeking access to clinical trials may be accommodated by research protocols that recognize the importance of voluntary and uncoerced consent for research taking place in a prison setting. To determine the best treatment for the HIV-positive inmate, a clinician must take into account what will work best biologically, what will be most tolerable to the inmate-patient, and what will gain his or her maximum adherence to the treatment plan.

Legal and Ethical Considerations

The U.S. Supreme Court ruled in *Estelle v. Gamble* that inmates have a right to be free of "deliberate indifference to their serious health care needs" under the provisions of the Constitution's Eighth Amendment. According to the National Commission on Correctional Health Care (NCCHC), "deliberate indifference" often takes the form of denied or unreasonably delayed access to a physician for diagnosis and treatment, failure to administer treatment prescribed by a physician, and the denial of a professional medical judgment.

NCCHC identified some specific legal and ethical considerations associated with the provision of medical care. Maintaining rights to privacy has also been proven to be very difficult in a correctional setting where HIV infection is still feared and stigmatized; where medical information may be deduced from an inmate's movement, a cell search,

or a pattern of scheduled visits; and where differing opinions may exist regarding who has a "need to know" someone's HIV status. Correctional staff and inmates have been implicated in breaches of confidentiality in many institutions. These breaches suggest a need to hold prison administrators more accountable for their confidentiality policies. Additional issues relate to the nature of the provider-patient relationship in a prison—the inmate cannot seek treatment elsewhere and the provider cannot refuse to treat the patient-inmate—and the right of a mentally competent adult to refuse treatment.

Women With HIV Infection

Factors such as drug use, race, poverty, having a partner who uses drugs, and having a history of sex work or physical or sexual victimization that place women at increased risk for incarceration also put women at increased risk for HIV infection. HIV infection rates are higher among women prison inmates than men inmates; 3.6% of all female inmates in state facilities were HIV infected compared to 2.2% of men. At the end of 2000, around 20,000 male inmates and 2,200 female inmates in state prisons were known to be HIV-positive. In six states and the District of Columbia, more than 5% of all female inmates were known to be HIV-positive. In two jurisdictions, more than 15% of all female inmates were known to be infected: the District of Columbia (41%) and New York (18.2%). As in the United States as a whole, women of color are overrepresented among those incarcerated who are infected with HIV.

Men and women HIV-positive inmates face similar problems such as the violation of their privacy rights, discrimination and stigma, unsanitary housing conditions, and difficulty accessing quality medical care. In addition, the HIV Education Prison Project reports that women inmates face the additional challenges of receiving HIV care from a doctor who not only has expertise but also recognizes the women-specific issues, such as gynecologic complications of HIV infections, management of the HIV-positive pregnant woman, and monitoring for toxicities of antiretroviral therapy. For example, women who are infected with HIV have high rates of STDs and cervical neoplasia; thus physical examinations should include pelvic exams (with Pap smear and STD screening), and laboratory evaluations should include screening for other bloodborne infections (e.g., hepatitis B and hepatitis C, tuberculosis), and other tests. Around one-quarter to one-third of all untreated pregnant women infected with HIV will pass the infection to the fetus during pregnancy or birth. If a woman can safely take AZT or Retrovir during pregnancy, labor, and delivery and she has a cesarean delivery, infection rates can be reduced to 1%.

Discharge Planning

In 1996, inmates comprised 35% of the U.S. population infected with tuberculosis and 17% of those infected with HIV. Releasing sick inmates—including those infected with HIV—with proper treatment and arrangements for follow-up care not only improves their health status but also reduces the potential threat they pose to public health. Inmates with HIV benefit most from a "continuum of care" encompassing early detection, effective medical and psychosocial support, prevention and risk-reduction counseling, hospice care and substance abuse treatment when appropriate, prerelease planning, and linkage to community-based services. Ideally, discharge planning for inmates with HIV disease and other health problems helps to ensure prisoners will be able to obtain their medications and adhere to their regimens. A 1997 NIJ/CDC study of discharge planning services found that inmates in most correctional systems are given referrals for services. Far fewer systems actually make appointments for inmates and provide additional support and assistance to ensure that inmates make contact and receive the services they need. For example, although 82% of state and federal systems made referrals for HIV medications, fewer than one in three made an appointment. Continuity of care is particularly difficult in jail settings since the time of discharge is often unanticipated and many jail inmates enter and exit the system frequently.

CONCLUSION

HIV/AIDS poses a complex set of legal, ethical, and practical challenges for prisons and jails, particularly in the areas of housing, medical care, education, and discharge planning. While many medical advances have been made in the treatment of HIV infection, efforts are still needed to ensure that inmates' privacy rights are protected and that the correctional system's response to HIV is based on the best epidemiological information available rather than prejudice and fear.

—*Jeanne Flavin*

See also Doctors; Eighth Amendment; *Estelle v. Gamble*; Health Care; Hospice; Physicians' Assistants; Solitary Confinement; Women's Health Care; Women Prisoners

Further Reading

AIDS Education and Global Information System (AEGIS). (2004). Retrieved form http://www.aegis.com

Anno, B. J. (2001). *Correctional health care: Guidelines for the management of an adequate delivery system.* Washington, DC: National Institute of Corrections.

The Body: An AIDS and HIV information service. (2004). Retrieved from http://www.thebody.com/whatis/prison.html

Centers for Disease Control and Prevention. (2001). *Providing services to inmates living with HIV.* Retrieved from http://www.cdc.gov/idu

Dolan, K. (1997/1998). Evidence about HIV transmission in prisons. *Canadian HIV/AIDS Policy & Law Newsletter, 3*(4)/4(1), 32–35. Retrieved from http://www.aidslaw.ca/Maincontent/otherdocs/Newsletter/winter9798/26DOLANE.html

Hammett, T. M., Harmon, P., & Maruschak. L. M. (1999). *1996–1997 update: HIV/AIDS, STDs, and TB in correctional facilities.* Washington, DC: National Institute of Justice.

Maruschak, L. M. (2001). *HIV in prisons and jails, 2000.* Washington, DC: Bureau of Justice Statistics.

Maruschak, L. M. (2002). *HIV in prisons, 2000.* Washington, DC: Bureau of Justice Statistics.

National Commission on Correctional Health Care. (2001, November 11). *Management of persons with HIV infection.* Chicago: Author.

Onorato, M. (2001). HIV infection among incarcerated women. *HEPP News, 4*(5). Retrieved from http://www.thebody.com/hepp/may01/incarcerated.html

Peiperl, L., & Volberding, P. (Eds.). (2003). *HIV InSite Knowledge Base.* San Francisco: University of California San Francisco and San Francisco General Hospital. Retrieved from http://hivinsite.ucsf.edu/InSite?page=KB

◪ HOME ARREST

Home arrest is a form of intermediate sanction that is used as an alternative to incarceration. This practice is known by many different names, including house arrest, home confinement, home detention, home incarceration, or home curfew. It comes in many forms and is used throughout the country for a diverse range of offenders. Typically, the decision to place someone on home arrest sentence is based on risk prediction involving factors such as the offender's past criminal record, the nature and circumstances of the current offense, history of good conduct, community and family witnesses, personal and family history, and drug or alcohol abuse history.

Home arrest allows the criminal justice system to reduce costs and some harmful effects of incarceration while allowing the offender access to rehabilitative opportunities in the community. Offenders under home arrest often serve their sentence (or some part of it) in the community, while remaining in their residence during certain defined hours of the day and night. As a result, they are often able to maintain employment. Where possible they are also required to pay some of the costs of monitoring house arrest, in addition to any restitution they may owe to victims.

Home arrest is administered at the frontend of the criminal justice system as a form of sentencing, but it can also be used at the backend of the criminal justice system as part of parole. It may be used for nonviolent offenders in lieu of prison or for violent offenders and/or repeat offenders as a form of intensive supervision after prison. In some instances, home arrest is used prior to conviction in the criminal justice system for pretrial release of offenders who cannot afford bail or for offenders who pose increased risk of flight or danger to the community.

HISTORICAL USE

Although some may think that home arrest an invention of the late 20th century, it was used as early as the 16th century when church authorities placed Galileo under house arrest for his heretical assertion that the earth revolved around the sun. In very early applications, an armed guard was placed outside the residence to enforce home arrest.

The first widespread use of home arrest in the U.S. criminal justice system occurred almost simultaneously in 1983 in two states, Florida and New Mexico. At the time, New Mexico's criminal justice system predominantly administered home arrest sentences to driving under the influence (DUI) and white-collar offenders, while Florida mainly sentenced DUI offender. Research from Florida indicated that 80% of offenders on home arrest were employed and half participated in restitution and community service programs. After Florida's success, the federal government started using home arrest in 1986 in concert with its early release and parole programs. The federal government in fact has made the most use of home arrest sentencing options.

CURRENT HOME ARREST PRACTICES

Home arrest is used in the United States in the pretrial phase of the criminal justice system, postconviction as a noncustodial sentencing alternative to incarceration, and postincarceration as an additional sanction after release from time served in a jail or prison facility. Offenders on home arrest are frequently required to stay within a few hundred feet of their residence. Some are mandated to remain at home 24 hours a day, while others are assigned curfew with authorization to leave during certain hours. Curfews are determined on a case-by-case basis by criminal justice officials according to the goals of supervision. Offenders typically are allowed to leave for work, medical appointments, appointments for rehabilitative programming, and other preapproved appointments. Compliance with curfews is verified by regular and random visits to the offender's residence and place of employment typically by a probation or parole officer.

Due to advances in cost and technology, electronic monitoring devices have become commonplace in home arrest sentencing to ensure compliance with curfew hours. Private companies, in contract with government or nonprofit agencies, generally make and operate electronic monitoring systems. Offenders are required to wear a monitoring device on their person, such as a bracelet on their ankle or wrist; these devices are often noticeable, but advances have been made so that some appear to be an ordinary watch or pager. Some advances have been made to detect tampering and to ensure compliance such as voice recognition devices and visual verification through video cameras connected to computers, which allow offenders and criminal justice officials to meet without traveling to the offenders' residence.

Modern technology advances have increased reliability of monitoring devices where initially telecommunication and radio signals were used; now some devices have the ability to track the exact location of the offender by using global positioning satellite (GPS). This is used particularly as an enhancement for dangerous offenders, such as sex offenders who are restricted from going near victims, schools, day care centers, and parks. There has even been discussion of surgical implantations of monitoring devices, although due to the intrusive nature of these devices it is unclear that this would be constitutionally permissible.

There are two types of electronic monitoring systems—passive monitors and active monitors. Passive monitors respond only to inquiries; for example, the offender responds to an automated call and then places the monitoring device near the monitoring receiver to verify his or her location. Active monitors send continuance signals to the monitoring device worn by the offender to a monitoring receiver. The monitoring company notifies criminal justice officials if there is any break in the signal or any curfew violations. Typically, probation or parole officers will review the logs of violations at a later date. Violations may be due to unauthorized absences from the residence or place of employment, failure to return to residence, late arrivals, early departures, equipment malfunctions, loss of electrical power or telephone service, or device tampering. Penalties or sanctions for violations vary and commonly rely on criminal justice officials' discretion; however, they can range from increased monitoring to incarceration.

BENEFITS OF HOME ARREST POLICIES

Home arrest policies were originally designed to reduce costs of incarceration and to alleviate overcrowding in jails and prisons. The average cost of incarceration in jail or prison ranges from $10,000 to $25,000 per person per year, while the average cost to administer home arrest ranges from $2,000 to $7,000. Even when electronic monitoring is added to home arrest the average cost ranges from $3,000 to $10,000. The savings appear to be plain and simple. In addition, offenders are often required to pay a portion or the entire cost of monitoring devices.

Home arrest may be particularly advantageous for offenders with special needs. People with physical or developmental disabilities, communicable diseases, terminal illnesses, or mental illness, along with pregnant women and elderly offenders, may benefit from this strategy because they are able to use family and other community resources.

Proponents attest that home arrest is more humane than jails and prisons and minimizes the trauma and stigma of incarceration with hardened criminals. This is particularly true for juvenile offenders. By design, home arrest policies for juveniles comply with federal legislation that requires juveniles to remain outside of sight and sound of incarcerated adult offenders. Home arrest also helps juveniles because it allows juveniles to stay in their current school and education programs, while the home arrest curfews keep juveniles out of trouble and reduce influence of delinquent peers.

Home arrest provides more rehabilitation opportunities, such as job/skill training, drug/alcohol treatment, mental health counseling, self-improvement programs, and general equivalency diploma (GED)/education programs. These types of programs are in more abundance in the community than in jails or prisons and provide a better opportunity to rehabilitate offenders, increasing their likelihood of not returning to a life of crime. Proponents go so far as to claim that even after a period of incarceration home arrest provides an easier transition or reintegration back to community because it provides more structure than regular probation or parole.

PROBLEMS WITH HOME ARREST POLICIES

The critiques of home arrest fall into four general categories. First, critics argue that home arrest results in increased punishment. Second, they contend that home arrest is actually more costly. Third, they suggest that home arrest is actually ineffective in terms of surveillance and public safety, while finally, some argue that home arrest violates offenders' civil rights.

Combining arguments one and two, critics point out that home arrest policies are often used for low-level offenders who otherwise would merely have been sentenced to probation. Due to the restrictions that are part of home arrest, such as curfew and victim restitution, it may be, in fact, more punitive than traditional sentencing particularly since those offenders who receive home arrest frequently need surveillance and rehabilitation opportunities the least. According to this argument, home arrest policies actually increase or "widen the net" of the criminal justice system because offenders on home arrest are monitored more intensively. Violations of conditions are more likely to be detected, which results in more jail or prison terms.

Others point out that for pretrial detainees or for those who violate conditions on home arrest, the time served on home arrest does not count toward time served once they receive their sentencing. In other words, pretrial offenders still have to serve their entire sentence with no credit for the home arrest program time. Last, in terms of cost, home arrest can be expensive to start because equipment must be purchased, monitoring companies must be paid, and probation or parole officers still have to be paid.

For some, home arrest is not effective in terms of surveillance or public safety. Some critics believe that home arrest does not ensure incapacitation of criminal activity, and it does not effectively punish offenders. In general, the purpose of home arrest is incapacitation with some rehabilitation programming, but critics contend that if life goes on as normal without severe consequences this punishment may not deter criminals from violating the law. Others point out the lack of reliability in monitoring systems due to false alarms, battery failures,

interruptions in service, and general lack of adequate technology. Offenders are able to commit crime while at home or in the community without violating any curfew and without the detection of a probation or parole officer. Offenders may keep associating with other criminal offenders and allow them to mastermind, control, or direct others to violate laws. Offenders may be able to continue drug sales, drug and alcohol abuse, conspiracy, and fencing of stolen property in their home. Also, because offenders are locked in the house with their family, home arrest may actually increase certain crimes such as assaults on family members including domestic violence and child abuse.

Despite the fact that staying at home may be somewhat of a luxury, offenders may come to hate their monitoring devices and surveillance officers. There is some concern, in other words, that home arrest may increase the likelihood of criminal activity due to "cabin fever," in which the desire to tamper with the monitoring device may become overwhelming. The effectiveness of home arrest may be reduced as some offenders become "stir crazy" and try to leave the residence. For this reason, many argue that home arrest should not last more than three to six months after which time the general effectiveness tends to wear off. Others contend that home arrest sets unrealistic goals and expectations of success because home arrest requires some level of self-discipline, but most criminals are impulsive by nature.

As mentioned above, concern exists about civil liberty issues in home arrest policies. By extending prison and punishment into the offender's own residence, criminal justice officials are said to be turning the offender's community into one big detention facility. Therefore, home arrest is unduly oppressive and grossly disproportionate to the criminal violations. Home arrest and electronic monitoring are likened to an Orwellian invasion with "big brother" watching over them in the privacy of their own homes. Opponents assert that home arrest is an abuse of monitoring that is so intrusive that it violates Fourth Amendment civil rights—especially those of family members in the same house who did not break any laws. In response, law enforcement points out that home arrest is voluntary and because they have violated laws and victimized others, offenders have diminished civil rights especially in terms of Fourth Amendment waivers.

RACE AND GENDER

The racial and class bias of home arrest policies was evident early in its administration process. In the beginning, house arrest sentences primarily involved mostly male, mostly white, and mostly middle-class offenders because criminal justice officials eliminated offenders with long criminal histories, violent criminal histories, no employment, and no ability to pay for monitoring devices or restitution to victims. In addition, offenders on home arrest often need to provide references from the community to testify as to their good character. As a result of other factors in society and in the criminal justice system, young urban, minority males often have long or violent criminal histories, often lack employment, lack good character witnesses, and lack ability to pay for monitoring or restitution, and many do not have a telephone, which is a requirement for some of the monitoring devices. Because of the policy decision to use house arrest mainly for DUI, white-collar, and other low-level offenders, poor and minority offenders are often excluded. Along with minorities, a larger percentage of unmarried females also lack employment and ability to pay for monitoring and restitution compared to middle-class males. One can imagine the amplified bias young, unmarried, poor, urban, minority females face.

Some criminal justice jurisdictions attempt to address the inherent bias by using a sliding scale for offender income, although this cannot help those who have no employment at all. Some jurisdictions also provide telephones to offenders who do not have them. Community service may be substituted in place of monetary restitution to victims.

CONCLUSION

Although there have been no large-scale studies of the effects of home arrest, some research suggests that those who are confined to their houses for first offenses generally reoffend at lower rates than those who receive other forms of punishment. Some say this success is mostly due to the fact that those offenders had employment, and because home arrest is often given to those offenders who posed little risk anyway.

Home arrest has been used internationally throughout Europe, Canada, and Australia, and it has been used in all 50 U.S. states and the federal system including Guam, Puerto Rico, and the Virgin Islands. It became particularly popular in the United States during the 1980s as a sentencing alternative to combat prison and jail overcrowding, although its popularity waned somewhat in the "get tough on crime" era of the 1990s. At the time of writing, home arrest is on the ascendancy once more because of budget crunches, jail and prison overcrowding, and a national trend of philosophy changes in community corrections from rehabilitation to surveillance. The general public tends to approve of home arrest policies because of the inherent accountability, victim compensation, and offender payment for costs of supervision while maintaining relative community safety.

—Darcy J. Purvis

See also Actuarial Justice; Community Corrections Centers; Electronic Monitoring; Intermediate Sanctions; Parole; Prisoner Reentry; Probation; Work-Release Programs

Further Reading

Ball, R. A., Huff, C. R., & Lilly, J. R. (1988). *House arrest and correctional policy: Doing time at home.* Newbury Park, CA: Sage.

Brown, M. P., & Elrod, P. (1999, Summer). Citizens' perceptions of a "good" electronic house arrest program. *Corrections Management Quarterly, 3*(3), 37–42.

Chicknavorian, E. D. (1990, Winter). House arrest: A viable alternative to the current prison system. *New England Journal on Criminal and Civil Confinement, 16*(1), 53–66.

Courtright, K. E., Berg, B. L., & Mutchnick, R. J. (1997, September). Cost effectiveness of using house arrest with electronic monitoring. *Federal Probation, 61*(3), 19–22.

Courtright, K. E., Berg, B. L., & Mutchnick, R J. (2000). Rehabilitation in the new machine? Exploring drug and alcohol use and variables related to success among DUI offenders under electronic monitoring—Some preliminary outcome results. *Criminology, 44*(3), 293–311.

Gainey, R. R., & Payne, B. K. (2000, February). Understanding the experience of house arrest with electronic monitoring: An analysis of quantitative and qualitative data. *International Journal of Offender Therapy and Comparative Criminology, 44*(1), 84–96.

Walker, J. L. (1990, June). Sharing the credit, sharing the blame: Managing political risks in electronically monitored house arrest. *Federal Probation, 54*(2), 16–20.

◪ HOMOSEXUAL PRISONERS

Current demographic estimates figure that approximately 3% to 9% of the general U.S. population are gay. Similar numbers are thought to live in the nation's penal system. As a result, at any given moment, there are believed to be anywhere from 60,000 to 180,000 gays being detained in U.S. prisons and jails. Though no longer subject to the harsh sodomy laws of the past, these men remain targets of discrimination, hate crimes, and sexual assault, inside and outside prison walls.

INCARCERATING HOMOSEXUALS

Until recently, sexual acts considered to be particularly associated with homosexuality have been against the law in many states. In Oklahoma, for example, persons found guilty of engaging in sodomy faced a maximum prison sentence of 20 years. This law and others like it tended to discriminate against gays as heterosexuals engaging in the same activity were rarely punished. This disparity continued until the landmark case *Lawrence and Garner v. Texas* (2003), in which the U.S. Supreme Court ruled 6–3 that sodomy laws were unconstitutional.

GENDER ROLES

Within single-sex environments such as prisons, normative gender role systems become complicated. For instance, because women are not housed with male prisoners, traditional divisions of gender do not exist there. Instead, interaction between inmates serves to establish a unique cultural hierarchy based on gender roles rather than gender itself. Researchers have attempted to understand the existing gender role system in prisons and to ascribe meaning to three specific observed roles. The roles of "men," "queens," and "punks" serve to stratify inmates into a power structure that is partly based on perceived gender roles from outside the institutional setting.

Men, Queens, and Punks

The majority of male prisoners are classified as "men," meaning that they uphold most traditional norms of masculinity. Regardless of their behavior, most other inmates and guards do not consider them to be homosexual. Most "men" exhibit heterosexual behavioral patterns before and after incarceration and it is only within the confines of the penal system that they may act out what outwardly appear to be homosexual acts. Conversely, "queens," also known as "bitches" or "ladies," are homosexuals whose behavioral patterns inside prison are similar to their actions on the outside. Within the prison subculture, they are essentially considered to be females and are strictly receptive in terms of penetrative sex.

"Queens" are generally submissive to the "men," and are usually not allowed to hold positions of obvious social power. In many correctional facilities, queens are systematically separated from the rest of the population to protect them from violent attacks and to reduce the occurrence of sexual activity and assault. This partitioning sometimes leads to discrimination against queens, and they are often denied inmate privileges, such as library and yard exercise rights. Effeminate gay men who enter the prison system are often pressured to assume a role because overt homosexuality is believed to be socially unacceptable. However, men are able to exist as openly gay without having to subscribe to these specific gendered identities. A small percentage of homosexuals pass as "men" by assimilating into this dominant subculture.

"Punks" are typically young, nonviolent, middle-class offenders. Because of these factors, they often find themselves as minorities in position of conflict within the social hierarchy. The relationships between queens and punks are often very tense, as punks usually far outnumber queens. More important, since the most coveted position is in partnership with a "man" who will protect his allies from the dangers of prison life, queens resent being passed up for punks. However, punks are also at higher risk of being raped by "men" and therefore occupy a marginalized role of their own.

SITUATIONAL HOMOSEXUALITY

Often mistakenly equated with homosexuality, situational homosexuality happens when heterosexual inmates participate willingly in homosexual relationships. Though it can simply be a response to loneliness and/or desire, situational homosexuality is often formulated around a hierarchy of power based on the sexual status of individual prisoners and the particular role they play within that hierarchy. This system is sometimes the source of sexual violence within prisons, when rape and assault are used as tools to maintain positions of authority among the prison population. Unfortunately, there is scant writing on situational homosexual activity before the 20th century, limiting attempts to trace its historical development. However, some evidence documents situational homosexuality, both consensual and coercive, in 19th-century prison systems.

Though difficult to gauge, researchers have been attempting to understand the prevalence of sexual activity within the penal system. One prominent recent study suggests that at least 80% of inmates perceive themselves to be heterosexual, whereas 8% report being homosexual. Of these, just under 19% are believed to have had a steady male partner. With regards to specific sexual acts during incarceration, 24% reported having touched or allowing their penis to be touched; while 23% had participated in oral sex. Twenty percent admitted to having had anal sex, and 8% had kissed or had been kissed by a fellow inmate.

THEORIES ABOUT SITUATIONAL HOMOSEXUALITY

A range of different explanations exist for why men who otherwise self-identify as heterosexual take part in homosexual activities remains unclear. For example, former inmate and prisoner rights activist Steven Donaldson has suggested that when a "man" sexually penetrates another inmate it is generally not viewed as a homosexual act. Instead, it serves to reinforce the "man's" masculine identity and power within the social hierarchy. Thus, within the confines of the prison, penetrating a "queen" or a "punk" is still considered to be heterosexual and to a certain extent, normal.

In contrast, proponents of the deprivation theory argue that prison homosexuality is specifically caused by the "pains of imprisonment." Based on the work of Gresham Sykes, these authors identify five specific pains prisoners face: the deprivation of liberty; deprivation of goods and services; deprivation of autonomy; deprivation of security; deprivation of physiological and emotional gratification associated with heterosexual relationships. Loss of these outside world comforts are then thought to cause inmates to seek gratification through alternative sources, usually through sexual relationships. Thus, prisoners can justify their transition to homosexual behavior because they are bored, needy, or lonely. Critics of this theory argue that sexual relationships established within the system often result in further victimization and exploitation. They also argue that it is difficult to measure deprivation because the individual inmates' perceptions of personal deprivation may not coincide with individual researchers' conceptualizations.

In contrast, followers of the importation theory believe that the behavior, both sexual and otherwise, of inmates is brought to the prison system from the outside. According to this theory, previous homosexual experience external to the prison setting is significant in predicting homosexual behavior while in prison. Thus, proponents of this theory suggest that inmates are sexually expressing themselves as they really are. Critics of this theory argue that most inmates' previous homosexual experience took place in jails, other reformatories, or incarceration programs. Thus, there is something unique about same-sex settings that seem to foster situational homosexuality.

HIV/AIDS

Individuals who participate in high-risk drug use, tattooing with dirty needles, unprotected sex, and sex work are at risk of contacting HIV/AIDS.

Specifically, those who engage in anal intercourse are at highest risk of contracting the deadly disease. Even though sexual activity is generally prohibited among inmates, it is undoubtedly a part of prison life. Prison officials are often tolerant of sexual relationships among inmates, and view them as an issue of minimal importance. Whether consensual or not, unprotected sexual relations put inmates at high risk for contracting HIV/AIDS. Despite the fact that sexual activity is acknowledged as a fact within prisons, in a majority of settings, condoms are considered to be contraband.

Not surprisingly, then, the current rate of confirmed HIV/AIDS cases is five times higher in state and federal prisons than among the general U.S. population, with African Americans and Hispanics being disproportionately affected. Because prisons have the nation's highest concentration of individuals with HIV/AIDS and are the population at highest risk for contracting it, heath experts refer to the circumstances as of epidemic proportions. Despite this, current research suggests that HIV transmission among prisoners is low and that most HIV-positive prisoners contracted the disease prior to incarceration. Regardless of these findings, any individual who engages in sexual activity, whether consensual or not, is at high risk for contracting the fatal illness while in prison.

VIOLENCE AGAINST GAY MEN

Violence against gay men is prevalent inside and outside of the prison setting. The torture and murder of Matthew Shepard in 1998 made national headlines and created widespread awareness of hate crimes against gays. Meanwhile, the prison setting has not been immune to such brutal attacks. In one well-known case, *Gregory v. Shelby* (2000), a known homosexual inmate was sexually assaulted and then murdered by a fellow prisoner.

SEXUAL ASSAULT

Sexual aggressors act out assaults for power rather than for sexual gratification. In men's prisons, inmate rape is generally committed by a "man" or group of "men" as an act of assertion of authority against one who wishes to preserve his heterosexual or homosexual autonomy. It is believed that sexual assault in male prisons reinforces the stereotypes associated with traditional societal gender roles. Thus, the largest influence of sexual assault is attributed to the "men," who are believed to be the ringleaders of social politics within the confines of prison.

Based on what is currently known about sexual assault in male prisons, race, class, and age appear to be significant factors for victimization. Middle- and upper-class prisoners are often more susceptible to sexual attacks because they are usually nonviolent and inexperienced in the prison's subculture. In addition, younger male inmates tend to be assaulted most often, as well as whites. In women's prisons, inmates tend to be assaulted by male prison guards, as opposed to other female inmates. Regardless of gender, victims are often discouraged from seeking help out of fear or shame. Even when sexual crimes are reported, disciplinary action is more likely to be imparted on known homosexuals than on known sexual aggressors.

Human rights groups have raised awareness of this sexual violence for both male and female prisoners, calling for significant policy changes. Proposals for reform include a tighter classification system based on the level of security needed to protect individual inmates, the legalization of consensual homosexual activity while still punishing rape, and the allowance of conjugal visits. Some institutions have abolished cell sharing, some house all "queens" and "punks" apart from the "men," and others punish any and all sexual activity. Others are developing educational campaigns to train guards to better handle situations of reported sexual assault. Perhaps most important, in 2003, the federal Prison Rape Elimination Act (HR 1707) was enacted calling national attention to the seriousness of sexual assault in prisons.

CONCLUSION

Just as a portion of the general population are homosexual, so also is a segment of the prison population.

While traditional homosexuality and situational homosexuality are often confused, same-sex intercourse can and does occur among both homosexuals and heterosexuals. However, gender roles and prison norms decidedly influence how each act is perceived by participants and by other inmates. For this, among other reasons, sexual assault within the penal setting is believed to be commonly used as a tool for reinforcing the hierarchical social order. Even consensual sexual relations can prove threatening as HIV/AIDS has become a more significant threat to inmates than to members of the outside population. Academics, activists, law enforcement agents, families, and inmates are all working toward creating sustainable solutions for these specific problems, and toward reaching out to homosexual inmates.

—Amy E. Desautels and Melissa J. Klein

See also Deprivation Theory; Stephen Donaldson; HIV/AIDS; Homosexual Relationships; Importation; Lesbian Prisoners; Lesbian Relationships; Prison Culture; Rape; "Stop Prisoner Rape"; Gresham Sykes; Violence

Further Reading

Donaldson, S. (1993). *A million jockers, punks, and queens: Sex among American male prisoners and its implications for concepts of sexual orientation.* Retrieved from www.spr.org

Hensley, C. (2000). Consensual homosexual activity in male prisons. *Corrections Compendium, 26*(1), 1–4.

Hensley, C. (Ed.). (2002). *Prison sex: Practice and policy.* Boulder, CO: Lynne Rienner.

Maruschak, L. M. (2001). HIV in prisons and jails, 1999. *Bureau of Justice Statistics Bulletin.* Retrieved from www.ojp.usdoj.gov/bjs/

U.S. Department of Justice. (2004). Bureau of Justice Statistics: Prison statistics. Retrieved from http://www.ojp.usdoj.gov/bjs/prisons.htm

West, D., & Green, R. (Eds.). (1997). *Sociolegal control of homosexuality: A multinational comparison.* New York: Plenum.

Legal Case

Gregory v. Shelby, 220 F. 3d 433 (6th Cir. 2000).

Lawrence and Garner v. Texas, 539 US 558 (2003).

◪ HOMOSEXUAL RELATIONSHIPS

In American prisons, heterosexual sexual activity is restricted. While regulations vary across states, some inmates may have access (either legally or through contraband) to pornographic materials. In a small number of jurisdictions, others may participate in conjugal visits. Finally, still others satisfy their heterosexual sex drives by engaging in sexual activity with prison staff, both consensually and nonconsensually. However, many inmates who seek sexual experiences are limited to homosexual encounters. These occur in both male and female correctional institutions, although there are gender differences in how these homosexual relationships develop. This entry will specifically examine homosexuality in male prisons; other entries in this volume address sexuality in female prisons.

Research on sex in prison has been limited. Studies in male correctional institutions have focused mainly on coerced sex, while much recent research has stressed the prevalence of sex in prison and the problems associated with the human immunodeficiency virus (HIV). However, much remains unknown about sexuality in prison, including how often voluntary sexual activity between two or more inmates occurs and how many prisoners actually engage in homosexual relationships.

It is important to conceptualize two types of homosexual activity. The first is dispositional homosexuality, best described as individuals who self-identify as gay or lesbian. Self-identified gays and lesbians are rare in prison. Those who are incarcerated are often at risk. In male prisons especially, homosexuals hold a low status in the prison culture and sometimes require protection. The second type of homosexual activity is situational. This occurs when the individual self-identifies as straight, but turns to homosexual activity due to a lack of heterosexual opportunities. Situational homosexuality comprises the majority of prison sex.

Research regarding bisexual or transgender inmates is scarce, but no doubt a study of them would further develop the topic of prison sexuality. A recent study of jail inmates in protective custody found that there were some differences between bisexual and gay inmates. Gay and bisexual prisoners reported feeling disrespect from their peers and from officers. However, gay inmates were less likely than bisexuals to change their behaviors while in jail, and were more likely to be harassed.

HOMOSEXUAL RELATIONSHIPS IN MALE PRISONS

Very little research has focused on consensual sex in male prisons, much less on relationships that form behind prison walls. However, there is a limited body of literature about the practice of exchanging sex for protection in what can amount to long-term relationships between male inmates. Anecdotal evidence, for instance, in Pete Earley's (1992) treatment of Leavenworth Penitentiary, *The Hot House,* is the most descriptive of this type of relationship. Essentially, a new, generally weak inmate (or "punk," in prison argot) makes the choice to partner with a stronger, more established man. The punk provides sexual favors, completes errands, and does other tasks as assigned by his partner. In return, he receives protection, so that it is understood that a conflict with the punk is tantamount to a conflict with his partner.

Whether or not these arrangements are consensual is debatable. On the one hand, some inmates choose to enter into these relationships. However, others may be pressured, by threat, intimidation, or actual force. Some individuals may feel as though becoming a punk is necessary for their own protection, so they do so voluntarily but without a true desire to be partnered with another man.

Entering into a relationship as a punk has long-term implications for an individual. Even if the initial relationship is short in duration, that inmate will carry the punk label and its implications of weakness with him throughout his prison stay. If the relationship ends, the prisoner may find it necessary to enter into a new relationship, or he may be physically coerced into doing so. If a relationship lasts, it is possible that the two inmates will transcend the simple exchange of sex for protection. Some men have reported caring relationships that have developed between the punk and his protector. However,

others may perceive the relationship as an undesirable necessity. It appears that the transaction of sex for protection is a key characteristic of these relationships, with other forms of emotional intimacy being secondary.

ATTITUDES REGARDING HOMOSEXUALITY IN PRISON

There is a small body of research concerning attitudes toward homosexual activity in prisons. This section will briefly address the attitudes that inmates, correctional officers, and gay activists organizations hold toward prison homosexuality.

A study of inmates examined what characteristics were related to feelings of homophobia. Being female, African American, or having previous homosexual sexual experiences were associated with lower levels of reported homophobia. These findings are consistent with research regarding attitudes toward homosexuality outside prison walls, lending support to importation theory—the idea that inmates bring their existing attitudes into prison.

Research on correctional officers has found that most believe that prison sexuality is motivated by situational homosexuality (as described above). Officers were less likely to discover incidents of rape than they were to happen upon incidents of consensual sexuality. However, an overwhelming majority of officers acknowledged that they found it difficult to determine whether acts were consensual or coercive by nature. As reported above, the line between consensual and coerced sexuality in prison is a blurry one. While a majority of officers felt that both consensual and coerced sexual acts should be prevented, they rated preventing consensual sexual activity as less important.

Finally, while there has not been specific research regarding the role of gay advocacy organizations in issues of prison sexuality, it is possible to note some trends. It appears as though groups on the outside of prison are willing to become involved through advocacy and public awareness with issues of prison homosexuality in a very limited way. Namely, such groups appear to become involved only when there are reports of abuse or failure to protect inmates. However, these circumstances appear to be rare—there does not appear to be much in the way of a permanent linkage between gay inmates and gay interest groups on the outside.

CONCLUSION

Homosexual relationships occur in all correctional institutions. However, there is limited research on consensual sex in prisons. Future scholars must work to clarify the nature of sexual activity, and attitudes toward it, within prisons.

—*Stephen S. Owen*

See also Argot; Bisexual Prisoners; Conjugal Visits; Contraband; Homosexual Prisoners; Importation; Lesbian Prisoners; Rape; Sex—Consensual; Sexual Relations With Staff; Transgender Prisoners; Women's Prisons

Further Reading

Alarid, L. (2000). Sexual orientation perspectives of incarcerated bisexual and gay men: The county jail protective custody experience. *The Prison Journal, 80,* 80–95.

Corrections Compendium. (2002, August). Inmate privileges and fees for service. *Corrections Compendium, 27,* 8–26.

Donaldson, S. (1996, August). The deal behind bars. *Harpers Magazine, 293,* 17–20.

Earley, P. (1992). *The hot house: Life inside Leavenworth Prison.* New York: Bantam.

Eigenberg, H. M. (2000). Correctional officers and their perceptions of homosexuality, rape, and prostitution in male prisons. *The Prison Journal, 80,* 415–433.

Gordon, G., & McConnell, E. H. (1999). Are conjugal and familial visitations effective rehabilitative concepts? *The Prison Journal, 79,* 119–135.

Hensley, C. (2000). Attitudes toward homosexuality in a male and female prison: An exploratory study. *The Prison Journal, 80,* 434–441.

Hensley, C., Struckman-Johnson, C., & Eigenberg, H. M. (2000). Introduction: The history of prison sex research. *The Prison Journal, 80,* 360–367.

Sykes, G. M. (1958). *The society of captives: A study of a maximum security prison.* Princeton, NJ: Princeton University Press.

Tewksbury, R., & West, A. (2000). Research on sex in prison during the late 1980s and early 1990s. *The Prison Journal, 80,* 368–378.

◪ HOOCH

Hooch, a term used to describe a fermented drink traditionally made by Native Americans of the Northwest, refers to any illicit alcohol manufactured by prisoners. As in the civilian world, alcohol or hooch is one of the common ways people deal with the boredom of their prison lives. Normally, hooch is made through a fermentation process of some combination of yeast, fruit, or sugar, but it can be made in many other ways, all of which are relatively easy, inexpensive, and can take from a few hours to a week. Fermented hooch requires only the basic ingredients of a fruit or starch base, a means of fermentation, a container, and a secure location to store the products away from staff or other inmates.

HOW IS IT MADE?

Although hooch can be made from any grain or fruit, the easiest and most common way of making it is with fruit juice, which can be obtained from sympathetic staff, kitchen personnel, or the commissary. Either by using yeast as a starter or by the more difficult way of attempting a natural fermentation, the concoction is distilled for a few days and then immediately consumed because of the short shelf life. This process requires practice and patience to perfect the timing and proportions of ingredients. Once some has been made to satisfaction, the starter can be saved for future batches. The fruity syrup in canned cherries or berries provides one of the best sources of making hooch. The heavy sugar content and fruit residue in the hands of a skilled practitioner provide a flavorful wine-like beverage with high alcohol content. Staff who have tested hooch made from this syrup during shakedowns claim that it contains as much as 10% alcohol, far higher than the more common 2% to 5% in hooch made from fruit juice or sugar-enhanced Tang.

A second way of obtaining alcohol is by filtering commissary or kitchen items, such as mouthwash or artificial food flavorings, through bread. The filtering helps remove impurities and concentrate the alcohol. Prisoners with access to refrigeration may also take mouthwash or similar products, freeze them several times, and pour off the alcohol, which does not freeze. If done successfully, this produces a high-content alcoholic liquid that can either be consumed directly or mixed. Although this method can produce some exemplary high-quality alcohol, it requires access to a freezer that is relatively secure from staff scrutiny for at least a few days to allow freezing. It is also expensive because of the costs of obtaining commissary items. However, because of the high alcohol content, it can be more easily stored, and its manufacture does not produce the fermentation odor that can alert staff.

Hooch can be made in any container, including individual-sized milk cartons or the preferred plastic gallon containers. Although open containers such as large cans be used, those with lids are far better in order to prevent impurities or insects from contaminating the product, and to reduce odor. Inexperienced hooch makers often ignore the need to make the product in sanitized, or at least clean, containers. Neglecting this detail risks disrupting proper fermentation and decreases the potability.

CONCEALMENT

Outsiders often wonder how prisoners can make alcohol in a controlled and tightly monitored correctional environment. Although there is considerable risk of discovery, which can lead to severe disciplinary sanctions such as segregation, loss of "good time" credits, and increased long-term surveillance by staff, the rewards of making hooch generally outweigh the costs of discovery, especially for long-term prisoners.

Most commonly, prisoners produce hooch in their cells, despite the risk of discovery either due to the occasional fermentation odor or during a shakedown. There are, however, some limitations to this method. In institutions that restrict prisoners' property only to that which can be contained in designated property boxes, there is little opportunity for hiding contraband in the cell. The confined area of a cell also limits the quantity that can be produced at one time. As a result, some hooch manufacturers hide the alcohol in concealed areas within the prison that staff and other inmates are unlikely to find. This strategy often requires collusion with sympathetic staff or with trusted peers who will help secure the area and not sample the beverage before completion. Workshop areas, secluded vegetation, or rarely used storage facilities are ideal.

HOOCH AND PRISON CULTURE

Hooch serves secondary functions beyond consumption. If made in quantity, it can be a valuable commodity in the prison economy, sold or traded for other scarce resources. Skilled producers also receive a measure of respect from other prisoners, which is also a valuable asset. On occasion, staff can use it as a control mechanism by gaining compliance or compromise from producers in return for allowing discrete production. When this occurs, there are generally tacit rules that, if violated by prisoners, lead to shakedowns, discipline, and temporary halt of production.

It is not necessarily the actual production or consumption of hooch that creates problems, but the derivative consequences created by competition over scarce and highly valuable resources. Although not as valuable as drugs, yeast is also a marketable commodity, and it can be easily smuggled in or obtained in-house and bartered. Some inmates who may not themselves make hooch are able to traffic in yeast smuggled in from the outside. Producers can take part of their fermentation and give it to others who are less skilled. But this also creates the risk of competition for "markets." This, in turn, may lead to turf conflicts or other disputes, because as a valuable commodity, hooch distribution—as it was outside prison during Prohibition in the 1920s—becomes profitable for those who control it.

CONCLUSION

Contrary to some observers who claim that prison hooch is invariably foul tasting, skilled prisoners can produce a potent and pleasant-tasting libation that ranges in taste from homemade beer to an after-dinner aperitif. Regardless of taste, prison hooch is a mainstay of the prison culture both for prisoners and—on occasion—staff.

—*Jim Thomas*

See also Commissary; Contraband; Deprivation; Governance; Importation; Prison Culture; Resistance

Further Reading

Cardozo-Freeman, I. (1984). *The joint: Language and culture in a maximum security prison.* Springfield, IL: Charles C Thomas.

Jones, R. A., & Schmid, T. (2000). *Doing time: Prison experience and identity among first-time inmates.* Greenwich, CT: JAI.

Marquart, J. W., & Roebuck, J. B. (1987, January). Institutional control and the Christmas festival in a maximum security penitentiary. *Urban Life, 3*(4), 449–473.

Sykes, G. M. (1958). *The society of captives: A study of a maximum security prison.* Princeton, NJ: Princeton University Press.

HOSPICE

Death is not the worst possible outcome of medical care. Death is not even the worst possible outcome of incarceration. Dying alone, in pain, without social, familial, and spiritual supports is the terrifying end that many prisoners and, indeed, most people fear. Unfortunately, it is too often the reality they experience.

—*Nancy Neveloff Dubler and Budd Heyman (1998, p. 355)*

WHAT IS HOSPICE?

Hospice is a form of end-of-life care that emphasizes palliative care services. *End-of-life care* refers to supportive services for individuals with advanced and potentially fatal illnesses. These services may include curative, life-prolonging, and palliative treatments. *Palliative care* includes comfort services designed to provide relief from symptoms without necessarily addressing or resolving underlying health problems. The intent is to provide relief from symptoms associated with serious, chronic, or terminal illness to improve quality of life, not to either extend or hasten the dying process. Hospice programs differ from other end-of-life care and palliative programs by specific patient enrollment requirements; they are limited to terminally ill patients with limited life expectancy. In addition, to be recognized as a hospice program, formal licensure or accreditation according to state regulations is required.

Hospice provides palliative or comfort care only to patients who have been diagnosed with terminal illness. Eligibility for inclusion in a hospice program varies by state and institution, but generally requires that the patient not only have a terminal diagnosis, for example, cancer or AIDS, but also a prognosis or life expectancy of less than six or 12 months to live. Determining a specific prognosis is very difficult and has proved to be a problem in hospice enrollment. Physicians are often reluctant to suggest that a patient has such a limited life span. Rather than requiring a definitive prognosis, enrollment in hospice may be based on a reasonable belief that a patient is likely to die within the next six months or year.

In addition to these eligibility requirements, patients may be required to have a "do not resuscitate" (DNR) order. This is a statement that allows health care professionals to forgo cardiopulmonary resuscitation (CPR) in the event that the patient's heart stops or other advance directives that limit life-sustaining treatment, for example, the use of ventilators, feeding tubes, or antibiotics. To be enrolled in a hospice program, patients must consent to the treatment approach and specific requirements. For those who are unable to consent themselves, for example, unconscious, comatose, or mentally incapacitated patients, a surrogate decision maker, usually a close family member, may consent on the patient's behalf.

Hospice is considered a concept or philosophy of care rather than a place. The concept dates back to medieval times and symbolizes care designed to comfort travelers and the sick. While hospice care may be provided in a particular place such as a unit in a hospital or a free-standing facility, it is more often provided in a patient's home or care setting (e.g., nursing home or assisted living facility), wherever it is most appropriate for the patient. The concept is one of comprehensive, interdisciplinary care for patients approaching the end of their lives. The emphasis is on palliative or comfort care rather than curative treatment, and usually includes emotional, spiritual, and practical support as well as physical treatment. Some curative treatments, such as hip replacement surgery or radiation therapy for cancer, may be offered to increase the patient's comfort. The goal is to offer personalized services to support patients comfortably through the dying process.

The services are designed to create a caring environment in which the biological and other aspects of care are integrated to enhance meaningful existence in the final phase of life for both the patient and his or her family. Palliation addresses distressing physical symptoms such as pain, shortness of breath, and fatigue; social, psychological, emotional, or spiritual issues such as grief, fear, and loneliness; and other needs identified by patients and their families. Services extend to grief counseling after the patient's death.

An interdisciplinary care team, usually directed by a physician, addresses the needs of the patient and family. These teams may consist of various arrays of physicians, nurses, health professional assistants, therapists, social workers, case managers, clergy, dietary professionals, pharmacists, psychologists, and administrators. Trained volunteers provide companionship and other nonmedical care and when possible, the family is involved. Hospices often coordinate with other services within the community, including inpatient medical services, ancillary medical services, and social service programs such as counseling. All services are readily available to patients based on identified needs. The total package of services is covered by Medicare for patients who qualify for Medicare (note, this does not include inmates) and meet the hospice eligibility requirements. The requirement for a limited prognosis stems from Medicare and other third-party payer coverage restrictions.

HISTORY OF THE CARE OF DYING INMATES

Health care practices within prisons generally became a matter for public concern and litigation in the 1970s, after a series of prison uprisings and public advocacy forced the issue. A landmark federal court decision, in *Newman v. State of Alabama,* addressed living conditions in the entire prison system. With regard to the adequacy of prison medical services, the court recognized conditions it deemed

constitutionally impermissible, including the use of unlicensed caregivers and instances of neglect and abuse. Other federal courts attempted to articulate a constitutional standard of care until the U.S. Supreme Court in the 1976 case of *Estelle v. Gamble* offered the basic constitutional standard of adequate health care:

Deliberate indifference to the serious medical needs of prisoners constitutes the unnecessary and wanton infliction of pain ... proscribed by the Eighth Amendment [in its protection against cruel and unusual punishment]. This is true whether the indifference is manifested by prison doctors in their response to the prisoner's needs or by prison guards in intentionally denying or delaying access to medical care or intentionally interfering with treatment once proscribed.

The provision of health care services, or lack thereof, is not to be used as part of an inmate's punishment. Since *Estelle v. Gamble,* other cases have provided substantive content to the requirement for adequate health care in prisons and jails, extending services available in the community to inmates. For example, the courts have ruled on the meaning of deliberate indifference, requirements for the provision of psychiatric care, inmate hospitalization, special medications or diets, emergency medical service training, contagious disease screening, and appropriate health care professionals. These rulings have been translated into standards for correctional health services, although such standards are limited to issues pertaining to specific legal cases and do not offer comprehensive guidelines.

The American Correctional Association (ACA) policy supports hospice services and mandates that health services provided within prisons be consistent with community health care standards. Historically, end-of-life care had not been a regular concern of correctional facilities. However, the development of hospice and palliative care programs in prisons was prompted by institutional changes, recognition of the needs of dying inmates, specific requests from prisoners, and the infrequency of compassionate release. Corrections officials began to recognize and respond to the need for special services to care for the dying among its aging prison population in the mid-1980s.

The early development of prison hospice may be traced to the work of a paraplegic, wheelchair-bound prisoner at the U.S. Medical Center for Federal Prisoners in Springfield, Missouri, in 1987. This inmate, Fleet Maull, was living on a hospital ward and recognized the increasing number of dying inmates, especially those with AIDS, and their special needs. He noted that they often died alone without support from family or friends either outside or within the prison. He began to visit a few dying inmate-patients and felt that the close relationships they developed with him in their final weeks and months made a significant difference in their lives. Based on this experience, he developed a formal proposal for an inmate-staffed hospice volunteer program. Maull went on to found the National Prison Hospice Association.

Institutional changes provided impetus for the continued development of prison hospice. These changes included an influx of seriously ill inmates, especially those with HIV/AIDS; the use of determinant sentences; "three strikes" laws; and limited compassionate release programs. The combination of increased numbers of seriously ill inmates and longer sentences ensure more deaths in prisons. Compassionate release or medical furlough programs, while available in the majority of states and the Federal Bureau of Prisons, are rarely used, also ensuring that inmates will die while incarcerated. Compassionate release refers to the release of seriously ill or dying inmates through procedures including the commutation of sentences through the department of corrections, executive clemency, or commutation; reduction of sentence through the courts; administrative leave or furlough; and parole. The judges, administrators, governors, and parole boards must weigh the needs of the ill and dying inmate against society's need for protection, retribution, and deterrence. The expense of providing the medical services an inmate needs may also affect the consideration. Despite the humanitarian goals of compassionate release programs and the limited threat to society from a terminally ill inmate, mandatory sentencing

requirements may make compassionate release impossible.

The first national survey on hospice and palliative care was conducted by the National Institute of Corrections in 1998. According to that study, the U.S. Bureau of Prisons and 11 states were operating prison hospice programs at one or more of their penal institutions. In addition, four more states, one municipal prison system, and the Correctional Service of Canada were developing formal hospice programs; nine states offered palliative care outside of a hospice program; and 11 states were considering the development of hospice programs. Further study since 1998 indicated that the numbers of palliative care and hospice programs continues to grow.

INMATE PALLIATIVE CARE AND HOSPICE PROGRAMS

Prison palliative care or hospice services mirror those available in community programs. Common program goals include the provision of appropriate and holistic care for dying inmates consistent with hospice philosophy, enhancement of the care available at the institution, and the assurance of "death with dignity." Palliative or hospice care services are provided to patients maintained within the general prison population, within prison hospital facilities, in special hospice beds, within independent licensed hospices, or in community hospitals (with prison supervision). Inmates are often transferred from one institution to another to gain access to these services.

Inmate eligibility for these services generally are they same as for community hospice; the inmate-patient must be terminally ill and have a prognosis of six months or less to live though some allow for a longer prognosis or require only physician referral or recommendation. Inmates, like other patients, are asked to consent to receive palliative services and may be required to sign DNR orders to participate in palliative care services. Palliative care or hospice services are available to all prisoners, male and female, where programs exist throughout the country.

Licensure or accreditation for hospice may be obtained from state agencies or national organizations. Prison hospices may be licensed by the same agencies as community hospice. To be licensed or accredited, an outside agency assesses a program for compliance with particular standards. Correctional health care is accredited according to standards from organizations such as the Joint Commission on Accreditation of Healthcare Organizations, the National Commission on Correctional Healthcare, and the ACA. These organizations are developing standards for prison hospice licensure. Until these are implemented, assessment is done according to community hospice standards.

Little is known about the cost of palliative care and hospice programs in total, per service, or per inmate, but existing programs report that their costs are covered by the general prison health care services budget. The average length of stay or use of palliative care services appears to be longer for inmates than for patients who are not incarcerated. The requirement for a limited prognosis may be relaxed in the prison setting as inmate health care is not affected by Medicare and other third-party payer restrictions.

The available services vary among existing programs but contain some consistent elements. Special visitation arrangements for friends, family, and fellow inmates are a key aspect of existing programs. Other elements include advance care planning; pain and symptom management (with adequate formularies); companionship from family, volunteers, or pastoral care services; bereavement services; and funerals or memorial services.

Interdisciplinary care teams are similar to those in community hospice programs, but in prisons also include security officials. Community hospices are involved with many of the programs in some capacity, such as program development, technical assistance, working with families, or discharge planning.

Programs may also use community volunteers, inmate family members, and prisoner volunteers. The inmate volunteers provide supportive services and companionship, but usually cannot be employed by the program and cannot provide medical services. Inmate volunteers can provide companionship; conversation; assistance with eating, hygiene, telephone calls, letter writing, and movement; reading and

activities; and spiritual support. The use of inmates remains difficult and controversial. Problems include concerns about protecting inmate-patient confidentiality, the potential for healthy inmates to victimize the weak, inmates violating or financially exploiting visiting family, unregulated inmate movement around an institution, and concerns about diversion or narcotics and other drugs used to treat the dying inmates. However, with careful screening, training, and supervision, institutions with inmate volunteer programs report success.

Through training, the inmates learn about the value of the program, the importance of confidentiality, and the consequences of any abuses. Including security personnel in the interdisciplinary team assists in the prevention of problems. Rather than creating problems, the inmate volunteers often become model prisoners, develop skills that will be useful when they are released from prison, experience increased compassion for others, work to protect the integrity of the program, feel comforted about the possibility of their own deaths in prison, and report appreciation for participation in the program. Prison personnel also report satisfaction with prison hospice programs and the use of inmate volunteers.

PRISON HOSPICE PROGRAM EVALUATION: BEST PRACTICES

The GRACE (Guiding Responsive Action in Corrections at End-of-Life) Project began in 1998 with the support of a grant from the Robert Wood Johnson Foundation. This collaborative of a number of correctional, research, and philanthropic organizations collected information on the state of end-of-life care organizations, aided in facilitating palliative care program development, and developed a set of best practices. Best practice program components include the use of

interdisciplinary teams, including physician, nurse, chaplain, and social worker, at a minimum;

increased visitation for families, including inmate family;

involvement of inmate volunteers;

comprehensive plan of care;

training in pain and symptom management;

advance care planning;

bereavement services; and

environmental adaptation for comfort.

SOME PROBLEMS WITH PRISON HOSPICE

Several characteristics of America's prisons combine to pose enormous challenges to achieving quality palliative or hospice care. Problems generally include balancing care and correction, notifying inmates about the availability of services, managing the program, and security concerns. Public opinion may not be supportive of programs to comfort inmates when prisons are designed to punish. Inmates are often in facilities far from home and may need to be transferred to access palliative services, making family involvement difficult. Prisons operate according to scale and promote conformity so that individual preferences and needs are difficult to address. Overcrowding interferes with the provision of services. Treatment plans are also be frustrated by inmate classification. Concerns about drug abuse and diversion constrain efforts to provide state-of-the-art pain management and symptom control. Pressure to avoid liability and litigation may result in the use aggressive treatment despite an inmate-patient's preference for palliative care. Communication and service delivery are complicated by the need to involve correctional personnel who must emphasize security and institutional efficiency.

In addition, a number of management problems are unique to older inmates, defined as those inmates at least 50 years of age. The geriatric population in prisons counts individuals younger than those in the outside population. Poor socioeconomic status, lack of access to medical care, lifestyle choices, and prison life combine to prematurely age inmates before and during incarceration. Management problems specific to this population include vulnerability to predatory abuse, difficulty mixing with younger inmates, need for accommodation for individual disabilities, requirements for special programming, and disproportionate consumption of health care services. Accessibility, safety, modified confinement conditions, classification procedures, and security are among the greatest challenges for those caring for elderly inmates and prison administrators.

End-of-life care programs in jails face many of the same difficulties as in prisons, but difficulties are exacerbated by short-term stays, rapid turnover, limited staff time and other resources, inadequate formularies, volunteers shortages, and security concerns. Yet some jail facilities are developing end-of–life care programs and transitional services. They are partnering with local hospices and working with prisons and community service providers.

CONCLUSION

Prison palliative care and hospice programs are growing throughout the United States in recognition of the needs of the increasing number of dying inmates. The programs reflect community-based hospice programs but are tailored to the unique needs of inmates, the physical setting of the prison, and security concerns. Overall, palliative care and hospice programs have overcome a number of difficulties and help many prisoners, correctional personnel, and institutions. Reported benefits for inmate-patients include increased comfort, appreciation, control, companionship, and family involvement. Inmate workers or volunteers also describe personal growth and appreciation for their participation in the programs. Benefits for institutional staff include help with workload, positive feelings toward the institution and inmate-patients, increased awareness of hospice and personal mortality, and improved care delivery. As standards for prison hospice develop, a number of health care and prison organizations continue to increase the quality of health care prisoners receive as they approach the end of life.

—Felicia Cohn

See also American Correctional Association; Compassionate Release; Determinate Sentencing; Elderly Prisoners; *Estelle v. Gamble*; Furlough; Health Care; HIV/AIDS; Increase in Prison Population; Women's Health Care

Further Reading

American Correctional Association public correctional policy on correctional health care, ratified by the American Correctional Association Delegate Assembly at the 117th Congress of Correction in New Orleans, LA, August 6, 1987, reviewed and amended at the Congress of Correction in Nashville, TN, August 23, 1996.

Dubler, N. N., & Heyman, B. (1998). End-of-life care in prisons and jails. In M. Paises (Ed.), *Clinical practice in correctional medicine* (pp. 355–364). St. Louis, MO: Mosby.

Faiver, K. L. (1997). *Health care management issues in corrections.* Lanham, MD: American Correctional Association.

GRACE, End-of-Life Care Standards of Practice in Correctional Settings. (2004). Retrieved from http://www.graceprojects .org/graceprojects/standards.htm

Maull, F. W. (1998). Issues in prison hospice: Toward a model for the delivery of hospice care in a correctional setting. *Hospice Journal, 12*(4), 57–82.

National Institute of Corrections. (1998). *Hospice and palliative care in prisons: Special issue in corrections.* Longmont, CO: Author.

Ratcliff, M. (2000). Dying inside the walls. *Journal of Palliative Medicine, 3,* 509–511.

Legal Cases

Estelle v. Gamble, 97 S. Ct. 285, 290, 429 U.S. 97, 104–105 (1976).

Newman v. State of Alabama. 349 F. Supp. 278, 503 F. 2d 1320, 5th Cir. (1974), *cert. denied* 421 U.S. 948 (1975).

◪ HOWARD, JOHN (1726–1790)

The origins of contemporary prison reform in the United States can be traced to an 18th-century English sheriff, John Howard. Howard, who was both a nonconformist and a social reformer, perhaps single-handedly changed the administration of English gaols and many of the habits of their inmates, rescuing prisoners from the conditions of neglect and filth in which they had long been held. Though Howard died more than 200 years ago, his legacy lives on. In the 21st century, his ideas are carried on through the work of several influential prison reform organizations in North America that currently bear his name, including the John Howard Association of Alberta, Canada, and the John Howard Association in Chicago, Illinois.

BIOGRAPHICAL DETAILS

At first glance, Howard seems an unlikely champion of prison reform. Born in 1726 in Enfield, England, to a comfortable middle-class family, Howard's childhood was disrupted by his poor health and by the death of his mother when he was 5 and of his father when he was 16. His subsequent years were spent in travel. On a trip to Portugal in 1756, his ship was captured by French privateers. Howard shared the sufferings of his fellow countrymen while on the ship, receiving little food or water while the ship sailed to a dungeon located in Brest, Belgium. Howard spent six days in the dungeon where treatment of prisoners was not much different than on the ship. He was further imprisoned at Morlaix, France, but was soon exchanged for a French officer. When he returned to England, he reported his experience to the Commissioner of Sick and Wounded Seamen of the British Royal Navy and was successful in receiving action to alleviate the conditions of the other English seamen.

After release, Howard married Henrietta Leeds, became a vegetarian, and turned to managing his landed estate. He also provided partial funding for a school for children that resided on his estate.

INSPECTOR OF PRISONS

In 1773, Howard was appointed sheriff of Bedford. One of his duties, neglected by his predecessors, was to inspect prisons. He soon found that in the three regional prisons for which he was responsible, prisoners were ill-treated. He also found that large numbers of men were confined simply because of their inability to pay various fees. For example, prisoners were required to pay their jailer, who received no other salary and, as a result, had little incentive to use any funds to improve conditions or to provide basic amenities. A previous unsuccessful attempt had been made to introduce legislation changing how jailers were paid. However, it was not until Howard made his case to the English Parliament that two Gaol Acts were passed in 1774. The first set all prisoners free who were held for nonpayment of jailer fees and authorized jailer salaries. The second bill addressed health in prisons by encouraging improvement of sanitary conditions.

At his own expense, Howard began touring the prisons of Europe for the purpose of promoting reform. He focused especially on prison architecture, noting that water, circulation, and light were generally inadequate. Combined with lack of fuel, inadequate clothing, poor hygiene, and lack of food, prisons were badly in need of reform. Howard especially drew attention to many prisons having inadequate water. Drawing from his observations in British and European prisons, in 1777 he published a pamphlet, *The State of Prisons in England and Wales,* which radically changed penal policy in England and abroad.

Shortly after publishing his second and final book, *Lazarettos,* in 1789, John Howard set off once more to inspect prisons in eastern Europe. After tending to a prisoner with typhus, he became ill and died in the Crimea on January 20, 1790.

REFORM

John Howard put forward a series of general and specific reforms in his writings and public lectures. In particular, he was concerned with reducing the filth that characterized most penal facilities of the time. He argued that prisons should improve sanitation, by removing human waste, keeping cells and other living areas clean, and providing prisoners with clean water, soap, and bathing opportunities. The proper circulation of fresh air, he asserted, would reduce outbreaks of contagious diseases that characterized early-modern penal establishments. Likewise, Howard advocated separation of sick prisoners and for providing health care facilities for them.

In addition to his concerns about the cleanliness of facilities and the health of their inmates, he urged classification of prisoners so that the more violent offenders, youths, and other special populations not be housed together. As with other penal reformers,

he strongly believed that prisoners should be kept occupied, rather than lying idle, and so he recommended various forms of penal labor. Finally, Howard advocated education to inform the public of the state of prisons.

CONCLUSION

Howard's works changed prisons in North America in several ways. First, his writings were widely read by reformers in Europe and North America. Second, the English reform acts based on his work provided model legislation for other countries including the United States. Reformers such as Jeremy Bentham drew from Howard's writings in redesigning prison architecture, and integrated Howard's emphasis on sanitation, air circulation, and natural light in their design. In the United States, Quakers drew heavily from Howard's writings in advocating humane prisons, in designing the Eastern State Penitentiary in Philadelphia. Finally, Howard's emphasis on making the public aware of prison conditions continues to be a primary goal of prison reform groups in the 21st century.

—Chris Schneider

See also Abolition; Bridewell Prison and Workhouse; Corporal Punishment; Critical Resistance; Angela Y. Davis; Elizabeth Fry; History of Prisons; Prison Monitoring Agencies; Pennsylvania System; Quakers; Walnut Street Jail

Further Reading

Forsythe, B. (Ed.). (2000). *The state of prisons in England 1775–1905.* London: Routledge.

Guy, W. A. (1875). John Howard's true place in history. *Journal of the Statistical Society of London, 38,* 430–437.

John Howard Society of Alberta. (1991). *John Howard: Portrait of a hero.* Retrieved from http://www.johnhoward.nf.ca/org/jh_hstry.HTM

Johnston, N. (2000). *Forms of constraint.* Chicago: University of Illinois Press.

Lewis, B. R. (1998). *John Howard.* Retrieved from http://www.britannia.com/history/biographies/jhoward.html

Sweeting, R. D. R. (1884). The experiences and opinions of John Howard on preservation and improvement of the health of inmates of schools, prisons, workhouses, hospitals, and other public institutions, as far as health is affected by structural arrangements relating to supplies to air and water, drainage, & c. *Journal of the Statistical Society of London, 47,* 25–141.

◪ HUNTSVILLE PENITENTIARY

Since 1849, Huntsville has served as the headquarters of the Texas state prison system, which is currently the largest in the United States. An imposing red-brick fortress known as "the Walls," Huntsville gained national prominence not only for hosting the spectacular Texas Prison Rodeo but for its grim history of conflict, including perennial scandals, endemic abuse, and prisoner uprisings. Today, the Walls is home to America's busiest death chamber.

FOUNDATION

Although Texans considered building a prison under Mexican rule, construction did not begin until after U.S. annexation in 1848. Its model was the industrial penitentiary at Auburn, New York, dedicated to regimented labor rather than solitary penitence. Through most of the 19th century, Huntsville's rule books required prisoners to march in drills, eat in silence, and put in long hours at the textile factory and other workshops. During the Civil War, Huntsville became a vital source of cloth for the Confederacy, so much so that officials imported runaway slaves to staff the mill.

CONVICT LEASING

The end of slavery transformed Huntsville. Before the Civil War, the prison confined only whites, as Texas law stipulated that free blacks and slaves were to be punished only by whipping, hard labor, or hanging. After emancipation, however, a rapid influx of African American prisoners—many of them convicted of petty offenses such as "stealing a cap"— soon crowded the Walls. Pressed for cash and reluctant to build another penitentiary, lawmakers responded in 1867 by hiring out prisoners to the highest bidder. Thus, like other southern states, Texas adopted the convict lease system—the most ignominious punishment regime in American history.

Photo 2   Huntsville rodeo clowns

As Texas's flagship institution, Huntsville provided a safer, generally less brutal punishment environment than other sites. While the state shipped out most black and Mexican convicts to isolated mining, railroad, and agricultural camps, Huntsville remained largely white and devoted to skilled industry. Moreover, enlightened administrators such as Thomas Jewett Goree, superintendent from 1877 to 1891, as well as a succession of physicians and chaplains, kept a close eye on its operations, ensuring that modest education and recreation programs developed.

Nevertheless, convict leasing generated its share of turmoil at Huntsville. In the 1870s, investigators discovered that juveniles as young as seven were languishing in its filthy cells and that lessees were engaging in "lascivious conduct" with black women prisoners. A group of federal soldiers held briefly at the Walls complained of spirit-breaking toil and a crude genital torture device called "the horse." Partly because Huntsville housed a number of well-educated prisoners, these wretched conditions engendered a literary protest movement around the turn of the 20th century. One convict writer complained that he was held in an "abject manner as a slave," while another described his time at the Walls as "fourteen years in Hell."

REFORM AND RETRENCHMENT

Huntsville underwent another dramatic transformation in 1910, when legislators abolished leasing after

Photo 3   *Huntsville electric chair*

a protracted campaign by labor leaders, muckraking journalists, and progressive clergymen. A new team of administrators dedicated to "order" and "humane treatment" reasserted state control and enacted far-reaching changes: new shower and laundry facilities, a new reformatory for women, convict wages, and the abolition of whipping. Within three years, however, budget cuts, combined with uncooperative guards and mutinous convicts, precipitated a fierce backlash and swept away many of these reforms.

This grim cycle of reform and retrenchment would forecast much of Huntsville's 20th-century history. In 1927, former suffragists and other Progressives seized leadership of the prison system and tried to implement the tenets of scientific penology, turning the Walls into the testing ground for a new classification scheme, medical program, and work regime. Borrowing from Thomas Mott Osborn's experiments with prison democracy at Sing Sing, authorities also allowed Huntsville prisoners to organize a Prison Welfare League, which attracted thousands of members, as well as an award-winning prisoner newspaper, *The Echo,* which remains in publication

today. As during the 1910s, however, parsimonious politicians and obstructionist guards, combined with a surge in prisoner escapes, ensured that most of these efforts were short lived.

More lasting changes were enacted after World War II under the leadership of Oscar Bryon Ellis (prison chief from 1948 to 1961), who came to power after an epidemic of prisoner self-mutilations. With a more generous budget than his predecessors, Ellis renovated Huntsville, modernized prison industries, and systematized education efforts. By enforcing rigid discipline and staff loyalty, Ellis and his protégés also made Texas's prison system into a national model of economy and order. Many believed the price of order was too high, however. In the 1960s, prisoners at Huntsville and nearby units began filing lawsuits, and in 1980 a federal judge declared Texas prisons unconstitutional. Thus began another reform effort that itself unraveled at the close of the 20th century.

HUNTSVILLE'S NOTORIETY

Through all of this administrative upheaval, Huntsville gained notoriety as a site of fierce conflict and public spectacle. Chronic conflagrations and periodic uprisings—including a death row breakout by members of the Bonnie and Clyde gang in 1934 and a bloody hostage crisis in 1974—kept the Walls in the news. More enduringly, the Texas Prison Rodeo, founded at Huntsville in 1931, evolved into one of Texas's major tourist attractions. Until 1986, tens of thousands of visitors streamed into Huntsville's stadium each fall to watch convicts get banged up in "the world's fastest and wildest" rodeo and to be entertained by celebrities, ranging from Tom Mix to Loretta Lynn. Between 1938 and 1946, a national radio show, "Thirty Minutes Behind the Walls," added to Huntsville's fame, while numerous Hollywood film productions, from *The Getaway* (1972) to *The Life of David Cole* (2003), have chosen Huntsville as their setting.

CAPITAL PUNISHMENT

Huntsville is also famous for its association with the death penalty. Executions began there on

February 8, 1924, when five young African American men were killed in the state's new electric chair. Texas executions had previously been handled at the county level. Huntsville's warden resigned, complaining that "reforming men and killing them can't be the same job," but his protest did little to slow the work of "Old Sparky," which dispatched 361 convicts between 1924 and 1964. The Walls's busiest execution era, however, began in 1982, when the state pioneered the technology of lethal injection. Since then, more persons have been executed at Huntsville than in any other state: 297 as of October 2002.

CONCLUSION

Although the exponential growth of Texas's prisons since the late 1960s has decreased its importance (in 2001, the Walls was but one of 105 Texas prisons and it housed just 1,544 of 144,981 inmates), Huntsville remains the centerpiece of the state's penal system. Top administrators live and work nearby. Because Huntsville operates a discharge center, many prisoners spend their last night in custody at the Walls. An assemblage of weather-worn brick fortifications and modern surveillance cameras, the prison stands as a monument to Texas's tortured past of enslavement, convict leasing, and arrested reform, even as it plays a key role in the state's colossal, bureaucratized punishment regime of our own time.

—*Robert Perkinson*

See also Auburn Correctional Facility; Auburn System; Capital Punishment; Convict Lease System; Death Row; Deathwatch; Plantation Prisons; *Ruiz* v. *Estelle*; Sing Sing Correctional Facility

Further Reading

Crouch, B. M., & Marquart, J. W. (1989). *An appeal to justice: Litigated reform of Texas prisons.* Austin: University of Texas Press.

George, A. L. (1893). *The Texas convict: Thrilling and terrible experience of a Texas boy.* Austin, TX: Ben C. Jones.

Hallinan, J. T. (2001). *Going up the river: Travels in a prison nation.* New York: Random House.

Lucko, P. (1999). *Prison farms, walls, and society: Punishment and politics in Texas, 1848–1910.* Unpublished doctoral dissertation, University of Texas, Austin.

Lyons, G. (1977). Stars and stripes. *Texas Monthly, 5*(2), 88–95, 143–148.

Marquart, J. W., Ekland-Olson, S., & Sorensen, J. R. (1994). *The rope, the chair, and the needle: Capital punishment in Texas, 1923–1990.* Austin: University of Texas Press.

Simmons, L. (1957). *Assignment Huntsville: Memoirs of a Texas prison official.* Austin: University of Texas Press.

Walker, D. R. (1988). *Penology for profit: A history of the Texas prison system, 1867–1912.* College Station: Texas A&M University Press.

I

ICE DETENTION FACILITIES

See INS DETENTION FACILITIES

IMMIGRANTS/ UNDOCUMENTED ALIENS

Many migrants attempt to enter foreign countries illegally every year. In a separate but often interconnected system, most countries have processes to enable refugees to remain in their country through claims of political asylum. Known as "asylum seekers," these refugees petition the government for protection from their native countries' oppressive political system and, if granted, they are allowed to stay.

The majority of countries hosting undocumented immigration have generally dealt with the problem through detention and/or deportation. Illegal immigrants are processed in the correction and prison system either when they are detected entering the country without authorization or when they are arrested for committing some other crime. Depending on jurisdiction, apprehended immigrants are either detained to serve out an imposed criminal sentence, returned to their native country, or a combination of both.

Although most developed countries face similar problems of unauthorized immigration, the nature of occurrence and particular methods of dealing with undocumented aliens vary. This entry focuses specifically on the U.S. experience. As is common, the terms *undocumented aliens*, *undocumented immigrants/migrants*, *unauthorized aliens*, *unauthorized immigrants/migrants*, *illegal aliens*, *illegal immigrants/migrants* are used interchangeably.

HISTORICAL TREATMENT OF ALIENS IN THE UNITED STATES

Over the course of the 20th century, the United States increasingly supervised and penalized illegal aliens, depending in part on their racial or ethnic background. At the beginning of the 21st century, laws surrounding immigration and asylum have become very restricted indeed.

Prior to the late 1800s, the United States maintained an open immigration policy. Most free people could come and claim a piece of land for settlement thereby taking citizenship. By the early 1900s, America began to codify immigration laws through the establishment of quota acts. Cycles of economic depressions in 1870, 1907, and later in 1921 fueled concerns of immigrants displacing Americans in the labor force. In response, the federal government began to restrict the number of immigrants allowed in the United States by setting limits on the number of legal entries. Fears of mass migration of the Chinese to the United States adding to labor shortages prompted the passage of the Chinese Exclusion act of 1882. This act prohibited Chinese from becoming U.S. citizens and prevented further Chinese immigration for a 10-year period. The terms of the act were extended three times before it was repealed in 1943 as a result of the U.S. and Chinese alliance during World War II.

In 1917, the first immigration act governing all migration to the United States was passed. This act required all foreigners to pass a literacy test and prohibited nonwhite immigration from most of Asia. In 1924, Congress passed and later amended the National Origins Act placing a ceiling on the number of allowable immigrants at 150,000 per year. It also established a quota for each nationality equal to 2% of that group already living in the United States according to the 1890 census. As the vast majority of the U.S. population was composed of people from Western and Northern Europe, considerable restriction was placed on entries from nations of Eastern and Southern Europe, Asia, Africa, and Latin America.

There are other instances where U.S. immigration policy has discriminated against people based on their ethnicity. In 1924, some 112,000 Japanese Americans were removed by force from their homes and placed in concentration camps. Likewise, illegal Mexican migrants were targeted during enforcement campaigns that removed them from the United States and returned them to Mexico. The first campaign was conducted from 1929 to 1934 and was called a "repatriation campaign." The second, referred to as "Operation Wetback" lasted from 1954 to 1958.

Over the next several decades, a series of immigration policy reforms were introduced that altered the landscape of legal immigration in response to the ebb and flow of geopolitical interests, economic conditions, and prevailing political ideology. Prior to the 1960s, immigration policy consistently specified

particular groups and races of people for exclusion. In 1965, the United States adopted a new approach that eliminated racial and ethnic exclusions for the first time in history, yet maintained a ceiling of total allowable entries. Referred to as the "preference system," the new act awarded immigration status based on relatives of the entrant who lived in the United States.

By the mid-1980s, concern over the number of illegal immigrants had grown once again. In response to pressures to control the size of the illegal alien population in the United States, the 1986 Immigration Reform and Control Act (IRCA) initiated three primary provisions: (1) It created sanctions for employers who knowingly hired undocumented aliens, (2) it increased enforcement along the U.S. borders, and (3) it legalized some of the then current illegal aliens residing in the United States. Just four years later, the 1990 Immigration Reform Act for the first time stipulated that all immigrants were subject to numerical restrictions, restricted criteria for entry, and liberalized conditions for exclusion. In 1996, the U.S. Congress passed the Illegal Immigration Reform and Immigrant Responsibility Act and the Antiterrorism and Effective Death Penalty Act. These two acts expanded the powers of the Immigration and Naturalization Service (INS) by allowing for the detention and deportation of any illegal and legal immigrant who has been charged with or convicted of a drug offense or who otherwise possesses a criminal record. In addition, they established measures to control U.S. borders and augmented enforcement of laws prohibiting businesses from employing illegal aliens.

EFFECTS OF THE SEPTEMBER 11 ATTACKS

The September 11, 2001, terrorist attacks in New York City and Washington, D.C., perpetrated by 19 hijackers, all of whom were Arab, initiated yet another chapter in immigration management and discriminatory policy. Soon after the terrorist attacks,

Congress formulated and passed the 2001 USA PATRIOT Act, which set out a wide range of provisions to strengthen the government's ability to prevent future acts of terrorism. Among its provisions it allowed for mandatory detention of asylum seekers from 33 Arab nations identified as sources of terrorists carried out in Operation Liberty Shield. Such individuals will be detained while their asylum requests are processed without opportunity for judicial review.

Consistently, the opportunity for legitimate entry into the United States has narrowed and the enforcement of those in violation strengthened. Such regulations have increased the number of aliens into the correctional system. Largely determined by prevailing domestic and international concerns, throughout the course of history immigration policy has selected people of different nationalities and ethnicities for differential treatment or exclusion.

THE NATURE OF UNDOCUMENTED ALIENS IN U.S. CORRECTIONS

The exact number of illegal aliens entering the United States every year is unknown. Estimates of the number of unauthorized immigrants living in the United States range from 7 million to more than 9 million (Reyes, Johnson, & Swearingen, 2002). While the exact number is elusive, during 1999 the INS and its patrol division, the U.S. Border Patrol, apprehended more than 1.7 million aliens who entered the country without inspection or had overstayed the term of their visa. Of those apprehensions, 90% were made along the U.S.-Mexico border.

Most apprehended aliens are deported to their country of origin voluntarily, while others are detained temporarily until their fate can be determined. Some, particularly those claiming political asylum, are processed then released into the United States pending immigration proceedings if they do not threaten national security or pose a risk of absconding.

Migrants managed by the U.S. correctional system are held in a variety of types of facility. Most detainees are held in federal and state prisons and local jails along with other criminal offenders. A smaller proportion are housed in INS-operated facilities specifically constructed for those charged with immigration-related offenses. Still others are held in privately managed facilities under exclusive contract with the INS.

CURRENT TRENDS

Over the past several decades, the United States has seen a marked increase in the enforcement, arrest, and incarceration of immigration-related offenses. At the end of year 2001, the INS held 19,137 detainees. Since 1985, the number of detainees has more than doubled and the number serving a sentence of imprisonment has increased almost nine times, from 1,593 to 13,676 (Scalia & Litras, 2002). Moreover, those convicted of an immigration offense are serving longer sentences. The average time served for an immigration offense has risen from 4 months in 1985 to 21 months in the year 2000.

In 2000, there were a total of 16,495 individuals referred to U.S. attorneys for immigration offenses. Of those, 75% were charged with unlawful entry or reentry, 20% were charged with smuggling or harboring unauthorized aliens, and the remaining 5% were charged with misuse of visas or other immigration infractions. Identified in Table 1, of those charged with an immigration offense in the federal system, 57% come from Mexico. The second largest group of noncitizens charged with an immigration offense came from Asia and Oceania with 4%. Another 3% and 2% came from Central America and the Caribbean, respectively. Those charged with an immigration offense also tend to be male and young. For the year 2000, the Bureau of Justice Statistics reported that 9 out of 10 charged with an immigration violation were male and more than half were under the age of 30.

Table 1   Nationality of Suspects in the U.S. Justice System for an Immigration Offense

Nationality	Number	Percentage (by region)
Total	16,495	
U.S. citizen	1,110	7
Mexico	9,425	57
Asia and Oceania	598	4
China	433	
Other	165	
Central America	428	3
Honduras	223	
El Salvador	113	
Guatemala	67	
Other	25	
Caribbean	388	2
Dominican Republic	190	
Other	198	
Europe	134	1
South America	111	1
Columbia	55	
Other	56	
Other countries or not indicated	4,652	

SOURCE: Scalia and Litras (2002).

PROBLEMS SURROUNDING UNDOCUMENTED ALIENS IN CORRECTIONS

The treatment of undocumented aliens is controversial, and there are several criticisms that can be leveled at the application of U.S. immigration policy. Some argue that the U.S. government unjustly discriminates, treating immigrants of various ethnicities differently. For instance, Haitians who are apprehended attempting unauthorized entry are systematically deported while immigrants from Cuba are allowed to remain in the United States if they make it to American shores. Others have claimed that the practice of indefinitely detaining convicted immigrants who are not accepted for deportation by their native country is a violation of civil rights. On June 28, 2001, the U.S. Supreme Court found this to be unconstitutional (*Zadvydas v. Davis,* 2001).

Still others have raised concerns over the physical and mental abuse of detainees held in local jails and other facilities. With limited space in INS-operated detention facilities, contained immigrants are often placed in jail and prison facilities where INS oversight has been limited. Lawsuits and accusations questioning the treatment of immigrants in these facilities has prompted the INS to implement rules that require visiting rights and access to proper food, medical care, recreation, and libraries for all detained foreign nationals. Critics are skeptical that these rules will be meaningfully enforced. Finally, there have also been concerns that federal agents engage in racial profiling when apprehending immigrants. In the wake of the September 11 terrorist attacks, such claims were made about the apprehension and detention of those of Middle Eastern descent. There have also been ongoing allegations of racial profiling of Mexicans along the southwestern border region.

CONCLUSION

Several developed countries face problems of managing both legal and illegal immigration traffic. Almost consistently, U.S. immigration policy has moved toward the position of restricting immigration flows through heightened enforcement. The consequence of this enforcement has been increasingly high levels of foreign nationals detained in the correctional and prison system. In spite of this increase in incarceration, there is little evidence that the flow of undocumented immigration has been curtailed. With the initiation of the Department of Homeland Security, into which the INS was merged in 2003, a new focus through the lens of national security is expected to reshape the nature of immigration enforcement. Until there is a shift away from the mass incarceration of immigration offenders, problems with their detainment are likely to continue.

—*Rob T. Guerette*

See also Asian American Prisoners; Cuban Detainees; Enemy Combatants; Habeas Corpus; Fourth

Amendment; INS Detention Facilities; Jails; Relocation Centers; USA PATRIOT Act 2001

Further Reading

Freilich, J. D., Newman, G., Shoham, S. G., & Addad, M. (Eds.). (2002). *Migration, culture conflict, and crime.* Burlington, VT: Ashgate.

Harrison, P., & Beck, A. (2002). *Prisoners in 2001.* Washington, DC: U.S. Department of Justice, Bureau of Justice Statistics.

Hayes, H. (2001). *U.S. immigration policy and the undocumented: Ambivalent laws, furtive lives.* Westport, CT: Praeger.

Reyes, B., Johnson, H., & Swearingen, R. V. (2002). *Holding the line? The effect of the recent border build-up on unauthorized immigration.* San Francisco: Public Policy Institute of California. Retrieved from www.ppic.org/publications/PPIC162/index.html

Scalia, J., & Litras, M. (2002). *Immigration offenders in the federal criminal justice system, 2000.* Washington, DC: U.S. Department of Justice, Bureau of Justice Statistics.

Tonry, M. (Ed.). (1997). *Ethnicity, crime, and immigration: Comparative and cross-national perspectives.* Chicago: University of Chicago Press.

Welch, M. (2002). *Detained: Immigration laws and the expanding I.N.S. jail complex.* Philadelphia: Temple University Press.

Legal Case

Zadvydas v. Davis, 533 U.S. 678 (2001).

IMPORTATION

To outsiders, the surface appearances of prisoner culture often may seem inexplicable and perverse. Two dominant models attempt to explain this culture. The first, variously called the importation or "negative selection" model, sees the culture as the reflection of a fairly preestablished set of norms, values, and behaviors imported into the prison from the streets.

The second, the deprivation or "functional" model, sees the culture as a reaction to what Gresham Sykes (1958) called the "pains of imprisonment." Critical evaluations of the deprivation model led some researchers, such as John Irwin and Donald Cressey (1962), to challenge the utility of the deprivation model in explaining the prison environment, and focused instead on the nature of prisoners themselves. The importation model shifts the focus away from responses to the deprivations of punishment as the source of inmate culture to the characteristics of prisoners themselves, which they bring with them into the prison.

Unlike deprivation theorists, who saw prisoner culture as arising from prisoners' attempts to create a normal existence by adapting to abnormal conditions, importation theorists attempt to explain prisoner culture as the mirror of attitudes and behaviors learned on the street and used as cultural building blocks in the prison. Focusing primarily on ultra-masculine male maximum-security institutions, proponents believe that violence, aggression, and other predatory behaviors that characterize prisoner culture, especially in maximum-security prisons, generally are not unique to, developed in, or caused by the prison environment. Instead, the culture is learned on the street and expressed in the prison environment.

WHAT IS IMPORTED?

In its simplest form, people who prey on others on the streets also prey on others in the prison. Prison culture reflects an off-balance dance between prey and predators and between predators and the staff who would control them. Inmates use a number of survival mechanisms, such as alliances between predators, and accommodations made between staff, prey, and other predators to establish a workable, if not harmonious, existence. These strategies result from several broad factors beyond the walls that shape prisoner culture. First, prisoners, by definition, have failed to comply with the rules of civil society. Therefore, they continue their resistance to rules and authority in prison. Second, prisoners are seen as possessing an excess of socially undesired characteristics, such as manipulation, willingness to use force to attain goals, low commitment to honesty or truth, and little respect for the well-being of others. Third, prisoners reflect the structure of the streets from which they come. The increase in street gang activity since the 1960s thus becomes the structure for much of prisoners' social organization, and the gangs compete for power and other resources inside the walls. Finally, prisoners also attempt to continue their street lifestyle in prisons. This results in an underground economy in which contraband such as drugs and alcohol are valued commodities, homemade weapons (shanks) become routine weapons for protection or assault, and inmate groups compete for control of resources.

The ultimate consequence of all these factors is a culture that facilitates the continued social values inside the walls for which the prisoners were originally incarcerated. Conning is valued, violence is condoned or even necessary, success in rule violations is valued, and disciplinary problems are high. Prisoners not only are not rehabilitated, but their original behaviors and values are enforced in the culture.

STRENGTHS

The importation model provides a number of useful insights into the sources of prisoner culture. If importation theorists are correct, then prisoner culture would be expected to shift in line with the characteristics of prisoners. These changes may reflect alterations in a demographic group, such as inner-city racial or ethnic minorities, or shifts in the broader society, such as awareness of civil rights.

There is considerable support for this view. Through the 1960s, for example, inmates were predominantly white, reflecting the racial composition of society. The demographics of prison populations created a dominant set of norms and values that were shared by most prisoners in the primarily white inmate population. As African Americans and Hispanics gradually outnumbered whites, the culture built on the experiences of inner-city males, whose norms and values were significantly different from those of white America. Blacks and Hispanics began to define themselves in terms of their racial and ethnic identities and less in terms of their prisoner status. Challenges to racial segregation and differential treatment were strengthened by court intervention into prison administration. As prisoners received more rights, the divisions within the inmate populations become more recognizable. Religious freedoms, influenced especially in the practice of Islam, increased for blacks and Native

Americans, providing them with new spiritual outlets.

The growth of street gangs also reshaped the prisoner culture. In addition to the importation of gang behaviors and goals, it also affected how prisoners did time. The old inmate code, "do your own time," shifted to "do our time" as gangs required and enforced compliance with its norms. As with their street counterparts, the norms of the gangs become the most important element in the lives of the members in imposing both obligations and providing rewards. Competition for members, control, and goods and services have become predominant factors in prison socialization. Violence was no longer driven by repudiation of the prison structure but an expression against rival gangs for control, reputation, and furtherance of their illegal enterprises or as internal discipline to control members.

External factors influenced the composition of the prison population and culture changed in other ways, providing evidence for the importation model. The war on drugs brought an increasing number of young, poor, and undereducated inner-city offenders into prison. Many of them had been convicted of violent offenses. Studies show that inmates convicted of violent offenses are more likely to engage in violence in prison.

The sentencing structure has also changed the composition of the prison population further highlighting the differences within the inmate culture. Society's "get tough on crime" policies create special groups of offenders with different values and norms imported into prisons. One example is the increasing number of younger inmates, who are more likely than older inmates to participate in disruptive behavior. Older inmates are more inclined to respect authority, if not always rules, and are less likely to be involved in expressive violence. Furthermore, with more prisoners serving time, prison construction has dramatically expanded. With more prisons, it becomes easier to classify offenders and distribute them into need-oriented and security-flexible specialized institutions, thus creating a more homogeneous population.

The importation model suggests that, if we are to make prisoner culture more stable and less dysfunctional, we should begin with rehabilitative programs that reduce the proclivity toward violence and predation and provide meaningful alternatives rewarded by changes in behavior. Prisons should be reorganized in ways that reduce the opportunities for and utility of predatory behavior. Importation theorists also suggest that many of the characteristics of prisoner culture are outside of direct administrative control, which creates an inevitable conflict between and among prisoners and staff. This, in turn, means that in addition to internal controls and reforms, the prisoner culture must also be addressed through wider social reforms that reduce the value of predatory behavior.

Finally, proponents of the model redirect the attention of researchers from inside the walls to the complex interplay of societal, legal, and other factors that facilitate what happens inside the walls. Prison culture cannot be perceived as something that emerges *sui generis*, as deprivation theorists emphasize, but are a complex interplay of factors on both sides.

LIMITATIONS

Despite its utility for offering insights into some of the sources of prisoner culture, the importation model remains somewhat limited. It is certainly not a profound observation that prisoner culture—any culture—reflects the characteristics of those who inhabit it. A commune of pacifists would be less likely to resemble prisoner culture than a commune of professional football players. Populations drawn from the same demographic backgrounds, whose members possess similar attributes and characteristics, are likely to translate their traditions into behaviors that lead to shared expectations, behaviors, and obligations. These shared ideas, in turn, lead to fairly invariant structures of collective meaning that we call culture.

Another serious problem is the gender bias. Despite several classic studies of the culture in women's prisons (e.g., Bosworth, 1999; Giallombardo, 1966; Heffernan, 1972; Owen, 1998; Ward & Kassebaum, 1965), studies of prisoner culture are overwhelmingly male oriented. The earliest studies

of women's prisons characterized the culture as recreating fictive families as women attempted to adapt, somewhat passively, to their conditions. These studies generally stressed the importance of close family ties and the importance of familial interactions that women imported into the prisons. Giallombardo emphasized homosexual relations, suggesting that there was a single-mindedness to women's socialization within the prison environment. Recent research, however, has found that there is no more homosexual activity among females in pseudofamilies than among other women in the prison population. These findings support the view that women who import strong family values into the prison are likely to form similar bonds within the correctional facility. Recognition of this has led some female facilities to develop programs to foster the need for child care and other family activities. This, in turn, suggests that by changing the nature of the prisons, we can also modify the influence of street culture in the prisons, demonstrating some utility in integrating the importation and deprivation models.

The importation model is further weakened by its inability to account for variations in different types of prisons. For example, it has been unsuccessful in explaining prisoner culture in medium- or minimum-security prisons, where the culture becomes increasingly "normal." As Galliher (1972) observed, while there is cultural consistency within types of prisons based on security level, there are dramatic cultural variations across security types. This suggests that not only are "bad guys" not all alike, but it reinforces the judgment that there is something about the nature of the institution that shapes the culture and the repertoire of prisoners' accommodation responses to it.

The model also overemphasizes homogeneity among prisoners. Just as in the outside culture, prisoner culture is not composed of a monolithic set of norms and values. It reflects diverse groups that may not share the same values. Prisoner subgroups vary dramatically in their responses to the culture, with racially based gangs, faith-based groups, and smaller cliques adapting in their own ways to the environment.

Although a less serious limitation, importation proponents do not examine the consistency in prisoner cultures across time. In could be argued that the basics of prisoner culture have not varied dramatically in maximum-security prisons over the decades, only the manner in which they are expressed. Violence, hustling, the tensions between staff and prisoners, and attempts to make time easier are relatively constant.

Finally, importation theorists tend to focus on the socially destructive aspects of prisoner culture, such as predatory behavior, resistance to authority, violence, and antisocial attitudes. But these characteristics are most common in maximum-security institutions, where gang behavior, resistance to tight control, and violent prisoners with long sentences prevail. This distorts outsiders' perceptions of prisons by creating an image of abnormally maladjusted and recalcitrant predators, which further stigmatizes them. Even in the most violent of prisons, prisoners show acts of humanity, caring, and kindness, and most prisoners just want to do their time and return to their communities.

CONCLUSION: FUTURE OF THE IMPORTATION MODEL

Despite John DiIulio's (1987) observation that prisoner research suffers from overemphasis on the "society of captives," few studies have addressed prisoner culture as a process, and there seems to be a declining interest in prisoner culture in recent years. Two recent cutting-edge critical studies (Bosworth, 1999; Jones & Schmid, 2000) have de-emphasized prisoner culture itself and focused instead on the relationship between prisoner identity formation and maintenance and culture. Neither study rejects the importation or deprivation models. Instead, both provide a third approach that addresses how prisoners resist and accommodate to prison life, drawing from their available social and cultural capital, to define and create a "self-as-prisoner" in a phenomenological experiential process.

The importation model will likely continue to be a viable approach in studying the "society of captives." However, it must first overcome its limitations and recognize the dialectical process between what prisoners import and how what is imported, in turn, provides resources for adapting to the deprivations. Unless this occurs, the model may still provide some utility, but will become increasingly irrelevant to our understanding of how prisons "make good guys bad and bad guys worse."

—*Jim Thomas and Patrick F. McManimon, Jr.*

See also Donald Clemmer; Deprivation; Gangs; Rose Giallombardo; Governance; Inmate Code; John Irwin; Prison Culture; Prisonization; Resistance; Riots; Gresham Sykes; Violence; Women's Prisons

Further Reading

Bosworth, M. (1999). *Engendering resistance: Agency and power in women's prisons.* Aldershot, UK: Ashgate.

Cao, L., Zhao, J., & Van Dine, S. (1997). Prison disciplinary tickets: A test of the deprivation and importation models. *Journal of Criminal Justice, 25,* 103–113.

Carroll, L. (1974). *Hacks, blacks and cons: Race relations in a maximum security prison.* Lexington, MA: D. C. Heath.

Clemmer, D. (1958). *The prison community.* New York: Holt, Rinehart & Winston. (Original work published 1940)

DiIulio, J. J., Jr. (1987). *Governing prisons: A comparative study of correctional management.* New York: Free Press.

Galliher, J. F. (1972, July). Change in a correctional institution: A case study of the tightening-up process. *Crime & Delinquency, 18,* 263–270.

Giallombardo, R. (1966). *Society of women: A study of a women's prison.* New York: John Wiley.

Heffernan, E. (1972). *Making it in prison: The square, the cool and the life.* New York: John Wiley.

Irwin, J. (1970). *The felon.* Englewood Cliffs, NJ: Prentice Hall.

Irwin, J., & Cressey, D. R. (1962, Fall). Thieves, convicts and the inmate culture. *Social Problems, 10,* 142–155.

Jones, R. A., & Schmid, T. J. (2000). *Doing time: Prison experience and identity among first-time inmates.* Greenwich, CT: JAI.

Owen, B. (1998). *"In the mix": Struggle and survival in a women's prison.* Albany: State University of New York Press.

Sykes, G. M. (1958). *The society of captives: A study of a maximum security prison.* Princeton, NJ: Princeton University Press.

Thomas, J. (2004): *Communicating prison culture.* Manuscript in progress, Northern Illinois University.

Ward, D. A., & Kassebaum, G. G. (1965). *Women's prison: Sex and social structure.* Chicago; Aldine.

INCAPACITATION THEORY

Proponents of the incapacitation theory of punishment advocate that offenders should be prevented from committing further crimes either by their (temporary or permanent) removal from society or by some other method that restricts their physical ability to reoffend in some other way. Incarceration is the most common method of incapacitating offenders; however, other, more severe, forms such as capital punishment are also used. The overall aim of incapacitation is to prevent the most dangerous or prolific offenders from reoffending in the community.

EXPLANATION

Incapacitation is a reductivist (or "forward looking") justification for punishment. Reductivism is underpinned by the theory of moral reasoning known as utilitarianism, which maintains that an act is defensible and reasonable if its overall consequences are beneficial to the greatest number of people. Thus, the pain or suffering imposed on an offender through punishment is justified if it reduces or prevents the further harm that would have been caused to the rest of society by the future crimes of that offender. The concern here is with the victim, or potential victim. The rights of the offender merit little consideration.

Incapacitation has long been a significant strategy of punishment. For example, in Britain during the 18th and 19th centuries, convicted offenders were often transported to Australia and the Americas. In the 21st century, the physical removal of offenders from society remains the primary method of incapacitation in most contemporary penal systems. This usually takes the form of imprisonment, although other methods of incapacitation are in operation.

The most severe and permanent form of incapacitation is capital punishment. Capital punishment is often justified through the concept of deterrence, but whether the death sentence actually deters potential offenders is highly contested. What is indisputable is that once put to death an individual is incapable of committing further offenses. Capital punishment is therefore undeniably "effective" in terms of its incapacitative function.

Other types of severe or permanent incapacitative punishments include dismemberment, which is practiced in various forms. For example, the physical or chemical castration of sex offenders has been used in some Western countries, notably North America. Less severe forms of incapacitation are often concerned with *restricting* rather than completely *disabling* offenders from reoffending. These include sentences such as disqualification from driving or curfews. In the United Kingdom, attendance center orders are used for individuals under the age of 21. Their aim is to restrict the leisure time of offenders by requiring them to attend a center in order to engage in some form of activity for a specified number of hours.

However, as mentioned above, the primary method of incapacitation is imprisonment. As with capital punishment, incapacitation in the form of imprisonment is considered to be a strategy that "works" because, for the duration of their prison sentence, offenders are restricted from committing crimes within the community.

So, according to this theory, punishment is not concerned with the nature of the offender, as is the case with rehabilitation, or with the nature of the offense, as is the case with retribution. Rather, punishment is justified by the risk individuals are believed to pose to society in the future. As a result, individuals can be punished for "hypothetical" crimes. In other words, they can be incarcerated, not for crimes they have actually committed but for crimes it is *anticipated* or *assumed* they will commit.

DEVELOPMENT AND DETAILS

Since the 1970s, and the demise of rehabilitation as a primary aim of punishment, incapacitation has become a significant goal of penal systems in both the United States and the United Kingdom. Two strategies have influenced penal policy and practice on both sides of the Atlantic: the "three strikes and you're out" policy and the practice of "selective incapacitation."

The three-strikes policy is partly informed by the theory of deterrence but is primarily underpinned by the concept of incapacitation. It has been influential in the United States since the early 1990s and aims to remove the most prolific or habitual offenders from society. Such offenders are given long sentences of up to life imprisonment for a third offense, regardless of the nature or gravity of that crime, if one or both of their previous offenses was a "serious" felony. In practice, this means that offenders can be given sentences that are disproportionately harsh for the offense committed. One of the most oft-cited examples of the severity of the three-strikes principle is the case of Jerry Williams, who, in 1995, was sentenced to life imprisonment without parole for stealing a piece of pizza.

The three-strikes principle has also had an impact on penal and criminal justice policy in the United Kingdom. The Crime Sentences Act (1997) proposed the use of harsh sentences, lengthier than the seriousness of the crime would normally warrant, for "serious" or prolific offenders. In addition, discretionary life sentences were introduced in the Powers of Criminal Courts (Sentencing) Act of 2000.

The second strategy, selective incapacitation, is concerned with identifying "risk" and predicting "dangerousness." This strategy emphasizes the proactive nature of incapacitative sentences. The aim is to incarcerate selectively those individuals who would pose a serious risk to the public if left within, or released back to, the community. Identifying risk is inherently problematic, and there have been many criticisms leveled at the subjectiveness of the methods and criteria used to predict future dangerousness. Indeed, as Norwegian sociologist Thomas Mathiesen has commented, many of the so-called aggravating factors often used to predict future behavior—such as previous periods of imprisonment, drug use, and unemployment—might actually be considered, by some, to be mitigating factors.

CRITIQUE

The use of incapacitation as a justification for punishment can be inherently problematic in both theory and practice. First, incapacitative sentences

such as the three-strikes principle effectively repunish individuals for previous crimes. Alternatively, sentences based on selective incapacitation punish individuals for crimes not yet committed. There is an inherent risk with selective incapacitation that some of the individuals who are identified as "dangerous," and thus incarcerated, would not have gone on to offend. However, even if the methods of prediction were accurate, there are naturally moral and ethical questions about incarcerating individuals for what they *may* do rather than what they have actually done.

Incapacitative sentences also maintain and legitimize structural divisions within society. U.S. sociologist Christian Parenti comments that the excessive use of incarceration in the United States is indicative of a growing class-based, racial intolerance. The three-strikes principle, as with imprisonment in general, is disproportionately applied to minorities and the poor. While African Americans make up only 7% of the Californian population, for example, they constitute 31% of the state prison population and 44% of its "three-striker" population.

At the same time, a penal strategy based around the concept of incapacitation places no emphasis on the crimes of the powerful. So white-collar, corporate, and environmental crimes, which are more costly and, some would argue, more harmful to society, are overlooked. The emphasis instead is placed on street crime, which is disproportionately committed by the young and the poor.

Finally, incapacitative sentences, which are frequently dispensed to young people, take no account of the fact that most individuals "grow out" of their criminal activity. Many "criminal careers" do not last beyond the late teen years. Thus, long sentences without the possibility of parole make no allowance for the transitory nature of much law breaking.

—Alana Barton

See also Civil Commitment of Sexual Predators; Corporal Punishment; Determinate Sentencing; Deterrence Theory; Increase in Prison Population; Indeterminate Sentencing; Just Deserts Theory; Life Without Parole; Megan's Law; Parole; Parole Boards; Prison Industrial Complex; Race, Class, and Gender of Prisoners; Rehabilitation Theory; Sentencing

Reform Act 1984; Sex Offenders; Three-Strikes Legislation; Truth in Sentencing; War on Drugs

Further Reading

Feeley, M., & Simon, J. (1992). The new penology: Notes on the emerging strategy of corrections and its implications. *Criminology, 30*(4), 449–470.

Mathiesen, T. (1990). *Prison on trial.* London: Sage

Parenti, C. (1999). *Lockdown America: Police and prisons in the age of crisis.* New York: Verso.

Zimring, F. E., & Hawkins, G. (1995). *Incapacitation: Penal confinement and the restraint of crime.* Oxford, UK: Oxford University Press.

Ⅻ INCREASE IN PRISON POPULATION

It would be no exaggeration to say that during the past two decades the U.S. prison system has been a growth industry. There are now more than 2 million people behind bars in America, with an incarceration rate above 700 per 100,000 (if we include jails), triple what it was 20 years ago. The United States is way ahead of other industrial democracies, whose incarceration rates tend to cluster in a range from around 55 to 120 per 100,000 population. Some countries have incarceration rates well below that range, such as Japan's rate of 37. Canada has a rate of only 115. The average incarceration rate for *all countries of the world* is around 80 per 100,000. Thus, America's incarceration rate is almost nine times greater than the average country.

Table 1 shows changes in the U.S. prison system during the past 75 years. Note that the most significant increases have occurred since the mid-1980s, when the war on drugs began to have its effects on jail and prison populations. Indeed, a recent estimate is that convictions for drugs accounted for almost *one half* of the increase in state prison inmates during the 1980s and early 1990s. Between 1988 and 1994, the number of prisoners who had been convicted of drug offenses went up by 155.5%. By comparison, only modest increases were seen for violent and property offenders. Between 1980 and 1992, court commitments to state prisons on drug charges alone increased by more than 1,000%.

The increase for women offenders has been even more striking. From 1925 to 1975, there was virtually no change in their rate of incarceration. Then, between 1975 and 2000, their incarceration rate increased by more than 600%, twice the rate of increase for males. Once again, this increase can be explained by drug policies, since the proportion of women sent to prison for drug offenses jumped from around 10% in the early 1980s to more than one third in the 1990s. In the federal system, the growth rate is even more dramatic. Whereas in 1984 a total of 28% of female offenders were drug offenders, by 1995 their percentage had more than doubled to 66%.

Table 1   The Growing Prison Population, 1925–1999 (rates per 100,000 in state and federal prison)

Year	Total	Rate	Male Rate	Female Rate
1925	91,669	79	149	6
1935	144,180	113	217	8
1945	133,649	98	193	9
1955	185,780	112	217	8
1965	210,895	108	213	8
1975	240,593	111	220	8
1985	480,568	202	397	17
1995	1,085,363	411	796	48
2000	1,321,137	478	915	59

SOURCE: Maguire and Pastore (2001, Table 6.27).

That the drug war has contributed to rising prison populations is further supported with data from U.S. district courts (federal system) showing that whereas in 1982 about 20% of all convictions were for drugs, by 1994 this percentage had increased to about 36. During this same period, the proportion of those convicted on drug charges who were sentenced to prison increased from 74% in 1982 to 84% in 1994, and their actual sentences increased from an average of 55 months in 1982 to 80 months in 1994. The average sentences for murder during this time actually *decreased* from 162 months to 117 months, while for all violent offenses the average sentence declined from 133 months to 88 months. At present, all of these changes have meant that on any given day, almost 60% of all federal prisoners are serving time for drug offenses; of these, 40% are African American.

As a result of the growing population behind bars, the actual *number of prisons* has increased, along with, in some cases, the *capacity within* the prison. These days, some "megaprisons" can hold from 5,000 to 10,000 inmates (Austin & Irwin, 2002, pp. 125–131). In 1990, there were a total of 1,287 prisons (80 federal and 1,207 state prisons); by 1995 there were a total of 1,500 prisons (125 federal and 1,375 state prisons), representing an increase of about 17%. The federal system experienced the largest increase, going up by 56%.

Of course, all such changes have not occurred evenly across the country. Some states have experienced a far greater expansion in imprisonment than others. In Texas, for example, the number of prisoners increased by more than 100,000 during the 1990s. Likewise, prison construction varied widely by state and region, with the largest increases occurring in the South, adding 95 prisons for an increase of 18%. Texas once again leads the way, adding 49 new prisons for an increase of 114%. Oklahoma added 17 new prisons for an increase of 74% (Mays & Winfree, 1998, p. 171). Texas currently leads the nation with 102 prisons, an increase of 155% from 1991 (Rush, 1997, p. 157). As of December 31, 2000, Texas had 163,190 prisoners, with 1 out of every 20 state residents behind bars, up from 1 out of every 25 in 1996. During the decade of the 1990s, almost one of every five new prisoners added in the United States was in Texas (18%). The Texas prison population tripled during this decade.

RACE

The modern prison system (along with local jails) has been described by many as a ghetto or poorhouse reserved primarily for the unskilled, the uneducated, and the powerless. African Americans, particularly males, are especially vulnerable. For example, in mid-year 2003, according to the Bureau of Justice Statistics, 12% of all black males in their 20s were in prison or jail. Moreover, if current trends continue, roughly one third of all black males born in 2003 will spend time behind bars. In some cities in

the United States, including the nation's capital, such figures have already been attained. Hispanics are also heavily overrepresented.

Many sentencing structures have a built-in class and racial bias. Drug laws, especially those for crack cocaine, illustrate this point most clearly. The penalty for possession and/or sale of crack cocaine is far greater than similar quantities for the powdered variety of cocaine. Recent scholarship has concluded that the evidence strongly suggests that such punishment has intentionally targeted African Americans, since this group is far more likely to use crack, while most users of the powdered cocaine are white and middle class.

Officially, this drug war was launched during the Nixon administration (according to Dan Baum [1997], Nixon's policy advisers specifically suggested that focusing on drugs would be a "legal" way to target blacks and hippies, whom they despised). The "war" was significantly escalated during the Reagan years when he promised that the police would attack the drug problem "with more ferocity than ever before." What Reagan did *not* say, however, was that the enforcement of the new drug laws would focus almost exclusively on low-level dealers in minority neighborhoods. Indeed, the police found such dealers in these areas mainly because *that is precisely where they looked for them,* rather than, say, on college campuses (Mauer, 1999, p. 142).

The results were immediate: The arrest rates for African Americans on drug charges shot dramatically upward in the late 1980s and well into the 1990s. During one period of time at the heights of the drug war, the proportion of admissions to prisons that were racial minorities increased from 42% to 51% between 1981 and 1991, while the proportion that were sentenced because of drug law violations increased from 9% to 25%. One study found that, between 1985 and 1987, of all the drug-trafficking defendants in the country, 99% were African American.

In fact, while African Americans constitute only around 12% of the U.S. population and about 13% of all monthly drug users (and their rate of illegal drug use is roughly the same as for whites), they represent 35% of those arrested for drug possession and 74% of those sentenced to prison on drug charges. The evidence of racial disproportionality in the drug war is overwhelming. For instance, drug arrest rates for minorities went from under 600 per 100,000 in 1980 to more than 1,500 in 1990, while for whites they essentially remained the same. Facts such as these have led such reputable scholars as Michael Tonry, William Chambliss, and Noam Chomsky to conclude that it was the *intent* of the Congress and the Senate to target minorities.

As far as prison sentences go, studies of individual states are telling. For instance, in North Carolina between 1980 and 1990, the rate of admissions to prison for nonwhites jumped from around 500 per 100,000 to almost 1,000, while in Pennsylvania, nonwhite males and females sentenced on drug offenses increase by 1613% and 1750%, respectively; in Virginia the percentage of commitments for drug offenses for minorities went from just under 40 in 1983 to about 65 in 1989, while for whites the percentage actually *decreased* from just over 60% in 1983 to about 30% in 1989 (Donziger, 1996, p. 115; Mauer, 1999; Tonry, 1995). Presently, the rate of incarceration for African Americans exceeds that for whites by a ratio of 8 to 1.

CONCLUSION

The growth of the U.S. prison system has been truly staggering in recent years and has far outpaced the growth of crime. One recent study found that, looking back over the 30-year period from 1971 to 2000, the overall crime rate remained roughly the same (4,124 per 100,000 in 2000 compared to 4,165 in 1971), while the rate of imprisonment increased almost fivefold. The billions of dollars in expenditures on the prison industry have had no effect on crime. Yet prisons continue to grow and continue to house more and more racial minorities.

—*Randall G. Shelden*

See also Abolition; Citizens for the Rehabilitation of Errants; Contract Facilities; Critical Resistance; Determinate Sentencing; Deterrence Theory; Drug Offenders; Families Against Mandatory Minimum Sentences; Hispanic/Latino(a) Prisoners; Incapacitation Theory; Indeterminate Sentencing; Jails; Just Deserts Theory; Life Without Parole; November Coalition; Overcrowding; Parole; Parole Boards; Prison Industrial Complex; Privatization; Privatization of Labor; Rehabilitation Theory; Sentencing Reform Act 1984; Race, Class, and Gender of Prisoners; Truth in Sentencing; War on Drugs; Women Prisoners; Women's Prisons

Further Reading

Austin, J., & Irwin, J. (2002). *It's about time: America's incarceration binge* (3rd ed.). Belmont, CA: Wadsworth.

Baum, D. (1997). *Smoke and mirrors: The war on drugs and the politics of failure.* Boston: Little, Brown/Back Bay Books.

Beck, A. J., & Brien, P. M. (1995). Trends in the U.S. correctional populations: Recent findings from the Bureau of Justice Statistics. In K. C. Haas & G. P. Alpert (Eds.), *The dilemmas of corrections* (3rd ed.). Project Heights, IL: Waveland.

Chambliss, W. (1999). *Power, politics, and crime.* Boulder, CO: Westview.

Currie, E. (1993). *Reckoning: Drugs, the cities, and the American future.* New York: Hill and Wang.

Currie, E. (1998). *Crime and punishment in America.* New York: Metropolitan Books.

Donziger, S. (1996). *The real war on crime: The report of the National Criminal Justice Commission.* New York: HarperPerennial.

Maguire, K., & Pastore, A. L. (Eds.). (1996). *Sourcebook of criminal justice statistics—1995.* Washington, DC: U.S. Department of Justice, Bureau of Justice Statistics.

Maguire, K., & Pastore, A. (Eds.). (2001). *Sourcebook of criminal justice statistics—2000.* Washington, DC: U.S. Department of Justice.

Mauer, M. (1999). *Race to incarcerate.* New York: New Press.

Mays, G. L., & Winfree, L. T., Jr. (1998). *Contemporary corrections.* Belmont, CA: Wadsworth.

Miller, J. (1996). *Search and destroy: African-Americans males in the criminal justice system.* New York: Cambridge University Press.

Pollock, J. M. (2002). *Women, prison, and crime* (2nd ed.). Belmont, CA: Wadsworth.

Reinarman, C., & Levine, H. G. (1997). *Crack in America.* Berkeley: University of California Press.

Rush, G. (1997). *Inside American prisons and jails.* Incline Village, NV: Copperhouse.

Shelden, R. G. (2001). *Controlling the dangerous classes: A critical introduction to the history of criminal justice.* Boston: Allyn & Bacon.

Shelden, R. G., & Brown, W. B. (2003). *Criminal justice in America: A critical view.* Boston: Allyn & Bacon.

Tonry, M. (1995). *Malign neglect: Race, crime, and punishment in America.* New York: Oxford University Press.

Ziedenberg, J., & Schiraldi, V. (1999). *The punishing decade: Prison and jail estimates at the millennium.* Washington, DC: Justice Policy Institute.

Ziedenberg, J., & Schiraldi, V. (2000a). *Poor prescription: The costs of imprisoning drug offenders in the United States.* Washington, DC: Justice Policy Institute. Retrieved from www.cjcj.org/drug

Ziedenberg, J., & Schiraldi, V. (2000b). *Texas tough? An analysis of incarceration and crime trends in the Lone Star State.* Washington, DC: Justice Policy Institute.

◪ INDETERMINATE SENTENCING

Indeterminate sentences operate when judges assign convicted offenders to terms of imprisonment identified only as a range—such as from one to five years—rather than naming a specific time period. In this context, indeterminacy refers to the unknown ultimate amount of the penalty (length of time) at sentencing. That is, one *cannot determine* at the time of sentencing the length of time that the convicted person shall actually serve. In fact, since indeterminate sentencing allows for a series of discretionary choices by prison officials leading to an eventual decision by a parole board, an individual may not be sure how long he or she has left in prison until near the end of the time actually served. Despite various movements toward determinacy beginning in the 1970s, indeterminate sentencing still prevails in the United States.

Debates over the case for and against indeterminacy or determinacy in sentencing raise complex questions about the purposes of criminal sentencing and corrections, what such regimes of control and surveillance achieve, and their political implications and consequences. Supporters of indeterminate sentencing typically believe that imprisonment can rehabilitate offenders, despite all of the known problems with penal facilities today.

HISTORY

Indeterminate sentencing dominated ideas about and practices of criminal sentencing and corrections in the United States from the late 19th to the late 20th centuries. It emerged in its modern form at the National Prison Association meeting in Cincinnati, Ohio, in 1870 as part of a series of social inventions spawned by reformers during the Progressive era, which ran from the late 1800s through the early 1900s. Throughout this time, rehabilitation prevailed as the official, professional, and reformist aim for corrections. Probation and parole emerged and developed as related institutions closely tied to the rehabilitative ideal and indeterminate sentencing.

Like other innovations or social inventions of the Progressive era, the indeterminate sentence grew out of reformers' faith in science, rationality, government benevolence, and human progress. Thus, the indeterminate sentence ideally would proceed via information gathering, prediction, treatment, and ongoing assessment and eventually would culminate in release of the prisoner after professional review of the evidence found him or her "cured." Reformers clearly saw utility in the less humane side of the indeterminate sentence as well; if never judged cured of their criminality, prisoners could languish in prison for the rest of their natural life.

Instead of the careful and thoughtful individualized treatment program envisioned by reformers, correctional institutions determined the actual experiences of inmates. In state after state during the Progressive era, indeterminate sentencing served as an expedient way of processing the dispossessed who had run afoul of the law. In particular, judges, prosecutors, wardens, and parole boards quickly adapted indeterminate sentencing to their own ends. Judges could appear tough on crime by pointing to the high end of the indeterminate range imposed. Prosecutors and defense attorneys could induce guilty pleas by emphasizing the possibility of early release. Wardens and correctional guards also had a ready means of eliciting inmate compliance with the reward of early release and the punishment of extended confinement contingent on institutional record, including discipline as well as program participation. Finally, parole boards depended for their existence on the whole mythology of indeterminacy and correctional treatment under coercion.

RECENT DEVELOPMENTS

Recent decades have witnessed the emergence of various challenges to indeterminate sentencing. The movement away from it and toward determinate sentencing began in the 1970s and has received considerable legislative, judicial, policy, and scholarly attention since then. As crime grew in the 1970s, forces on both sides of the political spectrum began to lose confidence in the possibility of reforming offenders. Given that indeterminate sentences were justified in large part by a belief that prisoners could be rehabilitated, this change in sentiment inevitably led toward determinate sentencing

Nevertheless, indeterminacy still characterizes most of the sentencing policy and practice in the United States. This remains true in the adult (criminal) as well as juvenile (delinquent) arena where the majority of offenders are sentenced to a range of time in prison, rather than a fixed number of years. In large part, the continuing existence of indeterminate sentencing reflects the more general failure of the progressive social movements of the late 20th century to achieve more far-reaching structural societal transformations. Yet it also has more specific sources in the dynamics of criminal justice policy.

Why is that? Why does convenience dominate still even with the decline of the rehabilitative ideal? In part, it may reflect a kind of intellectual and cultural exhaustion with this issue. It likely indicates too the power of institutionalization. Indeterminate sentencing has become too much a feature of the correctional landscape to disappear completely without sufficient political resources and bureaucratic alternatives to make reform critiques more effective. Yet we must recognize the significant inroads that determinacy has made. Even though most states retain indeterminate sentencing rhetoric and associated institutional arrangements, almost all have incorporated various forms of determinacy such as mandatory minimum incarceration, repeat-offender laws, and sentencing guidelines. Thus, indeterminacy stays on more as a vestige rather than an ideological center.

SOCIAL CLASS, ETHNICITY, AND GENDER

Part of the impetus of the 19th-century penal reformers in the United States in crafting the inter-related institutions of indeterminate sentencing, probation, and parole was to reduce social class biases associated with the previous system. Thus, for example, frequent use by governors of the power to pardon produced a system in which those with means and connections presumably had greater access to freedom via this route. The new system, built around the indeterminate sentence, should then work more fairly, creating more access by less privileged prisoners to the release decisions made by professionals based on scientific reasoning rather than political influence.

Yet the new system often failed to produce such laudable outcomes. This becomes especially apparent when noting that indeterminate sentencing developed along with probation. Operating under the same rehabilitative philosophy, probation was designed to serve offenders in their own communities when criminal justice professionals felt that they need not be imprisoned. In practice, however, probation tended to function as a substitute for the suspended sentence. Yet probation, unlike the suspended sentence, gave judges the means to supervise and monitor offenders. This meant greater control, including the distinct possibility of revocation followed by incarceration. Since probation developed much more rapidly in urban than rural areas, this meant that convicted criminals in cities, disproportionately the disenfranchised (e.g., impoverished, immigrant, black, Catholic), tended to fall under the enhanced supervision of the state.

Similarly, multiple opportunities for discretionary decision making under indeterminate sentencing enhanced the prospects that ethnic, social class, and gender discrimination would occur. Indeed, when attacks on indeterminate sentencing and associated institutions arose in the 1960s and 1970s, they highlighted such concerns.

In general, indeterminate sentencing has reinforced the tendency of the criminal justice system to reinforce existing patterns of race, gender, and class domination and privilege. This sentencing strategy exists within a broader context of social control and contributes to its regulatory and oppressive impacts. Sometimes this appears in patterns regarding social class and ethnicity, especially when recurrent low-visibility discretionary decisions allow bigotry room to affect individual fates. Likewise, indeterminacy often appears to institutionalize paternalistic treatment of women and girls, as female offenders who do not adhere to idealized gender norms frequently serve longer sentences than those who do.

CONCLUSION: INTERNATIONAL COMPARISONS

In criminal justice research literature and policy discourse, sentencing indeterminacy or determinacy remains largely a U.S. concern. Although its intellectual and cultural hegemony has characteristically influenced criminal justice discourse elsewhere, concerns about sentencing in Europe and in developing nations tend to center more on the broader themes of purposes, actual impact on persons, political consequences, and implications. In general, other nations have not embraced indeterminate sentencing to the same extent as in the United States.

—*Douglas Thompson*

See also Determinate Sentencing; Families Against Mandatory Minimums; Incapacitation Theory; Just-Deserts Theory; Parole; Prison Industrial Complex; Race, Class, and Gender of Prisoners; Rehabilitation Theory; Sentencing Reform Act 1984; Three-Strikes Legislation; Truth in Sentencing

Further Reading

Allen, F. (1964). *The borderland of criminal justice.* Chicago: University of Chicago.

American Friends Service Committee. (1973). *Struggle for justice.* New York: Hill and Wang.

Balbus, I. (1977). *The dialectics of legal repression: Black rebels before the criminal courts.* Chicago: University of Chicago.

Friedman, L. (1993). *Crime and punishment in American history.* New York: Basic Books.

Greenberg, D. (1993). *Crime and capitalism: Readings in Marxist criminology* (Expanded and updated ed.). Philadelphia: Temple University Press.

McKelvey, B. (1977). *American prisons: A history of good intentions.* Montclair, NJ: Patterson Smith.

Morris, N. (1974). *The future of imprisonment.* Chicago: University of Chicago Press.

Rothman, D. (1980). *Conscience and convenience: The asylum and its alternatives in Progressive America.* Boston: Scott, Foresman.

Tonry, M. (1999). Reconsidering indeterminate and structured sentencing. *Sentencing & Corrections Issues for the 21st Century* (Papers from the Executive Sessions on Sentencing and Corrections, No. 2). Washington, DC: U.S. Department of Justice.

Weinstein, J. (2003) *The long detour: The history and future of the American left.* Boulder, CO: Westview.

■ INDIVIDUAL THERAPY

Individual therapy attempts to transform an offender into a law-abiding citizen through one-on-one sessions with a counselor or psychiatrist. Unlike group therapy, individual therapy provides the clinical environment for treatment that can be targeted to each client differently. It also provides an opportunity for people who have difficulty participating in a group to be treated. In practice, individual therapy is often part of a group therapy program such as drug abuse or sex offender treatment. Despite challenges to the goal of rehabilitation in the current "get tough on crime" era, most correctional facilities continue to offer some form of individual therapy, ranging from an initial assessment with a prison psychologist to more extensive ongoing counseling throughout a person's sentence.

BACKGROUND

Those working in the field of mental health draw on a series of different traditions and ideas, all of which rest on a belief that people can change so long as they want to. There are more than 200 different theoretical therapy models, which can be reduced to four distinct categories—psychodynamic, humanistic, behavioral, and cognitive. Some therapists draw only on one set of ideas, while others use elements from a number of categories, combining them as they deem appropriate and effective in assisting in change. For example, some subscribe to ideas of psychoanalysis that developed from the work of Sigmund Freud. Others use methods of clinical psychology originating in the work of Lightner Witmer, who, in turn, was influenced by the experimental psychology of Wilhelm Wundt. Still others draw on the ideas of Frank Parsons, who first developed vocational guidance, in developing their individual counseling programs.

Educationally, practitioners of individual psychotherapy and individual counseling may hold a variety of degrees from a bachelor's degree to a doctorate (PhD, PsyD, or EdD). They may be psychiatrists, with medical degrees that entitle them to prescribe medications in treatment, or counselors who seek to help others manage their stress levels. Most states in the United States have licensing laws, which determine the minimal education and training for mental health counseling and the psychotherapeutic professions.

CURRENT PRACTICE

Authors of a report submitted to Congress that reviewed funded programs initiated in 1996 found that cognitive behaviorally oriented therapy, for both individuals and groups, appeared most effective (Sherman et al., 1998). This type of therapy attempts to change behavior by changing the ways individuals think. It addresses attitudes, beliefs, and thinking patterns, to shift people's moral reasoning and development as well as how they process information.

Anger management courses in prison are based on cognitive behaviorism. These courses, such as the Philadelphia Crime Prevention Program (PCPP), may be either individually focused or based on group work. The Philadelphia program tries both to change people's deviant behavior, to reduce their reoffending, and to alter their sense of self. Sex offender treatment programs are also generally based on cognitive behavioralism.

EFFECTIVENESS AND LIMITATIONS

The use and effectiveness of individual therapy in criminal rehabilitation have long been a source of heated debate because the element of personal choice that is so fundamental to therapy is severely compromised in prison. Inmates are often required to undergo psychological counseling as part of their sentence, and so do not choose of their own free will to embark on self-transformation. Others are offered a sentence reduction for participating in certain programs, which may be more important than the experience of therapy itself. Likewise, the therapeutic relationship between the individual inmate and the therapist is based on trust and confidentiality, which may be difficult to establish within an incarcerated population because the therapist is an employee of the justice system. Finally, not all institutions support individual therapy since it is both expensive and requires numerous staff. As a result, group therapy is more commonly offered.

SPECIAL NEEDS

As with the general population, those who are incarcerated are composed of clinical subgroups, each with common issues as well as special concerns that need individualized treatment. These subgroups are based on age, gender, and cultural backgrounds and types of crime. Unlike group therapy, individual therapy enables a practitioner to identify and then treat the particular issues that members of these subgroups demonstrate.

For example, female juvenile offenders are more often diagnosed with oppositional defiant disorder (American Psychiatric Association [APA], 1994), whereas male juveniles are more often diagnosed with conduct disorder (APA, 1994). Similarly juvenile offenders in general often require treatment for developmental issues due to their age. Both young offenders and adults often require counseling for learning disorders and sexual abuse. Female juveniles and adults report higher frequencies of sexual abuse victimization than males. Indeed, women may present a number of additional issues such as child custody, while some women arrive pregnant at the time of incarceration. Then there are the issues involving the status of child custody, both during incarceration and after release.

For all age classifications, there are the clinical issues of substance abuses and dependence by the individuals, and finally, there are the adjustments to being incarcerated, as well as various victimizations that may occur in prison. As far as types of offenses, two have been of major social concerns: sex offenses and violent offenses. With sexual offenders, the issues include perpetrating of the present offenses and possible past victimizations of the individual. In regards to violent offenses, there are the antisocial issues and anger management.

CONCLUSION

There are numerous conditions and situations in prison where individual therapy is clinically indicated and, when used appropriately, may be effective. To ensure and to further this effectiveness, continued research, development, and standardizing of techniques for the variety of offenders encountered in the prison population are required. This will require specialized training for the clinical professionals in working with this challenging population. Also, education of the criminal justice and juvenile justice enforcement community may increase their awareness of the potential individual therapy offers in order to increase their support and cooperation of this component of rehabilitation.

—*Richard L. McWhorter*

See also Drug Treatment Programs; Group Therapy; Juvenile Justice System; Juvenile Offenders; Medical Model; Mental Health; Psychological Services; Psychologists; Race, Class, and Gender; Rehabilitation Theory; Sex Offender Programs; Therapeutic Communities

Further Reading

American Psychiatric Association. (1994). *Diagnostic and statistical manual of mental disorders* (4th ed.). Washington, DC: Author.

Freud, S. (1971). *The psychopathology of everyday life.* New York: Norton.

Henning, K. R., & Frueh, B. C. (1996). Cognitive-behavioral treatment of incarcerated offenders: An evaluation of the Vermont Department of Corrections' cognitive self-change program. *Criminal Justice and Behavior, 23*(4), 523–542.

Lipsey, W. M. (1992). *The effects of treatment on juvenile delinquents: Results from meta-analysis.* Paper presented at the NIMH for Potential Applicants for Research to Prevent Youth Violence, Bethesda, Maryland.

Martinson, R. (1974). What works? Questions and answers about prison reform. *The Public Interest, 10,* 22–54.

Palmer, T. (1994). *A profile of correctional effectiveness & new directions for research.* Albany: State University of New York Press.

Parsons, F. (1989). *Choosing a vocation.* Garrett Park, MD: Garrett Park Press.

Patterson, C. H. (1986). *Theories of counseling and psychotherapy* (4th ed.). New York: Harper & Row.

Rogers, C. R. (1942). *Counseling and psychotherapy.* Boston: Houghton Mifflin.

Sherman, L. W., Gottfredson, D. C., MacKenzie, D. L., Eck, J., Reuter, P., & Bushway, S. D. (1998). *Preventing crime: What works, what doesn't, what's promising.* Washington, DC: U.S. Department of Justice, National Institute of Justice.

Sickmund, M., Snyder, H. N., & Poe-Yamagata, E. (1997). *Juvenile offenders and victims: 1997 update on violence.* Washington, DC: Office of Juvenile Justice and Delinquency Prevention.

Witmer, L. (1907). Clinical psychology. *Psychological Clinic, 1,* 1–9.

Wundt, W. M. (1974). *Principles of physiological psychology* (Vol. 1). Germantown, NY: Periodicals Service Company.

◪ INMATE CODE

Within the walls of prisons and underneath the formal rules of conduct mandated by each institution, inmates live by their own standards and rules. Isolated from the outside world, they create lives and meaning for themselves in conjunction with their peers in the institution. The inmate code dictates behavior and becomes the central point of reference for those immersed in the community of the prison.

The inmate code is an important element of the larger inmate subculture. It is, in a sense, a series of unwritten commandments, rules to live by, that are passed down from one generation to the next. The first and most important rule of the inmate code zis to "do your own time." To the extent possible, people should tolerate or ignore the behavior of others, keep their heads low, and not cause trouble. Inmates are expected to solve their own problems. They should never bring the guards into inmate business. The code suggests that if you have a problem, either fix it yourself or learn to live with it. Other important points from the inmate code include the following: keep your mouth shut and never be an informer or snitch; do not exploit other inmates; do not interfere in other people's business;

stay tough at all times and do not show weakness; and, whenever possible, remain loyal to your fellow prisoners.

ORIGINS

There are two general schools of thought as to how and why inmate subculture develops. Some scholars have suggested that the subculture present in any institution is of indigenous origin and develops in response to the specific conditions of confinement and the problems of adjustment posed by the pains of imprisonment. Sociologist Gresham Sykes (1958) outlined five major pains of imprisonment: rejection by the free community, lack of goods and services available in the outside world (and often replacement with inferior products), deprivation of sexual intimacy, deprivation of autonomy or a nearly complete lack of independence, and the loss of physical security. Sykes and others have argued that the inmate subculture and the corresponding inmate code developed as an adaptation to these pains of imprisonment and to the particular problems and challenges of life as an inmate.

Alternatively, John Irwin and Donald Cressey (1962) argued that the inmate subculture is not unique to prisons at all. They claimed "it seems rather obvious that the 'prison code'—don't inform on or exploit another inmate, don't lose your head, be weak, or be a sucker, etc.—is also part of a criminal code, existing outside of prison" (p. 145). This position is referred to as the direct importation model, which suggests that the personal identities, values, and loyalties that inmates bring into the institution from the outside give shape to the subculture. In this view, the inmate code is a version of the criminal code that many inmates had adopted and lived by for most of their lives before entering prison. As such, they come into the institutions valuing toughness, respect, and the ability to "take it." They have faced adversity in their lives and they have learned to keep their eyes open and their mouths shut. They understand, above all else, the importance of doing their own time and letting others do theirs.

THE INMATE CODE TODAY: RACE, GENDER, AND SECURITY LEVEL

There is some debate today whether the inmate code still exists as it was described by Sykes, Irwin, Cressey, and others. James B. Jacobs, for example, argued that divisions among racial groups

Inmate Code

The "inmate code" is a set of norms that allegedly guides how inmates should act toward each other in prison. It is similar to the unwritten bylaws of many other institutions and groups. In particular, it is like the police "code blue," where officers cover for another, wrong or right (usually wrong), or the "blue flu," where police stand united in calling off work by calling in sick to protest working conditions. Students, for example, usually do not "rat out" other students they see cheating. Professors may ignore violations by their peers.

The most important aspect of the inmate code is the "code of loyalty," which is intended to protect the prisoner from administrative punishment, whether the prisoner is wrong or right. This occurs, for example, when one inmate will not inform prison authorities or other parties about another inmate's actions. This is commonly referred to as "no snitching; no ratting; no dry snitching" (or intentionally or unintentionally revealing discrediting information in a joking or gossiping manner), no squealing; no "stool pigeoning." The unity many prisoners derived from the inmate code came under attack in the late 1970s and early 1980s, when the federal government implemented an unwritten policy in which accomplices could testify against their partners for immunity, the "undercover snitch program," a reduced sentence, or witness protections. This unwritten policy was commonly called "whoever got down first." This policy effectively made it OK to snitch. Although one may still be rewarded for silence and not "ratting" on partners or other inmates, in general, "not ratting" is just another old school value. As a result, the inmate code has taken a 180-degree turn. Today, whistle blowing is a public value. To be a whistle blower is to be a crime stopper, a "good fellow." This has filtered into the norms and ethics of potential (or soon-to-be) inmates, which transforms the old inmate code of "don't rat" into one in which "stool pigeon" is acceptable.

Geoffrey Truss
Dixon Correctional Center, Dixon, Illinois

in prison have played an important role in changing the inmate culture. According to Jacobs (1983), black and Latino/a inmates are generally better organized and more cohesive than whites; racially homogeneous prison gangs have thus been able to replace the original inmate code with codes of their own making, specific to their own needs and loyalties.

The inmate code also seems to be quite different in women's prisons. In general, the conditions and considerations of confinement are somewhat less threatening as women inmates tend to be less violent than males, posing less of a physical danger to staff members and fellow inmates. In her study of a large women's prison in California, Barbara Owen (1998) found that the inmate code among women is not nearly as important as it is among men. The desire, and need, for respect was one of the few values held by both the male and female inmate culture. Similar to their male counterparts, female inmates also felt the need to be ready to defend themselves, if necessary, but they generally tried to stay out of "the mix" and to avoid behavior that was likely to bring trouble and conflict with other prisoners or staff members. Owen also found that the current women prison culture seems to tolerate more "telling" or snitching than in the past—a key change from the traditional inmate code.

Finally, the inmate code may never be a facet of some of the newer supermaximum secure prisons where contact and communication between inmates are severely limited. With virtually no human contact in supermaximum secure prisons, a cohesive code amongst inmates is hardly necessary and is all but impossible to develop and maintain.

CONCLUSION

No discussion of life in prison is complete without consideration of the inmate code. While prisons exercise great power over the lives of those incarcerated within them, the hierarchy and leadership of inmates are frequently much more influential in their daily lives than the authority exerted by the correctional officers and the official rules of the institution. The inmate code dictates behavior and

helps to shape the experience of individuals living behind bars.

—*Michelle Inderbitzin*

See also Argot; Donald Clemmer; Deprivation; Gangs; Rose Giallombardo Importation; Prison Culture; Prisonization; Resistance; Gresham Sykes; Women's Prisons

Further Reading

Cloward, R. A. (1960). Social control in the prison. In *Theoretical studies in social organization of the prison.* New York: Social Science Research Council.

Irwin, J. (1970). *The felon.* Berkeley: University of California Press.

Irwin, J., & Cressey, D. R. (1962). Thieves, convicts and the inmate culture. *Social Problems, 10,* 142–155.

Jacobs, J. B. (1983). *New perspectives on prisons and imprisonment.* Ithaca, NY: Cornell University Press.

Owen, B. (1998). *"In the mix": Struggle and survival in a women's prison.* Albany: State University of New York Press.

Sykes, G. M. (1958). *The society of captives: A study of a maximum security prison.* Princeton, NJ: Princeton University Press.

Sykes, G. M., & Messinger, S. (1960). The inmate social system. In *Theoretical studies in social organization of the prison.* New York: Social Science Research Council.

◪ INMATE VOLUNTEERS

In recent years, prison administrators have made increasing use of inmate volunteers to run a range of inmate programs. By using prisoners to staff these activities, prisons are able to continue offering courses and programs that they would otherwise be unable to provide due to budgetary problems and overcrowding.

INMATE VOLUNTEER PROGRAMS

Prison education departments frequently make use of inmate volunteers. Since the demise of Pell grants, prison education departments have had their budgets severely reduced. As a result, they often turn to prisoners with advanced skills to volunteer as tutors. Across the country, prisoners instruct fellow inmates in reading, writing, and math, as well as in English as a second language. Some inmates hold advanced degrees and offer courses in business, history, creative writing, and so on.

Recreation departments also frequently rely on inmate volunteers to support many of the athletic programs. Prisoners volunteer to organize teams, to serve as referees and umpires, and to keep the detailed records of sporting activities required by the administration. Most facilities allow the volunteers to coordinate seasonal sporting events with several teams that compete against each other in softball, flag football, and basketball. Some institutions, such as San Quentin, even allow these inmate teams to contact and then play against similar teams from the community.

While many institutions have music rooms and even instruments, they may not be able to afford civilian instructors. Instead, they rely on individuals from the confined population to form bands to perform shows for the entire prison community. Inmate volunteers may also lead music theory classes and teach others to read music and play instruments.

Besides education and recreation programs, the psychology services department is another segment of the prison that extensively relies on inmate volunteers. One of the most important programs that runs under their supervision is the suicide watch program available in many institutions. When someone attempts to take his or her own life in the federal prison system, that person is taken out of the general population and placed on suicide watch. During this time, the individual is locked in an observation room where he or she can be monitored 24 hours a day. However, because there are not enough psychologists or correctional officers to be present all of the time, inmate volunteers take up the slack. The volunteers in the suicide watch program work in shifts, usually for four-hour intervals, sitting immediately outside the locked observation cell and recording the activities of the individual under the psychologist's care.

Psychologists also use inmate volunteers to participate in or even lead group counseling sessions designed to help new prisoners adjust to the complexities of confinement. Volunteers may also coordinate meetings for those prisoners who want to participate in the 12-step programs of Alcoholics Anonymous or Narcotics Anonymous. Chaplains too, invite inmates to contribute to spiritual programs in similar ways.

VOLUNTEER PROGRAMS ELSEWHERE

The United States is not alone in its use of inmate volunteers. In England and Wales and Northern Ireland, for example, a highly structured suicide prevention scheme exists in all prisons that depends entirely on inmate volunteers. Known as "listeners," inmates are first screened and then trained by members of the crisis help group, the Samaritans. Once accepted into the program, inmate volunteers then have greater freedom of movement around the facility, as they are meant to be available to listen to any other prisoner who needs help dealing with the strains of incarceration. British prisons also have traditionally used inmate volunteers to run programs within minimum-security prisons for mentally and physically disabled children. Some even volunteer to help with the aged in nearby homes for the elderly.

WHY PRISONERS VOLUNTEER

Just as administrators want to ensure that inmates are never idle, so too do most inmates eschew dead time. With so much time on their hands and nothing productive to do, many inmates find volunteering a solace. Volunteering programs not only fill their day but also give them something to think about and do.

CONCLUSION

As states face greater budgetary crises, they are reducing the funds made available to correctional institutions. However, the number of people being incarcerated is not slowing down. As a result, many prisons and jails are finding it difficult to offer programs in education, recreation, and religion. They also have problems providing adequate counseling services. Inmate volunteers, like community volunteers, help address some of the shortfall.

—*Michael Santos*

See also Alcoholics Anonymous; Chaplains; Contract Ministers; Drug Treatment Programs; Education; Psychological Services; Recreation Programs; Rehabilitation Theory; Suicide; Volunteers

Further Reading

Bayse, D. (1993). *Helping hands: A handbook for volunteers in prison.* Lanham, MD: American Correctional Association.

Bosworth, M. (2002). *The U.S. federal prison system.* Thousand Oaks, CA: Sage.

Liebling, A., & Ward, T. (Eds.). (1994). *Deaths in custody: International perspectives.* London: Whiting & Birch.

INS DETENTION FACILITIES

INS (Immigration and Naturalization Service) detention facilities hold non–U.S. citizens who have been convicted or accused of crime and are awaiting either trial or deportation. Since the 1990s, few federal agencies have grown more rapidly and become more controversial than the INS. With its new and expansive powers aimed at controlling illegal immigration, the INS has stepped up its commitment to detentions and deportations. Proponents of tough law-and-order tactics praise the INS for its campaign to rid the nation of criminal aliens; however, immigration advocates argue that the laws unfairly target immigrants who have had minor brushes with the law. Under the 1996 Illegal Immigration Reform and Immigrant Responsibility Act, numerous crimes were reclassified as aggravated felonies requiring detention and possibly deportation, including minor misdemeanors such as shoplifting and low-level drug violations (also see the 1996 Antiterrorism and Effective Death Penalty Act). Compounding the harshness of the revised statutes, enforcement was retroactive meaning that persons who had been convicted before 1996 also were subject to detention and deportation even though people previously convicted of those crimes rarely served jail terms and were placed on probation.

ORGANIZATIONAL STRUCTURE

The INS, which in 2003 was merged into the Immigration and Customs Enforcement (ICE), a bureau of the Department of Homeland Security, until recently operated within the U.S. Department of Justice. Its primary responsibility is enforcing the laws regulating the admission of foreign-born persons (i.e., aliens) to the United States and for administering various immigration benefits, including the naturalization of qualified applicants for U.S. citizenship. The INS also cooperates with the Department of State, the Department of Health and Human Services, and the United Nations in the admission and resettlement of refugees.

The operational and management functions of INS are administered through INS headquarters in Washington, D.C., that oversees approximately 29,000 employees through three regional offices and the headquarters-based Office of International Affairs. These offices are responsible for directing the activities of 33 districts and 21 Border Patrol sectors throughout the United States and three district offices and 39 area offices outside U.S. territory. INS field offices provide direct service to applicants for benefits under the Immigration and Nationality Act and implement INS policies to carry out statutory enforcement responsibilities in their respective geographic areas. Overseas offices, in addition, serve as important information channels between INS and U.S. Foreign Service officers and foreign government officials abroad. As its mission suggests, the INS is a unique agency because it has the duty both to enforce the law and to provide services to immigrants. The combination of these activities creates considerable strain for INS personnel as well as their clients.

Due in large part to problems caused by this dual mandate, the INS remained one of the most criticized agencies in the federal government. Specifically, it was often challenged over its controversial enforcement tactics and its difficulty to deliver services efficiently.

INCREASED FUNDING

At a time when Congress was cutting federal spending in the 1990s, it funneled increasingly greater funds and resources to the INS, making it the largest federal law enforcement agency. Between

1993 and 2001, the INS budget soared by more than 230% from $1.5 billion to $5.0 billion. During that period, spending for enforcement programs grew from $933 million to $3.1 billion, nearly five times as much as spending for citizenship and other immigrant services, which increased from $261 million to $679 million. The cost of shared support for the two missions increased from $525 million in 1993 to $1.1 billion in 2001. The INS also increased its full-time, permanent staff by 79% from 1993 (17,163) to 2001 (30,701). Most of that growth occurred in the enforcement programs, where the total number of employees, including officers, grew from 11,418 to 23,364. Border Patrol led the way with an increase of 7,962 employees or 159%. In addition, the agency designated funds to expand its detention sector.

INS DETENTION

Between 1995 and 2001, the INS more than doubled the number of detention bed spaces available, with the current capacity at about 20,000 beds; furthermore, the Detention and Deportation staff nearly doubled, growing to 3,475 full-time permanent staff. Although the INS allocated funds to improve services to immigrants, the lion's share of the budget was devoted to "strengthening its successful multi-year strategy to manage the border, deter illegal immigration, combat the smuggling of people, and remove criminal and other illegal aliens from the United States" (INS, 1999, p. 1). As of 2002, more than 20,000 undocumented immigrants (including asylum seekers) were detained by the INS.

With unprecedented power in dealing with immigrants, the INS has increased its reliance on detention and deportation, even though these policies are often fraught with contradictions and injustice. In particular, those violating revised immigration laws are unnecessarily detained for protracted periods of time. Many detainees are housed in harsh conditions of confinement exacerbated by overcrowding, inadequate health care, and in some instances assaults by staff or state detainees held on criminal charges. At the Krome Detention Center in Miami,

for example, many female INS detainees have been subject to physical and sexual assault.

Locked behind bars and fearing possible deportation, INS detainees are both physically and emotionally isolated. Cultural and language barriers merely complicate the experience of being detained. When detainees from the far reaches of the globe, such as Pakistan, China, Ecuador, or Afghanistan, find themselves in local jails around the United States, communication between jail officers and detainees is often impossible. Most jails holding detainees are located in rural parts of the country where staff may rarely have encountered non-English-speaking people before the INS began paying them to hold its detainees. Language barriers make everything from receiving medical attention to understanding jail rules extremely difficult. Without proper translation, detainees cannot understand legal services lists, call attorneys, make requests, or file grievances, all of which contribute to their isolation. Because INS detainees struggle to maintain contact with family, friends, and lawyers, they often lack basic emotional and legal support necessary to endure the lengthy administrative process. Frequent transfers to other facilities also compound their confusion and frustration. There are numerous reports of individuals being lost in the vast detention system; as a result, some detainees miss their court hearings because administrators cannot locate them in time.

A critical look reveals unsettling contradictions in INS detention practices, most notably the reliance on unnecessary and costly confinement that generates income for facilities renting their cells. In doing so, the INS abdicates its custodial responsibilities to local jails and private corrections companies, which the agency and concerned groups have difficulty monitoring. Despite cries from human rights groups, the business of detaining undocumented immigrants and asylum seekers has produced a vast network of more than 900 private and county jails nationwide, all eager to cash in on lucrative INS contracts that usually pay twice the cost of housing inmates charged with criminal offenses. Local jail administrators and private corrections firms have taken comfort in the fact that Congress remains deeply committed to its fight against illegal immigrants. The INS uses more than a third of its $900 million detention budget to rent cells, mostly in remote rural counties where the costs are low.

INS detainees are the fastest-growing segment of the nation's correctional population: 8,200 detainees were held by the INS in 1997, and by 2001, that figure leaped to more than 20,000 (INS, 2001). Opponents of INS detention practices also contend that the safety of undocumented immigrants and asylum seekers hangs in the balance when local jails and private correctional companies assume custody. Despite formal complaints and lawsuits over abuse and neglect, the INS has continued sending its detainees to facilities known for their mistreatment and deplorable conditions of confinement.

Recent rulings by the U.S. Supreme Court have shed light on the harsh detention policies of the INS, in particular its use of indefinite detention. As of 2002, there were 4,400 INS detainees convicted of deportable offenses who were detained indefinitely because the U.S. government did not have official diplomatic ties with their nation of origin, including Cambodia, Cuba, Gaza, Iran, Iraq, Laos, Vietnam, and former satellites of the Soviet Union. These men and women are held, despite the High Court ruling of 2001 that determined that immigrants who have committed crimes in the United States cannot be locked up indefinitely simply because the government has no place to send them (see Indefinite Detention Project, 2000; *Ma v. Ashcroft*, 2001; *Zadvydas v. Underdown*, 2001).

EFFECTS OF THE SEPTEMBER 11 ATTACKS AND THE USA PATRIOT ACT

The September 11, 2001, terrorist attacks on the World Trade Center and the Pentagon have given the debate over INS detention a new resonance. On October 26, 2001, President George W. Bush signed into law the USA PATRIOT Act (Uniting and Strengthening America by Providing Appropriate Tools Required to Intercept and Obstruct Terrorism). Whereas the PATRIOT Act received overwhelming bipartisan support, civil liberties and immigrants' rights organizations worry that the new law will

have unfair consequences for immigrants and foreign nationals visiting with valid visas. Chief among those concerns is mass detention shrouded in government secrecy.

In less than two months following the September 11 attacks, the government had rounded up and detained more than 1,200 persons of Middle Eastern descent. Although the PATRIOT Act expanded the powers of the Department of Justice and the INS, it limited the length of detention to seven days before the government must charge the detainee of a crime. Once charged under the new law, however, detainees found to be engaged in terrorist activities can be held for six months. Weeks after September 11, evidence surfaced of abuse and mistreatment against those detained, prompting tremendous concern among human rights advocates. In a year following the attacks, the government's dragnet had failed to link the vast majority of those detained to the terrorism investigation. Most of those who were swept up were charged on immigration violations, usually overstaying their visas.

Compounding the controversy over mass detention, the government has maintained a policy of secrecy. Attorney General John Ashcroft repeatedly denied access to basic information about many of those in detention, including their names and current location. Such secrecy has been denounced by human rights and civil liberties advocates as well as by news organizations and even some political leaders who have complained that the attorney general has failed to explain adequately the need for those drastic measures.

Reports that detainees have been subjected to solitary confinement without being criminally charged as well as being denied access to telephones and attorneys raises questions about whether detainees are being deprived of due process. Moreover, those deprivations clearly contradict assurances by the Justice Department that everyone arrested since September 11 has had access to counsel. Eventually, key members of Congress challenged the sweeps of aliens in search of terrorists, requesting from the attorney general detailed information on the more than 1,200 people detained since the terrorist attacks. Specifically, lawmakers asked for the identity of all those detained, the charges against them, the basis for holding those cleared of connection to terrorism, and a list of all government requests to seal legal proceedings, along with the rationale for doing so.

CONCLUSION

Unlike people charged criminally, INS detainees are not entitled to government-appointed counsel, thus many are not represented. Some civil rights advocates complain that law enforcement officials are charging people with INS violations, holding them in solitary confinement, and then interrogating them before they can consult attorneys who might advise them not to talk at all. In an effort to abolish the Justice Department's secrecy on detentions, a coalition of 21 news and civil liberties organizations filed a request under the Freedom of Information Act to release information about the people detained. In 2002, a federal appeals court declared that the Bush administration acted unlawfully in holding hundreds of deportation hearings in secret. The court issued stinging language criticizing the government's failure to recognize fundamental civil liberties. Months following the court's ruling, however, the Justice Department still refused to comply with the court order and continued its commitment to government secrecy.

—Michael Welch

See also Corrections Corporation of America; Cuban Detainees; Enemy Combatants; Foreign Nationals; Freedom of Information Act 1966; Privatization; Relocation Centers; Santería; USA PATRIOT Act 2001; Wackenhut Corrections Corporation

Further Reading

Calavita, K. (1992). *Inside the state: The bracero program, immigration, and the I.N.S.* New York: Routledge.

General Accounting Office. (1998). *Illegal aliens: Changes in the process of denying aliens entry into the United States.* Washington, DC: U.S. Government Printing Office.

Human Rights Watch. (1998). *Locked away: Immigration detainees in jails in the U.S.* New York: Author.

Human Rights Watch. (2002). *Presumption of guilt: Human rights abuses of post-September 11 detainees.* New York. Author.

Immigration and Customs Enforcement. (2004). ICE home page. http://www.ice.gov/graphics/about/organization/index.htm

Immigration and Naturalization Service. (1999). *Strengthening the nation's immigration system.* Fact sheet. Washington, DC: U.S. Government Printing Office.

Indefinite Detention Project. (2000, October–December). Indefinite Detention Project of the Catholic Legal Immigration Network Inc. *Quarterly Report for the Indefinite Detention Project.* Retrieved from www.cscd.org

Welch, M. (2000). The role of the Immigration and Naturalization Service in the prison industrial complex. *Social Justice: A Journal of Crime, Conflict & World Order, 27*(3), 73–88.

Welch, M. (2002). *Detained: Immigration laws and the expanding I.N.S. jail complex.* Philadelphia: Temple University Press.

Welch, M. (2003). Ironies of social control and the criminalization of immigrants. *Crime, Law & Social Change: An International Journal, 39,* 319–337.

Women's Commission for Refugee Women and Children. (2000). *Behind locked doors—Abuse of refugee women at the Krome Detention Center.* New York: Author.

Legal Cases

Ma v. Ashcroft, 257 F3d 1095 (2001).

Zadvydas v. Underdown, 185 F.3d 279 (5th Cir. 1999), 121 S. Ct. 876 (2001).

◪ INTERMEDIATE SANCTIONS

Intermediate sanctions are community-based corrections that are more restrictive than probation, but less restrictive than prison. Some intermediate penalties include intensive supervision probation, community residential corrections centers, and electronic home monitoring. Intermediate sanctions are designed to reduce incarceration and to lower the costs of holding offenders in the most restrictive environments. They are also meant to provide more supervision than that which can be offered through regular probation or a similar sanction. Finally, intermediate sanctions also offer incremental alternatives in resentencing probation and parole violators. Instead of sending or returning these violators to jail or prison, intermediate sanctions can be used to increase the supervision and services offered to probationers and parolees.

CURRENT PRACTICE

Though the various practices considered to be intermediate sanctions can be traced to the start of the use of community-based programs for offenders, the modern categorization of these sanctions began in the early 1980s when U.S. prison and probation populations grew dramatically. At this time, it was thought that intermediate sanctions could help lower the numbers of those confined or placed on probation. In practice, this has not been the case.

Intermediate sanctions are designed to (1) provide a wider variety of sentencing alternatives for offenders, (2) decrease the costs for the corrections system, (3) reduce the rate of reoffending, and (4) maintain community safety. Several intermediate punishments are often used in combination with one another or in addition to regular probation or parole. The most common of these sanctions are fines, restitution, community service, day reporting centers, intensive supervision probation or parole, home confinement, electronic monitoring, residential community corrections centers, and boot camps.

Fines, Restitution, and Community Service

The punitive nature of fines, restitution, and community service is all the same: financial. The amount someone is fined as punishment varies based on the level or seriousness of his or her offense. Often the fine may be part of a restitution program that repays victims for damages resulting from an offense. In contrast, community service does not involve an upfront payment of any sort. Instead, it requires an individual to participate in unpaid labor with public or private nonprofit agencies to benefits society in general.

As they stand alone, fines, community service, and restitution are not more restrictive than regular probation. However, when imposed in addition to probation and other intermediate sanctions such as home confinement or electronic monitoring, they fit within the definition of intermediate sanctions. In addition, in certain cases, imposing a fine or community service may provide an alternative to using overcrowded jails and prisons.

Day Reporting Centers, Intensive Supervision, Home Confinement, and Electronic Monitoring

Day reporting centers, intensive supervision, and home confinement provide surveillance without incarceration. Day reporting centers monitor offenders who live in their own homes. Individuals must report to the centers several times throughout a week, if not daily, for various activities, including drug treatment and drug testing, counseling services, and vocational and educational assistance. The first day reporting centers appeared in Connecticut and Massachusetts in the mid-1980s. By the mid-1990s, there were more than a hundred of such centers in several states.

Offenders who have been sentenced to intensive supervision probation are strictly monitored and supervised in lieu of going to prison. A variation on this is intensive supervision parole, which is similar to the program in probation, but provides supervision for offenders released on parole from prison who need greater supervision than that which is supplied with regular parole programs. Intensive supervision probation (ISP) was originally put into practice during the 1950s and 1960s, by reducing caseload sizes and increasing offender contacts. But it was not until 1982, when Georgia initiated the most stringent ISP at the time, that there was a nationwide movement to include ISP programs as an alternative to imprisonment. Every state had implemented a form of ISP for offenders by 1990.

Offenders on home confinement serve their sentences at their homes, rather than in jail or prison. They may be monitored by electronic devices to determine whether they are abiding by court orders, including remaining in their homes at specified times. Offenders in New Mexico who had been apprehended and punished for white-collar offenses or driving under the influence of altering substances were the first offenders to be required to use electronic monitoring. There are various forms of electronic monitoring in use, most commonly where the offender wears an ankle bracelet that transmits information with a device that remains in the home where the offender resides.

*Residential Community
Corrections Centers and Boot Camps*

Finally, residential community corrections centers and boot camps provide secure living without long-term incarceration in a prison or jail. Residential community corrections centers, also commonly referred to as halfway houses, are facilities where offenders reside instead of going to prison or jail, or after their release from prison or jail. Residents are allowed to leave the facility on a daily basis to work and attend school in the community. They may also earn the opportunity to receive overnight passes to the homes of family members. Some community corrections centers may offer specific services, such as drug abuse treatment.

Boot camps are a form of incarceration typically used for first-time, younger offenders that involve a military-based regimen over a short period. Boot camp inmates are then released to the community under some form of probation or parole supervision.

SUPPORT FOR INTERMEDIATE SANCTIONS

Several positive outcomes are attributed to intermediate sanctions. Their cost-effectiveness is typically one of their most attractive characteristics. Though they are generally more expensive than supervising an offender on regular probation or parole, intermediate sanctions cost less to operate per day than housing offenders in an institutional setting. Proponents point out that many prisoners are not a major threat to the community and could benefit more from serving their sentences as an intermediate sanction, with less cost to the public and less stigmatization of the offender. Offenders are less stigmatized by intermediate sanctions because they are allowed to live in the community at large without many people being aware of their offender status. Also, remaining in the community allows offenders to contribute to society and their victims by working to pay for their crime (i.e., restitution) and to defray the costs of their supervision.

Supporters also argue that individuals in intermediate sanctions are more able to become involved in treatment programs since there are more of these resources outside the prison than inside. Participating in treatment in the community allows the offenders to better practice the techniques they have learned. Treatment programs in prison, though warranted, do not often provide offenders the best opportunity to apply these skills in their ordinary surroundings. Thus, when released from prison, offenders may not be fully aware of how to relate their training to their real-world lives.

Last, intermediate sanctions resolve problems of reintegration into the community. Returning to a public life after serving a prison sentence can be difficult for some offenders. By eliminating the prison sentence, the difficulties of adjusting to life outside of prison is also eliminated.

SOME PROBLEMS WITH INTERMEDIATE SANCTIONS

Not everyone is in favor of intermediate sanctions. Though the cost-effectiveness of specific programs is not disputed by many, critics argue that intermediate sanctions are not cost effective if the use of institutional programs is not reduced. In this view, intermediate sanctions simply add to, thus increasing, the overall budget of the corrections system. Similarly, some argue that intermediate sanctions lead to "net widening" in the criminal justice system, whereby more people are sentenced to some form of correctional supervision simply because there is now a great range of options. Some offenders who would have received a probation sentence or less, for example, would now come under the control of stricter supervision requirements, though they may have been just as successful on regular probation or with no supervision at all. Once these programs exist, opponents of the use of intermediate sanctions contend that judges will find people to place in the programs, even if they are of no more benefit than less rigorous punishments.

Public safety as it relates to intermediate sanctions is another concern for critics. Some of the programs falling within the definition of intermediate sanctions require that offenders be those who would otherwise have been sentenced to prison. Though they have been screened out as offenders who are most obliging to strict community supervision, critics still believe these high-risk offenders would be better off in an institutional placement because community safety remains a concern. Finally, many are concerned about the effectiveness of intermediate sanction programs. Research conducted on intermediate sanctions such as boot camps, intensive supervision probation programs, monetary sanctions, and halfway houses do not show any less recidivism than when regular probation or prison are used as punishment.

CONCLUSION

Though there is more extensive use of intermediate sanctions today, the traditional community-based corrections methods of probation and parole are still the most widely used forms of community supervision. Even still, the implementation and use of intermediate sanctions are expected to rise due to continuing struggles with jail and prison crowding and sentencing practices. Due to conflicting views about their success rate and purpose, more research must be done to determine the effectiveness and legitimacy of the various intermediate sanctions.

—*Hillary Potter*

See also Boot Camp; Community Corrections Centers; Drug Treatment Programs; Electronic Monitoring; Fine; Furlough; Group Homes; Home Arrest; Parole; Prerelease Programs; Probation; Work-Release Programs

Further Reading

Byrne, J. M., Lurigio, A., & Petersilia, J. (Eds.) (1992). *Smart sentencing: The emergence of intermediate sanctions.* Newbury Park, CA: Sage.

Davies, M. (1993). *Punishing criminals: Developing community-based intermediate sanctions.* Westport, CT: Greenwood.

Klein, A. R. (1997). *Alternative sentencing, intermediate sanctions, and probation* (2nd ed.). Cincinnati, OH: Anderson.

Morris, N., & Tonry, M. (1990). *Between prison and probation: Intermediate punishments in a rational sentencing system.* New York: Oxford University Press.

Parent, D., Dunworth, T., McDonald, D., & Rhodes, W. (1997). *Key legislative issues in criminal justice: Intermediate sanctions.* Washington, DC: U.S. Department of

Justice, National Institute of Justice, Office of Justice Programs.

Tonry, M. (1997). *Intermediate sanctions in sentencing guidelines.* Washington, DC: U.S. Department of Justice, National Institute of Justice, Office of Justice Programs.

☑ IRISH (OR CROFTON) SYSTEM

The Irish system of penal discipline, developed by Sir Walter Crofton in Ireland from 1854 to 1862, was viewed by late-19th-century prison reformers as a model for prison administration. In the 1870s, supporters of the Irish system played a major role in formulating correctional policies and shaping the reformatory movement in the United States. Vestiges of Crofton's Irish system can be found even today in the centralization of correctional administration, contemporary classification, education and behavior modification programs, community corrections, and parole.

BACKGROUND

When transportation of convicts to Australia finally ceased in 1868, prisons throughout Britain became increasingly overcrowded and troublesome. At the same time, concern grew over the number of convicts being released into the community, some through "tickets of leave" developed in Australia as a form of parole for good behavior.

In famine-struck Ireland in 1854, the British government responded to serious conditions in Irish prisons by appointing Walter Crofton (1815–1897) chairman of the Irish Board of Directors of Convict Prisons. With a centralized colonial Irish government, Crofton and his directors began to construct the Irish convict system. In their work, they were greatly influenced by the ideas of Alexander Maconochie, who had been placed in charge of the Australian penal colony on Norfolk Island in 1840. At the time, Norfolk Island housed convicts who had committed crimes subsequent to their transportation to Australia and consequently were viewed as requiring the most punitive of conditions. Maconochie, convinced of the value of positive incentives, developed a "mark system" rewarding work and good behavior with earned amenities and early release. Though Maconochie's experiment lasted only a matter of years, since he was removed from his post in 1844, his philosophy of convict discipline and prison management was widely disseminated and adapted by Crofton. With almost 4,000 convicts, Crofton and his associates faced overcrowded housing, limited resources, inadequate staff, and malnourished and resistant inmates. Out of these conditions, Crofton organized and skillfully publicized the "Irish system" of penal discipline.

THE IRISH SYSTEM

Crofton set out to develop a system that could integrate both punishment and reformation. In it, as in the mark system, prisoners were required to complete three stages to be eligible for a sentence reduction and/or supervised release. The Irish system, as it came to be called, was made up of an initial punishment stage and two stages of increasing reformative incentives.

During the first or punishment stage, men were held in solitary confinement at Dublin's Mountjoy Prison, which had been built in 1850 and was thought to be a model cellular prison. Under Crofton's system, men were placed in separate cells, with a restricted diet. For eight or nine months they were held in spartan conditions and put to work at oakum picking. Women, viewed as more "sensitive," were held four months to the same regime. The goals of this part of the process were control and submission, a "deterrent" awareness of the consequences of crime, and after enforced idleness, desire for productive work.

During this period of punishment, Crofton asserted, the inevitable hostility that punitive and degrading practices evoke could be averted through strategies that sustained hope for liberty. Consequently, each convict was instructed that the successful completion of the later stages depended on their self-control as "arbiters of their own fate" who needed an active cooperative relationship with "those placed over them." Crofton demanded that staff maintain positive, fair, and model relationships with prisoners to reinforce the legitimacy of their rule. Secular and religious education was critical for reformation. Crofton enlisted the aid of the National Board of Education to provide licensed teachers and arranged for both Catholic and Protestant chaplains. The observations and recommendations of the teachers and chaplains, although sometimes disputed and censored, were included in the yearly reports.

At the successful completion of their first stage, male convicts were transferred to public work prisons while the women remained at Mountjoy, working in a common sewing room. "Benevolent Catholic and Protestant ladies" regularly visited the women and there was nursery space for children. For both women and men entering the second stage, there was a four-level system of classification. Earning a designated number of "marks" at each level, based on the "will to achieve" in discipline, school, and industry, brought increasing gratuities and privileges and a distinctive badge. Misconduct could bring the loss of marks, restricted diet, and for men, return to Mountjoy. Monthly rosters, meticulously kept for each convict, can still be viewed in the Irish National Archives.

After achieving the advanced second-stage level, at the third stage convicts, with the exception of political prisoners, moved from the ordinary prisons to the highly publicized "intermediate prisons." There, in Crofton's words, "individualization" with small numbers took place in an open environment. Descriptions stressed that the purpose was not only to test the assumed self-control and good conduct of the convict but through lectures and job placement to increase their chances for employment after release and lessen public fears by their visible presence in the community. At their intermediate-prison stage, women convicts were placed in two "houses of refuge"; at Goldenbridge the Sisters of Mercy administered a refuge for Catholic women, while Protestant ladies provided a smaller refuge in Dublin.

In 1857, only after the integrated three stages of the Irish system were in place, were "tickets of leave" issued providing the final incentive of a reduction of sentence and supervised release. With a well-organized and centrally controlled constabulary developed for Ireland under British rule, each released convict registered immediately and reported monthly to the local constabulary. Any irregularity or a new crime brought the convict back to prison, protecting the Irish use of tickets of leave from the public outcry in England.

The development of the Irish system met resistance not only from inmates, who smashed Mountjoy's cell fixtures, but also from within Crofton's staff, some of whom resented the strict discipline, frequent inspections, and low wages, as well as from his English colleagues. Joshua Jebb, Crofton's counterpart in England, aided by a disgruntled Presbyterian chaplain at the Cork Prison, reacted to the Irish system's acclaim and the implied failure of his efforts in England by launching attacks on the validity of Crofton's widely circulated reports. Some noted that employment in a depopulated Ireland rather than a system of prison discipline aided the successful integration of convicts and others warned of dangers to liberty in police surveillance. Pamphlet wars were waged between proponents and opponents of the Irish system. In the eight years before Crofton's retirement in 1862, however, the Irish system became the working model of the prison reform movement.

NETWORKS OF REFORM

During this period, in what has been described as a form of "penitentiary tourism," persons interested in prison reform visited prisons and met regularly in national and international prison congresses. Their motivations varied, including a mixture of belief in the new social sciences, a commitment to evangelical Christianity or humanitarian benevolence, a middle-class fear of the "dangerous classes," and governmental concerns with social disorder. Crofton was a frequent speaker at the yearly meetings of the National Association for the Promoting of the Social Sciences, and the Dublin meeting in 1861 brought visitors to the intermediate-stage prison at Lusk and the women's refuge at Goldenbridge, spreading the word of their successes internationally. Glowing descriptions of the total dedication of Lusk's James Organ to lecturing, finding employment, and constant supervision of male convicts modeled the role for future parole agents. Women reformers, including Rhoda Coffin, instrumental in 1873 in founding the first separate women's institution in the United States, visited and praised the Irish system's provision for

women. With their Dublin contacts, members of the New York Prison Association began planning with Zebulon Brockway for the first reformatory based on the mark system, opening at Elmira in 1876. Contacts with Crofton and his writings by the organizers of the 1870 National Prison Association meeting, held during a period of economic and political unrest, led to the call in the famous Declaration of Principles for the implementation of the "Irish or Crofton prison system" in the United States.

CONCLUSION

In the context of contemporary penal theory, the goals of the Irish system, to produce through individualized surveillance "an altered and reformed being," could be considered as a model for Michel Foucault's analysis of disciplinary power. Though Crofton's system was never developed in its entirety outside of Ireland, and even there existed only for a relatively short period, increasing centralization of correctional administration, the use of classification, forms of behavior modification, educational programs, community corrections, and parole have become integral components of correctional policy and practices.

—*Esther Heffernan*

See also Australia; Jeremy Bentham; Zebulon Reed Brockway; Chaplains; Classification; Community Corrections Centers; Discipline System; Education; Elmira Reformatory; Food; Michel Foucault; History of Prisons; History of Women's Prisons; Legitimacy; Alexander Maconochie; Parole; Rehabilitation Theory; Solitary Confinement

Further Reading

Carpenter, M. (1967). *Reformatory prison discipline as developed by the Rt. Hon. Sir Walter Crofton in the Irish convict prisons.* Reprint. Montclair, NJ: Patterson Smith. (Original work published 1872)

Carroll-Burke, P. (2000). *Colonial discipline: The making of the Irish convict system.* Dublin: Four Courts.

Dooley, E. (1981). Sir Walter Crofton and the Irish or intermediate system of prison discipline. *New England Journal of Prison Law, 575,* 72–115.

Eriksson, T. (1976). *The reformers: An historical survey of pioneer experiments in the treatment of criminals.* New York: Elsevier.

Foucault, M. (1977). *Discipline and punish: The birth of the prison.* New York: Vintage.

Hinde, R. (1977). Sir Walter Crofton and the reform of the Irish convict system, 1854–61. *The Irish Jurist,* 115–147, 295–337.

Morris, N. (2002). *Maconochie's gentlemen: The story of Norfolk Island and the roots of modern prison reform.* New York: Oxford University Press.

Pisciotta. A. (1994). *Benevolent repression: Social control and the American reformatory-prison movement.* New York: New York University Press.

Wines, E. C. (Ed.). (1970). *Transactions of the National Congress on Penitentiary and Reformatory Discipline.* Reprint. Washington, DC: American Correctional Association. (Original work published 1871)

⚑ IRWIN, JOHN (1929–)

John Irwin is a prison sociologist who has combined scholarship with activism throughout his intellectual career. His career, however, did not begin in the usual way. After developing a heroin habit and weaving in and out of the local jail system for short periods, Irwin was sentenced to a prison term at the California Training Facility in Soledad. While serving a five-year sentence, Irwin embarked on a program of self-study, maximizing the limited resources available in the prison library and developing work routines that guided his future achievements in sociology and criminology. Irwin's critique of this system and his experience with it can be found in his third book, *Prisons in Turmoil,* which was published in 1980.

EDUCATION

After his release, Irwin began his college studies at San Francisco State College (now University). He soon transferred to University of California, Los Angeles (UCLA), to finish his undergraduate degree, before commencing graduate work in sociology at the University of California, Berkeley, in the spring of 1963. Here he developed his long-standing association with Herbert Blumer, Erving Goffman, and David Matza.

After Berkeley, Irwin returned to San Francisco State, this time as a professor, where he remained for the next 27 years. Before his retirement in 1994,

Irwin developed a research program that critiqued the prison system from a perspective of justice and fairness. Works produced during his teaching career include *Scenes* (1977), *Prisons in Turmoil* (1980), and *The Jail* (1985) as well as numerous articles and presentations.

PRISON CULTURE

While a student at UCLA, Irwin enrolled in a graduate seminar on the sociology of prisons taught by Donald Cressey. During this class, Irwin took issue with the view that prison culture was a functional response to the pains or deprivations of imprisonment. Drawing from his own experience in prison, he suggested that other factors—specifically, preprison identity—created prison culture. Cressey challenged Irwin to develop a statement of his view and, together, they published the primary statement of the importation theory of prison culture in the seminal article "Thieves, Convicts and the Inmate Culture" (1962).

At Berkeley, Irwin completed his dissertation, subsequently published in 1970 as *The Felon.* This work remains a landmark in the study of prison culture and outlines the basic tenets of prison adaptation from a career perspective. In it, Irwin expands his earlier argument that forms of prison adaptation are closely tied to preprison orientations. He describes various ways prisoners adapt to incarceration depending on their preprison identities and self-definitions. These modes include "doing time" (closely associated with the thief identity); jailing (associated with the state-raised youths and those without any connection to conventional society); and gleaning (chosen by those who attempt to improve their life chances by developing new intellectual, vocational, or social skills while incarcerated). Irwin also describes the emerging importance of race and ethnicity in the convict world and foreshadows his later articulation of this phenomenon in *Prisons in Turmoil* (1980).

In *Prisons in Turmoil* (1980), Irwin continues his investigation of the prison social order. Beginning with sociological description of "The Big House: The Great American Prison," he reviews the history of American prisons and the evolution of prison social order through 1980. In this book, Irwin also describes the changing nature of male prisoner culture and the specific effects of tips and racial and ethnic membership on prison life.

ACTIVISM

As his academic career developed, Irwin also began to work as a prison activist. Along with other ex-prisoners, lawyers, prisoners' families, and community members, Irwin founded the Prisoner's Union, which was dedicated to elevating the interests of prisoners and developing their political influence in prison management. Albeit in a different form, the Prisoners Union continues to exist.

At this same time, Irwin was invited to work with the American Friends Service Committee and contributed to the publication *Struggle for Justice* (1971). In this influential volume, activists argued that the prison system reinforced existing inequalities in American society through the discretionary and arbitrary application of overly punitive sanctions. In particular, the discretion and bias inherent in indeterminate sentencing practices were defined as a major obstacle in any struggle for justice and fairness. These authors also advocated for a new restraint in the application of criminal justice practice. Irwin stated in the preface to *Prisons in Turmoil* (1980, p. xvi) that his work with the American Friends on *Struggle for Justice* "supplied me with a more thorough understanding of the criminal justice system and a philosophy of justice that has been my foundation, not only for this book, but for all my work in criminal justice."

CONCLUSION

At present, Irwin continues his work on prison scholarship and social change. With Jim Austin, he published *It's About Time* (2002), an analysis of American's imprisonment binge. His work has also been the primary influence on a new generation of ex-convict prison scholars, many of whom also completed their graduate work after serving a prison term. The work of these scholars, known collectively as *convict criminology,* continues John Irwin's

tradition of solid empirical work, critique of the justice system, and advocacy for the disenfranchised prisoner.

NOTE: Much of the information in this entry comes from an interview with John Irwin, Hermosa Beach, California, October 25, 2002.

—*Barbara Owen*

See also Activism; Convict Criminology; Deprivation; Fay Honey Knopp; Importation; Inmate Code; Anthony Platt; Prison Culture; Quakers; Gresham Sykes

Further Reading

American Friends Service Committee. (1971). *Struggle for justice: A report on crime & punishment in America.* New York: Hill and Wang.

Austin, J., & Irwin, J. (2002). *It's about time: America's incarceration binge* (3rd ed.). Belmont, CA: Wadsworth.

Irwin, J. (n.d.). *Rogue* (Autobiography of John Irwin). Unpublished manuscript.

Irwin, J. (1970). *The felon.* Englewood Cliffs, NJ: Prentice Hall.

Irwin, J. (1977). *Scenes.* Beverly Hills, CA: Sage.

Irwin, J. (1980). *Prisons in turmoil.* Boston: Little, Brown.

Irwin, J. (1985). *The jail: Managing the underclass in America society.* Berkeley: University of California Press.

Irwin J., & Cressey, D. (1962). Thieves, convicts and the inmate culture. *Social Problems, 10,* 142–155.

■ ISLAM IN PRISON

The religion of Islam has increased rapidly in the United States and its prisons over the past 40 years. There are currently an estimated 5 to 7 million Muslims in the United States, with the following ethnic distribution: 29% are African American, 29% are South Asian, and 20% are Arab. There are smaller percentages among African, European, and other Asian groups. When Malcolm X converted to Sunni Islam in 1964, there were an estimated 3,000 African American Sunni Muslims. By 2003, that number had grown to between 1 and 2 million. In federal and state correctional facilities, a sizable number of inmates have converted to Islam. For example, according to Imam Luqman Abdur Shahid, the former director of Ministerial Services of New York City Department of Corrections, in

1999 Islam replaced Catholicism as the religion of preference among the 17,000 daily inmates on Rikers Island. In New York state prisons, about 20% of the prison population are Muslims. Similar rates are found in the prison populations of the upper Midwest and the west coast in urban areas such as Chicago, Detroit, and Cleveland, the San Francisco Bay area, and Los Angeles. Only in the southern Bible Belt are the rates of Muslim conversion lower, about 10%.

The growth of Islam in the prison population of the United States was made possible by a series of court cases that eventually gave constitutional protection to Muslims and recognition of Islam as a legitimate religion. In the earliest cases, *Bratcher v. McGinnis* and *Cooper v. Pate,* the Nation of Islam paved the way for both orthodox Sunni Muslims and other Islamic sects such as Shiites and heterodox groups such as the Moorish Science Temple and the Nation of Gods and Earths or Five Percenters to be allowed to practice their faith while incarcerated. Other court cases led to Islamic inmates being allowed no-pork diets, to grow beards, to wear skull caps or kufis, and to pray at prescribed times five times a day as well as to own prayer rugs.

FUNCTIONS OF ISLAM IN PRISON: COPING, PROTECTION AND COMMUNITY, AND PERSONAL REHABILITATION

Many prisoners are attracted to Islam as a religion both because of its social aspect and because it provides protection and communal life. In his farewell speech in 632 C.E., the Prophet Muhammad Ibn Abdullah said that Muslims should treat each other as brothers and sisters. Within prisons in the United States and across the world, Muslims have formed brotherhood and sisterhood communities, which provides a sense of community and protection. For example, Sister Aisha at Rikers Island, one of the few African American Muslim women chaplains in the country, said that only Muslim women are allowed to wear a head covering or scarf at Rikers and at the women's maximum-security prison at Bedford Hills, New York. She claimed that the identifiable head coverings have provided Muslim women protection against homosexual rape and other forms of sexual abuse that occurs in women's prisons.

In contrast to prison gangs, Muslims provide protection for one another without the demand for extortion and violence. Islam does allow for an ethic of self-defense. Muslim prisoners can fight back if they are unjustly attacked. The willingness to defend themselves and to provide protection for their fellow Muslims have often been misinterpreted by correctional administrators who have tended to view Muslims as another gang. The ethics of Islam also prevent Muslim participation in any form of substance abuse.

The communal aspects of Islam in prison also include communal worship at Friday Jumu'ah prayer services and evening prayer in the prison's masjid or space set aside for worship. In some New York state prisons, the masjid space also includes offices for Muslim leaders and classrooms where Ta'leem classes are held for instruction in Arabic, Qur'anic study groups, and Islamic history. Islam encourages study, education, and the acquisition of knowledge about the Deen (religion). This separate sacred space in a prison setting also allows for the development of a calm, quiet, and peaceful atmosphere. Muslims take off their shoes before entering, a symbolic act that one has left the secular world (dar al Harb) behind and entered Islamic space (dar al Islam). The peacefulness of the masjid area stands in stark contrast to the noise of the cellblocks where several boom boxes are blasting and people have to shout to be heard. Praying five times a day, communal worship, and fasting during daylight hours for 30 days during the month of Ramadan also help inmates develop a strong internal discipline, which provides the foundation for personal rehabilitation.

Whatever rehabilitation that takes place behind the walls is often due to the personal motivation of individual inmates and the support of religious groups like Islam. Thus, for example, in some prisons, Muslims have also sponsored an Islamic Therapeutic Program, using Islamic principles to deal with drug and alcohol addiction. It is estimated that about 85%

of New York State prisoners have some form of drug or alcohol addiction. The treatment classes are similar to the 12-step programs of Alcoholic Anonymous or Narcotics Anonymous, using group therapy to help produce behavioral change.

OUTREACH MINISTRY TO PRISONERS AND EX-OFFENDERS BY MASJIDS

In a nationwide survey of 130 predominantly African American masjids, about 90% of them are actively involved in prison ministries and ministries to ex-offenders. However, in the Project 2000 survey of black churches by Gallup, about 46% of them claimed involvement in outreach to prisons. In comparison, about 20% of white churches were involved in prison ministries.

With America's inmate population at more than 2 million and another 5 to 7 million who have been released from prisons, Muslim groups have responded strongly in their ministry to prisoners and ex-offenders: 90% of the masjids have prison ministries in place, with 88% of them visiting prisons on a sustained basis, and 79% hold special programs at prisons during Muslim holidays. Thirty-eight percent of the imams also work as prison chaplains. Counseling (41%), meetings for ex-offenders (21%), and participation in a halfway house (13%) constitute the other activities. Within their communities, Muslim masjids are very active in programs against substance abuse because the religion strongly forbids the use of alcohol and drugs. Programs such as AMMAN, American Muslims Against Narcotics and Milatti Islami, a 12-step substance abuse program based on Islamic principles, have been popular in African American masjids.

When they are released, most former prisoners need housing and jobs. More than half of those returning from prison have already broken ties with their families so turning to them for shelter is often not an option. Even if they continued family ties, public housing laws do not allow ex-offenders to live there, thus continuing the discrimination and expanding the pool of the homeless. Employment discrimination also compounds the chances of ex-offenders in getting and retaining jobs. The 65% recidivism rate in New York state prisons is primarily due to the high unemployment rates of ex-offenders.

Occasionally, Muslim masjids will provide temporary shelter for those released from prison. Many masjids have a room for sleeping bags, bathroom facilities, and a kitchen. The Islamic tradition of allowing traveling Muslims to stay overnight at the masjid is sometimes extended to ex-offenders. Many African American imams have an understanding of the plight of the recently released because they have gone through the experience themselves.

The differential rate of participation in prison ministries between African American Muslim masjids (90%) and black churches (46%) is due primarily to a class difference. The majority of mainline black churches have a middle-class and working-class constituency, while African American Muslim masjids are predominantly working class and poor.

CONCLUSION

The religion of Islam has spread rapidly in American prisons over the past 40 years, reaching a level of 20% of the prison population in some state and federal facilities. Preliminary studies and interviews indicate that the majority of conversions occur in prison rather than in the streets. The reasons for attraction to Islam include the following: spiritual and theological dimensions of Islam; Islamic role models in prison; the emphasis on racial and social justice; criticism of Christianity; the emphasis on a brotherhood or sisterhood of Muslims; and protection from harm in a dangerous environment. The requirements of praying five times a day, reading the Qur'an, and fasting during the month of Ramadan contribute to the development of personal discipline, motivation, and rehabilitation. African American Muslim mosques are much more active in prison ministry than black churches.

—Lawrence H. Mamiya

See also African American Prisoners; Chaplains; Contract Ministers; First Amendment; Food; History of Religion; Judaism in Prison; Nation of Islam; Native American Spirituality; Race, Class, and Gender of Prisoners; Rehabilitation Theory; Religion in Prison; Resistance

Further Reading

Bagby, I., Perl, P., & Froehle, B. (2001). *The mosque in America: A national portrait.* Washington, DC: Council on American Islamic Relations.

Fuchs, M. (2002, September 21). After 9/11, inmates search for the true nature of Islam. *New York Times,* p. A16.

Jones, J. E. (1998). *Islamic prison ministry: Towards an effective chaplaincy at the Community Correctional Center in New Haven.* Unpublished thesis, Hartford Seminary, Hartford, Connecticut.

Lincoln, C. E., & Mamiya, L. H. (1990). *The black church in the African American experience.* Durham, NC: Duke University Press.

Mamiya, L. H. (1999). *Riker's Island study.* Unpublished preliminary survey.

Mamiya, L. H. (2002, Fall/Spring). Faith-based institutions and family support services among African American Muslim masjids and black churches. In J. Troutman (Ed.), *Journey inward, journey outward.* ITC/FaithFactor Project 2000 Study of Black Religious Life. Special book edition of *Journal of the Interdenominational Theological Center, 29*(1-2), 25–61.

Mamiya, L. H., & Bagby, I. (2003). *Casey study of African American Muslim mosques and programs for ex-offenders.* Ongoing research supported by the Annie E. Casey Foundation.

Mamiya, L. H., & Lincoln, C. E. (1998). *Islam in the African American experience.* National research project of African American mosques. Unpublished study.

Legal Cases

Cooper v Pate 378 US 546 (1964)

Bratcher v. Mc Ginnis (Attica State Prison) (WD NY, 9398)

J

◪ JACKSON, GEORGE (1941–1971)

George Jackson was one of the early pioneers of the prisoner rights movement. As a member of the Black Panthers and the founder of the prison-based Black Guerilla Family, he became a symbol for revolutionary organization and a soldier of the people against capitalist control and power. These days, Jackson is best remembered as the author of the prison letters in *Soledad Brother* and for his death at the hands of prison officers at San Quentin Penitentiary.

BIOGRAPHICAL DETAILS

George Jackson was born on September 24, 1941, in Chicago, Illinois, and grew up in a poverty-ridden industrial area just outside of the city. His childhood was characterized by risk taking, maladjustment, defiance, and delinquency. The family moved frequently around Chicago and eventually to Los Angeles. The enticements on the west coast were no fewer, however, and Jackson's involvement in delinquency progressed to gang involvement and more serious criminality. His contacts with the law grew more frequent, and he was eventually confined at the county jail and the California Youth Authority for breaking and entering, possession of stolen property, and robbery.

Jackson entered prison at the age of 18, convicted of a robbery that netted a total of $70. The inability or unwillingness to adjust that characterized his teenage years in Chicago carried over into his early years behind bars. During this time, he was often subjected to institutional discipline for disobeying policies and procedures. Incarcerated for an indeterminate sentence of one year to life, Jackson came before the parole board several times, only to be denied each time. Much of his time in prison was spent in solitary confinement.

While Jackson was serving his early years behind bars, Huey Newton and Bobby Seale were forming the Black Panther Party. From his prison cell, Jackson wrote to Newton requesting admittance into the party. Once he was granted full admission, this marked a turning point in his struggles against political repression in the institution. His membership in the Black Panther Party both legitimized and strengthened the prisoners' rights movement. It also provided a vehicle for the exchange of information between those inside the prison walls and those on the outside.

SOLEDAD BROTHERS

On January 16, 1970, Jackson and two other inmates were indicted in the murder of a white prison guard who was beaten to death and thrown over a railing to his death at Soledad Prison. Prison authorities charged that the convicts organized the killing in retaliation for an incident three days earlier in which a prison guard killed three black inmates during a fight in an exercise yard.

The case of the "Soledad Brothers" gained international recognition a year later when Jackson's younger brother, Jonathon, entered a Marin County (California) courtroom fully armed and intent on securing freedom for his brother and the other two inmates. The escape attempt failed when upon leaving the grounds of the courtroom, San Quentin guards and Marin County Sheriff's officers fired on the van and killed Jonathan and several others who were inside.

Soledad Brother

In 1970, Jackson published a book of his letters titled *Soledad Brother: The Prison Letters of George Jackson*. The book reveals the prolonged struggles of a man who desperately wanted his family members to comprehend their plight, to raise their awareness, and to mobilize their support of revolutionary black consciousness. His attempts to extract from them a black revolutionary mentality often seemed to tire and frustrate Jackson. In a December 1964 letter to his father, Jackson writes, "You see, I understand you people clearly. You are afflicted by the same set of principles that has always governed black people's ideas and habits here in the U.S. . . . My deepest and most sincerely felt sympathies go out to all of you who are not able to resolve your problems because of this fundamental lack of spirit" (pp. 40–41). Despite his disappointment, Jackson never stopped communicating with his family for any extended period of time.

Unfortunately, prison policies and procedures likely denied readers Jackson's most impassioned addresses, letters, and speeches. Not only do the readers of *Soledad Brother* not get to see his most intense letters, they also do not see the correspondence that came to Jackson while in prison. Despite the lack of context, the published letters reveal keen insights into the struggles and obstacles experienced by black prisoners.

CONCLUSION

It is clear through his correspondence with those he loved that Jackson truly believed that at some point he would again be free to carry on the struggle. Although much of the discourse about Jackson's life and book center on revolution, his story is also a symbol of the spiritual and intellectual transformation that can occur in prison. Unlike Malcolm X and other revolutionaries, however, he never had the opportunity to practice his newly developed tools as a free man. On August 21, 1971, Jackson was shot to death by prison guards in San Quentin in what most of his supporters believe was a prison conspiracy to effect his murder.

Considerable mystery shrouds the killing of Jackson, the circumstances leading up to his death, and the events that followed. The Attica Prison riots of 1971 occurred less than one month after his death, and according to several observers, was a direct result of the actions that occurred at San Quentin. One of the remarkable and little discussed sidebars of the Jackson story is the extensive network of information sharing and communication that existed within and between the nation's prisons. The publication and distribution of Jackson's letters gave prominence to the inhumane conditions of confinement faced by inmates in the nation's prisons.

One year after Jackson's death, his second book, *Blood in My Eye,* was published posthumously. Although this book also contains some of Jackson's letters, it is essentially a treatise on guerrilla warfare and the revolution to overthrow modern capitalist society. Along with the writings of Malcolm X, the books written by George Jackson raised the consciousness levels of inmates across the country and mobilized their fight against political repression. They also strengthened Jackson's political legacy as a black revolutionary intellectual.

—*David B. Taylor*

See also Abolition; Activism; African American Prisoners; Angela Y. Davis; Attica Correctional Facility; Attica Legal Brothers Defense Fund; Black Panther Party; Critical Resistance; Malcolm X; Nation of Islam; Riots

Further Reading

Davis, A. Y. (1974). *Angela Davis: An autobiography.* New York: Random House.

Jackson, G. (1971). *Soledad Brother: The prison letters of George Jackson.* New York: Coward-McCann.

Jackson, G. L. (1972). *Blood in my eye.* New York: Random House.

Nadelson, R. (1969). *Who is Angela Davis: The biography of a revolutionary.* New York: Peter H. Wyden.

Newton, H. P. (1973). *Revolutionary suicide.* New York: Harcourt Brace Jovanovich.

☑ JAILHOUSE LAWYERS

A jailhouse lawyer (JHL) is a prisoner knowledgeable in law who assists other prisoners with their legal needs. JHLs are often self-taught while incarcerated. Some perform their duties as part of their paid institutional job assignment in the prison. They advise other inmates who, unable to attain counsel or other professional help, come to the law library to find assistance with legal issues, such as preincarceration problems with landlords or employers, family problems (divorce, child custody), financial issues, name changes, and other civil disputes. Although they may specialize in particular areas, JHLs tend to focus most on postconviction complaints or with grievances against prison conditions, prison staff, and prison policy.

JHLs provide one of the few possible legitimate challenges by inmates to the conditions of their confinement. Their ability to help others with legal problems gives them influence and status within the prisoner culture, often allowing them to resolve nonlegal problems and disputes between and among inmates and staff. Prison officials, however, may see them as troublemakers and may attempt to discourage their activities through harassment, disciplinary threats, or other means that disrupt their work. In some cases, JHLs provide legal assistance for favors or gifts.

The intention of JHLs varies, often depending on whether the individual resides in a prison or jail, and whether the institution is for men or women. In jails, many need help with their bail reduction petitions. The JHL often guides the inmate in filling out the appropriate petition in order to get a lower bail, because private lawyers often claim they are too busy to do the necessary research. In women's prisons and jails, JHLs often help with domestic disputes dealing with relationships, children, child support, foster care, or divorce proceedings.

PRISONER LITIGATION

The term *prisoner litigation* typically connotes civil rights complaints or habeas corpus suits filed in federal court by prisoners in state and federal prisons and in jails. Habeas corpus petitions are "get me out of here" pleas, filed as state or federal habeas corpus challenges to continued incarceration. Complaints of staff abuse or of prison conditions are customarily filed as civil rights suits under 42 U.S.C. § 1983. Civil rights suits are the most controversial and have been significantly restricted by the 1995 Prison Litigation Reform Act (PLRA). Unless prisoners have access to outside attorneys, they must rely on the help of JHLs to put together their cases.

THE GENESIS OF PRISONER LITIGATION

Until the rise of the prisoners' rights movement in the 1960s, state and federal courts followed the "hands off" doctrine, holding that the judiciary has no business meddling in prison affairs. However, the foundations of prisoners' rights date to mid-19th-century legislation, beginning with the Fourteenth Amendment in 1868:

> No state shall make or enforce any law which shall abridge the privileges or immunities of citizens of the United States; nor shall any state deprive any person of life, liberty, or property, without due process of law; nor deny to any person within its jurisdiction the equal protection of the laws.

At the same time, Congress passed a civil rights act (Title 42 U.S.C. § 1983), which provides the basis for contemporary prisoner civil rights. Modified and renewed several times between 1866 and 1877, the relevant language remains essentially unchanged:

Every person who, under color of any statute, ordinance, regulation, custom, or usage, of any State or Territory, subjects, or causes to be subjected, any citizen of the United States or other person within the jurisdiction thereof to the deprivation of any rights, privileges, or immunities secured by the Constitution and laws, shall be liable to the party injured in an action at law, suit in equity, or other proper proceeding for redress.

Prisoners' rights expanded through broader civil rights activism in the 1960s. In prisons, Black Muslims were particularly effective in securing these changes, and after protracted court battles, they won a series of legal victories for religious recognition. Their successes, and even some failures, provided precedents that established the broader rights of prisoners.

In 1963, the Warren Court decision in *Monroe v. Pate* resurrected 19th-century civil rights legislation and provided the legislative justification for redressing state civil rights complaints in federal courts. A few years later, a federal appellate court extended to prisoners a First Amendment right to freely exercise their religion when it recognized the legitimacy of Black Muslims (*Cooper v. Pate,* 1967). More important, the *Cooper* decision for the first time explicitly allowed state prisoners to file federal litigation under the Civil Rights Act.

In one of the most significant decisions of the 1970s, the Supreme Court held in *Bounds v. Smith* (1977) that a state must provide prisoners with "adequate" access to courts and legal facilities. This translated into the requirement that the states and federal government either provide lawyers for inmates or set up a law library within the institution. Most states, faced with the cost factor, chose the latter. Since the *Bounds* decision, most prisons and jails allocate a portion of their regular library, or some space within the institution, to provide basic law books, typewriters/computers, a printer, supervising staff, and one or more law clerks. This decision provided the genesis for JHLs.

"MANIPULATIVE CON" OR "PRIMITIVE REBEL"?

Some observers ask whether the jailhouse lawyer is a social rebel who challenges prison conditions and who champions the disenfranchised, or is instead merely a manipulative self-interested power player. In our own research (Milovanovic & Thomas, 1989), we have concluded that JHLs can be viewed as "existential rebels" reacting to harsh prison conditions in one of the few ways available: litigation. With few exceptions, other than in class action suits, JHLs are not overtly political since they cannot articulate a coherent oppositional ideology in their legal challenges. Their goal is more limited, short run, and pragmatic. More often, where narrative frames are employed, their ideology is an eclectic borrowing from Marx, Muslim writings, newspaper clippings, stories of oppression, and an always present amorphous identification of a nebulous "they" as the victimizers of prisoners.

CONCLUSION: LITIGATION AS SELF-HELP AND DISCURSIVE PRACTICES

One irony of JHLs is that, even while helping to free prisoners from excessive control, they simultaneously function to legitimize it. JHLs are instrumental in translating the various stories of inmates into a legal discourse. One version of a constructed reality (from the "streets") is translated into a more cleansed, sterile, and categorical one (legal discourse). As a result, even though JHLs share a common background with other inmates, they often inadvertently participate in reinforcing the hegemonic domination of the law and its punitive practice. Similarly, prisoner litigation may also perpetuate the current penal system. Prisoners and staff both have an interest in maintaining effective, efficient, flexible, and stable prison communities, and prisoner litigation has been a significant factor in pursuing these shared goals.

Jailhouse lawyering is both a form of "primitive rebellion" and a form of dispute resolution by which prisoners attempt to resolve problems peacefully. Litigation alerts staff that complicity with street gangs is inappropriate, that ignoring critical safety hazards may mean liability, and that ignoring pleas for help during beatings and gang rapes will not be tolerated. Litigation also creates and expands rights and expectations of prisoners. Although staff are often able to subvert these rights, their incremental expansion is undeniable. More simply, jailhouse law has become a means of using the legal system for the purpose for which it has been designed, that of social maintenance. But for prisoners, social maintenance possesses a different meaning than for the public or for corrections officials. As a consequence, critics see cynical manipulation of the law where prisoner advocates perceive peaceful conflict resolution.

When Senator Bob Dole (1995) raised the specter of a "plague of litigation" contributed to by prisoners, he was partially correct. The number of prisoner civil rights petitions filed in federal court had increased annually increased in the previous two decades. However, from the early 1960s through the mid-1990s, the so-called explosion in prisoner litigation corresponded closely to the increase in prison population, while the rate of prisoner filings generally declined. The rate of state prisoner civil rights filings peaked in 1981 at 4.69 filings per 100 prisoners and gradually declined and then remained relatively stable into the mid-1990s. Since the passage of the Prison Litigation Reform Act in 1995, the rate of prisoner filings has plummeted from 4.1 filings per prisoner in 1995 to 1.6 in 2002.

Evidence also dispels the beliefs that prisoners generally file absurd (frivolous) cases or flood the courts with dozens of suits for each prisoner. Henry Fradella (1998) showed that most common examples of meritless prisoner petitions used by critics to curtail prisoners' access to courts were either falsely portrayed or erroneously misleading. His evidence also supported the view that most prisoners have a legitimate grievance motivating their petition. The overwhelming majority who file civil rights suits in federal court file only one petition, and less than 7% of petitioners file more than three. Most decisively, significant prison reforms that have resulted from prisoner litigation in the past 30 years have improved both the conditions and administration of prisons. Jailhouse lawyers have played a crucial role in helping inmates make their grievances known.

—Dragan Milovanovic and Jim Thomas

See also John J. DiIulio, Jr.; Fourteenth Amendment; Freedom of Information Act 1966; Habeas Corpus; Political Prisoners; Prison Litigation Reform Act 1996; Prisoner Litigation; Resistance; Section 1983 of the Civil Rights Act

Further Reading

Belbot, B. A., & Marquart, J. W. (1998, September). The political community model and prisoner litigation: Can we afford not to try a better way? *The Prison Journal, 78,* 299–329.

Dole, R. (1995). Hearings on Prison Litigation Reform Act. *Congressional Record,* September 27.

Fradella, H. F. (1998, December). A typology of the frivolous: Varying meanings of frivolity in Section 1983 Prisoner Civil Rights Litigation. *The Prison Journal, 78,* 465–491.

Jacobs, J. B. (1983). *New perspectives on prisons and imprisonment.* Ithaca, NY: Cornell University Press.

Milovanovic, D. (1988). Jailhouse lawyers and jailhouse lawyering. *International Journal of the Sociology of Law, 16,* 455–475.

Milovanovic, D., & Thomas, J. (1989). Overcoming the absurd: Legal struggle as primitive rebellion. *Social Problems, 36*(1), 48–60.

Thomas, J. (1988a, July). Inmate litigation: Using the courts or abusing them? *Corrections Today, 50,* 124–127.

Thomas, J. (1988b). *Prisoner litigation: The paradox of the jailhouse lawyer.* Totowa, NY: Rowman & Littlefield.

Thomas, J., McArthur, D., & McGee, T. (1999). Update: Reversing the pendulum of prisoners' rights. In D. Stephens (Ed.), *Perspectives: Corrections* (pp. 112–115). Madison, WI: Coursewise.

Thomas, J., & Milovanovic, D. (1999). Revisiting jailhouse lawyers: An excursion into constitutive criminology. In S. Henry & D. Milovanovic (Eds.), *Constitutive criminology at work: Applications to crime and justice* (pp. 227–246). Albany: State University of New York Press.

Legal Cases

Bounds v. Smith, 430 U.S. 817 (1977).
Cooper v. Pate, 382 F.2d 518, 7th Circuit (1967).
Monroe v. Pate, 365 U.S. 167, 961 (1963).

◪ JAILS

With a few exceptions, jails are operated and financed by local county or city governments. Typically, these institutions house four types of inmates: (1) those waiting for trial, known as pretrial detainees; (2) those sentenced to jail time who have been convicted of misdemeanors; (3) those awaiting transfer to state or federal institutions who are convicted felons; and (4) those convicted and waiting for sentencing who are also convicted felons. Some jails also hold material witnesses for safety and assurance purposes; however, this group comprises a small percentage of the jail population. Other offenders who may be found in local jails include probation, parole, and bail bond violators and absconders, juvenile detainees, and mentally ill persons awaiting transfer to mental health facilities. Jail time is also required in some circumstances as a condition of an offender's probation. He or she may have to serve a short period of time in jail, or to report to a jail facility for weekend confinement.

Despite their crucial role in the criminal justice system, jails tend to be the forgotten by penologists and policymakers. Instead, academic, political, and media attention is placed on prisons, which house felony offenders and are operated by state and federal governments.

HISTORY

Historically, jails have evolved in an attempt to meet the needs and demands of the criminal justice system, the offenders they serve, and the communities that use them for immediate control of crime as well as the apprehension of minor offenders. The first American jails in the colonial period were local institutions of confinement, operated by the local sheriff or one of his trusted staff, as places of confinement for both accused and sentenced offenders. The person expressly in charge of the day-to-day operation of the facility was called a jailer. Jails at this time were often the jailer's very own home, or portions of government buildings that were constructed for other purposes. Instead of being housed in cells, the accused usually shared rooms that were poorly ventilated and heated with sentenced offenders. Jailers charged inmates a fee for the provision of food and clothing, as well as for the firewood used to heat their rooms.

The Walnut Street Jail was the first purpose-built (i.e., built specifically for use as a prison or jail and not originally serving another purpose, such as barracks) jail on American soil. Opened in 1773 in Philadelphia,

Pennsylvania, the structure was originally intended to detain the accused prior to trial, as well as hold offenders awaiting sentencing. As the turn of the 19th century approached, the influence of Quaker reforms led to the addition of a penitentiary wing, which was built adjacent to the original physical structure. This wing, intended for sentenced offenders, attempted to establish silent, solitary penitence.

Throughout the 19th century, the number of convicted offenders serving time in local jails grew as the use of corporal punishment declined. At the same time, children began to be housed in separate jails or else placed in facilities for women to separate them from adult male offenders. Despite the advances made in treatment and classification, the architecture and physical environment of the mid- to late-19th-century jails made the reformation of offenders difficult. Jails built in the Midwest during this time period have been described as dark, dank, and barren. Many quickly became overcrowded as transient offender groups, such as bank robbers, grew in number.

During the post–Civil War years, jails, like prisons, sought to reform offenders through hard work. Many states, especially in the South, placed jail inmates in chain gangs and put them to work building roadways. Such activity not only was thought to reform the offender but also allowed local governments to exploit free inmate labor.

By the turn of the 20th century, most localities throughout the United States operated their own jail. As the number, and size, of these facilities increased, several problems related to inmate populations, offender programming, and the recruitment/training of detention officers began to emerge. Many of these issues are still prevalent in today's jail system.

TYPES OF JAILS TODAY

According to the most recent Census of Jails, there were more than 3,300 jails run by local governments across the United States in 1999. In addition, there were 11 federal jails operated by the Federal Bureau of Prisons in 1999 and approximately 47 privately operated jails. Typically, the sheriff's office operates one jail, which serves as the confinement facility for

Photo 1   *Martin Luther King Jr. in Jail at Jefferson County Courthouse, Birmingham, Alabama, 1967*

the entire county. This is the norm in the southern United States. In addition, local police departments operate some jails. This mode of operation is often found to be the case in large metropolitan areas, particularly in the Northeast.

Most jails are small. In fact, fewer than 10 jail systems in the United States have a capacity of more than 3,000 inmates. Almost one-half of the jails in the United States hold 50 or fewer inmates. However, according to the Census of Jails, the late 1990s saw an increase in the proportion of inmates housed in large jails and a decrease in the proportion that were held in the smallest jails. Smaller facilities tend to be located in the South, whereas larger facilities can be found in the North, as well as in large, metropolitan areas. Research has shown that small jail facilities tend to have poorly designed physical plants. They also tend to have fewer fiscal and personnel resources when compared to larger jail facilities.

Recently, some rural areas have decided to maximize their fiscal and organizational resources and open regional jails. Regionalization occurs when several counties jointly operate one jail facility. Regional jails are common in states west of the Mississippi, such as Oklahoma, Kansas, Nebraska, North Dakota, and South Dakota. In the South, smaller, outdated municipal jails have been consolidated into larger, countywide detention centers. Furthermore, Alaska, Connecticut, Delaware, Hawaii, Rhode Island, and Vermont each operate joint jail and prison systems. The jails found within such states are subsumed under the operation of state departments of correction. This practice is very common in the geographically smaller, northeastern states. Consolidation of jails into regional and state-level facilities contributed to a general decrease in the number of jails in operation in the United States during the 1980s. However, at least partly due to overcrowding, the number of jails rose during the mid- to late 1990s, generally keeping pace with the increase in the jail population.

JAIL POPULATIONS

In 2001, just over 40% of jail inmates had already been convicted of a crime, whereas almost 60% had not. As in prisons, men comprise the largest proportion of the jail population. However, the number of women in these facilities has increased recently rising to 12% of jail inmates in 2001. White and black inmates comprise approximately equal proportions of the jail population constituting just over 41% each.

Mentally Ill Detainees

Conservative estimates of the prevalence of mental disorders in jail institutions are that between 6% and 8% of jail inmates suffer from serious mental disorders. Due to the growing numbers of homeless persons housed in jails, as well as the use/abuse of alcohol and drugs by detainees, many critics argue that the number of detainees who experience mental illness is, in fact, much higher.

The presence of the mentally ill in jails poses a number of problems. First, detention officers must increase their surveillance of mentally ill inmates at admission, at the expense of their other duties, since such individuals have a much higher rate of suicide and self-harm when detained. Second, such officers are usually poorly equipped, both in terms of resources and training, to handle this special population. As a result, several commentators have recommended that nonviolent, mentally ill inmates be placed in specialized community programs. Such a policy change would reduce overcrowding as well as reallocate resources.

Women

Although women are a minority in the jail population, their numbers are currently growing at a faster rate than those of their male counterparts. Most female detainees come from disadvantaged backgrounds and often have very little job training/education and work experience. Because of their backgrounds and offense histories, females have specific needs and experience problems that are important to consider during incarceration. Thus, for example, close to half of the women housed in jails have experienced physical and/or sexual abuse. Women confined in jails are less likely than men to be charged with a violent offense. They are also more likely than their male counterparts to be charged with a substance abuse offense. The latter has implications for facility planning and programming, as special services are necessary to treat and care for women experiencing problems related to substance abuse.

JAIL DESIGN AND PHILOSOPHY

There are three general architectural designs for jail facilities: (1) traditional/first generation, (2) remote supervision/second generation, and (3) direct supervision/third generation. All three models can be found throughout the United States; however, recent emphasis has been placed on the development of the direct supervision philosophy. This model maximizes technological developments in the provision of a safe environment for inmates and jail staff.

Traditional/first-generation jails are similar in style to the first penitentiaries in the United States; they have long, linear hallways with cells lining both sides of each hallway. Observation of inmates occurs infrequently, and interaction is through bars that comprise the doors to each cell. Remote/second-generation jails are characterized by the physical design of the traditional/first-generation facilities; however, indirect surveillance of inmates occurs through technological devices such as closed-circuit televisions. Detention officers do not leave the control booth, and verbal interaction with inmates is infrequent.

Traditional/first-generation and remote supervision/second-generation facilities are often referred to as "hard" facilities due to their large, oppressive nature. These jails function to isolate persons being housed from each other as well as detention officers working in the facility. Traditional/ first-generation and remote supervision/second-generation jails tend to be large and difficult to manage. Space for programs and recreation is limited. Thus, it comes as no surprise that inmate and staff communication is restricted as well. Such environments often lend themselves to antisocial behavior. Subsequent consequences include violence, poor sanitation, and use of excessive force by detention officers to control jail inmates. Inmate litigation of the 1970s drew attention to such adverse conditions. At this time, jail advocates and correctional researchers began to devise alternatives to traditional design methods.

The design method developed in the late 1970s was different from both the traditional/first-generation and the remote supervision/second-generation facilities. The advent of the direct supervision/third-generation jail attempted to curb the building and operation of oppressive and unmanageable physical plants, to facilitate rehabilitation for inmates, and to promote safety among inmates as well as staff in the jail environment. Thus, in contrast to a "hard" characterization, direct supervision/third-generation jails have often been referred to as "soft" jails. In direct supervision/third-generation facilities, inmates are housed in small units called pods. Pods are single-occupancy rooms that surround a day room.

In theory, a pod holds between 24 and 36 inmates; however, most direct supervision/third-generation jails have pods that hold close to 100 inmates. Natural light is maximized, and the physical environment is softened with carpet and a lack of bars (as found in traditional jail designs). Detention officers are stationed in an open work area at all times to maximize inmate-staff interaction. It is hoped that this interaction facilitates positive relations among detention officers and inmates; in turn, rehabilitation of inmates as well as safety for inmates and staff becomes a realistic goal.

Another advantage to the direct supervision/third-generation jails is facilitation of classification and programming for special types of offenders. For example, the housing of and programming for one type of inmate (e.g., mentally ill) can be confined to a particular pod. In addition, preliminary studies of the direct supervision/third-generation philosophy show increases in inmate and staff safety and satisfaction. Despite these potential advantages, these facilities tend to be costly to build and maintain.

ISSUES THAT AFFECT JAILS

There are several issues that affect local jails. The first is local politics. A large portion of jail administrators in the United States are locally elected sheriffs. Since the sheriff is elected by popular vote, he or she is accountable to voters; in turn, he or she will allocate a limited amount of fiscal and personnel resources to the operation and management of the jail, since such facilities generally are not a pressing public concern. The local components of the criminal justice system often experience reduced funding when competing with local transportation and education initiatives. Within the criminal justice system, jails must compete with local courts as well as law enforcement and community correctional agencies for funding. Complicating matters further, with already limited funding, programming for special-needs inmates is difficult to implement and administer. To maximize limited budgets, some localities have turned to private agencies for the construction and management of jail facilities.

The second issue facing jails today concerns the administration, organization, and management of the facilities. Specifically, jails often do not have written standards or codes. If such standards do exist, they are often poorly written and vague, at best. Jails that have detailed and well-implemented standards have experienced optimal organization and smoother operations. To address this issue, many scholars are currently calling for the American Jail Association (AJA) to develop standards and actively support uniform accreditation for jail facilities.

The most pressing problem that jail administrators face today is that of overcrowding. Crowding is pervasive in each component of the criminal justice system, and jails are no exception. Often, jail facilities are hard to expand due to the lack of geographic space available for such endeavors. More specifically, jails are often located in the central business district of a city or county seat. Temporary strategies, such as the use of old warehouses and gymnasiums have been used; however, the problem of overcrowding in jails has yet to be addressed with long-term solutions.

At times, crowding has been problematic to the point that jails are unable to accept new admissions. When this happens, administrators, acting under court order, will not accept nonviolent misdemeanor offenders. Instead, these offenders will serve their sentence in the community while on standard probation or under other, more stringent forms of community control. Recently, advanced forms of electronic monitoring have proven effective in supervising and controlling misdemeanor offenders in the community.

In 2001, the Jails Division of the National Institute of Corrections (NIC) began offering technical assistance to local jurisdictions experiencing jail overcrowding. The purpose of such a program is that of information exchange via publications and symposiums. It is hoped that this program will facilitate a professional environment in which administrators and managers can share and analyze information related to the specific causes of crowding, as well as strategies for controlling crowding.

OTHER LOCAL DETENTION FACILITIES

There are several alternatives to jails, both at the pretrial and sanctioning stage of detention. Localities vary in their use of such facilities and programs, depending on resources, both fiscal and personnel, and availability. At the pretrial stage, police lockups have been used to detain offenders for a short period of time (usually less than 72 hours) until they can be questioned. Police lockups are typically found in a police station, although other facilities, such as rooms in abandoned gas stations, have been used. Furthermore, lockups are very common in large metropolitan areas, since it is often inefficient for the arresting officer to transport the accused to a centralized jail. Such facilities can be very dangerous due to the lack of supervision by and appropriate training of police officers and the volatility of those being detained. As a result, the International Association of the Chiefs of Police advocate that law enforcement agencies abandon the practice of lockup due to the potential dangers and liabilities associated with the practice.

Several alternatives to jails can be found at the sanctioning phase. Penal farms are common in the South for misdemeanants serving jail terms that are generally longer than eight months. While incarcerated at such facilities, men and women perform agricultural labor. These detention programs are praised for providing more rehabilitative services to inmates than do traditional facilities. Another alternative to placement in a local jail is weekend confinement. The terms of weekend confinement vary across jurisdictions; however, the basic premise is centered on the idea of incarceration for a period during the weekend days and release for occupational duty during the weekdays. Minimum-security-level facilities are often used for weekend confinement. At times, those serving sentences requiring weekend confinement may report to the local jail facility to serve this condition of their sentence.

Scholars and policymakers have questioned whether alternatives to jail facilities are effective. However, when considering alternative facilities used for sanctioning, general thoughts tend to lean toward the positive. Alternatives are seen as less expensive and as effective in preventing recidivism. Furthermore, alternatives can reduce jail overcrowding, thus alleviating the need for new construction. In turn, jurisdictions are able to maximize existing resources.

CONCLUSION

Jails in the United States are used for many purposes and house a diverse population of offenders who are at different stages of the criminal justice process. While there are some similarities in jails and their operation across different time periods, an examination of the history of such facilities reveals that they have also changed considerably in terms of design, function, and purpose. Such changes in the jail system are likely to persist as the numbers of jailed persons continues to increase. Increasing availability of alternative sanctions, and both political whims and availability of economic resources, are also likely to prescribe and necessitate change in the criminal justice system, including the use of jails.

—*Courtney A. Waid and Rhonda R. Dobbs*

See also American Correctional Association; Bridewell Prison and Workhouse; Electronic Monitoring; Federal Prison System; History of Prisons; Lockup; New Generation Prisons; Quakers; State Prison System; Walnut Street Jail

Further Reading

Beck, A. J., Karberg, J. C., & Harrison, Paige M. (2002). *Prison and jail inmates at midyear 2001.* Washington, DC: U.S. Department of Justice, Bureau of Justice Statistics.

Blomberg, T. G., & Lucken, K. (2000). *American penology: A history of control.* New York: Aldine de Gruyter.

Brennan, T., & Austin, J. (1997). *Women in jail: Classification issues.* Washington, DC: U.S. Department of Justice, National Institute of Corrections.

Collins, W. C., & Collins, A. W. (1996). *Women in jail: Legal issues.* Washington, DC: U.S. Department of Justice, National Institute of Corrections.

Elias, G. L., & Ricci, K. (1997). *Women in jail: Facility planning issues.* Washington, DC: U.S. Department of Justice, National Institute of Corrections.

Hutchinson, G. (2000, October). New initiatives from the NIC jails division. *Corrections Today, 62*(6), 30–31.

Kerle, K. E. (1998). *American jails: Looking to the future.* Boston: Butterworth-Heinemann.

Keve, P. W. (1986). *The history of corrections in Virginia.* Charlottesville: University of Virginia Press.

Miller, G. (2002, July). A SMART solution to jail crowding: Offender reintegration without compromising community safety. *Corrections Today, 62*(4), 72–74.

Moynahan, J. M., & Bunke, T. R. (1991, May/June). London's famous Newgate Gaol: 1188–1902. *American Jails,* pp. 76–77.

Moynahan, J. M., & Stewart, E. K. (1980). *The American jail—Its growth and development.* Chicago: Nelson-Hall.

Steiner, J. F., & Brown, R. M. (1927). *The North Carolina chain gang.* Chapel Hill: University of North Carolina Press.

Stephan, J. J. (2001). *Census of jails, 1999.* Washington, DC: U.S. Department of Justice, Bureau of Justice Statistics.

Wilber, H. B. (2000, October). The importance of jails. *Corrections Today, 62*(6), 8.

Zupan, L. L. (1991). *Jails: Reform and the new generation philosophy.* Cincinnati, OH: Anderson.

◪ JUDAISM IN PRISON

Jews make up a small minority of the population of the U.S. prison population. Partly because of their numbers, and partly because most prison personnel are not familiar with the religious and ritual requirements of Jewish inmates, it is often very difficult for observant Jews to practice their religion properly in prison. This entry gives a sense of some of the issues associated with Judaism in prison.

LEVELS OF OBSERVANCE

Jewish law imposes a duty on its adherents to ensure that all actions, including eating, drinking, talking, walking, sitting, dressing, transacting business, praying, studying, lying down, and rising up, are all performed in a certain way for the sake of, and in a manner worthy of, serving our Creator. Accordingly, the observant Jew's day is consumed with ritual, requiring such items as certain articles of clothing (e.g., a head covering such as a yarmulke, a prayer shawl (the tallis or tzitzit), prayer books, Torah volumes, and phylacteries.

Sabbath observances require grape juice, bread, and two candles. Specific Holy Day observances also require other occasional ritual items, for example, a ram's horn (the shofar) for Rosh Hashanah; a palm frond, citron, and a small booth for the Feast of Tabernacles (respectively, the lulav, etrog, and sukkah); and an eight-pronged candelabra and candles (the menorah) for Chanukah.

Observant Jews must consume only food or drink that is kosher (the word means "proper" or "fit"). Observant Jews believe that the slightest morsel of forbidden food taints not only the body but the soul itself. Accordingly, the availability of nutritionally sufficient kosher food for a Jew is not a luxury accommodation; it is an essential provision to allow that person to live. Courts have repeatedly recognized that the opportunity to obtain kosher food in prison is a right, not a privilege (see, e.g., *Ashelman v. Wawrzaszek,* 111 F.3d 676 [9th Cir. 1997]).

Kosher food can be made available to Jews in institutional environments in a variety of ways. It may be prepared on site with proper kitchen facilities under the direction of a qualified kosher food supervisor, or prepackaged meals from kosher food vendors around the country may be purchased. The use of disposable plastic or paper goods is an easy, cost-effective, and religiously acceptable alternative when providing kosher food in an institutional environment. Many common products and national brands are labeled with symbols signifying that they have been prepared under rabbinical supervision and comply with kosher dietary requirements.

Under Jewish law, every religious imperative stands separate and apart from one another. A Jew who does not observe one precept properly (e.g., rules of Sabbath) is not absolved from observing other religious rules. Accordingly, the fact that a Jew does not appear to observe all religious commandments (or does not appear to observe those commandments consistently) is not grounds to deny that person the opportunity to observe other precepts.

In the same vein, a Jew who violates a particular religious precept is still obligated to satisfy that precept the next time the opportunity presents itself. Accordingly, a Jewish inmate who "strays" to the mainline food line should not be precluded from fulfilling the religious obligation to eat kosher food the next time (see, e.g., *Young v. Lane,* 1990, 1991). Moreover, what might appear to the uninitiated to be a "violation" of religious laws may not, in fact, be one at all. For example, an inmate who participates in the mainline food line—for purposes of obtaining more variety, for example—by selecting kosher-labeled products and whole fresh fruits or vegetables—is not violating Jewish law.

On the other side, the ability to observe one precept does not absolve the Jew from following other precepts. Accordingly, the fact that a Jewish inmate may be permitted to pray and wear a yarmulke does not mean that person has been given "enough" opportunity to practice religion and then be denied other religious practices. Living Jewishly is a process: One observes whatever precepts one is able to and proceeds on a path of spiritual growth, observing more and more. As a practical matter, individual religious observances vary greatly.

PRISON CONDITIONS

By and large, prison personnel have little, if any, understanding of Jewish requests for religious materials or services. Though senior government officials and administrators of departments of corrections recognize the importance of allowing inmates to develop their spiritual side, firsthand accounts suggest that many rank-and-file staff and chaplains may accommodate requests for Christian religious materials, but will ignore or actively frustrate efforts by Jewish inmates to obtain religious materials or observe Holy Days or perform other ritual practices.

Religious issues are generally resolved when higher-ranking officials (e.g., wardens, associate wardens) take the time and initiative to address them. Unfortunately, in all too many cases violations appear to be ignored or condoned by higher-ranking prison officials, too, and are sometimes not resolved even when brought to the attention of executive-level staff at the department of corrections.

State departments of corrections have almost always fought any request to provide kosher food, notwithstanding that practically every court decision

has upheld the authorities' obligation to provide "nutritionally sufficient" meals that are "consistent with an inmate's religious beliefs" (see, e.g., *Ashelman v. Wawrzaszek,* 111 F.3d 674 [9th Cir. 1997]). In *Ashelman,* Arizona prison officials fought an inmate's request for three daily kosher meals for more than 12 years. Even those departments that purport to accommodate kosher requests often do so in a manner designed to deter them. In many cases, foods are offered in such small quantities, lack of variety, or poor quality that participation in the "kosher" line is effectively dissuaded.

One contributing factor may be that Jewish inmates almost always constitute an extremely small minority of the population at any given prison and are generally not perceived as a potentially violent threat to the security of the institution if their particular needs are not met. As a result, many religious requests from Jewish men and women are simply ignored, purposefully delayed in "channels," or dismissed out of hand. In the worst-case scenarios, Jewish individuals attempting to meet legitimate religious needs are treated with suspicion, contempt, and hostility and are even subjected to wrongful punitive actions.

CONCLUSION: RESOURCES FOR INSTITUTIONAL STAFF AND JEWISH INMATES

Some outside organizations exist to educate correctional officers about Judaism and to provide support for Jewish prisoners. For, example, the Aleph Institute, a national not-for-profit organization headquartered in Miami, Florida, acts as a consultant and resource for the Federal Bureau of Prisons and many state departments of corrections around the country to help meet the religious needs of Jewish men and women in prison. To solve the problem of institutional staff not "knowing" about Jewish needs, the *Aleph Advisory* newsletter gives wardens and chaplains sufficient notice of religious requirements for each Jewish holiday—and provides them with the opportunity to obtain whatever ritual items may be required. Aleph's *Institutional Handbook of Jewish Practice and Procedure* is a volume designed to advise wardens, chaplains, and institutional staff as to all of the minimum daily and holiday requirements for Jewish inmates.

—*Isaac M. Jaroslawicz*

See also Chaplains; Contract Ministers; Islam in Prison; Native American Spirituality; Rehabilitation Theory; Religion in Prison; Resistance; Santería; Satanism

Further Reading

Aleph Institute. (n.d.). *Institutional handbook of Jewish practice and procedure.* Miami, FL: Author. Retrieved from www.aleph-institute.org

Donin, H. H. (1972). *To be a Jew, A guide to Jewish observance in contemporary life.* New York: Basic Books, HarperCollins.

Ganzfried, S. (1993). *Code of Jewish law: Kitzur [Abridged] Shulhan Arukh, A compilation of Jewish laws and customs* (H. E. Goldin, Trans., annotated revised ed.). New York: Hebrew Publishing Company.

Legal Cases

Ashelman v. Wawrzaszek, 111 F.3d 674, 676 (9th Cir. 1997).

Young v. Lane, 733 F. Supp. 1205 (N.D. Ill. 1990), *revised on other grounds,* 922 F.2d 370 (7th Cir. 1991).

JUST DESERTS THEORY

The "just deserts" theory of sentencing advocates that punishment should be *proportionate* to the seriousness of the offense committed. Advocates of the just deserts philosophy emphasize the importance of due process, determinate sentences, and the removal of judicial discretion in sentencing practice. This philosophy became influential in the United States during the 1970s after publication of the book *Doing Justice* (1976) by Andrew von Hirsch, a leading proponent of the just deserts model. The book reported on the findings of the Committee for the Study of Incarceration and supported the replacement of the "treatment" model of punishment with a sentencing framework based on the principles of just deserts.

EXPLANATION

Just deserts is a *retributivist* theory of punishment. Unlike theories that are primarily concerned with preventing future offenses, such as deterrence, rehabilitation, and incapacitation, retributivist theories are only concerned with punishing crimes that have already been committed.

Historically, retribution has been associated with the biblical tenet of *lex talionis* or the law of vengeance. Epitomized by the phrase "an eye for an eye, a tooth for a tooth," this view of punishment argues that what happens to the offender should be *equivalent* to the crime he or she committed. However, modern retributivist theory is more concerned with seeking proportionality than with exacting vengeance. Proponents aim to ensure that offenders receive their *just deserts* for their wrongdoing and that their punishment is proportionate to the seriousness of their offense.

The just deserts model derives from the theories of Immanuel Kant. In his *Groundwork of the Metaphysics of Morals,* published in 1785, Kant argued that humans are free and rational agents. Therefore, everyone must recognize the consequences of his or her actions and accept the *deserts* of his or her deeds. Failure to punish the guilty, he argued, constitutes a violation of justice. However, he stated that *deserts* in the form of judicial punishment must only be inflicted to punish those who have committed a crime and not for any other purpose.

In keeping with this theory of moral reasoning, then, just deserts proponents argue that offenders should be punished, but only because they deserve it. They claim that although other positive benefits may occur as a result of punishment (such as, e.g., the prevention of further crimes) these are simply incidental effects and should not be seen as the *purpose* of punishment.

For the just deserts model to be feasible and effective, a scale or "tariff" of crimes and punishments is required. The underlying principle of the tariff system is that offenders receive a punishment that is proportionate to both the severity of the offense and the culpability, or blameworthiness, of the offender. To establish a tariff, crimes need to be ranked or categorized according to their relative seriousness and punishments should then be categorized alongside according to their relative unpleasantness. This is known as *ordinal proportionality.*

In addition, the severity of the whole scale or tariff needs to be standardized and fixed to ensure that offenders are not punished too severely or too leniently overall. This is the principle of *cardinal proportionality.*

Just deserts, and indeed retributivism in general, sets limits on the extent and the type of punishment an individual can receive. Proponents of the theory argue that these limits are absent in other theories such as rehabilitation—where an offender can receive an indeterminate prison sentence and may only be released when judged to be reformed or "cured." Alternatively, the theory of incapacitation can be used to endorse excessively long prison sentences on offenders in order to prevent future offending by the individual.

Another argument in favor of the just deserts model is that it offers a level of protection for the innocent that other philosophies, at least in theory, do not. For example, the punishment of the innocent could be theoretically justified within a strict general deterrence theory as long as the punishment deterred other potential offenders and was hence beneficial to society. As a retributivist theory, just deserts only sanctions the punishment of the guilty and considers the punishment of the innocent, regardless of any positive consequences that may be achieved, as inherently unjust.

HISTORY

The just deserts model became influential in the United States in the mid-1970s because of increasing concern about the discretionary and discriminatory practices inherent in the rehabilitation or treatment model, dominant at the time. In 1976, the Committee for the Study of Incarceration (with Andrew von Hirsch as director) reported that the just deserts model should replace the treatment model of sentencing. The committee argued that rehabilitative sentences were often excessively long and disproportionate to the offense committed. Rehabilitative theory is founded on the assumption that crime is the result of individual pathology, with little or no recognition of structural or social factors. Thus, the emphasis is on the *offender* rather

than the *offense.* In practice, this meant that sentences were individualized and as a result there were often inconsistencies between sentences given to different individuals for similar crimes. Furthermore, critics argued that proponents of the rehabilitation model often ignored the rights of the offender and the social context within which the offense was committed and this led to discriminatory treatment for minorities, women, and the poor.

SENTENCING GUIDELINES

The eventual abandonment of rehabilitation in favor of the justice model led to sentencing reforms aimed at increasing consistency in sentencing practice. The emphasis was now on dealing with the crime rather than the individual criminal, and the aim was for similar crimes to be dealt with in similar ways. In the United States, the Sentencing Reform Act of 1984 introduced federal guidelines that aimed to shift the emphasis away from rehabilitation and onto proportionality, equality, and justice. These guidelines, it was anticipated, would reduce the possibility of discriminatory treatment on the grounds of race, social class, gender, age, or any other structural or social division.

Essentially three types of sentencing guidelines were introduced. First, mandatory guidelines (such as those established in Arizona, Illinois, and California) meant fixed sentences for particular crimes and effectively allowed judges no discretion to take into account extra-legal factors such as the character and background of the offender or the levels of remorse shown. Second, presumptive guidelines (as introduced in Pennsylvania and Minnesota) were precise but did permit some flexibility and deviation under specific conditions. Finally, advisory guidelines (as were found in states such as Maryland and Michigan) were optional and judges could elect to follow them or not thus retaining full discretion.

Other countries, including Canada, Australia, Sweden, and the United Kingdom, also saw a shift toward a just deserts model of punishment, and sentencing frameworks were introduced accordingly. In the United Kingdom, the move to a just deserts philosophy culminated in the 1991 Criminal Justice Act. This act formally established retributivism and denunciation as the primary aims of sentencing and advocated proportionality and consistency within sentencing practice. Three broad categories of seriousness were established. Imprisonment was to be used only for the most serious offenses, while fines or discharges would be dispensed for the least serious crimes. Community penalties were recommended for those crimes that were serious but not so serious that they would warrant a prison sentence.

However, although the 1991 act claimed to be founded on the notion of just deserts, in reality UK policy was quite far removed from the original liberal deserts philosophy of the 1970s. The 1980s had witnessed a growing emphasis on a punitive law-and-order ideology, and consequently the 1991 act also ensured that violent or sexual offenders would go to prison for long periods, which in some cases might be greater than their offense might warrant. This practice of "incapacitating" particular offenders was completely inconsistent with a true justice model.

Throughout the 1990s, this punitive ideology, coupled with a growing emphasis on protecting the public, continued to flourish in both the United States and the United Kingdom. As a result the just deserts philosophy has been appropriated by the political right and the emphasis has shifted from proportionality to harsher punishments and longer sentences, thus sentences have become disproportionately severe. In the United States in particular, the justice model has been used to legitimize excessively long sentences for the sake of public protection. This indicates that, in addition to just deserts, other theories of punishment, in particular deterrence, incapacitation, and retribution, are underpinning sentencing practice.

CRITIQUE

In theory, the just deserts model appears to offer a fair and impartial sentencing system. It can restrict the power of the state in the use of disproportionate or exemplary sentences and it can serve to reduce or

eliminate inconsistent and discriminatory punishments. However, there have been several critiques made of the model as it works in theory and practice.

British criminologist Barbara Hudson has argued that just deserts, with its emphasis on treating similar crimes alike, takes no account of structural or economic factors such as poverty. She states that there is no acknowledgment of the inequalities in society and thus no room for mitigation on the grounds that some people have less opportunity to remain law-abiding. Thus, in this sense, a just deserts sentencing framework, which deals solely with the crime and makes no recognition of the background or circumstances of the offender, may simply perpetuate the discrimination against the poor, minorities, women, and the young that was inherent in the rehabilitative model. Indeed, in the United States some judges have complained that mandatory guidelines, which took no account of these relevant factors, compelled them to give what they considered to be *unjust* sentences.

Questions have also been raised about the political agenda that facilitated the shift away from rehabilitation and toward just deserts. Barbara Hudson claims that through this process the state was able to relinquish all responsibility for the rehabilitation and reintegration of offenders. Within the just deserts model, there is no place for rehabilitation-orientated practices, such as early release through parole or earned remission. Thus, this rejection of rehabilitation raises the question of how prisoners are expected to spend their time in custody. Just deserts provides a philosophical justification for punishment but does not adequately propose a rationalization for the use of custody as the primary method of punishment.

As discussed previously, the just deserts philosophy has been largely appropriated by the political right. In the right-wing version of "just deserts" there is also objection to the procedural safeguards that are promoted within a true "justice" philosophy. For example, although the death penalty can be justified through the *liberal* just deserts model, generic factors such as age or mental health would be considered as mitigating aspects when determining a sentence. However, under the current *hard-right* just deserts model, as employed in many U.S. states, the overriding concern is that punishment must "fit" the crime and thus such generic safeguards would be seen as measures that actually impede the ability of sentencers to give offenders their "just deserts." The rights of the offender are thus seriously undermined by this new right agenda.

Finally, in practice there has been some difficulty in establishing benchmarks for "seriousness." In the United States, states that have traditionally been more liberal (such as Minnesota) introduced moderate punishment scales, while states that have traditionally been more punitive (e.g., New Mexico) introduced much harsher scales. Consequently, there remain huge differences in the sentences that different individuals can receive for similar offenses.

CONCLUSION

The principles of "just deserts" could, in theory, ensure a fair and impartial system of justice. However, the desire for consistency and proportionality needs to be carefully balanced with a flexibility that allows for unique circumstances and the impact of structural inequalities on offending behavior and criminalization.

—*Alana Barton*

See also Deterrence Theory; Incapacitation Theory; Indeterminate Sentencing; Juvenile Death Penalty; *Parens Patriae*; Rehabilitation Theory; Sentencing Reform Act 1984; Three-Strikes Legislation; Truth in Sentencing

Further Reading

Hudson, B. (1987). *Justice through punishment.* London: Macmillan.
Hudson, B. (1996). *Understanding justice.* Buckingham, UK: Open University Press.
Kant, I. (1998). *Groundwork of the metaphysics of morals* (M. Gregor, Ed. & Trans.). Cambridge, UK: Cambridge University Press. (Original work published 1785)
von Hirsch, A. (1976). *Doing justice: The choice of punishments.* New York: Hill and Wang.
von Hirsch, A. (1986). *Past or future crimes: Deservedness and dangerousness in the sentencing of criminals.* Manchester, UK: Manchester University Press.
von Hirsch, A. (1996). *Censure and sanctions.* Oxford, UK: Oxford University Press.

◪ JUVENILE DEATH PENALTY

The juvenile death penalty, as defined by the U.S. Supreme Court, currently applies to capital defendants who have attained a minimum age of 16 years of age. However, a number of states have proposed lowering the age of executions to include those as young as 11. The United States is one of a small group of countries that executes juvenile offenders along with the Democratic Republic of Congo, Iran, Nigeria, and Saudi Arabia.

HISTORY

The earliest recorded juvenile execution occurred in the Plymouth Colony, Massachusettes, in 1642, when a young man by the name of Thomas Graunger was executed by hanging for having sex with animals. George Stinney was the youngest juvenile offender executed in the United States in the past hundred years. In 1944, he was put to death at the age of 14 for the murder of two South Carolina girls. In more recent times, since the 1976 reinstatement of the death penalty, 21 juveniles have been put to death, and some 80 currently await execution.

STATISTICS WITH REGARD TO STATE, RACE, AND GENDER

As the remainder of the world moves toward abolishing the death penalty for juveniles, the United States has maintained its commitment to this practice in 22 of its 50 states. Within these states, certain patterns arise. For example, Alabama, Arizona, Arkansas, Delaware, Idaho, Kentucky, Louisiana, Mississippi, Missouri, Nevada, Oklahoma, Pennsylvania, South Carolina, South Dakota, Utah, Virginia, and Wyoming all sentence juveniles to death for crimes committed when the defendant was as young as 16. In contrast, in Florida, Georgia, New Hampshire, North Carolina, and Texas, offenders must be at least 17 years old to receive a death sentence. Finally, as with adults, Texas has been responsible for more juvenile executions than any other state, putting to death 13 of the 21 juvenile offenders executed in the United States since 1976. Also like adults, the death penalty tends to be disproportionately applied to young men of color. Thus, two-thirds of the 80 young people currently awaiting execution belong to racial or ethnic minorities. Of the 13 young people put to death in Texas, 9 have been either African American or Latino and all have been male.

U.S. AGREEMENTS WITH THE INTERNATIONAL COMMUNITY

The international community has agreed on many basic human rights principles. One of these, the Fourth Geneva Convention, signed in 1949, Article 68, pertains to the execution of juvenile offenders. Here it states, "In any case the death penalty may not be pronounced against a protected person who was under eighteen years of age at the time of the offense." In 1970, a second declaration was signed confirming a person's basic right to life. Likewise, the American Convention on Human Rights, Article 4(5) affirms, "Capital punishment shall not be imposed upon persons who, at the time the crime was committed, were under eighteen years of age."

In 1992, the United States ratified Article 6 of the International Covenant on Civil and Political Rights (ICCPR) agreeing to prohibit the use of the death penalty for those under the age of 18. Soon afterward, however, the United States expressed reservations with this arrangement. Three years later, the United States refused to ratify the United Nations Convention on the Rights of the Child (Article 37 [a]), 1995, which reconfirmed the ICCPR's covenant, maintaining that capital punishment shall not be imposed on any person committing an offense below 18 years of age. Only Somalia also refused to agree to this contract.

In August 2000, the U.N. Sub-Commission on the Promotion and Protection of Human Rights determined that the execution of people under the age of 18 at the time the offense was committed "is contrary to customary international law." Customary

international law is binding on all countries, regardless of which treaties they have or have not ratified. Given the U.N.'s decision, the international community has asked the United States to respect the rights of the child and discontinue its current practice of executing juvenile offenders.

SUPREME COURT CASES

According to the Eighth Amendment to the U.S. Constitution, "Excessive bail shall not be required, nor excessive fines imposed, nor cruel and unusual punishments inflicted." Addressing the issue of cruel and unusual punishment, in *Thompson v. Oklahoma* (1988), the U.S. Supreme Court confirmed the constitutional relevance of the Eighth Amendment as it pertains to the minimum age required to be eligible for the death penalty. The Court held that executions of offenders ages 15 and younger at the time of their crimes are prohibited by the Eighth Amendment to the U.S. Constitution. The combined effect of the opinions by Justice John Paul Stevens and Justice Sandra Day O'Connor in *Thompson* means that no state without a minimum age in its death penalty statute can go below age 16 without violating *Thompson*. Within one year of *Thompson*, the issue of age was dealt with again in *Stanford v. Kentucky* (1989). In this case, the U.S. Supreme Court held that the Eighth Amendment to the U.S. Constitution does not prohibit the death penalty for crimes committed at ages 16 or 17 regardless of state statutory provisions. More recently, in *In re Stanford* (2002), the U.S. Supreme Court considered revisiting the issue of the juvenile death penalty, but decided not to take the case. The decision to not reexamine this matter was strongly opposed by Justices Stevens, Stephen Breyer, Ruth Bader Ginsburg, and David Souter. All four justices not only wanted to revisit the juvenile death penalty issue but also were ready to declare it unconstitutional and to "put an end to this shameful practice."

CONCLUSION

It is certain that the issue of the juvenile death penalty, at the very least, invokes debate. The United

States continues to defy all international conventions that forbid capital punishment for those convicted of crimes committed at less than 18 years of age. In fact, the United States leads the way worldwide with regard to total number of juvenile executions carried out this past decade. This has brought global attention to the debate surrounding the juvenile death penalty and has pushed it to the forefront of human rights discussions. Despite pressure from the international community to update its policy, the current U.S. position has remained unchanged.

—*Staci A. Cash*

See also Capital Punishment; Juvenile Offenders; Race, Gender, and Class; Juvenile Justice System; *Mens Rea*; *Parens Patriae*; Rehabilitation Theory.

Further Reading

Amnesty International. (2004). *The death penalty gives up on juvenile offenders*. Retrieved from http://www.amnestyusa .org/abolish/juveniles.html

Garofalo, A. (2000). *Brennan v. State*: The constitutionality of executing sixteen-year-old offenders in Florida. *Nova Law Review, 24*, 855.

International Justice Project. (2004). *International instruments— Juveniles*. Retrieved from http://www.internationaljusti ceproject.org/juvInstruments.cfm

Stolzenberg, L., & Alessio, S. J. D. (1999). *Criminal courts for the 21st century*. Upper Saddle River, NJ: Prentice Hall.

Streib, V. L. (1987). *Death penalty for juveniles*. Bloomington: Indiana University Press.

Streib, V. L. (2002). *The juvenile death penalty today: Death sentences and executions for juvenile crimes, January 1, 1973—June 30, 2003*. Retrieved from http://www.law.onu .edu/faculty/streib/juvdeath.htm

Wagman, M. (2000). Innocence lost: In the wake of green: The trend is clear—If you are old enough to do the crime, then you are old enough to do the time. *Catholic University Law Review, 49*, 643.

Legal Cases

In re Stanford, 123 S.Ct. 472 (October 21, 2002).
Stanford v. Kentucky, 492 U.S. 361 (1989).
Thompson v. Oklahoma, 487 U.S. 815 (1988).

◪ JUVENILE DETENTION CENTERS

Juvenile detention centers detain young offenders sentenced by a juvenile court as well as those awaiting trial. In principle, juvenile detention center sentences are reserved for the most dangerous offenders from whom society needs protection or for those who are most likely to escape before their case ever reaches the court. Nevertheless, judges often sentence youths who have merely breached probation orders or are in noncompliance with a court order. Most detention centers house an overrepresentation of ethnic minorities and are ill equipped to meet the unique needs of female young offenders.

Detention centers are the most durable feature of the juvenile justice system. Even before the creation of juvenile courts, institutions to detain young people such as houses of refuge, industrial schools, and reformatories were present. When separate centers of detention for juvenile offenders were inaugurated at the beginning of the 19th century, child savers and justice officials alike were confident that these carceral institutions were the antidote to juvenile deviance.

In 1998, there were 1,121 public and 2,310 private juvenile detention centers in the United States. These facilities admit approximately half a million juvenile offenders every year with the majority residing in public facilities. Between 1985 and 1995, the average daily population in American detention centers increased by 72% and the expense of detaining young offenders more than doubled to reach $820 million in operating costs. Despite increasing costs and greater attention devoted to alternatives to custody, detention continues to be a popular solution to juvenile deviance among justice officials, the public, and politicians.

HISTORY

For much of the 18th and 19th centuries, the majority of the American population lived in rural areas where communities were closely knit and citizens' lives were well integrated. The solidarity experienced in colonial America meant that criminal courts were unnecessary as justice was meted out by community members and was primarily directed not toward social exclusion (as is practiced today) but rather toward reintegration of the delinquent person into the community.

The primary mechanism to govern young offenders at this time was an informal network made up of church discipline, the family, and a strong network of community members. With the emergence of cities in the late 18th and early 19th centuries and the relative anonymity of the burgeoning urban context, informal social controls came to be less effective in dealing with juvenile misconduct. The influx of Western European immigrants and rural Americans migrating to cities in search of employment in the manufacturing sector created both a juvenile delinquent problem and a movement for its control.

To reclaim deviant youths, 19th-century reformers proposed centers of detention such as reformatories and industrial schools. Some institutions offered deviant boys disciplinary programs that emphasized education, athletics, drill, training in the habits of industry, and religious guidance designed to remake deviant them into respectable members of the working class who could fulfill their breadwinner roles, respect authority, attend church, and demonstrate self-control. Other institutions provided a disciplinary program designed to (re)make deviant girls into good, working-class women by training them in the values and manners of domesticity, femininity, and maternalism. Institutional officials encouraged girls to resist sexual temptations and attempted to make them into wives or chaste girls who could fill domestic roles in affluent homes.

As the turn of the 20th century approached, centers of detention for youths increasingly came to resemble adult prisons and to take on similar functions. By the late 19th century, institutionalizing deviant boys increasingly came under attack for creating an artificial environment that did not resemble society, promoted homosexual relations, and created a situation where older boys contaminated younger more impressionable inmates. In response, child savers began to promote community-based solutions such as probation. Initially designed to govern youths who had yet to spiral into a life of crime, the establishment of community-based practices such as probation effectively turned detention centers into dumping grounds for offenders hardened into a life a crime.

Another blow was dealt to the rehabilitative program of detention centers with the publication of the Martinson Report in the mid-1970s. Political officials and justice professionals alike understood Martinson's conclusion to be that "nothing works" when it came to rehabilitation. The debate over what works in correctional reform programming still rages today. Although commissions of inquiry and juvenile justice reformers have made several attempts to restructure centers of detention in the direction of rendering them more amenable to the needs of youths, in many ways these institutions have not progressed much beyond their early-19th-century arrangements. Many of the same problems reformers and child savers disputed more than a century ago continue to haunt the operation and environment of juvenile carceral institutions.

GENDER

Working-class girls were the clear losers in the movement toward establishing separate juvenile penal facilities. While first-time and nonserious male offenders received probation sentences, few similar programs were available for female offenders. Girls were also confined for different types of activities. Mary Odem and Steven Schlossman, for example, suggested that 93% of girls in 1920 who appeared in Los Angeles juvenile courts were arrested for status offenses with immoral sexual conduct being the offense of record in the majority of cases. Sentences for flouting socio-sexual norms for young adolescent females were extremely severe. In Chicago, half of all female delinquents and only 20% of male offenders were sentenced to training schools.

CURRENT PRACTICE AND BELIEFS

There seems to be no one antidote to the problem of youth crime. Nevertheless, the current crop of youth justice officials argues that through the application of modern case management techniques that defer to a risk management checklist the most appropriate residential treatment strategy can be devised. For example, Robert Hoge (2001) argued that the Youth Level of Service/Case Management Inventory is particularly relevant to case planning in institutional settings. The fundamental goals of the inventory are to provide broad assessments of risk and needs relevant to young offenders' patterns of offending and create a format for linking the assessment with decisions about treatment planning.

Whereas youths detained during the late 19th century were subjected to a sweeping reform program that promised an antidote to juvenile offending generally, contemporary research argues for more customized reform strategies. James Finckenauer (1992) suggested that effective treatment starts with rehabilitation programs that are constructed in conjunction with the offenders and tailored to their individual needs and particular risks. In recent years, some agreement has been reached about the success of programs that are matched to the needs and conditions of each offender.

The Dobbs Center in North Carolina, for example, offers many specialized programs and unique learning opportunities. In addition to the JROTC program and Boy Scouts, the institution offers youths an opportunity to take part in a vocational training program. Dobbs also boasts a broadcasting center that can be heard throughout the facility and a campuswide literary program that provides incentives for students to occupy their time with independent reading. Dobbs's innovative program aspires to facilitate inmates' reintegration into conforming society.

RACE, ETHNICITY, DIFFERENCE

Minorities of all kinds and the politically powerless continue to make up the class of offender who are most often detained in detention centers. Minority youths are currently incarcerated at rates that greatly exceed their representation in the U.S. population. A study of felony cases detained by juvenile court judges found that racial characteristics had a dramatic impact on judicial decisions to incarcerate minority offenders, even when weapon use, victim injury, and socioeconomic factors were controlled.

In Canada, the group that has been particularly hard hit by the pervasive youth incarceration addiction is Aboriginal peoples. That a colonial legacy continues to have dramatic effects for Aboriginal peoples is evident in the numbers of incarcerated Native youths. A Statistics Canada report for 1998–1999 on youths in custody confirmed that Aboriginal youths were overrepresented in detention.

While they account for only 5% of the total youth population in reporting jurisdictions across Canada, Aboriginal youths make up 24% of the total admissions to custody. The rates of incarceration of Aboriginal youths on the Prairies are far greater. In the prairie provinces of Manitoba and Saskatchewan, three quarters (75% for Manitoba and 74% for Saskatchewan) of youths sentenced to custody were identified as Aboriginal, while less than 20% of Manitoba's youth population, for example, is identified as Native (Statistics Canada, 2000). These facts not only are sobering reminders that colonialism is not a distant memory but also confirm that Aboriginal youths are considered the most punishable young offenders in Canada.

The conditions found inside many contemporary detention facilities seem to confirm 19th-century child savers' worst fears about institutionalizing young people. Many detention centers for juvenile delinquents today are practically indistinguishable from adult prisons. Slightly more than half of all detained youths live in overcrowded facilities that operate well beyond their design capacity. The conditions for incarcerated youths are often appalling with few work or education options and poorly trained staff.

While the conditions for male juvenile offenders are horrendous, adolescent girls' institutions are often neglected entirely by policymakers and politicians because adolescent females make up such a small percentage of the offending population. Girls in institutions remain "too few to count" and are the "forgotten few." This pattern of systemic disregard for the needs of young female offenders has created additional complexities that contribute to their subordination in the contemporary youth justice system. As a result of the small number of female offenders, very few programs have been designed to meet their unique needs. Instead, interventions and risk management tools that have been developed by men for boys are often applied to female offenders without reference to the gendered nature of adolescent development. Moreover, the small number of incarcerated girls is frequently invoked to deny them access to treatment programs.

CONCLUSION

The widespread optimism about strategies that promised to reform juvenile offenders during the early 19th century has been replaced in the current context by pervasive skepticism. During the 1990s and early 21st century, sentencing youths to custody was publicly popular and politically astute. While detention centers are supposed to be reserved for only the most dangerous juvenile offenders, reliance on custody to govern all categories of juvenile offenders has increased. In custodial facilities, ethnic minority groups are highly overrepresented and female young offenders are given short shrift.

Juvenile justice officials, politicians, the public, and the media have become almost zealous about the incidence of juvenile crime without at the same time highlighting the ways in which juvenile offenders have been socially produced through injurious conditions of life. By advertising the most heinous deeds of juvenile offenders, the media constructs all juvenile offenders as gun-toting gang bangers who, as a result of their violent disposition, require intrusive (read punitive) intervention to protect the public. Such an image that has captured public disdain and become the main focus of political campaigns is hardly characteristic of juvenile deviance. The majority of offenses that raise the ire of police, parents, and school officials are relatively minor ones, not the serious, violent offences emphasized by the media. However, when juvenile offenders are painted with one brush—as a serious problem requiring a serious solution—the result is an instinctive recourse to more punitive forms of intervention. In response to the question, "What should we do with bad kids?" the typical retort is, "Lock them up!" Despite the rising costs of incarcerating young offenders and the growing success of alternatives to custody, the popularity of custody among politicians, justice officials, and the public remains resolute.

—*Bryan Hogeveen*

See also Boot Camp; Meda Chesney-Lind; Child Savers; Detained Youth and Committed Youth; Juvenile Offenders; Race, Gender, and Class; Juvenile Justice System; Juvenile Reformatories; Jerome G. Miller; *Parens Patriae*; Patuxent Institution; Anthony Platt; Status Offenders; Youth Corrections Act

Further Reading

Adelberg, E., & Currie, C. (1987). *Too few to count: Canadian women in conflict with the law.* Vancouver, BC: Press Gang.

Bergsmann, I. (1989). The forgotten few: Juvenile female offenders. *Federal Probation, 58*, 73–78.

Chesney-Lind, M. (1997). *The female offender: Girls, women and crime.* Thousand Oaks, CA: Sage.

Feld, B. (1999). *Bad kids: Race and the transformation of the juvenile court.* New York: Oxford University Press.

Finckenauer, J. (1992). Juvenile criminals: Punishment or reform? In C. Hartjen & E. Rhine (Eds.), *Correctional theory and practice.* Chicago: Nelson-Hall.

Hoge, R. (2001). Case management instrument for use in juvenile justice systems. *Juvenile and Family Court Journal, 7*, 25–31.

Odem, M., & Schlossman, S. (1991). Guardians of virtue: The juvenile court and female delinquency in early 20th century Los Angeles. *Crime & Delinquency, 37*, 186–203.

Rothman, D. (1971). *The discovery of the asylum; social order and disorder in the new republic.* Boston: Little, Brown.

Rust, B. (1999). Juvenile jailhouse rocked. *AdvoCasey.* Anne E. Casey Foundation. Retrieved from www.aecf.org

Schwartz, I., & Willis, D. (1994). National trends in juvenile detention. In I. Schwartz & W. Barton (Eds.), *Reforming juvenile detention: No more hidden closets.* Columbus: Ohio State University Press.

Statistics Canada. (2000). *Youth in custody and community services in Canada, 1998/9.* Ottawa, ON: Canadian Centre for Justice Statistics.

U.S. Department of Justice. (1999). *Fact sheet, No. 96.* Washington, DC: Office of Juvenile Justice and Delinquency Prevention.

U.S. Department of Justice. (2000). *Fact sheet, No. 18.* Washington, DC: Office of Juvenile Justice and Delinquency Prevention.

Wald, P. (1976). Pretrial detention for juveniles. In M. Rosenheim (Ed.), *Pursuing justice for the child.* Chicago: University of Chicago Press.

Wordes, M., Bynum, T., & Corley, C. (1994). Locking up youth: The impact of race on detention decisions. *Journal of Research in Crime and Delinquency, 31*, 149–165.

JUVENILE JUSTICE AND DELINQUENCY PREVENTION ACT 1974

The Juvenile Justice and Delinquency Prevention (JJDP) Act was passed by the U.S. federal government in 1974. It served notice that juvenile justice was a national priority, and it placed a strong focus on prevention. The JJDP Act had two main components: the deinstitutionalization of status offenders, removing children whose offenses would not be crimes if committed by adults from secure custody; and the jail removal initiative that was intended to separate youths from adult offenders. To help facilitate these goals, the federal government provided funding to the states for community-based programs. The hope was that young offenders would be placed in the least restrictive program possible, reducing stigma and keeping youths in reasonable proximity to their families. Since its inception in 1974, the JJDP Act has been amended and reauthorized and states seeking federal funds must now address additional "core requirements," including providing services to girls within the juvenile justice system and reducing the disproportionate confinement of minority youths.

ORIGINS AND DEVELOPMENT OF THE JJDP ACT

Under the doctrine of *parens patriae,* juvenile reform schools or training schools (the youth equivalent to adult prisons) originally served any child thought to be in need. They housed in their confines dependent and neglected children, as well as juvenile delinquents. Thus, children who had committed no crime at all were often placed in the same institutions as serious young offenders and treated in the exact same fashion.

By the 1960s, critics argued that training schools had in effect become "crime schools," and many kids were coming out of them worse than when they had entered. Forced to live in the midst of more serious delinquents, noncriminal youths and status offenders were exposed to attitudes conducive to crime and they were presented with ample opportunities to learn techniques and skills used in committing crimes. When returning to the community, youths who had spent time in training schools were often labeled as delinquents and stigmatized, even when they had committed no crime.

Three influential groups—the President's Commission of Law Enforcement and the Administration of Justice, the National Council on Crime and Delinquency, and the National Advisory Commission on Criminal Justice Standards and Goals—noted the problems status offenders faced in the juvenile justice system and recommended significant changes. In 1974, the federal government of the United States passed the JJDP Act, tying federal funding to changes in the treatment of status offenders. States were encouraged to divert status offenders from incarceration and to create new community programs for the youths who needed treatment and a safe place to stay but who had not committed criminal acts.

In addition to its concern for status offenders, the JJDP Act included a jail removal initiative, which specified that children and adolescents should be removed from institutions where they would be exposed to adult offenders. Previous to this, juveniles in many areas were housed in jails alongside adults prior to their court hearings because there were no juvenile detention facilities in that particular area. At the time that the act was passed, there were approximately 3,000 juveniles held in adult jails on any given day. With the JJDP Act, the federal government passed deadlines for jail removal, rewarding states that complied with the promise of continued federal funding for juvenile justice initiatives. Congress amended the JJDP Act in 1980 to allow states more time to complete the removal of juveniles from adult jails and lockups; the deadline was extended several more times because so few states were able to comply. Even to this day, most states continue to resist full compliance of the jail removal initiative because local jurisdictions simply do not have the resources or the perceived need in the population to build separate detention facilities for juveniles.

Along with several amendments over the years, Congress reauthorized the JJDP Act in 1992, adding as a "core requirement" that states address the disproportionate confinement of minority youths in secure institutions. The reauthorization also provided specific guidelines requiring the provision of gender-specific services tailored to girls in the juvenile justice system. As a result of "challenge grants" offered by the Office of Juvenile Justice and

Delinquency Prevention, 23 states developed policies to prohibit gender bias and to create programs that would offer girls access to appropriate treatment and services.

RESULTS OF THE JJDP ACT

There is no question that the JJDP Act went a long way toward the goal of deinstitutionalizing status offenders and separating juvenile offenders from their adult counterparts in jails and correctional facilities. Girls particularly benefited from the reforms as they had always been more likely than boys to be incarcerated for status offenses; the incarceration of young women fell dramatically after the JJDP Act. Some judges responded to the limits on their discretion, however, by finding new ways to place status offenders in secure confinement. Status offenders were sometimes "bootstrapped" into delinquents if they violated a court order or if the judge issued a criminal contempt citation. In addition, status offenders have frequently been referred to private "semi-secure" facilities, including mental health facilities. This allows states and the judges working in them to follow the letter of the law in terms of diverting status offenders, but the youths still find themselves confined, often with the explanation that it is "for their own good."

As status offenders are now largely diverted from maximum-security juvenile institutions, there has been a "distilling effect" on state training schools. Home to the most serious juvenile offenders in the system, many training schools have prioritized accountability and punishment over the hopes of rehabilitation. They have become more similar to their adult prison counterparts in terms of both the characteristics of their populations and their intent in confining them.

Finally, some states used the changes brought forth by the JJDP Act as incentive to rethink and change their entire juvenile justice systems. Washington State, for example, rewrote the laws governing its juvenile justice system in 1978, implementing massive changes. It was one of the first states in the nation not only to deinstitutionalize status offenders but to go a step further and decriminalize status offenses. Status offenders were removed from the juvenile court's jurisdiction and became instead the responsibility of social service agencies in the community. The juvenile justice system was then free to focus on dealing with the punishment and control of more serious offenders.

CONCLUSION

With the Juvenile Justice and Delinquency Prevention Act of 1974 and the Juvenile Justice Amendments of 1977, 1980, and 1984, the federal government took an important step in creating uniform goals and more stringent standards for the incarceration of juveniles in secure institutions. The act greatly decreased the number of status offenders held in secure facilities. In 1975, well over 100,000 status offense cases involved detention; by 1992, the number was down to 24,300.

While most would agree that the JJDP Act was a step in the right direction, others—including many court officials—argue that status offenders are the best place to focus prevention, and without proper supervision and funding for care in the community, they are more likely to slip through the cracks of the system. The fear is that with their minor offenses unpunished, status offenders will be more likely to escalate into more serious crimes. Proponents of labeling theory would argue, however, that the majority of status offenders are likely to "age out" of their crimes and never go on to serious criminal careers if left alone. From this point of view, processing them through the juvenile justice system and subjecting them to the associated stigma would be likely to do more harm than good. Such disagreements are not likely to be resolved soon. One of the legacies of the JJDP Act is the opportunity to debate these issues and find the compromise that best serves young people, communities, and the juvenile justice system.

—*Michelle Inderbitzin*

See also Child Savers; Detained Youth and Committed Youth; Juvenile Reformatories; Jerome G. Miller; *Parens Patriae*; President's Commission on Law Enforcement and Administration of Justice; Status Offenders; Waiver to Adult Court

Further Reading

Bartollas, C., & Miller, S. J. (2000). *Juvenile justice in America* (3rd ed.). Upper Saddle River, NJ: Prentice Hall.

Chesney-Lind, M., & Shelden, R. G. (1998). *Girls, delinquency, and juvenile justice* (2nd ed.). Belmont, CA: Wadsworth.

Feld, B. C. (1999). *Bad kids: Race and the transformation of the juvenile court.* New York: Oxford University Press.

Jackson, M. S., & Knepper, P. (2003). *Delinquency and justice.* Boston: Pearson Education.

Mays, G. L., & Winfree, L. T., Jr. (2000). *Juvenile justice.* Boston: McGraw-Hill.

JUVENILE JUSTICE SYSTEM

Youthful offenders who are brought to the attention of the juvenile justice system by parents, school officials, or (most often) police are governed by a distinct set of practices and philosophies from those encountered by adults accused of crimes. Usually, unless they are waived to adult courts, they are processed by juvenile courts, and if sentenced to confinement, sent to juvenile detention centers. Specific beliefs underpin the juvenile justice system that have a history of their own, and differentiate the treatment of young offenders from their older counterparts.

Child savers established the first juvenile courts and justice system in the late 19th and early 20th centuries in North America. These reformers believed that a separate system of governance would reclaim delinquent youths and would function in their best interests. This view was premised on the philosophy of *parens patriae* where the state takes the role of guardian over delinquent youths. However, during the late 20th century many of the original philosophical underpinnings of the juvenile justice system were eroded as practitioners of juvenile justice abandoned rehabilitative beliefs based on the particular needs of youths in favor of punitive ones oriented toward coercive intervention. This shift in ideology is nowhere more apparent than in the United States where young people are incarcerated at a rate that has far surpassed many other industrial nations.

The juvenile court and correctional services are at the apex of modern juvenile justice systems, which operate on many levels carried out by social and legal agencies, schools, police departments, welfare agencies, and other nonjudicial organizations. In large urban centers in North America, juvenile justice systems are composed of the following elements:

Screening and intake

Detention

Probation

Record keeping and research

Psychological screening and mental health

Protective services

Medical services

Volunteer services

Court services (judges, district attorneys, etc.)

Aftercare

Unlike most other Western nations such as Canada that can boast a national or single juvenile justice system, American juvenile justice systems vary considerably by jurisdiction. Across the country separate systems controlled by state legislation differ in mission, scope, and procedure. Although these variations provide states with an opportunity to experiment with innovations in juvenile justice (while others observe the outcome), this configuration makes generalizing about the practices and procedures adopted in the United States difficult. In some jurisdictions, for example, rather than operating a separate juvenile court, special times are set aside in the adult court to hear matters related to young offenders. Whereas some states administer juvenile justice matters in a specialized courthouse with a large bureaucratic network, others operate in a single courtroom with only a skeleton crew. Despite state variation, the U.S. Constitution, federal policies, and legislation along with political and social pressures ensure that juvenile court processes share some degree of coherence across the country. This entry describes the emergence, shifts, alterations, developments, and current controversies evident in the U.S. juvenile justice system.

HISTORY

Before the first juvenile court was inaugurated in Illinois in 1899, juvenile offenders over the age of 7 were dealt with in much the same way as adults; that is, they were understood as, and adjudicated as, young adults. For most of the 19th century, the law was not directed toward reforming and reclaiming juvenile offenders; rather, legal processes attempted to proscribe behaviors through coercive punishments. Youthful transgressions against criminal law were managed through a generalized system of prohibitions and punishments. This retributive system of justice considered juvenile offenders to be rational and calculating actors. Consequently, findings of guilt were determined by the actions of the individual with little consideration for their situation, life experiences, social position, or mental state. When it came to governing juvenile offenders, justice officials held little regard for the individual's stage of life or for the conditions that may have led to the commission of his or her offenses. Children who committed crimes were believed to be acting with criminal intent and were consequently punished in much the same manner as adults.

While some evidence suggests that juries were often sympathetic to juvenile offenders, judges sometimes resorted to the use of capital punishment for youths convicted of relatively minor crimes, indicating that age was not always a mitigating factor. Nevertheless, the English Common Law tradition of *doli incapax* dictated that children under age 7 could not be held criminally responsible. It also assumed that youths between the ages of 7 and 14 should not be convicted of a criminal offense unless the prosecuting attorney could prove the offending party could form the necessary intent.

The development of a separate way of thinking about the governance and adjudication of deviant youth first appeared during the 19th century with the development of the reformatory and houses of refuge movement. Reformers believed that incarcerating young offenders in separate institutions from adults and providing them "a good dose of institutionalization could only work to the child's benefit" (Rothman, 1971, p. 209). As the 20th century

approached, carceral methods of governing deviant youths came under sustained attack by child savers. They were concerned about the negative elements of institutional confinement—the artificial environment and the lessons in crime and deviance to which children were exposed—and soon became convinced that community-based solutions were far superior.

Agreement among child savers about the importance of separate reform facilities for juvenile offenders ultimately led to the reformatory movement and the subsequent creation of separate institutions for boys and girls. Beliefs that families and environmental conditions caused juvenile crime created a uniquely American juvenile justice system. Reformers came to believe that youths who grew up in the seedy areas of town, who were not compelled by parents to attend school, were found begging on the street, associated with felonious peers, and were engaged in sexual immorality, could not be held accountable for their deviance in the same manner as adults. Instead, they thought that the deleterious conditions that surrounded them were to blame for their offending behavior and eclipsed any personal culpability that could be attached to deviant boys and girls. The wretchedness connected to the social milieu was so overpowering that moral crusaders came to see the deviant actions of youths as the result of immersion in such injurious environments. Moreover, reformers remained convinced that in the same way juvenile deviance was the product of immersion in regrettable social and economic conditions, so too could their wayward life be reversed. The causes of juvenile crime and delinquency, however, were not considered to be identical for boys and girls.

The concerns raised by child savers, justice officials, and parents over working-class boys' wayward character diverged from the anxieties these actors attached to delinquent girls. Feminist historians have observed that girls, unlike their male counterparts, were arrested and institutionalized for violations of virtuous feminine conduct and errant sexuality. The visibility of adolescent males' deviance became a troubling feature on city streets as early as the mid-19th century. While boys were not arrested and detained for violations of gender roles in the same way as girls, attempts were made to correct wayward working-class masculinity by juvenile courts, in institutions, on probation, or by social welfare agencies such as Big Brothers and the YMCA. Boys raised the concern of juvenile justice officials and deviated from working-class parents' understanding of respectable conduct when they were truant, refused to work, failed to revere adult authority, associated with felonious peers, and committed crimes.

A separate juvenile justice system was created first in Illinois in 1899 and shortly thereafter was quickly diffused throughout the United States and exported to Canada and Australia. By the 1920s, nearly every state had a juvenile court in operation that attempted to reform juvenile offenders in the community through programs such as probation. During the 1960s and 1970s, however, the philosophical underpinnings upon which 19th-century reformers erected the juvenile justice system came under intense scrutiny. As many historically disenfranchised groups—Native Americans, women, African Americans, gay and lesbian groups—demanded and eventually achieved legal and constitutional recognition, there was a remarkable increase in the acknowledgment of human and legal rights. In response, the assumption that suspending the rights of youths in order to assist them toward proper citizenship was rejected.

THE END OF REHABILITATION

The spread of rights discourse to juvenile justice was most evident in the U.S. Supreme Court cases of In re *Gault* (1967) and In re *Kent* (1966). In the 1966 *Kent* case, the Court highlighted a fundamental contradiction in the juvenile justice system when it stated: "The child receives the worst of both worlds . . . [they] get neither the protections accorded to adults nor the solicitous care and regenerative treatment postulated for children." A year later, the Court ruled in *Gault* that juvenile offenders were entitled to state-provided counsel and due process guarantees. During the 1980s, the informality of the court process—an essential feature of the original juvenile justice system—was severely circumscribed.

At about the same time as a rights discourse pervaded juvenile justice, the belief in the malleability of young offenders was increasingly held suspect. The 1974 Martinson report sent shock waves throughout the juvenile justice system as it called into question the juvenile justice system's very essence—to reform and to rehabilitate. When rehabilitation programs failed to achieve the lofty goals that 19th-century child savers had promised, juvenile justice officials and politicians alike were keen to refocus the intent of justice programs from the needs of offenders to their criminal conduct.

The questions about the efficacy and possibility of rehabilitation and the importance of young offenders' rights dramatically altered the administration of juvenile justice in the United States. Moreover, these movements forced juvenile justice officials, politicians, and academics to rethink the current structure and operation of the juvenile justice system. While some academics have called for the abolition of a specialized court for juvenile offenders arguing that it is an outmoded institution, others have attempted to reconfigure the system's objectives in line with changing times.

THE CONTEMPORARY SITUATION

The perception that an imminent crisis in youth crime calls for a "tougher" juvenile justice system backed by improved legislation is widely held by some juvenile justice officials, politicians, and members of the general public. The movement toward enacting tougher and more intrusive legislation is not confined to the U.S. context, but has spread throughout the Western world. Consequently, despite declining rates of youth crime since 1995, nations such as Canada and the United States continue to have exceedingly high rates of incarceration for young offenders. Irrespective of almost a century of evidence to the contrary, neoconservative politicians have argued that incidents of youth crime are declining as a result of more intensive and austere approaches to juvenile justice. For example, a headline from the Canadian *Alberta Report* boasted, "The tide of violence recedes and with a tougher youth policy the next one may be averted" (Anonymous, 1998, p.5).

The increasingly punitive mentality in juvenile justice today is reflected in the expansion of legislation designed to "get tough" with young offenders, the ease with which young people can be transferred to the adult system, and in the amplification of severe penalties. Federal statutes aimed at curbing youth crime through the youth justice system have proliferated. Similarly, each state has moved to enact statutes dealing with juvenile violence, often under "three strikes" policies. Municipalities and city governments that possess only modest lawmaking power have added their own legislative response to the already cramped arena of juvenile justice through instituting curfew ordinances, and anti-gang legislation. The most prominent feature of the majority of these measures is that they are directed toward the violent and hardened offender. That is, legislation, severe penalties, and transfer are intended not for the first-time and nonthreatening offender but for the gun-toting repeat offender.

The basic message delivered by legislative developments throughout the 1990s has been to "get tough" on youth crime and young offenders by giving the youth justice system "teeth." Canada, for example, has recently enacted the Youth Criminal Justice Act (YCJA) to replace the much maligned Young Offenders Act (1984). There is a contradiction involved when a government replaces one piece of legislation with another. High rates of juvenile crime through the early 1990s were taken as indicators that the juvenile justice system and the legislation upon which the system was based must have been somehow flawed. However, by enacting new legislation to bridge the gap left by ailing existing legislation the fundamental *cause* of a perceived problem is considered to be the *solution*. Legislative amendments that are leveled at the problem of youth crime are more often symbolic attempts by governments to quell public fears and demonstrate they are serious about protecting citizens from the risks associated with delinquent adolescents than

they are reasoned decisions based on evidence of the most successful interventions.

VIOLENT OFFENDERS

Since the emergence of the juvenile justice system, violent young offenders have presented serious problems for justice officials. The heinous crimes of a select few that invariably become highly publicized media events raise questions in the public's mind about the ability of the juvenile courts to govern offenders. To this end, all states in the United States have enacted legislation to provide for transfer of youths to adult courts. Despite preexisting transfer provisions that always allowed for certain, particularly violent young offenders to be tried in adult courts, in the past 10 years 40 of the 50 states have passed legislation to ease standards governing judicial waiver to adult court. Without exception, amendments have allowed juvenile court officials to expand the number and type of cases subject to transfer.

RESTORATIVE JUSTICE

Recent developments in juvenile justice have not been a one-way process of greater and more secure detention for all juvenile offenders. Instead, there has been a bifurcation in the contemporary juvenile justice approach where serious offenders are managed through more traditional, intrusive, and carceral programs, while first-time offenders are being governed through innovative community-based experiments. Since the 1990s, restorative justice initiatives have become implemented in many juvenile justice systems. Restorative justice comes from the idea that shaming criminal acts by community members allows for the reintegration of deviant actors back into the community once suitable redress has been made. The promise of this approach lies in its ability to bring large numbers of participants together to mend gulfs in community relationships, to create bonds between its members, to form a broader network for reintegrating the victim and offender into the community, and to educate the offender.

A growing body of research indicates that community-based alternatives to custodial treatment of offenders may also have great potential for effecting long-term change in the most serious offenders and difficult-to-treat youths. Several recent studies have confirmed that well-supervised after-school recreational programs substantially reduce recidivism among high-risk juvenile offenders. For example, day reporting centers that are characterized by high surveillance and diverse services and programs are receiving considerable attention as effective alternatives to custody for serious and high-risk offenders.

Photo 2   *Juvenile offenders gain computer skills in joint venture program, 1990*

RACE AND GENDER

The gendering of juvenile delinquency by the youth justice system did not end with the turn of the 20th century and the development of juvenile courts. Girls today are more likely to be arrested for status offenses (crimes that if committed by an adult would not draw legal, cultural, or social attention) and failure to comply with a disposition (what Reitsma-Street [1998], calls the new "status-like" offenses). They are also more likely to receive custodial sentences than their male counterparts (Reitsma-Street, 1998, p. 338).

In recent years, arrest statistics have pointed to a burgeoning "girl problem" where female youth crime is increasing faster than any other offender group. Media reports on growing female crime emphasize the size of the increase rather than the small number of incidents involved (compared to males). Perhaps, this says more about a change in the response of juvenile justice officials to girls' misdeeds than a change in their actual behavior. While detailed theoretical and substantive inquiry

into the extent and cause of this phenomenon is still inconclusive, the numbers of female offenders pale in comparison to their male counterparts. Nonetheless, headlines such as "Sugar and Spice and Veins as Cold as Ice: Teenage Girls Are Closing the Gender Gap in Violent Crime" fuel the perception that young women are out of control.

Conclusive evidence demonstrates that minority youths are overrepresented at all stages of the juvenile justice process. Such discrimination tends to be amplified the further minority youths are processed through the system. For example, in California, like most other states, African Americans are highly overrepresented in young offender detention centers. Of the 13,767 youths detained during 1992 in the state, 5,309 (37%) were of African American heritage compared to a mere 8.7% of the youth population (Austin, 1995). By contrast, Anglo Americans are underrepresented in California's incarcerated youth population. This trend is repeated across the United States.

The overrepresentation of indigenous youths in the juvenile justice system has become a source of concern to Native peoples, governments, and youth justice officials. Studies conducted in the United States, Australia, Canada, and New Zealand suggest that all social indicators (housing, income, health, crime) point to indigenous peoples being the most dispossessed population in Western society. In the Canadian province of Manitoba, for example, indigenous youths constitute 20% of the youth population and account for 75% of admissions to provincial detention centers (Statistics Canada, 2000).

CONCLUSION

The emergence of juvenile courts and the resulting juvenile justice system was shaped by Anglo-Celtic child savers and reform-minded elites during the late 19th and early 20th centuries. They promised that a separate system of governance for youths could reclaim delinquent youths and would function in their best interests. Today, the juvenile justice system in the United States only faintly resembles the early juvenile courts that focused primarily on the rehabilitative rather than retributive needs of youths. The recognition of offenders' rights and doubt cast on the reformability of the offender seriously called into question the very essence of a separate juvenile justice system and continues to shape its current configuration. Questions about the efficacy and possibility of rehabilitation and the importance of young offenders' rights dramatically altered the administration of juvenile justice in the United States. Moreover, these movements have forced juvenile justice officials, politicians, and academics to restructure the juvenile justice system.

The belief in an imminent crisis in youth crime has fueled calls for a "tougher" juvenile justice system and supported the enactment of new legislation. Recent developments in juvenile justice represent a twofold process of greater incarceration of serious and repeat juvenile offenders and a less intrusive, community-based strategy for first-time, nonserious offenders. How will such a bifurcated philosophy be translated into practice? While there has been much demonstrated success with nonintrusive, alternative measures and diversionary programs, it remains to be seen how the juvenile justice system will operate. Will officials continue to build more secure young offender facilities, or will they invest in new innovative strategies and prevention programs? Can a

return to the rehabilitative ideals and reform impulse characteristic of the early child savers be fostered in an environment of fiscal restraint, risk management, and public security, or will the juvenile justice system eventually mirror the adult system? At present, it seems like the situation could go either way, and thus only time, and more research, will tell.

—*Bryan Hogeveen and Joanne Minaker*

See also Meda Chesney-Lind; Child Savers; Determinate Sentencing; Gerald (Gerry) Gault; Incapacitation Theory; Indeterminate Sentencing; just deserts Theory; Juvenile Detention Centers; *Parens Patriae*; Patuxent Institution; Rehabilitation Theory; Restorative Justice; Status Offenders; Waiver of Juveniles Into the Adult Court system; Youth Correction Act 1950

Further Reading

Anonymous. (1998). The tide of violence recedes and with a tougher youth policy the next one may be averted. *Alberta Report, 25,* 5.

Austin, J. (1995). The overrepresentation of minority youth in the California juvenile justice system. In K. Kempf-Leonard, C. Pope, & W. Feyerherm (Eds.), *Minorities in juvenile justice* (pp. 153–178). Thousand Oaks, CA: Sage.

Chesney-Lind, M., & Sheldon, R. (1992). *Girls: Delinquency and juvenile justice.* Belmont, CA: Wadsworth.

Griffin, P., Torbet, P., & Szymanski, L. (1998). *Trying juveniles in adult court: An analysis of state transfer provisions.* Washington, DC: U.S. Department of Justice.

Reitsma-Street, M. (1998). Justice for Canadian girls: A 1990s update. *Canadian Journal of Criminology, 41,* 335–363.

Rothman, D. (1971). *The discovery of the asylum: Social order and disorder in the new republic.* Boston: Little, Brown.

Statistics Canada. (2000). *Youth in custody and community services in Canada, 1998/9.* Ottawa, ON: Canadian Centre for Justice Statistics.

Legal Cases

In re Gault, 387 U.S. 1, 87 S. Ct. 1248 (1967).
Kent v. United States, 383 U.S. 541 (1966).

◪ JUVENILE OFFENDERS: RACE, CLASS, AND GENDER

It is virtually impossible to discuss juvenile corrections without examining the issues of race, class, and gender. Where young people are placed by the courts, as well as the programs and facilities made available to them, is directly or indirectly associated with whether a juvenile is a member of a minority group, male or female, and/or working or middle class. Most public and scholarly attention has been devoted to the role of race and ethnicity in juvenile corrections, particularly to the overrepresentation and disparate treatment of minority youths (e.g., African American, Hispanic, Native American, and Asian American). Overrepresentation refers to situations in which a larger proportion of minority youths are involved in juvenile corrections than would be expected based on their numbers in the general population. Disparity describes a pattern of outcomes in which some racial groups are treated differently from others. Neither concept automatically implies discrimination since both can be the result of legal and extralegal factors. Biased decision making at earlier points in the juvenile justice system, however, increase the probability that racial and ethnic minority youths will experience juvenile corrections and that minority overrepresentation and disparity in juvenile corrections will occur.

OVERREPRESENTATION OF MINORITY YOUTHS

Minority youths are disproportionately represented at every stage of secure juvenile corrections. In 2001, minority youths accounted for approximately 60% of the residential placements of juveniles despite making up only roughly one-third of youths in the community. Of these young people, African American youths were the most overrepresented.

In 1999, the Office of Juvenile Justice and Delinquency Prevention published a detailed report about the racial composition of its juvenile institutions that cited numbers from 1997. This report provides the most recent figures currently available and is the basis for much of the following analysis. According to this report, in 1997 African American youths comprised 15% of the general adolescent population but made up 45% of detained youths, 40% of youths in secure confinement, and 60% of the youths under age 18 admitted to adult prisons.

Although their admission to adult prisons was equal to their representation in the population (15%), Hispanic youths were slightly overrepresented among detained or committed juveniles (18%). The failure to disaggregate ethnicity from race in data systems, however, results in many Hispanic youths being classified as white and the underreporting of Hispanic representation in the juvenile correctional population. Although African American youths also were overrepresented in probation placements, white youths were more likely to receive community-based treatment.

| Table 1 | Percentage of Juveniles in Population and in Residential Placement, 1997 |

Race/Ethnicity	In Population in 1997	Residential Placement October 29, 1997
Total	100%	100%
White	66	37
Minority	34	63
African American	15	40
Latino	15	18
Native American	1	2
Asian	4	2

SOURCE: Adapted from *Juvenile Offenders and Victims: 1999 National Report.* Office of Juvenile Justice and Delinquency Prevention (1999).

NOTE: Details may not add to totals due to rounding.

There is substantial evidence that the overrepresentation of minority youths in secure juvenile corrections is often the result of differential treatment rather than higher rates of criminal misbehavior. Research, for example, shows that nonwhite youths are more likely to be detained in secure custody prior to their hearing than white youths regardless of the delinquency offense. African American youths are six times more likely and Latino youths are three times more likely to be incarcerated than white youths even if both groups have no prior record and are charged with the same offense. Regional research also has indicated that racial and ethnic minority youths have a higher probability of receiving the harsher dispositions in juvenile corrections than white youths even when they are alike in terms of legal and extralegal factors. The greatest disparity in secure commitments is among African American and white youths for drug offenses for which African American youths were 5.3 times more likely to be committed to state prisons in 1997.

CAUSES OF OVERREPRESENTATION

Overrepresentation and disparity in secure juvenile corrections have been attributed to a variety of factors including the lack of private counsel, the lack of family or community resources to qualify racial and ethnic minority youths for alternatives to detention and other community-based treatment, and biased perceptions of juvenile justice personnel that result in majority youths being dealt with more sensitively and individually. Unlike majority youths, minority youths are often forced to rely on an indigent defense. Youths represented by private counsel are less likely to be convicted and are more likely to have their cases returned to juvenile court if they are originally prosecuted as adults. Juvenile justice officials also have been found to have a more negative view of the culpability of minority youths and the economic and social stability of minority families and communities, and to perceive that the juvenile justice system is a minority youth's best chance for treatment.

Family and community resources further influence the placement of minority youths in public or private correctional institutions. Although African American and Hispanic youths are overrepresented in both types of facilities, more than half (66%) of the juveniles in public facilities are minorities. While this may be partially related to the financial costs that are often associated with private correctional facilities, recent trends indicate that slightly more minority youths currently reside in private correctional institutions than in past years. Nevertheless, minority youths, in residential placements, especially African Americans and Hispanics, are more likely to be confined behind locked doors than nonminority youths.

GENDER AND CLASS

In comparison to race and ethnicity, far less attention has been devoted to the role of gender and class in juvenile corrections. Like their adult counterparts, males make up the majority of youths in the juvenile correctional system. Regardless of the seriousness of the offense, young women are less likely to experience detention or long-term out-of-home placement in secure institutional programs and facilities. Nevertheless, the number of female youths in some stages of juvenile corrections has increased more than for male youths in relative terms. Between 1989 and 1998, for example, the number of female youths given detention increased by 56% compared to a 20% increase in boys' detention (Chesney-Lind & Pasko, 2004, p. 69). This increase is partly associated with the growing number of young women in the juvenile justice system and the use of detention as a means of controlling the behavior of girls who are considered to be dangerous. Females, for example, are more likely than males to be detained for minor offenses that do not warrant detention and for technical violations of probation or parole in the absence of new offenses.

Female youths in residential placements tend to be younger than their male counterparts, to reside in private rather public facilities, and to be committed for shorter periods of time. Correctional institutions for female youths, however, are gendered in that they reinforce traditional female stereotypes and roles. Unlike juvenile male institutions, these facilities subject female youths to greater rule rigidity and control, offer fewer vocational and other correctional programs, and offer vocational and correctional programs that emphasize the traditional roles of wife, mother, and homemaker.

Researchers have long argued that the involvement of youths in juvenile justice is structured along class lines. Barry Feld (1999), for example, maintains that the juvenile court was originally intended and designed to regulate the behavior of poor and immigrant youths. The individualized treatment rendered by the juvenile court encouraged class disparity by allowing decisions to be based on social status and created a dual system of juvenile justice in which middle- and upper-class youths were treated (e.g., placed in community-based programs) and poor and immigrant youths were punished (e.g., placed in institutional facilities). Many argue that this pattern continues today with lower-class youths having a higher probability of experiencing juvenile corrections, especially secure placements, than their middle-class counterparts. Research further suggests that the general public is more willing to acknowledge disparate treatment of youths in the juvenile justice system on the basis of class rather than race. A national poll on youth and juvenile justice issues in 1999, for example, found that more than three-quarters of the public believed that wealthy youths received better treatment than poor youths, and more than 8 in 10 considered it was a serious issue if they were told that wealthy youths were less likely than poor youths to be locked up for the same crimes.

Overrepresentation and disparity in secure juvenile corrections also have been linked to the social and economic conditions that racial and ethnic minority youths face in the United States. African Americans, Hispanics, Native Americans, and other minority groups generally rank lower than whites on indicators of social and economic well-being (e.g., educational obtainment, employment, wealth). These contextual factors influence the ability of minority youths to afford the services of private mental health providers. Moreover, juvenile justice policies and practices that require youths and parents to be interviewed before making a recommendation to the state attorney negatively affect poor youths (who are often minorities), who are most likely not to have telephones or access to transportation. As a result, these youths tend to receive more formal and harsher dispositions rather than diversion or lesser sanctions.

COLLECTIVE EFFECTS

In recent years, researchers have stressed the importance of examining the collective effects of race, class, and gender on juvenile corrections. The basic argument is that the three variables operate independently and in combination with each other to influence juvenile correctional decisions. Youths, for example, who are involved in juvenile corrections, especially secure placements, are disproportionately minorities, male, and lower class. All three factors—race, class, and gender—independently and in combination with each other influence perceptions of perceived threat, culpability, and dangerousness that, in turn, result in very different correctional experiences between and within groups. Minorities, for example, were somewhat less disproportionate in the female residential placements than in the male residential placements in 1997. While whites accounted for the greatest proportion of females in residential placement (49%), African Americans accounted for the largest proportion of males in residential placement (41%). The custody rates for African American girls, however, were higher than for other racial and ethnic groups. The custody rates for African American males were three and a half times the rate for white males.

REMEDIES AND SOLUTIONS

Several recommendations have been proposed to reduce race, class, and gender disparities in juvenile correctional decisions. They include the following:

- Examine decision-making policies and practices of police, prosecutors, courts, and probation to identify where racial disparities occur in the system.
- Institute and require cultural and racial sensitivity training for all juvenile justice system personnel. This training should be geared toward debunking myths and stereotypes about racial and ethnic minorities.
- Establish funding to enable those youths with financial need to access private service providers.
- Address the root causes of crime with programs designed to improve social and economic conditions that contribute to delinquent behavior. This includes cultural educational programs and programs to address minority drop out, truancy, suspensions, and expulsions.
- Increase diversion programs for minority juveniles as well as the number of culturally appropriate juvenile services.

- Institute objective risk-screening criteria and objective needs assessments to reduce system bias where it may exist.
- Increase the involvement of minority communities and citizens in juvenile justice policy and the representation of minority staff in the juvenile justice system.
- Increase gender-specific programs and services that effectively address girls' diverse racial and cultural backgrounds and girls' innate strengths and resiliencies.

CONCLUSION

Few would argue that race, class, and gender do not affect juvenile correctional decision making. Nevertheless, there are still many unanswered questions. Much more research is needed to access the nature and extent of this issue both nationally and within local contexts. Through research, we can obtain a greater understanding of the independent and collective effects of the three factors in juvenile corrections and wider society and initiate effective policies and strategies to eliminate the bias treatment of minority youths.

—B. Tatumb

See also Meda Chesney-Lind; Child Savers; Juvenile Detention Centers; Juvenile Justice System; *Parens Patriae*; Race, Class, and Gender of Prisoners; Status Offenders; Waiver of Juveniles Into the Adult Court system

Further Reading

American Bar Association and the National Bar Association. (2001). *Justice by gender: The lack of appropriate prevention, diversion and treatment alternatives for girls in the justice system.* Chicago: American Bar Association.

Belknap, J. (1999). *The invisible women: Gender, crime, and justice.* Belmont, CA: Wadsworth.

Bridges, G., & Steen, S. (1998). Racial disparities in official assessments of juvenile offenders: Attributional stereotypes as mediating mechanisms. *American Sociological Review, 63,* 5–45.

Chesney-Lind, M., & Pasko, L. (2004). *The female offender: Girls, women, and crime* (2nd ed.). Thousand Oaks, CA: Sage.

Feld, B. (1999). *Bad kids: Race and the transformation of the juvenile court.* Chicago: University of Chicago Press.

Hoytt, R., Schiraldi, V., Smith, B., & Ziedenberg, J. (2001). *Reducing racial disparity in juvenile detention.* Baltimore, MD.: Annie E. Casey Foundation.

Office of Juvenile Justice and Delinquency Prevention. (1999). *Minorities in the juvenile justice system.* Washington, DC: U.S. Department of Justice, Office of Justice Programs.

Sickmund, M., Sladky, T. J., & Kang, W. (2004). *Census of juveniles in residential placement databook.* Retrieved September 2, 2004, from http://www.ojjdp.ncjrs.org/ojstatbb/cjrp

Sickmund, M., & Snyder, H. (2000). *Juvenile offenders and victims: 1999 national report.* Washington, DC: Office of Juvenile Justice and Delinquency Prevention.

Soler, M. (2001). *Public opinion on youth, crime and race: A guide for advocates.* Washington, DC: Building Blocks for Youths.

Yamagata, E. P., & Butts, J. (1996). *Female offenders in the juvenile justice system.* Washington, DC: Office of Juvenile Justice and Delinquency Prevention.

Yamagata, E. P., & Jones, M. A. (2000). *And justice for some: Differential treatment of minority youths in the justice system.* Washington, DC: Building Blocks for Youths.

◪ JUVENILE REFORMATORIES

Juvenile reformatories were once the juvenile equivalent of adult prisons. Originally opened to keep young offenders separate from the threat and influence of adult criminals, they were often used to house juvenile delinquents and children "for their own good" or for those in need of protection. Reformatories sought to aid and rehabilitate young people through teaching them the value of hard work. Great emphasis was placed on vocational skills that could lead to employment after release and on conforming to mainstream values in what was intended to be a wholesome environment. Juveniles were assigned to them without trial and with minimal legal requirements. Because the juvenile courts and the reformatories were acting in what they believed were the delinquents' best interests, the youths were given indeterminate sentences and left to be rehabilitated by the institution.

These days, delinquents are still generally kept in separate facilities from adult criminals, but reformatories are now known as training schools or juvenile correctional facilities. While many continue to embrace the goal of rehabilitation, these institutions are more explicitly concerned with protecting the community from juvenile criminals. They also seek to punish offenders and hold them accountable for their actions.

HISTORY

The first public reformatory, the New York House of Refuge, was opened in New York City in 1825 by the Society for the Prevention of Pauperism. It was soon followed by institutions in Boston, Philadelphia, Chicago, and other cities. These first reformatories varied in size, holding anywhere from 90 to 1,000 children. They were designed to maintain complete control and were often built with locked cells in order to hold the young people securely.

The New York House of Refuge was meant to be an alternative to the penitentiary for delinquent youths. In practice, however, it was not all that different from the prisons and jails of the time. Juveniles who had committed crimes were confined alongside orphans and poor or incorrigible children, without the benefit of a trial or concern for due process. The New York House of Refuge was used to house, school, and train poor children in an attempt to help them avoid becoming paupers as adults. Eventually, houses of refuges became clearing centers of sorts, collecting poor and delinquent children from the city streets and sending them to the west to work on farms as indentured servants. Boys were often sent there until their 21st birthday; girls were committed until their 18th birthday.

State reformatories or training schools were essentially a continuation of these houses of refuge, with slightly more focus on education. Massachusetts led the way, opening the Lyman School for Boys in 1847 and the Lancaster School for Girls in 1855. By the end of the century, all states had adopted the idea and opened their own reformatories. These institutions, whether in Massachusetts, New York, or elsewhere, were based on the guiding principle that strict discipline and vocational training could counteract the forces of poverty, unstable family lives, and an unhealthy, dangerous environment.

Reformatories were generally built in rural settings in order to remove children from the temptations of the city. The youths sent to them were closely supervised and expected to work and to learn vocational skills. Most reformatories were designed around a cottage system, with juveniles separated into a number of small living units. In these more intimate settings, house "parents" were able to focus on and supervise the youths in their care and to attempt to model conforming behavior and values. While many juvenile correctional facilities continue to use the cottage system, juvenile institutions also took on additional forms in the 20th century. Forestry camps and ranches became popular alternatives, and a number of larger training schools moved their populations under one roof and into a more custodial model.

Today, juvenile training schools and correctional facilities generally provide structured environments. Young inmates must attend school and participate in a range of activities including vocational training, individual and group counseling, regimented meals, and planned recreation, work, and chores. There are usually standard times for waking up, lights out, and showering. Privacy is almost nonexistent and children have few choices in the company they keep or how they spend their limited free time.

CHANGES AND CONTROVERSY

From the beginning, juvenile reformatories were criticized as overly punitive institutions, doing as much to punish children who had committed no crime as they did to help or "save" them. Immigrants and poor children were especially at risk of being taken to reformatories and housed there through their adolescence. Some have suggested that, by mixing delinquents and nondelinquents in the same institutions, these institutions created breeding grounds for learning criminal skills and values. In addition, youths who had committed no crime may have been stigmatized by spending time in reformatories and returning to their communities labeled as delinquent and treated as such. In turn, they may have faced diminished opportunities and actually been more likely to subsequently become delinquent.

Girls were in a particularly precarious position since they were vulnerable to abuse by a system all too willing to institutionalize them "for their own protection." Girls were frequently placed in the first reformatories for moral rather than criminal offenses, and many were brought in because of actions of their parents or family members rather than their own behavior. When institutionalized for delinquency, girls were most likely to have committed status offenses, or offenses that would not be crimes if committed by adults, such as running away, vagrancy, lewd conduct, or stubbornness.

Institutions for girls were often run more strictly than those for boys because administrators were very concerned about the morality and respectability of their female charges. They aimed to control the sexuality of adolescent girls from lower-class families in part by isolating them away from boys and out of trouble until they were of marriageable age. While boys in reformatories were trained in skills for higher-paying jobs such as auto mechanics and welding, girls in reformatories were subjected to gendered vocational training—they were taught cooking, sewing, and office skills. Through it all, the sexual double standard in incarceration was very much in place in early reformatories: Girls were much more likely to be held "for their own protection" and "for their own good" than boys.

The practice of holding girls and poor children who had committed no crime in reformatories for their own protection was challenged in the United States in the 1970s. In 1974, the federal government passed the Juvenile Justice Delinquency and Prevention (JJDP) Act. This act offered financial incentives for states to deinstitutionalize status offenders. Most states followed the federal government's lead, and nondelinquent youths were diverted to community agencies rather than confined in secure custody. The incarceration of girls fell dramatically after passage of the JJDP Act.

With status offenders largely out of the system, the next major problem to be addressed was the abuse that took place within reformatories. Juveniles in reform schools were frequently victimized by other inmates and by staff members. They were beaten, sexually abused, starved, drugged, forced to live their days in silence, subjected to demeaning rituals, put in restraints and in various versions of solitary confinement, and continuously threatened. Time served in reformatories was a painful, punitive process. In the 1970s, Jerome Miller (1998)

sent a Harvard University undergraduate into a Massachusetts training school undercover to document the abusive treatment of incarcerated youths. During the four days he spent in the institution, the young man watched a staff member hold a 12-year-old's head under water in a toilet; a 14-year-old boy was dragged by the legs over a urine-soaked floor; and other boys were beaten, hit about the face, and moved to isolation. The undercover Harvard student was himself hit in the face for a minor infraction, clearly illustrating that these institutions were places of pain and punishment.

As the director of youth services in Massachusetts in the early 1970s, Jerome Miller recognized that there were numerous problems plaguing juvenile institutions and although he began his tenure with the idea of improving the conditions of confinement, he chose, ultimately, to close all reform schools in the state. His decision was met with hostility, fear, and death threats, but he eventually managed to move both the children and the funding from the reform schools into a wide variety of community alternatives. The alternatives included both residential and nonresidential placements—options included boarding schools, art programs, group homes, universities, and specialized foster care.

One of the key components of this change in ideology was its flexibility. If a youth was placed in a program that did not work for him or her, the youth could request a new placement and be moved to a different environment that would, it was hoped, provide a better fit. To this day, Massachusetts has not reopened its reform schools ("an old-fashioned but honest name," according to Miller, 1998, p. xvii) or created new ones, and it does not suffer unusually high rates of juvenile crime. In fact, studies have shown that serious juvenile offenders have better results when sentenced to small, treatment-oriented facilities rather than the larger state-run juvenile prisons. The "Massachusetts experiment" illustrates that there are other options that can work at least as well as locking up adolescents in secure facilities; it serves as a reminder that there are other ways to think about how to best treat juvenile offenders.

CONCLUSION

Over the years, state reformatories were relabeled "vocational schools" or "training schools" to emphasize their focus on rehabilitation rather than punishment. Yet, for the youth confined to such institutions, the punitive climate continued to belie the soft words.

While federal lawsuits have curtailed the use of corporal punishment and blatantly cruel acts, state training schools still face criticism. In particular, concern exists about the racial and gender makeup of the populations of state training schools. According to critics, a two-tiered system of juvenile corrections has developed: private facilities that predominantly house white girls and boys—and those with the money to afford their costs—and state training schools that continue to house poor and minority delinquent youths. Another troubling trend can be found in the increasing numbers of girls placed in psychiatric units and private facilities. Youths can be locked in these facilities indefinitely "for their own good" and without meeting the legal standards of the juvenile courts. Total institutions seem to take on a life of their own, in spite of the best intentions of reformers and the particular individuals involved at any given time. Perhaps Jerome Miller (1998) said it best when he made the following point:

> Reformers come and reformers go. State institutions carry on. Nothing in their history suggests that they can sustain reform, no matter what money, staff, and programs are pumped into them. The same crises that have plagued them for 150 years intrude today. Though the casts may change, the players go on producing failure. (p. 18)

One reason to maintain a separate juvenile justice system is the belief that youths are more malleable than their adult counterparts and juvenile offenders have a chance to be resocialized by stints in training schools and shaped into more conforming

adults and humans. Yet, even with the best of intentions and using the best available materials and strategies, reform schools generally faced a losing battle in trying to turn the lives of delinquent adolescents around. While training schools may hold juvenile offenders captive for a time, outside forces are much stronger than the rules and the walls of institutions will ever be. Without creating real change in the communities, the families, and the opportunities that these youths will come home to, it is difficult to effect real change in their lives and to influence the choices each will make.

—*Michelle Inderbitzin*

See also Meda Chesney-Lind; Child Savers; Cottage System; Gerald (Gerry) Gault; Juvenile Justice and Delinquency Prevention Act 1974; Juvenile Offenders: Race, Class, and Gender of Prisoners; Massachusetts Reformatory; Jerome G. Miller; *Parens Patriae*; Patuxent Institution; Status Offenders

Further Reading

Bartollas, C., & Miller, S. J. (2001). *Juvenile justice in America* (3rd ed.). Upper Saddle River, NJ: Prentice Hall.

Bernard, T. J. (1992). *The cycle of juvenile justice.* New York: Oxford University Press.

Bortner, M. A., & Williams, L. M. (1997). *Youth in prison.* New York: Routledge.

Champion, D. J. (1998). *The juvenile justice system: Delinquency, processing, and the law* (2nd ed.). Upper Saddle River, NJ: Prentice Hall.

Chesney-Lind, M., & Shelden, R. G. (1998). *Girls, delinquency, and juvenile justice* (2nd ed.). Belmont, CA: Wadsworth.

Feld, B. C. (1999). *Bad kids: Race and the transformation of the juvenile court.* New York: Oxford University Press.

Miller, J. G. (1998). *Last one over the wall: The Massachusetts experiment in closing reform schools* (2nd ed.). Columbus: Ohio State University Press.

Platt, A. M. (1977). *The child savers: The invention of delinquency* (2nd ed., enlarged). Chicago: University of Chicago Press.

Wooden, K. (2000). *Weeping in the playtime of others: America's incarcerated children* (2nd ed.). Columbus: Ohio State University Press.

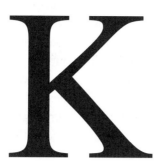

K

◼ KNOPP, FAY HONEY (1918–1995)

Little can be said with much authority about prison visiting, penal abolition, sex offender treatment, or "male survivor" movements in the United States without mention of Fay Honey Knopp. She was a Quaker and prison reformer, who championed penal reform and abolitionism.

BIOGRAPHICAL DETAILS

Fay Birdie Irving was born on August 15, 1918, to a Jewish dentist and his wife, both of Russian decent. Knopp was one of four children (two sisters and a brother). For much of her life, she was a middle-class businesswoman, who lived and worked in the fashion industry in Westport, Connecticut. She had two children and died of cancer on August 10, 1995 when she was 76 years old. In recognition of her reform work, Knopp received many awards for public service.

A QUAKER ACTIVIST AND PRISON REFORMER

Knopp's association with the Religious Society of Friends (Quakers) began in 1939, and she formally become a Quaker in 1962, as a "minister of record" to serve as prison visitor. Knopp was, at the time, one of only two people the Federal Bureau of Prisons allowed to visit any federal prison in the United States.

Knopp started visiting incarcerated conscientious objectors in 1955. She soon recognized the need to visit other prisoners. In response to what she saw on her visits, she formed the Prison Research Education Action Project (PREAP) in the mid-1970s. A penal abolition project, this group published *Instead of Prisons: A Handbook for Abolitionists* in 1976. PREAP subsequently became the Safer Society Project, which is now a leading international information center and publisher of materials for the prevention and treatment of sexual offending.

Instead of Prisons

Instead of Prisons puts forward a strategy for diminishing/dismantling the prison system that consisted of five stages: moratorium, decarceration, excarceration, restraint of the few, and building the caring community. The moratorium required communities to stop building prisons and jails while creating the space to develop nonpunitive programs, processes, policies, and philosophies. Decarceration strategies focused on depopulating jails and prisons. Excarceration meant a halt to putting people behind bars in the first place. Restraint of the few was defined as follows: "For the very *small* percentage of lawbreakers who need to be limited in movement for some periods of time in their lives, a monitoring and review procedure should be established with the goal of working out the least restrictive and most humane option for the shortest period of time" (Knopp et al., 1976, p. 63, emphasis in original). Building the caring community, the important end piece of this approach, was a method of providing the empowerment and support of prisoners through community support services, peer-assistant groups, victim assistance and restitution, and voting rights and constitutional guarantees.

A weakness of *Instead of Prisons,* Knopp felt, was its discussion of the dangerous few, including sex offenders, about whom little was then known. If prisons were abolished, she felt that incarceration, at least as we generally perceive it, should not be used for these offenders regardless of their potential or perceived dangerousness. However, their dangerousness, and their possible threat to personal as well as public safety, was of great concern to her, and she felt that the remedies to replace imprisonment of such offenders was described inadequately in *Instead of Prisons.* In typical fashion, she started to examine what could be done with this population, a project that only grew larger and was not completed before her untimely death.

CONCLUSION

Knopp's efforts to change the way we think about and response to criminal activity contributed to the historical and ongoing connection between Quakers and prison reform. The attrition model Knopp put forth for diminishing/dismantling the prison system was developed by a diverse group of ex-prisoners, prison reformers, prison visitors, families of prisoners, and prison teachers. As Knopp argued, "A successful movement to abolish prisons will grow thr(ough) the joining of those who have experienced the system from 'inside' the walls with those on the 'outside' who are willing to undertake the leap from palliative reform to abolition" (Knopp et al., 1976, p. 8).

—*Russ Immarigeon*

See also Abolition; Activism; Civil Commitment of Sexual Predators; Elizabeth Fry; Monitoring Agencies; Kate Richards O'Hare; Quakers; Sex Offenders; Sex Offender Programs

Further Reading

Knopp, F. H. (1982). *Remedial intervention in adolescent sex offences: Nine program descriptions.* Orwell, VT: Safer Society Press.

Knopp, F. H. (1984). *Retraining adult sex offenders: Methods and models.* Orwell, VT: Safer Society Press.

Knopp, F. H. (1985). *The youthful sex offender: The rationale and goals of early intervention and treatment.* Orwell, VT: Safer Society Press.

Knopp, F. H. (1991). Community solutions to sexual violence: Feminist/abolitionist perspectives. In H. E. Pepinsky & R. Quinney (Eds.), *Criminology as peacemaking* (pp. 181–193). Bloomington: Indiana University Press.

Knopp, F. H., et al. (Eds.). (1976). *Instead of prisons: A handbook for abolitionists.* Syracuse, NY: Prison Research Education Action Project.

Lust, M. (2002). *Living the spirit in the eye of the storm: Fay Honey Knopp—Rebel, heretic, housewife, saint.* Unpublished manuscript, Lincoln, VT.

L

◪ LABOR

Prison labor as a form of penal servitude originated in 1790 as one of the defining features of the "penitentiary house" in Philadelphia's Walnut Street Jail. Prior to the 18th century, prisons were used mainly for pretrial detention or for those awaiting execution of their corporal or capital sentences. Substituting productive labor for cruel and degrading punishments dramatically changed penal practice. Over the course of two centuries, prison labor came to serve various, often conflicting, objectives: (1) as a punitive element in detention and, conversely, as (2) a reward for good conduct, (3) a source of profit for entrepreneurs and revenue for state coffers, and (4) a form of rehabilitation.

Although the profit motive subsequently overcame the humanitarian potential of prison labor, prison industry provided a rationale and a means of rehabilitation. For better or worse, penal labor regimes also connected penology to the development of the America's industrial policy throughout the 19th century. Prisons became quasi-economic institutions, and their impact, directly and indirectly, on the wage and price market generated political controversy and conflict that would severely limit its reformative potential. Labor market changes and the evolution of industrial systems had a hand in shaping the history of penal labor and the transformation

of penal systems, but political pressure from labor groups and small manufacturers ultimately determined the viability of prison industry.

The penitentiary's immediate predecessor was the system of workhouses and houses of correction that first appeared in 16th-century London and Amsterdam as special types of disciplinary institutions for rogues and vagrants and other minor offenders. Among other tasks, inmates voluntarily worked at spinning, baking, and pin-making for which they were paid a wage. Holland's houses of correction are said to have been the inspiration for the provision in William Penn's Great Law of 1682 declaring that "all prisons shall be workhouses." The Crown soon abrogated the law, however, and a workhouse system did not materialize until after the Revolution. Even so, it established a precedent for a 1790 Pennsylvania law designating imprisonment as the prevailing criminal punishment and decreeing that all convicts must labor at the hardest and most servile work, "as far as may be consistent with their sex, age, health, and ability" (Barnes, 1921, p. 620). From 1790 to 1829, the penitentiary wing of the Walnut Street Jail set prisoners toiling in solitude at handicrafts under "piece-price" contracts arranged by merchant-capitalists, who provided the raw materials and paid a prearranged price for finished products. These entrepreneurs were crucial to any successful prison industry, providing the necessary capital for machinery and raw materials.

Likewise, prisons were helpful to the new economic system, as the merchant-capitalist added prison labor to the sweatshop and homework as sources of cheap labor. The jail keeper received 5% of all sales. Prisoner workers were also paid for their work; they got to keep half the profit after deductions for expenses, materials, and keep. Providing convicts with paid, productive, and dignified work was an astonishing statement of Quaker faith in personal renewal. Policy regarding prisoner compensation would regress over the next century, however, as conditions in the free labor market deteriorated. The future course of penal industry would have less to do with reformative ideals than with developments in America's industrial policy, business cycle swings, vicissitudes in the labor market, and politics.

Dignified and meaningful prison work has been especially hard to come by since the Great Depression. Today, productive prison labor is almost completely frustrated by chronic unemployment and a more-or-less permanent "surplus population" whose poor job skills make them redundant in a globalized and technologically advanced postindustrial economy. In a throwback to the late feudal period of penal history, harsh and degrading punishments aimed at deterrence are being reintroduced today. This new punitiveness includes a revival in several southern and western states of the highly symbolic slavelike chain gangs.

EARLY HISTORICAL FORMS

Even a cursory examination of ancient slavery can illuminate important facets of contemporary penal practice. Slavery's legacy has weighed heavily on European and American penal systems, directly and indirectly, symbolically and in practice. The earliest forms of penal servitude were chattel slavery and state penal slave systems of antiquity. Penal servitude originated as private exploitation of chattel slaves who were subject to domestic punishments, although it was the state that used penal slavery on a large scale. Ancient Greece, Egypt, and the Roman Empire sentenced war captives and criminals to slavery on public works (*opus publicum* or "public chains"), including mines and quarries, producing a penal serfdom of unimaginable brutality.

The Middle Ages formed a long interregnum between the ancient forms of state slavery and the return of penal labor in early modern Europe. Convict labor exploitation virtually disappeared by the ninth century because the sparsely populated peasant economy and the feudal relations of production were not conducive to forced gang labor. Penance and fines prevailed as official punishments, although vengeance and feud between rough social equals generally made criminal law unimportant in the early Middle Ages.

The rise of capitalism and the growth of population during the late Middle Ages helped to create dramatic class divisions, pauperism, crime, and social unrest. By the late 15th and early 16th centuries, a harsh system of corporal and capital punishment was in place as a deterrent. But what was once abundant became scarce, and compulsory penal labor made a dramatic reappearance with the development of mercantile economy and changing labor market conditions at end of 16th century. The establishment of colonies and the expansion of trade and foreign markets, combined with a dwindling population decimated by wars and disease, put pressure on wages. In the 16th and early 17th centuries, France, Spain, England, and Italy introduced four new basic forms of penal bondage to shore up labor supply: forced labor imprisonment, galley slavery, transportation, and public works. The establishment of London's Bridewell (1556) and Amsterdam's houses of correction (1596) introduced useful labor in confinement to combat labor shortages and wage inflation.

At the same time, to help satisfy its war and empire manpower needs, exploitation of penal labor was a central feature of the Spanish American colonial empire. In the Caribbean, prisoners were a source of coercive labor for private industry until the end of the 18th century, after which convicts were sent to the *presidios* to labor for the state. France, Spain, and England introduced galley slavery as a substitute for death (but which was really a gradual death sentence). Starting in the 17th century, Spain and England began transportation to the American colonies to dispose of surplus populations, and from 1787 to 1867, thousands of men and women petty criminals were transported to Australia.

Early-19th-century France and Spain adopted variants of the Auburn plan of rehabilitation requiring compulsory labor in prison, enabling them to maintain an efficient and productive penal manufacturing systems into the first half of the 19th century. The penitentiary as an alternative to torture and death elsewhere was predicated on labor market conditions favorable to exploiting the economic potential of convicts. Prisons were at least expected to be self-supporting. Unfortunately, labor scarcity would not last beyond the late 18th century. The introduction of labor-saving machinery during the Industrial Revolution and a rapidly growing population created a large pauperized body of unemployed, who drove down wages and made prison industry generally unprofitable.

During the 19th century in England, most prisoners were condemned to work in futility, as sheer torture. Mainly men, although sometimes joined by "ladybirds," these convicts were forced to turn a crank, walk in a treadwheel, or break rock from sunrise to sunset. With its growing "industrial reserve army" and widespread misery, these punishments were designed to deter the masses from crime. By contrast, employers in America suffered a chronic shortage of low-wage industrial workers, and prisons became busy factories. Indenture appeared as early as 1619 to help ease colonial labor shortages. When the British labor market became glutted and crime soared during late 17th century, a trickle turned into torrent of British convicts sent to the labor-starved American colonies. Transportation was an ideal mercantilist solution, allowing the mother country to export its social problems while contributing to colonial economic development.

STAGES IN THE DEVELOPMENT OF U.S. LABOR SYSTEMS

In its various forms—forced or voluntary, useful or futile, for private or public profit—prison labor has been one of the most significant and controversial penal practices of the modern era. Who should control the labor of prisoners? To what ends? Who should benefit from any profits? The type of work system and the prevailing methods of administering prison industry established the basic character of imprisonment in American history.

In his historical sketch of American prison labor policy, Northwestern University economist E. T. Hiller (1914–1915) identified four stages in the development of prison labor control methods based on the shifting nature of legal control, moving from public to private control and back again, with each period spelling a different combination of fortunes for the state, free industry, organized labor, and the prisoner. First is a period of *personal and local control,* based in indenture and personal servitude. From 1661 to 1700, as a substitute for execution, 4,500 men were transported as indentured servants to American colonies. Indenture reached its apex during the 18th century, with 50,000 convicts banished to America during the period 1718 to 1775. The second stage occurred during the rapid industrial development and growth of factory manufacture during the first quarter of the 19th century, which occasioned the Pennsylvania and Auburn prison discipline systems operated under *public control, public account.* Third were the contract, lease, and piece-price systems based in *private control and private account,* during last three-quarters of the 19th century.

The heyday of prison contracting was from 1835 to 1885, during which nearly every northern state adopted the Auburn plan for congregate employment under the private contract system. Auburn style contracting using machine production helped drive out free-world craft production (especially shoe making) in New York, but trade union workers mobilized a stronger resistance. Their complaints gained special resonance with the national depression that followed the Civil War. What was once a duty and a right became a privilege not accorded to prisoners. With the help of free manufacturers and penologists, trade unionists lobbied with increasing effectiveness against the unfair competition of the Auburn contract shops. The Knights of Labor in the 1870s and then the American Federation of Labor in the 1880s exerted considerable political pressure against prison contracting. Businesses representatives in the small manufacturing sector organized "anti-contract" associations, and together labor and business complained of false labeling, dumping, underselling, and false advertising. They were joined by penologists, criminologists, and reformers who decried the brutal treatment, improper management, and gross business interference in prison operations—the many instances of which were copiously documented by various government inquiries, including governmental reports of 1887, 1896, 1905, 1923, 1929, and 1932.

As early as June 13, 1883, the Pennsylvania Legislature became the first to abolish the contract system. The public-account method replaced the contract, but products had to be labeled "convict made." Then in 1897, after a series of late-century depressions destroyed prison markets, the Pennsylvania Legislature passed a law prohibiting machine production of prison-made goods. Elsewhere, union influence was not as powerful, and for disciplinary and revenue reasons other states maintained prison manufacturing but turned to public-account, piece-price (which split employer from supervisory personnel) and state-use systems as efforts to avert objections by penal reformers and business representatives.

In dramatic contrast, the southern states were free of an effective complaining sector regarding prison labor. They were able to maintain convict leasing operations without much opposition until the 1890s, when the spread of agricultural mechanization, the increased costs to lessees of complying with new state regulations, sharper lease bargaining by the state, and the end of the railroad boom culminated in its gradual abolition. In the fourth stage, from the 1900s, prisons moved back to *state-use systems under public control.*

Extending Hiller's 1914–1915 chronology farther into the 20th century demonstrates that state-use systems greatly expanded after the turn of the century to take up the slack from the diminution of contracting after 1905. By 1923, state-use accounted for the largest assignment, followed by public-account systems. By the end of the decade, there was an overall decline in work participation, with only 58% of state and federal prisoners productively employed by the late 1920s: 18% of these prisoner-workers were employed in state-use systems; 29% were working in open-market, state-account systems; 14% were involved in public works; contracting accounted for only about one-fifth of the job assignments; and the rest did institutional maintenance or unclassified work. Contracting was most popular in the Midwest, state-use was preferred in the eastern United States, and public works prevailed in the South, particularly in road building and agriculture.

The final blow to productive prison labor in the North came with the stock market crash. The passage of the Hawes-Cooper Act of 1929 terminated contract and piece-price systems in 17 northern or border states. By 1940, only 44% of state and federal prisoners were productively employed. With the exception of Federal Prison Industries, contract labor and other free-market industry did not survive the post–World War II period, and state-use production became an economic irrelevance and parody of free-world industry. This situation is the essence of the "less eligibility" principle that has influenced prison policy since its inception. Attributed to the 18th and early 19th century British philosopher Jeremy Bentham, the less eligibility principle states that the living conditions in prisons should never be more desirable (or "eligible") than the living situation for the poorest free person. This is a pretty straightforward dictum, and would be the bedrock of deterrence theory, except that the living conditions of the lowest social stratum historically have been so abysmal that a paradox immediately presented itself: On the one hand, popular sentiment demands that robbers and thieves be set to hard labor for public benefit, yet there is suspicion that this activity might in itself be a reward and construed as a privilege by prisoners.

POSTWAR CORRECTIONALISM SUPPLANTS WORK REGIMES

While the abolition of the lease system made little difference in the work lives of southern prisoners, elsewhere the demise of meaningful prison industry had tremendously deleterious consequences for convict morale and prison administration. From the early 19th century, prison reformers and penologists attacked the corruption and bribery of contractors and their foremen and complained that rehabilitation in general was being neglected in favor of production and profit. Criticism focused on the stint and overwork system, which allowed prisoners to work for their own small profit ("overwork") once they met the "stint," or daily quota set by the entrepreneur. This arrangement was perhaps not as bad as reformers made it out to be; it

Photo 1   *Prisoners work in Soledad State Prison, California*

at least had the virtue of being realistic, giving prisoner-workers a little bargaining muscle and control over the production process and in most cases setting limits on coercion. Without prison labor, institutional authorities had even less occasion to take notice of prisoners as individuals, furthering their objectification. The move from "hard labor" to "hard time" in the post-Depression era forced prison administrators to overhaul their management practices. Always authoritarian, prison wardens had to rely much more on pure regimentation, epitomized by the Big House of 1930s and 1940s. After a series postwar riots over intolerable conditions, rehabilitation programming based largely on the medical model was introduced.

From the 1950s on, midwestern and eastern states operated various institutional industries as vocational training, such as stamping license plates, manufacturing furniture, and making clothing for state use. In the South, prison farms accounted for the bulk of job assignments. Obviously, these work systems had little rehabilitative potential: While southern convicts were picking cotton by hand, their northern counterparts were struggling with obsolete shop equipment, antiquated technology, and irrelevant training, and their shops were generally unproductive and inefficient.

This dismal state of affairs was challenged in the 1970s by a group of penal reformers, backed by a national privatization movement and Congressional legislation in 1979 that created the Prison Industry Enhancement (PIE) program to "normalize" prison industry. This act sought to create a "realistic" work environment for prisoner-workers in self-supporting and profit-making businesses. The "factories with fences" concept of incarceration, promoted by U.S. Supreme Court Chief Justice Warren Burger and by former Attorney General Edwin Meese III, was legally enabled by passage of the "Percy amendment" to the Ashurst-Sumners Act of 1940 permitting conditional exception to the federal prohibition on interstate commerce in prison-made products. A precursor to the PIE program, the Law Enforcement Assistance Administration–funded Free Venture Prison Industries Program advanced innovative strategies in Minnesota, Illinois, and Connecticut. The Carter and Reagan administrations were very hospitable to privatization, and a number of states quickly followed under PIE certification.

By the 1990s, many southern and western states embraced private contracting, mostly in various Joint Venture forms meant to "repatriate" jobs lost to foreign competition (trying to find products for prisoners to produce that were primarily imported is an idea that goes back to the late 19th century). The economic boom of the late 1990s inspired a renewed initiative to privatize prison industry under various "repatriation" schemes. However, the privatization movement has collided with a deep recession that opened the 21st century. Coupled with the continued flight of manufacturing industries to cheaper foreign production sites, prison industrial privatization is again threatened with extinction. The acceleration of global competitiveness and the growing use of technology encourage large-scale factory relocations, downsizing, and a nationwide shift to lower-paying nonunion service industries. Millions of prime working-age blacks, Latinos, and poor whites have been unable or unwilling to make the labor market adjustment and are ending up in the prison circuit. Today, in the postindustrial United States, the poorly skilled face permanent exclusion from the work force, and therefore it would be difficult to see what occupational training a prison work system could have in the 21st century. For the foreseeable future, prisons will remain warehouses for the castoffs of the market economy.

WOMEN'S LABOR

Women have been forced to work at prison labor since the origins of the European workhouse, and American women have been required to work since the opening of the penitentiary house of the Walnut Street Jail in 1798. In the 19th-century prison, women were set to customary "female" tasks that emphasized women's traditional role in domestic occupations, sewing, spinning, weaving, cooking, and laundry. Vocational education was added during the women's reformatory movement, but it still focused on home economy. Today, the most meaningful and promising (in terms of postrelease preparation) occupational activities are on behalf of various joint venture commercial and industrial enterprises. While women at various state prison joint ventures work in light manufacturing, including computer chip production, they also work in telemarketing, airline reservations, data processing, and textile production and garment manufacturing.

Jostens, Inc. has a production facility at the Leath Correctional Facility in Laurens, South Carolina, where women perform the traditional work of sewing, inspecting, and packaging college graduation gowns. Third Generation and the Chesapeake Cap company in Somers, Connecticut, are other such companies that have chosen prisoner workers over off-shore production. One of the largest prison production systems to employ women is the PRIDE Enterprises of Florida, whose Broward Correctional Institution facility employs 54 maximum-security inmates in its Broward optical laboratory. The nation's largest women's penal facility, Valley State Prison for Women in California, focuses on work programming and has a Joint Venture Prison Industry work programming initiative that employs hundreds of prisoners in dry cleaning, office services, automotive repair, cabinetmaking, printings and graphic arts, and welding, as well as state-use employment in farm operation, eyewear manufacturing, laundry, and janitorial work. But women, like men, overall are not receiving the training and experience necessary to compete in the modern labor market.

CONCLUSION: CONTEMPORARY ISSUES AND FUTURE PROSPECTS

Overproduction and a surfeit of low-wage workers discourage meaningful employment or vocational training for prisoners throughout the world, not just in advanced market economies. While China and Japan maintain compulsory unpaid hard-labor systems (more for cultural or political than economic reasons), countries of the former Soviet Union abandoned after 1989 prison industries that gainfully employed nearly every able-bodied prisoner and have turned to warehousing them instead, often under the most deplorable conditions. Poland is a prime example. Under the Soviet regime, prison labor was an important element in Poland's planned economy, helping the central government to meet production targets while preparing convicts for social reintegration. Poland's once industrious prisons went from over 90% employment prior to the 1989 fall of communism to over 70% idleness today. Under their incipient free-market democracy, Polish citizens echo the centuries-old sentiment of

U.S. workers: "Why should criminals work when the law-abiding are unemployed?"

Prison labor is both oppressive and liberating. While liberals fret about exploitation and free-labor competition, meaningful work is absolutely vital to humane incarceration. The Scandinavian nations, whose prisons are models of free-labor equivalence, have grasped this insight. On the other hand, there are other schemes to integrate prison labor into the free market that are very controversial, most recently Mexico's program to get U.S. companies to open *maquiladora* workshops in prisons to assemble imported parts for duty-free export. Although U.S. laws ban the importation of goods made with prison labor, national news organizations have reported that prison-manufactured furniture has been shipped to Texas customers and that several other American companies have shown interest. Prison officials argue that prison maquiladoras will help stem the loss to Asia of foreign-owned assembly plants while training prisoners for factory jobs. The impact of these sweatshops on free labor in the United States and Mexico is obvious. But today's globalization gives the prison labor problem a new twist: U.S. prisoner-workers are in danger of losing jobs to even cheaper foreign prison labor (which at least is no loss to Texas prisoners, who are unpaid anyway). Just as the merchant-capitalist's quest for cheap labor in the prison shops initiated the Auburn system, today's contractors and subcontractors would be the handmaidens of a post-Fordist prison labor strategy of global competition.

—*Robert P. Weiss*

See also Ashurst-Sumners Act; Auburn System; Hard Labor; Hawes-Cooper Act; History of Prisons; Prison Industry Enhancement (PIE) Certification Program; Privatization of Labor; UNICOR; Vocational Training Programs; Walnut Street Jail; Womens's Prisons

Further Reading

Barnes, H. E. (1921). The economics of American penology as illustrated by the experience of the state of Pennsylvania. *Journal of Political Economy, 29*(8), 617–642.

Gildemeister, G. A. (1987). *Prison labor and convict competition with free workers in industrializing America, 1840–1890.* New York: Garland.

Gill, H. B. (1931). The prison labor problem. *The Annals, 157,* 83–101.

Grünhut, M. (1948/1972). Prison labor. In M. Grünhut, *Penal reform: A comparative study* (Chap. 9). Montclair, NJ: Patterson-Smith.

Hiller, E. T. (1914–1915, July). Development of the systems of control of convict labor in the United States. *Journal of the American Institute of Criminal Law and Criminology, 5,* 241–269.

Matthews, R. (1999). *Doing time: An introduction to the sociology of punishment.* London: Macmillan.

O'Brien, P. (1982). *The promise of punishment: Prisons in nineteenth-century France.* Princeton, NJ: Princeton University Press.

Parenti, C. (1999). *Lockdown America.* New York: Verso.

Rusche, G., & Kirchheimer, O. (1968). *Punishment and social structure.* New York: Russell & Russell. (Original work published 1939)

Sellin, T. (1965, October). Penal servitude: Origin and survival. *Proceedings of the American Philosophical Society, 109*(5), 277–281.

U.S. Commissioner of Labor. (1887). *Second annual report, 1886: Convict labor.* Washington, DC: U.S. Government Printing Office.

U.S. Industrial Commission. (1900). *Report . . . on prison labor.* Washington, DC: U.S. Government Printing Office.

U.S. Industrial Commission. (1923). *Report . . . on prison labor.* Washington, DC: U.S. Government Printing Office.

Van Zyl Smit, D., & Dunkel, F. (Eds.). (1999). *Prison labour: Salvation or slavery?* Aldershot, UK: Ashgate.

Weiss, R. P. (2001). "Repatriating" low-wage work: The political economy of prison labor reprivatization in the postindustrial United States. *Criminology, 39*(2), 253–291.

◪ LAWYER'S VISITS

Legal visitation enjoys special protections not afforded to social prison visits. The right to consult with one's lawyer is safeguarded by the attorney-client privilege and by the constitutionally recognized right of unrestricted access to the courts. While prison administrators may regulate lawyers' visits, confidential legal communication is a fundamental right, and any impositions placed on lawyers by prison officials must be reasonable. Recent antiterrorism legislation passed in the wake of the September 11, 2001, terrorist attacks in New York and Washington, D.C., however, has created significant exceptions to the typical right to confidential legal communications in the United States.

DERIVATION OF THE RIGHT TO A LAWYER'S VISIT

The right to consult with one's lawyer is derived from two sources: the doctrine of attorney-client privilege and the provisions of several constitutional amendments. The attorney-client privilege—the law's recognition that confidential attorney-client communications are necessary to promote full and frank disclosure and to foster effective advocacy—is the oldest recognized privilege in Anglo American common law. Because unrestricted communication between client and attorney is so fundamental to legal institutions, the attorney-client privilege extends to all legal correspondence, telephone calls, and visits—even in correctional settings. Until the September 11 terrorist attacks, all U.S. prisoners enjoyed the right to unencumbered communication with their attorneys; subsequent antiterrorism provisions, however, have authorized the monitoring of attorney-client communication in limited cases.

The right to meet with one's lawyer is also assured by the First, Fourth, Fifth, and Sixth Amendments of the U.S. Constitution. The First Amendment guarantees that the federal government "shall make no law . . . abridging the freedom of speech . . . and to petition the Government for a redress of grievances." The U.S. Supreme Court held in *Pell v. Procunier* that prisoners retain those First Amendment rights not inconsistent with their status as inmates or with the legitimate penological objectives of the corrections system. The Court further held in *Bounds v. Smith* that incarcerated individuals retain a right of access to the courts, inherent in which is the ability to seek and obtain the effective assistance of counsel. To be effective, lawyers must be able to communicate freely with their clients, by letter, telephone, or visit.

The Fourth Amendment ensures "the right of the people . . . against unreasonable searches and seizures." If an individual has an expectation of privacy that society would objectively recognize as reasonable, the government must obtain a warrant from a magistrate to conduct a search or seizure. Although the Supreme Court has concluded that prisoners have no reasonable expectation of privacy from searches in their cells, the Court has suggested that confidential relationships may be protected. In other words, because it could reasonably be expected that attorney-client communications were private, the "seizure" of privileged attorney-client conversations would typically violate the Fourth Amendment.

The Fifth Amendment of the U.S. Constitution guarantees that no person shall be "deprived of life, liberty, or property, without due process of law." Lower courts have construed this due process guarantee as including the right to have the effective aid of counsel. Because confidential communication lies at the heart of effective counsel, under the Fifth Amendment, lawyers must be free to communicate with their clients by letter, telephone, or visit. Legal communications may be monitored under new antiterrorism provisions (and are therefore no longer confidential under these circumstances), but even those individuals detained under antiterrorism regulations still retain the right to communicate with their attorneys.

The Sixth Amendment provides that "in all criminal prosecutions, the accused shall enjoy the right . . . to have the Assistance of Counsel for his defense." This right is so fundamental to the justice system that if the accused is indigent and facing a felony conviction or a misdemeanor conviction for which he or she could be jailed, the government must provide him or her with counsel. While there is no equivalent constitutional right to postconviction or postappeal counsel, prisoners who succeed in securing independent legal representation are protected by Sixth Amendment safeguards. The government cannot directly interfere with their attorney-client relationship, and except when authorized by antiterrorism provisions, their legal communications must remain free and unrestricted.

THE REGULATION OF LAWYER'S VISITS

Prison administrators must—above all else—maintain safe and secure correctional facilities, and they are accordingly allowed to regulate the visits of both jailhouse and licensed lawyers to realize that legitimate objective. However, under the doctrine of attorney-client privilege and Supreme Court precedent, all clients—even those who are incarcerated—enjoy largely unrestricted communication with their attorneys. U.S. courts have extended the right of access to attorneys to include (limited) access to public officials and advocacy organizations (such as the American Civil Liberties Union). This right of unrestricted legal communication does not, however, extend to communication with jailhouse lawyers. Because inmates who assist fellow inmates with their legal claims are not licensed officers of the courts and because they present unique security risks, they are not afforded the same relatively unchecked communication conferred on licensed professional attorneys.

Lawyers visiting incarcerated clients may face a number of administrative barriers: restrictive visiting hours, searches of attorneys and inmates, inspection of legal documents, or facilities that compromise lawyer-client confidentiality. U.S. courts have consistently held that lawyers must have access to their clients at reasonable times, and correctional institutions must attempt to accommodate them for extended periods and during evening visits when immediate client consultation is required. Lawyers are not, however, entitled to limitless visits, and hours may be limited or advance notice required. Even so, legal visits cannot be limited to the same extent that social visits may be. Any restrictions imposed by the prison must be reasonable and flexible.

It is generally permissible for both prisoners and lawyers to be searched prior to and after visits, but there are Fourth Amendment limits to these searches. While most courts have upheld pat-down searches for lawyers, other courts—finding no evidence of improper attorney conduct and emphasizing lawyers' professional status—have concluded that even a pat-down search is unjustified (e.g., *State ex rel. McCamic v. McCoy*, 1981). Searches cannot be so invasive that they deter attorney-client visiting. Requiring California lawyer Charles Lindner to remove his prosthetic leg before meeting with his incarcerated client was unreasonable (Goldberg, 1996), and subjecting an inmate to a body-cavity

search after each meeting with his attorney unconstitutionally restricted the inmate's right of access to the courts (*Sims v. Brierton*, 1980).

While a visiting attorney's legal documents may be visually inspected for contraband, correctional officials cannot read the contents. These materials are protected by the same attorney-client privilege that prohibits guards from reading legal mail or monitoring attorney-client telephone conversations.

The attorney-client privilege also mandates the confidentiality of visits. Officials are not required to provide an absolutely private room, but unless the client is one of the prisoners affected by antiterrorism regulations, prison administrators may not listen to or monitor legal conversations. Courts have held the presence of guards four feet away from a legal visit or a partitioned room that requires conversing at a level loud enough to be overheard to be unconstitutional. Lawyers are also generally entitled to contact visits. While noncontact social visits may be justified by security and contraband considerations, these concerns are less pronounced in visits with legal professionals. Noncontact visits impair the formation of the attorney-client relationship, making meetings impersonal and frustrating the attorney's efforts to assess a client's demeanor and credibility.

RECENT U.S. DEVELOPMENTS

In the past few years, significant exceptions to the attorney-client privilege have been enacted. On October 31, 2001, the U.S. attorney general promulgated a new amendment to the Code of Federal Regulations (C.F.R.) authorizing the Bureau of Prisons to monitor attorney-client communications in those cases where the attorney general has "reasonable suspicion" to "believe that a particular inmate may use communications with attorneys or their agents to further or facilitate acts of violence or terrorism." The order recognizes that these communications would "traditionally be covered by the attorney-client privilege."

Although the change to the C.F.R. includes procedural safeguards such as the use of "privilege teams" (prison personnel not involved in the investigation of the client), critics have noted that the amendment permits the Justice Department to decide unilaterally when to monitor the conversations of a person the Justice Department itself may be seeking to prosecute, with no form of judicial oversight. Furthermore, civil libertarians have noted that the regulations extend not only to convicted prisoners but also to anyone in the Bureau of Prison's jurisdiction, including pretrial detainees, people being held for immigration violations, and even witnesses who have not been charged with a crime.

Many attorneys involved with clients affected by the order have adopted an absolute "no phone conversations" rule, conduct their in-person conversations in whispers, and feel undermined by the abridgment of the attorney-client privilege. At least one attorney has been prosecuted under similar regulations. On April 8, 2002, Defense Attorney Lynne Stewart was arrested and indicted on four counts of aiding and abetting a terrorist organization. Stewart's prosecution is based on monitored conversations with her client, Sheik Omar Abdel-Rahman. If convicted, 62-year-old Stewart faces 40 years in prison.

CONCLUSION

Lawyer's visits, safeguarded by the attorney-client privilege and several constitutional amendments, enjoy protections not afforded to social visits. Prison officials may regulate attorney-client communications (including visits) but must maintain the inmate's right of access to the courts. Recent antiterrorism provisions have abridged the attorney-client privilege in some cases.

—J. C. Oleson

See also Contraband; First Amendment; Fourth Amendment; Jailhouse Lawyers; Prisoner Litigation; USA PATRIOT Act 2001; Visits

Further Reading

American Bar Association. (1981). *Standards for criminal justice: Legal status of prisoners* (2nd ed.). Washington, DC: Author.

Edwards, J. (2002, August 12). Struggling to keep client confidences: Lawyers in post–Sept. 11 "special interest" cases talk about how they are coping with often-intrusive government security measures. *New Jersey Law Journal*, 4.

Goldberg, D. (1996, September 12). Demand to remove artificial leg is found unreasonable. *Los Angeles Daily Journal*, 1.

Merritt, F. (1981). Corrections law developments: Attorney access to correctional institutions. *Criminal Law Bulletin, 17*, 607–613.

Palmer, J. W., & Palmer, S. E. (1999). *Constitutional rights of prisoners* (6th ed.). Cincinnati, OH: Anderson.

Legal Cases

Bounds v. Smith, 430 U.S. 817 (1977).
Pell v. Procunier, 417 U.S. 817 (1974).
Sims v. Brierton, 500 F. Supp. 813, 817 (N.D. Ill. 1980).
State ex rel. McCamic v. McCoy, 276 S.E.2d 534 (1981).

◾ LEAVENWORTH, U.S. PENITENTIARY

The United States Penitentiary (USP) Leavenworth is located just west of Kansas City, Kansas. The penitentiary, known as the "big top" or "hothouse," is the oldest and most famous USP. It is the flagship and geographic center of the Federal Bureau of Prisons. This maximum-security prison covers 1,583 acres with 22.8 acres inside the wall.

THE WALL

The prison walls are 35 feet high and extend 35 feet into the ground to prevent tunneling. They are 12 feet wide and protected by six gun towers, electric wire, and razor wire fences (a continuous stainless steel ribbon of razor blade). The stone walls are colored purple with day-glow paint that is reported to cover the clothes of escaping prisoners. The penitentiary is constructed of stone, concrete, and steel. For those men living inside these walls, there is no view of grass or trees. The sun rises late in the morning and sets early in the evening behind the walls.

CELLBLOCKS

This penitentiary can hold as many as 2,000 prisoners in four cell houses (A, B, C, D), each of which consists of five tiers stacked to a 150-foot-high ceiling. A fifth is dedicated to detainees, who are mostly Cubans held on immigration laws. A sixth is the Special Housing Unit (SHU) that confines prisoners for administrative detention and disciplinary segregation. This is also referred to as the "hole." Leavenworth has no air-conditioning in the cellblocks. The cell houses are also freezing cold in winter, with ice on the floor and walls.

THE CONVICTS

Leavenworth is a "mainline" maximum-security penitentiary that houses older prisoners (at least 26 years old) serving long sentences. The official rated capacity is approximately 1,200 convicts, with the daily count usually exceeding this by at least 50%. The prison population is diverse, including mafia gangsters, drug cartel soldiers, bikers, "hit men," political prisoners, and career criminals. Perhaps as a result, Leavenworth is known for the advanced training in criminal occupations that is available from old cons, including bank robbery, securities fraud, and counterfeiting currency.

HISTORY

Leavenworth was the first federal penitentiary. Construction began in 1895, when military prisoners were marched two and one-half miles from Fort Leavenworth to the site. The first prisoners occupied the prison in 1903. The construction of the prison took more than 30 years, with the dome added in 1926, and the shoe factory in 1928. The use of forced convict labor to build the penitentiary complicated and delayed the work. The prisoners also built and worked in the on-site sawmill, brick plant, and stone quarry used to fabricate construction materials. The entire construction site was enclosed in a heavy wood fence to prevent convict escapes.

CONVICT UNIFORMS

The early prisoners wore convict stripes. These were replaced in 1927 with dark-blue cotton uniforms. Following World War II, the prisoners were "dressed out" in worn out military fatigues. In recent years, the men have been issued kaki shirts and pants, and green army coats. The most famous apparel is the "Leavenworth boot," manufactured on site and consisting of a high-top shoe, brown on one side and black on the other. The unique color scheme was designed to identify convicts if they made it over the wall.

FEDERAL PRISON INDUSTRIES

Leavenworth operates the largest UNICOR factory operation in the federal prison system. Over the years, Leavenworth industries have produced many items for sale to government and the military, including shoes, paint, brushes, mailbags, and uniforms and mattresses at the satellite camp. The operation is so large the prison has its own UNICOR train parked on a railroad siding at the rear gate that may be used to deliver materials to the prison and production output to distance customers.

Today, UNICOR at Leavenworth includes three factories—textiles, furniture, and print—each of which, respectively produces, prison uniforms and sheets; wood and metal office chairs, desks, and bookcases; and government forms and documents. These factories employ over half of the convict population and generate tens of millions in sales and profits. In 2001, the furniture factory produced $12,168,920 in sales with a profit total of $1,254,056. The textile operation produced $6,340,082 in sales and $42,345 in profit. And the print shop produced $4,288,029 in sales with $1,210,808 in profit.

Prisoners employed at UNICOR receive better wages than those who work in food service, custodial duties (mopping floors, painting, cleaning cell houses), or grounds keeping (shoveling walks, cutting grass). These higher wages, which can reach $200 a month for "super grade pay" and overtime, allow the prisoners to purchase what they need at the commissary (prison store), pay for long-distance phone calls, send money home to their families, and save funds to support themselves when they return home upon release ("gate money").

More than 60 staff manage the factories at Leavenworth. They are also considered to be correctional officers (what convicts call "hacks"). These UNICOR officers wear a gray industrial type uniform that sets them apart from the mainline custodial personnel, who wear the standard uniform of gray pants, white shirt, blue blazer, and red tie. Women officers wear the same uniforms.

FEDERAL PRISON CAMP

Like many federal penitentiaries (maximum security) and correctional institutions (medium security), Leavenworth has a minimum-security camp. The Federal Prison Camp (FPC) Leavenworth, opened in 1960, is located outside the main walls and enclosed in its own fence. The facility was designed for 400, although it usually houses more in six dormitories. In general, camp prisoners are used to maintain the "prison reservation" (the grounds surrounding the penitentiary) and may be used as work crews repairing plumbing, air-conditioning in staff offices, and other maintenance inside the wall.

CONCLUSION

Leavenworth is the first and most famous federal penitentiary. Today, Leavenworth remains the center of a Federal Bureau of Prisons that has expanded to more than 160,000 prisoners and 102 institutions. Although many new maximum-security prisons have been built, none of them compare with the storied history of Leavenworth.

—*Stephen C. Richards and Jeffrey Ian Ross*

See also Jack Henry Abbott; ADX (Administrative Maximum): Florence; Auburn Correctional Facility; Corcoran, California State Prison; Correctional Officers; Federal Prison System; History of Prisons; Labor; Marion, U.S. Penitentiary; Maximum Security; Medium Security; Minimum Security; Prison Camp; San Quentin State Prison; Supermax Prisons; UNICOR

Further Reading

Abbott, J. H. (1981). *In the belly of the beast: Letters from prison.* New York: Random House.

Earley, P. (1993). *Hot house: Life inside Leavenworth Prison.* New York: Bantam.

Keve, P. W. (1991). *Prisons and the American conscience: A history of federal corrections.* Carbondale: Southern Illinois University Press.

Richards, S. C. (1990). The sociological penetration of the American gulag. *Wisconsin Sociologist, 27*(4), 18–28.

Roberts, J. W. (Ed.). (1994). *Escaping prison myths: Selected topics in the history of federal corrections.* Washington, DC: American University Press.

Ross, J. I., & Richards, S. C. (2002a). *Behind bars: Surviving prison.* New York: Alpha.

Ross, J. I., & Richards, S. C. (Eds.). (2002b). *Convict criminology.* Belmont, CA: Wadsworth.

U.S. Department of Justice. (2004). Federal Bureau of Prisons home page. Retrieved from http://www.bop.gov/

☑ LEGITIMACY

Prisons are places of great power inequalities. Rarely, however, does order have to be maintained within them through the overt use of force or weaponry. Though riots and other forms of violence do occur with some regularity in U.S. prisons, for the most part, everyday life goes on without such dramatic events; most prisoners follow most rules, most of the time.

In recent years, criminologists have explained this paradox that despite being held against their will, the majority of prisoners voluntarily submit to the rules or commands of prison officials, through the idea of legitimacy. According to these scholars, all institutions, including prisons, are best at regulating behavior when participants believe in their rules and accept their legitimacy. Prisoners must, in other words, believe that the commands, rules, and supervision of the prison staff are, overall, morally sound and fairly implemented. From this perspective, legitimacy operates as an important but subtle form of power that maintains a consensus between superiors and subordinates.

Nonetheless, scholars recognize that prison administrators and correctional staff face an uphill battle at building legitimacy. By design, correctional institutions are coercive environments in which a wide power disparity separates captors from captives. As a result, some wonder whether it is really possible to build legitimate authority when holding individuals against their will. In this view, prisoner compliance is based primarily on submission to force rather than legitimate authority. Prisons reduce disorder best by investing in surveillance mechanisms, limiting prisoners' individual due process rights, and reducing situational opportunities to engage in misconduct. This entry explores both sides of this debate about how order is maintained in prison.

BUILDING LEGITIMATE AUTHORITY

The overall number of prisoners, particularly when compared to officers, makes it difficult to maintain order based solely on a Hobbesian model of surveillance and force. There are simply too many prisoners in any facility to control them all through coercion and physical control alone. Thus, staff must somehow persuade inmates to want to follow the rules on their own free will. To do this, prison administrators and other correctional staff attempt to enforce discipline and order in such a way that (1) the rules can be defended through political and moral arguments, (2) administrator and staff authority is exerted consistently and fairly based on a set principles, and (3) administrators and staff recognize prisoners' citizenship and humanity.

In large part, views about legitimacy rest on beliefs about the causes of disorder within prisons. If disorder is assumed to result from a few antisocial individuals who cause trouble and lead others into noncompliant behavior, then a security model that limits prisoners' movements and ability to congregate logically follows. But if disorder is understood instead to be a group phenomenon—as the result of widespread perceived injustice—then attempts to build legitimacy would be the more reasonable response.

In *Prisons and the Problem of Order,* criminologists Richard Sparks, Anthony Bottoms, and Will Hay (1996) tested the assumption that legitimate authority was more efficient at securing order than force and sanctions by comparing the regimes of two English prisons. One institution relied on a situational crime prevention model, in which prisoners' movements were rigidly restricted (termed here

a *security model*). The other attempted to limit noncompliance by allowing prisoners greater mobility and autonomy (*legitimacy model*). While there were greater rates of minor noncompliance in the prison operating according to a legitimacy model, there also were fewer major disturbances. The researchers conclude that recognizing the need to improve social conditions helped build legitimate authority and thereby maintained order more efficiently than a security-only model.

RACE AND GENDER

Complicating matters, perceptions of injustice and legitimacy can vary based on gender and race. Women may interpret how they are governed differently than men. Because of gendered expectations, they may be more used to talking through decisions, rather than having rules anonymously applied. Likewise, prisoners of color may respond differently to officers of color.

Although not specifically concerned with race or gender, recent research by social psychologist Tom Tyler provides indirect support for the view that deference to authority and perceptions of legitimacy can vary by social location. In particular, Tyler examined why people voluntarily accept decisions made by legal authorities such as police and judges. He argued that community members will generally be satisfied with decisions made by legal authorities if two conditions are met: if they perceive that the procedures used to arrive at the decision are fair (referred to as procedural justice), and if they believe that the motives underlying the decision are benevolent (called motive-based trust). Tyler and Huo (2002) demonstrated that perceptions of procedural fairness and motive-based trust can vary by social group. For example, racial minorities may be more likely than whites to report that they are treated unfairly by the police, and less willing than whites to comply with directives from police officers.

POTENTIAL FUTURE PROBLEMS

Several recent trends in imprisonment have the potential to affect prison administrators' ability to build legitimate authority. Sentencing laws have increasingly limited the discretion of prisons and parole boards in deciding on release dates of prisoners. Laws such as "three strikes and you're out" that mandate life in prison without parole, and fixed sentencing regimes that do away with "good time" credits, limit the ability of correctional professionals to reward prisoners with time off for good behavior. As the powerful incentive of reduced time in prison becomes less available, it is possible that prisoners will be frustrated by fewer positive reinforcements for compliance and grow to perceive prison authority as less legitimate.

Another potentially problematic trend is the increasing use of private prisons. It remains to be seen whether the delivery of services and discipline in private prisons will suffer over the long term as private companies focus on building profits in addition to maintaining order. If private prison administrators attempt to save money by reducing rehabilitative or recreational services, or by lowering standards for security officers' training and qualifications, then they may run the risk of decreasing prisoners' perceptions of legitimacy in these prisons.

CONCLUSION

The concept of legitimacy refers to whether penal authority is just with regard to rules, delivery of services, and punishments. The key issue is not whether prisons are pleasant environments but whether prison administrators and correctional staff act fairly, consistently, and according to morally and politically defendable criteria.

Many believe that large-scale disorders such as riots are the result of groups of inmates reacting to unfair prison conditions, rather than the actions of a few dangerous prisoners. Thus, efforts to maintain legitimate authority, when coupled with efficient security practices, may help maintain order. Recent research supports this claim. Others, however, suggest that legitimacy is far less important than a prison's security climate and that limiting prisoner movement and privacy will help maintain order more efficiently.

—Aaron Kupchik and Joseph De Angelis

See also Actuarial Justice; Attica Correctional Facility; Correctional Officers; John J. DiIulio, Jr.; Good Time Credit; Governance; Managerialism; Privatization; Resistance; Riots; Security and Control; Violence; Women's Prisons

Further Reading

Beetham, D. (1991). *The legitimation of power.* London: Macmillan.

DiIulio, J. J., Jr. (1987). *Governing prisons: A comparative study of correctional management.* New York: Free Press.

Jacobs, J. (1976). *Stateville: The penitentiary in mass society.* Chicago: University of Chicago Press.

Sparks, R., & Bottoms, A. E. (1995). Legitimacy and order in prisons. *British Journal of Sociology, 46*(1), 45–62.

Sparks, R., Bottoms, A., & Hay, W. (1996). *Prisons and the problem of order.* Oxford, UK: Clarendon.

Sykes, G. M. (1958). *The society of captives: A study of a maximum security prison.* Princeton, NJ: Princeton University Press.

Tyler, T. R., & Huo, Y. J. (2002). *Trust in the law: Encouraging public cooperation with the police and courts.* New York: Russell Sage Foundation.

Weber, M. (1968). *Economy and society.* Berkeley: University of California Press.

◪ LESBIAN PRISONERS

Some women in prison form sexual and intimate relationships with one another. These sexual relationships may be consensual or forced. Lesbian prisoners may or may not have identified as homosexual prior to their experiences of incarceration. Though relatively little research exists on this topic, that which does speaks to issues surrounding prison culture; race, class, and gender; and the effects of imprisonment.

HISTORY

Until recently, relatively little was known about the history of lesbian prisoners because criminologists rarely studied them, and officials usually failed to mention them. However, recent historical studies along with some earlier primary source material document the presence of lesbians in penal institutions from at least the 19th century.

According to historian Estelle Freedman (1996), the first women to be identified as prison lesbians were predominantly African American. Ideas about race and gender intersected in the body of the prison lesbian, as black women were thought to be more masculine (and more criminal) than white women. Ideas of race and gender tended to prompt officials to report intimate relations between their female charges only when they were interracial. In particular, early-20th-century prison staff were concerned about the possible "contamination" of white women by predatory black inmates.

It was not until after World War II, Freedman reports, that white working-class prisoners became associated with an image of aggressive female homosexuality and that prison sociologists began studying women's sexual relationships behind bars. In response, prison wardens began to implement policies to control lesbian sexual relations in the institutions. Freedman determined that the greater attention afforded to prison lesbianism by scholars was based on the fear that the increase in prostitution arrests would lead to increased incidents of lesbian acts within the prison. Though researchers in the 1960s who studied issues of women in prison paid a considerable amount of attention to sexual relationships among women inmates, currently, criminologists tend to favor instead a more general study of women's lives in prison overall.

DEMOGRAPHICS

There are no reliable and consistent statistics on the incidence of homosexual activity among women inmates, or even data for similar relationships between male prisoners. Various studies suggest that anywhere between 2% and 65% of female and male inmates participate in consensual sexual relationships, while between 1% and 28% have admitted to being victims of coerced sex.

Research shows that lesbians tend to be given lengthier sentences than heterosexual women. They also experience more incidents of incarceration and have an earlier onset into the criminal justice system. Lesbians in prison are more likely to adhere to inmate subculture norms and exhibit higher levels of conflict with the administration. As a result, they are more likely to be written up for disciplinary

infractions. Finally, some research suggests that they are more likely to hold feminist beliefs and support of the idea of gender equality, both within and outside of the prison.

LESBIAN RELATIONSHIPS

Many women in lesbian relationships in prison identify as heterosexual prior to their confinement and may return to their heterosexual relationships upon their release. For these women, their relationships in prison may provide an entirely new experience and a particular means of coping with incarceration.

Though many of the sexual relationships between prisoners are based on companionship, support, and affection, not all sexual relationships among women are consensual and egalitarian. Nonconsensual, violent sexual acts may be perpetrated by women prisoners against other women prisoners. When a woman is raped in an all-female prison, there are typically multiple perpetrators involved. This situation is frequently exacerbated by the failure of correctional officers to respond to known sexual coercion and sexual assault among women prisoners. Even so, it is evident that such abuse occurs at a significantly lesser rate than in men's prisons and that women in prison remain more at risk from male officers than from one another.

Many intimate relationships in prison form between members of different racial or ethnic groups. In recent studies, African American women have been found to have higher rates of homosexual activity in prison and are more likely take on a "masculine" role that is characterized by aggression, leadership, power, and control within the relationship.

Finally, prison researchers have sometimes found that women inmates form "families" among the prison population in the United States. Members of the family play the roles of a traditional heterosexual family: mother, father, daughter, son, and so on. Each inmate is assigned one of these roles, either formally or informally. These individuals also connect to other family units who would be regarded as extended family members playing such roles as cousin, niece, and so on. Those playing the "daddy" function tend to present a stereotypical masculine persona.

CONCLUSION

Though lesbianism in prisons is not unique, the relationship dynamics among women prisoners are quite distinctive. Many women seek out constructive alliances to assist with adapting to prison life. This includes forming lesbian relationships, which may be part of make-believe families. Though some women identify as lesbian prior to entering prison, more appear to participate in homosexual relationships during their imprisonment, and return to heterosexuality upon their release. Some of the relationships formed among women prisoners are volatile, yet overall, these relationships are based more on companionship and affection than on sexual contact.

Prison lesbianism has been of interest to prison researchers for some time, but our understanding and awareness of these relationships and the extent to which they exist are considerably deficient. Relationships among female inmates, whether consensual or coerced, sexual or nonsexual, continue to be an important aspect of women's prison life. Accordingly, more research is certainly necessary in this area.

—*Hillary Potter*

See also Bisexual Prisoners; Deprivation; HIV/AIDS; Homosexual Prisoners; Importation; Lesbian Relationships; Prison Culture; Resistance; Sex—Consensual; Women in Prison

Further Reading

Freedman, E. B. (1996). The prison lesbian: Race, class, and the construction of the aggressive female homosexual, 1915–1965. *Feminist Studies, 22*(2), 397–424.

Giallombardo, R. (1966). *Society of women: A study of a women's prison*. New York: John Wiley.

Greer, K. R. (2000). The changing nature of interpersonal relationships in a women's prison. *The Prison Journal, 80*(4), 442–468.

Hart, L. (1994). *Fatal women: Lesbian sexuality and the mark of aggression*. Princeton, NJ: Princeton University Press.

Hensley, C. (2000). Attitudes toward homosexuality in a male and female prison: An exploratory study. *The Prison Journal, 80*(4), 434–441.

Nelson, C. (1974). *A study of homosexuality among women inmates at two state prisons*. Ph.D. dissertation, Temple University, Philadelphia.

Owen, B. (1998). *"In the mix": Struggle and survival in a women's prison*. Albany: State University of New York Press.

Pollock, J. M. (2002). *Women, prison, and crime* (2nd ed.). Belmont, CA: Wadsworth.

Struckman-Johnson, C., Struckman-Johnson, D., & Rucker, L. (1996). Sexual coercion reported by men and women in prison. *Journal of Sex Research, 33*(1), 67–76.

■ LESBIAN RELATIONSHIPS

Lesbian relationships refer to the emotional, physical, and sexual bonds formed between two women. It is not clear how many women participate in lesbian relationships in prison, although estimates from prison personnel and prisoners suggest that anywhere from 30% to 60% of women in prison are involved in same-sex relationships.

HISTORICAL DEPICTIONS OF LESBIAN RELATIONSHIPS IN PRISON

Studies about lesbian prison relationships conducted between 1913 and 1970 were primarily interested in three main areas: the "causes" and frequency of lesbian activity in prison, cross-racial lesbian relationships in U.S. women's prisons, and networks developed by women in American prisons called "play families" or "pseudofamilies." Researchers used personal observations and surveys distributed to prisoners to gather data about the frequency, causes, and nature of lesbian activity in prisons for women. The assumptions and interpretations inherent in these studies reflect the racial, sexual, and gender biases of the time.

For example, during the early to mid-20th century, researchers were interested in the prison subculture and the role and function of lesbian relationships. These studies viewed lesbianism as a gender inversion—a lesbian was someone who felt and behaved liked a man. Descriptions of lesbian prison relationships depicted masculine women ("butches") who adopted a "male" role, appearance, and demeanor. Butch women were described as turning traditionally feminine women ("femmes") into lesbians. Particularly in the United States, portrayals of lesbian relationships in prison also relied on racist stereotypes. Black women prisoners were considered "true" lesbians as racist imagery associated black women with masculinity. Black lesbian prisoners therefore were seen by early-20th-century prison administrators and criminologists to be butch lesbians who preyed on white femme women thus "turning them into" lesbians.

Studies conducted on lesbian relationships among juvenile offenders also concluded that the absence of males in the single-sex juvenile detention centers caused white girls to substitute black girls for their romantic partners. Black incarcerated girls and women were viewed as masculine and, consequently, as male "substitutions" in girls' and women's prisons.

The interest in roles, appearances, frequency, sexual practices, and causes of women prisoners' lesbian behavior continued in the 1960s through the 1980s. In the United States, researchers such as Rose Giallombardo (1966) and others described the existence of a play family or pseudofamily that consisted of a network of women who took on various heterosexual nuclear family roles. Researchers described these networks as including a mother, who adopted a traditional feminine appearance and qualities; a father, who adopted a traditional masculine role and appearance; and siblings, aunts, and uncles. However, in a 1972 study women prisoners who were subjects in the Giallombardo study said they did not recognize the characterization of their relationships as a parody of heterosexual family structures. The existence of these types of pseudofamilies has not been found in Canada or Great Britain.

CONTEMPORARY RESEARCH ON LESBIAN RELATIONSHIPS IN PRISON

Contemporary gender and sexuality theorists no longer consider lesbianism to be a gender inversion. In fact, the whole notion of fixed categories of gender and sexuality has been challenged, and many theorists acknowledge the fluidity of sexual identity.

Although contemporary criminology appears to be less interested in lesbian relationships in prison, as evident by the paucity of current literature on the topic, studies that do discuss lesbian prison relationships no longer reflect the same racial, gender, and heterosexist biases as earlier work. In addition, methodologies have expanded to include firsthand accounts from prisoners (Morgan, 1998) and qualitative research interviews with women prisoners (Owen, 1998).

Women prisoners themselves report that lesbian relationships in prison are complex and varied. It is inaccurate to characterize all lesbian relationships the same or to make universalizing statements about "causes" of lesbian relationships. This is consistent with contemporary scholarship about lesbian identities that suggested that there may be different pathways (biological or choice) to involvement in lesbian relationships. It seems clear from firsthand accounts and from contemporary qualitative research that some women involved in lesbian relationships in prison are lesbian-identified on the street and some are not. While incarcerated women may become involved in lesbian relationships for different reasons, the most common is the desire for emotional and physical connection and intimacy. Many report that lesbian relationships provide emotional support and companionship and help with the isolation and hostility of living in a prison environment.

What is less known is the degree to which women in lesbian relationships in prison continue to have same-sex relationships once released into the community. In Canada, lesbian relationships are tolerated in women's prisons and therefore may provide a relatively safe space for women to be involved in same-sex relationships. This tolerance is not as likely in the outside community, and thus the pressures of homophobia may prevent women from further involvement in lesbian relationships. These pressures may be compounded by other marginalizing factors such as the stigma of criminalization and/or racial oppression. Some women may be less likely to continue lesbian relationships outside of prison because of the multiple obstacles they already face in being accepted by mainstream society.

More recent studies of women's prison subculture have found lesbian relationships and prison families to be more multifaceted and complex than originally thought. Prisoners designated "mother" are often mature, serving longer sentences, and help guide, support, and teach younger members of the prison family. For some prisoners, this "maternal" relationship acts as a substitute for the lack of parental care in their lives. Shoshana Pollack (2000) found that in a Canadian prison some women formed bonds that they called "familial" but that the gender role playing found in American prisons did not exist. These prisoners were all gendered female and found that the nurturing, support, and autonomy achieved through these relationships helped them heal from past abuses in their family of origin and adult intimate relationships. The prison family may function as a protective and supportive network of friendships for women in prison.

MEANING OF LESBIAN RELATIONSHIPS IN THE PRISON CONTEXT

Lesbian relationships formed in prisons may or may not be a woman's first experience of same-sex relationships. The all-female prison environment and the general tolerance for lesbian relationships can provide a space for women to explore sexual and affective relationships with women. For some women, these relationships represent the first nonviolent intimate relationship they have experienced. In these cases, in addition to requiring affection and intimacy, women learn what a safe and caring relationship involves. Some women were lesbian-identified on the street and continue to be in lesbian relationships in the prison. These women are generally considered "true" lesbians in contrast to those who may participate in same-sex relationships only while in prison. For others, lesbian relationships replicate abusive dynamics by becoming either the aggressor or the victim in lesbian relationships. Given the high prevalence of child abuse and violence against women experienced by women prisoners, it is not surprising that some women repeat these patterns in their prison relationships.

However, sexual assault is a rare occurrence among women prisoners. Last, lesbian relationships in prison facilitate the development of a private and intimate sphere that is otherwise lacking in prisons. As such, lesbian relationships can function as a means of resistance to the pervasive scrutiny, control, and surveillance characteristic of prison life.

PRISON RESPONSE TO SAME-SEX RELATIONSHIPS

Historically, prison administrators have either ignored or tolerated lesbian prison relationships. Generally, there is more tolerance toward same-sex relationships in women's prisons than in prisons for men. Some prisons for women allow lesbian partners to live on the same unit or in the same cell, and lesbian prisoners are sometimes permitted to have commitment ceremonies to legitimize their relationships. However, although they may be unofficially tolerated, prison rules generally do not allow same-sex relationships. There are often regulations that forbid prisoners from visiting each other's cells or rooms, and in some prisons they can be charged for holding hands, kissing, or having sex. From a prison management perspective, lesbian relationships are seen as problematic when a relationship breaks up and conflict occurs or when women are competing for the same partner. On the other hand, lesbian relationships are sometimes advantageous to the prison administrators as the women provide a strong source of support for one another and can help manage each other's behavior.

CONCLUSION

Stereotypes about lesbian relationships are found in film, media, and television and in research studies about women's prisons. These stereotypes describe lesbians in prison as aggressive, masculine predators who prey upon heterosexual women. Ideas about sexual "deviance" are very closely linked to notions of women's criminal "deviance." Like those in the free world, lesbian relationships in prisons take on many forms and functions. Unlike the free world, women's prisons are female communities in which gender and sexual identity may be explored, challenged, and exploited. However, little is known about the impact of prison lesbian experiences once women are released from prison and if and how their identities as heterosexual, bisexual, or lesbian are reshaped in the outside community.

—*Shoshana Pollack*

See also Bisexual Prisoners; Donald Clemmer; Deprivation; Rose Giallombardo; Homosexual Prisoners; Importation; John Irwin; Lesbian Prisoners; Prison Culture; Sex—Consensual; Gresham Sykes; Women Prisoners; Women's Prisons

Further Reading

Bosworth, M. (1999). *Engendering resistance: Agency and power in women's prisons.* Aldershot, UK: Ashgate.

Damousi, J. (1997). *Depraved and disorderly: Female convicts, sexuality and gender in colonial Australia.* Cambridge, UK: Cambridge University Press.

Faith, K. (1993). Women confined. In *Unruly women: The politics of confinement and resistance* (Chap. 4.). Vancouver: Press Gang Publishers.

Freedman, E. (1996). The prison lesbian: Race, class, and the construction of the aggressive female homosexual, 1915–1965. *Feminist Studies, 22*(2).

Giallombardo, R. (1966). *Society of women: A study of a women's prison.* New York: John Wiley.

Hensley, C. (2002). *Prison sex: Practice and policy.* Boulder, CO: Lynne Rienner.

Morgan, D. (1998). Restricted love. In J. Harden & M. Hill (Eds.), *Breaking the rules: Women in prison and feminist therapy.* New York: Haworth.

Owen, B. (1998). *"In the mix": Struggle and survival in a women's prison.* Albany: State University of New York Press.

Pollack, S. (2000). *Outsiders inside: The social context of women's lawbreaking and imprisonment.* Unpublished doctoral thesis, Faculty of Social Work, University of Toronto.

Ward, D., & Kassebaum. G. (1965). *Women's prison: Sex and social structure.* Chicago: Aldine.

◪ LEXINGTON HIGH SECURITY UNIT

On October 29, 1986, the Federal Bureau of Prisons opened the first female High Security Unit (HSU) at the Federal Correctional Institution, Lexington, Kentucky. The mission of the Lexington HSU was to control and isolate women prisoners who posed a political threat to the United States or who were considered to be highly disruptive or an escape threat within the federal prison system. Lexington HSU was a 16-bed self-contained unit located in the subterranean level of the institution. It soon became a focus for national and international concern over human rights and was closed just two years after opening.

HISTORY OF THE LEXINGTON FEDERAL CORRECTIONAL INSTITUTION

Congress originally established the Lexington facility in 1929 as the first U.S. narcotics rehabilitation "farm" for the treatment of male addicts. In 1936, it became the U.S. Public Health Service Clinical Research Center and continued to treat drug addicts including those who were federal prisoners. At this time, the facility held 280 patients. In 1941, the Women's Building was constructed within the larger institution and the first female residents were admitted. In 1974, the U.S. Public Health Service's Clinical Research Center was finally transferred to the Federal Bureau of Prisons becoming a low-security coed correctional prison for inmates with drug or alcohol abuse problems.

THE WOMEN OF LEXINGTON

During its short period of existence, the Lexington HSU housed several women with long-standing political histories. The first two inmates placed in it were Alejandrina Torres and Susan Rosenberg. Torres had been sentenced to 35 years for seditious conspiracy in response to plotting bombings at U.S. military bases. Rosenberg, who was eventually granted clemency by President Bill Clinton in January 2001, received a maximum term of 58 years for possession of weapons, explosives, and false identification papers. The other women housed in the unit were Silvia Baraldini, Carol Manning, Lynette "Squeaky" Fromme, Sylvia Jean Brown, and Debra Denise Brown. These women's convictions varied from racketeering, armed robbery, kidnapping, and murder.

REVIEW AND CLOSURE OF THE CONTROL UNIT

In 1987, the National Prison Project, a wing of the American Civil Liberties Union, conducted a formal assessment of the Lexington HSU. Two National Prison Project staff attorneys, a correctional psychologist, and criminologists toured the facility and conducted interviews with five female prisoners confined to the unit, along with the warden, associate warden, and program staff. In their report, on the institution's medical and ethical correctional conditions, the panel determined that the women's rights had been violated in a number of ways. First, they had not been given proper administrative hearings prior to being transferred to the unit. Once incarcerated at Lexington, their visits were either curtailed completely or severely reduced. Their behavior was monitored at all times, even when they were showering, and they were strip searched after each outdoor exercise period. The panel also found that the prison did not provide adequate medical treatment or supervision.

The report concluded that the inmates in the Lexington HSU were dehumanized by their incarceration. Not only were they not allowed to personalize their living space, or allowed more than five books in their cell at one time, some were sexually abused and humiliated during their confinement. In response, the women were exhibiting numerous psychological disorders, including claustrophobia, chronic rage reactions, depression, hallucinatory symptoms, and defensive psychological withdrawal. Their physical and mental conditions were deteriorating as a result of loss of weight, loss of appetite, dehydration, insomnia, and acute anxiety syndrome.

Based on the findings of the report, it was recommended that the Lexington HSU be closed and the female inmates transferred to the general population of the Lexington facility. The HSU was permanently shut down in 1988.

CONCLUSION

Following the closing of the HSU in 1988, the prison briefly became a co-correctional facility again although by 1990 it was designated an administrative security-level facility for women only. Administrative security houses protective custody cases, inmates awaiting disciplinary hearings, inmates awaiting transfer to other institutions, and offenders who are separated from the general population because of security and/or safety reasons. In November 1991, it was designated as the Federal Medical Center (FMC), Lexington, and currently houses male inmates at the administrative level and houses females at an adjacent minimum-security camp.

—*Barbara Hanbury*

See also American Civil Liberties Union; Control Unit; Disciplinary Segregation; Health Care; Mental Health; Political Prisoners; Supermax Prisons; Women's Prisons

Further Reading

Elihu, R. (Ed.). (1996). *Criminal injustice: Confronting the prison crisis.* Boston: South End Press.

Freeman, A., Aiyetoro, A., & Korn, R. (1987). *Report on the High Security Unit for women, Federal Correctional Institution, Lexington, Kentucky.* Washington, DC: American Civil Liberties Union, National Prison Project.

Korn, R. (1987). *The effects of confinement at the H.S.U.: A follow-up.* Washington, DC: American Civil Liberties Union, National Prison Project.

Reuben, W., & Norman, C. (1987). The women of Lexington Prison. *The Nation, 244,* 25.

Rush, G. (1997). *Inside American prisons and jails.* Incline Village, NV: Copperhouse.

◪ LIFE WITHOUT PAROLE

The term "life without parole," sometimes called "LWOP" or "natural life," refers to a sentence of confinement in state or federal prison that lasts for the duration of an offender's life. A sentence of life without parole is generally given in instances of particularly serious crimes or in cases where the offender has a history of serious criminal activity. As opposed to other possible criminal sanctions, the primary goal of a sentence of life without parole is complete incapacitation.

TIME

While the concept of life without parole suggests that the offender will spend the rest of his or her life in prison, each jurisdiction implements this sentence in different ways (see Table 1). In some places, "life without parole" means that a certain number of years, as few as 10 years in Idaho and Montana or as many as 55 years in Indiana, must be served before the offender can be eligible for parole. In Oklahoma, those sentenced to life without parole are, in fact, eligible for parole after serving 45 years. In response, in 1994, an Oklahoma judge sentenced a convicted child molester with 14 prior felony convictions to six consecutive 5,000-year sentences in an effort to ensure that he would spend the rest of his life in prison.

Elsewhere, the term "life without parole" literally means that the individual will never be eligible for parole; he or she will die in prison. In some states (e.g., South Carolina and Vermont), the governor can commute a sentence of life without parole, while elsewhere (e.g., Alabama) the governor is prohibited from such action. In some jurisdictions, "life without parole" is the default sentence in capital cases where a guilty verdict is reached but the jury cannot reach a unanimous decision as to a sentence of death (see Table 1).

POPULATION CHARACTERISTICS

The vast majority of inmates serving life without parole are male (about 95%). However, in recent years, partly as a response to the so-called war on drugs and to "three strikes" laws that have been enacted at state and federal levels, the proportion of female inmates has been increasing. Overall, as with the general prison population, disproportionate numbers of men and women of color are serving this lengthy prison term.

Approximately 1.2% of all prisoners are doing life without parole, and it is thought that this proportion will grow substantially over the next two decades. For example, a recent Bureau of Justice Statistics analysis projects that by the year 2026, there will be approximately 30,000 persons serving sentences of 25 years to life in the state of California alone. Furthermore, about 83% of these (24,900 inmates in California) will be 40 years of age or older. Other estimates hold that as a result of sentencing changes in the 1980s and 1990s, over 10% of the prison population nationally will be over the age of 50 in coming years.

VIEWS FOR AND AGAINST

Generally, opponents of the death penalty are the strongest supporters of life without parole since they believe it is more cost effective (with primary savings in reduction of mandatory appeals) and allows possible errors to be corrected. Advocates also cite Gallup polls that indicate that national support for the death penalty drops when life without parole is given as an option to respondents. Opponents, however, argue that the growing numbers of sentences to life without parole is cause for concern. Research indicates that by the time people are imprisoned for a third strike or other repeat-offender statutes with a possible sentence of life without parole, they may be nearing the end of their criminal career. As such, the costs of long-term imprisonment may not outweigh the public benefits of reduced crime, since offenders are not likely to commit much crime in later years. Likewise, prison research documents that long-term prisoners are about half as likely to be involved in disciplinary actions as the general prison population lends further support to the "aging out" phenomenon in which deviant behavior declines with increasing age.

ELDERLY PRISONERS

The growing numbers of geriatric prisoners is a troubling consequence of life without parole. An aging prison population has additional health needs and requires increased basic prison services such as recreation and housing. Likewise, elderly prisoners eventually reach an age where they cannot work productively in the prison environment, nor can they continue living in regular cells. When this

Table 1   Life Without Parole (LWOP)–Most Serious Noncapital Sentence in U.S. Jurisdictions

Jurisdiction	*Most Serious Noncapital Sentence*
Alabama	LWOP; governor may not commute sentence
Alaska	20–99 years; prescribed minimum may not be reduced
Arizona	LWOP
Arkansas[1]	LWOP
California	Life with parole (15 to life or 25 to life) or LWOP
Colorado	LWOP
Connecticut[1]	LWOP
Delaware	LWOP
Dist. of Col.	LWOP
Federal[2]	Under sentencing guidelines. LWOP is possible for major drug traffickers.
Florida	Life = 25 years, no parole
Georgia	Murder: 25 years without parole for second life sentence, 20 years max for consecutive life sentences. Capital cases with mitigating circumstances = LWOP.
Hawaii[3]	Life without possibility of parole to be commuted after 20 years
Idaho	Life = 10 years without possibility of parole. LWOP is possible under parole statute.
Illinois	Minimum of 20, maximum of 60 if brutal or heinous. LWOP for second homicide.
Indiana	Life = 55 yrs, up to 10 added for aggravating circumstances 10 subtracted for mitigating. LWOP for third felony.
Iowa	Class A felony, LWOP
Kansas	Life, parole possible after 25 years
Kentucky	Life without parole for 25 years, life or a term of years not less than 20
Louisiana[1]	LWOP (only for habitual offenders)
Maine	LWOP of any term of years not less than 25
Maryland	LWOP or life. Life = 25 years.
Massachusetts	Life = 15 years. Murder in first degree, LWOP.
Michigan	Life = 15 years, no eligibility for parole (LWOP possible under parole statutes)
Minnesota	Life = 30 years, no eligibility for parole
Mississippi	LWOP (only for habitual offenders)
Missouri[1]	LWOP
Montana[4]	LWOP, life or a term of years not less than 10 nor more than 100
Nebraska	Life, indeterminate sentencing
Nevada	LWOP or life without parole for 20 years
New Hampshire[1]	Life without eligibility for parole
New Jersey[1]	30 years to life, no parole for 30 years
New Mexico	Life = no parole for 30 years
New York	LWOP
North Carolina[1]	LWOP
North Dakota	LWOP
Ohio	LWOP
Oklahoma	LWOP or life (for parole consideration purposes only, life is considered 45 years)
Oregon	LWOP or life. Life = 30 years

Pennsylvania	LWOP (contained in parole section)
Rhode Island	LWOP
South Carolina[1,5]	LWOP
South Dakota[1]	LWOP (person under life sentence not eligible for parole)
Tennessee	LWOP (no less than 25 full calendar years)
Texas[1]	Life, no parole for 35 years
Utah[1]	LWOP
Vermont[1]	LWOP
Virginia	Life
Washington[1]	LWOP
West Virginia	Life, indeterminate sentencing (with eligibility for parole)
Wisconsin	Life
Wyoming[1]	LWOP

SOURCE: Bureau of Justice Statistics (2000).

1. LWOP if no jury agreement on death sentence.

2. Federal: Prior to 1984 Life = 10 years before eligible for parole. Under sentencing reform, parole was abolished in favor of sentencing guidelines. Major drug traffickers face LWOP under 21 USC 848.

3. Hawaii: Minimum sentence, even in "life w/o parole," is determined by paroling authority.

4. Montana: Court may impose restriction that defendant be ineligible for parole. The court must state the reasons for this in writing as part of the judgment. LWOP may be applied to any felony, not just habitual offenders or first degree murder.

5. South Carolina and Vermont: Governor has the power to commute a LWOP sentence to a term of years.

happens, prisons must construct nursing home wings to meet the needs of the aging prison population. Finally, it is important to note the fiscal price of the aging prisoners serving sentences of life without parole. Housing an inmate over the age of 60 costs approximately $69,000 per year, approximately three times the national average cost for inmates overall.

CONCLUSION

A sentence of "life without parole" means different terms and conditions of confinement depending on the laws of the state where someone is convicted. Inmates sentenced to this term serve anywhere from 10 years to actual life in prison. They may be held in the general population—at least until they are too old to reside there any longer—or in administrative segregation/protective housing. They may be entitled to participate in optional work with pay or forced to labor without pay. Whatever their conditions or length of sentence, the numbers of women and men serving life without parole is growing and is destined to shape the prison experience for many years to come.

—*Connie Stivers Ireland*

See also Capital Punishment; Death Row; Deterrence Theory; Determinate Sentence; Elderly Prisoners; Incapacitation Theory; Indeterminate Sentence; Lifer; Maximum Security; Medium Security; Minimum Security; Parole; Supermax Prisons; Truth in Sentencing

Further Reading

Austin, J., & Irwin, J. (2001). *It's about time: America's imprisonment binge* (3rd ed.). Belmont, CA: Wadsworth/Thompson.

Clear, T. R., & Cole, G. F. (2003a). The death penalty. In *American corrections* (6th ed.). Belmont, CA: Wadsworth/Thompson.

Clear, T. R., & Cole, G. F. (2003b). Incarceration. In *American corrections* (6th ed.). Belmont, CA: Wadsworth/Thompson.

Cole, G. F., & Smith, C. E. (2001). Prisons: Their goal and management. In *The American system of criminal justice* (9th ed.). Belmont, CA: Wadsworth/Thompson.

Costanzo, M (1997). *Just revenge.* New York: St. Martin's.

Flanagan, T. J. (1991, Spring). Adaptation and adjustment among long-term prisoners. *Federal Prison Journal, 2,* 41–51.

King, R. S., & Mauer, M. (2000). Aging behind bars: "Three strikes" seven years later. *The Sentencing Project.* Retrieved November 22, 2002, from http://www.sentenc ingproject.org/

Seeking justice: Crime and punishment in America. (1997). New York: Edna McConnell-Lark Foundation.

Siegel, L. (2000). The judicatory process. In *Criminology* (7th ed.). Belmont, CA: Wadsworth/Thompson.

U.S. Department of Justice, Bureau of Justice Statistics. (1998). *State court organization.* Retrieved November 21, 2002, from http://www.ojp.usdoj.gov/bjs/pub/pdf/sc09807 .pdf

U.S. Department of Justice, Bureau of Justice Statistics. (2000). *Sourcebook of Criminal Justice Statistics.* Albany, NY: Hindelang Criminal Justice Research Center.

United Press. (1994, December 23). Oklahoma rapist gets 30,000 years. International wire services, southwest edition.

◪ LIFER

"Lifer" is a slang term referring to a prisoner who is serving a life sentence. There are two types of lifers, those who will spend the rest of their natural lives in prison waiting to die, and those who may someday be paroled or at least become eligible for parole. Over the past two decades, the composition of the population serving life sentences has changed. In the past, lifers were women as well as men convicted of the most serious and violent crimes. These individuals have now been joined by others who have been convicted of multiple nonviolent felonies such as drug offenses under increasingly punitive sanctions such as the "three strikes" laws and other mandatory minimum sentences.

Lifers are often individuals with little if any past criminal background. Most are not processed for parole until they meet certain predetermined time requirements (25 years as an example) imposed by the sentencing court. Generally, their good behavior will not play a role in reducing their sentence. However, when granted parole lifers seldom violate the conditions or return to prison. They are usually the most manageable and cooperative prisoners and are seldom involved in disciplinary infractions. Compared to other inmates, lifers take better advantage of the vocational and educational opportunities provided in prison.

LIFER CHARACTERISTICS

In the United States, approximately 65,000 people are serving life sentences. The Federal Bureau of Prisons confines slightly more than 5,000 inmates serving a life sentence. Lifers comprise approximately 3.3% of the federal inmate population.

Previously, lifers were the criminals that society portrayed as being the most dangerous and harmful. They were violent criminals, usually murderers. They were most commonly men in their 20s and 30s who had committed serious and violent crimes such as murder, armed robbery, and kidnapping. Female lifers were primarily involved in domestic homicides or as accomplices. Due to changes in sentencing policies in the United States, lifers in the federal system and many states are now composed of both violent and habitual offenders as well as violent criminals. In fiscal year 2001, criminal defendant sentenced in U.S. district courts to a term of life were predominantly drug traffickers. Violent felony offenders in that year comprised only 40% of those sentenced to life in prison. Ninety-six percent of the lifer population is male, and 4% is female. African Americans comprise 46% of those sentenced to life in prison, while whites comprise 38%, Hispanics 14%, and 2% are other races.

Lifers differ from "short termers" in many social and psychological ways. Unlike prisoners serving short-term sentences whose families often stand by to support them during their incarceration, lifers' networks of friends and families often disappear as the years go on. Psychological stresses arise during long-term incarceration. Lifers often try to focus on getting through their time by ending personal relationships on the outside, reasoning that their time will be more difficult to serve if they have to worry constantly about their loved ones on the outside. Lifers who stay in touch with their friends and family may develop anxiety and depression due to the lack of control they feel by not being able to be a part of, or intervene in, their loved ones' lives. Perhaps as a result, they are overrepresented as victims of suicide and homicide when compared to the general prison population.

WOMEN LIFERS

The numbers of women lifers have increased significantly in the past two decades. These women experience similar frustrations and limitations as their male counterparts. They exhibit an above average risk of being victims of suicide. Because of their sentences, they also are denied the prospect of programs and privileges. They are commonly prescribed psychotropic drugs to make them numb to their surroundings. Female lifers also experience an additional sense of guilt and depression caused by not being able to watch over and take care of their children as they grow up.

JUVENILE LIFERS

In the early 1990s, legislators responded to the sharp increase in juvenile violent crime by incorporating many punitive changes within the court system and penal processes. One result is that juvenile offenders are increasingly transferred from family and juvenile court to adult court, and at much younger ages. In addition, over the past 15 years increasing number of juveniles have been sentenced to life without parole. The Convention on the Rights of the Child, an international treaty passed by every member of the United Nations except Somalia and the United States, prohibits using life imprisonment without the possibility of parole for any crime committed by a minor. The United States did not sign this treaty.

The federal sentencing guidelines disallow "youthfulness" as a mitigating factor to reduce sentences outside the guidelines' range. According to the National Corrections Reporting Program, which describes admissions to state prisons in 38 states, an estimated 16 juvenile offenders were admitted to prison under a life-without-parole sentence in 1996. In the same year, an estimated 204 juvenile offenders began serving life sentences. That figure continues to rise.

LIFERS WITHOUT PAROLE

Parole eligibility varies from state to state as well as from country to country. Recently, there has been an increase in the numbers of men and women accorded life sentences without parole. Lifers without parole will be in prison until they die. Their release is possible through two conditions only: the use of clemency and, in some states, medical parole for the terminally ill. Both are used extremely infrequently. For these lifers, they live in the present; they try to survive each day, because they really do not have a future to look forward to.

There is no empirical evidence to date to indicate that inmates serving a sentence of life without parole are more likely to engage in major misconduct violations. In fact there are studies that show they are no more likely to engage in misconduct than their fellow inmates who are eligible for parole. In addition, a recent study indicates that "no hope of parole" actually reduces the likelihood of violent misconduct. With the growth of the no-parole option, future research is necessary to ascertain the effects of no parole on a younger lifer population.

LIFERS IN OTHER COUNTRIES

Lifers in England and Wales face similar sentence regulations as those in the United States. There are two types of life sentences in Britain and Whales: mandatory and discretionary. Mandatory lifers are those convicted of murder and are the majority of lifers in British correctional facilities. Most of these women and men will be eligible for parole after a certain amount of time—usually 15 years—although a small number will never be released.

Discretionary lifers are convicted of one of the following crimes: manslaughter, armed robbery, arson, rape, and kidnapping. In these cases, the judge has the discretion over the sentence and parole is possible if so ordered. The Crime (Sentences) Act 1997 requires the court to impose the sentence of life in prison with the possibility for parole for a person convicted of a second serious violent or sexual offense. The make-up of the lifer population in England and Wales is quite similar to the United States.

MANAGEMENT

Lifers are regarded as the most cooperative of prisoners by many prison officers and criminologists. Even so, at the initial stage of their incarceration they are viewed as maximum-security risks. They also receive few educational and vocational programs. This is especially true for lifers without parole eligibility. However, there are a variety of programs operated by lifers themselves, with the help of correctional staff. One of the more highly publicized lifers' groups is the Rahway Lifers Group Inc. at Rahway State Prison in New Jersey. The documentary *Scared Straight* chronicled the efforts of this group to turn troubled youths away from a life of crime. Today, the group maintains a Web site and continues to operate its youth tour program.

At Graterford State Prison in Pennsylvania, the lifers group recently hosted the first ever Crime Prevention Summit bringing together 100 Philadelphia civic leaders and police brass with lifers inside the prison walls. The goal of the conference was to discuss ways to end urban violence and drug distribution in the city of Philadelphia.

In the United Kingdom, lifers are assisted by both prison counseling services and Internet information to prepare them for their potential release. The Web site is comprehensive, addressing issues of anger management, parole release, and expectations, and other life skills' issues necessary to affect a positive outcome after release.

These programs share the common goal of promoting a positive self-image for lifers as well as providing opportunities for positive changes in individual offenders. Similar programs exist throughout the United States and the United Kingdom.

CONCLUSION

The changing demographics of lifers, the emerging juvenile and female lifers, and the nonviolent lifer illustrate the importance of reform in the correctional system. Lifers are becoming older requiring the prison systems to reexamine the needs of inmates. They have special needs in housing, recreation, and medical care that require special attention of prison administrators. Lifers have changed due to strict sentencing and penal policies and comprise an increasing percentage of the modern prison. This fact alone warrants review by administrators into operational changes.

—*Kimberly Albin and Patrick F. McManimon, Jr.*

See also Crime Control and Violent Crime Act 1994; Death Penalty; Deterrence Theory; Elderly Prisoners; Incapacitation Theory; Life Without Parole; Parole; Parole Board; Three-Strikes Legislation; Truth in Sentencing

Further Reading

Cohen, S., & Taylor, L. (1981). *Psychological survival.* London: Penguin.

Flanagan, T. (1999). *Long-term imprisonment: Policy, science, and correctional practice.* Thousand Oaks, CA: Sage.

Graham, E., Delnef, C., & Murphy, J. (2000). Long-term offenders. *Forum on Corrections Research, 12*(3).

◪ LITERACY

Literacy skills are important to people in prison for a number of reasons. Many prison jobs require prisoners to read instructions or order forms, and inmates are often required to write requests for belongings, items, or medical treatment. Reading and writing provide productive options for passing time while in prison. Letters to family and friends are a vital link to the outside world. Literacy skills are also important for those who will leave prison and attempt to reintegrate into the community. Jobs, continued education, and many social opportunities depend on the ability to read and write—regardless of whether an individual is in prison.

Research consistently demonstrates that quality education is one of the most effective forms of crime prevention since educational skills help deter people from committing criminal acts. One study, for example, indicated that those who benefited from correctional education recidivated 29% less often that those who did not have educational opportunities while in the correctional institution.

In the United States, however, a "get tough on crime" mentality has resulted in a push to incarcerate, punish, and limit the activities of prisoners. As part of this move, over the past 10 years political pressure has led to the elimination of funding for many corrections education programs. Many programs that have been demonstrated as extraordinarily effective have been completely eliminated.

Nonetheless, literacy programs continue in many correctional facilities, in part because they can be run at a relatively low cost. In addition, state and federal guidelines that encourage the development of literacy skills typically apply to all citizens, including prisoners. Prison literacy programs also benefit from volunteer efforts of organizations and individuals.

NEED FOR LITERACY PROGRAMS

Illiteracy is perhaps the greatest common denominator in correctional facilities. Data collected from the National Adult Literacy Survey (NALS) show that literacy levels among inmates are considerably lower than for the general population. For example, of the five levels measured by the NALS, 70% of inmates scored at the lowest two levels of literacy (below fourth grade). Other research suggests that 75% of inmates are illiterate (at the 12th-grade level) and 19% are completely illiterate. Forty percent are functionally illiterate. In real-world terms, this means that the individual would be unable to write a letter explaining a billing error. In comparison, the national illiteracy rate for adult Americans stands at 4%, with 21% functionally illiterate.

A related concern is that prisoners have a higher proportion of learning disabilities than the general population. Estimates of learning disability are as high as 75% to 90% for juvenile offenders. Low literacy levels and high rates of learning disabilities have contributed to high dropout rates. Nationwide, over 70% of all people entering state correctional facilities have not completed high school, with 46% having had some high school education and 16.4% having had no high school education at all. Since there is a strong link between low levels of education and high rates of criminal activity, it is logical to assume that high dropout rates will lead to higher crime rates.

PRISON LITERACY PROGRAMS

The correctional facility provides a controlled education setting for prisoners, many of whom are motivated students. However, the prison literacy educator faces many challenges. Students in these programs have varying levels of ability and have had a range of educational experiences. The educator's challenge is compounded by the uniqueness of prison culture and the need for security. Prisons adhere to strict routines, which may not be ideal in an educational setting. During their sentence, inmates are often moved from one facility to another. This movement interrupts, or ends, the individual's educational programming. These structural issues are accompanied by social factors that can further limit learning opportunities. Peer pressure may discourage attendance or achievement. Prison administrators usually only support education to varying degrees—especially if they see it as a threat to the primary functions of security and control.

In spite of the challenges, examples in the literature demonstrate that programs based on current thinking about literacy and sound adult education practices can be effective in prison settings. Successful prison literacy programs are learner centered, recognizing different learning styles, cultural backgrounds, and multiple literacies. Successful programs typically use learner strengths to help them shape their own learning. Historically, literacy education has been offered to the general population by two volunteer agencies: Literacy Volunteers of America (LVA) and Laubach Literacy International. (In 2002, these agencies merged to form ProLiteracy Worldwide.) These agencies train volunteers and staff who administer the programs in prison. Although the training emphasizes specific skills and curricula, educational programming in a correctional institution is always dependant on the philosophy and policies of the correctional facility. As such, it is difficult to ensure consistent delivery of literacy services from one institution to another.

TESTING AND CURRICULA

Several standardized reading tests are available to literacy instructors. Besides the Test of Adults in Basic Education (TABE), two other tests are commonly used. One, the Grey Oral Reading Test, measures the fluency and comprehension of the learner. For example, it determines the learner's ability to recognize common written words such as *car, be, house,* and *do* by sight or in context. A second commonly used test for literacy skills is the National Assessment of Adult Literacy (NAAL). This test is divided into five levels ranging from assessing the learner's ability to fill out a deposit slip (Level I), determining the difference in price between two items (Level II) to demonstrating proficiency in interpreting complex written passages (Level V). These tests can be used to assess needs, track progress, and demonstrate success to the learner and to administrators who may be called on to support the program.

Several literacy curricula are also available to prison educators. The National Institute for Literacy developed standards for literacy as a component of lifelong learning. This program focuses on skill acquisition in three areas: worker, family member, and citizen. The standards are broken down into four general areas with several subareas. For example, "communication" is broken into the following subareas: (1) reading with understanding, (2) conveying ideas in writing, (3) speaking so others can understand, (4) listening actively, and (5) observing critically. The curriculum uses activities that are relevant to the learner's life to develop skills in reading. Laubach Literacy offers curricula that can be used in classroom settings or in one-on-one instruction. "Reading Is Fundamental" and "Project Read" are examples of federally funded literacy programs that offer text-based curriculum.

Although there are similarities among each of these programs, data do not suggest a standardized delivery method for literacy programs in correctional facilities. The programs generally include reading, writing, calculating, listening, speaking, and problem solving as core parts of a literacy curriculum. In general, successful programs are learner centered, participatory, sensitive to the prison culture, and linked to postrelease services.

CONCLUSION

Since the 1970s, correctional philosophy has shifted from a rehabilitative to a punitive approach. Even so, correctional facilities remain responsible for addressing literacy problems among the corrections population. The logic behind providing literacy services in prison is that all of society benefits by allowing access to educational resources that are available to everyone else. As such, literacy programs should not be seen as "special treatment" for prisoners. The federal government encourages literacy skill improvement in all entities, including prisons, that receive federal aid and at least 26 states have enacted mandatory educational requirements for certain populations. These policies demonstrate the importance placed on efforts to improve literacy skills.

Although there are challenges, literacy programs can provide relatively inexpensive educational programs within correctional institutions. When we consider the high cost of imprisonment, coupled with a growing prison population, literacy programs provide a cost-effective opportunity to improve the job-related skills of incarcerated individuals. A large percentage of these individuals will be released from prison and will be expected to successfully, and lawfully, reintegrate in our communities. Literacy education provides a large payoff to the community in terms of crime reduction and employment opportunities for ex-offenders. Investments in these programs have been confirmed as wise, and cost-effective, public policy.

—Kenneth Mentor and Molly Wilkinson

See also Education; English as a Second Language; General Educational Development (GED) Exam and General Equivalency Diploma; Recidivism

Further Reading

American Corrections Association. (2004). ACA home page. Retrieved from http://www.aca.org

Bureau of Justice Statistics. (2002). *Key crime and justice facts at a glance.* Retrieved from http://www.ojp.usdoj.gov/bjs/glance.htm

Haigler, K. O., Harlow, C., O'Connor, P., & Campbell, A. (1994). *Literacy behind prison walls.* Washington, DC: National Center for Education Statistics.

Kerka, S. (1995). *Prison literacy programs.* Columbus, OH. (Eric Digest No. 159)

Kollhoff, M. (2002, June). Reflections of a Kansas corrections educator. *Journal of Correctional Education, 53*(2), 44–45.

Leone, P. E., & Meisel, S. (1997). Improving educational services for students in detention and confinement facilities. *Children's Legal Rights Journal, 17*(1), 2–12.

LoBuglio, S. (2001). Time to reframe politics and practices in correctional education. In J. Comings, B. Garner, & C. Smith (Eds.), *Annual review of adult learning and literacy* (Vol. 2). San Francisco: Jossey-Bass.

National Adult Literacy and Learning Disabilities Center. (1996, Fall). Correctional education: A worthwhile investment. In *Linkages: Linking literacy and learning disabilities* (Vol. 3, No. 2). Washington, DC: National Institute for Literacy.

National Institute for Literacy. (1999). *Equipped for the future standards.* Retrieved from http://www.nifl.gov/lincs/col lections/eff/eff.html

Newman, A. P., Lewis, W., & Beverstock, C. (1993). *Prison literacy.* Philadelphia: National Center on Adult Literacy.

Paul, M. (1991). *When words are behind bars.* Kitchener, ON: Core Literacy.

Project READ. (1978). To make a difference. In M. S. Brunner (Ed.), *Reduce recidivism and increased employment opportunity through research-based reading instruction* (pp. 20–27). Washington, DC: Office of Juvenile Justice and Delinquency Prevention.

ProLiteracy Worldwide. (2004). ProLiteracy Worldwide home page. Retrieved from http://www.proliteracy.org/about/index.asp

Quinn, M. M., Rutherford, R. B., & Leone, P. E. (2001). *Students with disabilities in correctional facilities.* (ERIC Digest No. E621).

Rutherford, R. B., Nelson, C. M., & Wolford, B. I. (1985). Special education in the most restrictive environment: Correctional special education. *Journal of Special Education, 19,* 59–71.

Steurer, S., Smith, L., & Tracy, A. (2001). *Three State Recidivism Study.* Prepared for the Office of Correctional Education, U.S. Department of Education. Lanham, MD: Correctional Education Association.

Tolbert, M. (2002). *State correctional education programs.* Washington, DC: National Institute for Literacy. Retrieved from http://www.nifl.gov/nifl/policy/st_correction_02.pdf

◪ LOCKUP

A lockup is a temporary holding facility for pretrial detainees, usually located within a courthouse or a police station. Lockups are also known as holding pens, bullpens, or tanks. They must be distinguished from jails, which are usually operated by county sheriff's departments. Typically, jail populations are composed of defendants awaiting trial who either did not make bail or who were not offered it, convicted misdemeanants who will spend all of their incarcerated term in jail, and convicted felons who are awaiting bedspace in a state prison. Lockups, on the other hand, are run by local police departments and are located within the police station. They may also be operated by the court and located in the basement of the courthouse.

Unlike the vast amount of scholarly work on corrections and jails in the United States, there is little literature, scholarly or otherwise, about lockups. The near academic and official silence over these institutions is surprising since the number of lockup facilities is almost four-and-one-half times larger than the number of local jails. Within the United States, there are more than 15,000 lockups but only about 3,400 local jails.

CURRENT PRACTICE

Detainees in a police lockup are individuals who have just been arrested and are awaiting their first court appearance, which may include informal charging and bail setting. While the Speedy Trial Act of 1974 (revised in 1979) does not specify the length of time from the point of arrest to the point of the first court appearance, states typically require that detainees must be brought to a judge, or an appropriate judicial officer, within 48 hours. The median time of holding is 22 hours. If detainees cannot make bail, they will await trial in a county-operated jail. In some jurisdictions where the jails are overcrowded, lockups may be used for longer periods of time.

Roughly 16% of all police departments in the United States operate lockup facilities, which are overnight holding facilities, while 19% administer holding cells, which are not for overnight detention. In jurisdictions with more than 1 million residents, 56% of the local police departments manage a lockup facility, while up to 42% of police departments in smaller jurisdictions do likewise. Most police departments with jurisdictions of more than 10,000 residents operate an adult lockup. The median capacity ranges from 70 detainees in jurisdictions with more than 500,000 residents to 3 in jurisdictions with fewer than 10,000 residents. Nationally, the number of adult detainees in local police lockups is approximately 41,000.

JUVENILES

Nationally, there are approximately 7,500 juvenile detainees held in lockup. One in seven police departments has a juvenile lockup facility, usually those located in the largest jurisdictions. The capacity of most institutions ranges from 16 in the largest jurisdictions to 1 in areas with fewer than 2,500 residents. Unlike adult detainees, the median time of holding for juveniles is six hours.

SOME PROBLEMS WITH LOCKUP

There are several areas of concern with regard to lockup. Of most importance is the lack of comprehensive standards for the treatment of detained persons in police lockups. In addition, the use of police officers rather than trained prison officers may cause problems for those who are held. Finally, conditions of confinement for detainees are often poor, and since so little academic attention is given to them, unlikely to change.

The need for comprehensive standards about the treatment of detained persons in police lockups is not specific to the United States. An examination of similar institutions in the Netherlands and other countries around the world reveals a similar problem. Recent efforts to create standards can be found in the United Nations' *Body of Principles for the Protection of all Persons Under Any Form of Detention or Imprisonment* (1988), *Standard Minimum Rules for the Treatment of Prisoners* (1955 and 1977), *The Convention Against Torture and Other Cruel, Inhuman or Degrading Treatment or Punishment* (1984), and *Basic Principles for the Treatment of Prisoners* (1990). However, only 10 of the rules

found in the *Standard Minimum Rules for the Treatment of Prisoners* address the treatment of detainees in lockup facilities. As a result, police departments implement custodial procedures and build cellblocks without proper guidance.

POLICE CULTURE AND ITS IMPACT ON LOCKUP

Understanding police culture and its values may help to explain the lack of interest in police lockups. Since its movement toward professionalism in the 1920s, the police have increasingly taken pride in keeping the peace and fighting crime. As a result, the caregiving aspect of the custodial role that police are required to take on when operating lockups is unfamiliar to many officers. The difference in values and primary responsibilities between the police and correctional personnel may lead police and prison officers to treat inmates differently. Specifically, police tend to see criminals as liable for the consequences of their misconduct while prison officers take on the more human services approach, combining the roles of counselor, diplomat, caretaker, caregiver, and disciplinarian.

Finally, the conditions of confinement pose a number of problems. Although, as has already been stated, little is known about the experiences people have in lockup, the United Nations' *Convention Against Torture and Other Cruel, Inhuman or Degrading Treatment or Punishment* (1984) has drawn increased attention to the conditions under which detainees are held in any institution. Research has found that police stations around the world have denied prisoners communication, recreational activity, and basic necessities such as blankets, health care, and adequate nutrition. Furthermore, it is common for hardened criminals and prisoners under trial to be housed together. At worst, cases of torture and killings of inmates at the hands of police officers within lockup have been documented by Amnesty International. These are all violations of basic human rights as specified by the United Nations.

One well-known example of poor conditions in the United States was found in New York City's criminal court lockup. The Visiting Committee of the Correctional Association of New York began its visits to the court lockup in 1989. The committee found it to be overcrowded, with broken toilets and sinks, no medical care, and inadequate or missed meals. There were no operating standards for cell capacity, food, health care, and access to family and legal counsel. As a result, the Midtown Community Court holding pen was created. Instead of bringing suspects to central booking and holding them at the police station, police now transport suspects directly to the court lockup or to the Midtown North Precinct. This current practice has minimized holding time of detainees and has allowed the city to monitor the conditions of lockup. The lockup was found to be clean and bright with glass panels instead of bars.

CONCLUSION

Lockup facilities have tended to be ignored by researchers as well as by criminal justice administrators. The low priority given to these facilities is a result of (1) the small numbers of inmates housed in these facilities, (2) the short periods of time inmates are kept at these facilities, and (3) the lack of fit of the custodial role into police culture. In addition, the operation of lockup facilities by police departments or courts is far from ideal. Police officers report that lockups in their stations create congestion problems within the stationhouse itself and report feelings of resentment and betrayal for being required to engage in custodial activities. Many police officers also feel unqualified for the task. Finally, lockup facilities are not subjected to the same operating standards as jails and prisons. This problem, both nationally and internationally, creates situations where violations of international standards are more likely to occur.

—*Venessa Garcia*

See also American Correctional Association; Correctional Officers; Detained Youth and Committed Youth; Jails; Pretrial Detainees; State Prison System

Further Reading

Blaauw, E., Vermunt, R., & Kerkhof, A. (1997). Detention circumstances in police stations: Towards setting the standards. *Policing and Society, 7*, 45–69.

Das, D. K., Light, S. C., & Verma, A. (2001). Using police as custodial officers: An analysis from the perspective of international human rights standards. *Police Quarterly, 4*, 215–232.

Hickman, M. J., & Brian A. R. (2001). *Local police departments 1999.* Washington, DC: Bureau of Justice Statistics.

Reaves, B. A., & Goldberg, A. L. (2000). *Local police departments 1997.* Washington, DC: Bureau of Justice Statistics.

Reich, I. (1994). *A citizen crusade for prison reform.* New York: Correctional Association of New York.

Speedy Trial Act of 1974, 18 U.S.C.A. 3161–3174.

United Nations. (1957, 1977). *Standard minimum rules for the treatment of prisoners.* Adopted with Res. 663 C (XXIV) on July 31, 1957, and Res. 2076 (LXII) on May 13, 1977.

United Nations. (1984). Convention against torture and other cruel, inhuman or degrading treatment or punishment. In *Yearbook of the United Nations 1984.* New York: Author.

United Nations. (1988). *Body of principles for the protection of all persons under any form of detention or imprisonment.* Adopted without a vote with GA. Res. 43/137 on Dec. 9, 1988.

United Nations. (1990). *Basic principles for the treatment of prisoners.* Adopted and proclaimed by General Assembly resolution 45/111 of December 14, 1990.

Welch, M. (1996). *Corrections: A critical approach.* New York: McGraw-Hill.

◪ LOWELL, JOSEPHINE SHAW (1843–1905)

The life of philanthropist and social reformer Josephine Shaw Lowell is something of an enigma. She demanded that the poor take responsibility for themselves at the same time that she promoted a wide range of social services, including antipoverty programs. She called on capitalists to pay workers fair wages and the state to pursue full employment. She advocated eugenics through preventive incapacitation, yet condemned retribution and fought for the rehabilitation of prisoners. A leader in the scientific charity movement, she combined principles of public duty, social responsibility, and civic materialism with an ardent pro-labor and anti-imperialist stance. Lowell was a complex personality.

Like many privileged reformers of her day, Lowell was influenced by her class position, social-cultural context, and historical conjuncture. Born in West Roxbury, Massachusetts, on December 16, 1843, to affluent parents, Sarah Sturgis and Francis George Shaw, Josephine traveled the world, attending schools in Europe as well as in the United States. Her parents were abolitionists and Unitarians; their circle of associates included feminists, communitarians, and transcendentalists. In 1863, she married Charles Russell Lowell, Jr., who, while serving in the Second Massachusetts Cavalry, died after sustaining injuries on a Virginia battlefield. She also lost her brother, Robert Gould Shaw, in an attack on Fort Wagner. He was leading a regiment of black soldiers.

Adding to the chaos of the Civil War (which drew republican women to the public sphere) was the Industrial Revolution, the abolition of slave labor, and waves of immigrants arriving on America's shores. The industrial reserve swelled, cities became overcrowded, crime increased—especially among women and immigrants—and the middle class grew fearful of the "dangerous classes," the working poor, the unemployed, the racialized, and the foreign. Simultaneously, and somewhat paradoxically, the relentless and unbridled force of the industrial bourgeoisie during the Gilded Age projected an image of American liberty built on economic freedom and individual autonomy.

OF CHARITY, PENITENTIARIES, EUGENICS, AND REFORM

Lowell's vision of social action was forged in this crucible. Charity was not supposed to ameliorate suffering, she argued, but fundamentally to transform the recipient, converting irresponsible paupers into hardworking and economically independent citizens. Her secular ideology thinly disguised a Protestant ethic that was rooted in a religious conception of human nature. In her book, *Public Relief and Private Charity* (1884), she argued that human nature is such that if individuals receive assistance without working for it, moral degradation inevitably results. Perhaps worse, when people see others receiving public relief, they cannot help but covet the same seemingly carefree life. On the basis of this, she emphasized work requirements as a prerequisite for charitable gifts, and, to make sure recipients were indeed working, surveillance of their habits.

Lowell's approach to social reform was labor intensive and paternalistic. She urged practitioners to enter homes to teach poor mothers how to rear their children. When the poor found their way into penal institutions, she demanded the development of educational and vocational programs behind prison walls.

In 1876, Lowell was appointed to the New York Board of Charities. This role brought her into contact with the harsh realities of the penitentiary. An adherent of the "new penology," articulated by such figures as Zebulon Brockway and the American Prison Association, Lowell campaigned for separate women's prisons, reformatories to rehabilitate minor offenders, and the indeterminate sentence, a measure believed essential for keeping persons in custody while they received treatment. Impressed by Richard Dugdale's notorious study of degeneracy, *The Jukes* (1875), she joined the eugenics movement. Dugdale's findings (which were fraudulent) told the story of a promiscuous woman responsible for a generation of criminals, inebriates, and miscreants. To prevent proliferation of undesirables, Lowell advocated preventative incapacitation and viewed crime control as prophylactic. To achieve this end, she established the Newark Custodial Asylum for Feebleminded Women.

Despite these views, Lowell eventually recognized that crime and poverty were the result of structural conditions and dedicated herself to the struggle for higher wages and improved working conditions for women. Thus, her story is a lesson in how experience can change point of view and practice.

CONCLUSION

Lowell's work remains relevant to contemporary debates surrounding welfare reform and the future of antipoverty programs. Those seeking to end programs for the poor have, in large measure, selectively co-opted Lowell's themes, such as personal responsibility and hostility toward welfare dependence, successfully eliminating Aid to Families with Dependent Children (AFDC), the major federal cash transfer program for poor children. Perhaps this would have pleased Lowell, who argued against "mothers' pensions" in favor of "widows' pensions" on grounds that the former would repeat the sin of abandonment. At any rate, for the history of corrections in America, Lowell is a central figure in the evolution of women's prisons and reformatories. Her work links charitable approaches to reformation rooted in organized religion to the emerging effort to address social problems through the application of rational scientific principles and social control.

—Andrew Austin

See also Zebulon Reed Brockway; Dorothea Lynde Dix; History of Women's Prisons; Incapacitation Theory; Indeterminate Sentencing; Massachusetts Reformatory; Rehabilitation Theory; Women Prisoners; Women's Prisons

Further Reading

Boyer, P. (1978). *Urban masses and moral order, 1820–1920.* Cambridge, MA: Harvard University Press.

Bremner, R. H. (1988). *American philanthropy* (2nd Ed.). Chicago: University of Chicago Press.

Colvin, M. (1997). *Penitentiaries, reformatories, and chain gangs.* New York: St. Martin's.

Ginzberg, L. D. (1990). *Women and the work of benevolence.* New Haven, CT: Yale University Press.

Katz, M. B. (1986). *In the shadow of the poorhouse: A social history of welfare in America.* New York: Basic Books.

Lowell, J. S. (1971). *Public relief and private charity.* New York: Arno. (Original work published 1884)

Olasky, M. (1992). *The tragedy of American compassion.* Washington, DC: Regnery.

Rafter, N. H. (1985). *Partial justice: Women in state prisons, 1800–1935.* Boston: Northeastern University Press.

Waugh, J. (1998). *Unsentimental reformer: The life of Josephine Shaw Lowell.* Cambridge, MA: Harvard University Press.

M

⬛ MACONOCHIE, ALEXANDER (1787–1860)

Alexander Maconochie is an important figure in penal history, known as the originator of the "marks" system. Maconochie developed this strategy of incentives and privileges at the Norfolk Island penal colony in the mid-1800s as a means of managing men who had been deemed uncontrollable. In the United States, a version of the marks system was most famously applied at Elmira Reformatory by Zebulon Brockway. Although Maconochie was ultimately forced to leave his position as warden of the Norfolk Island prison, echoes of his highly structured system of prison management can be found in prisons throughout the world today.

HISTORY

In 1840, the notorious prison on Norfolk Island (a penal colony in the Pacific Ocean hundreds of miles northeast of Sydney) was sent a new governor, Captain Alexander Maconochie. He had requested this post. Norfolk Island was a place of secondary punishment for convicts who reoffended in the British colony of New South Wales. It was distinguished by a regime of brutality designed to strike terror in the hearts and minds of all transported felons. Here, men were starved at the slightest infringement of rules and were confined in small fetid cells. Here, too, they could be flogged until their bones were revealed. Norfolk Island was a place where hope was removed from prisoners' lives, and where death was eagerly awaited.

Maconochie, a former soldier, had been employed in Van Diemen's Land as a private secretary to Governor Sir John Franklin before he sought this new employment. He was a prison reformer, concerned to establish a process of improvement even in the most brutal prison of the antipodes. Inspired, in part, by his Christian beliefs, Maconochie thought it necessary to build new, healthier prisons with strict, regulated regimes that would persuade inmates not to reoffend. These institutions would also equip prisoners with skills to support themselves with honest labor once back in the world.

THE MARKS SYSTEM

Maconochie's contribution to prison reform lay in his introduction of a scale of "marks" that prisoners could earn for good behavior. Once an individual achieved a certain number of marks, his living conditions would improve. An accumulation of marks would also result in an early form of parole known as a "ticket of leave" that allowed a person to be released from prison under license.

Maconochie experimented on Norfolk Island with these ideas and, to his mind at least, achieved some notable results. He altered inmates' lives by allowing them to hope. Unfortunately for the Norfolk Island convicts, the ticket of leave could only be permitted on the island itself. They had little chance of returning to the mainland and even less of returning to England. Maconochie could not achieve miracles, but he could and did permit a level of humanity to return to the men's lives.

Convicts in this system had been brutalized. One man's treatment had included a period of time chained to a rock in Sydney Harbor, where he became an object of mockery for those who could reach him and throw bread or less savory items at him. His life sentence was to be served out on the island, and by the time Maconochie reached it the convict could barely make himself understood. He was removed from the prison and sent to live by himself in a small hut where he was permitted to cultivate a garden and was supplied by convict stores. In this way, Maconochie believed he had retrieved an individual who was thought to be beyond help of any kind but God's.

MACONOCHIE CHALLENGED

Not everyone wished to see convicts reform themselves. Many proponents of the penal system firmly believed that a place of secondary punishment had to strike terror rather than hope in the malefactor's heart. They did not necessarily share a belief in the inherent goodness of man as a being created in God's image, which was the foundation of much reformist thought.

The first assessments of the marks system to reach London were negative, and in 1844 the colonial secretary ordered Sir George Grey to remove Maconochie from his post. A few weeks after this order had been received in Sydney, the home office received reports of a very different kind about Maconochie's successes. It was too late. Maconochie was recalled to live his life out in unrewarding positions in which he was briefly permitted to introduce

his system of marks and then dismissed as too radical. Norfolk Island reverted to its former brutal regime. Yet Maconochie's ideas remained influential within the British convict system, and were imported to the Irish system and ultimately to the United States in the 1870s. In Australia, marks were instituted in Fremantle Convict Establishment, a large prison built for 1,000 inmates, in the 1850s. They remained in the system until the 20th century, although their implementation became more and more debased and further and further from the Christian ideals of their founder.

CONCLUSION

Marks gave convicted criminals the opportunity to alter some part of their sentence by behaving well within the prison structure of rules and regulations. They worked in Fremantle while men labored outside the walls, where their activities could be noted and recorded by an interested public. Behind prison walls, however, marks easily became dependent upon the goodwill of the recording officer, with increased chances of corruption or poor assessment. Despite such problems, a structured system of incentives and privileges was introduced to the English prison system in the 1990s that in many respects is a modern application of Alexander Maconochie's 19th-century ideas.

—Michal Bosworth

See also Alcatraz; Australia; Cesare Beccaria; Jeremy Bentham; Zebulon Brockway; Corporal Punishment; Deterrence Theory; Disciplinary Segregation; Elmira Reformatory; England and Wales; Flogging; History of Prisons; John Howard; Irish System; Norval Morris; Panopticon; Parole; Quakers; Rehabilitation Theory; Solitary Confinement; Supermax Prisons

Further Reading

Barry, J. V. (1958). *Alexander Maconochie of Norfolk Island.* Melbourne: University of Melbourne Press.

Clay, J. (2000). *Maconochie's experiment: How one man's extraordinary vision saved transported convicts from degradation and despair.* London: Murray.

Morris, N. (2003). *Maconochie's gentlemen: The story of Norfolk Island and the roots of modern penal reform.* New York: Oxford University Press.

Morris, N., & Rothman, D. J. (Eds.). (1997). *The Oxford history of the prison: The practice of punishment in Western society.* New York: Oxford University Press.

MALCOLM X (1925–1965)

The prison experiences of Malcolm X proved to be the turning point in his life and career. During his years of incarceration, he underwent a profound spiritual conversion that transformed him from a petty criminal into the principal spokesperson for the Nation of Islam.

BIOGRAPHICAL DETAILS

Malcolm Little was born on May 19, 1925, in Omaha, Nebraska. His childhood could not have been more troubled. Malcolm's father, Earl, was an ardent advocate of the United Negro Improvement Association, the militant black organization established by Marcus Garvey. Earl's uncompromising politics aroused the enmity of the Ku Klux Klan, which repeatedly terrorized the family. The Littles abandoned Omaha and settled first in Milwaukee, Wisconsin, and then Lansing, Michigan. Trouble awaited them with every move. When the family moved into an otherwise all-white neighborhood in Lansing, they were served with an eviction notice. After Earl refused to relinquish the property, local whites burned it to the ground. On September 28, 1931, Earl was killed when he fell under the wheels of a streetcar. The circumstances surrounding his death are clouded in confusion. According to some, Earl was murdered by white supremacists known as the Black Legion; in the opinion of others, he died as the result of a drunken fall.

Whether or not the cause of his death was an accident, the impact on the rest of the family was catastrophic. Earl's widow, Louise, struggled unsuccessfully to support her children. Malcolm became increasingly unruly at school. He also started to steal. In January 1939, exhausted by strain, Louise Little was admitted to the Michigan State Mental Hospital. Malcolm was sent to live with an adoptive family. Expelled from school, he was then admitted to a detention home.

Malcolm found temporary reprieve when he moved to Roxbury, Massachusetts, under the legal guardianship of his half-sister, Ella Little-Collins. However, he soon descended into a life of petty crime. Under the alias "Detroit Red," Malcolm worked the streets of Harlem as a pimp, drug dealer, and number runner. In November 1944, he received a three-month suspended sentence and one year of probation for pawning a stolen coat. Four months later, he was arrested for a robbery in Detroit but failed to attend the trial hearing.

IMPRISONMENT

Eventually, the law caught up with him. On January 12, 1946, Malcolm was arrested when he attempted to reclaim a stolen watch left for repair at a jewelry store. The police then uncovered a cache of stolen goods in his apartment. Malcolm stood trial along with the other members of his small gang in February 1946. Two of his accomplices, a white woman Malcolm had dated, along with her sister, received minor sentences. Malcolm and his friend Shorty were advised to plead guilty on the assumption that they would each receive a maximum of two years' imprisonment. However, the judge had other plans and handed down sentences of eight to ten years. On February 27, 1946, Malcolm entered the Charlestown State Prison. Prisoner 22843 was still only 20 years old.

Yet prison was to prove Malcolm's salvation. There he befriended a fellow inmate, John Bembry ("Bimbi"), who encouraged him to study. In January 1947, Malcolm was transferred to the Concord Reformatory, where he received a letter from his brother Philbert, who had converted to the Nation of Islam. Further letters followed from other family members who had also become Black Muslims. By the time of his transfer to the Norfolk Prison Colony in 1948, Malcolm was himself a disciple of the Nation of Islam. Malcolm Little became Malcolm X. His new identity symbolized the African name that he never knew, stripped from his forebears who had been enslaved by white Christian masters. Through the teachings of Elijah Muhammad, spiritual leader of the Nation of Islam,

Malcolm learned that the "original man" who founded human civilization was black, but that this had been deliberately concealed by whites who distorted the texts of holy scripture. Malcolm started to practice the strict code of personal discipline demanded by the Nation of Islam, refraining from the consumption of pork, alcohol, tobacco, and narcotics. He also embraced the political doctrine of the Black Muslims: racial pride, self-determination, and the establishment of an independent black republic. Malcolm's success in recruiting and converting other inmates to the Nation of Islam eventually led to his being placed under FBI surveillance.

CONCLUSION

Malcolm was paroled on August 7, 1952. He did not look back. Rapidly working his way through the ranks of the Nation of Islam, Malcolm established himself as an outstanding spokesman for the poor and oppressed black masses. The experience of incarceration had proved crucial in determining his new identity and calling. In the years ahead, Malcolm's own tale of crime, imprisonment, and spiritual conversion served as inspiration to the black underclass who formed the core membership of the Nation of Islam.

—Clive Webb

See also Activism; African American Prisoners; Black Panther Party; Critical Resistance; Angela Y. Davis; Education; George Jackson; Nation of Islam; Racism

Further Reading

Goldman, P. (1973). *The death and life of Malcolm X.* New York: Harper & Row.

Malcolm X, & Haley, A. (1965). *The autobiography of Malcolm X.* New York: Grove.

Natambu, K. (2002). *Malcolm X.* Indianapolis, IN: Alpha.

Perry, B. (1991). *Malcolm: The life of a man who changed black America.* Barrytown, NY: Station Hill.

◪ MANAGERIALISM

Managerialism is an ideology. As such, it is a set of values, ideas, and beliefs about the state of the world that provides justification for action. At the heart of managerialism lies the belief that with better management, we can solve economic and social problems, including crime and crime control. Managerialist thought fostered and has been nourished by the development of actuarial justice and its expression in corrections: new penology.

CONTEXT AND DEFINITION

In Western societies in the 1980s, a consensus emerged that governments were regulating, owning, and owing too much, and that the welfare state was not working as planned. People wanted to be taxed less and were expecting others to become more self-reliant. Privatization and deregulation became popular. At the beginning of the 21st century, when globalization is increasing at ever-greater pace, governments are immersed in neo-liberalist philosophy: privatization of programs, deregulation of corporate behaviors, reducing government debts, participating in free trade agreements, and providing fewer social services at a lesser quality.

At the same time that this shift in philosophy occurred, the public sector has been transformed by the emergence of the "New Public Management." The trend, initiated in New Zealand and the United Kingdom, has appeared in the United States and Canada since about 1995. New Public Management is a paradigm that promotes a decentralized and performance-oriented culture in the public sector. More precisely, New Public Management can be identified through a number of features:

- Providing high-quality services that citizens value
- Demanding, measuring, and rewarding improved organizational and individual performance
- Advocating managerial autonomy, particularly by reducing central agency controls
- Recognizing the importance of providing the human and technological resources managers need to meet their performance targets, and
- Maintaining receptiveness to competition and open-mindedness about which public purposes should be performed by public servants as opposed to the private sector (Borins, 2002, p. 3).

Managerialism emerged from the New Public Management trend.

To understand managerialism, *management* has to be distinguished from *administration*. *Administration,* the traditional concept and set of practices, refers to the review and decision making within public services. In contrast, *management* means the search for the best use of resources in pursuit of stated objectives (Politt, 1993, p. 5). This whole enterprise revolves around the tasks of better planning, organizing, staffing, directing, coordinating, and budgeting. Of course, the pursuit of best management often involves transferring many of the values, principles, and practices of the private sector (performance indicators, audit, etc.) to the public sector.

As with many of these trends, managerialism hit the education system, health care, and social services first, and only slowly penetrated criminal justice. Because New Public Management and managerialism developed first in these parts of the world, it is not surprising to find that it has been documented in criminological research mainly in Australia, New Zealand, and the United Kingdom. Traces of it can nevertheless be found in the United States, Canada, and other Western criminal justice systems.

MANAGERIALISM IN THE CRIMINAL JUSTICE SYSTEM

The Representation of Criminal Justice

The mere fact of conceiving of police departments, courts, probation, prison, and parole offices, all organizations with very different goals and logics, as a "system" reflects ideas of managerialism. Justice is no longer to be represented by a blind woman holding a scale. The external "justice" point of view has been replaced by an internal "system" point of view, namely a chart: the criminal justice funnel. This "system" is made of "interconnected" agencies among which information must flow. Bottlenecks must be avoided for faster throughput. This conception of the criminal justice system directly reflects the preoccupation with efficient processing of case and files. Along the same line, the criminal justice system is redefined as a service industry that has to satisfy its customers rather than as the regulatory role of government as it was understood in the past. This redefinition is vivid

when, for example, state-employed parole officers call parolees "clients."

Policing

Within the police force, managerialism induces what Chan (1999) calls a "new accountability." Traditionally, police accountability was conceived with reference to values such as the rule of law and responsible government. Police practices were governed centrally by laws and rules that were enforced by the courts and the police hierarchies. The new accountability has involved a shift from this centralized control to self-regulation and external controls: record keeping by each police officer, monitoring by electronic tracking system and cameras in the patrol cars, auditing, and so on. As a result, some police officers specialize in dealing with accountability requirements while others do the "regular" work. Also, individual police officers as well as the organization become mostly preoccupied with the accountability measures, which now become a measure of their performance.

Tribunals

In accordance with the managerialist trend, productivity and cost efficiency is more and more a preoccupation for the courts. In Britain, for example, a policy has been put in place to encourage a wider use of police cautioning, a practice that has been found as effective as prosecution but less time and resource consuming both for the police and the courts (Raine & Wilson, 1997). For the same reason, policies are put in place to allow a large number of minor offenses to be dealt with by the police through fixed penalties. In Canada, the federal government is even considering doing so for possession of small amount of cannabis. The numeric importance of these cases and their congestion effect on the courts are not alien to the current discussions.

Probation and Parole

The traditional role of parole and probation officers, namely therapeutic intervention, has been seriously shaken in the last decades as it has been colonized by managerialist values and practices.

Accountability and administrative management have replaced rehabilitation as the primary goal of probation and parole. Parole and probation officers are now case managers, and their main tools are restriction of liberty and increased surveillance (Simon, 1993). An interest in the causes of behavior has been replaced by a focus on behavior control and prediction. Likewise, the goal of developing a meaningful relationship between professionals and service users has been replaced by the careful administration of standardized questionnaires and scales. Rehabilitation and individual relationships do not lend themselves easily to performance indicators; control does. Hence, the professionals have something tangible to show for their work (number of contacts, proper forms filled out, etc). Despite official policies, though, some studies showed that both the workers and the service users resist the attrition of the therapeutic relationship.

Prison

With the increasing spread of managerialism, prison workers find themselves in the same situation as probation and parole officers. Their discretion has been limited, and their attempts to reform prisoners curtailed. In both areas of the criminal justice system, the consequences of managerialism varies depending on the population under consideration. Governors (wardens) of women's prisons in England and Wales, for example, find that complying with procedures designed for the guidance, regulation, and performance of men is often difficult. Supposedly gender-neutral regulations are not always appropriate for women prisoners, yet wardens are not allowed to stray from policy. Whereas they had been able to rely on their long-term expertise in order to meet their goals as prison administrators—namely to make prison legitimate to a number of groups (different segments of the public, politicians, academics, etc.) whose demands are often incompatible—now prison governors are often forced to implement codes that may be inappropriate for their population. Moreover, due to the procedural nature of managerialism, the governors themselves are evaluated not only on the outcome of their policies but also on the process itself, which must be clearly documented when any decision is made.

CONCLUSION

Among other things, managerialism in criminal justice emphasizes better standards and greater accountability. A priori, these are positive contributions. However, acting in the name of greater efficiency can also cause neglect of human rights and due process. Moreover, the fetishism of better management should not hide the fact that the assumptions of managerialism are value laden and contestable. For example, whose standards are being imposed? Performance and efficiency for whom? As a result, it is important to ask whether managerialism is appropriate to organizations like those in the criminal justice system that are engaged in meeting public need and performing public services rather than producing consumer goods.

—*Dominique Robert*

See also Actuarial Justice; England and Wales; David Garland; Deterrence Theory Governance; Incapacitation Theory; Legitimacy; New Zealand Parole; Probation; Rehabilitation Theory; Women's Prisons

Further Reading

Barry, M. (2000). The mentor/monitor debate in criminal justice: "What works" for offenders. *British Journal of Social Work, 30,* 575–595.

Borins, S. (2002). New public management, North American style. In K. McLaughlin, S. P. Osborne, & E. Ferlie (Eds.), *The New Public Management: Current trends and future prospects* (pp. 1–21). London: Routledge.

Brownlee, I. (1998). New labour—new penology? Punitive rhetoric and the limits of managerialism in criminal justice policy. *Journal of Law and Society, 25*(3), 313–335.

Carlen, P. (2002). Governing the governors: Telling the tales of managers, mandarins and mavericks. *Criminal Justice, 2*(1), 27–49.

Chan, J. B. L. (1999). Governing police practice: Limits of the new accountability. *British Journal of Sociology, 50*(2), 251–270.

Pollitt, C. (1993). *Managerialism and the public services: Cuts or cultural change in the 1990s?* Oxford, UK: Blackwell.

Raine, J. W., & Wilson, M. J. (1997). Beyond managerialism in criminal justice. *The Howard Journal, 36*(1), 80–95.

Simon, J. (1993). *Poor discipline: Parole and the social control of the underclass, 1890–1990.* Chicago: University of Chicago Press.

☑ MARION, U.S. PENITENTIARY

U.S. Penitentiary (USP) Marion is located 300 miles south of Chicago and 120 miles from St. Louis in the southern tip of Illinois. Marion is a small penitentiary used to isolate high-security male prisoners. The prison has no wall, but is surrounded by a high-security fencing wrapped in razor wire, protected by gun towers, with multiple cellblocks divided by a maze of security grills and doors.

Marion, like all Federal Bureau of Prisons (BOP) prison facilities, is federal property situated on a U.S. government reservation, not that different from a Native American reservation or military base. Legally, USP Marion is not part of Illinois, since it is beyond state jurisdiction.

THE FEDERAL BUREAU OF PRISONS

The BOP uses an "inmate classification system" as a means to segregate, punish, and reward prisoners. This is a "classification ladder" with maximum security at the top and minimum security at the bottom. The classification designations have changed over the years to accommodate the dramatic growth in BOP prisons and population.

The old system had six security levels, with 6–5 being maximum security, 4–2 being medium, and 1 being minimum. USP Marion was the only Level 6 institution. U.S. Penitentiaries were Level 5 (e.g., USP Atlanta, USP Leavenworth, USP Lewisburg, USP Lompoc); the Federal Correctional Institutions (FCI) ranged from 4 to 2 (e.g., FCI Talladega, FCI Sandstone, FCI Oxford); and the Federal Prison Camps (FPC) were 1. Security levels 6 through 2 were "in" custody, which meant inside the fence or wall. Level 1 was "out" custody, which meant they were federal camps and do not have fences. Level 1 "community custody" referred to prisoners in camps who were eligible for community programs, work assignments, or furloughs.

In the 1990s, the BOP collapsed these six security designations into five: high, medium high, medium low, minimum, and administrative. The BOP prisoner population is approximately 10% high (USP), 25% high medium (FCI), 35% low medium (FCI),

and 25% minimum (FPC), with the rest not assigned a security level; many of these men and women are in administrative facilities (detention or medical), in transit, or are held in local jails or private prisons. "Administrative" refers to Administrative Detention Max (ADX) Florence (Colorado), the highest-security prison in the country; FTC Oklahoma City, a medium-security transport prison; and the federal medical centers, which may be maximum, medium, or minimum security.

The federal prisoner population can further be described as 92% male and 50% white, with the rest being black, Hispanic, Asian, Native American, or "other." The BOP reports that 70% of prisoners are American citizens, with 20% being Mexican, Colombian, or Cuban, and 10% unknown or from other countries. Seventy-five percent of these men and women are serving sentences longer than five years, with nearly 50% doing 10 years or more. Fifty-eight percent are doing time for drug convictions. The average age of a federal prisoner is 37 years. The federal prison system has no parole; all prisoners are required to serve at least 85% of their sentence before release to community supervision.

All federal penitentiaries (maximum security) and correctional institutions (medium security) have disciplinary or administrative detention cellblocks that hold hundreds of prisoners for weeks or months at a time. In comparison, USP Marion and ADX Florence are used to isolate individual prisoners for years at a time. These prisons are used to segregate maximum-security male prisoners who are escape risks, political problems, a threat to the order of other institutions, or have assaulted or murdered prisoners or correctional staff. Today, Marion serves as a model for the construction of similar federal and state facilities.

HISTORY

USP Alcatraz served as the nation's highest-security prison until it closed in 1963. As Alcatraz was decommissioned, the prisoners were transferred to large maximum-security penitentiaries, like USP Leavenworth, USP Atlanta, USP Lewisburg, and USP Lompoc. These are "mainline" penitentiaries; they each hold several thousand prisoners. In these penitentiaries, the prisoners sleep in locked cells but are allowed to travel to the dining hall, work station, and yard through a controlled movement that happens once an hour.

In 1963, the BOP built USP Marion as a smaller prison to house the Alcatraz convicts and others. Some of these were political prisoners who were associated with the Black Panthers, Japanese Red Army, anarchist groups, and the American Indian Movement. In 1973, the "control unit" cellblocks were first created at Marion. These consisted of segregation cells, where prisoners were locked in their cells but were allowed out for limited activities. In 1979, Marion was designated the only Level 6 institution. At this time, Marion became the primary destination for federal prisoners considered by the BOP to be disruptive or dangerous.

In 1983, Marion erupted in violence, when during a six-day period two officers and one prisoner were killed, while two other officers were seriously injured. To restore order, additional officers were brought into the prison. It is reported that the officers retaliated by brutally beating prisoners. Since that time, Marion has had a history of unrelenting warfare between convicts and correctional staff.

Since 1983, the prison has been in permanent lockdown. Prisoners confined in control unit cellblocks are confined 22–24 hours a day in their one-man cells and are not allowed any physical contact with other inmates. They are fed in their cells and are subject to intense security procedures.

THE "MEAN" LITTLE HOUSE

Marion is known for having some of the most violent prisoners in the BOP. Some of these are spies, terrorists, and political activists sent there directly from court. Most of the men who are transferred to Marion from other institutions have become violent after years of brutal survival in other federal or state penitentiaries. The minimum success of Marion has been keeping some of these dangerous individuals locked up securely. The BOP claims isolating violent prisoners at USP Marion and ADX Florence has lowered the rate of assault in the rest of the federal prison system.

Nevertheless, research suggest that only a small number of federal prisoners require the close supervision provided by USP Marion's control unit design. Furthermore, critics argue that Marion and other supermax penitentiaries are systematically socializing prisoners to be more violent. Sensory deprivation, physical and mental deterioration of prisoners, in addition to high rates of suicide and murder seem intended to bend, break, and destroy prisoners. Those who are not broken get even stronger and more dangerous.

THE PRISONERS

Marion has housed political prisoners, organized gangsters, drug cartel members, spies, terrorists, gang leaders, government informants in need of protection, and foreign officials. Some of the most famous individuals have been convicts who have become "legends in their own time" among federal prisoners. These are those men who have defied federal prison authorities by disrupting the orderly operation of different penal institutions or masterminding prison demonstrations or rebellions.

By BOP standards, Marion has a small population. For example, the inmate count at Marion is only 357, and its rated capacity is 440, as compared to "big house" penitentiaries like USP Atlanta with 2,151 and USP Leavenworth with 1,200. All prisons count their prisoner population several times a day. "Big house" refers to full-scale penitentiaries with tall walls and gun towers, many of which were built in the 19th or early 20th centuries.

Some prisoners, especially those serving long sentences, may be difficult to manage in large institutions, where prisoners live two or more men to a cell and walk corridors on the way to the dining hall, work station, or recreational yard. The BOP sends prisoners to Marion when they have been designated as unable to live in "general population" prisons.

PRISON STAFF

The officers at Marion are recruited from both the local community and from bureau staff nationwide. Federal correctional officers must transfer to distant institutions to climb the BOP career ladder. Many officers would prefer to work in minimum- or medium-security facilities rather than at penitentiaries or high-security facilities like Marion. In general, the higher the security level, the more violence and assaults against staff. As Marion is a special prison with severe security procedures, the BOP prefers that prison staff be reassigned to other prisons after three years of service. Nonetheless some officers employed at Marion may be compelled to remain at the institution, and forego promotions, because of family obligations.

CONTROL UNIT

Marion is the first experiment by the federal government with high-security administrative detention. "Disciplinary detention" refers to prisoners being confined in solitary confinement when found in violation of prison rules. In comparison, "administrative detention" is based on the dictates of the prison administration and does not require a disciplinary charge, hearing, or conviction. In effect, prison authorities may use administrative detention to isolate individual prisoners.

Marion control units do not have "controlled movement" of the prison population every hour. There is minimal movement by prisoners within the institution. The convicts are locked in their cells 22–24 hours a day, where they receive all meals, and they are not allowed to talk or socialize with one another. Marion has separate control unit cellblocks reserved for violent prisoners, a high-security unit for protective custody prisoners, and additional units that, while restrictive, provide a gradual increase in institutional privileges.

Generally, after one or more years of good conduct reports, prisoners may be moved to less restrictive cellblocks where they are gradually allowed more privileges. These may include eating in a dining hall, federal prison industry work, commissary access, and social activities.

PROGRAMS AND SERVICES

Marion has had few programs or services for rehabilitation. The BOP officially repudiated rehabilitation

in 1976. Still, most federal prison facilities do have education, usually limited to adult basic education (ABE; 8th grade) and general equivalency diploma (GED; 12th grade); job training programs, for example, grounds and building maintenance or food service; and short courses on anger management, stress reduction, parenting, and substance abuse.

Marion prisoners have few program opportunities until they reach the less restrictive cellblocks. Even then their options are limited to self-study to pass ABE or GED, television, and reading. As they are not allowed outside the building, there is no opportunity to engage in outdoor activities or work. Since 1968, Marion prisoners have been subjected to behavior modification experiments that include intense group pressure, thought reform techniques, and transactional analysis. It is also reported that prisoners are forced to take medication. Once Marion prisoners have graduated from the control units, they work in the Federal Prison Industries (UNICOR) prison cable factory. UNICOR Marion produces electronics communication cables for the military used in tanks, armored personnel carriers, and helicopters. During the Gulf War, the prisoners were compelled to do overtime production. Larger factories producing the same military hardware operate at FCI Oxford and FMC Lexington. Marion prisoners are required to work in the small prison factory before they are transferred back to "mainline" penitentiaries or are released to the street.

PRISONERS RELEASED FROM USP MARION

What happens when prisoners locked down in control units, after years of brutal conditions and socialization, are released to the "free world" without the benefit of programs, services, furloughs, or halfway houses? Marion prisoners, like those released from most maximum-security prisons, go straight to the street when their sentences are completed because they are too hardcore to live in halfway houses. The outcome is often sadly predictable. One famous example can be seen in Jack Henry Abbott, whose book *In the Belly of the Beast* (1981) became a national best-seller. Abbott, who served 25 years in prison, did 15 years in solitary confinement. He stabbed a waiter to death on a Manhattan sidewalk within six weeks of his release from Marion.

FEDERAL PRISON CAMP

The federal prison reservation includes a satellite minimum-security camp immediately adjacent to the prison. These Marion campers work doing grounds keeping and food service inside the main institution.

USP MARION AND COMPARABLE SUPERMAX PENITENTIARIES

USP Marion represents the blueprint for building super-secure federal and state facilities. For example, many federal medium-security facilities or correctional institutions have recently built new administrative segregation cells for solitary confinement.

States have recently turned to the use of "supermax" units or institutions to control the most disruptive or potentially troublesome prisoners. A survey conducted by the National Institute of Corrections in 1997 found at least 57 supermax facilities, with more than 13,500 beds in the United States, and 10 jurisdictions were developing 3,000 additional supermax beds. Roy King updated these figures in 1999 to 34 states with nearly 20,000 cells. Still, the figures are only an estimate, as "supermax" is defined differently by many prison systems. At the very least, we know that across the country there are a growing number of prisoners confined in high-security cellblocks. The conditions of confinement in these prisons are more restrictive than those on death row. Supermax prisons have no educational or vocational programs, with prisoners provided only limited visiting time with family, phone communication, or access to law library, and confined for the duration of their stay in austere 60–80-square-foot cells. These new high-security facilities are expensive, costing the taxpayers additional monies per square foot and bed space. Scarce public resources are squandered on concrete and steel structures rather than spent on education and job training for prisoners. The BOP constructed a new supermax in 1994.

Administrative MAX (ADX) Florence is one of four federal prisons in the Florence Correctional Complex built in southern Colorado. It is now the highest-security prison in the United States. This prison was built not only to eliminate escapes but also to defend from outside attack. At medium- and maximum-security facilities, an "outrider" is a correctional officer who patrols the prison perimeter in a pickup truck, armed with a shotgun, outside the fence or wall. The Florence outrider is a white armored personnel carrier. There are 550 permanent lockdown one-man cells, but only half of these are occupied at any given time. The empty cells are for prisoners who may be transferred in from rebellious or rioting institutions. In 1998, Ray Luc Levasseur (1998a, 1998b), a prisoner at ADX Florence, wrote about four-point spread eagle restraints, forced feedings, cell extractions, mind control medications, and chemical weapons used to incapacitate prisoners.

TRANSFER OF HIGH-SECURITY PRISONERS

High-security prisoners may be transferred back and forth between USP Marion, ADX Florence, and segregation cellblocks in mainline federal penitentiaries. Some of these are prisoners sentenced by state courts that have been moved into federal custody. The BOP uses transfers to further isolate high-security prisoners who are suspected of planning escapes or insurrections.

CONCLUSION

We know very little about these supermax facilities and the long-term consequences of this form of severe prison conditions on prisoners. We do recognize that penitentiary convicts assigned to administrative segregation and supermax facilities may spend years in these units before being released. We also know that some portion of this population is released directly from prison to the streets and, in some cases, with no parole supervision, assistance, or plan for their reentry to the community.

—Stephen C. Richards

See also Jack Abbott; ADX Florence; Alcatraz; Control Unit; Convict Criminology; Corcoran; California State Prison; Disciplinary Segregation; Federal Prison System; History of Prisons; Maximum Security; Medium Security; Minimum Security; New Generation Prisons; Riots; State Prison System; Supermax Prisons; Violence

Further Reading

Abbott, J. H. (1981). *In the belly of the beast: Letters from prison*. New York: Random House.

Abbott, J. H., & Zack, N. (1987). *My return*. Buffalo, NY: Prometheus.

Austin, J., Bruce, M. A., Carroll, L., McCall, P. L., & Richards, S. C. (2001). The use of incarceration in the United States. American Society of Criminology National Policy Committee. *Critical Criminology: An International Journal, 10*(1), 17–41.

Keve, P. W. (1991). *Prisons and the American conscience: A history of federal corrections*. Carbondale: Southern Illinois University Press.

Levasseur, R. L. (1998a). From USP Marion to ADX Florence (and back again): The fire inside. In D. Burton-Rose, D. Pens, & P. Wright (Eds.), *The celling of America: An inside look at the U.S. prison industry* (pp. 200–205). Monroe, ME: Common Courage.

Levasseur, R. L. (1998b). Trouble coming everyday: ADX, one year later. In D. Burton-Rose, D. Pens, & P. Wright (Eds.), *The celling of America: An inside look at the U.S. prison industry* (pp. 206–211). Monroe, ME: Common Courage.

Ross, J. I., & Richards, S. C. (Eds.). (2002). *Behind bars: Surviving prison*. New York: Alpha.

Ross, J. I., & Richards, S. C. (Eds.). (2003). *Convict criminology*. Belmont, CA: Wadsworth.

☙ MARTINSON, ROBERT

Robert Martinson was a correctional researcher who became famous following the publication of a provocative 1974 article on correctional treatment entitled "What Works? Questions and Answers About Prison Reform," in which he concluded that nothing works to reform and rehabilitate criminals. Although the phrase "Nothing works" became synonymous specifically with Martinson, he was actually a member of a research team that included Douglas Lipton and Judith Wilks, themselves well-regarded scholars in the field of corrections.

THE RESEARCH

These authors analyzed 231 studies of rehabilitation and treatment programs conducted over a 22-year period from 1945 to 1967. The study was sanctioned by the New York State Governor's Special Committee on Criminal Offenders and was funded through the Omnibus Crime Control and Safe Streets Act. Although final revisions for the report were completed in 1971, for political reasons associated with the nature of the findings, the publication of the full report was withheld by the Governor's Committee for more than four years. Following a district court case in Bronx, New York, however, Martinson was able to publish, reportedly without the authorization of his coauthors, the first official account of this research in the widely recognized and distributed magazine *Public Interest*.

Known as the Martinson Report, his article contains one of the most oft-cited statements in the history of criminal justice: "With few and isolated exceptions, the rehabilitative efforts that have been reported so far have had no appreciable effect on recidivism" (Martinson, 1974, p. 25). In the matter of just one sentence, Martinson challenged the conventional wisdom about rehabilitation that had prevailed for nearly a century. His article also provoked criticisms of the effectiveness and viability of parole, early release, and indeterminate sentencing.

IMPACT AND CONSEQUENCES

The rehabilitative model that for so long had dictated sentencing policy shifted during the 1970s to a crime-control model focused almost entirely on retribution and deterrence. Of course, this change came about not simply because of one article. Instead, the ready acceptance of Martinson's conclusions was as much due to the political context of the time as it was to the substance of his claims. A number of high-profile prison revolts, including events at San Quentin and Attica, brought to light the deplorable conditions of U.S. prisons. There was also a spike in crime rates and a growing climate of political conservatism. This combination of factors set the stage for Martinson's report and commenced the demise of the rehabilitation paradigm.

THE ACADEMIC RESPONSE

Many direct challenges have been made against the "Nothing works" doctrine in the three decades since the publication of Martinson's article. Though some conclude that the body of evidence is now robust enough to proclaim that Martinson's report has been discredited and that his extreme pessimism was unfounded, most reappraisals of Martinson's original thesis are usually prefaced with such qualifying phrases as "guardedly optimistic," "cautious hopefulness," and "'promising." Given the fervor in energy and resources devoted to the search to prove Martinson wrong, such tempered statements do little to justify with a high level of confidence that Martinson was simply wrong. There are, however, enough modest success stories to suggest that the bleak outlook may have been premature. Indeed, Martinson himself provided a retraction to his originally pessimistic view in a 1979 article in the *Hofstra Law Review*. Nonetheless, his later modification of his extreme position did little to dispel the acceptance of the original thesis or to curb the enthusiasm of those who saw Martinson's original conclusion as politically appealing.

More recent and sophisticated analyses of treatment have concluded that many programs work, as long as they are offender specific, sufficiently funded, well designed, and well implemented. In this, they follow Ted Palmer's original reply to Martinson in 1975, in which he asserted that, rather than asking what works best for offenders as a whole, we should ask, "Which methods work best for which types of offenders, and under what conditions or in what types of setting?" (Palmer, 1975, p. 150).

CONCLUSION

The Martinson report brought to light the glaring lack of sophistication of then-current research methodologies and evaluation techniques, forcing researchers to develop meaningful evaluation criteria and to articulate clear and consistent definitions of recidivism. It also raised questions about the proper role of science in informing policy and the capacity of outside forces (e.g., funding agencies) to control the direction and dissemination of scientific research.

While Martinson had his critics, there is no denying the substantial contributions that he made to the field of corrections. Along with the impact he had on correctional policy and philosophy, Martinson also single-handedly influenced the research agendas and professional careers of many scholars. Despite his influence, Martinson's career was cut short when he committed suicide in 1980. At the time he was working with Judith Wilks on a research program assessing the impact of various programs on recidivism at the Center for Knowledge in Criminal Justice Planning. A collection of Martinson's papers and correspondence is maintained in the Lloyd Sealy Library at the John Jay College of Criminal Justice in New York City.

Possibly no one person had more of an impact on the field of correctional treatment than Robert Martinson. If Martinson himself was attracted to the "Nothing works" doctrine because it had the potential to lead to a decrease in the use of imprisonment, he would be sorely disappointed. He likely would not have predicted, certainly based upon his research findings, the dramatic growth in prisons as the almost exclusive means of social control.

—*David B. Taylor*

See also Attica Correctional Facility; Deterrence Theory; John DiIulio, Jr.; Incapacitation Theory; Just Deserts Theory; Parole; Rehabilitation Theory; Riots; San Quentin State Prison; Truth in Sentencing

Further Reading

Cullen, F., & Applegate, B. (Eds.). (1998). *Offender rehabilitation*. Brookfield, VT: Dartmouth Publishing.

Duguid, S. (2000). *Can prisons work? The prisoner as object and subject in modern corrections*. Toronto: University of Toronto Press.

Lipton, D., Martinson, R., & Wilks, J. (1975). *The effectiveness of correctional treatment: A survey of treatment evaluation studies*. New York: Praeger.

Martinson, R. (1974). What works? Questions and answers about prison reform. *Public Interest, 35*, 22–54.

Martinson, R. (1979). New findings, new views: A note of caution regarding sentencing reform. *Hofstra Law Review, 7*, 243–258.

Palmer, T. (1975). Martinson revisited. *Journal of Research in Crime and Delinquency, 12,* 133–152.

Sarre, R. (2001). Beyond "what works?" A 25 year jubilee retrospective of Robert Martinson's famous article. *The Australian and New Zealand Journal of Criminology, 34,* 38–46.

☑ MASSACHUSETTS REFORMATORY

The history of the Massachusetts Reformatory at Concord provides an instructive case study of the changing perceptions and uses of imprisonment. Beginning as an Auburn-style penitentiary in 1878, it was converted in 1884 into the Massachusetts Reformatory for Men, which was patterned on the much more famous Elmira Reformatory in New York that opened in 1876. In the 1920s, it shifted in use to a juvenile and youthful offender facility, while in the 1950s it became the Massachusetts Correctional Institution at Concord. It is now a medium-security facility that serves as the Massachusetts Department of Correction's Reception and Diagnostic Center.

HISTORY

The first Massachusetts Prison, designed by Charles Bulfinch, was built in Charlestown in 1806 and reorganized in the 1820s as a model penitentiary. The rules and regulations of the facility provided for an initial period of solitary confinement for each inmate to ensure reflection and remorse, to be followed until the end of their sentence by "hard labor" in silence, augmented if necessary by the use of the whip. As described by one warden in an 1829 report, the inmates moved and acted "like machines" under the discipline of the penitentiary. Under labor contracts, the productive labor of the prisoners was assumed not only to provide for the costs of the prison but also provide a profit for the state, a goal retained but frequently not met.

With the aging of the Massachusetts Prison at Charleston, in 1878 a new facility, considered a model prison for the time, was built at Concord, with individual cells lit by large windows. In 1884, in the midst of controversy over both the profitability of its vocational shops and the desire that Massachusetts respond to the recommendations of the 1870 Principles of the National Congress of Penitentiary and Reformatory Discipline, the governor signed a bill that returned the prisoners held at Concord to Charleston and established the Massachusetts Reformatory for Men. Rejecting the systems of isolation, lockstep, and fear, the principles emphasized that the goals of prison discipline were to reward good conduct, industry, and educational efforts—to resocialize, retrain, and reform offenders, especially the youthful offender. One consequence of these goals was the movement to indeterminate sentences, with release from prison based on the individual efforts of the prisoner.

Massachusetts had already responded to the reformatory movement after successful agitation by influential women within the state, with the construction of the Reformatory Prison for Women at Sherborn (later renamed Framingham) in 1877—one of the first reformatories for women in the United States. Containing large work- and schoolrooms, the reformatory offered the hope that with disciplined work and education, and incentives of increased privileges and conditional release, vagrants, prostitutes, drunkards, and "idle and disorderly women" would be reformed. Women convicted of more serious offenses continued to be sentenced to the penitentiary.

THE MEN'S REFORMATORY AT CONCORD

In an effort to bring the 1870 principles into practice in Massachusetts for male inmates, in December 1884, the name of the Concord Prison was changed to become the Massachusetts Reformatory for Men. The initiative was based on the widely heralded New York Reformatory for Men in Elmira, founded by Zebulon Brockway. However, like Elmira, it did not live up to its promise, facing, as did the New York facility, major overcrowding as well as other difficulties. In the first nine months of operation it held more than 700 prisoners.

Following the movement for indeterminate sentences, on July 24, 1886, a new law was passed that would allow for sentencing with no fixed duration.

A prisoner could be sentenced for a maximum of five years (for crimes like breaking and entering or larceny) but could be released on parole within two or less. Those sentenced to a maximum of two years for drunkenness could also be released on parole considerably earlier. Ideals were often distant from practice.

The Concord Reformatory was underfunded. In 1892, for example, there were still only seven police officers who served as guards for 700 to 1,000 prisoners. For many years the age composition was mixed, with prisoners from 14 to 60 years of age or older housed at the reformatory. These men were separated from one another and put to work on the basis of elaborate rules of classification. Inmates were employed in cloth- or furniture-making industries inside as well as on extensive prison farms. Another 9% worked outside the prison in local factories.

With the subsequence changes in mission and administration that occurred through the years at Concord and Framingham, both reformatories tended in time to resemble ordinary prisons, with systems of discipline equally harsh and limited resources to prepare their inmates for release. In Sheldon and Eleanor Glueck's famous and controversial recidivism studies of the "graduates" of the two institutions in the 1930s, the researchers found that some 80% of inmates were again found guilty of crimes and returned to some form of imprisonment, usually jails. Their conclusion that the reformatories failed to reform was not unexpected (Glueck & Glueck, 1930, 1934).

CONCLUSION

Having started as a general reformatory for men of all ages, the Massachusetts Reformatory at Concord became a juvenile and young adult facility after World War I. The earlier high hopes placed in the reformatory movement were not realized because lack of funding, difficulty in recruiting adequate staff, and frequent overcrowding made it difficult to carry out the intensive classification, retraining, and education that was assumed necessary for the goals of the reformatory to be achieved. The later Glueck

studies (1930, 1934) made officials aware of the need for modifications such as age segregation and greater attention to relevant training, but overall their research found that only a relatively small percentage of young men (and young women) could be considered to have been truly reformed.

—*Hans Bakker*

See also Auburn System; Zebulon Brockway; Elmira Reformatory; Framingham, MCI; History of Prisons; Indeterminate Sentencing; Patuxent Institution

Further Reading

Freeman, E. B. (1981). *Their sisters' keepers: Women's prison reform in America*. Ann Arbor: University of Michigan Press.

Glueck, S., & Glueck, E. T. (1930). *500 criminal careers*. New York: Knopf.

Glueck, S., & Glueck, E. T. (1934). *500 delinquent women*. New York: Knopf.

Laub, J. H., & Vaillant, G. E. (2000). Delinquency and mortality: A 50-year follow-up study of 1,000 delinquent and non-delinquent boys. *American Journal of Psychiatry, 157*(1), 96–102.

Massachusetts Commissioners of Prisons. (1878, 1882, 1883, 1886, 1887, 1890, 1899). *Annual Reports*. Boston: Wright & Potter, State Printers; Rand, Avery & Co. and other "Printers to the Commonwealth."

Pelligrew, F. G. (1895). *A manual for prison officials; Commonwealth of Massachusetts rules and regulations for the government of the Massachusetts Reformatory* (approved March 11, 1891). Boston: Wright & Potter Publishers, State Printers.

◪ MAXIMUM SECURITY

Prison inmates and institutions are given security classifications. Most classification systems divide prisoners and facilities into minimum, medium, and maximum levels. Many states and the federal system now also have supermaximum secure prisons; however, under ordinary circumstances, "maximum security" refers to the highest level of inmate classification and institutional security.

Maximum-security facilities are designed to allow prison administrators total physical control over all aspects of inmates' conduct for extended periods of time. Prisoners classified as maximum security are placed in these facilities, where they are usually housed in their cells for most of the day. The cells are typically built to house one inmate, although prison crowding has sometimes forced two inmates into a cell.

HISTORY

The idea of a maximum-security facility grew from the practice of solitary confinement that formed the roots of American penal practice. In the late 1700s and early 1800s, citizens in Philadelphia reorganized the Walnut Street Jail and introduced solitary confinement as a means of reforming convicted felons. They believed that convicts incarcerated in isolation could more readily reflect on their sins, work out their own paths to salvation, and thus revitalize the inner light of God's grace. Their beliefs inspired authorities to construct single- and separate-cell prisons in Pennsylvania and elsewhere. This strategy became known as "the Pennsylvania system" and shaped prison practice in most places until it was replaced in the mid-19th century by the Auburn system.

In the early 19th century, a newly organized Auburn Prison in New York State began operation. Prisoners in this institution worked together in workshops and ate together in dining halls; however, at night they slept in separate cells. The undergirding ideology of this incarceration practice was the Puritan premise that criminals were innately depraved. All society could hope to do was bend the convict to its will through relentless discipline and punishment. Ironically, the workshops helped teach the inmates skills and trades; consequently they inadvertently opened the door to inmate rehabilitation. This prison style became known as "the Auburn system."

The Pennsylvania system ultimately failed because prison operators did not take into account the devastating effects of isolation on the sanity of many inmates. Rehabilitation attempts under such conditions proved to be unsuccessful. As a result, at the end of the 19th century, the Auburn system became the major penological practice in America. This approach to prison management sought to create a skilled and disciplined workforce. Though it

embraced some rehabilitation and reform-oriented practices, compliance in the Auburn system was enforced through swift and severe punishment. In the early 20th century, the Auburn system was also replaced, this time by a more limited vision of prison management in which inmates were simply warehoused in new fortress-like maximum-security prisons. Order was enforced with swift, violent force. Prisoners in these facilities often sat idle; they merely passed time. As a result, they commonly lost their physical and mental alertness. Alcatraz, commonly known as "the Rock," was one of the most notorious of these new-style maximum-security penitentiaries.

SECURITY AND CLASSIFICATION

The security rating assigned to a prison affects a range of structural and environmental features, such as the type of housing it offers and its inmate: staff ratio. Other conditions, including whether the institution has a mobile patrol and/or a gun tower, what type of perimeter barriers it has, and what its internal security and detection devices are like, also determine the security rating.

The security level of an inmate is usually based on his or her potential risk to the community. Other factors that are taken into account include an inmate's sentence length; security of the victim, witnesses, and the general public; and other judicial recommendations. The classification process starts once an offender has been convicted and sentenced by the courts and continues when the person arrives at a specific prison. Usually prisoners' security levels are reconsidered at regular intervals throughout their time behind bars. In the federal system, for example, the first reassessment of a person's classification level usually occurs around seven months after arrival in a facility. Reviews then occur on an annual basis. In these security reviews, many different factors are taken into account, including sentence length, escape attempts, history of violence, drug and alcohol abuse, mental or psychological stability, frequency and nature of disciplinary reports, a demonstration of financial responsibility (meaning the ability to pay fines, restitution, or family support), and family stability. Reevaluations may increase or decrease an inmate's security level and may sometimes cause an individual to be moved to a different establishment.

THE FEDERAL SYSTEM

Only individuals who are defined as "assaultive, predacious, riotous, serious escape risks, or seriously disruptive to the orderly running of an institution" are given the rating of "maximum." All men with this security level are usually sent to a penitentiary or, if deemed particularly dangerous or difficult to control, to USP Marion or ADX Florence. The rare woman labeled "maximum" may be held at a special high-security unit at FMC Carswell. A security rating of maximum not only affects where a prisoner resides but also determines in what occupation he or she may take part, because prisoners with this rating are subject to "maximum control and supervision."

U.S. penitentiaries (USPs) such as Marion and Leavenworth have walls or reinforced fences and close staff supervision. Prisoners in them are held in both single-occupant and cell housing. There is no penitentiary for women.

RACE AND GENDER

Research suggests that disproportionate numbers of minorities tend to be given higher security levels. This may reflect their greater history of confinement. The practice is also, in some cases, connected to the war on drugs or to a person's involvement in a gang. In the federal system, for example, the length of sentence is one of the determinants of a person's security level. Since drug offenders tend to receive particularly long sentences, they are more likely to be placed in higher-security facilities, even if it was their first offense and involved no violence. Likewise, in most prison systems, gang affiliation results in a higher security classification level.

In contrast, few women are given the rating of maximum security. In the federal prison system, the small number of maximum-security women are concentrated in part of FMC Carswell. Before Carswell, such women were housed at the notorious control unit in FMC Lexington. Other prison systems, like Connecticut's, rate their sole women's facility as inclusive of all security levels. This practice means that women of lower security live under restricted conditions due to the presence of a small number of maximum-security-rated offenders.

EFFECTS OF MAXIMUM SECURITY

Higher-security-level facilities are typically characterized by higher rates of officially reported disciplinary infractions when compared to lower-security facilities. Critics argue that the inmates act out as a result of the inhumane nature of high-security establishments. In contrast, proponents of maximum-security facilities contend that the increased number of incidents reflects the nature of those who are housed in maximum-security institutions. Contradicting both views, self-report studies have revealed less total misconduct in the higher-security institutions because of the reduced opportunities that result from the increased supervision and structure of such places.

Several other consequences of imprisonment in maximum-security institutions have emerged in the literature. Some studies have linked serious mental health problems to the social deprivation suffered by the inmates who are housed in some of these facilities. In addition, the lack of rehabilitation programs and contacts with community or family members often reduces the opportunities that the prisoners will have for correcting the behavior that was the reason for their incarceration. As such, maximum-security inmates released into the community typically have high rates of recidivism.

CONCLUSION

In most prison systems, a security or classification rating of maximum security represents the highest and most restricted level of institutions and inmates. Maximum-custody facilities are those that are most often portrayed in movies and on television. However, only about 40% of all prisons in the United States are maximum-security facilities. In operating these facilities, the progressive goals of rehabilitation or reintegration are typically not a part of the higher-custody institution's scheme. Instead, the facilities are geared toward supervision and control. More often, the goal of these facilities that house maximum-security inmates is solely incapacitation.

—*Benjamin Steiner*

See also ADX Florence; Attica Correctional Facility; Auburn Correctional Facility; Auburn System; Classification; Disciplinary Segregation; Discipline System; Eastern State Penitentiary; History of Prisons; Incapacitation Theory; Marion Penitentiary; Medium Security; Minimum Security; Pelican Bay State Prison; Pennsylvania System; Quakers; Rehabilitation Theory; San Quentin State Prison; Solitary Confinement; Supermax Prisons; Violence; Walnut Street Jail

Further Reading

Abbott, J. H. (1981). *In the belly of the beast.* New York: Vintage.

Bosworth, M. (2002). *The U.S. federal prison system.* Thousand Oaks, CA: Sage.

Fleisher, M. (1989). *Warehousing violence.* Newbury Park, CA: Sage.

Fox, J. (1982). *Organizational and racial conflict in maximum-security prisons.* Lexington, MA: Lexington Books.

Human Rights Watch. (2000). *Out of sight: Super-maximum security confinement in the United States.* New York: Human Rights Watch.

Irwin, J., & Austin, J. (1997). *It's about time: America's imprisonment binge* (2nd ed.). Belmont, CA: Wadsworth.

Johnson, R. (2002). *Hard time* (3rd ed.). Belmont, CA: Wadsworth.

May, J. P. (Ed.). (2000). *Building violence.* Thousand Oaks, CA: Sage.

Sykes, G. (1958). *The society of captives.* Princeton, NJ: Princeton University Press.

◼ McVEIGH, TIMOTHY (1968–2001)

Timothy McVeigh was convicted and executed for the 1995 bombing of the Alfred P. Murrah Building in Oklahoma City. The "deadliest terrorist attack in United States history" (Kittrie & Wedlock, 1998, p. 776) to that time killed 168 people, including children in the day care center that was located directly above the blast. McVeigh's motivations appear to have been rooted in an antigovernment ideology fueled by the government's killing of Randy Weaver's wife and child at Ruby Ridge, Idaho, and 76 Branch Davidians (including children) at Waco, Texas—an event occurring exactly two years prior to the Oklahoma City bombing.

In a letter from death row, McVeigh explained, "The bombing was a retaliatory strike: a counterattack, for the cumulative raids (and subsequent violence and damage) that federal agents had participated in over the preceding years (including, but not limited to, Waco)" (Vidal, 2001, p. 410). He believed government actions were growing "increasingly militaristic and violent, to the point where at Waco, our government—like the Chinese—was deploying tanks against its own citizens," so the Oklahoma City bombing represented for him the "moral and strategic equivalent of the U.S. hitting a government building in Serbia or Iraq" (p. 410).

BIOGRAPHICAL DETAILS

McVeigh is described as having a high IQ and a relatively normal childhood involving comic books, football, student council, computer hacking, and a job at Burger King. He played war with the children he baby-sat and enjoyed variations like *Star Wars:* "What seemed to attract him was the battle of good and evil" in which McVeigh 'always took the side of the good guys' (Michel & Herbeck, 2001, p. 26). In a pattern consistent through his later years, he could be charming when he wanted, but he rarely dated. His growing fascination with guns and survivalism led him to enlist in the Army in 1998. He excelled in basic training, where he met Terry Nichols and Michael Fortier, both of whom were also convicted for participating in the Oklahoma City bombing. While in the military, McVeigh first read the *Turner Diaries* (McDonald, 1996), a fictional racist account of Earl Turner's resistance to the "Zionist Occupied Government" that overtakes the United States and disarms white citizens. McVeigh claims he did not share the book's racism, but identified with "the *Diaries'* obsession with guns and explosives and a final all-out war against the 'System'" (Vidal, 2001, p. 409).

THE FIRST GULF WAR

During Operation Desert Storm, the military decorated McVeigh with a Bronze Star for valor, among other commendations (Hamm, 1997, p. 149). After the Persian Gulf War, he failed Special Forces training. With a "postwar hangover," posttraumatic stress, and possibly Gulf War Syndrome, McVeigh spent the next years leading up to the bombing traveling the gun show circuit, making contacts in the survivalist right, discussing the *Turner Diaries*, spending time with Nichols and Fortier, and taking methamphetamine.

THE CASE

Police arrested McVeigh near Oklahoma City because his car had no license plate and the officer found several weapons. McVeigh was wearing a shirt with a quote attributed to Thomas Jefferson: "The Tree of Liberty must be refreshed from time to time with the blood of patriots and tyrants." While he was held, authorities connected him to the bombing, and the trial would be shown via closed circuit TV to an overflow crowd of survivors of the bombing and victims' relatives. The jury convicted him on all 11 counts after four days of deliberations, and after the hearings in the penalty phase, the jury deliberated two more days before handing down the death sentence.

DETENTION AND EXECUTION

While awaiting execution, McVeigh was first held at the supermax federal facility in Florence, Colorado. He was on "Bomber's Row" with Ted Kaczynski ("the Unabomber") and Ramzi Yousef (convicted in the 1993 World Trade Center bombing). McVeigh was transferred in July 1999, "when the government decided it had enough death-row inmates—twenty was the magic number—to make it cost effective" to open the only federal death row in Terra Haute, Indiana (Michel & Herbeck, 2001, p. 373).

McVeigh claimed, "My objective was a state-assisted suicide," so he waived his appeals to hasten the execution date (Michel & Herbeck, 2001, pp. 358, 374). The Bureau of Prisons made arrangements to show his lethal injection via closed circuit TV to victims back in Oklahoma, in the same way as his trial. McVeigh requested that his execution be broadcast more publicly, and the Internet Entertainment Group unsuccessfully sued to be allowed to Webcast the event. As he had throughout his trial and sentencing, McVeigh remained expressionless and offered no apologies for what he had done.

CONCLUSION

McVeigh's trial for 168 deaths was the largest murder case in U.S. history. His execution was the first conducted by the federal government since 1933, when Victor Fuguer was hanged for kidnapping and murder. The execution thus represents the first experience of the federal government with lethal injection and the first use of the new facilities at Terra Haute. The closed circuit broadcast was the first time an execution had been televised, even to a limited audience, but in a manner consistent with federal prohibitions on making a photographic record of an execution.

—Paul Leighton

See also Aryan Brotherhood; Aryan Nations; Capital Punishment; Death Row, Deathwatch; Enemy Combatant; Federal Prison System; Terre Haute Penitentiary Death Row; USA Patriot Act

Further Reading

Hamm, M. (1997). *Apocalypse in Oklahoma*. Boston: Northeastern University Press.

Kittrie, N., & Wedlock, E. (Eds.). (1998). *The tree of liberty: A documentary history of rebellion and political crime in America, Vol. 2* (rev. ed.). Baltimore: Johns Hopkins University Press.

Leighton, P. (2001). Why is a photographer at an execution a criminal? Retrieved from http://www.paulsjusticepage.com/cjethics/6-emergingissues/lappin-critique.htm

McDonald, A. (1996). *The Turner diaries: A novel* (2nd ed.). Fort Lee, NJ: Barricade Books.

Michel, L., & Herbeck, D. 2001. *American terrorist*. New York: HarperCollins.

Vidal, G. (2001, September). The meaning of Timothy McVeigh. *Vanity Fair*, pp. 347–415.

◪ MEDICAL EXPERIMENTS

The use of inmates for medical experiments is a part of American prison history that tells us as much about society's attitudes toward prisoners as it does about prisoners' willingness to take part in any activity that might enhance their terms of confinement, despite the apparent danger. Despite doctors swearing to the Hippocratic Oath and widespread professional recognition of the ethical mandates of the Nuremberg Code of 1947 (fashioned after the atrocities of Nazi concentration camp experiments were exposed), thousands of inmates throughout the United States participated in hundreds of medical experiments between 1900 and the 1970s. It has been reported that more than 42 institutions participated in major research efforts. It has also been estimated that prisoners were used in the testing of at least 85% of all new drugs invented during these decades.

Many inmates were directly or indirectly misled to believe that their participation would affect their future in the system, win them favor with administrators, or influence an upcoming parole hearing. In addition, the "pains of imprisonment"—the loneliness and the deprivations of incarceration—caused some individuals to desire the rewards offered by research studies. Most inmates had no money for cigarettes or toiletries, simple items that would make their existence tolerable, and many experiments paid between $1 and $5 per day. The price was usually set in terms of the pain or inconvenience rather than the medical risk involved. For example, prices for participation in the Upjohn and Parke-Davis experiments in the 1970s in Southern Michigan State Prison ranged from 25 cents for a fingertip blood sample to $12 for a spinal tap. In 1976, 74 inmates at that facility earned more than $32,520, an average of about $439 each for their involvement in medical research.

THE ETHICS OF EXPERIMENTATION

Initially, there were no guidelines or regulations for medical experiments or experimental drug tests, and there was no supervision by agencies such as

the Food and Drug Administration (FDA). It was not prisoner research specifically that led to closer government scrutiny and participant protections. Instead, reforms were most often initiated following the disclosure of high-profile projects conducted in communities where poor, uneducated, and mostly minority subjects were involved, such as the Tuskegee syphilis study. In this case, between 1932 and 1972, poor sharecroppers in rural Alabama were injected with this serious venereal disease to test the utility of drugs at all stages of infection. Half, the control group, were left untreated, and others were given medicine only in the advanced stages of the disease so that researchers could study the drugs' effect on the most serious cases. Although cases such as this have received much media attention, particularly in recent years, culminating in presidential apologies and compensation programs, less focus has been given to the many varied medical research projects involving prisoners.

The reform of medical research procedures outside prisons eventually carried over into these facilities as well. Over the years, the FDA as well as a number of other regulatory agencies set up guidelines to ensure that all experiments would be approved and monitored by an independent institutional review board (IRB). In addition, research that involves prisoners must also pass a special layer of scrutiny in contemporary research settings. In most cases, an inmate representative or an advocate who reviews proposals on behalf of the inmates, such as a chaplain or a staff attorney, is also included in the funding or approval-granting process. These days, anyone wishing to use prisoners in a research project must obtain the prisoners' informed consent. All researchers are required to establish that the people participating in their study understand what the experiment involves. "Informed consent" implies that someone is intellectually able to assess the risks surrounding the research endeavor. This usually precludes a significant number of inmates who, because of a language barrier, developmental or physical disability, illiteracy, or mental impairment, would be limited in their ability to evaluate meaningful information offered about the research and its possible effects. Participants may not be coerced into participating in the study, nor should they have unrealistic or false perceptions of the potential rewards that may or may not be attached to participation. Finally, the research should not involve deception. Therefore, subjects may not be given false information about the nature of the experiment, treatment, drug, or information they are receiving for the purpose of achieving some other goal that is withheld from the participant. Although some researchers have argued that for some investigations, it is important that their subjects be uninformed and thus unbiased in their subsequent behaviors, there are always serious ethical risks to this type of inquiry.

SPONSORSHIP AND CONDUCT

In addition to other ethical problems, critics have revealed racism and corruption in prison medical experiments. For example, documenting the long and sordid history of medical experiments at Philadelphia's Holmesburg Prison, Allen Hornblum (1998) relates that higher-paying and less dangerous projects were targeted for white prisoners. Inmates with clerical connections could direct their friends toward the most profitable and low-risk assignments. Some "confederate" inmates even wore fake bandages to give themselves credibility when they told potential recruits that they themselves had participated in the experiments and that the procedures were easy and harmless.

In most cases, the experiments were carried out by large drug manufacturing companies, although from time to time local physicians or researchers working on grants for research institutes or the government were also involved. For example, the National Institute of Allergy and Infectious Diseases of the U.S. Public Health Service tested malaria in the federal prison at Atlanta in 1944. The U.S. Army's Surgeon General also sponsored a similar program at the Illinois State Penitentiary the following year: hundreds of prisoners were exposed to hungry disease-carrying mosquitoes. Infected inmates suffered fevers, chills, and the aches of the disease as they were measured, probed, wired, and watched as the disease ran its course. While some

received medications, for comparison purposes others did not. Some received treatment only in the latest stages of the illness, to test the effectiveness of the medications in subsequent phases. This particular experimental project was in operation for more than 25 years. Most of the prisoners received only five days reduction to their sentences and $50.

THE THREE PHASES OF DRUG TESTING

Often drug testing takes place in three phases. In Phase I, a drug is given to 100 or so subjects who are normal, healthy, with no obvious signs of any disease. Researchers simply monitor the effect of the drug on the body, tracking its absorption and its bioavailability and measuring any side effects or toxic reactions. Prisoners were often used in this type of research, including early experiments on LSD.

Phase II testing uses small groups of patients, or those purposefully infected with the disease or condition. In many prison research cases, the medical problem had to be created or induced. The zeal of medical experimenters was epitomized in Dr. Joseph Goldberg, who, having determined that the painful inflammatory disease of pellagra was caused by poor nutrition, set about to induce a dozen male convicts at Mississippi's Parchman Prison. The inmates, all healthy, white laborers in 1915 when the experiment began, were promised pardons in return for six months in diet-deprived isolation. Goldberg, known for also voluntarily contracting the diseases he was studying, was elated when the men began to manifest the symptoms of rashes, joint pain, and weight loss. Although the prisoners described the tortuous experiment as hellish and some begged to be withdrawn, all later recovered and were released as promised.

In 1962, 200 inmates in Ohio were injected with cancer cells by researchers associated with the Sloan Kettering Cancer Center, funded by the National Cancer Institute and the American Cancer Society. At that time researchers were still unsure whether cancer could be transmitted from one person to another and wanted to see if cancer cells would be rejected or would grow in otherwise healthy tissue.

The director of this project was later put on probation by the New York State Board of Regents for conducting these same experiments on his regular (outside) patients without their knowledge.

Phase III drug testing involves giving the medication to large groups of ill people who live under normal, everyday circumstances out in society. That is the final step in the testing process, and it allows researchers to see the way the drug functions under routine conditions. Obviously, inmates would not be used in this final phase.

INCENTIVES

Money was not the only incentive for participation in medical experiments. Other benefits included reassignment to more spacious living areas with television and exercise rooms, the use of phones, and extended visiting privileges. Subjects were also given cigarettes, books, and better food. Many simply enjoyed the medical attention and the interest paid to their health. In some cases, the research initiatives or surgical procedures appealed to the conscience of the prisoners to "do good" for society. Federal prisoners in Tallahassee voluntarily drank DDT to study its effects on the body, and more than 1,000 inmates at an Ohio prison donated skin to save the life of a badly burned nine-year-old girl. In 1943, an Army bomber plane was named after an inmate who died in the medical experiment that tested drugs needed by soldiers.

From a medical standpoint, inmates were easy-to-control research subjects. They were healthy, had regular diets, were relatively free of alcohol or drugs, and were unlikely to wander away or lose interest in participating. Most prisons allowed inmates to earn money or credit toward time served for donating blood. Prisoners frequently donated as often as allowed. Until the early 1980s, inmate records at the Texas Department of Corrections still reflected the good-time credit or "blood time" earned through the donation system.

In addition to the incentives received by the inmate participants, the facilities and their administrators also received substantial rewards or compensation for cooperation with the drug companies. When

Eli Lilly experimented on its early forms of the painkiller Darvon with inmates at Indiana State in 1972, the prison received a dishwasher, a remodeled hospital, high school supplies, library books, and recreational equipment. At the Oregon State Penitentiary, a group of inmates volunteered for bilateral testicular biopsies. In these experiments, researchers were testing the effects of steroids and sex hormones on sperm production and reproductive health. Tissue was removed from the testes of each subject and was examined, before and after the administration of the chemicals. In return, the prison received pharmacy services and some emergency medical equipment.

However, not all relationships with outside researchers were positive for the penal institution. In the early 1960s, Timothy Leary, the famous drug guru from Harvard University, was experimenting with psilocybin, a narcotic similar to LSD in hallucinogenic properties. Leary believed that the drug could reduce criminal tendencies, so he administered it to inmates at the Concord State Prison in Massachusetts. After extensive testing, the program was canceled because state officials believed that Leary was creating internal tensions and inciting inmates to rebel. Leary was eventually fired from the university when his extensive personal experimentation with hallucinogenic drugs and his advocacy of such use became public.

CRITIQUE

Medical experiments conducted during the Cold War, when the United States feared nuclear attack, have only recently been uncovered in detail. In addition to prisoners, the homeless, mentally ill, and unhealthy poor were often subjected to secret tests involving highly radioactive substances. In a 1963 memo, one radiologist (Healy, 1994, p. A12) explained that "I'm for support at the requested level, as long as we are not liable. I worry about possible carcinogenic effects of such treatments."

Many of the experiments conducted on inmates were extremely dangerous and caused serious permanent damage. Between 1963 and 1973, 131 prisoners in Washington and Oregon had their genitals irradiated by X-rays or their testicles dangled in irradiated water in order to study the effects of radiation on reproduction. These experiments were funded by the Atomic Energy Commission, a fore-runner of the Nuclear Regulatory Commission. Participants were paid $5 per month. After these tests the men were directed to receive vasectomies to "eliminate the possibility of defective offspring"; several of the participants changed their minds at that point, however, and did not have the vasectomy.

Around that same time a physician in Alabama conducted a plasma separation experiment in which blood samples, minus the plasma, were injected back into the donors. This process was repeated up to 16 times per month on some inmates. Unfortunately, the project was conducted in such unsanitary conditions with unsterile equipment that more than 500 cases of serum hepatitis resulted. Three inmates died from this experiment, and yet no formal complaints were ever filed. Because the research experiments did not track participants over a long period of time or conduct later follow-ups, it is difficult to say exactly how much permanent physical damage was caused by these projects. Prison records and experimental data were often destroyed, and former prisoners are characteristically difficult to locate once released.

THE DEMISE OF DRUG EXPERIMENTS

Legal and societal changes over the past 20 years have greatly reduced if not eliminated medical testing in prisons. The negative publicity attached to lawsuits and federal investigations convinced states to abandon such activities and to formulate policies against it. Concern over the coercive implications of participation, legal liabilities, and sophisticated government regulations regarding testing procedures has discouraged related practices. By 1980, the Department of Health, Education, and Welfare had stopped funding medical research that involved inmates. The Federal Bureau of Prisons and other federal agencies also stopped participating in such efforts. Finally, the American Correctional Association enacted a ban on medical research with prisoners as a criterion for obtaining accreditation.

CONCLUSION

The practice of widespread deception and exploitation in drug trials and medical experiments has been significantly limited by commitment to ethical guidelines and the control of "watchdog" agents in our society. Today, inmates are less likely to be considered suitable subjects for medical research. With high rates of serious health problems, HIV, hepatitis, hypertension, and histories of intravenous drug abuse, prisoners are better served with medical care rather than medical experiments.

—*Marilyn McShane*

See also American Civil Liberties Union; Doctors; Eighth Amendment; *Estelle v. Gamble; Habeas Corpus*; Health Care; History of Prisons; HIV/AIDS; Prison Litigation Reform Act; Prisoner Litigation; Physicians' Assistants; Privatization; Section 1983 of the Civil Rights Act

Further Reading

Bettag, O. (1957). Use of prison inmates in medical research. *American Journal of Correction*, *19*(3), 4–6, 26–29.

Gettinger, S., & Krajick, K. (1979). The demise of prison medical research. *Corrections, 5*(4), 4–14.

Healy, M. (1994). Science of power and weakness. *Los Angeles Times*, January 8, pp. A1, A12.

Hornblum, A. M. (1998). *Acres of skin: Human experiments at Holmesburg Prison*. New York: Routledge.

Krajick, K., & Moriarty, F. (1979). Life in the lab: Safer than the cellblocks? *Corrections, 5*(4), 15–20.

Mills, M., & Morris, N. (1974). Prisoners as laboratory animals. *Society, 11*(5), 60–66.

Oshinsky, D. M. (1996). *"Worse than slavery": Parchman Farm and the ordeal of Jim Crow justice*. New York: Free Press.

◪ MEDICAL MODEL

The *medical model* dominated prison philosophy and practice during the mid-20th century. Its proponents viewed criminality as a type of illness curable by various psychiatric or psychological interventions. They argued that prisoners were not responsible for their crimes and therefore should be treated through medical and psychological interventions rather than punished.

Support for the medical model waned during the late 1960s and 1970s in response to growing criticism that it could neither explain nor effectively treat crime. Nonetheless, its influence remains today, through, for example, various rehabilitation programs and in the field of biological criminology. The main difference is that current manifestations of the medical model are much less likely to mitigate responsibility and oppose punishment.

HISTORY

In order to understand the medical model of criminality, we must examine the medical model itself more generally. The medical model, which claimed to be rational, objective, and value-free, became the dominant method of health care within the West during the 19th century. Shaped by the scientific method, it was based on five key assumptions. The first, *mind-body dualism,* sees a clear division between the mind and the body. This view diminishes patients' own accounts and management of their illnesses and encourages the "clinical gaze," whereby the body is thought to be something that may be observed, manipulated, and treated by an expert. The second assumption, *physical reductionism,* reduces illness to physical or organic causes while omitting social, psychological, and spiritual aspects.

Specific etiology, the third pillar of the medical model, proposes that every disease has one specific, identifiable cause, such as a parasite, virus, or bacterium. It dismisses the complexity of illness as well as broader contributing factors. The fourth supposition, *mechanical metaphor,* views the body as a machine whose periodic breakdown or malfunction results in disease. Finally, due to the *technological imperative*, practitioners usually seek to cure illnesses rather than prevent them. This view also underpins the use of drugs, surgery, and other medical interventions.

THE MEDICAL MODEL OF CRIME

During the 19th century, the medical model became increasingly applied to an expanding number of social problems. In particular, at this time, both madness and crime came to be understood as diseases requiring medical treatment. Thus, one of the earliest applications of ideas from the medical model in the criminal justice system was with offenders thought to be insane. It was argued that since this group was mad, they could not be held accountable for their crimes and therefore deserved treatment rather than punishment. Alienists (nascent psychiatrists) established their field, in part, through their legal testimonies regarding the sanity and dangerousness of accused criminals and their professed expertise in classifying, understanding, and treating the criminally insane. In response, jurisdictions began to found specialized institutions for the criminally insane. In the United States, the first of these was established in 1855, adjacent to the Auburn State Prison in New York.

The application of the medical model to crime was also apparent in the work of various 19th-century scholars who linked physical attributes to criminal behavior. The most famous of these was Cesare Lombroso. In his 1876 study of Italian prisoners, he concluded that criminals had particular physical traits that signaled their "atavism" or reversion to a primitive state of evolution. Likewise, he proposed that they were subject to "degeneration," in which their criminality indicated that they were reverting to a racially primitive state of development.

Other adherents of biological explanations of crime emphasized heredity. For example, Robert Dugdale's 1877 study of one "degenerate" American family, the "Jukes," brought him to the conclusion that crime was inherited. Many also argued that crime was a consequence of "feeble-mindedness." This term was used loosely and interchangeably with others such as "moral imbecile" and "defective delinquent," each of which identified inborn low intellect as a primary cause of criminal behavior. All of these explanations reflected and perpetuated the eugenicist, and thereby racist and sexist, views and ideas of class of the time. In a number of cases, such ideas caused criminals and others deemed socially undesirable, such as people of color and the mentally ill, to be sterilized and/or institutionalized.

During the 20th century, the medical model of criminality persisted, albeit in a somewhat different form. While many of the earlier ideas remained, some took on a new shape due to scientific developments in burgeoning fields such as neurology and genetics. Of great influence here were theories linking different chromosomal anomalies (such as males with an XYY chromosomal constitution) and crime. Psychologically oriented theories increasingly came to exist alongside and be incorporated with biologically based theories. This change of approach largely reflected the influence of Sigmund Freud and his followers, who believed that the repression of internal impulses, such as sex and aggression, created mental symptoms. Freud advocated psychoanalysis, or the "talking cure," which attempted to treat mental symptoms by reliving and resolving past conflict. His ideas informed various psychological explanations of crime as well as its treatment. An example of this is the notion of the psychopathic personality who could be treated through therapy and drugs.

PSYCHIATRY AND CRIME

Psychiatry has been the most influential medical subdiscipline upon our understanding and treatment of crime. Gerry Johnstone (1996) identifies two separate approaches to crime within psychiatry: medical-somatic and social-psychological. The first assumes the existence of an organically rooted disorder typically located in the brain. Treatment closely mirrors physical medicine: surgery is performed and/or drugs are administered. Experts must be medically trained. Because of their knowledge, these experts are entitled to make all the decisions about their patients, who in turn are typically passive and have little say over what is done to them.

In contrast, advocates of a social-psychological approach assume that individuals are physically healthy, becoming ill only in response to their environment. As such, deviant behavior is typically perceived to be the consequence of psychological or emotional damage caused by neglect, abuse, or some other trauma. However, the focus is not on the environmental or situational causes but on the

psychological injuries they inflict. Because the disorder is manifested "subjectively" or within the psyche, patients are expected to take an active part in their treatment. Medical expertise is not mandatory, and treatment is therefore provided by a range of experts and even nonexperts, including occupational therapists, religious instructors, and prison guards.

Both the medical-somatic and social-psychological approaches individualize crime. Whether the cause of crime is located in the mind or the body, the focus is on the individual rather than the social structure. Therefore, the two approaches reinforce and strengthen one another.

Throughout the 20th century, psychiatry and its related disciplines shaped the "rehabilitative ideal," which increasingly dominated Western prisons following World War II. The rehabilitative ideal institutionalized the medical model through official acceptance that prisoners could be reformed by various medical-somatic and social-psychological interventions. While it was claimed the introduction of the medical model into prisons would make penal institutions more humane, in practice it led to compulsory and indeterminate sentencing on rehabilitative grounds and the implementation of a vast range of interventions, many of which were harmful. These included plastic surgery, castration, drug therapy, electroconvulsive treatment, psychosurgery, gas, psychotherapy, group counseling, individual counseling, therapeutic communities, aversion therapy, operant conditioning, and token economies.

CRITICISMS

During the mid-1960s, a series of criticisms was directed toward the medical model of crime and the rehabilitative ideal it introduced. First, it was maintained that physical illnesses are fundamentally different from offending behavior, since they exist independent of judgments made by others. Criminality, on the other hand, exists only because of judgments made by other people. Second, it was argued that while illness is not the result of a rational, deliberate choice, crime is. The medical model of crime fails to consider the inner, subjective meanings of offenders and thus fails to address their motivations. Third, illness and crime have different causes; while illness has a physical etiology, crime does not. The search for physical causes of crime is thus a pointless exercise that further serves to obscure the social causes of crime.

Fourth, many critics claimed that the introduction of the medical model created harm, both in deflecting attention away from social-structural issues and through the invasive treatments it inspired. In viewing offenders as "sick," they were also seen as irrational, helpless, and pitiful. This conceptual stripping of agency created conditions in which numerous harmful, invasive, and often compulsory interventions were carried out, including experimentation. Such practices furthermore reflected racist, sexist, and classist assumptions. Because they held scientific status and were conducted in the name of treatment, however, they were claimed to be benevolent and just. A final attack, coming from a different ideological position, maintained that the medical model of rehabilitation was "soft on criminals."

Various forms of prisoner resistance, including litigation, the civil rights movement, and intellectual developments such as anti-psychiatry, reinforced these criticisms. Most important, a series of research projects indicated that few interventions had any impact upon reoffending. Most famously, in 1974, Robert Martinson's examination of 231 studies led to the broad conclusion that none of the treatments introduced into prisons worked to reduce offending. Though Martinson himself later dissociated himself from this interpretation of his work, his article nonetheless created a climate of doubt that offenders could be rehabilitated. In response, the United States moved away from the rehabilitative ideal toward a hard-line law-and-order approach toward crime.

THE MEDICAL MODEL OF CRIME TODAY

Though the medical model of crime was seriously challenged, it did not disappear from prisons. Indeed, in some places, rehabilitation is currently undergoing a revival through the implementation of cognitive-behavioral strategies that reduce reoffending as well as because of the popularity of ideas within biological criminology. Cognitive behavioralism is essentially a social-psychological model. Practitioners claim that it is prisoners' faulty thinking that causes them to engage in crime, and thus that offenders need largely to be taught how to think differently. Such views have been most influential in Canada and Britain, although they are also present within the United States. They underpin numerous prison programs that seek to address "offending behavior."

At the same time as psychologists seek to retrain how offenders think, a new biological criminology, informed by genetics and evolutionary psychology, is advancing various medical explanations of crime. Whereas previous manifestations of the medical model assumed that prisoners should not be held accountable for their crimes, current variants no longer exonerate prisoners from responsibility. Consequently, there is concern that they may contribute to the growing prison population and punitive penal practices.

CONCLUSION

Supporters of the medical model hoped that it would not only contribute to a more humane environment, but would cure prisoners of their criminality. However, its narrow assumptions as well as the severe limitations imposed by the carceral environment meant that these prospects largely failed. Though it is no longer the official primary justification of punishment, many of the central ideas of the medical model of crime remain current in the U.S. prison system. In particular, the belief that the source and cure for crime lies within individual prisoners continues to shape a range of policy from drug rehabilitation programs to education and individual therapy.

—Kathleen Kendall

See also Doctors; Group Therapy; Health Care; Indeterminate Sentencing; Individual Therapy; Medical Experiments; Mental Health; Patuxent Institution; Psychiatric Care; Psychological Services; Psychologists; Rehabilitation Theory; Therapeutic Communities; Women's Health Care

Further Reading

Conrad, P. & Schneider, J. (Eds.). (1992). *Deviance and medicalization* (exp. ed.). Philadelphia: Temple University Press.

Johnstone, G. (1996). *Medical concepts and penal policy.* London: Cavendish.

Kittrie, N. (1971). *The right to be different: Deviance and enforced therapy.* Baltimore: Johns Hopkins University Press.

Rose, N. (2000). The biology of culpability. *Theoretical Criminology, 4*(1), 5–34.

◪ MEDIUM SECURITY

"Medium security" may refer either to the security of the penal facility or to the classification level of an inmate. Medium-secure prisons, which are often called correctional institutions, house one-third of all state prisoners. These institutions allow individual freedom of movement for the inmates within a secure perimeter. Inmates with a security classification of "medium" may work outside the security fence only under armed supervision.

CLASSIFICATION

In the early 20th century, in response to changing ideas in the behavioral sciences and an increased faith in the possibility of educating and reforming offenders, correctional administrators began examining alternatives to maximum-security prisons for the confinement of criminal offenders. At the same time, a classification system was being developed to determine the level of security and treatment inmates required and to identify special populations such as high risk, or the mentally ill, in order to house them in purpose-built institutions. Jails and pretrial detention centers were also being separated from those facilities that housed convicted felons.

Most classification systems are based on four different levels of security: maximum, medium, minimum, and open. Correctional facilities are then built to match a particular level of security, for both the facility and inmate population. "Security," in this sense, refers to the type of physical structure needed to hold the inmates, the internal structure that determines the scope of prisoner movement within the facility, and how much supervision each inmate needs.

TODAY'S MEDIUM-SECURITY FACILITY

The majority of correctional facilities built since the mid-20th century have been medium security. Though the predominant consideration in the design of these prisons is still security, increasingly the internal control features are hidden to create a more humane environment. Indeed, many of today's medium-security facilities, at both the federal and state levels, are patterned after the university or college campus. Examples include the Federal Correctional Institute at Glenville, West Virginia; the Texas Department of Criminal Justice Medium Security Facility at Amarillo; and the Virginia Women's Multi-Custody Correctional Facility at Fluvanna City. Inmates in these facilities may be housed either in dormitory-style rooms or in individual cells that are built around congregated living areas. In both designs, people share common and readily accessible showering and toilet areas.

External barriers are pivotal to all penal institutions. Those in medium-secure facilities typically begin with a double chain-link fence topped with barbed or razor wire. The area between the fences may contain electronic devices, such as motion or infrared sensors. Towers overlooking the institution are staffed by armed correctional officers, while other guards patrol the perimeter on foot or in vehicles.

In addition to such external barriers, medium-secure institutions rely on a number of internal measures. Most institutions, particularly those that have recently been built, rely on electronic surveillance in addition to locks and bars. Other strategies, such as clear separation of activities, highly defined movement paths, and officer training are all pivotal to the maintenance of order and control in all prisons.

THE MEDIUM-SECURITY INMATE

Approximately one-third of all state inmates are currently housed in medium-security facilities. Individuals assigned to medium-security facilities are classified as low escape and behavioral risks. They typically wear institutional clothing but may also be granted the opportunity to wear civilian clothing during recreational or free time. Inmates in medium-security facilities have less restricted movement than those in maximum-security, and they are searched and counted less frequently.

Medium Security for Women

Women currently account for nearly 7% of the entire prison population, and their number is increasing at a faster rate than men's. Female inmates are housed in either all-women facilities or in co-correctional facilities. Currently, there are 104 women's correctional facilities at the state and federal level. Of these, 36, or one-third, are medium security facilities. Of the 84 co-correctional facilities located throughout the country, 40% are medium security.

A medium-security classification for a female inmate indicates that she will live in a dormitory within the correctional institution. When examining all levels of inmate classification, a pattern emerges for female correctional facilities. If a facility serves only women, it will merit a lower security rating than comparable co-correctional or all-male facilities. This is because women are not considered high security risks, nor are they considered to be great risks to themselves or other inmates, since they are not as violent as men.

CONCLUSION

The classification system used to determine the level of security and type of prison programs for inmates created four levels of security. Medium security is a correctional design that is physically secure while providing some freedom of movement for the inmates. In the 1990s, more than 400 new correctional facilities were built in the United States. Of those, approximately 55% were medium security. With the continuing prison construction boom, any new correctional facility built in the 21st century will most likely be a medium-security facility.

—Douglas Neil Robinson and
Deborah Mitchell Robinson

See also Campus Style; Classification; Maximum Security; Minimum Security; New Generation Prisons; Supermax Prisons

Further Reading

Allen, H. E., & Simonsen, C. E. (2001). *Corrections in America: An introduction*. Upper Saddle River, NJ: Prentice Hall.

Carter, R. M., Glaser, R., & Wilkins, L. T. (1977). *Correctional institutions*. Philadelphia: Lippincott.

Champion, D. J. (2001). *Corrections in the United States: A contemporary perspective*. Upper Saddle River, NJ: Prentice Hall.

Mays, G. L., & Winfree, L. T. (2002). *Contemporary corrections*. Belmont, CA: Wadsworth/Thomson Learning.

Reid, S. T. (2001). *Criminal justice* (6th ed.). Cincinnati, OH: Atomic Dog.

Roberson, C. (1997). *Introduction to corrections*. Incline Village, NV: Copperhouse.

◪ MEGAN'S LAW

Megan's Law is an attempt by state and federal legislatures to notify the public about and protect them from recently released sexual offenders. The legislation was named in commemoration of seven-year-old Megan Kanka of Hamilton Township, New Jersey, who was sexually assaulted and strangled to death by a former sex offender, Jesse Timmendequas. After the police found Kanka's body in a nearby park, neighbors and community members held vigil and petitioned for legislation that would notify community members of a sexual offender's location. "Megan's Law" resulted from this community action.

NATIONAL ADOPTION OF MEGAN'S LAW

In 1994, then-Governor Christine Todd-Whitman signed Megan's Law into New Jersey legislation, only two months after the untimely death of Kanka. In 1996, Republican presidential candidate Bob Dole proposed national legislation providing states with two years to enact their own state version of Megan's Law or risk the loss of their state funding. Then-President Bill Clinton subsequently signed the federal version of the law into action in 1996. Presently, all 50 states have some version of Megan's Law. This legislation amended the previous Jacob Wetterling

Act of 1990 and has a number of provisions that vary by state. With few exceptions, such as an offender's age and/or type of sexual offense, Megan's Law applies to all sex offenders convicted after the state or federal enactment of the statute.

Megan's Law seeks to protect the community from released sexual offenders by increasing the public's awareness of their whereabouts and by providing local authorities with a pool of possible suspects. The law operates with a number of conditions, including the registration, notification, and civil commitment of sexual offenders, the possible use of the death penalty or life imprisonment, the development of a central database, lifetime supervision of offenders, DNA, fingerprinting, and the right to refuse "good time" credits. The two most well-known provisions of Megan's Law are sex offender registration and community notification.

SEX OFFENDER REGISTRATION

Sex offender registration is the less controversial of the two provisions. It is a practice that dates prior to Megan's Law and was the foundation of the Jacob Wetterling Act, which differs from Megan's Law mainly by not requiring dissemination of information. Under sex offender registration provisions, sex offenders are allocated a time frame, generally 72 hours, upon release from prison to register their information with the local authorities where they plan to reside. Offenders register on an annual basis for at least 10 years, and if deemed necessary, they register for life. The information that offenders provide includes their full name, their address, date of birth, Social Security number, a physical description, photographs, DNA, fingerprints, a place and address of employment if available, and a court or therapist's assessment of future dangerousness. Failure to comply results in criminal penalties, which often result in the offender's return to prison for a technical violation. In most states this is a crime of the fourth degree.

COMMUNITY NOTIFICATION

Notification of a sexual offender's residence has attracted much controversy. This procedure is intended to inform the community and past victims that a sexual offender is living nearby. The hope is that community members will protect themselves and their children accordingly. Generally speaking, although this varies slightly by state, the tier that an offender is placed into determines the level of notification. There are three tier levels. Tier 1 represents the lowest-risk sexual offenders and only requires notice to the police and the victims that the offender is likely to be encountered around their residence. Offenders are considered low risk if they are under probation or parole, are receiving therapy, are employed, and are alcohol- and drug-free. Tier 2 represents moderate-risk sex offenders; these people have difficulty complying with authority and supervision, lack employment, deny their offenses with no remorse, abuse alcohol and drugs, and have a history of violent behavior. These behaviors are believed to put an offender at a higher risk for recommitting a sexual offense; therefore their notification is broader. This level requires notification to organizations, educational institutions, day care centers, and summer camps.

Tier 3 sex offenders are the offenders who are most at risk for reoffending. This category has generated the most resistance. The entire community that may encounter the offender—usually a particular radius is chosen—is notified through posters, pamphlets, and possible door-to-door visits from the local authorities. Tier 3 offenders have the same risk factors as Tier 2 offenders, but Tier 3 includes an increased likelihood of reoffending because their behavior is deemed repetitive and compulsive. These offenders often have a sexual preference for children and refuse to be treated. Only a small number of offenders—approximately 5%—are placed into a Tier 3 classification.

LEGAL CHALLENGES

Megan's Law has survived a number of legal challenges from both state and federal courts. The first criticism is that it can be considered double jeopardy (multiple prosecution or punishment for the same offense) because offenders have already served their time in prison. Offenders claim that they have fulfilled the punishment requirement while incarcerated and that placement under a Megan's Law statute can be considered cruel and unusual punishment under the Eighth Amendment. This argument has fueled a number of legal challenges, but courts have avoided this claim by incorporating the requirement of sex offender registration and notification into the initial sentence.

Megan's Law statutes have also faced due process or Fourteenth Amendment challenges. The Fourteenth Amendment states that no person shall be deprived of life, liberty, or property without due process. Offenders claim that Megan's Law statutes infringe on their right to privacy and travel. In addition, it has been argued that offenders should be able to challenge their tier placement because of the heavy implications these tiers carry. Significant due process safeguards were considered to prevent infringements. These precautions included an offender's ability to challenge his tier placement and subsequent notification level. Right to privacy and arguments do not hold up; the courts have stated that the public's right to safety outweighs the offender's right to privacy. Additional challenges to the implementation of Megan's Law have included the vigilante actions of neighbors and community members living in the radius of sexual offenders. Although these vigilante actions are not widely reported, community members have protested outside the homes of registered sexual offenders, and in more serious circumstances have physically assaulted offenders. It is a punishable crime if citizens are found to have used sexual offender registries to commit a criminal offense against the offender. These community members are subject to both monetary fines and potential criminal charges.

SEXUAL OFFENDER REGISTRIES

All 50 states and the District of Columbia have some form of centralized sexual offender registries. Various departments ranging from the department of public safety to the local police departments and bureaus of identification maintain these centralized registries. To date, more than two-thirds of all states make their sexual offender registries available to the public, either in an offender-searchable format or in a more general information format. The number of sexual offenders registered in each state varies proportionally to the state's population. Larger states like California have approximately 33,000 sexual offenders included in their registries, while smaller states like Connecticut have 2,075 sexual offenders registered. Washington State, the first state to develop and maintain a sexual offender registry, has approximately 16,500 sexual offenders registered; this is a similar number to the 14,500 registered in New York State. Compilations are available online for each states' number of registered sexual offenders.

The compliance rate of registering under sexual offender statutes poses a serious problem in some states. Because many states mandate that sexual offenders register within 72 hours of their release from incarceration, a number of sexual offenders have been noncompliant with the requirement of registering. In a recent article it was noted that California has lost track of one-third of their released sexual offenders, while the majority of other states claim that they simply don't know their offenders' compliance rates. A minority of states have been successful in tracking their compliance rates, including Connecticut, Oregon, and Pennsylvania, with compliance rates ranging from 85% to nearly 95%.

CONCLUSION

Despite some legal challenges made to it, public response to Megan's Law has been fairly favorable. Many community members believe that Megan's Law's stipulations should be required of all sexual offenders, irrespective of the possibility that such a law penalizes individuals beyond their prison sentence. They have demanded to know who was living in their neighborhoods, and the government has agreed.

—Kristen Marie Zgoba

See also Civil Commitment of Sexual Predators; Incapacitation Theory; Parole; Parole Boards; Psychological Services; Psychologists; Sex Offender Programs; Sex Offenders; Therapeutic Communities; Truth in Sentencing

Further Reading

Adams, D. (1999). *Summary of state sex offender registry dissemination procedure* (NCJ 177620). Washington, DC: Bureau of Justice Statistics.

Brooks, A. (1996). Megan's Law: Constitutionality and policy. *Criminal Justice Ethics, 15*(1), 56–66.

Matson, S., & Lieb, R. (1997). *Megan's Law: A review of state and federal legislation* (pp. 1–20, 27–29). Olympia: Washington State Institute for Public Policy.

Rudin, J. (Fall, 1996). Megan's Law: Can it stop sexual predators, and at what cost to constitutionality? *Criminal Justice,* 3–6, 60–63.

Stop Sex Offenders. Retrieved from http://www.stopsexoffenders.com

◪ *MENS REA*

Mens rea is a Latin term meaning "guilty mind," criminal intent, or the mental state of an individual committing an act. Criminal law generally requires that *corpus delicti*, a Latin-based phrase meaning "the body of the crime," be proven before an individual can be found guilty of any unlawful activity. *Corpus delicti* is comprised of three basic elements of the crime: (1) *actus reus*, or the guilty act; (2) *mens rea*, or the guilty intent; and (3) concurrence, or the amalgamation of the guilty act and the guilty intent. *Mens rea* is an integral facet of the criminal justice legal process.

HISTORY

A belief that an individual must have a "guilty mind" in order for his or her action to count as a crime has existed for hundreds of years, dating as far back as the Roman Empire. The term *mens rea* was not utilized in English common law, however, until around the mid-18th century. The basic premise underlying this concept is that in order for an individual to be found guilty of a criminal act, the perpetrator must have acted with a guilty mind, or *mens rea*. This is articulated by the Latin *maxim actus not facit reum nisi mens sit rea* ("an act does not make one guilty unless his mind is guilty").

Ideas about *mens rea* found their way into American law in the latter part of the 18th century. By the time of the writing of the U.S. Constitution, the principles behind *mens rea* had already been integrated into general American law. As states gradually defined statutory law, *mens rea* was assumed; although it was not typically defined in the writings of the law, it was understood as common law.

During the Industrial Revolution, *mens rea* was incorporated in general law in public welfare offenses. Before this time, lawmakers and law officials were not concerned with why an individual committed a criminal act, but simply with the act itself. Additionally, they were not concerned with the intent of the offender, but that the prohibited act had been committed. With the implementation of various industry-related jobs and the dangers associated with them, however, society geared its public opinion toward the *why* instead of the *how*.

By the turn of the 20th century, an individual could be found to be criminally liable only if he or she was aware of the potential impact of his or her behavior. Thus, an injury caused without *mens rea* might be grounds for civil liability, but not for criminal prosecution. Even so, when the offense involves crimes such as violations of liquor laws and/or anti-narcotic laws, motor vehicle laws, traffic-related laws, sanitary and building codes and regulations, and factory laws, offenders are held to be strictly liable, and proof of intent is not required.

Mens rea is an integral part of the criminal justice systems throughout the nation. In all 50 states and Washington, D.C., it is part of every criminal code. In the instance of premeditated murder, both *mens rea* and *actus reus* must be present to establish a guilty verdict. This can be clearly understood by examining the standards of *mens rea* and its components.

THE *MENS REA* STANDARD

The phrase *mens rea* denotes the prerequisite that there exist a "culpable state of mind." Most crimes, according to state and federal statutes, necessitate a condition of mind that is certainly guilty, while additional crimes only call for sheer "recklessness" or "negligence." There are very few crimes that have no *mens rea* requirement. The U.S. Supreme Court has categorized the *mens rea* requirement into three categories: crimes including (1) "general intent," (2) "specific intent," and (3) "recklessness" or "negligence" ("strict liability" is sometimes utilized as a fourth requirement for *mens rea*).

For the "general intent" requirement, it must be shown that the defendant desired to perpetrate the act that served as the *actus reus*, or guilty act. The next requirement, "specific intent," holds that while the defendant had the desire to carry out the act, he or she also had the desire to do something further relating to the crime. Finally, an example of the "recklessness" or "negligence" requirement can be found in instances of crimes resulting from intoxication or mistake. For intoxication, the general intent requirement is seldom vacated; however, the specific intent requirement may be vacated for a particular crime. A mistake of fact is more probable to vacate the specific intent requirement of *mens rea*. While all of these listed requirements for *mens rea* are necessary to prove the intent of the crime, the intent cannot stand alone in criminal liability; the act and the intent must be present in singularity and in concurrence.

CORPUS DELICTI

As stated previously, the *corpus delicti*, or body of the crime, includes three basic elements: (1) *mens rea*, (2) *actus reus*, and (3) concurrence. The *mens rea*, or guilty intent, has been discussed; however, *actus reus* is an important component as well. The *actus reus* requirement establishes the need for the actual occurrence of a criminal act. Additionally, for the act to be criminal, it must be voluntary. In some situations where criminal intent is present, but the act did not occur, liability may be decreased; conspiracy is, in some instance, an example of this decrease in liability. To prove certain degrees of a crime as defined by most criminal statutes and the Model Penal Code, both *actus reus* and *mens rea* must be present, which becomes the concurrence of the two requirements for *corpus delicti*.

CONCLUSION

Ideas about criminal responsibility have been prevalent throughout history and can be traced back

in America to early common law. By the time of the writing of the U.S. Constitution, the principle of *mens rea* had already been integrated into general American law. The era of the Industrial Revolution witnessed the implementation of the *mens rea* requirement in public welfare issues involving civil liability. Eventually, this requirement could be found in every state code as well as the Model Penal Code. Generally, *mens rea*, or guilty intent, must be accompanied by *actus reus*, the criminal act, and the mergence of these two makes up the *corpus delicti*, or body of the crime.

—*Kristi M. McKinnon*

See also Cesare Beccaria; Child Savers; Gerald Gault; Juvenile Justice System; Medical Model; War on Drugs

Further Reading

Murphy, J. G., & Coleman, J. L. (1990). *Philosophy of law: An introduction to jurisprudence*. Boulder, CO: Westview.
Robinson, P. H. (1997). *Structure and function in criminal law*. Oxford, UK: Oxford University Press.
Swanson, K. A. (2002). Criminal law: Mens rea alive and well. *William Mitchell Law Review 28*(3), 1265–1282.

Legal Cases

Liparota v. United States, 471 U.S. 419 (1985).
Morrissette v. Unites States, 342 U.S. 246 (1952).
Staples v. United States, 511 U.S. 400 (1994).

◩ MENTAL HEALTH

The emotional and psychological well-being of convicts in correctional facilities is of considerable concern for prison officials, the courts, the psychiatric community, and society in general. While counseling and treatment services are available in many correctional institutions, these facilities are often ill equipped to deal with persistent and severely mentally disordered offenders and those persons identified as dangerous and psychiatrically ill. In those instances where treatment is uneven, absent, or otherwise ineffective, questions remain about whether the correctional milieu is itself responsible for breeding and sustaining long-term mental illness and dysfunctional prison behavior.

HISTORY

In the Western world, criminal (and civil) confinement of persons with mental disorders dates back many centuries. Historically, different cultures have had an uneasy relationship with how best simultaneously to address the needs of mentally ill citizens who engaged in criminal wrongdoing while also protecting the public from the likelihood of future harm. Within the United States, four progressive reform strategies can be identified, dating back to the colonial period.

The first reform occurred during the period of colonial jurisprudence. It was termed the "moral treatment movement." It emphasized hard work and penitence in the asylum rather than confinement in the correctional setting. During the moral treatment era, the conviction was that with enough religion, prayer, and labor, persons with mental disorders would be saved, and, therefore, would eventually refrain from criminal and delinquent transgressions.

The second reform emerged in the mid-1800s. It was termed the "mental hygiene movement." Discoveries in science, advances in psychopharmacological therapies, and a commitment to curing mental disease or defect meant that the promise of treatment was the source of change. Psychopathic hospitals displaced the asylums of the past, and mentally ill offenders were subjected to various experimental drug regimens and other unproven procedures (including lobotomies).

The third reform movement surfaced in the 1950s. It was termed the period of "deinstitutionalization." Disappointed by the failings of the mental hygiene era and outraged by the deteriorating, debilitating, and prison-like conditions in which persons with psychiatric disorders lived in psychopathic hospitals, progressive-minded politicians and social activists sought to validate the identity and affirm the (constitutional) liberties of persons with mental illness. This was the period of patients' rights. As such, during the 1950s and 1960s there was a massive deinstitutionalization movement, and psychiatric patients were placed in less restrictive community-based environments.

The fourth reform movement emerged in the 1980s and continues into the early 21st century.

Some researchers refer to this period as a time of "abandonment" in the care and treatment of persons with mental disorders. Others regard this period as a time during which various community mental health practices have been implemented with varying degrees of success. Deinstitutionalization produced a massive exodus from many state psychiatric facilities. This exodus raised a host of practical questions about how best to address the needs of persons with mental illness in community settings. Most critics agree that the limits of the fourth reform movement include cyclical or "revolving door" psychiatric treatment, homelessness, incarceration, and even death for some street dwellers with acute and/or chronic psychiatric disorders. Current efforts at progressive reform attempt to respond to each of these social problems.

Despite all progressive efforts at reform, each movement includes some serious limitations. These shortcomings have always produced a strong reaction, culminating in significant philosophical or policy changes. However, notwithstanding these well-intentioned, reform-minded efforts, each successive strategy has always given way to prison or related confinement practices.

CURRENT TRENDS AND STATISTICS

Two criminal law issues impact how persons with mental disorders are funneled through the criminal justice system and how they are dealt with by systems of confinement. First, some defendants can be found incompetent to stand trial (IST). Under these conditions, defendants are sent to a psychiatric facility unit until such time as they are competent to proceed to trial. IST determinations are prospective; that is, they question the mental state of the defendant at the time of the trial's commencement. However, the IST finding does not rule out a subsequent prison sentence, especially if the person becomes competent following appropriate psychiatric treatment, proceeds to trial, and is found guilty of the criminal charges.

Second, some defendants can be found not guilty by reason of insanity (NGRI). Under these conditions, the defendant is acquitted. NGRI defenses are retrospective; that is, they question the mental state of the defendant at the time the crime occurred. More recently, several state jurisdictions have implemented guilty but mentally ill (GBMI) statutes. These legislative enactments specify that, notwithstanding psychiatric disorder, a person can be found guilty and subsequently sentenced to a prison term. Of all those persons incarcerated, experts generally agree that approximately 20% experience problems with mental illness in one form or another. This figure rises considerably when focusing specifically on "Axis II" or personality disorders (e.g., borderline personality disorder, paranoid personality disorder, antisocial personality disorder). Estimates for persons with mental illness in local lockups, country jails, or secure holding facilities vary according to state or county jurisdiction. Researchers generally agree, however, that the incarceration of the mentally ill is on the rise. This is especially the case for dangerous mentally ill offenders, including sexually violent predators and psychopathic mentally ill offenders. So far, the clinical treatment of such dangerous mentally ill offenders in correctional settings has not produced promising success rates. Thus, in 18 state jurisdictions, civil confinement is ordered following the completion of one's prison term as a convicted sexually violent predator.

PROBLEMS

Typically, convicted mentally ill offenders receive a sentence of probation. They are treated in the community or some other less restrictive environment for their psychiatric disorder. However, given the absence of an adequate release or discharge plan, short-term civil commitment, bouts of homelessness, and temporary confinement to a jail or local lockup often follow.

When persons experiencing psychiatric illness are placed in correctional facilities, there are several problems that surface. Access to and quality of treatment vary across types of prisons. For example, approximately 41% of jail detainees receive some form of mental health treatment; approximately 60% of prison convicts receive some form of psychiatric care. Overwhelmingly, the correctional facility's treatment of choice for both groups is drug therapy,

with 36% of those in jail and 50% of those in prison receiving this treatment. In both instances, the presence of counseling personnel and services is often uneven, fragmented, or inadequate.

Researchers also question what the long-term emotional effects are for individuals placed in solitary confinement. To date, empirical evidence indicates that exposure to short bouts of prison seclusion is not psychologically crippling or debilitating. Investigators caution, however, that more research is needed in order to understand what the specific psychological effects are for repeated and/or long-term exposure to solitary confinement. Women in prison are diagnosed with personality disorders more frequently than their male counterparts. They also are more likely to be administered drug therapy. Prolonged bouts of depression, persistent and severe mood swings, and prison adjustment and socialization difficulties regularly result in personality disorder diagnoses for women. Researchers estimate that these diagnoses are assigned to women at a rate that is two to three times greater than that for their male imprisoned counterparts.

Women also experience sexual abuse while confined and are at risk of self-harm. Conservative estimates for the rate of sexual victimization of women in prison indicate that nearly 30% will experience some form of unwanted sex while confined. Researchers report that this figure also includes correctional officer-on-convict sexual abuse. Self-injurious behavior is a routine occurrence in many female correctional facilities. Examples include body mutilation and attempted suicide. Investigators have linked the incidence of sexual victimization and self-harm to prison conditions and to the woman's inability to be with and care for family, especially her children. Life on death row also raises important issues about the emotional well-being of convicts. Some studies suggest that the presence of impending death, the ongoing and protracted appellate process, and one's incessant exposure to the grief, anxiety, and remorse of others on death row, create a culture of psychological disorganization and social disequilibrium. In other words, waiting to die along with others has a profound negative effect on one's emotional health.

Life on death row also includes persons who are mentally ill awaiting execution. The U.S. Supreme

Court has ruled that one cannot be put to death if one is mentally incompetent. Moreover, the court has stipulated that medicating someone for the sole purpose of competency restoration violates both the right to privacy clause of the First Amendment and the cruel and unusual punishment clause of the Eighth Amendment. However, several federal appellate courts have concluded that under certain circumstances, restoring one's competency for purposes of execution is permissible. In these instances, the safety of the correctional personnel and/or the safety of the mentally ill death row convict must be jeopardized by the individual's psychiatric disorder, necessitating mental health (i.e., drug therapy) intervention. These decisions are further complicated when a mentally incompetent death row convict exercises his or her right to refuse treatment, thereby forestalling (potentially) prospects for competency restoration.

CONCLUSION

The relationship between prison facilities and mental health is unmistakable. This association implicates the legal and psychiatric communities as well as the public at large. While most crimes are not committed by mentally ill persons, the history of progressive reform in the United States indicates that these citizens often find themselves confined, in one setting or another. Not surprisingly, then, critical researchers question the basis for this confinement—whether in jails, prisons, or psychiatric hospitals. Some have suggested that what is at stake is the territorialization or the vanquishing of difference in the name of conformity. In these instances, one's *status* as mentally ill is synonymous with one's *identity* as dangerous, deviant, diseased. Thus, critical scholars examine how the state's efforts to contain, corral, or otherwise correct human expressions of difference represent institutional expressions of punishment.

Notwithstanding the concerns raised by critical commentators, correctional facilities directly confront issues of mental health for convicts in a myriad of ways. Treatment needs and counseling services are real concerns. The effects of solitary confinement and life on death row are real problems. Competency restoration for psychiatrically disordered offenders awaiting execution is a complex

ethical dilemma. These matters signal just how much the correctional environment implicates the emotional well-being of offenders. They also challenge us to reconsider whether, and to what extent, the prison culture nurtures, grows, and sustains maladaptive and dysfunctional convict behavior.

—Bruce Arrigo

See also Civil Commitment of Sexual Predators; Constitutive Penology; Death Row; Drug Treatment Programs; Eighth Amendment; First Amendment; Group Therapy; Individual Therapy; Medical Model; *Mens Rea*; Psychiatric Care; Psychological Services; Self-Harm; Solitary Confinement; Suicide; Therapeutic Communities; Women's Health Care; Women Prisoners

Further Reading

Arrigo, B. A. (2002). *Punishing the mentally ill: A critical analysis of law and psychiatry*. Albany: State University of New York Press.

Arrigo, B. A., & Fowler, C. R. (2001). The "death row" community: A community psychology perspective. *Deviant Behavior, 22*(1), 43–71.

Arrigo, B. A., & Tasca, J. J. (1999). The right to refuse treatment, competency to be executed, and therapeutic jurisprudence: Toward a systematic analysis. *Law and Psychology Review, 23,* 1–47.

Bardwell, M. C., & Arrigo, B. A. (2002). *Criminal competency on trial: The case of Colin Ferguson*. Durham, NC: Carolina Academic.

Ditton, P. (1999). Mental health and treatment of inmates and probationers. Washington, DC: Bureau of Justice Statistics.

Foucault, M. (1965). *Madness and civilization: A history of insanity in the age of reason*. New York: Pantheon.

Foucault, M. (1977). *Discipline and punish: The birth of the prison*. New York: Pantheon.

Haney, C. (1997). Psychology and the limits to prison pain: Confronting the coming crisis in Eighth Amendment law. *Psychology, Public Policy and Law, 3*(4), 499–588.

Roberts, J. V., & Gebotys, R. J. (2001). Prisoners of isolation: Research on the effects of administrative segregation. *Canadian Journal of Criminology, 43*(1), 85–97.

Steadman, H. J., & Cocozza, J. (Eds.). (1993). *Mental illness in America's prisons*. Seattle, WA: National Coalition for the Mentally Ill in the Criminal Justice System.

Legal Cases

Ford v. Wainwright, 477 U.S. 399 (1986).
Kansas v. Hendricks, 117 S. Ct. 2072 (1997).
Perry v. Louisiana, 498 U.S. 38 (1990).
Washington v. Harper, 494 U.S. 210 (1990).

◪ METROPOLITAN CORRECTIONAL CENTERS

Metropolitan correctional centers (MCCs) and metropolitan detention centers (MDCs) are high-rise correctional facilities that house inmates in dense urban environments. These institutions are generally designed to hold prisoners and pretrial detainees temporarily while awaiting transport, trials, or court hearings. Although their major function is the detention of criminal defendants in order to secure their presence at trial, the centers may also hold witnesses for appearances before grand juries or trials. Some also house noncitizens awaiting the outcome of U.S. Immigration and Customs Enforcement (ICE) proceedings. Some inmates may be detained overnight, while others are held for months. In rare cases, individuals may be confined in metropolitan correctional centers for more than a year while awaiting termination of court processes, and may also serve out sentences in excess of one year while providing labor for the facilities.

Urban detention centers serve all the major purposes of correctional facilities found elsewhere but concentrate on one primary feature: integration with court facilities and attorneys in urban settings. As federal criminal prosecutions have grown greater in number, the U.S. Justice Department has had increasing incentives to construct federal detention facilities in major cities to complement regional jails that already existed.

FEDERAL METROPOLITAN DETENTION AND CORRECTIONAL CENTERS

While the designation "metropolitan correctional center" may suggest various urban jail and prison facilities operated by state and local jurisdictions, the term represents a specific category of correctional institution at the federal level. Metropolitan correctional centers and metropolitan detention centers are important components in the U.S. Federal Bureau of Prisons system of correctional institutions. There are presently three federal MCCs (in downtown Chicago, San Diego, and New York City) and a half-dozen MDCs (at Los Angeles,

Brooklyn, Guaynabo, Puerto Rico, Honolulu, Seattle-Tacoma, and Philadelphia). Each of these institutions is located at the heart of a major city in close proximity to other government buildings.

The MCCs house both male and female inmates and are classified as administrative detention institutions. This means that they have special detention missions and can hold inmates of all four federal security classifications. In practice, the facilities generally hold most nontrustee inmates under high-security conditions, regardless of their individual classifications. All three metropolitan correctional centers were built in the mid-1970s during a period when corrections planners were experimenting with new approaches to the architecture and management of prison facilities.

Metropolitan detention centers are essentially federal jails. They are not appreciably distinct from the MCCs in their overall physical plants and operations, but they are designed to accomplish a more narrow set of correctional missions. Intended to provide short-term incarceration for approximately 500 federal pretrial detainees each, they are all beyond capacity today. Most are also classified as administrative and hold inmates of all federal security levels. Where MDCs exist, they displace the need of the U.S. Justice Department to lease cell space from city and county jails operated by local jurisdictions.

ARCHITECTURE

Urban skylines have long been graced by correctional facilities, but the modern metropolitan detention centers are distinguishable by their deliberately unobtrusive, relatively attractive, noncorrectional appearance. In fact, most of the federal MCCs and MDCs could easily be mistaken for metropolitan office buildings, and some have won architectural awards for their designs. The centers have no visible razor wire fences, thick block structures, or corner guard towers. There are also no detectable prison bars and no obvious armed patrols circling the facilities. This last feature helps the institutions avoid the cagelike appearance of traditional prison structures. Entrances to the buildings exhibit no obvious indicia of high security, because transportation of inmates to and from them takes place in large underground sally-port parking driveways, where buses and vans pick up and drop off inmates.

MDC PHILADELPHIA

Visitors to downtown Philadelphia might easily mistake the city's Federal Metropolitan Detention Center for an elegant hotel or a high-tech office building. Typical of the metropolitan detention centers, MDC Philadelphia is situated directly across the street from a federal courthouse and adjacent to other government buildings. It is also close to historic 19th-century buildings such as the Mellon Bank Center. Designers of the Philadelphia MDC intended the building's function not to be apparent to casual passers-by. Built in 1999 at a cost of $68 million, the 11-story concrete structure was constructed with 800 precast concrete panel walls. The designers' goal was to make the structure attractive and well suited to the historic downtown neighborhood. The contractor built a 120-foot-long tunnel from the basement of the detention center to the federal courthouse across the street. The 14-foot-wide tunnel, 30 feet below the street, was dug by hand due to space restrictions. The Philadelphia Metropolitan Detention Center contains 628 housing cells, each measuring 80 square feet and including a slit window. Although one of the newest MDCs, it is similar in its interior layout and operation to the MDCs found elsewhere.

MCC SAN DIEGO

MCC San Diego, first exhibited in 1974, rises 21 stories above a two-block "green belt" among a group of federal government buildings in San Diego. It was the first high-rise correctional institution completed for the U.S. Bureau of Prisons and was designed to hold 500 inmates and 160 staff. Like the metropolitan correctional centers at Chicago and New York, it has a large recreation yard on the top level and has its intake, administrative, and medical facilities on the first three floors. The remaining floors house inmates in modular two-story New Generation-style accommodations.

MCC CHICAGO

Chicago's Metropolitan Correctional Center, built in 1975 as a "skyscraper prison" has an extremely narrow sharp triangular shape, jutting out from the Chicago Federal Center Complex. With 27 floors rising above Chicago's Van Buren Street, MCC Chicago provides a picturesque addition to the city's skyline. The facility was designed to hold 411 detainees and 160 staff but now houses nearly 600. A U.S. magistrate courtroom occupies the second level, and a U.S. federal district court is situated one block away. The upper half of the building contains inmate cells that open into a two-tier multipurpose dayroom. The exercise yard is located on the roof and is hemmed in by 30-foot concrete walls with fenced openings.

MCC NEW YORK

MCC New York is an 11-story facility connected to the offices of the U.S. attorney and the U.S. Courthouse near the Manhattan financial district. When it opened in 1975, MCC New York was intended for 480 detainees and 160 staff. Today it generally holds more than 700 inmates. The three interconnected facilities (the MCC, the U.S. Courthouse, and the U.S. Attorney's Office) are integrated into a single complex with similar styling and materials used for the construction of each. Just as in MCC San Diego and MCC Chicago, inmates are housed in New Generation-style living units with 40 to 100 individuals living in small rooms along two tiers clustered around an open multipurpose dayroom.

INTERIORS

Designers of the MCCs and MDCs sought to "normalize" the character of both the exterior and interior physical environments. Thus the interiors of all the federal metropolitan centers lack traditional symbols of incarceration. They also have exterior windows, carpeting, and bright interior colors to encourage inmates to care for their living areas. Comfortable furniture and wood paneling instead of steel are intended to soften the effect of incarceration on the inmates' minds.

In each center, the lower floors are set aside for administrative offices, admissions, and medical facilities. The outer walls provide a secure perimeter, while central areas of the building are occupied by security control areas for staff. Inmates are housed in New Generation-style settings, with groups of 30 to 100 inmates kept in small modular units with access to larger common areas. All inmate activities in the dayrooms take place behind large glass panels, visible to staff at any angle, either directly or by closed-circuit camera.

MANAGEMENT AND OPERATION

Both metropolitan detention and correctional centers are capable of functioning as long-term prisons for federal inmates. In practice, however, the facilities hold people for relatively short periods of time. Metropolitan correctional and detention centers in cities like San Diego, New York, and Chicago are situated on costly real estate where space is at a premium. Inmates are rarely held for purposes other than trials or court appearances.

Metropolitan detention facilities complement suburban and rural federal prisons with different correctional missions. Each metropolitan facility is located on a federal prison transportation route that connects institutions from all over the United States. Airplanes and buses that travel along the route make regular drop-offs and pick-ups of inmates being transferred to and from the various federal prisons for different purposes. Each of the facilities have built-in vehicle sally-port intake and release areas on or below the ground floor. These are enclosed, secure areas from which inmates can be safely moved to and from transport vehicles.

TRENDS

When the three MCCs were constructed in the mid-1970s, some analysts predicted that metropolitan prison institutions would be a growing trend. Only a handful of similar prisons have been built in the intervening years, however. Like the U.S. correctional system in general, metropolitan detention centers have become crowded holding facilities as the federal prison population has grown. Each center now operates with inmate populations far in excess of its intended capacity. The U.S. Bureau of Prisons (BOP) as well as most state correctional agencies has opted to build their largest facilities in suburban or even remote rural settings to take advantage of opportunities for greater expandability.

CONCLUSION

Metropolitan correctional centers and detention centers provide correctional space in dense downtown areas where inmates and staff have easy access to court facilities, attorneys, and government administrators. Since the mid-1970s, inmate populations held by the U.S. federal prison system have increased dramatically, and the U.S. government has opted to construct its own jail facilities in some downtown environments instead of renting bed space from local jails. Evaluations of these metropolitan correctional and detention centers find that the attitudes of staff and inmates toward the centers can be described as more favorable than their attitudes toward traditional correctional institutions. Inmates in the centers are apparently more active, less violent, and more likely to engage in constructive activities.

—*Roger Roots*

See also Campus Style; Cottage System; Classification; Federal Prison System; High-Rise Prisons; Jails; New Generation Prisons; Panopticon; Trustee

Further Reading

Bosworth, M. (2002). *The U.S. federal prison system*. Thousand Oaks, CA: Sage.

Fairweather, L., & McConville, S. (2000). *Prison architecture: Policy, design and experience*. Oxford, UK: Architectural Press.

Farbstein, J. (1986). *Correctional facility planning and design*. New York: Van Nostrand Reinhold.

Krasnow, P. (1998). *Correctional facility design and detailing*. New York: McGraw-Hill.

Mays, G. L., & Winfree, L. T., Jr. (2002). *Contemporary corrections*. Stamford, CT: Wadsworth.

National Institute of Corrections. (1985). *Designs for contemporary correctional facilities*. Washington, DC: National Institute of Corrections.

Phillips, T. S., & Griebel, M. A. (2003). *Justice facilities*. Hoboken, NJ: Wiley.

Rush, G. E. (1997). *Inside American prisons and jails*. Incline Village, NV: Copperhouse.

◪ MILITARY PRISONS

Military prisons have been housing offenders from each branch of service since the early 1870s. The system replaced corporal punishment practices and was meant to standardize the treatment of military offenders in correctional facilities. It was designed to separate them from the "influences" of civilian offenders and facilities, decrease rates of desertion from service, and prepare military offenders for return to active duty or to a productive civilian life.

The Department of the Army acts as the Corrections Executive Agent for the Department of Defense and oversees all of the armed services correctional facilities and programs. While each service still operates penal facilities of its own, some are under the guidance of more than one branch. Consequently, the confinement experience varies according to programming and everyday practice, depending on service and facility. The facility on which there is the most available literature is the military's only maximum-security, long-term facility, the U.S. Disciplinary Barracks (USDB) at Fort Leavenworth, Kansas, which houses offenders from all branches and all sentenced officers. Although military prisons continue to differ from civilian federal and state prisons in inmate population characteristics and somewhat in structure, the correctional philosophy of the former is increasingly permeating the walls of the latter. One distinguishing characteristic of the military corrections system is its "restoration to duty" option, where an offender may be sentenced without discharge from service. This is seen by many as both a successful rehabilitative technique, by providing a working goal for the offender while incarcerated, and a form of release preparation. As a result, former military inmates may not experience the extensive stigma and difficulties obtaining employment and housing, upon release, as their civilian counterparts, which may account for decreased recidivism rates.

HISTORY

In 1871, then-Judge Advocate Major Thomas F. Barr began to evaluate the experience of military prisoners living among different stockades and state correctional facilities across the nation. He found that their treatment varied considerably, particularly concerning disciplinary measures. Prior to the formation of separate military prisons, minor infractions tended to be addressed harshly, with punishments such as flogging, shackling, tattooing, branding, solitary confinement, and execution. In a letter to the Secretary of War, William W. Belnap, Major Barr expressed his concerns about the U.S. system and requested that research be conducted on the British Military Prisons in Canada as a comparison.

British Military Prisons ran according to a mission based on three goals: to maintain discipline, reform offenders, and reduce the rate of military reoffending. These facilities were run systematically, with consistent use of discipline and prisoner classification. Authority was highly valued, as long as it was humane and effective in the goals of the overall mission. The findings of this research lead to a legislation submitted by the U.S. Congress in January 1872, establishing the first American military prison, also the first federal penal institution. The bill was written with specifications for the prison to be at Rock Island Arsenal, Illinois. This site, already guarded and situated between two rivers, provided opportunity for prisoner labor in the form of assembly and repair of small arms. Its location was soon criticized, however, as the bordering rivers would necessitate intensified security measures to protect both the arsenal itself and its new residents. In addition, the form of labor would require time-intensive training measures not conducive to the high turnover rate of inmates. Thus, an amendment to the bill in May 1874 led to the establishment of the first military prison at its present location: Fort Leavenworth, Kansas.

The founders of the military prison hoped to regulate the standard treatment of inmates, decrease rates of desertion and other military crimes, separate criminals with more rehabilitation potential, and finally, return the service personnel to a productive military or civilian life upon release from confinement. The establishment of a military prison system led to the abolition of many of the previous disciplinary measures, with the exception of solitary confinement. Military prisoners could now be segregated from civilian offenders and facilities, and the addition of training while incarcerated would allow them to continue to improve upon basic military principles. These changes were made to reconcile the correctional experience and the overall interests of military service.

MILITARY FACILITIES TODAY

The U.S. Armed Forces is governed by laws specified by the Uniform Code of Military Justice (UCMJ), part of the Manual for Courts-Martial. The corrections system of the Department of Defense consists of institutions organized by tier levels differing by mission and length of sentence. Tier I facilities house inmates confined pretrial and those with sentences of up to 90 days. The majority of military prisoners are housed in Tier II facilities, where sentences range from 91 days to 5 years. Each branch of service has at least one institution under the first two tiers, and usually inmates are housed by the service in which they serve. The U.S. Disciplinary Barracks (USDB) is the only Tier III and maximum-security correctional institution, where those serving terms of five years to life and death sentences are confined.

Facilities run by each branch are generally divided between four security levels: maximum, close (between maximum and medium), medium, and minimum. Prisoners may be as young as 17 years old, the minimum enlistment age. Since 1987, military prisoners include those who have committed any offense on active duty, whether or not service related. The traditional hierarchical ranks among the convicted are not upheld. That is, generally military prisoners are not distinguished by military rank with regard to correctional treatment and daily privileges. Inmates maintaining officer status upon entry may be segregated from enlisted inmates in their own housing units at the USDB only, and upon official dismissal from service they abandon these rights and are required to live within the general inmate population.

DEPARTMENT OF THE AIR FORCE

The Air Force Security Forces Center (AFSFC) has many roles in the correctional process. It seeks to aid in individual problem solving and behavior correction, as well as reformation for specific court-martialed offenders who may return to duty. This organization also conducts transfers of all U.S. Air Force (USAF) inmates and those inmates with sentences longer than three months. In addition, the AFSFC oversees 54 correctional facilities internationally and three Tier II regional correctional facilities. The USAF assists other branches of the military in the operation of three separate facilities: the USDB at Fort Leavenworth, Kansas, and the two Naval Consolidated Brigs in Miramar, California, and Charleston, South Carolina.

DEPARTMENT OF THE NAVY

In the early 1980s, an extensive study of the naval correctional system lead to significant attempts to improve the poor conditions that had plagued small facilities since the closing of the 80-year-old naval prison in Portsmouth, New Hampshire. Two consolidated brigs were built at Miramar, California, and Charleston, South Carolina, to serve as the Navy's new major confinement facilities. Consolidated brigs are direct-supervision facilities housing inmates with sentences ranging from 30 days to one year. They also provide training to prepare inmates for return to active duty or civilian life or hold them until they are ready to transfer to a long-term facility. Each facility has the capacity to house 450 prisoners but instead maintains full capacity at 360 to comply with the accreditation standards of the American Corrections Association (ACA).

The study resulted in a reconstruction of the naval correctional system into a three-tier system of waterfront brigs for detainees awaiting trial and inmates with relatively short sentences, consolidated brigs, and the option to transfer long-term inmates to the Federal Bureau of Prisons. Currently, the Department of the Navy operates six shore brigs, five pretrial confinement facilities, 20 shipboard brigs, and 10 detention spaces worldwide. The Department of the Navy also manages the Naval Corrections Academy, founded in 1976, located at the Lackland Air Force Base, Texas, where correctional personnel are trained. Finally, as of 1995, the department established a detachment that serves the USDB at Fort Leavenworth, Kansas.

U.S. MARINE CORPS

Before 1968, the U.S. Marine Corps corrections program was under the direction of the Department of the Navy correctional facilities, although staffed by Marine Corps personnel. In 1970, the Marine Corps created their own formal correctional program, including specific corrections Military Occupations of Specialty. By the early part of the decade, policy for the Navy and Marine Corps brigs was standardized in a publication of the Naval Corrections Manual. The closing of the Naval Disciplinary Command in Portsmouth, New Hampshire, saw the transfer of many Marine Corps inmates to the USDB. The end of the Vietnam conflict resulted in a decrease in the inmate population; thus, the need for Marine Corps correctional personnel declined. Six Marine Corps brigs were reclassified as detention facilities by the end of the decade. At the same time, the responsibility for apprehending absentees and deserters moved from the Federal Bureau of Prisons to the newly formed Marine Corps Absentee Collection Unit.

Today, the Marine Corps operates five brigs and two detention facilities in several states. Programs at each brig emphasize the retraining and readaptation of military standards and expectations. Physical training supplements recreational activities, work, and counseling programs.

DEPARTMENT OF THE ARMY

Four regional correctional facilities (medium-security level), two Army confinement facilities (minimum-security), and the USDB (the central maximum-security prison) and three facilities overseas make up the U.S. Army Corrections System. The Regional Corrections Facilities (RCFs) and the USDB implement several custodial and correctional treatment programs for military prisoners across branches of service. Short-term inmates can be found in the Army confinement facilities that provide services and programs on a smaller scale. Reform is the central focus of the official correctional policy, as stated by the Department of the Army and the Department of Defense in 1970. The concept of punishment remains relatively absent from the policy, as it is considered to already be intrinsically part of the nature of correctional confinement.

THE UNITED STATES DISCIPLINARY BARRACKS

The United States Disciplinary Barracks (USDB) is the only all-service, long-term confinement option for military offenders. For the most part, all inmates from every branch serving sentences longer than five years are sent to the USDB. Academy students and officers from each branch also serve their time here regardless of sentence length.

Established in 1874, it was called the U.S. Military Prison until 1915. Less than 20 years after the military prison was founded, the federal government determined that it too needed a federal prison system for civilian offenders who were serving time in various state and local facilities and were experiencing similar problems to those motivating the original establishment of the military prison system. The passage of the Three Prisons Act of 1891 transformed the USDB into the first federal civilian prison (USP Leavenworth), leaving the Army again without its own penal institution. The federal government became unsatisfied with the facility shortly afterward and built a new one nearby, to which the civilian federal prisoners moved. Control of the USDB has alternated between the U.S. Department of Justice as a federal prison and the Department of the Army as a military prison several times, but has remained under the Army since October 1940. Still, military prisoners may be transferred to federal civilian institutions for several reasons, including if the offender is proving harmful to the rehabilitation of other, potentially successful, military inmates.

In 1988, the USDB was the first military institution to be accredited by the American Corrections Association. Today, the facility struggles with deteriorating physical conditions as well as budgetary and staffing constraints due to lack of technological advancement. Thus a new facility is currently under construction.

SECURITY AT USDB

The acting warden of USDB is the Commandant and is ranked a Colonel (0-6) Military Police officer. Even though the prison is classified as a maximum-security institution, only a small percentage of inmates are classified at this level. The level of discipline and subsequent living conditions vary significantly among each level. Maximum custody only includes those serving sentences for severe crimes and/or those with a history of escape attempts. Most inmates are classified as medium custody upon entry. A custody level (Minimum Inside Only), unique to the USDB, exists between medium and minimum levels. At this level, inmates may enjoy minimum-custody privileges inside the facility, while movement outside the facility requires them to undergo medium-security measures. The Trustee Unit houses those reporting to work and other responsibilities without supervision.

Officially, control at USDB is to be achieved with the least amount of force possible, with correctional training as the ultimate goal. Military prisons experience lower rates of internal violence than do its civilian counterparts. A Discipline and Adjustment Board (D&A) is used to maintain discipline in the USDB. The board reviews aspects of each alleged violation of institutional rule or of the UCMJ. Disobedience, rule violations, threatening conduct, and staff harassment are the most frequent offenses appearing before the D&A.

INMATE POPULATION

The inmate population at the USDB has changed significantly in the past century. For most of the 20th century, the most common offenses for which sentences were being served were desertion, fraudulent enlistment, larceny, and assault. By 1996, however, fewer than 1% were serving sentences for traditional military offenses, and a great increase was evident in crimes against persons. Patterns in sentencing length have also changed dramatically. In the mid-1990s, the USDB facility operated at 80% capacity. As in civilian prisons, a steady increase began in 1979 and continued into the early 1980s. This expansion was due, in large part, to the change in average sentence length of those housed at the USDB, where the minimum was six months in the early 1980s and reached five years in 1994. By the late 1990s, the average sentence length had increased to 13.4 years. Inmates serving sentences at all military correctional institutions, however, are not likely to serve the entire term. Good conduct time (GCT), work abatement (WA), or special abatement (SA) in addition to clemency and parole can contribute to shortening the confinement stay.

As of 1999, the majority of all prisoners under military jurisdiction were white (non-Hispanic) (1,262 out of the total 2,279 prisoners) with the next most represented ethnic group black (non-Hispanic) inmates (674). The same year, the total inmate population included only 84 females. This inmate population is different than that of the average civilian prison, in that prisoners are older, more educated, and most often, first-time offenders. The number of inmates awaiting death by lethal injection as of the mid-1990s was under 10.

MILITARY CORRECTIONAL PROGRAMS

Title 10 of the United States Military Code requires that all correctional facilities include educational, training, and rehabilitation opportunities. Programs offered in the Military Corrections System vary across facilities according to service. The mission of military corrections is one of rehabilitation, not punishment, at every stage, from reception to release.

The most extensive correctional training program of all the facilities in the military corrections system is found at the USDB, where the motto is "Our Mission: Your Future." The Directorate of Training is divided into two divisions: academic and vocational. Few inmates are in need of basic education courses and can take a relevant course as needed; a higher education program option is available. In fact, the average inmates can expect to increase their academic level up to two grade levels with participation in this program. The Vocational Division includes 15 programs wherein a significant portion of the labor products benefits the military in some way. In addition, a large farm with animals and crops acts as a place of work for minimum-security inmates. Finally, counseling programs meant to prepare inmates for reintegration upon release, including job preparation and other workshops, are available. A work-release program, started in November 1970, operates to aid in this process and has shown to be successful. To participate, the inmate needs only to be classified as minimum security and be within two years of parole eligibility. The type of crime for which the individual is confined is irrelevant for eligibility in military work-release programs.

Finally, at the USDB, inmate treatment programs and correctional psychological research projects are the basis of the Directorate of Treatment Programs (DTP). The DTP is divided among three divisions: Treatment Planning, Rehabilitation, and Mental Health.

THE CASE FOR AND AGAINST A SEPARATE MILITARY SYSTEM

To its critics, the military corrections system no longer serves the same unique purposes for which it originated. Restoration-to-duty rates have declined significantly since the Vietnam conflict. This is due both to restrictions of eligibility as well as the ease at which new military personnel may be recruited from the community. Goals of decreasing military crimes have long since been reached, leaving less differentiation between civilian and military sentenced criminals.

For its supporters, however, military crimes not acknowledged by state and federal penal codes need a place for enforcement, and the assembly of military populations would prove useful should military need arise in a time of crisis. Finally, low rates of prison violence, the absence of overcrowding, and lower recidivism rates demonstrate that greater knowledge of the management of military prisons

may provide valuable information toward the improvement of civilian correctional facilities suffering from those problems.

CONCLUSION

The military corrections system holds criminal offenders obligated to a given military jurisdiction. While it shares some qualities with other penal systems, particularly the federal one, it is unique in many ways. Criminological research on this part of U.S. corrections is sparse, since access is often denied to anyone not associated with some part of the armed forces. As a result, it is difficult to know whether military prisons are effective, humane, or even completely necessary.

—*Jennifer Macy Sumner*

See also Enemy Combatants; Federal Prison System; Leavenworth, U.S. Penitentiary; Prisoner of War Camps; Trustee; USA Patriot Act 2001

Further Reading

Acorn, L. (1992). Military cares for its own with one-of-a-kind facility. *Corrections Today, 54*(1), 50.

American Correctional Association. (2002). *2002 directory: Adult and juvenile correctional departments, institutions, agencies, and probation and parole authorities.* Lanham, MD: Author.

Brodsky, S. L., & Eggleston, N. E. (Eds.). (1970). *The military prison: Theory, research, and practice.* Carbondale: Southern Illinois University Press.

Department of the Army. (1994). *Army Regulation 190–47: The Army corrections system.* Washington, DC: Author.

Handling offenders the military's way. (1992, February). *Corrections Today, 54*(1).

Herrod, R., Lt. Col. (1960). The United States Disciplinary Barracks system. *Military Law Review*, 35–72.

Leeson, B. A. (1997). The United States Disciplinary Barracks and military corrections. In R. Gregory Lande, D.O. (Ed.), *Principles and practice of military forensic psychiatry* (pp. 239–268). Springfield, IL: Charles C. Thomas.

Manos, A. M. (1992). *Inmate behavior and internal recidivism at the United States disciplinary barracks: Predictor variables, discipline and adjustment board procedures.* Doctoral dissertation, University of Kansas.

Morris, L. J., Lt. Col. (1996). Our mission, no future: The case for closing the United States Army Disciplinary Barracks. *Kansas Journal of Law and Public Policy 6,* 1–44.

◪ MILLER, JEROME G. (1931–)

Jerome G. Miller has served as a corrections administrator, reformer, and advocate in the United States since the 1970s. Best known for closing the juvenile reformatories in Massachusetts in the early 1970s, he also established and directs the National Center on Institutions and Alternatives and has written two influential books: *Last One Over the Wall: The Massachusetts Experiment in Closing Reform Schools* (1991) and *Search and Destroy: African-American Males in the Criminal Justice System* (1997).

Educated as a psychiatric social worker, Jerome Miller spent 10 years as a clinician in the U.S. Air Force. This experience, together with training in the therapeutic community concepts of Maxwell Jones, greatly influenced his view of institutionalization and care. After a stint as a social work professor at Ohio State University, he received an unexpected appointment as commissioner of youth services in Massachusetts in 1969. It provided him the opportunity to put into practice his progressive views of juvenile institutionalization.

THE "MASSACHUSETTS EXPERIMENT"

The customary difficulties of providing humane and effective treatment in coercive institutional settings stood in the way of Miller's reforming the juvenile facilities. He also encountered major political and bureaucratic obstacles in his attempts to move the reform schools in the direction of the therapeutic community ideal. He benefited, however, from strong support from Governor Francis Sargent, who very much wanted juvenile correctional reform. In addition, Miller found some talented and supportive staff and a lack of preparation and coordination on the part of his foes. Most of all, he was willing to take risks and to sacrifice his appointment if necessary. Both of these characteristics became necessary after he systematically closed all of the state's reformatories.

In 1970, after a year of thwarted efforts to transform them, Miller abruptly began closing the state's reform schools. In March 1972, he and staff closed the Lyman School for Boys, the seventh and final of these institutions. The previous residents of these institutions were not to be forgotten. Instead Miller had developed networks of community-based services throughout the state that were designed to help those who had been released from the institutions. Meant to address a variety of youth needs and to allow for flexible responsiveness in programming, these community-based services ranged from advocacy and mentoring through alternative education and vocational training to foster care and group homes. A residential psychiatric unit housed the small proportion of youth requiring such intervention.

Contemporaneous and subsequent research indicates the effectiveness and appropriateness of the Massachusetts Experiment. The state experienced no significant increase in serious juvenile delinquency. The most developed local systems of care more adequately met youth need without inflicting the harms associated with incarceration. Today, more than 30 years after this major project in juvenile corrections deinstitutionalization, Massachusetts continues to have one of the nation's lowest levels of juvenile institutionalization.

CAREER AFTER LEAVING MASSACHUSETTS

In 1973, Miller accepted an appointment as director of the Illinois Department of Children and Family Services (IDCFS). At about the same time, Governor Daniel Walker appointed David Fogel, a progressive from California by way of Minnesota, as director of the Illinois Department of Corrections (IDOC). As friends and allies, Miller and Fogel came as a package deal with a plan to reform youth services and juvenile corrections in a significant way. The plan, endorsed by the governor, who viewed it as a centerpiece for his administration, would transfer the juvenile division of IDOC to IDCFS. Miller then would establish something like the Massachusetts Experiment, closing juvenile reformatories while developing networks of community-based services for youth. Fogel would concentrate on ensuring that adult prisons operated constitutionally and that field services focused on effective reintegration of former prisoners into their communities. The plan fell apart when the Illinois Senate defeated Fogel's nomination, due to an unrelated battle between Walker and Chicago's powerful mayor, Richard J. Daley. Subsequently, Miller found himself stymied in intended major reform efforts. As he succeeded in overseeing implementation of the more modest Unified Delinquency Intervention Services (UDIS) project, he became enmeshed in various child welfare controversies and left the state in 1976.

Subsequently, Jerome Miller became commissioner of children and youth in Pennsylvania, where his efforts contributed to removing a thousand youths from adult prisons. He cofounded the National Center on Institutions and Alternatives, which has advanced client-specific sentencing advocacy, and where he serves as clinical director of its Augustus Institute. He also has served as a jail and prison monitor in Florida, under federal court appointment, and as receiver of the District of Columbia's child welfare system.

—*Douglas Thompson*

See also Zebulon Brockway; Child Savers; Cook County, Illinois; Elmira Reformatory; Incapacitation Theory; Juvenile Detention Centers; Juvenile Offenders: Race, Class, and Gender; Juvenile Reformatories; Robert Martinson; *Parens Patriae*; Rehabilitation Theory; Therapeutic Communities

Further Reading

Coates, R., Miller, A., & Ohlin, L. (1978). *Diversity in a youth correctional system: Handling delinquents in Massachusetts.* Cambridge, MA: Ballinger.

Krisberg, B., & Austin, J. (1993). *Reinventing juvenile justice.* Beverly Hills, CA: Sage.

Miller, A. (1985). *Delinquent and community: Creating opportunities and controls.* Beverly Hills, CA: Sage.

Miller, J. G. (1991). *Last one over the wall: The Massachusetts Experiment in closing reform schools.* Columbus: Ohio State University.

Miller, J. G. (1997). *Search and destroy: African-American males in the criminal justice system.* New York: Cambridge University Press.

◧ MINIMUM SECURITY

"Minimum security" refers both to those prisoners who pose the least risk of harm to the public as well as to the institutions in which they are housed. Minimum-security prisoners are typically afforded greater freedoms than their counterparts with greater custody classifications; they may be placed in facilities without perimeter barriers, and they often have limited access to the community. Minimum-security prisons have lower staff-to-inmate ratios. The low level of risk to public safety that minimum-security prisoners pose has led many to argue about whether it makes sense to incarcerate such offenders or instead whether they should be placed in the community with structured supervision and support.

CLASSIFICATION CONSIDERATIONS

Factors that weigh in security designation and custody classification vary among correctional systems. However, a minimum-security inmate is typically an offender who presents (1) with no or an insignificant prior criminal record; (2) with no history of violence, particularly no recent threatening or assaultive behavior; (3) with no history of escape or escape attempts; (4) with no gang or organized crime affiliations; and (5) with no outstanding detainers. Other considerations that can affect an inmate's classification include the seriousness of the offense for which the term of imprisonment is being served, the inmate's age and gender. Younger inmates are viewed as more prone to violence and disruption, while women are thought to be generally less aggressive and, therefore, more secure than men. Also, a person's education level, employment history, and the length of sentence to be served are taken into account. Better-educated inmates and those with a stable employment history or shorter sentences to serve are all seen as more reliable.

While the existence of one of the foregoing risk factors can alone preclude minimum-security designation, most classification systems recognize the need for graduated measures that allow for subjective judgments. In other words, correctional officials review classifications on a case-by-case basis. All the elements are added, resulting in a final rating. Correctional officials managing thousands of individuals in volatile settings tend to err on the side of caution and place prisoners in higher-security institutions should there be any question about potential risk of harm to staff or other inmates.

Because, as noted previously, women are considered to be safer than men, many correctional systems employ separate standards for classifying female inmates. It is thus more likely that a female prisoner will be housed at a minimum-security institution than a similarly situated male. In contrast, non–U.S. citizens are often ineligible for minimum-security placement regardless of their respective backgrounds due to immigration consequences of their convictions and related detainers placed by the U.S. Immigration and Customs Enforcement (ICE) to secure attendance at removal hearings. Indeed, many foreign prisoners are released to ICE custody after completing their sentences only to be held indefinitely pending a removal hearing and deportation should it be so ordered.

HOUSING

Minimum-security housing varies depending on a correctional system's structure and available resources. As an example, some jurisdictions permit the placement of low-risk offenders sentenced to short terms of confinement (e.g., 18 months or less) in community-based facilities, such as halfway houses or work release centers. Such places afford opportunities for daily release into the community to attend to employment, medical, religious, or other obligations. In them, offenders may only leave the institution for preapproved activities and times and are otherwise confined.

However, the most common form of minimum-security confinement is the prison camp, a correctional institution that employs less rigorous supervision over inmate activities and movement than traditional prisons (e.g., penitentiaries). Consistent with the understood level of risk, there are generally fewer perimeter security measures in place at camps, such as fences or walls, fewer patrol officers and towers, and prisoners bunk in either open cells or dormitories instead of locked cells. Work assignments regularly entail duties away from the institution, such as landscaping government

property, and minimum-security prisoners might be afforded access to a wider range of rehabilitative programming. For instance, in some correctional systems, an inmate must be classified as minimum security to participate in a boot camp program—a physically rigorous, shortened period of incarceration for offenders perceived as lacking life structure or discipline.

Irrespective of whether it is a camp or work release center, minimum-security housing is designed to promote change in individuals by teaching to them live independently while respecting the rights of others. Accordingly, minimum-security inmates are still subject to most of the same rules, regulations, and policies that govern a correctional system as a whole. Rules violations, disruption of institutional operations, and threatening behavior toward staff or other inmates can result in a minimum-security prisoner's brief period of detention within an administrative segregation unit (i.e., solitary confinement) or transfer to a higher-security institution. Conversely, higher-security inmates who demonstrate positive institutional adjustment through program participation, infraction-free conduct, or contributions to the institution or inmate population can achieve reductions in classification that lead to minimum-security placement and preparation for eventual release. Ultimately, minimum-security placement is considered a gateway toward community reintegration.

MINIMUM SECURITY FACILITIES IN THE FEDERAL PRISON SYSTEM

The Federal Bureau of Prisons has a number of minimum-security prison camps (FPCs) as well as three intensive confinement centers (ICCs) in Lewisburg, Lompoc, and Bryan. Reflecting their security classification, most of these facilities have no fences, and there is a low staff: inmate ratio. To be admitted to an ICC, prisoners should have either no history of incarceration or only a minor one and must agree to participate in a six-month program that is tailored to each inmate. These centers are like boot camps and have limited amenities. Drug treatment is a prominent part of the daily routine.

Usually, a term of confinement in one of these institutions is followed by some time in a ICC.

In contrast to those housed briefly in ICC, residents of prison camps may stay there for many years. Individuals may be either sent to the camps directly from the court or transferred from other higher-security facilities. They are usually housed in open dormitories. Though there is more freedom of movement in these institutions, they generally offer fewer opportunities for education and recreation because they are primarily work-oriented institutions. This is particularly the case for those prison camps located next to higher-security facilities. In the federal correctional centers (FCCs), which the bureau has built since the 1980s, camps are merely part of a series of other institutions, including correctional institutions and penitentiaries. Some prisoners argue that in this arrangement the inmates of the prison camp lose out since "the camp plays second fiddle to the needs of the bigger sister with regard to staff, supplies, requests, and recreational facilities" (Tayoun, 1997, p. 17).

THE CASE FOR AND AGAINST MINIMUM-SECURITY FACILITIES

Critics of minimum-security institutions deride them as insufficiently punitive "country clubs" that are more akin to college than the retributive desire for harsh penalties. Such objections are grounded in unsubstantiated concepts of deterrence that equate the severity of punishment with lower recidivism rates. Indeed, in recent years, states facing budget shortfalls have approved the release of large numbers of minimum-security prisoners, given the estimated annual cost—$22,000—to house and care for a single minimum-security prisoner.

There is a growing call to keep nonviolent, first-time offenders (i.e., minimum security) in the community. Structured community-based sanctions, such as day reporting centers, weekends in jail, house arrest, and community service, provide meaningful, cost-effective punishment while accounting for an individual's background. When an otherwise minimum-security prisoner is kept in the community, there is greater opportunity for treatment,

training, and satisfaction of restitution and court costs with an associated reduced drain on taxpayers.

CONCLUSION

As growing numbers of states face deepening fiscal crises and as state and federal prisons become increasingly overcrowded, the treatment of minimum-security prisoners and the form and purpose of minimum-security prisons are being reevaluated. At the same time that people are calling for changes in policy that would enable certain minimum-security inmates to serve out their sentences in the community, minimum-security prisons are increasingly being asked to hold well-behaved offenders with higher security levels in order to reduce the pressure on other institutions. What the long-term effects of these two changes will be is, as yet, unclear.

—Todd Bussert

See also Actuarial Justice; Boot Camp; Celebrities in Prison; Classification; Community Corrections Centers; Deterrence Theory; Home Arrest; Maximum Security; Medium Security; Probation; Rehabilitation Theory; Unit Management

Further Reading

American Correctional Association. (Ed.). (1993). *Classification: A tool for managing today's offenders.* Laurel, MD: American Correctional Association.

Carp, S., & Davis, J. (1989). *Design considerations in the building of women's prisons.* Washington, DC: National Institute of Corrections.

Farr, K. A. (2000). Classification for female inmates: Moving forward. *Crime and Delinquency, 46,* 3–17.

Petersilia, J. (Ed.). (1999). *Community corrections: Probation, parole and intermediate sanctions.* New York: Oxford University Press.

Tayoun, J. (1997). *Going to prison?* Brunswick, ME: Biddle.

Witke, L. (Ed.). (1999). *Planning and design guide for secure adult and juvenile facilities.* Lanham, MD: American Correctional Association.

◪ MORRIS, NORVAL RAMSDEN (1923–2004)

Norval Morris was one of the world's preeminent legal scholars, criminologists, and penal reformers. His work on prisons, sentencing, punishment theory, and mental health continues to be influential in both academic and public policy realms.

BIOGRAPHICAL DETAILS

Born in Auckland, New Zealand, in 1923, Morris received his law degrees at Melbourne University and a PhD in Law and Criminology at the University of London. He held several academic posts before serving as the Japan-based Director of the United Nations Institute for the Prevention of Crime and Treatment of Offenders from 1962 to 1964. From 1964 until 1994 Morris was on the faculty of the University of Chicago Law School. He served as Dean of the Law School from 1975 to 1978.

For more than 50 years, Morris worked to advance both the theoretical understanding of his field and to further its effective practice by teaching and mentoring generations of lawyers, policy makers, and scholars. He provided counsel to various components of the criminal justice system, including acting as a federal court's Special Master concerning issues of protective custody at Stateville Penitentiary (Illinois), and serving for more than 25 years on the Advisory Board of the National Institute of Corrections (and as chairman from 1986 to 1989).

EARLY WORK

Morris began his academic career exploring the question of recidivism. He expressed concern about preventative detention and the relevance of prison behavior to the prison release decision. He ultimately asserted that "at the time of sentencing as good a prediction as to when the prisoner can be safely released can be made as at any later time during confinement" (Morris, 2001, p. 186). In the 1950s, Morris also addressed the problem of unjustified sentencing disparity, and argued in favor of systematic, scientific studies on questions of crime and punishment, an approach that was not widely followed at the time.

THE DEVELOPMENT OF PENAL GOALS

Morris was one of the early advocates for punishment limited by principles of just desert. According to him, *desert* is "an essential link between crime and punishment. Punishment in excess of what is seen by that society at that time as a deserved punishment is tyranny" (Morris, 1974, p. 76). While Morris has contended that equality should merely be a guiding principle in part because of finite resources, he has strenuously argued that desert is a limiting principle—an absolute requirement—of just punishment. The punishment must be deserved, or, in Morris's term, it must be within the range of potential punishments that are not undeserved. To further determine an appropriate sentence, Morris has suggested following the concept of parsimony, which requires that the "least restrictive (punitive) sanction necessary to achieve defined social purposes should be imposed" (Morris, 1974, p. 59).

Despite his rejection of rehabilitation as a justification for imprisonment, and contrary to much of the scholarly and political rhetoric of recent decades, Morris repeatedly argued that rehabilitative programs remain crucial to both the theory and practice of incarceration and other sanctions. The important point is that such programs should be voluntary and should not be used to increase the length of an inmate's sentence.

In conjunction with his views of desert, Morris explored the proper role of predictions of dangerousness in the law, particularly in setting a defendant's sentence. Initially he believed that predictions could not properly be considered at sentencing, although he later came to argue that there was a narrow but legitimate purpose for predictions of dangerousness. Morris asserted that predictions of dangerousness cannot justify a more severe punishment than would be permissible without such a prediction. Yet within the array of punishments that satisfy the limiting principle of just deserts, Morris reasoned that reliable predictions of substantially greater than typical dangerousness may appropriately alter sentencing determinations. Morris investigated the relationship between law and mental illness, both in terms of criminal responsibility and sentencing. He objected to the amalgamation of the criminal justice and mental health systems, and strongly criticized various legal approaches to the mentally ill defendant, including the insanity defense.

Never content with isolated abstract arguments, Morris also described how a prison for recidivist criminals might be structured. The Federal Bureau of Prisons designed the programming and management at FCI Butner, North Carolina, based on Morris's description.

RETHINKING PENALTIES AND PRISON

In the 1990s, Morris turned his attention to the question of intermediate punishments. He and Michael Tonry argued that both prison and probation were overused and that a gap existed between those punishments:

> We are both too lenient and too severe; too lenient with many on probation who should be subject to tighter controls in the community, and too severe with many in prison and jail who would present no serious threat to community safety if they were under control in the community. (Morris & Tonry, 1990, p. 3)

Morris also used his skill as an author and stylist to confront basic problems of crime and punishment, and to bring these questions to a broader audience. In his classic work *The Brothel Boy and Other Parables of the Law* (1996), he brought to life the fictional Burmese experiences of police officer and magistrate Eric Blair, who later gained fame as the author George Orwell. Morris created engaging stories set in 1920s Burma built around challenging legal and moral questions of criminal and mental health law.

CONCLUSION

Morris continued to produce provocative works until he died. Such works included *Maconochie's Gentlemen* (2001), which uses a quasi-fictional form to study the emergence of the modern prison in the 1840s on Norfolk Island, 1,000 miles off the Australian coast. Morris's rich and subtle punishment theory—skeptical about state power, modest in its claims about society's ability to effectively redress criminality, yet hopeful with respect to the human character—permeates the book, and has informed much of his work. "Punishment may avenge, and restraint may, to a certain limited extent, prevent crime; but neither separately, nor together, will they teach virtue" (Morris, 2001, p. xx).

—*Steven L. Chanenson and Marc L. Miller*

See also Meda Chesney-Lind; John DiIulio, Jr.; David Garland; Incapacitation Theory; Intermediate Sanctions; Just Deserts Theory; Legitimacy; Alexander Maconochie; Mental Health; Jerome Miller; National Institute of Corrections; Nicole Hahn Rafter; Recidivism; Rehabilitation Theory; Stateville Correctional Center; Supermax Prisons.

Further Reading

Morris, N. (1951). *The habitual criminal*. New York: Longmans, Green.

Morris, N. (1974). *The future of imprisonment*. Chicago: University of Chicago Press.

Morris, N. (1983). *Madness and the criminal law*. Chicago: University of Chicago Press.

Morris, N. (1992). *The brothel boy and other parables of the law*. New York: Oxford University Press.

Morris, N. (2001). *Maconochie's gentlemen: The story of Norfolk Island and the roots of modern prison reform*. New York: Oxford University Press.

Morris, N., & Hawkins, G. (1970). *The honest politician's guide to crime control*. Chicago: University of Chicago Press.

Morris, N., & Tonry, M. (1990). *Between prison and probation: Intermediate punishments in a rational sentencing system*. New York: Oxford University Press.

◪ MOTHERS IN PRISON

The female prison population in the United States doubled during the 1990s and is continuing to rise. This increase affected minority women disproportionately, with black and Hispanic females far more likely than whites to be in prison. Two-thirds of the women in prison have one or more minor children. By the end of 1999, more than 53,000 mothers of minor children were incarcerated in state or federal prisons. This resulted in approximately 126,000 minor children with a mother in prison in 1999, almost double the number in 1990. Twenty-two percent of the children with a parent in prison were under five years old.

Unlike prisoner fathers, mothers in prison were often living with their children immediately prior to incarceration. In 1997, nearly 65% of the mothers in prison reported living with one or more of their minor children prior to their arrest. In the federal prison system, about 63% of women prisoners reported one or more minor children in the home prior to incarceration. As a result, in 1999 there were more than 35,000 women incarcerated who had resided with their children prior to arrest. Minority women and their children are particularly affected by the high incarceration rates of women. In state prisons, nearly half of the incarcerated parents were black, and nearly 1 in 5 were Hispanic. In the federal system, 44% were black, and 30% Hispanic. Several important issues have arisen as a result. The problems include placement of the children, contact between the prisoner mother and her children, the effects on the mothers, and the effects on the children. Furthermore, pregnancy during incarceration is becoming an increasing issue. A growing number of women enter prison pregnant, with some children born while they are incarcerated. Finally, some programs are being developed to address the problems of mothers in prison and their children.

PLACEMENT OF CHILDREN

Because nearly two-thirds of prisoner mothers lived with one or more of their minor children prior to incarceration, placement of the children is a serious issue. Almost half of the mothers in prison were the only parent in the home prior to arrest, and almost one-third of them lived alone with their children prior to incarceration. The children, therefore, must be placed in another household or setting.

While the children of prisoner fathers usually remain with the other parent during incarceration, the majority of children of prisoner mothers do not. The father becomes the caretaker in only about 1 out of 4 cases. Instead, the most common placement of these children is with the prisoner's family, usually with her relatives. The prisoners' parents are most

likely to become the caretakers, and siblings are the second most likely. On average, women in state prisons have 2.38 children. In many cases, the children are separated from each other as well as from their mothers. Additionally, they may be moved from one family member to another during the course of the mother's imprisonment. Most incarcerated mothers hope to resume their parenting responsibilities upon release. However, when children are placed in foster care or state custody, it is not uncommon for parental right to be terminated. Therefore, mothers in prison try to avoid nonfamily placement, fearing permanent loss of custody.

CONTACT BETWEEN INCARCERATED MOTHERS AND THEIR CHILDREN

The majority of incarcerated mothers report regular contact with their children. There are three common forms of interaction: telephone calls, mail, and visits. Approximately 60% of mothers in prison report weekly communication with their children, and nearly 80% report monthly contact. The most common form of contact is through letters. Telephone calls are also common. Visiting is the least common method of staying in touch, with only 24% of prisoner mothers reporting monthly visits from their children, and more than half reporting never receiving a visit from their children.

Writing letters to children helps maintain family bonds. However, many of the prisoners' children are under the age of five. For the youngest, letters may not be an effective way to preserve their relationship with their mother. Telephone contact is the next most common form, with nearly 40% of the mothers in prison reporting weekly telephone contact. However, since prisoners must call collect, the toll charges may be prohibitive, and it may be difficult for the mother to call at times convenient for the family.

Prison visits are the least common form of mother-child contact. Visiting is often problematic because of the locations of women's prisons. Because of the smaller number of women prisoners compared to men, there are fewer women's prisons. These are frequently located in remote areas. Therefore, a woman is often incarcerated at considerable distance from her family. In fact, most are housed at least 100 miles from where they lived prior to incarceration. Women in some states are warehoused in prisons located in other states, creating further difficulties. Visiting is difficult, due to the cost and the time involved. Furthermore, some women do not want their children to see them in prison and discourage visits. However, maintaining the mother–child relationships increases the mental health of both the mothers and the children. Children who are able to visit their mothers are more likely to be able deal with their separation anxiety as well as their fears for their mothers' safety. Furthermore, successful reunification after the woman's release is enhanced by ongoing contact. With less contact, the relationship between the mother and the child weakens, creating problems upon release.

EFFECTS ON THE MOTHERS

Separation from children may be linked to depression in mothers in prison. For many of them, the maternal role is one of few positive roles available. Self-esteem is decreased by the disruption of the relationship. Prisoner mothers may try to minimize emotional pain by distancing themselves from their children, further straining the relationships.

Mental health services for women in prison are limited. The majority of administrators indicate a need for increased mental health services in women's prisons, particularly programs designed to increase self-esteem. There are also some counseling programs available for women to help them deal with separation from their children. However, screening and assessment of women prisoners is frequently accomplished using instruments designed for men, resulting in the needs of women prisoners being overlooked. Few correctional facilities assess the need for counseling related to separation from their children.

EFFECTS ON THE CHILDREN

When a mother is incarcerated, the family unit is disrupted. Children are separated from their mothers and often from their siblings. Furthermore,

the relationships of children and their mothers become strained. Children may fear for their mothers' safety, and depression is a common reaction in all age groups. School attendance and performance is frequently affected as well, often resulting in older children dropping out of school. Finally, the children of imprisoned mothers may engage in law-violating behaviors themselves, resulting in arrest and punishment. While the mothers may receive some mental health services while in prison, most states do not provide services for the children of incarcerated parents or for their caretakers.

Placement of a minor child with the mother's family, while usually the mother's preference, may not always be in a child's best interest. The majority of women prisoners have histories of physical and/or sexual abuse. Therefore, children who live with family members of the prisoner may be placed in potentially abusive situations. Furthermore, the additional responsibility of the child or children adds to the economic and emotional strain on families that have limited resources. Some research has suggested that nonfamily placements are associated with higher-quality care, both material and emotional. However, fear of loss of custody leads women to place the children with family, despite the potentially negative consequences.

PREGNANT PRISONERS

More than 5% of women prisoners are pregnant at the time of incarceration, with nearly 1,400 children born to incarcerated mothers in the United States in 1998. Pregnancies in prison are frequently high risk, due to the lifestyles of the women prior to incarceration. Homelessness, poverty, substance abuse, and histories of abuse all increase the potential for problematic pregnancies and births. Moreover, few prisons have the specialized types of care needed to ensure good birth outcomes.

Pregnancy may increase the stress faced by prisoners. In addition to the difficulties of incarceration, the pregnant prisoner must deal with the impending separation from her child, ill-fitting prison uniforms, and decisions about placement of the child. Additionally, her health care will be limited. Often the pregnant prisoner may be placed in a maximum-security prison, regardless of her own security level, because of the need for medical care. Furthermore, only 15% of state prisons provide a special diet for pregnant prisoners.

Despite these problems, birth outcomes for pregnant prisoners are often better than for those whose children were born outside of prison, since incarcerated women may receive better medical care than they received on the street. Slightly fewer than half of the women's prisons in the United States offer specific prenatal care services, while another 40% provide prenatal services from community agencies. Women who were homeless or living in poverty prior to prison at least have shelter and adequate nutrition in prison, further increasing the likelihood of a positive birth outcome. Alcohol and drug consumption is less likely as well. Thus, the reduction in risk factors can contribute to better birth outcomes for both the mothers and their infants. Prison policies differ in regard to delivery of the infant. In most prisons, the mother is transferred to a local hospital to deliver. Policies concerning restraint of pregnant prisoners vary. In some states, it is illegal to shackle a pregnant prisoner during the move to the hospital for birth. However, in other states, restraints are allowed during the transfer, and in some states they are even used on pregnant prisoners during labor and delivery. In most jurisdictions, the policy is to use the least restrictive measures allowable in the situation.

Policies also vary concerning the contact allowed between the prisoner mother and her newborn. In some jurisdictions, virtually no contact is allowed. The mother may see the infant briefly at birth, then not again until after release. More commonly, the mother may spend time with the infant until she is discharged from the hospital, usually 1–2 days. Finally, some jurisdictions allow the mother to keep her infant with her in prison for about 18 months.

PROGRAM NEEDS AND AVAILABILITY

Mothers in prison and their children have special needs. In a number of prisons, programs have been developed to address those needs. Since the goal of most mothers is reunification with their children after they are released, institutions usually try to deal with the problems faced by prisoner mothers, including development of parental skills, substance abuse treatment, and life skills development. In a recent study, prison administrators reported a need to increase available mental health services for women prisoners, including parenting programs designed to strengthen the women's nurturing and discipline skills.

While there are some mental health services available for mothers in prison, fewer are available to their children and the children's caretakers. A few programs have been developed to ensure that the children are given needed treatment, although they are limited. Substance abuse is also a problem. Mothers in prison are likely to have serious drug abuse histories. More than half the mothers in state prisons reported drug use in the month prior to incarceration, and only slightly less than half committed their offense while under the influence of drugs.

Lack of contact between mothers and their children is another problem, leading to the development of programs to increase mother–child contact. In some locales, transportation is provided to the prison by either the state or a community or church organization. Other prisons have introduced innovative programs utilizing computers to allow "virtual visits." Others have mother–child programs to increase contact, including programs such as "Girl Scouts Beyond Bars" and family visits. In a few correctional systems, programs have been put into place that allow overnight visitation between mother and child. The most innovative programs for mothers in prison are those that allow the children to remain with the mother. The most well-known program, Bedford Hills Correctional Facility Children's Center in New York, not only allows infants to remain with the mothers the first year but also teaches the mothers parenting skills. This program also provides services to children outside of the program and facilitates visitation. The program utilizes prisoners as peer counselors to increase its effectiveness. Eleven states and the Federal Bureau of Prisons have instituted programs that allow infants and mothers to remain together from 3 months to 18 months after birth.

Finally, there are a few innovative programs that assist in the reunification process. The Women's Prison Association in New York City has a multiphase program that starts with visiting. When the mothers are deemed ready, the children join them in a halfway house setting, where both mothers and children receive services. Finally, the program assists the family with obtaining housing, employment, and social services. They receive follow-up services for one year after completion of the program. Other jurisdictions have implemented community-based programs that allow mother and children to remain together as an alternative to incarceration.

CONCLUSION

While mothers in prison face a wide range of problems, some programs are being instituted to address those problems. The most effective programs are those that deal with multiple issues in a holistic fashion. Successful reunification of mothers and their children is a difficult task. However, through addressing underlying mental health issues, substance abuse issues, life skills, and parenting skills, the chance of success is increased.

—*Susan F. Sharp*

See also Bedford Hills Correctional Facility; Children; Children's Visits; Fathers in Prison; Foster Care; Gynecology; Parenting Programs; Prison Nurseries; Termination of Parental Rights; Women Prisoners; Women's Health; Visits

Further Reading

Beck, A. J., & Karberg, J. C. (2001). *Prison and jail inmates at midyear 2000.* Washington, DC: U.S. Department of Justice.

Bloom, B., & Steinhart, D. (1993). *Why punish the children?* San Francisco: National Council on Crime and Delinquency.

Daane, D. (2003). Pregnant prisoners: Health, security and special needs issues. In S. F. Sharp (Ed.), *The incarcerated woman: Rehabilitative programming in women's prisons* (pp. 61–72). Upper Saddle River, NJ: Prentice-Hall.

Enos, S. (2001). *Mothering from the inside: Parenting in a women's prison.* Albany: State University of New York Press.

Greenfeld, L. A., & Snell, T. L. (1999). *Women offenders: Bureau of Justice Statistics Bulletin.* Washington, DC: U.S. Department of Justice.

Morash, M., Bynum, T., & Koons, B. A. (1998). *Women offenders: Programming needs and promising approaches.* Washington, DC: U.S. Department of Justice.

Mumola, C. J. (2000). *Incarcerated parents and their children.* Washington, DC: U.S. Department of Justice, Bureau of Justice Statistics.

Owen, B. (1998). *In the mix: Struggle and survival in a women's prison.* Albany: State University of New York Press.

Sharp, S. F. (2003). Mothers in prison: Issues in parent-child contact. In S. F. Sharp (Ed.), *The incarcerated woman: Rehabilitative programming in women's prisons* (pp. 151–165). Upper Saddle River, NJ: Prentice-Hall.

Sharp, S. F., & Marcus-Mendoza, S. T. (2001). It's a family affair: Incarcerated women and their families. *Women and Criminal Justice, 12*(4), 21–49.

◪ MUSIC PROGRAMS IN PRISONS

Music programs are used in prisons as part of the rehabilitation process. Advocates point to the therapeutic nature of music, the positive outlet of energy, and the stimulation of the creative processes as reasons to support the continuation and proliferation of music programs. Music programs emphasize cooperation and provide a skill that can be used outside of prison—if not as a source of income, then as a productive hobby.

PROGRAM CONTENT

Music programs have traditionally been offered in all kinds of facilities, from lower-security to maximum-security places like Angola and San Quentin. Prison music includes music lessons, playing and performing in groups or bands, and the opportunity to make recordings and/or perform live on radio and television. Historically, prison bands existed in many states in the early 1900s. Today, prison groups and bands sometimes travel outside the prison to perform in parades and at local festivals; others are limited to performing inside the institution for their convict peers only. They have played at rodeos in Texas and still perform at Louisiana's Angola Rodeo. Instruction varies from hiring professional music instructors to volunteers to prisoner teachers. At Angola, Louisiana, in the 1970s, Charles Neville of the Neville Brothers had full-time work duty in the music room as a convict music teacher.

Music programs can be part of larger overall arts programs that include theater, dancing, and painting, while sometimes they are part of other self-help groups organized by the prisoners themselves. They also can be free-standing music programs and/or part of the prisons' recreational program.

SUPPORT FOR PROGRAMS

Art and music program advocates believe that such classes restore a sense of humanity and safety that is vital to rehabilitation. The sense of completion and of contribution to the creation of something that society values can help inmates increase their self-esteem and recapture a sense of pride and satisfaction in themselves and their work. Other benefits can include relearning responsibility and discipline through individual and group practice and performance. As part of an all-around rehabilitation program, Superintendent Fred Jones appointed Wendell Cannon as Parchman's first director of music in 1960, although prison bands had existed at Parchman, Mississippi, since the 1940s. Cannon was empowered to exempt his choice of convict-musicians from the field and thus lured the black convicts into the music program; only white convicts had participated in the prison bands to date.

Music and art programs also have been shown to reduce recidivism rates. They provide an alternative to traditional education programs, to which inmates who have had negative experience with schooling in the past may be averse. The open structure of these programs also helps them bring together diverse groups of individuals from different racial, ethnic, geographical, and class backgrounds into a harmonious cooperative atmosphere. As part of a multi-faceted program to promote tolerance and mutual respect among its inmates, Ohio's Marion Correctional Institution created "Music in the Air." One successful participant of a music program observed, "I traded a pistol for a trumpet!" Music programs have even been used as a form of

psychotherapy to develop the relationship between the therapist and the client. Therapists believe that music can help individuals who would otherwise have a difficult time expressing themselves. Evaluation of a music therapy program implemented in a female correctional facility concluded that music therapy reduced tension and anxiety while also increasing motivations and ties with reality for the women convicts. Art and music programs have also been used in the treatment of sexual offenders against children.

Examples

Goals other than rehabilitation prompt prison systems to create music programs. In the late 1930s, the Texas radio program, *Thirty Minutes Behind the Walls* was created to gain favorable publicity for the prison system and to offset the negative publicity surrounding a recent rash of escapes, beatings, and gun fights within the prison. Not only male prison systems initiate music programs. Women prisoners at the Goree, Texas, prison farm for women created a band in the early 1940s because they believed that they might get the attention of then-Governor O'Daniel and be able to play their way out of prison. The women not only performed at rodeos and on the prison radio program; the "Goree Girls" also traveled extensively around the state. None of the women were paroled out of prison because of their singing abilities, but the notoriety of the prison radio show certainly declined when the last and most popular member of the band was paroled in 1943. By 1944, the prison radio show was no more.

Some states provide funding for prison music programs; in others, funding may be left to private foundations that support the arts and have an interest in correctional facilities. Prominent foundations and groups include "Art Behind Bars" in Florida and "Irene Taylor Trust" in England. Inmates have even requested to be transferred to prisons with well-known music programs, including the State Correctional Institution Graterford in Pennsylvania. At this prison, inmates are graded and must receive at least a C in order to get credit as a student in the music program.

Drawbacks

One drawback to music programs is the potential they may provide for smuggling contraband into the prison. In the past, for example, SCI Graterford experienced increased violence and drug overdoses that led to a temporary suspension of the program. Another current stumbling block has to do with negative publicity over such programs, which are viewed by many critics as being "soft" on criminals. A recent VH1 television series that highlighted various states' music programs, *Music Behind Bars,* brought such negative publicity from victims' family members and Bill O'Reilly of *The O'Reilly Factor* that Pennsylvania's Governor Schweiker canceled all prison music programs for murderers in Pennsylvania.

Less controversially, there can be a problem of consistency. Since prisoners are frequently moved from one institution to another during their confinement, they may find that they are unable to continue studying or playing music if they are moved to an institution that does not provide the necessary equipment. Accordingly, music may become yet another source of prison frustration rather than rehabilitation. Even with such positive support for prison programs, musical instruments are expensive and are often difficult to obtain and maintain. Access to them can become a problem for security. Finally, by definition, prison music programs operate as part of the overall system of social control that conflicts with goals of rehabilitation. Prisoners' ability to participate in such programs is not based simply on talents but on one's "good" prison behavior, and in Pennsylvania, the nature of one's crime. "Dark Mischief," one of the current bands at Graterford, must perform regularly. If the convicts do not like the show, the men lose their playing privileges.

CONCLUSION

Music programs, at least in the form of bands, have existed in prisons throughout the country since the early 1900s. Music programs offer a constructive and creative rehabilitation method for the correctional industry. While some may view these types of programs as a luxury that prisoners do not deserve, research supports their positive effects. As long as funding is available, either through the government or private foundations, music programs will continue to offer a piece to the rehabilitation puzzle. However, correctional budgets are being cut in many states across the nation, and prison music programs are suffering. Many bands do not travel anymore, instruments are not repaired, and music rooms are closed in an effort to cut costs.

—*Gregory Lobo-Jost*

See also Art Programs; Creative Writing Programs; Drama Programs; Education; Furlough; Labor; Parchman Farm, Mississippi State Penitentiary; Plantation-Style Prisons; Prison Literature; Prison Music; Rehabilitation Theory

Further Reading

Art Behind Bars. Retrieved from http://www.artbehindbars.com

Burton-Rose, D., Pens, D., & Wright, P. (Eds.). (1998). *The celling of America: An inside look at the U. S. prison industry.* Monroe, ME: Common Courage.

Daveson, B. A., & Edwards, J. (2001). A descriptive study exploring the role of music therapy in prisons. *Arts in Psychotherapy, 28*(2), 137–141. Retrieved from http://www.elsevier.com/inca/publications/store/8/3/3/

Hollandsworth, S. (2003). O sister, where art thou? *Texas Monthly, 31*(5), 136–147.

Irene Taylor Trust Brochure. Retrieved from mg.carltononline.com/citysurvival/programmes/Irene%20Taylor%20Trust.pdf

Menees, T. (2002). Cellblock cues: On the inside, prison music, and theater programs have positive powers. *Pittsburgh Post-Gazette*, November 4, 2002.

Money, C. (1999). A taste for tolerance fuels prison culture. *Corrections Today, 61*(3), 99–100.

Naitove, C. E. (1988). Using the arts therapies in treatment of sexual offenders against children. In S. Sgroi (Ed.), *Vulnerable populations: Evaluation and treatment of sexually abused children and adult survivors* (Vol. 1, pp. 265–298). New York: Free Press.

Taylor, W. B. (1999). *Down on Parchman Farm.* Columbus: Ohio State University Press.

N

◪ NARCOTICS ANONYMOUS

Offenders with substance abuse problems make up a minimum of 75% of the U.S. inmate population. Despite this alarming figure, currently fewer than half of U.S. prisons offer targeted substance abuse programming. Those programs that are offered most commonly include self-help programs such as Narcotics Anonymous. Narcotics Anonymous (NA) is a nonprofit organization made up of recovering addicts who meet regularly to support one another in the recovery process. The NA program developed from the Alcoholics Anonymous framework in the late 1940s. The organization grew slowly through North America until the 1980s, when they published their *Basic Text,* which became highly influential. The NA program is centered on complete abstinence from all drugs, although anyone with the desire to stop using may participate.

PROGRAM FRAMEWORK

Narcotics Anonymous is based on the premise that addicts are in the best position to help others through the process of substance abuse recovery. Peer support is considered key to reform; members can rely on others who have been through the same process to help them survive through cravings, deal with their emotions, and build a drug-free lifestyle.

New members are encouraged to seek a more experienced person as a sponsor—an individual guide and counselor. Recovering addicts are guided through the recovery process by NA's 12 steps. Addicts must admit that they have a problem and seek help. The other parts of the healing process involve moving through self-examination, self-disclosure, making amends, and finally helping others with their addictions.

The 12 steps also require addicts to acknowledge God in their own terms, as a higher spiritual power key to the recovery process. NA has no religious affiliation; the emphasis is on bringing people to a spiritual awakening that is meaningful to them and on the adoption of a moral code of honesty and responsibility.

PROGRAM DELIVERY IN THE CORRECTIONAL SETTING

Narcotics Anonymous operates within the correctional setting through Hospitals and Institutions (H&I) meetings and presentations. Volunteers from the community, in cooperation with the facility, conduct these meetings and presentations. NA does not employ service delivery professionals; all volunteers are program members. H&I provides presentations introducing the principles of NA and sharing early recovery stories to inmates in short-term (less than one year) facilities. In longer-term facilities, regular meetings with increased participation and sharing are encouraged as the recovery process takes place within the institution.

NA meetings are usually open discussions facilitated by volunteers. Members share their stories of relapse and recovery and receive support from their peers. Meetings do vary and may include, for example, guest speakers, a book study, or a focus on a particular topic of concern, such as dealing with drugs within the prison environment. The frequency of meetings depends on the availability of volunteers and space within the facility, but usually ranges from one to two meetings per week.

BENEFITS AND CONCERNS

Narcotics Anonymous programs are extremely low cost and require few facility resources to operate. Established NA groups can provide members with a subculture that is separate from the drugs, alcohol, and contraband within the institution. Unintentionally, however, they may also provide a concentrated source of potential clients for narcotics dealers.

ROLE IN THE TREATMENT CONTINUUM

The Federal Bureau of Prisons requires that nonresidential treatment programs be available in all institutions. However, 12-step programs such as NA do not qualify as nonresidential treatments under the Bureau of Prisons' classification; therefore they are usually accompanied by other treatment options. Although 12-step programs can be extremely powerful and successful for some inmates, they are not universally applicable and are best used in conjunction with more intensive interventions. Inmates may, for example, be required to attend NA meetings as follow-up to participation in treatment communities, detoxification, or counseling.

CONTINUITY THROUGH THE RELEASE PERIOD

One of the primary benefits of NA in the correctional setting is its continuity. Men and women approaching release are provided with meeting directories and phone numbers in order to establish contact with an NA group in the community. This outreach provides a source of familiarity and stability for inmates in the community while continuing the substance abuse recovery process. Members are encouraged to find a sponsor immediately upon release to provide an individual source of support through the transition period.

CONCERNS WITH SPECIAL POPULATIONS

The NA framework may be inapplicable or alienating to some prisoner groups. Most women with substance abuse problems have issues relating to self-esteem, emotional expression, and victimization that may interfere with or even be intensified by the open presentation and discussion process of NA. Members of minority ethnic or religious groups may feel alienated by the concepts of God and spirituality presented in NA literature. The required goal of freedom from all substance use may also prevent the participation of inmates with substance abuse problems who see abstinence as unattainable or unnecessary.

CONCLUSION

Narcotics Anonymous provides a low-cost option for a system in need of vastly increased substance abuse programming. The efficacy of NA alone as a solution to substance abuse among inmates remains contentious. However, evidence does indicate that NA can be an important contributing factor within a comprehensive substance abuse program. Support provided by the program within the institution and particularly throughout the release process can be a valuable part of the recovery and reintegration process.

—*Rebecca Jesseman*

See also Alcoholics Anonymous; Drug Offenders; Drug Treatment Programs; Federal Prison System; Group Therapy; Health Care; HIV/AIDS; Individual Therapy; Overprescription of Drugs; Psychological Services; Therapeutic Communities; Volunteers; War on Drugs; Women's Health

Further Reading

Leukefeld, C. G., Tims, F., & Farabee, D. (2002). *Treatment of drug offenders: Policies and issues.* New York: Springer.

Narcotics Anonymous. (1988). *Narcotics Anonymous.* Van Nuys, CA: Narcotics Anonymous World Service Office.

Narcotics Anonymous World Services. Retrieved July 23, 2003, from http://www.na.org

Ronel, N. (1998). Narcotics Anonymous: Understanding the "bridge of recovery." *Journal of Offender Rehabilitation, 27*(1/2), 179–197.

Wilson, D. J. (2000). *Drug use, testing, and treatment in jails.* Bureau of Justice Statistics Special Report. Washington, DC: U.S. Department of Justice. Retrieved July 23, 2003, from http://www.ojp.usdoj.gov/bjs/abstract/duttj.htm

◪ NATION OF ISLAM

The Nation of Islam was established by Wallace D. Fard in Detroit, Michigan, during the summer of 1930. When Fard mysteriously disappeared three years later, Elijah Muhammad (nee Poole) assumed his position as spiritual leader. Under the direction of Muhammad, the Nation of Islam espoused a black separatist doctrine at odds with the integrationist aims of mainstream civil rights organizations. Muhammad prophesied that the imminent destruction of the white race would allow black people to claim their rightful inheritance to the Earth. Throughout its history, the Nation of Islam has drawn not only much of its grassroots support but also some of its most important leaders from the African American prison population.

ORIGINS OF THE PRISON MINISTRIES

The efforts of the Nation of Islam to recruit the support of black prison inmates occurred largely as a result of the Second World War. Opposing what it perceived as a war of white imperialist aggression, the Nation attempted to claim conscientious objector status for its members who were threatened with enlistment in the U. S. Army. In 1942, Elijah Muhammad was convicted with more than 60 other Black Muslims for draft evasion, and was sentenced to three years' imprisonment.

During his incarceration, Muhammad reflected on the failure of civil rights leaders to recruit support from the black prison population. Following his release in 1946, he set out to establish prison ministries across the United States. These ministries attempted to rehabilitate African American inmates through a process of physical and spiritual transformation. Prison converts were instilled with a strict moral code of discipline, abandoning drugs and alcohol and cultivating the habits of thrift and hard work. Their personal redemption was accomplished by cleansing themselves in body and in mind of the destructive influences of the ghetto. To encourage a new sense of purpose and belonging, prison converts were provided with employment at one of the Nation's temples upon their release.

The most famous prison convert to the Nation of Islam was a petty criminal called Malcolm Little. Malcolm experienced his spiritual conversion while an inmate at the Charleston Penitentiary in Massachusetts. By the time of his release in 1952, Malcolm Little had become Malcolm X, a name that symbolized the rejection of the Christian surname imposed on his forefathers by white slave masters. Malcolm's brilliant oratorical skills swiftly established him as the preeminent spokesperson of the Nation of Islam. His status as a reformed inmate made him an ideal role model for other prison converts to the Nation.

THE FREEDOM OF RELIGIOUS PRACTICE IN PRISONS

The prison outreach programs of the Nation of Islam have received numerous awards. Despite such accolades, the ministries have suffered persistent opposition from prison authorities. Officials often perceive Black Muslim inmates as potential risks to prison security because of their supposed incitement of racial hatred. Converts to the Nation of Islam are also said to create an administrative burden because they demand exceptional treatment, such as the provision of special diets, days of worship, and religious instruction from their own ministers. These tensions have resulted in Black Muslims becoming the targets of harassment, intimidation, and violence. In response, the Nation of Islam has taken legal action on a number of occasions to secure the protection of its supporters' right to practice their religion under the First Amendment to the U.S. Constitution. Although the courts have not been entirely consistent, they have in broad principle established the freedom of religious practice in prisons.

CONCLUSION

Under the leadership of Minister Louis Farrakhan, the Nation of Islam launched a renewed prison recruitment campaign in 1984 with considerable success. It is not possible to determine the precise number of prison inmates who convert to the Nation of Islam, since the sect does not disclose statistics. More research is needed on the Black Muslims' prison ministries, especially their presence within women's institutions, a subject that has received scant attention from scholars. Prisons certainly continue to be a rich recruiting ground for the Nation of Islam. Although African Americans constitute only 13% of the total U.S. population, nearly half of all prison inmates in the early 21st century are black. The disproportionately large black prison population will likely continue to provide a fertile source of converts for the Nation of Islam.

—Clive Webb

See also Activism; Attica Correctional Facility; African American Prisoners; Black Panther Party; Angela Y. Davis; Deprivation; Importation; Islam in Prison; George Jackson; Malcolm X; Racial Conflict Among Prisoners; Religion in Prison; Resistance; Riots

Further Reading

Gardell, M. (1996). *In the name of Elijah Muhammad: Louis Farrakhan and the Nation of Islam.* Durham, NC: Duke University Press.

Marsh, C. E. (2000). *The lost-found Nation of Islam in America.* Lanham, MD, & London: Scarecrow.

◪ NATIONAL INSTITUTE OF CORRECTIONS

The National Institute of Corrections (NIC) is a subdivision of the Federal Bureau of Prisons in the Department of Justice. The NIC was created in response to a keynote address by Justice Warren E. Burger to the National Conference on Corrections in Williamsburg, Virginia. Justice Burger suggested that an agency should be created to handle national training, promote research and knowledge, develop professional guidelines and standards, and facilitate the exchange of ideas in corrections. His recommendations led to the formation of the NIC in 1974.

Today, a director appointed by the U.S. Attorney General administrates the NIC in conjunction with a 16-member advisory board. The NIC also utilizes staff employed by state and local governments who are appointed for two-year periods. The NIC has two offices in Washington, D.C., and Longmont, Colorado, that coordinate training, technical assistance, policy and program development, and provide information to federal, state, and local correctional agencies. The NIC provides direct assistance in the form of training, program development, and information to adult correctional agencies and personnel. It does not work with juvenile correctional agencies, but it does collaborate with other federal agencies on juvenile corrections, sex offender programs, and the 1994 Crime Bill.

The NIC uses many strategies to meet the goals set forth by local, state, and federal correctional agencies. Jails, prisons, and community-based correctional agencies can utilize information provided by the NIC on planning and management services, education, training and professionalism, and program development. The NIC also provides research opportunities on programs and policies that improve the organizational structure and operation of correctional agencies. Finally, the NIC works to provide programming that holds offenders accountable for their actions, emphasizes public safety and the safety of inmates, and facilitates responsible behavior among corrections staff and inmates.

DIVISIONS AND SPECIAL PROJECTS

The NIC is divided into five divisions and four offices. The Academy Division is primarily responsible for training programs in leadership, management, and training for trainers. It trains local, state, and federal correctional staff in a variety of locations throughout the United States and its territories. It also provides videoconferences and technical assistance in curriculum development and systems management.

Probation, parole, and community-based sanctions are the focus of the Community Corrections Division. This section of the NIC works with more than 2,500 probation and parole offices and 1,200 community residential facilities to promote diverting offenders from jail, to develop programs for high-risk offenders, and to investigate sentencing policies for female offenders. The Community Corrections Division is also involved in updating and facilitating the use of Interstate Compact for the Supervision of Parolees and Probationers and in providing publications on issues in probation, parole, and community treatment.

The NIC also contains a Jails Division that provides technical assistance to more than 3,000 local, state, and federal jails in the United States and its territories. The Jails Division's mission is to provide training, technical assistance, and resources in jail development, management, and operations. Its main areas are in administration, management of the facility and inmates, mentally ill inmates, the building of new jails, and working with local officials in the understanding of the importance of jails.

The Prisons Division operates in a similar manner to the Jails Division, providing technical assistance and training to more than 1,400 state prisons and 50 departments of corrections in the United States and its territories. Publications in areas of special interest to prisons are also developed within the Prisons Division. Some of the more recent Prisons Division publications include information on male sex offenders, classification and assessment procedures, prevention and detection of infectious diseases inside the institution, and overcrowding. The Prisons Division also produces handbooks for institution administrators on female offenders, staff management, health care issues, and substance abuse problems.

The last NIC division is the Special Projects Division. This office does not focus on one specific aspect of corrections but instead works to secure funding and cooperative relationships with other local, state, and federal governmental offices on all issues of interest to corrections. Some of the programs sponsored by the Special Projects Division include an assessment of children who have incarcerated parents, the planning and implementation of new juvenile facilities, mental health programs, and drug intervention programs. The Special Projects Division has also focused attention on women offenders in the criminal justice system in large part because of the dramatic growth of the female population in every sector of corrections. As a result, the NIC now offers programs in women's facility planning, classification, sentencing, and diversion and treatment.

OFFICES

The four offices found in the NIC are the Administration Office, the Office of International Assistance, the Office of Correctional Job Training and Placement, and the Information Center. The Administration Office houses the NIC director and deputy director along with the NIC advisory board. These individuals are directly responsible for financial management, personnel decisions, and publications associated with the NIC. The International Assistance Office and the Information Center have related duties.

As a result of the Violent Crime Control and Law Enforcement Act of 1994, an Office of Correctional Job Training and Placement (OCJTP) was created in the NIC to improve federal, state, and local job training programs and placement opportunities for offenders and ex-offenders. The goal of the office is to improve offender job training and placement in order to reduce recidivism rates in local, state, and federal jails and prisons. The OCJTP offers these services to correctional agencies through publications, on-site and satellite training programs, and through technical assistance. Some current initiatives of this office include a 36-hour basic training program that develops skills for staff who work with job assistance programs for inmates and a multiyear study of offender job retention. The OCJTP also offers a 108-hour program to five-person teams to improve programs in offender workforce development and to expand relationships with offender employment service providers. Staff may use the skills gained through many of the OCJTP training programs toward undergraduate or graduate credit hours at participating universities.

CONCLUSION

The NIC provides a variety of services to local, state, and federal correctional agencies in the United States, its territories, and internationally. All information is offered free of charge. Trainings are held at the NIC office, at various locations across the country, and by satellite through teleconferences. NIC staff members are willing to provide agencies, both private and public, with professional consultation on many topics, especially in the areas of agency management and administration. Administrators in need of assistance may contact the NIC for advice on facility planning, offender classification and programs, facility operations, physical plant operations, and pretrial and court services. Administrators may also use the information provided by the NIC to familiarize themselves with common practices in other states and facilities and to become acquainted with systemwide policies and programs. Because of the variety of services offered by the NIC, agency managers do not have to rely on in-house or local trainings but may request technical assistance from the NIC corrections specialists.

—*Jennifer M. Allen*

See also Accreditation; American Correctional Association; Bureau of Justice Statistics ; Community Corrections Centers; Federal Prison System; Managerialism; National Prison Project; Probation; Professionalization of Staff; Violent Crime Control and Law Enforcement Act of 1994; Work-Release Programs

Further Reading

Alexander, J., & Austin, J. (1992). *Handbook for evaluating objective prison classification systems*. Washington, DC: National Institute of Corrections.

Burke, P., & Adams, L. (1991). *Classification of women offenders in state correctional facilities: A handbook for practitioners*. Washington, DC: National Institute of Corrections.

Greenfield, L. A., & Snell, T. L. (1999). *Women offenders*. Bureau of Justice Statistics Special Report. Washington, DC: Bureau of Justice.

National Institute of Corrections. (2002). Retrieved from http://www.nicic.org

National Institute of Corrections Information Center. (1989). *Overview of substance abuse treatment programs in correctional settings*. Washington, DC: National Institute of Corrections.

◪ NATIONAL PRISON PROJECT

The National Prison Project (NPP) of the American Civil Liberties Union (ACLU) is the only nationwide, private sector organization with a primary mission to litigate on behalf of prisoners. It is based in Washington, D.C., and for the past 30 years has been at the forefront of all major legal battles to make prisons safer and more humane. During the 1990s, the NPP argued five cases in the U.S. Supreme Court and provided technical support to a national network of prisoner rights attorneys.

HISTORY

The NPP was founded in 1972 during a time when the federal courts were just beginning to address prison conditions. In the previous 10 years, the Supreme Court had made a series of decisions favorable to granting prisoners access to the federal courts. For example, in *Robinson v. California* (1962), the Court ruled that the Eighth Amendment ban on cruel and unusual punishment applied to state and local governments. The Court also ruled, in *Cooper v. Pate* (1964), that prisoners could file lawsuits under a federal civil rights law (U.S. Code 42, §1983).

DUE PROCESS, PRISON CONDITIONS, AND ACCESS TO LEGAL ADVICE

The NPP's initial strategy was to target the lack of due process in prison and parole hearings. Two years later, the Supreme Court granted due process rights in disciplinary proceedings and declared, "There is no iron curtain drawn between the Constitution and the prisons of this country" (*Wolff v. McDonnell,* 1974). As encouraging as this was, the NPP was still faced with two major problems: a lack of meaningful change in the treatment of prisoners, and a lack of resources.

Attaining procedural due process did not guarantee fair treatment. According to Alvin Bronstein, a former executive director of the NPP, corrections officials provided what appeared to be fair hearings but they still made arbitrary, unfair decisions. Bronstein realized that what was needed was a more profound change. In order to achieve this, the NPP had to expand its litigation strategy. For the rest of the 1970s and all of the 1980s, the project focused on prison and jail conditions. Project attorneys challenged the constitutionality of a broad range of prison conditions. They also criticized the lack of parity in the treatment of male and female prisoners. Unfortunately, the NPP was simply too small to provide sufficient legal representation. Even though inmates had access to the federal courts, there were, and still are, no court-appointed attorneys available to prisoners who file civil rights lawsuits. Nor did the incarcerated population, in the early 1970s, have access to prison law libraries. In a 1968 Supreme Court decision (*Johnson v. Avery*), inmates were given the right to confer with each other on civil rights cases, but without formally trained legal advocates or law libraries, the opportunities for success were extremely limited.

A major breakthrough came in 1976 with the passage of the Civil Rights Attorney's Fees Award Act. This federal law guaranteed the recovery of reasonable attorney fees to those who were successful in prisoner civil rights cases. Somewhat predictably, this policy increased the number of private attorneys willing to take prisoner rights cases, as well as providing a source of funding that allowed the NPP to expand.

RECENT DEVELOPMENTS

By 1995, the NPP Washington, D.C., office had a staff of 30 and an operating budget of $2 million per year. The office is busier than ever before, since there are so many prisoners requesting legal assistance, now that the prison population has grown from 200,000 in 1972 to more than 1.5 million in 2001.

The federal appellate courts and the Supreme Court have also become increasingly conservative. Prison crowding and judicial conservatism have put enormous pressure on the NPP to protect inmate rights and to ensure that the reforms it had negotiated in out-of-court settlements known as "consent decrees" were implemented. The NPP, however, experienced a major setback in 1996 when Congress passed the Prison Litigation Reform Act (PLRA).

The PLRA places substantial limits on the amount of attorney's fees that can be recovered in prison civil rights cases. This forced the NPP to reduce its staff and budget. Because the PLRA also discourages federal judges from appointing professional monitors or "special masters" to oversee prison reform, the NPP also lost an important source of support. For many years, project attorneys had worked closely with monitors who filed extensive reports on the progress of court-ordered or agreed-upon reforms. Other provisions of the PLRA severely limit the types of relief federal judges can grant in prison conditions lawsuits, and set two-year limits on court-ordered reform. In 1999, the constitutionality of the PLRA was challenged. The Supreme Court upheld the act and made it clear that even prison reform and consent decrees entered into before the act was passed were subject to the two-year limitation (*Miller v. French*, 1999). Many reform agreements the NPP had negotiated and worked on for years would be terminated.

By the late 1990s, the NPP had begun to adjust to a more restrictive environment. It was putting a greater emphasis on creating networks of prison reform activists. These networks were designed to focus on specific issues such as the treatment of HIV-positive inmates, the lack of appropriate medical care for female inmates, and the prevention of sexual assault. Litigation has also begun to focus on specific issues rather than broad prison conditions. For example, in April 2002, the NPP and the ACLU of Colorado filed a jail lawsuit over the treatment of mentally ill prisoners. In May 2002, the project filed suit against Texas prison officials, charging that they failed to protect an inmate they knew was highly vulnerable to sexual assault.

CONCLUSION

Over the past 30 years, the NPP has played an essential role in the reform of correctional institutions and practices. Due largely to the work of this organization, prisons and jails are more humane and safer than they were in the past. Despite the passage of the PLRA, the growth of conservatism among judicial and legislative branches, and continued prison crowding, the NPP and other reform groups continue to try to ensure that imprisonment in the United States is just, fair, and humane.

—*Agnes Baro*

See also Activism; American Civil Liberties Union; Eighth Amendment; Freedom of Information Act 1966; Jailhouse Lawyers; Overcrowding; Prison Litigation Reform Act of 1996; Prison Monitoring Agencies; Prisoner Litigation

Further Reading

ACLU National Prison Project. (n.d.). *Prisoners' rights*. Retrieved October 26, 2002, from http://www.aclu.org/issues/prisons/npp_missionl.html

Berkman, H. (1996). Proud and wary, prison project director bows out. *The National Law Journal, 18*(19), A12.

Robertson, J. E. (2001). Prison reform, a Faustian bargain: Commentary on prospective Relief before and after Miller v. French. *Criminal Law Bulletin, 37*(2), 195–209.

Legal Cases

Cooper v. Pate, 378 U.S. 546 (1964).
Johnson v. Avery, 393 U.S. 483 (1969).
Miller v. French, 529 U.S. 1051 (2000).
Robinson v. California, 370 U.S. 660 (1962).
Wolff v. McDonnell, 418 U.S. 539 (1974).

◾ NATIVE AMERICAN PRISONERS

American Indians and Alaskan Natives who constitute the indigenous peoples of North America were colonized by the British, the Russians, and finally by the European Americans. In the process, their societies were devastated by conquest, war, and disease. European American policies of "Christianizing the savage" and "manifest destiny" promoted forced assimilation, the destruction of traditional social structures, the creation of an economic dependency, and an overall marginalization of these indigenous groups within the dominant culture. These days, disproportionate numbers of Native Americans inhabit U.S. penal facilities.

POPULATION CHARACTERISTICS

On April 1, 2000, there were 2,475,956 American Indians and Alaskan Natives living in the United States, with about 40% of American Indians residing in rural areas. More than half the American Indians and Alaskan Natives live in 10 states, with Oklahoma, California, and Arizona each having populations of more than 200,000 American Indians. An estimated 63,000 American Indians are under the custody, control, or care of the criminal justice system on an average day, amounting to about 4% of the American Indian population aged 18 or older (Greenfeld & Smith, 1999, p. viii). Consequently, on a per capita basis, American Indians are incarcerated at a rate about 38% higher than the national rate.

American Indians have higher per capita rates of violent criminal victimization than whites, blacks, or Asians. While American Indians make up less than 1% of the U.S. population, they suffer a rate of violent victimization of 124 per 1,000 persons aged 12 or older as compared to a rate for all races of 50 per 100,000, or about 2 1/2 times the national rate. In rural areas, the crime rate for American Indians is more than double that of rural whites or blacks, and the urban crime rate is more than three times that found among whites. Alcohol and drug use are a factor in more than half of violent crimes against American Indians, and American Indian murder victims were more likely to have been killed during a brawl involving alcohol or drugs (13%) than whites (6%), blacks (4%), or Asians (2%).

The violent crime rate for American Indian males in 1999 was 153 per 100,000 and for females 98 per 100,000. This compares to a rate of 40 per 100,000 for white females and 56 per 100,000 for black females. At midyear 2000, the incarceration rate for American Indians was about 15% higher than the overall national rate (Minton, 2001, p. 2). Finally,

American Indians have a rate of arrest for alcohol violations more than double the national rate.

In a study undertaken in the mid-1980s, authors Michael Phillips and Thomas Inui (1986) found that Alaskan Natives were 2.2 times more likely to be arrested, 3.3 times more likely to be arrested for a violent felony, 2.9 times more likely to be hospitalized for psychiatric reasons, and 6.9 times more likely to be treated in alcohol treatment centers. Between 1979 and 1992, homicide rates for American Indians were twice those of U.S. national rates, and suicide rates were about 1.5 times higher. Between 1990 and 1992, homicide and suicide alternated as the second and third leading causes of death for American Indian males aged 10 to 34. For American Indian females aged 15 to 34, homicide was the third leading cause of death.

WOMEN

Few studies document indigenous women's experiences of incarceration. However, from the small amount of existing research it is possible to see that American Indian women, like the majority of women in prison, have been victimized through sexual and physical abuse and often suffer from drug and alcohol dependency. Indigenous incarcerated women often have a background of family dislocation, including sexual abuse as a child or teenager, a high rate of violent death in the family, and depression and loneliness. They also have a history of alcohol consumption at an early age, of being placed in and running away from foster homes or from home, of suffering domestic violence and physical abuse, of being placed in state custody as children, and of drug and alcohol abuse at the time of arrest and jailing.

During their incarceration, indigenous women are disproportionately likely to be prescribed medication for what is considered depression. They also complain of being allocated low-status positions such as cleaning floors and toilets, in contrast to the white women who are given higher-status positions. Finally, American Indian women are disproportionately represented in maximum security and are not allowed visits from family and friends when on that status.

Writing about indigenous women's incarceration in Montana, Luana Ross (1998, pp. 86–87) notes an increase over the past decade in the average sentence length for all women and a trend to incarcerate rather than use alternative sanctions. A typical American Indian woman incarcerated in Montana is 30 years old, single or divorced with two children, with a history of violent victimization, unemployed, an eighth grade education, and is convicted of a crime that is alcohol or drug related and is serving an average sentence of 19.1 years (Ross, 1998, p. 88).

During imprisonment, many women experience sexual intimidation, are overprescribed psychotropic drugs, are placed in lockup for extended periods, and are separated from their children. However, an additional punishment for American Indian women is the denial of their culture. The Montana Women's Correctional Center is located five hours from the nearest Indian reservation, and with the exception of an American Indian woman who conducts therapy sessions with American Indian prisoners, all the staff are white. Women here cope with family separation and cultural dislocation by uniting together in their culture and by forming a close-knit group that is often perceived as threatening by prison staff, who classify some of the women as troublemakers.

While American Indian women benefit from counseling with an American Indian woman counselor whose clients in the prison are wholly American Indian, there are no other culturally specific programs, and prison staff indicate that American Indian women refuse to participate in other programs. The women complain that prison rules prevent them having adequate access to their spiritual leaders and that prison authorities refuse to allow them a sweat lodge, though they are permitted to burn sweet grass during prayer time.

In researching the experience of Alaskan Native women in an Alaskan prison, Cyndi Banks (2002), like Ross, found that many Alaskan Native women offenders had been brought up in foster homes and had family histories involving drug and alcohol abuse. Staff in this institution often perceived the silence of the Native women during counseling and group treatment as a denial of their responsibility for their criminality and as resistance to treatment, instead of recognizing it as a cultural tendency first to observe unfamiliar events rather than instantly and actively to participate in them. Many staff seemed to resent the women's quietness and unwillingness to display the emotional patterns characteristic of European American women.

MENTAL HEALTH

Disproportionate numbers of Native Americans in prison are diagnosed with and treated for mental health problems, leading some to argue that prisons have become an alternative treatment option for American Indians. In a study based in New York State, for example, the authors discovered that more than half of the American Indians seen at mental health clinics were diagnosed with antisocial personality disorder compared to 25% of white patients. Yet, interviews with American Indian inmates, including women, revealed that the inmates often believed there was no basis for their referrals for mental health treatment. According to them, referrals were most likely if you acted in a "strange" manner, defined, they believed as "not behaving as most white Americans would behave" (Earle, Bradigan, & Morgenbesser, 2001, p. 127).

RELIGION

As a result of litigation concerning First Amendment rights, particularly the right to practice religion, the correctional system has been forced to accommodate American Indian beliefs, adjust to their rituals and religions as well as to their approaches to rehabilitation. In states like Nebraska, which has a substantial American Indian population, Indians living on reservations often speak their indigenous language as their first language and are usually familiar with aspects of their culture, including spiritual concerns, while prisoners from urban areas are likely to be less familiar with culture and religion. Imprisonment can serve as a cultural unifier for rural and urban American Indian prisoners because both are drawn into cultural and religious activities conducted within the prison system.

Religious activity among American Indian prisoners includes attendance at sweat ceremonies and sweat lodges, and these have become the single most important and widespread religious activity among these prisoners. However, despite a degree of acceptance by the correctional authorities, American Indians continue to feel that their cultural practices do not receive the same respect as, for example, the practice of a Western religion, and their access to sweat lodges continues to be impeded even though these structures are now found at nearly all facilities incarcerating American Indians.

CONCLUSION

The existing but scant research on indigenous women and men in prison reveals a number of issues, including the (mis)reading of Native culture by prison staff, the unfamiliarity of many indigenous groups (especially those in rural areas or on reservations), with the values, beliefs, and expectations of the European American culture, as well as how to cope with a prison sentence, and the necessity for culturally specific treatment programs. Few prisons offer cultural programs for American Indians, but those institutions that do rely mainly on Native Americans from the community willing to volunteer their time. Special items required for these programs are frequently viewed as "security risks" and are often denied by the prison authorities. The legacy of colonialism is evident in the incarceration rates and treatment of indigenous peoples, especially in the form of European American cultural dominance, which continues to inform many of the practices imposed on the indigenous incarcerated woman.

—*Cyndi Banks*

See also African American Prisoners; Asian American Prisoners; Drug Offenders; Health Care; Immigrants/ Undocumented Aliens; Mental Health; Native American Spirituality; Race, Gender, and Class of Prisoners; Religion in Prison; Resistance; Women Prisoners; Women's Prisons

Further Reading

Banks, C. (2002). Doing time in Alaska: Women, culture and crime. In R. Muraskin (Ed.), *It's a crime: Women and justice* (3rd ed.). Upper Saddle River, NJ: Prentice Hall.

Duran, E., & Duran, B. (1995). *Native American postcolonial psychology.* Albany: State University of New York Press.

Earle, K., Bradigan, B., & Morgenbesser, L. (2001). Mental health care for American Indians in prison. *Journal of Ethnic and Cultural Diversity in Social Work, 9*(3/4), 111–132.

Greenfeld, L., & Smith, S. (1999). *American Indians and crime* (Vol. NCJ 173386). Washington, DC: U.S. Department of Justice.

Grobsmith, E. (1994). *Indians in prison: Incarcerated Native Americans in Nebraska.* Lincoln & London: University of Nebraska Press.

Kunitz, S., & Levy, J. (Eds.). (2000). *Drinking, conduct disorder, and social change: Navajo experiences.* Oxford & New York: Oxford University Press.

LaPrairie, C. (1987). Native women and crime: A theoretical model. *Canadian Journal of Native Studies, VI*(1), 121–137.

Marsh, R., & Cox, V. (1996). The practice of Native American spirituality in prison: A survey. *The Justice Professional, 8*(2), 79–95.

Minton, T. (July 2001). *Jails in Indian Country, 2000* (Vol. NCJ 188156). Washington, DC: U.S. Department of Justice.

Pedersen, P., Draguns, J., Lonner, W., & Trimble, J. (Eds.). (1989). *Counseling across cultures.* Honolulu: University of Hawaii Press.

Phillips, M., & Inui, T. (1986). The interaction of mental illness, criminal behavior and culture: Native Alaskan mentally ill criminal offenders. *Culture, Medicine and Psychiatry, 10*, 123–149.

Razack, S. (1998). *Looking white people in the eye: Gender, race, and culture in courtrooms and classrooms.* Toronto, Buffalo, London: University of Toronto Press.

Ross, L. (1998). Inventing the savage: The social construction of Native American criminality. Austin: University of Texas Press.

◪ NATIVE AMERICAN SPIRITUALITY

Native spirituality speaks of the world as one spirit, referring to the creator of all things as the "Great Spirit." Mainstream religions might use words such as *God, Allah,* or *Mind* to describe this metaphor. In Native spirituality, every aspect of life is sacred, including the spirit that lives inside every human being. Sacred or holy teachings are often passed on through storytelling and the wisdom of the Elders or medicine men; such teachings, most often, include an intrinsic connection to land, tradition, and culture. Native spirituality is a highly ceremonial and experiential religion, with the ceremonies and traditions varying from tribe to tribe.

For traditional Native Americans, there is no separation between the sacred and the ordinary, nor any special day set aside for religious practices. Every act, every thought, every feeling walks hand in hand with Spirit. Rather than going to church, the traditional Native might attend a sweat lodge; rather than accepting bread from the Holy Priest, they may smoke a ceremonial pipe to come into Communion with the Great Spirit; and rather than kneeling with their hands placed together in prayer, they may let sweetgrass be feathered over their entire being for spiritual cleansing and allow the smoke to carry their prayers into the heavens.

With the arrival of the Europeans, the Native way of life and its connection to the land, culture, ceremonies, language, and to the Creator began to dissolve. Tens of millions of Native Americans died due to sickness, ill-advised government programs, persecution, greed, and the dogma of the Christian clergy. Many would say that the Natives lost their self-esteem because all they knew was forcibly removed from their life. They were also impoverished, as they had not functioned in a mercantile economy before. As a result, many ended up in prison. In the 1940s and later, the Native population in prisons grew disproportionately to the rest of the population. Prisons are often called "Iron Fences" or "Iron Houses" by Natives.

SUPPRESSION OF RELIGIOUS RIGHTS

Historically, only Christian beliefs were endorsed by prison administration and clergy, with the result that Native religion was suppressed inside of prisons. Today, despite federal laws guaranteeing the freedom of religious rights, Native Americans often face many difficulties in practicing their faith in U.S. prisons. For example, in 1999, the Brothers of Chillicothe Correctional Institution in Ohio started a campaign to fight for their Native rights. In this prison, they had been denied even the basic tenets of their spirituality, and are continually harassed during their prayer circles and private meditations. They had filed numerous grievances and Religious Accommodation Forms requesting the possession of certain medicine tools, a designated area of the yard for prayer, and recognition as an authentic religious group.

Prejudice and persecution exists elsewhere, too. For example, Canadian prisons have only recently allowed Native sweat lodge ceremonies in every province; approximately half the states in the United States allow Native sweat lodge ceremonies. Often, these sweat lodges and other Native spiritual ceremonies are the only spiritual and psychological sustenance that Native American inmates receive.

As the strength and political awareness of the Native people increases, Native organizations, such as Native American Prison Support (NAPS) and the Ik8ldimek Legal Clinic have fought to ensure the basic human, civic, and religious rights for all Native American prisoners, as guaranteed by the U.S. and Canadian Constitutions. These groups, and others like them, have been fairly successful. As a result, sweat lodges, talking circles, sacred pipes, Elders, and other forms of traditional healing are gradually becoming more available in many correctional institutions.

GENDER AND NATIVE AMERICAN SPIRITUALITY

Native women are incarcerated mostly from crimes involving drugs, alcohol, or child abuse. Outside prison, some Native American women will only practice their religion with women, while others celebrate their traditions in a nonsegregated environment. Few Native American women helpers work in prisons. Most of the spiritual advisors are male, and they are not allowed to conduct a sweat lodge ceremony for the female inmates. Instead, Native women often gather together with leaders elected as spokespersons to conduct talking circles, which often include opening prayers, smudging, and the keeping of minutes of what they talk about.

CONCLUSION

A belief in the critical role of religion in the rehabilitation of prisoners was integral to the development of penal systems in the United States. While most clearly articulated in the early penitentiary movement, themes of spiritual reformation have been central as a goal of prison discipline. Controversy has continued to center on whose voices are to be heard in a system that has been dominated historically by those of evangelical Christianity. There has been limited recognition that spiritual reformation could occur through other Christian traditions and rituals, and even less awareness of the healing presence for those whose experience of spiritual truth is rooted in the beliefs and practices of Islam, Judaism, and Native spirituality. While an increasing awareness is reflected in the efforts to provide for the diversity of beliefs present within the prison populations, there are still a number of barriers facing Native Americans who wish to practice their spirituality in prison.

—*Harry Derbitsky*

See also Chaplains; Contract Ministers; Islam in Prison; Judaism in Prison; Native American Prisoners; Religion in Prison

Further Reading

Neihardt, J. G. (1979). *Black Elk speaks.* Lincoln: University of Nebraska Press.

Ross, L. (1998). *Inventing the savage: The social construction of Native American criminality.* Austin: University of Texas Press.

Various Native authors. (1985). *The sacred tree.* Lethbridge, UK: Four Worlds Development Press.

◼ NEW GENERATION PRISONS

Since the late 1970s, most new prison construction in the United States has been modeled according to "New Generation" prison designs. These buildings are intended to maximize security and efficiency by means of easy observation and electronic surveillance of inmates. Such patterns utilize advancements in electronic communications and shatterproof glass materials to replace steel bars and stone blocks, creating a lighter, more comfortable environment that is also very secure.

New Generation prison architecture is largely a response to the rapidly changing penal population of the past three decades. New Generation prisons, along with methods of correctional management that deemphasize patrolling staff, have streamlined corrections operations at the same time as they have increased security. The early prototypes for these designs were the metropolitan correctional centers (MCCs) built by the Federal Bureau of Prisons in the 1970s and Minnesota's Oak Park Heights facility constructed in 1982.

CONTRASTS WITH OLD GENERATION PRISONS

According to British criminologist Roy King (1999), New Generation prisons represent the third major stage in Western prison architectural development. The first generation prisons were generally built with long rows of cagelike cells arranged in tiers, intermittently patrolled by guards. They tended to mimic fortresses in their pronounced size and scale of exterior stonework with imposing turrets and gates. Large slabs of stone, immense Gothic gateways, and castle-like styling gave the impression of institutional imperviousness. Second generation prisons, for the most part, kept this same architectural style, but withdrew staff and introduced remote supervision by closed-circuit television.

In contrast to these older styles, New Generation prisons are designed to fit in with surrounding structures or landscapes, or to appear like college campuses or office buildings. The high-rise federal MCC complexes in downtown Chicago and New York, for example, cannot easily be distinguished from the bank and office towers that surround them.

DESIGN

Most New Generation prisons borrow from the radial "Panopticon" design developed by Jeremy Bentham in the early 19th century. They position observation stations at central locations surrounded by inmate units. Large floor-to-ceiling aquarium-style windows allow guards an unrestricted view of inmate cells, living quarters, and recreation areas. Prisoners generally live in standardized cells within self-contained modular units of 30 to 100 inmates.

New Generation units are often segmented into triangular living quarters, with two or more stories of cells along two sides overlooking an open association area. The large floor-to-ceiling shatterproof windows provide the third side. Observation

stations generally appear outside the glass, providing a distinctive fish-tank-like appearance and allowing officers a full view of all inmate sleeping and living areas.

"LABOR REPLACEMENT TECHNOLOGY"

New Generation prisons are a product of sociological and psychological research that claims that people function most comfortably when they are housed in small groups. They are also influenced by the free-market competition among architectural firms and private prison firms for the most cost-effective designs. New Generation prisons are, in other words, designed for penal and fiscal efficiency.

In many cases, the mass incarceration trends of the 1980s and 1990s were accompanied by fiscal restraint among lawmakers, so prison designers had to incorporate cost-saving mechanisms into their proposed structures. Because salaries usually account for the majority of an institution's budget, New Generation layouts have been designed to minimize staff requirements. Closed-circuit TV surveillance and two-way communication devices have reduced the need for face-to-face encounters. Electronic door controls and computerization of many inmate operations allow for smooth inmate movements and strict adherence to daily schedules. Subdivided recreation pens connected to each block or unit instead of large facility-wide yards increase security by segregating populations into manageable groups. New Generation window designs allow one or two officers to monitor and control 200 to 300 prisoners.

STANDARDIZATION OF DESIGN

Since the 1970s, there has been a movement toward increased uniformity of cell and cellblock architecture. Cell segments are now standardized to allow for ease of remodeling and additions. In both Europe and the United States, designs have become so similar that separate facilities are often undistinguishable from each other. In the United Kingdom, for example, a single New Generation prison design has been identically repeated at several locations.

Some manufactures are now fabricating prison cells in factories rather than constructing them in the field, allowing sections of units to be transported and assembled on site. These trends have greatly increased the speed of delivery and installation of new cell space.

MANAGEMENT STYLE

New Generation prisons involve more than simply architecture. They encompass management techniques developed in response to the massive increases in penal populations of the past quarter-century. Their primary objective is to deliver recreation, work, exercise, sleeping, and eating to the inmate in as efficient a manner as possible. New Generation prisons tend to attempt cost cutting by reducing or downgrading staff, switching procurement from public to private sectors, and in some cases inviting wholesale privatization.

Unit management is also standardized. Inmates generally spend their nights in the smaller cells and are released into the larger dayrooms during the day. In the dayrooms, the inmates have access to shower facilities, game tables, television viewing, and pharmacy call. Meals can be delivered to the dayroom or to each individual cell. During counts, lockdowns, and whenever necessary, all inmates in a unit can be directed and locked in their individual cells.

WOMEN'S PRISONS

These trends in prison management and construction have also affected women's prisons. Standardized "unisex" architecture has taken the place of the small reformatory cottage-style women's housing. Indeed, most women's prisons now look more like prisons for men than ever before. New women's facilities, like FCI Victorville in California, are large, with central mess halls and multiple-person cells or dormitories.

MEASURABLE BENEFITS

New Generation designs have greatly decreased the costs of penal administration, enabling jurisdictions to incarcerate more inmates than ever before. Cost savings have in some cases been substantial; the state of California, for example, reported in 1995 that its substitution of electrified fencing instead of teams of snipers at its Calipatria Prison saved the state $2 million in labor costs per year.

Escape rates have also decreased considerably. The separation of inmates into self-contained living segments has made it easier for guards to track and monitor inmates designated to each unit. Abolition of opportunities for inmates of different blocks to mix with each other in dining halls and recreation yards have limited the means by which inmates can evade counts and identity checks.

New Generation proponents have also touted the safety improvements that have come with the new architectural designs. There are fewer edges, corners, and "ligature points" upon which inmates might hang themselves or others. It appears that New Generation prisons have decreased suicides as well as suicide attempts.

CRITICISMS

Not all observers however, support New Generation institutions. The facilities have been criticized for violating prisoners' privacy by exposing all inmate activities to observation at all times. Such institutions have also tended to move perceptively toward greater security than may be necessary. Some New Generation prisons have been deliberately modeled so that every inmate can be reduced to "supermax" security levels with relative ease. Some extreme examples of New Generation facilities, like the county jail in San Rafael, California—which is 60 feet below ground—seem to offer security far in excess of institutional needs. New Generation management style is also criticized for neglecting interpersonal interaction between inmates and staff, intelligence gathering, and direct communication between prisoners and staff.

Above all, New Generation prisons have helped fuel the move toward mass incarceration by making penal administration more efficient and cost effective. Critics maintain that these "improvements" are actually detriments to sound criminal justice policymaking and that they promote incarceration above rehabilitation.

CONCLUSION

Almost every large prison or detention center constructed in the United States since the 1980s has incorporated elements of New Generation design. Many European countries have also adopted New Generation concepts in their new facilities. Such designs have been popular with prison purchasers because of increased labor efficiency, and also because they complement hardened attitudes toward crime control.

—Roger Roots

See also Campus Style; Contract Facilities; Cottage Style; High-Rise Prisons; Increase in Prison Population; Metropolitan Correctional Centers; Panopticon; Privatization; Supermax Prisons; Telephone Pole Design; Unit Management; Women's Prisons

Further Reading

Davis, M. (1995). Hell factories in the field: A prison-industrial complex. *The Nation*, February 20, p. 229.

Fairweather, L., & McConville, S. (Eds.). (2000). *Prison architecture: Policy, design and experience*. Oxford, UK: Architectural Press.

Farbstein, J. (1986). *Correctional facility planning and design*. New York: Van Nostrand Reinhold.

Kerle, K. E. (1998). *American jails: Looking to the future*. Woburn, MA: Butterworth-Heinemann.

King, R. D. (1999). The rise and rise of Supermax. *Punishment & Society, 1,* 163–186.

Pollock, J. M. (2002). *Women, prison and crime*. Belmont, CA: Wadsworth.

◪ NEW MEXICO PENITENTIARY

Built in 1957, the Penitentiary of New Mexico has until recently served as the state's primary prison. Designed to house 850 inmates, it has long been plagued by poor administrative practices, inadequate security, and the absence of basic amenities. The penitentiary first gained national notoriety when a class-action suit was filed in 1979 in which its inmates alleged that confinement at the penitentiary violated their constitutional rights. In 1980, a large-scale riot at the prison brought the problems identified by the prisoners to the fore. Their suit, which later became the basis for the Duran Consent Decree, identified 14 areas of the penitentiary needing improvement. These areas included legal correspondence, food and medical services, and classification and disciplinary processes. The decree mandated court oversight of all medium- and maximum-security prisons operated by the New Mexico Corrections Department.

STAFF AND INMATE INTERACTION

For most of the penitentiary's history, staff maintained institutional control by cooperating with inmate leadership. However, as the 1970s ended, the relationship between staff and prisoners turned increasingly hostile. Administrative personnel eventually wrestled much of the power away from the well-established inmate leadership. To accomplish this, they increasingly relied on the use of physical coercion, segregation, and inmate informants. Ultimately, the relationship between staff and the inmate population turned mutually antagonistic and violent.

Compounding the problems existing between staff and prisoners, the penitentiary experienced five different administrations from 1975 to 1980. This turnover increased anxiety within the institution, leading to heightened levels of distrust and violence. Ultimately, these conditions culminated in a full-scale riot.

THE 1980 RIOT

On February 2, 1980, the penitentiary was the site of one of the bloodiest prison riots in American history. In a matter of minutes, prisoners overpowered four correctional officers and gained access to the penitentiary's control center. Once the control center was breached, keys permitted prisoners to gain access to most areas. Following the riot, investigations revealed that approximately 150 inmates had actively participated. During the 36-hour disturbance,

33 inmates were murdered. Two hundred additional inmates were raped or otherwise brutalized.

In addition to the enormous loss of life, the riot left the education, kitchen, and administrative areas gutted. The cost of facility repair was estimated to be between $70 and $100 million. The attorney general later reported that crowding, understaffed security, correctional officer misconduct, and classification inadequacies were contributory factors.

TODAY'S PENITENTIARY COMPLEX

Following the riot, the state legislature appropriated nearly $88,000,000 for the construction of new institutions. Today's penitentiary consists of three additional facilities located adjacent to the original building. With the addition of these three prisons, the original building was designated the main unit. In September 1985, the north unit was opened to house administrative segregation and close- and medium-security inmates. In April 1988, the south unit began operation and was designed to house medium-custody inmates. In September 1990, the minimum-restrict unit began operation holding inmates with the two lowest levels of security classification, minimum and minimum restrict. The addition of these facilities ensures that those offenders deemed to be the most dangerous are segregated from those who are less serious or violent.

Conditions at the penitentiary, though improved, have remained a concern of inmate advocacy groups and legislators. In 1997, authorities at the main unit discovered a 30-foot tunnel, complete with kitchen, tools, and riot plans. This discovery led the governor to declare an institutional emergency. Many others called for the prison's permanent closure. In 1998, the main unit was closed due to its dilapidated condition. Furthermore, the Corrections Department saw closure of the main unit as an opportunity to disassociate itself from its bloody and storied history. Recent debate has centered on leasing the now-vacant facility to a private correctional contractor for the housing of federal prisoners. The main, north, south, and minimum-restrict units are referred to, in their entirety, as the Penitentiary of New Mexico at Santa Fe.

CONCLUSION

The Penitentiary of New Mexico is an example of a prison historically plagued by a lack of basic amenities, mismanagement, and administrative turnover. More recently, the penitentiary provides a case study in how to effectively operate a contemporary prison complex with a concern for staff and inmate safety. This concern is reflected in the establishment of the nation's first accredited correctional training academy as well as in the operation of modern facilities that ascribe to well-established penological principles.

—Curtis R. Blakely

See also Attica Correctional Facility; Contract Facilities; Correctional Officers; Disciplinary Segregation; Governance; Managerialism; Maximum Security; Medium Security; Minimum Security; Overcrowding; Riots; Security and Control; Violence

Further Reading

Blakely, C. R. (1997). Santa Fe—17 years later: The status and effect of the Duran Consent Decree. *Corrections Today, 2,* 66–68.

Colvin, M. (1982, June). The 1980 New Mexico prison riot. *Social Problems, 25,* 449–463.

Dilulio, J., Jr. (1991). *No escape: The future of American corrections.* New York: Basic.

Johnson, R. (2002). *Hard time* (3rd ed.). Belmont, CA: Wadsworth.

Montgomery, R., & Crews, G. (1998). *A history of correctional violence: An examination of reported causes of riots and disturbances.* Lanham, MD: American Correctional Association.

Nash, J. R. (1990). *Encyclopedia of world crime.* Wilmette, IL: Crime.

Reid, S. (1981). *The correctional system: An introduction.* Austin: Holt, Rinehart & Winston.

Rolland, M. (1997). *Descent into madness: An inmate's experience of the New Mexico State Prison riot.* Cincinnati: Anderson.

Silverman, I. (2001). *Corrections: A comprehensive view.* Belmont, CA: Wadsworth.

Useem, B., & Kimball, P. (1989). *States of siege: U.S. prison riots, 1971-1986.* New York: Oxford University Press.

◪ NEW ZEALAND

New Zealand is a nation of 3.9 million people, located in the South Pacific approximately 1,200 miles southeast of Australia. The country consists of two main islands, known simply as the North and the South Islands. The North Island has more than twice the population of the South Island. Native or part-native New Zealanders, known as *Maori,* constitute about 14% of the total population. Inhabited by Europeans from 1792, New Zealand became a British colony in 1840. Although it has been fully independent since 1907, in its statutory development, New Zealand has often modeled that of England, and its early prison system reflected the same influence.

CORRECTIONS HISTORY

Before 1880, New Zealand's prisons were ineptly and often corruptly administered by local authorities, but in 1880 the system started to become centralized, and Captain Arthur Hume, an English prison deputy governor, was appointed as the country's first Inspector General of Prisons. Hume created a harsh regime similar to that of Victorian Britain, and he instituted an ambitious prison building program. The most enduring legacy of this program is Mt. Eden Prison, a radial-style institution designed in 1882 from plans shipped out from London. Mt. Eden still operates today and is one of the country's oldest surviving prisons (see Figure 1).

New Zealand has a long history of liberalism in corrections. Although Hume himself was an authoritarian, in 1886 New Zealand developed the world's first national probation system. After Hume's retirement in 1909, reflecting the country's growing reliance on farm exports, a vigorous agricultural program was pursued. Between 1910 and 1922, tens of thousands of acres of rural land were purchased and turned into prison farms or forests. Many of these enterprises still operate today. After 1909, security was deemphasized. By 1913, the issuing of firearms to guards had ceased at most prisons, and distinctive arrow markings had been removed from prisoners' clothing. Between 1910 and 1923, the percentage of inmates employed in outside work schemes grew from 8% to 70%. Segregation of young offenders began in 1910, and a system of juvenile reformatories, known as "Borstals" after their British counterparts,

Photo 1   *Entrance to Mt. Eden Prison in the 1950s; a "Black Maria" (prisoner escort vehicle) is in the foreground*

commenced in 1917. Borstal Training for juveniles continued until 1980, when, due to high recidivist rates, it was abolished.

Between 1840 and 1935, 76 men and one woman were hanged in New Zealand (all but one for murder), but in 1935 executions ceased, and in 1941 capital punishment for murder, along with corporal punishment, was legally repealed. Hanging for murder was reintroduced in 1951, and eight more men were executed before the penalty was struck out again in 1961. Hanging remained for crimes such as treason but was repealed completely in 1989.

The 1950s and 1960s were periods of great experimentation in New Zealand corrections. During the 1950s, full-time welfare officers were appointed to all prisons, hours of lockup were reduced, education services were improved, and opportunities for recreation were extended. In 1950, centralized training for prison officers commenced. In 1961 the first "boot camps" for juveniles—known initially as Detention Centers after their British counterparts and renamed Corrective Training Centers in 1981—were established and remained until high recidivism prompted their closure in 2002. In 1961 a work-release scheme was started, and in 1965 weekend furloughs for low-risk inmates began. Today, minimum-security prisoners (more than half of all inmates) are eligible to apply for a 72-hour "home leave," plus traveling time, every two months.

The 1960s also saw the beginning of experimentation with alternatives to incarceration. The most successful was periodic detention, launched in 1963. Periodic detention started as weekend incarceration in a work center for juveniles, but was extended to adults in 1966. In 1980, due to cost, Periodic detention became restricted to day attendance only, but its popularity as a sentencing option continued to grow. In 2002, periodic detention and a sentence called community service, which had been created in 1980, were merged under a new sentence named "community work." Approximately 29,000 offenders are sentenced to community work every year.

PRISONS TODAY

New Zealand operates 15 male and three female prison facilities, which cater to a total of approximately 6,000 inmates. Because it is an island nation from which escape is difficult, security levels are low. Of all classified inmates, just 2.5% are classified maximum security, 15% are high-medium, and 28.3%, are low-medium. The remainder, 53.8%, are minimum security. Apart from the Auckland Central Remand Prison (discussion following), there are no jails in the American sense. Arrested persons may be held overnight in police cells, but if bail is denied, they are transferred to special "remand" sections within local prisons, where they await trial and sentence.

In 1994, following international trends, New Zealand legislated for the contracting of prison services to private enterprise. The move was highly controversial, and political opposition held up the tendering process for a number of years. However, in July 2000, Australasian Correctional Management Pty. Ltd., a subsidiary of the U.S. Wackenhut group, began operating a purpose-built, 275-bed remand prison in Auckland. Known as Auckland Central Remand Prison (ACRP), it is the only privately run correctional facility in use in New Zealand. There are currently no plans for the contracting of any more.

Prisons in New Zealand range from the archaic and decrepit to the modern and new. Seven of the 15 male prisons have buildings that are more than 70 years old, and facilities in these institutions are run down and extremely limited. They cater principally to prisoners classified as high-medium security risks, and inmates in these prisons often have to share their cells with another prisoner. There are no dormitories. There are also a number of modern medium-security institutions, all of which have single-cell accommodation and facilities such as playing fields and gymnasiums. An innovation over the past decade or so has been the building of cheap but effective 60-bed units for low-medium- and minimum-security prisoners. In fact, today the majority of prisoners live in units of this type. Inmates in 60-bed units all have their own cells, which are equipped with flush toilets, hot and cold running water, and a heating pipe. Cells are of wooden or concrete block construction, with a pleasant interior, and are set in a rectangle that looks out onto a grass compound with a tennis or basketball court in the center. The units are self-contained, with a visiting room, education rooms, a weight room, flower gardens, and often a vegetable garden and a kitchen. They are surrounded by a double mesh wire fence, but many prisoners work outside the wire, and most have permission to play sport outside as well.

There is one maximum-security prison in New Zealand, located at Paremoremo, 14 miles north of Auckland, the country's largest city. Officially known as Auckland Prison (East Division), the facility is more commonly referred to as Paremoremo Maxi (see Figure 2). Modeled on America's USP Marion, Paremoremo Maxi was opened in 1969 and normally holds no more than 200 men. Only about two-thirds of Paremoremo's inmates are actually classified as maximum security; the rest are high-mediums awaiting transfer elsewhere or inmates with special needs such as psychiatric or medical problems. In the 1970s, Paremoremo was a showpiece of correctional liberalism, with numerous programs and activities for prisoners. However, in the 1980s, fighting between gangs—which, typically for New Zealand, was not of a racial nature—necessitated closure of many of these. In the late 1990s, radical changes in administrative philosophy saw a further tightening of security, with a dramatic increase in lockup hours and the virtual abandonment of reformative efforts.

There are three institutions for females. The oldest and largest is Arohata, near the capital city of Wellington. Opened during the Second World War and catering mainly to low-security inmates, Arohata is set in a semirural area where some inmates are able to work outside. The principal female prison is Christchurch Women's Prison, commonly known as Paparua Women's. Opened in 1974, Paparua Women's has a small maximum-custody unit, but deals principally with 80 or so female prisoners with medium- and minimum-security classifications. The facility is badly situated—in the South Island and 600 miles from Auckland, where most women prisoners come from. Because of this, a women's division at Mt. Eden Prison in Auckland has been expanded and upgraded, currently holding about 45 inmates at a time. Occasionally the construction of a new women's prison nearer to Auckland has been mooted (proposed), but with female inmate numbers having grown only by about 120 in the past 20 years and with existing facilities often operating below capacity, the expense is difficult to justify.

SENTENCES

Compared with America, sentences in New Zealand are short. Although average terms have increased by 75% since 1981, in 2000, 79% of all inmates were given seven years or less, and the average prisoner served about eight months. The average American inmate who is released spends about 30 months in prison. Apart from murder, the longest sentences are given for rape (average 96 months), attempted murder (average 88 months), and manslaughter (average 69 months). Approximately 8.6% of the New Zealand prison population is serving non-determinate sentences of life imprisonment for murder or selling Class A drugs (such as heroin, LSD, and cocaine; 6.5%), or preventive detention for repeated violent or sexual offending (2.1%). The standard nonparole period for murder is 10 years, and for preventive detention it is five years. The majority of prisoners serving life sentences will be released after about 12 years. Since 1987, judges have had discretion to sentence those with life

Photo 2   *Aerial photo of Auckland Maximum Security Prison (Paremoremo)*

sentences and preventive detainees to minimums that are longer than 10 years, and in 2002 the Sentencing Act mandated a 17-year minimum for all murders committed with certain aggravating features. Although the figures will no doubt increase as a result of the new law, in 2002 only 25 inmates in the entire country had done more than 12 years on their current terms, and only four had done more than 15 years. In 1995, the longest nonparole period ever was given—25 years, for serial rape. The longest nonparole period awarded for murder is 20 years, given to a man in 2002 who had killed his wife and daughter with an axe.

Since July 2002, there has been no automatic release on "good time" for inmates serving more than two years. Those doing two years or less are released automatically at half-sentence, and all others, provided they are not subject to a nonparole minimum, are eligible to apply for parole after serving one-third of their sentences or 10 years, whichever is the lesser. Prisoners released on parole may be recalled to prison if they reoffend or commit significant breaches of parole conditions. In recent years, 28% of parolees have been found to have breached the conditions of their parole. Many of these have been dealt with by a warning, and not all have been recalled to prison.

A recent innovation in New Zealand has been home detention. First proposed in 1991, legislated in

1993, and piloted for two years beginning in 1995, home detention originally allowed the electronic monitoring of certain offenders in their homes toward the end of their sentences. In 1999, legislation was passed enabling courts to grant offenders serving two years or less leave to apply for home detention immediately after sentencing. Prisoners serving terms of more than two years may apply to the parole board for release on home detention, for up to two years, prior to final discharge. At the end of 2001, approximately 200 offenders were serving prison sentences under conditions of home detention.

THE PRISON POPULATION

The primary purpose of home detention, like the liberalization of the parole laws, was to reduce the prison population. As happened in the United States, the prison population of New Zealand increased steadily after the Second World War. From 1,000 inmates in 1950, the average inmate population (including remands) reached 2,000 in 1967, 3,000 in 1984, 4,000 in 1991, and 6,000 in 2002. This last figure equates to a ratio of 154 per 100,000 mean population. Principal causes of the increases have been jumps in youthful crime in the 1950s, the advent of recreational drug use in the 1970s, and leaps in serious violent offending in the 1980s. Average sentences for violent offending almost doubled between 1985 and 1998, and between 1987 and 2002, violent offenders were ineligible for parole. This led to an accumulation of violent offenders in prison. Today, 62% of all inmates are doing time for violence, compared with 42% in 1987. The next largest group of offenders in prison are there for property damage (21%), followed by drug offences (7.5%).

Liberalizations in parole for nonviolent offenders, which allowed parole at half-sentence in 1985 and then at one-third-sentence in 1993, had only a temporary effect on prison populations. This was largely a result of high recidivist rates. In New Zealand, 58% of all prison releases are reconvicted within a year, and 86% are reconvicted within five years. More than half of all prisoners are reimprisoned within five years of release.

MAORI PRISONERS

Maori and part-Maori, who, as noted, represent about 14% of New Zealand's total population, are overrepresented in crime statistics and in the country's prisons. Maori are significantly more likely than the overall population to be unemployed, to have problems with heavy alcohol use, to come from single-parent families, and to experience physical and sexual abuse at the hands of adults when they are children. As adults, they are far more likely than non-Maori to be convicted of crimes involving serious violence such as aggravated robbery, injurious assault, rape, and homicide. They are also much more likely than non-Maori to belong to outlaw gangs, and the largest gangs by far are the Maori gangs. As a result, Maori are grossly overrepresented in prisons. More than half of all inmates are Maori: 3.7 times what would be expected on the basis of population. Recidivist rates of Maori are also higher than for non-Maori.

WOMEN

There are three institutions in New Zealand that cater to women prisoners, one in each of the three major urban centers. Numbering 233 in 1999, or 4% of the male inmate population, women prisoners are less likely than men to be serving terms of more than three years. Compared with men, women are more likely to be imprisoned for crimes involving drugs, property, and serious traffic violations, but are equally likely to be doing time for nonsexual violence. There is good evidence to suggest that, even when relevant sentencing factors are held constant, women are less likely than men to be imprisoned, and if imprisoned, their terms tend to be shorter. Recidivism figures for women are lower than men's, despite the fact that the proportion of female inmates that are Maori, at almost 60%, is higher than for men.

JUVENILES

In New Zealand, young people under the age of 17 cannot be prosecuted other than for purely indictable offences such as murder, manslaughter, rape, or dealing in Class A drugs. Children aged 10 to 13 can only be prosecuted for murder or manslaughter. The youngest killer ever prosecuted for murder was 12 when he committed the offence. He was convicted of manslaughter in 2002 and sentenced to seven years.

Most juveniles who are sentenced to imprisonment serve their sentences in facilities administered by the Department of Child, Youth, and Family Services (CYFS) until they turn 17, when they are transferred to prison. Teenagers are normally segregated from adults in special sections of adult prisons. In addition, since 1999 four dedicated youth offender units catering for about 150 inmates have opened, which deliver special programs designed to address the specific needs of pre-adults. Three of these units are smoke-free, and positive drug test returns are close to zero. In 1999 there were 435 inmates aged 15 to 19 in New Zealand prisons—9% of the adult sentenced population.

PRISON PROGRAMS

For nearly 100 years, New Zealand has had a comparatively progressive approach to correctional reform. One consequence, with small prisons and high wages for staff, is that incarceration costs are high. In New Zealand, where the local spending power of the New Zealand dollar is about equivalent to that of the U.S. dollar, it costs an average of approximately $60,000 to keep an inmate in prison for a year—almost three times the American figure. About one-eighth of the corrections budget is spent on rehabilitative services and programs. In 1990, an experiment known as *He Ara Hou* ("A New Way") commenced, emphasizing rehabilitation as an equivalent to custody in the administration of prisons. A serious attempt was made to reduce authoritarianism and break down the barriers that exist between staff and inmates. Formal systems of unit management and case management were installed, and unit managers were given considerable discretion in running their units. Inmates were actively encouraged to participate in programs.

He Ara Hou was partially successful in achieving its objectives. Inmates report that tension with staff

did decline in the early 1990s, and many officers took a personal interest in their welfare. Enrolments in educational and other programs increased, and there was an apparent decline in assaults, escapes, and suicides. But the new initiatives were never systematically analyzed, nor were they properly monitored. Lax procedures at some institutions led to irregularities in financial and general management, abuse of some prisoners, and corrupt relationships between some inmates and staff. By 1992, a series of embarrassing scandals had commenced, involving drugs, sex, money, escapes, and abuse of prisoners. The gravity of these matters prompted the resignation of the Assistant Secretary for Justice at the end of 1993, followed by the Secretary for Justice himself in 1994. Thus, *He Ara Hou* came to an end.

In 1995 the Department of Justice, which administered prisons, ceased to exist. A Ministry of Justice was created as a partial replacement, but the task of prison management fell to a new department known as the Department of Corrections. Under this title, a fresh experiment in rehabilitation commenced, known as Integrated Offender Management (IOM). Unlike its predecessor, IOM was systematically planned and gradually phased in over a five-year period. It consists of a sophisticated computerized offender recording program and a psychological approach to rehabilitation based in a series of "interventions" designed to address an inmate's "criminogenic needs." Central to the plan is an intense 10-week tailored program administered toward the end of an offender's sentence.

Although IOM has been introduced in all prisons, high running costs have restricted its applicability. Initially, the department anticipated that nearly all inmates would be exposed to IOM and that it would reduce reoffending between 10% and 15%. But the scheme has been more expensive and less effective than hoped. In 2001, only 18% of eligible inmates were able to receive IOM, despite $12 million in expenditure. Moreover, to date, those exposed to IOM have exhibited recidivist rates that are not significantly different from those not exposed to it. However, with the program still in its infancy, in 2002 the department still remained optimistic of being able to cut recidivism rates by up to 10%.

PRISONER SOCIETY AND CULTURE

There has never been a study of female convict culture in New Zealand, but among men, the social code of inmates is highly similar to that described by Sykes and Messinger (1975) in their landmark study. The male prisoner community is traditionalistic in its notions of masculinity. Men are expected to be strong, stoical, principled, and honest. The ideal man handles his problems on his own and without complaint. He does not bully the weak, nor does he compromise with bullies. He protects his dignity and is prepared to use violence when necessary: for example, when threatened, when abused, or when dealing with thieves and informers. Thieves ("tealeaves") and informers ("grasses") are the lowest form of life in a prison, and no self-respecting prisoner has anything to do with them. The ideal convict does not fraternize with staff; he sees them as a necessary nuisance, but otherwise of little consequence in his life.

Of course, such ideals are seldom realized, but men who approximate them achieve high respect. In truth, staff frequently receive information from prisoners, the weak are always at risk of being bullied, there are numerous disputes over stolen property or unpaid debts, and long-term inmates are often on friendly, first-name terms with long-term staff. That said, however, prisoner society in New Zealand is markedly different in certain respects from that reported elsewhere, particularly the United States. There is little inmate stratification in New Zealand prisons. As a general rule, a high level of egalitarianism prevails, and it is unusual for an inmate or a cabal of inmates to have power over others. Related to this is the fact that homosexuality is rare and homosexual rape is almost unheard of. There are a number of reasons why this is so.

First, prisons are small, units are restricted to about 60, and most inmates have their own cells. It is difficult for any individual or group to dominate in such an environment without being noticed by staff and transferred to a more secure setting.

Second, sentences are fairly short. Population turnover is high, making it difficult for any group to stabilize its membership and consolidate power.

Third, prisons are well staffed and staff are well paid. This renders the cooptation of inmate leaders for administrative purposes unnecessary and removes the incentive of staff to support or ignore the activities of power groups. Conversely, powerful inmates have little to gain and much to lose (e.g., privileges and parole chances) by attempting to "stand over" other inmates.

Finally, in New Zealand itself, class structure is less pronounced than in many capitalist countries. Wealthy entrepreneurs and workers often mix together in pubs, in clubs, and in other recreation. Exploitation of the rich by the poor is adulterated. New Zealand is a compassionate society, with a relatively generous welfare system, which generates few homeless and no beggars. Linked to this, particularly in the working classes, is a strong egalitarian ethic. Class and racial tension is largely dormant, and there is popular contempt for authority. The rich and the powerful are tolerated, but only as long as they act like "ordinary blokes."

This same culture is clear in prisons. Here, racial conflict is rare, and inmates who attempt to dominate others are denounced as "standovers," "screws," and "coppers." Doing one's own time and minding one's own business are highly valued. Those who do not risk ostracism, abuse, assault, and general hostility from the body of inmates as a whole. As a result, there is high incentive in New Zealand prisons, supported by management, the custodial environment, and years of social conditioning, for the preservation of equality among the incarcerated.

CONCLUSION

New Zealand is a country that, like many others, has faced rising prison numbers in recent decades. With some success, it has attempted to address the problem by creating alternatives to imprisonment and by liberalizing parole. It has also attempted to reduce recidivism, and for many years has had a humane approach to the treatment of criminals. Sentences are relatively short, prison conditions are generally good. Sincere efforts are made to assist inmates to discard the criminal lifestyle. So far, the results of these efforts have been disappointing, and recidivist rates are high. But one positive spin-off of this liberalism is that prison society itself is comparatively nonexploitive and the experience of living in custody is relatively benign.

—Greg Newbold

See also Australia; Canada; Community Corrections Centers; England and Wales; Furlough; Juvenile Justice System; Maximum Security; Native American Prisoners; Parole; Privatization; Prison Culture; Probation; Gresham Sykes; Wackenhut Corporation; Women Prisoners; Work-Release Programs

Further Reading

Jeffries, S. (2002). Just or unjust?: Problematising the gendered nature of criminal justice. *Women's Studies Journal, 18*(1), 24–41.

Newbold, G. (1982). *The Big Huey.* Auckland, NZ: Collins.

Newbold, G. (1989a). Criminal subcultures in New Zealand. In D. Novitz & B. Willmott (Eds.), *Culture and identity in New Zealand.* Wellington, NZ: GP.

Newbold, G. (1989b). *Punishment and politics: The maximum security prison in New Zealand.* Auckland, NZ: Oxford University Press.

Newbold, G., & Eskridge, C. (2003). History and development of modern correctional practices in New Zealand. In C. B. Fields & R. H. Moore (Eds.), *Comparative criminal justice: Traditional and non-traditional systems of law and control.* Prospect Heights, IL: Waveland.

Sykes, G. M., & Messinger, S. L. (1975). The inmate social system. In R. A. Cloward, D. R. Cressey, G. H. Grosser, R. McCleery, L. E. Ohlin, G. M. Sykes, & S. L. Messinger (Eds.), *Theoretical studies in social organization of the prison.* Millwood, NY: Kraus.

◪ NEWGATE PRISON

Newgate Prison was authorized by the Connecticut General Assembly in 1773 to utilize incarceration as a punishment for crime, the same year that construction began on the more famous Walnut Street Jail in Philadelphia. All male offenders who were not under sentence for a capital crime were to be imprisoned at Newgate. Prior to this time, most crimes, other than those deemed to be capital crimes, were punished through specific acts, such as branding, flogging, the stocks, fines, public shaming, and banishment. Unlike the Walnut Street Jail, Newgate was not influenced by the movement for reform as advocated by the Quakers or by individuals such as Benjamin Rush and Thomas Eddy.

THE INSTITUTION

Newgate Prison was constructed within an abandoned copper mine in East Granby, Connecticut. Prisoners worked, lived, and were housed in huts and cabins that were constructed inside the underground caverns and shafts of the mine.

The underground structure of the prison and installation of an iron door over the entrance shaft were at first believed to be escape-proof. Consequently, few if any guards would be required to run the prison. Captain John Viets, Newgate's first keeper, appointed by the Connecticut General Assembly, initially provided the only security for the institution. However, within three weeks, the first prisoner had escaped (with assistance) through a mineshaft. Although additional security measures were implemented by new legislation from the General Assembly, escapes were frequent and sometimes violent.

In addition, overcrowding became a serious issue over time. In one instance, 32 men were housed in an area only 21 feet by 10 feet by 7 feet. As well as escaping, prisoners also regularly burned any structures that were built over the mine. All of these problems were exacerbated by a combination of untrained staff and poor management. Ultimately, the difficulties with security would contribute to the closing of Newgate.

THE PRISONERS

Initially, the Connecticut General Assembly only dictated imprisonment for males convicted of five offenses: robbery, burglary, horse theft, counterfeiting, and forgery. However, it eventually included women, murderers, political prisoners, and prisoners of war. Newgate also housed Tories during the American Revolutionary period.

Prison labor was one of the core components of life at Newgate. Although at first prisoners worked in the mines, it quickly became evident that they lacked the training and skills necessary to make the venture profitable. Instead, they were set to work making nails, barrels, shoes, and wagons as well as doing farm work.

The prisoners housed at Newgate worked in close quarters with one another and were housed collectively, in contrast to the solitary system proposed in the Pennsylvania model. They were allowed to congregate after the workday to gamble and trade their rations for the day. These rations included a pound of meat, a pound of bread, a pint of cider, and potatoes. Additionally, those who had money from working or other sources had access to a tavern near the prison in the evenings. Such close contact between the inmates provided some savings on the cost of imprisonment, but it also made it easier for violence, riots, and insurrections to occur.

PROBLEMS

It was evident almost immediately that Newgate would have serious problems. Riots, uprisings, and escapes became commonplace. During many escapes and escape attempts, the inmates would burn, vandalize, and attempt to destroy the prison. After each incident, additional security measures were added, and new guards were hired. This became a problem especially when the prison was used to house Tories during the Revolutionary Period. As Durham (1990) notes, "The combination of these prisoners and the traditionally weak security of the prison were causes for local alarm" (p. 311). The result was an order by the Council on Safety that oversaw the prison to increase the number of guards. However, the repeated increases in the number of guards securing the prison ultimately defeated the purpose of using the abandoned mine, with its unique structure, as a prison in order to limit operational costs.

It was not merely the increased cost of running the prison that forced its abandonment in 1827. The effect of the prison on the inmates, evident upon release, also became a major factor. The prison environment further corrupted the inmates and helped to breed "cruelty, riots, insurrections, vice and crime" (Lewis, 1967, p. 67). Amplifying this problem was the use of measures including flogging, the stocks,

the treadmill, and the hanging of an inmate by the heels as a punishment for unruly behavior, escapes, and riots. Furthermore, as noted previously, the congregation of the inmates enabled many to learn additional criminal skills from each other, thereby increasing their abilities and skills.

CONCLUSION

Despite its shortcomings, Newgate was still believed to be the preeminent prison in the United States until it closed in 1827, when the last prisoner was transported to Wethersfeld Prison in Connecticut. Even so, the legacy and impact of Newgate on the evolving penal theories was not great. These days, it is remembered most commonly as one the first institutions to utilize imprisonment as a form of punishment in the U.S.

—Sarah Conte

See also Alderson, Federal Prison Camp; Auburn System; Eastern State Penitentiary; Framingham, MCI; History of Prisons; Pennsylvania System; Philadelphia Society for Alleviating the Miseries of Public Prisons; Benjamin Rush; Quakers; Solitary Confinement; Walnut Street Jail

Further Reading

Barnes, H. E. (1920, October). *The historical origin of the prison system in America*. Paper presented at the annual meeting of the New York State Historical Society, Bear Mountain Park, NY.

Durham, A. M. (1989). Newgate of Connecticut: Origins and early days of an early American prison. *Justice Quarterly, 6*(1), 89–116.

Durham, A. M. (1990). Social control and imprisonment during the American Revolution: Newgate of Connecticut. *Justice Quarterly, 7*(2), 293–323.

Lewis, O. F. (1967). Newgate of Connecticut. In Lewis, *The development of American prisons and prison customs 1776–1845* (pp. 64–67). Montclair, NJ: Patterson-Smith.

Phelps, R. H. (1969). *A history of Newgate of Connecticut*. New York: Arno Press and the *New York Times*.

◪ NORFOLK PRISON

Massachusetts Correctional Institution (MCI) Norfolk was the first "community-based" prison in the United States. It was designed to be a community, with a central quadrangle, similar to that of many traditional colleges. Dormitories lined the longer sides of the quadrangle. A community services building and an education center were located at either end. Industry buildings were placed outside the quadrangle. Though it has grown beyond this layout, the central quadrangle is still the focal point of the institution today.

HISTORY

Howard Belding Gill (1890–1989), a Harvard MBA with an interest in prison reform, was first superintendent of the Prison Colony at Norfolk. He was appointed in 1927 and directed the completion of work on the prison. The first prisoners came to the site in 1927 from the Charlestown State Prison. They finished building much of the prison complex itself, including the construction of the perimeter wall.

Gill considered Norfolk to be one of the first examples of "a new prison discipline." In contrast to the traditional Auburn prison model, which he believed was designed to "break the spirit of the criminal," Gill envisioned a community with an emphasis on education and industry (Gill, 2001, p. 49). Norfolk prisoners would not wear traditional prison uniforms. They were granted a stake in the management of the institution through participation in an advisory council.

Gill's philosophy depended upon classification. At its simplest, this entailed sorting the tractable from the intractable. He argued that the traditional view that "every prisoner should be treated alike" (2001, p. 51) could not be supported in light of the recent psychological studies by such criminological pioneers as William Healy (1915) and Bernard Glueck (1916). "Tractable prisoners," he proposed, should be housed in cottages or dormitories, rather than "massive, monolithic monkey cages" (Gill, 2001, p. 51) and provided with "work, education, medical care religion, recreation [and] family welfare . . . designed to *adjust the offender to the society to which he will return*, i.e. acculturation" (Gill, 2001, p. 52; italics in original).

After four inmates escaped from the colony, Gill came under fire from the Massachusetts legislature, and following a controversial hearing in 1934, he was removed as superintendent (Johnsen, 1999).

The second superintendent, Maurice N. Winslow, continued many of Gill's policies, though he instituted uniforms and did not allow prisoners to own dogs. Norfolk maintained a reputation as a progressive institution, supporting such diverse activities as poetry reading, debating society, and an academic quiz team.

Perhaps the most famous alumnus of the Norfolk Prison Colony was Malcolm Little (Malcolm X), who lauded the "culture" of the institution as he found it in 1948 and credited the educational support he received there with enabling him to achieve a level of fluency that far surpassed his formal eighth grade education. According to Malcolm X:

> The Norfolk Prison Colony's library was in the school building. A variety of classes were taught there by instructors who came from such places as Harvard and Boston universities. The weekly debates between inmate teams were also held in the school building. You would be astonished to know how worked up convict debaters and audiences would get over subjects like "Should Babies Be Fed Milk?"
>
> As you can imagine, especially in a prison where there was heavy emphasis on rehabilitation, an inmate was smiled upon if he demonstrated an unusually intense interest in books. There was a sizable number of well-read inmates, especially the popular debaters. Some were said by many to be practically walking encyclopedias. They were almost celebrities. No university would ask any student to devour literature as I did when this new world opened to me; of being able to read and understand. (Malcolm X, 1992, pp. 199–200)

TODAY

Today, MCI Norfolk houses more than 1,400 prisoners. It is the largest medium-security prison in Massachusetts. It has a 19-foot-high maximum-security perimeter wall that is 5,000 feet long surrounding 18 dormitory-type units and two modular units. Current educational programs include those offered through the MCI Norfolk School: adult basic education through general equivalency diploma and vocational programs including barber school, computer technology, culinary arts, welding, and the Boston University college program. Treatment programs include Correctional Recovery Academy, Sex Offender Treatment Program, and Security Threat Group Program.

CONCLUSION

The vision of the prison community established in the planning of Norfolk did not come to pass. However, many of the reforms espoused in the "modern penology" of the 1920s have been instituted and accepted throughout correctional systems: classification, full-time schooling, treatment programs, and meaningful vocational study are the norm. As Gill stated in the State House hearing in 1934, "You seek to remind me that the men at Norfolk are criminals; I seek to remind you that the criminals at Norfolk are men" (Janusz, 1990, p. 57).

—Robert T. Cadigan

See also ADX Florence; Attica Correctional Facility; Auburn Correctional Facility; Corcoran, California State Prison; Malcolm X; Marion, U.S. Penitentiary; San Quentin State Prison; Sing Sing Correctional Facility

Further Reading

Gill, H. B. (2001). A new prison discipline. In E. J. Latessa, A. Holsinger, J. W. Marquart, & J. R. Sorensen (Eds.), *Correctional contexts* (2nd ed., pp. 49–55). Los Angeles: Roxbury.

Glueck, B. (1916). *Studies in forensic psychiatry*. Boston: Little, Brown.

Healy, W. (1915). *The individual delinquent*. Boston: Little, Brown.

Janusz, L. (1990, Fall). Voter rights. *Odyssey: Creative Alternatives in Criminal Justice*, 56–57.

Johnsen, T. C. (1999, September–October). Howard Belding Gill: Brief life of a prison reformer: 1890–1989. *Harvard Magazine*. Retrieved September 2, 2004, from http://www.harvardmagazine.com/issues/so99/vita.html

Malcolm X. (1992). *The autobiography of Malcolm X* (as told to Alex Haley). New York: Ballantine.

Massachusetts Department of Correction. (n.d.). Retrieved from http://www.state.ma.us/doc/default.htm

◼ NOVEMBER COALITION

The *November Coalition* is a nonprofit, grassroots organization that seeks to educate the public about the war on drugs. According to their Web site, the coalition includes

a growing body of citizens whose lives have been gravely affected by our government's present drug policy. We are prisoners, parents of those incarcerated, wives, sisters, brothers, children, aunts, uncles and cousins. Some of us are loving friends and concerned citizens, each of us alarmed that drug war casualties are rising in absolutely horrific proportions. (November Coalition, n.d.)

It is one of a number of prison reform groups lobbying to rescind current federal and state laws on drugs.

WHAT DOES THE NOVEMBER COALITION DO?

Formed in 1997, the November Coalition uses real-life examples to illustrate how a drug arrest can become a "frightening introduction to conspiracy statutes, government's liberal use of informants, guideline-sentencing laws, and the nightmare usually leaves defendant and family confused and full of despair." Through individual accounts, they show how long-term imprisonment has dramatic effects on personality and personal relationships. Prisoners suffer from severe restrictions on their human and constitutional rights, and all of these difficulties exact a personal toll on offenders and those who love them.

The November Coalition seeks to rehumanize prisoners by telling their stories. This strategy reveals the damaging impact of mandatory minimum sentencing on individuals and their families. Autobiographical accounts help to demonstrate that many drug offenders are regular people, good citizens and neighbors, whose lives have been derailed by a misguided sentencing policy. Some of these stories remind us that those in prison are children who are also victimized—in part by the actions of their parents, and in part by the draconian measures used to fight drug use. Other stories share the painful experiences of aging parents who have lost their children due to the long sentences they must serve. The firsthand accounts document the disparate impact that drug policies have on different races and social classes. These stories also relay feelings about politicians who have escalated the drug war even though they have admitted past drug use that could have sent them to prison rather than to the White House.

The November Coalition argues that the discriminatory impact of drug policies, in which members of minority communities far outnumber whites in prison, should have been predicted. If that were not possible, then the discriminatory impacts are certainly clear to today's policymakers. According to the coalition, drug policies have created a situation in which the most vulnerable are least able to defend themselves against injustice. Such policies do not constitute a war on drugs; they have become a war on people. The coalition also points out the similarities between alcohol prohibition of the 1920s and drug prohibition today. Drug users have been dehumanized through demonizing propaganda, in particular "the crack epidemic," that dominated national media during the late 1980s.

PUBLICATIONS

The coalition produces a newsletter called *The Razor Wire* to report on drug policy reform efforts, legislative updates, and news about drug law vigils and meetings. This publication also includes letters from prisoners and others who have been victimized by the war on drugs. The organization also puts out *The Wall,* which is an online collection of prisoner photos and stories that document the impact of the war on drugs. *The Razor Wire* and *The Wall* can be found on the November Coalition Web site. The Web site also includes essays, statistics, and other information that supports efforts toward changing prisons and our views toward punishment. In addition to educating people about the necessity of penal reform, the coalition has demonstrated that the Internet can be an effective tool for information sharing and for organizing those who share an opposition to a policy that has shaped our justice system and filled our prisons.

CONCLUSION

The November Coalition provides an example of the effectiveness of grassroots challenges to policy. Working with limited resources, the group has made great progress in their efforts to educate the public and policymakers about problems associated with current legislation for drug crimes. The November Coalition succeeds in providing an arena where prisoners' voices and stories can be heard. These stories and voices are invaluable in the effort of challenging the status quo.

—*Kenneth Mentor*

See also Activism; American Civil Liberties Union; Drug Offenders; Families Against Mandatory Minimums; Federal Prison System; National Prison Project; Prison Monitoring Agencies; Stop Prisoner Rape; War on Drugs

Further Reading

Bonczar, T., & Glaze, L. (1999). *Probation and parole in the United States.* Washington, DC: U.S. Department of Justice, Bureau of Justice Statistics.

Common Sense for Drug Policy. (n.d.). Retrieved from http://www.csdp.org/

Criminal Justice Policy Foundation. (n.d.). Retrieved from http://www.cjpf.org/

Drug Policy Alliance. (n.d.). Retrieved from http://www.drugpolicy.org/

Harrison, P. M., & Beck, A. J. (2002). *Prisoners in 2001.* Washington, DC: U.S. Department of Justice, Bureau of Justice Statistics.

Irwin, J., Schiraldi, V., & Ziedenberg, J. (1999). *America's one million nonviolent prisoners.* Washington, DC: Justice Policy Institute.

Journey for Justice. (n.d.). Retrieved from http://www.journeyforjustice.org/

Media Awareness Project. (n.d.). Retrieved from http://www.mapinc.org/

National Drug Strategy Network. (n.d.). Retrieved from http://www.ndsn.org/

November Coalition. (n.d.). Retrieved from http://www.november.org

Students for Sensible Drug Policy. (n.d.). Retrieved from http://www.ssdp.org/

◪ OAK PARK HEIGHTS, MINNESOTA CORRECTIONAL FACILITY

Oak Park Heights, in Minnesota, is one of the first "New Generation" prisons constructed after the demise of the medical model in penology, which saw the role of imprisonment as the diagnosis, treatment, and cure of criminal behavior. It represents one of three fundamental changes in Minnesota penal policy in the 1970s and early 1980s: the introduction of a new sentencing system, an alternative to incarceration initiative, and the decision to build a new high-security prison.

OVERVIEW

The new sentencing system specified the number of months to be served for specific offenses and designated those crimes that would result in confinement in state prison and those that could be dealt with by alternatives to incarceration. Under the Sentencing Guidelines, only offenders convicted of crimes against persons (e.g., murder, assault, armed robbery, rape, child molestation) and drug trafficking, as well as those who had failed in the various alternatives to imprisonment, would be sent to state prison. Once in prison, they must serve two-thirds

of their sentences in prison and one-third on supervised release. The second change, the Community Corrections Act, provided state funds to enable Minnesota counties to keep nonviolent offenders in their jails, under probation supervision, or placed in community-based facilities and programs. The third new direction in penal policy was the decision to build a high-security prison to replace the State Penitentiary at Stillwater built in 1914. This decision was influenced by a series of inmate homicides (3 in 1975) and suicides (11 between 1971 and 1974), an increase in assaults on inmates and on staff, and allegations of drug trafficking that led to a legislative investigation.

In 1976, the Joint House-Senate Committee on Minnesota State Prison issued a detailed report that found that the state's only penitentiary for adult males was seriously mismanaged, that staff and inmates feared for their safety, and that dangerous prisoners were not effectively separated from the general inmate population. The investigation concluded that controlling prisoners in giant cell halls that were four tiers high, each containing 512 cells, made visual surveillance of inmate activity "impossible."

A new Commissioner of Corrections, Kenneth F. Schoen, replaced the warden at Stillwater with the Department of Corrections' Inspector of Jails, Frank W. Wood. With a promise of no interference from departmental headquarters, Wood introduced

645

Photo 1   *Oak Park Heights, administrative building in the foreground*

Photo 2   *Oak Park Heights security facility, Minnesota*

a proactive strategy to restore order in the prison. He greatly restricted and controlled all inmate movement, initiated random lockdowns and shakedowns of inmate cells, work and recreation areas, built walls to divide the large cell blocks into more manageable spaces, and replaced most of the administrative staff. Wood's management philosophy was summed up in words that have become widely quoted in penology: "If you gave me the choice between this place [the new prison] with a dishonest, incompetent staff and a tent with honest, competent staff, I'd take the tent" (King, 1991).

While Wood was bringing Stillwater Prison under control, planning moved ahead for the construction of the new high-security prison at Oak Park Heights (OPH). The new institution was to employ a nontraditional design to house a relatively small population of violent and predatory prisoners. Wood was appointed warden and began outlining security and staffing needs, along with inmate programs and services. With Wood's management strategy in place, Oak Park Heights began receiving prisoners in March 1982.

DESIGN

Oak Park Heights is an earth-sheltered maximum-security prison built into a hillside overlooking the St. Croix River Valley (Photos 1–3). From a nearby road and residential area, all that is visible of the

facility is a one-story brick administration building. Because it lies 30 feet or more under the ground, OPH has been able to achieve significant economies in heating and cooling costs. Double parallel fences with razor ribbon between them and equipped with electronic motion detection devices provide perimeter security.

OPH is comprised of nine separate 52-man units arranged in a U-shape; the units are connected by two separate traffic corridors, one for prisoners, the other for staff. Except for disciplinary segregation units, each unit has its own eating and indoor recreation areas and a heavy wire mesh enclosed outdoor recreation yard. A larger institution yard can accommodate prisoners from up to, but not more than, two units for softball, handball, and other sports. An unusual feature of these units is the use of wood covers on railings.

In each unit, an officer in a secure control "bubble" is able to observe other staff interacting with prisoners as well as inmates moving in the adjacent corridor. As a result, prisoners can move from one part of OPH to another without a staff escort. Two staff in each unit rotate every two hours with the officer in the bubble. In the event of trouble, the control officer records the names and actions of prisoners and calls for assistance.

The nine units serve a variety of custodial and program functions within the same physical perimeter. One provides the medical needs for the entire department of corrections; while another houses mental health cases. There is an educational unit, an industries unit, and an honor unit. There is also a disciplinary segregation unit for short-term punitive confinement and two special housing units (SHU) for inmates who are permitted to leave their cells only for individualized exercise. The ninth unit, recently completed and operational, offers a long-term control or "supermax" function. Here a prisoner cannot leave his cell without wrist and leg restraints and under the escort of several officers.

Inmate cells, called rooms, range in size from 70 square feet to 153 square feet for medical and mental health rooms. Standard cells have horizontal concrete slabs to hold a foam mattress and to double as a desk or table during the day; a vertical concrete configuration built into the wall contains shelves, storage space, and a flat surface for a television set. Toilets and wash basins are made of stainless steel and are set in concrete. Showers in all units are individually enclosed, locked stalls. Rooms have narrow, vertical windows providing natural light and looking into the large interior yard; from second-floor rooms inmates can see the river valley. OPH has never been crowded, since all cells were designed for one person.

STAFFING

Oak Park Heights opened with a staff complement of 289, of whom 234 had no previous experience working in prisons; the plan was to avoid hiring, in Warden Wood's words, "people with bad habits." Only 55 had worked in other Minnesota correctional facilities. Thirty of the new staff were women. Almost half of the new recruits had four-year college degrees—compared to 15% at nearby Stillwater Prison. The new staff were trained to deal with prisoners, as Wood said, in a "nonabrasive way," and they continue to receive 40 hours of in-service training each year. The absence of violence has been the measure of this strategy. Recently, however, 30 of the original positions have been eliminated due to state budget cuts, with the result that prisoners now remain in their cells during weekends. What effect this change will have on inmate violence is, as yet, unclear.

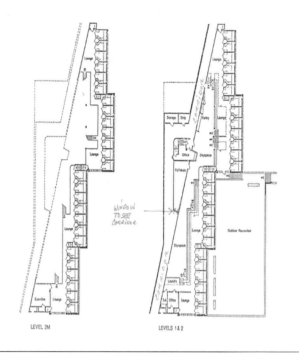

Photo 3   *Oak Park Heights diagram*

INMATE POPULATION AND PROGRAMS

Oak Park Heights' population is comprised of Minnesota's most violent offenders, who are serving long sentences, as well as prisoners who have been designated as escape risks or are viewed as management problems in other Minnesota prisons. Individuals who have committed violent crimes against others, including murder, assault, criminal sexual assault, kidnapping, and robbery, constituted 86.5% of the population in February 2003.

For the past 20 years, prisoners from the high-security federal prison at Marion, Illinois, have been accepted as "boarders." Almost all of these transfers, serving long sentences for serious crimes, have engaged in violence in prison, often associated with the major federal prison gangs that do not have a significant presence in Minnesota. Other boarders are interstate transfers. In exchange, the Department of Corrections has sent some Minnesota prisoners to other jurisdictions for purposes of protective custody. Oak Park Heights inmates who may engage in physical confrontations with rap partners, witnesses, or other inmates can be readily separated by transfer to another unit within the prison—as can prisoners observed or reported to be forming a gang or any illegal organized activity.

Job options at OPH include working as an orderly, joining the kitchen crew, or other maintenance and recreation services. Educational programs include classes and self-study courses. Courses in anger management and critical thinking skills are also offered. Prisoners can take remedial classes to obtain a general equivalency diploma (GED), and, if they pay for courses themselves, they can earn a BA degree. Religious and recreational activities are also available, as is access to legal resources. Inmates are allowed up to 16 hours of contact visits each month—although those in disciplinary segregation may have only noncontact visits. All inmate telephone calls are monitored and tape recorded.

MANAGEMENT PHILOSOPHY

The importance of the management philosophy that goes with a new design is fundamental in understanding how Oak Park Heights has functioned since 1982. Remarkably, five wardens, including the current warden Lynn Dingle, have continued the Wood strategy that was first employed at Stillwater and carried over to Oak Park Heights. All gained their prison experience working under Wood at Stillwater, Oak Park Heights, or both.

In addition to the points already noted, the management philosophy at OPH includes the following guidelines: At least one officer will always be stationed in each unit's protected control bubble so that staff can call for assistance in the event of any altercation or disruption of normal activities. Forty out of 200 custodial staff are women; they are assigned to all units because experience at OPH has shown that they have often helped deescalate problems. The institution also maintains a high ratio of staff to inmates. Prisoners will be frequently "pat-searched" to condition them to submit to staff authority, as well as to detect weapons or contraband. Any prisoner not assigned to a job or involved in an educational or treatment program will be locked in his cell. No protective custody unit will be established; such cases are transferred to other prisons.

Only such physical force as is necessary will be used to control prisoners who are acting out. Staff who are assaulted will be restrained and allowed no "payback," since they cannot preach nonviolence to prisoners and solve their own problems with violence. State or federal transfers will be given a fresh start at arrival but will be required to sign a contract agreeing to abide by facility rules; violation of the contract will lead to their prompt return to the jurisdictions from which they came.

A variety of services and program offerings will be made available to inmates, because going to prison *is* the punishment. OPH is not responsible for rehabilitating prisoners, but it is responsible for maintaining an environment that is conducive to change for those who are so inclined. The regimen at OPH is intended to reduce the frequency, scope, and seriousness of the inevitable incidents that will occur in a high-security prison. The regimen is not intended to aggravate the conditions of confinement under the mistaken belief that it will make inmates averse to coming back.

CONCLUSION

Essential measures of the success of the penal principles at Oak Park Heights relate to the control of violence and the protection of inmate rights. Since the prison opened, no inmate or staff member has been killed, nor have there been any escapes—not even any attempts—and no riots or major disturbances that have involved as much as an entire unit. The Federal District Court has had no case in which OPH has been found to violate the constitutional rights of any prisoner, and the prison received a 100% compliance score from the American Correctional Association the first time it applied for accreditation.

—*David A. Ward*

See also Correctional Officers; Cottage System; Maximum Security; Medium Security; Minimum Security; New Generation Prisons; Security and Control; Supermax Prisons; Telephone Pole Design; Unit Management

Further Reading

King, R. D. (1991). Maximum-security custody in Britain and the USA: A study of Gartree and Oak Park Heights. *The British Journal of Criminology, 31*(2), 126–152.

Ward, D. A. (1987). Control strategies for problem prisoners in American penal systems. In A. E. Bottoms & R. Light (Eds.), *Problems of long term imprisonment* (pp. 74–96). Aldershot, UK: Gower.

Ward, D. A., & Schoen, K. F. (1981). *Confinement in maximum custody: New last resort prisons in the United States and Western Europe.* Lexington, MA: Lexington Books.

◤ OFFICER CODE

Correctional officers form a distinct subculture within prisons, with their own beliefs and informal code of conduct that set them apart from inmates, administrators, and the world outside. The *officer code* is organized principally around ideas of solidarity within the subculture. The strength of the officer subculture within different prisons can be measured by the degree to which officers adhere to the code and by the severity and certainty of consequences imposed on those who violate the code.

CENTRAL NORMS OF THE OFFICER SUBCULTURE

Norm 1: Don't Rat

The prohibition against informing against others is fundamental to most codes of solidarity. In law enforcement, the manifestation of this norm is commonly referred to as "the blue wall of silence." In the prison world, the injunction is strongest in regard to testifying against a fellow officer for abuse of an inmate or informing on an officer to an inmate.

Testifying against a fellow officer is the most obvious and flagrant violation of the officer code. An officer who violates this norm in effect forfeits his or her membership in the subculture and the protection it provides within the prison world. It is a sanction that in most prisons cannot be borne. As an officer working in a maximum-security prison noted, "If nothing else, you do believe that you

need, you *know* you need, the rest of the officers in order to perform, and if you're alone, you can't last in a place like that a long time." Even officers who might be secretly sympathetic to a fellow officer who testified would turn their backs "because of that unwritten code that says that I violated them or I violated their code and I'm a *correctional officer*" (Kauffman, 1988, p. 98).

Events at Corcoran Prison in California during the 1990s illustrate the strength of this norm. Over a five-year period, some officers at the prison staged "gladiator fights" between inmates belonging to rival gangs. The fights frequently ended with officers shooting the inmates. Of 50 who were shot, seven died. By comparison, only eight other inmates in the entire California prison system were killed by officers during the same time period. When two Corcoran officers eventually blew the whistle on their fellow officers, they were threatened and harassed to the point that they felt compelled to resign. Ratting out an officer to an inmate, for example, by revealing the identities of officers who beat up an inmate or tore up an inmate's cell, is also a serious offense in the officer subculture, because doing so may endanger the lives of the officers involved. "Payback" is a constant threat within the prison world where antagonists can put little distance between themselves, and few distractions from long-standing grudges exist.

Norm 2: Always Go to the Aid of an Officer in Distress

The most important positive obligation under the officer code is to go to the aid of any fellow officer in distress, except in those rare instances when an officer has forfeited his or her membership in the officer subculture (see Norms 1 and 3). The obligation to provide immediate, unquestioned assistance to fellow officers in danger lies at the heart of the officer code. It is the norm on which positive feelings of officer solidarity are based. This norm is so important that those who consistently uphold it can sometimes violate other parts of the officer code without fear of reprisal.

For obvious reasons, the injunction to aid a fellow officer is strongest at those prisons in which employees perceive themselves to be in the greatest danger. Officers, especially rookies, who consistently violate this norm at prisons where tensions are high between staff and inmates are likely to be ostracized by their fellow officers, thus making their own situation at the prison untenable.

Norm 3: Don't Deal Drugs With Inmates

The prohibition against dealing drugs with inmates is based not on negative attitudes toward drugs per se, but rather on fear of the increased danger to officers presented by inmates under the influence of drugs. Officers who violate this norm risk ostracism, harassment, and the threat of physical harm by fellow officers. The norm is taken so seriously in some prisons that, if an officer persists in dealing drugs with inmates, the norm against ratting no longer applies.

Despite the vehemence with which officers may espouse this norm, drugs are plentiful in many prisons, and officers suspect one another of involvement. Demand is great, making incentives strong. Dealing drugs not only offers economic rewards, but it also can offer at least temporary respite from fear and threat of violence by inmates who can trade protection as well as money in exchange for drugs. Because the incentives to violate this norm are strong, informal sanctions for violating it are severe.

Norm 4: Always Support a Fellow Officer in a Dispute With an Inmate

Officers strive to maintain solidarity against inmates in appearance as well as in fact. Whether they agree with the actions of a fellow officer or not, they should never make another officer look bad in front of an inmate. Any disagreements between officers should be handled out of prisoners' hearing and sight. Officers are not supposed to act as impartial arbiters in disputes between inmates and fellow officers. Instead, the code mandates that they provide immediate and unquestioning support for one another as long as prisoners are present.

The expectation that officers will back one another is sufficiently strong in some prisons that officers will sign disciplinary reports as witnesses to events for which they were not, in fact, present. In its most extreme form, this norm calls for officers to support informal sanctions imposed by fellow officers on inmates, including acts of violence against inmates. Especially in prisons with sustained levels of conflict between officers and inmates, many officers believe that the only way to deter violence is to punish violence with violence. Those who refuse to support such sanctions (passively, by not participating; less commonly, by interceding) risk ostracism and harassment. Although seasoned officers who abide by other norms of the officer code can often abstain from violence without fear of censure, younger officers are more vulnerable. The norm mandating unquestioned support for officers in disputes with inmates, combined with the norm against ratting against fellow officers, promotes and protects the development of a violent officer subculture in some prisons.

Norm 5: Don't Fraternize With Inmates

The officer subculture is shaped by its opposition to the inmate subculture. The role of the officer, as defined by the subculture, is to neither help nor befriend inmates. It is, instead, to maintain order and security within the prison and protect fellow officers. The norm against fraternization may even prohibit expressions of sympathy or support regarding inmates made in private conversation with other officers.

Officers who are too lenient or too popular with inmates can jeopardize the safety of more hard-line officers, or at the very least make their jobs more difficult. Those who fraternize with inmates also attract suspicion that they are dealing drugs with inmates or cannot be relied upon in disputes with them.

Sanctions for violating this norm vary widely from prison to prison and often from shift to shift or unit to unit within prisons. But as long as officers uphold all other norms mandating solidarity vis-à-vis inmates, they rarely risk more than mild censure and harassment by their peers if they interact too closely with inmates.

Norm 6: Maintain Solidarity Versus All Other Groups

Officers ideally maintain solidarity versus anyone who is not an officer, including prison administrators, social workers, government officials, and, perhaps most of all, representatives of the news media. Officers typically view prison administrators, even those who have come up through the ranks, as pandering to inmates and unwilling to back officers in the difficult and dangerous work that they do. They have no illusions about how those outside the prison world see them: violent, power hungry, corrupt, racist, a "breath away from being inmates themselves." Members of news and entertainment businesses seem to revel in contrasting the depths and variety of the inmate experience with the stereotypical image of the brutal "screw." The beliefs, expectations, and obligations embodied in the officer code are designed in part to shield officers from these negative images, to allow them to reject their rejecters. As a result, the correctional officer subculture rivals, and in many prisons exceeds, police adherence to a code of silence versus the world outside.

Norm 7: Show Positive Concern for Fellow Officers

This last norm represents a behavioral ideal subscribed to, if not carried out, by most officers. That ideal prescribes consideration for fellow officers on the job—not leaving the person on the next shift with a problem, taking time to share important information with colleagues, covering for each other. It also prescribes—but does not require—concern for fellow officers off the job, especially if an officer or family member is injured or ill.

The officer code mandates no sanctions for those who fail to show positive concern for fellow officers. Yet the close bonds and tight-knit community that are the hallmark of the officer subculture in numerous prisons are for many officers the most rewarding aspects of their job.

CONCLUSION

Important variables affecting the nature and strength of the officer code at each individual prison include the security level of the prison, history of violence at that institution, size and nature of the inmate population (adolescent, geriatric, insane, etc.), and gender of the inmates and staff. Thus, large maximum-security facilities for men like Corcoran Prison tend to have far stronger officer subcultures and codes than do small, low-security prisons for women, where relatively congenial relations between officers and inmates may exist and neither officers nor inmates are fearful for their lives. Little has been written about the officer code, least of all by officers themselves. Those who study prisons have paid scant attention to varieties and intricacies of the officer subculture, in sharp contrast with rich detail provided about inmate subcultures. Yet, the prison world is largely defined by dynamic interaction between these two subcultures and the norms of behavior that each group mandates for its members.

—*Kelsey Kauffman*

See also Corcoran, California State Prison; Correctional Officers; Correctional Officer Unions; John DiIulio, Jr.; Governance; History of Prison Officers; Legitimacy; Managerialism; Prison Culture; Race Relations

Further Reading

Conover, T. (2000). *Newjack: Guarding Sing Sing*. New York: Vintage.
Kauffman, K. (1988). *Prison officers and their world*. Cambridge, MA: Harvard University Press.
Quinn, T. (Ed.). (1999). *Maximum security university: A documentary history of death and cover-up at America's most violent prison*. San Francisco: California Prison Focus.

O'HARE, KATE RICHARDS (1877–1948)

Kate Richards O'Hare, known by many as "Red Kate" because of her outspoken socialist beliefs, her political activism for the rights of women, workers, and children, and her vocal opposition to the United States' entry into World War I, was imprisoned for her political beliefs in 1919. Following her experience as a federal prisoner in the Missouri State Prison, she actively advocated for the reform of prisons. Her life story demonstrates the manner in which the government may use prisons to control public dissent. It also shows how individuals may effect changes in penal practices and beliefs.

BIOGRAPHICAL DETAILS

Kate Richards was born in Ada, Kansas, on March 26, 1877. She attended school in Nebraska for a short period of time before becoming an apprentice machinist working alongside her father in a Kansas City, Missouri, shop. Richards joined the International Order of Machinists union and, on her own time, devoted herself to temperance work through the Women's Christian Temperance Union.

POLITICAL INFLUENCES

During her tenure as a machinist, Richards became interested in the writings of many radical authors, including Henry George, Ignatius Donnelly, and Henry Demarest Lloyd. However, it was a speech made by Mary Harris "Mother" Jones and a meeting with Julius Wayland, the editor of *Appeal to Reason,* that ultimately converted Richards to socialism.

Richards joined the Socialist Labor Party in 1899, and two years later moved to the more moderate Socialist Party of America. She then enrolled in the first class of the International School of Socialist Economy in Girard, Kansas. This school was founded by the influential journalist Julius Wayland and was designed to train socialist organizers. Richards met and married Francis O'Hare while attending school in 1902. They spent their honeymoon lecturing on socialism and continued their efforts for 15 years. Their journeys on their lecture tours reached from the Great Plains states to places as far away as Britain, Canada, and Mexico.

In 1904, Kate O'Hare successfully published a socialist novel titled, *What Happened to Dan?*, later revised and reprinted as *The Sorrows of Cupid* in

1911. The O'Hares then became copublishers and coeditors of the radical weekly publication *National Rip-Saw,* published in St. Louis, which they subsequently renamed the *Socialist Revolution* in 1917. In 1910, Kate O'Hare unsuccessfully ran for the Kansas Congress on the Socialist ballot. In 1917, she became chair of the Committee on War and Militarism and toured the country to speak against the United States' entry into World War I. Shortly after her coast-to-coast travels, the Federal Espionage Act was passed that made it a federal offense to make speeches undermining the war effort.

IMPRISONMENT AND PENAL REFORM

In July 1917, Kate O'Hare was indicted under the new Federal Espionage Act for making an antiwar speech in North Dakota, and was convicted and sentenced to five years in prison. The trial judge acknowledged that the United States was a nation of free speech, but reminded all that war was also a time of sacrifice when people should not weaken the spirit or destroy faith or confidence of the people. Two years later, in April 1919, after her appeals failed, Richards became a federal prisoner, joining anarchist Emma Goldman in the women's section in the Missouri State Penitentiary, at the time the largest prison in the country.

O'Hare's prison confinement made a lasting impression on her. She immediately began to write widely circulated letters that were collected and published as *Kate O'Hare's Prison Letters* (1919) and *In Prison* (1923). Her protests about the absence of treatment for syphilitic women, the unhealthy living conditions and the inadequate food, the silent system, and more significantly, the illegal use of the contract labor of the federal prisoners by the Oberman Manufacturing Company, led to the visit by the federal inspector of prisons, Joseph Fishman. In his subsequent report he demanded that the prison officials remedy some of the more flagrant abuses. In 1920, her prison sentence was commuted after a nationwide campaign by socialist and civil libertarians. Later that year, she later received a full pardon from President

Woodrow Wilson and immediately sent to him a 63-page report on the conditions for federal women prisoners at the Missouri State Prison, likening their conditions to slaves stripped of their human rights, yet affirming that within the prison she found the opportunity for social service.

In 1922, Kate O'Hare recommenced her political activities, concentrating on various aspects of prison reform. First, she organized and lead a march on Washington called the Children's Crusade. The march was headed by children of antiwar agitators who were still in prison to demand immediate amnesty for all. Two years later, O'Hare began a national survey of prison labor in 1924 that took two years to complete. She increasingly spoke on the need for prison reform in her numerous public lectures, focusing on the inhumanity of the prison system and reaffirming the call she had made in her published memoir, *In Prison* (1923), that the federal government should build a federal prison for women that would be the model for all state prisons. Her voice became one of many that resulted in the development of the Federal Reformatory for Women at Alderson, West Virginia. Following also from her prison experience, she began to speak and write on the outrage of convict labor contracts where prison-made goods produced under abusive conditions competed with the work of free labor. While supporting the discipline of work for prisoners, she argued for fair wages and working conditions.

After her divorce from Frank O'Hare in 1928, she married again and moved to California, and initially thought she would remove herself from an active political life. However, her efforts at prison reform had not come to an end. As a result of her reputation and political connections, with the election of a Democratic governor interested in bringing significant change to an archaic penal system, a new director of penology was appointed, and O'Hare was appointed his assistant. During her tenure from late 1938 to 1940, she headed a major investigation that resulted in the dismissal of all of the members of the boards of directors for incompetence and neglect, the greater centralization of the prison system, the initial development of the first

minimum-security facility for men at Chino, and the appointment of the famous Clinton T. Duffy as warden of San Quentin State Prison. When she retired from the position after one year, California was on the way to developing one of the most progressive penal systems in the United States. In appreciation of her services, she was invited to attend the sessions of the State Crime Commission, and she continued to be present until the year of her death in 1948.

CONCLUSION

Kate Richards O'Hare stands out among historical U.S. prison reformers because of her socialist beliefs and activities. Her personal experience of incarceration was clearly important in shaping her consequent dedication to challenging the inhumanity of the prison system while actively working for change in practices and policies. Though rarely remembered these days in discussions of imprisonment, O'Hare demonstrates the importance of free speech, the way in which an individual may challenge the power of the state, and the ongoing need for changes to this nation's prison system.

—Kimberly L. Freiberger

See also Activism; Alderson, Federal Prison Camp; Critical Resistance; Angela Y. Davis; Enemy Combatants; First Amendment; Elizabeth Gurley Flynn; Fay Honey Knopp; Prison Monitoring Agencies; Resistance; USA Patriot Act 2001 Women's Prisons

Further Reading

Foner, P. S., & Miller, S. M. (Eds.). (1982). *Kate Richards O'Hare: Selected writings and speeches*. Baton Rouge: Louisiana State University Press.

Franklin, H. B. (1998). *Prison writing in 20th century America*. London: Penguin.

Gorn, E. J. (2001). *Mother Jones: The most dangerous woman in America*. New York: Hill & Wang.

Miller, S. M. (1993). *From prairie to prison: The life of social activist Kate Richards O'Hare*. Missouri Biography Series, William E. Foley (Ed.). Columbia: University of Missouri Press.

O'Hare, K. R. (1977 [1923]). *In prison*. Seattle: University of Washington Press.

Sassoon, D. (1998). *One hundred years of socialism: The west European left in the twentieth century.* New York: New Press.

◪ OPTOMETRY

In the 2003 standards for jail and prison medical care issued by the National Commission on Correctional Health Care (NCCHC), there is no specific standard for optometry. Yet, the NCCHC requires a full health assessment of all inmates entering the facility, which comprises a systematic review of all bodily systems, including inmates' visual needs. Inmates must be referred to specialists when they require consultation or care beyond the capabilities of the correctional facility, and they are entitled to eyeglasses if a physician deems them necessary for proper functioning.

EYE CARE AND THE LAW

Eye care is guaranteed to all prisoners in the United States both through the U.S. Constitution and through state constitutions and state laws. However, optometry services do not have to be the best available or even very good to meet legal requirements. Instead, the courts have merely set a threshold for the minimally acceptable ophthalmologic care that inmates are to receive.

Federal Law

Under the U.S. Constitution, prison officials must practice eye care that is not deliberately indifferent to serious medical needs (*Estelle v. Gamble*, 1976). Ordinary negligence in providing optometric treatment and/or differences of opinion as to matters of medical judgment does not lead to successful lawsuits under the Eighth Amendment (*Keyes v. Strack*, 1997). Courts have ruled that it is constitutionally permissible to prescribe an inmate with eyeglasses for a serious eye condition that the inmate thinks requires further treatment and evaluation (*Perkins v. Pelican Bay State Prison*, 1994), provided that the glasses are an appropriate treatment for the inmate's condition (*Dunville v. Morton*, 2000).

Under the deliberate indifference standard, even incompetent care may not be actionable under Title 42, U.S. Code §1983. Medical personnel must do the best they can, acting on their professional medical opinion. Even an inmate with a detached retina who complained about his blurred vision and worsening eye condition but who did not get timely treatment until months later may not be able to show deliberate indifference as long as prison officials continued to rely on their medical judgment and provide some treatment, even if substandard (*Keyes v. Strack*, 1997). As long as eye care is consistent with professional medical opinion (*Hodge v. Coughlin*, 1994), dissatisfaction with the treatment provided is inactionable under Section 1983 (*Grove v. Prison Health Services*, 1990).

Liability may, however, result if prison officials house inmates in such a way that contagious conditions are spread among cellmates. Thus, in *Freeman v. Lockhart* (1974), the inmate was placed in a prison cell with a cellmate whom prison authorities knew was infected with tuberculosis. After contracting tuberculosis in his eyes, the inmate received eye drops instead of undergoing the surgery suggested by an optometrist. The court ruled that the prisoner might be able to prove the allegations stated in the Section 1983 lawsuit.

Denial of eye care for serious eye conditions may invoke liability, including when a doctor refuses to provide eyeglasses to an inmate at the state's expense. In *Ennis v. Dasovick* (1993), for example, an inmate who wore glasses for 28 years was denied a new pair of eyeglasses by prison medical officials. The North Dakota Supreme Court found that the doctor may be liable for refusing to provide new eyeglasses to the inmate at the state's expense. Similarly, delay of care for serious eye conditions might also invoke liability, including actions that delay the time before an inmate can be seen by an ophthalmologist. Thus, in *Brady v. Attygala* (2002), an inmate with a serious eye injury repeatedly requested to be seen by a specialist outside of the prison facility. When he finally saw an ophthalmologist several weeks later, the physician informed him "his eye was infected, that it could not be saved, and that his vision could not be restored"

(p. 1018). The court ruled that the inmate might be able to recover damages for officials' deliberate indifference to serious medical needs.

State Law

Under state law, the standard for liability is medical malpractice. Courts have ruled that eye care given to inmates must meet acceptable standards of professional competence; care that falls below professional standards is negligence. An optometrist may violate a national standard of care by not immediately referring an inmate with a serious eye injury to an ophthalmologist. Such was the case in *Moss v. Miller* (1993), in which an inmate suffered serious eye injuries, but the two examining physicians and the optometrist did not refer him to an ophthalmologist for treatment of an orbital fracture or blowout fracture of the eye socket. Over the next two months, the inmate was examined 10 times and arrangements were made for the inmate to receive X-rays and an eye patch. Eight weeks after the injury, he was referred to an ophthalmologist who attempted corrective surgery, but the double vision remained a permanent disability. A jury found that the optometrist violated a national standard of care by not referring the inmate immediately to an ophthalmologist.

Delaying the proper diagnosis and treatment of a serious eye condition for two years might also result in medical malpractice. In addition, inappropriately treating eye infections with non-efficacious doses of antibiotics may be medical malpractice. In *Jacques v. State* (1984), after nasal surgery an inmate developed a serious infection of the eye area. The inmate received antibiotics, suffered pain, underwent subsequent surgery, and was permanently scarred under the eye. The Court of Claims of New York held that the "failure to use antibiotics post-surgery constituted medical malpractice" (p. 466).

CONCLUSION

Delivering eye care to prisoners is complicated by the specialties involved, the equipment needed, and the lack of optometric expertise in most correctional health care facilities. It is also sometimes compromised by the relatively scarce information available about specific eye ailments in jails and prisons. Data are not systematically collected on these issues, and very few studies have been written on the topic. Eye care for inmates frequently involves much more than providing glasses for poor vision. There are ailments that result from diabetes, high blood pressure, and other chronic diseases that adversely impact vision. There are also violent prison encounters that damage prisoners' eyes and require treatment and referral to specialists. Getting eye specialists to practice inside the prison walls or transporting inmates to and from free-world specialists presents security and logistical concerns for correctional administrators. While most facilities do a reasonable job of providing this basic medical service to inmates, given the lack of expertise among correctional health care personnel and the contractual nature of most optometry in prison settings, even well-intentioned personnel find it challenging to deliver quality eye care to inmates.

—*Michael S. Vaughn*

See also Doctors; Eighth Amendment; *Estelle v. Gamble*; Health Care; Pelican Bay State Prison

Further Reading

National Commission on Correctional Health Care. (2003a). *Standards for health services in jails.* Chicago: National Commission on Correctional Health Care.

National Commission on Correctional Health Care. (2003b). *Standards for health services in prisons.* Chicago: National Commission on Correctional Health Care.

Vaughn, M. S., & Carroll, L. (1998). Separate and unequal: Prison versus free-world medical care. *Justice Quarterly, 15,* 3–40.

Verma, S. B. (1989). Optometric services in the prison system. *Optometry and Vision Science, 66,* 6–8.

Legal Cases

Brady v. Attygala, 196 F.Supp.2d 1016 (C.D. Cal. 2002).

Butler v. Legesse, Lexis 16660 (E.D. Pa. 1990).

Dunville v. Morton, Lexis 21990 (7th Cir. 2000).

Ennis v. Dasovick, 506 N.W.2d 386 (N.D. 1993).

Estelle v. Gamble, 429 U.S. 97 (1976).

Freeman v. Lockhart, 503 F.2d 1016 (8th Cir. 1974).

Grove v. Prison Health Services, Lexis 14519 (E.D. Pa. 1990).

Hodge v. Coughlin, Lexis 13409 (S.D. N.Y. 1994).
Jacques v. State, 487 N.Y.S.2d 463 (Ct. Cl. 1984).
Keyes v. Strack, Lexis 4858 (S.D. N.Y. 1997).
Moss v. Miller, 625 N.E.2d 1044 (Ill. App. 4 Dist. 1993).
Perkins v. Pelican Bay State Prison, Lexis 34541 (9th Cir. 1994).

◪ OVERCROWDING

Determining whether a correctional facility is overcrowded involves consideration of a facility's rated capacity, operational capacity, and design capacity. The *rated capacity* refers to the number of beds or inmates assigned by a rating official to institutions within a specific jurisdiction. *Operational capacity* is the number of inmates who can be accommodated based on an institution's staff and existing programs and services. Finally, the *design capacity* refers to the number of individuals that planners or architects intended the facility to hold.

Overcrowding is not distributed evenly throughout the country. For example, according to the Bureau of Justice Statistics, the California prison system has a design capacity of nearly 80,000, however, by the end of 2001, it had an inmate population of more than 150,000—or almost 100% more than its design capacity. That same year, 21 additional states and the federal system were operating at or above their design capacity. Despite such figures, the situation seems to be improving as the number of state facilities ordered to limit population dropped from 216 in 1995 to 119 in 2000.

POPULATION GROWTH AND ITS CAUSES

By the end of 2002, more than 1.4 million inmates were incarcerated in federal and state prisons, compared to 1.0 million in 1995. After dramatic increases in the 1980s and 1990s, the incarceration rate has leveled off in recent years, though it is still growing. From 2001 to 2002, the prison population grew 2.6%, which was less than the average annual increase of 3.6% since 1995. More than half of the increase in the prison population since 1995 has been due to increased convictions for violent offenses.

One reason for the increase in inmate population is that the response to certain types of offenses and certain types of offenders (e.g., repeat offenders, drug offenders, violent offenders, immigration violators, and those convicted of drunk driving or weapons offenses) has become harsher. In the 1980s, the Reagan administration ushered in a "Get tough on crime" era that still influences sentencing practices today. In 1986, Congress enacted mandatory sentencing laws, which required judges to impose fixed sentences to those convicted of certain crimes in an effort to deter and incapacitate offenders. Currently, all 50 states have adopted one or more types of mandatory sentences. Then, in 1994, Congress passed stricter penalties for repeat offenders under the Violent Crime and Control Law Enforcement Act. The act mandated life imprisonment for individuals convicted of two or more felonies, serious violent felonies, and serious drug crimes. Many states responded by passing similar legislation. In March 1994, for example, Governor Pete Wilson of California signed the nation's first "three-strikes" law. Bill 971 ordered judges to impose a sentence of at least 25 years to life, or three times the normal sentence attached to the crime— whichever entailed the longer sentence—on offenders who were convicted of selected serious felonies or who had previously been convicted of any two felonies. In 2003, 26 states and the federal government had laws similar to California's, typically allowing a prison term or something close to it for someone convicted of a third felony.

Another reason for overcrowding is that convicted inmates are remaining incarcerated for a larger portion of their prison sentence. Traditionally, judges had discretion in sentencing an offender under felony class guidelines. Following the mandatory sentencing laws of 1986, however, states began implementing minimum sentence requirements for certain crimes. If a crime under these guidelines called for a minimum of 10 years and no greater than 30 years, the offender must serve at least 10 years. For crimes that have mandatory minimum requirements, judges may not pass alternative sentences to ease already crowded conditions in state prisons. In addition, truth-in-sentencing laws require offenders to serve 85 percent of their allotted time.

Although these laws satisfied legislators and lobbyists seeking "get tough" on crime approaches, by effectively abandoning parole, they have filled and often overfilled many state prison systems, since prisoners no longer circulate through them as rapidly as they once did. Other factors that contribute to overcrowding include high rates of recidivism and the difficulties associated with accurately projecting the inmate population.

CONSEQUENCES

Prison overcrowding strains resources and contributes to budgetary problems and a lack of programs. As states are forced to expand their correctional budget each year, other state-funded programs like public assistance programs and education suffer. Budgetary problems have made it difficult to offer programs such as drug and alcohol rehabilitation, education, and recreation. Given that an estimated 97% of those incarcerated will eventually be released to the mainstream society, the absence of such offerings is problematic. For example, most prisoners come from low-income families and have little education and few marketable job skills. Since the 1960s, the number of industrial-sector jobs (which historically have provided work to unskilled or uneducated workers) has been cut in half, making a significant impact on local employment opportunities. As more facilities operate at and above capacity, however, funding to provide prisoners with marketable job skills becomes harder to secure as resources become scarcer. Also, in order to accommodate more prisoners, many administrators are retrofitting classrooms, gymnasiums, and recreation rooms into large dormitories. Many newly constructed facilities designate minimal space for education and recreation programs. Consequently, prisoners must cope with greater idleness, which in turn contributes to greater stress and possibly greater violence.

RESPONSES

Three popular responses to overcrowding are prison construction, selective incapacitation, and the control of populations. The construction strategy responds to prison overcrowding by adding beds and building new facilities. The number of federal, state, and private facilities increased 14%, from 1,464 in 1995 to 1,668 in 2000. While this strategy is popular throughout the United States, it is very expensive. Nationwide, it costs an average of $54,000 to construct one bed space in a prison. In addition, the average cost of housing an inmate for one year ranges from $30,000 to $60,000. Many states are suffering large budget deficits as a result of the rapid growth of their prison system. California, for example, between 1980 and 1990 spent more than $5 billion building new prisons. The cost of financing the new prisons runs another $5.2 billion. Across the nation, prison construction has outpaced the construction of new schools. Moreover, while construction addresses overcrowding, it has no impact on reducing prison populations and may actually contribute to growing incarceration rates. States such as California, Texas, and Florida have spent millions of dollars on new prison construction, yet their prison populations continue to swell. Critics argue that the construction strategy is based upon an "If you build it, they will come" philosophy; that is, the more prisons that are built, the more inmates will be found to fill them.

Advocates of selective incapacitation hold that judges should only incarcerate a select group of offenders (i.e., repeat, violent offenders) whom they deem dangerous to society. Nonviolent offenders could be sentenced to community correctional facilities, probation, or rehabilitation programs. The idea is to free up bed space while keeping the public safe from the violent offenders. In reality, however, the passage of mandatory sentences such as Three-Strikes Laws, mandatory minimums, and truth-in-sentencing provisions have limited judges' discretion, as they must adhere to sentencing guidelines.

According to the population sensitive flow-control strategy, judicial districts are allotted a certain number of prison beds to which they may sentence offenders. Once that number is reached, the judge of that particular district must pursue alternative means of sentencing. Intensive Supervision Programs (ISP) developed as a popular type of alternative or intermediate sanction. After its introduction in the late 1960s and early 1970s, however, ISP was abandoned, based on research that it did not lower arrest rates for those participating. In 1982, Georgia modified ISP for use with first-time offenders or people convicted of less serious crimes. States across the nation soon followed Georgia's lead and developed similar ISP programs. ISP soon became a tool in easing prison crowding conditions when state prisons were near or at the designed capacity. ISPs involve more frequent contact between offenders and their supervising officers and more restrictions compared to regular probation. Studies of their effectiveness have had mixed results with some research suggesting that ISPs have not succeeded either in reducing correctional costs or in preventing crime.

Another possible means of reducing prison overcrowding is to make greater use of community corrections. Community corrections refer to programs designed to punish, supervise, or treat offenders within the community. The most popular forms are probation and parole. Other programs include pretrial diversion, dispute resolution and restitution, community service, day fines and probation fees, work-release programs, halfway houses, and electronic monitoring. The same goals and philosophies that apply to institutional corrections also apply to community corrections. Although much less expensive than incarceration, community corrections programs are still costly.

CONCLUSION

Greater reliance on incarceration combined with longer and mandatory sentences have contributed to the crowding problem facing many state and federal prison systems. Historically, the public has not supported policies that are perceived as "soft" on crime. The situation, however, is changing. Declining crime rates have made people less concerned about street violence and more concerned about issues such as education, the economy, and health care. Currently, state governments are grappling with the high costs of maintaining prisoners in a poor economy. Consequently, legislators have been prompted to reexamine some of the most

stringent laws, such as those imposing mandatory minimum sentences and forbidding early parole. This may signal the beginning of a reversal in a 20-year trend toward more punitive anticrime measures, which in turn may reduce the use of incarceration and reduce crowding (Flavin & Rosenthal, 2003).

—*Kristi M. McKinnon*

See also Community Corrections Centers; Deterrence Theory; Federal Prison System; Home Arrest; Incapacitation Theory; Increase in Prison Population; Indeterminate Sentencing; Intermediate Sanctions; Just Deserts Theory; Parole; Probation; Riots; Sentencing Reform Act 1984; Three-Strikes Legislation; Truth in Sentencing; Violent Crime Control and Law Enforcement Act 1994; War on Drugs

Further Reading

Bureau of Justice Statistics. (1999). *Truth in sentencing in state prisons*. Washington, DC: U.S. Department of Justice.

Bureau of Justice Statistics. (2002). *Prisoners in 2001*. Washington, DC: U.S. Department of Justice.

Bureau of Justice Statistics. (2003). *Census of state and federal correctional facilities, 2000*. Washington, DC: U.S. Department of Justice.

Cook, J. R. (2001). *Asphalt justice: A critique of the criminal justice system in America*. Westport, CT: Praeger.

Flavin, J., & D. Rosenthal. (2003). La Bodega de la Familia: Supporting parolees' reintegration within a family context. *Fordham University Urban Law Journal, 30*(5), 1603–1620.

Gottfredson, S. D., & McConville, S. (1987). *America's correctional crisis: Prison populations and public policy*. Westport, CT: Greenwood.

Harrison, P. M., & Beck, A. (2003). *Prisoners in 2002*. Washington, DC: U.S. Department of Justice.

Welch, M. (2003). *Corrections: A critical approach*. New York: McGraw-Hill.

◪ OVERPRESCRIPTION OF DRUGS

The issues around control and regulation of offenders through medical practice have provoked considerable debate. In particular, much controversy has centered on the extent and ethics of using psychotropic drugs for disciplinary and control purposes in prisons.

The use of psychotropic medications as a means of controlling inmate populations is not new. Prisoners in the 19th and early 20th centuries were known to be given "sleeping draughts" to alter their behavior. However, the emergence of the drug industry involving multinational companies, the large-scale manufacture and availability of powerful new combinations of chemicals, the worsening prison crisis, and increasing concern for order and security in prison meant that the prescription of drugs took on a new significance in the postwar period.

ORDER AND CONTROL

Prison reports and accounts from ex-prisoners, ex-governors, and prison doctors and other medical workers in Britain from the 1950s and 1960s provided some evidence of the use of psychotropic drugs to control "difficult" or "unruly" prisoners and those with various mental disorders, including schizophrenia and dementia. As the crisis of containment intensified and a small number of subversive prisoners were blamed for the increasing number of prison disturbances in the 1970s, so the allegations became stronger that drugs were being used for disciplinary purposes. Similarly, in the United States, there is evidence to suggest that psychotropic drugs were used in prisons and jails since at least the 1970s as a "quick, cheap, and effective" solution to warehousing increasing numbers of inmates into smaller spaces, while using fewer support services. "Healthy" inmates are frequently medicated without diagnosis or proper psychiatric and physical assessments. In *Liles v. Ward* (1976), a group of female inmates in a New York state prison were transported to a state mental hospital because they were deemed to be "disciplinary problems" by the correctional staff and placed on psychotropic medications (sometimes by force) in order to maintain peace and tranquility on the ward.

GENDER

The overprescription of psychotropic drugs has to be understood in the context not only of wider concerns about prison (dis)order but also of the differential understandings of male and female criminality. Medical professionals and other criminal justice experts have traditionally sought to analyze, categorize, judge, and treat female offenders differently than men. The medicalization of female deviance, the drive to normalize women's behavior according to particular ideals of femininity, and the tendency of medical professionals to overprescribe mood-altering drugs for women are common practices. In the United States, significantly more women than men receive prescriptions for antidepressants, tranquilizers, and sedatives. They are also given them for different reasons. Within correctional facilities, the use of psychotropic medications on male inmates is often justified with reference to "problems of institutional control," while female inmates tend to be drugged in the name of "treatment" in an attempt to correct their deviant behavior in a psycho-physiological manner.

There is some evidence to suggest that psychotropic drugs have been used disproportionately in terms of the rate of prescription per head of the female prison population. In their research study in Britain, Genders and Player (1987) found that large doses of antidepressants, sedatives, and tranquilizers were dispensed to women in prison, proportionately five times as many doses of this type of medication as men received in prison. A recent debate in Parliament also rekindled concerns that neuroleptics and other heavy tranquilizers are routinely prescribed to young women prisoners who mutilate themselves, and that medical drugs are used as pacifiers that move prisoners from nonaddictive illegal drugs to highly addictive medicinal drug use. In the U.S. context, Auerhahn and Dermody Leonard (2000) also found that it is the combined effect of being female and exhibiting behavior inconsistent with the normative requirements of the feminine ideal that often triggers the use of medication in their sample of inmates. Furthermore, they argued that the drugging of female prisoners and jail detainees can lead to disproportionately harsh outcomes for these offenders, including inability to participate fully in their own defense and to receive due process of the law.

RACE

Another important dimension in the debate around the overprescription of drugs has been the assessment and treatment of ethnic minorities. Critics argue that many medical and criminal justice professionals tend to operate on the basis of ethnocentric assumptions or racist stereotypes and view acute stress reactions in black people as symptoms of mental disorder, especially schizophrenia. One result is that black psychiatric in-patients are more likely than whites to be defined as "aggressive," placed in secure units, and subjected to harsh and invasive forms of treatment such as intramuscular medication and electroconvulsive therapy. More specifically, there were a number of cases involving black prisoners in Britain during the 1980s that raised issues around the psychiatric assessment of these prisoners, the inappropriate and/or inadequate medical treatment they received, the question of force-feeding, the use of drugs as controlling mechanisms, and their certification as either mentally ill or insane, which meant that they could be transferred to mental hospitals.

RESISTANCE AND LITIGATION

Medical practices in the prison system have not gone unchallenged. In Britain, the formation of prisoner rights campaign groups in the 1970s provided a forum for prisoners to articulate their concerns. At the time, concern over the disciplinary role of prison doctors in general and emerging allegations about the overprescription of drugs in prisons in particular led to an alliance between various prison reform groups, drug agencies, and mental health campaign groups and the setting up of the Medical Committee Against the Abuse of Prisoners by Drugging in 1977.

Resistance has also taken the form of litigation by prisoners over enforced medical treatment with mixed results. In the United States, the Eighth Amendment, which protects citizens from cruel and unusual punishment, has been used to challenge inadequate medical care in prison and, perhaps more significantly, to challenge a requirement to participate in treatment programs and/or be subjected to involuntary injection of psychotropic drugs. For example, the court held that the use of aversive drug therapy, which caused temporary painful and frightening medical problems as a way of "encouraging" better behavior, could constitute cruel and unusual punishment; this decision was upheld in *Knecht v. Gillman* (1973). The Fourteenth Amendment, with its equal protection clause, and the due process clause have also been used in prisoner rights suits in this area. In *Harper v. State* (1988), the Washington Supreme Court held that prison inmates had the right to refuse to take antipsychotic drugs prescribed by prison authorities, and that this right could be overridden only when the state proves a compelling state interest to administer medication. However, the U.S. Supreme Court reversed this ruling in *Washington v. Harper* (1990) and found that psychotropic drugs can be administered to unwilling prisoners if the prison and medical staff can show that medicating the inmate is related to "legitimate penological interests," including the maintenance of prison order.

CONCLUSION

It has become increasingly difficult for prisoners to challenge the appropriateness of medication they receive against a background of a worsening prison crisis. To the extent that the courts are prepared to defer to the expertise of prison administrators in the management of prisons and medical intervention into the lives of some of the most vulnerable prisoners, there is a danger that the emphasis on prison security and control will prevail at the expense of prisoner rights. While some prisoners may genuinely require certain prescription drugs, the historical precedence of overprescription of certain kinds of drugs for certain sections of the inmate community, along with various more recent legal challenges about the provision of medications, suggests that this practice is vulnerable to misuse.

—*Maggy Lee*

See also Doctors; Drug Offenders; Eighth Amendment; *Estelle v. Gamble*; Health Care; Medical Experiments; Prisoner Litigation; Psychiatric Care; Women's Prisons

Further Reading

Allen, H. (1987). *Justice unbalanced*. Milton Keynes, UK: Open University Press.

Auerhahn, K., & Dermody Leonard, E. (2000). Docile bodies? Chemical restraints and the female inmate. *Journal of Criminal Law and Criminology, 90*(2), 599–634.

Bhat, A., Carr-Hill, R., & Ohri, S. (1988). *Britain's black population: A new perspective*. Aldershot, UK: Gower.

Carlen, P. (1983). *Women's imprisonment*. London: Routledge & Kegan Paul.

Genders, E., & Player, E. (1987). Women in prison: The treatment, the control and the experience. In P. Carlen & A. Worrall (Eds.), *Gender, crime and justice* (pp. 161–175). Milton Keynes, UK: Open University Press.

Genders, E., & Player, E. (1995). *Grendon: A study of a therapeutic prison*. Oxford, UK: Clarendon Press.

Mandaraka-Sheppard, A. (1986). *The dynamics of aggression in women's prisons in England*. Aldershot, UK: Gower.

Prison Reform Trust. (Ed.). (1985). *Prison medicine: Ideas on health care in penal establishments*. London: Prison Reform Trust.

Sim, J. (1990). *Medical power in prisons: The prison medical service in England 1774–1989*. Milton Keynes, UK: Open University Press.

Legal Cases

Harper v. State, 759 P.2d 358 (Wash. 1988).

Knecht v. Gillman, 488 F.2d 1136 (8th Cir. 1973).

Liles v. Ward, 424 F. Supp. 675 (S.D.N.Y. 1976).

Washington v. Harper, 494 U.S. 210 (1990).